International Series in Quantitative Marketing

Series Editor

Jehoshua Eliashberg
The Wharton School
University of Pennsylvania
Philadelphia, PA, USA

More information about this series at http://www.springer.com/series/6164

Peter S. H. Leeflang • Jaap E. Wieringa
Tammo H. A. Bijmolt • Koen H. Pauwels
Editors

Advanced Methods for Modeling Markets

Springer

Editors
Peter S. H. Leeflang
Department of Marketing
University of Groningen
Groningen, The Netherlands

Aston Business School
Birmingham, UK

Tammo H. A. Bijmolt
Department of Marketing
University of Groningen
Groningen, The Netherlands

Jaap E. Wieringa
Department of Marketing
University of Groningen
Groningen, The Netherlands

Koen H. Pauwels
Department of Marketing
D'Amore-McKim School of Business
Northeastern University
Boston, USA

BI Norwegian Business School
Oslo, Norway

ISSN 0923-6716 ISSN 2199-1057 (electronic)
International Series in Quantitative Marketing
ISBN 978-3-319-53467-1 ISBN 978-3-319-53469-5 (eBook)
DOI 10.1007/978-3-319-53469-5

Library of Congress Control Number: 2017944728

Printed on acid-free paper

This Springer imprint is published by Springer Nature
The registered company is Springer International Publishing AG
The registered company address is: Gewerbestrasse 11, 6330 Cham, Switzerland

Preface

In 2015, we published our book *Modeling Markets* (MM). In MM, we provide the basics of modeling markets along with the classical steps of the model building process: specification, data collection, estimation, validation, and implementation. We spend much attention to models of the aggregate demand, the individual demand, and we give examples of database marketing models. The table of contents and the subject index of MM can be found at the end of this volume. However, in MM, we did not cover a number of advanced methods that are used to specify, estimate, and validate marketing models. Such methods are covered in the present volume: *Advanced Methods for Modeling Markets* (AMMM).

MM is particularly suitable for students in courses such as "models in marketing" and "quantitative analysis in marketing" at the graduate and advanced undergraduate level. AMMM is directed toward participants of Ph.D. courses and researchers in the marketing science discipline.

In AMMM, we consider—after an introduction (Part I)—the following topics:

- Models for advanced analysis (Part II):

  (Advanced) individual demand models
  Time series analysis
  State space models
  Spatial models
  Structural models
  Mediation
  Models that specify competition
  Diffusion models

  In addition, we present models with latent variables, including the estimation methods that they require (Part III):

- Specification and estimation models with latent variables:

  Structural equation models
  Partial least squares
  Mixture models
  Hidden Markov models

In the part that deals with specific estimation methods and issues, we discuss (Part IV):

- Generalized methods of moments
- Bayesian analysis
- Non-/semi-parametric estimation
- Endogeneity issues

In the final two chapters of this book (Part V), we give an outlook to the future of modeling markets, where we spend explicit attention to machine learning models and big data.

Each chapter of AMMM contains the following elements:

- An introduction to the method/methodology
- A numerical example/application in marketing
- References to other marketing applications
- Suggestions about software

We, as editors, would like to thank the 24 authors (affiliated to universities in eight different countries) who contributed to this book. Our colleague in Groningen Peter C. Verhoef came up with the idea to make this book an edited volume and invite authors to contribute their expertise. We thank him for this great idea. We thank the authors for their contributions and cooperation. The four editors contributed to chapters but also reviewed the chapters in cooperation with a number of other reviewers, namely Keyvan Dehmamy, Maarten Gijsenberg, Hans Risselada, and Tom Wansbeek, who are all affiliated to the University of Groningen, the Netherlands. We owe much to Linda Grondsma and Jasper Hidding who helped us tremendously in getting the chapters organized.

Groningen, The Netherlands — Peter S. H. Leeflang
Groningen, The Netherlands — Jaap E. Wieringa
Groningen, The Netherlands — Tammo H. A. Bijmolt
Boston, USA — Koen H. Pauwels
June 2017

Contents

Contributors

Paulo Albuquerque Faculty of Marketing, INSEAD Fontainebleau, Fontainebleau, France

Hans Baumgartner Department of Marketing, Smeal College of Business, The Pennsylvania State University, University Park, PA, USA

Tammo H. A. Bijmolt Department of Marketing, Faculty of Economics and Business, University of Groningen, Groningen, The Netherlands

Bart J. Bronnenberg Department of Marketing, Tilburg School of Economics and Marketing, Tilburg University, Tilburg, The Netherlands

Peter Ebbes Department of Marketing, HEC Paris, Jouy-en-Josas, France

J. Paul Elhorst Department of Economics, Econometrics and Finance, University of Groningen, Groningen, The Netherlands

Fred M. Feinberg Ross School of Business, University of Michigan, Ann Arbor, MI, USA

Elea McDonnell Feit LeBow College of Business, Drexel University, Philadelphia, PA, USA

Dennis Fok Econometric Institute, Erasmus School of Economics, Erasmus University Rotterdam, Rotterdam, The Netherlands

Harald J. Van Heerde Department of Marketing, School of Communication, Journalism and Marketing, Massey University, Auckland, New Zealand

Jörg Henseler Department of Design, Production and Management, University of Twente, Enschede, The Netherlands

Raoul V. Kübler Department of Marketing, Özyeğin University, Istanbul, Turkey

Peter S. H. Leeflang Department of Marketing, Faculty of Economics and Business, University of Groningen, Groningen, The Netherlands and Aston Business School, Birmingham, UK

Peter J. Lenk Ross School of Business, University of Michigan, Ann Arbor, MI, USA

Oded Netzer Columbia Business School, Columbia University, New York, NY, USA

Ernst C. Osinga Lee Kong Chian School of Business, Singapore Management University, Singapore, Singapore

Leo J. Paas Department of Marketing, School of Communication, Journalism and Marketing, Massey University, Auckland, New Zealand

Dominik Papies School of Business and Economics, University of Tübingen, Tübingen, Germany

Koen H. Pauwels Department of Marketing, Northeastern University, Boston, USA and BI Norwegian Business School, Oslo, Norway

Rik Pieters Department of Marketing, Tilburg School of Economics and Marketing, Tilburg University, Tilburg, The Netherlands

Jeroen K. Vermunt Department of Methodology and Statistics, Tilburg University, Tilburg, The Netherlands

Tom J. Wansbeek Department of Economics, Econometrics and Finance, Faculty of Economics and Business, University of Groningen, Groningen, The Netherlands

Bert Weijters Department of Personnel Management, Work and Organizational Psychology, Ghent University, Ghent, Belgium

Jaap E. Wieringa Department of Marketing, Faculty of Economics and Business, University of Groningen, Groningen, The Netherlands

Part I
Introduction

Chapter 1
Advanced Methods for Modeling Markets (AMMM)

Peter S.H. Leeflang, Jaap E. Wieringa, Tammo H.A. Bijmolt, and Koen H. Pauwels

1.1 Introduction

Over the last six decades, marketing concepts, tools, and knowledge have gone through tremendous developments. A general trend toward *formalization* has affected decision making and has clarified the relationship between marketing efforts and performance measures. This evolution has received strong support from concurrent revolutions in data collection and research methods (Leeflang 2011). In this book we discuss many of these research methods.

This monograph is the follow-up of *Modeling Markets* (*MM*) (Leeflang et al. 2015), also denoted as Vol. I. In Chap. 1 we will briefly discuss the most relevant concepts which have been discussed in *MM*. We also briefly discuss the topics that are discussed in *AMMM*.

Table 1.1 gives a brief and structured overview of the topics that are discussed in this book and relates these to corresponding topics discussed in Vol. I. = *MM*.

Section 1.2 discusses basic concepts. In Sect. 1.3 we briefly discuss the structures of the model *specifications* which have been frequently used in marketing. These are the demand models at the aggregate and the individual level. We then discuss how these models deviate from other specifications which are discussed in this book, such as advanced individual demand models (Chap. 2), structural models (Chap. 7), models for competitive analysis (Chap. 9) and diffusion models (Chap. 10). Specifying relationships using a mediator is discussed in Chap. 8.

P.S.H. Leeflang (✉) • J.E. Wieringa • T.H.A. Bijmolt
Department of Marketing, Faculty of Economics and Business, University of Groningen, Groningen, The Netherlands
e-mail: p.s.h.leeflang@rug.nl

K.H. Pauwels
Department of Marketing, Northeastern University, Boston, USA

P.S.H. Leeflang et al. (eds.), *Advanced Methods for Modeling Markets*, International Series in Quantitative Marketing, DOI 10.1007/978-3-319-53469-5_1

Table 1.1 Classification of topics discussed in MM (Vol. I) and AMMM (Vol. II)

Specification	Vol. I. (Leeflang et al. 2015)	Vol. II. (This book: Leeflang et al. 2016)	**Specification**
Specification issues	Chap. 2	Sect. 1.3	Recap
Individual demand models	Chap. 8	Chap. 2	Advanced individual demand models
Aggregate demand models	Chap. 7	Sect. 1.3.1	Recap
Database marketing models	Chap. 9	–	–
		Sect. 1.3.2, Chap. 7	Structural models
		Sect. 1.3.3, Chap. 9	Modeling competitive response and game-theoretic models
		Sect. 1.3.4, Chap. 10	Diffusion and adoption models
Mediation	Sect. 2.5	Sect 1.3.5, Chap. 8	Mediation
Specification and estimation			**Specification and estimation**
		Sect. 1.4.2.1, Chaps. 3, 4	Times series models
		Sect. 1.4.2.2, Chap. 5	State space models
		Sect. 1.4.2.3, Chap. 6	Spatial models
			Modeling with latent variables:
Simultaneous systems of equations	Sect. 6.5	Sect. 1.5, Chap. 11	Structural equation models
		Sect. 1.5, Chap. 12	Partial least squares
		Sect. 1.5, Chap. 13	Mixture models
	Sect. 8.2.4.2	Sect. 1.5, Chap. 14	Hidden Markov models
Estimation			**Estimation**
General linear model (GM)	Chap. 4	Sect. 1.4.1	GM—Recap
Generalized least squares	Sect. 6.2	Sect. 1.4.1	GLS—Recap
Maximum likelihood estimation (MLE)	Sect. 6.4	Sect. 1.4.2	MLE—Recap
Instrumental variables	Sect. 6.6	Sect. 1.1.6, Chaps. 15 + 18	Method of moments
Endogeneity	Sect. 6.7	Chap. 18	Endogeneity issues and IV estimation
Bayesian estimation	Sect. 6.8	Chap. 16	Bayesian estimation
		Chap. 17	Non- and semiparametric regression models
Data			**Data**
Data	Chap. 3	Chap. 19	Big data (and machine learning)
Dashboards and metrics	Sect. 10.5		

In Sect. 1.4 we recap two frequently used estimation methods viz. the General Linear Model (GM) and Maximum Likelihood Estimation (MLE). Sect. 1.4 also discusses sets of models which (1), at least in principle, can be estimated by GM and/or MLE but which have a specification which deviates from the specifications which are discussed in Sect. 1.3 and (2) require other statistical criteria for identification and validation than those which are usually applied using GM/MLE. We briefly introduce time series methods, state space models and spatial models, which are discussed in more detail in Chaps. 3–6.

Many variables of considerable interest are unobservable. Examples are attitude, buying intention, subjective norms, internal and external role behavior, etc. *Unobservable* or *latent* variables may be distinguished from observable variables or indicators. In this book, we spend ample attention to models that include latent variables: Chaps. 11–14. These models are briefly introduced in Sect. 1.5.

In Sect. 1.6 we briefly discuss a number of "other" estimation methods and spend some attention to endogeneity. These topics are discussed in more detail in Chaps. 15–18. Finally, in Sect. 1.7 we briefly introduce machine learning methods.

1.2 Modeling Markets: Basic Concepts

In Vol. I and in this book we consider models that can be used to support decision-making in marketing. "The most important elements of a perceived real world system" (the definition of a *model*) can be represented in a number of ways. We consider "*numerically specified models*" in which the various variables that are used to describe markets and their interrelations are quantified. Marketing models can be classified according to purpose or intended use reflecting the reason why a firm might want to engage in a model-building project. Different purposes often lead to different models. We distinguish between *descriptive, predictive,* and *normative (prescriptive)* models. Descriptive models are intended to describe decisions of suppliers and customers. The main purpose of predictive models is to forecast or predict future events. Normative models have as one of its outputs a recommended course of action.

Models can also be distinguished accordingly to the level of demand. We distinguish between models for individual demand and models for aggregate demand. Aggregate demand may refer to:

1. The total number of units of a product category purchased by the population of all spending units. The corresponding demand model is called an *industry sales*, or *product class sales* model.
2. The total number of units of a particular brand bought by the population of all spending units. The demand model is then a *brand sales model.*
3. The number of units of a particular brand purchased, relative to the total number of units purchased of the product class, in which case the demand model becomes a *market share* model.

We can define the same measures at the segment level and at the level of the *individual consumer* leading to models with different levels of aggregation: market, store, segment, household and so on. Thus we define, for example:

1. category purchases for a given household;
2. brand purchases for the household;
3. the proportion of category purchases accounted for by the brand, for the household ("share of wallet").

In Vol. I we distinguished 10 steps in the model building process.[1] After the identification of the *opportunity*, how a model can improve managerial decisions making, the *purpose* of the model has to be defined. The specification of a model is based on the *availability of data*. Revolutionary developments in data collection offer many opportunities for advanced model building and the application of advanced research methods (Leeflang et al. 2014, 2015, p. 71; Verhoef et al. 2016). Much attention is nowadays given to "Big Data" (see also Chap. 19). However, many managers in firms struggle to identify which data to use to improve their decision-making. The specification of marketing models is an excellent tool to define which data have to be collected to specify and estimate models that support decision-making. This is one side of the medal. The other side is that data are needed to obtain numerical specifications. Not all data are relevant and/or useful to this end. Data sets should contain "good data", where "good" encompasses availability, quality, variability, quantity and relevance.

The most important next steps of the model-building process are (1) *specification*, (2) *estimation*, and (3) *validation*. We discuss these topics in more detail in Sect. 1.3 and Sect. 1.4 respectively. We will first recap the most important issues discussed in Vol. I and then indicate how this topic receives attention in the present volume.

Steps that follow specification, estimation and validation refer to the implementation (*use*) and *updating* of the model.

1.3 Model Specification

1.3.1 Recap

Part II of this present volume deals with specification. *Specification* is the expression of the most important elements of a real-world system in mathematical terms. This involves two major steps:

a. Specifying the variables to be included in the model, and making a distinction between those to be explained (the dependent or criterion variables), and those providing the explanation (the explanatory, independent or predictor variables).

[1] See Leeflang et al. (2015, pp. 18–21).

b. Specifying the functional relationship between the variables. For example, the effects of the explanatory variables can be linear or non-linear, immediate and/or lagged, additive or multiplicative, etc.

In this book we spend explicit attention to the specification and estimation of models that are not linearizable (see Chap. 17).

Experience in model-building has led to model specification criteria that relate to model structure (Little 1970). Models should be:

1. *simple*;
2. *complete* on important issues;
3. *adaptive* to new phenomena on markets and/or new data;
4. *robust*, which means that the model structure constrains answers to a meaningful range of answers.

Another issue that deals with the specification of a good model is to link the criteria "simple" and "complete". It has been suggested to build models in an *evolutionary way*, i.e. starting simple and expanding in detail as time goes on.

The *demand* models which have been specified in the past usually have the following structure:

$$d_{it} = f\ (marketing\ instruments,\ environmental\ variables) \tag{1.1}$$

where d_{it} = the demand of brand or product category i in time period t. Eq. (1.1) may contain the own marketing instruments and the marketing instruments of competitive brands/products. Demand can be measured at the individual level (d_{ijt} = demand of unit (brand/product) i by consumer j at time t), at the segment (d_{ist}= demand of i in segment s at time t) or at the aggregate level. In Eq. (1.1) it is assumed that a specification can be estimated using time series data. There are, however, other data structures that can be used. The most important data structures are:

- cross-sectional data;
- time series data;
- pooled cross-sectional data, and
- panel data.

A *cross-sectional* data set consists of a sample of customers, firms, brands, regions or other units taken at a single point in time. Demand is represented by the variable d_{ij}, where i is the brand index and j is the index of the individual consumer.

Time series data sets consist of observations on a variable or several variables *over time* that are measured for a single unit. One feature that distinguishes time series data from cross-sectional data is that observations of a time series have a natural, temporal, ordering. In many cases time series observations are related to earlier observations and are not independent across time i.e., they exhibit serial correlation. The criterion variable is d_{it}.

Data sets may have both cross-sectional and time series features. For example, a researcher has access to different sets of cross-sectional data that refer to January 2017 and January 2018. A *pooled cross section* is formed by combining the observations of these months, which increases the sample size. In this case, demand can be represented by d_{ij1} and d_{ij2} where 1 refers to January 2017 and 2 to January 2018.

A *panel* data (or longitudinal data) set consists of a time series of *each* cross-sectional member in the data set (Wooldridge 2012, p. 10). The key feature of panel data that distinguishes them from pooled cross-sectional data is that the *same* cross-sectional units are followed over a given time period. The demand variable can be represented by d_{ijt} in this case.

The individual demand models are used to specify customer decisions as:

- whether to buy;
- what to buy;
- how much to buy; and
- when to buy.

Binary and multinomial choice models such as logit, probit and Markov models are developed for the first two decisions. Purchase quantity models such as count models are used to obtain answers for the third question whereas hazard models have been used to answer the question when to buy. Models that answer a number of these questions simultaneously are known as integrated models. Examples are (Type-1 and Type-2) Tobit models.

In Chap. 2 we first recap the choice models that were discussed in Vol. I, such as logit and probit models, and then discuss more advanced individual demand models, including nested logit, ordered logit and probit models, and models for censored variables and corner solutions.

Most (classical) marketing models have a structure as in Eq. (1.1). Below we introduce other structures/specifications such as:

- structural models;
- competitive response models;
- diffusion and adoption models,

which are discussed in Chaps. 7, 9, and 10 respectively.

1.3.2 Structural Models

Albuquerque and Bronnenberg (Chap. 7) define structural models as econometric representations of decision-making behavior. The equations of a structural model are based on (economic) theory. The models do not only represent quantities of sales (d_{it}) as outcomes of goal-directed decision-making by customers, but also explicitly consider outcomes of goal-directed decision-making by other agents such as suppliers (firms, retailers, etc.). Examples are prices, advertising budgets, number of distribution outlets visited by sales representatives, etc. Hence, in structural models also the supply side is explicitly modeled. As an example we specify (1.2):

$$p_{it} = g\ (\textit{competitive prices, lagged prices, sales,} \\ \textit{competitive sales, manufacturer variable cost, etc.}) \tag{1.2}$$

where p_{it} is the price of brand i at t. For each decision of the agent a function such as (1.2) can be specified, at least in principle. In addition goal-functions are defined such as, for example, a profit function. As an example we specify the profit function of a firm h:

$$\pi_h = \sum_{i \in M_h} (p_i - mc_i)\ D\ s_i\ (p_i) - F_h \tag{1.3}$$

where

$$\begin{aligned} \pi_h &= \text{profit function of firm } h, \\ p_i &= \text{price of brand } i, \\ M_h &= \text{product line of firm } h, \\ mc_i &= \text{marginal cost of } i, \\ D &= \text{total market size}, \\ s_i(p_i) &= \text{share of brand } i, \\ F_h &= \text{fixed cost of firm } h. \end{aligned}$$

However, the functions in structural models are usually much more complicated. The structural models are closely connected to the game-theoretic models which are briefly introduced in Chap. 9. Usually demand is obtained through aggregation of individual-level choices.

In many cases instrumental variables (Chaps. 7, 15, and 18) and the Generalized Method of Moments (Chap. 15) are used to estimate a system of relations such as (1.1)–(1.3).

1.3.3 Competitive Response Models

These models are more or less similar to Eq. (1.2). The starting point is that the outcome of a decision, such as price, is explained at a minimum by competitive prices (simple competitive reactions), but also by other marketing instruments than price which are used by competitors (multiple competitive reactions), lagged own prices, cost variables, demand feedback and current and lagged own marketing instruments other than price (e.g. Nijs et al. 2007). Demand-functions complete competitive response functions in a number of empirically tested models. To this end one specifies sets of simultaneous equations. Vector Autoregression (VAR) models (Chap. 4) are specific examples of these sets.

1.3.4 Diffusion and Adoption Models

These models differ from (1.1) in at least two ways:

- the "demand" is measured in number of people that have adopted the product, instead of sales;
- among the predictors are unique variables such as the number of potential adopters and the number of adopters at a certain time.

In adoption models the different steps from adoption to (repeat) purchase are explicitly specified. These models "zoom in" at the individual consumer level: *micro-micro models*.

1.3.5 Mediation

Oftentimes, the relationship between three variables *X*, *M* and *Y* can be presented as shown in Fig. 1.1. The explanatory variable *X*, has an effect on the dependent variable *M* (labelled as mediator), where the mediator *M* also has an effect on *Y*. This can be written as:

$$Y = intercept + cX + bM + \varepsilon_1 \tag{1.4}$$

$$M = intercept + aX + \varepsilon_2. \tag{1.5}$$

Hence, *X* has a direct effect *c* and an indirect effect (through *M*) $a \times b$ on *Y*, and the total effect of *X* on *Y* is equal to $c + a \times b$. The degree of mediation can be computed as $(a \times b)/(c + a \times b)$: indicating which percentage of the total effect of *X* on *Y* is due to the indirect effect, mediated through *M*.

Statistical significance of the indirect effect can be tested by means of the Sobel test, which is a *t*-test comparing the estimated values of *a* and *b* to the pooled standard error:

$$t = \frac{ab}{\sqrt{(b^2\sigma_a^2) + (a^2\sigma_b^2)}} \tag{1.6}$$

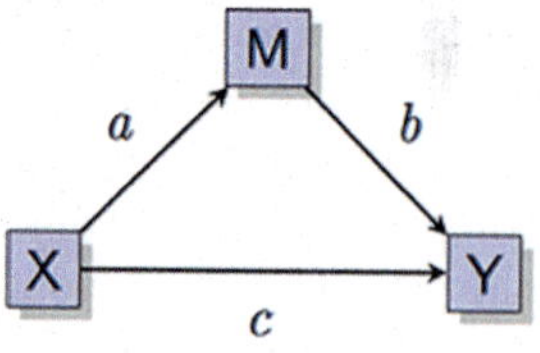

Fig. 1.1 Schematical representation of a mediation model

where σ_a^2 and σ_b^2 are the variances of a and b respectively. The basic mediation model can be extended to include multiple (parallel and/or sequential) mediators, and to combine mediation and moderation or interaction effects. Furthermore, the Sobel test has several problems and limitations, and more complex testing procedures have been developed. Finally, Eqs. (1.4) and (1.5) assume a linear model, and mediation methods have been developed for non-linear and other more complex models. Excellent discussions of basic and advanced methods for mediation analysis are available in Hayes (2013) and MacKinnon (2008).

Chapter 8 of this volume deals with challenges encountered by a researcher applying mediation analysis in a controlled experiment, while some of these challenges will occur also in other empirical settings. These challenges relate to among others measurement errors in the variables and omitted variables in the model specification. Chapter 8 discusses conditions for valid causal inferences on the mediation relationships, potential consequences if these conditions are not met, and possible solutions.

1.4 Model Estimation[2]

In this section, we first recap the principles of two sets of estimation methods: the General Linear Model (GM) and Maximum Likelihood Estimation (MLE) (Sect. 1.4.1). We then discuss models that can be estimated using these methods but *use other statistical criteria for identification and validation* than the models discussed so far in Vol. I in Sect. 1.4.2. The assumptions about the disturbances of these models also deviate from the "usual assumptions".

1.4.1 Recap

1.4.1.1 General Linear Model (GM)

We consider the following specification:

$$y_t = \alpha + \beta_1 x_{1t} + \beta_2 x_{2t} + \cdots + \beta_k x_{kt} + \varepsilon_t \tag{1.7}$$

where y_t is the criterion variable in t and x_{kt} is the value of the kth predictor variable, $k = 1, \ldots, K$. We can rewrite the relations in Eq. (1.7) as:

[2] The text of this section is based on Leeflang et al. (2015, Chaps. 4–6).

$$\begin{pmatrix} y_1 \\ y_2 \\ \vdots \\ y_T \end{pmatrix} = \begin{pmatrix} 1 & x_{11} & x_{21} & \dots & x_{K1} \\ 1 & x_{12} & x_{22} & \dots & x_{K2} \\ \vdots & \vdots & \vdots & \ddots & \vdots \\ 1 & x_{1T} & x_{2T} & \dots & x_{KT} \end{pmatrix} \begin{pmatrix} \alpha \\ \beta_1 \\ \beta_2 \\ \vdots \\ \beta_K \end{pmatrix} + \begin{pmatrix} \varepsilon_1 \\ \varepsilon_2 \\ \vdots \\ \varepsilon_T \end{pmatrix} \tag{1.8}$$

which in matrix notation becomes:

$$y = X\beta + \varepsilon \tag{1.9}$$

where

y = a column vector of size T with values of the criterion variable,
X = a matrix of dimensions $(T \times K + 1)$ with a column of ones and values of the K predictor variables,
β = a column vector of $K + 1$ unknown parameters, and
ε = a column vector of T disturbance terms.

When Ordinary Least Squares (OLS) is employed to obtain estimates of the parameters of (1.9), we obtain expression (1.10):

$$\widehat{\beta} = \left(X'X\right)^{-1}X'y. \tag{1.10}$$

When OLS is employed to obtain estimates of the parameter in a model, several assumptions about the model elements in (1.8) need to be satisfied. Four of these concern the disturbance term:

1. E $(\varepsilon_t) = 0$ for all t;
2. $\text{Var}(\varepsilon_t) = \sigma^2$ for all t;
3. $\text{Cov}(\varepsilon_t, \varepsilon_{t'}) = 0$ for $t \neq t'$;
4. ε_t is normally distributed.

Two other assumptions are:

5. There is no relation between the predictors and ε_t, i.e. Cov $(x_t, \varepsilon_t) = 0$ (one variable case). In other words the x_t are nonstochastic, exogenous or "fixed". For the K-variable case this implies Cov $(X', \varepsilon) = 0$, in which case we have E $(\varepsilon|X) = \text{E}(\varepsilon) = 0$. If the covariance between the disturbance term and an independent variable is not zero, we encounter the problem of endogeneity (Chap. 18).
6. For the K-variable case, the matrix of observations X has full rank, which is the case if the columns in X are linearly independent. This means that none of the independent variables is constant, and that there are no exact linear relationships among the independent variables.

If conditions 2 and 3 are both satisfied, Var(ε) has the following structure:

$$\text{Var}(\varepsilon) = \sigma^2 I \tag{1.11}$$

where I is a $T \times T$ – identity matrix. If assumptions 1 and 5 hold, the OLS estimate for β is unbiased, which means that its expected value equals β. The OLS-estimator of β is "optimal" if the assumptions 1–6 are satisfied. Violations of any of the assumptions leads to invalid statistical inferences. In these cases, we need other estimator methods such as Generalized Least Squares (GLS): GLS-methods allow for more general disturbance characteristics. Specifically GLS can accommodate violations of at least one of the assumptions 2 and 3. Consider again model (1.9). We modify (1.9) into (1.12):

$$y = X\beta + u \tag{1.12}$$

where we now use u instead of ε to denote the disturbances to indicate that the assumptions may not all be satisfied. The variance-covariance matrix of the disturbances is now defined as:

$$\text{E}\left(uu'\right) = \Omega \tag{1.13}$$

where

$$\Omega = \begin{pmatrix} \omega_{11} & \cdots & \omega_{1T} \\ \vdots & \ddots & \vdots \\ \omega_{T1} & \cdots & \omega_{TT} \end{pmatrix} = \sigma^2 \Omega^*$$

which is a positive definite symmetric $T \times T$ matrix with full rank T, and where the ω_{ij} are the covariances of the disturbances. Assumptions 2 and 3 are satisfied if $\Omega^* = I$, where I is a $T \times T$ identity matrix. However, if this is not the case, we obtain the following expression for the generalized least squares estimator of β:

$$\widehat{\beta}_{GLS} = \left(X'\left(\Omega^*\right)^{-1}X\right)^{-1} X'\left(\Omega^*\right)^{-1} y. \tag{1.14}$$

This model and estimation method are "generalized" because other models can be obtained as special cases. The ordinary least squares estimator is one such special case in which $\Omega = \sigma^2 I$. If Ω is unknown, as it is in empirical work, we replace Ω by $\widehat{\Omega}$ and use an Estimated Generalized Least Squares (EGLS) estimator (also called Feasible Generalized Least Squares (FGLS) estimator). This estimator is usually a two-stage estimator. In the first stage, the OLS-estimates are used to define residuals, and these residuals are used to estimate Ω. This estimate of Ω is used in the second stage to obtain the EGLS estimator denoted by $\widehat{\beta}_{GLS}$.

GLS can be applied when the disturbances are *heteroscedastic* and/or *autocorrelated*. *Heteroscedasticity* means that a subset of the observations have variance σ_1^2

and another subset has a different variance σ_2^2. Such a setting is often encountered when data from different cross-sections are used.

A second special case of GLS, *disturbance autocorrelation*, is typical for time series data. In this case, the covariances, $\mathrm{Cov}(u_t, u_{t'})$, $t \neq t'$ differ from zero (but we assume that the disturbances are homoscedastic). We consider the case that the disturbances are generated by a first-order autoregressive scheme, also called a first-order stationary (Markov) scheme, as in (1.16):

$$u_t = \rho u_{t-1} + \varepsilon_t, \qquad t = 1, \ldots, T, \qquad |\rho_j| < 1 \tag{1.16}$$

where the ε_t are independent normally distributed random variables with mean zero, and variance equal to σ_ε^2. We also assume ε_t to be independent of u_{t-1}. When time series of multiple cross-sections are available, the autoregressive parameter (ρ) will probably differ across the cross sections and each cross section will have a unique ρ_i, $i = 1, \ldots, N$, where N is the number of cross-sections. Specification and estimation of a specific matrix Ω and applying GLS will lead to unbiased and consistent parameter estimates.

One may also relax the assumption that the disturbances are independent between the cross sections, which implies that there is contemporaneous correlation between the disturbances. Hence, if we assume:

$$\mathrm{E}\left(u_{it}^{\,2}\right) = \sigma_i^2 \text{ for all } t, \text{ (heteroscedasticity)} \tag{1.17}$$

$$\mathrm{Cov}\left(u_{it}, u_{js}\right) \neq 0 \text{ for all } t \neq s \text{ and al } i \text{ and } j, \text{ (autocorrelation)} \tag{1.18}$$

$$\mathrm{Cov}\left(u_{it}, u_{jt}\right) = \sigma_{ij} \text{ for all } t \left(= \sigma_i^2 \text{ if } i = j\right). \tag{1.19}$$

We obtain the following specification of the variance-covariance matrix of the disturbances:

$$\mathrm{E}\left(uu'\right) = \Omega = \begin{pmatrix} \sigma_1^2 P_{11} & \sigma_{12} P_{12} & \ldots & \sigma_{1N} P_{1N} \\ \sigma_{21} P_{21} & \sigma_2^2 P_{22} & \ldots & \sigma_{2N} P_{2N} \\ \vdots & \vdots & \ddots & \vdots \\ \sigma_{N1} P_{N1} & \sigma_{N2} P_{N2} & \ldots & \sigma_N^2 P_{NN} \end{pmatrix} \tag{1.20}$$

where u now has dimension $NT \times 1$, Ω is a $NT \times NT$ matrix, and

$$P_{ij} = \begin{pmatrix} 1 & \rho_j & \ldots & \rho_j^{T-1} \\ \rho_i & 1 & \ldots & \rho_j^{T-2} \\ \vdots & \vdots & \ddots & \vdots \\ \rho_i^{T-1} & \rho_i^{T-2} & \ldots & 1 \end{pmatrix} \quad \textit{for } i, j = 1, \ldots, N.$$

Until now we only discussed violations of the 2nd and 3rd assumption. Violation of assumption 4 (the ε_t are normally distributed) requires usually a transformation of y_t (ln y_t or other transformations by Box and Cox 1964) and so-called robust regression methods are applied.

Violation of the 5th assumption (correlation between predictors and disturbances) leads to endogeneity, which leaves the least squares parameter estimates biased and inconsistent. In Chaps. 15 and 18 we discuss endogeneity in more detail and propose remedies, where the use of Generalized Method of Moments (GMM) and Instrumental Variables estimation (IV) are frequently used estimation methods.

Finally, we discussed the consequences of violations of assumption 6 (no exact relation between the predictors) in Vol. I, Sect. 5.2.6. These consequences, known as multicollinearity problems, can be addressed by several procedures which are discussed in Vol. I, Sect. 5.2.6.

1.4.1.2 Maximum Likelihood Estimation (MLE)

The principle of Maximum Likelihood, due to Fisher (1922), provides a statistical framework for assessing the information available in the data. The principle of maximum likelihood is based on distributional assumptions about the data.

Suppose that we have N random variables $\{Y_1,\ldots,Y_N\}$ with observations that are denoted as $\{y_1,\ldots, y_N\}$, such as purchase frequencies for a sample of N subjects. Let $f(y_i|\theta)$ denote the probability density function for Y_i, where θ is a parameter characterizing the distribution (we assume θ to be a scalar for convenience).

The Maximum Likelihood principle is an estimation principle that finds an estimate for one or more unknown parameters (say θ) such that it maximizes the likelihood of observing the data $y = \{y_1, \ldots, y_N\}$. The Likelihood of a model (L) can be interpreted as the probability of the observed data y, given that model. A certain parameter value θ_1 is more likely than another, θ_2, in light of the observed data, if it makes observing those data more probable (Cameron and Trivedi 2009, p. 139). In that case, the θ_1 will result in a larger value of the likelihood than θ_2: so that $L(\theta_1) > L(\theta_2)$. In the discrete case, this likelihood is the *probability* obtained from the probability mass function; in the continuous case this is the density.

The probability of observing y_i is provided by the *pf* or *pdf*: $f\,(y_i \mid \theta)$. When the variables for the N subjects are assumed independent, the joint density function of all observations is the product of the densities over i. This gives the following expression for the likelihood:

$$L(\theta) = \prod_{i=1}^{N} f\,(y_i|\theta)\,. \tag{1.21}$$

Note that we present the likelihood as a function of the unknown parameter θ; the data is considered as given.

This formulation holds for both discrete and continuous random variables. *Discrete random variables* are for example 0/1 choices, or purchase frequencies, while market shares and brand sales can be considered as continuous random variables. Important characteristics of these random variables are their expectations and variances. In the purchase frequency example usually a (discrete) Poisson distribution is assumed (see Chap. 2):

$$Y_i \sim f\ (y_i|\lambda) = \frac{e^{-\lambda}\lambda^{y_i}}{y_i!}. \tag{1.22}$$

The expectation of the Poisson variable in (1.22) can be shown to be $E(Y_i) = \lambda$, and its variance is $Var(Y_i) = \lambda$.

One of the well-known *continuous* distributions is the exponential distribution:

$$Y_i \sim f\ (y_i|\mu) = \mu e^{-\mu y_i}. \tag{1.23}$$

The mean and variance of the exponential random variable in (1.23) are $E(Y_i) = 1/\mu$ and $Var(Y_i) = 1/\mu^2$. This distribution is frequently used for interpurchase times.[3] The functions in (1.22) and (1.23) are known as the probability function (*pf*) and probability density function (*pdf*), respectively. Both the exponential and the Poisson distributions belong to the Exponential Family, which is a general family of distributions that encompasses both discrete and continuous distributions.[4]

If f belongs to the exponential family, the expression for the likelihood in (1.21) simplifies considerably after taking the natural logarithm. The product in (1.21) is replaced by a sum:

$$l(\theta) = \sum\nolimits_{i=1}^{N} \ln f\ (y_i|\theta). \tag{1.24}$$

Since the natural logarithm is a monotonic function, maximizing the log-likelihood $l(\theta)$ in Eq. (1.24) yields the same estimates as maximizing the likelihood $L(\theta)$ in Eq. (1.21).

In the Poisson example, the log-likelihood takes a simple form, as the Poisson distribution belongs to the exponential family:

$$l(\lambda) = \ln\left(\prod_{i=1}^{N} \frac{e^{-\lambda}\lambda^{y_i}}{y_i!}\right) \tag{1.25}$$

$$= -N\lambda + \ln\lambda \sum_{i=1}^{N} y_i - \sum_{i=1}^{N} \ln\ (y_i!). \tag{1.26}$$

---

[3]Gupta (1991). See also Vol. I, Sect. 8.4 and Chap. 2.

[4]Cameron and Trivedi (2009, pp. 147–149). See also Vol. I, Sect. 6.4.1 and Chap. 2 in this volume.

The ML estimator of λ is obtained by setting the derivatives of the log-likelihood equal to zero:

$$\frac{\delta l(\lambda)}{\delta\lambda} = -N + \frac{1}{\lambda}\sum_{i=1}^{N} y_i = 0. \tag{1.27}$$

Solving (1.27) provides the Maximum Likelihood Estimator (MLE) for λ:

$$\widehat{\lambda} = \frac{1}{N}\sum_{i=1}^{N} y_i \tag{1.28}$$

which is the sample mean.

Similarly, in the example of the exponential distribution, the log-likelihood is:

$$l(\mu) = N \ln \mu - \mu \sum_{i=1}^{N} y_i. \tag{1.29}$$

Setting the derivative of (1.29) with respect to μ to zero, and solving to μ yields the estimator:

$$\widehat{\mu} = \frac{N}{\sum_{i=1}^{N} y_i} \tag{1.30}$$

which is the inverse of the sample mean.

One of the benefits of MLE is that it has attractive large sample properties. Under fairly general conditions, MLEs:

1. are consistent;
2. have asymptotically minimum variance;
3. are asymptotically normal.

1.4.2 Estimation Methods that Use "Other" Identification and Validation Criteria

The models that we discuss below can be estimated, at least in principle, by OLS/GLS and MLE. The identification and validation of these models differs substantially from those which are usually used to test error-term and other model assumptions. We introduce briefly

- time series;
- state space models;
- spatial models.

See also Table 1.2.

Table 1.2 Estimation and specification

GLM (General Linear Model)			
OLS	$y = X\beta + u$	$\longleftrightarrow$	u satisfies 6 conditions
(1) *GLS*	$y = X\beta + u \quad u_t = \rho\, u_{t-1} + \varepsilon_t$	$\longleftrightarrow$	Autocorrelation $\longrightarrow$ GLS
(2) *GLS*	$(1) + \sigma_i^2 \neq \sigma_j^2$	$\longleftrightarrow$	Heteroscedasticity $\longrightarrow$ GLS
(3) *GLS*	$(1) + \text{Cov}\,(u_{it}, u_{jt}) \neq 0$	$\longleftrightarrow$	SUR $\longrightarrow$ GLS
Dynamic Models			
(4) *Univariate time series*	$y_t = \mu + \Phi\, y_{t-1} + \varepsilon_t$		
(5) *Multivariate time series*	$y_t = c + \sum_{i=1} \rho_i\, y_{t-1} + \sum_{j=1} x_{t-j} + u_t$		
(6) *Spatial models*	$y = \partial W y + X\beta + W x\theta + u \quad u = \lambda W u + \varepsilon$		
MLE (Maximum Likelihood Estimation)			
State Space Models	$y_t = \alpha + \beta_{1t}\, x_{it} + \beta_{2t}\, y_{t-1} + u_t$ $\beta_{1t} = \beta_{2,t-1} + v_t$ $\beta_{2t} = \beta_0 + \beta_3\, x_{2t} + \mu_t$, *etc.*	$\longleftarrow$	Kalman filters Kalman smoothers

1.4.2.1 Time Series

We discuss time series in two chapters of this volume. In Chap. 3 we consider the single-equation, i.e. "traditional" time series models and Chap. 4 discusses multiple-equation, i.e. "modern" time series models. The traditional time series deal with the specification and estimation of individual (univariate and multivariate) relations. Multiple time series models constitute dynamic systems of relations.

Time series models are uniquely suited to capture the time dependence of both a criterion variable (e.g. sales) and predictor variables (marketing actions) and how they relate to each other over time. The difference between dynamic models that model lag and lead effects (see Vol. I, Sect. 2.8) and time series models is that the latter models are able to choose the model that best fits the data, often combined with the principle of parsimony (i.e. using the simplest model) (Pickup 2015). In the univariate models the patterns in data on a criterion variable (y_t) as a function of its own past are described. As an example we specify Eq. (1.31):

$$y_t = \mu + \varphi y_{t-1} + \varepsilon_t \tag{1.31}$$

where μ is a constant and ε_t is a disturbance term.

This model states that sales (y_t) in period t are determined by sales in the previous period t-1. In principle, this model can be estimated by OLS or GLS. In time series analyses, however, this co-called ARIMA model is identified from the data, using important statistics such as the autocorrelation function (ACF) and partial autocorrelation function (PACF). Hence time series models are identified and also validated using other statistical criteria.

Eq. (1.31) can be extended including (R) endogenous variables (x_{rt}, $r = 1, \ldots, R$), which also may have their own dynamic history.

In multiple time series models,

1. dual causalities between "predictor" and "criterion" variables;
2. feedback effects;
3. relations between endogenous variables, etc.,

i.e. dynamic systems, are modeled. These systems of relations are known as VAR, VARX and Vector Error Correction models. Moreover, these models are *estimated* using *GLS-methods*, but again here the statistical criteria to identify and validate these systems that are used differ from other specifications that also deal with simultaneous equation systems (see Vol. I, Sect. 6.5).

1.4.2.2 State Space Models

The state space model is mostly used to specify time series. Where the time series models (Chap. 3) remove trend(s), seasonal influences, interventions, etc., state space models explicitly model these components along with other relevant influences. We give a brief introduction of these models using a modification of Eq. (1.7) as a starting point. To this end we specify (1.32):

$$y_t = \alpha + \beta_{1t} x_{1t} + \beta_{2t} y_{t-1} + \varepsilon_t. \tag{1.32}$$

Eq. (1.7) assumes that all parameters are constant. In state space models such as Eq. (1.32) one may that β_{1t} is dynamic and can be specified as:

$$\beta_{1t} = \beta_{1,t-1} + v_t \tag{1.33}$$

where v_t is a random disturbance term. Additionally we may assume that β_2 is a time-varying parameter and depends on another variable, which in its turn is explained by a third predictor, etc. Hence we get:

$$\beta_{2t} = \beta_0 + \beta_3 x_{2t} + \mu_t \tag{1.34}$$

where μ_t is a random disturbance term. In Chap. 5 it is demonstrated how the state space model can be cast in state space form. Usually a distinction is made between the *observation* or *measurement* equation and *state* or *transition* equation. Eq. (1.32) is an example of an observation equation and (1.33) and (1.34) are examples of transition/state equations.

The state space models are estimated using so-called Kalman filters and Kalman smoothers which are iterated *log-likelihood estimation methods*. The state space models offer several advantages over and above specifications such as (1.7). They allow:

- univariate and multivariate indicators (like the VAR/VARX models);
- for missing values;
- unequally spaced time series observations;
- unobserved variables;
- time-varying coefficients, and
- non-stationarity.

We discuss and illustrate state space models in Chap. 5.

1.4.2.3 Spatial Models

Spatial models are based on "the first law of geography" that "everything is related to everything else but near things are more related to each other". This violates the assumption of OLS that observations are independent of one another. Violations lead to biased and inconsistent parameter estimators with wrong estimated standard deviations.

An econometric model becomes spatial if the behavior of one economic agent (y_i) is determined by that of others (y_j, $j \neq i$). This can be done through criterion variables, predictors and/or the error term, as is explained in more detail in Chap. 6. Examples of economic agents are suppliers (firms, retailers, etc.) and customers.

The mutual relationships between economic agents is commonly modeled by the spatial weights matrix W. A full model capturing all types of spatial interaction effects takes the form:

$$y = \delta Wy + X\beta + WX\theta + u \tag{1.35}$$

$$u = \lambda Wu + \varepsilon \tag{1.36}$$

which is an extension of (1.9) with the following terms:

δWy = represents the relation between the criterion variables of different agents,
$WX\theta$ = the relation between predictors of other agents on y, and
λWu = represents the interaction effects among the disturbance terms of the different units.

The parameters δ are known as spatial autoregressive coefficients and λ represents the spatial autocorrelation coefficient.

As an example, δWy may represent the interactions between the (buyer) behavior of different customers who buy a certain brand. The part of (1.34) which is represented by $WX\theta$ represents for example the prices of the brands paid by the "other" consumers. Relation (1.35) represents the effects of omitted variables which are connected to different agents.

The system of relations (1.35) and (1.36) nests a number of specific spatial models for which δ and/or θ and/or λ are zero. Spatial models are estimated using MLE and Bayesian estimation methods.

The attention for spatial models has been increased in the past 15 years due to the interest in the effects of word-of-mouth among customers, neighborhood effects, contagion, imitation, network diffusion and the explicitation of interdependent preferences.

1.5 Modeling with Latent Variables

Four chapters in this book deal with latent variables (Part III). We first discuss structural equation modeling (SEM). Structural equation models are models for the analysis of relationships among observed and unobserved/latent variables. Examples of latent variables are intentions, attitudes, subjective norms, satisfaction, gratitude, etc. Many concepts that are of interest to researchers (in marketing, but also many other researchers) can only be assessed indirectly through fallible observed measures and underlying constructs. SEM offers the opportunity to connect latent variables to observed measures. Researchers investigating possibly complex patterns of relationships between multiple constructs across several layers can use SEM to test the plausibility of their theories based on empirical data. SEM has two major branches:

- covariance-based SEM (CBSEM) which is discussed in Chap. 11;
- variance-based SEM (PLS, see Chap. 12).

We first briefly introduce CBSEM. The relationships among the observed (manifest) variables are reflected in the covariances among them.[5] Those covariances form the basis for the estimation of a SEM that describes the relations among variables according to a set of hypotheses. Importantly CBSEM focuses on describing the covariances between the variables, which are described in the matrix $\sum$.

The structural equation model attempts to reproduce the covariances among the variables as accurately as possible with a set of parameters, θ, where the fundamental hypothesis is: $\sum = \sum(\theta)$. $\sum(\theta)$ is called the *implied covariance matrix*.

The structural equation model comprises two submodels. The first is called *measurement model*, the second the *structural model*. The measurement model relates the observed indicators to a set of unobserved, or latent variables. This part of the model is also called a confirmatory factor model, if it is considered in isolation. The measurement models for the endogenous and exogenous indicator variables are formulated in a general form respectively as:

$$y = \Lambda_y \eta + \varepsilon \tag{1.37}$$

$$x = \Lambda_x \xi + \delta \tag{1.38}$$

where

y = a $(p \times 1)$ vector of manifest endogenous variables,
η = a $(m \times 1)$ vector containing the latent endogenous variables (i.e. the variables that are explained within the model),
Λ_y = the $(p \times m)$ matrix of loadings, showing which manifest variable loads on which latent exogenous variable,
ε = a vector of error terms with expectation zero, and uncorrelated with η,
x = a $(q \times 1)$ vector of manifest exogenous variables,
ξ = a $(n \times 1)$ vector of latent exogenous variables (i.e. variables that explain the model),
Λ_x = the $(q \times n)$ matrix of loadings, showing which manifest variable loads on which latent exogenous variable, and
δ = a vector of error terms uncorrelated with ξ and expectation zero.

The y and x-vectors contain the same variables as y and X in (1.9). The variables in (1.9) are now connected to latent variables.

The *structural part* of the model captures the relationships between exogenous and endogenous variables:

$$\eta = B\eta + \Gamma\xi + \zeta. \tag{1.39}$$

---

[5] This text is based on Leeflang et al. (2000, pp. 442–444).

The $(m \times m)$ matrix B specifies the relationships among the m latent endogenous variables. Its diagonal equals zero (since the endogenous variables cannot affect themselves). If B is a lower triangular matrix, there are no reciprocal causal effects (e.g. η_1 influences η_2 but not vice versa), and the structural model is said to be recursive. The $(m \times n)$ matrix Γ captures the effects of the exogenous variables on the endogenous variables, and ζ is a vector of disturbances with expectation zero and uncorrelated with the endogenous and exogenous latent variables. The error terms may be correlated and have a $(m \times m)$ covariance matrix denoted by ψ.

The sample covariances between the observed variables (y, x) are used as an estimate of $\sum$, and $\sum\left(\widehat{\theta}\right) = \widehat{\sum}$ is the estimate of the covariance matrix $\sum(\theta)$ obtained from the parameter estimates. Although several estimation procedures are available, *maximum likelihood estimation* based on the assumption of *multivariate normality* of the observed variables is often the default method of choice (see Chap. 11). ML estimation does also assume that the sample size is substantial. Partial Least Squares (PLS) (Chap. 12) is an alternative estimation technique that relaxes these assumptions.

PLS is a variance-based SEM that combines factor analysis *and* multiple *regression analysis*. Compared to covariance-based SEMs, PLS-SEM allows for non-normal data and smaller samples.

PLS is also said to be a powerful method of analysis because of the minimal demands on measurement scales (i.e. do measures need to be at an interval or ratio level?) (Chin 1998).

PLS is also the method of choice if the hypothesized model contains composites (see Chap. 12).It has been proven that CBSEM outperforms PLS in terms of parameter consistency and is preferable in terms of parameter accuracy as long as the sample exceeds a threshold of 250 observation (Reinartz et al. 2009). PLS analysis should be preferred when the emphasis is on theory development and prediction. Reinartz et al. (2009) demonstrate that the statistical power of PLS is always larger than or equal to that of CBSEM and that already 100 observations can be sufficient to achieve acceptable levels of statistical power given a certain quality of the measurement model.[6]

Heterogeneity has become a very important topic in the marketing literature. Hete. particularly refers to differences in consumer behavior among consumers but also to suppliers (brands, retailers) in the sense that offers can be considered as competitive and non-competitive. A very common categorization concerns the allocation of customers to different segments, where needs and wants differ across segments (Wedel and Kamakura 2000). Mixture models are models that assume the existence of a number of (unobserved: "latent") heterogeneous groups of individuals in a population. These groups differ with respect to the parameters of a statistical model. These unobserved groups are referred to as mixture components or *latent* classes. In Chap. 13 we discuss several mixture model where most attention is given

[6]There is much debate about advantages and disadvantages of CBSEM and PLS. See, e.g., McIntosh et al. (2014) and Rönkkö et al. (2016).

to so-called mixture regression models. These models simultaneously allow for the classification of a sample into groups, as well as for the estimation of a regression model within each of these groups.

The fourth topic that deals with "latent variables" is Hidden Markov-Models, which have already been briefly introduced in Vol. I, Sect. 8.2.4.2. In these models one models the transitions of customers from "state" to "state". States may refer to the relation customers have with a brand/retailer ranging from very weak to very strong, or from awareness via awareness, interest, desire to action. These states are unobserved (or *latent*). Hidden Markov Models are able to estimate states and state transitions using a Maximum Likelihood or Markov Chain Monte Carlo (MCMC) hierarchical Bayes estimation procedure (see Chap. 16) Given the recent attention in marketing for the description and prediction of customer journeys these models become highly relevant.

1.6 "Other" Estimation Methods

In the preceding sections we briefly touched on a number of estimation methods which go beyond GM and MLE, such as Kalman filters and Kalman smoothers, which are iterated ML-estimation methods. In Part IV of this book we discuss a number of "other" estimation methods.

We start (Chap. 15) with the General Method of Moments (GMM). GMM estimates m parameters of a model using m moment conditions. The idea of GMM is to estimate the sample mean, the variance, the 3rd, 4th, ..., mth moment and solve the system of m equations to obtain parameters. Although (as is pointed out in Chap. 15) MLE is "the gold standard" in estimation. GMM is used when researchers are not able to confidently specify the entire model completely. MLE delivers estimators that are consistent, asymptotically normal and asymptotically efficient, and MLE gives more precise results than GMM does. Researchers have to make a trade-off between GMM and MLE because of the higher precision offered by MLE and the inconsistency of estimators when some elements of the model happen to be misspecified. GMM is a quite general estimation method and nests many special cases such as SEM and Instrumental Variables (IV) estimation.

Bayesian analysis (Chap. 16) allows decision makers to bring (prior/subjective) knowledge to the analysis that goes beyond the (observed/objective) data. Unlike most other statistical approaches, Bayesian analysis can be performed sequentially with regular model updates as new data arrive. In Chap. 16 attention is spent to:

- hierarchical modeling and hierarchical Bayes;
- Markov Chain Monte Carlo (MCMC) methods (including Gibbs sampling).

The beauty of Bayesian analysis is that the approach of combining a priori beliefs about phenomena with observed data can be applied to nearly any model and estimation method that we discuss in this monograph: SEM, choice models, state space models, instrumental variables, SUR models, mixture models, etc.

Many models in marketing are "parametric": Parametric models impose a mathematical function that links the variables, and this mathematical function contains parameters that have to be estimated. The most common types of mathematical terms are[7]:

1. linear in both parameters and variables;
2. nonlinear in the variables, but linear in the parameters;
3. nonlinear in the parameters and linearizable;
4. nonlinear in the parameters and not linearizable.

The last set of (intrinsically nonlinear) relations can be estimated by nonlinear estimation techniques.[8] Even the non-linearizable models may be inappropriate to represent relations between endogenous and exogenous variables.

To explore the functional form it may be useful to consider non- and semi-parametric regression models in these cases. We discuss these opportunities in Chap. 17. Other semi-parametric approaches are discussed in Chap. 15 (GMM).

Endogeneity results from a correlation between predictors and the disturbance term in Eqs. such as (1.7). Endogeneity results from a violation of assumption 5, specified in Sect. 1.4.1.1. The correlation between the error term and regressors will lead to inconsistent estimates of the regression coefficients and potentially erroneous conclusions.

The standard approach to deal with endogeneity is to use: (1) the instrumental variable approach (IV).[9] To introduce IV estimation formally, we return to (1.8). When we use IV estimation the matrix X is substituted by a matrix Z such that $E(Z'\varepsilon) = 0$. Thus, every column of the new matrix Z is uncorrelated with ε, and every linear combination of the columns of Z is uncorrelated with ε. The instrumental variables in Z are, however, correlated with the endogenous regressors. If Z has the same number of predictor variables as X, the IV estimator is:

$$\widehat{\beta_{IV}} = \left(Z'X\right)^{-1}Z'y. \tag{1.40}$$

There are several options to choose Z. Of all the different linear combinations of Z that we might choose:

$$\widehat{X} = Z\left(Z'Z\right)^{-1}Z'X \tag{1.41}$$

turns out to be the most efficient:

$$\widehat{\beta_{IV}} = \left(\widehat{X}'\widehat{X}\right)^{-1}\widehat{X}'y. \tag{1.42}$$

---

[7]See Vol. I, Sect. 2.4.

[8]See, for example Judge et al. (1985, Sect. 15.7).

[9]We closely follow Leeflang et al. (2015, pp. 205–206).

This procedure to obtain an IV estimator is also known as Two-Stage Least Squares (2SLS/TSLS).

1. Other estimation approaches that are used to reduce endogeneity are;
2. the Control Function approach;
3. the Limited Information Maximum Likelihood (LIML) approach, which estimates simultaneously a set of equations;
4. latent instrumental variables (LIV);
5. Gaussian copulas (adding a copula term to the model that represents the correlation between the endogenous regressor and the error term);
6. spatial models (Chap. 6).

The IV-related methods (1)–(3) perform equally well as is demonstrated through simulation in Chap. 18. The IV-free methods (4)–(6) rely on different conditions that are not always satisfied and they may be appropriate for specific problems.

1.7 Machine Learning Methods

In Chapter 19 we focus on several estimation methods that are gaining popularity in data-rich environments. These estimation methods, originating from computer science, are collectively indicated as Machine Learning methods. Machine learning methods include several methods that were discussed in Vol. I and in the present book, such as regression, logit models, etc., but also include procedures that are relative new to our field, such as Support Vector Machines, Neural Networks and Random Forests.

In Chap. 19 we focus those Machine learning algorithms that were not discussed in other parts of this book or in Vol. I. The algorithms that are discussed in Chap. 19 deviate from the other models in the book on a couple of dimensions. First of all, these models typically have a prediction focus only. For several of these models, the researcher is typically not interested in explaining why certain variables are affecting the dependent variable, or how strong this effect is. The goal is to maximize the prediction accuracy. Secondly, we focus on models that are used for classifying objects (in most applications customers) into groups, for example distinguishing customers that are churning from customers that stay with a focal company. Thirdly, not all models have a statistical bases. Several of the models classify objects based on deterministic algorithms. The chapter concludes with a practical example where we compare the performance of eight Machine Learning algorithms.

References

Box, G.E.P., Cox, D.R.: An analysis of transformations. J. R. Stat. Soc. B. **26**, 211–252 (1964)

Cameron, A.C., Trivedi, P.K.: Microeconometrics Using Stata. Stata Press, College Station (2009)

Chin, W.W.: Commentary: Issues and opinion on structural equation modeling. MIS Q. **22**, 7–16 (1998)

Fisher, R.A.: On the mathematical foundations of theoretical statistics. Philos. Trans. R. Soc. Lond. **222**, 309–368 (1922)

Gupta, S.: Stochastic models of interpurchase time with time dependent covariates. J. Mark. Res. **28**, 1–15 (1991)

Hayes, A.F.: Introduction to Mediation, Moderation, and Conditional Process Analysis: A Regression-Based Approach. The Guilford Press, New York (2013)

Judge, G.G., Griffiths, W.E., Hill, R.C., Lüthkepohl, H., Lee, T.C.: The Theory and Practice of Econometrics, 2nd edn. Wiley, New York (1985)

Leeflang, P.S.H., Wittink, D.R., Wedel, M., Naert, P.A.: Building Models for Marketing Decisions, pp. 442–444. Kluwer Academic, Boston (2000)

Leeflang, P.S.H.: Paving the way for distinguished marketing. Int. J. Res. Mark. **28**, 76–88 (2011)

Leeflang, P.S.H., Verhoef, P.C., Dahlstrom, P., Freundt, T.: Challenges and solutions for marketing in a digital era. Eur. Manag. J. **32**, 1–12 (2014)

Leeflang, P.S.H., Wieringa, J.E., Bijmolt, T.H.A., Pauwels, K.H.: Modeling Markets. Analyzing Marketing Phenomena and Improving Marketing Decision Making. Springer, New York (2015)

Little, J.D.C.: Models and managers: the concept of a decision calculus. Manag. Sci. **16**, 1–466 (1970)

MacKinnon, D.P.: Introduction to Statistical Mediation Analysis. Lawrence Erlbaum Associates, New York (2008)

McIntosh, C.N., Edwards, J.R., Antonakis, J.: Reflections on partial least squares path modeling. Organ. Res. Methods. **17**, 210–251 (2014)

Nijs, V.R., Srinivasan, S., Pauwels, K.H.: Retail-price drivers and retailer profits. Mark. Sci. **26**, 473–487 (2007)

Pickup, M.: Introduction to Time Series Analysis. Sage, Los Angeles (2015)

Reinartz, W., Haenlein, M., Henseler, J.: An empirical comparison of the efficacy of covariance-based and variance-based SEM. Int. J. Res. Mark. **26**, 332–344 (2009)

Rönkkö, M., McIntosh, C.N., Antonakis, J., Edwards, J.R.: Partial least squares path modeling: time for some serious second thoughts. J. Oper. Manag. **47–48**, 9–27 (2016)

Verhoef, P.C., Kooge, E., Walk, N.: Creating Value with Big Data Analytics. Rootledge, New York (2016)

Wedel, M., Kamakura, W.A.: Market Segmentation: Conceptual and Methodological Foundations. In: International Series in Quantitative Marketing, vol. **8**, Springer, New York (2000)

Wooldridge, J.M.: Introductory Econometrics: A Modern Approach, 5th edn. Cengage Learning, Mason (2012)

Part II
Specification

Chapter 2
Advanced Individual Demand Models

Dennis Fok

2.1 Introduction

Decisions of individuals are central to almost all marketing questions. In some cases, it is most sensible to model these decisions at an aggregate level, for example, using models for sales or market shares (see, for example, Chap. 7 in Vol. I). In many other cases, it is the behavior of the individuals themselves that are the key object of interest. For example, we can think of modeling the decisions of customers at a retailer (Mela et al. 1997; Zhang and Wedel 2009), modeling the behavior of website visitors (Montgomery et al. 2004), or modeling choices made by customers of an insurance firm (Donkers et al. 2007).

In this chapter we focus on models that are useful to describe, understand, and predict demand at the individual level. Underlying the individual-level demand of a customer are several decisions: what product to buy, what brand to choose, and how much to buy. The models discussed in this chapter can be used to describe such decisions by themselves, or several decisions in combination. We will use the word "demand" in a broad sense. The models also apply to settings where the decisions that are made do not directly correspond to purchases. For example, the decision to click on a certain banner advertising or not can also be modeled using the techniques discussed in this chapter. Chap. 8 in Vol. I discusses individual demand models at a more introductory level. This chapter continues the discussion about these models at a more advanced level.

This chapter is organized as follows. In Sect. 2.2 we first give a recap of the logit and probit model, as these are the basic building blocks in many more advanced models. In this section we in turn discuss the binary logit, binary probit, and

D. Fok (✉)
Econometric Institute, Erasmus School of Economics, Erasmus University Rotterdam, Rotterdam, The Netherlands
e-mail: dfok@ese.eur.nl

P.S.H. Leeflang et al. (eds.), *Advanced Methods for Modeling Markets*,
International Series in Quantitative Marketing, DOI 10.1007/978-3-319-53469-5_2

multinomial choice models. Section 2.3 develops the nested logit model and the generalized nested logit model. In order to discuss the latter model, we also present the theory behind the class of Generalized Extreme Value models. In Sect. 2.4 we deal with ordered dependent variables, that is, cases where the dependent variable can take on only few distinct values and where there is a clear ordering in these values. The two most popular models here are the ordered logit and ordered probit model. Sections 2.5 and 2.6 discuss models for variables that have a discrete as well as a continuous aspect. These models have three types of applications: correcting for sample selection, dealing with censored dependent variables, and describing corner solutions. An example of the latter case is a model to describe the decision to buy something together with the decision of how much to buy. For almost all models a detailed example is also presented. All these examples are based on the literature. In Sect. 2.7 we mention some related topics and in Sect. 2.8 we briefly discuss available software.

2.2 Recap of Choice Modeling[1]

2.2.1 *Binary Logit and Probit Models*

The basic choice model describes whether a customer does or does not do something. This can refer to various decisions, such as canceling a contract, buying a product, or donating to a charity. For simplicity, we will discuss the models in the context of buying a product. In general, the dependent variable is denoted by Y_i, where $Y_i = 1$ indicates that customer i bought the product, and $Y_i = 0$ indicates that she did not buy the product. In principle repeated observations over time can be available for the same individual. However, in the notation we will stick to a single index i.

The two most popular models are the logit and probit model. Keeping in mind the more advanced models that are discussed in later sections, it is best to consider the so-called latent variable representation for these models. In both models, it is assumed that an unobserved, latent, variable U_i drives the buying decision of individual i. This latent variable can be interpreted as the (indirect) utility of the product. The utility follows a linear specification:

$$U_i = \alpha + x_i'\beta + \varepsilon_i \tag{2.1}$$

where x_i is a vector of characteristics of the product or customer, α is the intercept, β is a vector of coefficients, and ε_i represents the error term, that is, the unexplained part of the utility. The vector of characteristics usually contains the price of the product. The utility U_i and the decision Y_i are linked to each other by the following rule:

[1] See also Sect. 8.2 in Vol. I.

$$Y_i = \begin{cases} 0 \text{ if } U_i \leq 0 \\ 1 \text{ if } U_i > 0. \end{cases} \tag{2.2}$$

It is important to note that the error term is a part of the utility that is known to the customer. So, from the customer's point of view the decision in Eq. (2.2) is not stochastic. However, for someone who is analyzing the decisions, ε_i is not observed and we therefore treat the decision as a random variable.

If we assume that ε_i is independently distributed according to distribution function $F(\cdot)$, we can write the probability of observing customer i buying the product as:

$$\begin{aligned} \Pr[Y_i = 1] &= \Pr[U_i > 0] = \Pr\left[\alpha + x_i'\beta + \varepsilon_i > 0\right] \\ &= \Pr\left[\varepsilon_i > -\alpha - x_i'\beta\right] = 1 - F\left(-\alpha - x_i'\beta\right). \end{aligned} \tag{2.3}$$

There are two common choices for the distribution of ε_i. One typically either assumes that ε_i has a logistic distribution, or one assumes a normal distribution. The distribution function of the logistic distribution equals:

$$\Lambda(z) = \frac{\exp(z)}{1 + \exp(z)}. \tag{2.4}$$

The distribution function for the normal can only be written in the form of an integral without a closed-form solution. For the standard normal the distribution function equals:

$$\phi(z) = \int_{-\infty}^{z} \frac{1}{\sqrt{2\pi}} \exp\left(-\frac{x}{2}\right) dx. \tag{2.5}$$

The densities of the normal and the logistic distribution are both symmetric around 0. Therefore, for these distributions it holds that $F(z) = 1 - F(-z)$ for all values of z. With this in mind we can write the probability of observing a 1 for the logit model as:

$$\Pr[Y_i = 1] = \Lambda\left(\alpha + x_i{}'\beta\right) = \frac{\exp\left(\alpha + x_i'\beta\right)}{1 + \exp\left(\alpha + x_i'\beta\right)} \tag{2.6}$$

and for the probit model as:

$$\Pr[Y_i = 1] = \Phi\left(\alpha + x_i'\beta\right) = \int_{-\infty}^{\alpha + x_i'\beta} \frac{1}{\sqrt{2\pi}} \exp\left(-\frac{z}{2}\right) dz. \tag{2.7}$$

Both models in the end specify a particular functional form for the dependence of the probability of a purchase on the explanatory variables x_i. Both models satisfy the logical consistency requirement that the probability is always between 0 and 1.

The parameters in the logit and probit models are somewhat difficult to interpret directly. If a parameter is positive, we do know that an increase in the corresponding variable will go together with an increase in the probability. We do not know how large this change will be. To shed more light on the effect sizes we can calculate marginal effects, that is, the derivative of the probability with respect to an explanatory variable. For the logit model we obtain:

$$\frac{\partial \Pr\left[Y_i = 1\right]}{\partial x_{ik}} = \left[\frac{\exp\left(\alpha + x_i'\beta\right)}{\left(1 + \exp\left(\alpha + x_i'\beta\right)\right)} - \frac{\exp\left(\alpha + x_i'\beta\right)^2}{\left(1 + \exp\left(\alpha + x_i'\beta\right)\right)^2}\right]\beta_k$$
$$= \Pr\left[Y_i = 1\right]\left(1 - \Pr\left[Y_i = 1\right]\right)\beta_k \qquad (2.8)$$

and for the probit we obtain:

$$\frac{\partial \Pr\left[Y_i = 1\right]}{\partial x_{ik}} = \frac{\partial \Phi\left(\alpha + x_i'\beta\right)}{\partial x_{ik}} = \phi\left(\alpha + x_i'\beta\right)\beta_k \qquad (2.9)$$

where $\Phi(z)$ is the density function of the standard normal distribution.

To obtain marginal effects we therefore need to multiply the coefficients with a certain factor. This factor depends on x_i and therefore on the individual that we consider. From the formulas it is clear that the marginal effect will be almost 0 if we consider an individual who has a probability close to 1 or close to 0, that is, when $\left|\alpha + x_i'\beta\right|$ is very large. If we consider an individual with a certain probability $\Pr[Y_i = 1]$ it is straightforward to calculate the marginal effect for the logit, see Eq. (2.8). For the probit a bit more work is necessary, given a certain probability $\Pr[Y_i = 1] = p$ we know that $\alpha + x_i'\beta = \Phi^{-1}(p)$ such that the multiplication factor in Eq. (2.9) becomes $\phi(\Phi^{-1}(p))$. In Fig. 2.1 we show the multiplication factor that appears in the formula for the marginal effects for the logit and the probit model as a function of the probability $\Pr[Y_i = 1]$.

From Fig. 2.1 it is clear that the marginal effects will be largest when $\Pr[Y_i = 1] = 0.5$. The fact that the scale of the multiplication factor for the logit and probit are quite different, is the main reason that the estimated parameter values for logit and probit differ when applied to the same data set. The marginal effects however are usually similar. Differences in marginal effects between logit and probit are mainly expected when the range of the predicted probabilities is wide as the two functions in the graph are not proportional.

2.2.2 *Identification in the Logit and Probit Model*

In the discussion above, we have used the standard logistic distribution and the standard normal distribution. The scale or variance parameters of both distributions have implicitly been set to 1. The reason for this is that the variance of the error term ε_i cannot be identified together with the scale of the β parameters.

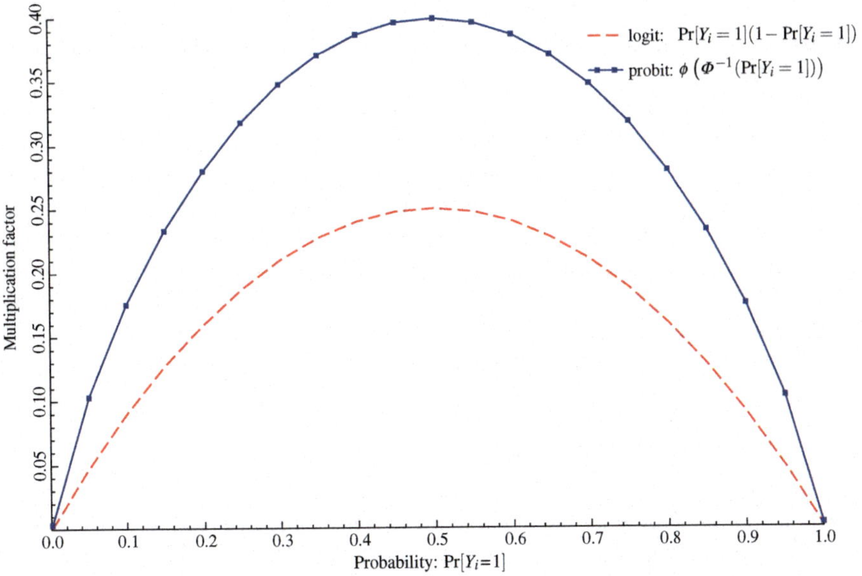

Fig. 2.1 Multiplication factor to calculate marginal effects at a certain value of $\Pr[Y_i = 1]$ in the logit and probit model

The easiest way to see this is to note that only the sign of the latent utility matters in the data generating process in Eqs. (2.1) and (2.2). If we were to increase or decrease the scale of all latent utilities, all customers would still make the same decisions, see Eq. (2.2). In other words, we can never infer the scale of the utilities from observed data. Therefore the researcher needs to somehow fix this scale. In the logit and probit models this is done by restricting the variance of the error term to a fixed value. This value is 1 for the probit model and 1/3 π^2 for the logit model. These values are chosen such that the formulas for the probabilities in Eqs. (2.6) and (2.7) are as simple as possible.

A more formal argument goes as follows. Suppose that we would assume that ε_i has a normal distribution with variance σ^2. The probability of observing $Y_i = 1$ would now be:

$$\Pr[Y_i = 1] = \Pr\left[\varepsilon_i > -\alpha - x_i'\beta\right] = \Pr\left[\varepsilon_i \leq \alpha + x_i'\beta\right]$$

$$= \Pr\left[\frac{1}{\sigma}\varepsilon_i \leq \frac{\alpha}{\sigma} + x_i'\left(\frac{1}{\sigma}\beta\right)\right] = \Phi\left(\frac{\alpha}{\sigma} + x_i'\left(\frac{1}{\sigma}\beta\right)\right). \quad (2.10)$$

This follows from the simple fact that $\frac{1}{\sigma}\varepsilon_i$ will have a standard normal distribution. Equation (2.10) shows that only the transformed parameters $\frac{\alpha}{\sigma}$ and $\frac{1}{\sigma}\beta$ determine the probabilities. Therefore, the scale of α and β cannot be estimated together with the variance σ^2. For example, increasing the variance by a factor 4 can be compensated by changing the scale of α and β by a factor 2 without any impact on the probabilities.

As said, identification in the logit and probit model can be obtained by restricting the variance. However this is not the only option. We can also decide to restrict the value of one of the elements of β and keep σ^2 as an unknown parameter to estimate. This will also lead to a model with identified parameters. However, the downside of this is that the latter also restricts the sign of one of the explanatory variables. In these cases the coefficient of price is often set to -1 (see for example, Sonnier et al. 2007). This simplifies the interpretation as all other coefficients can then be interpreted in monetary terms, that is, in terms of the willingness to pay.

2.2.3 *Multinomial Choices*

Given the above setup with latent variables we can easily extend the binary choice model to models that allow for a *multinomial* choice. The typical example here is choosing a particular brand from a set of brands. In these cases, the number of available brands is relatively small.

If we denote the brand choice by $Y_i \in \{1, 2, \ldots, J\}$, where J gives the number of brands, we can generalize our models by introducing a latent (indirect) utility for each brand. The utility as perceived by customer i for brand j is specified as:

$$U_{ij} = V_{ij} + \varepsilon_{ij} = \alpha_j + x'_{ij}\beta + w'_i\gamma_j + \varepsilon_{ij} \tag{2.11}$$

where V_{ij} denotes the explained part of the utility, x_{ij} is a vector of explanatory variables that differ across brands (and perhaps across customers) and w_i is a vector of variables that do not differ across brands. For example, x_{ij} may contain the price of product j as perceived by individual i, while w_i may contain the age and gender of the individual. Note that the parameters for w_i are specified to be brand specific, this allows the utility of an option relative to another one to depend on the individual-specific characteristics.

The latent utilities are linked to the actual decisions by assuming that a customer maximizes utility. Therefore if $Y_i = j$, then alternative j gave the highest utility. More formally, the customer's decision rule specifies:

$$Y_i = \text{argmax}_k U_{ik} \tag{2.12}$$

that is, Y_i equals the index k that maximizes the utility. As before there are two common choices for the distribution of the unexplained utility terms ε_{ij}. One either chooses these to be Type-1 Extreme Value (also known as Gumbel) distributed or to be normally distributed. In the former case we obtain the multinomial logit model, while in the latter case we obtain the multinomial probit model.[2]

These multinomial models are strongly related to the binary logit and probit models. In fact when $J = 2$, the multinomial logit (probit) model reduces to the binary logit (probit) model. The main result needed to show this is that the difference of two (independent) Extreme Value distributed variables has a logistic distribution, and that the difference of two normally distributed variables has a normal distribution.

We can write the probability that we see individual i buying brand j as:

$$\begin{aligned}
&\Pr[Y_i = j] = \Pr[\text{argmax}_k U_{ik} = j] = \Pr\left[U_{ij} \geq U_{ik}, \forall k \neq j\right] \\
&= \int_{-\infty}^{+\infty} \int_{-\infty}^{u_{i,j}} \cdots \int_{-\infty}^{u_{i,j}} f(u_{i,1}, u_{i,2}, \ldots, u_{i,J})\, du_{i1} \ldots du_{i,j-1} du_{i,j+1}, \ldots du_{i,J} du_{i,j} \\
&= \int_{-\infty}^{+\infty} \left(\int_{x_k=-\infty \cdots u_{ij}(k \neq j)} f\left(x_1, \ldots, u_{ij}, \ldots, x_J\right) dx_1 \ldots dx_{j-1} dx_{j+1}, \ldots dx_J \right) du_{i,j}
\end{aligned} \tag{2.13}$$

where $f(u_{i1}, \ldots, u_{iJ})$ denotes the joint density of all J utilities evaluated at $u_{i1}, \ldots, u_{iJ}$. The third line illustrates that we can first integrate over all "other" utilities and finally over the utility of brand j. A convenient way to rewrite this is:

$$\Pr[Y_i = j] = \int_{-\infty}^{+\infty} F_j\left(u_{ij}, \ldots, u_{ij}\right) du_{ij} \tag{2.14}$$

where $F_j(\cdot)$ denotes the derivative of the joint distribution function with respect to argument j. To see that this holds, we can simply work out the derivative of the distribution as:

$$\begin{aligned}
F_j(u_{i1}, \ldots, u_{iJ}) &= \frac{\partial F(u_{i1}, \ldots, u_{iJ})}{\partial u_{ij}} \\
&= \frac{\partial}{\partial u_{ij}} \int_{-\infty}^{u_{i1}} \int_{-\infty}^{u_{i2}} \cdots \int_{-\infty}^{u_{iJ}} f(x_1, \ldots, x_J)\, dx_1 \ldots dx_J \\
&= \int_{x_k=-\infty \cdots u_{ik}(k \neq j)} \frac{\partial}{\partial u_{ij}} \int_{-\infty}^{u_{ij}} f(x_1, \ldots, x_J)\, dx_1 \ldots dx_J \\
&= \int_{x_k=-\infty \cdots u_{ik}(k \neq j)} f\left(x_1, \ldots, u_{ij}, \ldots, x_J\right) dx_1 .. dx_{j-1} dx_{j+1} \ldots dx_J .
\end{aligned} \tag{2.15}$$

[2]A distinction is sometimes made between the multinomial logit/probit model and the conditional logit/probit model. The former model contains only constants and the x_{ij} variables, while the latter model only contains constants and the w_i variables (Franses and Paap 2001). In practice however both models tend to be combined. Many refer to the resulting model simply as the multinomial logit/probit model. In this chapter we follow this tradition.

Now it is easy to see that the last line also appears in Eq. (2.13), such that Eq. (2.14) is indeed correct.

Under the logit assumption, the integrals turn out to evaluate to an easy expression for the probability of buying product j, that is,[3]

$$\Pr[Y_i = j] = \frac{\exp(V_{ij})}{\sum_{k=1}^{J} \exp(V_{ik})} = \frac{\exp\left(\alpha_j + x_{ij}'\beta + w_i'\gamma_j\right)}{\sum_{k=1}^{J} \exp\left(\alpha_k + x_{ik}'\beta + w_i'\gamma_k\right)}. \tag{2.16}$$

Under the probit assumption we cannot simplify the integrals much. One can only reduce the dimension of the integrals by one, by working with differences of the utility with respect to some brand. If J is very small, one can evaluate the probabilities for the probit model using numerical approximations of the multivariate normal distribution function. Such functions are available in many programming languages. For larger values of J one needs to resort to simulation. The so-called Geweke, Hajivassiliou, and Keane [GHK] simulator is the most popular simulation method. Train (2003) provides a text book treatment of this simulator.

2.2.4 *Identification in the Multinomial Choice Models*

Similar to the binary models, we cannot identify all parameters in the multinomial choice model. First, the overall level of utility is not identified. Customer's decisions are only affected by *relative* utilities. This implies that we cannot estimate all α_j and all γ_j parameters. To obtain an identified model, we restrict α and γ to 0 for one of the brands. In this chapter, we choose to set $\alpha_J = 0$ and $\gamma_J = 0$. Next, the overall scale of the error terms is not identified, just as in the binary model. In the multinomial logit this is solved by using the *standard* extreme value distributions, that is, by restricting the variance of the error terms.

In the multinomial probit model, things are a bit more complicated as one can also specify the unobserved utility terms to be correlated. For exposition let's consider the trinomial probit model. As only relative utilities are identified, we impose $\alpha_3 = 0$ and $\gamma_3 = 0$ and look at the utility differences relative to brand 3, that is,

$$\begin{aligned} U_{i1} - U_{i3} &= \alpha_1 + (x_{i1} - x_{i3})'\beta + w_i'\gamma_1 + \varepsilon_{i1} - \varepsilon_{i3} \\ U_{i2} - U_{i3} &= \alpha_2 + (x_{i2} - x_{i3})'\beta + w_i'\gamma_2 + \varepsilon_{i2} - \varepsilon_{i3}. \end{aligned} \tag{2.17}$$

If $U_{i1} - U_{i3} > U_{i2} - U_{i3} > 0$ the customer will choose brand 1, if $U_{i2} - U_{i3} > U_{i1} - U_{i3} > 0$ she chooses 2 and if neither inequality is true she chooses brand 3. From this it is clear that we can at most estimate the 2×2 covariance matrix of $(\varepsilon_{i1} - \varepsilon_{i3})$ and

[3]See Train (2003) for a derivation.

$(\varepsilon_{i2} - \varepsilon_{i3})$, not the full 3×3 covariance matrix of ε_{i1}, ε_{i2} and ε_{i3}. However, as the scale of utility is also not identified, we at least need to restrict the variance of one of the elements to a fixed value. We therefore end up with the following covariance matrix to estimate:

$$\text{Var}\left[\begin{pmatrix} \varepsilon_{i1} - \varepsilon_{i3} \\ \varepsilon_{i2} - \varepsilon_{i3} \end{pmatrix}\right] = \begin{pmatrix} 1 & \sigma_{12} \\ \sigma_{12} & \sigma_2^2 \end{pmatrix}. \tag{2.18}$$

It turns out that in principle both unknown parameters in this matrix are identified as long as the model includes at least one variable that varies across customers (Heckman and Sedlacek 1985). This will be true in most marketing applications. However, Keane (1992) argues that although these parameters are theoretically identified it may be very difficult to empirically identify them. The covariance parameters are only well identified in practice if the model contains exclusion restrictions, that is, variables that affect the utility of one brand without affecting the other. In our notation this means that we need the presence of x_{ij} variables that differ across the brands. In many brand choice settings this is satisfied as the price of a brand is likely to be among these variables. We can then estimate the covariance parameters as long as the model does not allow a direct impact of the price of one brand on the utility of the other. Intuitively, this is also obvious as the covariance matrix captures substitution patterns. To identify such substitution we need to observe a driver of substitution (eg. price) and the changes in behavior due to this factor must not be included elsewhere in the model.

These results also generalize to models for more alternatives. Given variables that differ across brands, the covariance matrix of the utility differences is identified up to the variance of one of the elements.

2.2.5 *Marginal Effects in the Multinomial Logit and Multinomial Probit Models*

As in the binary models, it is not straightforward to interpret the coefficients directly. Parameters can of course be directly interpreted in terms of the underlying utilities. However, it is not easy to directly translate this to choice probabilities. One way to interpret the coefficients in a multinomial logit is to consider the ratios of choice probabilities, so called odds ratios. See Franses and Paap (2001) and Sect. 8.2.2.4 in Vol. I for a discussion. Below we will work out the (cross) marginal effects for the multinomial logit. For a discussion the multinomial probit model there are no easy formulas available for these effects.

To derive the marginal effects in the multinomial logit it is easiest to first consider how the probability of alternative j changes if the explained part of the utility of j, that is, V_{ij}, changes. The corresponding derivative gives:

$$\frac{\partial \Pr[Y_i = j]}{\partial V_{ij}} = \frac{\exp(V_{ij})}{\sum_k \exp(V_{ik})} - \frac{\exp(V_{ij})^2}{\left(\sum_k \exp(V_{ik})\right)^2} = \Pr[Y_i = j](1 - \Pr[Y_i = j]). \tag{2.19}$$

In a similar way we can obtain a cross effect:

$$\frac{\partial \Pr[Y_i = j]}{\partial V_{ik}} = -\frac{\exp(V_{ij})\exp(V_{ik})}{\left(\sum_k \exp(V_{ik})\right)^2} = -\Pr[Y_i = j]\Pr[Y_i = k], \text{ for } j \neq k. \tag{2.20}$$

From Eqs. (2.19) and (2.20) we can now obtain the own marginal effect of x_{ij}, that is,

$$\frac{\partial \Pr[Y_i = j]}{\partial x_{ij}} = \frac{\partial \Pr[Y_i = j]}{\partial V_{ij}} \frac{\partial V_{ij}}{\partial x_{ij}} = \Pr[Y_i = j](1 - \Pr[Y_i = j])\beta \tag{2.21}$$

the cross marginal effect,

$$\frac{\partial \Pr[Y_i = j]}{\partial x_{ik}} = \frac{\partial \Pr[Y_i = j]}{\partial V_{ik}} \frac{\partial V_{ik}}{\partial x_{ik}} = -\Pr[Y_i = j]\Pr[Y_i = k]\beta, \text{ for } j \neq k \tag{2.22}$$

and the marginal effect of w_i

$$\frac{\partial \Pr[Y_i = j]}{\partial w_i} = \sum_k \frac{\partial \Pr[Y_i = j]}{\partial V_{ik}} \frac{\partial V_{ik}}{\partial w_i} = \Pr[Y_i = j]\left(\gamma_j - \sum_k \Pr[Y_i = k]\gamma_k\right). \tag{2.23}$$

For the final result, note that w_i affects all utilities such that we need to sum over all brands.

The first equation can be used to obtain, for example, the own price effect; the second for a cross-price effect. The final equation gives the impact of individual specific characteristics. An important detail is that the sign of this latter marginal effect cannot be determined based on the estimated coefficients alone.

2.2.6 Estimation and Validation

In the standard setup of the binary and multinomial choice models discussed above, estimation of the model parameters is typically done by maximum likelihood. Given observed decisions $y_1, y_2, \ldots, y_N$, the log likelihood is simply given by:

$$\log L(\alpha, \beta, \gamma) = \sum_{i=1}^{N} \log(\Pr[Y_i = y_i]). \tag{2.24}$$

Maximizing this log likelihood over α, β, and γ yields the maximum likelihood estimator. As no closed-form solution is available for this problem, the maximization needs to be done numerically. Standard errors can straightforwardly be obtained using the matrix of second order derivatives of the log likelihood function. The variance matrix of the estimators can be estimated as:

$$\mathrm{Var}\left[\widehat{\theta}\right] = \left[-\left.\frac{\partial^2 \log L}{\partial \theta \partial \theta'}\right|_{\theta=\widehat{\theta}}\right]^{-1} \tag{2.25}$$

where $\widehat{\theta}$ denotes the Maximum Likelihood estimator.

Calculating the likelihood function for the multinomial probit model is difficult as each probability evaluation requires simulation. To estimate the parameters in this model one often uses Simulated Maximum Likelihood (Train 2003) or Bayesian methodology (see Albert and Chib 1993; McCulloch et al. 2000; and Chap. 16).

Various tests are available to validate the performance of the models, for this we refer the reader to Franses and Paap (2001), Wooldridge (2002), and Sect. 8.2.2.4 in Vol. I.

2.2.7 Example Multinomial Logit: Spillover Effects of Brand Extensions

Brand extensions are new products that are released under an existing brand name. The common rationale for launching brand extensions is that the new brand will benefit from the already known brand name. However, usually there is also an impact on the already existing products of the brand name, the so-called parent brand. Balachander and Ghose (2003) study this so-called reciprocal spillover impact by considering the effect of advertising of child brands on parent brands. They apply various multinomial logit based models on two product categories, namely yoghurts and detergents. Below we present the results of one of their MNL models on the yoghurt category.

Balachander and Ghose (2003) consider nine different brands in the yoghurt category. Some of these brands are "child brands". The utilities of the nine brands are related to a baseline preference (intercept), display exposure, feature exposure, price, coupons, own-advertising, advertising of child brands, and advertising of parent brands. Finally, the utility specification contains a constructed loyalty variable as introduced by Guadagni and Little (1983). For household i and brand j, this loyalty variable at time t is defined as:

$$L_{ijt} = \alpha L_{ij,t-1} + (1-\alpha)\, Y_{ij,t-1} \tag{2.26}$$

where $0 \leq \alpha \leq 1$ is a parameter and $Y_{ij,t-1} = 1$ if brand j was bought at time $t-1$ by household i. This loyalty variable indicates how attached a household is to a

Table 2.1 MNL parameter estimates of variables that determine brand choice

	Estimate	*t*-value
Brand loyalty	4.716	38.645
Display	1.109	3.565
Feature	0.578	3.648
List price (dollars/ounce)	−31.912	−6.397
Coupon value (dollars/ounce)	55.388	8.929
Own advertising	0.185	1.305
Child-advertising	0.3775	2.752
Parent-advertising	−0.3698	−0.782

Source: Balachander and Ghose (2003, p. 9)

brand. If α is close to 0, only the last purchase matters; if α is close to 1 all previous purchases define the loyalty. Balachander and Ghose (2003) set $\alpha = 0.8$. An initial (pre-sample) number of purchases is used to initialize brand loyalty. Advertising stock variables are defined in an analogous way to allow for a long-run impact of advertising.

The smoothing parameter for the advertising stock is estimated to equal 0.5, that is, the advertising stock equals the average of past advertising stock and current advertising. The parameter estimates are given in Table 2.1, where the brand specific intercepts are omitted to save space.

As expected, the estimation results show a very strong impact of brand loyalty as households tend to be quite persistent in their brand choices. The parameters of the marketing instruments display, feature, price, and coupon all have the expected sign and are all significantly different from 0. Display has a much larger impact compared to feature. Coupons have a large and significant impact on the brand choices. As often found in the literature own advertising does not significantly influence the utility. However, the authors do find a positive and significant effect of child advertising. These results therefore support the idea of the reciprocal spillover effect. Advertising expenditures on the child brand also benefit the parent brand. Finally, the coefficient for parent advertising is negative, but not significantly different from 0. So parent advertising does not hurt (or benefit) the child brand.

To interpret the size of the estimated parameters we can consider some marginal effects. As an example we look at the impact of coupons. Suppose that we consider brand *Nordica low fat* for a customer whose choice probability equals the average choice share in the sample, that is, 18.5%. The marginal effect of the coupon value of *Nordica low fat* therefore equals $0.185 \times (1 - 0.185) \times 55.388 = 8.35$, see Eq. (2.21). This implies that an increase in coupon value of 1 cent/ounce would increase the choice probability by 0.0835, or by about 8 percentage points. Note that the average price per ounce equals only 0.065 for this brand, so a 1 cent/ounce coupon corresponds to quite a large relative price change. The cross effect of such a change on another brand depends on the choice probability of the competing brand. Suppose that the choice probability of the competing brand *Dannon low-fat* also equals its population average, that is, 11.77%. In this case, the cross effect will equal $-0.185 \times 0.1177 \times 55.388 = -1.206$. The same 1 cent/ounce coupon would therefore reduce the choice probability of *Dannon low-fat* by 0.01206 or about 1.2 percentage points. In other words, of the total gain in probability for *Nordica low-fat* a substantial proportion of about 14.4% (=1.206/8.35) is taken away from *Dannon low-fat*.

2.3 Nested Logit Models

2.3.1 *Motivation and Marginal Effects in the Multinomial Logit Model*

Above we have introduced the multinomial logit and probit models to describe the situation where customers choose one brand from a set of brands. From the discussion it is obvious that the multinomial logit [MNL] is far easier to work with than the multinomial probit [MNP]. In the MNL, the probabilities are easier to calculate and the estimation can simply be done using maximum likelihood. On the other hand, MNL does not allow us to specify the covariance matrix of the unexplained utilities. So, why is this covariance matrix relevant?

To answer this question we need to consider the implied cross-effects of marketing instruments in the MNL model in more detail. Suppose that one of the x_{ij} variables is the price of alternative j as seen by customer i (denoted by p_{ij}). Next, consider the impact of changing the price of brand k on the probability of brand j. For the MNL, this cross-effect was be shown to equal:

$$\frac{\partial \Pr[Y_i = j]}{\partial p_{ik}} = -\beta_p \Pr[Y_i = j] \Pr[Y_i = k], \text{for } j \neq k \tag{2.27}$$

where β_p denotes the price parameter. As we expect the price parameter to be negative, this relation implies that an increase in the price of brand k leads to an increase in the probability of brand j. Moreover, the increase is proportional to the probability that j was chosen. So, by construction, competitors with large shares gain more from a price increase by k, than competitors with a small share. This substitution property is built into the MNL model! The cross-brand impact of coupon usage in the example in Sect. 2.2.7, is therefore also completely a result of the assumptions in the MNL. The 14.4% calculated in the example, could actually also be obtained without the model using only the choice probabilities.[4]

Another way to highlight the restrictive substitution pattern of MNL is by calculating the cross-price elasticity, that is,

$$\frac{\partial \Pr[Y_i = j]}{\partial p_{ik}} \frac{p_{ik}}{\Pr[Y_i = j]} = -\beta_p p_{ik} \Pr[Y_i = k]. \tag{2.28}$$

This equation shows that the cross-elasticity is the same for all brands $j \neq k$.

[4] In the example: Probability Dannon/(1 – Probability Nordica) = 0.1177 / (1–0.1851) = 0.144.

The above properties are a direct consequence of the so-called Independence of Irrelevant Alternatives [IIA] property that the MNL has. This property states that the ratio of the probability of brand j to the probability of brand k does not depend on the properties or presence of any other brand. It is exactly this property that the MNP tries to alleviate by treating the covariance matrix as an unknown parameter.

There are also other models that alleviate the IIA property, while staying within the logit framework. The clear advantage of such models is the mathematical tractability. Furthermore, the structure of such models may be interesting from a theoretical point of view. The class of models that we consider here is the class of generalized nested logit models. To set the stage we first present the most well-known example in this class, that is, the standard nested logit model. In Sect. 2.3.5 we will next describe the class of Generalized Extreme Value (GEV) models of which the generalized nested logit is a special case.

2.3.2 *Standard Nested Logit*

The key idea in the nested logit model is to group the available alternatives in so-called nests. Within each nest the alternatives are rather similar, while across nests they are different. The nesting structure may also be hierarchical such that a particular nest is subdivided into other nests. For ease of notation we stick to one level of nesting. A discussion of more general nesting structures can be found in Ben-Akiva and Lerman (1985), Foekens et al. (1997) and Leeflang et al. (2000, Sect. 14.5).

As a leading example, let us consider the choice between eight different cars. Furthermore we assume that the choice set contains cars of four different brands (A, B, C, and D) and three different sizes (small, midsize, and large). Not all brands and size combinations exist. One way to nest the different alternatives is by size as shown in Fig. 2.2.

The nesting structure suggests that customers first decide on the size of the car and given this choice they decide on the brand. However, when deciding on the size, customers will of course take into account the exact models available in that category. We will later see that the nested logit model accounts for such dependence.

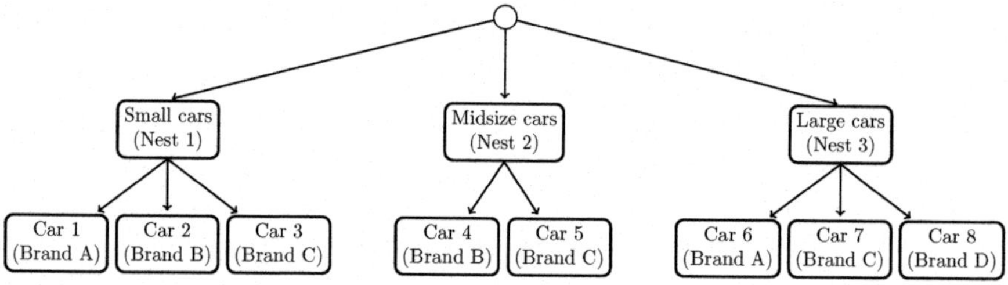

Fig. 2.2 Example of a nesting structure for the nested logit model

The size classes (nests) may differ in the number of available cars. Moreover, specific brands may be available in multiple nests.

To present the nested logit model, we need to introduce some notation. As before we number the alternatives (eg. cars) from 1 to J. Each nest can now be represented by a set of numbers. For nest m this set is given by $\mathcal{C}_m$. In the example of Fig. 2.2 we have $\mathcal{C}_2 = \{4, 5\}$. We denote the nest to which alternative j belongs as $m(j)$, so in the example, $m(7) = 3$. We continue to denote the chosen product by individual i as Y_i. Additionally we denote by C_i the nest that is chosen by i.

In the nested logit the utility for product j which is located in nest $m = m(j)$ is written as:

$$U_{i,jm} = V_{i,m} + V_{i,j|m} + \varepsilon_{i,m} + \varepsilon_{i,j|m} \tag{2.29}$$

where the $V_{i,m}$ gives the explained utility for nest m (a particular car size), $V_{i,j|m}$ gives the explained utility of the j-th alternative (a specific car) given that nest m is chosen. This utility component is only defined for $j \in \mathcal{C}_m$. Both terms $V_{i,m}$ and $V_{i,j|m}$ will be related to observed explanatory variables using parameters. The two ε terms give the associated unexplained utility terms.

Now suppose that we know that a customer selects a product in nest m. Given this information we can work out the probability that product $j \in \mathcal{C}_m$ is chosen. Given that nest m is chosen, product j needs to yield the highest utility within nest m. To the researcher, the probability of this event equals:

$$\Pr\left[Y_i = j | \, C_i = m\right] = \Pr\left[U_{i,jm} \geq U_{i,km}, \forall k \in \mathcal{C}_m, k \neq j\,\right] \text{for } j \in \mathcal{C}_m. \tag{2.30}$$

If $j \notin \mathcal{C}_m$ this probability is obviously 0. This probability can be simplified by observing that the nest specific utility components in Eq. (2.29) do not matter. Therefore the probability can be written as:

$$\begin{aligned}
&\Pr\left[Y_i = j | \, C_i = m\right] = \\
&\Pr\left[V_{i,m} + V_{i,j|m} + \varepsilon_{i,m} + \varepsilon_{i,j|m} \geq V_{i,m} + V_{i,k|m} + \varepsilon_{i,m} + \varepsilon_{i,k|m}, \forall k \in \mathcal{C}_m, k \neq j\right] = \\
&\Pr\left[V_{i,j|m} + \varepsilon_{i,j|m} \geq V_{i,k|m} + \varepsilon_{i,k|m}, \forall k \in \mathcal{C}_m, k \neq j\right] \ \text{for } j \in \mathcal{C}_m.
\end{aligned} \tag{2.31}$$

If we assume a Type-1 Extreme Value distribution for $\varepsilon_{i,j|m}$, this expression is very much like the probability in a standard MNL, see Eq. (2.13). As the relative variance of $\varepsilon_{i,m}$ versus $\varepsilon_{i,j|m}$ will matter, we assume that $\varepsilon_{i,k|m}$ has an Extreme Value distribution with scale parameter μ_m^p, where the superscript p stands for "product". Given this distribution, we almost have a standard MNL for the choice given a nest. Therefore we can show that:

$$\Pr\left[Y_i = j | \, C_i = m\right] = \frac{\exp\left(V_{i,j|m}\mu_m^p\right)}{\sum_{k \in \mathcal{C}_m} \exp\left(V_{i,k|m}\mu_m^p\right)} \ \text{for } j \in \mathcal{C}_m. \tag{2.32}$$

The only difference with the standard MNL expression in Eq. (2.16) is that the scale parameter explicitly appears in the expression, whereas for the standard MNL we have set the scale parameter equal to 1.

In a similar way we can work out the probability that the customer chooses nest m. A utility maximizing individual will choose nest m if the best product in nest m has the highest utility of all products, that is,

$$\Pr\left[C_i = m\right] = \Pr\left[\max_{k \in C_m} U_{i,km} \geq \max_{k' \in C_{m'}} U_{i,k'm'}, \forall m' \neq m\right]. \tag{2.33}$$

Using the utility specification in Eq. (2.29) this probability can be rewritten as:

$$\Pr\left[\max_{k \in C_m}\left\{V_{i,m}+V_{i,k|m}+\varepsilon_{i,m}+\varepsilon_{i,k|m}\right\} \geq \max_{k' \in C_{m'}}\left\{V_{i,m'}+V_{i,k'|m'}+\varepsilon_{i,m'}+\varepsilon_{i,k'|m'}\right\}, \forall m' \neq m\right] \tag{2.34}$$

or

$$\Pr\left[V_{i,m}+\varepsilon_{i,m}+\max_{k \in C_m}\left\{V_{i,k|m}+\varepsilon_{i,k|m}\right\} \geq V_{i,m'}+\varepsilon_{i,m'}+\max_{k' \in C_{m'}}\left\{V_{i,k'|m'}+\varepsilon_{i,k'|m'}\right\}, \forall m' \neq m\right]. \tag{2.35}$$

The term $\max_{k \in C_m}\left\{V_{i,k|m} + \varepsilon_{i,k|m}\right\}$ gives the maximum utility that can be obtained within nest m. As $\varepsilon_{i,k|m}$ has an extreme value distribution with scale μ_m^p, we can show that this maximum utility also has an Extreme Value distribution with scale μ_m^p, but with location[5]:

$$V'_{i,m} = \frac{1}{\mu_m^p} \log \sum_{k \in C_m} \exp\left(V_{i,k|m}\mu_m^p\right). \tag{2.36}$$

Therefore we can replace $\max_{k \in C_m}\left\{V_{i,k|m} + \varepsilon_{i,k|m}\right\}$ by $V'_{i,m} + \varepsilon'_{i,m}$, where $\varepsilon'_{i,m}$ has an Extreme Value distribution with location 0 and scale parameter μ_m^p. Equation (2.35) can now be written as:

$$\Pr\left[V_{i,m} + V'_{i,m} + \varepsilon_{i,m} + \varepsilon'_{i,m} \geq V_{i,m'} + V'_{i,m'} + \varepsilon_{i,m'} + \varepsilon'_{i,m'}, \forall m' \neq m\right]. \tag{2.37}$$

To complete the nested logit specification we need to add one final distributional assumption. We assume that $\varepsilon_{i,m} + \varepsilon'_{i,m}$ is iid extreme value distributed with scale

[5]See Ben-Akiva and Lerman (1985).

parameter μ^n, where now the superscript n stands for "nest". Given this assumption, the probability of choosing nest m becomes a standard logit expression and:

$$\begin{aligned} &\Pr\left[C_i = m\right] \\ &= \Pr\left[V_{i,m} + V'_{i,m} + \varepsilon_{i,m} + \varepsilon'_{i,m} \geq V_{i,m'} + V'_{i,m'} + \varepsilon_{i,m'} + \varepsilon'_{i,m'}, \forall m' \neq m\right] \\ &= \frac{\exp\left(\left(V_{i,m} + V'_{i,m}\right)\mu^n\right)}{\sum_{m'=1}^{M} \exp\left(\left(V_{i,m'} + V'_{i,m'}\right)\mu^n\right)}. \end{aligned} \tag{2.38}$$

The probability of choosing a particular product in a particular nest can now be obtained by collecting the results in Eqs. (2.32) and (2.38),

$$\begin{aligned} &\Pr\left[Y_i = j\right] = \Pr\left[Y_i = j | C_i = m(j)\right] \Pr\left[C_i = m(j)\right] = \\ &\frac{\exp\left(V_{i,j|m(j)}\mu^p_{m(j)}\right)}{\sum_{k\in C_{m(j)}} \exp\left(V_{i,k|m(j)}\mu^p_{m(j)}\right)} \frac{\exp\left(\left(V_{i,m(j)} + V'_{i,m(j)}\right)\mu^n\right)}{\sum_{m'=1}^{M} \exp\left(\left(V_{i,m'} + V'_{i,m'}\right)\mu^n\right)}. \end{aligned} \tag{2.39}$$

Plugging in the definition of $V'_{i,m}$ we obtain:

$$\begin{aligned} \Pr\left[Y_i = j\right] = &\frac{\exp\left(\mu^p_m V_{i,j|m(j)}\right)}{\sum_{k\in C_{m(j)}} \exp\left(\mu^p_m V_{i,k|m(j)}\right)} \times \\ &\frac{\exp\left(\mu^n V_{i,m(j)} + \frac{\mu^n}{\mu^p_{m(j)}} \log \sum_{k\in C_{m(j)}} \exp\left(V_{i,k|m(j)}\mu^p_{m(j)}\right)\right)}{\sum_{m'=1}^{M} \exp\left(\mu^n V_{i,m'} + \frac{\mu^n}{\mu^p_{m'}} \log \sum_{k\in C_{m'}} \exp\left(V_{i,k|m'}\mu^p_{m'}\right)\right)}. \end{aligned} \tag{2.40}$$

As the terms $V_{i,m}$ and $V_{i,k|m}$ are not known and are typically specified using explanatory variables and unknown coefficients, the two scale parameters cannot both be identified. It is convenient to set $\mu^n = 1$. Denoting $\frac{1}{\mu^p_m} = \lambda_m$ we then finally obtain:

$$\begin{aligned} \Pr\left[Y_i = j\right] = &\frac{\exp\left(V_{i,j|m(j)}/\lambda_{m(j)}\right)}{\sum_{k\in C_{m(j)}} \exp\left(V_{i,k|m(j)}/\lambda_{m(j)}\right)} \times \\ &\frac{\exp\left(V_{i,m(j)} + \lambda_{m(j)} \log \sum_{k\in C_{m(j)}} \exp\left(V_{i,k|m(j)}/\lambda_{m(j)}\right)\right)}{\sum_{m'} \exp\left(V_{i,m'} + \lambda_{m'} \log \sum_{k\in C_{m'}} \exp\left(V_{i,k|m'}/\lambda_{m'}\right)\right)}. \end{aligned} \tag{2.41}$$

The term $\log \sum_{k\in C_m} \exp\left(V_{k|m}/\lambda_m\right)$ is called the *inclusive value* of nest m and relates to the expected maximum utility within this nest, see Eq. (2.36). A large inclusive value implies that one expects to obtain a high utility in the corresponding nest.

The coefficient λ_m can be shown to be related to the (positive) correlation between utilities within a nest (Ben-Akiva and Lerman 1985), that is,

$$\lambda_m = \sqrt{1 - \text{corr}\left(U_{jm}, U_{j'm}\right)} \text{ for } j, j' \in \mathcal{C}_m \text{ and } j \neq j'. \tag{2.42}$$

From this it follows that λ_m should be between 0 and 1. If λ_m equals 1, one can obtain that the nested logit reduces to the normal MNL. In some cases one can obtain values of λ_m larger than 1. However in this case one cannot interpret the model in terms of correlated utilities anymore. The model does give well defined choice probabilities and is therefore still useful.

To see how the nested logit affects the competitive structure we consider the odds-ratios of two brands. Let us first consider two brands j and k that are within the same nest m. It holds that:

$$\begin{aligned}\frac{\Pr[Y_i = j]}{\Pr[Y_i = k]} &= \frac{\Pr[Y_i = j|C_i = m] \Pr[C_i = m]}{\Pr[Y_i = k|C_i = m] \Pr[C_i = m]} = \frac{\Pr[Y_i = j|C_i = m]}{\Pr[Y_i = k|C_i = m]} \\ &= \frac{\exp\left(V_{i,j|m}/\lambda_m\right)}{\exp\left(V_{i,k|m}/\lambda_m\right)}.\end{aligned} \tag{2.43}$$

The ratio does not depend on any other brand's valuation. Therefore, within a nest the *IIA property* still holds in the nested logit. *Across nests this is not the case.*

Let us now consider brands j and k that are in different nests, that is, $m(j) \neq m(k)$. For these brands we have:

$$\begin{aligned}\frac{\Pr[Y_i = j]}{\Pr[Y_i = k]} &= \frac{\Pr[Y_i = j|C_i = m(j)] \Pr[C_i = m(j)]}{\Pr[Y_i = k|C_i = m(k)] \Pr[C_i = m(k)]} \\ &= \frac{\exp\left(V_{i,m(j)} + V_{i,j|m(j)}/\lambda_{m(j)} + \left(\lambda_{m(j)} - 1\right) \log \sum_{l \in C_{m(j)}} \exp\left(V_{i,l|m(j)}/\lambda_{m(j)}\right)\right)}{\exp\left(V_{i,m(k)} + V_{i,j|m(k)}/\lambda_{m(k)} + \left(\lambda_{m(k)} - 1\right) \log \sum_{l \in C_{m(k)}} \exp\left(V_{i,l|m(k)}/\lambda_{m(k)}\right)\right)}.\end{aligned} \tag{2.44}$$

If $\lambda_{m(j)} \neq 1$ or $\lambda_{m(k)} \neq 1$ this odds ratio will depend on the valuation of other brands in the nests of j and/or k. Therefore IIA does not hold across nests in the nested logit.

Given the expressions for the choice probabilities in Eq. (2.41), the parameters of the nested logit model can straightforwardly be estimated using maximum likelihood. In this procedure all parameters are estimated at the same time. Alternatively, one may consider a two-step procedure where the parameters in the nest-specific models are estimated first and given these estimates the parameters in the nest-choice model are estimated. Such a procedure is not efficient, but may be useful to speed up the estimation procedure.

2.3.3 Marginal Effects in the Nested Logit

When applying the nested logit it is useful to be able to judge how probabilities change due to a change in one of the utility components. Moreover, it is important to know how the nesting structure affects the competitive structure implied by the model. To this end, we derive marginal effects of changing brand-specific utility components $V_{i,k|m(k)}$.

We first consider the own effect, that is, how the probability of brand j changes when the utility component $V_{i,j|m(j)}$ changes. The chain rule of derivatives allows us to split this marginal effect as:

$$\frac{\partial \Pr[Y_i = j]}{\partial V_{i,j|m(j)}} = \frac{\partial \Pr[Y_i = j|C_i = m(j)]}{\partial V_{i,j|m(j)}} \Pr[C_i = m(j)] + \Pr[Y_i = j|C_i = m(j)] \frac{\partial \Pr[C_i = m(j)]}{\partial V_{i,j|m(j)}}. \tag{2.45}$$

After some algebra we can show that this can be written as:

$$\frac{\partial \Pr[Y_i = j]}{\partial V_{i,j|m(j)}} = \Pr[Y_i = j] \times \left\{(1 - \Pr[Y_i = j]) + \left(\frac{1}{\lambda_{m(j)}} - 1\right)(1 - \Pr[Y_i = j|C_i = m(j)])\right\}. \tag{2.46}$$

Note that if $\lambda_{m(j)}$ is between 0 and 1, the marginal effect above will be larger than in a corresponding MNL model.

For the cross-effect of brand k on the probability of j we need to distinguish between the case where j and k are in the *same nest* versus the case where they are in different nests. If they are in the same nest, that is, $m = m(j) = m(k)$ it holds:

$$\begin{aligned}\frac{\partial \Pr[Y_i = j]}{\partial V_{i,k|m}} &= \frac{\partial \Pr[Y_i = j|C_i = m]}{\partial V_{i,k|m}} \Pr[C_i = m] + \Pr[Y_i = j|C_i = m] \frac{\partial \Pr[C_i = m]}{\partial V_{i,k|m}} \\ &= -\Pr[Y_i = j]\Pr[Y_i = k|C_i = m]\left\{\left(\frac{1}{\lambda_m} - 1\right) + \Pr[C_i = m]\right\}.\end{aligned} \tag{2.47}$$

This can be rewritten to:

$$\frac{\partial \Pr[Y_i = j]}{\partial V_{i,k|m}} = -\left[\Pr[Y_i = j]\Pr[Y_i = k] + \left(\frac{1}{\lambda_m} - 1\right)\Pr[Y_i = j|C_i = m]\Pr[Y_i = k|C_i = m]\Pr[C_i = m]\right]. \tag{2.48}$$

From the above it is easy to see that the expression simplifies to the MNL expressions in Eqs. (2.19) and (2.20) when $\lambda_m = 1$.

If brands j and k are in *different nests* the marginal effect is given by:

$$\begin{aligned}\frac{\partial \Pr[Y_i = j]}{\partial V_{i,k|m(k)}} &= \frac{\partial \Pr[Y_i = j|C_i = m(j)]}{\partial V_{i,k|m(k)}} \Pr[C_i = m] \\ &\quad + \Pr[Y_i = j|C_i = m(j)] \frac{\partial \Pr[C_i = m(j)]}{\partial V_{i,k|m(k)}} \\ &= \Pr[Y_i = j|C_i = m(j)] \frac{\partial \Pr[C_i = m(j)]}{\partial V_{i,k|m(k)}}. \end{aligned} \quad (2.49)$$

This can be worked out to be:

$$\begin{aligned}\frac{\partial \Pr[Y_i = j]}{\partial V_{i,k|m(k)}} &= \Pr[Y_i = j|C_i = m(j)] (-\Pr[C_i = m(j)] \Pr[C_i = m(k)] \\ &\quad \Pr[Y_i = k|C_i = m(k)]) = -\Pr[Y_i = j] \Pr[Y_i = k]. \end{aligned} \quad (2.50)$$

This expression is exactly equal to to the MNL expression, no matter what the values of the λ_m parameters are.

In practice we will specify $V_{ij|m}$ to be a function of observed variables and parameters, for example, $V_{ij|m} = x_i'\beta$, where x_{ij} is a vector that includes variables that relate to marketing instruments. With this specification, the marginal effect of the n-th variable of brand k (x_{ikn}) on brand j is given by:

$$\frac{\partial \Pr[Y_i = j]}{\partial x_{ikn}} = \frac{\partial \Pr[Y_i = j]}{\partial V_{ik|m(k)}} \frac{\partial V_{ik|m(k)}}{\partial x_{ikn}} = \frac{\partial \Pr[Y_i = j]}{\partial V_{ik|m(k)}} \beta_n. \quad (2.51)$$

From Eqs. (2.48) and (2.50) it is clear that the cross-effects depend on the nesting structure of the model.

We motivated the nested logit model using an example where customers first choose the size of a car and next choose a specific model. Of course, it could also be that customers follow the reverse process: they first select a brand and only next choose a size. In the latter case, one would end up with a *different* nested logit model.[6] Instead of having a random term in Eq. (2.29) that refers to the sizes, one would have a random component that represents the brands. Model selection procedures could be used to select the best performing specification.

[6] See for example Foekens et al. (1997).

2.3.4 Example of the Nested Logit Model

It is also possible to specify the nesting structure per customer. An example is given by Kamakura et al. (1996). In their paper they consider brand and product-form choices of consumers over time. In their application there are four brands of peanut butter (Peter Pan, Jif, Skippy, and Store brand) and each brand sells two different product forms (Creamy and Crunchy). Of course one could use a MNL to model the choices between the eight available products. However, such a model would impose the, in this context, rather implausible assumption of Independence of Irrelevant Alternatives. For example, IIA implies that an increase in the choice share of one product is proportionally taken from all other products. It may be more realistic that the cross impact is larger for competing products of the same product form. In other words a nested logit structure may be more appropriate. In this setting there are two ways to construct the nesting, at the first level we can consider the four brands or the two product forms. A priori it is difficult to indicate which one of the two is more appropriate. At the same time, it may also be that the MNL structure does explain behavior properly.

Kamakura et al. (1996) specify a mixture model to allow for different groups of customers. These groups may differ in the type of model that best describes their behavior (structural heterogeneity) or only in the parameters that best describe them (preference heterogeneity). In the end there turns out to be 8 different groups of customers in their data. Some customers always buy the same product (14%), these are described as hard-core loyal customers. Of the other customers, the largest group consists of customers whose choices are best described by a nested logit based on product form (29% of the non-hard core loyal group). For three groups a nested logit by brand works better (in total 47% of non-hard core loyal). These three groups differ in their parameter values. Three groups are found where the inclusive value parameter (also called dissimilarity coefficient) λ_m is not significantly different from 1. This implies that the MNL model describes the behavior in these groups (24%).

For illustrative purposes, we highlight the parameter estimates for the segment where the nesting is done according to product form. The nested logit model as used by Kamakura et al. (1996) does not have any parameters at the nest level, that is, $V_{i,m}$ does not appear in the model, next it does not scale the explained utilities within a nest using the inclusive value parameter as in Eq. (2.32). Stated differently, this factor is absorbed in the explained utility component. In order to calculate marginal effects using the formulas in this chapter, one therefore has to multiply the parameters obtained by Kamakura et al. (1996) by $\lambda_m = 1/\mu_m$.

Table 2.2 shows the parameter estimates. To be able to identify all parameters the intercept for "Peter Pan Crunchy" has been set to 0. The price and display coefficients have the expected signs: price negatively influences utility while display increases the utility. The inclusive value coefficient is estimated to be 0.8. This implies that the correlation in unexplained utility between any two brands of the same product form equals $1–0.8^2 = 1–0.64 = 0.36$. The products Peter Pan Creamy, Jif Creamy, and Skippy Creamy have relatively large intercepts. As a consequence the creamy products are in general preferred over the others in this segment. Another

Table 2.2 Parameter estimates for a nested logit on brand choices of peanut butter

Variable	Parameter estimates
Brand-specific intercept:	
Peter Pan Creamy	3.6[a]
Peter Pan Crunchy	0
Jif Creamy	2.8[a]
Jif Crunchy	−1.6[a]
Skippy Creamy	2.4[a]
Skippy Crunchy	−4.4[a]
Store Creamy	−1.8[a]
Store Crunchy	−4.9[a]
Price	−6.1[a]
Display	2.9[a]
Dissimilarity coefficient (λ_m)	0.8[a]

[a]Significantly different from 0 at 5% significance level
Source: Kamakura et al. (1996, p. 165)

way to state this is that the inclusive value of the creamy nest will be larger than that of the crunchy nest (at equal prices and display activity). Within the creamy nest, the brand Peter Pan dominates as it has the largest intercept. This is also reflected by the reported average choice shares by Kamakura et al. (1996). Within this segment, Peter Pan Crunchy has an average choice share of 69%. The total choice share of the crunchy nest is only 13%.

Using the parameter estimates and some information on the overall choice shares we can calculate the marginal impact of price within the customer segment we consider here. First we consider the marginal effect of the price of Peter Pan Creamy on its own probability. We will evaluate this at the average probabilities. The overall choice share of this product in this segment is equal to 69%. The share within the nest equals 80% (numbers are obtained from Fig. 1 in Kamakura et al. 1996). Formula (2.46) now evaluates to:

$$\begin{aligned}\frac{\partial \Pr[Y_i = j]}{\partial V_{i,j|m(j)}} &= \Pr[Y_i = j]\left\{(1 - \Pr[Y_i = j])\right.\\ &\quad \left. + \left(\frac{1}{\lambda_{m(j)}} - 1\right)(1 - \Pr[Y_i = j | C_i = m(j)])\right\}\\ &= 0.69\left\{(1 - 0.69) + \left(\frac{1}{0.8} - 1\right)(1 - 0.80)\right\} = 0.25. \qquad (2.52)\end{aligned}$$

Therefore the marginal effect of own price equals:

$$\frac{\partial \Pr[Y_i = j]}{\partial p_{ij}} = \frac{\partial \Pr[Y_i = j]}{\partial V_{ij|m(j)}} \frac{\partial V_{ij|m(j)}}{\partial p_{ij}} = 0.25 \times (-6.1 \times 0.8) = -1.22. \qquad (2.53)$$

This means that a price increase of 10 cents decreases the choice probability of Peter Pan Creamy by about 0.12. Note that the final multiplication by 0.8 is due the fact that the explained utility contains the dissimilarity coefficient in Kamakura et al. (1996). The cross effect of this price change on another creamy product, say Skippy Creamy (choice share within segment equal to 13% and within the nest 15%), can be obtained using the formula in Eq. (2.48):

$$\begin{aligned}\frac{\partial \Pr[Y_i = j]}{\partial V_{i,k|m}} &= -\Bigg[\Pr[Y_i = j]\Pr[Y_i = k] \\ &\quad + \left(\frac{1}{\lambda_m} - 1\right)\Pr[Y_i = j|C_i = m]\Pr[Y_i = k|C_i = m]\Pr[C_i = m]\Bigg] \\ &= -\left[0.13 \times 0.69 + \left(\frac{1}{0.8} - 1\right) \times 0.15 \times 0.80 \times 0.86\right] = -0.116,\end{aligned} \tag{2.54}$$

where 0.86 equals the choice share of the creamy nest. The marginal cross effect becomes $-0.116 \times (-6.1 \times 0.8) = 0.566$. If Peter Pan Creamy would increase its price by 10 cents, the choice share of Skippy Creamy would increase by 0.056. Note that this is a larger impact than what would be expected based on cross-effects that are proportional to choice shares as in the MNL. The cross effect on a product in the other nest uses formula (2.50). Considering the impact on Peter Pan Crunchy (choice share 8%) we obtain $\frac{\partial \Pr[Y_i=j]}{\partial V_{i,k|m(k)}} = -\Pr[Y_i = j]\Pr[Y_i = k] = -0.69 \times 0.08 = -0.055$ and for the marginal effect $-0.055 \times (-6.1 \times 0.8) = 0.268$. So the choice share of this product increases by 0.0268 for a 10 cents price increase of Peter Pan Creamy.

2.3.5 *Generalized Extreme Value*

The MNL and the nested logit model are both members of the same family of models. This family is known as the class of Generalized Extreme Value [GEV] models (McFadden 1978). This class can actually generate an infinite number of models. However, the two best known models are MNL and nested logit.

The basis for GEV models is still a random utility specification. For customer i alternative j has utility $V_{ij} + \varepsilon_{ij}$ and the marginal distributions of ε_{ij} are type-1 extreme value with scale parameter μ. The joint distribution of all error terms however is governed by a function $G(z_1, \ldots, z_J)$, where z_j simply denotes one of the arguments of this function. Different members of the class of GEV models are obtained by specifying different functions. However, to be consistent with utility maximization the function G needs to satisfy a number of properties for $z_1, \ldots, z_J \geq 0$[7]:

[7]See Ben-Akiva and Lerman (1985) for a more extensive discussion.

1. G is non-negative;
2. G is homogenous of degree $\mu > 0$, that is, $G(\alpha z_1, \ldots, \alpha z_J) = \alpha^{\mu} G(z_1, \ldots, z_J)$;
3. $\lim_{z_j \to \infty} G(z_1, \ldots, z_J) = \infty$ for $j = 1, \ldots, J$;
4. the l-th partial derivative of G with respect to any combination of l distinct z_j's is non-negative if l is odd and non-positive if l is even.

Given an appropriate function $G()$ the cumulative distribution function of the errors is given by:

$$F(\varepsilon_{i1}, \varepsilon_{i2}, \ldots, \varepsilon_{iJ}) = \exp\left(-G\left(\exp\left(-\varepsilon_{i1}\right), \ldots, \exp\left(-\varepsilon_{iJ}\right)\right)\right) \tag{2.55}$$

which is a well-defined cumulative distribution function and where the marginal distribution of ε_{ij} is extreme value.

If a function G satisfies the mentioned properties we can show that the probability of a customer choosing brand j equals:

$$\begin{aligned} \Pr[Y_i = j] &= \frac{\exp\left(V_{ij}\right) G_j\left(\exp\left(V_{i1}\right), \ldots, \exp\left(V_{iJ}\right)\right)}{\mu G\left(\exp\left(V_{i1}\right), \ldots, \exp\left(V_{iJ}\right)\right)} \\ &= \frac{\exp\left(V_{ij} + \log G_j\left(\exp\left(V_{i1}\right), \ldots, \exp\left(V_{iJ}\right)\right)\right)}{\sum_{k=1}^{J} \exp\left(V_{ik} + \log G_k\left(\exp\left(V_{i1}\right), \ldots, \exp\left(V_{iJ}\right)\right)\right)} \end{aligned} \tag{2.56}$$

where $G_j(z_1, \ldots, z_J)$ denotes the derivative of $G(z_1, \ldots, z_J)$ with respect to z_j. The first equality is proven in McFadden (1978) using the result in Eq. (2.14) and the mentioned properties of G. The second equality follows from differentiating the μ-homogeneity definition of G with respect to α and next setting $\alpha = 1$, this leads to:

$$\mu G(z_1, \ldots, z_J) = \sum_j z_j G_j(z_1, \ldots, z_J). \tag{2.57}$$

Now it is time to consider some special cases in the GEV family of models. If we set the function G to be $\sum_j z_j^{\mu}$ we have $\log G_j(z_1, \ldots, z_J) = \log(\mu) + (\mu - 1)\log(z_j)$ and we obtain:

$$\Pr[Y_i = j] = \frac{\exp\left(V_{ij} + \log\mu + (\mu - 1) V_{ij}\right)}{\sum_{k=1}^{J} \exp\left(V_{ik} + \log\mu + (\mu - 1) V_{ik}\right)} = \frac{\exp\left(\mu V_{ij}\right)}{\sum_{k=1}^{J} \exp\left(\mu V_{ik}\right)} \tag{2.58}$$

which obviously is very similar to the MNL model. The only difference is that the explained part of the utilities V_{ij} is scaled by μ. As the μ parameter reflects the scale of the error distribution we know that it is not separately identified from the scale of the parameters that appear in V_{ij}. Under the identification restriction $\mu = 1$, we obtain the standard MNL model.

On the other hand we obtain the nested logit if we set:

$$G(z_1, \dots, z_J) = \sum_{m=1}^{M} \left(\sum\nolimits_{k \in C_m} (z_k)^{1/\mu} \right)^{\mu} \tag{2.59}$$

with the earlier introduced definition of the set C_m. It can be shown that this function satisfies all requirements if $0 < \mu \leq 1$. A detailed exposition of this is also provided in Cameron and Trivedi (2005). The log derivative is given by:

$$\log G_j(z_1, \dots z_J) = (\mu - 1) \log \left(\sum\nolimits_{l \in C_{m(j)}} (z_l)^{\frac{1}{\mu}} \right) + \left(\frac{1}{\mu} - 1 \right) \log z_j \tag{2.60}$$

where, as before, $m(j)$ gives the nest to which j belongs. Plugging this in Eq. (2.56) gives:

$$\Pr[Y_i = j] = \frac{\exp\left(V_{ij} + (\mu - 1) \log \left(\sum\nolimits_{l \in C_{m(j)}} \exp(V_{il})^{\frac{1}{\mu}} \right) + \left(\frac{1}{\mu} - 1 \right) V_{ij} \right)}{\sum_{k=1}^{J} \exp\left(V_{ik} + (\mu - 1) \log \left(\sum\nolimits_{l \in C_{m(k)}} \exp(V_{il})^{\frac{1}{\mu}} \right) + \left(\frac{1}{\mu} - 1 \right) V_{ik} \right)}$$
$$= \frac{\exp\left(\mu \log \sum\nolimits_{l \in C_{m(j)}} \exp(V_{il}/\mu) \right) \frac{\exp(V_{ij}/\mu)}{\sum_{l \in C_{m(j)}} \exp(V_{il}/\mu)}}{\sum_{k=1}^{J} \left[\exp\left(\mu \log \sum\nolimits_{l \in C_{m(k)}} \exp(V_{il}/\mu) \right) \frac{\exp(V_{ik}/\mu)}{\sum_{l \in C_{m(k)}} \exp(V_{il}/\mu)} \right]}. \tag{2.61}$$

The denominator can be simplified by noting that the sum over all options can be written as a sum over all nests, and within each nest over the products in the nest. We then obtain:

$$\Pr[Y_i = j] = \frac{\exp\left(\mu \log \sum\nolimits_{l \in C_{m(j)}} \exp(V_{il}/\mu) \right) \frac{\exp(V_{ij}/\mu)}{\sum_{l \in C_{m(j)}} \exp(V_{il}/\mu)}}{\sum_m \exp\left(\mu \log \sum\nolimits_{l \in C_m} \exp(V_{il}/\mu) \right) \frac{\sum_{k \in C_m} \exp(V_{ik}/\mu)}{\sum_{l \in C_m} \exp(V_{il}/\mu)}}$$
$$= \frac{\exp(V_{ij}/\mu)}{\sum\nolimits_{l \in C_{m(j)}} \exp(V_{il}/\mu)} \frac{\exp\left(\mu \log \sum\nolimits_{l \in C_{m(j)}} \exp(V_{il}/\mu) \right)}{\sum_m \exp\left(\mu \log \sum\nolimits_{l \in C_m} \exp(V_{il}/\mu) \right)}. \tag{2.62}$$

If we would further split V_{ij} into a nest and product specific part we would obtain the same type of expression as in Eq. (2.41). Nest-specific inclusive value parameters are obtained by specifying μ to depend on m in Eq. (2.59).

2.3.6 Generalized Nested Logit

In Sect. 2.3.2 we have seen that the nested logit alleviates the IIA property by allowing for a specific form of correlation between the unexplained utility components of products that are in the same nest. However, the derived marginal effects show that the competitive structure in the nested logit is still quite restrictive. The generalized nested logit [GNL] model (Wen and Koppelman 2001) solves this.

The main idea in the GNL is that a product can *partly* belong to a certain nest. The fraction with which product $j = 1, \ldots, J$ belongs to nest $m = 1, \ldots, M$ is given by α_{jm}, where $\alpha_{jm} \geq 0$ and $\sum_m \alpha_{jm} = 1$ for all products j. The GNL is a particular case of a GEV model and is obtained by using:

$$G(z_1, \ldots, z_J) = \sum_{m=1}^{M} \left(\sum_{j=1}^{J} (\alpha_{jm} z_j)^{\frac{1}{\mu_m}} \right)^{\mu_m} \tag{2.63}$$

where μ_m is the logsum or dissimilarity parameter for nest m and statisfies $0 < \mu_m \leq 1$. It can be checked that this function satisfies all requirement of the GEV model.

If we, as usual, set the explained part of the utility of alternative j for individual i to V_{ij} we obtain[8]:

$$\Pr[Y_i = j] = \sum_{m=1}^{M} \Pr[C_i = m] \Pr[Y_i = j | C_i = m]$$

$$= \sum_{m=1}^{M} \left(\frac{\left(\sum_{k=1}^{J} (\alpha_{km} \exp(V_{ik}))^{\frac{1}{\mu_m}}\right)^{\mu_m}}{\sum_{m'=1}^{M} \left(\left(\sum_{k=1}^{J} (\alpha_{km'} \exp(V_{ik}))^{\frac{1}{\mu_{m'}}}\right)^{\mu_{m'}}\right)} \frac{(\alpha_{jm} \exp(V_{ij}))^{\frac{1}{\mu_m}}}{\sum_{j'=1}^{J} (\alpha_{j'm} \exp(V_{ij'}))^{\frac{1}{\mu_m}}} \right). \tag{2.64}$$

The first term in the multiplication gives the probability of choosing nest m, this probability can be rewritten in terms of inclusive values as we did for the (standard) nested logit, that, $\Pr[C_i = m]$ can be written as:

$$\Pr[C_i = m] = \frac{\exp\left(\mu_m \log \sum_{j=1}^{M} (\alpha_{jm} \exp(V_{ij}))^{\frac{1}{\mu_m}}\right)}{\sum_{m'=1}^{M} \exp\left(\mu_{m'} \log \sum_{j=1}^{M} (\alpha_{jm'} \exp(V_{ij}))^{\frac{1}{\mu_{m'}}}\right)}. \tag{2.65}$$

The above expressions give the GNL in its most general form. In practice one will choose a particular parameterization of V_{ij}. Furthermore, one may impose some

[8]See Wen and Koppelman (2001).

restrictions on the α_{jm} parameters. If, for each j, we set only one of the $\alpha_{j1}, \ldots, \alpha_{jM}$ parameters to 1 and the others to zero, we obtain the standard nested logit with one level. If we create a nest for each possible pair of brands and set the corresponding α's to ½ and all others to zero, we obtain the so-called paired combinatorial logit model (Chu 1989; Koppelman and Wen 2000). If we restrict all μ_{m} to be equal we obtain the cross-nested logit model (Vovsha 1997). The Ordered Generalized Extreme Value model (Small 1987) and the Product Differentiation model (Bresnahan et al. 1997) set the nesting structure based on observable product dimensions or characteristics. Wen and Koppelman (2001) provide a detailed discussion of these restricted versions of the GNL. They also describe how the GNL closely approximates the standard nested logit with multiple levels. Other information, such as expert knowledge on the market structure, may also be used to set a number of α parameters to zero. Although this restricts the flexibility of the GNL, this will lead to a reduction in parameter uncertainty.

Restrictions on the α parameters have a direct impact on the cross-effects of marketing instruments. To see this we first look at the impact of a change in the V_{ij} value on the probability that individual i chooses brand j. The marginal effect of changing the valuation of brand j on its own probability can be shown to equal (Wen and Koppelman 2001):

$$\frac{\partial \Pr[Y_i = j]}{\partial V_{ij}} = \sum_{m=1}^{M} \Pr[C_i = m] \Pr[Y_i = j | C_i = m] \times$$
$$\left(1 - \Pr[Y_i = j] + \left(\frac{1}{\mu_m} - 1\right)(1 - \Pr[Y_i = j | C_i = m])\right). \quad (2.66)$$

The cross effect of the valuation of brand k on the probability of brand j equals:

$$\frac{\partial \Pr[Y_i = j]}{\partial V_{ik}} = -\left[\Pr[Y_i = j] \Pr[Y_i = k]\right.$$
$$+ \sum_{m=1}^{M} \left(\frac{1}{\mu_m} - 1\right) \Pr[Y_i = j | C_i = m] \Pr[Y_i = k | C_i = m]$$
$$\left.\Pr[C_i = m]\right], \text{for } j \neq k. \quad (2.67)$$

Comparing these two equations to the corresponding equations for the standard nested logit in Eqs. (2.46), (2.48) and (2.50) reconfirms that the GNL is indeed a generalization of the standard nested logit. Through the probability $\Pr[C_i = m]$ in the expression above, the cross effects depends on the characteristics of all other brands l that are in the same nests as j and k. Note that if a brand k does not appear in nest m ($\alpha_{km} = 0$) the probability $\Pr[Y_i = k | C_i = m]$ will be zero. The expression in Eq. (2.67) also illustrates that the GNL solves the IIA property.

The GNL contains three sets of parameters, the logsum parameters μ_m, the allocation parameters α_{jm} and the parameters β that relate to the explained utilities V_{ij}. All three sets of parameters need to be estimated. Oftentimes, some of the α's will be restricted to 0. The remaining parameters can be estimated using maximum likelihood. It is obvious that no closed form expression exists for the maximum likelihood estimates. Instead, we need to numerically maximize the log likelihood over the parameters. During this optimization, the α parameters and μ_m parameters need to be restricted between 0 and 1 and for the α parameters we also require that $\sum_m \alpha_{jm} = 1$ for all j.

2.3.7 Example of Generalized Nested Logit

Below we reproduce the application of the Generalized Nested Logit as presented in Wen and Koppelman (2001). Another interesting application of the Generalized Nested Logit in the marketing literature can be found in Guyt and Gijsbrechts (2014).

Wen and Koppelman (2001) study the demand for a high-speed rail connection in Canada. The data is obtained through a survey in which respondents need to choose between different modes of transportation in hypothetical situations. The considered modes are air, train, bus and car. Across different choice tasks the researchers manipulated the frequency, costs, in-vehicle travel time and out-of-vehicle travel time. Within one choice task multiple alternatives of the same mode may be present.

Different models are considered to describe the consumer preferences. The MNL model is clearly rejected in favor of models with a nesting structure. Across a number of nesting models the Generalized Nested Logit performs best. The authors apply an exploratory analysis to find the best nesting structure. The best performing model has as nests: Train-Car, Air-Car, Train-Air-Car, Train only, Car only, Bus only. Table 2.3 shows the parameter estimates for this model.

The parameter estimates confirm that alternatives are indeed spread over different nests in the Generalized Nested Logit model. For example, the car alternative belongs for 41% to the Air-Car nest, and for about 20% to the Car nest. Over the different nests the allocation parameters sum to 1, as can be checked in the table. This allocation allows for a very flexible substitution pattern. In this chapter we will not work out any examples of cross effects, however, they can straightforwardly be obtained from Eqs. (2.66) and (2.67).

A goal of studies like this one is to obtain the willingness to pay for certain characteristics. From the results above we can obtain the willingness to pay for the in-vehicle travel time for example. A decrease of 60 minutes travel time, increases the utility by $60 \times .0031 = .186$ utility units. This increase can exactly be compensated by a price increase of $0.186/0.0173 = 10.75$, or about C$ 11. In other words, individuals will be willing to pay C$ 11 for a one hour decrease in in-vehicle travel time. Likewise the out-of-vehicle travel time is valued at C$ 38 per hour.

Table 2.3 Parameter estimates for generalized nested logit for choice of transportation mode

	Estimate	Standard error
Mode constants		
Air	6.264	(0.321)
Train	4.981	(0.285)
Car	5.133	(0.253)
Bus	0[a]	
Frequency	0.0288	(0.002)
Travel costs (C$)	−0.0173	(0.002)
In-vehicle time	−0.0031	(0.0002)
Out-of-vehicle time	−0.0110	(0.001)
Logsum parameter		
Train-Car	0.0146	(0.002)
Air-Car	0.2819	(0.032)
Train-Car-Air	0.01	(−)[b]

Allocation	Air	Train	Car	Bus
Train-Car nest		0.272 (0.033)	0.106 (0.012)	
Air-Car nest	0.606 (0.040)		0.418 (0.046)	
Train-Car-Air nest	0.394 (0.041)	0.529 (0.031)	0.274 (0.029)	
Train nest		0.200 (0.025)		
Car nest			0.202 (0.032)	
Bus nest				1

[a]Restricted to zero for identification
[b]Could not be obtained due to correlations between inclusive value variables and allocation parameters
Source: Wen and Koppelman (2001, p. 638)

2.4 Ordered Logit and Probit

2.4.1 *Introduction*

In the models discussed so far, customers choose a particular brand out of an unordered set of available brands. As said these models also apply to other settings where the dependent variable is categorical. The discussed models consider all alternatives as being a priori the same. However, in quite many cases there is a particular ordering in the alternatives. The most straightforward example is where individuals choose a particular value on a Likert scale in a survey. For example, a respondent in a survey may choose between (1) completely dissatisfied, (2) dissatisfied, (3) neutral, (4) satisfied, or (5) completely satisfied on a question whether she is satisfied with the service of a company. This could be seen as a standard categorical choice and the MNL could be applied. However, it makes sense to explicitly account for the ordering of the answer categories. We will present two models that do this: the ordered logit and the ordered probit model (McKelvey and Zavoina 1975). Both models assume that there is a one-dimensional latent construct that relates to the outcome categories.

2.4.2 Model Specification

To formalize things, suppose that there are M different ordered outcome categories. In some sense outcome category m is lower on a certain underlying scale than category $m+1$, for $m = 1, \ldots, M-1$. The decision of individual i is denoted by Y_i. We introduce a latent variable Y_i^* that gives individual i's position on the latent scale. This latent variable is related to an intercept and a vector of individual-specific variables x_i, that is,

$$Y_i^* = \alpha + x_i'\beta + \varepsilon_i, \text{ with } \mathrm{E}[\varepsilon_i] = 0. \tag{2.68}$$

The latent variable has a direct and deterministic relation with the chosen category Y_i according to:

$$Y_i = \begin{cases} 1 \text{ if } \tau_0 < Y_i^* \leq \tau_1 \\ 2 \text{ if } \tau_1 < Y_i^* \leq \tau_2 \\ \vdots \\ j \text{ if } \tau_{j-1} < Y_i^* \leq \tau_j \\ \vdots \\ M \text{ if } \tau_{M-1} < Y_i^* \leq \tau_M \end{cases} \tag{2.69}$$

where τ_j, for $j = 0, \ldots, M$ are threshold values on the latent scale and $\tau_{j-1} < \tau_j$ for $j = 1, \ldots, M$. We set $\tau_0 = -\infty$ and $\tau_M = \infty$ such that every possible value of Y_i^* corresponds to one of the response categories. In other words we define a latent scale and we use the thresholds τ_j to divide this scale into M different regions. The probability of observing individual i choosing category j is therefore equal to the probability that the latent variable is in between the thresholds τ_{j-1} and τ_j, that is,

$$\Pr[Y_i = j] = \Pr\left[\tau_{j-1} < Y_i^* \leq \tau_j\right] = \Pr\left[Y_i^* \leq \tau_j\right] - \Pr\left[Y_i^* \leq \tau_{j-1}\right]. \tag{2.70}$$

Using the linear specification for Y_i^* in Eq. (2.68) and denoting the distribution function of ε_i by $F(\cdot)$, we obtain:

$$\Pr\left[Y_i^* \leq \tau_j\right] = \Pr\left[\alpha + x_i'\beta + \varepsilon_i \leq \tau_j\right] = F\left(\tau_j - \alpha - x_i'\beta\right). \tag{2.71}$$

The probability of observing category j therefore becomes:

$$\Pr[Y_i = j] = \begin{cases} F\left(\tau_1 - \alpha - x_i'\beta\right), \text{for } j = 1 \\ F\left(\tau_j - \alpha - x_i'\beta\right) - F\left(\tau_{j-1} - \alpha - x_i'\beta\right), \text{for } j = 2, \ldots, M-1 \\ 1 - F\left(\tau_{M-1} - \alpha - x_i'\beta\right), \text{for } j = M. \end{cases} \tag{2.72}$$

For the first and the last line we have used that $F(-\infty) = 0$ and $F(\infty) = 1$.

Similar to the brand choice models, different variants of the model can be obtained by choosing a functional form for F. The two most popular choices are the logistic distribution and the normal distribution. When we choose the logistic distribution ($F = \Lambda$, see Eq. (2.4)) we obtain the ordered logit model. When the normal distribution is used ($F = \Phi$, see Eq. (2.5)) we have the ordered probit model. Both models tend to perform rather similarly. The ordered logit model has the advantage of leading to easier expressions for probabilities and marginal effects. The ordered probit model is sometimes easier in more complex models where correlations between different choices need to be modeled. The parameters of the ordered logit or probit can straightforwardly be estimated using Maximum Likelihood methods.

From Eq. (2.72) it is clear that we cannot identify all threshold parameters and the intercept. Only the difference between the thresholds and the intercept matters for the probabilities. This is due to the fact that the level of the latent scale that we have introduced is not observed. For the same reason the variance of the error term ε_i cannot be identified. Several identifying restrictions are possible, the most common restriction is to set $\alpha = 0$ and to also restrict the variance of ε_i. Alternatively, one may arbitrarily set one threshold to 0 and keep the intercept. The variance of ε_i can also be estimated if another threshold is set to a fixed number, for example 1. The identification restriction that is chosen has no impact on the quality or performance of the model. If a Bayesian estimation method is used it is advisable to use as few threshold parameters as possible. The intuitive reason for this is that sampling the parameters that appear in the Y_i^* equation is easy, while sampling the threshold parameters is difficult. For maximum likelihood estimation, the choice of the identifying restriction is less important.

2.4.3 Interpretation

The parameters in the ordered logit/probit model can only be directly interpreted in terms of the latent scale Y_i^*. If the dependent variable gives the response on a Likert scale measuring satisfaction with a company, the latent variable can easily be interpreted as the underlying (continuous) satisfaction. If a parameter β is positive, this then implies that if the corresponding x-variable increases, the customer becomes more satisfied. Of course, this does not imply that the probability of this individual choosing a certain level on the Likert scale also increases. To see this, let us consider the impact of one of the explanatory variables (say x_{ik}) on the probability of observing customer i choosing category j.

From Eq. (2.72) it follows that:

$$\begin{aligned}\frac{\partial \Pr[Y_i = j]}{\partial x_{ik}} &= \frac{\partial F\left(\tau_j - \alpha - x_i'\beta\right)}{\partial x_{ik}} - \frac{\partial F\left(\tau_{j-1} - \alpha - x_i'\beta\right)}{\partial x_{ik}} \\ &= -\left(f\left(\tau_j - \alpha - x_i'\beta\right) - f\left(\tau_{j-1} - \alpha - x_i'\beta\right)\right)\beta_k\end{aligned} \tag{2.73}$$

where $f()$ denotes the density function of ε_i. For the ordered logit this density equals $\lambda(z) = \Lambda(z)(1 - \Lambda(z))$. For the ordered probit the density is $\phi(z) = \frac{1}{\sqrt{2\pi}} \exp\left(-\frac{z}{2}\right)$. The sign of the marginal effect in Eq. (2.73) is not directly clear as the difference between the two density functions may be positive or negative. Only for the first category ($j = 1$) and the final category ($j = M$) we know the sign of the marginal effect. This follows from the fact that $f(z) \geq 0$, for all z and $f(-\infty) = f(\infty) = 0$. Therefore for $j = 1$ the marginal effect has the opposite sign of β_k, while for $j = M$ the marginal effect has the same sign.

The above also makes sense intuitively. In the satisfaction example, if β_k is positive an increase in x_{ik} implies that the underlying satisfaction increases. This decreases the probability of reporting completely dissatisfied and increases the probability of reporting completely satisfied. However, without further information we cannot say whether the probability for the neutral category increases or decreases. This completely depends on the initial satisfaction of the customer.

The ordered logit model is also sometimes interpreted in terms of odds ratios (see Franses and Paap 2001 and Vol. I, Sect. 8.2). The odds ratio is then defined in the terms of the probability of observing outcome category j or lower versus higher than outcome category j, that is,

$$\frac{\Pr[Y_i \leq j]}{\Pr[Y_i > j]} = \frac{\Pr\left[Y_i^* \leq \tau_j\right]}{1 - \Pr\left[Y_i^* \leq \tau_j\right]} = \frac{\Lambda\left(\tau_j - \alpha - x_i'\beta\right)}{1 - \Lambda\left(\tau_j - \alpha - x_i'\beta\right)} = \exp\left(\tau_j - \alpha - x_i'\beta\right). \tag{2.74}$$

In other words, the log odds ratio is linear in x_i. If $\beta_k > 0$ this odds ratio will decrease if x_{ik} increases and the probability of a low category also decreases.

2.4.4 *Example of the Ordered Probit Model: Customer Satisfaction*

In their paper Kekre et al. (1995) use an ordered probit model to study the determinants of the overall satisfaction of customers with different software products and service support for mainframes and workstations. The main dependent variable is an overall satisfaction score, denoted by OS, which is measured on a 5 point scale where a 5 indicates very satisfied. The goal of the analysis is to figure out how certain features of the software affect the overall satisfaction. The following features are considered: reliability (REL), capability (CAP), usability (USE), installability

Table 2.4 Parameter estimates for full ordered probit model for product satistisfaction

	Estimate	*t*-value
Intercept	−10.421	−388.39
REL	0.209	8.22
CAP	0.940	35.80
USE	0.524	19.56
INS	0.068	2.36
MNT	0.152	5.62
PFC	0.344	12.37
DOC	0.083	3.29
Network product	−0.002	−0.07
Mainframe product	−0.127	−4.56
Expert programmer	−0.083	−3.04
End-user	0.015	0.57
Network product*REL	0.271	10.18
Network product*MNT	0.012	0.45
Network product*PFC	0.227	8.64
Mainframe product*REL	0.139	5.21
Mainframe product*MNT	0.016	0.60
Mainframe product*PFC	0.205	9.63
Expert programmer*REL	0.195	9.48
Expert programmer*CAP	0.231	8.81
End user*USE	1.052	37.21
End user*DOC	0.512	18.13
Threshold 2 vs. 3	2.647	92.74
Threshold 3 vs. 4	3.755	133.30
Threshold 4 vs. 5	5.438	195.21

Source: Kekre et al. (1995, p. 1463)

(INS), maintainability (MNT), performance (PFC), and documentation (DOC). We refer to Kekre et al. (1995) for an exact definition of these features. As additional explanatory variables the authors use the type of product (network, mainframe, or other) and the type of user (expert programmer, end user, or other). In the analysis also the interactions between some software features and product/user type are considered.

As identification restriction, the authors choose to set the first threshold to zero and include a constant in the equation for the latent satisfaction Y_i^*. The model with interactions is tested against restricted models without interactions and found to be superior. The parameter estimates for this model as reported by Kekre et al. (1995) are given in Table 2.4.

As expected all the product features have a positive main effect on the underlying satisfaction score. This is as expected given that these features are all formulated in a positive sense. The capabilities of the software (CAP) seem to have the largest impact. All these effects should be interpreted for a product and a user in the "other" category, as these levels are chosen as baseline in the dummy coding. The interaction effects in the model indicate how the effects are different for different products or users. With these interactions in mind it is difficult to directly interpret the coefficients for the variables that code the types of users and software.

The estimation results identify some very clear interaction effects. The strongest interaction effect is found for end users and the usability of the software. End users tend to value the usability much more than other users. For expert programmers and other users, the impact of the usability score equals 0.524 while for end users it equals $0.524 + 1.052 = 1.576$. As another example, the results show that expert programmers especially value the capabilities of the software.

The estimated thresholds allow us to judge the effect sizes of the various features and the distances between outcomes. The threshold that distinguishes the category very dissatisfied from dissatisfied has implicitly been set to 0. The value for the threshold between categories 2 and 3 ($= 2.647$), indicates that there is a rather large distance between the very dissatisfied category and the neutral category. The distance between the largest two thresholds is about 1.7. This means that to move someone from the border between neutral and satisfied to the border between satisfied and very satisfied the latent score needs to increase by 1.7. Given the estimate for CAP ($= 0.940$), this means that to achieve this increase the capabilities of the software would need to improve by $1.7/0.94 = 1.8$ (for an expert programmer a change of $1.7/1.576 = 1.08$ would be enough).

Using the model, Kekre et al. (1995) perform a sensitivity analysis to measure the impact of increasing one of the product features scores by $+1$ on the overall satisfaction. Such an analysis is very similar to calculating marginal effects. Improving the capabilities (CAP) is shown to have the largest impact on the number of very satisfied customers. Improving the installability (INS) has the smallest impact. For all features the number of very satisfied customers goes up, while the number of very dissatisfied customers goes down. This corresponds to the positive sign of the respective parameters. For the intermediate categories the signs of the change cannot be related to the sign of the parameters. However, in this specific case the proportion of all intermediate categories decrease as a result of a $+ 1$ change in a product feature. This result is mainly driven by the very large proportion of customers that is already very satisfied.

2.5 Models for Censored Variables and Corner Solutions

2.5.1 *Introduction*

The models described sofar in this chapter all deal with a discrete dependent variable. In many cases in marketing the dependent variable has a discrete as well as a continuous aspect. Broadly speaking there are two possible situations in which this happens. In one situation there is a process that censors or selects the data in some way; in the other the decision problem of the individual allows the existence of corner solutions (Wooldridge 2002). The class of models that deal with sample selection issues is very related. These models are discussed in Sect. 2.6. In the current section we focus on models for censored variables and corner solutions. However, before we go into details we further describe the situations in which these two classes of models are useful.

First, there may be a true censoring process, that is, for some observations we can only observe a censored version of the dependent variable. The typical example is modeling the demand for a concert where the venue has a capacity constraint of, say, 250 people. We are interested in modeling the demand, but we only observe the number of tickets sold. As long as the demand is below 250 there is no problem, the demand equals the number of tickets sold. However, when the number of tickets sold equals 250 we only know that the demand was equal to or larger than 250. Because of this censoring process one cannot use a simple linear regression model in order to describe the demand.

The existence of corner solutions is also very common in marketing and economics. In this case there is an economic agent (say a consumer) who solves a utility maximization problem subject to certain constraints. For example, consider a customer who chooses the amount of money to spend on travel by solving a utility maximization problem. In principle, the amount spent should be treated as a continuous variable. However, this amount is restricted to be larger or equal to zero. Dependent on the utility function, the utility-maximizing solution may be in the corner of the allowed solution space, that is, the optimal amount may be exactly equal to 0. This implies that there is a non-trivial probability that the amount equals 0 exactly. The dependent variable is therefore a mixture of a continuous and a discrete variable. As another example, the dependent variable may be the amount of money someone donates to charity (Van Diepen et al. 2009), or the number of loyalty points collected by a member of a loyalty program (Dorotic et al. 2014). In both cases, the dependent variable will be 0 for some individuals in a particular period, while for others it is a positive number.

If the dependent variable is censored or subject to corner solutions, a model for such a variable needs to capture the discrete and the continuous aspect of the variable. Although similar models may be used for both cases, the applicability and interpretation of the models will differ. Below we discuss the most commonly used reduced-form models for these settings. Formal utility-maximization based (structural) models are very briefly discussed in Sect. 2.7.3, a more thorough discussion is also available in Chap. 7.

2.5.2 *Type-1 Tobit*[9]

The most straightforward model for censored variables or corner solutions is called the Type-1 Tobit model (Amemiya 1985; Tobin 1958). This model may be applied for various processes. However, it is most common to present the model for the case of censoring from below at 0.

[9]Vol. I, Sect. 8.5.2 gives a short introduction of Tobit models.

The Type-1 Tobit model simply specifies a latent variable that can take on any value. If this latent variable is negative, the observed dependent variable equals 0. If the latent variable is positive, the dependent variable is equal to the latent variable. In the context of donations, we can think of the latent variable as the willingness to donate. Again we will denote the latent variable for consumer i by Y_i^*. For this latent variable we specify a standard linear model, that is,

$$Y_i^* = x_i'\beta + \varepsilon_i, \text{ with } \varepsilon_i \sim N\left(0, \sigma^2\right) \tag{2.75}$$

where the vector x_i now also contains a constant term. The Tobit-1 model then links the latent variable to the dependent variable by specifying:

$$Y_i = \begin{cases} 0 \text{ if } Y_i^* \leq 0 \\ Y_i^* \text{if } Y_i^* > 0. \end{cases} \tag{2.76}$$

One can see the Tobit-1 model as a mix between a probit model for the events $Y_i = 0$ versus $Y_i > 0$ and a linear regression model, where the parameters in both models are assumed to be the same. From this observation we can work out a number of interesting quantities. First, the probability of a positive response equals:

$$\Pr\left[Y_i > 0\right] = \Pr\left[Y_i^* > 0\right] = \Pr\left[\frac{1}{\sigma}\varepsilon_i > -x_i'\beta/\sigma\right] = 1 - \Phi\left(-x_i'\beta/\sigma\right) = \Phi\left(x_i'\beta/\sigma\right). \tag{2.77}$$

Note that because we also observe the non-zero Y_i's, we can identify the scale of β and the variance σ^2 in the Tobit-1 model. The expectation of Y_i conditional on it being positive equals:

$$\mathrm{E}\left[Y_i | Y_i > 0\right] = \mathrm{E}\left[Y_i^* | Y_i^* > 0\right] = x_i'\beta + \mathrm{E}\left[\varepsilon_i | \varepsilon_i > -x_i'\beta\right] = x_i'\beta + \sigma \frac{\phi\left(x_i'\beta/\sigma\right)}{\Phi\left(x_i'\beta/\sigma\right)} \tag{2.78}$$

where the latter ratio follows from properties of the normal distribution and is usually called the inverse Mills ratio. This ratio is denoted by $\lambda_i = \lambda\left(x_i'\beta/\sigma\right) = \phi\left(x_i'\beta/\sigma\right)/\Phi\left(x_i'\beta/\sigma\right)$. Using these results the unconditional expectation becomes:

$$\mathrm{E}\left[Y_i\right] = \Pr\left[Y_i > 0\right] \mathrm{E}\left[Y_i | Y_i > 0\right] = \Phi\left(\frac{x_i'\beta}{\sigma}\right)\left(x_i'\beta + \sigma\lambda_i\right). \tag{2.79}$$

Using (2.79) we can derive the marginal effect of explanatory variable k. A straightforward (but tedious) derivation shows that:

$$\frac{\partial \mathrm{E}\left[Y_i\right]}{\partial x_{ik}} = \Phi\left(x_i'\beta/\sigma\right)\beta_k. \tag{2.80}$$

The sign of this marginal effect is therefore equal to the sign of β_k and the maximum marginal effect is obtained for customers whose probability of a positive outcome is close to 1. Conversely, for individuals whose probability of a positive outcome is almost 0 the marginal effect will also be close to 0.

To estimate β and σ^2 we cannot just regress the observed dependent values on x_i. This would erroneously assume that the expectation of Y_i equals $x_i'\beta$ and introduce a substantial bias. Instead we rely on maximum likelihood estimation. Given observations $y_1, \ldots, y_n$ we specify the log likelihood function as:

$$\log L\left(\beta, \sigma^2\right) = \sum_{i:y_i=0} \log\left(1 - \Phi\left(x_i'\beta/\sigma\right)\right) + \sum_{i:y_i>0}\left(-\frac{1}{2}\log\sigma^2 + \log\phi\left(\frac{y_i - x_i'\beta}{\sigma}\right)\right). \tag{2.81}$$

The first sum in this likelihood is over all observations equal to 0 and the likelihood contribution equals the log of the probability of an outcome equal to 0. The second sum deals with all non-zero observations and the contribution of a single observation equals the log density at the non-zero observed value.

The Tobit-1 model perfectly fits the situation where the dependent variable is subject to a true censoring process. In this case one is actually interested in modeling the latent variable instead of the observed dependent variable. The assumptions of the Tobit-1 then perfectly make sense. Furthermore, in this case one will likely be most interested in the marginal effects of a variable on Y_i^*, which simply equals β.

The Tobit-1 may also be useful to model a variable subject to corner solutions. However, the assumptions of the Tobit-1 may not always hold in such a case. For example, the Tobit-1 assumes that the "yes/no decision" and the "amount decision", that are both present in Y_i, are driven by a single latent variable. This implies that if a variable positively affects the probability of $Y_i > 0$ it also positively affects the conditional expectation $\mathrm{E}[Y_i \mid Y_i > 0]$. This may not always be true. A variable may for example negatively influence the likelihood to donate, but may have a positive influence on the donated amount conditional on donation. Furthermore, the Tobit-1 model cannot well handle the case where there are observations equal to 0, but hardly any observations close to 0. This will happen for example, when some people do not donate but when someone donates she donates a substantial amount.

2.5.3 Example of a Tobit model

Bell et al. (2011) study unplanned buying in a retailing context. In-store marketing is used heavily by retailers to try to induce customers to buy products that they did not plan to buy. Bell et al. (2011) study the rate at which customers buy unplanned items and relate this to, among other things, pre-shopping factors. One of the models they consider is a Tobit model. The main dependent variable in this model is the so-called rate of unplanned buying of household h at shopping trip t, y_{ht}, defined as the ratio of the number of unplanned purchases by the log of the time spent in the store. This rate has a natural lower bound at 0 for those households who do not buy any

Table 2.5 Parameter estimates of a Tobit model for the rate of unplanned purchases

	Estimate	Significance
Overall shopping trip goal		
Fill-in trip, daily essentials, top-up shopping	0.222	*
Major trip, weekly or less often	0.522	***
Store choice goals		
Low prices	0.148	**
Store offers one-stop shopping	0.131	**
Interaction between out-of-store exposure and in-store marketing[a]		
Special offers seen in the leaflet delivered to home	0.252	*
Special offers seen on television, heard on radio, seen in coupons, or communicated by friends and family	0.571	*
Control variables		
Travel to store by bicycle or scooter	0.147	*
Travel to store by car or taxi	0.377	***
Primary shopper is female on current trip	0.332	**
Log number of planned category purchases	−0.330	***
Special offers seen at the shelf	0.377	***
Special offers seen on display away from shelf	0.456	***
I wanted the shopping trip to be fast and efficient	−0.671	***

*, **, *** significantly different from 0 at 5%, 1%, 0.1%

[a]All out-of-store exposure variables are interacted with a dummy indicating whether the household "stays informed about special offers through the leaflet inside the store"

Source: Bell et al. (2011, p. 39)

unplanned items. The data for this study is based on a panel of households who were asked to record after every purchase trip what was bought and whether the purchase was planned beforehand.

The Tobit model that is applied by Bell et al. (2011) contains household-specific fixed effects and a number of household/trip specific explanatory variables. Although also more advanced estimation methods are applied, we will report the findings based on standard maximum likelihood estimation.[10] Table 2.5 gives the obtained parameter estimates, for ease of exposition, we omit all estimates that are not significant at 5%.

The explanatory variables that are used in the model are rather self-explanatory. Most of the variables are 0/1 variables indicating whether a certain statement applies to the focal shopping trip. Interestingly, compared to other trips, both in fill-in trips and in major shopping trips households tend to have a high unplanned buying rate, holding other things constant. Out-of-store marketing exposure does not directly influence the unplanned buying rate significantly. However, it does show a significant interaction effect with in-store promotions.

[10]As Bell et al. (2011) mention standard maximum likelihood estimation is not consistent due to the incidental parameters problem generated by the presence of the household fixed effects.

2.5.4 Two-Part or Hurdle Model

The earlier mentioned problems of the Tobit-1 for variables subject to corner solutions, are solved in the so-called two-part or hurdle model (Cameron and Trivedi 2005; Cragg 1971; Wooldridge 2002). As the name suggests, these models contain two parts. One part deals with the probability of observing a strictly positive outcome, while the second part describes the outcome conditional on knowing that it is positive. In the two-part model we typically specify a logit or probit model with parameters α to describe $\Pr[Y_i > 0]$. For the second part of the model we need to ensure that only (strictly) positive outcomes are possible. Therefore conditional on $Y_i > 0$ we specify either a truncated normal model (Cragg 1971) or a log-linear model. Here we will focus on the version of the model with a log-linear specification,[11] that is,

$$\log Y_i = x_i'\beta + \varepsilon_i, \text{ given } Y_i > 0 \tag{2.82}$$

where $\varepsilon_i \sim N(0, \sigma^2)$.

The parameters in the two-part model are quite easy to estimate as both parts of the model can be treated separately. So, one uses the standard logit or probit techniques to estimate α and straightforward least-squares estimation for β.

For the same reason, parameter interpretation is straightforward. To calculate marginal effects with respect to the expectation of Y_i we need to combine both parts of the model using the chain rule of derivatives to obtain:

$$\frac{\partial \mathrm{E}[Y_i]}{\partial x_{ik}} = \frac{\partial \Pr[Y_i > 0]}{\partial x_{ik}} \mathrm{E}[Y_i|Y_i > 0] + \frac{\partial \mathrm{E}[Y_i|Y_i > 0]}{\partial x_{ik}} \Pr[Y_i > 0]. \tag{2.83}$$

Assuming that the logit model is used for the event $Y_i > 0$ and observing that $\mathrm{E}[Y_i|\, Y_i > 0] = \exp\left(x_i'\beta + \frac{1}{2}\sigma^2\right)$ for the log-linear specification in Eq. (2.82), we obtain:

$$\begin{aligned}\frac{\partial \mathrm{E}[Y_i]}{\partial x_{ik}} &= \frac{\exp(x_i'\alpha)}{1+\exp(x_i'\alpha)} \exp\left(x_i'\beta + \frac{1}{2}\sigma^2\right)\left(\left(1 - \frac{\exp(x_i'\alpha)}{1+\exp(x_i'\alpha)}\right)\alpha_k + \beta_k\right) \\ &= \mathrm{E}[Y_i]\left((1 - \Pr[Y_i > 0])\,\alpha_k + \beta_k\right).\end{aligned} \tag{2.84}$$

Note that if $\Pr[Y_i > 0]$ approaches 1, the marginal effect corresponds to the marginal effect of the log-linear model.

[11]The advantage of using a Truncated Normal is that the resulting model is a generalization of the Tobit-1, that is, under certain parameter restrictions this model reduces to the Tobit-1 model. The log-linear specification is however easier to use.

2.5.5 Example of a Two-Part Model

Dorotic et al. (2014) study the impact of reward redemption in a loyalty program [LP]. Among other things, the paper studies the impact that redemption of rewards has on purchases and future redemptions within the loyalty program. Two different two-part models are used in this study. Both models a built up from a probit part and a log-linear part.

One of the models considers the redemption decision. Under the condition that they have collected enough loyalty points, LP members can decide to redeem in each period. If they redeem, they also decide on the number of points to redeem. Dorotic et al. (2014) formulate the amount decision in terms of the fraction of available points that is redeemed. This setting corresponds to the corner-solution situation mentioned above. There is one decision (redemption amount), but in many periods the redeemed amount equals 0.

The other two-part model deals with the purchase decision. Again in each period the LP member may decide to make a purchase, and if a purchase is made she decides how much to buy. The incidence decision is captured using a probit model and the amount using a log-linear specification. Below we will only consider this purchase model. However, the purchase and redemption models are closely connected through an imposed heterogeneity distribution and the balance of points that a LP member has available at the beginning of a period.

Table 2.6 shows the estimation results dealing with the purchase decision in a model without interaction effects. The explained part of the model is split into several components: a baseline, a time trend, the impact of an approaching redemption threshold (points pressure), the redemption momentum (related to an upcoming redemption), post-reward effects, (mental) accessibility of the loyalty program which gets enhanced once a purchase is made, the log balance, and a (lagged) impact of mailings that were sent to the LP members. For the baseline and trend the model reported in Table 2.6 allows for interaction with certain member characteristics as well as a random member-specific effect. For all the other factors only an interaction with the average number of mailings received is allowed. This latter interaction is included to correct for a possible endogeneity of the mailing decisions made by the LP. All member-specific characteristics have been standardized for ease of interpretation. For more details on the model and estimation results see Dorotic et al. (2014).

The results in Table 2.6 show that the baseline purchase incidence rate is positively related to the age and number of membership years of the LP member. However, quite a lot of the member-to-member variation in the baseline incidence is not explained (see the large estimated variance of the random effect). The trend in the incidence is negative overall, and especially so for older people who have been a member for a long time. As expected all other main factors have a positive impact on the purchase incidence decision. If members feel points pressure, when a redemption is approaching, when they have just redeemed or purchased something, when they have many LP points, or when they have just received a mailing they tend to be more likely to make a purchase. There is an especially strong impact of the redemption momentum.

Table 2.6 Estimation results for two-part model to explain purchases in a loyalty program context

		Purchase incidence	Log(purchase amount)
Baseline	Constant	1.037***	−5.784***
	Average income	0.004	0.076***
	Age	0.052***	−0.040***
	Membership yrs.	0.066***	−0.044***
	Avg. no. mailings	0.059***	0.106***
	Variance of random effect	0.418***	0.539***
Trend	Constant	−0.068***	−0.251***
	Average income	0.005	0.000
	Age	−0.033***	−0.018**
	Membership yrs.	−0.036***	0.035***
	Avg. no. mailings	−0.034***	−0.022***
	Variance of random effect	0.113***	0.143***
Points pressure	Constant	0.053***	0.002
	Avg. no. mailings	−0.012	0.008
Redemption momentum	Constant	1.763***	0.325***
	Avg. no. mailings	−0.548***	−0.020**
Post-reward effect	Constant	0.033***	0.031***
	Avg. no. mailings	−0.006	0.002
Accessibility due to purchase	Constant	0.282***	0.064***
	Avg. no. mailings	−0.031***	0.000
Log balance	Constant	0.040***	0.015***
	Avg. no. mailings	−0.016***	0.006
Mailing decay	Constant	0.021***	0.003**
	Avg. no. mailings	−0.012***	0.007***

*,**,***: significant at 10%, 5%, 1% (formally: 0 not in the 90, 95, 99% highest posterior density region)
Source: Dorotic et al. (2014, p. 348)

All results in the final two columns correspond to the log purchase amount conditional on a purchase being made. This is also positively related to the various variables just mentioned. Only the points-pressure mechanism turns out to be insignificant. Based on the results we can calculate marginal effects. For example, we can consider the marginal effect of a redemption (post-reward effect) on future purchase behavior. The marginal effect on the purchase incidence is given by:

$$\frac{\partial \Pr\left[\text{Purchase}_{it} = \text{yes}\right]}{\partial x_{itk}} = \frac{\partial \Phi\left(x_{it}'\alpha\right)}{\partial x_{itk}} = \phi\left(x_{it}'\alpha\right)\alpha_k \tag{2.85}$$

where $x_{it}'\alpha$ denotes the explained part of the probit model. Let us consider an individual who has 10% probability of making a purchase, for this person $x_{it}'\alpha = \Phi^{-1}(0.1) = -1.28$ such that for this individual the marginal effect equals $\phi(-1.28) \times 0.033 = 0.176 \times 0.033 = 0.0058$ (see also Fig. 2.1 and Eq. (2.9). In other words, if this person would have redeemed a reward her purchase probability would have been about 10.5%, keeping other things fixed. The coefficient for the purchase amount equation indicates that, conditional on a purchase, the purchase amount increases with an additional redemption by about 3%. We can take these together to calculate the percentage increase in the expected purchase amount by noting that:

$$\begin{aligned}
\%\text{increase} &= \frac{\partial \mathrm{E}\left[\text{Purchase amount}\right]/x_{itk}}{\mathrm{E}\left[\text{Purchase amount}\right]}\\
&= \frac{1}{\Phi\left(x_{it}'\alpha\right)\exp\left(x_{it}'\beta+\frac{1}{2}\sigma^2\right)}\frac{\partial \Phi\left(x_{it}'\alpha\right)\exp\left(x_{it}'\beta+\frac{1}{2}\sigma^2\right)}{\partial x_{itk}}\\
&= \frac{1}{\Phi\left(x_{it}'\alpha\right)}\frac{\partial \Phi\left(x_{it}'\alpha\right)}{\partial x_{itk}} + \frac{1}{\exp\left(x_{it}'\beta+\frac{1}{2}\sigma^2\right)}\frac{\partial \exp\left(x_{it}'\beta+\frac{1}{2}\sigma^2\right)}{\partial x_{itk}}\\
&= \frac{\phi\left(x_{it}'\alpha\right)\alpha_k}{\Phi\left(x_{it}'\alpha\right)} + \beta_k \qquad (2.86)
\end{aligned}$$

which for our example of a person with 10% purchase probability evaluates to 0.0058/0.10 + 0.031 = 0.089 or 8.9%. So the redemption event increases the expected purchase quantity by almost 9%. Of course, for different base purchase probabilities we will obtain different effect sizes.

2.6 Sample Selection Models[12]

The class of sample selection models very much resembles the two-part model discussed above. In the sample selection models the dependent variable also has features of a discrete and a continuous variable. One of the best known model is the Tobit-2 model. This model however describes a very different process compared to the Tobit-1 and two-part models. In Sect. 2.6.4 we will discuss these differences.

2.6.1 Specification of the Type-2 Tobit

The classical example of the Type-2 Tobit model (Amemiya 1985) concerns explaining the wage of individuals. If the sample also contains individuals who are not employed, the dependent variable looks like a censored variable. The wage equals 0 for those who are not employed and attains a positive value for all others. The interest of a researcher may especially be in explaining the wage *offer*, or

[12]See also Vol. I, Sect. 8.5.2.3.

potential wage, that a person could get. This wage offer is of course unobserved for those who do not work. This introduces a sample selection model.

The assumptions of the Tobit-1 model are likely invalid. First, the impact of an observed characteristic of an individual may have a different impact on the probability to work (wage > 0), than it has on the (potential) wage itself. Furthermore, conditioning on being employed, the wage is unlikely to be close to 0.

The two-part model on the other hand could be also used. A logit (or probit) model can be specified for the probability to work, and conditional on work we can specify a (log)linear model for the wage. However, what clearly distinguishes this example from the charitable giving (corner solution) example is that in this case there are actually *two* decisions coded in the dependent variable that we want to model. First, there is the decision to work or not (in the simplest setting made by the individual itself). Next, there is the wage offer (made by the employer). In the charitable giving example on the other hand, there is clearly only one decision maker. In other words, the observed wage is not the solution of a straightforward utility maximization problem subject to corner solutions. Next, in the wage example, it can very well be that the two decisions are related to each other. A person decides not to work because she expects a low wage. As said, in this context, researchers often want to be able to predict the potential wage that a currently unemployed person could get. The relation between the two decisions is captured in the Tobit-2 model.

The Tobit-2 specifies a latent variable Y_i^* that relates to the selection equation (say, decision to work), for this variable we specify a linear expression:

$$Y_i^* = x_i'\alpha + \varepsilon_{1i}, \text{with } \varepsilon_{1i} \sim N(0, 1). \tag{2.87}$$

Next the observed Y_i (say, wage) is described in the outcome equation:

$$Y_i = \begin{cases} 0, & \text{if } Y_i^* \leq 0 \\ x_i'\beta + \varepsilon_{2i}, & \text{if } Y_i^* > 0. \end{cases} \tag{2.88}$$

The second error term has $\varepsilon_{2i} \sim N(0, \sigma^2)$. So far, the model is very much like the two-part model. The differences are that the selection, or participation, is typically modeled as a probit and that a linear instead of a log-linear model is used conditional on the selection. A more substantial difference between the two models comes from the assumption that ε_{1i} and ε_{2i} may be correlated with correlation coefficient ρ. The rationale for this correlation is that there may be unobserved characteristics of individual i that not only influence the selection decision, but also the amount decision. In the wage example, this captures the fact that those with a low propensity to participate in the job market may be especially those who would otherwise earn a low wage. This would be captured by a positive ρ.

The expectation of Y_i again can be split in two parts. Using the assumption on the joint distribution of the error terms and the rules of conditional expectations we can show that:

$$\mathrm{E}\left[Y_i|Y_i^* > 0\right] = x_i'\beta + \sigma\rho\lambda\left(x_i'\alpha\right) \tag{2.89}$$

where λ is again the inverse Mills ratio (see Franses and Paap 2001, for some more intermediate steps). The marginal effect conditional on participation equals:

$$\frac{\partial \mathrm{E}\left[Y_i|Y_i^* > 0\right]}{\partial x_{ik}} = \beta_k - \sigma\rho\lambda\left(x_i'\alpha\right)\left(x_i'\alpha + \lambda\left(x_i'\alpha\right)\right)\alpha_k \tag{2.90}$$

where we use that:

$$\frac{\partial \lambda(z)}{\partial z} = -\lambda(z)\left(z + \lambda(z)\right). \tag{2.91}$$

Next the probability of participating equals:

$$\Pr\left[Y_i^* > 0\right] = \Pr\left[\varepsilon_i > -x_i'\alpha\right] = 1 - \Phi\left(-x_i'\alpha\right) = \Phi\left(x_i'\alpha\right) \tag{2.92}$$

such that the unconditional expectation becomes:

$$\mathrm{E}\left[Y_i\right] = \Pr\left[Y_i^* > 0\right]\mathrm{E}\left[Y_i|Y_i^* > 0\right] = \Phi\left(x_i'\alpha\right)\left(x_i'\beta + \sigma\rho\lambda\left(x_i'\alpha\right)\right). \tag{2.93}$$

The unconditional marginal effect therefore equals:

$$\begin{aligned}\frac{\partial \mathrm{E}\left[Y_i\right]}{\partial x_{ik}} &= \phi\left(x_i'\alpha\right)\alpha_k\left(x_i'\beta + \sigma\rho\lambda\left(x_i'\alpha\right)\right)\\ &\quad + \Phi\left(x_i'\alpha\right)\left(\beta_k - \sigma\rho\lambda\left(x_i'\alpha\right)\left(x_i'\alpha + \lambda\left(x_i'\alpha\right)\right)\alpha_k\right)\\ &= \beta_k\Phi\left(x_i'\alpha\right) + \alpha_k\left(\phi\left(x_i'\alpha\right)x_i'\left(\beta - \sigma\rho\alpha\right)\right)\end{aligned} \tag{2.94}$$

where we have used that $\Phi(z)\lambda(z) = \phi(z)$. Both the unconditional as the conditional marginal effects are complicated functions of the parameters α and β. It is important to recognize that β cannot directly be interpreted in terms of either of these effects. Instead the coefficients indicate the marginal effect on a *hypothetical* outcome. It is the impact on the amount irrespective of the (self)selection process. In the wage example, β would give the impact on the wage that someone could earn. For large values of $x_i'\alpha$ the expression in Eqs. (2.90) and (2.94) both converge to β_k as the selection probability will approach 1.

2.6.2 Parameter Estimation in Tobit-2

The parameters of the Tobit-2 model can be estimated using Maximum Likelihood or other techniques such as Bayesian estimation. Here we will only consider ML estimation. As in the Tobit-1 model we can split the (log) likelihood in two parts. One part that deals with the observations equal to 0, and a part that deals with the non-zero observations. For these latter observations, the likelihood contribution equals:

$$\begin{aligned} f\left(Y_i = y_i | Y_i^* > 0\right) \Pr\left[Y_i^* > 0\right] &= \int_0^\infty f\left(Y_i = y_i, Y_i^* = z\right) dz \\ &= \int_0^\infty f\left(Y_i^* = z | Y_i = y_i\right) f\left(Y_i = y_i\right) dz \\ &= f\left(Y_i = y_i\right) \int_0^\infty f\left(Y_i^* = z | Y_i = y_i\right) dz \end{aligned} \tag{2.95}$$

where $f()$ denotes a general density function. As Y_i^* and Y_i have a bivariate normal distribution, the density of Y_i^* given Y_i is a normal with mean $x_i'\alpha + \frac{\rho}{\sigma}\left(y_i - x_i'\beta\right)$, and variance $1 - \rho^2$. We refer to Franses and Paap (2001) and Wooldridge (2002) for some more intermediate steps. Eq. (2.95) therefore becomes:

$$f\left(Y_i = y_i | Y_i^* > 0\right) \Pr\left[Y_i^* > 0\right] = \frac{1}{\sigma} \phi\left(\frac{y_i - x_i'\beta}{\sigma}\right) \Phi\left(\frac{x_i'\alpha + \frac{\rho}{\sigma}\left(y_i - x_i'\beta\right)}{\sqrt{1 - \rho^2}}\right) \tag{2.96}$$

and the log likelihood reads:

$$\begin{aligned} \log L\left(\alpha, \beta, \sigma^2, \rho\right) = &\sum_{i: y_i = 0} \log\left(1 - \Phi\left(x_i'\alpha\right)\right) \\ &+ \sum_{i: y_i > 0} \left(- \frac{1}{2}\log \sigma^2 - \log \phi\left(\frac{y_i - x_i'\beta}{\sigma}\right) \right. \\ &\left. - \log \Phi\left(\frac{x_i'\alpha + \frac{\rho}{\sigma}\left(y_i - x_i'\beta\right)}{\sqrt{1 - \rho^2}}\right)\right). \end{aligned} \tag{2.97}$$

Numerically maximizing this log likelihood over its parameters yields the ML estimates.

As an alternative method, the so-called Heckman (1976) two-step procedure can be used. This procedure relies on the following observations. First, we can consistently estimate the probit parameters α by only considering the selection part of the model. Given the estimates $\widehat{\alpha}$ we can focus on the non-zero observations and estimate the parameters of the linear model:

$$y_i = x_i'\beta + \gamma\lambda\left(x_i'\widehat{\alpha}\right) + \eta_i, \text{for } y_i > 0. \tag{2.98}$$

The OLS estimator of β will also be consistent.

In general one must be careful when applying this two-step procedure. First, the method is not efficient as it relies on two separate steps. Second, the error term η_i is not homoskedastic. Therefore, the straightforward OLS standard errors should not be used. A White correction for these standard errors is available, see for example Franses and Paap (2001).

2.6.3 *Identification in Tobit-2*

All presented parameters in the Tobit-2 model are theoretically identified. However, in practice it may turn out to be difficult to identify the correlation parameter. This is especially the case if the selection and the outcome equation have exactly the same explanatory variables, that is, there are no exclusion restrictions. The identification is complicated even further if there are few observations with extreme selection probabilities.

To see this we first note that identification of α is trivial. As discussed in the Heckman two-step procedure, one can easily estimate α by applying a probit to the selection decision. The observed amounts have to provide the information to estimate the other parameters. The information that these observations bring to estimate ρ can be seen from Eqs. (2.89) and (2.90), for ease of reference we copy these equations below:

$$\mathrm{E}\left[Y_i|Y_i^* > 0\right] = x_i'\beta + \sigma\rho\lambda\left(x_i'\alpha\right)$$

$$\frac{\partial \mathrm{E}\left[Y_i|Y_i^* > 0\right]}{\partial x_{ik}} = \beta_k - \sigma\rho\lambda\left(x_i'\alpha\right)\left(x_i'\alpha + \lambda\left(x_i'\alpha\right)\right)\alpha_k. \tag{2.99}$$

The expected value for non-zero observations and the marginal effect conditional on a non-zero observation depends on the inverse Mills ratio $\lambda(\cdot)$. The magnitude of this dependence is driven by the unknown parameter ρ. Figure 2.3 shows the contribution of (functions of) the inverse Mills ratio to the conditional expectation and the marginal effect as a function of $x_i'\alpha$. Additionally, the figure shows the probability that $Y_i^* > 0$ as a function of $x_i'\alpha$.

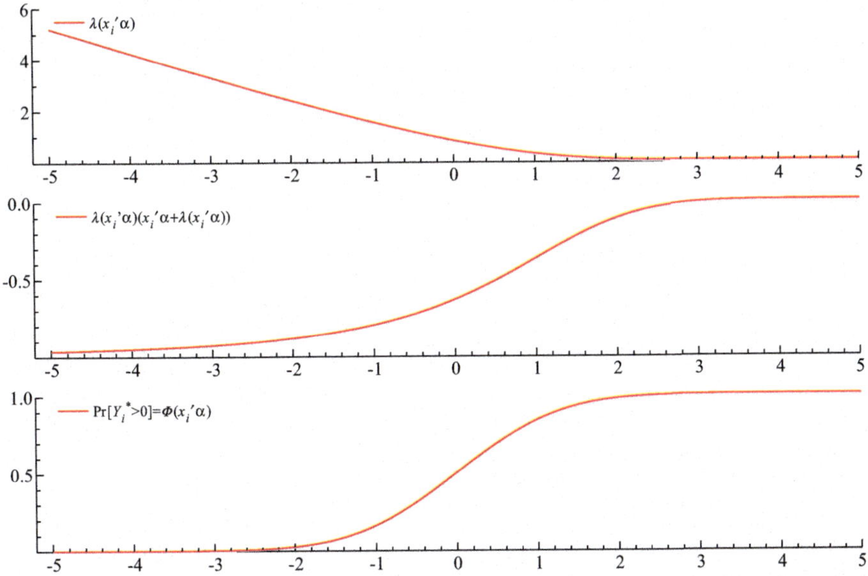

Fig. 2.3 (Functions) of the inverse Mills ratio and the probability of $Y_i^* > 0$ as a function of $x_i'\alpha$ on the horizontal axis

From Fig. 2.3 it is clear that λ_i converges to zero as $x_i'\alpha$ increases. Therefore the conditional expectation of Y_i equals $x_i'\beta$ for large values of $x_i'\alpha$. For these values of $x_i'\alpha$, observations will be included with very high probability as the bottom graph shows. In other words, the selection process does not play a role here. The conditional marginal effect equals β for those observations. If observations are available with large positive values of $x_i'\alpha$, we can easily identify β. The identification of σ is then also straightforward.

On the other extreme of the $x_i'\alpha$ scale, the selection does play an important role. The probability of a positive response is very small, and this has a clear influence on the expectation and conditional marginal effect. The equations show that the conditional marginal effect approaches $\beta + \sigma\rho\alpha$. So, observations on this end of the scale should provide information on ρ. Theoretically, the ρ parameter is therefore identified. However, in practice the problem is that there will not be many non-zero observations at this end of the $x_i'\alpha$ scale. The lower graph in Fig. 2.3 clearly shows that the probability of observing such values is very small. So, in the range where ρ is easy to identify, we tend to have only few observations. This complicates the empirical identification substantially. With only observations with an intermediate value of $x_i'\alpha$ it is difficult to disentangle the effects of α, β and ρ. This is due to the fact that $\lambda(\cdot)$ is close to linear for this range of values, such that the conditional amount equation will suffer from a multicollinearity problem, see also Wooldridge (2002, Sect. 17.4, p. 564).

Adding *exclusion restrictions* helps. Suppose that we have a variable of which we know that it affects the selection process, but not the outcome process. Any impact of this variable on the subset of non-zero observations that we can find will help to identify ρ. In other words, in this case the λ function will not be strongly correlated with the explanatory variables in the amount equation.

2.6.4 Sample Selection Versus Corner Solutions

If we set the correlation coefficient in the Tobit-2 model to zero, we obtain a variant of the two-part model. The main difference is that in the two-part model we usually use the log of the amount as dependent variable, whereas the Tobit-2 uses the amount itself. Strictly speaking this means that the Tobit-2 model also allows the dependent variable to be negative. In any case, it is clear that the two-part model and the Tobit-2 are closely related.

When deciding which model to use it is important to consider whether one or two decision processes underlie the dependent variable and which marginal effects are most interesting: marginal effects conditional on a non-zero outcome, unconditional marginal effects, or marginal effect on hypothetical outcomes.

As said, the prototypical example for the Tobit-2 model is labor participation and wages. Clearly, there are two underlying processes. The first is the decision to participate or not while the second is the determination of the wage. Furthermore, a key object of interest is indeed the marginal effects of certain variables on hypothetical wages.

An example related to marketing could be explaining the number of loyalty points collected by customers of a loyalty program. Naturally not all customers will be a member of the loyalty program such that some will collect 0 points. These are also two different decisions: participate yes or no, and separately from this how much to spend. Note that the spending may happen even if the customer is not a member. Again here it could make sense to consider marginal effects on the hypothetical number of points collected, irrespective of the actual participation in the loyalty program.

In marketing there are many other examples where the amount spent is modeled (for example, Dorotic et al. 2014). If the amount equals zero the respective product is not bought. In this example there is only one decision. The zeros appear in the data because of the restriction that the amount cannot be negative. In such a case the two-part model is more appropriate if one clearly wants to distinguish the purchase incidence decision from the amount decision conditional on a purchase. Marginal effects on hypothetical purchase amounts may be less relevant in this context.

2.6.5 Example of a Tobit-2 model

Van Heerde et al. (2008) study the impact of a price war in the Dutch grocery retail industry. This price war was initiated by the market leader at the end of 2003. Van Heerde et al. (2008) use advanced models based on the Tobit-2 idea to measure the impact of this price war on store visits and store spending. They also consider the impact of the price war on the sensitivity of visits and spending with respect to marketing instruments.

The basic Tobit-2 setup as discussed above is used as the core of the methodology. The selection equation describes the household's decision to visit a particular store or not. The amount equation describes the spending within the store. The authors choose to use the log spending as the dependent variable in this equation. The basic Tobit-2 model is extended to allow for household heterogeneity and competition among retailers. The latter is achieved by considering a multivariate extension of the Tobit-2 model. In the presentation below we will ignore the heterogeneity (by only discussing the results for the median household) and the multivariate setting. The parameters are estimated using Bayesian techniques (see Chap. 16).

The data used by Van Heerde et al. (2008) combines household-specific purchase records over a period of 4.5 years and household-level survey data on store perception. From this survey the authors define measures of the price image and the produce quality of the different stores. To capture state dependence the model contains lags of the dependent variables as explanatory variables. Four lags are used, for the store visit equations lagged visits are used while lagged log spending is used for the amount equation. To capture the long-term impact of the price war, the model contains the variable PWRound. This variable equals the cumulative number of products that were permanently reduced in price since the start of the price war (in 1000s of products). The variable Pulse_PWRound gives the first difference of this number, that is, the number of products that get a price reduction at a certain point in time. This variable captures the short-run impact of the price war. The other explanatory variables used in the model are rather self-explanatory. Mean-centering has been applied to some variables to allow for an easy interpretation. This is especially relevant for the log(price) and PriceImage variables that also appear in interaction terms.[13] Table 2.7 shows the main parameter estimates for the median household. Details on retailer-specific effects are not reported here.

From Table 2.7 it is clear that an exclusion restriction is imposed in the model. As discussed in Sect. 2.6.3 this ensures the empirical identification of the correlation coefficient between the error term in the selection equation and the amount equation. Feature activity is assumed to only influence the store visit decision, while (in-store) display activity is assumed to only influence the amount decision. These exclusion restrictions clearly make sense in this context.

[13]For further details we refer to Van Heerde et al. (2008).

Table 2.7 Parameter estimates for the Multivariate Tobit-2 model to explain store visits and expenditures (results correspond to the median household)

	Store visits	Log(spending)
Price image	0.009*	0.008*
Produce quality	0.011*	0.010*
Log(store surface)	0.155*	0.098*
Feature	0.002*	
Display		0.003*
Lagged dependent 1	0.235*	0.002*
Lagged dependent 2	0.298*	0.009*
Lagged dependent 3	0.283*	0.010*
Lagged dependent 4	0.264*	0.009*
Log(distance)	−0.502*	−0.116*
Log(price)	−0.097*	0.282*
Week 1	−0.458*	−0.217*
Week 51	0.040*	0.127*
Week 52	−0.107*	0.025*
Easter	0.073*	0.128*
PWRound	−0.011*	−0.004*
Pulse_PWRound	0.020*	0.008*
PWRound × log(price)	0.009	−0.026*
PWRound × PriceImage	0.005*	0.004*
Pulse_PWRound × log(price)	−0.058*	−0.084*
Pulse_PWRound × PriceImage	0.004*	−0.002
Promweek	0.024*	−0.007*
Promweek × ln(Price)	−0.350*	−0.026*
Promweek × PriceImage	0.009	0.002

*Significant at 5% (formally: 95% posterior interval does not contain 0)
Source: Van Heerde et al. (2008, p. 511)

The results for the store visit equation show that the price image, produce quality, size of the store and feature activity all positively, and significantly, impact the probability of a store visit. This perfectly matches expectations. Next, there tends to be a significant persistence in the store visit decisions, all four lagged store visit variables have a significant effect. The signs for the coefficients for distance, price and the seasonal effects are also according to expectation. For the impact of the price war the authors find a significantly positive short-run impact of the price war (see the Pulse_PWRound coefficient). The long-run impact is significantly negative. However, at the same time the store visit decision becomes more sensitive to price image (long-run effect) and price itself (short-run effect). So as more products get reduced in price, the store's price image becomes more and more important.

For the amount equation the authors find some similar effects for price image, quality, distance and persistence as above. Remarkably the price coefficient is positive, indicating a small but positive effect of price on the quantity bought. Note that this price elasticity refers to the period before the price war. The short-run impact of the price war is positive, however, the long-run impact is again negative and significant. Furthermore, due to the price war households have become more price-sensitive.

Note that one should consider the above results on the spending *unconditional* on the actual store choice decision. In other words the coefficients in the spending equation describe the spending in the hypothetical case that the household visits the store. The effects can be different for the subset of weeks in which the household actually visits the store. The marginal effects for these weeks should be seen conditional on the store visit decision, and follow from Eq. (2.90). Van Heerde et al. (2008) do not report details on the estimated variances and correlations. Therefore the marginal effects conditional on a visit cannot be obtained. In case one is mainly interested in estimating the marginal effects conditional on a visit, a (multivariate) two-part model could also be used as an alternative.

2.7 Related Topics

2.7.1 Treatment Effect Models

In the sample selection setting there are two decisions: a selection decisions and an amount or outcome decision. We only observe a non-zero outcome if the customer selects herself (or is selected through some other process). There are also settings where the outcome is also observed even if the customer does not select herself. An example in marketing is the impact of membership of a loyalty program on sales. Sales can be observed for customers inside and outside the loyalty program. Furthermore, the customer herself decides whether to be a member or not. In the literature the models corresponding to this case are called treatment effect models. In the loyalty program example the treatment would be the loyalty program membership. Models for treatment effects have a strong link with the Tobit-2 model.

In the treatment literature the focus is usually on estimating the causal impact of the treatment (eg. loyalty program membership) on the outcome (e.g. sales). When doing this one needs to acknowledge that the 0/1 treatment dummy is an endogenous variable in a regression of the outcome on this dummy and other variables. Proper estimation methods therefore need to correct for this endogeneity. For more on this topic see Chap. 18 or Wooldridge (2002).

2.7.2 Heterogeneity

All models discussed in this chapter deal with the behavior of individuals. Not all individuals will be the same: some individuals may be very likely to choose a certain brand while others are very unlikely to do so. These differences are usually referred to as heterogeneity. Part of the heterogeneity can be explained using explanatory variables that code certain customer characteristics. These explained differences are called *observed heterogeneity*.

There may also be differences that cannot be explained, so-called, *unobserved heterogeneity*. Given suitable data we are often able to estimate the differences between individuals by extending the basic models as described in this chapter. There are two popular approaches. In the first approach one assumes that there are segments in the populations. The behavior of customers will differ across segments, while within a segment all customers behave the same. In the model this means that we assign a different vector of parameters to each segment. This methodology is referred to as mixture modeling (Wedel and Kamakura 2000 and Chap. 13).

In the alternative approach, we specify a model with different parameters for each individual. There are no segments and all customers will be at least a bit different. To allow the estimation of individual-specific parameters we usually assume a population distribution from which all individual level parameters are assumed to be generated. This population distribution is usually chosen to be a normal distribution.[14]

In general, to estimate the parameters of a model including unobserved heterogeneity we need to have multiple observations per customer. There are cases where a single observation per customer is enough. For example, when the dependent variable is continuous and heterogeneity with respect to the intercept in a linear model is specified using a mixture approach. In this case, the heterogeneity is identified by contrasting the discrete aspect of the mixture to the continuous error term in the linear model. However, if the dependent variable itself is discrete we need to be very careful. If the dependent variable is binary and only a single observation per customer is available one may end up with a model where the heterogeneity completely explains the observed choices. In a mixture model context (see also Chap. 13), we may obtain a segment of customers who buy the product and a segment of customers who do not. Clearly this is not a useful model. If customers are tracked over time and panel data is available, the identification of heterogeneity becomes easier. Observed persistence in behavior over time can be directly attributed to the heterogeneity.

Parameter estimation for models including heterogeneity requires specific techniques. For the mixture approach the Expectation-Maximization algorithm is often used. We refer to Wedel and Kamakura (2000) for a marketing-based introduction of this algorithm and McLachlan and Krishnan (1997) for a more detailed and technical discussion. For the approach with individual-specific coefficients, Bayesian estimation methods are often applied (Allenby and Rossi 1999). Therefore this approach is often combined with models of the probit type. This topic is discussed in more detail in Chap. 16.

---

[14]Note that if we assume that the population distribution is discrete in the sense that it only assigns non-zero probability to a small number of points we obtain the segment-based specification of unobserved heterogeneity.

2.7.3 Formal Utility-Based Models and Multivariate Corner-Solution Models

In marketing and economics choice models are often derived or motivated based on the assumption that customers are maximizing a particular utility function. The observed decisions are then a result of formal utility maximization. Not all models discussed in this chapter can be motivated from a utility maximization perspective.

The binary and multinomial logit/probit models and the nested models are not difficult to present in a formal utility maximization context. This is not the case for the ordered logit and probit model. However, in many applications of those models it also does not make sense to talk about utility maximization. This is especially the case when these models describe outcome categories on a Likert scale. For the case of censored variables it also does not make much sense to view the model in the context of utility maximization.

On the other hand, for the models that are intended to describe corner solutions it is relevant to consider whether they can be cast into a utility framework. Wooldridge (2002) shows a utility function that matches a particular version of the Tobit-1 model. To be precise, this version of the Tobit-1 has $\log(1 + q_i)$ as dependent variable, where q_i gives the observed quantity that individual i buys. The two-part and Tobit-2 models can in general not be motivated from an utility maximization perspective.

The corner solution models presented in Sect. 2.6 can be extended to a situation where multiple products are considered at the same time. If multiple products can be bought at the same time, the models should capture the variety of products that are chosen and for each chosen product the purchased quantity. The two-part model can be extended in this direction by building on the Multivariate Probit (Ashford and Sowden 1970; Chib and Greenberg 1998; Edwards and Allenby 2003) or Multivariate Logit model (Cox 1972; Russell and Petersen 2000) in the two-part setting. The Tobit-1 and Tobit-2 can also be extended to a multivariate setting by specifying multivariate normal distributions for the error terms. Van Heerde et al. (2008) apply such a multivariate Tobit-2 to describe the shopping behavior of consumers across retailers.

As said, such models cannot easily be interpreted in the context of utility maximization. There is a separate literature where utility-based models are developed for this purpose. Such models start with a suitable utility function and derive the first order conditions for optimal decisions. The observed choices should satisfy these conditions and this provides the basis for parameter estimation. Such models are also referred to as "multiple discreteness models" or "discrete-continuous models". Examples of such models are Bhat (2005, 2008); Dubé (2004) and Kim et al. (2002, 2007). The paper by Dubé (2004) is based on the idea that when making decisions the customer anticipates a number of (unobserved) consumption occasions. The papers by Kim et al. and Bhat do not consider such occasions but obtain a discrete-continuous model by using a non-linear utility function. Kim et al. (2002, 2007) use normally distributed error terms, while Bhat (2005, 2008) uses extreme-value distributed errors. It should be no surprise that the latter model is more tractable.

2.8 Software

For almost all of the models presented in this chapter the parameters can be estimated using maximum likelihood estimation. Most standard models are available in commonly used software such as STATA, EViews and SPSS. R packages for these models are also widely available. For some of the more complicated models, such as the generalized nested logit standard software will most likely not be readily available. However, given the specification of the likelihood function as presented in this chapter and general purpose numerical maximization routines it is straightforward to obtain maximum likelihood estimates.

Acknowledgements The author wants to thank Bas Donkers, Richard Paap, Jaap Wieringa, Peter Leeflang, and Hans Risselada for very helpful comments and discussions.

References

Albert, J.H., Chib, S.: Bayesian-analysis of binary and polychotomous response data. J. Am. Stat. Assoc. **88**, 669–679 (1993)

Allenby, G.M., Rossi, P.E.: Marketing Models of Consumer Heterogeneity. J. Econ. **89**, 57–78 (1999)

Amemiya, T.: Advanced Econometrics. Harvard University Press, Cambridge (1985)

Ashford, J.R., Sowden, R.R.: Multi-variate probit analysis. Biometrics. **26**, 535–546 (1970)

Balachander, S., Ghose, S.: Reciprocal spillover effects: a strategic benefit of brand extensions. J. Mark. **67**(1), 4–13 (2003)

Bell, D.R., Corsten, D., Knox, G.: From point of purchase to path to purchase: how preshopping factors drive unplanned buying. J. Mark. **75**(1), 31–45 (2011)

Ben-Akiva, M., Lerman, S.R.: Discrete Choice Analysis: Theory and Application to Travel Demand, MIT Press Series in Transportation Studies, vol. 9. MIT, Cambridge (1985)

Bhat, C.R.: A multiple discrete–continuous extreme value model: formulation and application to discretionary time-use decisions. Transp. Res. B: Methodol. **39**, 679–707 (2005)

Bhat, C.R.: The multiple discrete-continuous extreme value (MDCEV) model: role of utility function parameters, identification considerations, and model extensions. Transp. Res. B: Methodol. **42**, 274–303 (2008)

Bresnahan, T.F., Stern, S., Trajtenberg, M.: Market segmentation and the sources of rents from innovation: personal computers in the late 1980s. RAND J. Econ. **28**, 17–44 (1997)

Cameron, A.C., Trivedi, P.K.: Microeconometrics: Methods and Applications. Cambridge University Press, New York (2005)

Chib, S., Greenberg, E.: Analysis of multivariate probit models. Biometrika. **85**, 347–361 (1998)

Chu, C.A.:Paired combinatorial logit model for travel demand analysis. In: Proceedings of the Fifth World Conference on Transportation Research, vol. 4, pp. 295–309, Ventura, CA (1989)

Cox, D.R.: The analysis of multivariate binary data. J. R. Stat. Soc.: Ser. C: Appl. Stat. **21**, 113–120 (1972)

Cragg, J.C.: Some statistical models for limited dependent variables with applications to the demand for durable goods. Econometrica. **39**, 829–844 (1971)

Donkers, B., Verhoef, P.C., de Jong, M.G.: Modeling CLV: a test of competing models in the insurance industry. Quant. Mark. Econ. **5**, 163–190 (2007)

Dorotic, M., Verhoef, P.C., Fok, D., Bijmolt, T.H.A.: Reward redemption effects in a loyalty program when customers choose how much and when to redeem. Int. J. Res. Mark. **31**, 339–355 (2014)

Dubé, J.P.: Multiple discreteness and product differentiation: demand for carbonated doft drinks. Mark. Sci. **23**, 66–81 (2004)

Edwards, Y.D., Allenby, G.M.: Multivariate analysis of multiple response data. J. Mark. Res. **40**, 321–334 (2003)

Foekens, E.W., Leeflang, P.S.H., Wittink, D.R.: Hierarchical versus other market share models for markets with many items. Int. J. Res. Mark. **14**, 359–378 (1997)

Franses, P.H., Paap, R.: Quantitative Models in Marketing Research. Cambridge University Press, Cambridge (2001)

Guadagni, P.M., Little, J.D.C.: A logit model of brand choice calibrated on scanner data. Mark. Sci. **2**, 202–238 (1983)

Guyt, J.Y., Gijsbrechts, E.: Take turns or march in sync? the impact of the national brand promotion calendar on manufacturer and retailer performance. J. Mark. Res. **51**, 753–772 (2014)

Heckman, J.J.: the common structure of statistical models of truncation, sample selection and limited dependent variables and a simple estimator for such models. Ann. Econ. Soc. Meas. **5**, 475–492 (1976)

Heckman, J.J., Sedlacek, G.: Heterogeneity, aggregation, and market wage functions: an empirical model of self-selection in the labor-market. J. Polit. Econ. **93**, 1077–1125 (1985)

Kamakura, W.A., Kim, B.D., Lee, J.: Modeling preference and structural heterogeneity in consumer choice. Mark. Sci. **15**, 152–172 (1996)

Keane, M.P.: A note on identification in the multinomial probit model. J. Bus. Econ. Stat. **10**, 193–200 (1992)

Kekre, S., Krishnan, M.S., Srinivasan, K.: Drivers of customer satisfaction for software products: implications for design and service support. Manag. Sci. **41**, 1456–1470 (1995)

Kim, J., Allenby, G.M., Rossi, P.E.: Modeling consumer demand for variety. Mark. Sci. **21**, 229–250 (2002)

Kim, J., Allenby, G.M., Rossi, P.E.: Product attributes and models of multiple discreteness. J. Econ. **137**, 208–230 (2007)

Koppelman, F.S., Wen, C.-H.: The paired combinatorial logit model: properties, estimation and application. Transp. Res. B. **34**, 75–89 (2000)

Leeflang, P.S.H., Wittink, D.R., Wedel, M., Naert, P.A.: Building Models for Marketing Decisions. Kluwer Academic Publishers, Dordrecht (2000)

McCulloch, R.E., Polson, N.G., Rossi, P.E.: A Bayesian analysis of the multinomial probit model with fully identified parameters. J. Econ. **99**, 173–193 (2000)

McFadden, D.: Modeling the choice of residential location. In: Karlquist A. et al. (eds.) Spatial Interaction Theory and Residential Location, North-Holland, Amsterdam, pp.75–96 (1978)

McKelvey, R., Zavoina, W.: A statistical model for the analyst of ordinal level dependent variables. J. Math. Sociol. **4**, 103–120 (1975)

McLachlan, G.J., Krishnan, T.: The EM Algorithm and Extensions. Wiley, New York (1997)

Mela, C.F., Gupta, S., Lehmann, D.R.: The long-term impact of promotion and advertising on consumer brand choice. J. Mark. Res. **34**, 248–261 (1997)

Montgomery, A.L., Li, S., Srinivasan, K., Liechty, J.C.: Modeling online browsing and path analysis using clickstream data. Mark. Sci. **23**, 579–595 (2004)

Russell, G.J., Petersen, A.: Analysis of cross category dependence in market basket selection. J. Retail. **76**, 367–392 (2000)

Small, K.: A discrete choice model for ordered alternatives. Econometrica. **55**, 409–424 (1987)

Sonnier, G., Ainslie, A., Otter, T.: Heterogeneity distributions of willingness-to-pay in choice models. Quant. Mark. Econ. **5**, 313–331 (2007)

Tobin, J.: Estimation of relationships for limited dependent variables. Econometrica. **26**, 24–36 (1958)

Train, K.E.: Discrete Choice Methods with Simulation. Cambridge University Press, New York (2003)

Van Diepen, M., Donkers, B., Franses, P.H.: Dynamic and competitive effects of direct mailings: a charitable giving applications. J. Mark. Res. **46**, 120–133 (2009)

Van Heerde, H.J., Gijsbrechts, E., Pauwels, K.H.: Winners and losers in a major price war. J. Mark. Res. **45**, 499–518 (2008)

Vovsha, P.: The cross-nested logit model: application to mode choice in the Tel-Aviv metropolitan area. In Transportation Research Record 1607, TRB, National Research Council, Washington, DC, pp. 6–15 (1997)

Wedel, M., Kamakura, W.A.: Market Segmentation: Conceptual and Methodological Foundations, International Series in Quantitative Marketing, vol. 8. Springer, Berlin (2000)

Wen, C.-H., Koppelman, F.S.: The generalized nested logit model. Transp. Res. B. **35**, 627–641 (2001)

Wooldridge, J.M.: Econometric Analysis of Cross Section and Panel Data. The MIT Press, Cambridge (2002)

Zhang, J., Wedel, M.: The effectiveness of customized promotions in online and offline stores. J. Mark. Res. **46**, 190–206 (2009)

Chapter 3
Traditional Time-Series Models

Koen H. Pauwels

3.1 Introduction

Marketing and performance data often include measures repeated (typically at equally spaced intervals) over time. In Chap. 2 of Vol. I, we captured market dynamics with lagged effects for predictor variables and distributed lags on the criterion variable, y. In this chapter, we refine and extend this treatment of market dynamics by means of time-series models. Time-series models are uniquely suited to capture the time dependence of both a criterion variable (e.g. sales performance) and predictor variables (e.g. marketing actions, online consumer behavior metrics), how they relate to each other over time.

Time series models come in different forms, and we distinguish between "traditional" time series models (the univariate and multivariate time series models popularized in the 1970s and 1980s) and the "modern" time series models (the multiple time series models popularized in the last three decades). Table 3.1 compares how 5 key dynamic marketing phenomena are treated in the conventional models (Chap. 2 of Vol. I), traditional time series models (this Chap. 3) and modern time series models (Chap. 4).

The role of theory and data in time series models is important to clarify at this point. Because marketing (and economic) theory is typically more informative on *which* variables affect each other than on the *timing* of these effects, time series models typically use theory to suggest the variables, but the data patterns themselves

Parts of this chapter are based on Hanssens et al. (2001) and Sect. 17.8 in Leeflang et al. (2000). We like to thank Michel Wedel for his efforts to compose this section in Leeflang et al. (2000).

K.H. Pauwels (✉)
Department of Marketing, Northeastern University, Boston, USA
e-mail: k.pauwels@northeastern.edu

P.S.H. Leeflang et al. (eds.), *Advanced Methods for Modeling Markets*,
International Series in Quantitative Marketing, DOI 10.1007/978-3-319-53469-5_3

Table 3.1 Comparing conventional, traditional and modern time series models

Dynamic marketing concept	Conventional model (Distributed lag, Chap. 2, Vol. I)	Traditional time series (Multivariate: this Chap. 3)	Modern time series (Multiple equation: Chap. 4)
Delayed response to Marketing action (Little 1979)	Koyck + extensions: Fixed decay pattern Temporary effect	Impulse response simulation: wear-in, wear-out from data Permanent effects possible	
Negative lagged effects such as post promotion dips (Blattberg and Neslin 1990)	Requires additional modeling	Shows up as such in impulse response	
Customer holdover (Leeflang et al. 1992; Parsons 1976)	Add lags of performance	Unit root allows for (partial) hysteresis in performance	
Performance-marketing feedback (Dekimpe and Hanssens 1999)	Partial adjustment		Granger causality Marketing explained by past sales Vector error-correction
Competition and Intermediary Decision Rules (Pauwels 2004, 2007)	Can be separately modeled, but only shown in their effect on company performance, not explained by its marketing, performance		May influence and be influenced by marketing/business performance

suggest the appropriate lags (or leads), the direction of causality and the presence of feedback loops. For instance, a company's paid search ad gets higher click-through if it is placed higher on the consumer's screen, but the search engine also prefers to give these prime locations to companies that had higher-clicked ads in the past (marketing-performance feedback). A flexible, data-driven approach to causality and to lag structure allows researchers to separate short-term (temporary) from long-term (lasting) effects, to discover wear-in and wear-out of marketing impact, and to empirically demonstrate and quantify company, intermediary and competitive marketing decision rules. Its data-driven nature reflects Sims' (1980) philosophy that alternative models often have to place "incredible" identifying restrictions on how key variables are allowed to behave and influence each other over time. If this holds true in economics, which typically assumes human rationality and often perfect information, marketing settings add several potential violations of these assumptions.

The remainder of this chapter details the analysis steps, interpretation and marketing insights from traditional time series models. We start with with the univariate treatment of each separate marketing time series in evolution/stationarity tests and ARIMA models (Sect. 3.2). Next, we consider the over-time relation of multivariate time series in transfer functions and intervention analysis (Sect. 3.3). We then give an elaborative marketing application (Sect. 3.4) and discuss helpful software (Sect. 3.5).

3.2 Evolution, Stationarity, and ARIMA for Each Separate Marketing Series

3.2.1 Introduction

Why would we be interested in the time series properties of a separate variable, such as sales performance? First, both managers and economic policy makers mind if a performance change is temporary (short-term) or lasting (long-term). If GDP has declined dramatically this quarter, will it soon rebound to its historic mean + upward trend? Or will it not, in which case government action may be called for? Likewise, some marketing actions are often considered "tactical" tools, such as price promotions to boost sales - but may hurt brand performance in the long run (Mela et al. 1997; Pauwels et al. 2002). Other marketing actions, such as investments in product updates and advertising may only be justified by promises of future benefits (Aaker and Keller 1990). The distinction between short-term and long-term marketing effectiveness permeates discussions on dealing with recessions, on retailer category and store performance (Srinivasan et al. 2004) and on manufacturer brand equity (Keller 1998).

Second, we are often interested in decomposing a marketing time series into its relevant components. For instance, a retailer price series may be decomposed into a constant term, a deterministic time trend, seasonality fluctuations, and past prices (indicating the extent of inertia in retail price setting). Forecasting future prices by this retailer is considerably easier and more accurate when retail price is mostly driven by deterministic components, as opposed to environmental changes that have yet to happen at the time of the forecast.[1]

Forecasting was indeed the main objective of the first explosion in time series models in the 1970s. They are known as ARIMA models, an abbreviation for AutoRegressive-Integrated-Moving Average models, as we discuss in detail in the following pages. Important statistics in building ARIMA models are the autocorrelation function (ACF) and partial autocorrelation function (PACF). To illustrate, let y_t be the sales of a brand in period t. The ACF at lag k is simply the correlation $\rho(y_t, y_{t-k})$. The PACF is the coefficient of y_{t-k} in the regression of y_t on all lagged values of y up to y_{t-k}. In general, the type of time series model to be fitted to the data is identified from plots of the ACF and PACF against the lag k. Specific types of models correspond to specific autocorrelation functions, as explained below.

In our discussion of ARIMA models, we start with autoregressive models in which, say, sales are explained by sales levels in a previous period. We then describe moving average processes, in which it is assumed that random shocks in sales carry over to a subsequent period. This is followed by a discussion on ARMA models that combine the effects in the previous two models. Finally we put the "I" in ARIMA by discussing unit root tests to determine whether the series is stationary or evolving, and formulate integrated models that accommodate non-stationarity.

3.2.2 Autoregressive Processes

Let y_t be the sales of a brand in period t. A common and fairly simple way to describe fluctuations in sales is with a first-order autoregressive; i.e. an AR(1) process. In this process it is assumed that sales at $t-1$ affect sales at t:

$$y_t = \mu + \varphi y_{t-1} + \varepsilon_t \tag{3.1}$$

where μ is a constant and ε_t is a disturbance term. This model states that sales in period t are determined by sales in the previous period $t-1$. Depending on the value of φ we distinguish three situations:

1. If $|\varphi| < 1$, the effect of past sales (and thus any "shock" that has affected past sales) diminishes as we move into the future. We call such time series *stationary*, i.e. it has a time-independent mean and variance. This situation is typical for the market performance of established brands in mature markets (e.g. Bass and Pilon 1980; Nijs et al. 2001).

[1] See, for example, Chap. 9.

2. If $|\varphi| = 1$, the effect of sales in y_{t-1} has a permanent effect on sales. Sales will not revert to a historical level but will *evolve*. This situation has been demonstrated for smaller brands and in emerging markets (Pauwels and Dans 2001; Slotegraaf and Pauwels 2008).
3. If $|\varphi| > 1$, the effect of past sales (and thus of past shocks) becomes increasingly important. Such explosive time series behavior appears to be unrealistic in marketing (Dekimpe and Hanssens 1995a, p. 5). Exceptions are typically stock variables, such as the stock of cars in a country (Franses 1994).

How do we recognize an AR(1) process from the time series? Our main tools are the AutoCorrelation Function (ACF) and Partial AutoCorrelation Function (PACF), calculated from sample data. To derive these functions, let's start from the expected value of y at any time t, which for the AR(1) process is given by:

$$\mathrm{E}\left(y_t\right) = \mu / \left(1 - \varphi\right). \tag{3.2}$$

Therefore, the autocovariance at lag k is given by:

$$\begin{aligned} \gamma_k &= \mathrm{E}\left(\left[y_t - \mathrm{E}\left(y_t\right)\right]\left[y_{t-k} - \mathrm{E}\left(y_{t-k}\right)\right]\right) \\ &= \varphi \mathrm{E}\left(\left[y_{t-1} - \mathrm{E}\left(y_{t-1}\right)\right]\left[y_{t-k} - \mathrm{E}\left(y_{t-k}\right)\right]\right) + \mathrm{E}\left(\varepsilon_t\left[y_{t-k} - \mathrm{E}\left(y_{t-k}\right)\right]\right) \\ &= \varphi \gamma_{k-1}. \end{aligned} \tag{3.3}$$

The autocorrelation function (ACF) shows the autocorrelation at each lag k, which is:

$$\begin{aligned} \rho_1 &= \frac{\gamma_1}{\gamma_0} = \varphi \\ \rho_2 &= \frac{\gamma_2}{\gamma_0} = \frac{\varphi\gamma_1}{\gamma_0} = \varphi^2 \\ &\vdots \\ \rho_k &= \varphi^k. \end{aligned} \tag{3.4}$$

Thus, when $\varphi > 0$, the ACF dies out towards zero, as shown in Fig. 3.1. When $\varphi < 0$, the ACF oscillates towards zero, as shown in Fig. 3.2.

Note that ρ_1 is correlated with ρ_3 but only through their relation with ρ_2. If we control for that relation through ρ_2, the correlation disappears. This is a key feature of the AR(1) process, which is visualized through the partial autocorrelation function (PACF).

Formally, the partial autocorrelation function of kth order is the correlation between two time series observations (e.g. x_1 and x_3) that are k lags apart, holding constant all $(k-1)$ intermediate observations (e.g. x_2). Let's denote the correlation between x_1 and x_3 as ρ_{13}, between x_1 and x_2 as ρ_{12} and between x_2 and x_3 as ρ_{23}. The PACF between x_1 and x_3, holding constant x_2 (ρ_{132}) is defined as:

$$\rho_{132} = \left(\rho_{13} - \rho_{12}\rho_{23}\right) / \sqrt{\left(1 - \rho_{12}^2\right)\left(1 - \rho_{23}^2\right)}. \tag{3.5}$$

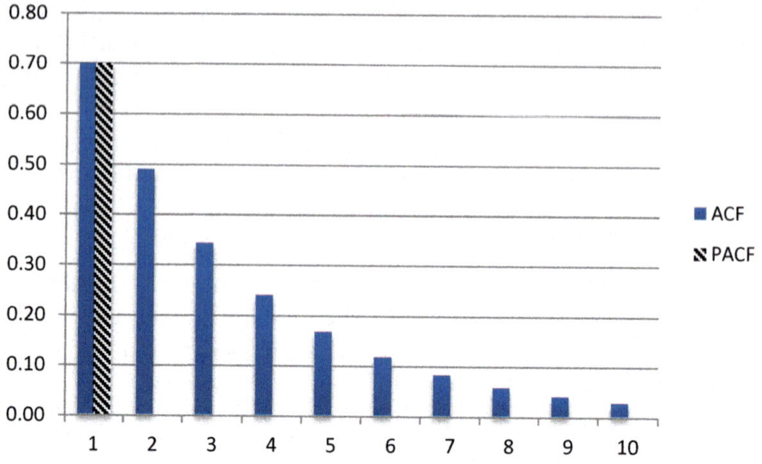

Fig. 3.1 ACF and PACF patterns of an AR(1) process with $\varphi = 0.7$

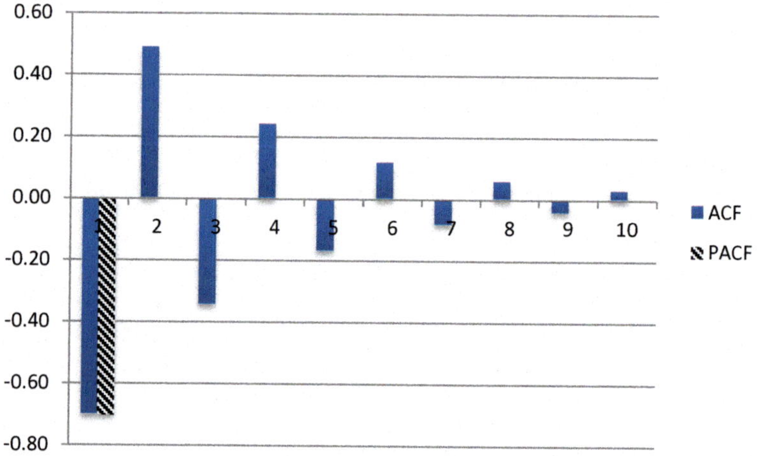

Fig. 3.2 ACF and PACF patterns of an AR(1) process with $\varphi = -0.7$

Because a stationary time series ($|\varphi| < 1$) has time-independent autocorrelation ($\rho_{12} = \rho_{23}$), Eq. (3.5) simplifies to:

$$\begin{aligned}\rho_{132} &= \left(\rho_2 - \rho_1^2\right) \Big/ \sqrt{\left(1 - \rho_1^2\right)\left(1 - \rho_1^2\right)} \\ &= \left(\rho_2 - \rho_1^2\right) \Big/ \left(1 - \rho_1^2\right).\end{aligned} \tag{3.6}$$

For the AR(1) process, Eq. (3.1), $\rho_2 = \rho_1^2$ and thus $\rho_{132} = 0$. The same holds for the partial autocorrelation at higher order lags. In other words, the PACF of an AR(1) time series only shows 1 spike (equal to ρ_1, which equals φ), and then becomes 0.

Combining the ACF and the PACF information, we can recognize an AR(1) process by observing an exponential ACF decay and a PACF with only 1 spike. Figs. 3.1 and 3.2 visualize such ACF and PACF patterns for the cases where φ is respectively positive or negative, with numerical values of 0.7 and −0.7.

More generally, an AR(p) process is an autoregressive process with the order (p) the highest lag of y_t that appears in the model. The p-order AR process is written as:

$$\varphi_p(B)y_t = \mu + \varepsilon_t$$

where

$$\varphi_p(B) = \left(1 - \varphi_1 - \varphi_2 B^2 - \cdots - \varphi_p B^p\right) \tag{3.7}$$

and where B is the backshift operator defined by $B^k y_t = y_{t-k}$. For example, for an AR(2) process $\varphi_2(B) = (1 - \varphi_1 B - \varphi_2 B^2)$, so that $(1 - \varphi_1 B - \varphi_2 B^2)y_t = \mu + \varepsilon_t$, which leads to:

$$y_t = \mu + \varphi_1 y_{t-1} + \varphi_2 y_{t-2} + \varepsilon_t. \tag{3.8}$$

Why would marketing time series display such auto-regressive behavior? First, increased sales in this period (e.g. because of new customers) may partially persist in the future because these new customers continue buying. Second, negative autoregression may be due to purchase acceleration: customers decide to buy now instead of later, so that increased sales today mean lower sales tomorrow. Finally, the sales impact of marketing such as advertising may be very slow to decay: once included in customer long-term memory, the communicated message may continue to influence behavior for a long time.

3.2.3 *Moving Average Processes*

A first-order moving average process assumes that a random shock at $t-1$ affects sales levels at time t:

$$y_t = \mu - \theta\varepsilon_{t-1} + \varepsilon_t. \tag{3.9}$$

This model is indicated as MA(1). Note that the past random shock does not come from y_{t-1}, as in the AR(1) model, but it stems from the random component of y_{t-1}. The ACF and PACF for the MA(1) model are depicted in Figs. 3.3 and 3.4. Here, the ACF shows a spike at lag 1, which is positive if $\theta < 0$ (Fig. 3.3) and negative if $\theta > 0$ (Fig. 3.4) while the PACF shows exponential decay in the former case, or a damped wavelike pattern in the latter.

An MA process is stationary for all values of θ. Hence, unlike AR processes, there are no stationarity restrictions required. The reason why the parameters of an

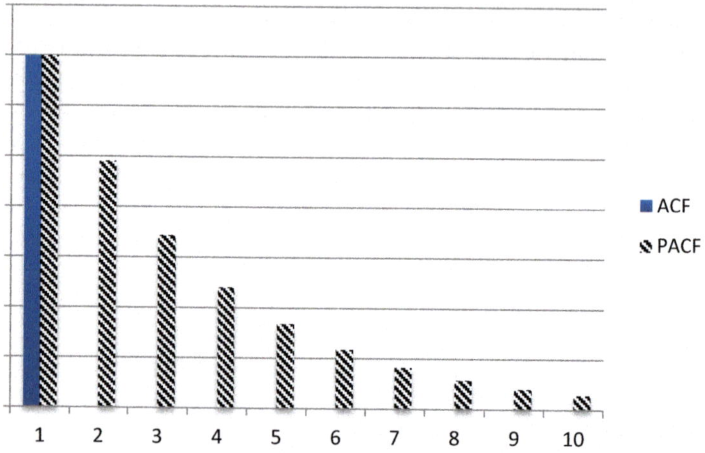

Fig. 3.3 ACF and PACF of an MA(1) process with $0 < \theta < 1$

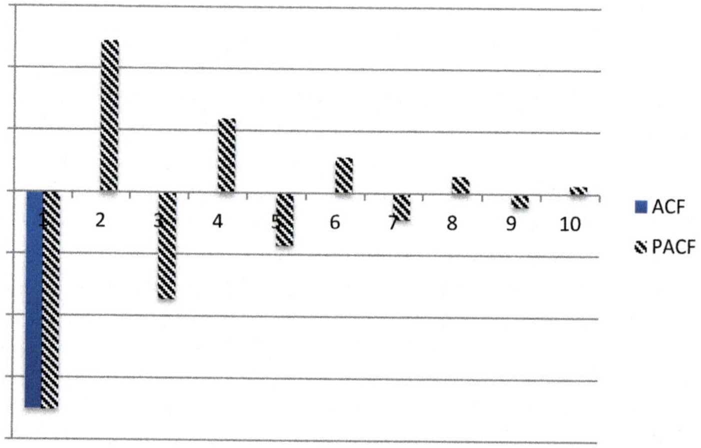

Fig. 3.4 ACF and PACF of an MA(1) process with $-1 < \theta < 0$

MA process are typically restricted becomes apparent when we consider the ACF of an MA(1) process with parameter θ: $\rho_1 = \frac{-\theta}{1+\theta^2}$, and $\rho_k = 0$ for $k > 1$. However, an MA(1) process with parameter $1/\theta$ leads to the same ACF. To overcome this issue, an MA(1) process needs to satisfy the so-called invertibility restriction: $|\theta| < 1$.

The general q-order MA process is written as:

$$\begin{aligned} y_t &= \mu + \theta_q(B)\varepsilon_t \\ \theta_q(B) &= \left(1 - \theta_1 B - \theta_2 B^2 - \cdots - \theta_q B^q\right) \end{aligned} \tag{3.10}$$

where B is the backshift operator defined as before. The invertibility restriction for higher order MA processes requires that the roots of $\theta_q(B)$ lie outside the unit circle. Specifically, for a MA(2) process, where $\theta_2(B) = (1 - \theta_1 B - \theta_2 B^2)$, leading to $y_t = \mu + (1 - \theta_1 B - \theta_2 B^2)\varepsilon_t$, we have:

$$y_t = \mu - \theta_1 \varepsilon_{t-1} - \theta_2 \varepsilon_{t-2} + \varepsilon_t. \tag{3.11}$$

Why would marketing time series ressemble a moving average process? A key reason is that variables omitted from the model (e.g. the weather) continue to affect marketing performance for several periods. For instance, if beer sales today are unexpectedly high because of a heat wave, they are likely to still be high tomorrow as the heat wave continues. Negative moving averages may be caused by equilibrium-seeking of supply and demand. For instance, if wheat production is lower than expected this year because of a natural disaster, farmers will take the resulting higher prices into account and seed too much wheat for next year's demand. In that next year, when prices are lower than expected, farmers will then decide to seed less, etc. If a model does not include the natural disaster, both wheat sales and prices will show negative moving averages in their time series.

The patterns observed for AR(1) and MA(1) in Figs. 3.1 to 3.4 generalize to AR(p) and MA(q) processes. Specifically, we can recognize AR(p) and MA(q) processes based on the ACF and PACF patterns:

1. an AR(p) process is characterized by an exponentially declining ACF and a PACF that cuts off after lag p;
2. an MA(q) process is characterized by an ACF that cuts off after lag q and an exponentially declining PACF.

The combination of both patterns is called an ARMA process, to which we turn next.

3.2.4 Autoregressive Moving Average (ARMA) Processes

The AR and MA processes can be combined into a single model to reflect the idea that both past sales and past random shocks affect y_t. For example, the ARMA(1,1) process is:

$$y_t = \varphi y_{t-1} + \theta \varepsilon_{t-1} + \varepsilon_t. \tag{3.12}$$

This ARMA(1,1) model is by far the most common of the mixed models, and the ACF and PACF patterns are each a function of both the AR and the MA coefficients. First, both the ACF and the PACF at the first lag is given by:

$$\rho_1 = \frac{(1 + \varphi\theta)(\varphi + \theta)}{1 + \theta^2 + \varphi\theta}. \tag{3.13}$$

For instance, when both coefficients equal 0.5, the first lag ACF and PACF equal 0.71 (Fig. 3.5). When both equal −0.5, the first lag ACF and PACF equal −0.71 (Fig. 3.6) Next, the ACF shows exponential decay (with factor φ), while the PACF dies out in more complex patterns, as illustrated in Figs. 3.5 and 3.6. We refer to Enders (2010, p. 65) for the identification of mixed ARMA models from the ACF and PACF functions.

The mixed processes need to satisfy stationarity conditions. The orders (p, q) of an ARMA process are the highest lags of y_t and ε_t, respectively that appear in the model. The general ARMA(p, q) process is formulated as follows:

$$\varphi_p(B)y_t = \mu + \theta_q(B)\varepsilon_t \tag{3.14}$$

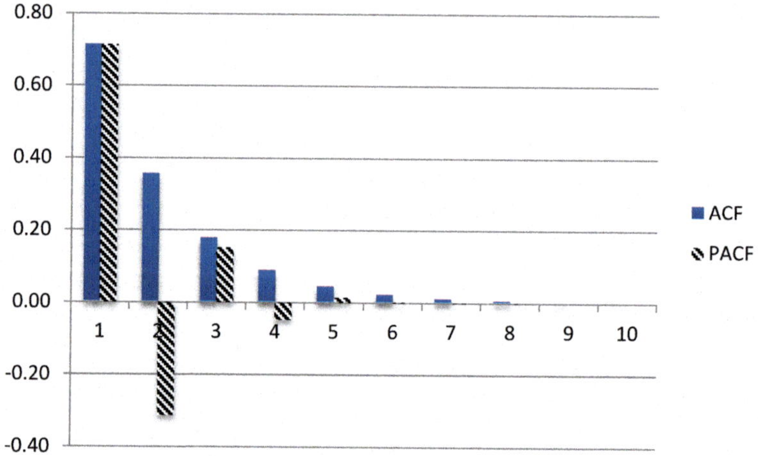

Fig. 3.5 ACF and PACF patterns of an ARMA(1,1) process with $\varphi = \theta = 0.5$

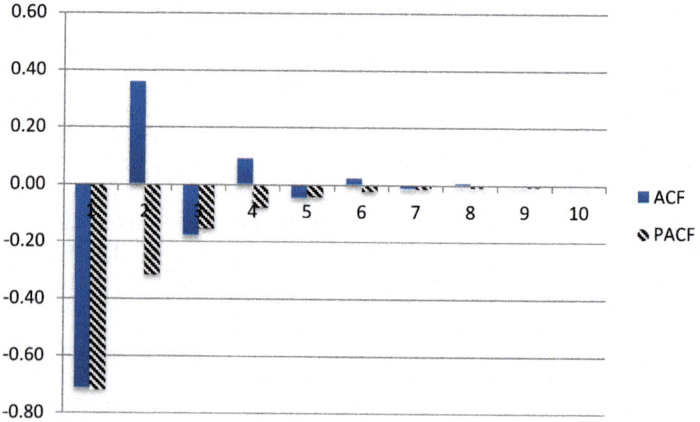

Fig. 3.6 ACF and PACF patterns of an ARMA(1,1) process with $\varphi = \theta = -0.5$

with $\varphi_p(B)$ and $\theta_q(B)$ as defined above. As an example, for an ARMA(2,2) process, $\varphi_2(B) = (1 - \varphi_1 B - \varphi_2 B^2)$ and $\theta_2(B) = (1 - \theta_1 B - \theta_2 B^2)$, so that:

$$y_t = \mu + \varphi_1 y_{t-1} + \varphi_2 y_{t-2} - \theta_1 \varepsilon_{t-1} - \theta_2 \varepsilon_{t-2} + \varepsilon_t. \tag{3.15}$$

As to marketing applications, Dekimpe and Hanssens (1995b) provide an overview of published univariate time series results. They identify 44 studies between 1987 and 1994 that have published results from such models, on a wide variety of durable (trucks, airplanes, furniture), nondurable food (cereal, catsup, beverages) and nonfood (detergents, toothpaste, cleaning aids) product categories and services (holidays, passenger transit, advertising).

3.2.5 *Testing for Evolution Versus Stationarity*

Stationarity is the tendency of a time series to revert back to its deterministic components; such as a fixed mean (mean-stationary) or a mean and trend (trend-stationary). Stationary processes have a finite variance and their future values are relatively easy to predict. In contrast, evolving series do not return to a fixed mean (+ trend); shocks to these series persist in the future. In the context of ARIMA processes, we can formally define the related concepts of stationarity versus unit root (evolution). Stationarity requires that the roots of $\varphi_p(B)$ lie outside the unit circle. Invertibility requires that the roots of $\theta_q(B)$ are outside the unit circle. For the AR(2) process this implies solving $(1 - \varphi_1 B - \varphi_2 B^2) = 0$ and for the MA(2) process solving $(1 - \theta_1 B - \theta_2 B^2) = 0$. In practice, a numerical routine can be used to solve these characteristic equations (if $p > 2$ or $q > 2$).

For example, for an AR(1) process $p = 1$. Then, $(1 - \varphi_1 B) = 0$ is the characteristic equation. The root equals $1/\varphi_1$, which is greater than one in absolute value if $\varphi_1 < 1$. Thus, the null-hypothesis for testing nonstationarity is that $\varphi_1 = 1$. This test is called a unit root test. We redefine the AR(1)-model Eq. (3.1) as follows:

$$\begin{aligned} z_t &= \mu + \gamma y_{t-1} + \varepsilon_t \\ z_t &= y_t - y_{t-1}, \quad \text{and} \quad \gamma = \varphi_1 - 1. \end{aligned} \tag{3.16}$$

Then the unit root null hypothesis is H_0: $\hat{\gamma} = 0$.

The reparameterized model Eq. (3.16) applied to data yields a t-statistic for $\hat{\gamma}$, which can be used to test H_0. This test is known as the Dickey-Fuller test. However, the t-statistic that is obtained cannot be evaluated with the regular tables of the t-distribution. Instead, special tables need to be used. The generalization of the Dickey-Fuller test to an AR(p) process yields the Augmented Dickey-Fuller test. This test is based on a reformulation of the AR(p) process as:

$$z_t = \mu + \gamma y_{t-1} + \delta_1 z_{t-1} + \delta_2 z_{t-2} + \cdots + \delta_p z_{t-p} + \varepsilon_t. \tag{3.17}$$

The Augmented Dickey-Fuller (ADF) test can be used to test the null hypothesis $\gamma = 0$. A large number of lagged first differences should be included in the ADF regression to ensure that the error is approximately white noise. In addition, depending on the assumptions of the underlying process, the test may be performed with or without the μ term in the model. Enders (2003) offered an iterative procedure to implement these different test specifications, as implemented in several recent marketing papers (e.g. Slotegraaf and Pauwels 2008; Srinivasan et al. 2004).

While the Augmented Dicky Fuller (ADF) method is the most popular unit root test in marketing, it is only one of the many developed in light of the low power of the test under certain conditions (see Madalla and Kim 1996 for an excellent elaborate discussion). Because a unit root is the null hypothesis of the ADF-test, particularly appealing are alternatives that have stationarity as the null hypothesis, such as the Kwiatkowski et al. (1992): KPSS test. Unfortunately, Maddalla and Kim (1996) find little convergence of test results for the typical series analyzed in economics research. In contrast, the two applications in marketing (Pauwels and Weiss 2008; Pauwels et al. 2011) show that the ADF and the KPSS test most often lead to the same conclusion for marketing and performance variables, which strengthens the confidence in the variable classification. Pauwels and Weiss (2008) show convergence for all 8 studied cases (4 stationary, 4 evolving series) in the unit root test without time trend, and 7 out of 8 studied cases in the unit root test with time trend (Table 4 in Pauwels and Weiss 2008). In the one exception, the ADF test indicates stationarity around a time trend, while the KPSS test indicates evolution.

Evidently, further research is needed to verify whether this convergence of unit root tests results holds up across marketing variables and settings. Moreover, other test specifications should be compared. The initial evidence is encouraging: Ouyang et al. (2002) find convergence of the ADF and the Perron (1989) test for 9 out of 10 sales series and 9 out of 10 advertising series of Chinese brands. A final important point of convergence is that the results of unit root tests do not depend on the temporal aggregation of the data (Noriega-Muro 1993).

Specific issues in the data generating process have been addressed with special versions of unit root tests. First, it is important to account for structural breaks such as regulatory shifts, and the introduction of new products and channels (see the next section). Second, unit root test may be sensitive to outliers, such as data recording errors. Franses and Paap (2001) developed an outlier-robust unit root test. The logical consistency requirement when modeling market shares has been incorporated in unit root tests by Franses and Paap (2001).

Why would marketing performance show evolution versus stationarity? Building on Dekimpe (1992), Pauwels (2001) classifies the reasons for performance evolution and stationarity as depicted in Table 3.2 The first two groups of reasons deal with general technology and economic factors. The next two groups of reasons deal with actions of specific market players; distinguishing consumers and retailers from management decision making by the firm and its competitors.

Table 3.2 Reasons for evolution and stationarity in performance

Evolution	Stationarity
Technology diffusion factors	
Technological breakthroughs (D'Aveni 1994)	Lack of technological innovation (Pauwels and D'Aveni 2016)
Growth stage in the product life cycle (Day 1981)	Maturity stage in the product life cycle (Lilien and Yoon 1988)
Changing marketing effectiveness over product life cycle (Arora 1979)	Stable marketing effectiveness over product life cycle (Wildt 1976)
Macroeconomic and regulation factors	
Co-movements of performance with economy boosts, recessions and disruptions (Deleersnyder et al. 2007)	Performance isolated from economic ups and downs or related to stable economy
Regulations that open markets and stimulate competition	Regulations that limit company growth and/or bankruptcy options
Behavior of consumers and channel partners	
Consumer learning (Alba et al. 1991)	Consumer forgetting (Little 1979)
Changing customer tastes/base (Abell 1978)	Consumer inertia (Ehrenberg 1988)
Retail distribution and performance positive feedback loop (Ataman et al. 2008; Bronnenberg et al. 2000)	Retailer inertia and assortment commitment (Broniarczyk et al. 1998)
Competitive behavior	
Performance feedback in evolving business practice (Dekimpe and Hanssens 1999)	Normative marketing decision models
Error-correcting behavior towards desired performance (Salmon 1982, 1988)	Satisficing managers (March and Simon 1958)
Competitive quest for more (Hunt 2000) incorporated in budgets	Fixing marketing budgets as sales ratios in mature markets
Breakthrough changes in marketing strategy or practices, which are not quickly matched by competitors (Hermann 1997)	Interdependent adaptation with competitors (Johnson and Russo 1994) enables fast competitive cancellation of marketing effects (Bass and Pilon 1980)

Table 3.3 Evolution and stationarity of 220 time series

Model-type	Evolving		Stationary	
Sales	122	(68%)	58	(32%)
Market share	9	(22%)	31	(78%)
Total	131		89	

Source: Dekimpe and Hanssens (1995b, p. G114)

Dekimpe and Hanssens (1995b) apply unit root tests and other time-series methods to identify empirical generalizations about market evolution. Based on data from hundreds of published studies, their meta-analysis for performance measures is given in Table 3.3.

The models are classified into sales models and market share models. The results show that evolution occurs for a majority of brand sales series, and that a vast majority of the market share time-series models is stationary. This is consistent with arguments of Bass and Pilon (1980) and Ehrenberg (1988) that many markets are in a long-run equilibrium. The relative position of the brands is only temporarily affected by marketing activities. Even for brand sales (and category sales) series, later studies suggest that stationarity, and not evolution is the norm for mature brands in mature categories (e.g. Nijs et al. 2001; Pauwels et al. 2002). Emerging markets and brands show a substantially higher potential for evolution (Osinga et al. 2010; Pauwels and Dans 2001; Slotegraaf and Pauwels 2008).

3.2.6 Unit Root Tests with Structural Breaks

The earliest unit root tests assume no structural break in the time series; i.e. if a unit root is found, it is assumed that any shock to the series has a permanent effect. In contrast, it could be that most (small) shocks have no permanent effect, while one or a few big shocks do (Perron 1989). Such big shocks are called "structural breaks" and may be wars and oil price shocks in economics (ibid) or regulatory shifts, and the introduction of new products and channels in marketing (Deleersnyder et al. 2002; Kornelis et al. 2008; Pauwels and Srinivasan 2004). Researchers define a structural break in terms of a parameter change in the deterministic part of the model, i.e. in the slope and/or intercept of the deterministic growth path (Kornelis et al. 2008; Perron 1989).

Even if the typical, smaller shocks do not persist, the presence of such a large shock biases the standard unit root tests towards reporting evolution. This topic has been much discussed in the econometrics literature, which provides tests for known and unknown breaks, and for single and multiple breaks (e.g. Bai and Perron 1998; Perron 1990; Zivot and Andrews 1992).

Known structural breaks represent obvious shifts in the data generating process, such as a product harm crisis (Leeflang et al. 2000, pp. 472–473), introducing a new brand (Pauwels and Srinivasan 2004) or channel (Kornelis et al. 2008) or changing the pricing structure from free to fee (Pauwels and Weiss 2008). Perron (1990) developed the most widely used test for a single break, which has been the focus of most marketing applications (Deleersnyder et al. 2002; Lim et al. 2005; Nijs et al. 2001; Pauwels and Srinivasan 2004)

Unknown structural breaks are the more common scenario, as Zivot and Andrews (1992) critized Perron (1990) for pretesting; i.e. eyeballing the time series for where a structural break should be and then testing for it. Such pretesting biases the finite-sample and asymptotic distributions of the known break test statistics (Christiano 1992; Zivot and Andrews 1992). Instead, they advocate scanning for unknown structural breaks throughout the time series. This procedure also has the advantage of not assuming that a known break occurs at a specific time; e.g. consumers could take a while to react to a product improvement or recall, so that the sales break comes at an unknown time. If players anticipate changes, they may even react before the time the researcher dates the event (Doyle and Saunders 1985; Pauwels and Srinivasan 2004, p. 368), which will also be picked up by unknown structural break tests.

In marketing, Pauwels and Dans (2001) use unknown structural breaks when analyzing the daily dynamics of online news, i.e. visits, page views and brand choice for each newspaper. The total number of online news visits initially evolves, but later stabilises. In contrast, page views continue to evolve as usage depth increases over time. Finally, brand choice is stable and proportional to the brand equity borrowed from the printed newspaper. Thus, evolutionary growth first comes from freeriding on the wave of increasing online news readership, but then needs to come from increases usage depth, which is brand specific.

What if there may be more than one structural break? The testing procedure by Ben-David and Papell (2000) tests, for consecutive values of M, the null hypothesis of M breaks against the alternative hypothesis of $M + 1$ breaks. This testing follows the spirit of Chow (1960) tests for parameter stability (see Sect. 5.4.3 in Vol. I), and aims to identify any remaining "irregular" events that could change a part of the model (Ben-David and Papell 2000). However, because Ben-David and Papell (2000) stop once stationarity is established, Kornelis et al. (2008) propose the identification of all unknown breaks as the stopping rule. They quantify the impact of entrants in the Dutch TV advertising market, and find that the steady-state growth of incumbents' revenues was slowed by these entries.

3.2.7 Integrated Processes

The ARMA processes described above are processes for series with a stationary mean. In these processes the mean value of y_t does not change over time. However, in marketing we often see that sales variables evolve (see Table 3.3) which implies nonstationarity. Nonstationary series can be formulated as ARMA processes for differenced series, $z_t = y_t - y_{t-1}$. The differencing operation removes a trend from the data. The corresponding model is called an ARIMA (Integrated ARMA) model.

As an example, consider an ARIMA(1,1,1) model:

$$z_t = \mu + \varphi_1 z_{t-1} - \theta_1 \varepsilon_{t-1} + \varepsilon_t \tag{3.18}$$

where

$$z_t = y_t - y_{t-1}.$$

The ACF of a nonstationary process decays very slowly to zero. Therefore it is difficult to determine the AR and MA components from the ACF and PACF. However these functions for z_t (i.e. after differencing), display the typical patterns for ARMA processes, as illustrated above. In order to formulate the general ARIMA(p,d,f)

process, integrated of order d, we define the differencing operator $\Delta^d = (1-B)^d$. For example, if $d = 1$ this amounts to taking $z_t = (1-B)y_t = y_t - By_t = y_t - y_{t-1}$. For $d = 2$ we have quadratic differencing $z_t^2 = (1-B)^2 y_t = (y_t - y_{t-1}) - (y_{t-1} - y_{t-2})$. Trends in marketing are often linear and sometimes quadratic, so that d is rarely greater than 2. The ARIMA(p,d,q) process can then be defined as:

$$\varphi_p(B)\Delta^d y_t = \mu + \theta_q(B)\varepsilon_t. \tag{3.19}$$

3.2.8 Extent of Persistence

The above discussion of evolution versus stationarity may give the impression that marketing series are either one or the other – which is why this issue is treated in most marketing applications. However, persistence can also be considered a matter of *degree*; and the resulting insights can be profound, as demonstrated in Hanssens (1998). Instead of the extremes of 100% versus 0% of a shock to the series persisting over time, an intermediate value of e.g. 30% may persist. In the ARIMA-framework, this may be obtained with an ARIMA(0,1,1) model as shown below:

$$y_t = y_{t-1} + \varepsilon_t - 0.7\varepsilon_{t-1} = \varepsilon_t + 0.3\varepsilon_{t-1} + 0.3\varepsilon_{t-2} + 0.3\varepsilon_{t-3} + \cdots \tag{3.20}$$

For instance, in the setting of Wiesel et al. (2011), an unexpected boost in profits by 3000 euros today, would result in a 1000 euros higher profit tomorrow, and the day after, etc. For a computer peripheral product, Hanssens (1998) reports that monthly orders are evolving, but with a persistence degree of only 12%. In contrast, retail sales have a much higher persistence of 68%. The author concludes that signals coming from end-users have longer-lasting demand effects than those coming from retailers.

3.2.9 Seasonal Processes

Many series of sales data in marketing display seasonal patterns, resulting from variation in weather and other factors. As a result sales fluctuate systematically around the mean level, such that some observations are expected to have values above and other observations below the mean. For example, sales of ice cream in Europe tend to be highest in the spring and summer and lowest in winter periods. The seasonal effects can be of the AR, the MA or the Integrated types, depending on whether sales levels or random shocks affect future sales, and on whether nonstationary seasonal patterns exist. Therefore a seasonal model may apply, with orders P, D, and Q respectively for the AR, I and MA components, denoted by ARIMA(P,D,Q)$_s$, with s the lag of the seasonal terms.

To illustrate, suppose there exists a seasonal pattern in monthly data, such that any month's value contains a component that resembles the previous year's value in the same month. Then a purely seasonal ARIMA(1,1,1)$_{12}$ model is written as:

$$z_t^{12} = \mu + \varphi_{12} z_{t-12}^{12} - \theta_{12}\varepsilon_{t-12} + \varepsilon_t \tag{3.21}$$

where

$$z_t^{12} = \nabla^{12} y_t = y_t - B^{12} y_t = y_t - y_{t-12}, \quad \text{and} \quad \nabla^{12} = \left(1 - B^{12}\right).$$

The ARIMA(0,1,1)$_s$ is the most common seasonal model, and it provides an exponentially weighted moving average of the data. This simple model is written in two equivalent forms:

$$\begin{aligned} y_t &= \mu + y_{t-s} - \theta_s \varepsilon_{t-s} + \varepsilon_t, \text{ and} \\ \nabla^s y_t &= \mu + (1 - \theta_s B^s)\,\varepsilon_t. \end{aligned} \tag{3.22}$$

Seasonal processes can be identified from the ACF and PACF functions, similarly to the nonseasonal ARIMA processes above, except that the patterns occur at lags s, $2s$, $3s$, etc., instead of at lags 1, 2, 3, etc. Thus, for these purely seasonal processes:

1. the ACF decays slowly at multiples of s in case of seasonal differencing of order s;
2. the ACF decays at multiples of lag s and the PACF has spikes at multiples of lag s up to lag $P \times s$, after which it is zero, for seasonal AR processes;
3. the ACF has spikes at multiples of lag s up to lag $Q \times s$, after which it is zero, and the PACF decays at multiples of lag s, for purely seasonal MA processes.

In practice, *seasonal* and *nonseasonal* processes occur together. However, an examination of ACF and PACF may suggest patterns in these functions at different lags. This general process is indicated as an ARIMA(p,d,q)(P,D,Q)$_s$ process:

$$\varphi_P\left(B^s\right)\varphi_p(B)\nabla^D\Delta^d y_t = \mu + \theta_Q\left(B^s\right)\theta_q(B)\varepsilon_t. \tag{3.23}$$

In practice, the orders p, d, q, and P, D, Q, are small, ranging from 0 to 2 in most cases.

An application of an ARIMA model is provided by Blattberg and Neslin (1990, p. 249). They model warehouse withdrawal sales data for a packaged good on 25 four-week periods in order to estimate incremental sales generated by a promotion. Examination of the series and the ACF and PACF functions yielded a ARIMA(2,1,0)(0,1,0)$_{13}$ model. That is, sales are affected by sales two (4-week) periods back, with linear trends in 1- and 13-period intervals. The estimated model is:

$$\left(1 + 0.83B + 0.58B^2\right)(1 - B)\left(1 - B^{13}\right) y_t = -3686 + \varepsilon_t \tag{3.24}$$

or

$$y_t = 0.17y_{t-1} + 0.25y_{t-2} + 0.58y_{t-3} + y_{t-13} - 0.17y_{t-14} - 0.25y_{t-15} - 0.58_{t-16} - 3686 + \varepsilon_t. \tag{3.25}$$

Despite initially widespread practice to deseasonalize data before including it in a model, Ghysels et al. (1994) have shown that such procedure may mask relations between variables. As a result, most time series techniques instead use dummy variables to control for seasonal effects, leaving the original variables of interest intact. Still, researchers should examine the robustness of unit root test inferences by using different specifications (e.g. Maddala and Kim 1998). One such specification is the recent study by Gijsenberg (2017). He uses the Christiano and Fitzgerald (2003) random-walk filter to uncover intra-year seasonal cycles in category demand, brand sales, advertising and pricing – without the need of a priori specifying peak and/or valley periods. Applying this method across 61 fast moving consumer good categories, he finds an average volatility of category demand of 0.083, from a low of 0.041 for washing machines to a high of 0.296 for spirit-based drinks. Moreover, both advertising effectiveness and observed advertising are stronger at demand peaks. Surprisingly, consumer reactions to price decreases are weaker at demand peaks, while reactions to price increases remain unchanged.

3.3 Relating Marketing to Performance: Multivariate Time Series

A strategic perspective on marketing decisions requires a dynamic understanding of the conditions for performance growth and of the role marketing actions play in this process. Section 3.2 covered the first aspect; but to answer the second question we need to relate time series of marketing activity with time series of performance. Two popular techniques are transfer function analysis, which extends the ARIMA approach to multivariate time series analysis and intervention analysis, where the effects of predictor variables take the form of steps or pulses.

3.3.1 Transfer Functions

So far we have restricted the discussion to time series models to predict a single variable of interest such as sales, as a function of past sales. In marketing, we are typically also interested in explaining by variables such as price and advertising, which themselves may be subject to time series patterns. We can include these variables in the model through a *transfer function*. To illustrate, assume there is just one explanatory variable, indicated by x_t. Often, the transfer function takes the form of a linear distributed lag function. Such a distributed lag function is a linear combination of current and past values of the explanatory variable (x_t, $x_{t-1,\ldots}$). Thus, these models postulate that sales may respond to current and previous values of x, as is often the case for advertising. Suppose advertising affects sales as follows:

$$y_t = \mu + \nu_0 x_t + \nu_1 x_{t-1} + \varepsilon_t. \tag{3.26}$$

In this model sales in each period is affected by advertising in that period (x_t), and by advertising in the previous period (x_{t-1}). The general dynamic regression model formulation for one variable is:

$$y_t = \mu + \nu_k(B) x_t + \varepsilon_t \tag{3.27}$$

where

μ = a constant,
$\nu_k(B) = \nu_0 + \nu_1 B + \nu_2 B^2 + \cdots + \nu_k B^k$, the transfer function,
B = the backshift operator, and
k = the order of the transfer function, which is to be determined.

The transfer function is also called the impulse response function, and the ν-coefficients are called the impulse response weights. In the example, if sales do not react to advertising in period t, but only to lagged advertising, $\nu_0 = 0$. In that case, the model is said to have a "dead time" (or "wear-in time") of one. In general, the dead time is the number of consecutive ν's equal to zero, starting with ν_0.

Before we discuss how the order of the impulse response function can be determined, we consider a well-known special case: the Koyck model (see Vol. I, Sect. 2.8.2). In this model, the impulse response weights are defined by $\nu_i = \alpha\nu_{i-1}$, for $i = 1,\ldots,\infty$. Thus, the response is a constant fraction of the response in the previous time period, and the weights decay exponentially. It can be shown that Koyck's model is equivalent to:

$$y_t = \nu_0 x_t + \alpha y_{t-1} + \varepsilon_t \tag{3.28}$$

or an AR(1) model with one explanatory variable of lag zero. Now, bringing the term involving the lagged criterion variable to the left-hand side of Eq. (3.28) results in:

$$(1 - \alpha B)\, y_t = \nu_0 x_t + \varepsilon_t \tag{3.29}$$

which can be rewritten as:

$$y_t = \frac{\nu_0 x_t + \varepsilon_t}{(1 - \alpha B)}. \tag{3.30}$$

This formulation is called the (rational) polynomial form of the Koyck model. In general, rational polynomial distributed lag models comprise a family of models.

Equation (3.31) represents such models by defining terms that generalize those in Eq. (3.30):

$$\nu_{k,l}(B) = \frac{\omega_k(B)B^d}{\alpha_l(B)} \tag{3.31}$$

where

$\omega_k(B) = \omega_0 + \omega_1 B + \omega_2 B^2 + \cdots + \omega_k B^k$, which contain the direct effects of changes in x or y over time,
$\alpha_l(B) = \alpha_0 + \alpha_1 B + \alpha_2 B^2 + \cdots + \alpha_l B^l$, which show the gradual adjustment of y to x over time, and
B^d = the dead time (i.e. $d = 0$ corresponds to dead time of $B^0 = 1$).

For the identification of these models from data, two problems arise. The first is to find a parsimonious expression for the polynomial $\nu_{k,l}(B)$, and the second is to find an expression for the time structure of the error term, in the form of an ARIMA model. An important tool in the identification of transfer functions is the cross-correlation function (CCF), which is the correlation between x and y at lag k: $\rho(y_t, x_{t-k})$. The CCF extends the ACF for the situation of two or more series (those of x and of y), with similar interpretation: spikes denote MA parameters (in the numerator in Eq. (3.31)), and decaying patterns indicate AR parameters (in the denominator in Eq. (3.31)).

We note that the simultaneous identification of the transfer function and the ARIMA structure of the error in Eq. (3.28) is much more complex than it is for a single ARIMA process. An example that occurs frequently in marketing is one where the original sales series shows a seasonal pattern, for which an ARIMA(1,0,1)(1,0,0)$_{12}$ model is indicated. However, if temperature is included as an explanatory variable in the model, an ARIMA(1,1,0) may suffice. Thus, the identification of the ARIMA error structure in Eq. (3.28) depends on the exogenous variables included in the model. Procedures that have been proposed for that purpose are the *LTF* (linear transfer function) method and the double prewhitening method. The core of these methods involves fitting univariate time series to the individual series, after which the estimated white noise residuals are used for multivariate analyses. This is called the prewhitening of variables.[2]

An alternative strategy that is useful especially with several input variables is the ARMAX procedure, which is an ARMA model for an endogenous variable with multiple exogenous variables. Franses (1991) applied this procedure to an analysis of the primary demand for beer in the Netherlands. Based on 42 bimonthly observations from 1978 to 1984, using ACFs and model tests, Franses obtained the following model:

[2]See Sect. 5.4.3 in Vol. I.

$$\ln y_t = 0.17 y_{t-6} - 0.06\delta_1 + 2.30\delta_2 + 2.34\delta_3 + 2.51\delta_4 + 2.30\delta_5 + 2.37\delta_6 - 3.98\Delta^1 p_t + 2.27\Delta^1 p_{t+1} - 0.54 y_{t-1} + \varepsilon_t. \quad (3.32)$$

In this model, δ_1 to δ_6 are bimonthly seasonal dummies, p_t is the price, Δ^1 is a first-order differencing operator, and p_{t+1} is a price expectation variable that assumes perfect foresight. The model contains a lagged endogenous variable, a moving average component, seasonal effects (modeled through dummies rather then through differencing) and current price and future price effects. Substantively, Franses concluded that tax changes may be effective if one wants to change the primary demand for beer, given the strong price effect. The positive effect of future prices suggests some forward buying by consumers. Advertising expenditures did not significantly influence the primary demand for beer.

In the transfer functions we consider the relations between criterion (y) and predictor variables (x). The variables y and x may both be *integrated* of order d_y and d_x respectively, where $d_y \neq 0$, $d_x \neq 0$. We discuss the relevance of this below. In the regression model:

$$y_t = \beta x_t + \varepsilon_t \quad (3.33)$$

there is a presumption that the ε_t are white noise series. However, this is unlikely to be true if $d_y \neq 0$ and/or $d_x \neq 0$. Generally, if two series are integrated of different order, i.e. $d_y \neq d_x$, linear combinations of them are integrated to the higher of the two orders ($\max(d_x, d_y)$). If y_t and x_t are integrated to the *same* order ($d_y = d_x$) then it is possible that there is a β such that:

$$\varepsilon_t = y_t - \beta x_t \quad (3.34)$$

is $I(0)$ (i.e. integrated to the order zero=white noise). Two series that satisfy this requirement are said to be *cointegrated*. We will return to cointegration in Chap. 4.

3.3.2 Intervention Analysis

Apart from traditional marketing variables such as price and advertising, we can accommodate discrete events in models of sales. Examples include a new government regulation, the introduction of a competitive brand, a catastrophic event such as poisoning or disease relevant to food products, and so on. Intervention analysis extends the transfer function approach described above for the estimation of the impact of such events. Intervention analysis in fact extends dummy-variable regression to a dynamic context. The interventions may have two different effects: a pulse effect, which is a temporary effect that disappears (gradually), or a step effect that is permanent once it has occurred. A strike could have a pulse effect on the production or distribution of a product. The introduction of a new brand may permanently change sales of an existing brand. The dummy variables for these two types of effects can be represented as follows:

1. pulse effect: $x_t^p = 1$ in the time periods of the intervention ($t = t'$), and $x_t^p = 0$ in all other periods ($t \neq t'$);
2. step effect: $x_t^s = 1$ in the time periods in which the event occurs and *all subsequent time periods* ($t \geq t'$), and $x_t^s = 0$ at all time periods before the event ($t < t'$),

where t' denotes the time of the intervention.

For intervention analysis the model defined by Eq. (3.31) applies, with the x-variable defined as above. The form of Eq. (3.31) determines the nature of the *pulse* interventions. If $\nu_p(B)x_t^p = \frac{\omega_0 x_t^p}{(1-\alpha B)}$ then y_t shows a single spike at time t. In Fig. 3.7 we show a number of pulse interventions. In Fig. 3.7a, y_t has a *stationary* mean except for the effect of the pulse intervention at $t = t'$. During $t = t'$, y_t shifts upward. Immediately after $t = t'$, the series returns to its previous level. For a series with a *nonstationary* mean, a pulse intervention might appear as shown in Fig. 3.7b. After $t = t'$, in which there is a downward shift, the series returns to the level determined by its nonstationary character. The transfer function part is again $\omega_0 x_t^p$ as in Fig. 3.7a.

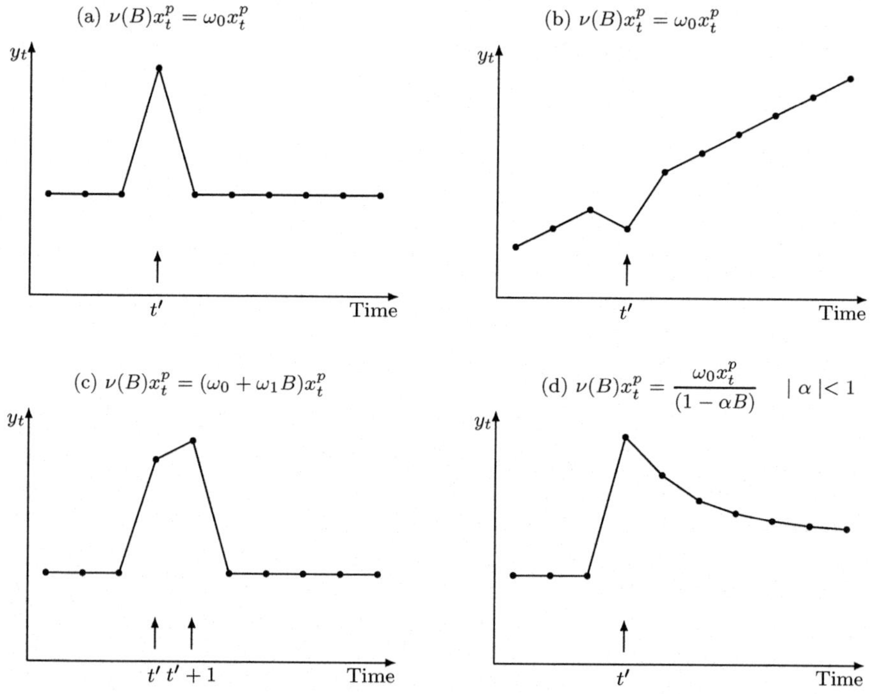

Fig. 3.7 Examples of pulse interventions
Source: Pankratz (1991, pp. 256–257)

Figure 3.7c shows a pulse intervention at $t = t'$ and $t = t' + 1$, i.e., a multiperiod temporary response. The transfer function part in $t = t'$ is $\omega_0 x_t^P$ and in $t = t' + 1$ it is $\omega_1 B x_t^P$. Hence $v(B)x_t^P = (\omega_0 + \omega_1 B)\, x_t^P$. Notice that these effects are not cumulative; the response of $\omega_0 x_t^P$ after $t = t'$ is zero, and the "secondary" response of $\omega_1 B x_t^P$ is zero after $t = t' + 1$. If $v_p(B)x_t^P = \frac{\omega_0 x_t^P}{(1-\alpha B)}$, the effect is a spike at $t = t'$, which decays subsequently (if $|\alpha| < 1$). The series in Fig. 3.7d shows a continuing dynamic response following period t'. Each response after $t = t'$ is a constant fraction α of the response during the previous period. The specification of $v(B)x_t^P$ is a Koyck model; $\omega_0 x_t^P$ is the initial response of $t = t'$ and α is the retention rate.

In Fig. 3.8 we show some *step* interventions, i.e. *permanent* changes on y_t. Figure 3.8a shows a permanent effect that is immediate. Here $v(B)x_t^S = \omega_0 x_t^S$, $x_t^S = 0$ for $t < t'$ and $x_t^S = 1$ for $t \geq t'$. Figure 3.8b shows that a step intervention can be semi-permanent. Here $x_t^S = 1$ for $t = t'$, $t' + 1$, $t' + 2$. Figure 3.8c illustrates a step intervention for a series with a nonstationary mean. A step intervention with dynamic effects is shown in Fig. 3.8d. The transfer function of Fig. 3.8d is $(\omega_0 + \omega_1 B)\, x_t^S$, where $\omega_0 x_t^S$ captures the step during $t' - 1$ and t'.

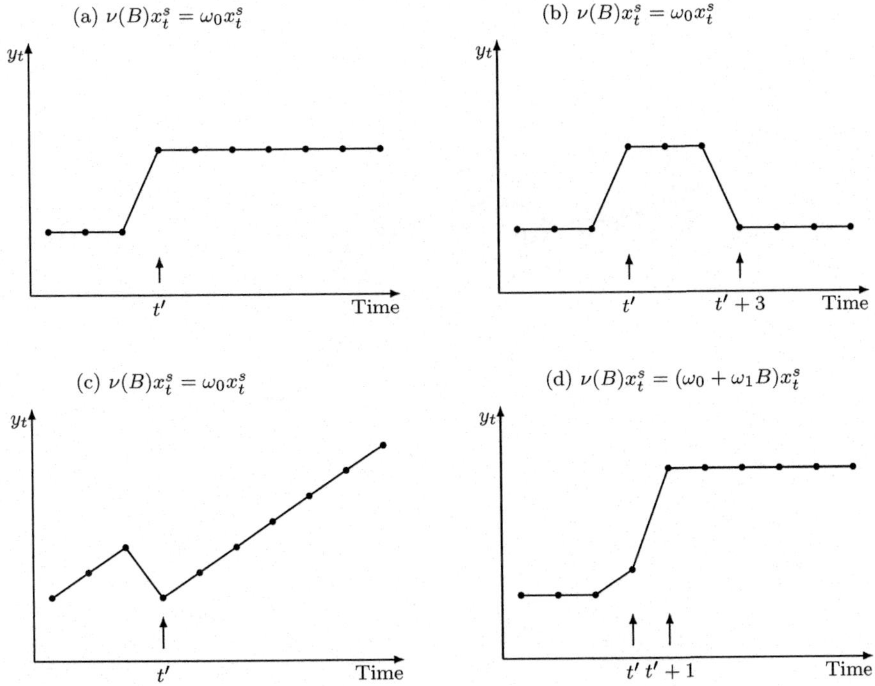

Fig. 3.8 Examples of step interventions
Source: Pankratz (1991, pp. 261–262)

3.4 Marketing Application

We provide an application of intervention analysis to the analysis of sales for a fast-moving consumer good.[3] The manufacturer of this product incurred two successive catastrophic events both of which affected the product's sales. We show a graph of the product's market share in Fig. 3.9. The actual market share values and the time periods are disguised for reasons of confidentiality. Data were collected by a market research agency and are shown in periods of four weeks. The total length of the series is 52 (four-weekly) periods (4 years).

For this problem, no data on marketing variables were available, and the model was calibrated on market shares (y_t) only. The interventions occurred in periods 28 and 29. First, an ARIMA model was identified on the series up to the first intervention ($t \leq 27$). The ACF and PACF suggested an AR(1) model. There is no evidence of a seasonal pattern. The Dickey-Fuller unit root test indicated that the series is stationary. The estimates of the AR(1) model are presented below:

$$y_t = 27.20 + 0.36y_{t-1} + \varepsilon_t. \tag{3.35}$$

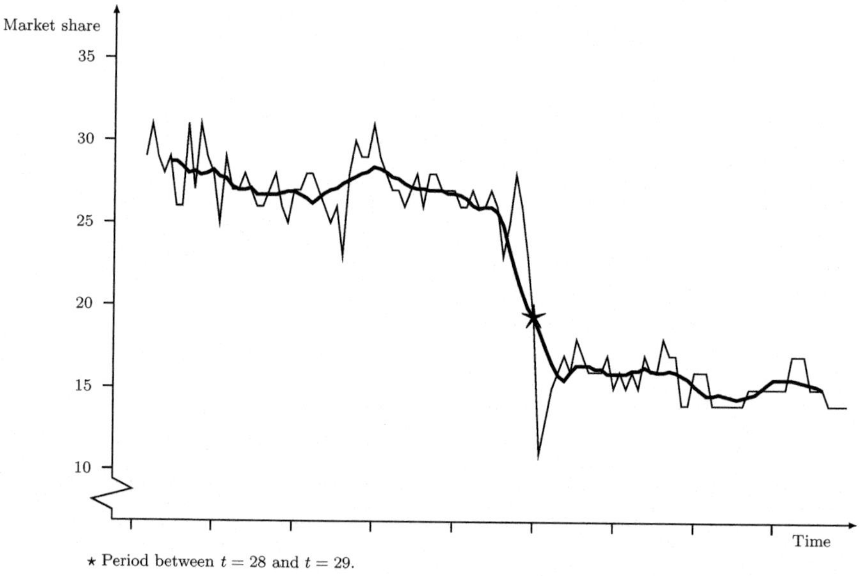

Fig. 3.9 Market share of a brand subject to two catastrophic events

[3]This example is based on an unpublished study by Leeflang and Wedel. See Leeflang et al. (2000, pp. 472–473).

In this model, the AR(1) coefficient is significant. Next, we model the interventions. Based on our observation of the data, we assume step functions for the two interventions Because the two interventions occur in two subsequent time periods, we estimate only a simple transfer function. The two intervention dummies are $x_{1t} = 0$ for $t = 1,\ldots,27$ and $x_{1t} = 1$ for $t > 27$, and $x_{2t} = 0$ for $t = 1,\ldots,28$ and $x_{2t} = 1$ for $t > 28$, respectively. The estimated intervention model is:

$$y_t = 27.18 + 0.44y_{t-1} - 5.83x_{1t} - 5.77x_{2t} + \varepsilon_t. \tag{3.36}$$

The R^2 of this model is 92.4 percent. The estimated standard error of each of the intervention effects is about 1.5, indicating that both effects are highly significant. The estimated standard error of the AR term is 0.1, so that this term is significant as well. The model appears to fit the data quite well. The residuals do not show any remaining autocorrelation and are approximately normal. The step function specification of the interventions thus seems appropriate. The analysis suggests that both interventions have affected the market share of the brand permanently over the time period considered in the study and it quantifies the magnitudes of the effects as about equal.

In summary, transfer function analysis and intervention analysis are interesting techniques to analyze the over time effect of marketing on peformance. A first benefit of transfer functional analysis is that it is a straightforward extension of the well-understood univariate (ARIMA) approach. Moreover, compared to the traditional regression model, which is a special case of the transfer function, it (1) allows for a response parameter that is polynomial in time and (2) allows for systematic behavior in the error term. While the x-series needs to be a continous time series, intervention analysis allows examination of the dynamic effects of discrete events. However, a major limitation of transfer function analysis is that causality is assumed to flow only from the x variables (typically marketing by the firm and/or its competitors) to a single y-variable (typically performance, such as sales or profits). Over the last decade, Granger Causality tests have demonstrated the presence of marketing-performance feedback (e.g. Dekimpe and Hanssens 1999), causality patterns among marketing variables of the focal firm (e.g. Pauwels 2004), causality patterns among own and competitive marketing actions (e.g. Steenkamp et al. 2005), and causality patterns among intermediate performance metrics such as purchase funnel stages (e.g. Wiesel et al. 2011). In such case, it is better to estimate a full dynamic system, in which both marketing and peformance series are treated as endogenous variables – as discussed in the next chapter.

Additional applications of traditional time series models can be found in Bass and Pilon (1980), Doyle and Saunders (1985), and Leone (1983).

3.5 Software Packages

Forecast Pro and Eviews are specialized software programs for forecasting time series, including the ARIMA processes discussed in Sect. 3.2. For transfer function and intervention analysis, both R and SAS offer excellent options.

References

Aaker, D.A., Keller, K.L.: Consumer evaluations of brand extensions. J. Mark. **54**(1), 27–41 (1990)

Abell, D.F.: Strategic windows. J. Mark. **42**(3), 21–26 (1978)

Alba, J., Chattopadhyay, A. W., Wesley Hutchinson, J., Lynch, J.G., Jr: Memory and decision making. In: Robertson, T.S., Kassarjian, H.H. (eds.) Handbook of Consumer Behavior, pp. 1–49. Prentice-Hall, Englewood Cliffs, NJ (1991)

Arora, R.: How promotion elasticities change. J. Advert. Res. **19**(3), 57–62 (1979)

Ataman, M.B., Mela, C.F., Van Heerde, H.J.: Building brands. Mark. Sci. **27**, 1036–1054 (2008)

Bai, J., Perron, P.: Estimating and testing linear models with multiple structural changes. Econometrica. **66**, 47–78 (1998)

Bass, F.M., Pilon, T.L.: A stochastic brand choice framework for econometric modeling of time series market share behavior. J. Mark. Res. **17**, 486–497 (1980)

Ben-David, D., Papell, D.H.: Some evidence on the continuity of the growth process among the G7 countries. Econ. Inq. **38**, 320–330 (2000)

Blattberg, R. C., Neslin, S. A.: Sales promotion: Concepts, Methods, and Strategies. Prentice Hall, Englewood Cliffs, NJ (1990)

Broniarczyk, S.M., Hoyer, W.D., McAlister, L.: Consumers' perceptions of the assortment offered in a grocery category: the impact of item reduction. J. Mark. Res. **35**, 166–176 (1998)

Bronnenberg, B.J., Mahajan, V., Vanhonacker, W.R.: The emergence of market structure in new repeat-purchase categories: the interplay of market share and retailer distribution. J. Mark. Res. **37**, 16–31 (2000)

Chow, G.C.: Tests of equality between sets of coefficients in two linear regressions. Econometrica. **28**, 591–605 (1960)

Christiano, L.J.: Searching for a break in GNP. J. Bus. Econ. Stat. **10**, 237–250 (1992)

Christiano, L.J., Fitzgerald, T.J.: The band pass filter. Int. Econ. Rev. **44**, 435–465 (2003)

D'Aveni, R.: Hypercompetition: Managing the Dynamics of Strategic Marketing. The Free Press, New York (1994)

Day, G.S.: The product life cycle: analysis and applications issues. J. Mark. **45**(4), 60–67 (1981)

Dekimpe, M. G.: Long-run modeling in marketing. PhD-thesis, University of California, Los Angeles (1992)

Dekimpe, M.G., Hanssens, D.M.: The persistence of marketing effects on sales. Mark. Sci. **14**, 1–21 (1995a)

Dekimpe, M.G., Hanssens, D.M.: Empirical generalizations about market evolution and stationarity. Mark. Sci. **14**(supplement), G109–G121 (1995b)

Dekimpe, M.G., Hanssens, D.M.: Sustained spending and persistent response: A new look at long-term marketing profitability. J. Mark. Res. **36**, 397–412 (1999)

Deleersnyder, B., Geyskens, I., Gielens, K., Dekimpe, M.G.: How cannibalistic is the Internet channel? A study of the newspaper industry in the United Kingdom and the Netherlands. Int. J. Res. Mark. **19**, 337–348 (2002)

Deleersnyder, B., Dekimpe, M.G., Steenkamp, J-B.E.M., Koll, O.: Win–win strategies at discount stores. J. Retail. Consum. Serv. **14**, 309–318 (2007)

Doyle, P., Saunders, J.: The lead effect of marketing decisicions. J. Mark. Res. **22**, 54–65 (1985)

Ehrenberg, A.: Repeat-Buying: Facts, Theory and Applications. Griffin, London (1988)
Enders, W.: Applied Econometric Time Series, 2nd edn. Wiley, New York (2003)
Enders, C.K.: Applied Missing Data Analysis. The Guildford Press, New York (2010)
Franses, P.H.: Seasonality, non-stationarity and the forecasting of monthly time series. Int. J. Forecast. **7**, 199–208 (1991)
Franses, P.H.: Modeling new product sales; an application of cointegration analysis. Int. J. Res. Mark. **11**, 491–502 (1994)
Franses, P.H., Paap, R.: Quantitative Models in Marketing Research. Cambridge University Press, Cambridge (2001)
Ghysels, E., Lee, H.S., Siklos, P.L.: On the (mis)specification of seasonality and its consequences: an empirical investigation with US data. In: Dufour, J.-M., Raj, B. (eds.) New Developments in Time Series Econometrics, pp. 191–204. Physica-Verlag HD, Heidelberg (1994)
Gijsenberg, M.J.: Riding the waves: Revealing the impact of intra-year category demand cycles on advertising and pricing effectiveness. J. Market. Res. **54**, 171–186 (2017)
Hanssens, D.M.: Order forecasts, retail sales and the marketing mix for consumer durables. J. Forecast. **17**, 327–346 (1998)
Hanssens, D.M., Parsons, L.J., Schultz, R.L.: Market Response Models. Springer, US (2001)
Hermann, S.: Hysteresis in marketing—A new phenomenon? MIT Sloan Manag. Rev. **38**(3), 39 (1997)
Hunt, S.D.: A General Theory of Competition: Resources, Competences, Productivity, Economic Growth. Sage, Thousand Oaks (2000)
Johnson, E.J., Russo, J.E.: Competitive decision making: Two and a half frames. Mark. Lett. **5**, 289–302 (1994)
Keller, K.L.: Brand equity. In: Dorf, R. (ed.) The Technology Management Handbook, pp. 12.59–12.64. CRC Press, Boca Raton (1998)
Kornelis, M., Dekimpe, M.G., Leeflang, P.S.H.: Does competitive entry structurally change key marketing metrics? Int. J. Res. Mark. **25**, 173–182 (2008)
Kwiatkowski, D., Phillips, P.C., Schmidt, P., Shin, Y.: Testing the null hypothesis of stationarity against the alternative of a unit root: how sure are we that economic time series have a unit root? J. Econ. **54**, 159–178 (1992)
Leeflang, P.S.H., Mijatovic, G.M., Saunders, J.: Identification and estimation of complex multivariate lag structures: a nesting approach. Appl. Econ. **24**, 273–283 (1992)
Leeflang, P.S.H., Wittink, D.R., Wedel, M., Naert, P.A.: Building Models for Marketing Decisions. Kluwer Academic Publishers, Boston (2000)
Leone, R.P.: Modeling sales-advertising relationships: An integrated time series-econometric approach. J. Mark. Res. **20**, 291–295 (1983)
Lilien, G.L., Yoon, E.: An exploratory analysis of the dynamic behavior of price elasticity over the product life cycle: an empirical analysis of industrial chemical products. In: Devinney, T.M. (ed.) Issues in Pricing, pp. 261–287. Lexington Press, Lexington, MA (1988)
Lim, J., Currim, I.S., Andrews, R.L.: Consumer heterogeneity in the longer-term effects of price promotions. Int. J. Res. Mark. **22**, 441–457 (2005)
Little, J.D.C.: Aggregate advertising models: the state of the art. Oper. Res. **27**, 629–667 (1979)
Maddala, G.S., Kim, I.M.: Structural change and unit roots. Journal of Statistical Planning and Inference. **49**, 73–103 (1996)
Maddala, G.S., Kim, I.M.: Unit Roots, Cointegration, and Structural Change. Cambridge University Press, Cambridge (1998)
March, J.G., Simon, H.A.: Organizations. Wiley, New York (1958)
Mela, C.F., Gupta, S., Lehmann, D.R.: The long-term impact of promotion and advertising on consumer brand choice. J. Mark. Res. **34**, 248–261 (1997)
Nijs, V.R., Dekimpe, M.G., Steenkamp, J-B.E.M., Hanssens, D.M.: The category-demand effects of price promotions. Mark. Sci. **20**, 1–22 (2001)
Noriega-Muro, A.E.: Nonstationarity and Structural Breaks in Economic Time Series. Avebury Publishers, New York (1993)

Osinga, E.C., Leeflang, P.S.H., Wieringa, J.E.: Early marketing matters: a time-varying parameter approach to persistence modeling. J. Mark. Res. **47**, 173–185 (2010)

Ouyang, M., Zhou, D., Zhou, N.: Estimating marketing persistence on sales of consumer durables in China. J. Bus. Res. **55**, 337–342 (2002)

Pankratz, A.: Forecasting with Dynamic Regression Models. John Wiley and sons, Canada (1991)

Parsons, L.J.: A rachet model of advertising carryover effects. J. Mark. Res. **13**, 76–79 (1976)

Pauwels, K.H.: Long-term marketing effectiveness in mature, emerging and changing markets. PhD thesis, University of California, Los Angeles (2001)

Pauwels, K.H.: How dynamic consumer response, competitor response, company support, and company inertia shape long-term marketing effectiveness. Mark. Sci. **23**, 596–610 (2004)

Pauwels, K.H.: Price war: what is it good for? Store visit and basket size response to the price war in Dutch grocery retailing. Marketing Science Institute, Report 07-104 (2007)

Pauwels, K.H., D'Aveni, R.: The formation, evolution and replacement of price–quality relationships. J. Acad. Mark. Sci. **44**, 46–65 (2016)

Pauwels, K.H., Dans, E.: Internet marketing the news: leveraging brand equity from marketplace to marketspace. J. Brand Manag. **8**, 303–314 (2001)

Pauwels, K.H., Hanssens, D.M., Siddarth, S.: The long-term effects of price promotions on category incidence, brand choice, and purchase quantity. J. Mark. Res. **39**, 421–439 (2002)

Pauwels, K.H., Leeflang, P.S.H., Teerling, M.L., Huizingh, K.E.: Does online information drive offline revenues?: only for specific products and consumer segments! J. Retail. **87**, 1–17 (2011)

Pauwels, K.H., Srinivasan, S.: Who benefits from store brand entry? Mark. Sci. **23**, 364–390 (2004)

Pauwels, K.H., Weiss, A.: Moving from free to fee: how online firms market to change their business model successfully. J. Mark. **72**(3), 14–31 (2008)

Perron, P.: The great crash, the oil price shock, and the unit root hypothesis. Econometrica. **57**, 1361–1401 (1989)

Perron, P.: Tests of joint hypotheses in time series regression with a unit root. In: Rhodes, G.F., Fomby, T.B. (eds.) Advances in Econometrics: Co-integration, Spurious Regression and Unit Roots, vol. 8, pp. 135–159. JAI Press, Greenwich CT (1990)

Salmon, M.: Error correction mechanisms. Econ. J. **92**(367), 615–629 (1982)

Salmon, M.: Error correction models, cointegration and the internal model principle. J. Econ. Dyn. Control. **12**, 523–549 (1988)

Sims, C.A.: Macroeconomics and reality. Econometrica. **48**, 1–48 (1980)

Slotegraaf, R.J., Pauwels, K.H.: The impact of brand equity and innovation on the long-term effectiveness of promotions. J. Mark. Res. **45**, 293–306 (2008)

Srinivasan, S., Pauwels, K.H., Hanssens, D.M., Dekimpe, M.G.: Do promotions benefit manufacturers, retailers, or both? Manag. Sci. **50**, 617–629 (2004)

Steenkamp, J-B.E.M., Nijs, V.R., Hanssens, D.M., Dekimpe, M.G.: Competitive reactions to advertising and promotion attacks. Mark. Sci. **24**, 35–54 (2005)

Wiesel, T., Pauwels, K.H., Arts, J.: Marketing's profit impact: Quantifying online and off-line funnel progression. Mark. Sci. **30**, 604–611 (2011)

Wildt, A.R.: The empirical investigation of time dependent parameter variation in marketing models. In: Bernhardt, K.L. (ed.) AMA Educators' Proceedings, pp. 466–472. American Marketing Association, Chicago (1976)

Zivot, E., Andrews, D.W.K.: Further evidence on the great crash, the oil-price shock, and the unit-root hypothesis. J. Bus. Econ. Stat. **10**, 251–270 (1992)

Chapter 4
Modern (Multiple) Time Series Models: The Dynamic System

Koen H. Pauwels

4.1 Introduction

While Chap. 3's univariate models capture dynamic patterns of a single variable, and multivariate models allow us to analyze the dynamic effect of marketing actions on performance, they leave several interesting phenomena unexplored. These include:

1. dual causality among marketing and performance, which could be tied in a long-term equilibrium;
2. explaining competitive marketing activity and predicing competitive reaction, and
3. uncovering decision rules of key market players, such as retailers (Dekimpe and Hanssens 1999).

As shown in the last 3 rows of Table 3.1, we need multiple equation time series models to flexibly model such phenomena. These multiple equations constitute a dynamic system, whose estimates may be used to track complex feedback loops over time and uncover not just performance reaction to marketing, but also the reactions of other marketing actions, of competitors, and of retailers (Pauwels 2004). Note the difference between multivariate time series (more than one variable, but only one equation) and multi equation time series (more than one equation).

Modern time series analysis emerges from the marriage of econometric developments in the late 1980s and traditional time series methods. In the words of Franses (1991, p. 240):

K.H. Pauwels (✉)
Department of Marketing, Northeastern University, Boston, USA
e-mail: k.pauwels@northeastern.edu

P.S.H. Leeflang et al. (eds.), *Advanced Methods for Modeling Markets*,
International Series in Quantitative Marketing, DOI 10.1007/978-3-319-53469-5_4

"econometric time series analysis combines the merits of econometrics, which focuses on the relationship between variables, with those of time series analysis, which specifies the dynamics in the model".

Multiple time series models have the power to capture intricate short-term and long-term relationships among variables without strong prior knowledge, and have been shown to outperform multivariate time series models in parameter efficiency, goodness-of-fit measures and forecasting performance (Horváth et al. 2005; Takada and Bass 1998).

In this chapter, we focus on the "frequentist" approach to multiple time series models. Combining this chapter with Chap. 16 on Bayesian analysis should give the reader enough background to start reading about the "Bayesian" approach to dynamic system models, including Bayesian VARs and the Dynamic Linear Model (Chap. 5)

Our structure for this chapter is inspired by the "persistence modeling framework" (Dekimpe and Hanssens 1995), which has been successfully applied across industries and marketing settings, and has seen several extensions in the last decade. Table 4.1 outlines the six methodological steps and relevant literature.

Table 4.1 Methodological steps in extended persistence modeling framework

Methodological step	Relevant literature	Research question
1. Granger Causality tests (Sect. 4.2)	Granger (1969) Trusov et al. (2009)	Which variables are temporally causing which other variables?
2. Unit root & cointegration Augmented Dickey-Fuller Test Cointegration test With structural breaks (Sect. 4.3)	Enders (2004) Engle and Granger (1987) Johansen et al. (2000)	Are variables stationary or evolving? Are evolving variables in long-run equilibrium?
3. Model of dynamic system Vector Autoregressive model VAR in Differences Vector Error Correction model (Sect. 4.4)	Baghestani (1991) Dekimpe and Hanssens (1999)	How do performance and marketing interact in the long run and short run, accounting for the unit root and cointegration results?
4. Policy simulation analysis Unrestricted impulse response Restricted policy simulation (Sect. 4.5)	Pauwels (2004) Pauwels et al. (2002) Pesaran and Shin (1998)	What is the dynamic impact of marketing on performance? Which actors drive the dynamic impact of marketing?
5. Drivers of performance Forecast Variance Error Decomposition (FEVD) Generalized FEVD (Sect. 4.6)	Hanssens (1998) Nijs et al. (2007) Srinivasan et al. (2004)	What is the importance of each driver's past in explaining performance variance? Independent of causal ordering?
6. Policy recommendations (Sect. 4.7)	Franses (2005) Sims (1986)	How do model results yield advice to policy makers?

4.2 Granger Causality Tests: Do We Need to Model a Dynamic System?

In essence, Granger causality tests the traditional market response assumption that performance is driven by marketing actions (Vol. I, Sect. 5.4.3). In contrast, marketing actions could be driven by past performance (Baghestani 1991), by competitive marketing actions (Hanssens 1980), and by other marketing actions of the same company (Pauwels 2004) or its retailer (Pauwels and Hanssens 2007). Franses (1998) notes that not accounting for this marketing endogeneity may lead to substantially wrong conclusions about marketing effectiveness.

Faced with the possibility of causal relations, we could, in principle, specify all possible interactions among marketing and performance variables in complex simultaneous equation models. Unfortunately, marketing (and economic) theory is typically insufficient for correct a priori specification of such models, and their identification thus requires the "incredible identifying restrictions" to which Sims (1980) objected. In the absence of strong theoretic rationale to exclude specific directions of causality, he prefers to establish them empirically using the available data.

Specifically, we test for the presence of endogeneity among all variables with Granger causality tests (Granger 1969). This "temporal causality" is the closest proxy for causality that can be gained from studying the time series of the variables (i.e., in the absence of manipulating causality in controlled experiments). In words, a variable x is Granger causing a variable y if knowing the past of x improves our forecast for y based on only the past of y. Formally, x Granger causes y if, at the 5% significance level:

$$Q\left(y_t|y_{t-1},\ldots,y_{t-k},x_{t-1},\ldots,x_{t-m}\right) < Q\left(y_t|y_{t-1},\ldots,y_{t-k}\right) \tag{4.1}$$

with $Q =$ mean squared forecast error and k and m the maximum lags for y and x (compare to Eq. (5.31), Vol. I).

We note this is a rather tough test to pass because only the past of x, not its present value is allowed to predict the present value of y. This is especially important when data are sampled at long intervals (e.g. annually or quarterly in economics), and less when the data are sampled more frequently—as typical in marketing. For instance, scanner panel data contain weekly retail prices and sales in a context where manufacturers need to negotiate retail prices weeks ahead and thus cannot observe sales and change prices within the same week (Leeflang and Wittink 1996). We can lift this constraint by considering Granger instantaneous causality (Layton 1984), but this merely demonstrates a nonzero correlation, which is problematic to interpret as causality (Lütkepohl 1993, p. 41). Moreover, marketing applications often use data sampled so frequently that the direction of instantaneous causality is not in doubt. Examples include weekly scanner data where brand sales can react to prices, but brand managers cannot change prices within the same week (Leeflang and Wittink 1992), daily marketing mix data where managers cannot change marketing spending day-by-day (Wiesel et al. 2010) and hourly advertising data (Tellis et al. 2005).

An important caveat is that Granger causality tests are pairwise, i.e. an independent variable x is Granger causing y while instead they are both being driven (x earlier than y) by a third variable z. Thus, Granger causality does not mean that x is the "ultimate" causing variable of interest; the researcher should further consider what Granger causes x to develop a full understanding of the web of Granger causality and how performance can be affected. The most common test procedure for Granger causality goes back to Granger (1969) himself, running the regression (compare to Eq. (5.32) in Vol. I):

$$y_t = c + \sum_{i=1}^{\infty} \rho_i y_{t-i} + \sum_{j=1}^{\infty} \beta_j x_{t-j} + u_t. \tag{4.2}$$

Variable x is said to be Granger causing y if any of the β_j coefficients significantly differ from zero. In most software packages (e.g. Eviews, see Sect. 4.7), the researcher is asked to specify the number of lags j. This choice is important, because the wrong choice for the number of lags in the test may erroneously conclude the absence of Granger causality (e.g. Hanssens 1980). Therefore, recent marketing applications test for all plausible lags, e.g. 26 weeks for weekly data (e.g. Lautman and Pauwels 2009) and 30 days for daily data (Wiesel et al. 2011). Other test procedures include Sims (1972) regression, which simultaneously tests for x Granger causing y and y Granger causing x, and the double prewhitening method (Haugh 1976; Pierce and Haugh 1977). While all three procedures are asymptotically identical (Geweke et al. 1983), the Granger (1969) regression combines higher power in finite samples (against double prewhitening) with ease of implementation against both alternatives (Nelson and Schwert 1982). See also Vol. I, Sect. 5.4.3.

Intriguing findings from marketing applications of Granger Causality tests include:

- *Which marketing actions drive performance?* Coca-Cola includes "Granger Causality" in the 2 × 2 marketing effectiveness matrix they share throughout the company (see also Pauwels 2014). For two fast moving consumer goods, Pauwels and Joshi (2016) find that Granger causality tests reduce a set of 99 potential "key performance indicators" to only 17 performance-leading indicators.
- *Which social media metrics drive performance?* Luo et al. (2013) find that specific social media metrics drive stock market performance, while Pauwels et al. (2016) find that social media discussion topics regarding ad love, brand love and purchase drive sales performance.
- *Does offline marketing spending drive online marketing?* Trusov et al. (2009) find that offline events organized by a large social media company increased the number of online friend referrals they received. Therefore, these organized events actually had a higher total ROI than would be calculated from their direct performance effects. In contrast, Wiesel et al. (2011) find that offline flyers and

faxes by a furniture company does not Grange cause Google Adwords spending. A possible explanation for these different findings is that the social media events were aimed at brand building in an industry where awareness and social context is important, while the furniture company's direct marketing called for immediate action in an industry where customers only need the product infrequently. Still, further research is needed to test this assertion.

- *Do managers react to performance when setting marketing actions (performance feedback)?* The direction of this feedback may go both ways: high sales may induce more marketing spending because more money is available—or low sales may induce management to take corrective action. The former is demonstrated in the classical Lydia Pinkham case (Baghestani 1991), with sales Granger causing advertising, and the latter in Wiesel et al. (2010), where slow sales induce managers to run another marketing campaign. When researchers have access to managers, it is worthwhile to ask them whether they agree with these observed patterns and whether they are aware of them. The resulting discussion would give direct insights into marketing decision making rules. Moreover, Horváth et al. (2005) consider the relative importance of feedback performance in their model (see Chap. 9).
- *Which competitors react to each other and in which temporal pattern?* Surprisingly few papers have explicitly used Granger causality tests for this purpose. Hanssens (1980) applied Granger causality tests to sort out patterns of competitive interactions in the airline industry and Putsis and Dhar (1998) discuss their usefulness. Other examples can be found in Leeflang and Wittink (1992, 1996). In nowadays' information economy, companies face potential competition from countries around the world and a wide variety of brick-and-mortar, bricks-and-clicks, and online-only providers. Future research can analyze which of these providers react to the company's marketing changes—and which of these reactions have any effect on the performance of the initiating company (Steenkamp et al. 2005). Likewise, many firms are affected by the reaction of other market players, such as intermediaries, (retailers), partners, suppliers and the government. Studying Granger causality in such web of interactions appears worthwhile.

4.3 Unit Root and Cointegration Tests: Strategic Scenarios of Long-Term Effectiveness

4.3.1 Test Specifics

In the second step, we test for the time series properties of the variables regarding *unit roots* and *cointegration*. The results of these unit root and cointegration tests determine how the variables enter into the model of dynamic interactions (see Dekimpe and Hanssens 1999). We covered unit root tests in Chap. 3, and focus in this section on cointegration.

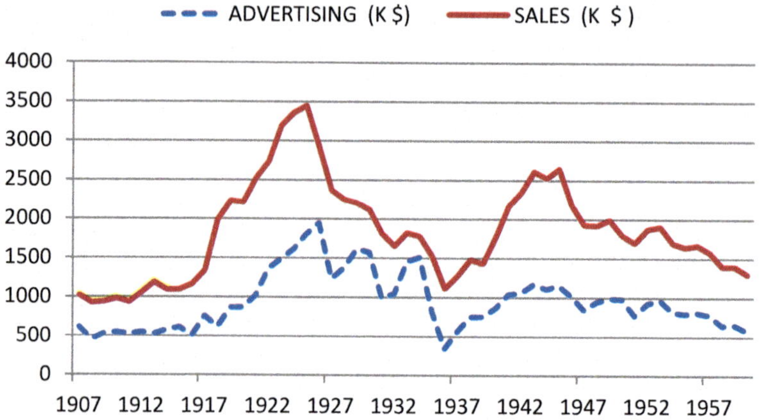

Fig. 4.1 Long-term equilibrium between Lydia Pinkham's advertising and sales

Cointegration between two (or more) evolving variables means that they are bound in a long-term equilibrium, from which they only temporarily deviate. The analogy is a drunk walking her dog (Murray 1994): although each variable by itself seems to be wandering aimlessly, they won't stray far from each other. Figure 4.1 shows a classic example of cointegration between annual advertising spending and sales revenues for Lydia Pinkham 1907–1960.

In the case of cointegration, we can predict the level of one variable by knowing the level of the other variable Therefore, we would throw information away by including the variables only in differences in our dynamic system model. The cointegrating equation quantifies this equilibrium, e.g. between the two variables x and y, as:

$$y_t = a + b \times x_t + \varepsilon_t \tag{4.3}$$

with ε representing the equilibrium error, which needs to be stationary (mean-reverting) and will be included as a variable in the dynamic system model. In a scatterplot of x and y, cointegration shows up as a straight line capturing most of the variation. While two seperately evolving variables need be shown in 2 dimensions, cointegrating variables can be summarized rather well in 1 dimension (a line). Figure 4.2 shows the scatterplot for the Lydia Pinkham advertising-sales data graphed over time in Fig. 4.1.

Just as most of the points in Fig. 4.2 are not right on the regression line, the long-term equilibrium may not hold exactly in any given period. In that case, the dynamic system tends to reduce the distance from the long-term equilibrium (the equilibrium error ε) by adjusting one or more of the cointegrating variables. The speed of such adjustment often yields interesting information beyond the existence and estimation of the long-term equilibrium relationship itself.

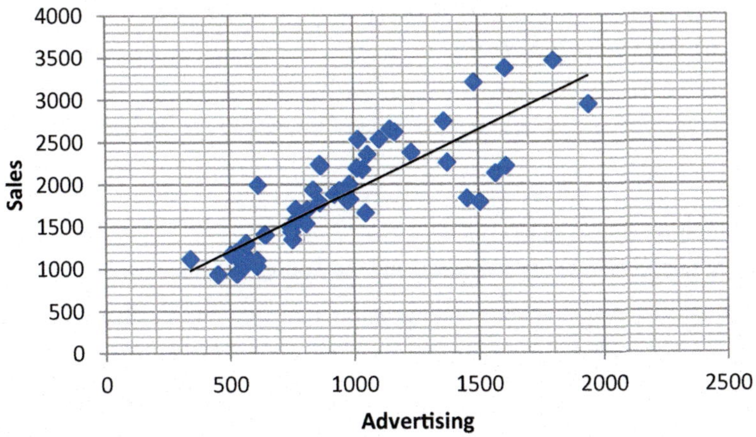

Fig. 4.2 Scatterplot of Lydia Pinkham advertising and sales

Cointegration tests come in several procedures. Engle and Granger (1987) estimate Eq. (4.3) with Ordinary Least Squares, and then test the error for evolution. This procedure is straightforward and consistent, but can be biased in small samples and is not possible with more than 1 cointegrating vector. Johansen's (1988) Full Information Maximum Likelihood (FIML) test does not suffer from these limitations, and has been the more popular test in marketing applications. It is a multivariate generalization of the Dickey-Fully unit root test:

$$\Delta y_t = (A_i - I)\, y_{t-1} + \varepsilon_t \tag{4.4}$$

with y_t the $n \times 1$ vector of variables, I the $n \times n$ identity matrix and A_i the $n \times n$ matrix of parameters. The Johansen test checks the rank of $(A_i - I)$, which equals the number of cointegrating vectors. Maximum likelihood estimation obtains these cointegrating vectors, and the trace and maximum eigenvalue statistics are used to test sequentially for no cointegrating vectors, at most one, at most 2, etc.

Finally, the Johansen et al. (2000) cointegration test allows for structural breaks in the relationship among the variables. Its use is recommended when the unit root tests have revealed that the analyzed variables contain structural breaks (see Chap. 3).

Early applications of the Engle and Granger (1987) cointegration tests in marketing include Baghestani (1991) analysis of the advertising-sales relationship for the Lydia Pinkham data and Powers et al.'s (1991) analysis of the adjustment in narcotics abuse to changes in methadone administration. Early applications of the Johansen (1988) cointegration test in marketing include Franses' (1994) analysis of new car sales and prices in the framework of a Gompertz growth model, and Dekimpe and Hanssens' (1995) advertising media effectiveness analysis. Kireyev et al. (2016) use the Johansen et al. (2000) test allowing for structural breaks in the relationship between online display and online search clicks.

4.3.2 Which Variables Are Likely to be Cointegrated in Marketing Settings?

We distinguish three types of cointegration of interest to researchers and decisions makers:

- cointegration among performance variables;
- cointegration among marketing variables, and
- cointegration between performance and marketing variables.

Cointegration among performance variables indicates the need to monitor one variable to predict the future of another (typically the performance variable of most interest to the decision maker). Examples include cointegration among industry sales and own brand sales, and among factory orders and end-user demand. For Hewlet-Packard printers, factory orders and end-user demand are cointegrated (Hanssens 1998), so it is important to monitor the development of both for the purpose of sales forecasting and marketing-mix intervention. For online newspaper growth, Pauwels and Dans (2001) show that growth in page views is first driven by visit growth (cointegration between page views and visits), while it is later driven by usage growth (cointegration between page views and pages per visit). Newspapers stop growing when both cointegration relations break down. A promising area for future research is when such cointegration windows hold more generally between intermediate and final performance variables. Pauwels (2001) proposes that emerging brands should grow awareness, and then distribution in the initial stages, when both are cointegrated with sales, and then focus on temporary promotions when this cointegration breaks down. To the best of our knowledge, this assertion still needs to be empirically validated.

Cointegration among marketing variables may appear because of company profit pressures to e.g. raise prices when advertising budgets increase in the car industry. Other company decision rules may include raising/cutting spending simultaneously across, for example, online and offline marketing, or detailing and direct-to-consumer ads in the pharmaceutical industry. Marketing actions of one firm may be cointegrated with competitive marketing actions, especially in changing markets. In emerging economies, rival firms may grow their marketing spending in a race for market share.

Cointegration between marketing and performance variables may occur due to explicit and implicit budgeting rules. For example, Lydia Pinkham appeared to be setting advertising as a percentage of past sales (Baghestani 1991). Hendry (1995) derives the theoretical rationale for cointegration when managers observe the difference between their target and their performance, and aim to reduce that difference. Such explanations provide a supply-side rationale for marketing-performance cointegration. From the demand side, prices and sales may be cointegrated if a price drop increases sales, but needs to be maintained for sales to remain at the higher level. For instance, the combination of high product utility with low disposable income in many countries implies that lowering prices of cars and computers may greatly increase demand, which again evaporates if prices return to a higher level. For marketing communication, the theory of information disuse (Bjørk and Bjørk 1992) posits that need-brand connections in customer brains may be replaced with competing brand connections. Thus, higher share of voice may lead to higher market share, but needs to be sustained in order to maintain the market share increase. This behavior has been observed in the automobile market, where competitors are hesitant to reduce share of voice, for fear of loosing the customers in the market for a new vehicle. Pauwels and Hanssens (2007) demonstrated how marketing regimes changes drive performance regime changes, and Hanssens et al. (2016) distinguish periods of stationary, intrinsically evolving and marketing-induced performance. In both cases, windows of opportunity (such as positive consumer reviews) open during which managers can obtained sustained growth at low cost.

4.3.3 Strategic Scenarios of Long-Term Marketing Effectiveness

Combining unit root tests with cointegration tests for both marketing and performance, Dekimpe and Hanssens (1999) offer four strategic scenarios for long-term marketing effectiveness, as depicted in Table 4.2. First, *business-as-usual* combines stationary performance with stationary marketing. In this case, one-shot marketing campaigns (e.g. a temporary increase in advertising spending or a temporary price reduction) have only temporary effects on performance. This scenario is the most typical situation for established markets and brands, often the ones analyzed by marketing academics (e.g. Nijs et al. 2001; Pauwels et al. 2002; Srinivasan et al. 2004). In contrast, cointegration among marketing and sales implies the *evolving business* scenario. While increased marketing spending may permanently lift performance, it needs to be maintained at that higher spending level to sustain the lift. Dekimpe and Hanssens (1999) demonstrate this phenomenon in the pharmaceutical industry, Kireyev et al. (2016) in the online display and search behavior of banking customers.

The remaining two scenarios combine an evolving variable with a stationary variable (which by definition can not be cointegrated). *Hysteresis* implies that the one-shot marketing campaign has permanent performance effects—identifying and exploiting these scenarios constitutes the holy grail of long-term marketing effectiveness. Hysteresis is more often found in emerging markets (Osinga et al. 2010; Pauwels and Dans 2001), for recently introduced (Dekimpe et al. 1999;

Table 4.2 Strategic scenarios of long-term marketing effectiveness

		Marketing effort	
		Temporary	*Sustained*
Sales Response	*Temporary*	Business-as-Usual	Escalation
	Permanent	Hysteresis	Evolving business practice

Pauwels et al. 2002), for smaller brands (Slotegraaf and Pauwels 2008), and when the external environment changes substantially, for instance because of government intervention (Hermann 1997). Hanssens et al. (2016) develop long-term profit maximizing allocation rules when marketing has hysteric effects on sales. While the past focus has been on identifying and exploiting positive hysteresis (Hermann 1997), it may be at least as important to detect negative hysteresis.

On the flip side, *escalation* combines evolving marketing spending with stationary performance—typically caused by competitors driving up marketing costs without any lasting performance benefit. Such scenario is rampant during price wars, as diagnosed in pharmaceuticals (Dekimpe and Hanssens 1999), automobiles (Pauwels et al. 2004b) and grocery store retailers (Van Heerde et al. 2007).

A more recent paper uncovers these four strategic scenarios at the individual physician level, classifying their prescription behavior in the four cells with unit root tests and panel VAR models (Sismeiro et al. 2012). The largest group of U.K. physians combined stationary prescribing behavior with sustained marketing increases (escalation), which makes them less attractive for pharmaceutical companies.

4.4 Dynamic System Model: Vector Autoregression and Vector Error-Correction

4.4.1 Motivation for a Dynamic System Model

When multiple variables need to explained by a time series model, we need to specify multiple equations in a dynamic system model, such as a Vector ARMA (VARMA), a Vector Autoregressive Model (VAR) or a Vector Error Correction Model (VEC). As discussed earlier, a typical reason to estimate such models is that the researcher is interested in explaining more than one variable. For instance, competitive marketing actions may be explained and forecasted by their historical patterns and their reaction to competitive performance (performance feedback) and/or to the focal firm's actions. Likewise, some of the focal firm's marketing actions may be driven by its performance and/or its other marketing actions. For instance, a higher click-through and thus spending on Google Adwords may be induced by the firm's offline marketing actions and/or by higher sales in previous periods, e.g. due to positive word-of-mouth by previous customers (Wiesel et al. 2010). In turn, word-of-mouth referrals may be driven by the firm's paid marketing actions (Trusov et al. 2009).

4.4.2 Vector Autoregressive Moving Average (VARMA) and Vector Autoregression (VAR)

The VARMA model extends univariate time series analysis (Chap. 3) to a system of equations for any n number of time series variables (e.g. $n = 2$ for the Lydia Pinham advertising and sales data):

$$\left(I - \Phi_1 B - \Phi_2 B^2 - \cdots - \Phi_p B^p\right) y_t = \mu + \left(I - \Theta_1 B - \Theta_2 B^2 - \cdots - \Theta_q B^q\right) \varepsilon_t \tag{4.5}$$

with y_t the $n \times 1$ vector of the j time series, and ε_t the $n \times 1$ vector of white noise errors, which are typically interdependent and identically distributed as multivariate normal. To identify te model, researchers extend the univariate analysis with similar tools:

1. cut-offs in the sample cross-correlation matrix indicate moving-average parameters (Θ), while dying-out patterns suggest autoregression (Φ), and
2. partial autocorrelation matrices, interpreted in the same way as the PACF in univariate time series analysis.

To the best of our knowledge, the only marketing applications of VARMA include Moriarty (1985), who illustrates the relative value of objective versus judgment forecasts, and Takada and Bass (1998), who analyze competitive marketing behavior and detect causality of marketing mix variables and sales. Key drawbacks of the VARMA models are that:

1. different restrictions lead to the same relationship among endogenous variables (identification problem);
2. the model contains non-linear moving average terms that require conditional or exact likelihood procedures;
3. it is hard to interpret the estimated parameters to generate marketing insights, and
4. the model is not particularly useful to analyze common stochastic trends or cointegration (Franses 1998; Hanssens et al. 2001).

All these drawbacks are overcome by the more popular Vector Autoregressive (VAR) Model, which is a VARMA model in which the moving-average terms are inverted and moved to the autoregressive side of the equation, yielding:

$$\left(I - \Phi_1 B - \Phi_2 B^2 - \cdots - \Phi_p B^p\right) y_t = \mu + \varepsilon_t. \tag{4.6}$$

In fact, Zellner and Palm (1974) show that any simultaneous equation model with one or more lagged endogenous variables leads to a VAR-model, while Pauwels and Weiss (2008) show the forecasting superioriy of VAR over simultaneous equations for their online services data. Besides Eq. (4.6), there are three interesting alternative ways to write the dynamic system:

1. its *structural form* (Eq. (4.7)) is most appropriate to understand contemporaneous effects and impose restrictions;
2. its *reduced form* (Eq. (4.10)) plays a key role in its estimation and in the derivation of impulse response functions;
3. its *moving average form* (Eq. (4.12)) plays a key role in deriving the forecast error variance decomposition.

We discuss in turn these different ways to write the dynamic system.

4.4.3 Structural Vector Autoregressive Model

The structural VAR (SVAR) is displayed in Eq. (4.7):

$$B_0 y_t = c_0 + B_1 y_{t-1} + B_2 y_{t-2} + \cdots + B_p y_{t-p} + \varepsilon_t. \tag{4.7}$$

The $n \times 1$ vector of n endogenous variables y is regressed on constant terms (which may include a deterministic time trend and seasonality terms) and on its own past, with p the number of lags and B the $n \times n$ coefficient matrix of a given lag. Note that the contemporaneous effects are captured in the B_0 matrix; as a result the structural errors ε are uncorrelated (orthogonal) across equations. For instance, a bi-variate VAR of order 1 (i.e. $n = 2$ and $p = 1$) is displayed in Eq. (4.8):

$$\begin{bmatrix} 1 & B_{0;1,2} \\ B_{0;2,1} & 1 \end{bmatrix} \begin{bmatrix} y_{1,t} \\ y_{2,t} \end{bmatrix} = \begin{bmatrix} c_{0;1} \\ c_{0;2} \end{bmatrix} + \begin{bmatrix} B_{1;1,1} & B_{1;1,2} \\ B_{1;2,1} & B_{1;2,2} \end{bmatrix} \begin{bmatrix} y_{1,t-1} \\ y_{2,t-1} \end{bmatrix} + \begin{bmatrix} \varepsilon_{1,t} \\ \varepsilon_{2,t} \end{bmatrix}. \tag{4.8}$$

This structural form of the VAR model is directly interesting for decision makers, as it generates predictions of results of various kinds of actions (the orthogonal errors) by calculating the conditional distribution given the action (Sims 1986). It is also the appropriate form for imposing restrictions, typically on the B_0 matrix. Amisano and Giannini (1997) present an excellent overview of different ways of exposing such restrictions, which leads to four different classes of structural VARs:

1. The Wold Causal ordering uses theory-based arguments for why one group of variables should not cause another group of variables (e.g. Bernanke 1986; Blanchard and Watson 1982). The imposed block exogeneity restrictions obtain a lower triangular B_0 matrix. For instance, Sims (1986) separates monetary from real economy variables.
2. The K-model, which premultiplies Eq. (4.8) with a matrix K to induce transformation of the errors by generating a vector or orthonormalized errors (i.e.with covariance matrix $= I =$ the identity matrix).
3. The C-model, which does not implicitly model contemporaneous effects but instead models the set of orthonormal disturbances. For instance, Blanchard and Quah (1988) distinguish temporary from permanent disturbances by finding another variable that gets no permanent effect of either variable in their dynamic system.

4. The *AB*-model, which nests both the *K* and the *C* model. For instance, Keating (1990) bases himself on rational expectations models to impose a set of nonlinear restrictions on the off diagonal elements of B_0.

Note that none of these impose restrictions on the number of lags or the exact form of dynamic effects; practices typical for dynamic structural models in economics. A key critique of such restrictions is that economic theory is uninformative on lags and that it is heroic to assume that effects decay with the same fraction over time (Amisano and Gianninni 1997; Sims 1980). Instead, VAR-modelers appear more willing to impose restrictions on the contemporaneous relations and the error covariance matrix.

Structural VARs have seen many applications in economics, but few till recently in marketing (DeHaan et al. 2016; Freo 2005; Gijsenberg et al. 2015; Horváth et al. 2005; Kang et al. 2016). Freo (2005) applies the *AB* model to study the response of store performance to sales promotions. He causally orders the variables by decreasing Granger exogeneity test statistics and deleting coefficients not significantly different from 0. He finds that promotions in heavy household items increase store revenues, but promotions in the textile category decrease them instantaneously. Horváth et al. (2005) show that the inclusion of competitive reaction and feedback effects matters a lot in the tuna category but not in the shampoo category, where competitive interactions are more limited due to distinct brand positioning. More recently, Kang et al. (2016) use a structural panel VAR to show that corporate social responsibility actions are not driven by slack resources, but by an (only partially successful) attempt to make up for past social irresponsibility.

Gijsenberg et al. (2015) develop a Double-Asymmetric Structural VAR (DAS-VAR) model that allows for asymmetric effects of increases versus decreases, and for a different number of lags in each equation. In their analysis of the effect of service on customer satisfaction, they find that losses (service failures) not only have stronger (the first asymmetry), but also longer-lasting (the second asymmetry) effects on satisfaction than gains.

DeHaan et al. (2016) test and find support for their proposed restriction of both immediate and dynamic feedback loops within the online funnel of a retailer (i.e. increase in product page visits increase checkouts, but not vice versa). These restrictions enable a model with many marketing variables affecting each funnel metric over time, leading to the insight that content-integrated online advertising brings in better customers than content-separated advertising does.

At least two reasons explain the scarcity of Structural VAR applications in marketing. First, the high degree of multicollinearity among lagged variables complicates the exclusion assessment of the estimated coefficients (Ramos 1996). Second, if we follow the test results, the re-estimation of the (appropriately restricted) VAR-models may still induce omitted-variable bias to the other parameter estimates (Faust 1998; Sims 1980). One approach to overcome this issue is to estimate several restricted VAR models and to compare their results (Horváth et al. 2001). Such procedure quickly becomes very elaborate however, and no statistical significance criteria exist to compare the effect estimates across different models.

As a general strategy, many econometric researchers prefer to impose restrictions on the long-run, structural impulse responses (Enders 2004). Pauwels (2004) adheres to this strategy of restricted impulse response functions, which we discuss in the next section.

4.4.4 Reduced-Form Vector Autoregressive Model

In the absence of imposed restrictions, we can write the structural VAR of Eq. (4.7) in reduced form by premultiplying each term by B_0^{-1} to obtain:

$$y_t = B_0^{-1}c_0 + B_0^{-1}B_1y_{t-1} + B_0^{-1}B_2y_{t-2} + \cdots + B_0^{-1}B_py_{t-p} + B_0^{-1}\varepsilon_t \tag{4.9}$$

which can be written as:

$$y_t = c + A_1y_{t-1} + A_2y_{t-2} + \ldots + A_py_{t-p} + e_t \tag{4.10}$$

with the residual variance-covariance matrix:

$$\Omega = \mathrm{E}\left(e_te_t'\right) = \mathrm{E}\left(B_0^{-1}\varepsilon_t\varepsilon_t'\left(B_0^{-1}\right)'\right) = B_0^{-1}\Sigma\left(B_0^{-1}\right)'. \tag{4.11}$$

Note that the residual variance-covariance matrix is no longer diagonal; the reduced-form errors are contemporaneously correlated as they do not capture the contemporaneous effects among the endogenous variables. Thus, the researchers needs to identify the model, i.e. assert a connection between the reduced form and the structure so that estimates of reduced form parameters translate into structural parameters. In the words of Sims (1986, p. 2):

> "Identification is the interpretation of historically observed variation in data in a way that allows the variation to be used to predict the consequences of an action not yet undertaken".

The important advantage of the reduced-form model is that all right-hand-side (RHS) variables are now predetermined at time *t*, and the system can be estimated without imposing restrictions or a causal ordering (this identification issue will come back though when calculating impulse response functions in the next section). Moreover, because all RHS variables are the same in each equation, there is no efficiency gain in using Seemingly Unrelated Regression (SUR) estimation. Even if the errors are correlated across equations, ordinary least squares (OLS) estimates are consistent and asymptotically efficient (Srivastava and Giles 1987, Chap. 2). Thus, we can perform OLS estimation equation by equation. This feature is especially valuable in marketing applications with many endogenous variables. For example, a 12-equation VAR model requires estimation of $12 \times 12 = 144$ parameters more for each lag added to the model. This does not bode well for the typical weekly scanner panel data of 104–156 observations. In contrast, OLS estimation equation by equation implies that only 12 additional parameters have to be estimated for each equation.

Another strategy for reducing the number of estimated coefficients is to include variables as exogenous instead of endogenous (e.g. Nijs et al. 2001). Adding exogenous variables to the VAR is technically straightforward and leads to a VARX (Vector Autoregressive Model with eXogenous variables). However, this is only recommended after the appropriate tests on endogeneity and exogeneity, as detailed in the next section.

In general, two important decisions for the researcher involve:

1. which variables to include as endogenous versus exogenous, and
2. how many lags to include.

We discuss these in turn.

4.4.5 Endogeneity and Exogeneity

First, it is consistent with the orginal philosophy of dynamic system models to treat each variable as endogenous until proven exogenous. Considering a regression of a variable y on a variable x, the question of exogeneity of x to y depends on the purpose of the analysis. There are several possibilities:

1. to make inferences about the estimated effect of x on y (weak exogeneity);
2. to forecast y conditional on x (strong exogeneity);
3. to test whether the regression of y on x is structurally invariant to change in the marginal distribution of x (super exogeneity).

Weak exogeneity implies that the parameters of interest can be expressed uniquely in terms of parameters of the conditional distribution. Strong exogeneity combines weak exogeneity with the absence of Granger Causality, while super exogeneity implies that the estimated effect is invariant to changes in market players' decision rules—the core of the Lucas (1976) critique. In marketing applications, we would require at least strong exogeneity due to the importance of conditional forecasting (e.g. "if I double my advertising spending, what will the sales level be?"). Testing for strong exogeneity requires both a test for weak exogeneity (eg the Wu-Hausman test or Engle's Lagrange multiplier test) and Granger Causality (Johnston and Dinardo 1997, Chap. 8). Evidently, such stringent tests may leave the researcher with many variables to treat as endogenous (Dekimpe and Hanssens 1999). One approach, followed by Nijs et al. (2001) is to estimate a basic VAR-model with less important variables as exogenous (in their case, feature and display), and then enter these one-by-one as endogenous to the model.

4.4.6 Lag Selection in VAR

Lag selection is important, as the accuracy of VAR forecasts varies across alternative lag structures (Hafer and Sheehan 1989). Adding more lags yields higher explanatory power and better white noise properties of the residuals, but the added complexity comes at a high price. Indeed, Hafer and Sheehan (1989) and Lütkepohl (1985) find that short-lagged models predict more accurately on average than longer-lagged specifications. Moreover, shorter lag models allow the researcher to include more endogenous variables in the model—a key advantage in marketing applications, which often feature more than 10 endogenous variables.

A straightforward way to determine the lag order p is to test for zero restrictions on the coefficients of the next lag $p + 1$. This leads to Likelihood Ratio (LR) statistic of:

$$\lambda(\text{LR}) = 2\ [\ln \text{Likelihood}\,(\delta_u) - \ln \text{Likelihood}\,(\delta_r)] \tag{4.12}$$

where δ_u is the unrestricted Maximum Likelihood estimator for parameter vector δ and δ_r is the restricted Maximum Likelihood estimator when the restrictions are imposed. In our case of lag order restriction, the VAR coefficient restrictions are linear and thus the LR statistic has an asymptotic χ^2- distribution with the number of restrictions as its degrees of freedom. Thus, lag order can be determined by a series of Likelihood Ratio tests comparing each order p with order $p + 1$ (order of 0 versus 1, 2 versus 1, etc.) and settling on a p-order if the Null Hypothesis (that the higher lag order has significantly better Likelihood than the lower lag order) is rejected. Fortunately, time series software packages such as Eviews automatically include the LR test for lag order selection (the researcher does have to specify a maximum number of lags to check). Unfortunately, this testing procedure still has a chance of choosing an incorrect lag order—even when the number of observations is large (Lütkepohl 1993). Moreover, researchers may have different goals for lag order selection, such as the highest predictive accuracy. For these reasons, information criteria have become more popular to determine the order of VARs.

Information criteria for lag order selection differ in their main goal:

1. predictive accuracy, or
2. consistent selection of the correct order of the data generating process.

If the main goal is predictive accuracy, it makes sense to start from the 1-step ahead Mean Squared Error, and turn it into a scalar criterion (Akaike 1969). Based on this rationale, Akaike (1969) proposes the Final Prediction Error (FPE) for a VAR of lag order p:

$$\text{FPE}(p) = \left[\frac{T + Kp + 1}{T - Kp - 1}\right]^K |\text{ML Cov}(p)| \tag{4.13}$$

with T the sample size, K the number of endogenous variables, p the lag and $|\text{ML Cov}(p)|$ the determinant of the Maximum Likelihood estimator of the residual

Covariance Matrix at lag p. Note that this determinant decreases with increasing lag p (i.e. our residuals get closer to representing white noise) while the ratio in the first part of Eq. (4.13) increases (i.e. our punishment for adding more lags). The lag p that yields the lowest value of the FPE therefore gives us the best balance between these two parts. Other information criteria such as the Akaike Information Criterion (AIC) for a VAR with lag p has a similar structure, but propose a different "punishment" for adding more lags (Akaike, 1973):

$$\mathrm{AIC}(p) = \ln |\mathrm{ML\ Cov}(p)| + \frac{2}{T} pK^2. \tag{4.14}$$

With all variable labels as before, and the square of the number of endogenous variables K^2 also known as the number of freely estimated paramaters (adding a lag requires the estimation of K^2 more parameters). Lütkepohl (1993, p. 129) shows the exact relation between AIC and FPE and concludes that they are equivalent for moderate and large T. Indeed, experience shows that both criteria typically select the same lag order p in marketing applications.

When the main researcher goal is selecting the correct VAR order p, the FPE and AIC have the issue that they are not consistent; i.e. they do not uncover the correct lag order p as the number of time series observations goes to infinity (see Quinn 1980 for the proof). Consistent information criteria were developed by Schwartz (1978) and by Hannan and Quinn (1979).

Schwartz (1978) derives his criterion from a Bayesian perspective, it is hence often called the Bayesian Information Criterion (BIC). The BIC criterion for a VAR of lag order p is given by:

$$\mathrm{BIC}(p) = \ln |\mathrm{ML\ Cov}(p)| + \frac{\ln(T)}{T} pK^2. \tag{4.15}$$

Compared to the AIC, the BIC has a stronger punishment for increasing lag order p, because $\ln(T) > 2$ in virtually any time series application. Finally, the Hannan-Quinn (HQ) criterion for a VAR of lag order p is given by:

$$\mathrm{HQ}(p) = \ln |\mathrm{ML\ Cov}(p)| + \frac{\ln[\ln(T)]}{T} pK^2. \tag{4.16}$$

Thus, Hannan-Quinn yields a stronger punishment than the AIC does, but a lesser punishment than the BIC does for increasing the lag order. In typical applications (moderate to large T), the BIC and the HQ criteria will choose a similar lag order, with the BIC sometimes choosing a smaller lag order than the HQ. Lütkepohl (1993, p. 132) shows the BIC and the HQ criteria are consistent, i.e. select the correct lag order p as the number of observations T goes to infinity.

In practice though, researchers may care more about small-sample properties than about the asymptotic properties of the lag selection criteria. Simulations for $T = 30$ and $T = 100$ show that all criteria, but especially the BIC, tend to underestimate the true lag order (set to $p = 1$ or $p = 2$) of the model (Lütkepohl

1993, p. 136). However, the forecasting accuracy of the BIC-selected lag was superior to all alternatives. Overall, the BIC criterion does well in both selecting the correct VAR model and in obtaining the best forecasting accuracy (Lütkepohl 1985). However, the AIC may give better forecasting accuracy for an infinite order VAR model. Therefore, we recommend to:

- compare the different criteria values and their suggested optimal lag orders, and
- to estimate the VAR-model with different reasonable lag orders as a robustness check.

What should the lag order of the "focus" model be in the presence of such robustness checks? Of course the researcher can choose to stick to a specific information criterion based on the above mentioned benefits. Alternatively, the researcher can consider all criteria, and choose a lag order that performs rather well on each, typically in between the FPE/AIC recommended and the BIC recommended "optimal" lag.

In marketing applications, most researchers follow the BIC advice by Hafer and Sheehan (1989) as it yields shorter-lagged models. Horváth et al. (2005) use the Forecast Prediction Error for lag selection. The remaining marketing researchers typically use the AIC criterion to ensure against residual autocorrelation (e.g. Naik and Peters 2009) or check whether additional lags do not improve the model nor lead to different conclusions (e.g. Nijs et al. 2001).

The trade-off between accuracy and degrees of can also be addressed in different ways, such as pre-selecting endogenous variables and estimating submodels (e.g. Srinivasan et al. 2004) and/or setting some of the model's parameters to zero. As to the latter, Gelper et al. (2016) adapt the Lasso technique (Ren and Zhang 2013; Tibshirani 1996), which minimizes the least squares criterion penalized for the sum of the absolute values of the regression parameters. They demonstrate the superior model performance (compared to Bayesian methods in a simulation study) and forecasting accuracy of this sparse VAR estimation of cross-category marketing effects (Gelper et al. 2016). Such techniques hold much promise as the number of potential variables continues to grow, whether in the form of many brands and categories or in the form of detailed customer level data online and in transactional databases (see the Big Data Chap. 19 in this volume).

4.4.7 Vector Error Correction

When (some) variables are evolving, but not cointegrated (see Sect. 4.3), we estimate the VAR model in differences, i.e. taking first differences of the evolving variables (e.g. Bronnenberg et al. 2000). For instance, in the Lydia Pinkham case discussed in Sect. 4.3, we would model the effects of a change in advertising to the change in sales. However, in case of cointegration, both the levels and the differences of the cointegrated variables contain useful information on their relations. To preserve this information, a vector error correction (VEC) model relates variables both in differences and in levels. Specifically, we specify the following VEC model with n endogenous variables and K lags:

$$\Delta y_t = C + \sum_{k=1}^{K} \Gamma_k \Delta y_{t-k} + \alpha e_{t-1} + u_t \tag{4.17}$$

where C is the $n \times 1$ vector of constants, Γ_k the $n \times n$ vector of coefficients for each lag k, α the $n \times 1$ vector of adjustment coefficients, e_{t-1} the $n \times 1$ vector of last period's error from long-term equilibrium, and u_t the $n \times 1$ vector of errors. Importantly, the changes to each endogenous variable are not just driven by these usual suspects (see the VAR model in Eq. (4.9)), but also by adjusting (with coefficient α) to reduce last period's error (e_{t-1}) from the long-term equilibrium (formulated in levels of the variables). Equation (4.17) clearly shows that the Vector Error Correction model is a VAR in differences, while adding the adjustment factor αe_{t-1}. This factor captures the speed with which each variable adjust to restore the equilibrium. Thus, VEC models are particularly interesting from a substantive perspective, because they quantify learning and adjustment behavior by market players such as manufacturers, retailers, competitors and (prospective) customers (Kireyev et al. 2016; Pauwels 2001). Buyers learn from marketing stimuli and adjust their behaviour, while sellers observe these behavioral outcomes and adjust their marketing stimuli.

Examples of marketing applications that employ VEC modelling investigate the relationship between: advertising and sales (Baghestani 1991), narcotics abuse and methadone administration (Powers et al. 1991), advertising, price differential and prescriptions (Dekimpe and Hanssens 1999), brand sales and category sales (Srinivasan and Bass 2000), sales and advertising for seven Chinese brands (Ouyang et al. 2002), price and sales (Fok et al. 2006), online display and search (Kireyev et al. 2016). For instance, in the case of Lydia Pinkham, we learn that advertising has a stronger adjustment coefficient than sales while restoring the equilibrium that advertising budgets are half of sales revenues (Baghestani 1991).

An extension of the VEC model is the Hierarchical Bayesian VEC model by Horváth and Fok (2013). At the first level of the hierarchy, they measure cross-price promotional effects, which they then relate to moderators at the second level. Estimated with Markov Chain Monte Carlo (MCMC) sampling, the model finds evidence for asymmetric and neighbourhood price effects in long-term competitive price response across 33 categories in 5 stores.

4.4.8 Seasonality in VAR/VEC models

Many marketing and performance series exhibit seasonality. Econometrics offers several ways to account for this phenomenon, including deseasonalizing the data and including seasonal dummy variables in the model. The former approach is standard in macro-economics, which typically assumes seasonality is some form of uninformative data contamination (Franses 1998). In business however, we typically want to foreast the seasonal series itself, and thus the analysis of seasonally adjusted data is not useful. Hylleberg (1994) shows several technical drawbacks of deseasonalizing, including altering the time series nature of the data. Shocks to seasonally adjusted series tend to be more persistent than those to the raw data (Jaeger and Kunst 1990) and seasonal filters bias unit root tests to non-rejection of the unit root hypotheis (Ghysels and Perron 1993). As a result, most marketing applications follow Ghysels (1994) recommendation to instead model the raw data and include seasonal dummies.

How many seasonal dummies should be included? For the typical weekly scanner data, researchers balance forecasting accuracy with degrees of freedom by chosing 4-weekly dummies (e.g. Nijs et al. 2001; Pauwels et al. 2002; Srinivasan et al. 2004), using the first 4 weeks of the year as the hold-out. For the daily data so common on the Internet, day-of-week seasonality is often captured by daily dummies, using Friday as the hold-out day (e.g. Pauwels and Dans, 2001; Pauwels and Weiss 2008; Trusov et al. 2009).

4.4.9 Extensions to VAR/VEC models

The recent decade has seen many extensions to VAR-models, mostly to overcome the key challenges laid out in Pauwels et al. (2004a, b):

- the assumptions of linear, monotone response;
- the assumption of time-independent response;
- the explosion of parameters when the number of entities becomes large.

The first issue is addressed in Smooth Threshold AutoRegression (STAR) models, such as those applied in Pauwels et al. (2016). For the top 4 brands in 20 product categories, they find evidence of thresholds in sales response to price, which are asymmetric for price gains versus price losses. Gijsenberg et al. (2015) develop a double asymmetric structural VAR model to show how service losses both matter more and matter longer than service gains.

The second issue is addressed by making the impulse response functions depend on the timing and/or the history of the impulse. As to the former, Yoo (2003) computes the conditional expectation and standard errors with the Monte Carlo technique in Koop et al. (1996). As to the latter, Gijsenberg et al. (2015) use the approach of Kilian and Vigfusson (2011) to first define a set of histories and then to evaluate the effect of the impulse response against these histories to obtain to obtain the impulse response at a certain time dependent on a certain history.

The third issue is addressed in Factor VAR models, as demonstrated in Pauwels et al. (2004a, 2004b). They propose and apply factor structure estimation of VAR-models to reduce the dynamic complexity and thus enable consideration of more endogenous variables and lags. This procedure yields an efficient determination of the number of factors with a confirmatory factor analysis, grounded in marketing theory.

4.5 Impulse Response Functions

4.5.1 Quantifying the Over-Time Impact of Marketing on the Full Dynamic System

Because of their sheer number and multicollinearity, it is infeasible to interpret the estimated VAR-coefficients directly (Ramos 1996; Sims 1980). The main interest of VAR-modelers therefore lies in the net result of all the modeled actions and reactions over time, which can be derived from the estimated coefficients through the associated impulse-response functions. These impulse-response functions (IRF) simulate the over-time impact of a change (over its baseline) to one variable on the full dynamic system (Bronnenberg et al. 2000; Litterman 1984).

Starting from the reduced-form model specification in Eq. (4.9), we can substitute each lag of each endogenous variable by the same equation and thus express the right hand side as a function of only current and lagged values of the error terms. This yields the Vector Moving Average (VMA) representation of Eq. (4.18):

$$y_t = \mu + \left(I - \Phi_1 B - \Phi_2 B^2 - \cdots - \Phi_p B^p\right)^{-1} \varepsilon_t. \tag{4.18}$$

In words, each endogenous variable is explained by a weighted average of current and past errors or "shocks" both to itself and to the other endogenous variables. Therefore, we operationalize a change to a variable (e.g. a one-time price discount) as a shock to the variable series (e.g. to price). An impulse response function then tracks the impact of that shock to each variable in the system (price, sales, competitive price, . . .) during the shock (typically denoted as period 0) and for each period thereafter. In case the affected variable is evolving (has a unit root), the shock may (but does not need to) have a permanent impact, i.e. the variable does not return to its pre-shock level. In the typical case of stationary variables, these shock effects die out, i.e. the permanent impact is 0 and the variable returns to its steady-state, i.e. pre-shock level. To illustrate both cases, Figs. 4.3 and 4.4 (Figs. 3 and 4 in Slotegraaf and Pauwels 2008) show such impulse response functions for the sales elasticity to a price promotion of a mature toothpaste brand (Close-up in the 1990s) and an emerging toothpaste brand (Rembrandt in the 1990s)

Mature brand Close-up obtains a higher immediate (i.e. same-week) effect of a price promotion because it has higher brand penetration (i.e. consumers who tried it at least once before) than emerging brand Rembrandt. However, Close-up does not enjoy a permanent sales benefit of its price promotion; sales eventually return to their baseline level. The cumulative effect (the area under the curve in Fig. 4.2) is much smaller than the immediate effect because the post promotion

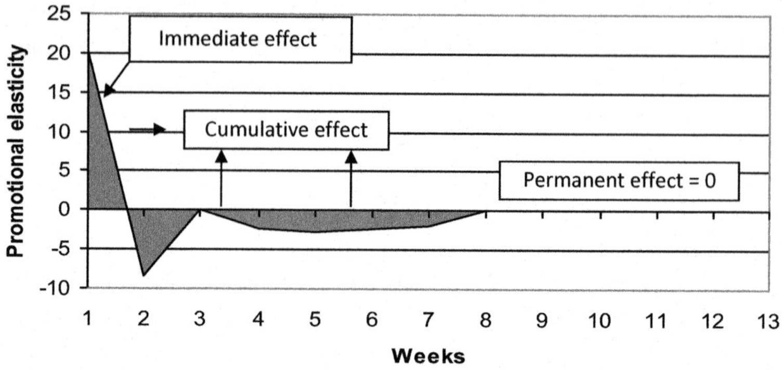

Fig. 4.3 Impulse response of price promotion on sales for mature brand Close-up

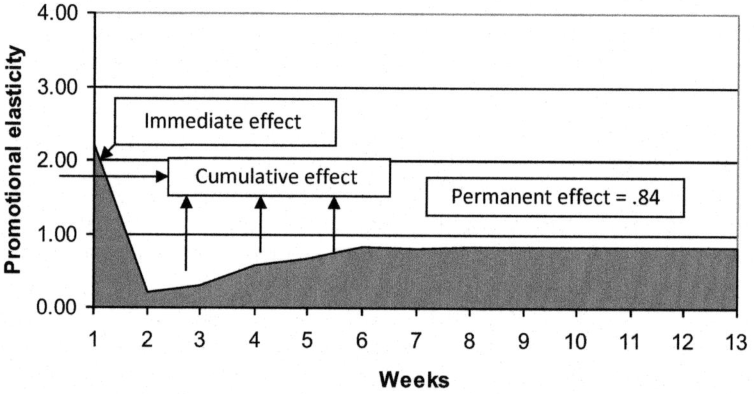

Fig. 4.4 Impulse response of price promotion on sales for new brand Rembrandt

dip (likely due to consumer stockpiling and then using Close-up toothpaste for several months without having to buy again) is almost as large as the immediate sales boost. In contrast, the emerging brand Rembrandt enjoys higher sales after the price promotion—likely due to first-time consumers having tried the brand due to the price promotion and being satisfied enough to buy again at regular price (see Slotegraaf and Pauwels 2008). This sales benefit is even permanent; i.e. the baseline of sales has increased.

For a more detailed understanding of the impulse response function, we start from the VAR-system in Dekimpe and Hanssens (1999) and Pauwels (2004) with log sales (*s*), log of focal marketing action (*fm*), log of other own marketing actions (*om*) and log of competitor marketing actions (*cm*). Changes to sales represent consumer action and changes to competitive marketing represent competitive action, while changes to focal marketing and other marketing represent how the company respectively sustains and support the focal marketing action. If all variables are stationary, we may write our model in terms of deviations from the steady-state means:

$$(s_t, fm_t, om_t, cm_t)' = \sum_{k=0}^{K} \Phi_k (S - \mu_S, FM - \mu_{FM}, OM - \mu_{OM}, CM - \mu_{CM})'_{t-k} + (u_{St}, u_{FMt}, u_{OMt}, u_{CMt})' \tag{4.19}$$

where *S*, *FM*, *OM*, and *CM* stand for the current realizations of respectively "sales", "focal marketing action", "other marketing actions", and "competitive marketing actions". Deducting their mean values, we arrive at the steady-state deviations for sales (*s*), the focal marketing action (*fm*), other marketing actions (*om*), and competitor marketing actions (*cm*). The unconditional forecasts for these steady-state deviations are zero for any forecast period.

Now, we are interested in the forecast for the sales deviation conditional on the knowledge that a focal marketing variable changes by one unit ($u_{FM,t} = 1$). Focusing on the sales equation of the VAR system in (Eq. 4.19)[1] the conditional sales forecast ($\widehat{s}$) for *p* periods ahead is:

$$\widehat{s}_{t+p} = \beta_{12}^0 fm_{t+p} + \beta_{13}^0 om_{t+p} + \beta_{14}^0 cm_{t+p} + \beta_{11}^1 s_{t+p-1} + \beta_{12}^1 fm_{t+p-1} + \ldots \tag{4.20}$$

Starting from the steady state, the updated forecast for the sales deviation at time *t* becomes:

$$\widehat{s}_t = \beta_{12}^0 fm_t + \beta_{13}^0 om_t + \beta_{14}^0 cm_t \tag{4.21}$$

and the forecast for the sales deviation one period in the future:

$$\widehat{s}_{t+1} = \beta_{12}^0 fm_{t+1} + \beta_{13}^0 om_{t+1} + \beta_{14}^0 cm_{t+1} + \beta_{11}^1 s_t + \beta_{12}^1 fm_t + \beta_{13}^1 om_t + \beta_{14}^1 cm_t. \tag{4.22}$$

A plot of these forecasts against time yields the impulse response function; allowing all endogenous variables to respond according to the historically observed reaction patterns, as captured by all estimated VAR-coefficients. How can IRFs show permanent effects if the VAR-model can only include stationary variables? If the performance variable (e.g. sales) is evolving, we indeed include it in the model in first differences, i.e. in *changes* to the variable. Therefore, the impulse response function on this variable (change in sales) will die out, as shown in the bottom part

[1]The VAR-system can also be represented as:

$$\begin{bmatrix} s_t \\ fm_t \\ om_t \\ cm_t \end{bmatrix} \begin{bmatrix} 0 & \beta_{12}^0 & \beta_{13}^0 & \beta_{14}^0 \\ \beta_{21}^0 & 0 & \beta_{23}^0 & \beta_{24}^0 \\ \beta_{31}^0 & \beta_{32}^0 & 0 & \beta_{34}^0 \\ \beta_{41}^0 & \beta_{42}^0 & \beta_{43}^0 & 0 \end{bmatrix} + \sum_{k=0}^{K} \begin{bmatrix} \beta_{11}^k & \beta_{12}^k & \beta_{13}^k & \beta_{14}^k \\ \beta_{21}^k & \beta_{22}^k & \beta_{23}^k & \beta_{24}^k \\ \beta_{31}^k & \beta_{32}^k & \beta_{33}^k & \beta_{34}^k \\ \beta_{41}^k & \beta_{42}^k & \beta_{43}^k & \beta_{44}^k \end{bmatrix} \begin{bmatrix} s_{t-k} \\ fm_{t-k} \\ om_{t-k} \\ cm_{t-k} \end{bmatrix} + \begin{bmatrix} u_{St} \\ u_{FMt} \\ u_{OMt} \\ u_{CMt} \end{bmatrix}.$$

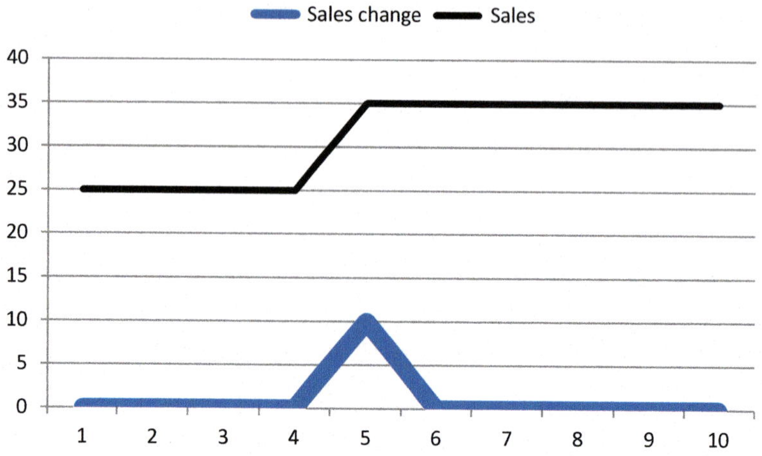

Fig. 4.5 Full hysteresis in sales change and how it translates into sales

of Fig. 4.5. To derive the effect on sales itself, we have to accumulate the IRF values starting from the first period, as shown in the top part of Fig. 4.5.

In this case of "full hysteresis" (Hanssens et al. 2001), only the immediate effect on sales *change* is significant, i.e. the only impact occurs at the time of the marketing action (period 5 in Fig. 4.5). This translates into a permanent increase of the same magnitude on sales *level* (e.g. from 25 to 35 in Fig. 4.5).

In a more typical case, we observe some negative dynamic effects on sales change, but these do not fully outweigh the positive immediate effects. Hanssens et al. (2001) call this "partial hysteresis" i.e. only part of the immediate impact becomes permanent as market players adapt (e.g. consumers become less excited and/or competitors imitate the marketing action). Fig. 4.6 illustrates this pattern, with the immediate effect of 10, and a negative effect in the next period of −7, leading to a net permanent sales increase of 3. Note that accumulating the impulse response function coefficients for sales change ($10 - 7 = 3$) gives us the net permanent effect on sales. Wieringa and Horváth (2005) note that the results of the IRFs do not have a direct interpretation when the variables are log transformed before the VAR model is estimated. They present explicit expressions for computing impulse response functions that are expressed in the levels of the variables, given a log-log transformed VAR model.

What happens when the impulse (i.e. marketing) is the evolving variable? Again, we include the marketing action (e.g. price) in first differences in the model, and its IRF therefore shows the performance impact not of a temporary shock but of a permanent change (e.g. reduction in regular price). We need to keep this in mind when interpreting the result.

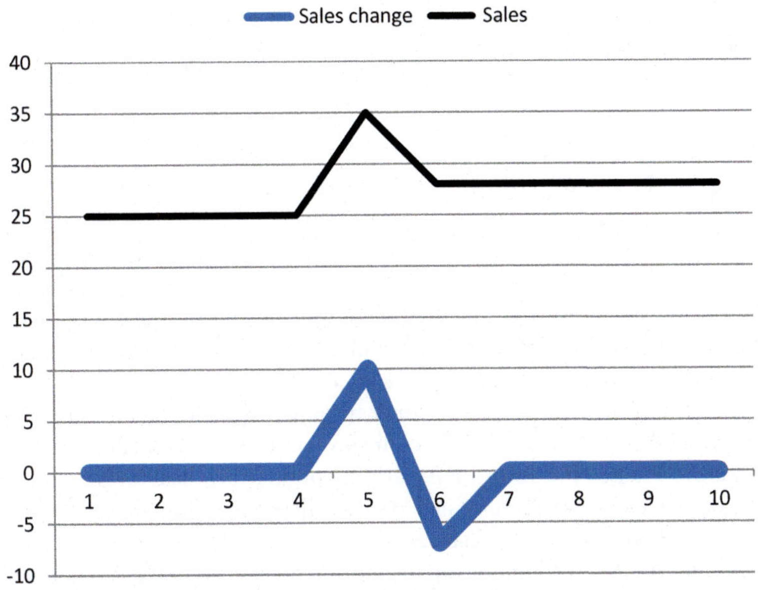

Fig. 4.6 Partial hysteresis in sales change and how it translates into sales

4.5.2 Restricted Impulse Response Function

Instead of imposing restrictions on the VAR model itself (Structural VAR), several authors believe it makes more sense to estimate an unrestricted VAR and impose restrictions on the impulse response functions instead. First, leaves the response of real GDP to monetary policy free but imposes sign restrictions on the impulse responses of the other variables for five periods. Second, Pauwels (2004) decomposes the net performance impact of a marketing action into the actions of consumers, retailers, competitors and own performance feedback.

The answer depends on the endogenous variables that we allow to be affected. If we allow only consumer (sales) response, we restrict future own and competitive marketing actions to remain in steady state, i.e. to have zero deviations ($fm_{t+p} = 0$ for $p > 0$ and $om_{t+p} = cm_{t+p} = 0$ for $p \geq 0$). In that case (4.21) and (4.22) simplify to respectively:

$$\widehat{s}_t = \beta_{12}^0, \text{ and} \tag{4.23}$$

$$\widehat{s}_{t+1} = \beta_{11}^1\, \beta_{12}^0 + \beta_{12}^1. \tag{4.24}$$

These updated forecasts, plotted as a function of forecast period p, represent the restricted policy simulation of sales to the marketing change, allowing only for consumer response (restricted simulation 1). Similarly, we add competitor response by allowing deviations from the steady state of the competitor marketing actions (simulation 2), resulting in the forecasts:

$$\widehat{s}_t = \beta_{12}^0 + \beta_{14}^0 \beta_{42}^0 \tag{4.25}$$

$$\widehat{s}_{t+1} = \beta_{14}^0 \left(\beta_{41}^1 \, \beta_{12}^0 + \beta_{41}^1 \, \beta_{14}^0 \beta_{42}^0 + \beta_{42}^1 + \beta_{44}^1 \, \beta_{12}^0\right). \tag{4.26}$$

In a similar fashion, company inertia and company support are added to consumer response.

Comparing these restricted impulse response functions shows that consumer response significantly differs from the net effectiveness of product line extensions, price, feature and advertising. In particular, net sales effects are *up to five times* stronger and longer-lasting than consumer response. Second, this difference is not due to competitor response, but to company action. For tactical actions (price and feature), it takes the form of *inertia*, as promotions last for several weeks. For strategic actions (advertising and product line extensions), *support* by other marketing instruments greatly enhances dynamic consumer response. This company action negates the post-promotion dip in consumer response, and enhances the long-term sales benefits of product line extensions, feature and advertising.

4.5.3 Generalized Impulse Response Function

An initial issue with impulse response functions is that they required a researcher-imposed causal ordering for the contemporaneous (same-period) effects. For instance, in the restricted impulse response functions above, we have assumed that marketing actions can affect sales, but not vice-versa in the same period. The need for this identification arises because we are estimating a reduced-order model, and thus need to find a way to deduct the structural VAR coefficients of Eq. (4.7). An alternative to the researcher-imposed ordering is to calculate from the data the expected contemporaneous shock in the residual variance-covariance matrix (Evans and Wells 1983; Pesaran and Shin 1998). As explained with marketing examples in Dekimpe and Hanssens (1999) and Nijs et al. (2001), we can now calculate generalized IRFs (GIRFs), which do not depend on a causal ordering. As verified in later marketing applications, these GIRFs give the same answer as IRFs in which the causal ordering is clear (e.g. retail prices that cannot be changed by manufacturers for weeks; Leeflang and Wittink 1992, 1996). GIRFs are especially important when prior theory or observation does not suggest a clear causal ordering, e.g. among different marketing actions, competitors or online customer actions (DeHaan et al. 2016). Not surprisingly, most marketing papers in the last decade use GIRFs.

4.6 Forecast Error Variance Decomposition

While impulse response functions track the effect of one shock to the full system, forecast error variance decomposition (FEVD) reveals how the forecast error variance in one variable (e.g. sales) can be explained by its own past shocks and all the shocks of the other endogenous variables. Analogous to a "dynamic R^2", it shows the relative importance of each variable in having contributed to the variation in the performance variable. An important issue in standard FEVD is the need to impose a causal ordering for model identification purposes (see Hanssens 1998 for a marketing application of FEVD). Similar to the Generalized Impulse Response function, the Generalized FEVD (Pesaran and Shin 1998) does not require such a priori causal ordering. The GFEVD is given in Eq. (4.27):

$$\theta_{ij}(n) = \frac{\sum_{l=0}^{n} \left(\psi_{ij}(l)\right)^2}{\sum_{l=0}^{n} \sum_{j=0}^{m} \left(\psi_{ij}(l)\right)^2}, i, j, = 1, \ldots, m \tag{4.27}$$

where $\psi_{ij}(l)$ is the value of a Generalized Impulse Response Function (GIRF) following a one standard-error shock to variable j on variable i at time l. In the GFEVD approach, an initial shock is *allowed* to (but *need not*, depending on the size of the corresponding residual correlation) affect all other endogenous variables instantaneously. To evaluate the accuracy of the GFEVD estimates, Nijs et al. (2007) obtain standard errors using Monte Carlo simulations (see Benkwitz et al. 2001 for an equivalent procedure to estimate the standard errors for IRFs).

(Generalized) Forecast Error Variance Decomposition always sums up to 100%, with typically the own past of the focal variable explaining most of its variance. In some marketing applications, that % of "inertia" is of special importance, e.g. indicating price inertia in Nijs et al. (2007) and Srinivasan et al. (2008). In most others though, it is the least interesting of % categories, and thus gets reduced from the 100% to yield the % of performance explained by the other groups of variables. For instance, Srinivasan et al. (2010) and Pauwels et al. (2013) show how adding mindset metrics improves the % of the GFEVD not explained by sales' own past, while Pauwels and Van Ewijk (2013) and Srinivasan et al. (2015) show how adding online behavior metrics (owned, earned and paid) does the same.

4.7 Policy Analysis Based on Modern Time Series Models and the Lucas Critique

As several papers in economics and marketing have shown, modern time series models do a particularly good job in describing the data generating process and in forecasting out of sample (Dekimpe and Hanssens 1999; Pauwels and Weiss 2008; Sims 1980). However, are they useful for policy analysis and advice (Franses 2005; Sims 1986; Van Heerde et al. 2005).

Modern time series models yield both unconditional ("what will happen") and conditional forecasts ("what wil happen if we change a marketing action"), which are widely used by policy makers in practice (Sims 1986). However, several academics object to this practice, claiming that such evidence-based (reduced form) models are mere descriptions of the data in the observed sample, and thus can not be trusted to inform policy. Well-known proponents of such perspective include Sargent (1984) and Lucas (1976, p. 41), who states that:

> ..."given that the structure of an econometric model consists of optimal decision rules of economic agents, and that optimal decision rules vary systematically with changes in the structure of series relevant to the decision maker, it follows that *any change in policy will systematically alter the structure of econometric models*" (emphasis added).

Underlying their argument is the idea that agents are forward rather than backward looking, and adapt their expectations and behavior to the new policy (Lindé 2001, p. 986). In contrast, the modern time series models discussed in this chapter are backward-looking summaries of past correlational patterns that are assumed to persist in the future, regardless of policy changes (Lindé 2001). Van Heerde et al. (2005) correctly argue that the Lucas critique is not worrysome for "any change in policy" (managers typically consider only incremental actions, such as adding or dropping price promotions or direct mail in their marketing plan), but *only* for a major policy change such as P&G "Value Pricing" strategy substantially cutting price promotions (Ailawadi et al. 2005) or Albert Heijn announcing a permanent regular price reduction across categories (Van Heerde et al. 2008).

But even for major policy changes, it is important to realize that the above critique does not necessarily disqualify forecasing models for policy analysis; instead we should compare their identifying interpretations from those of alternatives (Sims 1986). A currently popular alternative to data-driven (reduced form) models are assumption-driven models, also known as "structural models" (Chap. 7). Not to be confused with "structural VARs" (Sect. 4.3), economic models are called "structural" to the extent that they formalize and estimate parameters of "objective functions of agents", described as characterizing the agents' "tastes and technologies" invariant to the policy under consideration (Hansen and Sargent 1980). In marketing applications, the meaning of "structure" has been narrowed to consumers and managers "making optimal decisions based on a maximimition of an objective function subject to constraints" (Bronnenberg et al. 2005, p. 23). To be able to predict reactions to policy changes, the claim is that the structural model specification reflects all relevant aspects of these tastes and technologies. For any model, the more the contemplated action differs from those undertaken in the past, the more difficult it is to predict its consequences (Sims 1986).

So how can the researcher address these issues? As detailed in Franses (2005), any model used for policy analysis should first pass the tests for descriptive and forecasting models. In addition, models for policy simulation should have a constant-parameter equation for the policy instrument—in which case the Lucas critique does not hold (Ericsson and Irons 1995). If there are any changes in the parameters of the instrument model, such as due to an announced permanent change in price, the model for price should include such level shift, as should the model for sales (Franses 2005). Likewise, an assumption-driven model can be formulated to explicitly incorporate expectations and endogeneity (Bronnenberg et al. 2005). In the end though, the proof of the pudding is in the eating:

> "the true test is predictive validity for data in which there is a major change in policy" (Van Heerde et al. 2005, p. 16).

Ailawadi et al. (2005) do so by showing how their game-theoretic predictions outperform those of reaction function models after P&G Value Pricing policy change. Likewise, Wiesel et al. (2011) re-estimate their VAR-model after the company agreed to a field experiment where it increased paid search spending by 80% and reduced direct mail (its main marketing activity) by 56%. The parameter estimates of the experimental period are similar to those from the earlier period, with the exception that direct mail has a stronger impact when it was reduced (as expected given diminishing returns). An important research opportunity is to perform such an exercise directly contrasting the predictive accuracy and outcomes of an assumption-driven versus an evidence-based model. For instance, in macroeconomics, virtually no evidence is found in support of the empirical relevance of the Lucas critique (Ericsson et al. 1998).

In sum, the modeler faces the trade-off between strong identifying assumptions (which typically reduce forecasting performance) and the benefits of explicit and theory-derived primitives of rational consumers and managers (such as forward looking behavior). After understanding their relative strenghts and weaknesses, the choice basically comes down to personal preference and model purpose. For instance, New Empirical Industrial Organization (NEIO) models (Chap. 9) allow us to uncover the company's costs (which are typically not available to researchers) from its actions, if we are willing to assume profit maximizing behavior and a rather extensive information set from the decision makers. As Bronnenberg et al. (2005), p. 23 state, assumption-driven (structural) models are expected to have worse forecasting performance than evidence-based models, but the latter:

> ... "do not ensure that predictions are immune to the Lucas critique".

However, neither does any estimated "structural" model, because the structure can be misspecified. For instance, specification error in the supply side (management and competitive behavior) can lead to substantial biases in the demand-side estimates (Bronnenberg et al. 2005), which is likely if we know little about the actual nature of dynamic marketing behavior. In such typical case, Sims (1986) would rather use a model

> ... "which aims to uncover a conditional distribution of important outcomes given policy actions, without detailing all the dynamic optimization underlying that conditional distribution" (Sims 1986, p. 8).

Likewise, Bronnenberg et al. (2005) call for more attention to uncovering manager's heuristic decision rules. As we explained in Sect. 4.3, a benefit of the VAR model is to make explicit both the observed decision rules and the connection of the structural model to the reduced form forecasting model. Moreover, the impulse response function is explicit in considering the effect of an unexpected "shock"; i.e. a small change (such as having seven instead of the historical six price promotions a year), which does not alter the nature of the underlying data generating process (e.g. Srinivasan et al. 2004, p. 627).

4.8 Software

Modern time series packages are included in many general-purpose softwares such as Stata, Matlab, Gauss and R. Dedicated software packages include Time Series Processor (TSP), OX/PcGive, Eviews and JMulTi. All these packages have distinct advantages. While Stata has the most commonly used time series functions and models, Matlab has embedded functions not available in Stata but requires more coding. R is free and has many useful time series functions. TSP and JMulTi are entirely dedicated to time series.

While the other softwares are better for your own coding, Eviews and OX/PcGive offer alow-threshold click-and-find software. Moreover, Eviews has the most typical option as the default in its software and updates regularly, adding the most recent tests and deleting those found to be less desirable.

References

Akaike, H.: Fitting autoregressive models for prediction. Ann. Inst. Stat. Math. **21**, 243–247 (1969)

Akaike, H.: Maximum likelihood identification of Gaussian autoregressive moving average models. Biometrika. **60**, 255–265 (1973)

Ailawadi, K.L., Kopalle, P.K., Neslin, S.A.: Predicting competitive response to a major policy change: combining game-theoretic and empirical analyses. Mark. Sci. **24**, 12–24 (2005)

Amisano, G., Giannini, C.: Topics in structural VAR economics. Springer-Verlag, Berlin (1997)

Baghestani, H.: Cointegration analysis of the advertising-sales relationship. J. Ind. Econ. **39**, 671–681 (1991)

Benkwitz, A., Lütkepohl, H., Wolters, J.: Comparison of bootstrap confidence intervals for impulse responses of German monetary systems. Macroecon. Dyn. **5**, 81–100 (2001)

Bernanke, B.S.: Alternative explanations of the money-income correlation. Carn. Roch. Conf. Ser. **25**, 49–99 (1986)

Bjørk, R.A., Bjørk, E.L.: A new theory of disuse and an old theory of stimulus fluctuation. In: From Learning Processes to Cognitive Processes: Essays in Honor of William K. Estes, vol. 2, pp. 35–67 (1992)

Blanchard, O.J., Quah, D.: The dynamic effects of aggregate demand and supply disturbances, NBER paper series (1988)

Blanchard, O.J., Watson, M.W.: Bubbles, rational expectations and financial markets. *Working paper* (945), National Bureau of Economic Research (1982)

Bronnenberg, B.J., Mahajan, V., Vanhonacker, W.R.: The emergence of market structure in new repeat-purchase categories: the interplay of market share and retailer distribution. J. Mark. Res. **37**, 16–31 (2000)

Bronnenberg, B.J., Rossi, P.E., Vilcassim, N.J.: Structural modeling and policy simulation. J. Mark. Res. **42**, 22–26 (2005)

DeHaan, E., Wiesel, T., Pauwels, K.H.: The effectiveness of different forms of online advertising for purchase conversion in a multiple-channel attribution framework. Int. J. Res. Mark. **33**, 491–507 (2016)

Dekimpe, M.G., Hanssens, D.M.: Sustained spending and persistent response: a new look at long-term marketing profitability. J. Mark. Res. **36**, 397–412 (1999)

Dekimpe, M.G., Hanssens, D.M.: The persistence of marketing effects on sales. Mark. Sci. **14**, 1–21 (1995)

Dekimpe, M.G., Hanssens, D.J., Silva-Risso, J.M.: Long-run effects of price promotions in scanner markets. J. Econ. **89**, 269–291 (1999)

Enders, W.: Applied Econometric Time Series. John Wiley & Sons, New York (2004)

Engle, R.F., Granger, C.W.: Co-integration and error correction: representation, estimation, and testing. Econometrica. **55**, 251–276 (1987)

Ericsson, N.R., Irons, J.S.: The Lucas critique in practice: theory without measurement. In: Hoover, K.D. (ed.) Macroeconometrics: Developments, Tensions and Prospects. Kluwer Academic, Dordrecht (1995)

Ericsson, N.R., Hendry, D.F., Mizon, G.E.: Exogeneity, cointegration, and economic policy analysis. J. Bus. Econ. Stat. **16**, 370–387 (1998)

Evans, L., Wells, G.: An alternative approach to simulating VAR models. Econ. Lett. **12**, 23–29 (1983)

Faust, J.: The robustness of identified VAR conclusions about money. Carn. Roch. Conf. Ser. **49**, 207–244 (1998)

Fok, D., Horváth, C., Paap, R., Franses, P.H.: A hierarchical Bayes error correction model to explain dynamic effects of price changes. J. Mark. Res. **43**, 443–461 (2006)

Franses, P.H.: Seasonality, non-stationarity and the forecasting of monthly time series. Int. J. Forecast. **7**, 199–208 (1991)

Franses, P.H.: A multivariate approach to modeling univariate seasonal time series. J. Econ. **63**, 133–151 (1994)

Franses, P.H.: Time Series Models for Business and Economic Forecasting. Cambridge University Press, Cambridge (1998)

Franses, P.H.: Diagnostics, expectations, and endogeneity. J. Mark. Res. **42**, 27–29 (2005)

Freo, M.: The impact of sales promotions on store performance: a structural vector autoregressive approach. Stat. Method Appl. **14**, 271–281 (2005)

Gelper, S., Wilms, I., Croux, C.: Identifying demand effects in a large network of product categories. J. Retail. **92**, 25–39 (2016)

Geweke, J., Meese, R., Dent, W.: Comparing alternative tests of causality in temporal systems: Analytic results and experimental evidence. J. Econ. **21**, 161–194 (1983)

Ghysels, E.: On the periodic structure of the business cycle. J. Bus. Econ. Stat. **12**, 289–298 (1994)

Ghysels, E., Perron, P.: The effect of seasonal adjustment filters on tests for a unit root. J. Econ. **55**, 57–98 (1993)

Gijsenberg, M.J., Van Heerde, H.J., Verhoef, P.C.: Losses loom longer than gains: Modeling the impact of service crises on perceived service quality over time. J. Mark. Res. **52**, 642–656 (2015)

Granger, C.W.: Investigating causal relations by econometric models and cross-spectral methods. Econometrica. **37**, 424–438 (1969)

Hafer, R.W., Sheehan, R.G.: The sensitivity of VAR forecasts to alternative lag structures. Int. J. Forecast. **5**, 399–408 (1989)

Hannan, E.J., Quinn, B.G.: The determination of the order of an autoregression. J. Roy. Stat. Soc. B. **41**, 190–195 (1979)

Hansen, L.P., Sargent, T.J.: Formulating and estimating dynamic linear rational expectations models. J. Econ. Dyn. Control. **2**, 7–46 (1980)

Hanssens, D.M.: Market response, competitive behavior, and time series analysis. J. Mark. Res. **17**, 470–485 (1980)

Hanssens, D.M.: Order forecasts, retail sales, and the marketing mix for consumer durables. J. Forecast. **17**, 327–346 (1998)

Hanssens, D.M., Parsons, L.J., Schultz, L.: Market Response Models: Econometric and Time Series Analysis. Springer Science & Business Media, New York (2001)
Hanssens, D.M., Wang, F., Zhang, X.-P.: Performance growth and opportunistic marketing spending. Int. J. Res. Mark. **33**, 711–724 (2016)
Haugh, L.D.: Checking the independence of two covariance-stationary time series: a univariate residual cross-correlation approach. J. Am. Stat. Assoc. **71**, 378–385 (1976)
Hendry, D.F.: Dynamic Econometrics. Oxford University Press on Demand, Oxford (1995)
Hermann, S.: Hysteresis in marketing: A New Phenomenon? MIT Sloan Manage. Rev. **38**(3), 39 (1997)
Horváth, C., Fok, D.: Moderating factors of immediate, gross, and net cross-brand effects of price promotions. Mark. Sci. **32**, 127–152 (2013)
Horváth, C., Leeflang, P.S.H., Wieringa, J.E., Wittink, D.R.: Competitive reaction-and feedback effects based on VARX models of pooled store data. Int. J. Res. Mark. **22**, 415–426 (2005)
Horváth, C., Leeflang, P.S.H., Wittink, D.R.: Dynamic analysis of a competitive marketing system, Working Paper (2001)
Hylleberg, S.: Modelling seasonal variation. In: Nonstationary Time Series Analyses and Cointegration. Oxford University Press, Oxford (1994)
Jaeger, A., Kunst, R.M.: Seasonal adjustment and measuring persistence in output. J. Appl. Econ. **5**, 47–58 (1990)
Johansen, S., Mosconi, R., Nielsen, B.: Cointegration analysis in the presence of structural breaks in the deterministic trend. Econ. J. **3**, 216–249 (2000)
Johansen, S.: Statistical analysis of cointegration vectors. J. Econ. Dyn. Control. **12**, 231–254 (1988)
Johnston, J., DiNardo, J.: Econometric Methods. McGraw Hill, New York (1997)
Kang, C., Germann, F., Grewal, R.: Washing away your sins? corporate social responsibility, corporate social irresponsibility, and firm performance. J. Mark. **80**(2), 59–79 (2016)
Keating, J.W.: Identifying VAR models under rational expectations. J. Monet. Econ. **25**, 453–476 (1990)
Kilian, L., Vigfusson, J.: Are the responses of the US economy asymmetric in energy price increases and decreases? Quant. Econ. **2**, 419–453 (2011)
Kireyev, P., Pauwels, K.H., Gupta, S.: Do display ads influence search? attribution and dynamics in online advertising. Int. J. Res. Mark. **33**, 475–490 (2016)
Koop, G., Pesaran, M.H., Potter, S.M.: Impulse response analysis in nonlinear multivariate models. J. Econ. **74**, 119–147 (1996)
Lautman, M.R., Pauwels, K.H.: Metrics that matter. J. Adv. Res. **49**, 339–359 (2009)
Layton, A.P.: A further note on the detection of Granger instantaneous causality. J. Time Ser. Anal. **5**, 15–18 (1984)
Leeflang, P.S.H., Wittink, D.R.: Diagnosing competitive reactions using (aggregated) scanner data. Int. J. Res. Mark. **9**, 39–57 (1992)
Leeflang, P.S.H., Wittink, D.R.: Competitive reaction versus consumer response: Do managers overreact? Int. J. Res. Mark. **13**, 103–119 (1996)
Lindé, J.: Testing for the Lucas critique: a quantitative investigation. Am. Econ. Rev. **91**, 986–1005 (2001)
Litterman, R.B.: Forecasting and policy analysis with Bayesian vector autoregression models. Q. Rev., 30–41 (1984)
Lucas, R.E.: Econometric policy evaluation: a critique. Carn. Roch. Conf. Ser. **1**, 19–46 (1976)
Luo, X., Zhang, J., Duan, W.: Social media and firm equity value. Inf. Syst. Res. **24**, 146–163 (2013)
Lütkepohl, H.: Comparison of criteria for estimating the order of a vector autoregressive process. J. Time Ser. Anal. **6**, 35–52 (1985)
Lütkepohl, H.: Introduction to Multiple Time Series. Springer Verlag, Berlin (1993)
Murray, M.P.: A drunk and her dog: an illustration of cointegration and error correction. Am. Stat. **48**, 37–39 (1994)

Moriarty, M.M.: Transfer function analysis of the relationship between advertising and sales: a synthesis of prior research. J. Bus. Res. **13**, 247–257 (1985)

Naik, P.A., Peters, K.: A hierarchical marketing communications model of online and offline media synergies. J. Interact. Mark. **23**, 288–299 (2009)

Nelson, C.R., Schwert, G.W.: Tests for predictive relationships between time series variables: a Monte Carlo investigation. J. Am. Stat. Assoc. **77**, 11–18 (1982)

Nijs, V.R., Srinivasan, S., Pauwels, K.H.: Retail-price drivers and retailer profits. Mark. Sci. **26**, 473–487 (2007)

Nijs, V.R., Dekimpe, M.G., Steenkamp, J-B.E.M., Hanssens, D.M.: The category-demand effects of price promotions. Mark. Sci. **20**, 1–22 (2001)

Osinga, E.C., Leeflang, P.S.H., Wieringa, J.E.: Early marketing matters: a time-varying parameter approach to persistence modeling. J. Mark. Res. **47**, 173–185 (2010)

Ouyang, M., Zhou, D., Zhou, N.: Estimating marketing persistence on sales of consumer durables in China. J. Bus. Res. **55**, 337–342 (2002)

Pauwels, K.H.: Long-term marketing effectiveness in mature, emerging and changing markets. Doctoral dissertation, UCLA (2001)

Pauwels, K.H.: How dynamic consumer response, competitor response, company support, and company inertia shape long-term marketing effectiveness. Mark. Sci. **23**, 596–610 (2004)

Pauwels, K.H.: It's Not the Size of the Data: It's How You Use It: Smarter Marketing with Analytics and Dashboards, American Management Association (2014). ISBN: 9780814433959

Pauwels, K.H., Z. Aksehirli, A. Lackmann: Like the ad or the brand? Marketing stimulates different electronic word-of-mouth content to drive online and offline performance. Int. J. Res. Mark. **33**, 639–655 (2016)

Pauwels, K.H., Currim, I., Dekimpe, M.G., Hanssens, D.M., Mizik, N., Ghysels, E., Naik, P.: Modeling marketing dynamics by time series econometrics. Mark. Lett. **15**, 167–183 (2004a)

Pauwels, K.H., Dans, E.: Internet marketing the news: leveraging brand equity from marketplace to marketspace. The J. Brand Manage. **8**, 303–314 (2001)

Pauwels, K.H., Erguncu, S., Yildirim, G.: Winning hearts, minds and sales: How marketing communication enters the purchase process in emerging and mature markets. Int. J. Res. Mark. **30**, 57–68 (2013)

Pauwels, K.H., Hanssens, D.M.: Performance regimes and marketing policy shifts. Mark. Sci. **26**, 293–311 (2007)

Pauwels, K.H., Hanssens, D.M., Siddarth, S.: The long-term effects of price promotions on category incidence, brand choice, and purchase quantity. J. Mark. Res. **39**, 421–439 (2002)

Pauwels, K.H., Joshi, A.: Selecting predictive metrics for marketing dashboards: an analytical approach. J. Mark. Behav. **2**, 195–224 (2016)

Pauwels, K.H., Silva-Risso, J., Srinivasan, S., Hanssens, D.M.: New products, sales promotions, and firm value: The case of the automobile industry. J. Mark. **68**(4), 142–156 (2004b)

Pauwels, K.H., Van Ewijk, B.: Do online behavior tracking or attitude survey metrics drive brand sales? an integrative model of attitudes and actions on the consumer boulevard. Mark. Sci. Inst., 13–118 (2013)

Pauwels, K.H., Weiss, A.: Moving from free to fee: how online firms market to change their business model successfully. J. Mark. **72**(3), 14–31 (2008)

Pesaran, H.H., Shin, Y.: Generalized impulse response analysis in linear multivariate models. Econ. Lett. **58**, 17–29 (1998)

Pierce, D.A., Haugh, L.D.: Causality in temporal systems: characterization and a survey. J. Econ. **5**, 265–293 (1977)

Powers, K., Hanssens, D.M., Hser, Y.I., Anglin, M.D.: Measuring the long-term effects of public policy: the case of narcotics use and property crime. Manag. Sci. **37**, 627–644 (1991)

Putsis, W., Dhar, R.: The many faces of competition. Mark. Lett. **9**, 269–284 (1998)

Quinn, J.F.: Labor-force participation patterns of older self-employed workers. Soc. Sec. Bull. **43**, 17 (1980)

Ramos, F.F.: Forecasting market shares using VAR and BVAR models: a comparison of their forecasting performance. Faculdade de Economia, Universidade do Porto (1996)

Ren, Y., Zhang, X.: Model selection for vector autoregressive processes via adaptive lasso. Commun. Stat. Theor. Methods. **42**, 2423–2436 (2013)

Sargent, T.J.: Autoregressions, expectations, and advice. Am. Econ. Rev. **74**, 408–415 (1984)

Schwartz, G.: Estimating the dimension of a model. Ann. Stat. **6**, 461–464 (1978)

Sims, C.A.: Money, income, and causality. Am. Econ. Rev. **62**, 540–552 (1972)

Sims, C.A.: Macroeconomics and reality. Econometrica. **48**, 1 (1980)

Sims, C.A.: Are forecasting models usable for policy analysis? Fed. Bank Min. **10**, 2–16 (1986)

Sismeiro, C., Mizik, N., Bucklin, R.E.: Modeling coexisting business scenarios with time-series panel data: a dynamics-based segmentation approach. Int. J. Res. Mark. **29**, 134–147 (2012)

Slotegraaf, R.J., Pauwels, K.H.: The impact of brand equity and innovation on the long-term effectiveness of promotions. J. Mark. Res. **45**, 293–306 (2008)

Srinivasan, S., Bass, F.M.: Cointegration analysis of brand and category sales: Stationarity and long-run equilibrium in market shares. Appl. Stoch. Model. Bus. **16**, 159–177 (2000)

Srinivasan, S., Pauwels, K.H., Hanssens, D.M., Dekimpe, M.G.: Do promotions benefit manufacturers, retailers, or both? Manag. Sci. **50**, 617–629 (2004)

Srinivasan, S., Pauwels, K.H., Nijs, V.: Demand-based pricing versus past-price dependence: a cost-benefit analysis. J. Mark. **72**, 15–27 (2008)

Srinivasan, S., Rutz, O.J., Pauwels, K.H.: Paths to and off purchase: quantifying the impact of traditional marketing and online consumer activity. J. Acad. Mark. Sci. **44**, 1–14 (2015)

Srinivasan, S., Vanhuele, M., Pauwels, K.H.: Mind-set metrics in market response models: an integrative approach. J. Mark. Res. **47**, 672–684 (2010)

Srivastava, V.K., Giles, D.E.: Seemingly unrelated regression equations models: estimation and inference, vol. 80. CRC Press, New York (1987)

Steenkamp, J-B.E.M., Nijs, V.R., Hanssens, D.M., Dekimpe, M.G.: Competitive reactions to advertising and promotion attacks. Mark. Sci. **24**, 35–54 (2005)

Takada, H., Bass, F.M.: Multiple time series analysis of competitive marketing behavior. J. Bus. Res. **43**, 97–107 (1998)

Tellis, G.J., Chandy, R.K., MacInnis, D.J., Thaivanich, P.: Modeling the microeffects of television advertising: Which ad works, when, where, for how long, and why?. Mark. Sci. **24**, 359–366 (2005)

Tibshirani, R.: Regression shrinkage and selection via the lasso. J. R. Stat. Soc. B. **58**, 267–288 (1996)

Trusov, M., Bucklin, R.E., Pauwels, K.H.: Effects of word-of-mouth versus traditional marketing: findings from an internet social networking site. J. Mark. **73**(5), 90–102 (2009)

Van Heerde, H.J., Dekimpe, M.G., Putsis Jr., W.: Marketing models and the Lucas critique. J. Mark. Res. **42**, 15–21 (2005)

Van Heerde, H.J., Gijsbrechts, E., Pauwels, K.H.: Winners and losers in a major price war. J. Mark. Res. **45**, 499–518 (2008)

Van Heerde, H., Helsen, K., Dekimpe, M.G.: The impact of a product-harm crisis on marketing effectiveness. Mark. Sci. **26**, 230–245 (2007)

Wieringa, J.E., Horváth, C.: Computing level-impulse responses of log-specified VAR systems. Int. J. Forecast. **21**, 279–289 (2005)

Wiesel, T., Pauwels, K.H., Arts, J.: Marketing's profit impact: quantifying online and off-line funnel progression. Mark. Sci. **30**, 604–611 (2011)

Wiesel, T., Skiera, B., Villanueva, J.: My customers are better than yours! on reporting customer equity. GfK MIR. **2**, 42–53 (2010)

Yoo, S.: Essays on customer equity and product marketing. Doctoral dissertation, UCLA, United States of America (2003)

Zellner, A., Palm, F.: Time series analysis and simultaneous equation econometric models. J. Econ. **2**, 17–54 (1974)

Chapter 5
State Space Models

Ernst C. Osinga

5.1 Introduction

The state space model is a very general model, mostly used to specify structural time-series models. Structural time-series models explicitly specify trends and seasonality along with other relevant influences. Under the classical Box-Jenkins time-series approach, in contrast, trends and seasonal influences are removed before estimating the core model. At the heart of state space models is the specification of one or more unobserved time series α, the states, to describe observed time series y. States can serve several purposes in state space models. For example, one may use states to capture unobserved trends in the observed time series y, to model unobserved (latent) variables such as goodwill, or to specify unobserved time-varying response parameters. Given the increasing availability of time-series data in marketing (Pauwels et al. 2004 and Chaps. 3 and 4), the importance of hard-to-measure variables such as goodwill (e.g., Naik et al. 1998), and the knowledge that response parameters may change dramatically over time (e.g., Osinga et al. 2010), state space models are highly relevant for marketing.

In this chapter, we provide an introduction to state space models. We proceed as follows. In Sect. 5.2, we discuss examples of marketing models that are facilitated by a state space approach: time-varying parameter and goodwill models. Next, we introduce the state space model and show how time-varying parameter and goodwill models can be cast as state space models (Sect. 5.3). In Sect. 5.4, we introduce the Kalman filter and Kalman smoother. We explain how state space models can be estimated by a combination of Kalman filtering and maximum likelihood. We continue by discussing statistical inference and model selection. In Sect. 5.5, we

E.C. Osinga (✉)
Lee Kong Chian School of Business, Singapore Management University, Singapore, Singapore
e-mail: ecosinga@smu.edu.sg

P.S.H. Leeflang et al. (eds.), *Advanced Methods for Modeling Markets*,
International Series in Quantitative Marketing, DOI 10.1007/978-3-319-53469-5_5

briefly discuss optimal control theory. We end by providing a detailed empirical application of state space models and describe software that can be used to estimate state space models in Sects. 5.6 and 5.7, respectively. This chapter aims to introduce the reader to state space models and their applications in marketing. For an in-depth discussion of state space models, we refer to Durbin and Koopman (2001).

5.2 Marketing Applications

5.2.1 Introduction

Many marketing models are estimated on time-series data, i.e. the variables are observed over time (Vol. I, p. 66). For example, sales in week t may be explained by weekly prices and advertising expenditures, which, when modeled as a linear regression model, gives:

$$Sales_t = \beta_0 + \beta_1 Price_t + \beta_2 Advertising_t + \varepsilon_t \tag{5.1}$$

with $\varepsilon_t \sim N\left(0, \sigma_\varepsilon^2\right)$. Equation (5.1) makes two important assumptions. First, the constant β_0 as well as the response parameters β_1 and β_2 are assumed time-invariant. This assumption may be invalid. For example, baseline sales may slowly decrease because a brand is getting out of fashion, price responsiveness may change over a brand's life cycle, and the advertising effect may depend on the (unobserved) quality of the ad campaign. Second, advertising expenditures in time period t affect week t sales, i.e. the advertising effect is strictly immediate. It is, however, well known that advertising effects build up over time in a (goodwill) stock variable (Nerlove and Arrow 1962). Such a stock variable is unobserved. One may predefine the stock variable with assumed carryover parameter λ by $Stock_t = \lambda Stock_{t-1} + Advertising_t$. This specification requires a value for λ, which may, for example, be obtained by using a grid search approach, and (most likely) incorrectly assumes that the stock variable can be defined without error. Hence, standard regression techniques are not well suited to models with parameters that change and stocks that build up over time. To accommodate time-varying parameters and goodwill stocks, more advanced techniques have to be used. In this chapter, we introduce one such technique: state space models estimated by a combination of Kalman filtering and maximum likelihood. After elaborating on time-varying parameter and goodwill models, we introduce the state space model and show how time-varying parameter and goodwill models can be cast as state space models.

5.2.2 Time-Varying Parameter Models

The marketing literature is rich with examples where time-varying parameter models are required. For example, Osinga et al. (2010) find support for a decline in the effectiveness of physician-oriented marketing efforts for branded drugs over the drug's lifecycle.

The parameters in Eq. (5.1) can be made time-varying in several ways. For example, if one wishes to allow for a time-varying advertising effect, a simple approach is to include an interaction of advertising with t. However, such an approach only allows for a parameter that changes linearly over time. A more flexible form is obtained by considering a random walk model for the parameter. Focusing again on the advertising parameter, a random walk model gives:

$$\beta_{2t} = \beta_{2t-1} + \nu_t \tag{5.2}$$

with $\nu_t \sim N\left(0, \sigma_\nu^2\right)$. After plugging Eq. (5.2) into Eq. (5.1), we obtain:

$$Sales_t = \beta_0 + \beta_1 Price_t + \beta_{2t} Advertising_t + \varepsilon_t \tag{5.3}$$

with $\varepsilon_t \sim N\left(0, \sigma_\varepsilon^2\right)$. Equation (5.2) allows β_2 to change over time in a pattern that best fits the data. More complicated specifications are possible. For example, Osinga et al. (2010) specify a random walk with drift model for the time-varying parameters, i.e. a parameter at time t is equal to its lagged value plus a random error and a non-zero drift term, which we discuss in detail in Sect. 5.6. Also, covariates may be added if the source of temporal variation in the parameter(s) is known, or hypothesized.

5.2.3 Goodwill Models

Advertising builds goodwill which, in turn, may translate into sales. We observe advertising expenditures and sales but not goodwill, i.e. goodwill is a latent variable (see also Chaps. 11 and 12). Goodwill, as indicated above, can be modeled by:

$$Stock_t = \lambda Stock_{t-1} + \beta_3 Advertising_t + \xi_t \tag{5.4}$$

with $\xi_t \sim N\left(0, \sigma_\xi^2\right)$, and where λ captures the decay rate of the goodwill stock, β_3 indicates to what extent advertising expenditures help to replenish the goodwill stock and where ξ_t captures unobserved disturbances to the goodwill stock. The goodwill stock can be related to sales by simply specifying:

$$Sales_t = \beta_0 + Stock_t + \varepsilon_t \tag{5.5}$$

where $\varepsilon_t \sim N\left(0, \sigma_\varepsilon^2\right)$. We note that, in Eq. (5.5), a response parameter for the stock variable is redundant. The goodwill model can be extended in several ways.

Naik and Raman (2003) introduce a model that allows the formation of three goodwill stocks, one for television advertising, one for print advertising, and one for the synergy between TV and print advertising. The different media may have differential replenishment parameters and decay rates may differ. Also, instead of specifying a single intermediate step from advertising expenditures towards sales, i.e. the goodwill stock, we may use latent factors to capture the think-feel-do hierarchy - cognition (*C*), affect (*A*), and experience (*E*) - of intermediate steps towards sales. Many market response models focus on the direct effect of advertising on sales without explaining the role of intermediate effects in building brands. Bruce et al. (2012) propose a dynamic factor model of advertising to capture the effect of advertising on both sales and brand building. Based on the classical hierarchy of effects, Bruce et al. (2012) assume that advertising initiates a sequence, where the final component drives sales. For example, Eqs. (5.6)–(5.9) specify an $E \rightarrow C \rightarrow A$ sequence triggered by advertising and culminating in sales. More precisely, the advertising effect, γ_4, triggers experience E_t, after which prior experience E_{t-1} drives current cognition C_t via γ_3, prior cognition C_{t-1}, in turn, affects current affect A_t via γ_2, and, finally, prior affect A_{t-1} gives brand sales S_t via γ_1. The square root of advertising is used to capture diminishing returns to advertising. The model is described by the following equations:

$$Sales_t = \gamma_1 A_{t-1} + w_{1t} \tag{5.6}$$

$$A_t = \gamma_2 C_{t-1} + w_{2t} \tag{5.7}$$

$$C_t = \gamma_3 E_{t-1} + w_{3t} \tag{5.8}$$

$$E_t = \gamma_4 \sqrt{Advertising_t} + w_{4t} \tag{5.9}$$

with, for $j = 1, \ldots, 4$, $w_{jt} \sim N\left(0, \sigma_{w_j}^2\right)$. We note that the *E*, *C*, and *A* labels for the states are arbitrary if data on these variables are unavailable. If data are available, one can label the states with more certainty and test the temporal order by which advertising and the intermediate metrics affect sales (see Bruce et al. 2012).

5.3 The Linear Gaussian State Space Model

In this section, we introduce the linear Gaussian state space model and indicate how time-varying parameter and goodwill models can be cast in state space form.

5.3.1 Definition and Notation

The state space model consists of two equations, the *observation* (or *measurement*) *equation* and the *state* (or *transition*) *equation*. The observation Eq. (5.10) connects the state vector α_t to the observation vector y_t:

$$y_t = Z_t\alpha_t + c_t + \varepsilon_t, \quad \varepsilon_t \sim N(0, H_t) \tag{5.10}$$

and the state Eq. (5.11) describes the dynamics of the state vector α_t:

$$\alpha_t = T_t\alpha_{t-1} + d_t + \eta_t, \quad \eta_t \sim N(0, Q_t). \tag{5.11}$$

We indicate the number of observed variables in y_t by m and the number of unobserved states in α_t by n. Typically, m and n are different, i.e. matrix Z_t which links α_t to y_t is rectangular. Table 5.1 provides an overview of the names and dimensions of all vectors and matrices in Eqs. (5.10) and (5.11).

As indicated by the time subscripts, all vectors and matrices in Eqs. (5.10) and (5.11) are allowed to be time-varying. Covariates can influence the mean via c_t or d_t, Z_t, or T_t. For example we can specify $c_t = X_t\gamma$, or, to obtain the same effect, we can include X_t in Z_t and specify γ as a state with a transition parameter of one and zero variance. Covariates can also influence the variance, for example, we may model heteroscedasticity by specifying $H_t = \exp(X_t\gamma)$.

Table 5.1 Names and dimensions for vectors and matrices in state space models

Notation	Name	Dimension
Vectors		
y_t	Observation vector	$m \times 1$
α_t	State vector	$n \times 1$
c_t	Observation drift vector	$m \times 1$
d_t	Transition drift vector	$n \times 1$
ε_t	Observation errors	$m \times 1$
η_t	Transition errors	$n \times 1$
Matrices		
Z_t	Link matrix	$m \times n$
T_t	Transition matrix	$n \times n$
H_t	Observation error covariance matrix	$m \times m$
Q_t	Transition error covariance matrix	$n \times n$

5.3.2 Casting the Time-Varying Parameter and Goodwill Model in State Space Form

Now that we have introduced the general equations for the linear Gaussian state space model, we can illustrate how to cast the previously introduced time-varying parameter and goodwill models in state space form. We start with the time-varying parameter model given by Eqs. (5.2) and (5.3). For this particular model, we specify $y_t = Sales_t$, $Z_t = Advertising_t$, $\alpha_t = \beta_{2t}$, $c_t = \beta_0 + \beta_1 Price_t$, $H_t = \sigma_\varepsilon^2$ and $T_t = 1$, $d_t = 0$, and $Q_t = \sigma_\nu^2$. Additional time-varying parameters can be included by expanding α_t. Other extensions include the specification of a deterministic drift in the state equation by assuming non-zero d_t, a stochastic drift by specifying an additional state variable that influences β_{2t}, or to allow for heteroscedasticity in the state and/or observation equation by letting Q_t and H_t vary over time. For examples of studies that specify stochastic drift components in the state equation and allow for heteroscedasticity in the observation equation, we refer to Osinga et al. (2010) and Osinga et al. (2011), respectively.

To cast the goodwill model given by Eqs. (5.4) and (5.5) in state space form, we specify $y_t = Sales_t$, $Z_t = 1$, $\alpha_t = Stock_t$, $c_t = \beta_0$, $H_t = \sigma_\varepsilon^2$ and $T_t = \lambda$, $d_t = \beta_3 Advertising_t$, and $Q_t = \sigma_\xi^2$.

The goodwill model with intermediate factors given by Eqs. (5.6)–(5.9) requires four state variables: lagged affect denoted by S and A, C, and E. To cast this model in state space form, we specify the observation equation:

$$Sales_t = [\gamma_1 \;\; 0 \;\; 0 \;\; 0] \begin{bmatrix} S_t \\ A_t \\ C_t \\ E_t \end{bmatrix} + w_{1t}, \quad w_{1t} \sim N\left(0, \sigma_{w_1}^2\right) \tag{5.12}$$

and state equation:

$$\begin{bmatrix} S_t \\ A_t \\ C_t \\ E_t \end{bmatrix} = \begin{bmatrix} 0 & 1 & 0 & 0 \\ 0 & 0 & \gamma_2 & 0 \\ 0 & 0 & 0 & \gamma_3 \\ 0 & 0 & 0 & 0 \end{bmatrix} \begin{bmatrix} S_{t-1} \\ A_{t-1} \\ C_{t-1} \\ E_{t-1} \end{bmatrix} + \begin{bmatrix} 0 \\ 0 \\ 0 \\ \gamma_4 \sqrt{Advertising_t} \end{bmatrix} + \begin{bmatrix} 0 \\ w_{2t} \\ w_{3t} \\ w_{4t} \end{bmatrix} \tag{5.13}$$

where $w_{jt} \sim N\left(0, \sigma_{w_j}^2\right)$ for $j = 2 - 4$.

The transition matrix in Eq. (5.13), i.e. the matrix containing γ_2 and γ_3, can be easily manipulated to change the sequence of effects. Also, the specification is easily extended to allow for correlated errors w_{jt}, where $j = 2 - 4$.

5.3.3 Advantages of the State Space Approach

As the examples above illustrate, time-varying parameter and goodwill models are nested in the state space form given by Eqs. (5.10) and (5.11). The ease with which time-varying parameters and unobserved variables, such as goodwill, can be accommodated provides an important advantage to state space models. The state space form, however, is not limited to these models. In fact, any Markovian dynamic model[1] can be specified as a state space model, including dynamic spatial models (see, e.g., Aravindakshan et al. 2012). Importantly, all state space models can be estimated by using a common approach based on the Kalman filter and maximum likelihood. The generality of the state space form and the common estimation approach offers another compelling advantage for using state space models. Instead of viewing models such as AR(1), MA(1), and exponential smoothing as distinct models with their own estimation approach, the state space approach unifies these models and offers a common estimation strategy (see Durbin and Koopman 2001, pp. 49–51, for an interesting discussion on the equivalence of exponentially weighted moving average, ARIMA, and simple state space models). State space models offer several additional advantages, including:

- both multivariate and univariate outcomes can be specified through y;
- missing values can be easily handled by setting the forecasting error and Kalman gain matrix to zero for these observations (Durbin and Koopman 2001, pp. 92–93);
- time-series observations can be unequally spaced (Durbin and Koopman 2001, pp. 57–59);
- non-stationarity can be easily accommodated (see, for example, the empirical application presented in Sect. 5.6);
- correlated residuals across equations are easily specified in H_t and Q_t and serially correlated errors can be specified by incorporating the errors in the state vector.

5.4 Estimation

5.4.1 Introduction

Estimation of state space models requires the estimation of (1) the states and (2) the parameters. We rely on the Kalman filter for state estimation. The Kalman filter, which is widely applied in engineering, is named after Rudolf E. Kalman, whose work led to its development. State space models are estimated by iteratively estimating states and parameters until convergence. For example, for Eqs. (5.2) and (5.3), state estimation gives estimates for β_{2t} and parameter estimation gives σ_v^2,

[1] See Vol. I, Sect. 8.2.4.

β_0, β_1 and σ_ε^2. In state estimation, we assume model parameters as given and use the Kalman filter to obtain updated state estimates. We assume these updated state estimates as given in parameter estimation. We use log-likelihood maximization to improve our parameter estimates, where we update the states when we obtain new parameter values. The states given by the Kalman filter can be improved by applying the Kalman smoother which, as the name suggests, gives state estimates that are smoother over time and that have smaller variances. As we will see in Sect. 5.4.4, the likelihood function that is used for parameter estimation only requires the filtered states provided by the Kalman filter and not the smoothed states from the Kalman smoother. Below, we describe the Kalman filter and smoother used to obtain state estimates (Sects. 5.4.2 and 5.4.3, respectively). Then, in Sect. 5.4.4 we describe the maximum likelihood procedure for obtaining parameter estimates. Finally, we discuss statistical inference (Sect. 5.4.5) and model selection (Sect 5.4.6). The estimation procedure described below pertains to the linear Gaussian state space model in Eqs. (5.10) and (5.11).

5.4.2 *The Kalman Filter*

5.4.2.1 Derivation of the Kalman Filter

The matrices in Eqs. (5.10) and (5.11) depend on the parameter vector θ, or more formally we have $Z_t(\theta)$, $T_t(\theta)$, $c_t(\theta)$, $d_t(\theta)$, $H_t(\theta)$, and $Q_t(\theta)$. In state estimation, we assume given values for θ and use the Kalman filter to derive the best estimate of the state vector α_t based on information up to time $t-1$.

We denote $a_{t|t-1} = \mathrm{E}[\alpha_t | I_{t-1}]$ to be the mean of the state vector at time t based on *information up to and including time* $t-1$, where I_{t-1} represents the set of information from observations up to $t-1$. Also let $a_t = \mathrm{E}[\alpha_t | I_t]$ denote the mean of the state vector at time t based on information available at time t. Similarly, we denote the covariance matrices of the state vector based on information up to $t-1$ and t by $P_{t|t-1} = \mathrm{Var}[\alpha_t | I_{t-1}]$ and $P_t = \mathrm{Var}[\alpha_t | I_t]$, respectively.

The expectation of Eq. (5.11) at time $t-1$ is $\mathrm{E}[\alpha_t|I_{t-1}] = T_t\mathrm{E}[\alpha_{t-1}|I_{t-1}] + d_t + \mathrm{E}[\eta_t|I_{t-1}]$, which gives:

$$a_{t|t-1} = T_t a_{t-1} + d_t. \tag{5.14}$$

Similarly, applying the variance operator to Eq. (5.11) at time $t-1$ gives $\mathrm{Var}\,[\alpha_t\,|I_{t-1}] = T_t\mathrm{Var}[\alpha_{t-1}\,|I_{t-1}]\,T_t' + \mathrm{Var}\Big[\eta_t\,|I_{t-1}]$, which yields:

$$P_{t|t-1} = T_t P_{t-1} T_t' + Q_t. \tag{5.15}$$

At time t we receive information from the new observation y_t. Specifically, using the new information, we can calculate the forecasting errors $y_t - \mathrm{E}[y_t| I_{t-1}] = y_t - Z_t a_{t|t-1} - c_t = v_t$. The forecasting errors are used to update the states. We are interested in determining $a_t = \mathrm{E}[\alpha_t|I_t] = \mathrm{E}[\alpha_t|\, I_{t-1}, \nu_t]$. To do so, we present a lemma in multivariate normal regression theory (for a proof we refer to Durbin and Koopman 2001, p. 37):

$$\mathrm{E}\,[x|b,c] = \mathrm{E}\,[x|b] + \mathrm{Cov}\,[x,c]\,[\mathrm{Var}\,[c]]^{-1}c \tag{5.16}$$

$$\mathrm{Var}\,[x\,|b,c] = \mathrm{Var}\,[x\,|b] - \mathrm{Cov}\,[x,c]\,[\mathrm{Var}\,[c]]^{-1}\mathrm{Cov}[x,c]' \tag{5.17}$$

where x, b, and c are random vectors that are normally distributed, c has mean zero and is uncorrelated with b, and where $\mathrm{Cov}[x, c]$ indicates the covariance matrix of x and c. By applying Eq. (5.16), we obtain:

$$a_t = \mathrm{E}\,[\alpha_t|I_{t-1},\nu_t] = \mathrm{E}\,[\alpha_t|I_{t-1}] + \mathrm{Cov}\,[\alpha_t,\nu_t]\,[\mathrm{Var}\,[\nu_t]]^{-1}\nu_t. \tag{5.18}$$

By setting $\mathrm{Cov}[\alpha_t, \nu_t] = M_t$, $\mathrm{Var}[\nu_t] = F_t$, we obtain:

$$a_t = a_{t|t-1} + M_t F_t^{-1}\nu_t. \tag{5.19}$$

Next, we derive M_t and F_t:

$$\begin{aligned} M_t = \mathrm{Cov}\;[\alpha_t,\nu_t] &= \mathrm{E}\left[\mathrm{E}\left[\alpha_t\left(Z_t\alpha_t + \varepsilon_t - Z_t a_{t|t-1}\right)'|I_{t-1}\right]\right] \\ &= \mathrm{E}\left[\mathrm{E}\left[\alpha_t\left(\alpha_t - a_{t|t-1}\right)'Z_t'|I_{t-1}\right]\right] = P_{t|t-1}Z_t' \end{aligned} \tag{5.20}$$

and

$$F_t = \mathrm{Cov}\left[Z_t\alpha_t + \varepsilon_t - Z_t a_{t|t-1}\right] = Z_t P_{t|t-1} Z_t' + H_t. \tag{5.21}$$

By defining the Kalman gain matrix as $K_t = M_t F_t^{-1}$ we obtain:

$$a_t = a_{t|t-1} + K_t\nu_t. \tag{5.22}$$

Intuitively, a_t is adjusted in the direction of the forecasting error, ν_t, if $\mathrm{Cov}[\alpha_t, \nu_t] = M_t$ is positive, and the adjustment is larger if the uncertainty around the forecasting error, $\mathrm{Var}[\nu_t]$, is smaller.

With the new information that becomes available at time t, we can also update the state covariance matrix by determining $P_t = \mathrm{Var}[\alpha_t|I_t] = \mathrm{Var}[\alpha_t|\, I_{t-1}, \nu_t]$. By using Eq. (5.17) and (5.20), we obtain:

$$\begin{aligned} P_t = \mathrm{Var}\,[\alpha_t|I_{t-1},\nu_t] &= \mathrm{Var}\,[\alpha_t|I_{t-1}] - \mathrm{Cov}\,[\alpha_t,\nu_t]\,[\mathrm{Var}\,[\nu_t]]^{-1}\mathrm{Cov}[\alpha_t,\nu_t]' \\ &= P_{t|t-1} - M_t F_t^{-1} M_t' = P_{t|t-1} - K_t M_t' = P_{t|t-1}(I - K_t Z_t)' \end{aligned} \tag{5.23}$$

where I without time subscript is the identity matrix, not to be confused with I_t, the information set at time t. Equations (5.22) and (5.23) form the Kalman filter for the linear Gaussian state space model as defined in Eqs. (5.10) and (5.11).

5.4.2.2 Summary of the Kalman Filter

For easy reference, below, we restate the linear Gaussian state space model along with a summary of the Kalman filter just derived.

Observation equation: $$y_t = z_t\alpha_t + c_t + \varepsilon_t, \quad \varepsilon_t \sim N(0, H_t) \tag{5.10'}$$

State equation: $$\alpha_t = T_t\alpha_{t-1} + d_t + \nu_t, \quad \nu_t \sim N(0, Q_t). \tag{5.11'}$$

The optimal time-path of the distribution of the state vector, based on information up to and including time t is given by the Kalman filter that we derived above.

Prior state means: $$a_{t|t-1} = T_t a_{t-1} + d_t \tag{5.24}$$

Prior state covariances: $$P_{t|t-1} = T_t P_{t-1} T_t' + Q_t \tag{5.25}$$

Forecasting errors: $$\nu_t = y_t - Z_t a_{t|t-1} - c_t \tag{5.26}$$

Kalman gain matrix: $$K_t = M_t F_t^{-1} \tag{5.27}$$

with $M_t = P_{t|t-1} Z_t'$ and $F_t = Z_t P_{t|t-1} Z_t' + H_t$

Posterior state means: $$a_t = a_{t|t-1} + K_t\nu_t \tag{5.28}$$

Posterior state covariances: $$P_t = P_{t|t-1}(I - K_t Z_t)'. \tag{5.29}$$

These filter recursions are initiated by the initial state distribution $\alpha_0 \sim N(a_0, P_0)$ and then run forward over time. In case of a nonstationary state, where the initial state distribution cannot be derived, P_0 is often set to an identity matrix multiplied by a large number, i.e. we assume large initial state variance. Unfortunately, assuming large initial state variances while applying the standard Kalman filter may result in large rounding errors (Durbin and Koopman 2001, p. 101). Koopman (1997) therefore presents exact initialization routines for the Kalman filter that hold when we let the initial state variances go to infinity. For an application of exact initialization in marketing we refer to Osinga et al. (2010).

5.4.3 The Kalman Smoother

5.4.3.1 Introduction

The Kalman filter provides the mean a_t and covariance P_t of the state vector based on information *up to and including time t*. We could, however, improve our state estimates by also *utilizing future information*, i.e. observations from time $t+1, \ldots, T$. The question then is, how do we optimally update the state mean and covariance if we use future information? This question is answered by the Kalman smoother. The Kalman smoother yields "smoother" time plots than the Kalman filter because we use more information. Three types of smoothing estimators exist: the fixed-interval smoother, fixed-point smoother, and fixed-lag smoother.

In fixed-interval smoothing, we improve all the filtered states by using information from the entire observation span T at every time t, the estimate $a_{t|T}$. Here, the time span T remains fixed, i.e. the states at each time t are improved based on the same complete information set. In fixed-point smoothing, we improve the estimate of the state vector at a fixed time point s as future information arrives, i.e. we are interested in determining $a_{s|s+1}, a_{s|s+2}, \ldots$. Finally, in fixed-lag smoothing, we seek improvement in the filtered estimates τ periods ago, i.e. $a_{t|t+\tau}$.

In marketing, to our knowledge, the last two smoothing concepts have not been used. Hence, we focus our discussion on fixed-interval smoothing. Fixed-interval smoothing is performed after the filtering cycle is complete, and typically, after the parameter vector θ has been estimated. Fixed-point and fixed-lag smoothing can be applied in real-time, although with a delay, i.e. we can apply these smoothers as soon as the Kalman filter provides the required "future" information which occurs before the filter reaches T.

5.4.3.2 Derivation of the Kalman Smoother

We are interested in obtaining expressions for $a_{t|T}$, the smoothed state means, and $P_{t|T}$, the smoothed state covariances. We first focus on the fixed-interval smoother for the state means. To derive this Kalman smoother, we again rely on Eqs. (5.16) and (5.17). We note that $a_{t|T} = \mathrm{E}[\alpha_t | I_T] = \mathrm{E}[\alpha_t | I_t, v_{t+1}, \ldots, v_T]$, i.e. we decompose the full information set in the information set up to and including t and the future forecasting errors $v_{t+1}, \ldots, v_T$. We can now apply Eq. (5.16) to obtain:

$$a_{t|T} = \mathrm{E}\left[\alpha_t \left| I_t, v_{t+1}, \cdots, v_T\right.\right] = a_t + \sum\nolimits_{jt+1}^{T} \mathrm{Cov}\left[\alpha_t, v_j\right] F_j^{-1} v_j. \tag{5.30}$$

Equation (5.30) requires $\mathrm{Cov}[\alpha_t, v_j]$ which we can rewrite as:

$$\mathrm{Cov}\left[\alpha_t, v_j\right] = \mathrm{E}\left[\alpha_t v_j'\right] = \mathrm{E}\left[\alpha_t \left(Z_j\left(\alpha_j - a_{j|j-1}\right)\right)'\right] = \mathrm{E}\left[\alpha_t\left(\alpha_j - a_{j|j-1}\right)'\right] Z_j'. \tag{5.31}$$

Equipped with Eqs. (5.30) and (5.31) we can further derive the state smoother. We note that the summation in Eq. (5.30) renders the expression impractical. Fortunately, as we show below, we can obtain a (backwards) recursive algorithm that does no longer contain the summation. To do so, we use Eqs. (5.30) and (5.31) to obtain our first smoothed state means.

We first observe that a_T, the posterior filtered state mean at time T, is equal to $a_{T|T}$, the smoothed state mean, because a_T is based on the complete information set I_T. The first unknown smoothed state mean is $a_{T-1|T}$. To obtain $a_{T-1|T}$ we need to determine $\mathrm{E}\left[\alpha_t(\alpha_j - a_{j|j-1})'\right]Z_j'$ for $j = 1$ which is done by using Eq. (5.24) from the Kalman filter:

$$\begin{aligned}\mathrm{E}\left[\alpha_t(\alpha_{t+1} - a_{t+1|t})'\right]Z_{t+1}' &= \mathrm{E}\left[\mathrm{E}\left[\alpha_t(\alpha_{t+1} - a_{t+1|t})'|I_T\right]\right]Z_{t+1}' \\ &= \mathrm{E}\left[\mathrm{E}\left[\alpha_t(T_{t+1}\,(\alpha_t - \alpha_t))'|I_T\right]\right]Z_{t+1}' = P_tT_{t+1}'Z_{t+1}'. \end{aligned} \tag{5.32}$$

We insert the final expression of Eq. (5.32) at time T in Eq. (5.30) to obtain $a_{T-1|T}$, the smoothed state mean at time $T-1$:

$$\begin{aligned} a_{T-1|T} &= \mathrm{E}\left[\alpha_{T-1}|I_{T-1}, \nu_T\right] = a_{T-1} + P_{T-1}T_T'Z_T'F_T^{-1}\nu_T \\ &= a_{T-1} + P_{T-1}T_T'P_{T|T-1}^{-1}\left(a_T - a_{T|T-1}\right) \end{aligned} \tag{5.33}$$

where we make use of Eqs. (5.27) and (5.28). Before moving on to the smoothed state mean at time $T-2$, we first re-express the smoothed state mean at time $T-1$, Eq. (5.33), to obtain an expression that will prove extremely useful below. Using Eq. (5.28), we first replace a_{T-1} by $a_{T-1|T-2} + K_{T-1}\nu_{T-1}$. Also, based on Eq. (5.29), we write $P_{T-1|T-2}(I - K_{T-1}Z_{T-1})$ instead of P_{T-1} and use Eq. (5.27) to rewrite the first instance of K_{T-1}:

$$\begin{aligned} a_{T-1|T} &= a_{T-1} + P_{T-1}T_T'Z_T'F_T^{-1}\nu_T \\ &= a_{T-1|T-2} + K_{T-1}\nu_{T-1} + P_{T-1|T-2}(I - K_{T-1}Z_{T-1})'T_T'Z_T'F_T^{-1}\nu_T \\ &= a_{T-1|T-2} + P_{T-1|T-2}Z_{T-1}'F_{T-1}^{-1}\nu_{T-1} \\ &\quad + P_{T-1|T-2}(I - K_{T-1}Z_{T-1})'T_T'Z_T'F_T^{-1}\nu_T \\ &= a_{T-1|T-2} + P_{T-1|T-2}\left(Z_{T-1}'F_{T-1}^{-1}\nu_{T-1}\right. \\ &\quad \left. + \,(T_{T-1} - T_{T-1}K_{T-1}Z_{T-1})'Z_T'F_T^{-1}\nu_T\right). \end{aligned} \tag{5.34}$$

Finally, we rearrange Eq. (5.34) to obtain:

$$P_{T-1|T-2}^{-1}\left(a_{T-1|T} - a_{T-1|T-2}\right) = Z_{T-1}'F_{T-1}^{-1}\nu_{T-1} + (T_T - T_TK_{T-1}Z_{T-1})'Z_T'F_T^{-1}\nu_T. \tag{5.35}$$

Next, we derive $a_{T-2|T}$, the state mean at time $T-2$. Equation (5.30) shows that we require $\mathrm{E}\left[\alpha_t(\alpha_j - a_{j|j-1})'\right] Z_j'$ for $j=1$, which is given by Eq. (5.32), and for $j=2$, which we derive below, by employing Eqs. (5.24), (5.28) and (5.32):

$$\begin{aligned}
\mathrm{E}\left[\alpha_t(\alpha_{t+2} - a_{t+2|t+1})'\right] &= \mathrm{E}\left[\mathrm{E}\left[\alpha_t(\alpha_{t+2} - a_{t+2|t+1})'|I_T\right]\right] Z_{t+2}' \\
&= \mathrm{E}\left[\mathrm{E}\left[\alpha_t(T_{t+2}(\alpha_{t+1} - a_{t+1}))'|I_T\right]\right] Z_{t+2}' \\
&= \mathrm{E}\left[\mathrm{E}\left[\alpha_t(T_{t+2}(T_{t+1}\alpha_t - (a_{t+1|t} + K_{t+1}v_{t+1})))'|I_T\right]\right] Z_{t+2}' \\
&= \mathrm{E}\left[\mathrm{E}\left[\alpha_t(T_{t+2}(T_{t+1}\alpha_t - (T_{t+1}a_t + K_{t+1}v_{t+1})))'|I_T\right]\right] Z_{t+2}' \\
&= \mathrm{E}\left[\mathrm{E}\left[\alpha_t(T_{t+2}(T_{t+1}(\alpha_t - a_t) - K_{t+1}v_{t+1}))'|I_T\right]\right] Z_{t+2}' \\
&= \left(P_t T_{t+1}' T_{t+2}' - P_t T_{t+1}' Z_{t+1}' K_{t+1}' T_{t+2}'\right) Z_{t+2}' \\
&= P_t T_{t+1}'(T_{t+2} - T_{t+2}K_{t+1}Z_{t+1})' Z_{t+2}'.
\end{aligned} \tag{5.36}$$

We now have all the ingredients to obtain the expression for $a_{T-2|T}$. We plug the expressions obtained in Eqs. (5.32) and (5.36) into Eq. (5.30) to obtain, for $t=T-2$,

$$\begin{aligned}
a_{T-2|T} &= \mathrm{E}\left[\alpha_{T-2}|I_{T-2}, v_{T-1}, v_T\right] \\
&= a_{T-2} + P_{T-2}T_{T-1}'Z_{T-1}'F_{T-1}^{-1}v_{T-1} \\
&\quad + P_{T-2}T_{T-1}'(T_T - T_T K_{T-1}Z_{T-1})'Z_T'F_T^{-1}v_T \\
&= a_{T-2} + P_{T-2}T_{T-1}'\left(Z_{T-1}'F_{T-1}^{-1}v_{T-1} + \left(T_T - T_T K_{T-1}Z_{(T-1)}\right)'Z_T'F_{T-1}^{-1}v_T\right).
\end{aligned} \tag{5.37}$$

The last part of the right-hand side of Eq. (5.37) is equal to the right-hand side of Eq. (5.35). We can thus replace the last part of Eq. (5.37) with the left-hand side of Eq. (5.35) to arrive at a convenient and concise expression for $a_{T-2|T}$:

$$a_{T-2|T} = a_{T-2} + P_{T-2}T_{T-1}'P_{T-1|T-2}^{-1}\left(a_{T-1|T} - a_{T-1|T-2}\right). \tag{5.38}$$

We note the similarity between Eqs. (5.38) and (5.33). In fact, for all t, it holds that the smoothed state means can be obtained by using the following backward recursive algorithm:

$$a_{t|T} = a_t + P_t T_{t+1}' P_{t+1|t}^{-1}\left(a_{t+1|T} - a_{t+1|t}\right) \tag{5.39}$$

which is part of the fixed-interval Kalman smoother.

Smoothed state variances can be derived in similar fashion. Applying Eq. (5.17), we obtain the following expression for the state variances based on the complete information set:

$$P_{t|T} = \mathrm{Var}\left[\alpha_t | I_t, \nu_{t+1}, \ldots, \nu_T\right] = P_t + \sum_{j=t+1}^{T} \mathrm{Cov}\left[\alpha_t, \nu_j\right] F_j^{-1} \mathrm{Cov}\left[\alpha_t, \nu_j\right]'. \quad (5.40)$$

We immediately note that we have already derived the building blocks for Eq. (5.40). Also, we note that P_T is equal to $P_{T|T}$ as both are based on the complete information set. The expression for the smoothed state variances at time $T-1$ can be determined by using Eq. (5.32):

$$\begin{aligned} P_{T-1|T} &= \mathrm{E}\left[P_{T-1} | I_{T-1}, \nu_T\right] = P_{T-1} + P_{T-1} T_T' Z_T' F_T^{-1} Z_T T_T P_{T-1} \\ &= P_{T-1} + P_{T-1} T_T' P_{T|T-1}^{-1} K_T Z_T T_T P_{T-1} \\ &= P_{T-1} + P_{T-1} T_T' P_{T|T-1}^{-1} \left(P_T - P_{T|T-1}\right) P_{T|T-1}^{-1} T_T P_{T-1} \end{aligned} \quad (5.41)$$

where the last two lines follow from Eqs. (5.28) and (5.29). The expressions for the smoothed state variances at time $T-2$ can be derived based on the result in Eq. (5.36). Again we would find that a backward recursive algorithm can be used to obtain smoothed state variances. The routine is given by:

$$P_{t|T} = P_t + P_t T_{t+1}' P_{t+1|t}^{-1} \left(P_{t+1|T} - P_{t+1|t}\right) P_{t+1|t}^{-1} T_{t+1} P_t. \quad (5.42)$$

Eqs. (5.38) and (5.42) together form the fixed-interval Kalman smoother.

5.4.3.3 Summary of the Kalman Smoother

Below, for easy reference, we restate the linear Gaussian state space model and fixed-interval Kalman smoother.

Observation equation: $y_t = z_t \alpha_t + c_t + \varepsilon_t, \quad \varepsilon_t \sim N(0, H_t)$ (5.10′)

State equation: $\alpha_t = T_t \alpha_{t-1} + d_t + \nu_t, \quad \nu_t \sim N(0, Q_t).$ (5.11′)

The Kalman smoother utilizes all information available up to and including time T to give the unique and optimal time-path of the distribution of the state vector. The smoother is given by the following routines that we derived above:

Smoothed state means: $a_{t|T} = a_t + P_t T_{t+1}' P_{t+1|t}^{-1} \left(a_{t+1|T} - a_{t+1|t}\right)$ (5.39′)

Smoothed state covariances: $P_{t|T} = P_t + P_t T_{t+1}' P_{t+1|t}^{-1} \left(P_{t+1|T} - P_{t+1|t}\right) P_{t+1|t}^{-1} T_{t+1} P_t.$ (5.42′)

The Kalman smoother recursions start at time $t = T$ and then *run backwards*. The recursions are initiated by the state distribution at time T, $\alpha_T \sim N(a_T, P_T)$, which is provided by the Kalman filter.

5.4.4 Parameter Estimation

We estimate the parameters of state space models, given the filtered states, by maximum likelihood. To do so, we first write the likelihood function for observing the data $\{y_1, \ldots, y_T\}$ sequentially over time. The likelihood function is given by:

$$L(\theta | \{y_1, y_2, \ldots, y_T\}) = p(y_1, y_2, \ldots y_T; \theta) = \prod_{t=1}^{T} p(y_t | I_{t-1}; \theta) \tag{5.43}$$

where we obtain the final expression by rewriting the likelihood function as the product of conditional densities. Because $y_t | I_{t-1}$ is normally distributed with mean $Z_t a_{t|t-1} - c_t = v_t$ and variance F_t, i.e., $y_t | I_{t-1} \sim N(v_t, F_t)$, we can further simplify (5.42) to obtain the log-likelihood function:

$$\begin{aligned} LL(\theta) &= \ln\left(\prod_{t=1}^{T} p(y_t | I_{t-1}; \theta)\right) = \sum_{t=1}^{T} \ln(p(y_t | I_{t-1}; \theta)) \\ &= -\frac{mT}{2} \ln(2\pi) - \frac{1}{2} \sum_{t=1}^{T} \left(\ln(\det(F_t)) + v_t' F_t^{-1} v_t\right) \end{aligned} \tag{5.44}$$

where ln denotes the natural logarithm and det denotes the determinant. Intuitively, the likelihood provides a tradeoff between the forecasting errors, v_t, and their variance, F_t. By making the states more flexible, we can obtain smaller forecasting errors which, in isolation, increase the likelihood. However, more flexible states require larger state variances, P_t, which, in turn, give larger forecasting error variances, F_t, thus decreasing the likelihood through the determinant term. Equation (5.44) immediately shows that we only require the Kalman filter, and not the smoother, to calculate the likelihood of a linear Gaussian state space model because both v_t and F_t are given by the filter. We evaluate the natural logarithm of the likelihood function because the resulting numbers are easier to handle. We note that the likelihood and log likelihood both reach their maximum at $\theta*$. Matrices of the state space model may be specified as nonlinear functions of θ without affecting the likelihood function. The score vector, however, may become a complicated function and may make parameter estimation computationally intensive. Hence, we recommend to numerically maximize Eq. (5.44) using numerical solvers, (e.g., BFGS, BHHH) and are available in commercial software (e.g., Matlab's fminunc or Gauss' Optmum) and free open source software (e.g., optimx in R).

To avoid local maxima and obtain faster convergence, re-scaling of the data such that the various elements of θ have comparable magnitudes is advised. Good starting values θ_0 can be found by using derivative-free optimization. For example, to obtain starting values for a time-varying parameter model, one can first estimate a static model by OLS. Finally, multiple starting values should be used to test robustness of the parameter estimates.

5.4.5 Statistical Inference

To assess significance of our parameter estimates, $\theta*$, we need an estimate of the variance-covariance matrix of $\theta*$, Var($\theta*$). We base our estimate of Var($\theta*$) on the curvature of the likelihood function at the maximum. More specifically, we use the second derivative of the likelihood function. For a parameter vector θ of length k, we determine the $k \times k$ matrix of second partial derivatives, the Hessian matrix. The Hessian matrix is defined by $\mathscr{H} = \frac{\partial^2 L(\theta)}{\partial\theta\partial\theta'}$. Next, we determine the Fisher information matrix:

$$\mathfrak{I} = \mathrm{E}\left[-\mathscr{H}\right] \tag{5.45}$$

which we use as an estimate for the variance-covariance matrix of $\theta*$. Standard errors for each parameter in $\theta*$ are given by the square root of the diagonal elements of $\mathfrak{I}$.

5.4.6 Model Selection

In practical situations, we may wish to specify and estimate several competing models. For example, we may specify time-varying parameter models with and without stochastic drift in the state equation. Model selection literature offers metrics to select that model that is parsimonious while fitting the data well (Vol. I, pp. 157–159).

A good model is (a) simple to allow for easy understanding and (b) complete to give accurate forecasts. It is easy to see that these two criteria conflict: simple models (e.g., intercept only) do not predict well, whereas complete models and their results may be too complex to understand. To find a balance between simplicity and completeness, we use information criteria, such as AIC (Akaike Information Criterion), $\mathrm{AIC_C}$ (corrected AIC), and BIC (Bayesian Information Criterion), see also Vol. I, Sect. 5.6:

$$\mathrm{AIC} = -2LL^* + 2k \tag{5.46}$$

$$\mathrm{AIC_c} = -2LL^* + \frac{n\,(n+k)}{n-k-2} \tag{5.47}$$

$$\mathrm{BIC} = -2LL^* + k\ln(n). \tag{5.48}$$

In Eqs. (5.46)–(5.48), LL^* denotes the maximum log likelihood, and k and n are the number of parameters and sample size, respectively. All criteria are based on the same idea that a better fit lowers and a larger number of parameters increases its values, i.e. we strive for the lowest value possible. The criteria differ only in the size of the "penalty" that is imposed for each additional parameter.

When we consider multiple competing models, we compute a score for each model and select the model that has the lowest score on the chosen information criterion. In the ideal situation, all three criteria point to the same model as "the winner"; we then achieve convergent validity. We may, however, encounter situations where different criteria favor different models as the best one. In those situations, we need to choose which criterion to rely on. The AIC and AIC_C are preferred in settings where models involve many parameters while being estimated on small samples (i.e., large k/n ratio). The AIC_C outperforms the AIC as the k/n ratio increases. For models with few parameters that are estimated on large sample sizes (i.e., small k/n ratio) we prefer the BIC. For more information on the properties of the various criteria, we refer to McQuarie and Tsai (1998, p. 3) and Naik et al. (2007).

5.5 From Descriptive to Normative Insights

In the previous sections, we explained state space model specification, estimation, statistical inference and model selection. The parameter estimates and significance levels of the selected model provide important descriptive insights to managers. For example, a manager may learn about the effect of advertising dollars on sales, or even the differential sales effects of different advertising media. Other examples include insights about the effect of price on product trial and the effect of distribution on sales. Although these insights can be of great importance to managers, it does not inform them about the optimal course of action based on the findings. A great advantage of state space models is that they can be linked to optimal control theory to provide normative insights. For example, one may use optimal control theory to determine the future allocation of the advertising budget across different media that optimizes profits. For a discussion of optimal control theory for state space models, we refer to Naik (2015).

5.6 Empirical Application and Further Reading

5.6.1 Introduction and Model Specification

To illustrate the practical use of state space models in marketing, we provide an example of an empirical application. The example is derived from Osinga et al. (2010) who use a state space model to determine the time-varying effects of pharmaceutical marketing efforts on drug sales.

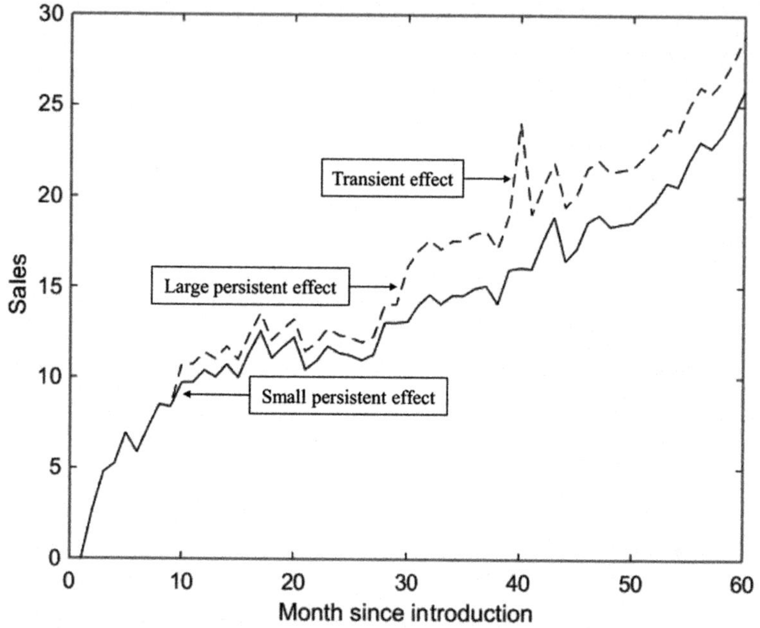

Fig. 5.1 Graphical illustration of persistent and transient marketing effects

Osinga et al. (2010) distinguish between persistent and transient marketing effects. Persistent effects represent an enduring influence of marketing efforts on sales (or a different metric), i.e. a positive persistent effect means that sales are increased by a marketing effort and remain at a higher level when the marketing effort is stopped. Marketing efforts that produce a transient effect yield (relatively) short-lived sales increases, i.e. after the marketing effort is stopped, sales soon fall back to the original level. In Fig. 5.1, we illustrate the distinction between persistent and transient effects. Figure 5.1 depicts the first 60 months of a simulated sales series. The solid line represents the sales series in the absence of marketing efforts. The dashed line shows how marketing efforts with persistent and transient effects impact the sales curve. More specifically, in month 10, we introduce a small positive persistent marketing effect, which shifts the sales curve upward. Here it must be noted that the upward shift applies to all time periods to come. In month 30, we introduce a larger positive persistent effect which creates an even larger distance between the solid and the dashed line for the months to come. Finally, in month 40, we apply a positive transient effect. The transient effect gives a temporary sales boost which only applies to month 40 and not to subsequent months. Managers would ideally allocate their budget to periods in which strong persistent effects might be expected. Therefore, it is of great importance to understand how persistent marketing effects evolve over time.

To empirically distinguish between persistent and transient effects, Osinga et al. (2010) use the following time-varying parameter model for drug i at time t:

$$\ln(Sales_{it}) = \mu_{it} + \beta_{1it} \ln(DTP_{it-1}) + X_{1it}\gamma_{1i} + \varepsilon_{it} \tag{5.49}$$

$$\mu_{it} = \mu_{it-1} + \beta_{2it-1} \ln(DTP_{it-1}) + X_{2it}\gamma_{2i} + \xi_{it} \tag{5.50}$$

where direct-to-physician marketing efforts are indicated by the variable *DTP*, X_1 and X_2 contain control variables, μ_{it} is the time-varying intercept, and β_{1it} and β_{2it} are time-varying marketing effects. Transient effects are captured by β_{1it} because the effect on sales disappears when marketing efforts are reduced. Because μ_{it} is a direct function of its own lag, the effect of direct-to-physician marketing efforts captured by β_{2it-1} is absorbed in μ_{it} and thus persistent, i.e. the effect persists after marketing efforts are stopped. Osinga et al. (2010) assume local linear trend, or random walk with random walk drift, specifications for the time-varying parameters (Durbin and Koopman, 2001, p. 39). A local linear trend specification provides a good trade-off between a large degree of flexibility and the number of parameters. They thus specify:

$$\beta_{1it} = \beta_{1it-1} + \pi_{1it-1} + \eta_{1it} \tag{5.51}$$

$$\beta_{2it} = \beta_{2it-1} + \pi_{2it-1} + \eta_{2it} \tag{5.52}$$

$$\pi_{1it} = \pi_{1it-1} + \eta_{3it} \tag{5.53}$$

$$\pi_{2it} = \pi_{2it-1} + \eta_{4it}. \tag{5.54}$$

All error terms, ε_{it}, ξ_{it}, and all η terms, are assumed normally distributed. Equations (5.49)–(5.54) can be easily rewritten in state space form by specifying states for μ_{it}, both marketing effects (β_{1it} and β_{2it}) and all drift factors π.

5.6.2 Data and Estimation

Equations (5.49)–(5.54) are estimated on data for 89 prescription drugs from 39 categories. All of these 89 drugs are introduced between the beginning of 1993 and the end of 2000, have a 2000 annual sales level of $25 million or more in the United States and a minimum of 50 observations. For these drugs, Osinga et al. (2010) observe drug sales, direct-to-physician marketing efforts (*DTP*) and control variables.

For each individual drug, the model given by Eqs. (5.49)–(5.54) is estimated by a combination of Kalman filtering and maximum likelihood as outlined above. Because of the abundant use of time-varying parameters that follow a random walk, Osinga et al. (2010) pay particular attention to the initialization of the filtering routine. They rely on exact initialization (Koopman, 1997), which is more accurate than naive methods and computationally more efficient than the augmented Kalman filter (Koopman, 1997). Finally, Osinga et al. (2010) determine the smoothed coefficients, given by the fixed-interval Kalman smoother.

5.6.3 Results

In Fig. 5.2, we provide an overview of the results obtained by Osinga et al. (2010). We present the means of the significant smoothed persistent (solid line) and transient (dashed line) effects across all brands as well as twice the standard error of the means (gray lines). Figure 5.2 clearly demonstrate that the average size of both persistent and transient effects declines with the number of months a drug has been on the market. Importantly, we observe that the mean of the significant persistent effects across all brands is positive and significantly different from zero during approximately the first two years after a drug's introduction. Transient effects remain significant over the first five years after introduction. These results correspond with the marketing expenditure patterns observed in practice: direct-to-physician marketing expenditures are highest after introduction; approximately two years after the introduction, expenditures start to fluctuate around a stable level.

These results not only illustrate that state space models can be successfully applied to empirical data; the results also illustrate the importance of accommo-

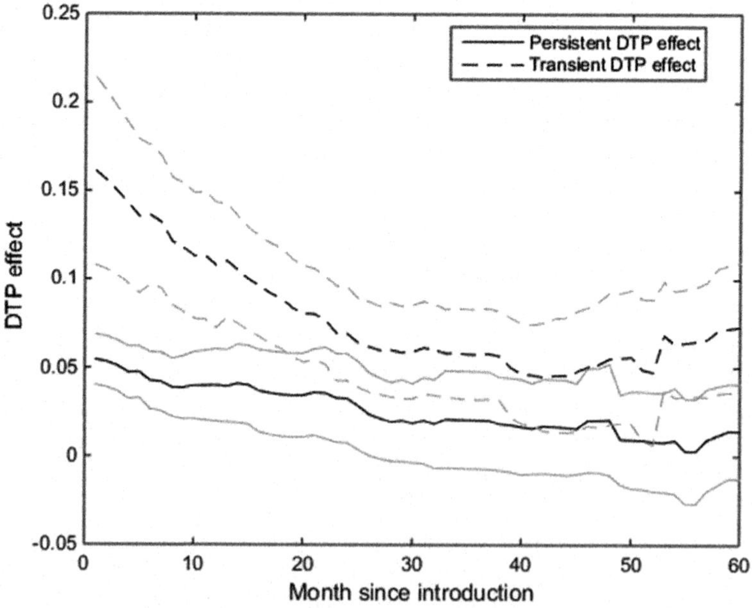

Fig. 5.2 Time-varying persistent and transient effects of DTP efforts

dating time-varying effects. A model specification with time-invariant parameters is unlikely to provide support for the presence of persistent marketing effects unless persistent effects occur during the entire observation period.

5.6.4 *Further Reading*

The marketing literature is rich with interesting applications of state space models. In Table 5.2 we provide an overview of selected studies that specify state space models. For each study, we indicate the substantive use of latent states as well as specific methodological features. We see that states are often used to specify time-varying parameters but also to capture unobserved trends and variables. The methodological features show that the state space models and estimation techniques that we presented above can be extended in many exciting ways. We refer the reader to the mentioned papers and references therein for more details on these methodological features. For an introduction to a Bayesian treatment of state space models, we highly recommend West and Harrison (1997).

Table 5.2 Selected applications of state space models in marketing

Study	Substantive use of states	Methodological feature(s)
Du and Kamakura (2012)	Latent trends	Dynamic factor analysis
Jap and Naik (2008)	Latent price distribution	Focus on forecasting
Kolsarici and Vakratsas (2010)	Several time-varying components, including the unobserved number of trials and renewals	Continuous time—discrete observations
Liu and Shankar (2015)	Time-varying advertising effectiveness and product recall response	Bayesian estimation, integration with random coefficient demand model
Naik et al. (1998)	Time-varying ad quality and awareness stock	Normative insights regarding pulsing schedules
Osinga et al. (2010)	Time-varying marketing effectiveness	Exact initialization
Osinga et al. (2011)	Time-varying CAPM beta	Time-varying error variance
Van Heerde et al. (2004)	Time-varying marketing mix parameters	Bayesian estimation
Xie et al. (1997)	Product diffusion	Continuous time—discrete observations

5.7 Software

Several software options are available for estimating state space models. For example, Stata and Eviews have built-in routines for specifying and estimating state space models. Alternatively, one may rely on dedicated software such as STAMP. Free packages are available for several programming languages. An example is the KFAS package for R. For users familiar with coding, we highly recommend to write custom functions. The Kalman filter and smoother are relatively easy to code and the coding exercise helps to obtain a thorough understanding of the filtering and smoothing routines. Moreover, custom-built functions allow for greater flexibility than built-in routines.

Acknowledgements The author gratefully acknowledges the support of the Netherlands Organisation for Scientific Research (NWO) under grant number 016.135.234. Also, the author thanks Prasad Naik for commenting on an earlier version of this chapter and for sharing his extensive set of materials on state space models.

References

Aravindakshan, A., Peters, K., Naik, P.A.: Spatiotemporal allocation of advertising budgets. J. Mark. Res. **49**, 1–14 (2012)

Bruce, N.I., Peters, K., Naik, P.A.: Discovering how advertising grows sales and builds brands. J. Mark. Res. **49**, 793–806 (2012)

Du, R.Y., Kamakura, W.A.: Quantitative Trendspotting. J. Mark. Res. **49**, 514–536 (2012)

Durbin, J., Koopman, S.J.: Time Series Analysis by State Space Methods. Oxford University Press, Oxford (2001)

Jap, S.D., Naik, P.A.: Bidanalyzer: a method for estimation and selection of dynamic bidding models. Mark. Sci. **27**, 949–960 (2008)

Kolsarici, C., Vakratsas, D.: Category-versus brand-level advertising messages in a highly regulated environment. J. Mark. Res. **47**, 1078–1089 (2010)

Koopman, S.J.: Exact initial Kalman filtering and smoothing for nonstationary time series models. J. Am. Stat. Assoc. **92**, 1630–1638 (1997)

Liu, Y., Shankar, V.: The dynamic impact of product-harm crises on brand preference and advertising effectiveness: an empirical analysis of the automobile industry. Manag. Sci. **61**, 2514–2535 (2015)

McQuarie, A., Tsai, C.: Regression and Time Series Model Selection. World Scientific, Singapore (1998)

Naik, P.A.: Marketing dynamics: a primer on estimation and control. Foundations and Trends® in Marketing. **9**, 175–266 (2015)

Naik, P.A., Mantrala, M.K., Sawyer, A.: Planning pulsing media schedules in the presence of dynamic advertising quality. Mark. Sci. **17**, 214–235 (1998)

Naik, P.A., Raman, K.: Understanding the impact of media synergy in multimedia communications. J. Mark. Res. **40**, 375–388 (2003)

Naik, P.A., Shi, P., Tsai, C.: Extending the Akaike information criterion to mixture regression models. J. Am. Stat. Assoc. **102**, 244–254 (2007)

Nerlove, M., Arrow, K.: Optimal advertising policy under dynamic conditions. Economica. **29**, 129–142 (1962)

Osinga, E.C., Leeflang, P.S.H., Srinivasan, S., Wieringa, J.E.: Why do firms invest in consumer advertising with limited sales response? A shareholder perspective. J. Mark. **75**(1), 109–124 (2011)
Osinga, E.C., Leeflang, P.S.H., Wieringa, J.E.: Early marketing matters: a time-varying parameter approach to persistence modeling. J. Mark. Res. **47**, 173–185 (2010)
Pauwels, K.H., Currim, I., Dekimpe, M.G., Hanssens, D.M., Mizik, N., Ghysels, E., Naik, P.A.: Modeling marketing dynamics by time series econometrics. Market. Lett. **15**, 167–183 (2004)
Van Heerde, H.J., Mela, C.F., Manchanda, P.: The dynamic effect of innovation on market structure. J. Mark. Res. **41**, 166–183 (2004)
West, M., Harrison, J.: Bayesian Forecasting and Dynamic Models. Springer, New York (1997)
Xie, J.X., Song, M., Sirbu, M., Wang, Q.: Kalman filter estimation of new product diffusion models. J. Mark. Res. **34**, 378–393 (1997)

Chapter 6
Spatial Models

J. Paul Elhorst

6.1 Introduction

Since the turn of the century, the interest for spatial models in marketing science has increased significantly. An econometric model becomes spatial if the behavior of one economic agent is codetermined by the dependent variable, the explanatory variables, and/or the error term observed on other economic agents, known as respectively the spatially lagged dependent variable, spatially lagged explanatory variables, and the spatially lagged error term, or shortly spatial lags. Except for these spatial lags, the degree of codetermination also depends on the set of agents affecting the focal agent; these mutual relationships among economic agents is generally modeled by the so-called spatial weights matrix W. It should be stressed that the term spatial needs to be read here in the broadest sense of the word, since spatial models are synonymous to several alternative terminologies used in marketing science, among which social interactions, word of mouth, peer effects, neighborhood effects, contagion, imitation, network diffusion and interdependent preferences.

The aim of this chapter is to provide an overview of the rationale behind the different spatial extensions of a standard econometric model, the various descriptions and model names that are circulating in the literature, and the basics behind the matrix W. To provide a better understanding of the link between the spatial econometrics literature and marketing science, each of these extensions is illustrated by one or more marketing studies. Spatial econometric models can be estimated by different data sets and by different methods. The pros and cons of these data sets and methods are also briefly pointed out. A final aim is to discuss two

J.P. Elhorst (✉)
Department of Economics, Econometrics and Finance, University of Groningen, P.O. Box 800, Groningen 9700AV, The Netherlands
e-mail: j.p.elhorst@rug.nl

P.S.H. Leeflang et al. (eds.), *Advanced Methods for Modeling Markets*,
International Series in Quantitative Marketing, DOI 10.1007/978-3-319-53469-5_6

scientific fundamentals developed in the spatial econometrics literature that hardly got any attention up to now in the marketing literature: the concept of spillover effects and identification problems.

The setup of this chapter is as follows. Section 6.2 sets out the basic spatial econometric model. It defines and distinguishes the three types of spatial lags, it explains different methods of estimation, it discusses the strengths and weaknesses of different specifications nested within the basic spatial econometric model based on the direct and indirect (or spatial spillover) effects that can be derived from them, and finally it pays attention to identification problems. To illustrate the importance of controls for spatial lags, but also of identification problems, Sect. 6.3 provides and further works out a numerical example taken from Halleck-Vega and Elhorst (2015) based on Baltagi and Li (2004) cigarette demand model. Section 6.4 continues with four popular extensions of the basic spatial econometric model in marketing science: higher-order spatial processes, spatial panels, dynamic spatial panels, and binary choice data. The discussion of software that can be used to apply these models is integrated within the different sections.

6.2 Basic Spatial Econometric Model

6.2.1 Spatial Lags

The basic spatial econometric model is a linear regression model extended to include spatial lags. Three types of lags may be considered. The first is a spatially lagged dependent variable, which refers to the situation where the behavior of agent *A* depends on the behavior of other agents, including say agent *B*, and vice versa:

$$\text{Dependent variable } y \text{ of agent } A \leftrightarrow \text{Dependent variable } y \text{ of agent } B. \tag{6.1}$$

A spatially lagged dependent variable is typically considered as the formal specification for the equilibrium outcome of a spatial or social interaction process, in which the value of the dependent variable for one agent is jointly determined with that of neighboring agents. Pinkse et al. (2002) offer a striking example. They develop an economic-theoretical model to show that price-setting behavior of one firm depends on that of others in close proximity. In addition, they propose a method of estimating proximity that places minimal structure on the problem. Bradlow et al. (2005) describe a spatially lagged dependent variable as a spatial lag (given the similarity with a time lag in the time-series literature) based on the idea that individuals are directly affected by the known decisions of others, but this designation might be too short since spatial lags can also be taken of the explanatory variables and the error term. Studies considering a spatially lagged dependent variable will be indicated by the abbreviation "SAR" in this chapter, which stands for spatial autoregressive model.

The second type of interaction effects are spatially lagged explanatory variables; the behavior of a particular agent depends on explanatory variables observed on other agents:

$$\text{Explanatory variable } x \text{ of agent } B \rightarrow \text{Dependent variable } y \text{ of agent } A. \quad (6.2)$$

Katona et al. (2011) explain the adoption process of network membership of a country-specific social network site by variables characterizing people who already adopted this site. These variables include both demographics and characteristics that describe the adopter's network position. Bronnenberg (2005) delineates a model in which local sales depend on local promotion levels, which in turn are based on existing base-line outputs with a spatial structure, as a result of which local sales are eventually codetermined by base-line outputs in neighboring locations. Studies considering spatially lagged explanatory variables will be indicated by "SLX", which is an abbreviation for spatial lag of X.

The third type of spatial lag occurs when the error terms of different agents are jointly determined:

$$\text{Error term } u \text{ of agent } A \leftrightarrow \text{Error term } u \text{ of agent } B. \quad (6.3)$$

A spatially lagged error term does not require a theoretical model for a spatial or social interaction process, but instead, is consistent with a situation where agents (partly) share the same variables omitted from the model, and with a situation where unobserved shocks follow a spatial pattern. Bronnenberg and Mahajan (2001) are among the first considering this specification in the marketing literature, in combination with serial autocorrelation. A more recent study is of Chen et al. (2013). They investigate whether the method of sampling individuals from a larger population affects the parameter estimates of a regression model if these people are involved in a social network; is a person's attitude to a brand influenced by the attitudes of his or her friends toward the same brand, and does it matter whether the social network is large, dense or even unknown to the researcher? Studies considering a spatially lagged error term will be indicated by the abbreviation "SEM", which stands for spatial error model.

A full linear regression model capturing all types of spatial lags takes the form:

$$Y = \delta WY + \alpha \iota_N + X\beta + WX\theta + u \quad (6.4a)$$

$$u = \lambda Wu + \varepsilon \quad (6.4b)$$

where Y denotes an $N \times 1$ vector consisting of one observation on the dependent variable for every agent in the sample ($i = 1, \ldots, N$), ι_N is an $N \times 1$ vector of ones associated with the constant term parameter α, X denotes an $N \times K$ matrix of exogenous explanatory variables whose impact is measured by the corresponding $K \times 1$ vector β, and $\varepsilon = (\varepsilon_1, \ldots, \varepsilon_N)^T$ is a vector of disturbance terms. The ε_i are independently and identically distributed error terms for all i with zero mean and variance σ^2. W is a nonnegative $N \times N$ (weight) matrix describing the arrangement of the agents in the sample. A more detailed explanation follows shortly. The variable WY denotes the spatially lagged dependent variable (one spatial lag), WX the spatially lagged explanatory variables (K spatial lags), and Wu the spatially lagged error term (one spatial lags). δ is called the spatial autoregressive coefficient, λ the spatial autocorrelation coefficient, while θ, just as β, represents a $K \times 1$ vector of fixed but unknown parameters. Summing up, a total of $K + 2$ spatial lags is possible. Table 6.1 gives an overview of all spatial econometric models with different combinations of spatial lags that have been considered in the spatial econometrics literature, including their designations and abbreviations.

Table 6.2 provides an overview of 29 marketing studies based on spatial econometric models. These studies are selected by systematically searching the main marketing journals. Based on references made in these studies, this list was further extended to include other relevant studies. We also made use of Bradlow et al. (2005), Bronnenberg (2005) and Hartmann et al. (2008), who are among the first to review spatial models in marketing science on a wider scale. Table 6.2 shows that most marketing studies focus on SAR, SEM or SLX models with only one type of spatial lag: *WY*, *Wu* or *WX*. Exceptions are Aral and Walker (2011) who combine the spatially lagged dependent variable *WY* with the spatially lagged error term *Wu*, Yang et al. (2006) who combine spatially lagged explanatory variables *WX* with the spatially lagged error term *Wu*, and Nair et al. (2010) who combine the spatially lagged dependent and the spatially lagged explanatory variables *WY* and *WX* with the spatially lagged error term *Wu*. In the spatial econometrics literature these combinations are better known as respectively the SAC, SDEM and GNS model, as reported in Table 6.1.

The study of Nair et al. (2010) is exceptional since it is one of the few studies, both in Table 6.2 and in the spatial econometrics literature, considering all types of spatial lags. Elhorst (2014), who analyzes this model in more detail, explains why. The main reason is overfitting. Even though the parameters of these spatial lags are formally identified, they have the tendency either to blow each other up or to become insignificant due to overlap, similar as to multicollinearity, as a result of which this

Table 6.1 Spatial econometric models with different combinations of spatial lags

Type of model	Type(s) of spatial lag(s)
SAR, spatial autoregressive model or spatial lag model	*WY*
SEM, spatial error model	*Wu*
SLX, spatial lag of X model	*WX*
SAC, spatial autoregressive combined model, also known as SARAR or Clifford model	*WY*, *Wu*
SDM, spatial Durbin model	*WY*, *WX*
SDEM, spatial Durbin error model	*WX*, *Wu*
GNS, general spatial nesting model	*WY*, *WX*, *Wu*

Table 6.2 Overview of marketing studies using spatial modeling techniques

(1) Study	(2) Econometric model	(3) W	(4) Data	(5) Estimation method
Zhang et al. (2015)	SEM–COV	ED, estimated	Cross-sectional	Lasso/ML
Verhelst and Van den Poel (2014)	Dynamic SAR	BC	Panel, CFE + TFE	Bias corrected ML
Haenlein (2013)	0/1 lagged SAR	BC	Cross-sectional	ML
Chen et al. (2013)	SEM	BC	Cross-sectional	ML
Bollinger and Gillingham (2012)	Dynamic lagged SAR	Group interaction	Panel, CFE + TFE + CFE*TFE	OLS/FD
Aravindakshan et al. (2012)	Dynamic lagged SAR, serial autocorrelation	BC	Panel, spatial heterogeneous	ML
Du and Kamakura (2011)	0/1 second order lagged SAR	q-nearest neighbors, non-q-nearest neighbors	Panel, CRE (higher level)	ML
Katona et al. (2011)	0/1 SLX	"BC"	Panel, CRE	ML
Iyengar et al. (2011)	0/1 lagged SAR	BC	Panel, TFE	ML
Aral and Walker (2011)	0/1 lagged SAC–COV	BC	Cross-sectional	ML
Choi et al. (2010)	Second-order lagged SAR	ED, demographic	Panel, time heterogeneous	Bayesian
Nair et al. (2010)	GNS	Leader, group interaction	Panel, CFE + TFE	2SLS/IV
Hartmann (2010)	0/1 lagged SAR	BC	Cross-sectional	Bayesian
Korniotis (2010)	Dynamic lagged SAR	Distance, urbanization, group interaction	Panel, CFE	Bias corrected ML
Bezawada et al. (2009)	Third-order SEM–COV (different levels)	Placement in store	Panel, pooled	Bayesian
Albuquerque et al. (2007)	Third-order lagged SAR	Distance, trade, culture	Panel, spatial heterogeneous	Bayesian
Bell and Song (2007)	0/1 lagged SAR	BC	Panel, CFE (higher level)	Not specified
Jank and Kannan (2006)	0/1 SEM–COV	ED, estimated	Panel, pooled	EM

(continued)

Table 6.2 (continued)

(1) Study	(2) Econometric model	(3) W	(4) Data	(5) Estimation method
Yang et al. (2006)	0/1 SDEM	BC, estimated	Panel, pooled	Bayesian
Bronnenberg (2005)	Dynamic lagged SAR SEM, SLX	Exogenous	Cross-sectional, pooled	Focus on ML
Jank and Kannan (2005)	0/1 SEM–COV	Matérn family—distance, estimated	Panel, pooled, product heterogeneous	EM
Bradlow et al. (2005)	SAR, SEM	Geo, demo and psychometric	Cross-sectional, pooled	Focus on ML
Van Dijk et al. (2004)	SEM	BC	Cross-sectional, Panel CFE	ML
Bronnenberg and Mela (2004)	0/1 second order lagged SAR	BC	Panel, CRE	Bayesian
Yang and Allenby (2003)	0/1 second order lagged SEM	Geographic, demographic	Cross-sectional	Bayesian
Pinkse et al. (2002)	SAR	Estimated, distance-dependent	Cross-sectional	2SLS
Ter Hofstede et al. (2002)	SEM–COV	Spatial clustering	Cross-sectional	Bayesian
Bronnenberg and Sismeiro (2002)	SEM–COV, serial autocorrelation	Estimated, distance-dependent	Panel, CFE	Bayesian
Bronnenberg and Mahajan (2001)	SEM, serial autocorrelation	BC	Panel, CRE/RCM	ML

Note: Explanation of terminology in main text

model does not help to test for simpler models with a smaller number of spatial lags. Another reason is related to the specification of W, but before explaining this, this matrix needs to be spelled out in more detail.

W symbolizes a nonnegative $N \times N$ matrix describing the arrangement of the agents in the sample:

$$W = \begin{pmatrix} 0 & w_{12} & . & w_{1N} \\ w_{21} & 0 & . & w_{2N} \\ . & . & . & . \\ w_{N1} & w_{N2} & . & 0 \end{pmatrix}. \tag{6.5}$$

In most studies W is specified as a matrix of known constants with zero diagonal elements, since an agent cannot affect itself or cannot be viewed as its own neighbor. A non-zero off-diagonal element in row i and column j indicates that agent i is affected by agent j, and a zero element that agent i is not. In addition, most studies use a distance metric to specify its elements: (1) p-order binary contiguity (BC) matrices (if $p = 1$ only first-order neighbors are included, if $p = 2$ first and second order neighbors are considered, and so on); (2) inverse distance (ID) or exponential distance (ED) decay matrices (with or without a cut-off point); (3) q-nearest neighbor matrices (where q is a positive integer); (4) block diagonal or group interaction matrices where each block represents a group of agents that interact with each other but not with agents belonging to other groups. Column (3) of Table 6.2 shows that BC matrices are the most popular; 13 of the 29 studies adopt this specification. Distance decay matrices are considered in seven studies, while only two studies consider a group interaction matrix, and just one a q-nearest neighbor matrix. Finally, many studies initially assume that the spatial weight matrix is different for different spatial lags, i.e., W_l for $l = 1, \ldots, K+2$, but eventually they impose the restriction $W_1 = \cdots = W_{K+2}$ in their Monte Carlo simulation experiment(s) or their empirical analysis. However, when the same specification of W is used for all spatial lags, the overlap between them might increase, which is the second explanation for overfitting in the GNS model. The study of Nair et al. (2010) is again exceptional, since they do consider different spatial weights matrices.

Nair et al.'s model consists of two equations. The first equation explains prescription behavior of general practitioner physicians. They assume that there is a group of opinion leaders, i.e., specialist physicians organized around specific disease conditions and therapeutic treatment options (Hartmann et al. 2008, p. 94), who affect the prescription behavior of their colleagues, but not vice versa. This setup of the spatial weights is different from that in Eq. (6.1) and known as a leader matrix. It is important that Nair et al. (2010) consider several leaders. If everybody would follow one common leader, one column of W would exist of $N - 1$ ones only (except the diagonal element), which consequently is not uniformly bounded if N, representing the number of physicians, goes to infinity. Uniformly boundedness of the rows and columns of W is one of the pre-conditions to get consistent parameter estimates (Kelejian and Prucha 1998, 1999; Lee 2004). However, by assuming that there are numerous leaders and that every leader is followed by a limited number of individuals this condition is satisfied again.

In the second equation of their model, Nair et al. (2010) pose that the prescription behavior of opinion leader j of physician i is affected by the mean prescription behavior of all other physicians operating in physician's i zip code. In other words, the mutual relationship denoted in (6.1) is restored: opinion leaders affect physicians and physicians affect opinion leaders, though in a different and thus asymmetric way. In addition, they add the mean value of explanatory variables D (calculated over each zip code), which are part of their first equation, to the second equation in their study. This variable can therefore be seen as a spatially lagged explanatory variable. Although not obvious from their mathematical formulation, this implies that Nair et al. (2010) adopt a generalized spatial nesting (GNS) type of model. The reason why it is not obvious is because they specify two rather than one equation and use two different symbols rather than one for the same type of behavior (y for the prescription behavior of practitioner physicians and x for that of specialist physicians). It should be clear, however, that their model may be reformulated as a single equation model, as in (6.4), with an asymmetric spatial weights matrix W, where practitioner physicians follow their leaders and these leaders respond to practitioners operating in certain zip code areas.

The fact that distance metrics are so popular in setting up spatial weights matrices does not imply that it is necessarily the best choice. Spatial econometrics originated from regional science, which explains the emphasis on distance, but in principle W can take any form to model mutual relationships between agents, dependent on the type of discipline. Rather than a geographic map, Bradlow et al. (2005) point out that W may also be based on a demographic or psychometric map to describe the relationships among agents. Choi et al. (2010) investigate imitation behavior and pose that the likelihood of imitation is greater among agents who are similar, where similarity is measured by demographic characteristics (education, age, ethnicity and income). Comparable demographic characteristics are used in Yang and Allenby (2003) to analyze automobile purchases. Van Dijk et al. (2004) posit that the sales of a brand in a particular store depend on its shelf space. One of the approaches suggested in their paper to deal with potential endogeneity of this explanatory variable, is to filter out a common observable, which takes the form of a spatial error model (SEM) in which W is based on a set of household and competitor characteristics of the store. Other studies using non-spatial measures are of Korniotis (2010) and Albuquerque et al. (2007). Perhaps the most advanced approach is of Ter Hofstede et al. (2002). They assume that consumers are nested within regions and that regions are nested within clusters (in their study called segments). Each cluster of regions has its own regression parameters. They develop a method to determine to which cluster each region belongs. The method has similarities with the group interaction matrix, the difference being that the regions belonging to each group are not necessarily contiguous and that the group composition is determined endogenously. The authors cluster the regions based on culture, geodemographic, and lifestyle variables and point out that in this respect it is more likely that Paris,

New York, and Tokyo form a cluster than a set of adjacent regions. To further stress this, they also account for a spatial lag among the error terms, thereby investigating which cluster concept outperforms others: spatial independence, binary contiguity, groups consisting of regions within countries, or their more general proposed clustering of regions.

Instead of estimating the degree of interaction among the error terms of different agents by one parameter λ, as in (6.4b), one can also estimate the full N by N covariance matrix. In the first case the covariance matrix takes the form $\sigma^2[(I - \lambda W)^T(I - \lambda W)]^{-1}$, which in addition to σ^2 requires the estimation of one common parameter, while in the second case the covariance matrix becomes $\sigma^2\Sigma$, where $\Sigma = [\sigma_{ij}]$. Since the covariance matrix is symmetric, this requires the estimation of $1/2N(N + 1)$ parameters. It is obvious that the latter approach is only possible when N is small, as a result of which it is hardly used. An alternative is to join homogeneous agents within groups. Froot (1989) suggests this approach in the accounting and finance literature in order to deal with cross-sectional time series data of firms. In addition, one can choose between spatial dependence among the observations within groups (as in Froot 1989), or spatial dependence between groups. Let P denote the number of groups and N_p $(p = 1,\ldots,P)$ the number of agents in each group, so that $\Sigma_p N_p = N$. Then, the number of parameters for spatial dependence within groups in the spatial error model reduces to $\Sigma_p ½N_p(N_p + 1)$. In the case of spatial dependence between groups, the number of parameters reduces to $½P(P + 1)$. One example is Aral and Walker (2011). They consider three groups of people and estimate the elements of the covariance matrix $\Sigma = [\sigma_{ij}]$ based on the error terms within these groups. Studies such as Aral and Walker (2011) in which the covariance matrix is estimated, seven in total, are indicated by the term "COV" in column (2) of Table 6.2.

Except for pre-specifying the matrix W, the extent of distance decay can also be estimated by parameterizing its elements. Zhang et al. (2015) model the elements of the covariance matrix between different brands in different markets by an exponential distance decay matrix based on a limited set of additional parameters. Jank and Kannan (2005) follow a similar approach but adopt a more flexible correlation function taken from the so-called Matérn family of which the exponential distance decay function is a special case. These and other studies directly parameterizing the variance-covariance matrix are indicated by the term "estimated" in column (3) of Table 6.2. As pointed out by Anselin (2003), one problem overlooked in these studies is that the null hypothesis of no spatial autocorrelation does not correspond to an interior point of the parameter space, which is one of the regular pre-conditions specified in Kelejian and Prucha (1998, 1999) and Lee (2004) for commonly used estimators (GMM and ML, respectively) to be consistent. For example, if the elements of W are parameterized by an exponential distance decay function $w_{ij} = \exp(-\gamma d_{ij})$, where d_{ij} measures the mutual distance between agents i and j, there is no interior point for γ such that $w_{ij} = 0$, as a result of which one cannot test whether this spatial model is significantly different from a non-spatial model and thus whether considering a simpler model without a spatial lag among the error terms suffices. This problem does not occur when adopting the basic spatial econometric model in (6.4b), since the existence of a spatial lag in this model can be tested by the hypothesis H_0: $\lambda = 0$.

6.2.2 Estimation

Spatial econometric models can be estimated by maximum likelihood (ML), quasi-maximum likelihood (QML), instrumental variables (IV), generalized method of moments (GMM) or by Bayesian Markov Chain Monte Carlo methods (Bayesian MCMC, Chap. 16). Ord (1975) was among the first to consider the log-likelihood function of the SAR and SEM models for cross-sectional data. The log-likelihood of the model in (6.4a) and (6.4b) takes the form:

$$L(\kappa) = -\frac{N}{2}\ln\left(2\pi\sigma^2\right) + \ln\|I - \delta W\| + \ln\|I - \lambda W\| - \frac{1}{2\sigma^2}e^T e \tag{6.6}$$

where $\kappa = (\delta, \alpha, \beta^T, \theta^T, \lambda, \sigma^2)^T$, $e = Y - \delta WY - \alpha\iota_N - X\beta - WX\theta$, I, W, Y and X are matrices and e, ι_N, β and θ are vectors. The error terms are assumed to be normally distributed. The log-likelihood functions of simpler models as specified in Table 6.1 are obtained by setting the corresponding parameters to zero. It is especially the term $\ln\|I - \delta W\|$ that has led to a lot of discussion and contributions to the spatial econometrics literature. To understand this term, we consider the reduced form of Eqs. (6.4a) and (6.4b), which yields:

$$Y = (I - \delta W)^{-1}\left(\alpha\iota_N + X\beta + WX\theta + [I - \lambda W]^{-1}\varepsilon\right). \tag{6.7}$$

This equation demonstrates that $\ln\|I - \delta W\|$ represents the Jacobian term of the transformation from ε to Y taking into account the endogeneity of WY, the fact that according to (6.1) the dependent variables of different agents affect each other mutually. Ignoring this Jacobian term causes biased coefficients estimates. In the past, some studies carried out the matrix multiplication of the $N \times N$ matrix W and the $N \times 1$ vector Y in advance, storing the resulting $N \times 1$ vector in a database together with the X variables, so as to be able to read in the data in a regular econometric computer software program and to estimate the model by OLS. This method is known as spatial OLS, but should be discouraged since it ignores the endogeneity of WY.

The Jacobian term $\ln\|I - \delta W\|$ is important because it also determines the interval on which the spatial autoregressive parameter δ is defined. Ord (1975) shows that the Jacobian term can be calculated by $\ln\|I - \delta W\| = \Sigma_i \ln(1 - \delta\omega_i)$, where ω_i $(i = 1, \ldots, N)$ denote the characteristic roots of W. Since the natural log is not defined if its argument is zero or negative, it follows that $1/\omega_{\min} < \delta < 1/\omega_{\max}$, where $\omega_{\min}$ denotes the smallest (i.e. most negative) and $\omega_{\max}$ the largest real characteristic root of W. Generally, W is normalized such that its largest root equals unity, as a result of which the interval becomes $1/\omega_{\min} < \delta < 1$. If W happens to be asymmetric, it may have complex characteristic roots. LeSage and Pace (2009, pp. 88–89) demonstrate that in that case δ is an interior point of the interval $(1/r_{\min}, 1)$, where $r_{\min}$ equals the most negative purely real characteristic root of W.

To estimate the parameters of the spatial econometric model in (6.4a) and (6.4b), or one of its counterparts in Table 6.2, two-step or iterative procedures have been developed in which β, θ and σ^2, given δ and λ, and vice versa, are alternately estimated until convergence occurs. This is because β, θ and σ^2 can be solved analytically from their first-order maximizing conditions, whereas δ and/or λ cannot and thus need to be determined numerically. These procedures are well described in Anselin (1988) and LeSage and Pace (2009) for cross-sectional data, and in Elhorst (2010, 2014) and Lee and Yu (2010) for panel data.

In addition to the likelihood function of a spatial econometric model, the Bayesian methodology also considers prior distributions of the model parameters, capturing the prior beliefs of the researcher about these parameters, and the posterior distribution, summarizing all of the available information by multiplying the likelihood function of the model by the prior distributions of its parameters. An introduction of the Bayesian methodology to spatial econometric modeling and estimation for cross-sectional data is provided by LeSage and Pace (2009), Chap. 5, and for panel data by LeSage (2014). The main strength of the Bayesian approach is that it offers the Bayesian posterior model probability as an additional criterion to select models. Whereas tests for significant differences between log-likelihood function values, such as the LR-test, can formally not be used if models are non-nested (for example, if based on different spatial weights matrices), Bayesian posterior model probabilities do not require nested models to carry out these comparisons. The basic idea is to set prior probabilities equal to $1/S$, making each model equally likely a priori, to estimate each model by Bayesian methods, and then to compute posterior probabilities based on the data and the estimation results of this set of S models.

One huge computational problem is the storage of the $N \times N$ spatial weights matrix W and matrix manipulations involving W, notably the calculation of the Jacobian term $\ln||I - \delta W||$ and the inversion of the matrix $(I - \delta W)$ if N grows large, partly because numerical procedures are needed to determine δ and λ. This is also the reason why many commercial econometrics software packages do not offer any facilities to estimate spatial econometric models. The interested researcher has to turn to Stata, GeoDa, R or Matlab, since only these computer programs offer the opportunity to work with so-called sparse matrix algorithms and so do not require the storage of the whole W matrix. Suppose a researcher has a medium-sized data set of 1000 observations. This problem already requires 1,000,000 memory places if the full matrix W would be stored. However, often no more than 5% of its elements are non-zero, for example, since the matrix is based on the first-order binary contiguity principle. In the previous section we saw that it concerns 13 of the 29 studies reported in Table 6.2. From a computational viewpoint, it is much more efficient to store the non-zero elements only, in the mentioned example 50,000 of the 1,000,000 elements, since this will speed up computation time considerably.

These computational difficulties was one of the reasons for Kelejian and Prucha (1998, 1999) to develop IV/GMM estimators (see Chap. 15). Instead of accounting for the Jacobian term $\ln||I - \delta W||$ in the log-likelihood function, the endogenous regressor *WY* may also be instrumented. The advantages are that the Jacobian term no longer needs to be determined, that *WY* may be determined in advance, see the explanation above, and that commercial econometric software packages may be used again. As instruments Kelejian et al. (2004) suggest $[X \ \ WX \ \ \cdots \ \ W^g X]$, where g is a pre-selected constant that needs to be at least one if *WX* (SAR specification) is excluded and two if included (SDM specification). Gibbons and Overman (2012), however, point out that a weak instrumental problem might occur in the latter case. Not many spatial econometric studies provide test results to show that these instruments are relevant, exogenous and have no explanatory power in the model itself. In the marketing literature this topic did not receive much attention either, but this is because only a fraction of all studies recorded in Table 6.2 employed IV/GMM estimators. Pinkse et al. (2002) is one exception. One explanation for the moderate interest in this estimator might be that another awkward side effect of not utilizing the Jacobian term $\ln||I - \delta W||$ is the possibility of ending up with a coefficient estimate for δ outside its parameter space and thus a model that is unstable.

The ML, Bayesian, as well as the IV/GMM estimator is based on the assumption that the disturbances ε_i are independently and identically distributed for all i with zero mean and variance σ^2 (Chaps. 15 and 16). The difference is that the ML and Bayesian estimators also require that the error terms are normally distributed, whereas the IV/GMM estimator does not, which is often argued to be an advantage. However, Lee (2004) proves that the normality assumption when applying ML can be dropped if the first four moments are available. He designates this estimation procedure quasi-ML (QML). In practice, however, this procedure is hardly used.

The decision which estimator to use gets more complicated if in addition to *WY* also some of the explanatory variables are endogenous. Since IV is the primary goal to deal with the endogeneity of *WY*, the IV/GMM also seems to be the proper estimation method to deal with endogeneity of other regressors. For this reason, it is widely used in the spatial econometrics literature. In this case, the set of instruments must be limited to $[X^{\text{ex}} \ \ WX^{\text{ex}} \ \ \cdots \ \ W^d X^{\text{ex}}]$, where "ex" denotes the *X* variables that are exogenous. In addition, this set should be used to instrument the additional endogenous explanatory variables, X^{end} and WX^{end}, where "end" denotes the variables that are endogenous. If the number of instruments is too small or if these instruments suffer from a weak instrument problem, the instrument set should be augmented by other exogenous variables expected to be part of the reduced form of the system, as recently pointed out in an overview paper of Drukker et al. (2013) on the IV/GMM estimator. Notwithstanding the preference for the IV/GMM estimator in the spatial econometrics literature, Murphy and Topel (1985) already proved mathematically in the 1980s that IV estimation of potential endogenous regressors in the first stage, in this case of X^{end} and WX^{end}, and ML estimation of the estimation equation in the second stage, using the predicted values of X^{end} and WX^{end}, is another possibility. In this case, ML estimation in the second stage can be used to account for the additional endogeneity of WY. Since for one reason or another this alternative ML approach became forgotten, it is an interesting topic for further research.

6.2.3 Direct, Indirect and Spatial Spillover Effects

If the spatial econometric model in (6.4a) and (6.4b) is rewritten to its reduced form (6.7), the matrix of partial derivatives of the expectation of Y, E(Y), with respect to the kth explanatory variable of X in unit 1 up to unit N can be seen to be an $N \times N$ matrix:

$$\begin{bmatrix} \frac{\partial \mathrm{E}(Y)}{\partial x_{1k}} & \cdots & \frac{\partial \mathrm{E}(Y)}{\partial x_{Nk}} \end{bmatrix} = (I - \delta W)^{-1} \left[\beta_k I_N + \theta_k W \right] \tag{6.8}$$

whose diagonal elements represent the impact on the dependent variable of unit 1 up to N if the kth explanatory variable of the own agent changes, while its off-diagonal elements represent the impact on the dependent variable if the kth explanatory variable of other agents change. The error term drops out due to taking expectations. LeSage and Pace (2009) define the direct effect as the average diagonal element of the full N by N matrix expression on the right-hand side of (6.8), and the indirect effect as the average row or column sums of the off-diagonal elements of that matrix expression. A more appealing synonym for the indirect effect is spatial spillover effect, a term that will mainly be used in the remainder of this chapter.

These spillover effects can be further subdivided into local and global ones. Local spillovers occur when $\delta = 0$, $\theta \neq 0$, and agents are connected to each other. If two agents i and j are unconnected, i.e., if $w_{ij} = 0$, a change in X of agent i cannot affect the dependent variable of agent j, and vice versa. By contrast, global spillovers occur when $\delta \neq 0$ and $\theta = 0$, no matter whether agents are connected or unconnected. This is because a change in X of any agent i due to the spatial multiplier matrix $(I - \delta W)^{-1}$ is transmitted to all other agents, also if $w_{ij} \neq 0$. Unfortunately, it is not possible to decompose spatial spillover effects in local and global effects if both δ and θ are nonzero. Finally, it should be stressed that the choice between local and global spillovers is also related to the specification of W. A spatial weights matrix that is sparse—a matrix in which only a limited number of elements is non-zero, such as a binary contiguity matrix—is more likely to occur in combination with a global spillover model ($\delta \neq 0$), whereas a spatial weights matrix that is dense—a matrix in which all off-diagonal elements are non-zero, such as an inverse distance matrix—is more likely to occur in combination with a local spillover model ($\delta = 0$, $\theta \neq 0$).

One limitation of the SAR, SAC and SDM models is that the spillover effects are global by construction ($\delta \neq 0$), while global spillovers are often more difficult to justify than local spillovers (see Halleck-Vega and Elhorst 2015; and the references therein). In this respect, the SLX and SDEM models whose spillover effects are local ($\delta = 0, \theta \neq 0$) and simply defined by the coefficient estimates θ, are generally overlooked. Table 6.2 counts only two of these studies: Katona et al. (2011) and Yang et al. (2006). Another limitation of the SAR and SAC models is that the ratio between the spillover effect and direct effect is the same for every explanatory variable. If $\theta = 0$ the β_k in the numerator and the β_k in the denominator of this ratio cancel each other out, which implies that the magnitude of this ratio only depends on the spatial autoregressive parameter δ and the specification of the spatial weights matrix W. In many empirical applications, this is not very likely. One limitation of the SEM model is that the spillover effects are zero by construction ($\delta = 0, \theta = 0$). The direct effect, i.e. the effect of a change to a particular explanatory variable of one agent on the dependent variable of that agent, is the only information provided.

Generally, it is harder to find empirical evidence in favor of significant spillovers than in favor of significant spatial lags. This is because the former depend on three parameters (δ, β_k, θ_k), among which two parameters that correspond to spatial lags. If already one of these three parameters happens to be insignificant, the spillover effect might become insignificant too. For this reason, empirical studies tend to find only a fraction of their K explanatory variables to produce significant spillover effects. In contrast to general belief, this is not a weakness of these studies, but a validation that the hypothesis that a change to one of the determinants of an agent affects the dependent variable of other agents is a strong one.

6.2.4 *Identification Problems*

By far the biggest problem when analyzing spatial econometric problems is the research strategy to find out whether WY, WX, Wu or a combination of these spatial interaction effects need to be included and to choose between different specifications of W, especially if no reference is made to specific economic theories. Consequently, too many empirical studies follow a statistical approach driven by data-analytic considerations and only consider the SAR and/or SEM model with one type of spatial lag. Moreover, many of these studies are further limited to one or a few pre-specified W matrices. Stakhovych and Bijmolt (2009), for example, find that first-order binary contiguity matrices perform better in detecting the true model than other spatial weights matrices, but they only test the SAR and SEM specifications against each other.

A minority of empirical studies go a step further by considering the SAC and SDM models with two types of spatial lags, but again based on one or a few pre-specified W matrices. If these studies already provide a well-founded background for certain spatial lags, they often lack guidance of how the spatial weights matrix should be specified. Most often, spatial weights matrices are used whose appeal seems to lie in the frequency of their use. For these reasons many empirical studies, including many of the marketing studies recorded in Table 6.2, can easily be criticized, such as in the special theme issue of the Journal of Regional Science

(Vol. 52, Issue 2); see Partridge et al. (2012) for an overview of the contributing papers. Up to now, the spatial econometrics literature offers two solutions.

According to Halleck-Vega and Elhorst (2015), the SLX model can be best taken as point of departure when an underlying theory is lacking. The first reason is that it represents the simplest spatial econometric model producing flexible spatial spillover effects. According to the previous section, the SAR, SAC and SEM models are of limited use in empirical research due to initial restrictions on the spillover effects they can potentially produce. By contrast, the spillover effects produced by the SLX, SDM and SDEM models can take any value. Since both SDM and SDEM are extensions of the SLX model, the latter is the simplest one of this family of models. The second reason is that in contrast to other spatial econometric models, the spatial weights matrix W in the SLX model can be parameterized. Suppose a researcher wants to use a simple parametric approach applied to the elements of an inverse distance matrix $w_{ij} = 1/d_{ij}^{\gamma}$, where d_{ij} measures the mutual distance between agents i and j, and γ is a parameter to be estimated, so as to obtain more information on the strength of interdependencies among the cross-sectional observations at each point in time t, rather than to impose one of the popular pre-specified matrices discussed in Sect. 6.2.1 in advance. A nonlinear estimation technique can then be used to estimate the parameters of the SLX model. The larger the distance parameter γ, the smaller the impact of observations at distant locations. An obstacle to parameterizing the W in models with a spatial lag in the dependent variable and/or the error term instead of the explanatory variables is the perfect solution problem (see Halleck-Vega and Elhorst 2015, for details). A final advantage of the SLX model over other spatial econometric models is that nonspatial econometric techniques can be used to test for endogeneity among the explanatory variables. The attention for endogenous regressors (other than the spatial lag WY_t) is important since researchers face uncertainty about the endogeneity not only of the explanatory variables X_t themselves, but also of their spatial lags WX_t (see next section).

The second solution is offered by LeSage (2014), who demonstrates that a Bayesian comparison approach considerably simplifies the task of selecting an appropriate model and appropriate spatial weights matrix simultaneously. He posits that there are only two spatial econometric models that need to be considered: the spatial Durbin model (SDM) and the spatial Durbin error model (SDEM). The first model implies that spillover effects are global and the second that they are local. His Bayesian comparison approach then determines Bayesian posterior model probabilities of these two model specifications in combination with different specifications of the W matrix, such that the combination with the highest probability may be considered the best performing one.

6.3 Example: Cigarette Demand and the Bootlegging Effect

To illustrate the importance of controlling for spatial lags, but also the identification problems set out in the previous section, we take and further work out a numerical example from Halleck-Vega and Elhorst (2015) based on Baltagi and Li (2004) cigarette demand model. In this model, which is used more often for illustration purposes in the spatial econometrics literature, real per capita sales of cigarettes (S_{it}, i denotes one of 48 U.S. states, and $t = 1963, \ldots, 1992$) is regressed on the average retail price of a pack of cigarettes (p_{it}) and real per capita disposable income (I_{it}). In addition, variables are in logs. This rather basic equation can be obtained from maximizing a utility function depending on cigarettes and other consumer goods subject to a budget constraint (Chintagunta and Nair 2011). The model is aggregated over individuals since the objective is to explain sales in a particular state. If the purpose would be to model individual behavior (e.g., the reduction in the number of smokers or teenage smoking behavior) then this is better studied using micro data. Blundell and Stoker (2007) provide a review and propositions to bridge the gap between micro and macro level research and point out that both approaches have a role to play. We use state-level data mainly due to our illustration purposes. Spatial and time fixed effects are controlled for based on test results in Elhorst (2014, p. 63).

The reason to consider this data set is because consumers may be expected to purchase cigarettes in nearby states, both legally and illegally, if there is a price advantage, known as the bootlegging effect. A popular approach to test for this is to specify W as a binary contiguity matrix, whose elements are 1 if two states share a common border and 0 if they do not (before W is row-normalized), and to estimate a spatial autoregressive model with WY. However, there are two objections to this approach. First, this would imply that consumption in one state is directly affected by consumption in another state. This is difficult to justify, just because it is expected that the change in consumption behavior is caused by a price change. To test for this, one better considers a spatial lag of the price of cigarettes (WX). Furthermore, when controlling for WY rather than WX the spillover effects will be global, which would mean that a change in price in a particular state potentially impacts consumption in all states, including distant states that according to W are unconnected. Second, one better employs a simple parametric approach applied to the elements of an inverse distance matrix $w_{ij} = 1/d_{ij}{}^{\gamma}$, where d_{ij} measures the distance between state capitals and γ is a parameter to be estimated, so as to obtain more information on the strength of connectedness among states, including states that do not share a common border.

Table 6.3 reports the estimation results when taking the SLX model as point of departure. The first column gives the estimation results when using the binary contiguity matrix, the second column when using the inverse distance with the distance decay parameter γ set equal to one in advance, and the third column when the distance decay parameter is estimated. Remarkably, whereas the price spillover effect is negative and strongly significant when adopting the binary contiguity matrix, it becomes insignificant when adopting the inverse distance matrix, and it changes sign, becomes significant and, above all, consistent with the bootlegging effect hypothesis when the distance decay parameter is estimated. The estimate of this distance decay parameter amounts to 2.938 and is also significant. This makes sense because only people living near the border of a state are able to benefit from lower prices in a neighboring state on a daily or weekly basis. If the distance decay effect at 5 miles from the border is set to 1, it falls to 0.130 at 10 miles, 0.040 at 15 miles, and 0.017 at 20 miles. People living further from the border can thus

Table 6.3 SLX model estimation results explaining cigarette demand and the parameterization of W

	BC	ID ($\gamma = 1$)	ID	ID + $\lambda W_{BC}u$	2SLS
Price	−1.017 (−24.77)[a]	−1.013 (−25.28)	−0.908 (−24.43)	−0.902 (−24.22)	−1.246 (−16.32)
Income	0.608 (10.38)	0.658 (13.73)	0.654 (15.39)	0.645 (14.70)	0.591 (13.34)
$W \times$ Price	−0.220 (−2.95)	−0.021 (−0.34)	0.254 (3.08)	0.298 (3.94)	0.192 (3.00)
$W \times$ Income	−0.219 (−2.80)	−0.314 (−6.63)	−0.815 (−4.76)	−0.819 (−6.57)	−0.750 (−14.14)
$W_{BC}u$				0.164 (4.58)	
γ			2.938 (16.48)	2.904 (21.36)	3.141 (11.11)
R^2	0.897	0.899	0.916	0.916	0.484
Log$L$	1668.4	1689.8	1812.9	1819.2	
Prob. SDM	0.7266	0.0000	0.0000		
Prob. SDEM	0.2734	1.0000	1.0000		

[a] t-statistics in parentheses; coefficient estimates of WX variables in the SLX represent spillover effects

only benefit from lower prices if they visit states for other purposes or if smuggling takes place by trucks over longer distances. It are these results which explain why the parameterized inverse distance matrix gives a much better fit than the binary contiguity matrix; the degree of spatial interaction among states on shorter distances falls much faster and on longer distances more gradually than according to the binary contiguity principle. This is corroborated by the R^2, which increases respectively from 0.897 to 0.899 and to 0.916, and the log-likelihood function value, which increases from 1668.2 to 1689.8 and to 1812.9.

Turning to the income spillover effects in Table 6.3, the estimates are negative and highly significant across all different functional forms. The main difference is that under the third column, the estimate is higher. These results indicate that increases in own-state per capita income decrease cigarette sales in neighboring states. An explanation is that higher income levels reduce the necessity or incentive to purchase less expensive cigarettes elsewhere. In sum, not testing for the best specification of the spatial weights matrix may lead to wrong inferences.

Table 6.3 also reports the results of LeSage (2014) Bayesian comparison approach to investigate statistically whether a local spillover model specification is more likely than a global one. The global spillover specification (SDM) seems to be more likely than the local one when adopting the rejected binary contiguity specification of the spatial weights matrix; the corresponding Bayesian posterior model probabilities of this sparse matrix amount to 0.73 and 0.27, respectively. Conversely, when the pre-specified or parameterized inverse distance is adopted, a dense matrix, this proportion changes into 0 to 1. This indicates that the local spillover specification outperforms the global one not only from a theoretical, but also from a statistical viewpoint.

Due to this evidence in favor of SDEM, the SLX model is re-estimated in the fourth column of Table 6.3 extended to include a spatial lag among the error terms, though with a different matrix than the parameterized inverse distance matrix used to model the spatial lags in the explanatory variables. The main reason to adopt a different matrix is methodological. Potentially, the spatial weight matrix (W) used to model the spatial lags in the explanatory variables might still be different from the true matrix (W^*). If so, the misspecification in these spatial lags $(W - W^*)X$ is transmitted to the error term specification, as a result of which it loses its property of being distributed with $\mathrm{Var}(\varepsilon) = \sigma^2 I$. Instead, the error term specification will follow a spatial autoregressive process with spatial weights matrix V different from W and $\mathrm{Var}(u) = \sigma^2[(I - \lambda V)^T(I - \lambda V)]^{-1}$. A Hausman test based on Pace and LeSage (2009, Sect. 3.3.1) can be used for comparing SLX and SDEM estimates. Using $V = W_{\mathrm{BC}}$, we find that this test statistic amounts to 0.9267, which follows a chi-squared distribution with 4 degrees of freedom equal to the number of regression parameters under test. The corresponding p-value is 0.9207. Since the Hausman test whether the SLX and SDEM estimates are the same cannot be rejected, but the spatial autocorrelation coefficient nonetheless appears to be significant (0.164 with t-value 4.58), the conclusion must be that the SDEM re-specification of the SLX model leads (at the very most) to an efficiency gain.

A final issue is whether or not cigarette prices are endogenous. For this purpose, the Hausman test for endogeneity in combination with tests for the validity of the instruments are performed, namely to assess if they satisfied the relevance and exogeneity criterions. As instrumental variables the cigarette excise tax rate, state compensation per employee in neighboring states, and income and income in neighboring states (the latter two which are already part of the SLX model) are used. Details can be found in Halleck-Vega and Elhorst (2015), who find that the price of cigarettes observed in neighboring states may be used as an exogenous determinant of cigarette demand in the U.S., whereas the price of cigarettes observed in the own state may not. Apparently, consumption has feedback effects on the price in the own state, but if consumers decide to buy more cigarettes in neighboring states due to a price increase in their own state this has no significant feedback effects on prices there too.

In conclusion, we may say that a significant price spillover effect of 0.254 is found when using the SLX model with a parameterized inverse distance matrix, of 0.298 when using the more efficient SDEM specification, and of 0.192 when treating price in the own state as endogenous. In addition, the distance decay effect is found to fluctuate around 3.

6.4 Extensions of the Basic Spatial Econometric Model

6.4.1 Higher-Order Spatial Processes

Except for first-order lags, as illustrated in (6.4a) and (6.4b), second or higher-order spatial processes in the dependent variable, explanatory variables and/or the error term have been considered. An overview of these studies in the spatial econometrics literature, and its ins and outs, can be found in Elhorst et al. (2012). The basic principles of this extension can be explained by considering a second-order spatial autoregressive process in the dependent variable, which takes the form:

$$Y = \delta_1 W_1 Y + \delta_2 W_2 Y + \varepsilon \tag{6.9}$$

where W_1 and W_2 represent different spatial weights matrices that are assumed to be normalized. Table 6.2 contains five marketing studies that adopted higher-order spatial processes.

Du and Kamakura (2011) take individual adoptions of new consumer packaged goods to depend on the number of prior adopters, thereby, distinguishing both the q-nearest and the non-q-nearest neighbors of each consumer.

Choi et al. (2010) and Yang and Allenby (2003) also explain adoption rates by two spatial lags, one based on an exponential distance decay matrix and one based on demographic characteristics, the difference being that the former adopts a SAR and the latter a SEM specification.

Albuquerque et al. (2007) and Bezawada et al. (2009) go one step further by considering three lags respectively in the dependent variable and the error term. The study of Bezawada et al. (2009) also distinguishes itself from other studies in that it tries to explain the sales shares of brands in a particular product category dependent not only on the display placement in the store of the brands themselves, but also on that of related brands and product categories. It corroborates the view that spatial econometric models can be used in a wide variety of applications.

Due to similarities with the time-series literature—a first-order serial autoregressive process $y_t = \rho y_{t-1} + \varepsilon_t$ with T observations is stationary if ρ lies in the interval $(-1, 1)$—many spatial econometric studies assume that δ in a first-order spatial autoregressive process $Y = \delta WY + \varepsilon$ with N observations also lies in the interval $(-1, 1)$. This tendency seems innocent; although the lower bound of this interval is smaller ($1/\omega_{\min} < -1$), negative values smaller than -1 are unlikely both from a theoretical and an empirical viewpoint. For similar reasons, some studies also assume that $|\delta_1| + |\delta_2| < 1$ in a second-order spatial autoregressive model. However, whereas the restriction of δ in a first-order spatial process to the interval $(-1, +1)$ is rather innocent, Elhorst et al. (2012) and Lee and Yu (2014) demonstrate that its counterpart in a second-order spatial process is anything but innocent, since it leads to both the exclusion of feasible parameter combinations and the inclusion of infeasible ones.

6.4.2 Spatial Panels

In recent years, the spatial econometrics literature has exhibited a growing interest in the specification and estimation of econometric relationships based on spatial panels. This interest can be explained by the increased availability of data sets in which a number of agents are followed over time, and by the fact that panel data offer researchers extended modeling possibilities compared to the single equation cross-sectional approach (see Baltagi 2005, Sect. 1.2). The extension of the spatial econometric model for a cross-section of N observations, presented in (6.4a) and (6.4b), to a space-time model for a panel of N observations over T time periods can be obtained by adding a subscript t, which runs from 1 to T, to the variables and the error terms of that model. Table 6.2 lists six studies that have pooled the data using this setup (indicated by "pooled" in column 4). However, the main objection to pooling is that the resulting model does not account for spatial and temporal heterogeneity. Economic agents are likely to differ in their background variables, which are usually cross-sectional specific time-invariant variables that do affect the dependent variable, but which are difficult to measure or hard to obtain. Failing to account for these variables increases the risk of obtaining biased estimation results. One remedy is to introduce a variable intercept μ_i representing the effect of the omitted variables that are peculiar to each agent considered. In sum, cross-sectional specific effects control for all time-invariant variables whose omission could bias the estimates in a typical cross-sectional study. Similarly, the justification for adding time-period specific effects, denoted by ξ_t below, is that they control for all cross-sectional invariant variables whose omission could bias the estimates in a typical time-series study (Baltagi 2005). The counterpart of the cross-sectional model presented in (6.4a) and (6.4b) extended to a space-time data set with cross-sectional specific and time-period specific effects reads as:

$$Y_t = \rho W Y_t + \alpha \iota_N + X_t \beta + W X_t \theta + \mu + \xi_t \iota_N + u_t \tag{6.10a}$$

$$u_t = \lambda W u_t + \varepsilon_t \tag{6.10b}$$

where $\mu = (\mu_{1,\ldots,}\mu_N)^T$. The cross-sectional ($\mu$) and time-period ($\xi$) specific effects may be treated as fixed effects or as random effects. In the fixed effects model, a dummy variable is introduced for each cross-sectional unit and for each time period (both sets of fixed effects are assumed to sum up to zero to avoid perfect multicollinearity mutually or with the intercept α), while in the random effects model, μ_i and ξ_t are treated as random variables that are independently and identically distributed with zero mean and variance σ_μ^2 and σ_ξ^2, respectively. Furthermore, it is assumed that the random variables μ_i, ξ_t and ε_{it} are independent of each other.

Table 6.2 captures four studies that control for cross-sectional fixed effects and four that control for cross-sectional random effects, one study that controls for time-period fixed effects, and two studies that control for both type of effects. Two of these studies control for either cross-sectional fixed or random effects at a higher scale level than the units of observations. This is indicated by "(higher level)" in column (4). Finally, there is one study that also considers interaction effects between the controls for cross-sectional and time period fixed effects (Bollinger and Gillingham 2012). One of the arguments sometimes used to augment the regression model with a broad range of fixed or random effects is to "control for endogenous group formation" (Hartman et al. 2008, p. 294; see also Bollinger and Gillingham 2012; Nair et al. 2010) or to control for sorting, i.e., agents with similar tastes may tend to form social groups or co-locate. This may produce a positive correlation of the dependent variable among economic agents not caused by pure spatial lags. However, the idea that controls for fixed or random effects help to solve these identification problems is based on a misunderstanding. The reason to control for fixed or random effects in both space and time is because their omission could bias the parameter estimates of the remaining variables. For example, using Monte Carlo simulation experiments, Lee and Yu (2010) show that ignoring time-period fixed effects may lead to large upward biases (up to 0.45) in the coefficient of the spatial lag of the dependent variable. The right question to be asked is therefore whether spatial lags remain significant after fixed or random effects in both space and time have been controlled for, since their magnitude might become smaller due to these controls. But if they remain significant, which needs to be tested, ignoring them still leads to wrong inferences.

Instead of capturing heterogeneity by a different intercept for different agents and/or time periods, a natural generalization would be to let the slope parameters of the regressors vary as well. This principle is applied in four studies. In Aranvindakshan et al. (2012) and Albuquergue et al. (2007) the coefficients are different for different regions. The former study subdivides Germany into seven regions and therefore is able to report the coefficient estimates for every single region. The latter study employs a random coefficients model based on data of 59 countries and only reports the common-mean coefficients. In Choi et al. (2010) the coefficients are different for different time periods. Since they have 45 months of data, they only provide a graphical presentation of the estimation results. Finally, Jank and Kannan (2005) report separate parameter estimates for two product categories: printed and electronic books.

If the cross-sectional model in (6.4a) and (6.4b) is extended to a space-time data set with cross-sectional specific and time-period specific effects as in (6.10a) and (6.10b), the log-likelihood in (6.6) also needs to be extended. We explain this extension in two steps. For the space-time model with spatial fixed effects only, we get:

$$L(\kappa) = (T-1)\Big[-\tfrac{N}{2}\ln\left(2\pi\sigma^2\right) + \ln\|\,I-\delta W\,\| + \ln\|\,I-\lambda W\,\|\Big] - \tfrac{1}{2\sigma^2}\textstyle\sum_{t=1}^{T-1} e_t^{*T} e_t^{*} \tag{6.11}$$

where $e_t^* = (I-\lambda W)^{-1}\left(Y_t^* - \delta W Y_t^* - X_t^*\beta - W X_t^*\theta\right)$ and a vector or matrix with superscript *, say p_t^*, is obtained by the transformation $p_t^* = p_t F_{T,T-1}$. In the panel data literature, variables tend to be demeaned (Baltagi 2005, Sects. 2.2 and 3.2). In the case of spatial fixed effects, the time demean operator $J_T = (I_T - T^{-1}\tau_N \tau_N^T)$ can be used. However, due to the additional right-hand side term WY_t and/or Wu_t in spatial econometric models and the fact that W is time invariant in most applications, the resulting error terms would be linearly dependent over the time dimension. To avoid this, Lee and Yu (2010) introduce the orthonormal decomposition $[F_{T,T-1}, T^{-0.5}\tau_T]$, where the $F_{T,T-1}$ matrix represents the eigenvector matrix of the time demean operator J_T corresponding to the eigenvalues of one ($T-1$ in total). This transformation reduces the number of degrees of freedom by one for each time period. Alternatively, one may apply the time demean operator J_T and then bias-correct the parameter estimates afterwards (see Elhorst 2014, Sect. 3.3.3).

If the model also contains time-period fixed effects, each vector or matrix should, in addition to the transformation $F_{T,T-1}$, also be transformed by $F_{N-1,N}$, the orthonormal eigenvector matrix of the spatial demean operator $J_N = (I_N - N^{-1}\iota_T \iota_T^T)$, where ι_T is a vector of ones, to get $p_t^* = F_{N-1,N} p_t F_{T,T-1}$. The log-likelihood of this model is:

$$L(\kappa) = (T-1)\left[-\tfrac{N-1}{2}\ln\left(2\pi\sigma^2\right) + \ln\|I-\delta W\| + \ln\|I-\lambda W\|\right] + \ln(1-\delta) + \ln(1-\lambda) - \tfrac{1}{2\sigma^2}\textstyle\sum_{t=1}^{T-1} e_t^{*T} e_t^{*}. \tag{6.12}$$

Whereas the Stata routine XSMLE (version 2013) at the time of writing this chapter covers the correction specified in (6.11), it does not cover the correction in (6.12).

This is remarkable, since tests whether spatial and time period fixed effects are jointly insignificant must be rejected in many cases.

If the spatial specific effects are random rather than fixed and the spatial lag among the error terms is left aside, the log-likelihood function in (6.11) changes into:

$$L(\kappa) = -\frac{NT}{2}\ln\left(2\pi\sigma^2\right) + \ln \| I - \delta W \| + \frac{N}{2}\ln\left(\phi^2\right) - \frac{1}{2\sigma^2}e_t^{*T}e_t^* \qquad (6.13)$$

where the symbol * now denotes the transformation $p_t^* = p_t - (1-\varphi)\bar{p}$, where $\bar{p}$ is the average over the entire time period. This expression shows that one additional parameter (φ) needs to be estimated. It measures the weight attached to the cross-sectional variation in the data. In the fixed effects model, this weight equals zero. Time-specific effects may also be added to this model, but generally they are treated fixed rather than random. If T is small, as in most samples, these time dummies can then be treated as regular explanatory variables. Note that Eq. (6.4a) contains an intercept $\alpha\iota_N$ but not its spatial lagged value $W\alpha\iota_N$. This is because most empirical studies normalize W such that every row sums to unity. This yields $W\alpha\iota_N = \alpha\iota_N$, as a result of which the regressor $W\alpha\iota_N$ needs to be removed so as to avoid perfect multicollinearity. A similar result applies to time dummies, implying that the spatial lagged values of time dummies should also be left aside.

If instead of the spatial lag among the error terms, the spatial lag among the dependent variables is left aside, the log-likelihood takes the form (Anselin 1988; Baltagi 2005; Elhorst 2003):

$$\begin{aligned} L(\kappa) = &-\tfrac{NT}{2}\ln\left(2\pi\sigma^2\right) - \tfrac{1}{2}\log|V| + (T-1)\ln\|B\| \\ &-\tfrac{1}{2\sigma^2}e^T\left(\tfrac{1}{T}\iota_T\iota_T^T \otimes V^{-1}\right)e - \tfrac{1}{2\sigma^2}e^T\left(I_T - \tfrac{1}{T}\iota_T\iota_T^{T'}\right)\otimes\left(B^TB\right)e \end{aligned} \qquad (6.14)$$

where $V = (T\sigma_\mu^2/\sigma^2)I_N + (B^TB)^{-1}$, $B = I_N - \lambda W$ and $e = Y - X\beta$. This model distinguishes itself from previous models in that various transformations or mathematical simplifications to speed up computation time are not applicable here. Therefore, all the more remarkable is that so many marketing studies reported in Table 6.2 are mainly focusing on a spatial lag among the error terms, sometimes using even more complicated mathematical forms than presented in this overview chapter. Simpler models would be obtained by shifting the attention towards fixed effects models and towards spatial lags in the deterministic regression equation rather than the stochastic error term specification.

Reasons to consider fixed effects models, other than just mathematical ones, are the following. First, rather than drawing a random sample from a particular population, researchers tend to sample the whole population, otherwise the impact of neighboring agents cannot be consistently estimated. But if the whole population is sampled by a fixed sample design, it is also entirely logical to adopt a fixed effects model in line with this. Second, in most cases the random effects model is rejected in favor of the fixed effects model when using the Hausman test, since the assumption that the random effects are uncorrelated with the X variables does not hold.

Reasons to focus on spatial lags in the deterministic regression equation rather than the stochastic error term specification are related to the spatial spillover effects, a topic discussed in Sect. 6.2.3. The main motivation to apply spatial econometric models is to investigate whether the behavior of one economic agent is codetermined by that of others. Up to now, most marketing studies used the coefficient estimates of a spatial econometric model to test the hypothesis as to whether or not spillover effects exist, i.e., whether the impact of changes to explanatory variables of one agent i affects the dependent variable values of other agents j ($\neq i$). In Sect. 6.2.3 it was shown that a partial derivative interpretation of the impact from changes to the variables represents a more valid basis for testing this hypothesis, and related to that that models with a spatial lag among the error terms provide no information about the spatial spillover effects.

The formula behind the calculation of the direct and spatial spillover effects presented in (6.8) does not change when considering the static model panel data model in (6.10a) and (6.10b). This is because this formula is independent of the time dimension, provided that the spatial weights matrix W is constant over time. If W also happens to change over time, the direct and indirect effects may be determined by not only taking averages over the agents but also over time.

6.4.3 Dynamic Spatial Panels

A dynamic extension of the spatial panel data model, presented in (6.10a) and (6.10b), is obtained by adding time lags of the variables Y_t and WY_t, to get:

$$Y_t = \tau Y_{t-1} + \rho WY_t + \eta WY_{t-1} + \alpha \iota_N + X_t\beta + WX_t\theta + \mu + \xi_t\iota_N + u_t. \quad (6.15)$$

This model, indicated by "Dynamic SAR" in column (2) of Table 6.2, is considered by Verhelst and Van den Poel (2014), though without spatial lags in WX. Studies denoted by "Dynamic lagged SAR" are of Korniotis (2010) and Bronnenberg (2005); this description has been chosen since they leave the contemporaneous spatial lag in the dependent variable (WY_t) aside. Korniotos (2010) applies this model to explain annual consumption growth in U.S. states over the period 1966–1998 and interprets the coefficients of the temporal and space-time lags of the dependent variable as measures of internal and external habit persistence. This terminology is borrowed by Verhelst and Van den Poel (2014). Instead of making the deterministic regression model dynamic, one can also make the error term specification dynamic:

$$u_t = \eta u_{t-1} + \lambda Wu_t + \varepsilon_t. \quad (6.16)$$

This specification is considered in Bronnenberg and Mahajan (2001). Alternatively, Aranvindakshan et al. (2012) mix space and time by specifying the deterministic regression equation as a dynamic lagged spatial autoregressive model and the error term specification as a serial autocorrelation model.

If the dynamic spatial panel data model in (6.15) is taken as point of departure, initial estimates of the parameters can be obtained by maximizing the log-likelihood function in (6.11) or (6.13), dependent on whether or not time fixed effects are included. The difference is that the residuals take the form:

$$e_t^* = Y_t^* - \tau WY_t^* - \delta WY_t^* - \eta WY_{t-1}^* - X_t^*\beta - WX_t^*\theta \tag{6.17}$$

and that the pre-multiplication by the matrix $(I - \lambda W)^{-1}$ is left aside since dynamic spatial panel data models that also contain a spatial lag among the error terms have not been considered yet in the literature. In the second step, the parameter estimates can be bias-corrected, though these corrections are more complicated than in a static spatial panel data model, since it should also cover the Nickell (1981) bias: the problem that lagged values of the dependent variable (Y_{t-1}) and spatial fixed effects are correlated with each other. Detailed specifications of these bias corrections are in Yu et al. (2008, (17) and (18)) and Lee and Yu (2010). Jihai Yu also made a set of Matlab routines available to estimate this model (including some variants) that are freely downloadable from www.regroningen.nl/elhorst/software.shtml (Code Regional Science and Urban Economics paper 2010) (Elhorst 2010).

When the dynamic spatial panel data model in (6.13) is adopted, Eq. (6.8) can be used to calculate direct and indirect effects in the short term, whereas the long-term direct and indirect effects can be calculated using the expression:

$$\left[\frac{\partial \mathrm{E}(Y)}{\partial x_{1k}} \cdots \frac{\partial \mathrm{E}(Y)}{\partial x_{Nk}}\right] = \left[(1-\tau)I - (\delta+\eta)\,W\Big)\right]^{-1}[\beta_k I_N + \theta_k W]. \tag{6.18}$$

6.4.4 Binary Choice Data

A dynamic but much simpler and also popular diffusion model of consumer adoption is obtained if adoption at time t is explained by the number of adopters at time $t-1$:

$$Y_t^* = \eta WY_{t-1} + X_t\beta + \mu_t. \tag{6.19}$$

In this model, the observed choices whether consumer i adopts a particular product at time t, y_{it}, is linked to the unobserved element y_{it}* of vector Y_t* by the rule: $y_{it} = 0$ if $y_{it}* \leq 0$ and $y_{it} = 1$ if $y_{it}* > 0$. If a consumer already adopted a particular product in the past, it is usually assumed that $y_{it} = 1$, although one might question whether these observations should not be removed from the sample, just as in the duration literature (see Elhorst et al. 2016). Depending on the distribution function of the error term, the model can then be estimated using a logit or probit approach.

The binary diffusion model in (6.19) is widespread in the marketing literature; Table 6.2 counts four of these studies. They are indicated by the description "0/1" in column (2) of Table 6.2 to denote that they focus on binary choices, and by the description “lagged SAR” in the same column to denote that they focus on the spatial econometric model in (6.19). If instead of SAR another spatial econometric model is considered, this is indicated by one of the other abbreviations presented in Table 6.2, such as the SLX binary response model in Katona et al. (2011) and the SEM binary response model in Jank and Kannan (2005). Bollinger and Gillingham (2012) use a so-called dynamic lagged SAR model to explain the diffusion of solar panels. The terminology “lagged SAR” is used to indicate that the dependent variable is taken to depend on WY_{t-1}, and “dynamic” since they also control for serial correlation. Since they do not employ individual data, but the fraction of owner-occupied households in each zip code that had not previously adopted solar panels, their dependent variable remains continuous.

Perhaps the most difficult models to estimate are spatial probit and logit models. This is best illustrated using the spatial error probit model:

$$Y^* = \delta WY^* + X\beta + u, \quad u = \lambda Wu + \varepsilon \tag{6.20}$$

where the symbol * in this section denotes that the dependent variable is unobservable.

The basic problem that needs to be solved in estimating this model is that the likelihood function cannot be written as the product of N one-dimensional normal probabilities as is the case with the standard (non-spatial) probit model. This is because the individual error terms ε_i $(i = 1, \ldots, N)$ are dependent on each other, as a result of which the likelihood function:

$$L(\beta, \lambda | Y) = \int\limits_{Y^*} \frac{1}{(2\pi)^{N/2} \mid \Omega_\lambda \mid^{1/2}} \exp\left(-\frac{1}{2}\varepsilon^T \Omega_\lambda^{-1} \varepsilon\right) \tag{6.21}$$

is an N-dimensional integral, where $\Omega_\lambda = [(I - \lambda W)^T (I - \lambda W)]^{-1}$ and $\sigma^2 = 1$ since it cannot be separately identified. Other spatial econometric models reported in Table 6.2, except for the SLX model, have been shown to face the same problem of this N-dimensional integral (Elhorst et al. 2016).

The expectation-maximization (EM) algorithm adapted by McMillen (1992) is one of the earliest attempts to deal with the multidimensional integration problem. The main shortcoming of this algorithm is that the individual unobserved value of y_i^* is determined conditional on the observed value y_i of the agent itself, while it should be determined conditional on the observed values of all other agents. Consequently, this algorithm produces inconsistent parameter estimates.

A similar objection applies to the Bayesian MCMC estimation procedure originally developed by LeSage (2000). This procedure is based on sequentially drawing model parameters from their conditional distributions. This process of sampling parameters continues until the distribution of draws converges to the targeted joint posterior distribution of the model parameters. The key problem is to sample Y^*. In LeSage (2000), the individual elements y_i^* are obtained by sampling from a sequence of univariate truncated normal distributions, but in later work this shortcoming has been fixed (LeSage and Pace 2009, p. 285).

A third estimation method is the Generalized Method of Moments (GMM), initially proposed by Pinkse and Slade (1998) (see also Chap. 15). Similar techniques have been used to estimate the spatial logit model (Klier and McMillen 2008). Since GMM estimators in contrast to Bayesian and ML estimators do not specify the distribution function of the error terms, they also do not solve the multidimensional integration problem. They take into account that the diagonal elements of the covariance matrix are different from one agent to another, often labeled as heteroscedasticity, but they do not take into account that the off-diagonal elements of this matrix are also non-zero. Consequently, they overrule the basic notion underlying spatial econometric models that agents cannot be treated as independent entities. In other words, although these studies are right that the ML and Bayesian methods rely on the potentially inaccurate assumption of normally distributed error terms, they in turn ignore the spatial lag among the error terms.

The last estimation method is Maximum Likelihood. Starting from McMillen (1992), Beron and Vijverberg (2004) developed a Simulated Maximum Likelihood (SML) estimator. This simulation method is also known as Recursive-Importance-Sampling (RIS) and relies on Monte Carlo simulation of truncated multivariate normal distributions, as discussed by Vijverberg (1997). The advantage of this estimation method is that it provides a feasible and efficient algorithm to approximate the N-dimensional truncated normal density function needed to maximize the log-likelihood function. The only problem is that this algorithm is rather slow. Two recent studies developed estimation routines to speed up computation time of the SML estimator, to begin with Pace and LeSage (2011) by exploiting the fact that often only a fraction of the elements of the spatial weight matrix W is different from zero. Following Pace and LeSage (2011), Liesenfeld et al. (2013) use sparse matrix algorithms, but instead of the RIS simulator they propose Efficient Importance Sampling (EIS), a high-dimensional Monte Carlo integration technique, based on simple least-squares (LS) approximation, designed to maximize numerical accuracy of the SML estimator. Full details are in their studies.

Most marketing studies reported in Table 6.2 avoid these problems by considering Eq. (6.19), where the right-hand side variable WY is taken from the previous time period and thus can be observed, and by assuming that the error terms are independent of each other.

Finally, when having a spatial probit model of the form $Y^* = \delta WY^* + \alpha\iota_N + X\beta + WX\theta + u$, the matrix of partial derivatives in (6.8) changes into:

$$\left[\frac{\partial \mathrm{E}(Y)}{\partial x_{1k}} \cdots \frac{\partial \mathrm{E}(Y)}{\partial x_{Nk}}\right] = diag\,[\phi\,(\varsigma)]\,(I - \delta W)^{-1}\,[\beta_k I_N + \theta_k W] \tag{6.22}$$

where the additional diagonal matrix on the right-hand side is of order N, whose nonzero diagonal elements φ represent the normally distributed probabilities that the dependent variables take their observed values, dependent on the observed values of the other agents in the sample, which in turn is represented by $\varsigma = (I - \delta W)^{-1}(\alpha\iota_N + X\beta + WX\theta)$ (LeSage et al. 2011).

References

Albuquerque, P., Bronnenberg, B.J., Corbett, C.J.: A spatiotemporal analysis of the global diffusion of ISO 9000 and ISO 14000 certification. Manag. Sci. **53**, 451–468 (2007)

Anselin, L.: Spatial Econometrics: Methods and Models. Kluwer, Dordrecht (1988)

Anselin, L.: Rao's score test in spatial econometrics. J. Stat. Plann. Infer. **97**, 113–139 (2003)

Aral, S., Walker, D.: Creating social contagion through viral product design: a randomized trial of peer influence in networks. Manag. Sci. **57**, 1623–1639 (2011)

Aravindakshan, A., Peters, K., Naik, P.A.: Spatiotemporal allocation of advertising budgets. J. Mark. Res. **49**, 1–14 (2012)

Baltagi, B.H.: Econometric Analysis of Panel Data, 3rd edn. Wiley, Chichester (2005)

Baltagi, B.H., Li, D.: Prediction in the panel data model with spatial autocorrelation. In: Anselin, L., Florax, R.J.G.M., Rey, S.J. (eds.) Advances in Spatial Econometrics: Methodology, Tools and Applications. Springer, Berlin, pp. 283–295 (2004)

Bell, D.R., Song, S.: Neighborhood effects and trial on the internet: evidence from online grocery retailing. Quant. Mark. Econ. **5**, 361–400 (2007)

Beron, K.J., Vijverberg, W.P.M.: Probit in a spatial context: a Monte Carlo analysis. In: Anselin, L., Florax, R.J.G.M., Rey, S.J. (eds.) Advances in Spatial Econometrics: Methodology, Tools and Applications. Springer, Berlin, pp. 169–195 (2004)

Bezawada, R., Balachander, S., Kannan, P.K., Shankar, V.: Cross-category effects of aisle and display placements: a spatial modeling approach and insights. J. Mark. **73**(3), 99–117 (2009)

Blundell, R., Stoker, T.M.: Models of aggregate economic relationships that account for heterogeneity. In: Heckman, J.J., Leamer, E. (eds.) Handbook of Econometrics, vol. 6A. Elsevier, Amsterdam, pp. 4609–4663 (2007)

Bollinger, B., Gillingham, K.: Peer effects in the diffusion of solar photovoltaic panels. Mark. Sci. **31**, 900–912 (2012)

Bradlow, E.T., Bronnenberg, B., Russel, G.J., Arora, N., Bell, D.R., Duvvuri, S.D., Ter Hofstede, F., Sismeiro, C., Thomadsen, R., Yang, S.: Spatial models in marketing. Mark. Lett. **16**, 267–278 (2005)

Bronnenberg, B.J.: Spatial models in marketing research and practice. Appl. Stoch. Model. Bus. **21**, 335–343 (2005)

Bronnenberg, B.J., Mahajan, V.: Unobserved retailer behavior in multimarket data: joint spatial dependence in market shares and promotion variables. Mark. Sci. **20**, 284–299 (2001)

Bronnenberg, B.J., Mela, C.F.: Market roll-out and retailer adoption for new brands. Mark. Sci. **23**, 500–518 (2004)

Bronnenberg, B.J., Sismeiro, C.: Using multimarket data to predict brand performance in markets for which no or poor data exists. J. Mark. Res. **39**, 1–17 (2002)

Chen, X., Chen, Y., Xiao, P.: The impact of sampling and network topology on the estimation of social intercorrelations. J. Mark. Res. **50**, 95–110 (2013)

Chintagunta, P.K., Nair, H.S.: Discrete-choice models of consumer demand in marketing. Mark. Sci. **30**, 977–996 (2011)

Choi, J., Hui, S.K., Bell, D.R.: Spatiotemporal analysis of imitation behavior across new buyers at an online grocery retailer. J. Mark. Res. **47**, 75–89 (2010)

Drukker, D.M., Egger, P., Prucha, I.R.: On two-step estimation of a spatial autoregressive model with autoregressive disturbances and endogenous regressors. Econ. Rev. **32**, 686–733 (2013)

Du, R.Y., Kamakura, W.A.: Measuring contagion in the diffusion of consumer packaged goods. J. Mark. Res. **48**, 28–47 (2011)

Elhorst, J.P.: Specification and estimation of spatial panel data models. Int. Reg. Sci. Rev. **26**, 244–268 (2003)

Elhorst, J.P.: Spatial panel data models. In: Fischer, M.M., Getis, A. (eds.) Handbook of Applied Spatial Analysis. Springer, Berlin, pp. 377–407 (2010)

Elhorst, J.P.: Spatial Econometrics: From Cross-Sectional Data to Spatial Panels. Springer, Heidelberg (2014)

Elhorst, J.P., Lacombe, D.J., Piras, G.: On model specification and parameter space definitions in higher order spatial econometrics models. Reg. Sci. Urban Econ. **42**, 211–220 (2012)

Elhorst, J.P., Heijnen, P., Samarina, A., Jacobs, J.: State transfers at different moments in time. J. Appl. Econ. **2016**, 1 (2016)

Froot, K.A.: Consistent covariance matrix estimation with cross-sectional dependence and heteroskedasticity in financial data. J. Financ. Anal. **24**, 333–355 (1989)

Gibbons, S., Overman, H.G.: Mostly pointless spatial econometrics? J. Reg. Sci. **52**, 172–191 (2012)

Haenlein, M.: Social interactions in customer churn decisions: the impact of relationship directionality. Int. J. Res. Mark. **30**, 236–248 (2013)

Halleck-Vega, S., Elhorst, J.P.: The SLX model. J. Reg. Sci. **55**, 339–363 (2015)

Hartmann, W.R.: Demand estimation with social interactions and the implications for targeted marketing. Mark. Sci. **29**, 558–601 (2010)

Hartmann, W.R., Manchanda, P., Nair, H., Bothner, M., Dodds, P., Godes, D., Hosanagar, K., Tucker, C.: Modeling social interactions: identification, empirical methods and policy implications. Mark. Lett. **19**, 287–304 (2008)

Iyengar, R., Van den Bulte, C., Valente, T.W.: Opinion leadership and social contagion in new product diffusion. Mark. Sci. **30**, 195–212 (2011)

Jank, W., Kannan, P.K.: Understanding geographical markets of online firms using spatial models of customer choice. Mark. Sci. **24**, 623–634 (2005)

Jank, W., Kannan, P.K.: Dynamic e-targeting using learning spatial choice models. J. Interact. Mark. **20**, 30–42 (2006)

Katona, Z., Zubcsek, P.P., Sarvary, M.: Network effects and personal influences: the diffusion of an online social network. J. Mark. Res. **48**, 425–443 (2011)

Kelejian, H.H., Prucha, I.R.: A generalized spatial two stage least squares procedure for estimating a spatial autoregressive model with autoregressive disturbances. J. Real Estate Financ. Econ. **17**, 99–121 (1998)

Kelejian, H.H., Prucha, I.R.: A generalized moments estimator for the autoregressive parameter in a spatial model. Int. Econ. Rev. **40**, 509–533 (1999)

Kelejian, H.H., Prucha, I.R., Yuzefovich, Y.: Instrumental variable estimation of a spatial autoregressive model with autoregressive disturbances: large and small sample results. In: LeSage, J.P., Pace, K. (eds.) Spatial and Spatiotemporal Econometrics. Elsevier, Amsterdam, pp. 163–198 (2004)

Klier, T., McMillen, D.P.: Clustering of auto supplier plants in the United States: generalized method of moments spatial logit for large samples. J. Bus. Econ. Stat. **26**, 460–471 (2008)

Korniotis, G.M.: Estimating panel models with internal and external habit formation. J. Bus. Econ. Stat. **28**, 145–158 (2010)

Lee, L.F.: Asymptotic distribution of quasi-maximum likelihood estimators for spatial autoregressive models. Econometrica. **72**, 1899–1925 (2004)

Lee, L.F., Yu, J.: Some recent developments in spatial panel data models. Reg. Sci. Urban Econ. **40**, 255–271 (2010)

Lee, L.F., Yu, J.: Efficient GMM estimation of spatial dynamic panel data models with fixed effects. J. Econ. **180**, 174–197 (2014)

LeSage, J.P.: Bayesian estimation of limited dependent variable spatial autoregressive models. Geogr. Anal. **32**, 19–35 (2000)

LeSage, J.P.: Spatial econometric panel data model specification: a Bayesian approach. Spat. Stat. **9**, 122–145 (2014)

LeSage, J.P., Pace, R.K.: Introduction to Spatial Econometrics. Taylor and Francis, Boca Raton (2009)

LeSage, J.P., Pace, R.K., Lam, N., Campanella, R., Liu, X.: New Orleans business recovery in the aftermath of hurricane Katrina. J. R. Stat. Soc. A. **174**, 1007–1027 (2011)

Liesenfeld, R., Richard, J.-F., Vogler, J.: Analysis of discrete dependent variable models with spatial correlation. Available at SSRN: http://ssrn.com/abstract=2196041 (2013)

McMillen, D.P.: Probit with spatial autocorrelation. J. Reg. Sci. **32**, 335–348 (1992)

Murphy, K.M., Topel, R.H.: Estimation and inference in two-step econometric models. J. Bus. Econ. Stat. **3**, 370–379 (1985)
Nair, H.S., Manchanda, P., Bhatia, T.: Asymmetric social interactions in physician prescription behavior: the role of opinion leaders. J. Mark. Res. **47**, 883–895 (2010)
Nickell, S.: Biases in dynamic models with fixed effects. Econometrica. **49**, 1417–1426 (1981)
Ord, K.: Estimation methods for models of spatial interaction. J. Am. Stat. Assoc. **70**, 120–126 (1975)
Pace, R.K., LeSage, J.P.: Fast simulated maximum likelihood estimation of the spatial probit model capable of handling large samples. Available at SSRN: http://ssrn.com/abstract=1966039 (2011)
Partridge, M.D., Boarnet, M.G., Brakman, S., Ottaviano, G.: Introduction: whither spatial econometrics? J. Reg. Sci. **52**, 167–171 (2012)
Pinkse, J., Slade, M.: Contracting in space: an application of spatial statistics to discrete-choice models. J. Econ. **85**, 125–154 (1998)
Pinkse, J., Slade, M.E., Brett, C.: Spatial price competition: a semiparametric approach. Econometrica. **70**, 1111–1153 (2002)
Stakhovych, S., Bijmolt, T.H.A.: Specification of spatial models: a simulation study on weights matrices. Pap. Reg. Sci. **88**, 389–408 (2009)
Ter Hofstede, F., Wedel, M., Steenkamp, J-B.E.M.: Identifying spatial segments in international markets. Mark. Sci. **21**, 160–177 (2002)
Van Dijk, A., Van Heerde, H.J., Leeflang, P.S.H., Wittink, D.R.: Similarity-based spatial methods to estimate shelf space elasticities. Quant. Mark. Econ. **2**, 257–277 (2004)
Verhelst, B., Van den Poel, D.: Deep habits in consumption: a spatial panel analysis using scanner data. Empir. Econ. **47**, 959–976 (2014)
Vijverberg, W.P.M.: Monte Carlo evaluation of multivariate normal probabilities. J. Econ. **76**, 281–307 (1997)
Yang, S., Allenby, G.M.: Modeling interdependent consumer preferences. J. Mark. Res. **40**, 282–294 (2003)
Yang, S., Narayan, V., Assael, H.: Estimating the interdependence of television program viewership between spouses: a Bayesian simultaneous equation model. Mark. Sci. **25**, 336–349 (2006)
Yu, J., de Jong, R., Lee, L.: Quasi-maximum likelihood estimators for spatial dynamic panel data with fixed effects when both n and T are large. J. Econ. **146**, 118–134 (2008)
Zhang, Q., Song, Y., Liu, Q., Chandukala, S.R., Qian, P.Z.G.: Modeling brand correlation through iterative sparsity search. Kelly School of Business Research 15. Available at SSRN: http://ssrn.com/abstract=2557037 (2015)

Chapter 7
Structural Models

Paulo Albuquerque and Bart J. Bronnenberg

7.1 Introduction

7.1.1 What Is a Structural Model?

Structural models are econometric representations of decision-making behavior. Their key characteristic is that they frequently represent quantities of sales and price data as outcomes of goal-directed decision-making by agents. A litmus test of the structural nature of an empirical model is therefore answering the question "where in the model are the agents' decisions?" or in short "who maximizes what?".

In a marketing context, the decision makers in structural models are typically consumers who solve consumption problems (e.g., purchasing products, deciding on optimal variety, etc.) or marketing managers who solve firm problems (e.g., setting prices, product-line length, promotional activities, making distribution decisions, etc.) or both.

What are the benefits of modeling data as the outcome of explicit optimization problems by consumers and marketing managers? Two stand out. First, the structural approach offers a direct link between the observed data and the behavior of consumers and managers. More specifically, structural models estimate the determinants or primitives of the agent's behavior. Examples of primitives that

P. Albuquerque (✉)
Faculty of Marketing, INSEAD Fontainebleau, Fontainebleau, France
e-mail: paulo.albuquerque@insead.edu

B.J. Bronnenberg
Department of Marketing, Tilburg School of Economics and Marketing, Tilburg University, The Netherlands, and Centre for Economic Policy Research, London, UK

P.S.H. Leeflang et al. (eds.), *Advanced Methods for Modeling Markets*,
International Series in Quantitative Marketing, DOI 10.1007/978-3-319-53469-5_7

drive consumer decision-making are price sensitivity or the preference for certain product features, while examples of primitives that drive the behavior of marketing managers are marketing costs or the productivity of sales representatives. Second, the underlying decision primitives of consumers and managers do not depend on any particular strategy. In other words, the decision primitives are immutable to the strategies of firms. For instance, the sensitivity to price, when estimated correctly, drives the behavior of consumers in response to observed prices in the same way that it does for alternative counterfactual prices. Equipped with these decision primitives, a structural model can be used to evaluate how consumers adjust their behavior in response to a counterfactual marketplace in which prices have changed (e.g., Bronnenberg et al. 2005) or how marketing managers change their pricing strategy as a function of entry by more firms. Hence, structural models help forecast how demand and supply systems adjust to changes in the marketing environment.

Reiss (2011, p. 951) writes that "structural models combine mathematical, economic, or marketing models of behavior with statistical assumptions to derive estimable empirical models." The "structure" in structural empirical models thus comes from behavioral theories, developed in marketing, economics, and psychology, that are combined with a statistical approach. In this understanding, the *behavioral* component of structural models usually contains agents who explicitly optimize along an objective function, i.e., a consumer who maximizes utility, a marketing manager who maximizes profit, or a social planner who maximizes welfare. In addition, the behavioral model can involve a theory of how agents interact with each other, socially or competitively, or it may contain rules for how agents deal with incomplete information – for example, a consumer who does not know future prices in a dynamic demand problem, or a firm that does not observe the advertising plans of its competitors. Structural models further specify how decision makers incorporate such missing information, for instance by treating future prices as stochastic and allowing consumers to base their decisions on the characteristics of these stochastic variables, e.g., their mean and variance.

Next, the *statistical* component of a structural model specifies how discrepancies between model predictions and observations are generated. The main explanation for such discrepancies in structural models is measurement error by the marketing analyst or decision or optimization error by the demand and supply agents.

7.1.2 A Typology of Structural Models in Marketing

Structural models in marketing are not a recent phenomenon. The first to use the term "structural model" in a marketing paper, at least to our knowledge, was Frank M. Bass. He and Len Parssons (Bass 1969; Bass and Parssons 1969) modeled advertising and sales as a simultaneous equation system and used estimates of the structural parameters in the model to simulate counterfactual scenarios.

In the intervening decades, especially in the recent ones, structural models have become mainstream econometric tools to describe the actions of consumers and

Table 7.1 Structural models in marketing, typology and selected examples

Demand	Static	Single Agent	Consumer search	Kim et al. (2010)
			Product replacement	Gordon (2009)
			Preferences and learning	Shin et al. (2012)
		Multiple Agent	Innovation diffusion	Nair et al. (2010)
			Social interactions	Hartmann (2010)
	Dynamic	Single Agent	Identifying discount rates	Yao et al. (2012)
			Identifying discount rates	Dubé et al. (2014)
			Promotion effects	Chan et al. (2008)
		Multiple Agent	Adoption of innovation	Ryan and Tucker (2012)
			User generated content	Ahn et al. (2016)
Supply	Static	Single Agent	Brand alliances	Yang et al. (2009)
			Dealership network decisions	Albuquerque and Bronnenberg (2012)
		Multiple Agent	Static discrete games	Su (2014)
			Spatial competition	Thomadsen (2005, 2007)
			Entry with complementarities	Vitorino (2012)
	Dynamic	Single Agent	Sales force compensation	Misra and Nair (2011)
			Product launches	Hitsch (2006)
			Retailing	Holmes (2011)
		Multiple Agent	Network externalities	Goettler and Gordon (2011)
			Dynamic competition	Dubé et al. (2010)

marketing managers alike, and their role in shaping marketing thought in academics is significant. In terms of classifying the large body of work in structural models in marketing, we introduce three characteristics of structural models to organize the existing literature: demand vs. supply agents, static vs. dynamic decision making, and single agent vs. multiple agent models. Table 7.1 provides examples of recent work in marketing of each structural model type.

The aim of this chapter is to discuss the main building blocks of structural models along the lines of this typology and illustrate the process of building a structural model. We do this in Sect. 7.2, discussing where some of the obstacles lie, especially with respect to identification of model parameters, and its reliance on structure and/or data variation. We explain structural methods using examples of the marketing literature from 2006 to 2015 in Sect. 7.3. We next give a detailed description of the structural approach implemented in Albuquerque and Bronnenberg (2012), who study the automobile industry during the Great Recession of 2008–2009 in Sect. 7.4. Section 7.5 gives a few (personal) notes on the use of software. Section 7.6 specifies some further reading and the state-of-the-art of structural models. To the reader interested in the large volume of pre-2006 structural work in marketing, we refer to the reviews by Bronnenberg et al. (2005) and Chintagunta et al. (2006).

7.2 Structural Models of Demand

7.2.1 Introduction

Marketing applications of structural demand analysis typically seek to answer questions about the demand effects of marketing variables, such as price, display, feature, price-promotions, shelf-space availability, or advertising. The structural methods employed in this area were heavily influenced by the literature on multinomial choice models in marketing (e.g., Chintagunta et al. 1991; Guadagni and Little 1983), which represent demand data as the outcome of individual consumer optimization problems.[1] However, variation in price (and other marketing elements) is not random in empirical data, as it is reasonable to expect managers to raise price in response to positive demand shocks. Demand estimation therefore needs to account for the actions of the supply side or for omitted marketing variables (see e.g., Bruno and Vilcassim 2008) to avoid omitted variable and endogeneity biases. Hence, in the intervening years, the choice modeling literature has been advanced by (1) providing a more formal treatment of unobserved demand shocks, (2) accounting for the role of the strategic nature of firm actions, such as pricing and advertising, and (3) extending the static consumer problem into dynamic decision making and multiple agent problems.

7.2.2 The Consumer Problem

7.2.2.1 Basic Setup

In the basic setup, consumers make purchase or consumption decisions that maximize their utility. There are two approaches used in the marketing literature to specify the consumer's utility function. First, the analyst can specify how utility depends *directly* on quantities q of a vector of goods and quantities q_0 of outside goods. The consumer problem takes the form:

$$\max_{q,q_0} U(q, q_0), \text{ such that} \tag{7.1}$$

$$Y = p\,q + p_0\,q_0 \tag{7.2}$$

where the constraint on income Y defines the set of feasible choices, and p and p_0 represent the prices of inside and outside goods respectively. This *direct utility approach* allows for continuous quantities or multiple discreteness, i.e., each choice may include several alternatives in a product category or multiple units of the

[1]See also Chap. 2 and Chap. 8 in Vol. I.

same alternative. Hence, it is a natural framework to model demand for variety (e.g. Bronnenberg 2015; Kim et al. 2002). It is also a natural vehicle to investigate how shifts in income translate into shifts in consumption.

A second approach specifies utilities *indirectly* on quantities, by making utilities a function of prices, $U(p, p_0)$, and sometimes also income, $U(p, p_0, Y)$. A formal link between the two approaches is easy to establish. The result from the direct utility maximization, Eq. (7.1), are quantities as a function of prices also called Marshallian demand, $q(p, p_0, Y)$. When these are substituted into the utility function $U(q, q_0)$, the *indirect* utility function $U(p, p_0, Y)$ is obtained. This function depends on prices and income. The choice between the direct or indirect utility models is often guided by context and research questions. In a discrete choice framework, where individual quantities are of secondary interest, the use of indirect utility models is standard and often takes place even without reference to an underlying direct utility model.

7.2.2.2 Utility Formulation

We illustrate this basic set up and its estimation using the indirect utility approach in a discrete choice context. Seminal works in the development of such structural demand models include Berry (1994), Berry et al. (1995) (henceforth BLP), and Nevo (2001) among others. These models are founded on a static utility maximization problem and represent market level data as aggregations of individual level choices. As an illustrative example, similar to the model of BLP, consider that the utility that consumer i has for alternative j, with characteristics x_j, is given by:

$$U_{ij} = x_j\beta_i - \alpha_i p_j + \xi_j + \epsilon_{ij} \tag{7.3}$$

where x_j are the product characteristics of alternative j.

The utility model accounts for individual level preferences, α_i and β_i. It also accounts for demand shocks ξ_j, which the analyst does not observe. But, to estimate the demand parameters, the analysts want to account for the possibility that the demand shocks are taken into account by marketing managers when setting prices or other marketing variables.

The consumer chooses the alternative that maximizes utility, i.e., chooses the alternative j for which the following inequalities are true:

$$U_{ij} > U_{ik}, \text{for } k = 0, 1, \ldots, J, k \neq j. \tag{7.4}$$

Next, define the support set of alternative j:

$$R_j\left(X, p, \xi\right) = \left\{\beta_i, \alpha_i, \epsilon_{ij} | U_{ij} > U_{ik}\right\} \tag{7.5}$$

as the region of consumer characteristics (β_i, α_i, *and* ϵ_{ij}), for which alternative j is preferred. For inexpensive products, this set might represent consumers who have a high price sensitivity; for products with a high level of performance, the set includes many consumers who share a taste for high performance, etc.

7.2.2.3 Demand

Market-level demand is obtained through the aggregation of individual-level choices. In the simple case of a discrete choice setting with unit demand at the consumer level, this is equal to the mass of the support set. If consumer preferences have density *f*, then aggregate shares (s_j) are equal to:

$$s_j(X, p, \xi; \theta) = \iiint_{R_j(X,p,\xi)} f(d\alpha, d\beta, d\epsilon) \tag{7.6}$$

where θ contains the parameters of the distributions of the demand parameters.

A special case emerges when the utility shocks ϵ_{ij} are identically and independently distributed according to an Extreme Value Type-I distribution, i.e., $\epsilon_{ij} \sim EV_I$. In this case, the ϵ shocks can be integrated out and the demand Eq. (7.6) becomes:

$$s_j(X, p, \xi; \theta) = \int_{-\infty}^{\infty}\int_{-\infty}^{\infty} \frac{\exp(x_j\beta_i - \alpha_i p_j + \xi_j)}{1 + \sum_k \exp(x_k\beta_i - \alpha_i p_k + \xi_k)} f(d\alpha_i, d\beta_i) \tag{7.7}$$

which represents aggregate market shares as an aggregation of logit behavior over the heterogeneity distribution of consumers $f(\alpha, \beta)$. In turn, $f(\alpha, \beta)$ can be any multivariate distribution, e.g., the multivariate normal distribution.

An important advantage of random effects logit models, such as the one in Eq. (7.7), is that they typically avoid the unrealistic implications of some aggregate models, in particular the homogeneous logit model, which predicts that substitution patterns and price elasticities only depend on market shares. Random effects models display aggregate substitution patterns that reflect similarity in characteristics space rather than in market shares, even when the ϵ_{ij} are extreme value distributed (and thus individual choice behavior follows a logit model).

7.2.2.4 Estimation

The estimation of random effects logit models of demand follows methods developed in Berry (1994) and BLP. These estimation procedures account for the non-randomness of certain product characteristics, in particular the possibility that prices are endogenously set by firms based on demand. Additionally, BLP account for differences in consumer tastes.[2]

BLP start from the assumption that the ϵ_{ij} are independent and identically distributed (IID) with an Extreme Value distribution, resulting in an individual-level demand model that, given any α_i and β_i, is of the logit form. Aggregate demand in this model is therefore the sum of individual logit machines, each with idiosyncratic preferences α_i, β_i, as in Eq. (7.7).

[2] See also Chap. 15.

The key to estimating the model is the condition that the aggregate demand shocks, ξ_j, although possibly correlated with marketing variables, like price, should be uncorrelated with variables that instrument for the endogenous variables. Therefore, to estimate the model one needs to solve the demand shocks, ξ_j, given the data and given a candidate of the model parameters. When the demand parameters α_i, β_i, are common to consumers (i.e., $\alpha_i = \alpha$, and $\beta_i = \beta$, $\forall\, i$), the demand shocks, ξ_j, can be solved analytically, as in Berry (1994). However, in the more general case of heterogeneous preferences, the demand shocks need to be computed non-analytically. BLP propose a contraction mapping to compute the demand shocks $\xi_j(S, X, p; \theta)$ as a function of the data (X, p, S) and the model parameters θ.

Next, the analyst needs a set of instrumental variables, Z, that are correlated to the endogenous variable but not to the demand shocks. Using the instruments in combination with the demand shocks, the unrelatedness of the instruments and the demand shocks leads to the following moment condition:

$$\mathrm{E}\left[\xi_j\left(S, X, p; \theta\right) \;|Z\right] = 0. \tag{7.8}$$

To set up an objective function for a moment estimator, the sample analog of this moment is computed as:

$$G(\theta) = \frac{1}{J}\sum_j \xi_j\left(\theta\right) \otimes Z_j \tag{7.9}$$

using the Kronecker product $\otimes$ to interact each of the instruments with the vector of demand shocks of each brand. This sample analog $G(\theta)$ is a column vector with as many elements as there are instruments. The population values of all these elements are zero. The final objective function is constructed by weighting the elements of the sample moments by the inverse of their variance-covariance matrix.[3] Calling this matrix W, the goal function to be minimized is:

$$G(\theta)' \; W \, G\left(\theta\right). \tag{7.10}$$

Minimization of this goal function gives the Generalized Method of Moments (GMM) estimates of the parameters θ (see Chap. 15). In the demand model of Eq. (7.7), these are the parameters in $f(\alpha, \beta)$, which could be for example the mean utility parameters and the variance terms of the heterogeneity distribution of consumers. Inference on the parameters and computation of their standard errors follows the procedure outlined in BLP and Nevo (2001).

---

[3]For computational details see, for example, Nevo (2001).

7.2.2.5 Refinements

There has been some concern about the identification of heterogeneous demand systems using aggregate level data. BLP themselves use supply side moments, in addition to the demand side moments in Eq. (7.9) to help identify the demand parameters. Albuquerque and Bronnenberg (2009), Berry (1994) and Petrin (2002) add micro moments to the estimation using data on brand switching, second choices, and demographic distributions to help identify the heterogeneity parameters.

7.2.3 *Additional Demand Primitives*

The demand model previously described accounts for unit demand and discrete choice in a full information environment. However, most marketing and economic problems are more complex, featuring interactions among agents, imperfect and costly information, and possibly forward-looking consumers. The extensions to the basic demand model explained above take some of these into account (see also Table 7.1.). We mention four important moderators of demand: (1) consideration and search, (2) consumer learning and experimentation, (3) stockpiling and forward buying, (4) peer effects and networked consumers.

7.2.3.1 Consideration and Search

Frequently, consumers do not know of all alternatives available to them in the market, possibly because of lack of awareness or availability, or because of costly search. In such cases, consumers choose among a subset of K choices from the universal set J. In this setting, the utility drawn from products is likely to stay the same as in Eq. (7.3) of the basic setup. However, the inequalities that define the chosen alternative in Eq. (7.4) change to:

$$U_{ij} \geq U_{ik}, \text{for } k \in K, K \subseteq J. \tag{7.11}$$

When the set of considered options is constrained by awareness or availability, their impact can be modeled by treating the awareness or availability as unknowns, which can be a function of advertising or proximity, and integrating out unobserved awareness or availability variables (see Bruno and Vilcassim 2008; Sovinski-Goeree 2008). When the set of considered options is constrained by the cost of search, we have a search model. Search can be assumed to be sequential or simultaneous: when search is assumed to be sequential, an often used model is presented in Weitzman (1979); when search is assumed to be simultaneous or fixed-sample, the original search model is Stigler (1961).

An advantage of using a structural model in this context is that the model makes explicit how search is guided by utility, uncertainty, and search cost arguments. For example, in Kim et al. (2010) consumers need to incur a cost c_{ij} to uncover the unobservable match value ϵ_{ij}. In other applications, they pay a cost to learn about prices (e.g., De Santos et al. 2012; Honka 2014; Seiler 2013).

7.2.3.2 Dynamic Demand Models

A decision maker's current actions can be guided by future consequences. For instance, a consumer might decide to sample brands now to learn about their quality and benefit from this information in future periods. Modeling consumers as dynamic decision makers allows for the estimation of quantities important to marketing researchers, such as consumer learning rates or their trade-off between short-term and long-term gains. Such quantities would be challenging to study, if not impossible, in a static perspective, but help make strategic decisions on promotions, price evolution, and new product introduction.

To represent demand data through the lens of dynamic decision-making, consumers are assumed to maximize the *net present value* of flows of utilities $U_{it}(X, a)$ over time, which depend on the state variables X and purchase decisions a. Typical state variables include quantities such as prices, advertising, etc., but also variables that evolve as a function of the household purchases, such as household inventory, product knowledge, brand awareness, etc. These variables determine how current choices impact future states and thus future choices. The utility from purchase decisions a is represented as:

$$U_i = \sum_t \delta^t U_{it}(X, a). \tag{7.12}$$

Utility in the future may be valued less than current utility, as reflected by the discount factor $0 \leq \delta < 1$.

The maximization of Eq. (7.12) with respect to purchase decisions a is a dynamic programming problem. Its solution can be expressed through a Bellman equation, which defines the value $V_i(X)$ of being in a particular state X as:

$$V_i(X) = \max_a \{U_{it}(X, a) + \delta V_i(T(X, a))\}. \tag{7.13}$$

The value $V_i(X)$ is the maximum—across all feasible current choices a—of the flow utility plus the discounted value of being in the transitioned state $T(X, a)$, which is reached from the current X given choices a. Ackerberg et al. (2007) discuss various econometric tools to solve the Bellman equation, which typically rely on nested fixed-point algorithms (Rust 1987) or a two-stage approach (Hotz and Miller 1993).

Demand models that account for dynamic decision-making face several challenges. An important problem to solve in dynamic demand models is the separate identification of utility functions, discount factors, and subjective beliefs about future market conditions (Magnac and Thesmar 2002). The literature has often addressed this by fixing the discount rate and treating it as common across consumers.

Two studies in marketing have made progress in relaxing this restriction. First, Dubé et al. (2014) model dynamic demand decisions by using survey data to estimate how consumers inter-temporally trade off gains. Their approach features choices made by consumers among options with different short-term and long-term gains. These choices reveal individual consumer discount rates. The paper implements this idea with two studies in cooperation with a large U.S. marketing research company on the dynamic adoption choices of Blu-ray players under different price predictions and availability of Blu-ray movies. In contrast to common beliefs and assumptions made in the literature, the authors find that the future is discounted heavily and that consumers differ greatly in their degree of discounting the future.

Second, Yao et al. (2012) use data from field studies to determine consumer discount rates. The authors observe consumers changing from a linear tariff to a three-part tariff for cell phone plans in a field experiment carried out by a cellphone service provider. They develop an economic model of minute usage under the two plans where the plan-induced change in optimal usage differs by discount rates. Hence, it is the use of theory—the structure of a dynamic demand problem—that allows Yao et al. (2012) to measure individual level discount rates from observed differences in minute usage in pre- versus post-switching of cell phone plans. Like Dubé et al. (2014), Yao et al. (2012) find that consumers discount the future much more than was heretofore assumed: in particular, rather than the typical weekly discount factor of 0.995, the estimated weekly discount factors are on the order of 0.81 and 0.91.

In terms of applications, a good context to discuss dynamic demand models is stockpiling, incentivized by promotions, consumers can buy large quantities for future consumption but doing so comes at a large short-term expenditure plus a stock-up cost. Chan et al. (2008) propose a structural dynamic model of consumer purchases *and* consumption decisions given past purchases. Compared to the extant literature on the effects of promotions (see, e.g., Bell et al. 1999, 2002), they use this model to decompose the promotion effect into business stealing, stockpiling, *and* endogenous consumption increases, whereby high inventory levels drive more consumption. Using their structural model, formulated as a dynamic single-agent utility maximization framework, the authors find support for the endogenous consumption hypothesis. Moreover, in the confines of their application, their finding of an endogenous consumption effect alters our views on the effects of promotional activities: stockpiling and increased consumption are found to be much more prevalent components of promotional consequences, in contrast to previous results that gave more prevalence to brand switching.

Finally, Seiler (2013) investigates the dynamic-demand trade-off between short-term costs and long-term gains resulting from the interaction between the storability of products and the willingness to incur search costs to find good deals. He considers the consumer problem with costly search for prices. The benefits of finding lower prices are larger when purchasing a storable good. Seiler (2013) uses a dynamic structural demand model of a two-stage choice process: (1) a search stage in which the consumer decides whether to look for prices based on the expected utility from purchasing and the cost of search and (2) a subsequent purchase decision, using a dynamic demand framework for a storable product. One of the main objects of interest in this study is the identification of the first stage in this process. Seiler finds that search costs are quantitatively important and that consumers do not search during approximately 70% of their shopping trips. For managers, this is relevant because if consumers are not aware of prices on most shopping trips, marketing tools such as price advertising and displays become strategic complements to price cuts.

7.2.3.3 Extension: Dependence Across Agents

The building of structural models also depends on whether decisions are related across agents. For instance, consumers may directly influence the product adoption of other consumers. If such influences are important, the maximization problem of the structural model that is "responsible" for the generation of demand or price data needs to reflect the interaction of agents. The benefit of models that allow for dependence of decision-making across agents is the capability to estimate the influence of subsets of agents on the remaining network. For instance, in a context of new product adoption with contagion, the social multipliers from contagion, if measured correctly, can be used to compute the total impact of an ad campaign as the initial effects spread from its direct recipients through the social network (Hartmann 2010).

In the presence of social contagion, the payoffs of agents are a function of other agents' choices or states. As pointed out in Hartmann et al. (2008), the analysis of structural models with social contagion is challenging and requires specific methods. One of the main challenges in this literature is the separation of causal contagion effects from positive correlation among agents. This identification problem is caused by:

- social groups organizing themselves along some unobserved variable or feature;
- other unobservables being positively correlated in a social group;
- simultaneous causation taking place among actors.

The separation of causal effects of consumers impacting each other's decisions from correlation driven by homophily or omitted variables generally requires panel data to control for unobservables. Disentangling simultaneous causation among peers requires applying methods that use instrumental variables and exclusion restrictions. The interested reader is referred to Nair et al. (2004), who offer an extensive discussion on these identification issues.

Decomposing the behavior of interacting agents into preferences versus contagion, Nair et al. (2010) model the prescription behavior of physicians as a function of the prescription behavior of doctors that are close in their social network. To separate contagion effects from mere correlation in preferences, the paper uses a rich specification of time and physician fixed effects to account for heterogeneity and common time trends. It also uses a change in the drug usage guidelines as an experiment in the data to trace prescription behavior back to specialist doctors in a physician's network. The paper finds that key opinion leaders have large contagion effects on the behavior of other doctors in their network.

In another example of consumer interactions, Hartmann (2010) models the decisions made by a group of customers as an equilibrium outcome of a discrete game, in a way that all group members are satisfied with their choice: the indirect utility of each individual's decision is not only a function of his own preferences, but also a function of the decisions of others in the group. Hartmann finds, that for a group of golfers, 65% of customer value is attributable to individual preferences, while the remaining 35% is created by the effect of the individual on members of his group.

7.3 Structural Models of Marketing Actions

7.3.1 Decision Motives and Assumptions

Structural supply-side models in marketing treat observations of marketing strategy, e.g., prices, advertising, promotions, product line length, etc., as being generated from goal-directed decision making by marketing managers. Most frequently, the objective is profit maximization (e.g., Thomadsen 2005), although sometimes the focus may chance, for example, to the maximization of sales or awareness (e.g., Hartmann and Klapper 2015). To fix ideas, consider the problem of the marketing manager who maximizes profits π with respect to strategic marketing variables, $V = \{\text{Price, Advertising, Promotion, etc.}\}$:

$$\max_{V} \pi\left(V, V_0\right) \tag{7.14}$$

where profits $\pi(V, V_0)$ can also depend on a set of exogenous shifters V_0. In some marketing applications, the profit function is constructed from *demand principles* (e.g., Dubé et al. 2010; Goettler and Gordon 2011), whereas in other applications profit functions are *indirect* or *descriptive* (see, e.g., Ellickson and Misra 2011; Vitorino 2012).

Critics of the structural modeling tradition question the premise of interpreting marketing actions as the outcome of optimization by marketing managers. There are two lines of defense to this criticism. First, even if marketing managers do not explicitly solve the firm's optimization problem, over time they are likely to get close to an optimal solution through a process of trial and error, mimicry, and, increasingly, the use of data analysis. Second, surviving firms in a competitive market do not likely leave important profit opportunities on the table. Hence, it seems a valuable starting point that firms are able to reach marketing decisions in proximity to optimal behavior. In addition, the criticism is also weakened by the fact that structural models, as behavioral models, can be formulated to account for behavior that is boundedly rational (see, e.g., Spiegler 2014) or prone to decision errors (see, e.g., Reiss and Wolak 2007).

We illustrate the different elements of the structural approach to modeling marketing strategies using two types of applications, each with their own modeling traditions.

7.3.2 *Price Competition*

7.3.2.1 Basic Approach

Structural models of price competition are of interest to marketing thought and practice for several reasons. First, understanding how firms compete on prices is central in assessing the appropriate level of entry or in assessing whether firms collude (see also Chap. 9). Second, firms set their price strategies based on consumer response and demand, e.g., price elasticities. Therefore, data on prices (or other supply side decisions) are informative about price sensitivity (or the sensitivity to other demand primitives) when studied through a structural lens. In this setting, this means that observations of prices, costs, and margins alone can teach us something about price sensitivity: when consumers are price sensitive optimal margins are smaller, while when consumers have a high willingness to pay margins are larger, all else equal. BLP put this in practice and use price and quantity data to improve the estimation of demand side parameters. Going a step further, Thomadsen (2005) presents an example where observed prices constitute the main source of information about demand side parameters in a model of spatial price competition.

To illustrate the approach, consider a choice-based random-effects logit demand system as defined in Sect. 7.2. To model price data, assume that observed prices are consistent with Bertrand-Nash price competition under such demand.[4] The objective of the analysis is to represent the observed price data as equilibrium outcomes of competition among multi-product firms. Define the profit function for firm h as:

$$\pi_h = \sum_{j \in \mathcal{M}_h} \left(p_j - mc_j\right) M s_j(p) - F_h \tag{7.15}$$

where mc_j is marginal cost, F_h is a fixed cost for firm h, M is total market size, $\mathcal{M}_h$ is the product line of the firm, and $s_j(p)$ is the share equation defined in Eq. (7.7). The marketing manager of each firm maximizes the total product-line profits and not the profits of each individual product, thus internalizing the profit impact of substitution patterns within each product line. The J prices that support a pure strategy Bertrand-Nash equilibrium must all satisfy the first-order equations:

[4]Our discussion here is based on Nevo (2001). See also Sect. 9.5.

$$s_j(p) + \sum_{k \in \mathcal{M}_h} (p_k - mc_k) \frac{\partial s_k(p)}{\partial p_j} = 0. \tag{7.16}$$

Prices can be solved by defining a dummy $I_{jk} = 1$ if j and k are both in the product line of the same firm (and 0 if not) and arranging the elements $-I_{jk} \times {}^{\partial s_k(p)}\big/_{\partial p_j}$ into a matrix $\Omega_{(J \times J)}$. This matrix contains the (cross)price effects of all product pairs that are part of the same product line and 0's for product pairs belonging to two separate competitors. This allows the first order conditions to be cast in matrix form,

$$s(p) - \Omega\,(p - mc) = 0. \tag{7.17}$$

Equilibrium margins are the solution to the matrix equation:

$$(p - mc) = \Omega^{-1} s(p). \tag{7.18}$$

Suppose that the analyst observes marginal costs with some degree of error. Now, Eq. (7.18) can be written as a price estimation equation:

$$p = \Omega^{-1} s(p) + mc + \eta. \tag{7.19}$$

This equation can be used in two ways. To start, if the researcher has estimates of the demand primitives in the matrix Ω, it is possible to estimate the marginal costs using the above regression. This might be the case when good demand side data exist. Nevo (2001) uses this approach to study competition in the breakfast cereal industry. Alternatively, if the researchers have data on the price-cost margins, then such data helps identify demand. BLP use this by defining a system of equations consisting of the demand equations in Eq. (7.7) and the price Eq. (7.19) and estimating the supply-demand system jointly. In short, a structural model of price competition can be used to measure costs and/or help estimate price sensitivity.

7.3.2.2 Extensions

Several extensions of modeling marketing competition exist. For instance, rather than maximizing short-term profits, as in Eq. (7.14) or (7.15), managers often realize that their current actions impact future profits. Thus a natural extension is to model marketing strategy in a dynamic optimization framework, acknowledging that marketing managers make certain decisions with an eye for their long run effects. Compare in this respect also Sect. 9.5.

Looking at marketing strategies using a dynamic structural model allows for a better understanding of time-varying marketing strategies or the nature of competition. For instance, advertising pulsing strategies or tacitly collusiveprice agreements are difficult to understand empirically, unless a dynamic decision framework is adopted where current advertising or price levels are set considering their future consequences.

We mention one example. Dubé et al. (2005) study advertising in a model where firms advertise to build a stock of goodwill which in turn shifts demand. The stock of goodwill depletes slowly and thus a firm's current investments have effects into the future. The approach advocated in Dubé et al. (2005) takes such effects into account and provides an empirical model of pulsing behavior, i.e., of switching between heavy advertising and no advertising at all.

7.3.3 Entry Models

7.3.3.1 Basic Approach

The competition models above contain both demand and supply primitives. In fact, the model in Berry et al. (1995) features both utility and profit maximization, i.e., optimization on the demand side as well as the supply side.

A next class of structural models on the supply side uses a less structural and more descriptive model on the demand side. The motivation for this choice is that the interest is primarily with the supply primitives, e.g., cost or productivity. We illustrate this approach analyzing entry data. Models of entry are important in a variety of questions about competition, barriers to entry, and market coverage.

A structural entry model might start from the assumption that if a store enters in a market, then the store manager can make a profit there. In turn, this places a bound on unobserved post-entry profits. Namely, if the store manager decides to enter a market, this must mean that post-entry profits are at least equal to the cost of entry. Using this revealed preference argument, entry data speak to the decision primitives of the store manager (such as the cost of entry).

Using a similar argument, Bresnahan and Reiss (1991) make a seminal contribution in studying static entry decisions with competitive interaction. The basic idea in this study is that if entry decisions are profit based, then one can infer important aspects of competition from observing the relation between entry and market size, for instance, when looking across a set of independent markets. The informativeness about competition comes from the observation that, in a (imperfectly) competitive market, the relation between market size and total industry profits (and hence entry) is affected by demand sharing *and* margin erosion. In contrast, in a market of monopolists, this relation is only impacted by demand sharing at a constant monopolist margin.

More specifically, Bresnahan and Reiss (1991) look at entry of services like dentists, or lawyers, etc. in towns in the United States. If the smallest market that supports a monopolist has, say, 100 K consumers, and the smallest market that supports duopolists has 300 K consumers, requiring more than double the population size to support two firms, this suggests the presence of margin erosion in the post-entry market in addition to demand sharing. Therefore, if, in a cross-sectional data set covering many markets, the smallest N-player market is disproportionally larger than the smallest $(N-1)$-player market, it stands to reason to conclude this market is (imperfectly) competitive. Bresnahan and Reiss (1991) find that, in professional service markets, the smallest two-player market is more than twice the size of the smallest one-player market, but that the relation between market size and entry becomes linear quickly after two players. This suggests that such markets are competitive but that the level of competition stays constant after a low number of entrants has entered.

We illustrate modeling entry data using a simple example, admittedly at the expense of conceptual richness. Assume for now that all potential entrants operate similar stores and suppose we observe the number of entrants N_s across a set of markets $s = 1, \ldots, S$, and nothing else. Assume profits are equal to:

$$\pi (N_s) = W (N_s, x_s, \theta) - F_s \tag{7.20}$$

with W being a descriptive model of gross profits, x_s being the characteristics of market s, F_s the fixed cost of entry, and θ the parameters of demand and supply. Firms know their entry cost, but the analyst observes these with some error. For instance, the analyst may assume that fixed costs follow a normal distribution, e.g.,

$$F_s \sim N \left(\mu, \sigma_F^2\right) \tag{7.21}$$

where μ is the mean entry cost and σ_F^2 its variance. Obviously, if cost shifters exist, those can be taken into account.

Firms enter when profits are positive. This means that, in a free-entry equilibrium, the last entrant makes profits above entry cost and the next entrant would make profits below entry cost. That is, modeling the observed N_s as the equilibrium outcome, it needs to be true that:

$$W (N_s, x_s, \theta) \geq F_s > W (N_s + 1, x_s, \theta) . \tag{7.22}$$

Given the distributional assumptions about entry costs, the probability that this is true at parameter values θ, μ, and σ_F^2 equals:

$$\Pr(N_s|x_s, \theta, \mu, \sigma_F^2) = \Phi \left(\frac{W (N_s, x_s, \theta) - \mu}{\sigma_F}\right) - \Phi \left(\frac{W (N_s + 1, x_s, \theta) - \mu}{\sigma_F}\right) \tag{7.23}$$

and the log likelihood of the observed entry data across markets s equals

$$LL(N_s|x_s, \theta, \mu, \sigma_F^2) = \sum_s \ln \left[\Pr(N_s|x_s, \theta, \mu, \sigma_F^2)\right] \tag{7.24}$$

assuming that the markets are independent. A maximum likelihood estimator of the cost parameters, μ and σ_F^2, and the profit parameters, θ, can then be obtained as the argmax of this log likelihood function.

The above illustration of entry models and method of inferring entry costs assumes homogenous firms, static decision-making, and no firm interaction. Various elaborations to this model relax these restrictions.

7.3.3.2 Extensions of Entry Models

The first set of extensions that relaxes the assumption of market independence includes models of competitive interaction. Thomadsen (2007) develops a structural model of firm location in the fast food industry. Starting from individual-level consumer primitives, he develops a model of demand for fast food at a specific outlet that depends on the distance between consumers and outlets. Outlets compete following a static two-stage Bertrand competition game, where outlets first set their locations, and then, holding these locations fixed, compete on price. Given a set of entry primitives for McDonald's and Burger King (estimated and discussed in Thomadsen 2005), the location and pricing decisions are solved in the model and compared with the respective actual decisions by firms. Thomadsen finds that the firm location equilibrium depends on market size: in small markets, McDonald's locates itself in the center of the market, and Burger King in the periphery. In larger markets, McDonald's and Burger King both prioritize spatial differentiation, locating on opposite sides of the market.

In a related paper, Vitorino (2012) studies store entry and exit, but addresses a different type of competitive interaction than Thomadsen (2007). Specifically, Vitorino (2012) considers that managers of similar stores may choose locations close to other stores. The trade-off for co-location is classic: on the one hand, co-location leads to increased attractiveness of a particular site to consumers, which increases demand for the site; on the other hand, co-location increases competition due to store proximity. Using shopping malls in the United States as a setting, Vitorino (2012) estimates an entry game[5] that allows for the possibility that mall membership of department stores causes other stores to locate themselves in the same mall, benefiting from the department-store driven shopper traffic. The paper finds strong complementarity effects consistent with the co-location argument. The structural estimates of the parameters in her model are used to justify that department stores function as "anchor-stores" and that mall-owners often give them better deals than to other stores, in terms of rent and location fees.

A second set of extensions moves from a static-decision making setting to a dynamic one. For example, Holmes (2011) studies the roll-out pattern of entry by Walmart stores across local markets in the United States from 1962 until

[5]In this paper, Vitorino also discusses and proposes a solution to the multiple-equilibria problem that is present in the entry literature.

2005. During this period, Walmart consistently opened stores radiating outward from its original location in Bentonville, Arkansas, maintaining high geographical concentration of stores throughout. Holmes (2011) proposes a single-agent dynamic structural model of entry to understand why Walmart preferred to enter with high store density despite sales cannibalization over entering in a more scattered pattern with no cannibalization. In this model, Holmes allows for the possibility that high store density provides economies of scale from resource sharing with respect to advertising and distribution. He then sets out to measure these economies using a revealed preference approach: opening an outlet nearer others and accepting stronger cannibalization of sales must be more profitable than locating it in other candidate locations with less or no cannibalization. Using methods described in Holmes (2011) and Pakes et al. (2015) generates a large number of moment inequalities from the condition that the observed path of opening stores maximizes the present value of profits. The intuition behind this approach is that the true parameters should be such that any other candidate path has a lower present value of forecasted profits than the chosen path. The study infers large economies of density to justify the geographic concentration in Walmart's store entry strategy.

Several other methods for analyzing entry data exist, each providing variations on the simple case explained above. Ellickson and Misra (2011) provide an overview of the state-of-the-art methods and approaches involved in entry models. Su (2014) discusses many of the computational aspects of these models under simple static interactions.

7.3.4 Other Marketing Strategy Decisions

The focus on price competition and entry models does poor justice to the literature on structural models of marketing actions. We selectively mention three important recent strands of literature.

Misra and Nair (2011) study effort by sales reps and the design of sales force contracts using a dynamic single-agent structural model. They start by investigating how the sales-force compensation schemes, including the presence of target quotas and time limits to achieve them, affect how much effort sales agents decide to put in over a contract period. Next, the paper uses the estimates from this exercise to improve existing compensation plans.

Existing contracts in the empirical example modeled by Misra and Nair (2011) consist of a fixed salary plus a marginal payment per additional sales between a floor and a ceiling of sales performance. The authors assume that sales agents maximize the net present value of a flow of utility, which in turn depends on per-period compensation. The dynamics in the decision problem are rooted in the nonlinearity of the compensation plan, which causes time-shifting of the sales effort. That is, the presence of a floor quota introduces the perverse incentive to postpone effort in this period once a sales agent realizes the infeasibility of reaching the minimum sales. Instead, the agent may lower current effort and "bank" current potential sales for a next period. In other words, lowering current effort now increases the chance that the pent-up demand will surpass the quota tomorrow. Similarly, ceilings do not incentivize effort beyond them.

Estimation of the model proceeds in two steps. First, the authors semi-parametrically[6] estimate the transitions of the state variables (e.g., sales per agent) and the policy function of each agent (how much effort to put in, taking into account the compensation contract and the state variables). This estimation is helped by having access to extensive sales force performance and compensation data at the individual level. Next, given the state transitions and the policy functions, the paper estimates the agent's risk aversion and cost of effort such that their observed behavior is rationalized. Estimation of these parameters is done agent by agent.

Next, the authors use the estimates of individual level parameters on risk aversion and time cost to test alternative redesigns of the sales force compensation contract. They conclude that the current contract is suboptimal and that the company should offer a payout based on monthly sales. This recommendation was subsequently implemented by the firm and resulted in strongly increased profits. Misra and Nair's (2011) study illustrates that structural models, including those with the additional complexity of dynamic optimization, can be highly practical and valuable.

In another application of single agent dynamic models, Hitsch (2006) develops a model that can be used to manage a product launch (or exit) when the true product performance or quality is unknown to the firm before entry and must be learned from sales. In this study, the marketing manager wants to maximize long-term profits with respect to pricing and advertising, and with respect to continuing the product or scrapping it. Signals from the market about the true product quality parameter are noisy. The estimation of the model requires the identification of initial beliefs that the decision makers have about product quality. The model estimation proceeds in two steps: in the first step, a demand model is estimated similarly to the procedure in Berry et al. (1995) using the generalized method of moments (GMM)[7]; next, with the demand parameters in hand, the dynamic firm model is estimated via maximum likelihood methods. The paper uses data on new product introductions in the consumer packaged goods industry between 1988 and 1990. The parameter estimates imply that managers can improve profits by being able to scrap bad products earlier when better information about the true quality of the products is available.

Finally, Goettler and Gordon (2011) estimate an equilibrium model of dynamic oligopoly in the market for computer chips. In particular, the authors represent observed product innovation and pricing data of the two leading computer chip manufacturers, AMD and Intel, as the equilibrium outcome of a two-stage product innovation and pricing game. The structural model in this paper portrays decision-makers maximizing long-term profits in a repeated game of investment and pricing decisions, and serving consumers who may postpone current purchases to wait

---

[6]See Chap. 17.

[7]See Chap. 15.

for better products and maximize a discounted flow of utilities. The authors find that the rate of innovation in the industry is *lowered* by competition. Unintuitive perhaps at first, this effect is consistent with the hypothesis that competition erodes profits required to finance innovation. This hypothesis traces back to Schumpeterian explanations about the incentives for innovation and creative destruction. For a more general perspective on this so-called Schumpeterian trade-off between low prices or innovation, see Nelson and Winter (1982).

7.4 Application: A Structural Model of the Effects of the Great Recession of 2008–2009 on the Automobile Industry

7.4.1 Research Problem and General Approach

For illustration purposes, we now provide a more elaborate example involving the various structural methods and models presented above. The example covers the structural model of consumer demand and channel decisions in the automotive industry proposed in Albuquerque and Bronnenberg (2012) published in marketing science, AB henceforth.[8]

AB (2012) study how a severe negative demand shock—such as the Great Recession of 2008–2009—impacts consumers, dealers, and manufacturers in the United States automobile industry. They also evaluate the impact of a three billion dollar subsidy on consumer prices, called the "Car Allowance Rebate System" (CARS) program, that the U.S. government implemented in 2009 to dull the impact of the Great Recession on the industry.

AB's approach first represents observed quantity, wholesale price and retail price data as demand- and supply-side optimization problems, and estimates the demand and supply primitives using pre-recession data. Next, AB use these primitives to simulate how the various agents change their behavior in response to (1) the Great Recession of 2008–2009 and (2) the Great Recession plus new prices resulting from the CARS program.

To simulate the channel's response to the recession, AB represent the Great Recession of 2008–2009 as a reduction to the demand for all alternatives in the market. More practically, AB calibrate an increase in the appeal of the outside good, i.e., in the appeal of *not buying* a car, to match the reduction in quantities during the Great Recession. After this calibration, the adjustment in behavior of consumers, retailers, and manufacturers is simulated in turn holding the behavior of other agents fixed until convergence. Schematically, this is represented in Fig. 7.1.

[8]The following text is based on Albuquerque and Bronnenberg (2012).

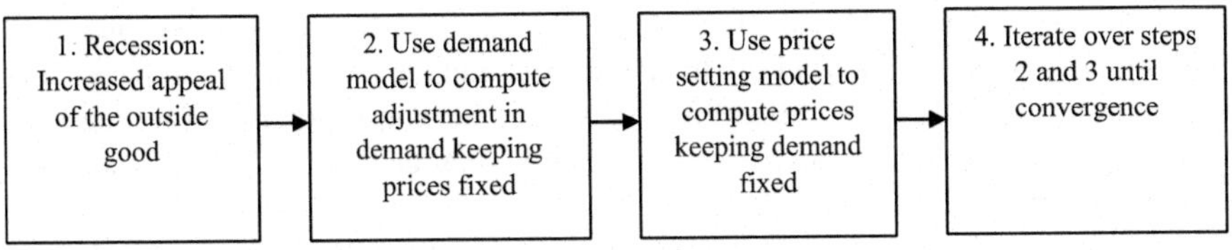

Fig. 7.1 Simulating the channel's response to a demand shock

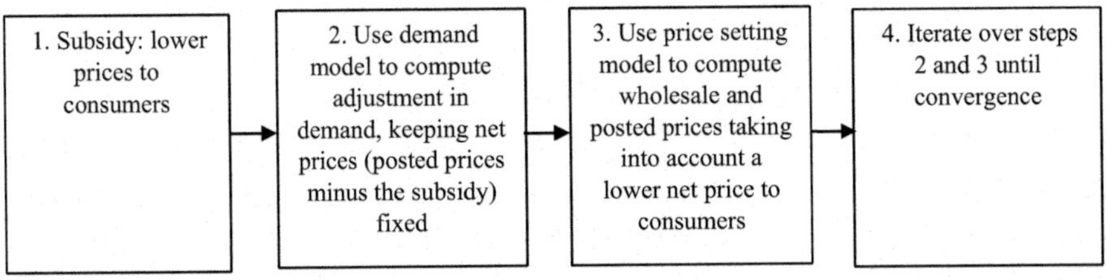

Fig. 7.2 Simulating the channel's response to a price subsidy

below. At convergence, this approach captures the adjusted equilibrium that fully incorporates the effects of the demand shock on all agents.

AB follow a similar approach to simulate the impact of the government subsidy that followed the recession. The U.S. government subsidized consumers buying a new car, offering them a rebate for the new car plus a scrap value for their trade-in vehicle. This subsidy therefore creates a difference between the prices charged by retailers and the prices paid by consumers. The reduction in the effective retail price was aimed to raise consumer demand for new vehicles. To evaluate the effect of the subsidy, it needs to be taken into account that the subsidy-driven boost in demand is likely to increase retail prices, as it may not be optimal for dealers to pass-through all the subsidy to consumers. The structural approach in AB takes this pass-through into account by allowing manufacturers and retailers to set prices given the gap between prices charged by sellers and net prices paid by consumers. Technically, AB iterate between forecasting demand at given prices minus the subsidy, and forecasting wholesale and final prices given the increased consumer demand under the subsidy, until convergence. AB interpret the result as a forecast of the new equilibrium with an endogenous pass-through rate. Fig. 7.2 shows this process schematically.

The approach followed in AB requires formulating a model of choice decisions by consumers and a model of price setting behavior among the channel members on the supply side of the market.

7.4.2 *The Demand Side of the Market*

AB model consumers making choices among combinations of car make, car type, and a specific dealership (including location). Although rooted in the original BLP demand framework, the approach is different by making a choice alternative a combination of a car and a dealership. This means that changes in the purchase conditions impact demand for both the chosen car and the location of purchase. This is important because some dealerships may become non-profitable in a recession and the model should be able to predict possible retailer closures when simulating market outcomes.

AB assume that there are M consumers in the market. Household i chooses to purchase car j at a dealership d, or use a different means of transportation or an old car (the outside good). AB use an indirect utility approach with the utility for consumer i of purchasing car j given by:

$$U_{ijt} = x_{jt}\beta_i - \alpha_i p_{jt} + \xi_{jt} + \epsilon_{ijt}. \tag{7.25}$$

Each purchase option j is a unique combination of a car of brand b, type m, and dealer d. The x_{jt} include observed characteristics, such as engine size, transmission type, and distance between the individual and dealer locations. The prices p_{jt} represent the average price for option j at the dealer in quarter t, and heterogeneity in the demand effects of price and other attributes is captured by observed consumer characteristics, for example, income at the zip code level. Finally, ξ_{jt} captures the impact of car attributes unobserved to the researcher but taken into consideration by consumers and supply agents. As discussed above, such demand shocks may create an endogeneity bias in the model estimates if unaccounted for.

In the automobile category, alternatives can be aggregated into subgroups based on car similarity, with competition being stronger within group that across groups. For example, a sport utility vehicle (SUV) is likely to strongly compete with other SUVs but much less so with compact cars. Because of this, the authors use a nested logit formulation,[9] with nests based on car type and brand in the unobservable term ϵ_{ijt} (Richards 2007). Dropping the t subscript momentarily to avoid cluttered notation, the choice probability of alternative j (a car of type m and brand b) becomes:

$$\Pr_i(j) = \Pr_i(j|b(m)) \times \Pr_i(b(m)|m) \times \Pr_i(m) \tag{7.26}$$

where $\Pr_i(m)$ is the probability of choosing the car type m or the outside good; $\Pr_i(b(m)|\, m)$ represents the probability of choosing brand b, given the choice of car type m; and finally $\Pr_i(j|\, b(m))$ is the probability of buying brand b and type m at the dealership corresponding to alternative j. Each component of Eq. (7.26) is given by:

$$\Pr_i(j|b(m)) = \exp\left(\frac{1}{(1-\sigma_B)(1-\sigma_M)} V_{ij}\right) \Big/ \sum\nolimits_{j' \in b(m)} \exp\left(\frac{1}{(1-\sigma_B)(1-\sigma_M)} V_{ij'}\right) \tag{7.27}$$

$$\Pr_i(b(m)|m) = \exp\left((1-\sigma_B)\, IV_{ib(m)}\right) \Big/ \sum\nolimits_{b' \in m} \exp\left((1-\sigma_B)\, IV_{ib'}\right) \tag{7.28}$$

[9]See Sect. 8.2.3.1 in Vol. I.

$$\Pr_i(m) = \exp\left((1-\sigma_M)\, IV_{im}\right) \Big/ 1 + \sum_{m'} \exp\left((1-\sigma_M)\, IV_{im'}\right) \tag{7.29}$$

where $IV_{ib(m)}$ and IV_{im} are the inclusive values given by:

$$V_{ib(m)} = \ln \sum_{j \in b(m)} \exp\left(\frac{1}{(1-\sigma_B)(1-\sigma_M)} V_{ij}\right) \tag{7.30}$$

and

$$IV_{im} = \ln \sum_{b \in m} \exp\left((1-\sigma_B)\, IV_{ib}\right). \tag{7.31}$$

7.4.3 The Supply Side of the Model

The supply side of the model accounts for two central aspects of selling automobiles previously discussed in Sects. 7.3.2 and 7.3.3 , respectively (1) price competition among manufacturers and retailers and (2) distribution, in particular manufacturer decisions about dealer networks and retailer decisions about entry and exit.

7.4.3.1 Pricing Decisions

For the pricing decisions of manufacturers and retailers, AB assume that manufacturers are Stackelberg leaders and take retailer price setting into account. The study also assumes that retailers engage in Bertrand-Nash price competition and the same is assumed for manufacturers.[10]

In particular, manufacturer k sets wholesale prices w_j of all car alternatives j under its portfolio, for each time period t (the subscript t is again dropped for clarity):

$$\pi_k = \sum_{j \in k} \left(w_j - mc_j\right) \cdot M \cdot s_j(p) - \left(x_k \rho_1 + \upsilon_k\right) n_k - F_k \tag{7.32}$$

where mc_j is the manufacturer variable cost. The total quantity for alternative j is the product of its market share $s_j(p)$ (which depends on retail prices) and market size M. The fixed costs incurred by the manufacturer have two components: a first part that depends on the dealership network, i.e., the number of dealerships inthe market n_k,

[10] See also Sect. 9.5.

with x_k being a vector of cost shifters and ρ_1 the respective parameters; and a second part not dependent on the network denoted by F_k. AB also allows for measurement error on fixed network costs v_k.

The manufacturer maximizes profits with respect to wholesale prices. Analogous to the methods developed in Sect. 7.3.2, the first order conditions that provide the optimal manufacturer prices are:

$$W - MC = {\Omega_w}^{-1} S. \tag{7.33}$$

In this formulation, element (j,j') of matrix Ω_w is equal to the negative of the derivative of shares with respect to manufacturer price, $-\frac{\partial s_{j'}}{\partial w_j}$, if j and j' are made by the same manufacturer and 0 otherwise. Because manufacturer prices influence retailer prices that in turn influence consumer demand, this derivative is obtained through the chain rule $\frac{\partial s_{j'}}{\partial w_j} = \sum_{j''} \frac{\partial s_{j'}}{\partial p_{j''}} \times \frac{\partial p_{j''}}{\partial w_j}$. AB show, drawing from Villas-Boas (2007), pp. 633–634, that the terms in the chain rule can be evaluated numerically, using the parameters from the demand side.

Dealers take manufacturer prices as given and choose final prices by maximizing the following profit function:

$$\pi_d = \sum_{j \in d} \left(p_j - w_j + \delta_j\right) \cdot s_j \cdot M - F_d. \tag{7.34}$$

The margin on each car is equal to the price p_j minus the manufacturer price w_j, plus any additional cash flows δ_j (for example, car service net revenues) that are estimated. AB assume that the δ_j are fixed quantities based on industry standards and are not strategically set. The term F_d denotes any fixed costs of dealer d. With the assumption of Bertrand-Nash competition among dealerships, and with coordination across all alternatives that belong to the same dealership, the dealer first-order conditions are:

$$p - w = \Delta + {\Omega_p}^{-1} S. \tag{7.35}$$

The vectors p and w include, respectively, the final consumer prices and the manufacturer prices. The term Δ of additional cash flows from future servicing a car is estimated. As above, Ω_p is a matrix of derivatives of share with respect to final price, where the element (j,j') of matrix Ω_p is $-\frac{\partial s_{j'}}{\partial p_j}$ if the pair of alternatives is sold through the same retailer, and 0 otherwise.

With estimates of the demand model in hand and observations of both wholesale and retail prices, the two price Eqs. (7.33) and (7.35) can be used to estimate manufacturer variable costs and retailer additional cash flows that impact the pricing of cars.

7.4.3.2 Manufacturer Decisions About the Dealership Networks

The second term on the right hand side of Eq. (7.32) measures the impact on profitability of manufacturers of having large or small networks. To identify the parameters related to the cost shifters, AB assume that manufacturers make optimal decisions regarding the size and location of the dealership network. This is used in estimation by requiring of the parameter values that the observed configuration is more profitable than alternative ones, similar to Eq. (7.22).

To find the network cost parameters for manufacturers, the authors assume that the profits associated with the observed network of n_k dealers must be higher than those associated with a configuration with $n_k + 1$ and $n_k - 1$ dealers:

$$\pi_k \left(\Lambda, n_k, n_{-k}\right) > \pi_k \left(\Lambda, n_k - 1, n_{-k}\right), \text{and} \tag{7.36}$$

$$\pi_k \left(\Lambda, n_k, n_{-k}\right) > \pi_k \left(\Lambda, n_k + 1, n_{-k}\right). \tag{7.37}$$

The term Λ summarizes all the data available for estimation. Using Eq. (7.32), this implies that:

$$x_k \rho_1 + v_k \leq R_k \left(\Lambda, n_k, n_{-k}\right) - R_k \left(\Lambda, n_k - 1, n_{-k}\right), \text{and} \tag{7.38}$$

$$x_k \rho_1 + v_k \geq R_k \left(\Lambda, n_k + 1, n_{-k}\right) - R_k \left(\Lambda, n_k, n_{-k}\right) \tag{7.39}$$

where

$$R_k \left(\Lambda, n_k, n_{-k}\right) = \sum_{j \in k} \left(w_j - mc_j\right) \cdot M \cdot s_j \left(p_k, n_k\right).$$

In estimation, evaluating these conditions involves running counterfactuals for one more and one less dealer in the market, thereby representing how changes in the dealer network affect market shares and prices. The variable profits of the observed network minus the fixed costs associated with the management of the network need to be higher than the counterfactual ones, or the manufacturers would have an incentive to deviate.

7.4.3.3 Fixed Costs of Dealers

A similar approach to the one just described can be used to estimate the setup costs of dealerships. The decision of dealerships is to continue their operations at a particular location. Hence, the optimization conditions are (1) that variable profits are larger than the fixed costs, and (2) that the net profit is largest at the observed locations. Therefore, given the configuration of dealerships, one boundary condition on parameter estimates is that any deviation from the observed configuration would lead to lower profits for any given dealership. With the assumption that the fixed costs take the functional form $F_d = x_d \rho_2 + v_d$, the authors formalize the optimization conditions (1) and (2) above, respectively as

$$R_d\left(\Lambda, d_z, -d_z\right) > x_d \rho_2 + \upsilon_d \tag{7.40}$$

$$R_d\left(\Lambda, d_z, -d_z\right) - \left(x_{d_z} \rho_2 + \upsilon_{d_z}\right) > R_d\left(\Lambda, d_{z'}, -d_z\right) - \left(x_{d_{z'}} \rho_2 + \upsilon_{d_{z'}}\right) \tag{7.41}$$

where $R_d\left(\Lambda, d_z, -d_z\right) = \sum_{j \in d_z} \left(p_j - w_j - \delta_j\right) \cdot s_j \cdot M$ represents the variable part of profits with the dealerships d and all other dealers $-d$ located at zip codes z. The alternative setting in the right hand side of Eq. (7.41) changes a focal dealer d from zip code z to zip code z', which leads to different market shares and equilibrium prices for all agents in the market.

7.4.4 Data

The core data in AB is an individual-level transactional data set covering the larger San Diego market from 2004 to 2006, i.e., pre-dating the recession. For each car transaction, the data include the car make and type, engine size, fuel, and transmission type, zip code of dealer where the transaction happened, and residential zip codes of the consumers.

AB also collect zip code level U.S. Census data on distributions of income and population density. The data set also covers the retail price net of discounts paid by consumers as well as the vehicle's wholesale price, net of any manufacturer rebate, which allows the researchers to observe the gross margin per car.

AB next collect data on manufacturer dealership networks and on the number and location (at the zip code level) of a large sample of dealers in the San Diego region. These are used in estimating the fixed costs of operating the network of dealers. Finally, AB collect data on cost shifters to dealerships and manufacturers such as distance from the port of San Diego and the size of the dealer.

Overall, the data cover 15,795 transactions, distributed across 22 different dealerships, 9 car makes, with a total of $J = 62$ alternatives. The analysis focuses on the top brands in the San Diego area: General Motors, Ford, Honda, Hyundai, Chrysler, Toyota, and Volkswagen. Variation across consumers, cars, dealers, prices, and other characteristics, combined with the assumption of optimality of decisions (and the functional form assumptions), allows for the identification of all model parameters.

7.4.5 Estimation

Estimation proceeds in three stages. To start, the detailed transaction and location data allow AB to estimate the demand parameters independently of other parameters. Next, using the demand parameter values, the supply-side first order conditions related to pricing can be evaluated and manufacturer marginal costs as well as retailer additional cash flows are estimated. Third, with the first two stages estimated, AB estimate the fixed costs for dealers and fixed costs for manufacturers directly related to managing a dealership network using the profit inequalities outlined above.

Since the demand model is fully identified from the choice data, AB estimate the demand side parameters without any assumptions on the behavior of dealers and manufacturers. They use the control function approach (Pancras and Sudhir 2007; Petrin and Train 2010) to control for endogeneity of prices. To account for heterogeneity, AB draw consumers from the empirical distributions of demographic characteristics for the zip code where they reside. Estimation of demand parameters is done using simulated maximum likelihood. The likelihood function takes the following form:

$$L = \prod_i \prod_j \prod_t \left(\Pr_{ijt} | \text{data}, \theta\right)^{y_{ijt}} \tag{7.42}$$

with y_{ijt} being an indicator variable that takes the value of 1 for the chosen alternative and zero otherwise. The vector θ contains the demand parameters to be estimated.

With the demand parameters, the derivatives of demand to prices can be obtained numerically, and can then be used in the first-order conditions of the pricing decision equations. For example, to estimate the variable costs of the manufacturers in Eq. (7.33), $W = MC + {\Omega_w}^{-1}S$, all terms on the right hand side are either observed or can be obtained through the demand side of the market, except for the variable costs MC.

Since the authors are also interested in testing different dealer network configurations and predicting closures in the recession, AB use the approach in Pakes et al. (2015) and estimate the dealership costs of manufacturers and retailers as a function of a set of observed cost shifters.

In practice, to estimate the parameters for dealership fixed costs, the authors relocate one dealer at the time to a different zip code, keeping all others constant. They choose 11 alternative locations for each dealer and obtain 20 dealers × 11 alternative locations = 220 inequalities. Additionally, the authors impose that the estimated fixed costs need to be higher than zero and that the profits of each dealer at their actual observed location, given by Eq. (7.34), needs to be non-negative, or else the dealership would close. This gives the authors a total of 260 inequalities to estimate the cost parameters by minimizing the sum of the absolute value of inequality violations, as in Pakes et al. (2015). A similar approach, outlined in detail in AB, can be used to estimate the manufacturer fixed costs that are dependent on the management of a network of dealers.

7.4.6 Results

As described at the beginning of Sect. 7.4.1, the two main counterfactuals that are included in the paper are (1) measuring the impact of the recession on final prices and demand and (2) investigating the final results and pass-through of a government subsidy—the Car Allowance Rebate System - intended to reduce the impact of the crisis.

AB find that in the Great Recession of 2008–2009, which led to a market size drop of about 30%, prices dropped by 13% and 11% for dealer and manufacturers respectively. This drop in prices counteracts the effect of the crises which otherwise would have led to even lower demand.

Relevant to policy makers, the Car Allowance Rebate System subsidy was reduced by retailers seeking to profit from the improved demand conditions that the subsidy caused. AB finds that in the presence of a $4500 Car Allowance Rebate System subsidy, retailers would raise their price by about $1500. Therefore, whereas $3000 is passed on to consumers, AB estimates that dealers optimally "pocket" $1500 of the CARS subsidy per vehicle.

AB discuss predictions of manufacturers reacting to the Great Recession by closing various dealerships in their network and show that their approach is informative about the location of the closed dealerships.

7.5 A Few Notes on Software

Although structural models have become mainstream econometric tools to analyze marketing problems, there is as of yet no standard or comprehensive econometric software for structural models in marketing. There are however many computation resources available to the interested researcher and marketing modeler. A few personal favorites are as follows.

The random effects logit model has become the natural starting point for researchers interested in structural (choice based) models of demand. The estimation of random effects logit models has been coded by Aviv Nevo in Matlab and is available at http://faculty.wcas.northwestern.edu/~ane686/supplements/rc_dc_code.htm. The late Che-Lin Su from the University of Chicago has published Matlab code on estimating the random effects logit demand model using constrained optimization methods. See http://faculty.chicagobooth.edu/che-lin.su/research/code.html. Chris Conlon from Columbia has Matlab code for dynamic demand models available at http://www.columbia.edu/~cc3264/code.html.

For entry models, and in particular dynamic entry models, Jaap Abbring has published Matlab code for Abbring and Campbell (2010), and extensions of that paper at http://jaap.abbring.org/research/oligopoly/18-theory.

7.6 Further Reading

Since Frank M. Bass modeled advertising and sales as a simultaneous equation system and used estimates of the structural parameters in the model to simulate counterfactual scenarios in the late 1960's, structural models in marketing and industrial organization were further developed early on by, among others, Kadiyali et al. (2000) and Villas-Boas and Winer (1999).

Since then the structural modeling approach has gained a lot of following. In the intervening years, significant progress has been made in computation, allowing for more realistic assumptions about consumers' and marketing managers' behavior. It has also benefitted from increased focus on identification. By now, structural models have become mainstream econometric tools to describe the actions of consumers and marketing managers, and their role in shaping marketing thought in academics has been and continues to be significant.

Structural methods to estimate demand and supply primitives are increasingly combined with (quasi) experimental methods making full use of new possibilities to conduct natural or randomized experiments at a large scale in online environments and more and more sophisticated panel data platforms.

To the enterprising researchers and Ph.D. students, we note that there are a number of useful readings about different aspects of the structural modeling method. Reiss and Wolak (2007) discuss elements of structural models, stochastic models, and models of competition. Ackerberg et al. (2007) discuss econometric tools for analyzing market outcomes, mostly from a structural perspective. Bronnenberg et al. (2005) and Chintagunta et al. (2006) cover the structural modeling literature in marketing until 2006. Finally, the five Structural Workshop Papers in the November–December 2011 issue of *Marketing Science* give overviews of selected aspects of structural models in a marketing context.

References

Abbring, J.H., Campbell, J.R.: Last-in first-out oligopoly dynamics. Econometrica. **78**, 1491–1527 (2010)

Ackerberg, D., Benkard, C.L., Berry, S., Pakes, A.: Econometric tools for analyzing market outcomes. In: Heckman, J.J., Leamer, E.E. (eds) Handbook of Econometrics, vol 6A. Elsevier B.V., pp. 4711–4276 (2007)

Ahn, D.-Y., Duan, J.A., Mela, C.F.: Managing user generated content: a dynamic rational expectations equilibrium approach. Mark. Sci. **35**, 284–303 (2016)

Albuquerque, P., Bronnenberg, B.J.: Estimating demand heterogeneity using aggregated data: an application to the frozen pizza category. Mark. Sci. **28**, 356–372 (2009)

Albuquerque, P., Bronnenberg, B.J.: Measuring the impact of negative demand shocks on car dealer networks. Mark. Sci. **31**, 4–23 (2012)

Bass, F.M.: A simultaneous equation regression study of advertising and sales of cigarettes. J. Mark. Res. **6**, 291–300 (1969)

Bass, F.M., Parssons, L.J.: Simultaneous-equation regression analysis of sales and advertising. Appl. Econ. **1**, 103–124 (1969)

Bell, D.R., Chiang, J., Padmanabhan, V.: The decomposition of promotional response: an empirical generalization. Mark. Sci. **18**, 504–526 (1999)

Bell, D.R., Iyer, G., Padmanabhan, V.: Price competition under stockpiling and flexible consumption. J. Mark. Res. **39**, 292–303 (2002)

Berry, S.T.: Estimating discrete-choice models of product differentiation. RAND J. Econ. **25**, 242–262 (1994)

Berry, S., Levinsohn, J., Pakes, A.: Automobile prices in market equilibrium. Econometrica. **63**, 841–890 (1995)

Bresnahan, T.F., Reiss, P.C.: Entry and competition in concentrated markets. J. Polit. Econ. **99**, 977–1009 (1991)

Bronnenberg, B.J.: The provision of convenience and variety by the market. RAND J. Econ. **46**, 480–498 (2015)

Bronnenberg, B.J., Rossi, P.E., Vilcassim, N.J.: Structural modeling and policy simulation. J. Mark. Res. **42**, 22–26 (2005)

Bruno, H.A., Vilcassim, N.J.: Structural demand estimation with varying product availability. Mark. Sci. **27**, 1126–1131 (2008)

Chan, T., Narasimhan, C., Zhang, Q.: Decomposing promotional effects with a dynamic structural model of flexible consumption. J. Mark. Res. **45**, 487–498 (2008)

Chintagunta, P.K., Jain, D.C., Vilcassim, N.J.: Investigating heterogeneity in brand preferences in logit models for panel data. J. Mark. Res. **28**, 417–428 (1991)

Chintagunta, P.K., Erdem, T., Rossi, P.E., Wedel, M.: Structural modeling in marketing: review and assessment. Mark. Sci. **25**, 604–616 (2006)

De los Santos, B., Hortacsu, A., Wildenbeest, M.R.: Testing models of consumer search using data on web browsing and purchasing behavior. Am. Econ. Rev. **102**, 2955–2980 (2012)

Dubé, J.-P., Hitsch, G.J., Manchanda, P.: An empirical model of advertising dynamics. Quant. Mark. Econ. **3**, 107–144 (2005)

Dubé, J.-P., Hitsch, G.J., Chintagunta, P.: Tipping and concentration in markets with indirect network effects. Mark. Sci. **29**, 216–249 (2010)

Dubé, J.-P., Hitsch, G.J., Jindal, P.: The joint identification of utility and discount functions from stated choice data: an application to durable goods adoption. Quant. Mark. Econ. **12**, 331–377 (2014)

Ellickson, P.B., Misra, S.: Estimating discrete games. Mark. Sci. **30**(6), 997–1010 (2011)

Goettler, R.L., Gordon, B.R.: Does AMD spur intel to innovate more? J. Polit. Econ. **119**, 1141–1200 (2011)

Gordon, B.R.: A dynamic model of consumer replacement cycles in the pc processor industry. Mark. Sci. **28**, 846–867 (2009)

Guadagni, P.M., Little, J.D.C.: A logit model of brand choice calibrated on scanner data. Mark. Sci. **2**, 203–238 (1983)

Hartmann, W.R.: Demand estimation with social interactions and the implications for targeted marketing. Mark. Sci. **29**, 585–601 (2010)

Hartmann, W.R., Klapper, D.: Super Bowl Ads. Working paper, Stanford University (2015)

Hartmann, W.R., Manchanda, P., Nair, H.S., Bothner, M., Dodds, P., Godes, D., Hosanagar, K., Tucker, C.: Modeling social interactions: identification, empirical methods and policy implications. Mark. Lett. **19**, 387–304 (2008)

Hitsch, G.J.: An empirical model of optimal dynamic product launch and exit under demand uncertainty. Mark. Sci. **25**, 25–50 (2006)

Holmes, T.J.: The diffusion of Wal-Mart and economics of density. Econometrica. **79**, 253–302 (2011)

Honka, E.: Quantifying search and switching costs in the u.s. auto insurance industry. RAND J. Econ. **45**, 847–884 (2014)

Hotz, V.J., Miller, R.A.: Conditional choice probabilities and the estimation of dynamic models. Rev. Econ. Stud. **60**, 497–529 (1993)

Kadiyali, V., Chintagunta, P., Vilcassim, N.: Manufacturer-retailer channel interactions and implications for channel power: an empirical investigation of pricing in a local market. Mark. Sci. **19**, 127–148 (2000)
Kim, J., Allenby, G.M., Rossi, P.E.: Modeling consumer demand for variety. Mark. Sci. **21**, 229–250 (2002)
Kim, J.B., Albuquerque, P., Bronnenberg, B.J.: Online demand under limited consumer search. Mark. Sci. **29**, 1001–1023 (2010)
Magnac, T., Thesmar, D.: Identifying dynamic discrete decision processes. Econometrica. **70**, 801–816 (2002)
Misra, S., Nair, H.S.: A structural model of sales-force compensation dynamics: estimation and field implementation. Quant. Mark. Econ. **9**, 211–257 (2011)
Nair, H.S., Chintagunta, P.K., Dubé, J-P.: Empirical analysis of indirect network effects in the market for personal digital assistants. Quant. Mark. Econ. **2**, 23–58 (2004)
Nair, H.S., Manchanda, P., Bhatia, T.: Asymmetric social interactions in physician prescription behavior: the role of opinion leaders. J. Mark. Res. **47**, 883–895 (2010)
Nelson, R.R., Winter, S.G.: The Schumpeterian tradeoff revisited. Am. Econ. Rev. **72**, 114–132 (1982)
Nevo, A.: Measuring market power in the ready-to-eat cereal industry. Econometrica. **69**, 307–342 (2001)
Pakes, A., Porter, J., Ho, K., Ishii, J.: Moment inequalities and their application. Econometrica. **83**, 315–334 (2015)
Pancras, J., Sudhir, K.: Optimal marketing strategies for a customer data intermediary. J. Mark. Res. **44**, 560–578 (2007)
Petrin, A.: Quantifying the benefits of new products: the case of the minivan. J. Polit. Econ. **110**, 705–729 (2002)
Petrin, A., Train, K.: A control function approach to endogeneity in consumer choice models. J. Mark. Res. **47**, 3–13 (2010)
Reiss, P.C.: Descriptive, structural, and experimental methods in marketing research. Mark. Sci. **30**, 950–964 (2011)
Reiss, P.C., Wolak, F.A.: Structural Econometric Modeling: Rationales and Examples from Industrial Organization. In: Heckman, J.J., Leamer, E.E. (eds.) Handbook of Econometrics, vol. 6A. Elsevier B.V., pp. 4277–4415 (2007)
Richards, T.J.: A nested logit model of strategic promotion. Quant. Mark. Econ. **5**, 63–91 (2007)
Rust, J.: Optimal replacement of gmc bus engines: an empirical model of Harold Zurcher. Econometrica. **55**, 999–1033 (1987)
Ryan, S., Tucker, C.: Heterogeneity and the dynamics of technology adoption. Quant. Mark. Econ. **10**, 63–109 (2012)
Seiler, S.: The impact of search costs on consumer behavior: a dynamic approach. Quant. Mark. Econ. **11**, 155–203 (2013)
Shin, S., Misra, S., Horsky, D.: Disentangling preferences and learning in brand choice models. Mark. Sci. **31**, 115–137 (2012)
Sovinski-Goeree, M.: Limited information and advertising in the US personal computer industry. Econometrica. **76**, 1017–1074 (2008)
Spiegler, R.: Bounded Rationality and Industrial Organization. Oxford University Press, Oxford (2014)
Stigler, G.J.: The economics of information. J. Polit. Econ. **69**, 213–225 (1961)
Su, C.-L.: Estimating discrete-choice games of incomplete information: simple static examples. Quant. Mark. Econ. **12**, 167–202 (2014)
Thomadsen, R.: The effect of ownership structure on prices in geographically differentiated industries. RAND J. Econ. **36**, 908–929 (2005)
Thomadsen, R.: Product positioning and competition: the role of location in the fast food industry. Mark. Sci. **26**, 792–804 (2007)
Villas-Boas, J.M.: Vertical relationships between manufacturers and retailers: inference with limited data. Rev. Econ. Stud. **74**, 625–652 (2007)

Villas-Boas, J.M., Winer, R.S.: Endogeneity in brand choice models. Manag. Sci. **45**, 1324–1338 (1999)

Vitorino, M.A.: Empirical entry games with complementarities: an application to the shopping center industry. J. Mark. Res. **49**, 175–191 (2012)

Weitzman, M.L.: Optimal search for the best alternative. Econometrica. **47**(3), 641–654 (1979)

Yang, Y., Shi, M., Goldfarb, A.: Estimating the value of brand alliances in professional team sports. Mark. Sci. **28**, 1095–1111 (2009)

Yao, S., Mela, C.F., Chiang, J., Chen, Y.: Determining consumers' discount rates with field studies. J. Mark. Res. **49**, 822–841 (2012)

Chapter 8
Mediation Analysis: Inferring Causal Processes in Marketing from Experiments

Rik Pieters

8.1 Introduction

Mediation analysis is applied to make causal inferences about the process that accounts for the effect that an intervention has on an outcome. Such an intervention can range from short-term tactics such as the content of a new on-line campaign or the size of a temporary price-cut, to far-ranging strategic interventions about customer loyalty programs, product introductions, brand extensions, retail chain mergers and so forth. Outcomes may involve any self-reported or observed state, trait, belief or action of consumers, managers, and firms. Mediation analysis is academically important because it enables tests of theories about causal processes, and it is policy relevant because improved insight into these causal processes might lead to more effective and efficient interventions. It has become an indispensable tool in the marketing researcher's toolbox because of this hope for insight into the causal process, and because of foundational publications on mediation analysis, the development of statistical procedures to test for mediation, and because of the availability of these procedures in common statistical software (e.g., Baron and Kenny 1986; Hayes 2012, 2013; MacKinnon 2008; Preacher et al. 2007; Rucker et al. 2011; Shrout and Bolger 2002; Zhao et al. 2010). Mediation analysis is central in many academic disciplines. It is considered:

> "...almost mandatory for new social-psychology manuscripts" (Bullock et al. 2010, p. 550)

R. Pieters (✉)
Department of Marketing, Tilburg School of Economics and Marketing, Tilburg University, Tilburg, The Netherlands
e-mail: pieters@uvt.nl

P.S.H. Leeflang et al. (eds.), *Advanced Methods for Modeling Markets*,
International Series in Quantitative Marketing, DOI 10.1007/978-3-319-53469-5_8

and the same seems to hold in marketing and consumer science. To illustrate, the majority of empirical articles in recent issues (2014–2015) of the Journal of Consumer Research made use of mediation analysis.

Yet, the popularity of mediation analysis for theory testing also holds dangers. Easy access to "canned" statistical tests for mediation can lead to a focus on the significance of 1 or 2 summary estimates rather than on understanding the causal process of key interest. This is important because causal inferences from statistical mediation analysis rely on fundamental conditions about the data generating mechanisms, and failure to satisfy these conditions leads to biased causal inferences. The discussion of these conditions and the potential biases is dispersed across a wide literature in epidemiology, methodology, psychology, sociology and elsewhere and is not readily accessible (Emsley and Dunn 2012; Imai et al. 2010a; Judd and Kenny 1981; Morgan and Winship 2007; Pearl 2000, 2009; Ten Have and Joffe 2010). In addition, some conditions have remained underemphasized. Also, much is still unknown about the severity of the biases when conditions are not met. These issues are even more pressing because some conditions can be empirically verified but others are inherently unverifiable, thus relying strongly on theory. Finally, the extent to which published mediation studies consider the conditions is largely unknown.

This chapter aims to contribute to closing these knowledge gaps. Section 8.2 introduces statistical mediation analysis, and describes a general condition for making valid causal inferences from mediation analysis. Section 8.3 describes four (additional) conditions, and identifies potential biases when the conditions are not met. That section also reports on the results of a literature survey of published mediation analyses. It finds that most of the additional conditions are ignored in published work. Section 8.4 summarizes the results of Monte Carlo experiments (Pieters 2016), which document severe biases in the size, significance and even sign of the mediation effects when conditions are not met. Section 8.5 provides recommendations to improve the validity of inferences about causal processes based on mediation analyses.

Although mediation analysis is standard in much of marketing research, the chapter focuses on its application in the context of experimental research. Experimental research with random assignment of units-of-observation to conditions is considered the "Gold Standard" of causal inference (Angrist and Pischke 2009). It is the main data collection procedure in consumer behavior research and increasingly in other areas of marketing science, and it is commonly used in tandem with mediation analysis to gain insight into causal processes. As such, random assignment to experimental conditions may provide a false sense of being shielded from the perils of causal inference that haunt other areas of marketing research. It is therefore useful to highlight its application in the context of experimental research. The challenges of making causal inferences from mediation analysis are even greater when marketing research needs to rely on non-experimental data all together to make causal inferences.

8.2 Causal Processes from Mediation Analysis

8.2.1 *Introduction*

Mediation analysis aims to make causal inferences by identifying the indirect effect that an input variable (*X*) has on an outcome variable (*Y*) via some intervening or mediator variable (*M*). Figure 8.1 graphs this situation, and Table 8.1 provides three typical scenarios for the correlations (as measures of effect size) between, respectively, the *X*, *M*, and *Y*, and omitted variables (*U*) which are discussed later. Our focus is on natural or controlled experiments that vary the *X* variable in several levels, typically in one or more intervention and control conditions, and

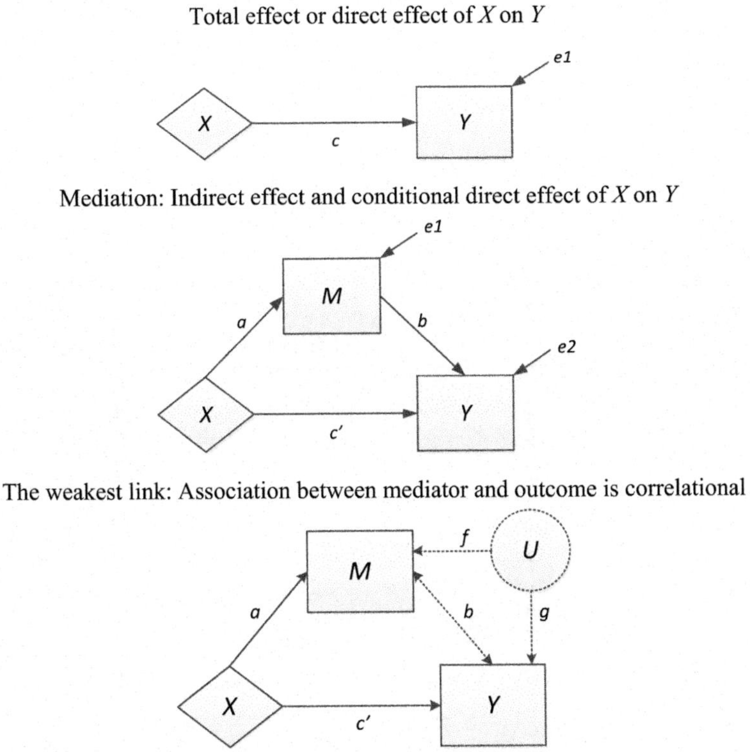

Fig. 8.1 Direct and indirect effects in mediation analysis
Note: The diamond (*X*) indicates an intervention with random assignment of participants to experimental conditions. Boxes are observed variables (*M* and *Y*). The circle indicates omitted "other variables" (*U*). Dotted lines indicate conditions of interest. Directionality is the direction of the *b*-path. Unconfoundedness are effects of omitted variables (*U*) expressed in the *f*- and *g*-arrows. Distinctiveness is reflected in the *b*-path, as it is a function of variance shared by mediator and outcome. Statistical power overarches this

Table 8.1 Mediation analysis: three scenarios

	Scenario 1: small total effect				Scenario 2: medium total effect				Scenario 3: large total effect			
X = Intervention		X	M	Y		X	M	Y		X	M	Y
M = Mediator	M	0.30			M	0.50			M	0.70		
Y = Outcome	Y	0.09	0.30		Y	0.25	0.50		Y	0.49	0.70	
U = Omitted variables	U	0.00	r	r	U	0.00	r	r	U	0.00	r	r
Effects	Estimate	Sample size for 80% power			Estimate	Sample size for 80% power			Estimate	Sample size for 80% power		
Omitted variables ($r = 0.00$):												
Indirect (*ab*)	0.09	128			0.25	<50			0.49	<50		
Direct (*c'*)	0.00	–			0.00	–			0.00	–		
Total (*ab* + *c'*)	0.09	983			0.25	131			0.49	<50		
Omitted variables ($r = 0.30$):												
Indirect (*ab*)	0.07	195			0.22	63			0.44	<50		
Direct (*c'*)	0.02	>1000			0.03	>1000			0.05	>1000		
Total (*ab* + *c'*)	0.09	944			0.25	120			0.49	<50		
Omitted variables ($r = 0.50$):												
Indirect (*ab*)	0.01	>1000			0.13	179			0.29	92		
Direct (*c'*)	0.08	>1000			0.13	500			0.20	275		
Total (*ab* + *c'*)	0.09	841			0.25	94			0.49	<50		

Note: r = the correlation between omitted variables (U) and, respectively, M and Y. The correlation between omitted variables (U) and the intervention is (X) 0.00 due to random assignment to experimental conditions. Sample size estimates are approximate and obtained from Monte Carlo analyses with stepwise increases in sample size (50, 100, 150, 250, 500, and 1000, with 1000 replication data sets for each), and interpolation between steps to determine the sample size for the threshold power of 80%

where participants are randomly assigned to the conditions. The terms intervention (*X*), mediator (*M*), and outcome (*Y*) denote the three key variables. The diamond box in Fig. 8.1 indicates that *X* is an experimental variable, from now on called "intervention." The square boxes in Fig. 8.1 indicate that *M* and *Y* are observational variables. The basic mediation analysis with a single intervention, mediator, and outcome can be readily generalized to situations with multiple mediators and/or outcomes.

8.2.2 *The Indirect Association Condition*

The central condition for causal inference based on mediation analysis is that there is a non-zero indirect association between the intervention and outcome via the mediator. To establish whether this is the case, one simultaneously estimates the influence that the intervention has on the mediator (*a*-path in Fig. 8.1 middle), and the association between mediator and outcome (*b*-path), while statistically controlling for the conditional direct effect that the intervention has on the outcome (*c*'-path). The product of the weights of the *a*- and *b*-path then indicates the size of the indirect effect (labeled $a \times b$ or *ab*), as originally proposed by Wright (1921), p. 563 in the context of path analysis. The total effect of the intervention on the outcome (c-path; Fig. 8.1 top) is the sum of the indirect effect (*ab*) and the conditional direct effect (c'-path). Thus: $c = ab + c'$. For instance, in scenario 1 in Table 8.1, the indirect effect (*ab*) between *X* and *Y* is 0.09 (namely 0.30 * 0.30), which is also the total effect (*c*) because the conditional direct effect (*c*') is 0.00.

The statistical significance, of the indirect effect is assessed using a joint significance test, Sobel test (see Sect. 1.3), bootstrapping (MacKinnon 2008; Preacher et al. 2007; Zhao et al. 2010), or Bayesian estimation (Zhang et al. 2009 and Chap. 16). Bootstrapping and Bayesian estimation allow for the possibility that the distribution of the indirect effect is skewed, which would lead to underpowered tests if a Normal distribution were assumed. If the indirect effect is statistically significant this is taken as evidence for mediation. Therefore, this type of mediation analysis is called statistical mediation analysis to differentiate it from experimental mediation analysis, in which case the mediator is also experimentally manipulated (Smith 1982).

When *X* is an intervention in a controlled or natural experiment, it may appear sufficient to have evidence about an indirect association between *X* and *Y* via *M* in order to make valid causal inferences about the causal process from *X* to *Y* via *M*. It is not sufficient. The problem lies in the *b*-path which links the mediator with the outcome. It is the weakest link when making causal inferences from statistical mediation analysis.

Experimental manipulation ensures that the intervention temporally precedes the mediator and the outcome, and random assignment of units-of-observation ensures that "other variables" cannot confound the relationship between, respectively, the intervention (*X*) and the mediator (*M*), and between the intervention (*X*) and the outcome (*Y*). Therefore, the statistical association between *X* and *M* (*a*-path), and between *X* and *Y* (*c*-path and *c*'-path) can be interpreted causally as the influence of the intervention on the mediator, and the influence of the intervention on the outcome. These are the "strongest links" in the causal chain. However both mediator and outcome are influenced by the intervention (reflected in the residuals, *e*1 and *e*2, in Fig. 8.1). Therefore the link between the mediator and outcome concerns a correlation between two observational variables, which is prone to various biases. This is rarely fully appreciated in mediation studies as Bullock et al. (2010) and Bullock and Ha (2011) point out. What is more, any bias in estimating the link between mediator and outcome (*b*-path) will lead to the opposite bias in estimating the link between intervention and outcome (*c*'-path), because the total effect (*c*-path) is given and is decomposed into the indirect path (*ab*) and the conditional direct path (*c*'). Therefore, one might say that bias in mediation models travels between the indirect effect and the conditional direct effect.

The link between mediator and outcome is the focus here. The next section describes four additional conditions—next to the indirect association condition—for valid causal inferences from statistical mediation analysis. Specifically, valid inferences about causal processes require

1. an indirect association between intervention and outcome via the mediator;
2. evidence that the direction of causal influence is from the mediator to the outcome;
3. unconfoundedness of the relationship between mediator and outcome;
4. distinctiveness of the mediator and outcome, and
5. sufficient statistical power to find the true effects.

Table 8.2 summarizes the five conditions and offers recommendations to ensure that they are satisfied. To explore how current mediation research deals with each of the conditions, we conducted a small-scale literature survey (more fully reported in Pieters 2016). A sample of recent articles that contained at least one mediation analysis was drawn from leading journals in marketing and social psychology, because these disciplines make extensive use of mediation analyses (Rucker et al. 2011; Zhao et al. 2010). Marketing articles ($n = 59$) were selected from, alphabetically, the International Journal of Research in Marketing (IJRM), Journal of Consumer Psychology (JCP), Journal of Consumer Research (JCR), Journal of Marketing (JM), and Journal of Marketing Research (JMR). The final set of 77 articles (after excluding articles that did not use mediation analysis in the context of an experiment) reported on a total of 191 mediation analyses (with a median sample size of 120 participants). All analyses reported on and discussed an indirect association between some intervention and outcome via a mediator. Results are comparable across disciplines and jointly described below.

Table 8.2 Mediation analysis: five conditions for valid inferences about the causal process

Assume:	X is an experimentally controlled variable with random assignment of participants to one or more interventions and/or control conditions ("intervention"), M is an observed process measure ("mediator), and Y is an observed outcome measure ("outcome").	
Aim:	Make inferences about the causal process that accounts for the effect that the intervention (X) has on the outcome (Y), by identifying whether and to what extent it is transferred via the mediator (M).	
Condition:	Description:	Recommendation:
1. Indirect Association	Product of the association between intervention and mediator, and mediator and outcome is non-zero	Report standardized effect sizes for all paths and for the indirect effect Report sufficient statistics (Means, *SD*s, correlations, reliabilities)
2. Directionality	Direction of influence is from mediator to outcome	a. Offer external evidence for the plausibility of the hypothesized causal direction vis-à-vis equivalent models b. Refrain from statistical mediation analysis without such evidence c. Conduct experimental mediation analysis d. Conduct instrumental variable (IV) analysis
3. Unconfoundedness	Unobserved variables do not confound the association between mediator and outcome	*Measurement Error*: Improve reliability of the measures Account for unreliability of the measures *Omitted Variable Bias*: Reduce common method bias See also 2c and 2d. Control for theory-based confounders Conduct sensitivity analysis
4. Distinctiveness	Mediator and outcome are distinct variables	Report evidence for discriminant validity of mediator vis-à-vis the outcome Refrain from statistical mediation analysis without such evidence Identify theoretically more meaningful mediator
5. Power	Statistical power is sufficient to identify true non null direct and indirect associations between intervention, mediator, and outcome	Provide evidence of sufficient statistical power to test for the indirect and conditional direct effect See also 3. Increase the sample size to have sufficient power

8.3 The Link Between Mediator and Outcome

8.3.1 The Directionality Condition

The directionality condition specifies that the most plausible direction of influence should be from the mediator to the outcome. By design, causal influence starts at the intervention and runs respectively to the mediator and to the outcome. However, the causal direction between the mediator and outcome is undetermined, because *correlation* does not imply *causation*. The double-headed arrow in the bottom part of Fig. 8.1 expresses this. That is, on statistical grounds it is equally likely that (*a*) the mediator influences the outcome, then that (*b*) the outcome influences the mediator, or that (*c*) mediator and outcome are two correlated consequences of the intervention. These three specifications of the association between mediator and outcome are "equivalent models" (Bollen 1989; Kline 2015; MacCallum and Austin 2000). Equivalent models have the same global statistical fit, in terms of CFI, BIC and similar information criteria. Therefore, the causal direction between mediator and outcome cannot be established on statistical grounds when only information about intervention, mediator, and outcome is available. The number of equivalent models quickly proliferates in models with multiple mediators. With a single mediator and outcome there are three equivalent models. With two mediators and one outcome there are already nine equivalent models, which all have the same global fit. Without strong evidence that the causal direction from mediator to outcome is most plausible, there is a threat of inferring a false causal chain or of falsely inferring a causal chain where none exists.

Although, equivalent models have the same global statistical fit, they may differ in local statistical fit criteria such as variance accounted for (VAF) and similar effect-size criteria when predicting the mediator and outcome. Take for example scenario 2 from Table 8.1. The correlation between X and the presumed Y is 0.25, and the correlations between the presumed M and X, and the presumed M and Y are both 0.50. All three equivalent models have the same global fit. The BIC is 643, for the median sample size of 120 in the literature survey. However, the model specifying X-to-M-to-Y reveals full mediation ($ab = 0.25$ and $c' = 0.00$, total effect $= 0.25$), the model specifying X-to-Y-to-M reveals partial mediation ($ab = 0.10$, $c' = 0.40$, total effect $= 0.50$), and the model specifying X-to-M-and-Y (a multivariate regression) does not test mediation but has the highest total effect (total effect $= 0.75$). It might thus be tempting in practice to run all equivalent models and then select-and-present the first model if full mediation was hypothesized, or the second if partial mediation is of interest. This is not a good idea. Correlation is an insufficient condition for causation, and local fit criteria cannot serve as evidence for the plausibility of one causal process over another (Roberts and Pashler 2000). Moreover, formulating a model after inspecting the correlations is a form of data snooping or hypothesizing after the results are known (Kerr 1998). It nullifies the informativeness of subsequent model testing and increases the likelihood of finding false positives (Simmons et al. 2011; Vul et al. 2009).

Frequently, as Meehl (1990, p. 229) put it:

> "The substantive theory has a host of alternatives, some of which are interesting theoretically, some of which are not, and most of which nobody has thought of but could in a morning's free-wheeling speculation."

Strong theoretical justification is required to select the proposed model over a statistically equivalent, alternative model. In spite of this, MacCallum and Austin (2000) observed in a literature survey of over 500 applications of structural equation modeling that most authors did not consider the possibility of equivalent models. Likewise, 67-out-of-68 relevant studies published in top management journals focused on a single model without considering possible equivalent models (Shook et al. 2004). In our survey of published mediation studies only a single article raised the possibility of "equivalent models" (Middlewood and Gasper 2014). Yet, it did not point out that statistical mediation analysis as such cannot establish the causal direction between mediator and outcome, nor did it provide strong theoretical or other evidence that the proposed causal direction was more plausible than alternatives.

8.3.2 The Unconfoundedness Condition

8.3.2.1 Unconfoundedness

The unconfoundedness condition specifies that *unobserved variables* do not systematically bias the association between mediator and outcome. Because the intervention is experimentally manipulated with random assignment of participants to conditions, unobserved variables cannot confound the relationship between, respectively, intervention and mediator, and intervention and outcome. However, because the association between mediator and outcome is observational rather than experimental, various unobserved variables can confound the association, by making it seem smaller or larger than it truly is. The lower part of Fig. 8.1 indicates the unconfoundedness condition by the circle (U) with arrows (f and g) to mediator and outcome. The literature variously terms this condition "no omitted variables," "(sequential) ignorability," "isolation," "(conditional) exchange-ability", "no-confounding," or "unconfoundedness" (Bollen 1989; Emsley and Dunn 2012; Imai et al. 2010b; Judd and Kenny 1981; Kline 2015; VanderWeele et al. 2012). The general term *unconfoundedness* is used here.

Notably, there are two different sources of confounding which have opposite effects on the association between mediator and outcome. Although both sources reflect omitted variables, they have a different origin and different effects. Therefore, they are treated under the common heading of unconfoundedness but described separately.

8.3.2.2 Unconfoundedness: Measurement Error

Measurement error is unique to each construct in the weakest link, mediator or outcome. It reduces the reliability of measures of constructs and this attenuates the size of the association between them. The lower the reliability of the measures of constructs is, the more the size of the observed association between them is biased downward, and the higher the likelihood of not identifying a true non-zero association between them (Type-II error). In the lower part of Fig. 8.2 (see Sect. 8.3.5) the f-arrow expresses measurement error in the mediator and the g-arrow expresses measurement error in the outcome.

Cronbach's coefficient alpha is a leading measure of scale reliability; it expresses the proportion of true variance extracted by a construct from its measures relative to the total variance of the measures. A reliability coefficient alpha is commonly considered satisfactory if it is 0.70, good if it is 0.80, and excellent if it is 0.90 (Peterson 1994). A meta-analysis across 1359 alpha coefficients for personality trait measures, and such measures have typically have undergone systematic scale construction efforts to increase their reliability, reported average values ranging between a satisfactory 0.73 and near good 0.78 (Viswesvaran and Ones 2000). A meta-analysis across 4286 alpha coefficients, 1030 samples, and 832 studies in marketing and psychology found average reliabilities ranging from 0.70 for values and beliefs, to 0.80 for emotion, and 0.82 for job satisfaction, with an overall mean of 0.77 (Peterson 1994). Estimates of the reliability of single-item measures of constructs can be in the same range (Bergkvist 2015; Wanous and Hudy 2001). Importantly, even when both mediator and outcome are measured with a "good" reliability of 0.80, the correlation between them is attenuated appreciably. If the true correlation between mediator and outcome were 0.50, then the observed correlation is 0.40: a 20% attenuation. Attenuation is larger when reliabilities are lower. Recall that the observed correlation between two variables is a function of the true correlation and the reliability of the measures of the variables (Spearman 1904, p. 90). That is: $\widehat{r}_{my} = r_{my}\sqrt{(r_{mm}r_{yy})}$, where $\widehat{r}_{my}$ is the observed correlation between mediator and outcome, r_{my} is the true correlation, and r_{mm} and r_{yy} are the reliabilities of respectively the mediator and outcome. When reliabilities approach unity (1.00), the observed and true correlation converge to the same value. When the mediator and outcome's reliability are 0.80, and true correlation is 0.50, the observed correlation is $0.40 = 0.50 * 0.80$. Although measurement error in mediator and outcome both reduce the observed correlation, measurement error in the mediator as the independent variable in the *b*-path is perhaps more problematic because it biases regression coefficients (Greene 2012, Sect. 4.7.5). Because bias in mediation models travels, an underestimated *b*-path due to a failure to account for measurement error leads to an overestimated *c'*-path. This raises the likelihood of falsely inferring partial mediation where full mediation exists (Type-I error).

It is well-known in the mediation literature that measurement error attenuates the indirect effect (Ledgerwood and Shrout 2011; VanderWeele et al. 2012). It is less well known that bias caused by measurement error travels in mediation models, and largely unknown what the extent of bias can be. The condition that the association between mediator and outcome is unconfounded by measurement error can be satisfied by estimating a structural equation model, which will be described in Chap. 11 (Bagozzi 1977; Bollen and Pearl 2013; Sawyer et al. 1995). Such models can be estimated when multiple and when single measures of mediator and outcome are available. However, until recently mediation research has relied on standard regression and path analysis techniques without controlling for measurement error, as documented by Iacobucci et al. (2007). In fact, in our survey of mediation studies, over half of the independent data sets in the studies (62% out of 177) assessed the mediator with multiple measures, and the others did with single measures, but none of the studies corrected for measurement unreliability.

8.3.2.3 Unconfoundedness: Omitted Variables

Omitted variables are not influenced by the intervention, and they do not influence the intervention themselves, but they influence both the mediator and the outcome. The lower part of Fig. 8.1 shows this as the *joint* paths of the omitted variable (*U*) to the mediator (f-path) and the outcome (g-path). Because these "other variables" are influential but omitted from the analysis, they confound the estimated association between mediator and outcome. Whereas measurement error is a source of bias that is unique to each construct, omitted variables are a source of bias that constructs share. Crucially, whereas measurement error *attenuates* the magnitude of the association between mediator and outcome, omitted variables, generally, *exaggerate* the magnitude of the association between mediator and outcome. That is, with an intervention (*X*), mediator (*M*), outcome (*Y*), and omitted variable (*U*), the (standardized) indirect effect (*ab*) between *X* and *Y* is the product of the simple correlation between *X* and *M*, and the partial correlation between *M* and *Y* while controlling for *X* and *U*. The indirect effect (*ab*) derived from the correlations between variables is (based on Cohen et al. 2003; Mauro 1990): $ab = r_{xm}\frac{r_{my} - r_{xy}r_{xm} - r_{um}r_{uy}}{1 - r_{xm}^2 - r_{um}^2}$. When the correlations between *U* and, respectively, *M* and *Y* are non-zero and have the same sign but are not accounted for (*U* is falsely assumed 0), the indirect effect is exaggerated.

Consider the three scenarios in Table 8.1 for a situation that omitted variables do not correlate with mediator and outcome ($r = 0.00$) up to a situation that they are correlated strongly with those ($r = 0.50$). Take scenario 2, with a medium total effect between intervention and outcome of 0.25 (0.50 * 0.50), in case omitted variables have no effect on mediator and outcome. If omitted variables would have a large effect ($r = 0.50$) on the mediator and outcome, and this effect would be accounted for, the "corrected" indirect effect would drop to almost 50% from 0.25 (first row in Table 8.1) to 0.13 (third row in Table 8.1). Because bias in mediation models travels, an exaggerated b-path due to omitted variables leads to an attenuated c'-path. This increases the likelihood of false inferring full mediation whereas only partial or even no mediation at all might exist (Type-I error). Thus, the conditional direct effect (*c'*) seemed to be not different from zero (0.00) but truly was 0.13. In severe cases of omitted variable bias in mediation models, the sign of effects can switch and truly negative indirect effects may appear to be positive. The implications for theory testing and policy recommendations could be serious.

Confounding from omitted variables can be due to methodological similarities between mediator and outcome, such as by using very similar item formats or response scales (number of responses, labels, spatial orientation, fonts, colors, sizes and so forth) for self-reports or from measuring mediator and outcome in close spatial or temporal proximity. Such method factors artificially increase the correlation between mediator and outcome. In a review of the method-bias literature, Podsakoff et al. (2012) report on two meta-analyses in which on average, respectively, about 45% and 56% of the correlation between measures of constructs was due to method factors. To appreciate this, if the simple correlation between mediator and outcome were 0.50, and both would be correlated 0.50 with omitted variables, the partial correlation between mediator and outcome controlling for omitted variables would be 0.33. Then, 34% of the simple correlation between mediator and outcome would be due to the omitted variables, and method bias can even be higher. As a case in point, the correlation between two items increased by 225% when these were measured consecutively rather than separated by six other items in the questionnaire (Podsakoff et al. 2012, p. 546).

Confounding from omitted variables can also be due to substantive similarities between mediator and outcome. Constructs that are conceptually similar are more likely to share the same set of omitted causes, or—when self-report measures used—are more likely to have the correlation between them artificially raised due to "halo effects". More generally, the "crud factor" is likely to confound the association between mediator and outcome, because in the social sciences,

> "everything correlates to some extent with everything" (Meehl 1990, pp. 204–208).

Such correlations are not surprising since most measured characteristics of observational units, be they consumers, firms, stores, or nations, are some complex function of other characteristics, and genetic, historic and environmental factors.[1] Thus, to the extent that the characteristics are (1) more substantively similar, (2) measured proximally in time and space, and with (3) similar measurement instruments, they are likely to be correlated due to omitted, other variables. None of the studies in our survey of published mediation research discussed the possibility of omitted variable bias, and none tried to explicitly rule out its effects theoretically or otherwise.

[1] See also Chap. 6.

8.3.3 The Distinctiveness Condition

The distinctiveness condition specifies that the intervention, mediator, and outcome themselves are theoretically and empirically distinct from each other. When measures of two constructs are empirically distinct they reflect discriminant validity. Without discriminant validity between intervention and mediator, and between mediator and outcome there is no basis for causal inference. Then, the mediator is either a very close manipulation check or an alternative measure of the outcome.

Fornell and Larcker (1981) proposed three general criteria for discriminant validity, which are relevant for mediation analysis as well. We focus on the association between mediator and outcome as the "weakest link" in causal inference, although the criteria hold for the association with the intervention as well, and we assume that mediator and/or outcome are assessed with multiple measures, although this is not a requirement (Pieters 2016). First (Fornell and Larcker 1981), the average variance that the latent variable (mediator or outcome) extracts from its purported measures should be at least 50%. Put differently, if the total variance of each of the measures (manifest variables) is 100%, the latent variable should extract on average more variance than what remains as measurement error. This criterion focuses on the relationship between the latent variable and its measures. The next two criteria emphasize the relationship between the two latent variables of interest and are more relevant. Second, the correlation between the measures of the mediator and outcome should be less than unity (1.00). In operational terms, a mediation model with the correlation between mediator and outcome fixed to one should fit worse that a model with this correlation freely estimated (as evidenced, for instance, by a likelihood ratio test). If this criterion is not met, it cannot be ruled out empirically that a single latent variable underlies the measures of the mediator and outcome. This is a weak criterion for discriminant validity which is comparatively easy to meet, since mediator and outcome are rarely correlated at unity. Third, the average variance that a latent variable (mediator or outcome) extracts from its measures should be larger than the average variance that the latent variable shares with other variables. This is a strong criterion for discriminant validity, since even if mediator and outcome are correlated less than at unity, they can still lack discriminant validity if they extract insufficient variance from their measures. In short, the first discriminant validity criterion holds that: $\frac{\sum \lambda_i^2}{\sum(\lambda_i^2+e_i^2)} > 0.50$, the second criterion holds that $r_{my} < 1$, and the third criterion holds that: $\frac{\sum \lambda_i^2}{\sum(\lambda_i^2+e_i^2)} - r_{my}^2 > 0$, with λ_i the loadings of each of the measures (i) on the mediator or outcome, e_i^2 the variance of the respective residuals, and r_{my}^2 the shared variance between mediator and outcome.

Without discriminant validity of the mediator vis-à-vis the outcome, there is no empirical basis for making causal inferences about the role of the mediator to begin with. In view of the principal role of discriminant validity in causal inference, it is quite surprising that the issue is rarely covered in the mediation literature, as Zhao et al. (2010) point out. In fact, this lack of attention to discriminant validity seems to holds more generally for the causal inference and structural equations literature (Bollen and Pearl 2013; Morgan and Winship 2007; Shook et al. 2004). In our survey of published mediation studies, only a single article (Seggie et al. 2013) assessed discriminant validity of the mediator and outcome. A next section summarizes the results of Monte Carlo analyses on discriminant validity between mediator and outcome.

8.3.4 The Power Condition

The statistical power of testing the indirect and direct effects should be sufficient to identity the true relationships between intervention, mediator, and outcome. Statistical power is the probability of identifying a true non-null effect, with 80% as a common benchmark. The directionality, unconfoundedness, and distinctiveness conditions are about construct validity, i.e., the truthfulness of the identified effects. The power condition is about statistical conclusion validity, i.e., the likelihood of identifying those effects given that they are true.

At least until recently, the statistical power of hypothesis testing in social and related sciences was often low (Ioannidis 2005; Maxwell 2004). As a case in point, Cashen and Geiger (2004), p. 160 reported in a literature survey of 53 articles from management journals:

> "Overall, only 4 studies in our sample had sufficient power to draw sound conclusions from the results of their null hypothesis tests."

Button et al. (2013) found a median power of 21% across 730 primary neuroscience studies summarized in 49 meta-analyses.

Statistical power depends on:

1. the chosen significance level;
2. the observed effect size, and
3. the sample size, with larger numbers improving power in all cases.

Correlation coefficients of 0.10 are deemed a small effect size, those of 0.30 are deemed moderate, and those of 0.50 or higher are deemed large (Hemphill 2003). The commonly small-to-moderate effect sizes and sample sizes in psychology, management and marketing research largely account for low statistical power. In a meta-analysis of 322 earlier meta-analyses in social psychology, representing over 25,000 studies on 8 million people, Richard et al. (2003) found an average effect size (correlation) of 0.21 (SD = 0.15). Only 5% of the effect sizes were larger than 0.50. A replication of 100 experimental and correlational studies published in three psychology journals (Open Science Collaboration 2015) found an average effect size (correlation) of 0.20 (SD = 0.26). A meta-analysis of 94 meta-analyses across domains in marketing found an average effect size (correlation) of 0.27 (SD = 0.17) (Eisend and Tarrahi 2014).

Statistical power is particularly relevant in statistical mediation analysis because the indirect effect is the product of two separate effect sizes (the *a*-path and *b*-path), and this can readily become small. It is also relevant because the intervention and the mediator are by definition multicollinear predictors of the outcome, because the a-path $\neq 0$. Multicollinearity increases the standard error of the parameter estimates, and thereby decreases the statistical power of testing that these are non-zero. The statistical significance of a regression coefficient β tested two-tailed at $\alpha < 0.05$ is given by (cf. Cohen et al. 2003): $t = \frac{\beta}{\mathrm{SE}_\beta} > |\ 1.96\ |$, with $\mathrm{SE}_\beta = \sqrt{\frac{1-R_Y^2}{n-k-1}} * \sqrt{\frac{1}{1-R_i^2}}$, where SE_β is the standard error of β, n is the sample size, k is the number of predictors in the model, R_Y^2 is the squared correlation of the target predictor with the criterion variable Y, and R_i^2 is the squared correlation of the other predictors with the target predictor. The second component of the SE captures inflation of the standard error due to multicollinearity. The larger the multicollinearity, the larger the standard error of β, and thus the smaller the t-statistic. For example, when $\beta = 0.50$, and $\mathrm{SE}_\beta = 0.25$, then $t = 2.00$ without multicollinearity. When, X and M correlate 0.50, t becomes 1.73, a drop of 0.27.

This leads to the counterintuitive implication that, at a given total effect (c-path) and sample size, larger correlations between intervention and mediator (a-path) reduce the likelihood of identifying true mediation (significance of b-path, and thus of ab). Increasing the sample size can offset power reductions caused by small effect sizes and multicollinearity.

Low statistical power, such as when effect sizes and sample sizes are small, reduce the likelihood of identifying true non-zero effects. This increases the likelihood of false negatives: incorrectly claiming a "zero" effect which is truly non-zero. Conversely, finding evidence of a non-zero effect when the statistical power is low, signals that the result might be a false positive (Simmons et al. 2011). Then,

> "... either you have been quite lucky, or there is something you have not told us about how the study was done that questions its validity" (Meyer 2015, p. 578),

both of which hamper scientific progress. For all these reasons, the early recommendation that investigators [should] use larger samples than they customarily do (Cohen's 1962, p. 153) still holds. Table 8.2 re-iterates the recommendation.

The median sample size of the 177 data sets in our survey of mediation studies was 120 (mean 151). At this median sample size an indirect effect of about 0.09 is sufficient to have 80% power (see Table 8.1, scenario 1). Although an indirect effect of 0.09 seems small, it is good to note that this requires effect sizes for the a- and b-path of 0.30 (or one of these correlations larger than 0.30 when the other is smaller), and these are larger effect sizes than the average effect sizes reported in meta-analyses in marketing and psychology. Moreover, 50% of mediation analyses in our survey had a sample size less than 120. On a different note, Kenny and Judd (2014) observed that the statistical power to identify a particular indirect effect (ab) is larger than the statistical power to identify an unconditional (c) or conditional direct effect (c') of the same size. Therefore, at a given sample, it is more likely to obtain empirical evidence for an indirect effect than to obtain evidence for a direct effect of the same size. Table 8.1 shows, for example, that an indirect effect (ab) of 0.09 requires a sample size of about 128 for 80% power, but a same-sized direct effect requires a sample size of over 800 in our example. This makes it even more important to conduct a power analysis to determine the required sample size for the indirect *and* for the direct effect before embarking in a mediation analysis.

None of the studies in the survey discussed the statistical power of the obtained effects. One reason for this might be the remarkably high 88% of all mediation analyses that found evidence for the hypothesized mediation effect. Discussion of statistical power is more common when hypothesized effects are not empirically supported. The high percentage of positive effect in mediation studies is consistent with the more general 86% of supported hypotheses across scientific domains, which expresses researchers' extra-ordinary aptitude to correctly predict the results of their own analyses (Fanelli 2012).

8.3.5 Relationships between Conditions

The five conditions for valid causal inference from statistical mediation analysis are ordered. The framework in Fig. 8.2 indicates this. It provides the key questions that each of the conditions poses, and the potential biases when the answers to the questions are ignored. Because a failure to meet the directionality condition renders statistical mediation analysis meaningless (Bias 1), it needs to be addressed first. Because measurement error biases the indirect association between mediator and outcome *downward* (Bias 2), and omitted variables generally bias the association *upward* (Bias 3). The distinctiveness condition can only be assessed once such sources of confounding are addressed. Failure to account for measurement error biases the observed correlation between mediator and outcome downward, and thus can lead to falsely inferring the presence of discriminant validity (Bias 4). Failure to address omitted variable bias biases the observed correlation between mediator and outcome upward, and thus can lead to falsely inferring absence of discriminant validity (Bias 5). And true absence of discriminant validity makes mediation analysis meaningless. Thus, although indirect association is the key condition, it can only be addressed meaningfully once the other conditions have been satisfied (Fig. 8.2). The power condition is the first and last to consider when planning and conducting a statistical mediation analysis. Taken together, this demonstrates how the seemingly uncontroversial indirect association condition to make causal inferences from mediation analysis is rooted in a set of four crucial additional conditions.

The five conditions are necessary but not sufficient to make valid causal inferences. For instance, the homogeneity condition specifies that the association between the mediator and the outcome does not depend on the level of the intervention (Imai et al. 2010a, 2010b; Judd and Kenny 1981). Although that condition can readily be tested (Preacher et al. 2007; model-1 moderation), there are as yet few published examples (Valeri and VanderWeele 2013). Likewise, the Stable Unit Treatment Value Assumption (SUTVA) specifies that knowledge of the intervention status of others does not influence participants' responses to their

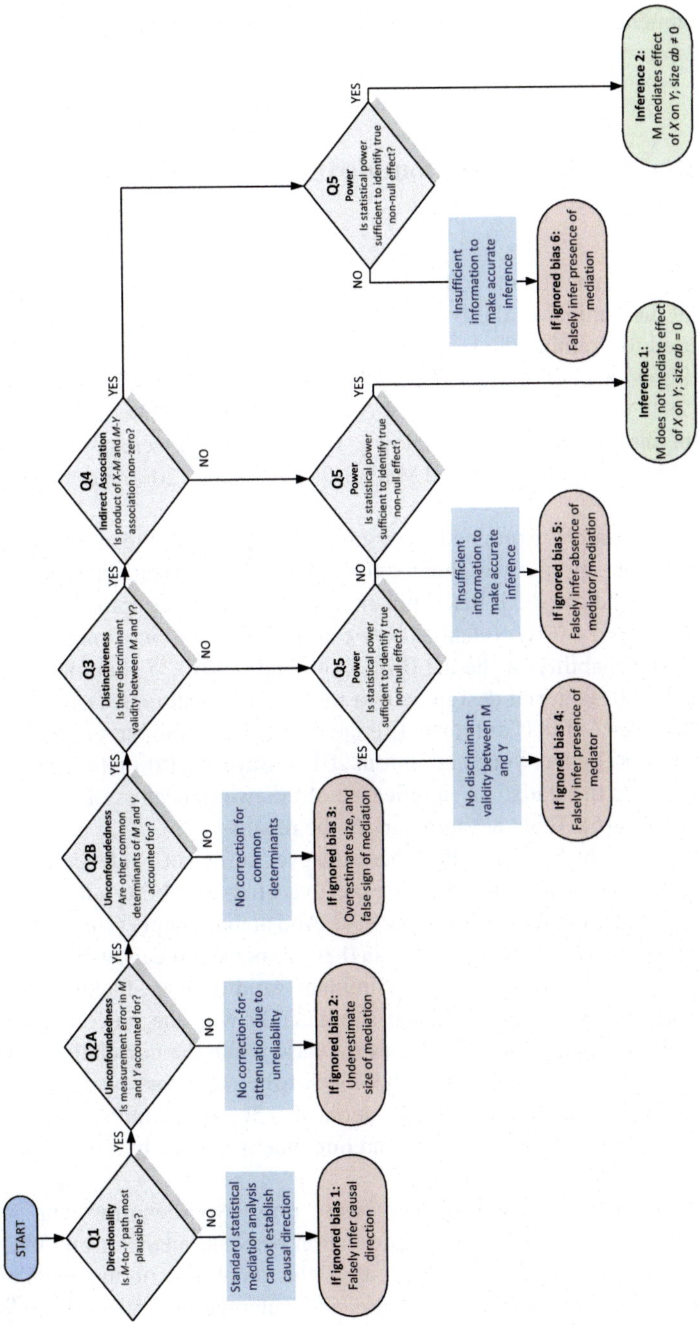

Fig. 8.2 Mediation analysis: five conditions for valid causal inference

assigned condition (Ten Have and Joffe 2010). This condition is often satisfied in controlled experiments but may be harder to satisfy in field or natural experiments where assignment conditions may be known or become known to participants over time.

8.4 Exploring Bias: Unconfoundedness, Distinctiveness, Power

Two Monte Carlo experiments followed-up on Zhao et al. (2010) call for research on the role of discriminant validity in mediation analysis. Monte Carlo experiments have been used to examine the sensitivity of mediation analyses (Fritz and MacKinnon 2007; Imai et al. 2010a, 2010b; Muthén and Asparouhov 2015; Ledgerwood and Shrout 2011), but the joint effects of conditions and in particular the effects of measurement unreliability are lesser known. The experiments were conducted using the MPlus 7.11 program (Muthén and Muthén 2014). Pieters (2016) provides further detail.

The first experiment examined discriminant validity of the mediator when measurement error is properly accounted for, and it examined statistical power. The strong and weak indicators of discriminant validity, described before, were used. The experiment used a 3 (correlations between mediator and outcome: 0.30, 0.50, and 0.70) × 3 (Reliability of the *M*: 0.70, 0.80, and 0.90) × 5 (Sample Size: 50, 100, 150, 250, 500) factorial design, with a total of 45 conditions each with 1000 replication samples (45,000 in total). The latent mediator was represented with 3 manifest measures (Ledgerwood and Shrout 2011). Bayesian estimation techniques were used to assess the statistical significance of the two indicators of discriminant validity (Pieters 2016). Table 8.3 summarizes the results.

At a sample size of 50 or smaller, there is never sufficient evidence for strong discriminant validity of the mediator, irrespective of its reliability and even if its correlation with the outcome is only a low 0.30. And at that sample size, correlations between mediator and outcome smaller than 0.30 are not significantly different from zero at 80% power. Even the weak discriminant validity index flagged only two scenarios where the mediator correlated significantly with the outcome, but was still empirically distinct from it. This was the case when the correlation between mediator and outcome was 0.50 and reliability of the mediator was 0.80 or 0.90. However, with lower reliabilities a correlation of 0.50, which indicates a "mere" 25% shared variance between mediator and outcome was already not discriminant valid, at this weak criterion.

Even at a sample size of 100, there were only two scenarios with strong discriminant validity and a significant correlation between mediator and outcome (scenario 7, 8 in Table 8.3). In these cases, the reliability of the mediator is 0.90 and the correlation between mediator and outcome is 0.50 or less. When correlations between mediator and outcome are 0.50 or higher, reliabilities over

Table 8.3 Conditions for causal inference: discriminant validity of mediator

					Statistical power of the correlation, and discriminant validity between mediator and outcome at the specified sample size														
	Reliability of	Correlation between mediator-	Discriminant validity criterion		$n = 50$			$n = 100$			$n = 150$			$n = 250$			$n = 500$		
Nr.	mediator	outcome	Strong	Weak	Corr	Strong	Weak	Corr	Strong	Weak	Corr	Strong	Weak	Corr	Strong	Weak	Corr	Strong	Weak
1	0.70	0.30	0.34	0.70	0.38	0.39	0.94	0.68	0.73	0.99	0.85	0.90	0.99	0.98	0.98	0.99	0.99	0.99	0.99
2	0.70	0.50	0.18	0.50	0.83	0.10	0.76	0.99	0.22	0.98	0.99	0.31	0.99	0.99	0.49	0.99	0.99	0.79	0.99
3	0.70	0.70	−0.06	0.30	0.99	0.04	0.37	0.99	0.06	0.74	0.99	0.05	0.91	0.99	0.08	0.99	0.99	0.12	0.99
4	0.80	0.30	0.47	0.70	0.44	0.66	0.97	0.75	0.95	0.99	0.91	0.99	0.99	0.99	0.99	0.99	0.99	0.99	0.99
5	0.80	0.50	0.31	0.50	0.90	0.23	0.81	0.99	0.54	0.99	0.99	0.75	0.99	0.99	0.93	0.99	0.99	0.99	0.99
6	0.80	0.70	0.07	0.30	0.99	0.03	0.38	0.99	0.05	0.78	0.99	0.06	0.93	0.99	0.09	0.99	0.99	0.14	0.99
7	0.90	0.30	0.65	0.70	0.48	0.89	0.98	0.81	0.99	0.99	0.93	0.99	0.99	0.99	0.99	0.99	0.99	0.99	0.99
8	0.90	0.50	0.49	0.50	0.94	0.52	0.82	0.99	0.89	0.99	0.99	0.98	0.99	0.99	0.99	0.99	0.99	0.99	0.99
9	0.90	0.70	0.25	0.30	0.99	0.10	0.39	0.99	0.29	0.81	0.99	0.48	0.95	0.99	0.75	0.99	0.99	0.97	0.99
Jointly sufficient power of mediator-outcome correlation, and for discriminant validity (p times)						0	2		2	5		4	9		5	9		6	9

Note: Mediator is a latent variable with three observed measures. Corr.: correlation between mediator and outcome. Discriminant validity criterion ranges from 0 (no) to 1 (maximum). Strong discriminant validity: average variance extracted by mediator (AVE) minus squared correlation between mediator and outcome. Weak discriminant validity: one minus correlation between mediator and outcome. Power based on 1000 replication samples per condition. Power estimates of 0.80 or better are bolded. Power 99% is 99% or larger. Graying of rows to facilitate inspection

0.80, and sample sizes over 250 are required to have sufficient evidence for strong discriminant validity. When correlations between mediator and outcome reach 0.70, sample sizes around 500 and reliabilities of 0.90 are needed for strong discriminant validity. In view of the median sample size of 120 in published mediation studies, there is reason to believe that a substantial proportion of them may not be able to express discriminant validity between mediator and outcome. The final section of the chapter returns to this.

Experiment 2 examined the implications of failing to account for measurement error in the mediator, and of omitted variable bias. It compared the 9 scenarios from Experiment 1 where the mediator was treated as a latent variable with three items, with the same 9 scenarios but now treating the mediator as an observed variable, by simply averaging across the three items. The latter is the default when not using a structural equation model, and used in all mediation studies covered in our literature survey. The 18 scenarios were compared for the situation with no versus small omitted variable bias ($U = 0.00$ or 0.30). A single sample size of 250 was used because at that size the majority of scenarios in the first experiment expressed strong and all expressed weak discriminant validity.

For all levels of reliability, treating the mediator as a latent variable correctly reconstructed the true indirect and conditional direct effects in the mediation model. However, systematic biases arose when failing to account for measurement error in the mediator. Overall, the indirect effect was underestimated, and the conditional direct effect was overestimated, and sometimes gravely so. Over- and underestimation of effects were larger when true correlations between mediator and outcome were larger and when the mediator's reliability was smaller. For instance, the estimated indirect effect was a mere 36% of the true effect when the true correlation between mediator and outcome is 0.70, the mediator is treated as an observed variable and its reliability is 0.70. When the reliability of the mediator rises to 0.90, the estimate was closer but still only 67% of the true effect. This reveals the *size bias* in all cases when failing to account for measurement error in the mediator. When the true indirect effect was small, namely 0.09, and the mediator was treated as an observed variable, the statistical power to test for the indirect effect dropped below the desired 80% level, even at a this comparatively large sample size of 250. Then, the indirect effect is likely to be considered not significantly different from zero although the true effect is (significance bias: Type-II error).

Once more, underestimating the indirect effects led to overestimating the conditional direct effects. For instance, when the correlation between mediator and outcome is 0.70, the mediator's reliability is 0.80, the true conditional direct effect is 0, but when measurement error in the mediator is not accounted for, the conditional direct effect is estimated to be 0.15 with 84% power. Then, the estimated conditional direct effect is likely deemed significantly different from zero although the true effect is not (significance bias: Type-I error).

To exacerbate matters, all cases where measurement error in the mediator was not accounted for and where the conditional direct effect was falsely considered positive, are also cases which lack strong discriminant validity between mediator and outcome—if the mediator would have been treated as a latent variable. Put differently, mediation analysis would be meaningless in these cases, because the mediator lacks discriminant validity. This meaningless of the mediation would remain undetected when not accounting for measurement error in the mediator. Moreover, these situations would also lead to the false inference that there is partial mediation. At the sample size of 250, correlations of mediator with intervention and outcome of 0.50, lead to size bias, but not to lack of discriminant validity or significance bias (Type-I or Type-II error). Yet, at smaller sample sizes, more correlations between mediator and outcome would lack discriminant validity, which would go undetected when treating the mediator as an observed variable. Ironically, increasing the sample size, aggravates the bias that is caused by not accounting for measurement error in the mediator: it increases the likelihood of "false positives" for the conditional direct effect.

8.5 Recommendations

This chapter described five conditions that need to be met in order to make valid causal inferences from statistical mediation analysis, even if such an analysis is conducted in the context of experiments with random assignment to conditions: (1) indirect association, (2) directionality, (3) unconfoundedness, (4) distinctiveness, and (5) power. The five conditions are essential, and known under various names across disciplines.

This makes the almost complete lack of consideration for them in published mediation research even more striking. Essentially, the presence of indirect association was the only condition considered, perhaps because the randomized experiment suggests that it is sufficient. It is useful to consider all five conditions when planning, analyzing, and reporting mediation analysis. Despite the belief that "mentioning limitations makes them go away" (Wells 1993, p. 493), it would be unfortunate when future mediation studies would only mention the conditions for causal inference in the limitations sections of their reports.

Table 8.2 and Fig. 8.2 summarize the conditions and the potential biases when conditions are not met, and they provide recommendations to improve mediation analysis practice.

8.5.1 Report More Details about the Mediation Process

It seems good advice to report standardized effect sizes for all three paths and for the indirect effect in the mediation analysis. Standardized regression or path weights are useful in their own right and can be readily converted into (partial) correlations. Other standardized effect size measures are available (Hayes 2012; MacKinnon 2008; Preacher and Kelley 2011). It is also good practice to report the means, standard deviations, and reliabilities of variables and the correlations between them in a summary table. Such information provides *sufficient statistics* to replicate standard mediation analyses and to accumulate knowledge across studies. Although bootstrapping and Bayesian analyses require the raw data and there are other complications, much can already be gleaned from the sufficient statistics.

Unfortunately, it is common practice in mediation studies to report only the confidence interval or significance level of the unstandardized indirect effect. In fact, 54% of the cases in the literature survey failed to report point estimates for each of the three paths and for the indirect effect, and 82% did not report standardized effect sizes. Such reporting practices hamper insight into the causal processes between intervention and outcome, and hinder knowledge accumulation across studies.

One might reason that standardized effect size measures are not very useful for theory development and testing because:

1. the prime goal there is to establish whether or not a particular process variable accounts for an effect rather than what the size of the effect is, or because
2. effect sizes are partly under experimental control and can thus be maximized, or
3. have a large error around them due to the typically small sample sizes in fundamental research.

Such arguments are moot. First, many phenomena in marketing and psychology are multi-determined (Meehl 1990). This makes it more interesting to examine the *extent* to which a mediator accounts for the outcomes-of-interventions rather than whether or not it does so. Moreover, developing more precise, quantitative theories and predictions may move marketing and social psychology research beyond the lamented null-hypothesis significance testing (Gelman and Carlin 2014; Meehl 1990). Indeed, as Lykken (1991, p. 33) pointed out for theories in psychology and the same seems to hold for marketing:

> "[They] may never be able to make point predictions, but at least, like say the cosmologists, we ought to be able to squeeze out of our theories something more than merely the prediction that A and B are positively correlated. If we took our theories seriously and made the effort, we should be able to make rough estimates of parameters sufficient to say, e.g., that the correlation ought to be greater than 0.40 but not higher than 0.80."

More complete reporting of standardized effect sizes in mediation analyses may help to achieve this for marketing. Second, being able to control effect sizes, when all data collection and analysis procedures are replicable and ethical, is a strength rather than a weakness, because it implies insight into the causal mechanisms of prime interest. Moreover, a focus on effect size does not imply a drive to maximize it, or that small effects are necessarily unimportant (Abelson 1985). Third, although effect sizes may have a large error component in individual studies, aggregating them across studies in meta-analyses increases precision, and allows knowledge accumulation. If only a single recommendation were to be taken to heart in future mediation studies, it would be to report more detail about the mediation process and to provide (standardized) effect sizes.

8.5.2 Refrain from Statistical Mediation Analysis

It is good advice to refrain from standard statistical mediation analysis when there is insufficient evidence that the hypothesized mediation model is more plausible than statistically equivalent, alternative models.

Only one of the studies in the literature survey considered the possibility of equivalent models, and it relied on local fit criteria to build a case in favor of one of the causal chains, which is not wise. Support for the directionality condition rests on a combination of logic, theory, prior research, experimental mediation analysis and instrumental variable estimation. These are all *external* to the basic statistical mediation analysis, and none is a "magic bullet." In case of experimental mediation analysis, a sequence of studies examines the influence of, respectively, the manipulated intervention on the mediator and outcome, the manipulated mediator on the outcome, and sometimes the manipulated outcome on the mediator (Imai et al. 2013; MacKinnon 2008; Spencer et al. 2005). Thus, each step in the causal chain after the intervention is manipulated and observed. Lee and Schwarz (2012) used this approach in research on embodied cognition of consumers. A major challenge is that often the mediator cannot be manipulated directly and strongly. Then, the manipulation can only be a weak proxy of the mediator of interest, with loss of efficiency and potential systematic bias as a result. Similar issues hold for instrumental variable (IV) estimation (Bollen 2012; Emsley and Dunn 2012; Larcker and Rusticus 2010; Rossi 2014; Zhang et al. 2009; and Chaps. 15 and 18).

8.5.3 Account for Unreliability of the Mediator

It is good advice to measure the mediator with high reliability, and to account for its remaining unreliability by using a structural equation model. This advice is neither recent (Bagozzi 1977) nor unique (Iacobucci et al. 2007). Still, none of the studies in the literature survey followed-up on it.

The default practice in mediation studies is to use the average scores across measures of the mediator and outcome. Perhaps this default practice is due to the belief that ignoring measurement unreliability leads only to a modest biases, and that it only makes tests of indirect effects more conservative. In contrast, biases can be severe, that they travel to worsen false causal inferences. It can lead to an estimated indirect effect which is only half of the true effect, and an estimated conditional direct effect which is misleadingly deemed significant. This can lead to the false inference that mediation is partial, and to a search for additional mediators, although mediation truly is full.

To make matters worse, increasing the sample size in a mediation study that does not control for measurement error in the constructs only worsens these biases. And even if the significance levels of indirect effects would be unaffected, biased estimates of the size of the indirect effects still hamper progress towards the more precise, quantitative theories that are called for (Gelman and Carlin 2014; Lykken 1991). Another reason to refrain from using a structural equation model might be the common use of single-item measures of the mediator (38% of the cases in the survey) and/or outcome. Yet, reliabilities of single-item measures can be assessed and readily accounted for in a structural equation model to provide accurate estimates. The availability of structural equation routines in all general-purpose statistics programs facilitates taking this recommendation to heart.

8.5.4 Minimize the Likelihood of Omitted Variable Bias

It is good advice to take measures to prevent omitted variable bias, to cope with it in the analyses, to build a case that it cannot unduly bias the statistical mediation analysis at hand, and to consider sensitivity analysis to support the case. None of the studies in the survey explicitly discussed the possibility of omitted variable bias or tried to cope with it.

It is hard to rule out that the association between mediator and outcome is confounded by other variables. But there are various ways to prevent and cope with it, although again none is a magic bullet (Bagozzi 2011; Richardson et al. 2009). First, omitted variable bias can be reduced by using different instruments, item types, and response scales to measure the mediator and the outcome, and by increasing the time interval between measuring the mediator and outcome (Podsakoff et al. 2012). Second and as for the directionality condition, *experimental* mediation analysis can ensure unconfoundedness by omitted variables. In that case, one would refrain from statistical mediation analysis. Third, instrumental variable (IV) estimation can increase the plausibility that the unconfoundedness condition is met. Fourth, adding potential confounder variables to the mediation model based on theory how these influence the mediator and outcome, independent of the intervention, can help to make the unconfoundedness condition more plausible (Fiedler et al. 2011; Pearl 2009; VanSteelandt 2012). Fifth, sensitivity analyses can be performed to assess how large the omitted variable bias can be before it substantially changes the estimated indirect and conditional direct effect (the summarized Monte Carlo experiments here made use of it) (Mauro 1990; Morgan and Winship 2007). Imai et al. (2010a, p. 315) even argue that:

> "... a mediation analysis is not complete without a sensitivity analysis." Causal inferences are more plausible to the extent that they are insensitive to scenarios with large omitted-variable effects.

8.5.5 Establish Discriminant Validity

It is good advice to provide empirical evidence for the mediator's discriminant validity when reporting on a statistical mediation analysis. Only a single study in the survey assessed the mediator's discriminant validity. Importantly, correlations between mediator and outcome much lower than 1.00, in fact as low as 0.30, could already imply lack of discriminant validity. The experiments found lack of strong discriminant validity, at the mean sample size of 150 in the survey, when correlations between mediator and outcome were 0.50 or higher, even when the mediator's reliability was good (0.80). At a sample size of 50, there is essentially never sufficient evidence for strong discriminant validity between mediator and outcome at 80% power, and such sample sizes are not uncommon in published research. Discriminant validity increases when constructs are measured with better reliability and for larger sample size. It is good advice to refrain from mediation analysis when there is no discriminant validity between mediator and outcome.

8.5.6 *Increase Sample Size*

It is good advice to conduct mediation studies with sufficient statistical power, which usually implies having substantially larger sample sizes than is currently customary. General rules of thumb about required sample sizes can easily mislead because sample sizes depend on the reliability of the measures, the effect size of the indirect and conditional direct effect, and on the required power to identify these. Still, our findings indicate that a minimum sample size of around 250 is required to make plausible causal inferences from a standard three-variable mediation analysis when the reliability of the mediator is 0.80 or lower and its correlation with the outcome is around 0.50 or higher. With smaller correlations and lower reliabilities, larger sample size are needed. Within-subjects and repeated-measures designs generally have higher power, and require smaller sample sizes.

None of the studies in the survey discussed the statistical power of testing for the hypothesized mediation effect. Yet, the majority of them seemed underpowered to identify a true non-zero indirect and conditional direct effect of low-to-moderate size, and those are typical in marketing and psychology. The sample size of many mediation analyses was probably too small to establish strong discriminant validity of the mediator. Resources are available to estimate the required sample size for a specific mediation analysis (Gelman and Carlin 2014; Muthén and Muthén 2014). The results of more recent work (Kenny and Judd 2014; Ledgerwood and Shrout 2011; Pieters 2016) and the current chapter can be a starting point for reasonable rules of thumb.

8.6 At Closing

The current chapter aimed to contribute to making statistical mediation analysis more meaningful by raising awareness about the "weakest link," and by offering recommendations to strengthen it. The aim was and is not to discourage researchers from conducting statistical mediation analysis all together, on the contrary. Surely, trying to satisfy the conditions for valid inferences about causal processes from mediation analysis might result in fewer mediation studies being conducted. Those studies will most likely have a larger sample size, mediators measured with high levels of reliability, analyzed with a structural equation model, with moderate-to-small correlations between the mediator and, respectively, the intervention and the outcome to ensure distinctiveness, and with stronger justification for the hypothesized causal direction. It is hard to satisfy all conditions simultaneously, but efforts to try are likely to make inferences about causal processes from statistical mediation analysis more meaningful. The first step is to report the results of the mediation analysis in detail and in a usable form, so that we can begin to gain insight and accumulate knowledge.

References

Abelson, R.P.: A variance explanation paradox: when a little is a lot. Psychol. Bull. **97**, 129–133 (1985)

Angrist, J.D., Pischke, J.-S.: Mostly Harmless Econometrics: An Empiricist's Companion. Princeton University Press, Princeton, Oxford (2009)

Bagozzi, R.P.: Structural equation models in experimental research. J. Mark. Res. **14**, 209–226 (1977)

Bagozzi, R.P.: Measurement and meaning in information systems and organizational research: methodological and philosophical foundations. MIS Q. **35**, 261–292 (2011)

Baron, R.M., Kenny, D.A.: The moderator-mediator variable distinction in social psychological research: conceptual, strategic, and statistical considerations. J. Pers. Soc. Psychol. **51**, 1173–1182 (1986)

Bergkvist, L.: Appropriate use of single-item measures is here to stay. Mark. Lett. **26**, 245–255 (2015)

Bollen, K.A.: Structural Equations with Latent Variables. John Wiley & Sons, New York (1989)

Bollen, K.A.: Instrumental variables in sociology and the social sciences. Annu. Rev. Sociol. **38**, 37–72 (2012)

Bollen, K.A., Pearl, J.: Eight myths about causality and structural equation models. In: Morgan, S. (ed.) Handbook of Causal Analysis for Social Research, pp. 301–328. Springer., Chapter 15, New York (2013)

Bullock, J.G., Green, D.P., Ha, S.E.: Yes, but what's the mechanism? (don't expect an easy answer). J. Pers. Soc. Psychol. **98**, 550–558 (2010)

Bullock, J.G., Ha, S.E.: Mediation analysis is harder than it looks. In: Druckman, J.N., Green, D.P., Kuklinski, J.H., Lupia, A. (eds.) Cambridge Handbook of Experimental Political Science, pp. 508–521. Cambridge University Press, Cambridge (2011)

Button, K.S., Ioannidis, J.P.A., Mokrysz, C., Nosek, B.A., Flint, J., Robinson, E.S.J., Munafo, M.R.: Power failure: why small sample size undermines the reliability of neuroscience. Nat. Rev. Neurosci. **1-12**, (2013)

Cashen, L.H., Geiger, S.W.: Statistical power and the testing of null hypotheses: a review of contemporary management research and recommendations for future studies. Organ. Res. Methods. **7**, 151–167 (2004)

Cohen, J.: The statistical power of abnormal-social psychology research: a review. J. Abnorm. Soc. Psychol. **65**, 145–153 (1962)

Cohen, J., Cohen, P., West, S.G., Aiken, L.S.: Applied Multiple Regression/correlation Analysis for the Behavioral Sciences, 3rd edn. Lawrence Erlbaum Associates, Mahwah, NJ (2003)
Eisend, M., Tarrahi, F.: Meta-analysis selection bias in marketing research. Int. J. Res. Mark. **31**, 317–326 (2014)
Emsley, R., Dunn, G.: Evaluation of potential mediators in randomised trials of complex interventions (psychotherapies). In: Berzuini, C., Dawid, P., Bernardelli, L. (eds.) Causality: Statistical Perspectives and Applications, pp. 290–309. John Wiley & Sons, Chicester (2012)
Fanelli, D.: Negative results are disappearing from most disciplines and countries. Scientometrics. **90**, 891–904 (2012)
Fiedler, K., Schott, M., Meiser, T.: What mediation analysis can (not) do. J. Exp. Soc. Psychol. **47**, 1231–1236 (2011)
Fornell, C., Larcker, D.F.: Structural equation models with unobserved variables and measurement error: algebra and statistics. J. Mark. Res. **18**, 382–380 (1981)
Fritz, M.S., MacKinnon, D.P.: Required sample size to detect the mediated effect. Psychol. Sci. **18**, 233–239 (2007)
Gelman, A., Carlin, J.: Beyond power calculations: assessing type s (sign) and type m (magnitude) errors. Perspect. Psychol. Sci. **9**, 641–651 (2014)
Greene, W.H.: Econometric Analysis, 7th edn. Pearson Education ltd, Boston (2012)
Hayes, A. F.: PROCESS: A Versatile Computational Tool for Observed variable Mediation, Moderation, and Conditional Process Modeling (2012), Retrieved from http://www.afhayes.com/public/process 2012.pdf
Hayes, A.F.: Introduction to Mediation, Moderation and Conditional Process Analysis: A Regression-Based Approach. New York: The Guilford Press (2013)
Hemphill, J.F.: Interpreting the magnitudes of correlation coefficients. Am. Psychol. **58**, 78–80 (2003)
Iacobucci, D., Saldanha, N., Deng, X.: A meditation on mediation: evidence that structural equations model perform better than regressions. J. Consum. Psychol. **17**, 140–154 (2007)
Imai, K., Keele, L., Tingley, D.: A general approach to causal mediation analysis. Psychol. Methods. **15**, 309–334 (2010a)
Imai, K., Keele, L., Yamamoto, T.: Identification, inference and sensitivity analysis for causal mediation effects. Stat. Sci. **25**, 51–71 (2010b)
Imai, K., Tingley, D., Yamamoto, T.: Experimental designs for identifying causal mechanism. J R Stat Soc A. **176**, 5–51 (2013)
Ioannidis, J.P.A.: Why most published research findings are false. PLoS Med. **2**, 696–701 (2005)
Judd, C.M., Kenny, D.: Process analysis: estimating mediation in intervention evaluations. Eval. Rev. **5**, 602–619 (1981)
Kenny, D.A., Judd, C.M.: Power anomalies in testing mediation. Psychol. Sci. **25**, 334–339 (2014)
Kerr, N.L.: HARKing: hypothesizing after the results are known. Personal. Soc. Psychol. Rev. **2**, 196–217 (1998)
Kline, R.B.: The mediation myth. Basic Appl. Soc. Psychol. **37**(4), 202–213 (2015)
Larcker, D.F., Rusticus, T.C.: On the use of instrumental variables in accounting research. J. Account. Econ. **49**, 186–205 (2010)
Ledgerwood, A., Shrout, P.E.: The trade-off between accuracy and precision in latent variable models of mediation processes. J. Pers. Soc. Psychol. **101**(6), 1174–1188 (2011)
Lee, S.W.S., Schwarz, N.: Bidirectionality, mediation, and moderation of metaphorical effects: the embodiment of social suspicion and fishy smells. J. Pers. Soc. Psychol. **103**, 737–749 (2012)
Lykken, D.T.: What's wrong with psychology anyway? In: Cicchetti, D., Grove, W.M. (eds.) Thinking Clearly about Psychology, Volume 1: Matters of Public Interest, pp. 3–39. University of Minnesota Press, Minneappolis (1991)
MacCallum, R.C., Austin, J.T.: Applications of structural equations modeling in psychological research. Annu. Rev. Psychol. **51**, 201–236 (2000)
Mauro, R.: Understanding L.O.V.E. (left out variables error): a method for estimating the effects of omitted variables. Psychol. Bull. **108**, 314–329 (1990)

Maxwell, S.E.: The persistence of underpowered studies in psychological research: causes, consequences, and remedies. Psychol. Methods. **9**, 147–163 (2004)
MacKinnon, D.P.: Introduction to Statistical Mediation Analysis. Lawrence Erlbaum Associates, New York (2008)
Meehl, P.E.: Why summaries of research on psychological theories are often uninterpretable. Psychol. Rep. **66**, 195–244 (1990)
Meyer, R.J.: Editorial: a field guide to publishing in an era of doubt. J. Mark. Res. **52**, 577–579 (2015)
Middlewood, B.L., Gasper, K.: Making information matter: symmetrically appealing layouts promote issue relevance, which facilitates action and attention to argument quality. J. Exp. Soc. Psychol. **53**, 100–106 (2014)
Morgan, S.L., Winship, C.: Counterfactuals and Causal Inference. Methods and Principles for Social Research. Cambridge University Press, Cambridge (2007)
Muthén, B., Asparouhov, T.: Causal effects in mediation modeling: an introduction with applications to latent variables. Struct. Equ. Model. **22**, 12–23 (2015)
Muthén, L., Muthén, B.O.: MPlus User's Guide, 7th edn. Muthén and Muthén, Los Angeles, CA (2014)
Open Science Collaboration: Estimating the reproducibility of psychological science. Science. **349**, 1–8 (2015)
Pearl, J.: Causality: Models, Reasoning, and Inference. Cambridge University Press, New York (2000)
Pearl, J.: Causal inference in statistics: an overview. Stat. Surv. **3**, 96–146 (2009)
Peterson, R.A.: A meta-analysis of cronbach's coefficient alpha. J. Consum. Res. **21**, 381–391 (1994)
Pieters, R.: Meaningful mediation analysis: strenghtening the weakest link in causal inference from experiments. Unpublished Report, Tilburg School of Economics and Management, Tilburg University, Tilburg, The Netherlands (2016)
Podsakoff, P.M., MacKenzie, S.B., Podsakoff, N.P.: Sources of method bias in social science research and recommendations on how to control it. Annu. Rev. Psychol. **63**, 539–569 (2012)
Preacher, K., Kelley, K.: Effect size measures for mediation models: quantitative strategies for communicating indirect effects. Psychol. Methods. **16**, 93–115 (2011)
Preacher, K., Rucker, D.D., Hayes, A.: Addressing moderated mediation hypotheses: theory, methods, and prescriptions. Multivar. Behav. Res. **42**, 185–227 (2007)
Richard, F.D., Bond Jr., C.F., Stoles-Zoota, J.: One hundred years of social psychology quantitatively described. Rev. Gen. Psychol. **7**, 331–363 (2003)
Richardson, H.A., Simmering, M.J., Sturman, M.C.: A tale of three perspectives: examining post hoc statistical techniques for detection and correction of common method variance. Organ. Res. Methods. **12**, 762–800 (2009)
Roberts, S., Pashler, H.: How persuasive is a good fit? a comment on theory testing. Psychol. Rev. **107**, 358–367 (2000)
Rossi, P.E.: Even the rich can make themselves poor: a critical examination of the use of IV methods in marketing. Mark. Sci. **33**, 655–672 (2014)
Rucker, D.D., Preacher, K.J., Tormala, Z.L., Petty, R.E.: Mediation analysis in social psychology: current practices and new recommendations. Soc. Personal. Psychol. Compass. **5**(6), 359–371 (2011)
Sawyer, A.G., Lynch Jr., J.G., Brinberg, D.: A Bayesian analysis of the information value of manipulation and confounding checks in theory tests. J. Consum. Res. **21**, 581–595 (1995)
Seggie, S.H., Griffith, D.A., Jap, S.D.: Passive and active opportunism in interorganizational exchange. J. Mark. **77**, 73–90 (2013)
Shook, C.L., Ketchen Jr., D.J., Hult, G.T., Kacmar, K.M.: An assessment of the use of structural equation modeling in strategic management research. Strateg. Manag. J. **25**, 397–404 (2004)
Shrout, P.E., Bolger, N.: Mediation in experimental and nonexperimental studies: new procedures and recommendations. Psychol. Methods. **7**, 422–445 (2002)

Simmons, J.P., Nelson, L.D., Simonsohn, U.: False-positive psychology: undisclosed flexibility in data collection and analysis allows presenting anything as significant. Psychol. Sci. **22**, 1359–1366 (2011)

Smith, E.R.: Beliefs, attributions, and evaluations: nonhierarchical models of mediation in social cognition. J. Pers. Soc. Psychol. **43**, 248–259 (1982)

Spearman, C.: The proof and measurement of association between two things. Am. J. Psychol. **15**, 72–101 (1904)

Spencer, S.J., Zanna, M.P., Fong, G.T.: Establishing a causal chain: why experiments are often more effective than mediational analyses in examining psychological processes. J. Pers. Soc. Psychol. **89**, 845–851 (2005)

Ten Have, T.R., Joffe, M.M.: A review of causal estimation of effects in mediation analyses. Stat. Methods Med. Res. **21**, 77–107 (2010)

Valeri, L., VanderWeele, T.: Mediation analysis allowing for exposure-mediator interactions and causal interpretation: theoretical assumptions and implementation with SAS and SPSS macros. Psychol. Methods. **18**, 137–150 (2013)

VanSteelandt, S.: Estimation for direct and indirect effects. In: Berzuini, C., Dawid, P., Bernardelli, L. (eds.) Causality: Statistical Perspectives and Applications, pp. 127–150. John Wiley & Sons, Chicester (2012)

VanderWeele, T.J., Valeri, L., Ogburn, E.L.: The role of measurement error and misclassification in mediation analysis. Epidemiology. **23**, 561–564 (2012)

Viswesvaran, C., Ones, D.S.: Measurement error in "big five factors" personality assessment: reliability generalization across studies and measures. Educ. Psychol. Meas. **60**, 224–235 (2000)

Vul, E., Harris, C., Winkielman, P., Pashler, H.: Puzzingly high correlations in fmri studies of emotion, personality, and social cognition. Perspect. Psychol. Sci. **4**, 274–291 (2009)

Wanous, J.P., Hudy, M.J.: Single-item reliability: a replication and extension. Organ. Res. Methods. **4**, 361–375 (2001)

Wells, W.D.: Discovery-oriented consumer research. J. Consum. Res. **19**, 489–504 (1993)

Wright, S.: Correlation and causation. J. Agric. Res. **20**, 557–585 (1921)

Zhao, X., Lynch Jr., J., Chen, Q.: Reconsidering Baron and Kenny: myths and truths about mediation analysis. J. Consum. Res. **37**, 197–206 (2010)

Zhang, J., Wedel, M., Pieters, R.: Sales effects of attention to feature advertisements: a Bayesian mediation analysis. J. Mark. Res. **46**, 669–681 (2009)

Chapter 9
Modeling Competitive Responsiveness and Game Theoretic Models

Peter S. H. Leeflang

9.1 Introduction

The study of competition and competitive responsiveness has a long tradition, involving a variety of models developed and applied in many different situations. In this chapter we give a brief survey of specific applications and methodologies used to model competitive responsiveness. In addition, we attend to the use of competitive response models for normative decision-making and introduce game theoretic models.

A brand's or firm's success depends on the degree to which its managers' decisions satisfy selected consumers' needs and preferences better than competing brands/firms do (Day and Reibstein 1997). Thus, firms' actions *and* reactions to competitive actions strongly influence their performance. In modern marketing, much attention has been devoted to competition. The intensity of competition may increase when markets show minimal growth. New product introductions and the reactions to these new entries may both result from and contribute to more intense competition. In more recent studies much attention is devoted to competitive reactions to the *entry* of new competitors,[1] either new brands or new

A part of this chapter is based on Leeflang (2008a, 2008b).

[1] Aboulnasr et al. (2008); Moe and Yang (2009).

P.S.H. Leeflang (✉)
Department of Marketing, Faculty of Economics and Business, University of Groningen, Groningen, The Netherlands
e-mail: p.s.h.leeflang@rug.nl

P.S.H. Leeflang et al. (eds.), *Advanced Methods for Modeling Markets*,
International Series in Quantitative Marketing, DOI 10.1007/978-3-319-53469-5_9

retailers,[2] particularly, Wal-Mart.[3] There are also studies that consider the reactions of *channels* to *brand* introductions.[4]

In this chapter we discuss which models can be used to capture competitive response. We first consider models in which the marketing instruments of brand j are a function of competitive marketing instruments and other variables (Sect. 9.4). The competitive response functions model responsiveness at the individual brand level (brand j).

Game theoretic approaches consider market equilibria and, particularly, how competitive actions and reactions may lead to new equilibria. In these models so-called "simultaneous solutions" (of all brands j, $j = 1, \ldots, n$) are considered.

We demonstrate that there are different niches for different model types. The different model types are connected. We use the evolutionary model approach (See Vol. I, Chap. 2) to connect the different competitive response models. We start to discuss the rationale to use competitive response models in Sect. 9.2. A classification of competitive response models is discussed in Sect. 9.3.

9.2 A Rationale to Account for Competitive Reactions

Research findings (Montgomery et al. 2005) demonstrate that although managers consider competitors in their decision-making, competitive considerations focus primarily on competitor's past or current behavior rather than on anticipated competitors' reactions. The low incidence of strategic competitor reasoning is due to perceptions of low returns from anticipating competitor reactions more than to the high costs of doing so. Hence efforts are needed to convince managers that models and methods can be fruitfully applied to predict competitive reactions and to define firms' future actions.

In this section we demonstrate how marketing decisions and marketing's contribution to profit can be improved if one accounts for competitive reactions. To this end we specify the following simple model:

$$\widehat{q} = \widehat{\beta}_0 + \widehat{\beta}_a \sqrt{a} + \widehat{\beta}_{a_c} \sqrt{a_c} \tag{9.1}$$

$$C = c\widehat{q} + FC + a \tag{9.2}$$

$$\widehat{\pi} = p\widehat{q} - C \tag{9.3}$$

[2]Cleeren et al. (2006); Cleeren et al. (2010).

[3]Ailawadi et al. (2010); Gielens et al. (2008); Singh et al. (2006).

[4]Sriram and Kadiyali (2009).

where

$\widehat{q}$ = the estimated demand of the focal brand (say brand j) in units,
a, a_c = advertising expenditures of the focal brand and the advertising expenditures of a competitor respectively,
C = total cost,
c = variable cost per unit,
FC = fixed cost, other than advertising,
π = profit.

We do not use indices j (brand) and t (time) to restrict the number of indices. We assume that the parameters $\widehat{\beta}_a$and $\widehat{\beta}_{a_c}$have been estimated through time series data. The effects of competitive actions are represented through $\widehat{\beta}_{a_c}$. Throughout we assume that $\widehat{\beta}_a > 0$, $\widehat{\beta}_{a_c} < 0$ and $p > c$. The reduced form of (9.1)–(9.3) is:

$$\widehat{\pi} = (p - c)\left(\widehat{\beta}_0 + \widehat{\beta}_a\sqrt{a} + \widehat{\beta}_{a_c}\sqrt{a_c}\right) - a - FC. \tag{9.4}$$

The optimal advertising budget is obtained by differentiating (9.4) with respect to a and equating this expression to zero. First we assume that there is no relation between a and a_c. Hence we get[5]:

$$a_{opt} = \frac{\left((p - c)\,\widehat{\beta}_a\right)^2}{4}. \tag{9.5}$$

The higher the margin (p-c), and the effectiveness of advertising, β_a, the higher the optimal advertising budget will be. We now assume that the competitor reacts with a_c on a:

$$a_c = \widehat{\alpha}_0 + \widehat{\alpha}_1 a \tag{9.6}$$

where we assume that $\widehat{\alpha}_1 > 0$. The effect of a change in a on q is now represented by:

$$\frac{\partial q}{\partial a} = \frac{\partial q_j}{\partial a} + \frac{\partial q_j}{\partial a_c} \cdot \frac{\partial a_c}{\partial a} \tag{9.7}$$

where $\frac{\partial q_j}{\partial a}$= the *direct* effect of advertising on demand and $\frac{\partial q}{\partial a}$ is the *total* effect of advertising on demand. Given (9.1) and (9.6) we have:

$$\frac{\partial q}{\partial a} = \frac{1}{2}\widehat{\beta}_a \cdot a^{-\frac{1}{2}} + \frac{1}{2}\widehat{\alpha}_1 \cdot \widehat{\beta}_{a_c} \cdot a_c^{-\frac{1}{2}}. \tag{9.8}$$

[5]To make sure this expression for a_{opt} corresponds to a maximum, second-order conditions are examined. We find that, given the assumptions about $\widehat{\beta}_a$, $\widehat{\beta}_{a_c}$, and p-c, the second-order condition is expected to be negative which leads to a maximum value of π.

Given that $\widehat{\beta}_{a_c} < 0$, the effect of brand j's advertising on q is lower than if there is no competitive reaction. This also means that the marginal revenue product of advertising $p \cdot \frac{\partial q}{\partial a}$ is lower, which has its implication for the optimal advertising expenditures and the optimal profit. The optimal advertising expenditures, and so the optimal profit, are a function of $\widehat{\beta}_{a_c}$, $\widehat{\alpha}_1$ and a_c:

$$a_{opt} = \frac{\left((p-c)\,\widehat{\beta}_a\right)^2 a_c}{\left(2\sqrt{a_c} - \widehat{\beta}_{a_c}\,\alpha_1\,(p-c)\right)^2}. \tag{9.9}$$

If managers do not account for competitive actions and instead determine their budget on Eq. (9.5), they will spend too much on advertising. This statement is conditional on the assumption that the estimates are unbiased. Biases in parameter estimates also lead to non-optimal decisions. Hence, manager's decision-making will benefit from anticipating competitors' reactions and estimating the values of $\widehat{\beta}_{a_c}$ and $\widehat{\alpha}_1$ and forecasting a_c. There are different opportunities to obtain these forecasts, ranging from naive methods such as $a_{ct} = a_{ct-1}$ or $a_{c_t} = 1.05a_{ct-1}$(competitive advertising increases with 5% over time) to more sophisticated methods using competitive reaction functions, such as those that are discussed in Sect. 9.3.[6]

9.3 Modeling Competitive Responsiveness; Model Classification

In this section we briefly sketch some opportunities for modeling competitive behavior. Many developed models and methods attempt to diagnose and predict competitive behavior (see also the special issues of Marketing Science (Vol. 24, nr. 1) and the International Journal of Research in Marketing (Vol. 18, nr. 1, 2; Vol. 27, nr. 2). The modeling of competitive responsiveness functions can be interpreted as an evolutionary process, as we depict in Fig. 9.1, in which we consider different steps involved and 12 sets of models.

The first step consists of building relatively simple models,[7] which subsequently may be expanded to incorporate additional elements and becoming more complex.

Day and Wensley (1988) dichotomize competitive response models into competitor-centered methods and customer-focused approaches. *Competitor-centered assessments* employ direct management comparisons between the firm and a few target *competitors* and often include determination of the relative strengths and weaknesses of each firm and the extent to which competitors quickly match marketing activities initiated by another firm. *Customer-focused assessments* start

[6]For a more in-dept. review, see for example Alsem and Leeflang (1994) and Alsem et al. (1989).
[7]Urban and Karash (1971).

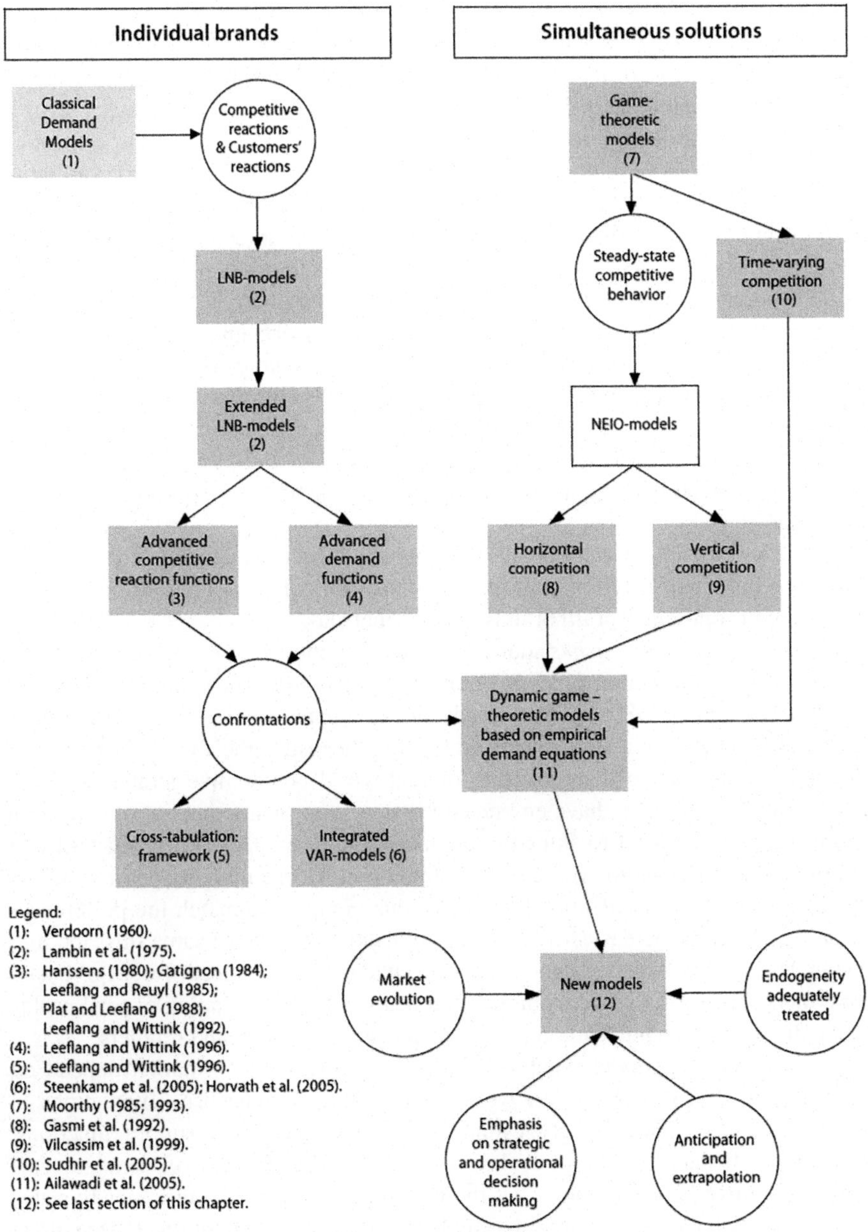

Fig. 9.1 Evolutionary model building in competitive responsiveness
Source: Leeflang (2008a, p. 327)

with detailed analyses of customer benefits within end-user segments and work backward from the *customer* to the company to identify the necessary actions that will improve performance. Customer-focused assessments become possible by calibrating demand models that include competitive marketing variables.

Classical micro-economic theory (see 1 in Fig. 9.1) considers the impact of competitive actions on demand on the basis of cross-elasticities.[8] However, more specific marketing models also include marketing-mix instruments other than price and use brand sales as the demand measure. In addition, demand equations may be supplemented by competitive reaction functions. For example, Lambin et al. (1975) calibrate competitive reaction functions (see 2 in Fig. 9.1) using data about a low-priced consumer durable good in West Germany. Extensions to their classical "LNB (Lambin/Naert/Bultez) model" include more *advanced competitive reaction functions* (3) and *demand functions* (4). Using a framework based on cross-tabulations, researchers have also studied reaction functions and demand functions simultaneously (5). Furthermore, *VARX models* provide a means to estimate advanced demand and competitive reaction functions simultaneously (6) (see Chap. 4).

These models (1–6) can be used to determine the optimal mix for *one* brand assuming particular reaction patterns by competitors. That is, they do not offer a simultaneous optimum for *all* brands in a product class.

Game-theoretic approaches address this issue, though most early game-theoretic models were theoretical and had no empirical applications.[9] (see 7 in Fig. 9.1).

Since the early 1980s, powerful advances in game theory have taken place, particularly in the area of dynamic games. As a result, the theory has become far more applicable to the modeling of real-world competitive strategies. Even more recently, marketers have embraced the new empirical industrial organization (NEIO)-based approach to infer the competitive behavior of firms[10] in terms of both horizontal (8) and/or vertical (9) competition. Horizontal competition occurs between brands or organizations (retailers) that compete to match the preferences of the customers, whereas vertical competition exists within the same (distribution) channel between different partners that have, at least in principle, different groups of customers. Therefore, vertical competition deals with the allocation of total profits in the distribution channel among manufacturers, wholesalers and retailers.

In the structural models such as these, price levels in the market depend on demand and cost conditions, as well as the nature of inter-firm interactions in the market (see Chap. 7). By estimating both demand and supply functions, this approach decomposes price levels in the unique effects of demand, cost and competitive behavior (note that these models typically assume "steady-state" competitive behavior). In models that study time-varying competition (10) the direct

[8] The numbers refer to the sets of models that we distinguish in Fig. 9.1.

[9] Examples are Friedman (1958); Krishnan and Gupta (1967).

[10] See Kadiyali et al. (2001) for a review.

effects of demand and cost changes on prices *and* the indirect effects on *competitive intensity* all come in to play.[11]

One of the most advanced models used to study competitive response (11)[12]:

- considers vertical *and* horizontal competition;
- is based on advanced empirical demand and competitive reaction functions and
- is dynamic.

Finally, new models of competitive response (12) satisfy various criteria and deal with many different issues such as endogeneity (Chap. 18) and market evolution (Soberman and Gatignon 2005). We discuss these issues in more detail in Sect. 9.5.

9.4 Competitive Response Models with a Focus on Individual Brands

9.4.1 Classical Demand Models

Incorporating competitive marketing instruments into a demand model offers opportunities to determine the effects of competitive actions in a relatively simple way. As an example we specify the following model:

$$\widehat{q} = \widehat{\alpha} + \widehat{\beta}_p p + \widehat{\beta_{p_c}} p_c + \widehat{\beta}_a a + \widehat{\beta_{a_c}} a_c \tag{9.10}$$

where

$\widehat{q}, a, a_c$ = as defined in Sect. 9.2, and
p, p_c = price of the focal brand and the competitive price respectively.

The effects of competitive actions on $\widehat{q}$ are represented through $\widehat{\beta_{p_c}}$ and $\widehat{\beta_{a_c}}$ and the effects of competitive actions on sales can be predicted by substituting the expected future values of p_c and a_c in the estimated relationship.[13]

This classical, simple model does not account for how the focal brand may react to competitive actions or how its competitor reacts in turn to the focal brand's actions, nor does it address how these reactions ultimately modify consumer demand. One of the first studies that explicitly models these competitive reaction effects is a study by Kotler (1965). Kotler's model has been modified in the so-called LNB-model.

---

[11]Examples are models developed by Ellison (1994) and Sudhir et al. (2005).

[12]The model of Ailawadi et al. (2005) has these features: see Sect. 9.5.3.

[13]See, for example, Alsem et al. (1989).

9.4.2 LNB Models

Consider the following functions for Q, product class sales, and m, a brand's market share:

$$Q = Q_T\ (p, a, k, p_c, a_c, k_c, ev) \tag{9.11a}$$

and

$$m = m_j\ (p, a, k, p_c, a_c, k_c) \tag{9.11b}$$

where

Q_T, m_j = *functional forms* for *T*otal *Q*uantity and brand *j*'s *m*arket share, respectively,
p, p_c = price of a brand (say, brand *j*) and an index of competitor's prices, respectively,
k, k_c = a quality measure for brand (*j*) and an index of competitor's quality measures, respectively,
a, a_c = advertising expenditure of brand (*j*) and an index of competitor's advertising expenditures, respectively, and
ev = a vector of environmental variables.

We do not use the index j for p, a, k and m. We will use j instead to make a distinction between direct effects and total effects: see below. The focal brand is brand *j*. A similar reasoning holds for Q, Q_T. Q is used to indicate the total effect, Q_T represents the direct effect of a marketing instrument (here advertising) on product class sales. Eqs. (9.11a) and (9.11b) also provide examples of equations that represent consumer's reactions to competitive actions (p_c, a_c, k_c).

Brand *j*'s sales elasticity with respect to its advertising ($\eta_{q,a}$) equals the total product class elasticity ($\eta_{Q,a}$) plus the total market share elasticity with respect to the focal brand's advertising ($\eta_{m,a}$):

$$\eta_{q,a} = \eta_{Q,a} + \eta_{m,a} \tag{9.12}$$

where the expression for the total product and market share elasticities are as given in Eqs. (9.15) and (9.16), respectively.

These elasticity measures capture the effect of advertising by one brand on consumer demand, but to capture *total* actual impact, we must consider how competitors react to brand advertising changes and how this reaction modifies consumer demand. The competitive reactions belong to the set of competitor-centered approaches. Specifically, we distinguish *direct* and *indirect partial effects* of brand *j*'s advertising on product class sales and on brand *j*'s own market share. An indirect partial effect captures the following scenario: If brand j changes its advertising expenditure level (∂a) competitors may react by similarly adapting their spending level (∂a_c) and a_c in turn influences Q and/or m. According to this explanation, as is usually assumed in oligopoly theory, competitors' react with the same marketing instrument as that which caused their reactions. Thus, competitors react to a change in price for j by changing their prices, to a change in advertising by an advertising response, and so forth. This type of reaction reflects the *simple competitive reactions* case. A more realistic approach consistent with the *concept of the marketing mix*, accommodates *multiple competitive reactions* such that a competitor may react to a price change by not just changing its price, but also changing its advertising and other such marketing instruments. These reactions are called indirect effects. Direct effects plus indirect effects lead to total effects.

With the general case of multiple competitive reactions we can write $\frac{\partial Q}{\partial a}$ and $\frac{\partial m}{\partial a}$ as follows[14]:

$$\frac{\partial Q}{\partial a} = \frac{\partial Q_T}{\partial a} + \frac{\partial Q_T}{\partial p_c}\frac{\partial p_c}{\partial a} + \frac{\partial Q_T}{\partial a_c}\frac{\partial a_c}{\partial a} + \frac{\partial Q_T}{\partial k_c}\frac{\partial k_c}{\partial a} \tag{9.13}$$

and

$$\frac{\delta m}{\delta a} = \frac{\delta m_j}{\delta a} + \frac{\delta m_j}{\delta p_c}\frac{\delta p_c}{\delta a} + \frac{\delta m_j}{\delta a_c}\frac{\delta a_c}{\delta a} + \frac{\delta m_j}{\delta k_c}\frac{\delta k_c}{\delta a}. \tag{9.14}$$

Multiplying both sides of Eq. (9.13) by $\frac{a}{Q}$ we obtain the product class elasticity, $\eta_{Q,a}$:

$$\eta_{Q,a} = \eta_{Q_T,a} + \left(\rho_{p_c,a}\right)\left(\eta_{Q_T,p_c}\right) + \left(\rho_{a_c,a}\right)\left(\eta_{Q_T,a_c}\right) + \left(\rho_{k_c,a}\right)\left(\eta_{Q_T,k_c}\right) \tag{9.15}$$

where

$\eta_{Q_T,a}$ = direct product class sales elasticity with respect to brand j's advertising,
η_{Q_T,u_c} = product class sales elasticity with respect to competitor's marketing instrument $u_c(=p_c, a_c,$ or $k_c)$, and
$\rho_{u_c,a}$ = reaction elasticity of competitor's instrument $u_c(=p_c, a_c,$ or $k_c)$ with respect to brand j's advertising expenditures.

Similarly, $\eta_{m,a}$ can be decomposed as follows:

$$\eta_{m,a} = \eta_{m_j,a} + \left(\rho_{p_c,a}\right)\left(\eta_{m_j,p_c}\right) + \left(\rho_{a_c,a}\right)\left(\eta_{m_j,a_c}\right) + \left(\rho_{k_c,a}\right)\left(\eta_{m_j,k_c}\right). \tag{9.16}$$

The LNB model can be fruitfully applied if a company

- is not particularly interested in the effects of individual competitors but rather in the effects of the aggregate of other brands/firms;
- does not face vertical competition, and
- specifies its marketing mix independently from retailers.

[14]In (9.13) and (9.14) $\frac{\partial Q_T}{\partial a}$, $\frac{\partial m_j}{\partial a}$ are the *direct* effects and $\frac{\partial Q}{\partial a}$, $\frac{\partial m}{\partial a}$ are the *total effects*.

Extended LNB models relax on one or more of these conditions. Hence, the extended LNB models are the result of the identification of opportunities to improve an earlier specification. They constitute the next generation of models of competitive market response.

Lambin et al. (1975) applied the concept of multiple competitive reactions to the market of a low-priced consumer durable good in West Germany. They used a multiplicative market share function:[15]

$$m_j = \alpha m_{j,-1}^{\lambda} (p^r)^{\beta_p} (\alpha^r)^{\beta_a} (k^r)^{\beta_k} \tag{9.17}$$

where $u^r = u/u_c$, $u = p, a, k$ and $m_{j,-1} = m_{j,t-1}$. Since $u^r = u/u_c$ it follows that:

$$\eta_{m_j,u^r} = \eta_{m_j,u} = -\eta_{m_j,u_c}. \tag{9.18}$$

If industry sales are insensitive to changes in marketing activities $\eta_{Q_T,u} = 0$. By using (9.17) we specify (9.12) as follows:

$$\eta_{q,a} = (1 - \rho_{a_c,a}) \left(\eta_{m_j,a^r}\right) - \left(\rho_{p_c,a}\right) \left(\eta_{m_j,p^r}\right) - \left(\rho_{k_c,a}\right) \left(\eta_{m_j,k^r}\right). \tag{9.19}$$

Estimation of (9.17) by Lambin et al. (1975) yielded the estimates:

$$\widehat{\eta}_{m_j,a^r} = 0.147, \widehat{\eta}_{m_j,p^r} = -3.726 \text{ and } \widehat{\eta}_{m_j,k^r} = 0.583.$$

The reaction elasticities were estimated from three multiplicative reaction functions,

$$u_c = \alpha_u p^{\rho_{u,p}} a^{\rho_{u,a}} k^{\rho_{u,k}} \tag{9.20}$$

where $u_c = p_c, a_c$ and k_c for the three equations respectively. The estimates of the reaction elasticities to advertising for brand j were $\widehat{\rho}_{a_c,a} = 0.273$, $\widehat{\rho}_{p_c,a} = 0.008$, $\widehat{\rho}_{k_c,a} = 0.023$.

Brand j's sales elasticity (here, the total market share elasticity, since $\eta_{Q_T,u} = 0$) can now be assessed by substituting the estimated market share and reaction elasticities in (9.19):

$$\widehat{\eta}_{q,a} = (1 - 0.273)\,(0.147) - (0.008)\,(-3.726) - (0.023)(0.583)$$

i.e., the total brand sales elasticity $\widehat{\eta}_{q,a}$ is 0.124 which compares with a direct (market share) elasticity of 0.147. Thus the net or total effect of advertising for brand j is smaller than the direct effect.

[15]The time is omitted for convenience. Some of the variables in the reaction functions were specified with a one-period lag.

9.4.3 *Extended LNB Models with Advanced Competitive Reaction Functions*

The LNB model assumes that the market consists of a leader that uses marketing instruments p, a and k and a follower, defined as the aggregate of other firms in the market. For example, $p_c = \sum_{r=2}^{n} \frac{p_r}{n-1}, p = p_1, a_c = \sum_{r=2}^{n} a_r, a = a_1$, and so forth, where n = total number of brands and "1" indicates the leading brand.

In extended LNB models, modelers make no distinction between leaders and followers, but rather consider all brands separately in what amounts to a decomposition of competitive interactions.

An example of an extended LNB model is Hanssens' (1980) approach[16]:

$$x_{\ell_{jt}} = h\left(x_{\ell' rt} - x_{\ell jt}\right), \ell, \ell' = 1, \ldots, L, r = 1, \ldots, n, j \neq r, t = 1, \ldots, T \quad (9.21)$$

where $x_{\ell_{jt}}$ is the value of the ℓ-th marketing instrument of brand j in period t.

Equation (9.21) allows for joint decision making when $j = r$, which summarizes the possibility that changes in one variable result in changes in one or more *alternative* variables for a given brand. These relations between different variables for the same brand are known as *intrafirm* activities.

In Eq. (9.21) the number of equations to be estimated is Ln and the many predictor variables can make its estimation difficult. For example, each equation may have (Ln-1) predictors, even if we do not consider time lags. Hence if we consider five ($L = 5$) marketing instruments of five brands ($n = 5$) we have 24 predictors. This implies that we need about (5 × 24) ≈100 observations to obtain reliable estimates. Given that the time horizon which is used for calibration should not be too long (say 2 years) we have to work with weekly data.

The data used to calibrate the reaction functions in these studies generally involve manufacturer's actions and reactions. In the past, researchers used monthly, bimonthly or quarterly data, but scanner data now offers ample opportunities to study competitive reactions. However, calibrating competitive reaction functions with weekly scanner data collected at the *retail level* involves its own problems, because changes in marketing activities may reflect the actions and reactions of retailers as well manufacturers. For example, ultimately price decisions about a brand are made by retailers (Kim and Staelin 1999), temporary price cuts, displays, refunds, and bonuses introduced at the retail level depend on the degree to which retailers accept (pass-through rates) promotional programs from manufacturers. Thus, especially with scanner data, researchers who estimate competitive reaction functions should create models that reflect the roles of both manufacturers and retailers. Another issue is the interpretation of the signs in the competitive reaction functions. The question is, for example, whether a negative sign is a reaction or just an association between two variables. Hence we touch on causality issues (see also Sect. 5.4.3 in Vol. I).

---

[16]In (9.21) the "subtraction" of $x_{\ell jt}$ means that instrument ℓ for brand j in period t is *not* a predictor variable.

Leeflang and Wittink (1992) develop models that explicitly account for the roles of manufacturers and retailers. In this chapter we do not discuss these roles but refer to Leeflang and Wittink (1992).

Using weekly scanner data that refer to 76 weeks and seven brands Leeflang and Wittink (1992) consider the following marketing instruments: price (*p*) sampling (free products and gifts)(*sa*), refunds (giving money back on, for example, a bank account) (*rf*) bonus offers (more content of a product at the same price) (*bo*) and featuring (retailer advertising) (*ft*). For each brand, they estimate competitive reaction functions for each marketing instrument and express the criterion variables in the competitive reaction functions as changes. For example, the logarithm of the ratio of prices in two successive periods represents price changes. Price changes for brands with different regular price levels are more comparable on a percentage rather than on an absolute basis. In this way they also circumvent price inflation issues.

Other promotional activities are specified in terms of simple differences, since zero values may occur in these cases, which imply the logarithms cannot be used. The authors specify the following competitive function to illustrate the price of brand j (p_{jt}):

$$\begin{aligned}\ln\left(p_{jt}/p_{j,t-1}\right) = \alpha_j &+ \sum_{r=1,r\neq j}^{n}\sum_{t^*=1}^{T^*+1}\beta_{jrt^*}\ln\left(p_{r,t-t^*+1}/p_{r,t-t^*}\right)\\ &+ \sum_{t^*=2}^{T^*+1}\beta_{jjt^*}\ln\left(p_{j,t-t^*+1}/p_{j,t-t^*}\right)\\ &+ \sum_{r=1}^{n}\sum_{t^*=1}^{T^*+1}\sum_{x=1}^{4}\tau_{xjrt^*}\left(x_{r,t-t^*+1}-x_{r,t-t^*}\right)+\varepsilon_{jt}\end{aligned} \quad (9.22)$$

for $j = 1,\ldots,n$ and $t = T^* + 2, \ldots, T$

where

$x = 1 = sa$, $x = 2 = rf$, $x = 3 = bo$, $x = 4 = ft$,
T^* = the maximum number of time lags ($T^* = 10$),
T = the number of observations available,
n = the number of brands,
ε_{jt} = a disturbance term.

Equation (9.22) also includes lagged endogenous variables, to account for the phenomenon that periods with heavy promotions are followed by periods with relatively low promotional efforts.

Table 9.1 Number of significant causal competitive reactions aggregated across all pairs of brands (with simple competitive reactions shown in italics and intrafirm reactions between brackets)

	Criterion variable					
Predictor Variable	Price	Samping	Refund	Bonus	Feature	Total
Price	*24*	4(1)	14 (2)	11	9 (5)	62 (9)
Samping	5 (1)	*14*	2	4	18 (13)	43 (4)
Refund	5 (3)	4(1)	*4*	6 (2)	7 (2)	26 (8)
Bonus	12	8(1)	3 (1)	*5*	9 (2)	27 (4)
Feature	13 (4)	14(2)	4 (2)	4 (2)	*18*	53 (10)
Total	59 (8)	44(5)	27 (6)	30 (4)	61 (12)	221 (35)

Source: Leeflang and Wittink (1992, p. 52)

Further inspection of Eq. (9.22) makes it clear that the number of predictor variables is so large that they easily exceed the number of observations.[17] Leeflang and Wittink (1992) therefore use bivariate causality tests to select potentially relevant predictor variables (see also Bult et al. 1997).[18]

For all variable combinations, we show in Table 9.1 the number of times pairs of brands are "causally" related, based on bivariate tests. The maximum number for each of the cells in this table is 42 (excluding causal relations between different variables for the same brand). The largest number, 24, pertains to price-price relations. The smallest number, 2, refers to sampling-refund relations.

There are 256 significant relations $(221 + 35)$ in Table 9.1, out of which 35 pertain to relations between variables for the same brand. These intrafirm activities are indicated in parentheses. Of the remaining 221 competitive reactions, 65 (29%) are simple (shown on the diagonal). This observed percentage is (significantly) different from an expected percentage of 20% if simple and other competitive relations are equally likely. Yet 156 (71%) of the estimated competitive reaction effects involve a different instrument. Thus, the results in Table 9.1 show that there is ample evidence of multiple competitive reactions.

9.4.4 *Extended LNB Models with Advanced Demand Functions*

In these models researchers relax the assumptions that a *limited number* of marketing instruments of *one* competitive brand affects the demand function, as

[17] For example, suppose that $n = 7$ (brands) each with five instruments, $T^* = 10$(lagged periods), and $T = 76$. Then we have 76 observations to estimate 391 parameters, under the assumption that all manufacturers use all marketing instruments.

[18] For a discussion of other models that calibrate competitive reaction functions, see Kadiyali et al. (1999) and Vilcassim et al. (1999). In all cases, the reaction functions attempt to capture the use of marketing instruments to react to changes in other instruments without regard to consumer responses.

in (9.10). A customer-focused approach relies on information about consumers' sensitivity to changes in marketing instruments; that is it considers estimated market response functions.

Leeflang and Wittink (1996) describe customer-focused assessments by estimating "asymmetric"[19] market share response functions. Their model is calibrated with the same data set discussed in Sect. 9.4.3 for the estimation of competitive reaction functions Eq. (9.22). The structure of the market response functions is similar to that used for the competitive reactions. The criterion variable is the natural logarithm of the ratio of market shares in successive periods for brand $j = 1, \ldots, n: \ln(m_{jt}/m_{j,t-1})$ which is a function of the natural logarithm of the ratio of prices in successive periods and the first differences of four promotional variables (refunds, bonus activities, sampling, featuring) of all brands $r = 1, \ldots, n$:

$$\begin{aligned} \ln\left(m_{jt}/m_{j,t-1}\right) &= \lambda_j + \sum_{r=1}^{n} \sum_{t^*=1}^{T^*+1} \gamma_{jrt^*} \ln\left(p_{r,t-t^*+1}/p_{r,t-t^*}\right) \\ &\quad + \sum_{r=1}^{n} \sum_{t^*=1}^{T^*+1} \sum_{x=1}^{4} \xi_{xjrt^*} \left(x_{r,t-t^*+1} - x_{r,t-t^*}\right) + u_{jt} \end{aligned} \tag{9.23}$$

where u_{jt} is a disturbance term and all other variables have been defined before.

We show in Table 9.2 the predictor variables with statistically significant effects for each brand's market share equation. In this study 13 own-brand effects are obtained, that is, in 13 cases when $j = r$, the marketing instrument of brand j has a statistically significant effect with the expected sign on the brand's own market share. Because

Table 9.2 Statistically significant effects[a] in market share response functions

Criterion variable	Relevant predictors for each brand[c]						
Market share[b]	1	2	3	4	5	6	7
m_1	*p*, *ft*	*ft*		*sa*		*sa*	
m_2		*p*, *bo*, *ft*	*ft*	*ft*	*p*	*p**	
m_3			*p*		*ft*		
m_4		*ft*	*ft**	*bo*, *ft*			*sa*
m_5	*p*			*bo**	*p*, *ft*	*sa*, *ft*	
m_6	*p*	*p*, *bo*	*sa*			*rf*, *sa*	
m_7	*ft*	*p*				*p**	*p*
Maximum possible number of effects per cell	2	4	3	5	4	5	5

Notes: [a]The letters are used for predictor variables that have statistically significant effects in the multiple regression; *p* price, *sa* sampling, *rf* refund, *bo* bonus, *ft* feature defined as in (9.22). If the sign of the coefficient for the next predictor in the multiple regression is counter to expectations, the letter has the symbol * next to it

[b]Market share: $\widetilde{m_j} = \ln\left(m_{jt}/m_{j,t-1}\right)$

[c]Own-brand effects are in the cells on the diagonal; cross-brands effects are in the off-counter cells

Source: Leeflang and Wittink (1996, p. 114)

[19]See for a discussion about modeling asymmetric competition: Foekens et al. (1997); Leeflang et al. (2000, Sect. 14.4) and Vol. I, Sect. 7.3.3.3.

each brand does not use all marketing instruments, the maximum possible number of own-brand effects varies between the brands (the maxima are shown in the last row). Across the brands the maximum number of own-brand effects is 28.

There are 18 cross-brand effects significant, with the expected sign, indicated as off-diagonal entries in Table 9.2. The maximum number of cross-brand effects equals 168. Thus, the proportion of significant cross-brand effects (18/168 or 11%) is much lower than the proportion of significant own-brand effects (13/28 or 46%). From Table 9.2 we can draw some conclusions about competition based on consumers' response function estimates. For example, brand 3's market share is affected only by feature advertising for brand 5. Brand 7 only affects brands 4's market share with sampling.

A more recent example of an extended LNB model with advanced demand functions can be found in Van Heerde et al. (2015).[20] These authors explore how media coverage of a price war affects customer, retailer and investor reactions (abnormal stock returns) over time. The authors find that (deep) price reductions trigger media coverage which sets off a chain of reactions. The model has been estimated using Hierarchical Bayes modeling (Chap. 16) where they use uninformative prices.

9.4.5 Framework and Cross Tabulations

The framework approach can enhance the congruence between competitor-oriented and customer-focused decision making, because the framework itself relates consumer response and competitive reaction effects and thus provides a basis for categorizing over- and underreactions by managers. Hence this approach combines advanced competitive reaction functions with advanced demand functions.

In the framework there are three kinds of elasticities: reaction elasticity, cross-elasticity and own elasticity. For simplification, the framework is restricted to the absence/presence of effects, such that the elasticities are either 0 or not, which results in eight possible combinations (see Fig. 9.2). We consider two brands: the defender brand i and the attacker brand j. Brand i uses marketing instrument ℓ to react to an attack of brand j.

In cell A of Fig. 9.2 all three effects are non-zero, which implies intense competition, so brand i uses marketing instrument ℓ to restore its market share, influenced by brand j's use of variable h. In the presence of a cross-brand market share effect, brand j cannot recover its loss of market share if:

- the own-brand market share effect is 0, as in cell B;
- there is no competitive reaction effect, as in cell C, or
- there is neither a competitive reaction effect nor an own-brand market share effect, as in cell D.

[20]This text is based on Van Heerde et al. (2015).

	Cross-brand market share effect[a]			
	YES $\frac{\delta m_i}{\delta u_{hj}} \neq 0$		NO $\frac{\delta m_i}{\delta u_{hj}} = 0$	
	Competitive reaction effect		Competitive reaction effect	
	YES $\frac{\delta u_{\ell i}}{\delta u_{hj}} \neq 0$	NO $\frac{\delta u_{\ell i}}{\delta u_{hj}} = 0$	YES $\frac{\delta u_{\ell i}}{\delta u_{hj}} \neq 0$	NO $\frac{\delta u_{\ell i}}{\delta u_{hj}} = 0$
Own-brand market share effect				
YES $\frac{\delta m_i}{\delta u_{\ell i}} \neq 0$	A Intense competition	C Underreaction Lost opportunity for defender[b]	E Defender's game	G No competition
NO $\frac{\delta m_i}{\delta u_{\ell i}} = 0$	B Spoiled arms for defender[b]	D Ineffective arms	F Overreaction Spoiled arms for defender[b]	H No competition

[a] i = Defender, j = Attacker
[b] Defender may lack information on own market share effects

Fig. 9.2 Cross-brand market share effect
Source: Leeflang et al. (2000, p. 214)

Cell B indicates the use of an ineffective instrument ("spoiled arms") chosen by i to react to j, cell C represents *underreactions*, such that brand i should defend its market share but does not react, even though instrument ℓ of the competitive brand is effective. We define this case as a lost opportunity for defender i. If there are no reaction effects and the own-brand market share elasticities equal 0, we recognize ineffective arms (cell D).

In case of no cross-brand market share effect, competitive reactions effects should not occur if the firm's objective is simply to preserve its market share. In the third column of Fig. 9.2, we identify some associated *overreactions*. In cell E (defender's game) the reactions include an instrument that has an own-brand effect, even though no cross-brand market share effect exists. Cell F involves (unnecessary) reactions with an ineffective instrument, which we call spoiled arms for the defender. Finally, cells G and H reflect no competition, because of the absence of both a cross-brand market share effect and a competitive reaction effect.

This framework suggests that knowledge about *cross- and own-brand* market share effects enables managers to prepare themselves better for competitor's activities in terms of whether and which reactions are desirable. Thus, a consumer-focused approach that captures consumers' responses to marketing helps management diagnose competition.

Leeflang and Wittink (1996) find that marketing managers of Dutch detergent brands tend to overreact, even though no reaction represents the dominant competitive response mode. In a replication study, Brodie et al. (1996) confirm their findings with New Zealand data.

Steenkamp et al. (2005) study simple and multiple reactions to both price promotions and advertising, including both short- and long-run effects. They also examine the moderating impact of *brand-* and *category*-related characteristics on competitive reaction elasticities. In contrast to Leeflang and Wittink (1992, 1996) and Steenkamp et al. (2005) distinguish two types of reactions: accommodations (i.e. reductions in marketing support after a competitive attack) and retaliations. On the basis of this differentiation they find that:

- the most common form of competitive reaction is a passive lack of "reaction";
- when reactions occur, they are more often in response to *price promotions* than to advertising;
- retaliation with a price promotion against price promotion attacks is more prevalent than any other action-reaction combination;
- simple competitive reactions are generally retaliatory, whereas multiple reactions are either retaliatory or accommodating;
- all forms of competitive reactions generally are restricted to short-run changes in brands' marketing spending that do not prompt permanent changes in spending behavior.

Because the most common form of competitive reaction is *no reaction* to an attack cells (C + D + G + H in Fig. 9.2), we must question whether this decision is managerially sound, in the sense that sales protection appears unnecessary. Steenkamp et al. (2005) find that responses to promotional attacks that fall into cells G + H constitute 82% of the time. Of these cases, no effects emerge for 78%, whereas in 22% positive cross-sales effects occur. In the 18% of all cases that suffer negative cross-sales effects (C + D), retaliation would have been ineffective 30% of the time, that is, in 30% $\times$ 18% $\approx$ 5% of *all* cases (cell D). This finding suggests that underreactions (cell C) occur in about 13% of all cases. These rarely occur in response to advertising attacks. Steenkamp et al. (2005) also find a substantial number of overreactions (cells E + F); across all cases and situations, 45% of defenders respond with a promotion to a promotion attack, even when the initial promotion has no effect on them (E + F/(E + F + A + B)).

Although the estimation of reaction matrices captures the nature of competitive reactions, it falls short of explaining reaction patterns. In other words, it fails to provide sufficient insight into the underlying reasons for the observed reactions (Kadiyali et al. 2001; Ramaswamy et al. 1994). Another drawback of competitive reaction models involves the understanding who is the defender and who is the attacker, i.e. the one who initiates a move. In response, researchers developed the VARX-models, as well as the NEIO-models that we discussed subsequently, to provide such insights. The availability of more data (scanner data at the store level) *and* new methodologies (VARX-modeling) determine this step in the evolutionary model-building process.

9.4.6 VARX-Models

Modern time-series analysis (TSA) offers the opportunity to use demand functions and reaction functions *simultaneously* to diagnose and predict competition: see Chap. 4. Vector AutoRegressive models with eXogeneous variables (VARX) may be applied in cases in which the marketer wants to:

- account for the dynamic effects of marketing instruments on the sales of individual brands in a market and when, or
- distinguish among *immediate* (instanteneous), *gross* and *net* effects.

The direct effects again refer to the unaltered influence of marketing actions on a performance measure; indirect effects capture their impact on performance through competitive (or other) reactions. Among the direct effects, we may distinguish between *immediate* effects and *gross* effects, or the sum of the direct and indirect effects measured during the same time horizon and therefore account for competitive reactions, whereas gross effects do not. To estimate immediate, gross, and net effects, impulse response analyses (IRA) are employed.

We illustrate the use of a VARX-model by discussing a model specified and calibrated by Horváth et al. (2005), which simultaneously considers advanced market response *and* advanced competitive reaction functions and relies on pooled *store* data for each of three brands of tuna fish for calibration.[21]

9.4.6.1 Response Functions

The ("advanced") demand functions *in this example* are adaptations of AC Nielsen's SCAN*PRO model (see Wittink et al. 2011, and Sects. 6.8.7 and 7.3.2.2 in Vol. I.) in which the variables of interest are the logarithms of the unit sales and price indices (ratio or actual to regular price) for brands at the store level. The SCAN*PRO model includes several own- and cross-brand promotional variables: price index, feature only, display only, and feature and display. Horváth et al. (2005) extend this model by including dynamic price promotion effects (delayed responses) and purchase reinforcement effects (through lagged sales).[22]

They define two types of price promotion variables: (1) own- and other-brand temporary discounts without support and (2) own- and other-brand temporary discounts with feature and/or display support. By definition, such promotion variables are minimally correlated. All parameters are brand specific and all lagged variables have unique parameters. Horváth et al. (2005) specify the market response function as:

[21]We closely follow Horváth et al. (2005). For a thorough discussion of VARX-models see also Dekimpe et al. (2008) and Chap. 4. Other examples of VARX-models that are used to model competitive response are Srinivasan et al. (2000); Takada and Bass (1998).

[22]They do not include separate lagged non-price instruments to reduce concerns about the degrees of freedom.

$$\ln S_{qi,t} = \alpha_{qi} + \sum_{k=1}^{2} \sum_{j=1}^{n} \sum_{t^*=0}^{P_{ijk}^{SP}} \beta_{PIijk,t^*} \ln PI_{qjk,t-t^*}$$
$$+ \sum_{j=1}^{n} \sum_{t^*=1}^{P_{ij}^{SS}} \varphi_{ij,t^*} \ln S_{qj,t-t^*} + \sum_{j=1}^{n} \beta_{Fij} F_{qj,t} \qquad (9.24)$$
$$+ \sum_{j=1}^{n} \beta_{Dij} D_{qj,t} + \sum_{j=1}^{n} \beta_{FDij} FD_{qj,t} + \varepsilon_{qi,t}$$

$$q = 1, \ldots, Q,\ i = 1, \ldots, n \text{ and } t = 1, \ldots, T$$

where

$\ln S_{qi,t}$ = the natural logarithm of sales of brand i in store q in week t,
$\ln PI_{qik,t}$ = log price index (actual to regular price) of brand i in store q in week t; ($k = 1$ denotes the feature/display-supported price cuts and $k = 2$ denotes price cuts that are not supported),
$F_{qj,t}$ = feature-only dummy variable for *non-price* promotions of brand j in store q at time t,
$D_{qj,t}$ = display-only dummy variable for *non-price* promotions of brand j in store q at time t,
$FD_{qj,t}$ = combined use of feature and display supports of *non-price* promotions of brand j in store q at time t,
α_{qi} = store-specific intercept for brand i and store q,
β_{PIijk,t^*} = (pooled) elasticity of brand i's sales with respect to brand j's price index,
φ_{ij,t^*} = (pooled) substitution elasticity of brand i's sales with respect to competitive (j) sales in week t ($i \neq j$),
$\beta_{Fij}, \beta_{Dij}, \beta_{FDij}$ = effects of feature-only (F), display-only (D), and feature and display (FD) on sales,
P_{ijk}^{SP} = number of lags for price index variable k of brand i included in the equation for brand j,
P_{ij}^{SS} = number of lags of the sales variable of brand i included in the equation for brand j,
n = the number of brands in the product category,
Q = number of stores, and
$\varepsilon_{qi,t}$ = disturbances.

Horváth et al. (2005) test for the equality of slopes across stores and fail to reject this null hypothesis; therefore the specification of the demand model does not allow for slope heterogeneity. This specification captures purchase reinforcements (φ_{ij,t^*}) immediate sales response (β_{PIijk,t^*} for $t^* = 0$), and delayed response (β_{PIijk,t^*} for $t^* > 0$).

9.4.6.2 Reaction Functions

In the preceding text, the competitive reactions are defined as the reactions of brand managers to the marketing activities of other brands, but this reaction is not the only possible type of reaction nor is it necessarily the most efficient one.

For example, managers often track market shares or sales, and a drop in either measure may prompt them to react with a marketing instrument. Similarly, they track other brand's performances and may interpret an increase as a competitive threat. Therefore, Horváth et al. (2005) incorporate these ideas as feedback effects in the reaction functions (compare also Kotler 1965). These reaction functions also include price indices as in Eq. (9.24). Although one may doubt whether these competitors react on price indices, Horváth et al. (2005) use these indices instead of regular or promotional prices because VARX-models require the same set of model variables. The reaction functions also account for inertia in decision-making and coordination between own-brand instruments (internal decisions):

$$\begin{aligned}\ln PI_{qi\ell,t} &= \delta_{qi\ell} + \sum_{t^*=1}^{P_{ii\ell\ell}^{PP}} \gamma_{i\ell,t^*} \ln PI_{qi\ell,t-t^*} + \sum_{t^*=1,k\neq\ell}^{P_{ii\ell k}^{PP}} \gamma_{ik,t^*} \ln PI_{qik,t-t^*}\\ &+ \sum_{k=1}^{2}\sum_{j=1,j\neq i}^{n}\sum_{t^*=1}^{P_{ij\ell k}^{PP}} \gamma_{i\ell jk,t^*} \ln PI_{qjk,t-t^*} \qquad (9.25)\\ &+ \sum_{j=1}^{n}\sum_{t^*=1}^{P_{ij\ell}^{PS}} \eta_{ij,t^*} \ln S_{qj,t-t^*} + \upsilon_{qi\ell,t}\end{aligned}$$

$$q = 1,\ldots,Q,\ i = 1,\ldots,n,\ \ell = 1,2 \text{ and } t = 1,\ldots,T,$$

where the variables are defined as in Eq. (9.24) and the $\upsilon_{qi\ell,t}$ respresent the disturbance terms. The super- and sub-indices of P indicate that the number of included lags may vary per equation and per variable. Equation (9.25) thus captures internal decisions (inertia in decisions making: $\gamma_{i\ell,t^*}$, intrafirm effects: : $\gamma_{ik,t^*}, k \neq \ell$) and own-brand ($\eta_{ii,t^*}$) and cross-brand ($\eta_{ij,t^*}\ j \neq i$) feedback effects, which refer to reactions to the consequence of an action. If marketing managers who track their own-brand market share or sales perceive a decrease in either measure, they may react by changing their marketing activities. In the same way, they may track and react to other brands' performance (cross-feedback effects).

Before we continue our discussion about the possibilities of modeling competitive behavior, we believe a wrap-up discussion is appropriate. Thus far, we have detailed six different approaches; we summarize their characteristics in Table 9.3.

Table 9.3 Characteristics of methods to model competitive response for individual brands

Method	Characteristics
(1) Classical demand models	Simple, no interactions among actions, reactions and responses
(2) Classical LNB model	Interactions, aggregation of competitive brands, horizontal competition, no effects of retailers' decisions
(3–5) Extended LNB models	Interactions, actions and reactions of/on individual brands, horizontal competition, accounting for effects of retailers' decisions, no simultaneous equation system(framework instead), no explanations of reactions
(6) VARX models	Interactions, individual brands, horizontal competition, accounting for retailers' decisions, simultaneous equation system with emphasis on dynamic effects, some explanation of competitive moves

The models (1)–(6) constitute a string of models that have been developed by "generations" of model builders in an evolutionary way. This "way" is covering a period of more than 40 years (1975–2015) and has not come to an end yet. We refer in this context to a recent study by Voleti et al. (2015) who study interproduct competition using Bayesian hierarchical clustering (Chap. 16) and spatial models (Chap. 5). The models we have discussed so far all assume that each manager treats the competitors' strategies as a given and computes his or her own best response. In the models that we will discuss next, managers achieve *simultaneous solutions* for, at least in principle, *all relevant brands* in the marketplace. Such simultaneous solutions call for game-theoretic approaches.

9.5 Game-Theoretic Models

9.5.1 Introduction

The preceding discussions make clear that in the market place, managers consider not only their perceptions of consumer responses, but also their expectations of competitor reactions to a potential marketing initiative. These complexities make the choice of an action in a competitive situation intractable, because the optimal choice for one brand depends on what other brands may do, which in turn depends on what the focal brand does, and so on. (Moorthy 1985). Game theory offers a means to study these interdependencies.[23] The game-theoretic models of competitive responsiveness result from applying existing approaches to "new" problems. Game-theoretic models are based on the assumption that competitors' strategies are given. In these models we are interested in the specification of optimal marketing decisions for all (relevant) brands.

The game-theoretic models origin from another branch of models than the models in (1–6) discussed so far. In other words, they do not result from previous steps in the evolutionary process we described above.

Game theory may distinguish into cooperative and non-cooperative categories. Cooperative game theory examines the behavior of *colluding firms* by maximizing a weighted average of all firms' profits. If we have two firms with profits π_1 and π_2 this means that:

$$\max_{x_{\ell j}} \pi = \lambda \pi_1 + (1 - \lambda)\, \pi_2 \tag{9.26}$$

[23]More complete treatments of game theory in a marketing context can be found in Hanssens et al. (2001, pp. 367–374); Moorthy (1985). A managerial treatment of game theoretic principles appears in Nalebuff et al. (1996). For a general introduction to modern game theory, see Fudenberg and Tirole (1991); Mass-Calell et al. (1995).

where

λ = the weight for firm 1, and
$x_{\ell j}$ = marketing instrument ℓ of firm j, $j = 1,2$, $\ell = 1,\ldots,L$.

In the empirical studies the weight λ is determined by the data. In the modern world, competition takes place among a few competitors with interdependent interests such that each competitor's actions affect the others. This situation is characterized by strategic competition, which requires non-cooperative game theory. The Nash (1950) equilibrium represents the central concept of non-cooperative game theory and involves a set of strategies, one for each competitor, defined such that no competitor wants unilaterally to change its strategy. In a Nash equilibrium, each strategy is a competitor's best option, given the best strategies of its rivals, where the meaning of "best" depends on specified objectives. If the objective is profit, Nash equilibriums are obtained for all ℓ and j:

$$\frac{\partial \pi_i}{\partial x_{\ell j}} = 0, \quad j = 1,\ldots,n, \ell = 1,\ldots,L \tag{9.27}$$

where $\pi_i = f(x_{\ell j})$.

Models that use game-theoretic principles date back to Cournot (1838), who argued that *quantity* (q) should be the choice variable, and Bertrand (1883), who posited *price* (p) as the choice variable. In Cournot's model, competitors conjecture the quantities supplied by other firms, and assume that other firms will act as necessary to sell those quantities, leading to a "Cournot-equilibrium". In the Bertrand model, price is the decision variable and creates a "Bertrand-equilibrium". For single-firm decision making under certainty, the choice of either price or quantity as a decision variable, is moot, but when solving for an equilibrium, each firm's conjecture about the other firm's strategy variable must be correct. Therefore, modelers must evaluate and specify different alternatives. For example, with two firms and quantity and prices serving as decision variables, four kinds of equilibriums may emerge: (price, price), (price, quantity), (quantity, price) and (quantity, quantity). Specifically, the (price, quantity) equilibrium results if firm 1 chooses price and conjectures that firm 2 sets quantity, while firm 2 sets quantity and conjectures that firm 1 sets price.

Non-cooperative game theory also provides a natural vehicle for models of oligopolistic competition (Moorthy 1985, p. 268). In a Stackelberg-leader follower game, one competitor's actions occur *independent* of the other's, but the other firm considers these actions during its decision-making.

The so-called conjectural variation approach, pioneered by Iwata (1974), estimates conjectures about *how* competitors will react to changes in their marketing mix from the data. Different equilibriums imply different conjectural variables (CV) estimates for the structural equation system of demand and supply equations. In the conjectural variation approach each firm (brand) believes that its choice of, for example, price (or some other strategic variable) will affect the price by its rival, and the rival's reaction can be captured by a single parameter (Iwata 1974). The CV ranges from a competitive value of -1, through 0 for Cournot duopoly, to $+1$ for (symmetric) collusive duopoly. We illustrate this approach in Sect. 9.5.2.

Most early game-theoretic models were theoretical and lacked empirical applications, but powerful advances in game theory, particularly in the area of dynamic games, have emerged since the early 1980s. As a result, game theory is more applicable to modeling real-world competitive strategies.[24]

9.5.2 *The New Empirical Industrial Organization (NEIO)-Based Approach: Horizontal Competition*

The move from theoretical, static game-theoretic models to empirical, dynamic models has shifted attention from normative models to *descriptive game theory*, which implies game-theoretic models to test whether marketplace data are consistent with model specifications. A rich tradition of empirical research in marketing strategy examines the impact of cost and competitive characteristics of a market on the profitability of a firm and generally follows the (market) structure ➔ conduct (marketing mix, entry of new products, R&D expenditures) ➔ performance (profitability)-paradigm (SCP paradigm) of empirical industrial organization (EIO) theory. Empirical studies use cross-sectional data across industries to find empirical regularities.

Research that applies advanced game theory also has led to the insights that conduct and performance are not merely functions of structural market characteristics such as concentration, growth, barriers to entry, and product differentiation, as used in SCP studies. These insights provide the basis for *new* empirical industrial organization (NEIO) literature, which focuses on developing and estimating structural econometric models of strategic, competitive behavior by firms, in which context:

- "structural" means that the firm's decisions are based on some kind of optimizing behavior,[25] and
- "econometric models'" reflect simultaneous equations of demand and supply of all relevant competitors.

Usually, an NEIO model contains the following ingredients:

- demand functions,
- cost functions,
- specifications for competitive interactions, and
- an objective function (usually a profit function).

Furthermore, the typical steps required to specify and estimate empirical game theory models are as follows:

1. specify demand functions (including competitive marketing instruments);
2. specify cost functions;
3. specify objective functions (usually profit functions);

[24]We closely follow Kadiyali et al. (2001).

[25]See also Chap. 5 on Structural Models.

4. specify the game;
5. derive the first-order conditions for optimal marketing instruments;
6. add observed variables to identify the system;
7. estimate the models.

Simultaneous equations models usually rely on a simultaneous equation instrumental variable approach for estimation, such as the three-stage least squares (3SLS), full information maximum likelihood (FIML), and generalized method of moments (GMM) approaches (see Chap. 15). Dubé et al. (2005) discuss various other computational and methodological issues, and Chintagunta et al. (2006) offer a review of structural modeling in marketing. Ample attention to this topic is also given in Chap. 5. The methods proposed in the NEIO-literature have been compared by Roy et al. (2006).

To serve as an example we discuss a study by Gasmi et al. (1992), who investigate the behavior of Coca-Cola and Pepsi using quarterly data covering 18 years from the United States about quantity sold, price and advertising. They estimate various model specifications to allow for the possible existence of both cooperative and non-cooperative strategic behavior in this industry ("the game"). Their work proceeds by specifying an objective function for each firm (profit function), as well as demand and cost functions. Using these specifications, they obtain a system of simultaneous equations based on assumptions about the firm's behavior. Throughout their work, they also assume a one-to-one assumption relation between firm j and brand j and therefore use those terms interchangeably. Gasmi et al. (1992) propose the following demand function for brand j:

$$q_j = \gamma_{j0} + \alpha_{jj}p_j + \alpha_{jr}p_r + \gamma_{jj}a_j^{1/2} + \gamma_{jr}a_r^{1/2}, \quad j \neq r, \ j, r = 1, 2 \tag{9.28}$$

where

q_j = quantity demanded from brand j,
p_j = price per unit for brand j,
a_j = advertising expenditure for brand j,
r = index for a competitive brand.

We omit an error term and a subscript t for time periods from Eq. (9.28) for convenience. To illustrate the use of this model, we assume the cost function is:

$$C_j(q_j) = c_j q_j \tag{9.29}$$

where c_j is the constant variable cost per unit of brand j.

The profit function therefore can be written as:

$$\pi_j = p_j q_j - C_j(q_j) - a_j = (p_j - c_j)\left(\gamma_{j0} + \alpha_{jj}p_j + \alpha_{jr}p_r + \gamma_{jj}\, a_j^{\frac{1}{2}} + \gamma_{jr}\, a_r^{\frac{1}{2}}\right) - a_j. \tag{9.30}$$

Gasmi et al. (1992) consider six games:

1. firms set prices and advertising expenditures simultaneously (naive static Nash behavior in price and advertising);
2. firm $j = 1$ is the leader in both price and advertising, and firm $r = 2$ is the follower;
3. firm $j = 1$ is the leader in price, but the two firms "behave Nash" in advertising;
4. total collusion exists, which maximizes Eq. (9.26), a weighted average of both firms' profits;
5. firms first collude on advertising, and later compete on prices;
6. firms collude on price, knowing that they will compete later on advertising expenditures.

The first three games are based on non-cooperating behavior, and the last three games consider tacit collusion.

Gasmi et al. (1992) include additional exogenous variables and specify functions for the demand intercepts (γ_{j0}) and marginal costs (c_j), which makes the system identifiable. These functions, together with the demand functions in Eq. (9.28), can be estimated as a system of simultaneous equations.

They thus derive a general model specification, which they use to test the six games. The empirical results suggest that, for the period covered by the sample (1968–1986), tacit collusive behavior prevailed in advertising between Coca-Cola and Pepsi in the market for cola drinks, though collusion on prices is not as well supported by the data. Thus, the results favor the specification for game 5.

The preceding studies deal with horizontal competition and collusion, but these models also can be extended to consider *vertical competition*/collusion between competitors/partners in the marketing system, which operate at other levels of the system. Examples of these partners are wholesalers and retailers (Jeuland and Shugan 1983). The structure of the demand equation (9.28) also appears in other game-theoretic models, such as studies by Kadiyali (1996) and Putsis and Dhar (1999). In the past decades, aggregate logit and probit models have become the prevalent demand functions.[26] This also follows an evolutionary approach where an earlier specification is improved over time.

We now illustrate the CV-approach using the system of (two) equations (9.28).[27] In (9.28) we assume that price is the strategic variable and we model the pricing game as a single-period game in which each firm (brand) attempts to maximize current period profits. If we consider the price competition, the parameters θ_{12} and θ_{21} where:

$$\partial p_{1t} \Big/ \partial p_{2t} = \theta_{12} \text{ and } \partial p_{2t} \Big/ \partial p_{1t} = \theta_{21}$$

[26]See, for example, Chintagunta and Rao (1996); Sudhir (2001); Sudhir et al. (2005); Zhu et al. (2009).

[27]We closely follow Roy et al. (2006).

represent the conjectural variations parameters. If $\theta_{12} = \theta_{21} = 0$, we infer a Nash competitive structure. If not, one may infer that one of the firms acts or as a price leader. Brand 1 is a price leader if $\theta_{12} \neq 0$ and $\theta_{21} = 0$. If both $\theta_{12} = \theta_{21} = 1$ then we have evidence of potential price collusion. The parameters θ_{12} and θ_{21}, in principle, can be easily obtained from a set of response functions, such as:

$$p_j = \beta_{0j} + \beta_{jr}p_r + \mu_{jr}a_r + \mu_{jj}a_j, \quad j = 1, 2 \tag{9.31}$$

where we omit disturbances and time subscripts for convenience. The derivation of the CV-estimates can be obtained by the specification of a profit function and differentiating this function to price and equating this expression to zero. See Roy et al. (2006) for technical details.

9.5.3 *NEIO-Based Approach: Vertical Competition*

The eight sets of models that we have discussed thus far deal primarily with horizontal competition and therefore cannot be applied if the focal company confronts vertical competition, which, in modern Western markets, usually refers to competition between manufacturers and retailers. Historically, retailers have been local, fragmented and technically primitive, so powerful multinational manufacturers, such as Coca-Cola and Procter & Gamble, behaved like branded bulldozers, pushing their products and promotion plans onto retailers, who were expected to accept them subserviently. Within the span of two or three decades, this situation has become history. The largest retailers (Carrefour, METRO, Tesco, Wal-Mart) enjoy global footprints that have shifted power structures and their global purchasing practices have brought enormous price pressures to bear even on leading consumer packaged good companies, which has increased vertical competition in the channels. This new situation also requires new specifications of equilibriums of Nash and Stackelberg games for example. This is worked out in detail by, for example, Draganska et al. (2010).

In a Vertical Nash game, prices are determined as follows[28]:

- retailers set their prices to maximize retail profits, without knowing wholesale prices;
- manufacturers set their prices to maximize profits without knowing retail prices, and
- manufacturers choose wholesale prices taking retail margins on their own products as given.

In a Vertical Manufacturer Stackelberg game, wholesale prices are set first and then retail prices are set after wholesale prices are observed.

[28]We closely follow Draganska et al. (2010).

Many game-theoretic models deal with vertical competition, especially pass-through in channels, i.e. how the amount of money offered by manufacturers that is intended to stimulate consumer demand is allocated to consumers by retailers. Models that consider vertical competition must optimize the objective functions of at least two partners simultaneously. Therefore, game theoretic approaches are applied to determine joint, simultaneous solutions. As an example, we discuss the (general) structure of a pass-through model developed by Moorthy (2005), who considers two retailers (1 and 2), each with two brands, 1 and 2, such that brand 1 is common to both retailers and brand 2 is a private label. If $i = 1{,}2, j = 1{,}2$ denotes brand *j*'s demand functions at retailer *i* the demand functions become the functions of all four retail prices: p_{11}, p_{21}, p_{12} and p_{22}. Then, retailer *i*'s $(i = 1{,}2)$ category profit function is given by:

$$\pi_i\left(\tilde{p}\right) = (p_{i1} - w_1 - c_{i1} - c_i - c)\, D_{i1}\left(\tilde{p}\right) + (p_{i1} - c_{i2} - c_i - c)\, D_{i2}\left(\tilde{p}\right), i = 1, 2 \tag{9.32}$$

where

$\tilde{p} = p_{11}, p_{21}, p_{12}, p_{22}$,
w_1 = the wholesale price of the national brand, usually assumed to be common to both retailers,
c_{i1}, c_{i2} = retailers i's non-brand-specific marginal operating costs, and
c = non-retailer-specific, non-brand-specific marginal operating costs.

Because brand 2 is a private label, the model provides no specific wholesale price for it. If the vector of marginal costs (w_1, c_{i1}, c_i, c) is taken as given and assuming that the demand functions are available, Moorthy is able to determine the optimal retail prices for both brands of both retailers. Solving the system of four first-order conditions leads to optimal price determinations, at least in principle.[29] Moorthy's study (2005) is a non-empirical study.

9.5.4 Time-Varying Competition

Normative models typically suggest that prices rise when demand and cost are higher, but in many markets, prices fall when demand or costs rise. This inconsistency occurs because normative models assume that competitive intensity is constant over time. In time-varying competition models the assumption about constant competitive intensity is relaxed. Time-varying competition models explicitly

[29] The system of equations should have a negative- definite Hessian matrix. See for a similar model Villas-Boas and Zhao (2005).

consider the so-called *indirect effects* of demand and cost changes on competition, which complement the *direct effects* of demand and cost on prices.[30]

The idea to integrate competitive intensity in a game-theoretic model can be illustrated as follows: Consider a profit function (π_{jt}) of brand j at t,

$$\max_{p_{jt}} \pi_{jt} = M_t \left(p_{jt} - c_{jt}\right) m_{jt} \tag{9.33}$$

where

M_t = potential size of the market at time t,
p_{jt} = price per unit at time t,
c_{jt} = cost per unit at time t, and
m_{jt} = market share of brand j at t.

Solving the first-order conditions for profit maximization under the assumption of Nash-Bertrand equilibrium, it is derived by Sudhir et al. (2005) that:

$$p_{jt} = c_{jt} - m_{jt} / \left(\frac{\partial m_{jt}}{\partial p_{jt}}\right). \tag{9.34}$$

Therefore, the so-called Bertrand margin is:

$$margin_{jt}^{Bertr.} = -m_{jt} / \left(\frac{\partial m_{jt}}{\partial p_{jt}}\right). \tag{9.35}$$

In addition, the indirect effect of changes in competitive intensity on price may be captured by introducing a multiplier w_{jt} on the Bertrand margin. The pricing equation then is specified as:

$$p_{jt} = c_{jt} + w_{jt}\, margin_{jt}^{Bertr}. \tag{9.36}$$

The multiplier w_{jt} is a function of the predictor variables that affect competitive behavior. The interpretation of w_{jt} is as follows: when w_{jt} >(<)1, firm j is pricing cooperatively (competitively) relative to the Bertrand equilibrium. At $w_{jt} = 0$, firm j prices at marginal cost. Sudhir et al. (2005) use quarterly dummy variables, which measure consumer confidence, costs of material and labor, and so forth, as predictor variables and thereby explicitly model the indirect effects of demand and cost changes on competition.

The last link in the evolutionary chain of building models of competitive response consists of dynamic, empirical, game-theoretic models.

[30] See Sudhir et al. (2005).

9.5.5 Dynamic, Empirical Game-Theoretic Models

The model developed by Ailawadi et al. (2005) encompasses the following equations:

- demand equations for all brands in a product category;
- the objective function of a retailer;
- the objective function of a competitive brand.

The context of the model Ailawadi et al. (2005) consider is the response to Procter & Gamble's (P&G) value pricing strategy, which entailed P&G making major cuts in promotions and providing a lower everyday price to retailers and consumers. Ailawadi et al. (2005) conduct their analysis for a local market and model the channel structure as a dynamic series of Manufacturer-Retailer Stackelberg games. In each period the manufacturer of brand 1 (P&G) is the leader and the retailer is the follower.

Ailawadi et al. (2005) generate predictions of competitor and retailer responses and test their accuracy. To this end they use weekly scanner data from stores in the Chicago market belonging to the Dominicks grocery store chain. The data represent sales, deal, prices, etc. of nine product categories and over 6 years.

Specifically, they compare the predictive ability of their model with the reaction function approach (Leeflang and Wittink 1992, 1996) and a dynamic model that assumes that the retailer is nonstrategic. The dynamic, empirical game-theoretic model offers better predictive ability than either benchmark model; thus, such models provide the means to account for *important changes* in competitive *strategy* (see also Shugan 2005) and are more consistent with strategic competitive reasoning than with the extrapolation of past reactions to the future.

This model is an evolution of a number of existing approaches and models, viz. NEIO-models in Fig. 9.1 with horizontal (Set 8) and vertical competition (Set 9), which is time-varying (Set 10). The models also combine advanced demand functions (4) with advanced competitive reaction functions (3). Hence the evolutionary steps are based on combinations of different research "models".

The models (7), (8), (9) and (11) constitute an evolutionary path that covers a time period of about 180 years! With the development of the empirical game-theoretic models in the past 20 years, these models have proven their value in the area of competitive responsiveness. We expect that the dynamic, empirical game-theoretic models can be improved in the near future through the application of Dynamic Linear Models (DLM).[31]

The next steps to model competition through game-theoretic models (12) involve:

- the development of competitive response models that are adequate tools to predict *strategic changes* (Montgomery et al. 2005);

[31] Ataman et al. (2007); Ataman et al. (2008); Van Heerde et al. (2004) and Chap. 5.

- tailored models to fit unique solutions (as an example we refer to a model developed by Roberts et al. (2005) which is a prelaunch diffusion model for evaluating market defense strategies in the telecom sector);
- more competitors, retailers, wholesalers, etc. that the analytical models developed so far (Ailawadi et al. 2005). We suggest in this respect to use simulation of these complicated demand and supply systems, to provide means to derive optimal decisions;
- modeling the simultaneous effects of strategic and operational (tactic) decisions (Holtrop and Wieringa 2017).

Furthermore, we believe that endogenizing competitive responses, for example, by adding more variables to the models is beneficial. Soberman and Gatignon (2005) suggest, in this respect, a link between competitive dynamic models and market evolution.

References

Aboulnasr, K., Narasimhan, O., Blair, E., Chandy, R.: Competitive response to radical product innovations. J. Mark. **72**(3), 94–110 (2008)

Ailawadi, K.L., Kopalle, P.K., Neslin, S.A.: Predicting competitive response to a major policy change: combining game-theoretic and empirical analyses. Mark. Sci. **24**, 12–24 (2005)

Ailawadi, K.L., Zhang, J., Krishna, A., Kruger, M.W.: When Wal-Mart enters: how incumbent retailers react and how this affects their sales outcomes. J. Mark. Res. **47**, 577–593 (2010)

Alsem, K.J., Leeflang, P.S.H: Predicting advertising expenditures using intention surveys. Int. J. Forecast. **10**, 327–337 (1994)

Alsem, K.J., Leeflang, P.S.H, Reuyl, J.C.: The forecasting accuracy of market share models using predicted values of competitive marketing behavior. Int. J. Res. Mark. **6**, 183–198 (1989)

Ataman, B.M., Mela, C.F., Van Heerde, H.J.: Consumer pckaged goods in France: national brands, regional chains, and local branding. J. Mark. Res. **44**, 14–20 (2007)

Ataman, B.M., Mela, C.F., Van Heerde, H.J.: Building brands. Mark. Sci. **27**, 1036–1054 (2008)

Bertrand, J.: Théorie Mathématique de la Richesse Sociale. Journal des Savants. 499–508 (1883)

Brodie, R.J., Bonfrer, A., Cutler, J.: Do managers ovȩrreact to each other's promotional activity? Further empirical evidence. Int. J. Res. Mark. **13**, 379–387 (1996)

Bult, J.R., Leeflang, P.S.H., Wittink, D.R.: The relative performance of bivariate causality tests in small samples. Eur. J. Oper. Res. **97**, 450–464 (1997)

Chintagunta, P.K., Rao, V.R.: Pricing strategies in a dynamic duopoly: a differential game model. Manag. Sci. **42**, 1501–1514 (1996)

Chintagunta, P.K., Erdem, T., Rossi, P.E., Wedel, M.: Structural modeling in marketing: review and assessment. Mark. Sci. **25**, 604–616 (2006)

Cleeren, K., Dekimpe, M.G., Verboven, F.: Competition in local-service sectors. Int. J. Res. Mark. **23**, 357–367 (2006)

Cleeren, K., Verboven, F., Dekimpe, M.G., Gielens, K.: Intra-and interformat competition among discounters and supermarkets. Mark. Sci. **29**, 456–473 (2010)

Cournot, A.A.: Recherches sur les Principes Mathématiques de la Théorie des Richesses par Augustin Cournot. L. Hachette (1838)

Day, G.S., Reibstein, D.J.: Wharton on Dynamic Competitive Strategy. Wiley, New York (1997)

Day, G.S., Wensley, R.: Assessing advantage: a framework for diagnosing competitive superiority. J. Mark. **52**(1), 1–20 (1988)

Dekimpe, M.G., Franses, P.H., Hanssens, D.M., and Naik, P.A.: Time-Series models in marketing. In: Wierenga, B. (ed.) Handbook of Marketing Decision Models, pp. 373–398. Springer, New York (2008)

Draganska, M., Klapper, D., Villas-Boas, S.B.: A larger slice or a larger pie? An empirical investigation of bargaining power in the distribution channel. Mark. Sci. **29**, 57–74 (2010)

Dubé, J., Hitsch, G., Manchanda, P.: An empirical model of advertising dynamics. Quant. Mark. Econ. **3**, 107–144 (2005)

Ellison, G.: Cooperation in the prisoner's dilemma with anonymous random matching. Rev. Econ. Stud. **61**, 567–588 (1994)

Friedman, L.: Game-theory models in the allocation of advertising expenditures. Oper. Res. **6**, 699–709 (1958)

Foekens, E.W., Leeflang, P.S.H., Wittink, D.R.: Hierarchical versus other market share models for markets with many items. Int. J. Res. Mark. **14**, 359–378 (1997)

Fudenberg, D. and Tirole, J.: Game Theory. Harvard University Press, Cambridge, MA, p. 393 (1991)

Gasmi, F., Laffont, J.J., Vuong, Q.: Econometric analysis of collusive behavior in a soft-drink market. J. Econ. Manag. Strateg. **1**, 277–311 (1992)

Gatignon, H.: Competition as a moderator of the effect of advertising on sales. J. Mark. Res. **21**, 387–398 (1984)

Gielens, K., Van de Gucht, L.M., Steenkamp, J-B.E.M., Dekimpe, M.G.: Dancing with a giant: the effect of Wal-Mart's entry into the United Kingdom on retailers. J. Mark. Res. **45**, 519–534 (2008)

Hanssens, D.M.: Market response, competitive behavior, and time series analysis. J. Mark. Res. **17**, 470–485 (1980)

Hanssens, D.M., Parsons, L.J., Schultz, R.L.: Market Response Models: Econometric and Time Series Analysis. Kluwer Academic Publishers, Dordrecht (2001)

Holtrop, N, and Wieringa, J.E.: Competitive reactions to strategic and tactical marketing actions. SOM Research Report, 16004, Mark, University of Groningen (2017)

Horváth, C., Leeflang, P.S., Wieringa, J.E., Wittink, D.R.: Competitive reaction-and feedback effects based on VARX models of pooled store data. Int. J. Res. Mark. **22**, 415–426 (2005)

Iwata, G.: Measurement of conjectural variations in oligopoly. Econometrica. **42**, 947–966 (1974)

Jeuland, A.P., Shugan, S.M.: Managing channel profits. Mark. Sci. **2**, 239–272 (1983)

Kadiyali, V.: Entry, its deterrence, and its accommodation: a study of the US photographic film industry. Rand J. Econ. **27**, 452–478 (1996)

Kadiyali, V., Sudhir, K., Rao, V.R.: Structural analysis of competitive behavior: New empirical industrial organization methods in marketing. Int. J. Res. Mark. **18**, 161–186 (2001)

Kadiyali, V., Vilcassim, N., Chintagunta, P.K.: Product line extensions and competitive market interactions: an empirical analysis. J. Econ. **89**, 339–363 (1999)

Kim, S.Y., Staelin, R.: Manufacturer allowances and retailer pass-through rates in a competitive environment. Mark. Sci. **18**, 59–76 (1999)

Kotler, P.: Competitive strategies for new product marketing over the life cycle. Manag. Sci. **12**, 104–119 (1965)

Krishnan, K.S., Gupta, S.K.: Mathematical model for a duopolistic market. Manag. Sci. **13**, 568–583 (1967)

Lambin, J.J., Naert, P.A., Bultez, A.: Optimal marketing behavior in oligopoly. Eur. Econ. Rev. **6**, 105–128 (1975)

Leeflang, P.S.H.: Modeling competitive reaction effects. Schmalenbach Bus. Rev. **60**, (2008a)

Leeflang, P.S.H.: Modeling Competitive Responsiveness. In: Wierenga, B (ed.) Handbook of Marketing Decision Models, pp. 211–251. Springer, New York, (2008b)

Leeflang, P.S.H., Reuyl, J.C.: Competitive analysis using market response functions. In: Rusch, R.F., et al. (eds.) Educators' Proceedings, pp. 388–395. American Marketing Association, Chicago (1985)

Leeflang, P.S.H., Wittink, D.R.: Diagnosing competitive reactions using (aggregated) scanner data. Int. J. Res. Mark. **9**, 39–57 (1992)

Leeflang, P.S.H., Wittink, D.R.: Competitive reaction versus consumer response: do managers overreact? Int. J. Res. Mark. **13**, 103–119 (1996)
Leeflang, P.S.H., Wittink, D.R., Wedel, M., Naert, P.A.: Building Models for Marketing Decisions, pp. 442–444. Kluwer Academic Publishers, Boston (2000)
Mass-Calell, A., Whinston, M.D., and Green, J.R.: Microeconomic Theory, 1st edn. Oxford University Press, New York (1995)
Moe, W.W., Yang, S.: Inertial disruption: the impact of a new competitive entrant on online consumer search. J. Mark. **73**(1), 109–121 (2009)
Montgomery, D.B., Moore, M.C., Urbany, J.E.: Reasoning about competitive reactions: evidence from executives. Mark. Sci. **24**, 138–149 (2005)
Moorthy, K.S.: Using game theory to model competition. J. Mark. Res. **22**, 262–282 (1985)
Moorthy, K.S.: Competitive marketing strategies: game-theoretic models. In: Eliashberg, J., Lilien, G.L. (eds.) Handbooks in Operations Research and Management Science: Marketing, vol. 5, pp. 143–192. North-Holland, Amsterdam (1993)
Moorthy, K.S.: A general theory of pass-through in channels with category management and retail competition. Mark. Sci. **24**, 110–122 (2005)
Nalebuff, B.J., Brandenburger, A., Maulana, A.: Co-opetition. Harper Collins Business, London (1996)
Plat, F.W., Leeflang, P.S.H.: Decomposing sales elasticities on segmented markets. Int. J. Res. Mark. **5**, 303–315 (1988)
Putsis Jr, W.P. and Dhar, R.: Category expenditure, promotion and competitive market interactions: Can private labels expand the pie. Working paper, London Business School, London (1999)
Ramaswamy, V., Gatignon, H., Reibstein, D.J.: Competitive marketing behavior in industrial markets. J. Mark. **58**(2), 45–55 (1994)
Roberts, J.H., Nelson, C.J., Morrison, P.D.: A prelaunch diffusion model for evaluating market defense strategies. Mark. Sci. **24**, 150–164 (2005)
Roy, A., Kim, N., Raju, J.S.: Assessing new empirical industrial organization (NEIO) methods: the cases of five industries. Int. J. Res. Mark. **23**, 369–383 (2006)
Shugan, S.M.: Comments on competitive responsiveness. Mark. Sci. **24**, 3–7 (2005)
Singh, V.P., Hansen, K.T., Blattberg, R.C.: Market entry and consumer behavior: an investigation of a Wal-Mart supercenter. Mark. Sci. **25**, 457–476 (2006)
Soberman, D., Gatignon, H.: Research issues at the boundary of competitive dynamics and market evolution. Mark. Sci. **24**, 165–174 (2005)
Srinivasan, S., Leszczyc Popowski, P., Bass, F.M.: Market share response and competitive interaction: the impact of temporary, evolving and structural changes in prices. Int. J. Res. Mark. **17**, 281–305 (2000)
Sriram, S., Kadiyali, V.: Empirical investigation of channel reactions to brand introductions. Int. J. Res. Mark. **26**, 345–355 (2009)
Steenkamp, J-B.E.M., Nijs, V.R., Hanssens, D.M., Dekimpe, M.G.: Competitive reactions to advertising and promotion attacks. Mark. Sci. **24**, 35–54 (2005)
Sudhir, K.: Competitive pricing behavior in the auto market: a structural analysis. Mark. Sci. **20**, 42–60 (2001)
Sudhir, K., Chintagunta, P.K., Kadiyali, V.: Time-varying competition. Mark. Sci. **24**, 96–109 (2005)
Takada, H., Bass, F.M.: Multiple time series analysis of competitive marketing behavior. J. Bus. Res. **43**, 97–107 (1998)
Urban, G.L., Karash, R.: Evolutionary model building. J. Mark. Res. **8**, 62–66 (1971)
Voleti, S., Kopalle, P.K., Ghash, P.: An interproduct competition model incorporating branding hierarchy and product similarities using store-level data. Manag. Sci. **61**, 2720–2738 (2015)
Van Heerde, H.J., Gijsbrechts, E., Pauwels, K.H.: Fanning the flames? How media coverage of a price war affects retailers, consumers, and investors. J. Mark. Res. **52**, 674–693 (2015)
Van Heerde, H.J., Mela, C.F., Manchanda, P.: The dynamic effect of innovation on market structure. J. Mark. Res. **41**, 166–183 (2004)

Verdoorn, P.J.: The Intra-block trade of Benelux. In Robinson, A. (ed.) The Economic Consequences of the Size of Nations, Appendix A, pp. 319–321. Palgrave Macmillan, London (1960)

Vilcassim, N.J., Kadiyali, V., Chintagunta, P.K.: Investigating dynamic multifirm market interactions in price and advertising. Manag. Sci. **45**, 499–518 (1999)

Villas-Boas, J.M., Zhao, Y.: Retailer, manufacturers, and individual consumers: modeling the supply side in the ketchup marketplace. J. Mark. Res. **42**, 83–95 (2005)

Wittink, D.R., Addona, M.J., Hawkes, W.J., and Porter, J.C.: SCAN*PRO: The estimation, validation, and use of promotional effects based on scanner data. In: Wieringa, J.E., Verhoef, P.C., Hoekstra, J.C. (eds.). Liber Amicorum in Honor of Peter S.H. Leeflang, Rijksuniversiteit Groningen. Faculteit Economie en Bedrijfskunde, Groningen, 135–162 (2011)

Zhu, T., Singh, V., Manuszak, M.D.: Market structure and competition in the retail discount industry. J. Mark. Res. **46**, 453–466 (2009)

Chapter 10
Diffusion and Adoption Models

Peter S. H. Leeflang and Jaap E. Wieringa

10.1 Introduction

In this chapter we discuss specific sets of models: diffusion models and adoption models. *Diffusion models* describe the spread of an innovation among a set of prospective adopters over time. A diffusion model depicts successive increases in the number of adopters and predicts the continued development of a diffusion process already in progress (Mahajan et al. 1993). The focus is generally on the generation of the product life cycle to forecast the first-purchase sales volume. Diffusion models are based on the assumption that the diffusion of a new product is a social process of imitation. For example, early adopters influence late adopters to purchase the new product. Positive interaction between current adopters and later adopters is assumed to bring about the (rapid) growth of the diffusion process.

Adoption models describe the stages of adoption processes at the individual level. Adoption processes represent the sequence of stages through which consumers progress from unawareness of an innovation to ultimate adoption. The adoption framework can be used by managers to determine the potential viability of a new product at pre-test market and test market stages of the new-product development process. By contrast, diffusion models are used to describe the early sales history of a new product and to forecast the time and the magnitude of peak sales at the aggregate or "macro" level.

We start to discuss the general structure of diffusion models in Sect. 10.2. In Sect. 10.3 we discuss modifications of these models. Section 10.4 spends attention to adoption models, which are also known as disaggregate diffusion models or

P.S.H. Leeflang (✉) • J.E. Wieringa
Department of Marketing, University of Groningen, Groningen 9700 AV, The Netherlands
e-mail: p.s.h.leeflang@rug.nl

P.S.H. Leeflang et al. (eds.), *Advanced Methods for Modeling Markets*,
International Series in Quantitative Marketing, DOI 10.1007/978-3-319-53469-5_10

models that represent diffusion at the individual level. Section 10.5 discusses in-depth examples of diffusion and adoption models.

10.2 Diffusion Models

Category sales for a new durable product such as televisions for high definition (HDTV) broadcasts can be pictured as in Fig. 10.1. Sales start out slowly but grow thereafter at an increasing rate, then continue to grow prior to t^* at a decreasing rate until a maximum is reached at t^*, after which sales decline. Sales do not tend to zero because new households (e.g., young couples) become potential buyers. Also, existing households will replace initial purchases and purchase additional units. Thus, once households purchase a second unit, or replace the first one, the interest in modeling goes beyond first-purchase sales volumes. The general shape of this curve has useful implications for the marketing and production of such products over their life cycle. The effectiveness of decisions depends on the availability of valid and reliable forecasts of the time (t^*) and the magnitude (Q_t^*) of peak sales (see for example Fischer et al. 2010).

Traditionally, diffusion models have been based on the model developed by Bass (1969), and assume the following:

1. the total number of potential adopters is fixed;
2. the values of the crucial parameters in the Bass model (p and q) are fixed throughout the life cycle of the innovation;

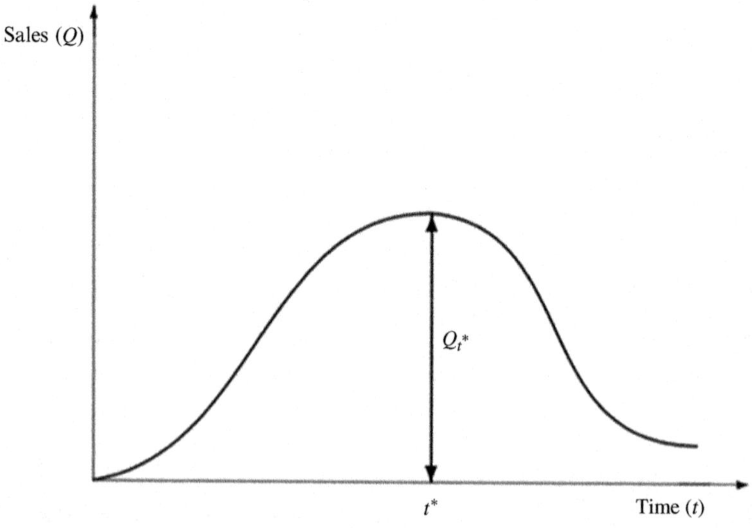

Fig. 10.1 Sales of a new consumer durable over time

Table 10.1 Past versus current research focus of diffusion modeling

Diffusion modeling 1960–1990	Diffusion modeling since 1990
Word-of-mouth as driver	Consumer interdependencies as drivers
Monotonically increasing penetration curve	Turning points and irregularities in the penetration curve
Temporal	Temporal and spatial
Industry-level analysis	Brand-level analysis
Aggregate or segment-based models	Individual-level models
Fully connected networks	Partially connected and small-world networks
Products	Services
Forecasting	Managerial diagnostics

Source: Muller et al. (2009, p. 4)

3. the marketing strategies supporting the innovation do not influence the diffusion process;
4. there are only two "consumer states", consumers who have adopted (i.e. made a first purchase) and consumers who have not (yet) adopted;
5. the purchase volume per buyer is one unit, i.e. there are no replacements or repeat purchases and no multiple adoptions.

Muller et al. (2009, p. 3) state that these models are no longer adequate to fully describe the diffusion process in many of today's markets. Therefore, these and a number of other assumptions are relaxed in (1) extended Bass models and (2) the diffusion models that are developed after 1990. Table 10.1 provides an overview of the most important recent changes.

The sales curve depicted in Fig. 10.1 has been replaced by curves with "turning points", "saddles" and other irregularities, particularly due to technological changes. Diffusion in a certain area or country is nowadays influenced by interactions with individuals in other countries taking the effects of social media explicitly into account. Hence spatial effects, such as explained in Chap. 6, play an important role in more modern diffusion models.

There is a trend from modeling aggregate behavior to the modeling of individual-level behavior as we also discussed in Chap. 1. This is also reflected in diffusion models at the individual level: adoption models.

In course of time the diffusion of pharmaceuticals and services has become more and more important. Finally, Muller et al. (2009, p. 5) mention that recent diffusion research places more emphasis on managerial diagnostics than (only) on forecasting the development of (aggregate) sales that represent the product life cycle.

In this section we discuss the classical Bass model. Some of its extensions are discussed in Sect. 10.3. In Sect. 10.4 we also discuss diffusion models that account for consumer interdependencies through (social) networks and irregularities in diffusion/adoption curves and models which are developed at a more disaggregate (brand) level.

The Bass model (Bass 1969) remains the most parsimonious model for diffusion processes in marketing literature and is widely accepted (Mahajan et al. 1990, 2000; Muller et al. 2009; Peres et al. 2010).[1] The empirical application of the Bass model has been tested on many different product categories, especially durable products (Sultan et al. 1990) but also on products such as franchising as an innovation of managerial organizations (Ruiz-Conde and Leeflang 2006), wind energy (Davies and Diaz-Rainey 2011), photovoltaic systems (Guidelin and Mortarino 2010) or scientific publications (Fok and Franses 2007). Many empirical examples of the Bass model have been discussed in Van den Bulte (2000) and Lilien et al. (2007, pp. 112–118).

The general structure of a diffusion model can be represented as:

$$\frac{dN(t)}{dt} = g(t)\left[\bar{N} - N(t)\right] = g\left(N(t)\right)\left[\bar{N} - N(t)\right] \tag{10.1}$$

where

$N(t)$ = cumulative number of adopters at time t,
$g(t)$ = the coefficient of diffusion, which is usually formulated as a function of $N(t)$,
$\bar{N}$ = the total number of potential adopters, e.g., consumers who ultimately adopt.

In the differential equation (10.1), the rate of diffusion of an innovation is assumed to be proportional to the difference between the total number of potential adopters $\bar{N}$and the number of adopters at that time. The term $\left[\bar{N} - N(t)\right]$ is often called the "untapped" potential, i.e., the remaining number of potential adopters. The proportionality coefficient is usually formulated as a function of the cumulative number of adopters:

$$g(t) = \alpha_0 + \alpha_1 N(t) + \alpha_2 (N(t))^2 + \ldots \tag{10.2}$$

In many diffusion models (10.2) is linear ($\alpha_2, \alpha_3, \ \ldots \ = 0$):

$$g(t) = \alpha_0 + \alpha_1 N(t). \tag{10.3}$$

Substituting (10.3) in (10.1) gives:

$$\frac{dN(t)}{dt} = \left(\alpha_0 + \alpha_1 N(t)\right)\left[\bar{N} - N(t)\right]. \tag{10.4}$$

For $\alpha_0, \alpha_1 > 0$, (10.4) is known as the *mixed-influence model.* An increase in $N(t)$ is modeled as the sum of two terms, each having its own interpretation. For $\alpha_1 = 0$, we obtain the (*single*) *external influence model* (10.5):

[1] We closely follow Ruiz-Conde et al. (2014).

$$\frac{dN(t)}{dt} = \alpha_0 \left[\bar{N} - N(t)\right] \tag{10.5}$$

where $\alpha_0 =$ the external conversion parameter.

The parameter α_0 represents the influence of a "change agent" in the diffusion process, which may capture any influence other than that from previous adopters. In (10.5) it is assumed that there is no interpersonal communication between consumers in the social system. Thus, the change in $N(t)$, $\frac{dN(t)}{dt}$, is assumed to be due to the effects of mass communications (advertising).

The *(single) internal influence* diffusion *model* (10.6) is based on a contagion paradigm that implies that diffusion occurs through interpersonal contacts:

$$\frac{dN(t)}{dt} = \alpha_1 N(t) \left[\bar{N} - N(t)\right]. \tag{10.6}$$

In Eq. (10.6) the rate of diffusion is a function of the interaction between prior adopters $N(t)$ and the (remaining) potential adopters $\left[\bar{N} - N(t)\right]$. The parameter α_1 can be interpreted as the word-of-mouth effect of previous buyers upon potential buyers.

The linear differential Eq. (10.4) can be solved to obtain:

$$N(t) = \frac{\bar{N} - \left[\alpha_0 \left(\bar{N} - N_0\right) / \left(\alpha_0 + \alpha_1 N_0\right)\right] \exp\left[-\left(\alpha_0 + \alpha_1 \bar{N}\right) t\right]}{1 - \left[\alpha_1 \left(\bar{N} - N_0\right) / \left(\alpha_0 + \alpha_1 N_0\right)\right] \exp\left[-\left(\alpha_0 + \alpha_1 \bar{N}\right) t\right]} \tag{10.7}$$

where $N_0 =$ the cumulative number of adopters at $t = 0$.

In the *external* influence model (10.5) $\alpha_1 = 0$. Substituting this value in (10.7) and setting $N_0 = 0$ gives:

$$N(t) = \bar{N}\left[1 - \exp\left(-\alpha_0 t\right)\right] \tag{10.8}$$

which is the continuous formulation of the penetration model developed by Fourt and Woodlock (1960).

In the *internal* influence model (10.6), $\alpha_0 = 0$. Substituting this value into (10.7) gives:

$$N(t) = \bar{N} / \left[1 + \left(\frac{\bar{N} - N_0}{N_0}\right) \exp\left(-\alpha_1 \bar{N} t\right)\right] \tag{10.9}$$

which is a logistic curve.

A specific mixed-influence model is the Bass model (Bass 1969). The model can be formulated in absolute terms (number of adopters, sales) or in relative terms (the fraction of potential adopters who adopted the product at time t: $F(t)$). In *absolute terms* the Bass model can be specified as:

$$\frac{dN(t)}{dt} = \left[p + \frac{q}{\bar{N}} N(t)\right] \left[\bar{N} - N(t)\right] \tag{10.10}$$

where

p = the coefficient of innovation,
q = the coefficient of imitation.

Relation (10.10) can also be written as:

$$n(t) = \frac{dN(t)}{dt} = p\left[\bar{N} - N(t)\right] + \frac{q}{\bar{N}}N(t)\left[\bar{N} - N(t)\right] \tag{10.11}$$

where $n(t)$ = number of initial purchases at t.

The first term in (10.11) represents adoptions due to buyers who are not influenced in the timing of their adoption by the number of people who have already bought the product ("innovators"). The second term represents adoptions due to buyers who are influenced by the number of previous buyers ("imitators").

The Bass model is usually specified in *relative terms*: $F(t)$ is the (cumulative) probability that someone in the market or in the target segment will adopt the innovation by time t, where $F(t)$ approaches 1 as t gets larger. Such a function is depicted in Fig. 10.2. The derivative of $F(t)$ is the probability density function (Fig. 10.3) which indicates the rate at which the probability of adoption is changing over time.

Relation (10.11) can also be written as:

$$n(t) = p\bar{N} + (q - p)\,N(t) - \frac{q}{\bar{N}}(N(t))^2. \tag{10.12}$$

The first-order differential Eq. (10.12) can be integrated to yield the S-shaped cumulative adopters distribution, $N(t)$ Once $N(t)$ is known, differentiation yields an expression for the non-cumulative number of adopters, $n(t)$, the time (t^*) and the magnitude of ($n(t^*)$ and $N(t^*)$) the peak of the adoption curve. We provide relevant expressions in Table 10.2.

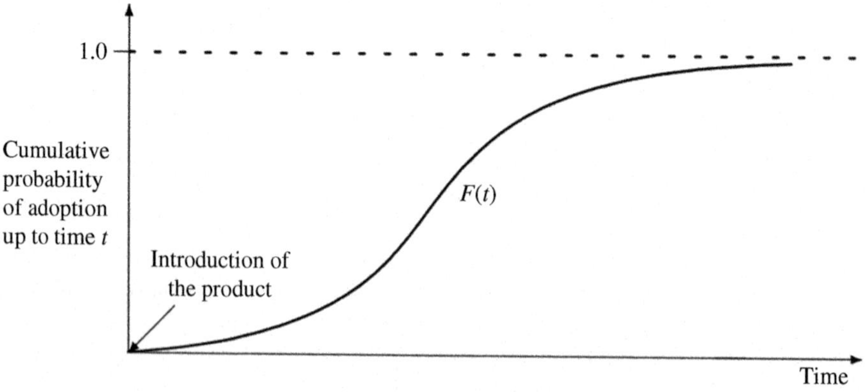

Fig. 10.2 Cumulative probability that a customer in the target segment will adopt the product before t
Source: Lilien and Rangaswamy (2003, p. 256)

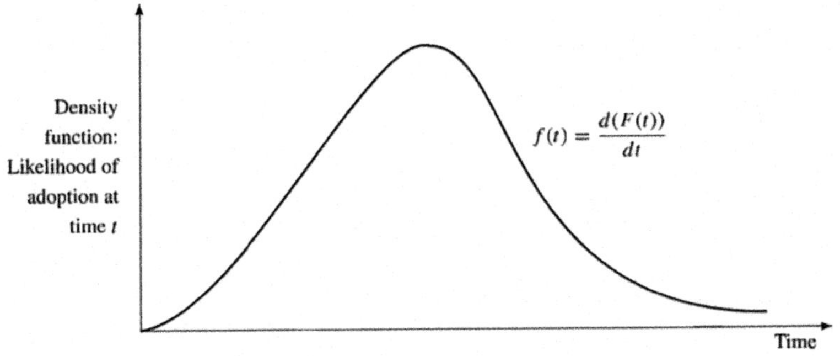

Fig. 10.3 Density function: likelihood that a consumer adopts the product at t
Source: Lilien and Rangaswamy (2003, p. 256)

Table 10.2 Analytical expressions for the Bass model

Item	Expression
Cumulative number of adopters	$N(t) = \overline{N}\left[\frac{1-e^{-(p+q)t}}{1+\frac{q}{p}e^{-(p+q)t}}\right]$
Noncumulative number of adopters	$n(t) = \overline{N}\left[\frac{p(p+q)^2e^{-(p+q)t}}{\left(p+qe^{(p+q)t}\right)^2}\right]$
Time of peak adoptions	$t^* = -\frac{1}{p+q}\ln\left(\frac{p}{q}\right)$
Number of adopters at the peak time	$n\left(t^*\right) = \frac{1}{4q}(p+q)^2$
Cumulative number of adopters at the peaktime	$N\left(t^*\right) = \overline{N}\left[\frac{1}{2} - \frac{p}{2q}\right]$
Cumulative number of adoptions due to innovators	$N_1(t) = \overline{N}\frac{p}{q}\ln\left[\frac{1+\frac{q}{p}}{1+\frac{q}{p}e^{-(p+q)t}}\right]$
Cumulative number of adoptions due to imitators	$N_2(t) = N(t) - N_1(t)$

Source: Mahajan et al. (1993, p. 354)

Relation (10.12) can also be written in a simpler format:

$$n(t) = \beta_0 + \beta_1 N(t) + \beta_2 (N(t))^2. \qquad (10.13)$$

Relation (10.13) can be discretized by replacing continuous time t by discrete time periods, where t is the current period, $t + 1$ is the next period, and so on. To reflect this, we replace $n(t)$ by n_t, and $N(t)$ by N_t. With this modification, the parameters of the following linear function can be estimated with ordinary least squares:

$$n_t = \gamma_0 + \gamma_1 N_{t-1} + \gamma_2 N_{t-1}^2 + u_t \qquad (10.14)$$

where u_t = a disturbance term.

The Bass model parameters p, q and $\bar{N}$ can be estimated from adoption data, usually by using non-linear least squares.[2] Sultan et al. (1990) estimated the average values of p and q for durable goods. These values were found to be $p = 0.03$ and $q = 0.38$.

10.3 Extensions of the Bass model

10.3.1 The Generalized Bass Model

10.3.1.1 Introduction

In this section we discuss extensions of the Bass model. We start to discuss the Generalized Bass Model (GBM) developed by Bass et al. (1994) that includes marketing decision variables.[3]

In Table 10.3 we present the framework that we use to classify how various researchers include marketing variables in macro-level diffusion models. Table 10.3 shows five possibilities. We distinguish between models including marketing variables in the diffusion model via a separable and via a non-separable function. We speak of a separable function if the marketing variables are specified to have a direct effect on sales, separate from the past that describes the diffusion process. In case of a non-separable specification, the marketing effects (variables) are assumed to moderate the diffusion process, so that both parts cannot be separately included in the model.

Many GBM's use option 3b of Table 10.1 to extend the classical Bass model. An example is Eq. (10.15) developed by Bass et al. (1994): they multiply the right hand side of (10.10) by:

$$f(p_t, a_t) = [1 + f_1(p_t) + f_2(a_t)] \tag{10.15}$$

where

$$f_1(p_t) = \delta_1 \frac{\Delta p_t}{p_{t-1}} \tag{10.16}$$

$$f_2(a_t) = \delta_2 \frac{\Delta a_t}{a_{t-1}} \tag{10.17}$$

and

p_t = price at time t,
a_t = advertising expenditures at time t.[4]

---

[2] Sultan et al. (1990).

[3] We closely follow Ruiz-Conde et al. (2006).

[4] Be aware that $p(t)$ is external influence and p_t is a price variable, whereas $\tilde{p}_t$ is the relative price in (10.19).

Table 10.3 Marketing variables in diffusion models[a]

Starting point: the fundamental diffusion model

$$n(t) = \frac{dN(t)}{d(t)} = \left(p + q\frac{N(t)}{\bar{N}}\right)\left[\bar{N} - N(t)\right] \quad (10.10)$$

Extensions: marketing variables affect...

1. External influence (non-separable function):
$p \equiv p(t) = f(\text{marketing variables}(t))$

2. Internal influence (non-separable function):
$q \equiv q(t) = f(\text{marketing variables}(t))$

3a. Both external and internal influence (non-separable function):
$p \equiv p(t) = f(\text{marketing variables}(t))$ and
$q \equiv q(t) = f(\text{marketing variables}(t))$

3b. Both external and internal influence (separable function):
Multiply the right hand side of (10.10) with $f(\text{marketing variables}(t))$

4. Potential market (non-separable function):
$\bar{N} = \bar{N}(t) = f\ (\text{marketing variables}(t))$

where

$n(t) = \frac{dN(t)}{dt}$ = non-cumulative number of adopters at time t or the rate of diffusion at time t,
$N(t)$ = cumulative number of adopters at time t,
$\bar{N}$ = potential market,
p = parameter of external influence,
q = parameter of internal influence,
marketing variables (t) = marketing variables at time t,
$f(\cdot)$ = functional shape of the influence of marketing variables.

[a]A similar table can be found in Parker and Gatignon (1994)
Source: Ruiz-Conde et al. (2006, p. 161)

Bass et al. (1994) test their model for three consumer durables and find that price and advertising have significant effects for room air conditioners and clothes dryers, but for color televisions only price has a significant effect. The effect of price on the size of the potential market ($\bar{N}$) is not significant or has the wrong sign.

Parker and Gatignon (1994) propose alternative specifications for brand-level first purchase diffusion models for different types of interpersonal influences and different levels of brand-level competition. Some of these specifications assume separable marketing effects (affecting the parameter of external or internal influence). They propose to include price and advertising via

$$f\left(p_t, a_t\right) = p_t^{\delta_1 + \delta_2 B_t} a_t^{\delta_3 + \delta_4 B_t}, \quad (10.18)$$

or

$$f\left(\widetilde{p}_t, \widetilde{a}_t\right) = \widetilde{p}_t^{\delta_1^* + \delta_2^* B_t} \widetilde{a}_t^{\delta_3^* + \delta_4^* B_t} \quad (10.19)$$

where

$\widetilde{p}_t$ = relative price,
$\widetilde{a}_t$ = advertising share, and
B_t = the number of brands in the category.

These response functions can affect external or internal influence. Parker and Gatignon (1994) analyze five different brands in the hair styling mousse product category. Based on their results, the authors conclude that there is not a unique diffusion model that captures the diffusion process of all the brands in the category best. Their results also demonstrate that marketing mix variables are critical to the diffusion of brands, but their effects are not identical across brands. The price effects remain constant or increase over time, but advertising sensitivity can be insignificant, increase or decrease over time, depending on the order of entry. In conclusion: the coefficients of the marketing variables have the expected sign in the latter two studies. Several options for incorporating price and advertising are investigated, but there is no dominant functional form.

Many other examples of macro-level diffusion models can be found in Ruiz-Conde et al. (2006).

10.3.2 Other Extensions: Recent Developments in Modeling Diffusion

We discuss the following modifications of the classical Bass model in this section:

- turning points and irregularities in the penetration curve;
- effects of technological changes;
- brand-level analysis and accounting for competition;
- cross-country effects;
- effects of externalities;
- services.

The effects of network externalities and consumer independencies are discussed in Sect. 10.5 where we discuss adoption models.

10.3.2.1 Turning Points and Irregularities

Figures 10.1, 10.2 and 10.3 describe the penetration of an innovation as a smooth curve, which increases monotonically until the entire market potential ($\bar{N}$) has adopted. In many real diffusion processes the diffusion curve does not look as smooth as in these figures. Figure 10.4 is an example of a much more realistic life cycle of a product.

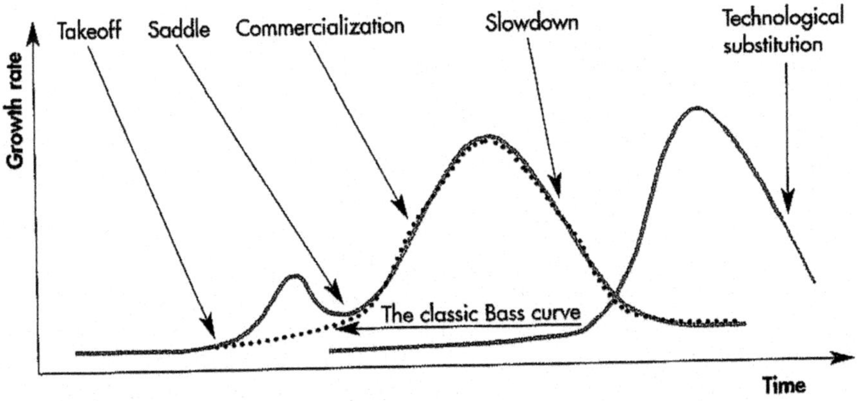

Fig. 10.4 Turning points in the product life cycle
Source: Muller et al. (2009, p. 19)

Golder and Tellis (1997, p. 257) define the takeoff point as

> "the time at which a dramatic increase in sales occurs that distinguishes the cutoff point between the introduction and growth stage of the product life cycle".

Muller et al. (2009, p. 24) consider the takeoff point as the interface between external and internal influences. External influences are more dominant before takeoff, and internal consumer interdependencies become more dominant after takeoff. Golder and Tellis (1997) and Tellis et al. (2003) use hazard models (Vol. I, Sect. 8.4.2) to determine takeoff points.

In many markets there is no monotonic increase in sales, up to the peak of growth. Goldenberg et al. (2002, p. 1) refer to this phenomenon as a saddle, and define it as

> "a pattern in which an initial peak predates a trough of sufficient depth and duration, followed by sales that eventually exceed the initial peak".

Saddles could be attributed to many causes including stockpiling, changes in technology, industry performance, external factors (macro-economic) and by social influencers.[5] Goldenberg et al. (2002) offer an explanation based on heterogeneity in the adopting population and its division into two separate markets: an early market and main market. This phenomenon can be modeled first modifying Eq. (10.10) as follows:

$$\frac{d\left(\frac{N(t)}{\bar{N}}\right)}{dt} = \left(p + q\frac{N(t)}{\bar{N}}\right)\left[1 - \frac{N(t)}{\bar{N}}\right] \tag{10.20}$$

or

$$\frac{d\widetilde{N}(t)}{dt} = \left(p + q\widetilde{N}(t)\right)\left[1 - \widetilde{N}(t)\right] \tag{10.21}$$

[5]We closely follow Muller et al. (2009, Chap. 4).

where $\widetilde{N}(t) = \frac{N(t)}{\bar{N}}$ = the adoption percentage at time t.

Equation (10.21) is then modified into (10.22) and (10.23):

$$\frac{d\widetilde{N}_1(t)}{dt} = \left(p_1 + q_1\widetilde{N}_1(t)\right)\left[1 - \widetilde{N}_{1t}\right] \tag{10.22}$$

$$\frac{d\widetilde{N}_2(t)}{dt} = \left(p_2 + q_2\widetilde{N}_2(t) + q_{12}\widetilde{N}_1(t)\right)\left[1 - \widetilde{N}_2(t)\right] \tag{10.23}$$

where p_1 and q_1 and p_2 and q_2 represent external and internal coefficients of the early market and main market respectively. The cross-market communication between both markets is denoted by q_{12}. Finally, $\widetilde{N}_1(t)$ is the percentage of adopters of the early market population and $\widetilde{N}_2(t)$ is the percentage of adopters of the main market population. The pattern of the product life cycle in Fig. 10.4 can be modified to account for seasonal effects. To this end, Peers et al. (2012) modify the Bass model in the following way:

$$S_t = \bar{N}\left[N(t) - N(t-1)\right] + \varepsilon_t \tag{10.24}$$

where S_t are the monthly sales of a new product. The disturbance ε_t is normal-distributed with mean zero and where the variable of the error term is proportional to the square of the fraction of current adopters. To model seasonal peaks and troughs (10.24) is modified into (10.25):

$$S_t = \bar{N}\left[N(t) - N(t-1)\right]\left[1 + \sum_{k \in K} \delta_k D_{kt}^{01}\right] + \varepsilon_t \tag{10.25}$$

where D_{kt}^{01} represents a 0/1 dummy for each month k in the set K, where K is usually (12–1) = 11 months, and the "1" in (10.25) represents the "base month".

10.3.2.2 Technological Changes

There are different opportunities to model the effects of technological changes that impact the shape of the product life cycle. First, one may model the impact of the market with the new technology on the existing market in a similar way as has been used in (10.22) and (10.23). Second, heuristics can be used to identify the time at which takeoff occurs for each technology generation (Stremersch et al. 2010; Tellis et al. 2003). Third, technological changes can be modeled through the "Meta-Bass"-model. Sood et al. (2009) use cross-sectional and longitudinal data to estimate the basic parameters $\bar{N}, p$ and q, of the classical Bass model (10.10). For each brand/product they estimate unique parameters $\bar{N}_i, p_i$ and q_i. Then they estimate the nonlinear additive model:

$$y_i = \alpha_0 + g_1\left(\bar{N}_i\right) + g_2\left(p_i\right) + g_3\left(q_i\right) + \varepsilon_t \tag{10.26}$$

where

y_i = the item to be predicted (sales of brand i, or sales in country i, or sales increases at the ith level),
p_i and q_i = external and internal influence,
g_1, g_2 and g_3 = smoothing spline functions (see Chap. 17).

Sood et al. (2009) compare this and other models to the predictive performance of models that are estimated using Functional Data Analyses (FDA). They demonstrate that FDA provides predictions that are superior to the classical and Meta-Bass models. This is also confirmed in a more recent study (Sood et al. 2012).

Jiang and Jain (2012) developed a model that accounts for multigenerations of products. The model accounts for consumers who adopt an old generation of the product and those who substitute an old product generation with a new generation. These models are also known as Norton-Bass models (Norton and Bass 1987).

10.3.2.3 Brand-level Analysis and Accounting for Competition

Bass-type models can also be used to model brand choice.[6] One may assume that a potential consumer adopts brand i as a result of the combination of two optional communication patterns:

- within brand communication with adopters of brand i, and/or
- cross-brand communication with adopters of brand j, $j \neq i$, $j = 1, \ldots, B$, where B is the set of competitive brands including i.

Cross-brand communication may be either positive or negative. A diffusion equation for multiple brands that explicitly presents both communication paths is (10.27):

$$\frac{dN_i(t)}{dt} = \left(p_i + q_i \frac{N_i(t)}{\bar{N}} + \sum_{j \neq i}^{B} \delta_{ij} \frac{N_j(t)}{\bar{N}} \right) [\bar{N} - N(t)] \tag{10.27}$$

where

$N(t) = N_i(t) + N_j(t)$ = total number of adopters,
δ_{ij} = cross-brand influences.

Studies have tried to examine systematically the distinction between within- and cross-brand communication. Examples are Parker and Gatignon (1994) (hair styling mousses) and Libai et al. (2009a) (cellular services). The model by Libai et al. (2009a) can be adjusted to account for different entry times.

Equation (10.27) demonstrates how, at least in principle, competition can be taken into account. In Eq. (10.27) the assumption is that firms compete for the

[6] We follow Peres et al. (2010).

same market potential. Parker and Gatignon (1994) relaxed the assumption of a joint potential and assume that brands can develop independently with each brand having its own market potential. In that case Eq. (10.27) should be specified as:

$$\frac{dN_i(t)}{dt} = \left(p_i + q_i\frac{N_i(t)}{\bar{N}_i} + \delta_{ij}\frac{N_j(t)}{\bar{N}_j}\right)\left[\bar{N}_i - N_i(t)\right] \tag{10.28}$$

where $\bar{N}_i$ and $\bar{N}_j$ are the market potentials for brand i and j, respectively.

10.3.2.4 Cross-Country Effects

Several studies have modeled multi-market diffusion with cross-country influences (Kumar and Krishnan 2002; Van Everdingen et al. 2005). A generic cross-country influence model may take the following form:

$$\frac{d\widetilde{N}_i(t)}{dt} = \left[p_i + q_i\widetilde{N}_i(t) + \sum_{j\neq i}^{C}\delta_{ij}\widetilde{N}_j(t)\right]\left[1 - \widetilde{N}_i(t)\right] \tag{10.29}$$

where

$\widetilde{N}_i(t) = \frac{N_i(t)}{\bar{N}_i}$ = the proportion of adopters in country i,
δ_{ij} = cross-country effect between countries i and j.

Cross-country effects result from adopters in one country who communicate with adopters form other countries ("weak ties", Wuyts et al. 2004). The level of acceptance in one country may also act as a signal to customers in other countries, reducing their perceptions of risk and increasing the legitimacy of using the new product: "signals" (Peres et al. 2010). Both effects are represented through the parameters δ_{ij}.[7]

10.3.2.5 Effects of Externalities

In a number of studies the effects of network externalities on the diffusion rate are explicitly taken into account. A distinction is made between direct network effects such as e-mail or other communication products that mediate adoption. Goldenberg et al. (2010) mention the number of DVD rental outlets, which is in turn a function of the number of adopters.

The effects of network externalities on product growth can be modeled through two approaches: a bottom-up approach which models individual adoption behavior (see Sect. 10.5) and an aggregate diffusion approach that enables an analysis using market-level data.

[7] An example of a sophisticated international diffusion model is Gelper and Stremersch (2014).

The effects of network externalities on the diffusion of a new product can be modeled by replacing the constant market potential $\bar{N}$ in Eq. (10.10) by a time varying market potential $\bar{N}(t)$. Network externalities affect the changing market potential $\bar{N}(t)$ by:

$$\bar{N}(t) = \text{prob}\left(H < \frac{N(t)}{\bar{N}^T}\right) \cdot \bar{N}^T \tag{10.30}$$

$$H \sim \text{Norm}\left(h, \sigma^2\right) \tag{10.31}$$

where

$\bar{N}(t)$ = market potential at time t;
$\bar{N}^T$ = total market potential;
H = the distribution of individual thresholds which is normally distributed with mean h and variance σ^2 which are both measured as percentages of the total market potential $\bar{N}^T$.

Taking the network effect into account the market potential is comprised of only those customers whose thresholds are lower than $\bar{N}(t)$. Compared to the classical Bass model two more parameters have to be estimated: h and σ. The classical Bass model is nested in (10.30) and (10.31) for $h = \sigma = 0$. Equations (10.30) and (10.31) can be estimated by the NLS estimation algorithm.

Goldenberg et al. (2010) do this for the diffusion of cellular phones, DVD-players, CD-players and fax machines which are all products for which the diffusion depends on network externalities. The diffusion of a new product is not only influenced by network externalities but might be affected by supply constraints. See, for example, Shen et al. (2011).

10.3.2.6 Services

Services differ from durable goods in several important aspects[8]:

- many services induce multiple purchases;
- recurrent purchase results in long-term relationships between customers and service providers;
- there is not only an inflow of new customers for a specific service but there is also an outward flow of departing customers.

Libai et al. (2009b) suggest a model that incorporates the attrition of new customers at both the category and firm levels. Their category-level model assumes that some customers leave the new service, but eventually return:

$$\frac{dN(t)}{dt} = \left(p + q\left(1 - \alpha_0\right)\frac{N(t)}{\bar{N}}\right)\left[\bar{N} - N(t)\right] - \alpha_0 N(t) \tag{10.32}$$

[8] We follow Muller et al. (2009).

where the parameter α_0 denotes the defection of customers from the category. Note that it also appears in the internal influence part of the model because the authors assume that that only those who did not disadopt spread positive word-of-mouth communications about the product.

For a competitive market which is specified at the firm/brand level (i), a brand can lose customers not only due to disadoption, but also due to churn to one of the competitors. This is expressed in the following diffusion model:

$$\frac{dN_i(t)}{dt} = \left(p_i + q_i\,(1-\alpha_i)\,\frac{N_i(t)}{\bar{N}}\right)\left[\bar{N} - N(t)\right] - (\alpha_i + c_i)\,N_i(t) + \sum_{j \neq i}^{B} \beta_{ij} c_j N_j(t) \tag{10.33}$$

where all parameters are indexed by i or j so that they are brand specific, c_i denotes the churn rate for brand i, and the β_{ij} denote the share of the churn of firm/brand level j that goes to firm/brand i.

10.4 Adoption Models

10.4.1 Introduction

Adoption models differ from diffusion models in a number of ways. Adoption models usually deal with frequently purchased items although there are also examples of these models which forecast the adoptions of durables.[9] Starting point for adoption models is that they are based on adoption processes conceptualized at the individual level. In these processes one may distinguish the following steps[10]:

1. *awareness*, in which the individual becomes cognizant of a new product in terms of its existence, but not necessarily with regard to the benefits offered by the product;
2. *interest*, the stage in which the individual is stimulated to seek more detailed information about the new product;
3. *evaluation*, in which the individual tries the new product;
4. *trial*, the stage in which the individual considers whether the new product provides sufficient value relative to its cost;
5. *adoption*, the stage in which the individual decides to make full and regular use of the new product.

The explicit specification of the fifth stage means that adoption models are particularly suited as *repeat purchase models*. In the early adoption models the *interactions*

---

[9]See Urban et al. (1990) and Urban (1993).

[10]These steps were identified by Rogers (1962).

between adopters are not explicitly considered, however, most interactions among individual customers are crucial in more recent adoption models.

We start to discuss the more classical adoption models in Sect. 10.4.2. These models are often represented in an aggregate manner, although they are based on assumptions and descriptions at the individual demand level. In Sect. 10.4.3 we will discuss more recently developed adoption models which are based on individual adoptions/diffusions of new products and which explicitly consider consumer interactions.

10.4.2 Classical Adoption Models

The marketing literature includes a large number of adoption models,[11] which may be due to the high costs and high risks inherent in the introduction of a new product. Particularly important contributions were made by Urban. First for new industrial products[12] and later for frequently purchased consumer goods,[13] Urban created a new-product evaluation model with modular structure called SPRINTER, which stands for Specification of PRofit with INTERaction. The interdependencies refer to the new brand and its relation to established brands in a product line of the firm that introduces the new brand. Although the SPRINTER model has been succeeded by other "more implementable" models, its structure is an excellent illustration of a macro flow adoption model.

In its simplest form this new-product model contains the elements in Fig. 10.5. Three consumer states or experience classes are distinguished. The *pretrial* class

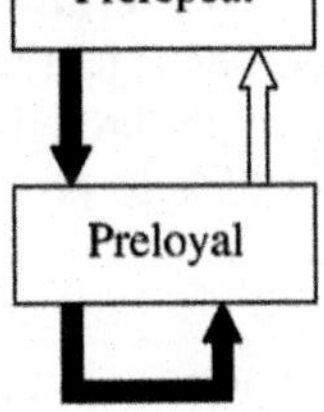

Fig. 10.5 Diagram of SPRINTER (Mod 1) *Source*: Nijkamp (1993, p. 120)

[11] See Mahajan et al. (2000).

[12] Urban (1968).

[13] Urban (1969, 1970) and Urban and Karash (1971).

consists of potential triers who have no experience with the new brand. In a specific time interval some people of the pretrial class buy the new brand and move to the prerepeat class, which consists of potential repeaters. These "purchases" are shown in black in Fig. 10.5. When these consumers buy the new brand again, they move to the preloyal class, the class of potentially loyal consumers of the new brand. They stay in this class when they repurchase the brand a second time, etc.

When consumers in an experience class purchase a competitive brand instead of a new brand, they move to the "preceding" experience class. This is denoted by the white arrows in Fig. 10.5.

Many adoption models have a similar structure (logical flow models). Most of these models have been developed since the early 1980s. Examples are BBDO's NEWS model,[14] the LITMUS[15] and ASSESSOR.[16]

ASSESSOR was initially marketed in the U.S. by Management Decision Systems, Inc. (MDS), then by Information Resources Inc. (IRI) and subsequently by M/A/R/C Inc.[17] In Europe ASSESSOR was introduced by NOVACTION.

As of 1997 both in Europe and in the USA, BASES accounts for the majority of pre-test-market new-product/concept evaluations. The services offered by BASES center around a system for consumer reactions to concepts or new products prior to test market or market introduction. The consumer reactions, along with planned media schedules, promotional activities and distribution, are used to predict sales volumes for the first 2 years. These predicted volumes are based on the information obtained from a sample of consumers who belong to the target market and who agree to participate after recruitment in a shopping mall. The consumers provide responses that allow BASES to estimate trial rates, repeat sales, transaction sizes and purchase frequencies. Importantly, due to the large number of commercial studies conducted, BASES uses its database to make various adjustments. For example, the first repeat rate, which is estimated from an after-use purchase intent, is adjusted for product-category specific and culture specific overstatements, price/value perceptions, intensity of liking perceptions, purchase cycle claims, etc. Thus, the usefulness of a service such as BASES is not indicated just by the quality of the modeling and the consumer responses. By linking actual new-product results to the consumer responses, based on factors such as product category and target market characteristics, one can improve the validity of market projections.

The ASSESSOR model is one of the few commercial models published in academic journals.[18] According to published results the success rate of new products that go through an ASSESSOR evaluation is 66%, compared with a success rate of 35% to products that do not undergo a formal pretest analysis.[19] By contrast,

[14]Pringle et al. (1982).

[15]Blackburn and Clancy (1980).

[16]Silk and Urban (1978).

[17]Urban (1993).

[18]Urban and Katz (1983).

[19]Lilien et al. (2007, p. 122).

only 4% of new products that "failed" in ASSESSOR, but were introduced in the market anyway, succeeded. Also, the correlation between predicted and actual market shares is reported to be very high (0.95).

ASSESSOR and other pre-test-market models can be useful for marketing decisions in several ways. One is that test markets are expensive, take a long time, and can provide insights to competitors such that ultimate results are reduced. Thus, pretest market models can sometimes be used instead of test markets. If the pretest market model is an additional step in the new-product development process, one benefit is the reduction in risk.

The ASSESSOR-model is based on two sub models:

- a trial and repeat model;
- a preference model.

The reason for having two models is that if these two models provide similar forecasts one can have more confidence in the forecasts. In case of differences in the forecasts, there is an opportunity to identify what unusual characteristics are present in the new product that require special attention. The trial-repeat model is estimated with consumer trials of products in a specially created store environment, and follow- up contacts to capture repeat in at-home use. The preference model is estimated from survey responses about the new product and established brands familiar to the respondents. Both models also use management judgment about variables such as brand awareness and -availability.

Consumers are typically screened in shopping malls. Given agreement to participate, they enter a testing facility. Participants complete a survey about awareness of existing brands and the consideration set of brands for purchases in the product category to which the new product might belong.[20] In addition, participants are asked about the brands in the product category they have purchased in the immediate past and their preferences for the brands in their consideration sets. The preference model transforms the measured preferences of the participants into choice probabilities.

Participants who do not choose the new brand in the store laboratory receive a small size sample of the new brand. In this manner, all participants have an opportunity to try the new product. After a short period, sufficiently long for most consumers to experience product usage, the participants are contacted at their homes. Many of the questions are the same as those asked in the store laboratory. In addition, consumers are asked about product usage and are given an opportunity to (re)purchase the new product. Having collected trial and repeat data, it is then possible to predict the new product's market share. Similarly, the preference data after product usage are used to obtain a second prediction of market share. Both of these predictions are adjusted based on available information on such aspects as consideration set, brand awareness and -availability.

[20] For detailed descriptions see Lilien and Rangaswamy (2003, pp. 264–271) and Silk and Urban (1978).

The (long-run) market share of the new product is predicted by the trial-repeat model as follows:

$$\widehat{m}_j = \frac{\widehat{N}(t)}{N*} \cdot \widehat{\pi} \cdot w \tag{10.34}$$

where

$\widehat{m}_j$ = the predicted value of the long-run market share of the new brand j,
$N(t)$ = the predicted cumulative number of adopters,
$N*$ = the size of the target segment,
π = the proportion of those trying the new product who will become long-run repeat purchasers of the new product,
w = relative usage rate, with $w = 1$ the average usage rate in the market.

This model was originally formulated by Parfitt and Collins (1968). In ASSESSOR the components $N(t)/N*$ and π are disaggregated in a number of macro flows:

$$\frac{\widehat{N}(t)}{N*} = F \cdot K \cdot D + C \cdot U - (F \cdot K \cdot D)\,(C \cdot U) \tag{10.35}$$

where

F = long-run probability of trial assuming 100% awareness and distribution,
K = long-run probability of awareness,
D = long-run probability of availability in retail outlets (weighted distribution fractions),
C = probability that a consumer receives a sample,
U = probability that a consumer who receives a sample uses the sample.

The first right-hand term in (10.35), $F \cdot K \cdot D$, is quantified by the proportion of consumers who will try the new product (laboratory store results), are aware of the new brand (management judgment), and have access to it in a store (management judgment). The second term $C \cdot U$, represents the fraction of target market consumers who receive a sample of the new brand (management judgment) and use it (home contact). The third term adjusts for double counting those who both purchase the new product in a store for trial and receive a sample (since in the marketplace these two events are not mutually exclusive).

The repeat rate π is calculated as the equilibrium share of a two-state Markov process. It can be shown that:

$$\widehat{\pi} = \frac{\widehat{p}_{on}}{1 - \widehat{p}_{nn} + \widehat{p}_{on}} \tag{10.36}$$

where

$\widehat{p}_{on}$ = the estimated probability that a consumer who purchases an_other brand in period t, purchased the _new brand in $t+1$,

$\widehat{p}_{nn}$ = the estimated probability that a consumer purchases the _new brand in t and in $t+1$.

$\widehat{p}_{on}$ is estimated from the proportion of consumers who did *not* "purchase" the new product in the test facility but say in the post-usage survey that they will buy the new product at the next purchase occasion. $\widehat{p}_{nn}$ is the proportion of consumers who purchased the new product in the test facility and say in the post-usage survey that they will buy the product again.[21]

We finally discuss an adoption model that has been developed by Hahn et al. (1994) which also has the form of a logical-flow model which in a later stage is transformed into a numerically specified model. Also, this model is an example of a macr-flow adoption model. It has been applied in pharmaceutical marketing research and explicitly considers physicians in different stages in the adoption process of a new prescription drug. Hahn et al. (1994) propose four segments: non-triers, triers, post-trial non-repeaters and post-trial repeaters.[22] Their framework is presented in Fig. 10.6.

In this model physicians are classified into four segments depending on where they are in the adoption process. The first segment consists of physicians that have not tried the new product; the second segment contains those physicians that have tried the new product only once. The third segment comprises those physicians that repeat the use of the innovation. The physicians who have tried the innovation but then used a competing product and not repeated their use of the innovation constitute the fourth segment. As a consequence of this definition of segments, physicians can neither switch back to the first segment (non-triers) if they have ever tried the product (segment two) nor can they go back to the second segment (triers of the innovation) if they were in segment three or four.

10.4.3 More Recently Developed Adoption Models

Diffusion modeling since 1990 is, amongst others, characterized by consumer interdependencies as drivers of diffusion. Innovation diffusion, nowadays, depends not only on word-of-mouth communications but on other social interactions of consumers, including functions and social signals and, as discussed in Sect. 10.3, network externalities.

[21]The derivation of (10.36) can be found in, for example, Sect. 8.2.4.1 in Vol. I.

[22]In Sect. 10.5.2 we extend this model.

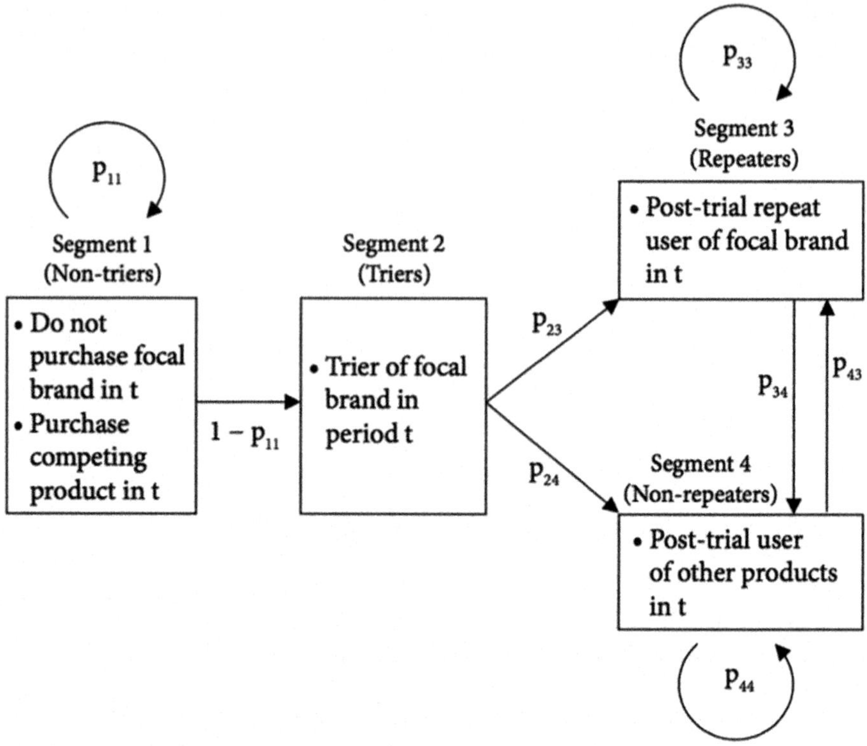

Fig. 10.6 Example of a (macro-flow) adoption model for prescribed drugs
Source: Hahn et al. (1994, p. 226)

Word-of-Mouth (WOM) communications has been facilitated by social media including participation in user groups/communities, crowd sourcing, etc.[23]

Functional signals contain information regarding the acceptance of the product in the social system, whereas social signals contain information on the social consequences of the product. Signals can be distinguished from word-of-mouth in that signals convey information about the product and market status other than personal information.[24]

In more recent adoption models one models these interactions with other customers at the individual level. In Sect. 9.7.2 in Vol. I we discussed already how WOM can be measured and used at an independent variable in a model to explain sales (see Godes and Mayzlin 2009).

There are different ways to model social interactions/social influence in adoption models. The most frequently used models are:

---

[23]See, for example, Tuten and Solomon (2015).

[24]Muller et al. (2009, p. 9).

- agent-based (simulation) models;
- hazard models;
- econometric models.

10.4.3.1 Agent-Based Models

In these models each unit represents an individual consumer *i*. The unit has a value of "0" if it has not yet adopted the product or brand, and a value "1" if adoption took place. It is assumed that units adopt as a result of external influence (p_i) and internal influence (q_i), like in the diffusion models. The probability of adoption by individual *i* at *t* ($\Pr_{\text{adoption}}(t)_i$) is:

$$\Pr_{adoption}(t)_i = 1 - (1 - p_i)\,(1 - q_i)^{N_i(t)}. \tag{10.37}$$

In Eq. (10.37) we distinguish between external influence and word-of-mouth ties. It is possible to build in spatial effects though the relative influence of strong and weak ties.[25] The model allows for heterogeneity by making p_i and q_i differ between units.

Libai et al. (2013) extended (10.37) assuming two brands, *A* and *B*, each having its own external influence δ_A and δ_B and internal influence q_{iA} and q_{iB} for each person in the network:

$$\Pr(A|t)_i = 1 - (1 - \delta_A)\,(1 - q_{iA})^{N_i^A(t)}, \tag{10.38}$$

and

$$\Pr(B|t)_i = 1 - (1 - \delta_A)\,(1 - q_{iB})^{N_i^B(t)} \tag{10.39}$$

where

$\Pr(A|\,t)_i$ = probability of at least one adopter of *A* successfully influencing *i* to consider brand *A*,

$N_i^A(t)$ = all consumers in *i*'s personal social network who have adopted *A*.

The probabilities of *i* adopting *A*, *B*, or neither are given by the following equations:

$$\Pr(adopt\,A|t)_i = \Pr(A|t)_i\,(1 - \Pr(B|t)_i) + \alpha_A \Pr(A|t)_i \Pr(B|t)_i \tag{10.40a}$$

$$\Pr(adopt\,B|t)_i = \Pr(B|t)_i\,(1 - \Pr(A|t)_i) + \alpha_B \Pr(A|t)_i \Pr(B|t)_i \tag{10.40b}$$

$$\Pr(adoptnone|t)_i = (1 - \Pr(B|t)_i)\,(1 - \Pr(A|t)_i) \tag{10.40c}$$

where $\alpha_A = \frac{\Pr(A|t)_i}{\Pr(A|t)_i + \Pr(B|t)_i}$ and $\alpha_B = 1 - \alpha_A$.

Other examples and specifications of agent-based models can be found in, for example, Dover et al. (2012), Trusov et al. (2013) and Van Eck et al. (2011).

[25] See, for example, Goldenberg et al. (2001).

10.4.3.2 Hazard Models

These models have been discussed in Sect. 8.4.2., Vol. I. Examples of models that are used in a product/brand adoption context are, for example, Hu and Van den Bulte (2014), Iyengar et al. (2011), Prins and Verhoef (2007), and Risselada et al. (2014).

Toubia et al. (2014) demonstrate that the discretized mixed influence model (10.4) may be obtained as a special case of their hazard model. Iyengar et al. (2011) and Iyengar et al. (2015) investigate social contagion, i.e. the notion of peer influence, on trials *and* repeats of a risky prescription drug by physicians by discrete-time hazard models. The parameters of the adoption and repeat model have been estimated using simulated maximum likelihood, where they account for correlated random effects of trial and repeat.

10.4.3.3 Econometric Models

Goldenberg et al. (2009) explore the role of people with an exceptionally large number of social ties (called: hubs) in diffusion and adoption through different regression analyses. Viard and Economides (2015) model the simultaneous determination of a country's content production in a language and adoption in that country by people wing that language, through the parameterization of a simultaneous system of stochastic equations.

10.5 Empirical Applications

10.5.1 Diffusion of Pharmaceuticals

We first illustrate the application of diffusion models using data from a therapeutic category on the US pharmaceutical market. Below we present a part of an empirical study in which the two authors of this chapter participated: see Ruiz-Conde et al. (2014).[26]

We use monthly US data pertaining to several brands in three categories of pharmaceuticals that belong to the "Top-10 markets" of prescription drugs in the United States in 2000: rhinitis (14 brands), osteoarthritis and rheumatoid arthritis (ORA—brands), and asthma (10 brands). The data describe brand sales and brand-level expenditures for detailing, medical journal advertising, physician meetings, and direct-to-consumer (DTC). The historical data come from syndicated secondary data sources.

[26]We closely follow Ruiz-Conde et al. (2014).

In this application we follow Hahn et al. (1994), and incorporate three components of new product buying behavior:

1. innovative behavior;
2. imitating behavior;
3. repeat buying.

We investigate six different options how marketing variables can affect the diffusion process, depending on whether the marketing variables affect external influence, internal influence, or both (options 1–3 in Table 10.3), and whether competitive marketing variables should be included in addition to own marketing variables. The specifications for the models can be found in Table 10.4.

In the models in Table 10.4, $s_{i,t}$ indicates unit sales of product i in month t, (i.e. the sum of trial and repeat purchases), $x_{ij,t}$ are own expenditures of brand i on marketing instrument j in month t, and $x_{cj,t}$ denote competitive expenditures on marketing instrument j in month t. The last term in all models, $\beta_{3i}q_{i,t-1}$, reflects the repeat purchase behavior, where $q_{i,t-1}$are potential sales to physicians in the post-trial segments (triers, repeaters, and buyers of competing brands that have tried brand i before, see Fig. 10.6), and is calculated as follows: $q_{i,t} - q_{i,t-1} = s_{i,t} - \beta_{3i}q_{i,t-1}$ (Hahn et al. 1994). The models in Table 10.4 are estimated using an iterative ordinary least squares procedure developed by Hahn et al. (1994).

We employ three criteria to select the most appropriate model specification: (1) the Akaike Information Criterion (AIC) to select the most parsimonious specification with the best goodness-of-fit, (2) the parameter stability measures proposed by Golder and Tellis (1997), and (3) the face validity of the estimates. We do not consider predictive validity because the intended use of all models is descriptive rather than predictive, and sales forecasts in any future period require knowledge of the size of the potential market in the same period, which in turn depends on the value of sales in that period.

Models 1EI and 2EI suffer from multicollinearity issues and are never selected as preferred model for any of the brands in our analyses. AIC is lowest for model 2E in about 50% of the cases (detailed results can be found in Ruiz-Conde et al. 2014). With regard to the second criterion, we conclude that an external specification leads to a slightly larger parameter stability than an internal specification, which is improved further to some extent when competitive marketing variables are included. The third criterion also prefers model 2E: 76% of all parameter estimates are in their expected range. We conclude that based on all three criteria, model 2E is the preferred model specification for the analyzed brands in our data set. We present the results of estimating model 2E for the 14 brands in the rhinitis category in Table 10.5.

The estimation results for Model 2E for the rhinitis category in Table 10.5 indicate that all estimates for β_{10i} are significant and positive. Furthermore, the effects of own marketing expenditures on the trial rate (β_{11i}) are (marginally) significant for 9 out of the 14 brands, and all of the corresponding estimates are positive except for brand 8. As expected, competitors' marketing expenditures

Table 10.4 Six Specifications of the diffusion model for the pharmaceutical application

Subset 1
External influence (Model 1E)
$s_{i,t} = \left[\beta_{10i} + \beta_{11i} \ln(x_{i\cdot t}) + \beta_{2i}\left[\frac{s_{i,t-1}}{m_t}\right]\right]\left[m_t - q_{i,t-1}\right] + \beta_{3i} q_{i,t-1}$
Internal influence (Model 1I)
$s_{i,t} = \left[\beta_{10i} + (\beta_{2i} + \beta_{21i} \ln(x_{i\cdot t}))\left[\frac{s_{i,t-1}}{m_t}\right]\right]\left[m_t - q_{i,t-1}\right] + \beta_{3i} q_{i,t-1}$
External and internal influence (Model 1EI)
$s_{i,t} = \left[\beta_{10i} + \beta_{2i}\left[\frac{s_{i,t-1}}{m_t}\right]\right](1 + \beta_{41i} \ln(x_{i\cdot t}))\left[m_t - q_{i,t-1}\right] + \beta_{3i} q_{i,t-1}$, where $x_{i\cdot t} = \sum_{j=1}^{4} x_{ij,t}$
Subset 2
External influence (Model 2E)
$s_{i,t} = \left[\beta_{10i} + \beta_{11i} \ln(x_{i\cdot t}) + \beta_{11ci} \ln(x_{c\cdot t}) + \beta_{2i}\left[\frac{s_{i,t-1}}{m_t}\right]\right]\left[m_t - q_{i,t-1}\right] + \beta_{3i} q_{i,t-1}$
Internal influence (Model 2I)
$s_{i,t} = \left[\beta_{10i} + (\beta_{2i} + \beta_{21i} \ln(x_{i\cdot t}) + \beta_{21ci} \ln(x_{c\cdot t}))\left[\frac{s_{i,t-1}}{m_t}\right]\right]\left[m_t - q_{i,t-1}\right] + \beta_{3i} q_{i,t-1}$
External and internal influence (Model 2EI)
$s_{i,t} = \left[\beta_{10i} + \beta_{2i}\left[\frac{s_{i,t-1}}{m_t}\right]\right](1 + \beta_{41i} \ln(x_{i\cdot t}) + \beta_{41ci} \ln(x_{c\cdot t}))\left[m_t - q_{i,t-1}\right] + \beta_{3i} q_{i,t-1}$, where $x_{i\cdot t} = \sum_{j=1}^{4} x_{ij,t}$ and $x_{c\cdot t} = \sum_{j=1}^{4} x_{cj,t}$

Table 10.5 Estimation results of Model 2E: Rhinitis category (insignificant estimates are omitted)

	Trial rate								
	External influence			Internal influence	Repeat rate	Average market share			
Brand code	$\widehat{\beta}_{10i}$	$\widehat{\beta}_{11i}$	$\widehat{\beta}_{11ci}$	$\widehat{\beta}_{2i}$	$\widehat{\beta}_{3i}$	(in units)	MAD	MAPE	r
10	0.04[a]			1.29[a]	0.01[a]	0.03	22.81	8.81	0.92
6	0.09[b]	0.02[c]	−0.07[a]		0.32[a]	0.20	47.74	3.56	0.99
13	0.03[a]	0.01[a]	−0.01[a]	1.47[a]	0.04[a]	0.03	7.17	3.65	0.99
7	0.07[a]	0.02[c]	−0.07[a]	1.47[a]	0.17[a]	0.13	42.48	5.01	0.98
9	0.06[a]	0.003[d]	−0.02[a]	0.63[a]	0.11[a]	0.09	13.53	2.41	0.99
11	0.01[a]	0.0004[a]	−0.0003[b]	0.99[a]	0.004[a]	0.01	0.76	1.99	0.99
4	0.01[a]			0.84[a]		0.01	1.66	2.54	0.95
15	0.05[a]			0.24[b]	0.13[a]	0.10	13.84	2.08	0.99
1	0.03[a]	0.01[b]	−0.01[b]		0.19[a]	0.11	19.59	2.66	0.99
8	0.02[a]	−0.001[d]	0.001[b]	0.53[a]	0.01[a]	0.02	1.74	1.53	0.98
16	0.01[a]			0.61[a]	0.05[a]	0.02	2.11	1.63	0.99
3	0.01[a]	0.002[b]	−0.003[d]	0.39[b]	0.02[a]	0.01	3.28	4.20	0.93
12	0.03[a]	0.002[b]		0.40[a]	0.09[a]	0.06	4.38	1.11	0.99
2	0.03[a]		−0.01[b]	0.61[d]	0.07[a]	0.05	9.01	2.57	0.95

[a]$p \le 0.0001$ [b]$p \le 0.05$ [c]$p < 0.1$ [d]$p \le 0.001$

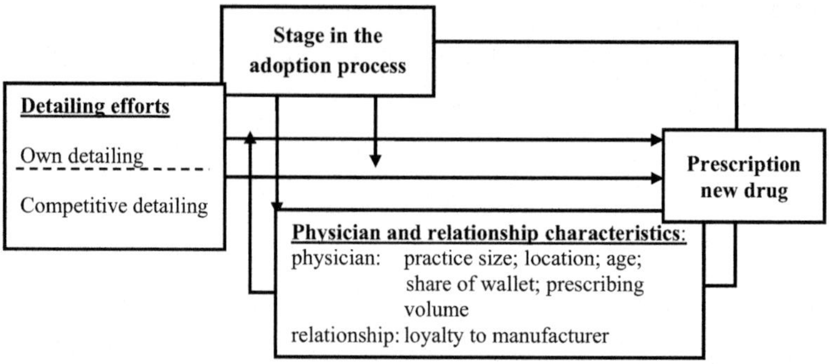

Fig. 10.7 Direct and indirect effects on prescriptions of a new drug
Source: Reber et al. (2013, p. 102)

generally have a negative effect on the trial rate ($\widehat{\beta}_{11ci} < 0$), but the estimate is insignificant for five brands. The significant estimates of β_{2i} are within the expected range. The estimates in Table 10.5 thus agree with outcomes of a meta-study by Sultan et al. (1990), who find that estimates for β_{10i} are positive and (much) smaller than the estimated internal influence coefficient ($\widehat{\beta}_{2i}$), as is the case for all brands in Table 10.5. Finally, the estimates for β_{3i} are significant, except for brand 4, and the values of $\widehat{\beta}_{3i}$ are very similar to the average market share, as we expected.

10.5.2 Drivers of New Drug Adoption by Physicians

Reber et al. (2013) use the framework in Fig. 10.6 to investigate the adoption process of physicians when a new drug enters the market. To this end, they study how the interplay between stage in the adoption process, marketing efforts, and physician characteristics affect new drug prescriptions, according to the conceptual framework of Fig. 10.7.

In line with this conceptual framework, they model π_{mijt}, the transition probability that physician m progresses from stage i to stage j in the adoption process at prescription occasion t using in a multinomial logit transformation:

$$\pi_{mijt} = \frac{\exp\left(\theta_{1mij} + \theta_{2mij} \times DET_{mt} + \theta_{3mij} \times CDET_{mt}\right)}{\sum \exp\left(\theta_{1mij} + \theta_{2mij} \times DET_{mt} + \theta_{3mij} \times CDET_{mt}\right)} \tag{10.41}$$

where DET_{mt} denotes own detailing effort (i.e. the number of detailing calls a physician received) for the drug during 6 months preceding prescription occasion t, and $CDET_{mt}$ denotes the number of competitive detailing calls during 6 month preceding prescription occasion t. Depending on the stages i and j, the parameter θ_{1mij} can be interpreted as the basic propensity to switch to the focal drug or as the basic propensity to switch to one of the competitive drugs, and $\theta_{2mij}(\theta_{3mij})$ as the sensitivity to (competitive) detailing. They allow θ_{1mij} and θ_{2mij} to vary with physician and relationship characteristics by considering them as drawings from a distribution with mean:

$$\begin{aligned}\mu_{\theta_{kmij}} &= \gamma_{k1ij} + \gamma_{k2ij} \times PRACTSIZE_m + \gamma_{k3ij} \times SOW_m + \gamma_{k4ij} \times AGE_m \\ &+ \gamma_{k5ij} \times LOYALTY_m + \gamma_{k6ij} \times REGION_m + \gamma_{k7ij} \times VOLUME_m\end{aligned} \tag{10.42}$$

for $k = 1{,}2$. The variables in Eq. (10.42) are defined as:

$PRACTSIZE_m$ = size of physician practice (number of GPs working in the practice);
SOW_m = share of wallet (the number of prescriptions a physician wrote in the category relative to the total number of prescription s/he wrote for any drug). This is an indicator of whether a GP is a "specialist" in the related disease area;
AGE_m = physician age;
$LOYALTY_m$ = loyalty to the manufacturer of the focal brand operationalized as the average share a physician prescribes from the company of that brand;
$REGION_m$ = dummy variable indicating whether the physician's practice is in a rural or an urban area (0 = rural, 1 = urban);
$VOLUME_m$ = category-level prescription volume that is the (absolute) number of prescriptions written in the category; an indicator of whether a physician is a heavy prescriber.

Using a random effect specification for θ_{3mij}, Reber et al. (2013) calibrate their model with a data set that covers 46,841 prescriptions written by 137 UK physicians for drugs in the antidepressant category over a period from September 1st, 1988 to July 31st, 1997. For their focal drug Prozac, they conclude that that doctors in smaller practices have a smaller propensity to switch. They explain this by noting that this could be due to a lack of easy-to-access information which is more likely to be the case in smaller practices because there are fewer professional colleagues and fewer intra-group contacts. Their results also show that switching to one of the competitive brands is less likely for doctors who are loyal to the focal pharmaceutical firm. They also find smaller switching propensities for heavy prescribers.

With regard to the sensitivity to detailing, the authors find that the effectiveness of detailing to generate repeat use is larger for doctors who are more "specialized" in the disease area (i.e., exhibit a higher category prescription share). Their outcomes also indicate that detailing is more effective in generating repeat for physicians who are loyal to the focal pharmaceutical firm. This could be due to synergy effects of other calls or combined calls for different products from the same manufacturer. Finally, they conclude that detailing is less effective to generate repeat for high-volume prescribers. Possibly, heavy prescribers are more inclined to use alternative, already existing antidepressant drugs which could explain their lower responsiveness to detailing as well as the negative relationship between prescribing volume and repeat rates.

The authors conduct a scenario analysis to illustrate the consequences of their findings. They identify five strategies for targeting physicians:

1. the selection of physicians that have so far received the most detailing calls for the innovator drug (base case);
2. a selection of physicians according to the criterion applied in pharmaceutical practice which is total category volume prescribed in the past (heavy prescriber);
3. a random selection of physicians (naive approach);
4. a selection of physicians who appeared to be most responsive to detailing according to the parameter estimates of the logit benchmark;
5. the selection of physicians with the highest change in prescriptions as predicted by our model.

For each scenario, they assume that the pharmaceutical firm has a budget for 30 detailing visits, and for each of the scenarios the expected (marginal) number of additional prescriptions due to the extra detailing visits is computed. The results are presented in Table 10.6.

The results of the scenario analysis show that targeting physicians according to the model of Reber et al. (2013) outperforms the alternative strategies, in both stimulating repeat use and attracting physicians away from competitive products. Although the logit benchmark performs reasonably well, companies can increase their profits even further when allocating their detailing efforts towards physicians whose expected number of additional prescriptions is largest. The current targeting strategy (base case), and most notably, the practice rule (i.e., targeting physicians based on their prescription volume) appear to be highly ineffective; they will result in fewer prescriptions.

Table 10.6 Expected number of additional prescriptions due to one additional detailing call

Base case (current targeting)	Heavy prescribers (practice rule)	Random selection (naive approach)	Logit benchmark	"Reber et al. (2013) model"
Stimulate trial				
−0.36	−0.59	−0.35	−0.49	−0.03
Stimulate repeat use				
−2.95	−5.90	−3.18	9.61	11.20
Attract from others				
−3.05	−5.31	−2.97	8.63	10.25

References

Bass, F.: A new product growth for model consumer durables. Manag. Sci. **15**, 215–227 (1969)

Bass, F., Krishnan, T.V., Jain, D.C.: Why the Bass model fits without decision variables. Mark. Sci. **13**, 203–223 (1994)

Blackburn, J.D., Clancy, K.J.: LITMUS: A new product planning model. In: Leone, R.P. (ed.) Proceedings: Market Measurement and Analysis, pp. 182–193. The Institute of Management Sciences, Providence, RI (1980)

Davies, S.W., Diaz-Rainey, I.: The patterns of induced diffusion: Evidence from the international diffusion of wind energy. Technol. Forecast. Soc. Change. **78**, 1227–1241 (2011)

Dover, Y., Goldenberg, J., Shapira, D.: Network traces on penetrations: Uncovering degree distribution from adoption data. Mark. Sci. **31**, 689–712 (2012)

Fischer, M., Leeflang, P.S.H., Verhoef, P.C.: Drivers of peak sales for pharmaceutical brands. Quant. Mark. Econ. **8**, 429–460 (2010)

Fok, D., Franses, P.H.: Modeling the diffusion of scientific publications. J. Econ. **139**, 376–390 (2007)

Fourt, L.A., Woodlock, J.W.: Early prediction of market success for new grocery products. J. Mark. **25**(4), 31–38 (1960)

Gelper, S., Stremersch, S.: Variable selection in international diffusion models. Int. J. Res. Mark. **31**, 356–367 (2014)

Godes, S., Mayzlin, D.: Firm-created word-of-mouth communications: Evidence from a field test. Mark. Sci. **28**, 721–739 (2009)

Goldenberg, J., Han, S., Lehmann, D.R., Hong, J.W.: The role of hubs in the adoption process. J. Mark. **73**(2), 1–13 (2009)

Goldenberg, J., Libai, B., Muller, E.: Talk of the network: A complex systems look at the underlying process of word-of-mouth. Mark. Lett. **12**, 211–223 (2001)

Goldenberg, J., Libai, B., Muller, E.: Riding the saddle: How cross-market communications can create a major slump in sales. J. Mark. **66**(2), 1–16 (2002)

Goldenberg, J., Libai, B., Muller, E.: The chilling effects of network externalities. Int. J. Res. Mark. **27**, 4–15 (2010)

Golder, P.N., Tellis, G.J.: Will it ever fly? Modeling the takeoff of really new consumer durables. Mark. Sci. **16**, 256–270 (1997)

Guidelin, M., Mortarino, C.: Cross-country diffusion of photovoltaic systems: Modelling choices and forecasts for national adoption patterns. Technol. Forecast. Soc. Change. **77**, 279–296 (2010)

Hahn, M., Park, S., Krishnamurthi, L., Zoltners, A.: Analysis of new product diffusion using a four-segment trial-repeat model. Mark. Sci. **13**, 224–247 (1994)

Hu, Y., Van den Bulte, C.: Nonmonotonic status effect in new product adoption. Mark. Sci. **33**, 509–533 (2014)

Iyengar, R., Van den Bulte, C., Valente, T.W.: Opinion leadership and social contagion in new product diffusion. Mark. Sci. **30**, 195–212 (2011)

Iyengar, R., Van den Bulte, C., Lee, J.Y.: Social contagion in new product trial and repeat. Mark. Sci. **34**, 408–429 (2015)

Jiang, Z., Jain, D.C.: A generalized Norton-Bass model for multigeneration diffusion. Manag. Sci. **58**, 1887–1897 (2012)

Kumar, V., Krishnan, T.V.: Multinational diffusion models: An alternative framework. Mark. Sci. **21**, 318–330 (2002)

Libai, B., Muller, E., Peres, R.: The role of within-brand and cross-brand communications in competitive growth. J. Mark. **73**(3), 19–34 (2009a)

Libai, B., Muller, E., Peres, R.: The diffusion of services. J. Mark. Res. **46**, 163–175 (2009b)

Libai, B., Muller, E., Peres, R.: Decomposing the value of word-of-mouth seeding programs: Acceleration versus expansion. J. Mark. Res. **50**, 161–176 (2013)

Lilien, G.L., Rangaswamy, A.: Marketing Engineering, 2nd ed. Prentice Hall, Upple Saddle River (2003)
Lilien, G.L., Rangaswamy, A., DeBruyn, A.: Principles of Marketing Engineering. Trafford Publishing, State College (2007)
Mahajan, V., Muller, E., Bass, F.M.: New product diffusion modes in marketing: A review and directions for research. J. Mark. **54**(1), 1–26 (1990)
Mahajan, V., Muller, E., Bass, F.M.: New-product diffusion models. In: Birge, J.R., Linetsky, V. (eds.) Handbooks in Operations Research and Management Science, vol. 5, 349–408 (1993)
Mahajan, V., Muller, E., Wind, Y.: New-Product Diffusion Models. Springer, New York (2000)
Muller, E., Mahajan, V., Peres, R.: Innovation Diffusion and New Product Growth. Marketing Science Institute, Boston (2009)
Norton, J.A., Bass, F.M.: A diffusion theory model of adoption and substitution for successive generations of high-technology products. Manag. Sci. **33**(9), 1069–1086 (1987)
Nijkamp, W.G.: New productmacroflow models – Specification and analysis. Unpublished Ph.D. thesis, Groningen, The Netherlands (1993)
Parfitt, J.H., Collins, B.J.K.: Use of consumer panels for brand-share prediction. J. Mark. Res. **5**, 131–145 (1968)
Parker, P., Gatignon, H.: Specifying competitive effects in diffusion models: an empirical analysis. Int. J. Res. Mark. **11**, 17–39 (1994)
Peers, Y., Fok, D., Franses, P.H.: Modeling seasonality in new product diffusion. Mark. Sci. **31**, 351–364 (2012)
Peres, R., Muller, E., Mahajan, V.: Innovation diffusion and new product growth models: A critical review and research directions. Int. J. Res. Mark. **27**, 91–106 (2010)
Pringle, G.L., Wilson, R.D., Brody, E.I.: NEWS: A decision-oriented model for new product analysis and forecasting. Mark. Sci. **1**, 1–29 (1982)
Prins, R., Verhoef, P.C.: Marketing communication drivers of adoption timing of a new e-service among existing customers. J. Mark. **71**(2), 169–183 (2007)
Reber, K., Wieringa, J.E., Leeflang, P.S.H. and Stern, P.: Marketing new pharmaceuticals: When should which doctors be detailed?, Working paper, University of Groningen (2013)
Risselada, H., Verhoef, P.C., Bijmolt, T.H.A.: Dynamic effects of social influence and direct marketing on the adoption of high-technology products. J. Mark. **78**(2), 52–68 (2014)
Rogers, R.: Diffusion of Innovations. The Free Press, New York (1962)
Ruiz-Conde, E., Leeflang, P.S.H.: Diffusion of franchising as an innovation of managerial organization. Mark Journal of Res. and Man. **2**, 65–75 (2006)
Ruiz-Conde, E., Leeflang, P.S.H., Wieringa, J.E.: Marketing variables in macro-level diffusion models. Journal für Betriebswirtschaft. **56**, 155–183 (2006)
Ruiz-Conde, E., Wieringa, J.E., Leeflang, P.S.H.: Competitive diffusion of new prescription drugs: The role of pharmaceutical marketing investment. Technol. Forecast. Soc. Change. **88**, 49–63 (2014)
Shen, W., Duenyas, I., Kapuscinski, R.: New product diffusion decisions under supply constraints. Manag. Sci. **57**, 1802–1810 (2011)
Silk, A.J., Urban, G.L.: Pre-test-market evaluation of new packaged goods: A model and measurement methodology. J. Mark. Res. **15**, 171–191 (1978)
Sood, A., James, G.M., Tellis, J.: Functional regression: A new model for predicting market penetration of new products. Mark. Sci. **28**, 36–51 (2009)
Sood, A., James, G.M., Tellis, G.J., Zhu, J.: Predicting the path of technological innovation: SAW vs. Moore, Bass, Gompertz, and Kryder. Mark. Sci. **31**, 964–979 (2012)
Stremersch, S., Muller, E., Peres, R.: Does new product growth accelerate across technology generations? Mark. Lett. **21**, 103–120 (2010)
Sultan, F., Farley, J.U., Lehmann, D.R.: A meta-analysis of applications of diffusion models. J. Mark. Res. **27**, 70–77 (1990)
Tellis, G.J., Stremersch, S., Yin, E.: The international takeoff of new products: The role of economics, culture, and country innovativeness. Mark. Sci. **22**, 188–208 (2003)

Toubia, O., Goldenberg, J., Garcia, R.: Improving penetration forecasts using social interactions data. Manag. Sci. **60**, 3049–3066 (2014)
Trusov, M., Rand, W., Joshi, Y.V.: Improving prelaunch diffusion forecasts: Using synthetic networks as simulated priors. J. Mark. Res. **50**, 675–690 (2013)
Tuten, T.L., Solomon, M.R.: Social Media Marketing. Sage Publications Ltd, London (2015)
Urban, G.L.: A new product analysis and decision model. Manag. Sci. **14**, 490–517 (1968)
Urban, G.L.: SPRINTER Mod. II: Basic new product analysis model. In: Morin, B.A. (ed.), Proceedings of the National Conference of the American Marketing Association, pp. 139–150 (1969)
Urban, G.L.: SPRINTER Mod. III: A model for the analysis of new frequently purchased consumer products. Oper. Res. **18**, 805–854 (1970)
Urban, G.L.: Pretest market forecasting. In: Eliashberg, J., Lilien, G.L. (eds.) Handbooks in Operations Research and Management Science 5, pp. 315–348, Marketing, North-Holland, Amsterdam (1993)
Urban, G.L., Hauser, J.R., Roberts, J.H.: Prelaunch forecasting of new automobiles: Models and implementation. Manag. Sci. **36**, 401–421 (1990)
Urban, G.L., Karash, R.: Evolutionary model building. J. Mark. Res. **8**, 62–66 (1971)
Urban, G.L., Katz, M.: Pre-test-markets models: Validation and managerial implications. J. Mark. Res. **20**, 221–234 (1983)
Van den Bulte, C.: New product diffusion acceleration: Measurement and analysis. Mark. Sci. **19**, 366–380 (2000)
Van Eck, P.S., Jager, W., Leeflang, P.S.H.: Opinion leaders' role in innovations diffusion: A simulation study. J. Prod. Innov. Manag. **28**, 187–203 (2011)
Van Everdingen, Y.M., Aghina, W.B., Fok, D.: Forecasting cross-population innovation diffusion: A Bayesian approach. Int. J. Res. Mark. **22**, 293–308 (2005)
Viard, V.B., Economides, N.: The effect of content on global internet adoption and the global "digital divide". Manag. Sci. **61**, 665–687 (2015)
Wuyts, S., Stremersch, S., Van den Bulte, C., Franses, P.H.: Vertical marketing systems for compley products: A triadic perspective. J. Mark. Res. **41**, 479–487 (2004)

Part III
Modeling with Latent Variables

Chapter 11
Structural Equation Modeling

Hans Baumgartner and Bert Weijters

11.1 Introduction

The term structural equation modeling (SEM) refers to a family of multivariate techniques concerned with the examination of relationships between constructs (conceptual or latent variables) that can generally be measured only imperfectly by observed variables. For example, a researcher may be interested in the determinants of consumers' use of self-scanning when buying groceries in a grocery store (Weijters et al. 2007). Although the actual use of a self-scanning device is directly observable, antecedents such as consumers' attitude toward self-scanning technology or specific beliefs about the benefits of using self-scanning (perceived usefulness, perceived ease of use, etc.) cannot be directly observed and have to be assessed indirectly via self-report or other means.

SEM has two important advantages over other, related techniques (e.g., exploratory factor analysis, regression analysis). First and maybe most importantly, SEM enables a sophisticated analysis of the quality of measurement of the theoretical concepts of interest by observable measures. When using SEM for measurement analysis, a researcher will usually specify an explicit *measurement model* in which each observed variable is linked to a theoretical concept of interest (conceived of as a latent variable of substantive interest) and measurement error. More complex measurement models in which other sources of systematic

H. Baumgartner (✉)
Department of Marketing, Smeal College of Business, The Pennsylvania State University, 482 Business Building, University Park, PA 16802, USA
e-mail: jxb14@psu.edu

B. Weijters
Department of Personnel Management, Work and Organizational Psychology, Ghent University, Henri Dunantlaan 2, Ghent 9000, Belgium

P.S.H. Leeflang et al. (eds.), *Advanced Methods for Modeling Markets*,
International Series in Quantitative Marketing, DOI 10.1007/978-3-319-53469-5_11

covariation between observed measures besides a common underlying construct are present can also be formulated. This is important because most conceptual variables of interest can only be measured with error (both random and systematic) and ignoring measurement error has undesirable effects on model estimation and testing. Second, SEM makes it possible to investigate complex patterns of relationships among the constructs in one's theory and assess, both in an overall sense and in terms of specific relations between constructs, how well the hypothesized model represents the data. The model describing the relationships between the constructs in one's theory is usually called the *latent variable (or structural) model.* For example, a researcher can test whether several perceived benefits of self-scanning technologies influence the actual use of such technologies directly or indirectly via attitudes toward these technologies (e.g., whether attitudes mediate the effects of beliefs on behavior), and one can also investigate whether the relationships of interest are invariant across gender or other potential moderators.

Initially, SEM was designed for linear relationships between continuous or quasi-continuous observed variables that originated from a single population and for which the assumption of multivariate normality was reasonable. However, substantial progress has been made in broadening the scope of SEM. The model has been extended to represent data from multiple populations (multi-sample analysis), and the heterogeneity can even be unobserved (mixture models; see Chap. 13). Observed variables need not be continuous (e.g., binary, ordinal, or count variables can be modeled), and the latent variables can also be discrete. Estimation procedures that correct for violations of multivariate normality are available, and Bayesian estimation procedures have been incorporated into some programs. Missing data are allowed and can be readily accommodated during model estimation. Models for nonlinear relationships (e.g., interactions between latent variables) have been developed. Traditional cross-sectional models have been supplemented with increasingly sophisticated longitudinal models such as latent curve models. Complex survey designs (e.g., stratification, cluster sampling) can be handled easily, and structural models can be specified at several levels in multi-level models.

Because of space constraints, the focus of this chapter will be on cross-sectional confirmatory factor models and full structural equation models combining a confirmatory factor model with a path model for the latent variables. We will emphasize models for continuous observed and latent variables, although we will briefly mention extensions to other observed variable types. After reviewing some general model specification, estimation, and testing issues (Sect. 11.2), we will discuss confirmatory factor models (Sect. 11.3) and full structural equation models (Sect. 11.4) in more detail. We will also present an empirical example to illustrate SEM in a particular context (Sect. 11.5). Finally, in Sect. 11.6 we briefly discuss common applications of SEM in marketing and provide an overview of computer programs available for estimating and testing structural equation models.

11.2 An Overview of Structural Equation Modeling

11.2.1 Specification of Structural Equation Models

A structural equation model can be specified algebraically or graphically. Since a graphical representation, if done correctly, is a complete formulation of the underlying model and often communicates the desired specification more intuitively, we will emphasize graphical models.

In order to make the discussion more concrete, we will consider a specific model. According to the model shown in Fig. 11.1, a consumer's attitude toward the use of self-scanning technologies (SST) is a function of five types of benefits: perceived usefulness (PU), perceived ease of use (PEU), reliability (REL), fun (FUN), and newness (NEW). Attitude toward the use of self-scanning (ATT), in turn, influences a consumer's actual use of self-scanning (USE). Because USE is a 0/1 observed dependent variable, a probit transformation of the probability of use of SST is employed so that the relationship of actual use with its antecedents is linear; a logit specification would be another possibility. The six unobserved constructs in this simple model are shown as ellipses (or circles), which signifies that they are the conceptual (latent) entities of theoretical interest. The five benefit constructs are called exogenous latent variables because they are not influenced by

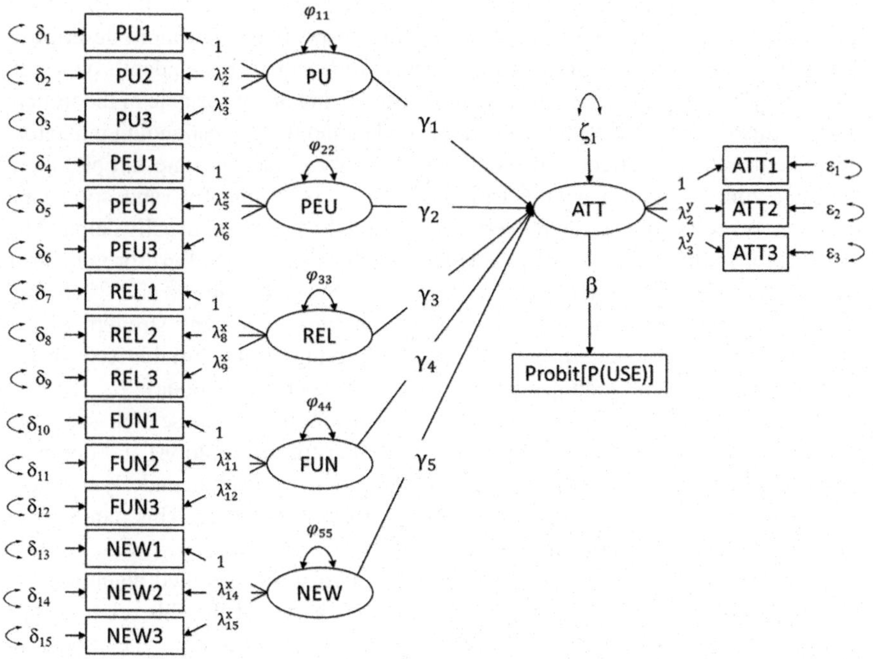

Fig. 11.1 Graphical illustration of a specific structural equation model

other latent variables in the model. In contrast, attitude and USE are endogenous latent variables (although USE is not really latent in the present case) because they depend on other constructs in the model. The Greek letters ξ (ksi) and η (eta) are sometimes used to refer to exogenous and endogenous latent variables, respectively, but more descriptive names are used in the present case. Directed paths from exogenous to endogenous latent variables are sometimes called γ (gamma) and directed paths from endogenous to other endogenous latent variables are called β (beta), although it is not necessary to make this distinction. The model assumes that the determinants of an endogenous latent variable do not account for all of the variation in the variable, which implies that an error term (ζ, zeta) is associated with each endogenous latent variable (a so-called error in equation or equation disturbance); there is no error term for Probit [P(USE)] since it is fixed in the present case. Curved arrows starting and ending at the same variable indicate variances, and two-way arrows between variables indicate covariances. For example, the curved arrows associated with the five belief factors are the variances of the exogenous constructs, which are denoted by φ_{ii} (phi). For simplicity, the variances of the errors in equations (which are usually denoted by ψ_{ii} or psi) and the covariances between the exogenous constructs (φ_{ij}) are not shown explicitly in the model; usually, non-zero covariances between the exogenous constructs are assumed by default.

If the constructs in one's theory are latent variables, they have to be linked to observed measures. Except for USE, each of the other six constructs is measured by three observed (manifest) variables or indicators, which are shown as rectangles (or squares). The letters x and y are sometimes used to refer to the indicators of exogenous and endogenous latent constructs, respectively, but more descriptive names are used in the present case. The model assumes that a respondent's observed score for a given variable is a function of the underlying latent variable of theoretical interest; this is called a reflective indicator model, and the corresponding indicators are sometimes called effect indicators. Since observed variables are fallible, there is also a unique component of variation, which is frequently (and somewhat inaccurately) equated with random error variance. The errors are usually denoted by δ (delta) for indicators of exogenous latent variables and ε (epsilon) for indicators of endogenous latent variables; the corresponding variances are θ^{δ} and θ^{ε} (theta), respectively (which are not shown explicitly in Fig. 11.1). The strength of the relationship between an indicator and its underlying latent variable (construct, factor) is called a factor loading and is usually denoted by λ (lambda).

The observed USE measure is a 0/1 variable in the present case (self-scanning was or was not used during the particular shopping trip in question) and one may assume that the observed variable is a crude (binary) measure of an underlying latent variable indicating a consumer's propensity to use self-scanning. This requires the estimation of a threshold parameter.

Of course, the model depicted in Fig. 11.1 can also be specified algebraically. This is shown in Table 11.1. In Table 11.1, it is assumed that all relationships between variables are linear. This is not explicitly expressed in the model in Fig. 11.1 (which could be interpreted as a nonparametric structural equation model), but relationships between variables are usually assumed to be linear (esp. when the

Table 11.1 Algebraic specification of the model in Fig. 11.1

Latent variable model:
$ATT = \gamma_1 PU + \gamma_2 PEU + \gamma_3 REL + \gamma_4 FUN + \gamma_5 NEW + \varsigma_1$
$\text{Probit}[P(USE)] = \beta ATT$
$VAR(\zeta_1) = \psi_{11}$
$VAR(\xi_i) = \varphi_{ii}$
$COV(\xi_i, \xi_i) = \varphi_{ij}$
Measurement model:
$PU1 = \lambda_1^x PU + \delta_1$
$PU2 = \lambda_2^x PU + \delta_2$
$PU3 = \lambda_3^x PU + \delta_3$
$PEU1 = \lambda_4^x PEU + \delta_4$
$PEU2 = \lambda_5^x PEU + \delta_5$
$PEU3 = \lambda_6^x PEU + \delta_6$
$REL1 = \lambda_7^x REL + \delta_7$
$REL2 = \lambda_8^x REL + \delta_8$
$REL3 = \lambda_9^x REL + \delta_9$
$FUN1 = \lambda_{10}^x FUN + \delta_{10}$
$FUN2 = \lambda_{11}^x FUN + \delta_{11}$
$FUN3 = \lambda_{12}^x FUN + \delta_{12}$
$NEW1 = \lambda_{13}^x NEW + \delta_{13}$
$NEW2 = \lambda_{14}^x NEW + \delta_{14}$
$NEW3 = \lambda_{15}^x NEW + \delta_{15}$
$ATT1 = \lambda_1^y ATT + \varepsilon_1$
$ATT2 = \lambda_2^y ATT + \varepsilon_2$
$ATT3 = \lambda_3^y ATT + \varepsilon_3$
$USE = 1$ if $\text{Probit}[P(USE)] > \nu$, where ν is a threshold parameter, $USE = 0$ otherwise
$VAR(\delta_i) = \theta_{ii}^x$
$VAR(\varepsilon_i) = \theta_{ii}^y$

model is estimated with commonly used SEM programs), unless a distribution other than the normal distribution is specified for a variable.

Note that the model in Fig. 11.1 or Table 11.1 is specified for observed variables that have been mean-centered. In this case, latent variable means and equation intercepts can be ignored. Although the means can be estimated, they usually do not provide important additional information. However, in multi-sample analysis, to be discussed below, means may be relevant (e.g., one may want to compare means across samples) and are often modeled explicitly.

The hypothesized model shown in Fig. 11.1 contains six relationships between constructs that are specified to be nonzero (i.e., the effect of the five belief factors on attitude, and the effect of attitude on USE). However, one could argue that the relationships that are assumed to be zero are even more important, because these restrictions allow the researcher to test the plausibility of the specified model.

The model in Fig. 11.1 contains several restrictions. First, it is hypothesized that, controlling for attitude, there are no direct effects from the five benefit factors on the use of self-scanning. Technically speaking, the model assumes that the effects of benefit beliefs on the use of self-scanning are mediated by consumers' attitudes (see Chap. 8). Second, the errors in equations are hypothesized to be uncorrelated. This means that there are no influences on attitude and use that are common to both constructs other than those contained in the model. Third, each observed variable is allowed to load only on its assumed underlying factor; non-target loadings are specified to be zero. Fourth, the model assumes that all errors of measurement are uncorrelated. Models in which at least some of the error correlations are nonzero could be entertained. Testing the model on empirical data will show whether these assumptions are justified.

Before a model can be estimated or tested, it is important to ascertain that the specified model is actually identified. *Identification* refers to whether or not a unique solution is possible. A unique aspect of structural equation models is that many variables in the model are unobserved. For example, in the measurement equations for the observed variables, all the right-hand side variables are unobserved (see Table 11.1). A first requirement for identification is that the scale in which the latent variables are measured be fixed. This can be done by setting one factor loading per latent variable to one or standardizing the factor variance to one. In Fig. 11.1, one loading per factor was fixed at one.

A second requirement is that the number of model parameters (i.e., the number of parameters to be estimated) not be greater than the number of unique elements in the variance-covariance of the observed measures. Since the number of unique variances and covariances is $(p)(p+1)/2$, where p is the number of observed variables (19 in the present case), and since $(p)(p+1)/2-r$ is the degrees of freedom of the model, where r is the number of model parameters, this requirement says that the number of degrees of freedom must be nonnegative. This is a necessary condition for model identification, but it is not sufficient. If the model in Fig. 11.1 did not contain a categorical variable, the number of estimated parameters would be 53 and the model would have 137 degrees of freedom. Because of the presence of the 0/1 USE variable, the situation is more complex, but the degrees of freedom of the model is still 137. Thus, the necessary condition for identification is satisfied.

There are no identification rules that are both necessary and sufficient and can be applied to any type of model. This makes determining model identification a nontrivial task, at least for certain models. However, simple identification rules are available for commonly encountered models and some of these will be described later in the chapter.

11.2.2 Estimation of Structural Equation Models

Estimation means finding values of the model parameters such that the discrepancy between the sample variance/covariance matrix of the observed variables (S) and the variance/covariance matrix implied by the estimated model parameters ($\widehat{\Sigma}$) is minimized. Although several estimation procedures are available (e.g., unweighted least squares, weighted least squares), Maximum Likelihood (ML) estimation based on the assumption of multivariate normality of the observed variables is often the default method of choice (see Sect. 6.4, Vol. I). ML estimation *assumes* that the observations are independently and identically multivariate-normally distributed and that the sample size is large.[1] The researcher has to ensure that these assumptions are not too grossly violated (e.g., that the skewness and kurtosis of the observed variables, both individually and jointly, is not excessive).

Although all estimation methods are iterative procedures, convergence is usually not a problem unless the model is severely misspecified or complex. Small sample sizes and a very small number of indicators per factor may also create problems. If ML estimation is appropriate, the resulting estimates have a variety of desirable properties such as consistency, asymptotic (large-sample) efficiency, and asymptotic normality. Missing values are easily accommodated as long as the missing response mechanism is completely random or random conditional on the observed data.

Unfortunately, data are often not distributed multivariate normally, and this is problematic if non-normal variables serve as dependent variables (or outcomes) in the analysis (i.e., if they appear on the left-hand side of any model equation). For example, the distribution of the observed variables may not be symmetric, or the distribution may be too flat or too peaked. If categorical or other types of variables are used in the analysis, normality is also violated. Although estimation procedures are available that do not depend on the assumption of multivariate normality (often called asymptotically distribution-free methods), they are frequently not practical because they require very large samples in order to work well. A more promising approach seems to be the use of various "robust" estimators that apply corrections to the usual test statistic of overall model fit and the estimated standard errors. An example is the Satorra-Bentler scaled (chi-square) test statistic and corresponding robust standard errors. Other correction procedures, which can also be used to correct for non-independence of observations, are available as well.

As mentioned earlier, a major advantage of SEM is that measurement error in the observed variables is explicitly accounted for. It is well-known that if observed variables that are measured with error are correlated, the resulting correlations are attenuated (i.e., lower than they should be). When multiple items are available to measure a construct of interest, using an average of several fallible indicators takes into account unreliability to some extent, and the correlation between averages of individual measures will be purged of the distorting influence of measurement error to some extent, but the correction is usually insufficient. SEM automatically controls for the presence of measurement error, and the correlations between the latent variables (factor correlations) are corrected for attenuation.

[1] See Chap. 12 for a discussion of alternative methods that relax these assumptions.

11.2.3 Testing Structural Equation Models

11.2.3.1 Testing the Overall Fit of Structural Equation Models

The fit of a specified model to empirical data can be tested with a chi-square test, which examines whether the null hypothesis of perfect fit is tenable. In principle, this is an attractive test of the overall fit of the model, but in practice there are two problems. First, the test is based on strong assumptions, which are often not met in real data (although as explained earlier, robust versions of the test are available). Second, on the one hand the test requires a large sample size, but on the other hand, as the sample size increases, it becomes more likely that (possibly minor and practically unimportant) misspecifications will lead to the rejection of a hypothesized model.

Because of these shortcomings of the chi-square test of overall model fit, many alternative fit indices have been proposed. Although researchers' reliance on these fit indices is somewhat controversial (model evaluation is based on mere rules of thumb, and some authors argue that researchers dismiss a significant chi-square test too easily), several alternative fit indices are often reported in practice. Definitions, brief explanations, important characteristics, and commonly used cutoffs for assessing model fit are summarized in Table 11.2.

We offer the following guidelines to researchers assessing the overall fit of a model. First, a significant chi-square statistic should not be ignored because of the presumed weaknesses of the test; after all, a significant chi-square value does show that the model is inconsistent with the data. Close inspection of the hypothesized model is necessary to determine whether or not the discrepancies identified by the chi-square test are serious (even if some of the alternative fit indices suggest that the fit of the model is reasonable). Second, surprisingly often, different fit indices suggest different conclusions (i.e., the CFI may indicate a good fit of the model, whereas the RMSEA is problematic). In these cases, particular care is required in interpreting the model results. Third, a hypothesized model may be problematic even when the overall fit indices are favorable (e.g., if estimated error variances are negative or path coefficients have the wrong sign). Fourth, a well-fitting model is not necessarily the "true" model. There may be other models that fit equally or nearly equally well. In summary, overall fit indices seem to be most helpful in alerting researchers to possible problems with the specified model.

11.2.3.2 Model Modification

If a model is found to be deficient, it should be respecified. Two tools are useful in this regard. First, a researcher can inspect the residuals, which express the difference between a sample variance or covariance and the variance or covariance implied by the hypothesized model. So-called standardized residuals are most helpful, because they correct for both differences in the metric in which different observed variables

Table 11.2 Summary of commonly used overall fit (or lack-of-fit) indices

Index	Definition of the index[a]	Characteristics[b]	Interpretation and use of the index
Minimum fit function chi-square (χ^2)	$(N-1)f$	BF, SA, NNO, NP	Tests the hypothesis that the specified model fits perfectly (within the limits of sampling error); the obtained χ^2 value should be smaller than χ^2_{crit}; note that the minimum fit function χ^2 is only one possible chi-square statistic and that different discrepancy functions will yield different χ^2 values
Root mean square error of approximation (RMSEA)	$\sqrt{\frac{(\chi^2-df)}{(N-1)df}}$	BF, SA, NNO, P	Estimates how well the fitted model approximates the population covariance matrix per df; Browne and Cudeck (1992) suggest that a value of 0.05 indicates a close fit and that values up to 0.08 are reasonable; Hu and Bentler (1999) recommend a cutoff value of 0.06; a p-value for testing the hypothesis that the discrepancy is smaller than 0.05 may be calculated (so-called test of close fit)
Bayesian information criterion (BIC)	$[\chi^2 + r\ ln\ N]$ or $[\chi^2 - df\ ln\ N]$	BF, SA, NNO, P	Based on statistical information theory and used for testing competing (possibly non-nested) models; the model with the smallest BIC is selected
Root mean squared residual (S)RMR)	$\sqrt{\frac{2\Sigma\Sigma(s_{ij}-\hat{\sigma}_{ij})^2}{(p)(p+1)}}$	BF, SA, NO or NNO, NP	Measures the average size of residuals between the fitted and sample covariance matrices; if a correlation matrix is analyzed, RMR is "standardized" to fall within the [0, 1] interval (SRMR), otherwise it is only bounded from below; a cutoff of 0.05 is often used for SRMR; Hu and Bentler (1999) recommend a cutoff value close to 0.08
Comparative Fit Index (CFI)		GF, IM, NO, NP	Measures the proportionate improvement in fit (defined in terms of noncentrality, i.e., $2-df$) as one moves from the baseline to the target model; originally, values greater than 0.90 were deemed acceptable, but Hu and Bentler (1999) recommend a cutoff value of 0.95
Tucker and Lewis nonnormed fit index (TLI, NNFI)	$\frac{\frac{\chi^2_n-df_n}{df_n}-\frac{\chi^2_t-df_t}{df_t}}{\frac{\chi^2_n-df_n}{df_n}}$	GF, IM, ANO, P	Measures the proportionate improvement in fit (defined in terms of noncentrality) as one moves from the baseline to the target model, per df; originally, values greater than 0.90 were deemed acceptable, but Hu and Bentler (1999) recommend a cutoff value of 0.95

[a]N = sample size; f = minimum of the fitting function; df = degrees of freedom; r = number of parameters estimated; p = number of observed variables; χ^2_{crit} = critical value of the χ^2 distribution with the appropriate number of degrees of freedom and for a given significance level; the subscripts n and t refer to the null (or baseline) and target models, respectively. The baseline model is usually the model of complete independence of all observed variables

[b]GF = goodness-of-fit index (i.e., the larger the fit index, the better the fit); BF = badness-of-fit index (i.e., the smaller the fit index, the better the fit); SA = stand-alone fit index (i.e., the model is evaluated in an absolute sense); IM = incremental fit index (i.e., the model is evaluated relative to a baseline model); NO = normed (in the sample) fit index; ANO = normed (in the population) fit index, but only approximately normed in the sample (i.e., can fall outside the [0, 1] interval); NNO = nonnormed fit index; NP = no correction for parsimony; P = correction for parsimony

are measured and sampling fluctuation. A standardized residual can be interpreted as a z-value for testing whether the residual is significantly different from zero. For example, if there is a large positive standardized residual between two variables, it means that the specified model cannot fully account for the covariation between the two variables; a respecification that increases the implied covariance is called for.

Second, a researcher can study the modification indices for the specified model. A modification index is essentially a Lagrange multiplier test of whether a certain model restriction is consistent with the data (e.g., whether a certain parameter is actually zero or whether an equality constraint holds). If a modification index (MI) is larger than 3.84 (i.e., 1.96 squared), this means that the revised model in which the parameter is freely estimated will fit significantly better (at $\alpha = 0.05$) and that the estimated parameter will be significant. Most computer programs also report an estimated parameter change (EPC) statistic, which indicates the likely value of the freely estimated parameter. Modification indices have to be used with care because there is no guarantee that a specification search based on MIs will recover the "true" model, in part because an added parameter may simply model an idiosyncratic characteristic of the data set at hand. For this reason, it is best to validate data-driven model modifications on a new data set. Often, quite a few MIs will be significant and it may not be obvious which parameters to add first (the final model is likely to depend on the sequence in which parameters are added). Finally, model modification should not only be based on statistical considerations, and strong reliance on prior theory and conceptual understanding of the context at hand is the best guide to meaningful model modifications.

11.2.3.3 Assessing the Local Fit of Structural Equation Models

Often, researchers will iterate between examining the overall fit of the model, inspecting residuals and modification indices, and looking at some of the details of the specified model. However, once the researcher is comfortable with the final model, this model has to be interpreted in detail. Usually, this will involve the following. First, all model parameters are checked for consistency with expectations and significance tests are conducted at least for the parameters that are of substantive interest. Second, depending on the model, certain other analyses will be conducted. For example, a researcher will usually want to report evidence about the reliability and convergent validity of the observed measures, as well as the discriminant validity of the constructs. Third, for models containing endogenous latent variables, the amount of variance in each endogenous variable explained by the exogenous latent variables should be reported. Finally, for some models one may want to conduct particular model comparisons. For example, if a model contains three layers of relationships, one may wish to examine to what extent the variables in the middle layer mediate or channel the relationships between the variables in the first and third layer. Or if a multi-sample analysis is performed, one may wish to test the invariance of particular paths across different groups. More details about local fit assessment will be provided below.

11.3 Confirmatory Measurement Models

11.3.1 Congeneric Measurement Models

Conceptual variables frequently cannot be measured directly and sets of individually imperfect observed variables are used as proxies of the underlying constructs of interest. SEM is very useful for ascertaining the quality of construct measurement because it enables a detailed assessment of the reliability and validity of measurement instruments, as described below. The analysis usually starts with a congeneric measurement model in which (continuous) observed variables are seen as effects of underlying constructs (i.e., the measurement model is reflective), each observed variable loads on one and only one factor (if the model contains multiple factors), the common factors are correlated, and the unique factors are assumed to be uncorrelated. These assumptions are not always realistic, but the model can be modified if the original model is too restrictive. An illustrative congeneric measurement model corresponding to the antecedent constructs in the model in Fig. 11.1 is shown in Fig. 11.2.

Although reflective measurement models are reasonable in many situations, researchers should carefully evaluate whether observed measures can be assumed to be the effects of underlying latent variables. Sometimes, constructs are better thought of as being caused by their indicators (so-called formative measurement models). For example, satisfaction with a product probably does not lead to satisfaction with particular aspects of a product, but is a function of satisfaction with these aspects. Chapter 12 discusses formative measurement models in more detail (see also Diamantopoulos et al. 2008).

Several simple identification rules are available for congeneric measurement models (see Bollen 1989). If at least three indicators per factor are available, a congeneric measurement model is identified, even if the factors are uncorrelated. If a factor has only two indicators, the factor has to have at least one nonzero correlation with another factor, or the model has to be constrained further (e.g., the factor loadings have to be set equal). If there is only a single indicator of a given "construct", the error variance of this measure has to be set to zero or another assumed value (e.g., based on the measure's reliability observed in other studies).

Provided that the congeneric measurement model is found to be reasonably consistent with the data, the following measurement issues should be investigated. First, the indicators of a given construct should be substantially related to the target construct, both individually and as a set. In the congeneric measurement model, the observed variance in a measure consists of only two sources, substantive variance (variance due to the underlying construct) and unique variance. If one assumes that unique variance is equal to random error variance (usually, it is difficult to separate random error variance from other sources of unique variance), convergent validity is the same as reliability and we will henceforth use the term reliability for simplicity.

Individually, an item should load significantly on its target factor, and each item's observed variance should contain a substantial amount of substantive variance.

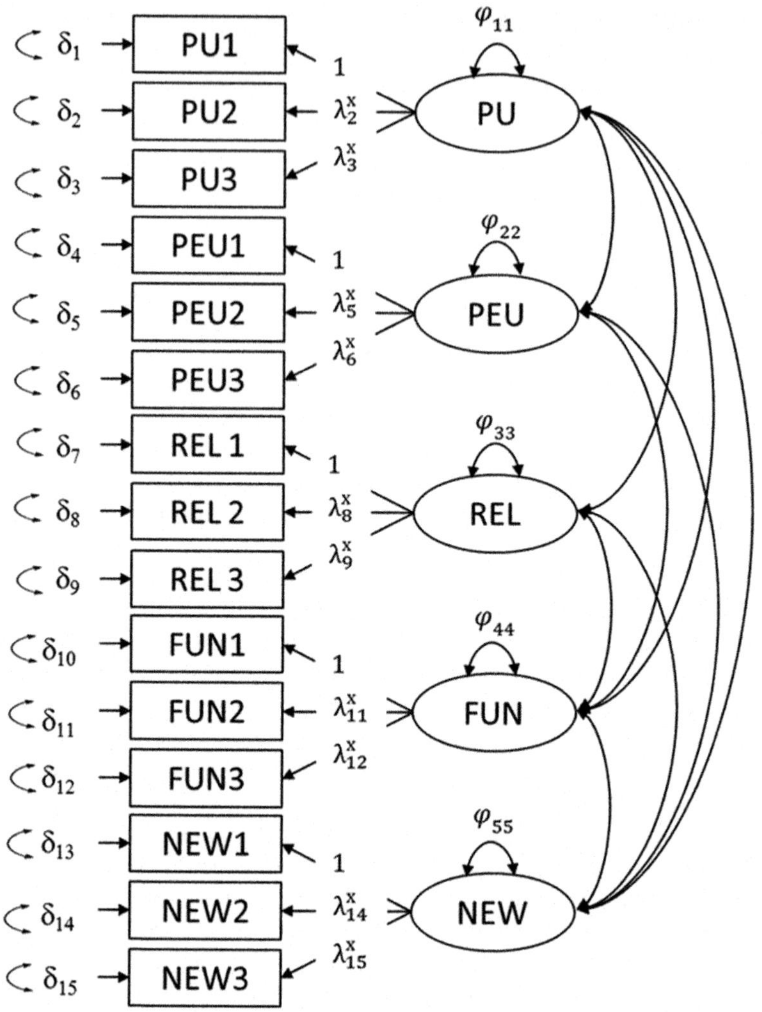

Fig. 11.2 An illustrative congeneric measurement model

One index, called individual-item reliability (IIR) or individual-item convergent validity (IICV), is defined as the squared correlation between a measure x_i and its underlying construct ξ_j (i.e., the proportion of the total variance in x_i that is substantive variance), which can be computed as follows:

$$\mathrm{IIR}_{x_i} = \frac{\lambda_{ij}^2 \varphi_{jj}}{\lambda_{ij}^2 \varphi_{jj} + \theta_{ii}} \tag{11.1}$$

where λ_{ij} is the loading of indicator x_i on construct ξ_j, φ_{jj} is the variance of ξ_j, and θ_{ii} is the unique variance in x_i. One common rule of thumb is that at least half of the total variance in an indicator should be substantive variance (i.e., IIR ≥ 0.5). One can also summarize the reliability of all indicators of a given construct by computing the average of the individual-item reliabilities. This is usually called average variance extracted (AVE), that is,

$$\mathrm{AVE}_{\xi_j} = \frac{\sum \mathrm{IIR}_{x_i}}{K} \tag{11.2}$$

where K is the number of indicators (x_i) for the construct in question (ξ_j). Similar to IIR, a common rule of thumb is that AVE should be at least 0.5.

As a set, all measures of a given construct combined should be strongly related to the underlying construct. One common index is composite reliability (CR), which is defined as the squared correlation between an unweighted sum (or average) of the measures of a construct and the construct itself. CR is a generalization of coefficient alpha to a situation in which items can have different loadings on the underlying factor and it can be computed as follows:

$$\mathrm{CR}_{\sum x_i} = \frac{\left(\sum \lambda_{ij}\right)^2 \varphi_{jj}}{\left(\sum \lambda_{ij}\right)^2 \varphi_{jj} + \sum \theta_{ii}}. \tag{11.3}$$

CR should be at least 0.7 and preferably higher.

Second, indicators should be primarily related to their underlying construct and not to other constructs. In a congeneric model, loadings on non-target factors are set to zero *a priori*, but the researcher has to evaluate whether this assumption is justified by looking at the relevant modification indices and expected parameter changes. This criterion can be thought of as an assessment of discriminant validity at the item level.

Third, the constructs themselves should not be too highly correlated if they are to be distinct. This is called discriminant validity at the construct level. One way to test discriminant validity is to construct a confidence interval around each construct correlation and check whether the confidence interval includes one. However, this is a weak criterion of discriminant validity because with a large sample and precise estimates of the factor correlations, the factor correlations will usually be distinct from one, even if the correlations are quite high. A stronger test of discriminant validity is the criterion proposed by Fornell and Larcker (1981). This criterion says that each squared factor correlation should be smaller than the AVE for the two constructs involved in the correlation. Intuitively, this rule means that a construct should be more strongly related to its own indicators than to another construct from which it is supposedly distinct.

Up to this point, the assumption has been that individual items are used as indicators of each latent variable. In principle, having more indicators to measure a latent variable is beneficial, but in practice a large number of indicators may not be practical (i.e., too many parameters have to be estimated, the required sample size becomes prohibitive, and it will be difficult to obtain a well-fitting model, etc.). Sometimes, researchers combine individual items into parcels and use the sum or average score of the items in the parcel as an indicator. Such a strategy may be unavoidable when the number of items in a scale is rather large (e.g., a personality scale may consist of 20 or more items) and has certain advantages (e.g., parceling may be used strategically to correct for lack of normality), but parceling has to be used with care (e.g., the items in the parcel should be unidimensional). Particularly when the factor structure of a set of items is not well-understood, item parceling is not recommended. An alternative to item parceling is to average all the measures of a given construct, fix the loading on the construct to one, and set the error variance to $(1-\alpha)$ times the variance of the average of the observed measures, where α is an estimate of the reliability of the composite of observed measures (such as coefficient α). However, the same caution as for item parceling is applicable here as well.

11.3.2 More Complex Measurement Models

The congeneric measurement model makes strong assumptions about the factor loading matrix and the covariance matrix of the unique factors. Each indicator loads on a single substantive factor, and the unique factors are uncorrelated.

It is possible to relax the assumption that the loadings of observed measures on nontarget factors are zero. In Exploratory Structural Equation Modeling (ESEM), the congeneric confirmatory factor model is replaced with an exploratory factor model in which the number of factors is determined *a priori* and the initial factor solution is rotated using target rotation (Marsh et al. 2014). The fit of the congeneric factor model can be compared to the fit of an exploratory structural equation model using a chi-square difference test (based on the difference of the two chi-square values and the difference in the degrees of freedom of the two models) and, ideally, the restrictions in the congeneric factor model will not decrease the fit substantially, although frequently the fit does get worse. An alternative method for modeling a more flexible factor pattern is based on Bayesian Structural Equation Modeling (BSEM) (Muthén and Asparouhov 2012). In this approach, informative priors with a small variance are specified for the cross-loadings (e.g., a normal prior with a mean of zero and a variance of 0.01 for the standardized loadings, which implies a 95 percent confidence interval for the loadings ranging from -0.2 to $+0.2$).[2] Although both methods tend to improve the fit of specified models and may avoid distortions of the factor solution when the congeneric measurement model is clearly inconsistent with the data, the two approaches abandon the ideal that an indicator should only be related to a single construct, which creates problems with the interpretation of hypothesized factors.

The assumption that the substantive factors specified in the congeneric measurement model are the only sources of covariation between observed measures is also limiting. Frequently, there will be significant modification indices suggesting that the covariation between certain unique factors should be freely estimated. However,

---

[2]See Chap. 16 on Bayesian Analysis.

there have to be plausible conceptual reasons for introducing correlated errors, because otherwise the resulting respecification of the model will come across as too *ad hoc*. As an example of a theoretically justified model modification, consider a situation in which some of the indicators are reverse-scored. There is extensive evidence showing that if some of the indicators are reverse-keyed, it is likely that the items keyed in the same direction are more highly correlated than the items keyed in the opposite direction. In this case, the specification of alternative sources of covariation besides substantive overlap seems reasonable (see Weijters et al. 2013).

There are two ways in which method effects have been modeled. The first approach is generally referred to as the correlated uniqueness model (Marsh 1989). This method consists of allowing correlations among certain error terms, but instead of introducing the error correlations in an *ad hoc* fashion, they are motived by *a priori* hypotheses. For example, correlated uniquenesses might be specified for all items that share the same keying direction (i.e., the reversed items, the regular items, or both)

The second approach involves specifying method factors for the hypothesized method effects. Sometimes, a global method factor is posited to underlie all items in one's model, but this is only meaningful under special circumstances (e.g., when both regular and reversed items are available to measure a construct or several constructs; see Weijters et al. 2013), because otherwise method variance will be confounded with substantive variance. More likely, a method factor will be specified for subsets of items that share a common method (e.g., reversed items). Of course, it is possible to model multiple method factors if several sources of method bias are thought to be present.

11.3.3 Multi-sample Measurement Models

Sometimes, researchers want to conduct a measurement analysis across different populations of respondents. This is particularly useful in cross-cultural research, where certain conditions of measurement invariance have to be satisfied before meaningful comparisons across different cultures can be performed. Multi-sample measurement models are also useful for comparing factor means across groups, and this requires incorporating the means of observed variables into the analysis.

Three types of measurement invariance are particularly important. First, at the most basic level, the same factor model has to hold in each population if constructs are to be compared across groups. This is sometimes called *configural invariance*. Second, one can test whether the factor loadings of corresponding items are the same across groups. This is referred to as *metric invariance*. Third, if the means of the variables are included in the model (which is important when the means of constructs are to be compared across groups), one can test whether the intercept of the regression of each observed variable on the underlying factor is the same in each group. This is called *scalar invariance* in the literature. As discussed by Steenkamp and Baumgartner (1998), if a researcher wants to investigate the strength of directional relationships between constructs across groups, metric invariance (equality of factor loadings) has to hold, and if latent construct means are to be compared across groups, scalar invariance (invariance of measurement intercepts) has to hold as well. It is not necessary that all loadings or all measurement intercepts are invariant across groups, but at least two indicators per factor have to exhibit metric and scalar invariance. For details, the interested reader is referred to Steenkamp and Baumgartner (1998).

Multi-sample measurement analysis may be thought of as an instance of population heterogeneity in which the heterogeneity is known. Multi-sample models are most useful when the number of distinct groups is small to moderate, and in this situation such fixed-effects models are a straightforward approach to test for moderator effects. As the number of groups gets large, a random-effects specification may be more useful, and if the moderator is continuous, a model with interaction effects is preferable (i.e., continuous moderators should not be discretized). It is also possible to estimate models in which the heterogeneity is unknown and the researcher tries to recover the population heterogeneity from the data. Unknown population heterogeneity is discussed in Chap. 13.

11.3.4 Measurement Models Based on Item Response Theory

Simulation evidence suggests that the assumption of continuous, normally distributed observed variables, while never literally true, is reasonable if the response scale has at least 5–7 distinct categories, the response scale category labels were chosen carefully to be equidistant, and the distribution of the data is symmetric. However, there are situations in which these assumptions are difficult to justify, such as when there are only two response options (e.g., yes or no).

An attractive approach that explicitly takes into account the discreteness of the data is item response theory (IRT; see Kamata and Bauer 2008). The IRT model can be developed by assuming that the variables that are actually observed are discretized versions of underlying continuous response variables. Therefore, the conventional measurement model has to be extended by specifying how the discretized variable that is actually observed is related to the underlying continuous response variable. In the so-called two-parameter IRT model, the probability that a person will provide a response of 1 on item i, given ξ_j, is expressed as follows:

$$P\left(x_i = 1|\xi_j\right) = F\left(a_i\xi_j + \nu_i\right) = F\left(a_i\left(\xi_j - b_i\right)\right) \tag{11.4}$$

where F is either the normal or logistic cumulative distribution function. Equation (11.4) specifies a sigmoid relationship between the probability of a response of 1 to an item and the latent construct (referred to as an item characteristic curve); a_i is called the discrimination parameter (which shows the sensitivity of the item to discriminate between respondents having different ξ_j around the point of inflection of the sigmoid curve) and b_i the difficulty parameter (i.e., the value of ξ_j at which the probability of a response of 1 is 0.5). The model is similar to logistic or probit regression, except that the explanatory variable ξ_j is latent rather than observed (Wu and Zumbo 2007). The IRT model for binary data can be extended to ordinal responses. The interested reader is referred to Baumgartner and Weijters (2017) for a recent discussion.

11.4 Full Structural Equation Models

A full structural equation model can be thought of as a combination of a confirmatory factor model with a latent variable path model. There is a measurement model for both the exogenous and endogenous latent variables, and the latent variable path model (sometimes called the structural model) specifies the relationships between the constructs in one's model. Since measurement models were discussed previously, this section will focus on the latent variable path model.

Two kinds of latent variable models can be distinguished. In recursive models, one cannot trace a series of directed (one-way) paths from a latent variable back to the same latent variable (there are no bidirectional effects or feedback loops), and all errors in equations (equation disturbances) are uncorrelated. In nonrecursive models, at least one of these conditions is violated. Although nonrecursive models can be specified, questions have been raised about the meaningfulness of such models when all the constructs are measured at the same point of time.

When proposing a full structural equation model, it is important to show that the model is identified. The so-called two-step rule is often used for this purpose, which is a sufficient condition for identification (Bollen 1989). In the first step, it is shown that the measurement model corresponding to the structural equation model (in which no structural specification is imposed on the latent variable model and the constructs are allowed to freely correlate) is identified. Identification rules for measurement models have already been discussed. In the second step, the latent variables can be treated as observed (since their variances and covariances were shown to be identified in the first step) and the remaining model parameters (the relationships between the latent variables and the variances and covariances of the errors in equations) are shown to be identified. If there are no direct relationships between the endogenous latent variables (i.e., there are no nonzero β's, see Sect. 11.2.1) or the latent variable model is recursive, the model is identified. If the model is nonrecursive, other identification rules may be applicable (e.g., the rank rule).

It is not always easy to show that a model is identified theoretically. Frequently, researchers rely on the computer program used for estimation and testing to alert them to identification problems. A preferred approach may be to start with a model that is known to be identified and to free desired parameters one at a time, provided the modification index for the parameter in question is significant. If a modification index is significant, the parameter in question is probably identified. If the modification index is zero, the parameter is probably not identified. If the modification index is non-significant, the freely estimated parameter is likely non-significant, so there should be little interest in freeing the parameter.

When assessing the overall fit of a model, one should not only assess the model's fit in isolation, but also compare the target model to several other models (Anderson and Gerbing 1988). The overall fit of the target model is a function of the fit of the measurement model and the fit of the latent variable model. On the one hand, a measurement model in which the latent variables are freely correlated provides an upper limit on the fit of the latent variable model because the latent variable model is saturated. Such a model assesses the fit of the measurement model only and if the measurement model does not fit adequately, the measurement model has to be respecified. On the other hand, a measurement model in which the latent variables are uncorrelated (the so-called model of structural independence) provides a baseline of comparison to evaluate how much the consideration of relationships between the constructs as hypothesized in the target model improves the fit of the model. Note that the model of structural independence is only identified if at least three indicators are available for each latent variable (unless one of the constructs is assumed to be measured perfectly by a single indicator or a certain amount of reliability is assumed). Ideally, the target model should fit much better than the baseline model of structural independence, and as well as (or nearly as well as) the saturated structural model, even though fewer relationships among the latent variables are estimated.

It should be noted that the issue of whether the specified model is able to account for the covariances between observed variables (covariance fit) is distinct from the issue of whether the specified model can account for the variation in each endogenous latent variable (variance fit). For example, it is possible that a model fits very well overall, but only a very small portion of the variance in the endogenous constructs is explained. Thus, it is necessary to provide evidence about the explained variance in each endogenous latent variable.

If a multi-stage latent variable model is specified (e.g., A→B→C), it is often of interest to test whether the effect of the antecedent (e.g., A) on the outcome (e.g., C) is completely (i.e., no direct effect of A on C) or at least partially mediated by the intervening variables (i.e., at least some of the total effect of A on C goes through B), and how strong the mediated effect is. Most computer programs provide estimates and statistical tests of direct, indirect, and total effects. Research has shown that normal-theory tests of the indirect effects are not always trustworthy and alternatives based on bootstrapping are available.

SEM was initially developed for models containing only linear relationships. For example, LISREL, the first commonly used program for SEM, stands for Linear Structural Relations (Jöreskog and Sörbom 2006). However, the model has been extended to accommodate nonlinear effects of latent variables, particularly interaction effects. Several different approaches are available; interested readers are referred to Marsh et al. 2013. The approach implemented in Mplus, based on the method proposed by Klein and Moosbrugger (2000), is very easy to use and has been shown to perform well in simulations.

Researchers are often interested in comparing structural paths across different populations. For example, it may be of interest to assess whether the effects of the perceived benefits of self-scanning on attitudes toward self-scanning, or the effect of attitude on the use of self-scanning, are invariant across gender. In order for such comparisons to be meaningful, the measurement model has to exhibit metric invariance across the populations to be compared. In other words, the factor loadings of corresponding items have to be the same across groups. Although full metric invariance is not required, at least two items per construct have to have invariant loadings. Since one loading per factor is fixed at one to set the scale of each factor, this implies that at least one additional loading has to be invariant. If at least two indicators per factor are constrained to be invariant, the modification indices on the loadings of the two items will show whether these constraints are satisfied. Provided that a sufficient number of items per factor is invariant (i.e., at least 2), the structural paths of interest can be compared across samples using a chi-square difference test.

11.5 Empirical Example

11.5.1 Introduction

As an empirical example, we analyze data that were collected from shoppers in stores of a grocery retail chain in Western Europe to study the determinants of consumers' use of self-scanning technology (SST). The self-scanners were hand-held devices that were made available on a shelf at the entrance of the store. Customers choosing the self-scanning option used the device throughout their shopping trip to scan the barcodes on all items they selected from the shelves. At check-out, self-scanner users then proceeded to separate "fast" lanes. Different teams of research associates simultaneously collected the data in six stores of the grocery retailer over the course of three days. Data collection consisted of two stages. In the first stage, research associates approached shoppers upon entering the store and, if shoppers agreed to participate, administered a questionnaire with closed-ended questions. The entry survey contained filter questions to screen out people who were unaware of self-scanning devices and to restrict the sample to customers with a loyalty card, given the retailer's policy of offering self-scanning devices only to loyal customers. The main questionnaire consisted of a series of items measuring attitudes toward SST as well as the perceived attributes of SST and some demographic background variables, including gender. The items are reported in Table 11.3. In the second stage of data collection, after customers had done their shopping and had checked out their purchases, respondents' use or non-use of self-scanning was recorded by matching unique codes provided to respondents in the entry and exit data.

A total of 1492 shoppers were approached for participation in the survey. Of these, 709 people responded favorably. Finally, 497 questionnaires contained complete data for customers who were eligible to participate in the study (i.e., they were aware of self-scanning, were in possession of a loyalty card, had purchased at least

Table 11.3 Questionnaire items for the empirical data

Perceived usefulness (PU)	PU1	Self-scanning will allow me to shop faster
	PU2	Self-scanning will make me more efficient while shopping
	PU3	Self-scanning reduces the waiting time at the cash register
Perceived ease of use (PEU)	PEU1	Self-scanning will be effortless
	PEU2	Self-scanning will be easy
	PEU3	Self-scanning will be user-friendly
Reliability (REL)	REL1	Self-scanning will be reliable
	REL2	I expect self-scanning to work well
	REL3	Self-scanning will have a faultless result
Fun (FUN)	FUN1	Self-scanning will be entertaining
	FUN2	Self-scanning will be fun
	FUN3	Self-scanning will be enjoyable
Newness (NEW)	NEW1	Self-scanning is outmoded—Self-scanning is progressive
	NEW2	Self-scanning is old—Self-scanning is new
	NEW3	Self-scanning is obsolete—Self-scanning is innovative
Attitude (ATT)	ATT1	Unfavorable—Favorable
	ATT2	I dislike it—I like it
	ATT3	Bad—Good

Note: All items were administered using a 5-point rating scale format and the instruction "What is your position on the following statements?", with the exception of the attitude scale, which contained the following question stem: "How would you describe your feelings toward using self-scanning in this store?"

one product, and their observed self-scanning use or non-use could be matched with their entry survey data). In this sample, 65% (35%) were female (male). Further, 63% had had education after secondary school. As for age, 1% were aged 12–19, 21% 20–29, 21% 30–39, 28% 40–49, 19% 50–59, 7% 60–69, 2% 70–79, and 1% 80–89 years. Finally, 36% used self-scanning during their visit to the store.

11.5.2 Analyses and Results

In what follows, we illustrate the use of SEM on the self-scanning data, roughly following the outline of the preceding exposition. Thus, we start with a CFA of the five belief constructs. Next, we test measurement invariance of this factor structure across men and women (multi-sample measurement). We then move on to full SEM, testing a two-group (men/women) mediation model where the five belief factors are used as antecedents of self-scanning use, mediated by attitude toward self-scanning use. All analyses were run in Mplus 7.4.

11.5.2.1 Measurement Analysis

Our first aim is to assess the factor structure of the five belief factors (PU, PEU, REL, FUN and NEW). Note that the factor models are intended as stand-alone examples of a measurement analysis. If a factor analysis were used as a precursor to a full structural equation model, it would be common to also include the endogenous constructs and their indicators in the measurement analysis. We start by running an exploratory factor analysis where the 15 belief items freely load on five factors using the default ML estimator with oblique GEOMIN rotation. This model shows acceptable fit to the data: $\chi^2(40) = 86.725$, $p < 0.001$; RMSEA $= 0.048$ (90% confidence interval (CI) $= [0.034, 0.062]$); SRMR $= 0.014$; CFI $= 0.989$; TLI $= 0.970$. Each of the five factors shows loadings for the three target items that are statistically significant ($p < 0.05$) and substantial (all loadings were greater than 0.50, although most loadings were greater than 0.80). There were also six significant cross-loadings, suggesting that the factor pattern does not have perfect simple structure. However, these six cross-loadings do not seem problematic as they are small (most are smaller than 0.10, and none are greater than 0.20).

We proceed to test a confirmatory factor analysis (CFA) of the five belief factors. Even though the CFA model fits the data significantly worse than the exploratory factor model (the two models are nested and can be compared with a chi-square difference test, $\Delta\chi^2(40) = 108.975$, $p < 0.001$), the fit of the CFA model is deemed acceptable, especially in terms of the alternative fit indices: $\chi^2(80) = 195.70$; RMSEA $= 0.054$ (90% CI $= [0.044,0.064]$); SRMR $= 0.037$; CFI $= 0.972$; TLI $= 0.963$. Closer inspection of the local fit of the model shows that five modification indices for factor loadings constrained to zero have a value greater than 10; these five modification indices are for the non-target loadings identified in the exploratory factor analysis. Although statistically significant, they are not large enough to warrant model modifications, as this would come at the expense of parsimony and replicability. Table 11.4 reports the CFA results for individual items and factors. Overall, the results are satisfactory, with the exception of two items that have problematic IIR values (less than 0.50). All AVE values are at least 0.50 and all CR values are larger than 0.70, in support of convergent validity. Table 11.5 evaluates discriminant and convergent validity by showing the AVE's and correlations for all factors. Discriminant validity is supported as the squared correlations between constructs are smaller than the AVE's of the constructs involved in the correlation.

Now that we have established a viable factor model, we can test for measurement invariance between male and female respondents. To this purpose, we use the same CFA model as before, but additionally specify gender as the grouping variable and run a sequence of three models with constraints corresponding to configural invariance, metric invariance and scalar invariance. Table 11.6 reports the model fit results.

The comparison of the metric invariance model with the configural invariance model shows no significant deterioration in fit, so metric invariance can be accepted. Strictly speaking, the χ^2 difference testing scalar invariance against metric

Table 11.4 CFA factor structure

		Standardized factor loading	IIR	AVE	CR
PU	PU1	0.79	0.63	0.50	0.75
	PU2	0.74	0.55		
	PU3	0.58	0.33		
PEU	PEU1	0.73	0.53	0.65	0.85
	PEU2	0.92	0.85		
	PEU3	0.75	0.57		
FUN	FUN1	0.93	0.87	0.88	0.96
	FUN2	0.98	0.96		
	FUN3	0.90	0.81		
REL	REL1	0.75	0.57	0.54	0.78
	REL2	0.80	0.64		
	REL3	0.64	0.40		
NEW	NEW1	0.79	0.62	0.64	0.84
	NEW2	0.76	0.57		
	NEW3	0.86	0.74		

Table 11.5 Factor correlations, composite reliability (CR) and average variance extracted (AVE)

	CR	PU	PEU	FUN	REL	NEW
PU	*0.75*	0.50	0.24	0.26	0.06	0.11
PEU	*0.85*	0.49	0.65	0.20	0.23	0.03
FUN	*0.96*	0.51	0.44	0.88	0.05	0.06
REL	*0.78*	0.24	0.48	0.22	0.54	0.01
NEW	*0.84*	0.33	0.17	0.25	0.12	0.64

Note: Values on the diagonal for PU through NEW represent AVE. Below-diagonal values are inter-factor correlations. Above-diagonal values are squared inter-factor correlations. CR refers to composite reliability

Table 11.6 Model fit indices for measurement invariance tests

Model	χ^2	*df*	$\Delta\chi^2$	Δdf	*p*	CFI	TLI	SRMR	BIC	RMSEA
Configural	287.3	160				0.970	0.961	0.043	20127.6	0.057
Metric	305.3	170	18.03	10	0.054	0.968	0.961	0.051	20083.6	0.057
Scalar	325.4	180	20.13	10	0.028	0.966	0.960	0.050	20041.6	0.057

invariance is significant at the 0.05 level, but there are good reasons to nevertheless accept scalar invariance: the χ^2 difference is small, and the alternative fit indices (CFI, TLI, SRMR, and RMSEA) do not deteriorate much, particularly the ones that take into account model parsimony (TLI and RMSEA). The information-theory based fit index BIC is lowest for the scalar invariance model. Moreover, closer inspection of the results shows that the modification indices are rather small (the highest modification index for an item intercept is 6.42). In sum, it is reasonable to conclude that the five beliefs related to self-scanning are measured equivalently among men and women, both in terms of scale metrics and item intercepts.

As a result, we can use the CFA model to compare factor means. To do so, we set the factor means to zero in the male group while freely estimating the factor means in the female group. None of the factor means are significantly different across groups, although two differences come close: the means of PEU ($t = -1.664$, $p = 0.096$) and REL ($t = -1.709, p = 0.088$) are somewhat lower for women than for men.

11.5.2.2 Full Structural Equation Model

To illustrate the use of full SEM, we test the model shown in Fig. 11.1, although we include gender as a grouping variable and test the invariance of structural paths across men and women. In order for comparisons of structural coefficients to be meaningful, we imposed equality of factor loadings across groups. It was already established that the belief items satisfy metric invariance, and additional analyses showed that metric invariance also held for the indicators of attitude. Table 11.7 reports the model fit indices for a partial mediation model in which the five belief factors influence USE (more specifically, the probit of the probability of use of SST) both directly and indirectly via attitude (model A) and a model with full mediation in which there are no direct effects of the five belief factors on USE (model B). Model B shows significantly worse fit than model A. Closer inspection of the results reveals a significant modification index for the direct effect of PEU on USE in the female group. In model C, we therefore release the direct effect of PEU on USE, and the resulting model does not show a deterioration in fit relative to model A. We can conclude that there are no direct effects of four of the belief factors (PU, REL, FUN, and NEW) on USE, but PEU has a direct effect for women. Figure 11.3 presents the unstandardized path coefficients estimated for model C. Note that the regressions of USE on ATT and on PEU are probit regressions, which means that

Table 11.7 Model fit indices for different models

	Exact fit			$\Delta\chi^2$								
	χ^2	*df*	*p*	χ^2	*df*	*p*	CFI	TLI	WRMR	RMSEA	Lo	Hi
A.	327.2	276	0.019				0.964	0.955	0.755	0.027	0.012	0.038
B.	353.4	286	0.004	23.74	10	0.008	0.952	0.943	0.819	0.031	0.018	0.041
C.	337.7	284	0.016	10.79	8	0.214	0.962	0.954	0.785	0.028	0.013	0.038

Note: Model A = partial mediation (direct and indirect effects); Model B = full mediation (no direct effects); Model C = full mediation with the exception of a direct effect of PEU on USE. The χ^2 difference tests are based on the DIFFTEST procedure in Mplus since the regular χ^2 difference test is not appropriate for the estimation procedure used in the present case (WLSMV due to the presence of the binary USE measure). A probit link is assumed for USE. Lo and Hi refer to the lower and upper bound of a 90% CI for RMSEA. WRMR is the weighted root mean square residual (for which the fit heuristics listed in Table 11.2 are not applicable)

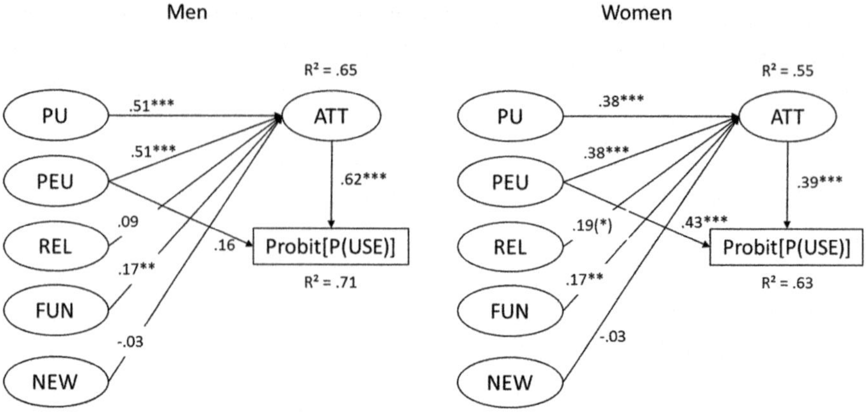

Fig. 11.3 Parameter estimates for model C
Note: Unstandardized path coefficients; *** $= p < 0.001$, ** $= p < 0.01$, * $= p < 0.05$, (*) $0.05 < p < 0.10$

the path coefficients are interpreted as the increase in the probit index (*z*-score) of the probability of USE of SST for a unit increase in attitude or PEU (as measured by a five point scale). Although the path coefficients are not identical for men and women, none of the coefficients were significantly different across groups (the chi-square difference test comparing a model with freely estimated coefficients and a model with invariant coefficients was $\Delta\chi^2(7) = 6.77$, $p = 0.45$). PU, PEU, and FUN have significant effects on ATT for both males and females and the effect of REL is marginal for women; the effect of NEW is non-significant for both men and women. PEU also has a direct effect on USE for women. In a bootstrap analysis based on 1000 bootstrap samples the effect of FUN on ATT for men is only marginal. The indirect effects of PU, PEU, and FUN are significant for both men and women, and the indirect effect of REL is marginal for women, based on a Sobel test. However, the indirect effects of PEU and FUN are fragile for men based on a bootstrap analysis with 1000 bootstrap samples (i.e., PEU is not significant and FUN is marginal), and the indirect effect of REL for women is nonsignificant. Note that the indirect effects are "naïve" indirect effects, not causally defined indirect effects (see Muthén and Asparouhov 2015). Figure 11.3 also reports the R^2's for the various endogenous constructs, which range from 0.55 to 0.71.

In summary, the findings show that perceptions of PU, PEU, and FUN determine consumers' attitude toward self-scanning technology, and that attitude influences actual use of self-scanning. PEU also has a direct effect on USE for women, but overall the structural model is largely invariant across genders.

11.6 Recent Applications of SEM and Computer Programs for SEM

Early reviews of SEM in marketing are provided by Baumgartner and Homburg (1996) and Hulland et al. (1996). An update of the Baumgartner and Homburg review, covering articles published in the major marketing journals until 2007, is available in Martínez-López et al. (2013). SEM is often used in scale development studies, and is particularly useful for examining measurement invariance of instruments in cross-cultural research (see Hult et al. 2008). SEM is also quite common in survey-based managerial research in marketing (see Homburg et al. 2013 for an example).

The empirical illustrations described in this chapter were estimated using MPlus 7.4 (https://www.statmodel.com). Several other programs exist and are commonly used for model estimation and testing, including:

- LISREL and SIMPLIS (http://www.ssicentral.com/lisrel);
- EQS (http://www.mvsoft.com);
- Mx (http://www.vcu.edu/mx).

Many popular general statistical modeling programs have modules for SEM, including:

- SPSS-Amos (http://www-03.ibm.com/software/products/en/spss-amos);
- Proc Calis in SAS (http://www.sas.com);
- SEM in Stata (http://www.stata.com);
- Lavaan in R (https://www.r-project.org).

All except Mx and R are commercial programs.

References

Anderson, J.C., Gerbing, D.W.: Structural equation modeling in practice: a review and recommended two-step approach. Psychol. Bull. **103**, 411–423 (1988)

Baumgartner, H., Homburg, C.: Applications of structural equation modeling in marketing and consumer research: a review. Int. J. Res. Mark. **13**, 139–161 (1996)

Baumgartner, H., Weijters, B.: Measurement models for marketing constructus. In: Wierenga, B., van der Lans, R. (eds.) Handbook of Marketing Decision Models, Springer, New York, forthcoming (2017)

Bollen, K.A.: Structural Equations with Latent Variables. Wiley, New York (1989)

Browne, M.W., Cudeck, R.: Alternative ways of assessing model fit. Sociol. Methods Res. **21**, 230–258 (1992)

Diamantopoulos, A., Riefler, P., Roth, K.P.: Advancing formative measurement models. J. Bus. Res. **61**, 1203–1218 (2008)

Fornell, C., Larcker, D.F.: Evaluating structural equation models with unobservable variables and measurement error. J. Mark. Res. **18**, 39–50 (1981)

Homburg, C., Stierl, M., Borneman, T.: Corporate social responsibility in business-to-business markets: how organizational customers account for supplier corporate social responsibility engagement. J. Mark. **77**(6), 54–72 (2013)
Hu, L.t., Bentler, P.M.: Cutoff criteria for fit indexes in covariance structure analysis: conventional criteria versus new alternatives. Struct. Equ. Model. **6**(1), 1–55 (1999)
Hulland, J., Chow, Y.H., Lam, S.: Use of causal models in marketing research: A review. Int. J. Res. Mark. **13**, 181–197 (1996)
Hult, G.T., Ketchen Jr., D.J., Griffith, D.A., Finnegan, C.A., Gonzalez-Padron, T., Harmancioglu, N., Huang, Y., Talay, M.B., Cavusgil, S.T.: Data equivalence in cross-cultural international business research: assessment and guidelines. J. Int. Bus. Stud. **39**, 1027–1044 (2008)
Jöreskog, K.G., Sörbom, D.: LISREL 8.8 for Windows [Computer Software]. Scientific Software International, Inc., Skokie, IL (2006)
Kamata, A., Bauer, D.J.: A note on the relation between factor analytic and item response theory models. Struct. Equ. Model. **15**(1), 136–153 (2008)
Klein, A., Moosbrugger, H.: Maximum likelihood estimation of latent interaction effects with the LMS method. Psychometrika. **65**, 457–474 (2000)
Marsh, H.W.: Confirmatory factor analyses of multitrait-multimethod data: many problems and a few solutions. Appl. Psychol. Meas. **13**, 335–361 (1989)
Marsh, H.W., Morin, A.J., Parker, P.D., Kaur, G.: Exploratory structural equation modeling: an integration of the best features of exploratory and confirmatory factor analysis. Annu. Rev. Clin. Psychol. **10**, 85–110 (2014)
Marsh, H.W., Wen, Z., Hau, K.-T., Nagengast, B.: Structural equation models of latent interaction and quadratic effects. In: Hancock, G.R., Mueller, R.O. (eds.) Structural Equation Modeling: A Second Course, 2nd edn, pp. 267–308. Information Age Publishing, Charlotte, NC (2013)
Martínez-López, F.J., Gázquez-Abad, J.C., Sousa, C.M.P.: Structural equation modelling in marketing and business research. Eur. J. Mark. **47**(1/2), 115–152 (2013)
Muthén, B., Asparouhov, T.: Bayesian structural equation modeling: a more flexible representation of substantive theory. Psychol. Methods. **17**(3), 313–335 (2012)
Muthén, B., Asparouhov, T.: Causal effects in mediation modeling: an introduction with applications to latent variables. Struct. Equ. Model. **22**, 12–23 (2015)
Steenkamp, J-B.E.M., Baumgartner, H.: Assessing measurement invariance in cross-national consumer research. J. Consum. Res. **25**, 78–90 (1998)
Weijters, B., Baumgartner, H., Schillewaert, N.: Reversed item bias: an integrative model. Psychol. Methods. **18**(3), 320–334 (2013)
Weijters, B., Rangarajan, D., Falk, T., Schillewaert, N.: Determinants and outcomes of customers' use of self-service technology in a retail setting. J. Serv. Res. **10**(August), 3–21 (2007)
Wu, A.D., Zumbo, B.D.: Thinking about item response theory from a logistic regression perspective. In: Sawilowsky, S.S. (ed.) Real Data Analysis, pp. 241–269. Information Age Publishing, Charlotte, NC (2007)

Chapter 12
Partial Least Squares Path Modeling

Jörg Henseler

12.1 Introduction

Structural equation modeling (SEM) is a family of statistical techniques that has become very popular in marketing. Its ability to model latent variables, to take various forms of measurement error into account, and to test entire theories makes it useful for a plethora of research questions. It does not come as a surprise that some of the most cited scholarly articles in the marketing domain are about SEM (e.g., Bagozzi and Yi 1988; Fornell and Larcker 1981), and that SEM is covered by two contributions within this volume. The need for two contributions arises from the SEM family tree having two major branches (Reinartz et al. 2009): covariance-based SEM (which is presented in Chap. 11) and variance-based SEM, which is presented in this chapter.

Covariance-based SEM estimates model parameters using the empirical variance–covariance matrix, and is the method of choice if the hypothesized model consists of one or more common factors. In contrast, variance-based SEM first creates proxies as linear combinations of observed variables, and then estimates the model parameters using these proxies. Variance-based SEM is the method of choice if the hypothesized model contains composites. Of the variance-based SEM methods, partial least squares path modeling (PLS) is regarded as the "most fully developed and general system" (McDonald 1996, p. 240), and is the subject of this contribution.

A distinguishing PLS characteristic is its ability to include both factors and composites in a structural equation model (Dijkstra and Henseler 2015a, 2015b). Factors can be used to model latent variables of behavioral research, such as

J. Henseler (✉)
Department of Design, Production and Management, University of Twente, Drienerlolaan 5, Enschede 7522 NB, The Netherlands
e-mail: j.henseler@utwente.nl

P.S.H. Leeflang et al. (eds.), *Advanced Methods for Modeling Markets*,
International Series in Quantitative Marketing, DOI 10.1007/978-3-319-53469-5_12

attitudes or personality traits. Another term for this type of model is reflective measurement. Composites can be applied to model abstractions of artifacts such as plans, strategies, value, portfolios, and marketing instruments in general (Henseler 2015). In this vein, Albers (2010) recommends PLS as the preferred statistical tool for success factor studies in marketing. Composites are the core of composite–formative measurement (Bollen and Diamantopoulos 2017).

Recently, PLS has undergone a series of serious examinations, and has been the topic of heated scientific debates (Henseler et al. 2016). Scholars have discussed the conceptual underpinnings (Rigdon 2012, 2014; Sarstedt et al. 2014), the strengths and weaknesses (Henseler et al. 2014; Rigdon et al. 2014), and the use of PLS as a statistical method (Hair et al. 2012a, 2012b). As a fruitful outcome of these debates, substantial contributions to PLS emerged, such as bootstrap-based tests of the overall model fit (Dijkstra and Henseler 2015a), consistent PLS with which to estimate factor models (PLSc, see Dijkstra and Henseler 2015b), and the heterotrait–monotrait ratio of correlations as a new criterion for discriminant validity (HTMT, see Henseler et al. 2015). These new developments call for updated guidelines on why, when, and how to use PLS in marketing research.

The purpose of this chapter is manifold. In Sect. 12.2, it provides an updated view on what PLS actually is and the algorithmic steps it has included since the invention of consistent PLS. In Sect. 12.3, it explains how to specify PLS path models, taking the nature of the measurement models (composite vs. factor), model identification, sign indeterminacy, and special treatments of categorical variables into account. In Sect. 12.4, it explains how to assess and report PLS results, including the novel bootstrap-based tests of model fit, the SRMR as an approximate measure of model fit, the new reliability coefficient rho_A, and the HTMT. In Sect. 12.5, we discuss the various publicly available software implementations. An example application of PLS to illustrate its use is given in Sect. 12.6. Finally, Sect. 12.7 provides a concluding discussion.

12.2 The Partial Least Squares Path Modeling Method

The core of PLS is a set of alternating least squares algorithms that emulates and extends principal component analysis, as well as canonical correlation analysis. Herman Wold (1974, 1982) invented the method, which has undergone various extensions and modifications, to analyze high dimensional data in a low-structure environment. In its most modern appearance (see Dijkstra and Henseler 2015a, 2015b), PLS path modeling can be understood as a full-fledged structural equation modeling method that can handle both factor models and composite models for construct measurement, can estimate recursive and non-recursive structural models, and conduct exact tests of model fit.

PLS path models are formally defined by two sets of linear equations: the measurement model (also called the outer model) and the structural model (also called the inner model). The measurement model specifies the relations between

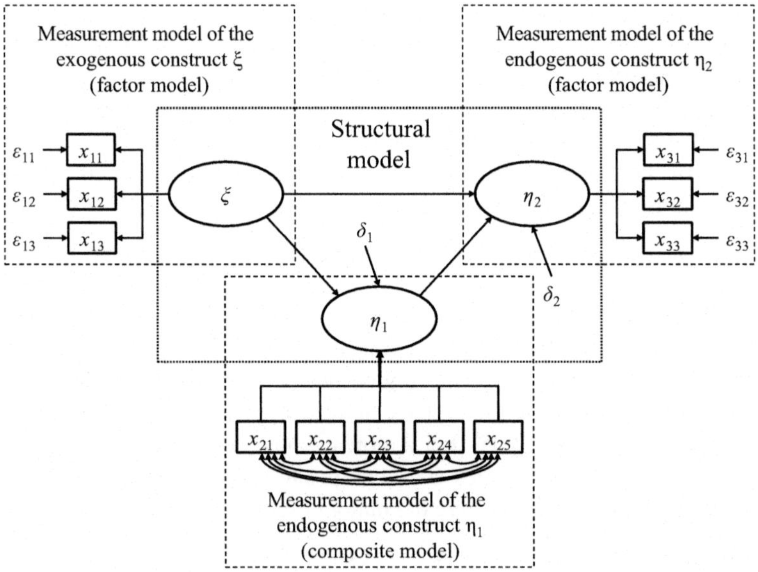

Fig. 12.1 PLS path model example

a construct and its observed indicators (also called manifest variables), whereas the structural model specifies the relationships between the constructs. Figure 12.1 depicts an example of a PLS path model.

The structural model consists of exogenous and endogenous constructs, as well as the relationships between them. The values of exogenous constructs are assumed to be given from outside the model. Thus, other constructs in the model do not explain exogenous variables, and no arrows in the structural model should point to exogenous constructs. In contrast, other constructs in the model explain endogenous constructs at least partially. Each endogenous construct must have at least one of the structural model's arrow pointing to it. The relationships between the constructs are usually assumed to be linear. The size and significance of path relationships are typically the focus of the scientific endeavors pursued in empirical research.

PLS path models can contain two different forms of construct measurement: factor models and composite models (see Rigdon 2012, for a nice comparison of both types of measurement models). The factor model hypothesizes that the existence of one unobserved variable (the common factor) and indicator-specific random error perfectly explain the variance of a block of indicators. This is the standard model of behavioral research. The term reflective measurement model is also often used. In Fig. 12.1, the exogenous construct ξ and the endogenous construct η_2 are modeled as factors. In contrast, composites are formed as linear combinations of their respective indicators. The composite model does not impose any restrictions on the covariances between indicators of the same construct, i.e., it relaxes the assumption that a common factor explains all the covariation between a block of indicators.

The estimation of PLS path model parameters is done in four steps: An iterative algorithm that determines the composite scores of each construct, a correction for attenuation of those constructs modeled as factors (Dijkstra and Henseler 2015b), parameter estimation, and bootstrapping for inference testing.

Step 1 For each construct, the iterative PLS algorithm creates a proxy as a linear combination of the observed indicators. The indicator weights are determined such that each proxy shares as much variance as possible with the proxies of causally related constructs. The PLS algorithm can be viewed as an approach to extend canonical correlation analysis to more than two sets of variables; it can emulate several of Kettenring's (1971) techniques for the canonical analysis of several sets of variables (Tenenhaus et al. 2005). For a more detailed description of the algorithm, see Henseler (2010). The proxies (i.e., composite scores), the proxy correlation matrix, and the indicator weights are the major output of the first step.

Step 2 Correcting for attenuation is a necessary step if a model involves factors. As long as the indicators contain random measurement error, so will the proxies. Consequently, proxy correlations are usually underestimations of factor correlations. Consistent PLS (PLSc) corrects this tendency (Dijkstra and Henseler 2015a, 2015b) by dividing a proxy's correlations with other proxies by the square root of its reliability (also known as the correction for attenuation). PLSc addresses the issue of what the correlation between constructs would be if there were no random measurement error. The major output of this second step is a consistent construct correlation matrix.

Step 3 Once a consistent construct correlation matrix is available, it is possible to estimate the model parameters. If the structural model is recursive (i.e., there are no feedback loops), ordinary least squares (OLS) regression can be used to obtain consistent parameter estimates of the structural paths. In the case of non-recursive models, instrumental variable techniques, such as two-stage least squares (2SLS), should be employed. Beside the path coefficient estimates, this third step can also provide estimates of loadings, indirect effects, total effects, and several model assessment criteria.

Step 4 Finally, the bootstrap is applied in order to obtain inference statistics for all the model parameters. The bootstrap is a non-parametric inferential technique based on the assumption that the sample distribution conveys information about the population distribution. Bootstrapping is the process of drawing a large number of re-samples with replacement from the original sample, and then estimating the model parameters for each bootstrap re-sample. The standard error of an estimate is inferred from the standard deviation of the bootstrap estimates.

The PLS path modeling algorithm has favorable convergence properties (Henseler 2010). However, as soon as PLS path models involve common factors, there is the possibility of Heywood cases (Krijnen et al. 1998), meaning that one or more of the variances that the model implies could be negative. An atypical, or too-small sample, may cause the occurrence of Heywood cases, or the common factor structure may not hold for a particular block of indicators.

PLS path modeling is not as efficient as maximum likelihood covariance-based structural equation modeling. One possibility is to further minimize the discrepancy between the empirical and the model-implied correlation matrix, an approach that efficient PLS follows (PLSe, see Bentler and Huang 2014). Alternatively, one could embrace the notion that PLS is a limited-information estimator and that model misspecification in some subparts of a model affects it less (Antonakis et al. 2010). Ultimately, there is no clear-cut resolution of the issues on this trade-off between efficiency and robustness with respect to model misspecification.

12.3 Specifying PLS Path Models

The analysts must ensure that the specified statistical model complies with the conceptual model intended to be tested, and further, that the model complies with the technical requirements such as identification, and with the data conforming to the required format and offering sufficient statistical power.

Typically, the structural model is theory-based and is the prime focus of the research question and/or research hypotheses. The specification of the structural model addresses two questions: Which constructs should be included in the model? And how are they hypothesized to be interrelated? That is, what are the directions and strengths of the causal influences between and among the constructs? In general, analysts should keep in mind that the constructs specified in a model are only proxies, and that there will always be a validity gap between these proxies and the theoretical concepts that are the intended modeling target (Rigdon 2012). The paths, specified as arrows in a PLS model, represent directional linear relationships between these proxies. The structural model and the indicated relationships among the constructs are regarded as separate from the measurement model.

The specification of the measurement model entails deciding on composite or factor models and assigning indicators to constructs. Factor models are the predominant measurement model for behavioral constructs such as attitudes or personality traits. Factor models are strongly linked to true score theory (McDonald 1999), the most important measurement paradigm in behavioral sciences. If a construct has this background and random measurement error is likely to be an issue, analysts should choose the factor model. In contrast composites help model emergent constructs, for which elements are combined to form a new entity (Henseler 2017). Composites can be applied to model strong concepts (Höök and Löwgren 2012), i.e., the abstraction of artifacts. Whenever a model contains this type of construct, it is preferable to opt for a composite model.

Measurement models of PLS path models may appear less detailed than those of covariance-based structural equation modeling, but some specifications are implicit and not visualized. For instance, neither the unique indicator errors (nor their correlations) of factor models, nor the correlations between the indicators of composite models are drawn. Structural disturbance terms are assumed to be orthogonal to their predictor variables, as well as to each other[1]; and correlations between exogenous variables are free. Because PLS does not currently allow either constraining these parameters, or freeing the error correlations of factor models, these model elements are, by convention, not drawn. No matter which type of measurement is chosen to measure a construct, PLS requires at least one indicator. Constructs without indicators, also called phantom variables (Rindskopf 1984), cannot be included in PLS path models.

Identification has always been an important issue for SEM, although it was previously neglected in the realm of PLS path modeling. It refers to the necessity to specify a model such that only one set of estimates exists that yields the same model-implied correlation matrix. A complete model might be unidentified, as might only parts of it. In general, it is not possible to derive useful conclusions from unidentified (parts of) models. In order to achieve identification, PLS fixes the variance of factors and composites to one. A nomological net is an important requirement of composite models. This means that composites cannot be estimated in isolation, but need at least one relation with another variable. Since PLS also estimates factor models via composites, this requirement extends to all factor models estimated by using PLS. If a factor model has exactly two indicators, it does not matter which form of measurement model is used—a nomological net is then required to achieve identification. If only one indicator measures a construct, this is called a single-indicator measurement (Diamantopoulos et al. 2012). The construct scores are then identical to the standardized indicator values. In this case, the amount of random measurement error in this indicator cannot be determined. If an indicator contains measurement error, the only possibility to account for the error is to utilize external knowledge about this indicator's reliability and to manually define this.

A typical characteristic of SEM, and factor-analytical tools in general, is sign-indeterminacy, in which the weight, or loading estimates, of a factor or a composite can only be unanimously determined regarding their value, but not regarding their sign. For example, if a factor is extracted from the strongly negatively correlated customer satisfaction indicators "How satisfied are you with provider X?" and "How much does provider X differ from an ideal provider?," the method cannot "know" whether the extracted factor should correlate positively with the first or with the second indicator. Depending on the sign of the loadings, the meaning of the factor would either be "customer satisfaction" or "customer non-satisfaction." To avoid this ambiguity, it has become practice in SEM to determine a particular indicator per construct, with which the construct scores are then forced to correlate positively.

---

[1]This assumption should be relaxed in the case of non-recursive models (Dijkstra and Henseler 2015a).

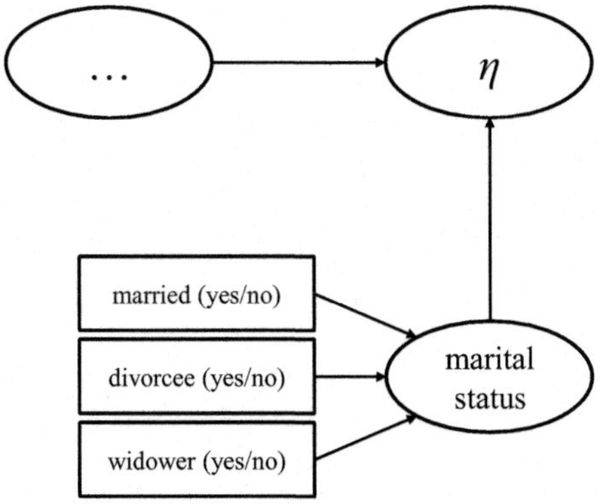

Fig. 12.2 Including a categorical variable in a PLS path model
Note: Marital status with the four categories "unmarried," "married," "divorcee," "widower"; the reference category is "unmarried"

Since this indicator dictates the orientation of the construct, it is called the dominant indicator. Whereas, in covariance-based structural equation modeling, this dominant indicator also dictates the construct's variance, in PLS path modeling the construct variance is simply set to one.

Like multiple regression, PLS path modeling requires metric data for the dependent variables. Dependent variables are the indicators of the factor model(s), as well as the endogenous constructs. Quasi-metric data stemming from multi-point scales, such as Likert scales or semantic differential scales, are also acceptable as long as the scale points can be assumed to be equidistant and there are five or more scale points (Rhemtulla et al. 2012). To some extent it is also possible to include categorical variables in a model. Categorical variables are particularly relevant for analyzing experiments (see Streukens et al. 2010), or for control variables. Figure 12.2 illustrates how a categorical variable "marital status" would be included in a PLS path model. If a categorical variable has only two levels (i.e., it is dichotomous), it can immediately serve as a construct indicator. If a categorical variable has more than two levels, it should be transformed into as many dummy variables as there are levels. A composite model is built from all but one dummy variable. The remaining dummy variable characterizes the reference level. Preferably, categorical variables should only play the role of exogenous variables in a structural model.

12.4 Assessing and Reporting PLS Analyses

PLS path modeling can be used for both explanatory and predictive research. The model assessment will differ depending on the analyst's aim—explanation or prediction. Since PLS applications in marketing mainly focus on explanation (Hair et al. 2012b), in the remainder, we concentrate on model assessment given that the analyst's aim is explanation.

12.4.1 Assessing Overall Model Fit

PLS results can be assessed globally (i.e., for the overall model) and locally (separately for the measurement model and the structural model). Since, in the form described above, PLS provides consistent estimates for factor and composite models, it is possible to meaningfully compare the model-implied correlation matrix with the empirical correlation matrix, which opens up the possibility to assess the global model fit.

The model's overall goodness of fit should be the starting point of model assessment. If the model does not fit the data, the data contain more information than the model conveys. The obtained estimates may be meaningless, in which case the conclusions drawn from them become questionable. The global model fit can be assessed in two non-exclusive ways: by means of inference statistics, i.e., tests of the model fit, or through the use of fit indices, i.e., an assessment of the approximate model fit. In order to have some frame of reference, it has become customary to determine the model fit for both the estimated model and the saturated model. Saturation refers to the structural model, which means that, in the saturated model, all the constructs correlate freely. Any lack of fit of the saturated model can only be attributed to the construct measurement. Hence, the saturated model is most suitable for assessing the measurement model, whereas the estimated model also allows to quantify the fit of the structural model.

Tests of the overall model fit of PLS path models rely on the bootstrap to determine the likelihood of obtaining a discrepancy between the empirical and the model-implied correlation matrix that is as high as the that obtained for the sample at hand, if the hypothesized model were indeed correct (Dijkstra and Henseler 2015a). Bootstrap samples are drawn from modified sample data. This modification entails an orthogonalization of all variables and a subsequent imposition of the model-implied correlation matrix. In covariance-based SEM, this approach is known as the Bollen–Stine bootstrap (Bollen and Stine 1992). If more than five percent (or a different percentage if an alpha level different from 0.05 is chosen) of the bootstrap samples yield discrepancy values above the ones of the actual model, the sample data are likely to stem from a population that functions according to the hypothesized model. The model thus cannot be rejected.

There is more than one way to quantify the discrepancy between two matrices, for instance, the maximum likelihood discrepancy, the geodesic discrepancy d_G, or the unweighted least squares discrepancy d_{ULS} (Dijkstra and Henseler 2015a), and there are consequently several tests of model fit. Monte Carlo simulations confirm that the tests of model fit can indeed discriminate between well-fitting and ill-fitting models (Henseler et al. 2014). More precisely, both measurement model misspecification and structural model misspecification can be detected by testing the model fit (Dijkstra and Henseler 2014). Since different tests might lead to different results, a transparent reporting practice should always include several tests.

Beside conducting model fit tests, the approximate model fit can also be determined. Approximate model fit criteria help answer the question of how substantial the discrepancy between the model-implied and the empirical correlation matrix is. This question is particularly relevant if this discrepancy is significant, or if a too small sample size and the subsequently low statistical power renders the model fit tests too liberal. Currently, in the context of PLS, the dominant approximate model fit criterion is the standardized root mean square residual (SRMR, Hu and Bentler 1998, 1999). As can be derived from its name, the SRMR is the square root of the sum of the squared differences between the model-implied and the empirical correlation matrix, i.e., the Euclidean distance between the two matrices. A value of 0 for the SRMR would indicate a perfect fit, and generally an SRMR value less than 0.05 indicates an acceptable fit (Byrne 2013). However, even entirely correctly specified PLS path models can yield SRMR values of 0.06 and higher (Henseler et al. 2014). Therefore, a cut-off value of 0.08, which Hu and Bentler (1999) propose, appears to be more adequate for PLS. Another useful approximate model fit criterion could be the Bentler–Bonett index, or the normed fit index (NFI, Bentler and Bonett 1980), which Lohmöller (1989) suggested using in connection with PLS path modeling. NFI values above 0.90 are considered acceptable for factor models (Byrne 2013). Thresholds for the NFI are still to be determined regarding composite models. Further, the NFI does not penalize the adding of parameters and should thus be used with caution for model comparisons. In general, the usage of the NFI is still rare.[2] The root mean square error correlation (RMS_{theta}, see Lohmöller 1989) is another promising approximate model fit criterion. While the RMS_{theta} can distinguish well-specified from ill-specified models (Henseler et al. 2014), the RMS_{theta} thresholds are yet to be determined, and PLS software has not yet implemented this approximate model fit criterion. Note that early suggestions for PLS-based goodness-of-fit measures, such as the "goodness-of-fit" (GoF, see Tenenhaus et al. 2004) or the "relative goodness-of-fit" (GoF_{rel}, proposed by Esposito Vinzi et al. 2010), are—contrary to what they seem to suggest—not informative about the goodness of the model fit (Henseler et al. 2014; Henseler and Sarstedt 2013). Consequently, there is no reason to evaluate and report them if the analyst's aim is to test or compare models.

12.4.2 Assessing Measurement Models

If the specified measurement (or outer) model does not have the minimum required properties of acceptable reliability and validity, the structural (inner) model estimates become meaningless. That is, a necessary condition before starting to assess the "goodness" of the inner structural model is that the outer measurement model should already demonstrate acceptable levels of reliability and validity. There must be a sound measurement model before one can begin to assess the "goodness" of the inner structural model, or can rely on the magnitude, direction, and/or statistical

[2]For an application of the NFI, see Ziggers and Henseler (2016).

strength of the structural model's estimated parameters. Factor and composite models are assessed differently.

Factor models can be assessed in various ways. The bootstrap-based tests of overall model fit (of the saturated model) can indicate whether the data are coherent with a factor model, i.e., it represents a confirmatory factor analysis. In essence, the test of model fit provides an answer to the question "Does empirical evidence negate the existence of the factor?" This quest for truth illustrates that the factor model testing is rooted in the positivist research paradigm. If the overall model fit test does not provide evidence negating the existence of a factor,[3] several questions regarding the factor structure emerge: Do the data support a factor structure at all? Can one clear factor be consistently extracted? How well has this factor been measured? Note that tests of overall model fit cannot answer these questions; specifically, entirely uncorrelated empirical variables do not necessarily lead to the factor model's rejection. To answer these questions, one should instead rely on various local assessment criteria regarding the reliability and validity of measurement.

The amount of random error in the construct scores should be acceptable; that is, the reliability of the construct scores should be sufficiently high. Nunnally and Bernstein (1994) recommend a minimum reliability of 0.7. The most important PLS reliability measure is rho_A (Dijkstra and Henseler 2015b), which is currently the only consistent reliability measure of PLS construct scores. The reliability measure rho_A is an estimate for the squared correlation of the PLS construct score with the (unknown) true construct score. Most PLS software also provides a measure of composite reliability (also called Dillon-Goldstein's rho, factor reliability, Jöreskog's rho, omega, or rho_c), as well as Cronbach's alpha. Both refer to sum scores, not composite scores. In particular, Cronbach's alpha typically underestimates the true reliability, and should therefore only be regarded as a lower boundary of the reliability (Sijtsma 2009).

The measurement of factors should also be free of systematic measurement error. This quest for validity can be fulfilled in several non-exclusive ways. First, a factor should be unidimensional, a characteristic that convergent validity examines. The dominant measure of convergent validity is the average variance extracted (AVE, Fornell and Larcker 1981).[4] If the first factor extracted from a set of indicators explains more than one half of their variance, there cannot be a second, equally important, factor. An AVE of 0.5 or higher is therefore regarded as acceptable. Sahmer et al. (2006) proposed a somewhat more liberal criterion: They find evidence of unidimensionality as long as a factor explains significantly more variance than the second factor extracted from the same block of indicators. Second, each pair

[3]Interestingly, the methodological literature on factor models hardly mentions what to do if the test rejects a factor model. Some researchers suggest considering a composite model as an alternative, because it is less restrictive (Henseler et al. 2014) and not subject to factor indeterminacy (Rigdon 2012). Others suggest allowing small deviations without principally questioning the factor model (see Asparouhov et al. 2015).

[4]The AVE must be calculated based on consistent loadings, otherwise the assessment of convergent and discriminant validity based on the AVE is meaningless.

of factors that represent theoretically different concepts should also be statistically different, which raises the question of discriminant validity. Two criteria have been shown to be informative about discriminant validity (Voorhees et al. 2016): The Fornell–Larcker criterion (proposed by Fornell and Larcker 1981) and the heterotrait–monotrait ratio of correlations (HTMT, developed by Henseler et al. 2015). The Fornell-Larcker criterion maintains that a factor's AVE should be higher than its squared correlations with all other factors in the model. The HTMT is an estimate of the factor correlation (more precisely, an upper boundary). In order to clearly discriminate between two factors, the HTMT should be significantly smaller than one. Third, the cross-loadings should be assessed to ensure that no indicator is incorrectly assigned.

The assessment of composite models is somewhat less developed. Again, the major point of departure should be the tests of model fit. The tests of the model fit of the saturated model provide evidence of the composites' external validity. Henseler et al. (2014) call this step a "confirmatory composite analysis." For composite models, the major research question is "Does it make sense to create this composite?" This question shows that testing composite models follows a different research paradigm, namely pragmatism (Henseler 2015). Once confirmatory composite analysis has provided support for the composite, it can be analyzed further. Some follow-up questions present themselves: How is the composite built? Do all the ingredients contribute significantly and substantially? To answer these questions, an analyst should assess the sign and the magnitude of the indicator weights, as well as their significance. If indicator weights have unexpected signs, or are insignificant, this can specifically be due to multicollinearity. It is therefore recommendable to assess the variance inflation factor (VIF) of the indicators. VIF values far higher than one indicate that multicollinearity might play a role. In this case, analysts should consider using correlation weights (PLS Mode A, see Rigdon 2012), or the best fitting proper indices (Dijkstra and Henseler 2011) to estimate the indicator weights.

12.4.3 Assessing Structural Models

Once the measurement model is deemed of sufficient quality, the analyst can proceed and assess the structural model. If OLS is used for the structural model, the endogenous constructs' R^2 values would be the point of departure. They indicate the percentage of variability accounted for by the precursor constructs in the model. The adjusted R^2 values take the model complexity and sample size into account, and are thus helpful to compare different models, or the explanatory power of a model across different datasets.

The path coefficients are essentially standardized regression coefficients, which can be assessed with regard to their sign and their absolute size. They should be interpreted as the change in the dependent variable if the independent variable is increased by one and all other independent variables remain constant. Indirect effects and their inference statistics are important for mediation analysis (Nitzl et al. 2016; Zhao et al. 2010), while total effects are useful for successful factor analysis (Albers 2010).

If the analyst's aim is to generalize from a sample to a population, the path coefficients should be evaluated for significance. Inference statistics include the empirical bootstrap confidence intervals, as well as one-sided or two-sided p-values. We recommend using 4999 bootstrap samples. This number is sufficiently close to infinity for usual situations, is tractable with regard to computation time, and allows for a unanimous determination of empirical bootstrap confidence intervals (for instance, the 2.5% [97.5%] quantile would be the 125th [4875th] element of the sorted list of bootstrap values). A path coefficient is regarded as significant (i.e., unlikely to purely result from sampling error) if its confidence interval does not include the value of zero, or if the p-value is below the pre-defined alpha level. Despite strong pleas for the use of confidence intervals (Cohen 1994), reporting p-values still seems to be more common in business research.

It makes sense to quantify how substantial the significant effects are, which can be done by assessing their effect size f^2. Effect size values above 0.35, 0.15, and 0.02 can be regarded as respectively strong, moderate, and weak (Cohen 1988).

Finally, recent research confirms that PLS is a promising technique for prediction purposes (Becker et al. 2013). Blindfolding is the standard approach used to examine if the model, or a single effect of it, can predict the values of reflective indicators (Tenenhaus et al. 2005). It is already widely applied (Hair et al. 2012b; Ringle et al. 2012). Criteria for the predictive capability of structural models have been proposed (see Chin 2010), but still need to be disseminated. Once business and social science researchers' interest in prediction becomes more pronounced, PLS is likely to face an additional substantial increase in popularity.

12.5 PLS Software

There is quite a variety of PLS software available, each of which has unique advantages and disadvantages. The first widely available PLS software was LVPLS (Lohmöller 1988), which did not yet contain a graphical user interface. The further development of the program was discontinued after the early death of the program author. Since the original code is no longer available, changes to the calculation of LVPLS are hardly possible. However, Wynne Chin substantially increased the usability of LVPLS by embedding it into a graphical user interface called PLS-Graph (Chin and Frye 2003). PLS-Graph was the dominant software at the end of the last millennium. Its limited improvement and extension possibilities motivated Christian Ringle and his team to develop a new PLS software, called SmartPLS, from scratch (Ringle et al. 2005). Later, other PLS applications emerged, such as PLS-GUI, WarpPLS, and XLSTAT-PLS.

When specifying the model, analysts should keep in mind that, in some PLS path modeling software (e.g., SmartPLS, PLS-Graph, and XLSTAT-PLS), the depicted direction of the arrows in the measurement model does not indicate whether a factor or composite model is estimated. Instead, the arrow directions indicate whether correlation weights (Mode A, represented by arrows pointing from a construct to its indicators) or regression weights (Mode B, represented by arrows pointing from indicators to their construct) should be used to create the proxy. Mode A uses a set of simple regressions to determine the indicator weights, whereas Mode B uses a multiple regression. PLS will estimate a composite model in both cases. Indicator weights estimated by Mode B are consistent (Dijkstra 2010), whereas indicator weights estimated by Mode A are usually not consistent. However, the latter excel at out-of-sample prediction (Rigdon 2012).

Of all the PLS programs with graphical user interface, SmartPLS 3.2 (Ringle et al. 2015) is currently the most comprehensive software. It contains many extensions of PLS, such as analysis of interaction effects (Henseler and Chin 2010; Henseler and Fassott 2010), analysis of nonlinear effects (Henseler et al. 2012a), multigroup analysis (Henseler 2012a; Sarstedt et al. 2011), assessment of measurement invariance (Jean et al. 2016), importance-performance matrix analysis (Ringle and Sarstedt 2016), and diagnostics for predictive research like blindfolding (Tenenhaus et al. 2005). However, if an analyst undertakes confirmatory research, SmartPLS is not optimally suitable, because the model fit tests are not implemented (version 3.2). Analysts may prefer ADANCO (Henseler and Dijkstra 2015), a new software for variance-based SEM, which also includes PLS path modeling. ADANCO has implemented all goodness-of-fit criteria presented in this contribution, including the tests of the overall model fit.

12.6 Empirical Application

A researcher wants to explore whether there is a relationship between customer focus and firm performance. The researcher has empirical data from 176 key informants. These data include six reflective indicators of the customer focus; measures of return on investment, the profit margin, the profit, and the market capitalization; and a categorical variable capturing the industry.

Figure 12.3 depicts the model as specified, using ADANCO 2.0. It consists of the endogenous construct firm performance as a composite of return on investment, the profit margin, the profit, and the market capitalization; the exogenous construct customer focus measured by the six reflective indicators; and a control variable industry composed of a set of dummy variables like the set proposed in Fig. 12.2. Figure 12.3 also shows the most relevant model estimates: path coefficients (and their significance), weights (of the composite models), and loadings (of the factor models).

The assessment of the construct measurement focuses on two major questions: Can we clearly extract one factor from our six customer focus indicators? And is it reasonable to create a firm performance composite as a linear combination of return on investment, the profit margin, the profit, and the market capitalization? The

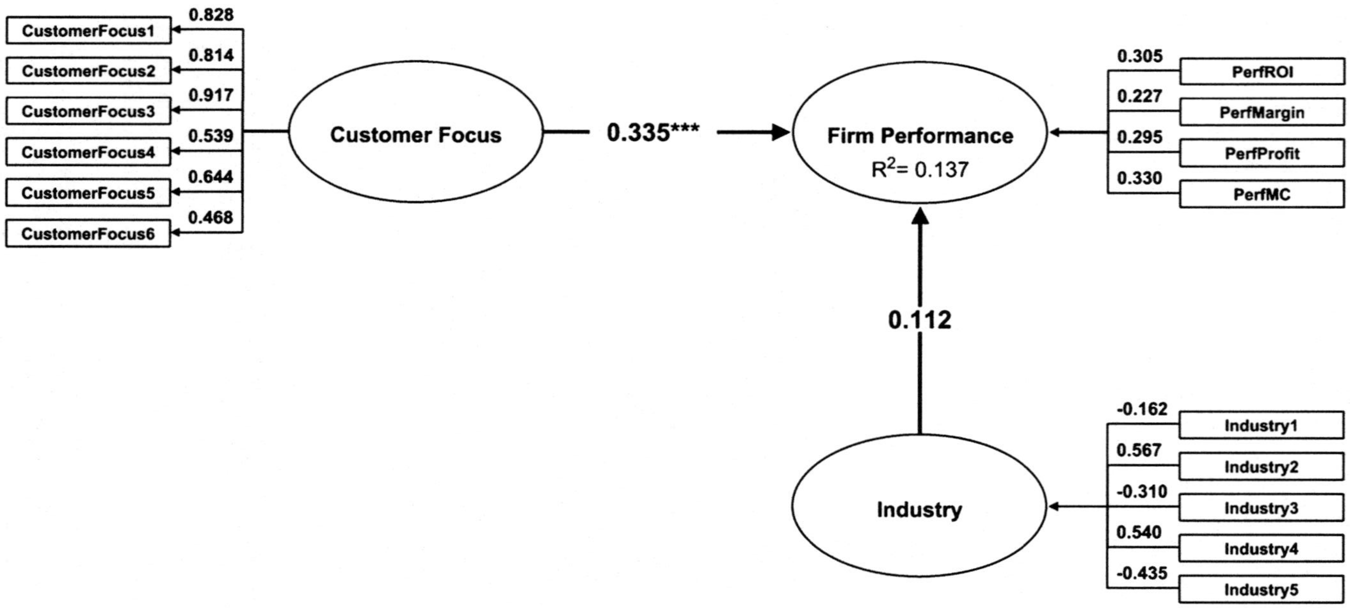

Fig. 12.3 Example model as specified, using ADANCO 2.0

overall model fit tests of the saturated model simultaneously conduct confirmatory factor analysis (to answer the first question) and confirmatory composite analysis (to answer the second question). ADANCO provides three measures of discrepancy between the empirical and the model-implied correlation matrix, together with the 95% quantile of its distribution if the model is correct (HI_{95}): an SRMR value of 0.069 ($HI_{95} = 0.100$), a d_{ULS} value of 0.575 ($HI_{95} = 1.192$), and a d_G value of 0.285 ($HI_{95} = 0.586$). All three measures of discrepancy are below their corresponding HI_{95} values, which means that the discrepancy between the empirical and the model-implied correlation matrix is not significant. This implies that the information loss owing to the composite of firm success is negligible, and can be defended to form this composite.

Since the customer focus construct is operationalized using a factor model, we can apply the criteria for reliability and construct validity. The reliability coefficient ρ_A is 0.890, which implies a high degree of reliability. This is higher than ρ_c (0.860) and α (0.869), which means that it is worth the effort to create the construct scores as a weighted sum of its indicators instead of pure sum scores. The average variance extracted is 0.519, which provides evidence of the unidimensionality of the customer focus construct. Since customer focus is the only construct operationalized using a factor model, neither the Fornell-Larcker criterion, nor the HTMT can be applied to assess discriminant validity. However, given the inter-construct correlations below 0.4, there is hardly any basis for doubts about the discriminant validity. Overall, the construct measurement can be deemed valid.

Once we have sufficient certainty about the quality of the construct measurement, we can assess the structural model. Because the structural model is saturated, the overall model fit of the estimated model equals that of the saturated model. This implies that the overall model fit does not inform about the structural model. However, this would only be a problem if the researcher's aim is confirmatory research. A local assessment of the structural model provides sufficient insight regarding exploratory research. First, we look at the coefficient of determination (R^2 value) of the endogenous variable, namely firm performance. While the obtained R^2 value of 0.137 may not be large, it is certainly worthwhile interpreting this value relatively to the R^2 values obtained in comparable studies, because normally achieved R^2 values tend to vary across disciplines and phenomena.

Inference statistics based on 4999 bootstrap samples indicate that the effect of customer focus on firm performance is significant ($p < 0.001$), whereas firm performance does not vary significantly across industries. The f^2 value of the effect of customer focus on firm performance is 0.127, which means that its effect size is small to moderate. The path coefficient of 0.335 means that if one of two firms in the same industry succeeds in increasing its customer focus by one standard deviation, it will gain an increase in firm performance of 0.335 standard deviations.

12.7 Further Applications and Outlook

Traditionally, national customer satisfaction indices have been the dominant field of PLS path model application in marketing. From the beginning, PLS path modeling has been the method of choice of the Swedish Customer Satisfaction Index (Fornell 1992), and continues to be the method of choice for successors, such as the American Customer Satisfaction Index (Fornell et al. 1996), the European Customer Satisfaction Index (Tenenhaus et al. 2005), and the Portuguese Customer Satisfaction Index (Coelho and Henseler 2012). However, the use of PLS is in no way limited to customer satisfaction indices. Hair et al. (2012b) identified hundreds of PLS path models reported in the leading marketing journals. Moreover, PLS is applied in various marketing subdisciplines, such as advertising (Henseler et al. 2012b) and international marketing (Henseler et al. 2009). Some studies are particularly worth naming:

- Rego (1998) reports the probably smallest PLS path model in the marketing literature. It consists of two constructs, market structure and market efficiency. This model provides evidence for both a negative linear and a negative quadratic effect of market structure on market efficiency.
- Hennig-Thurau et al. (2006) investigate to what extent two facets of employee emotions, namely service employees' display of positive emotions and the authenticity of their emotional labor, influence customers' assessments of service encounters. They use PLS to analyze the outcomes of an experiment. Bagozzi et al. (1991) show how PLS can be used to analyze marketing and consumer data obtained from experimental designs. Updated guidelines have been proposed by Streukens and Leroi-Werelds (2016).
- Ulaga and Eggert (2006) use PLS to develop and validate a higher-order construct "relationship value" in order to help firms differentiate in business relationships. This paper is also one example for the many papers in B2B marketing using PLS.
- In another B2B marketing paper, Smith and Barclay (1997) use PLS to analyze dyadic relationships to explore the role of trust in selling alliances.
- Johnson et al. (2006) use PLS to demonstrate that perceived value early in the customer life cycle affects loyalty intentions of mobile phone customers. Their paper is one of the relatively few who apply PLS to longitudinal data. Roemer (2016) offers a tutorial on how to analyze longitudinal data using PLS.

Marketing is not the only business research discipline that relies strongly on PLS as an analysis method. Neighboring disciplines, such as purchasing (Kaufmann and Gaeckler 2015), operations management (Peng and Lai 2012), and strategic management (Hair et al. 2012a; Hulland 1999), are also increasingly applying PLS path modeling.

The modularity of PLS path modeling, as introduced in the second section, opens up the possibility of replacing one or more steps with other approaches. For instance, the least squares estimators of the third step could be replaced with neural networks (Buckler and Hennig-Thurau 2008; Turkyilmaz et al. 2013). One could even replace the PLS algorithm in Step 1 with alternative indicator weight generators, such as principal component analysis (Tenenhaus 2008), generalized structured component analysis (Henseler 2012b; Hwang and Takane 2004), regularized generalized canonical correlation analysis (Tenenhaus and Tenenhaus 2011), or even plain sum scores. Since the iterative PLS algorithm would not serve as an eponym in these instances, one can no longer refer to PLS path modeling. However, it is still variance-based structural equation modeling.

Acknowledgments Major parts of this paper are taken from Henseler et al. (2016). The author acknowledges a financial interest in ADANCO and its distributor, Composite Modeling.

References

Albers, S.: PLS and success factor studies in marketing. In: Esposito Vinzi, V., Chin, W.W., Henseler, J., Wang, H. (eds.) Handbook of Partial Least Squares, pp. 409–425. Springer, Berlin (2010)

Antonakis, J., Bendahan, S., Jacquart, P., Lalive, R.: On making causal claims: a review and recommendations. Leadership Quart. **21**, 1086–1120 (2010)

Asparouhov, T., Muthén, B., Morin, A.J.S.: Bayesian structural equation modeling with cross-loadings and residual covariances: comments on Stromeyer et al. J. Manag. **41**, 1561–1577 (2015)

Bagozzi, R.P., Yi, Y.: On the evaluation of structural equation models. J. Acad. Mark. Sci. **16**, 74–94 (1988)

Bagozzi, R.P., Yi, Y., Singh, S.: On the use of structural equation models in experimental designs: two extensions. Int. J. Res. Mark. **8**, 125–140 (1991)

Becker, J.-M., Rai, A., Rigdon, E.E.: Predictive validity and formative measurement in structural equation modeling: embracing practical relevance. Paper presented at the International Conference on Information Systems, Milan, Italy (2013)

Bentler, P.M., Bonett, D.G.: Significance tests and goodness of fit in the analysis of covariance structures. Psychol. Bull. **88**, 588–606 (1980)

Bentler, P.M., Huang, W.: On components, latent variables, PLS and simple methods: reactions to Rigdon's rethinking of PLS. Long Range Plan. **47**, 138–145 (2014)

Bollen, K.A., Diamantopoulos, A.: In defense of causal–formative indicators: a minority report. Psychol. Methods. (2017). In print

Bollen, K.A., Stine, R.A.: Bootstrapping goodness-of-fit measures in structural equation models. Sociol. Methods Res. **21**, 205–229 (1992)

Buckler, F., Hennig-Thurau, T.: Identifying hidden structures in marketing's structural models through universal structure modeling. An explorative Bayesian neural network complement to LISREL and PLS. Mark. J. Res. Manag. **4**, 47–66 (2008)

Byrne, B.M.: Structural Equation Modeling with LISREL, PRELIS, and SIMPLIS: Basic Concepts, Applications, and Programming. Psychology Press, Hove (2013)

Chin, W.W.: Bootstrap cross-validation indices for PLS path model assessment. In: Esposito Vinzi, V., Chin, W.W., Henseler, J., Wang, H. (eds.) Handbook of Partial Least Squares: Concepts, Methods and Applications, pp. 83–97. Springer, Heidelberg (2010)

Chin, W.W., Frye, T.A.: PLS graph-version 3.0: Soft Modeling Inc. (2003)

Coelho, P.S., Henseler, J.: Creating customer loyalty through service customization. Eur. J. Mark. **46**, 331–356 (2012)

Cohen, J.: Statistical Power Analysis for the Behavioral Sciences. Lawrence Erlbaum, Mahwah, NJ (1988)
Cohen, J.: The earth is round (p<.05). Am. Psychol. **49**, 997–1003 (1994)
Diamantopoulos, A., Sarstedt, M., Fuchs, C., Wilczynski, P., Kaiser, S.: Guidelines for choosing between multi-item and single-item scales for construct measurement: a predictive validity perspective. J. Acad. Mark. Sci. **40**, 434–449 (2012)
Dijkstra, T.K.: Latent variables and indices: Herman Wold's basic design and partial least squares. In: Esposito Vinzi, V., Chin, W.W., Henseler, J., Wang, H. (eds.) Handbook of Partial Least Squares: Concepts, Methods and Applications, pp. 23–46. Heidelberg, Springer (2010)
Dijkstra, T.K., Henseler, J.: Linear indices in nonlinear structural equation models: best fitting proper indices and other composites. Qual. Quant. **45**, 1505–1518 (2011)
Dijkstra, T.K., Henseler, J.: Assessing and testing the goodness-of-fit of PLS path models. Paper presented at the 3rd VOC Conference, Leiden (2014)
Dijkstra, T.K., Henseler, J.: Consistent and asymptotically normal PLS estimators for linear structural equations. Comput. Stat. Data Anal. **81**, 10–23 (2015a)
Dijkstra, T.K., Henseler, J.: Consistent partial least squares path modeling. MIS Quart. **39**, 297–316 (2015b)
Esposito Vinzi, V., Trinchera, L., Amato, S.: PLS path modeling: from foundations to recent developments and open issues for model assessment and improvement. In: Esposito Vinzi, V., Chin, W.W., Henseler, J., Wang, H. (eds.) Handbook of Partial Least Squares: Concepts, Methods and Applications, pp. 23–46. Springer, Heidelberg (2010)
Fornell, C.: A national customer satisfaction barometer: the Swedish experience. J. Mark. **56**(1), 6–21 (1992)
Fornell, C., Johnson, M.D., Anderson, E.W., Cha, J., Bryant, B.E.: The American customer satisfaction index: nature, purpose, and findings. J. Mark. **60**(4), 7–18 (1996)
Fornell, C., Larcker, D.F.: Evaluating structural equation models with unobservable variables and measurement error. J. Mark. Res. **18**, 39–50 (1981)
Hair, J.F., Sarstedt, M., Pieper, T.M., Ringle, C.M.: The use of partial least squares structural equation modeling in strategic management research: a review of past practices and recommendations for future applications. Long Range Plan. **45**, 320–340 (2012a)
Hair, J.F., Sarstedt, M., Ringle, C.M., Mena, J.A.: An assessment of the use of partial least squares structural equation modeling in marketing research. J. Acad. Mark. Sci. **40**, 414–433 (2012b)
Hennig-Thurau, T., Groth, M., Paul, M., Gremler, D.D.: Are all smiles created equal? How emotional contagion and emotional labor affect service relationships. J. Mark. **70**(3), 58–73 (2006)
Henseler, J.: On the convergence of the partial least squares path modeling algorithm. Comput. Stat. **25**, 107–120 (2010)
Henseler, J.: PLS-MGA: a non-parametric approach to partial least squares-based multi-group analysis. In: Gaul, W.A., Geyer-Schulz, A., Schmidt-Thieme, L., Kunze, J. (eds.) Challenges at the Interface of Data Analysis, Computer Science, and Optimization (Studies in Classification, Data Analysis, and Knowledge Organization), pp. 495–501. Springer, Heidelberg (2012a)
Henseler, J.: Why generalized structured component analysis is not universally preferable to structural equation modeling. J. Acad. Mark. Sci. **40**, 402–413 (2012b)
Henseler, J.: Is the whole more than the sum of its parts? On the interplay of marketing and design research. Inaugural lecture, University of Twente (2015)
Henseler, J.: Bridging design and behavioral research with variance-based structural equation modelling. J. Adv. **46**(1), 178–192 (2017)
Henseler, J., Chin, W.W.: A comparison of approaches for the analysis of interaction effects between latent variables using partial least squares path modeling. Struct. Equ. Model. **17**, 82–109 (2010)
Henseler, J., Dijkstra, T.K.: ADANCO 2.0. Composite Modeling, Kleve (2015)
Henseler, J., Dijkstra, T.K., Sarstedt, M., Ringle, C.M., Diamantopoulos, A., Straub, D.W., et al.: Common beliefs and reality about PLS: Comments on Rönkkö and Evermann (2013). Organ. Res. Methods. **17**, 182–209 (2014)

Henseler, J., Fassott, G.: Testing moderating effects in PLS path models: an illustration of available procedures. In: Esposito Vinzi, V., Chin, W.W., Henseler, J., Wang, H. (eds.) Handbook of Partial Least Squares: Concepts, Methods and Applications, pp. 713–735. Springer, Heidelberg (2010)

Henseler, J., Fassott, G., Dijkstra, T.K., Wilson, B.: Analysing quadratic effects of formative constructs by means of variance-based structural equation modelling. Eur. J. Inf. Syst. **21**, 99–112 (2012a)

Henseler, J., Hubona, G., Ray, P.A.: Using PLS path modeling in new tech-nology research: updated guidelines. Ind. Manag. Data Syst. **116**, 2–20 (2016)

Henseler, J., Ringle, C.M., Sarstedt, M.: Using partial least squares path modeling in international advertising research: basic concepts and recent issues. In: Okazaki, S. (ed.) Handbook of Research in International Advertising, pp. 252–276. Edward Elgar Publishing, Cheltenham (2012b)

Henseler, J., Ringle, C.M., Sarstedt, M.: A new criterion for assessing discriminant validity in variance-based structural equation modeling. J. Acad. Mark. Sci. **43**, 115–135 (2015)

Henseler, J., Ringle, C.M., Sinkovics, R.R.: The use of partial least squares path modeling in international marketing. In: Sinkovics, R.R., Ghauri, P.N. (eds.) Advances in International Marketing, vol. 20, pp. 277–320. Emerald, Bingley (2009)

Henseler, J., Sarstedt, M.: Goodness-of-fit indices for partial least squares path modeling. Comput. Stat. **28**, 565–580 (2013)

Höök, K., Löwgren, J.: Strong concepts: intermediate-level knowledge in interaction design research. ACM Trans. Comput.-Hum. Interact. **19**, 23 (2012)

Hu, L.-T., Bentler, P.M.: Fit indices in covariance structure modeling: sensitivity to underparameterized model misspecification. Psychol. Methods. **3**(4), 424–453 (1998)

Hu, L.-T., Bentler, P.M.: Cutoff criteria for fit indexes in covariance structure analysis: conventional criteria versus new alternatives. Struct. Equ. Model. **6**, 1–55 (1999)

Hulland, J.: Use of partial least squares (PLS) in strategic management research: a review of four recent studies. Strateg. Manag. J. **20**, 195–204 (1999)

Hwang, H., Takane, Y.: Generalized structured component analysis. Psychometrika. **69**, 81–99 (2004)

Jean, R.-J., Sinhovies, R.R., Henseler, J., Ringle, C.M., Sarstedt, M.: Testing measurement invariance of composites using partial least squares. Int. Mark. Rev. **33**, 405–431 (2016)

Johnson, M.D., Herrmann, A., Huber, F.: The evolution of loyalty intentions. J. Mark. **70**(2), 122–132 (2006)

Kaufmann, L., Gaeckler, J.: A structured review of partial least squares in supply chain management research. J. Purch. Supply Manag. **21**, 259–272 (2015)

Kettenring, J.R.: Canonical analysis of several sets of variables. Biometrika. **58**, 433 (1971)

Krijnen, W.P., Dijkstra, T.K., Gill, R.D.: Conditions for factor (in)determinacy in factor analysis. Psychometrika. **63**, 359–367 (1998)

Lohmöller, J.-B.: The PLS program system: latent variables path analysis with partial least squares estimation. Multivar. Behav. Res. **23**, 125–127 (1988)

Lohmöller, J.-B.: Latent Variable Path Modeling with Partial Least Squares. Physica, Heidelberg (1989)

McDonald, R.P.: Path analysis with composite variables. Multivar. Behav. Res. **31**, 239–270 (1996)

McDonald, R.P.: Test Theory: A Unified Treatment. Lawrence Erlbaum, Mahwah, NJ (1999)

Nitzl, C., Roldán, J.L., Cepeda, G.: Mediation analyses in partial least squares structural equation modeling: helping researchers discuss more sophisticated models. Ind. Manag. Data Syst. **116**, 1849–1864 (2016)

Nunnally, J.C., Bernstein, I.H.: Psychometric Theory, 3rd edn. McGraw-Hill, New York (1994)

Peng, D.X., Lai, F.: Using partial least squares in operations management research: a practical guideline and summary of past research. J. Oper. Manag. **30**, 467–480 (2012)

Rego, L.L.: The relationship market structure-market efficiency from a customer satisfaction perspective. Adv. Consum. Res. **25**, 132–138 (1998)

Reinartz, W., Haenlein, M., Henseler, J.: An empirical comparison of the efficacy of covariance-based and variance-based SEM. Int. J. Res. Mark. **26**, 332–344 (2009)
Rhemtulla, M., Brosseau-Liard, P.E., Savalei, V.: When can categorical variables be treated as continuous? A comparison of robust continuous and categorical SEM estimation methods under suboptimal conditions. Psychol. Methods. **17**, 354–373 (2012)
Rigdon, E.E.: Rethinking partial least squares path modeling: in praise of simple methods. Long Range Plan. **45**, 341–358 (2012)
Rigdon, E.E.: Rethinking partial least squares path modeling: breaking chains and forging ahead. Long Range Plan. **47**, 161–167 (2014)
Rigdon, E.E., Becker, J.-M., Rai, A., Ringle, C.M., Diamantopoulos, A., Karahanna, E., Straub, D.W., Dijkstra, T.K.: Conflating antecedents and formative indicators: a comment on Aguirre-Urreta and Marakas. Inf. Syst. Res. **25**, 780–784 (2014)
Rindskopf, D.: Using phantom and imaginary latent variables to parameterize constraints in linear structural models. Psychometrika. **49**, 37–47 (1984)
Ringle, C.M., Sarstedt, M.: Gain more insight from your PLS-SEM results: the importance-performance map analysis. Ind. Manag. Data Syst. **11**, 1865–1886 (2016)
Ringle, C.M., Sarstedt, M., Straub, D.W.: Editor's comments: a critical look at the use of PLS-SEM in MIS Quarterly. MIS Quart. **36**, 3–14 (2012)
Ringle, C.M., Wende, S., Becker, J.-M.: SmartPLS 3. SmartPLS, Bönningstedt (2015). http://www.smartpls.com
Ringle, C. M., Wende, S., Will, A.: SmartPLS 2.0 (2005) www.smartpls.de
Roemer, E.: A tutorial on the use of PLS path modeling in longitudinal studies. Ind. Manag. Data Syst. **116**, 1901–1921 (2016)
Sahmer, K., Hanafi, M., Qannari, M.: Assessing unidimensionality within the PLS path modeling framework. In: Spiliopoulou, M., Kruse, R., Borgelt, C., Nürnberger, A., Gaul, W. (eds.) From Data and Information Analysis to Knowledge Engineering, pp. 222–229. Springer, Heidelberg (2006)
Sarstedt, M., Henseler, J., Ringle, C.M.: Multi-group analysis in partial least squares (PLS) path modeling: alternative methods and empirical results. Adv. Int. Mark. **22**, 195–218. Emerald, Bingley (2011)
Sarstedt, M., Ringle, C.M., Henseler, J., Hair, J.F.: On the emancipation of PLS-SEM: a commentary on Rigdon (2012). Long Range Plan. **47**, 154–160 (2014)
Sijtsma, K.: On the use, the misuse, and the very limited usefulness of Cronbach's alpha. Psychometrika. **74**, 107–120 (2009)
Smith, J.B., Barclay, D.W.: The effects of organizational differences and trust on the effectiveness of selling partner relationships. J. Mark. **61**(1), 3–21 (1997)
Streukens, S., Leroi-Werelds, S.: PLS FAC-SEM: an illustrated step-by-step guideline to obtain a unique insight in factorial data. Ind. Manag. Data Syst. **116** (2016)
Streukens, S., Wetzels, M., Daryanto, A., De Ruyter, K.: Analyzing factorial data using PLS: application in an online complaining context. In: Esposito Vinzi, V., Chin, W.W., Henseler, J., Wang, H. (eds.) Handbook of Partial Least Squares: Concepts, Methods and Applications, pp. 567–587. Springer, Heidelberg (2010)
Tenenhaus, M.: Component-based structural equation modelling. Total Qual. Manag. Bus. Excell. **19**, 871–886 (2008)
Tenenhaus, M., Amato, S., Esposito Vinzi, V.: A global goodness-of-fit index for PLS structural equation modelling. In proceedings of the XLII SIS scientific meeting. **1**, 739–742 (2004)
Tenenhaus, M., Esposito Vinzi, V., Chatelin, Y.-M., Lauro, C.: PLS path modeling. Comput. Stat. Data Anal. **48**, 159–205 (2005)
Tenenhaus, A., Tenenhaus, M.: Regularized generalized canonical correlation analysis. Psychometrika. **76**, 257–284 (2011)
Turkyilmaz, A., Oztekin, A., Zaim, S., Fahrettin Demirel, O.: Universal structure modeling approach to customer satisfaction index. Ind. Manag. Data Syst. **113**, 932–949 (2013)
Ulaga, W., Eggert, A.: Value-based differentiation in business relationships: gaining and sustaining key supplier status. J. Mark. **70**(1), 119–136 (2006)

Voorhees, C.M., Brady, M.K., Calantone, R., Ramirez, E.: Discriminant validity testing in marketing: an analysis, causes for concern, and proposed remedies. J. Acad. Mark. Sci. **44**, 119–134 (2016)

Wold, H.O.A.: Causal flows with latent variables: partings of the ways in the light of NIPALS modelling. Eur. Econ. Rev. **5**, 67–86 (1974)

Wold, H.O.A.: Soft modeling: the basic design and some extensions. In: Jöreskog, K.G., Wold, H.O.A. (eds.) Systems Under Indirect Observation, vol. 2, pp. 1–54. North-Holland, Amsterdam (1982)

Zhao, X., Lynch, J.G., Chen, Q.: Reconsidering Baron and Kenny: myths and truths about mediation analysis. J. Consum. Res. **37**, 197–206 (2010)

Ziggers, G.-W., Henseler, J.: The reinforcing effect of a firm's customer orientation and supply-base orientation on performance. Ind. Mark. Manag. **52**, 18–26 (2016)

Chapter 13
Mixture Models

Jeroen K. Vermunt and Leo J. Paas

13.1 Introduction

Marketing research literature, and most quantitative literature in other fields, addresses two main topics:

1. categorization, and
2. prediction.

Categorization can involve the following types of units: variables, companies, countries, consumers, customers, brands, websites, etc. For example, variables can be categorized using factor analysis or other techniques to assess the dimensionality underlying response patterns to the observed items (Paas and Sijtsma 2008). Categorization can also assess which brands may be competing for the same market of consumers and which brands can be considered as non-competitive, by allocating brands in groups (Rossiter and Bellman 2005). A very common categorization in the marketing research literature concerns the allocation of consumers or clients to different segments, where needs and wants differ across segments (Wedel and Kamakura 2000) and result in segment-specific strategies. This will be the emphasis of this chapter.

Consumer and client-base segmentation have received much attention (Wedel and Kamakura 2000) since the basic concepts were introduced by Smith (1956). Traditional heuristic-based clustering procedures have been used extensively for

J.K. Vermunt (✉)
Department of Methodology and Statistics, Tilburg University, Warandelaan 2, Tilburg 5037 AB, The Netherlands
e-mail: j.k.vermunt@tilburguniversity.edu

L.J. Paas
Department of Marketing, School of Communication, Journalism and Marketing, Massey University, Private Bag 102904, North Shore, Auckland 0745, New Zealand

P.S.H. Leeflang et al. (eds.), *Advanced Methods for Modeling Markets*,
International Series in Quantitative Marketing, DOI 10.1007/978-3-319-53469-5_13

Table 13.1 Typology of mixture models based other type of data structure

	Independent observations	Dependent observations or multilevel data	Longitudinal or panel data
Univariate response	1. Simple mixture model	2. Mixture regression model	3. Mixture growth model
Multivariate responses	4. LC model	5. Multilevel LC model	6. (Mixture) Latent Markov model

deriving segments from databases on clients or consumers. However, since the first application of latent class analysis, a type of mixture model, was reported in a marketing journal (Green et al. 1976), the model-based mixture modeling approach has been the preferred method for market segmentation (Leeflang et al. 2000). Interestingly, the marketing literature was early in adopting mixture modeling, two years after the seminal publication of the Goodman (1974) and even one year before the publication of the article on the EM-algorithm (Dempster et al. 1977), which made estimation of mixture models more feasible.

Mixture models are highly flexible, enabling the modeling of data with various types of structures (Leeflang et al. 2000). Table 13.1 summarizes the main types of data structures with the corresponding type of mixture model. Basically, we distinguish between data sets with either a single or multiple columns for the response variable(s), and with a single or multiple rows per observational unit, where for the latter we make a further distinction between an arbitrary and a meaningful (longitudinal) ordering of the rows. Simple mixture models are typically used only for density estimation and are of less interest for marketing applications. Mixture regression and mixture growth models are random-effects like models: the aim is to describe the heterogeneity in the regression or growth parameters by assuming that individuals belong to finite number of latent classes. These models will always contain predictors affecting the responses (in mixture growth models these are time-variables). In the second row, we see the more typical cluster analysis like applications of Latent Class (LC) analysis. Here one may also include predictors affecting the responses, yielding multivariate extensions of mixture regression and growth models.

In this chapter we further discuss the model types 4 and 5 in Table 13.1, starting with the basic idea of a simple mixture model (category 1 in Table 13.1) in Sect. 13.2.1. After that we focus on models for multivariate responses (Sect. 13.2.2), which correspond to cluster-analysis like applications of mixture models, i.e., the standard latent class model (category 4), with covariates, as well as its multilevel extension for situations in which lower-level observations (e.g. individuals) are nested within higher-level units (e.g. regions), and in which we wish to cluster/segment both lower- and higher-level units, i.e., the multilevel LC model (category 5). In Sect. 13.2.3 we discuss the restrictions that may be imposed on the observed responses. We discuss parameter estimation and model selection in Sects. 13.2.4 and 13.2.5. After this we discuss two special cases of the LC model for multivariate responses, LC analysis with concomitant variables and multilevel

LC analysis for accommodating data with lower- and higher-level units. Note that, (mixture) latent Markov models (category 6), which can be used for studying how individuals move between latent states, clusters, or segments over time, have been discussed previously in Vol. I, Sect. 8.2.4.2, and will also be addressed in detail in Chap. 14. We illustrate applications of the standard and multilevel LC models based on applications in international marketing in Sect. 13.3. We end with a discussion of statistical software implementing these models and a brief summary in Sect. 13.4, which also introduces other marketing applications of the LC model and the multilevel LC model.

13.2 Mixture Models

13.2.1 The Simple Mixture Model

The basic assumption of any type of mixture model is that the population consists of a finite number of unobserved groups which differ with respect to the parameters of a statistical model. These unobserved groups are referred to as mixture components or latent classes. The assumed statistical model within latent classes is typically rather simple; for example, a Poisson distribution for a count variable, a linear regression model with normal errors for a continuous outcome variables, or an independence model for a set of categorical variables.

Let us first look at a simple mixture model (category 1 in Table 13.1), say a count variable denoted by y_i, where i refers to one of the individuals in the sample and $1 \leq i \leq N$. The aim of the analysis is to describe the sample distribution of this variable assuming

1. there are C latent classes, and
2. y_i follows a Poisson distribution with mean μ_c within the classes, where c refers to a particular latent class.

The corresponding mixture model can be expressed as follows:

$$\mathrm{P}(y_i) = \sum_{c=1}^{C} \pi_c \mathrm{P}(y_i|c) = \sum_{c=1}^{C} \pi_c \frac{e^{-\mu_c} {\mu_c}^{y_i}}{y_i!}. \tag{13.1}$$

Here, π_c is the class proportion or the probability of belonging to class c, where $\pi_c > 0$ and $\sum_{c=1}^{C} \pi_c = 1$. As can be seen, the probability of observing a count value of y_i, $\mathrm{P}(y_i)$, is assumed to be a weighted average of the class-specific probabilities $\mathrm{P}(y_i|c)$, where class proportions are weights (McLachlan and Peel 2000). The $\mathrm{P}(y_i|c)$ are Poisson-distributions with means μ_c.

Table 13.2 illustrates an application of this model. It presents the observed frequency distribution of a count variable as well as its estimated frequency distributions under a standard and three-class Poisson model. As can be seen,

Table 13.2 Observed and estimated frequency distributions under a standard and 3-class mixture Poisson model

Count	Observed	Standard Poisson	3-Class Poisson
0	102	8.43	101.99
1	54	33.63	53.93
2	49	67.11	50.20
3	62	89.28	54.23
4	44	89.09	47.42
5	25	71.11	34.14
6	26	47.30	21.93
7	15	26.97	14.28
8	15	13.46	10.95
9	10	5.97	10.13
10	10	2.38	10.14
11	10	0.86	9.95
12	10	0.29	9.19
13	3	0.09	7.90
14	3	0.03	6.32
15	5	0.01	4.72
16	5	0.00	3.31
17	4	0.00	2.18
18	1	0.00	1.36
19	2	0.00	0.80
20	1	0.00	0.45

Note: In the standard model, the Poisson rate equals 3.99. In the 3-class model, the class-specific rates are 0.29, 3.48, and 11.22, and the class proportions are 0.28, 0.54, and 0.18, respectively

while the standard Poisson model does not fit the data, the observed distribution is approximated very well with three latent classes. This shows a general result: complex observed distributions can typically be approximated well using a mixture of simple distributions, which is why mixture models are well suited for density estimation.

13.2.2 *The Unrestricted LC Model for Multivariate Responses*

In the LC model (category 4), which can be considered as cluster- or segmentation-like applications of mixture models, we will typically have multiple responses per individual. We denote these responses by y_{ik}, where k denotes a particular response variable and K the number of response variables ($1 \leq k \leq K$). Denoting the full response vector of person i as y_i, an LC model can be defined as follows (Goodman 1974; Lazarsfeld 1950):

$$P(y_i) = \sum_{c=1}^{C} \pi_c P(y_i|c) = \sum_{c=1}^{C} \pi_c \prod_{k=1}^{K} P(y_{ik}|c). \tag{13.2}$$

As can be seen, similar to the simple mixture model presented above, we assume $P(y_i)$ to be a mixture of class-specific distributions $P(y_i|c)$. However, here we make a second important assumption, namely that the K responses are independent of one another conditional on a person's class membership. That is, we assume $P(y_i|c) = \prod_{k=1}^{K} P(y_{ik}|c)$. This is usually referred to as the local independence assumption. This assumption is also used in other types of latent variable models, such as in factor analysis and Item Response Theory (IRT) modeling, as well as in random-effects models, meaning that it is not specific for LC analysis. Note that IRT models will be discussed further in Sect. 13.2.3. As shown by Hagenaars (1988) and Oberski et al. (2013), this assumption can be tested and also be relaxed for some item pairs.

The specific form used for the class-specific probability density $P(y_{ik}|c)$ depends on the scale type of y_{ik}. Examples include a normal distribution for continuous y_{ik}, a Poisson distribution for count y_{ik}, a Bernoulli distribution for dichotomous y_{ik}, and a multinomial distribution for polytomous y_{ik}. Moreover, different forms can be combined within the same model (Vermunt and Magidson 2002). Let us look in more detail at the Bernoulli case, in which $P(y_{ik}|c) = {\pi_{kc}}^{y_{ik}}(1 - \pi_{kc})^{(1-y_{ik})}$, meaning that the class-specific parameters are the success probabilities π_{kc}. Table 13.3 presents a small illustrative data set consisting of three dichotomous responses from a hypothetical customer survey asking whether respondents own three types of electronic devices. Table 13.4 reports the parameter estimates (class proportions π_c and class-specific success probabilities π_{kc}) obtained with a 2-class model. For a subject belonging to the first latent class, the ownership probabilities equal 0.844, 0.912, and 0.730 for products 1–3, respectively. The local independence assumption implies, for example, that the probability of owning only the first two products equals $0.844 \times 0.912 \times (1 - 0.730) = 0.208$ in Latent Class one, and 0.091 in Latent Class two. Furthermore, a LC model defines the *overall* probability of having a particular response pattern, which turns out to be 0.161 for the owning of products 1 and 2. The latter number is obtained as a weighted average of the class-specific

Table 13.3 Small data set with three dichotomous responses

y_{i1}	y_{i2}	y_{i3}	Frequency	$P(y_i\|c=1)$	$P(y_i\|c=2)$	$P(y_i)$	$P(c=1\|y_i)$	$P(c=2\|y_i)$	Modal
0	0	0	239	0.004	0.272	0.111	0.020	0.980	2
0	0	1	101	0.010	0.102	0.047	0.128	0.872	2
0	1	0	283	0.038	0.271	0.131	0.175	0.825	2
0	1	1	222	0.104	0.102	0.103	0.605	0.395	1
1	0	0	105	0.020	0.092	0.049	0.248	0.753	2
1	0	1	100	0.054	0.035	0.046	0.703	0.297	1
1	1	0	348	0.208	0.091	0.161	0.774	0.226	1
1	1	1	758	0.562	0.034	0.352	0.961	0.039	1

Table 13.4 Parameters (class proportions and ownership probabilities) obtained with a 2-class model for the data in Table 13.3

Parameter	Class 1	Class 2
π_c	0.601	0.399
π_{1c}	0.844	0.252
π_{2c}	0.912	0.499
π_{3c}	0.730	0.273

joint response probabilities taking into account the class proportions (0.601 and 0.399); that is, $0.601 \times 0.208 + 0.399 \times 0.091 = 0.161$. The LC model was used in the first marketing application of mixture modeling reported by Green et al. (1976).

Similar to cluster analysis, one of the purposes of the LC model might be to assign individuals to latent classes (LCs). The probability of belonging to LC c given responses y_i—often referred to as the posterior class membership probability—can be obtained by the Bayes rule:

$$P(c|y_i) = \frac{\pi_c P(y_i|c)}{P(y_i)}. \tag{13.3}$$

Table 13.3 reports $P(c|y_i)$ for each answer pattern. For example, $P(c = 1|y_i)$ equals 0.774 for the (1,1,0) pattern, which is obtained as $0.601 \times 0.208/0.161$. The most common classification rule is modal assignment, which amounts to assigning each individual to the LC for which $P(c|y_i)$ is largest. The last column of Table 13.3 reports the modal assignments and shows that consumers that own at least two products are assigned to class 1 and the others to class 2.

The assigned class membership can among others be used to investigate the relationship between class-membership and external variables (for example, concomitant variables). Such variables can however also be included in the LC model itself. We discuss this in more detail in Sect. 13.2.6.

13.2.3 Some Restricted LC Models for Categorical Responses

Interesting types of restricted LC models for categorical items have been proposed, which involve imposing (linear) constraints on either the conditional probabilities or the corresponding logit coefficients. Of particular interest are probabilistic Guttman scaling models for dichotomous responses, which are LC models with $C=K+1$ classes, in datasets with K items. Various marketing papers presented applications of such restricted LC models, e.g., Bijmolt et al. (2004), Feick (1987) and Paas and Molenaar (2005).

The basic rationale on which Guttman scaling is based can be explained using Fig. 13.1, which is based on a hypothetical dataset in which five persons reacted to four items, e.g., survey questions. The line represents the underlying latent trait on which both persons and items are ordered. A latent trait could be brand knowledge, with low values representing a low level of knowledge and higher positions on the

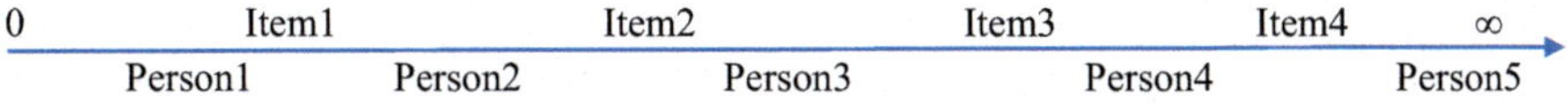

Fig. 13.1 Hypothetical Guttman scale

Table 13.5 Parameters (class proportions and ownership probabilities) obtained with a Proctor model for the data in Table 13.3

Parameter	Class 1	Class 2	Class 3	Class 4
π_c	0.160	0.155	0.126	0.559
π_{1c}	0.167	0.833	0.833	0.833
π_{2c}	0.167	0.167	0.833	0.833
π_{3c}	0.167	0.167	0.167	0.833

latent trait representing much knowledge on the focal brand. Person1 has the lowest position on the latent trait, a position below all items, implying this person possesses too little knowledge to answer any of the items correctly. Person2 is found between item1 and item2, implying Person2 will probably answer item1 correctly, but not the three other items. Person3's knowledge is likely to lead to correct answers on items 1 and 2, but not on the other items. Moving all the way up the latent trait will lead to Person5, who possesses sufficient brand knowledge for answering all items correctly.

The hierarchical ordering of items and persons implies that if a person answers a difficult brand knowledge item correctly, such as item 4, this person should also answer the easier items correctly, items 1–3 in this example. Stated more formally and in terms of LC models, apart from measurement error, class c should provide a positive answer to the $c-1$ easiest items and a negative answer to the remaining $K-(c-1)$ items. This rather basic Guttman scale model forms the fundamentals for various types of IRT models. Most relevant herein is that the answer patterns of respondents will not be deterministic, some answers maybe be inconsistent with the hierarchical ordering of items. In our hypothetical example a Guttman error occurs if a respondent answers the more difficult item4 correctly but not the easier item2. Probabilistic IRT models accommodate for the occurrence of such Guttmann errors in various ways. Refer to Hambleton and Swaminathan (1985) or Sijtsma and Molenaar (2002) for a more formal and elaborate description of item response theory. These different models can be represented in a LC model framework, as we will discuss briefly in this section.

The various types of probabilistic Guttman models differ in the constraints they impose on the measurement error. The simplest and most restricted model is the Proctor (1970) model. Table 13.5 presents the parameter estimates obtained when fitting the Proctor model to the data set in Table 13.3. As can be seen, the ownership probability is either 0.833 or $0.167 = 1 - 0.833$. The measurement error—or the probability of owning a product which is not in agreement with the class—is estimated to be equal to 0.167.

Whereas the Proctor model assumes that the measurement error is constant across items and classes, less restricted models can be defined, with different error probabilities across items, classes, or both (Dayton 1999).

Croon (1990) proposed a restricted LC model that similarly to a non-parametric Item Response Theoretical (IRT) model (Sijtsma and Molenaar 2002) assumes monotonic item response functions; that is, $\pi_{kc} \leq \pi_{k,c+1}$. A restricted version, in which not only classes but also items are ordered, is obtained by imposing the additional set of restrictions, $\pi_{kc} \leq \pi_{k+1\,.c}$; that is, by assuming double monotony. Vermunt (2001) discussed various generalizations of these models. In the marketing literature such model restrictions were applied for predicting consumer's future product acquisition using cross sectional data on ownership of financial products (Paas and Molenaar 2005).

Various authors described the connection between restricted LC models and parametric IRT modeling (see, for example, Heinen 1996; Lindsay et al. 1991; Rost 1990); that is, IRT models with a discrete specification of the distribution of the underlying trait or ability can be defined as LC models in which the response probabilities are parametrized using logistic equations with constraints on the logit parameters, where LC locations represent the C possible values of the discretized latent trait. These locations may be fixed a priori, for example, at -2, -1, 0, 1, and 2 in the case of $C = 5$, but may also be treated as free parameters to be estimated. Depending on whether the items are dichotomous, ordinal, or nominal, this yields a 2-parameter logistic, generalized partial credit, or nominal response model. Further restrictions involve equating slope parameters across items, yielding Rasch and partial credit models, and imposing across category and across item restrictions on intercept parameters as in rating scale models for ordinal items. Multidimensional variants can be obtained using what Magidson and Vermunt (2001) refer to as discrete factor models.

13.2.4 Parameter Estimation by Maximum Likelihood

The parameters of LC models are typically estimated by means of maximum likelihood (ML). The log-likelihood function that is maximized is based on the probability density $\mathrm{P}(y_i)$, that is,

$$\ln L = \sum_{i=1}^{N} \ln \mathrm{P}(y_i) \tag{13.4}$$

With categorical responses one will typically group the data and construct a frequency table as we did in Table 13.3. The log-likelihood function for grouped data equals:

$$\ln L = \sum_{m=1}^{M} n_m \ln \mathrm{P}(y_m). \tag{13.5}$$

where m is a data pattern, M the number of different data patterns, and n_m the cell count corresponding to data pattern m. Notice that only nonzero observed cell entries contribute to the log-likelihood function, a feature that is exploited by the more efficient LC software packages that have been developed over the last decades. These packages will be discussed in Sect. 13.4.

One of the problems in the estimation of LC models for discrete y_{ik} is that model parameters may be *nonidentified*, even if the number of degrees of freedom—the number of independent cells in the K-way cross-tabulation minus the number of free parameters—is larger than or equal to zero. Non-identification means that different sets of parameter values yield the same maximum of the log-likelihood function or, worded differently, that there is no unique set of parameter estimates. The formal identification check is via the Jacobian matrix (matrix of first derivatives of $P(y_i)$), which should be column full rank. Another option is to estimate the model of interest with different sets of starting values. Except for local solutions (see below), an identified model gives the same final estimates for each set of the starting values.

Although there are no general rules with respect to the identification of LC models, it is possible to provide certain minimal requirements and point to possible pitfalls. For an unrestricted LC model, one needs at least three responses (y_{ik}'s) per individual, but if these are dichotomous, no more than two latent classes can be identified. Consideration is required when analyzing four dichotomous response variables, in which case the unrestricted three-class model is not identified, even though it has a positive number of degrees of freedom. With five dichotomous items, however, even a five-class model is identified. Usually, it is possible to achieve identification by constraining model parameters.

A second problem associated with the estimation of LC models is the presence of local maxima. The log-likelihood function of a LC model is not always concave, which means that hill-climbing algorithms may converge to a different maximum depending on the starting values. Usually, we are looking for the global maximum. The best way to proceed is, therefore, to estimate the model with different sets of random starting values. Typically, several sets converge to the same highest log-likelihood value, which can then be assumed to be the ML solution. Some software packages have automated the use of multiple sets of random starting values to reduce the probability of getting a local solution.

Another problem in LC models is the occurrence of boundary solutions, which are probabilities equal to 0 (or 1) or logit parameters equal to minus (or plus) infinity. These may cause numerical problems in the estimation algorithms, occurrence of local solutions, and complications in the computation of standard errors and number of degrees of freedom of the goodness-of-fit tests. Boundary solutions can be prevented by imposing constraints or by taking into account other kinds of prior information on the model parameters.

The most popular methods for solving the ML estimation problem are the expectation-maximization (EM) and Newton-Raphson (NR) algorithms. EM is a very stable iterative method for ML estimation with incomplete data (Dempster et al. 1977). NR is a faster procedure that, however, needs good starting values to converge. The latter method makes use of the matrix of second-order derivatives of the log-likelihood function, which is also needed for obtaining standard errors of the model parameters.

13.2.5 Model Selection Issues

A challenging and fundamental decision for LC models and other categories of models, in Table 13.1, concerns model specification. With most available data sets model specifications can differ in various ways. Models may differ in the number of latent classes, the specification of the measurement model, freely estimated or restricted as discussed in Sect. 13.2.4, the relationship between the measured indicators and the latent classes, nominal, ordinal or metric, specification of the form of the covariate effects, nominal, ordinal or metric, etc.

The goodness-of-fit of such alternative formulation of LC models for categorical responses can be tested using Pearson and likelihood-ratio chi-squared tests. The latter is defined as:

$$G^2 = 2\sum_{m=1}^{M} n_m \ln {n_m} \Big/ (N \cdot \mathrm{P}\left(y_m\right)) \cdot \tag{13.6}$$

As in log-linear analysis, the number of degrees of freedom (df) equals the number of cells in the frequency table minus 1, minus the number of independent parameters (npar). In an unrestricted LC model,

$$df = \prod_{k=1}^{K} R_k - 1 - npar = \prod_{k=1}^{K} R_k - C \cdot \left[1 + \sum_{k=1}^{K} (R_k - 1)\right] \tag{13.7}$$

where R_k is the number of categories of the kth response variable. Although it is no problem to estimate LC models with 10, 20, or 50 indicators, in such cases, the frequency table may become very sparse and, as a result, asymptotic p-values can no longer be trusted. An elegant but time-consuming solution to this problem is to estimate the p-values by parametric bootstrapping. This procedure constructs the sampling distribution of the statistic of interested using Monte-Carlo simulation. More specifically, one generates M samples from the population defined by the estimated parameters and estimates the model with each of these M samples. The p-value is the proportion of samples in which the statistic is larger than in the original sample.

Another alternative for assessing model fit in sparse tables is to look at the fit in lower-order marginal tables (e.g., in the two-way marginal tables). An example is the bivariate residual, which is a Pearson chi-squared statistic for a two-way table divided by the number of degrees of freedom (Oberski et al. 2013); that is,

$$BVR_{kk'} = \sum_{r=1}^{R_k}\sum_{r'=1}^{R_{k'}} \frac{\left[n_{kk'(rr')} - N \cdot \mathrm{P}(y_k = r, y_{k'} = r')\right]^2}{N \cdot \mathrm{P}(y_k = r, y_{k'} = r')} / \left[(R_k - 1)(R_{k'} - 1)\right]. \tag{13.8}$$

Here $n_{kk'(rr')}$ is the observed number of persons with responses r and r' on item pair k and k', and $\mathrm{P}(y_k = r, y_{k'} = r')$ is the probability of this response pattern according to the estimated LC model. It can be computed by:

$$\mathrm{P}(y_k = r, y_{k'} = r') = \sum_{c=1}^{C} \pi_c \mathrm{P}(y_k = r|c)\mathrm{P}(y_{k'} = r'|c) \tag{13.9}$$

thus basically by applying the LC formula to an item pair. Larger BVR values point at possible violations of the local independence assumption for the item pairs concerned.

Even though LC models with C and $C + 1$ classes are nested, one cannot test them against each other using a standard likelihood-ratio test because it does not have an asymptotic chi-squared distribution. A way out to this problem is to approximate its sampling distribution using bootstrapping. But since this bootstrap likelihood-ratio method is computationally demanding, alternative methods are often used for comparing models with different numbers of classes. Most popular are information criteria, e.g., the Bayesian Information Criterion (BIC), the Akaike Information Criterion (AIC), and the AIC3 measure, defined as: $\mathrm{BIC} = -2\ln L + \ln(N)npar$, $\mathrm{AIC} = -2\ln L + 2npar$, and $\mathrm{AIC3} = -2\ln L + 3\,npar$. Lower values imply better fit and parsimony.[1]

Usually, we are not only interested in (relative) goodness-of-fit but also in how well class memberships can be predicted from the observed responses or, worded differently, how well classes are separated. This is can among other be quantified based on the estimated proportion of classification errors under modal classification, which equals:

$$\mathrm{CE} = \sum_{i=1}^{N} \frac{1}{N}\left[1 - \max \mathrm{P}(c|y_i)\right]. \tag{13.10}$$

This number can be compared to the proportion of classification errors based on the unconditional probabilities π_c, yielding a reduction of errors measure called Lambda:

$$\mathrm{Lambda} = 1 - \frac{CE}{1 - \max(\pi_c)}. \tag{13.11}$$

[1]Compare Sect. 5.6, Vol. I.

The closer this nominal pseudo R^2 measure is to 1, the better the model performs in terms of classification accuracy. Other types of R^2 measures have been proposed based on entropy and qualitative variance; that is, using $\sum_{i=1}^{N}\sum_{c=1}^{C} - \mathrm{P}(c|y_i) \ln \mathrm{P}(c|y_i)/N$ and $\sum_{i=1}^{N}\left[1 - \sum_{c=1}^{C}\mathrm{P}(c|y_i)^2\right]/N$ as measures for class separation.

Finally, there is a class of measures which are similar to information criteria, but which also take into account classification performance. In other words, these measures try to balance fit, parsimony, and classification performance. The best-known of these measures are AWE and ICL-BIC.

13.2.6 LC Analysis with Concomitant Variables

An important extension of the LC model involves inclusion of concomitant variables or covariates predicting class membership (Dayton and Macready 1988; Kamakura et al. 1994). Denoting a person's covariate vector by x_i, this extended LC model is defined as:

$$\mathrm{P}(y_i|x_i) = \sum_{c=1}^{C} \pi_{c|x_i} \mathrm{P}(y_i|c) = \sum_{c=1}^{C} \pi_{c|x_i} \prod_{k=1}^{K} \mathrm{P}(y_{ik}|c). \tag{13.12}$$

The main change compared to the LC model is that the class membership probabilities may now be dependent on x_i, whereas the definition of $\mathrm{P}(y_i|c)$ remains unchanged. Note that an additional assumption is made, namely that the effect of the x_i on the y_i is fully mediated by the latent classes. Section 13.3.1 provides an example of such a LC model, in which country of residence is the covariate of interest. It is possible to test this assumption using local fit measures similar to those discussed earlier, as well as to relax it by allowing for direct effects, which implies replacing $\mathrm{P}(y_{ik}|c)$ by $\mathrm{P}(y_{ik}|c, x_i)$ for one or more of the y_{ik}.

Typically, $\pi_{c|x_i}$ is modeled using a multinomial logistic specification; that is,

$$\pi_{c|x_i} = \exp\left(\gamma_{0c} + \sum_{p=1}^{P} \gamma_{pc} x_{ip}\right) \Big/ \sum_{c'=1}^{C} \exp\left(\gamma_{0c'} + \sum_{p=1}^{P} \gamma_{pc'} x_{ip}\right) \tag{13.13}$$

where γ_{0c} represents the intercept and γ_{pc} the slope for predictor x_{ip} for latent class c. For identification, we will typically assume parameters to sum to 0 across classes (effect coding) or to be equal to 0 for one class (dummy coding).

The simultaneous modeling of responses y_i and concomitant variables x_i may sometimes be impractical, especially when the number of possibly relevant concomitant variables is large. Therefore, researchers often prefer using a three-step analysis approach. This involves:

1. estimating a LC model without covariates;
2. obtaining the individuals' class assignment using the posterior membership probabilities, and
3. investigating how the class assignments are related to covariates.

The advantage of this approach is that it does not lead to a segmentation structure that is determined by the chosen covariates, only indicator variables influence this. This is particularly relevant when there is little theory on the relationship between covariates and latent class membership and possible direct effects of covariates on responses, which is often the case in the more or less exploratory clustering analyses conducted in marketing research.

However, as shown by Bolck et al. (2004), this yields downward biased estimates of the covariate effects. Based on the work of these authors, Vermunt (2010) proposed a simple method to adjust for this bias (see also Bakk et al. 2013). The adjustment is based on the following relationship between the class assignments w_i and the true class membership c:

$$P(w_i|x_i) = \sum_{c=1}^{C} \pi_{c|x_i} P(w_i|c). \tag{13.14}$$

Note that this is again a LC model, but with $\mathrm{w_i}$ as a single "response" variable. The adjustment proposed by Vermunt (2010) therefore involves estimating a LC model with x_i as concomitant variables and w_i as the single response variable, while fixing the $P(w_i|c)$ at the values computed using the parameter estimates from the first step.

13.2.7 Multilevel LC Analysis

Another important extension of the LC model concerns its adaptation for the analysis of multilevel data sets (Vermunt 2003). Description of this multilevel extension of the LC model requires expansion of our notation. We refer to a particular higher-level unit as j and to the response vector of a group and an individual within a group as y_j and y_{ji}, respectively. The number of individuals within a group is denoted by n_j, a group-level latent class or cluster by d, and the number of group-level clusters by D. The lower-level part of the multi-level LC model (category 5), a two-level LC model in this case, has the following form:

$$P(y_{ji}|d) = \sum_{c=1}^{C} \pi_{c|d} P(y_{ji}|c) = \sum_{c=1}^{C} \pi_{c|d} \prod_{k=1}^{K} P(y_{jik}|c) \tag{13.15}$$

which is the same as a LC model, except for the fact that the class proportions are allowed to differ across higher-level clusters. For $P(y_{ji}|c)$, as in the LC model, we assume local independence. The higher-level model equals:

$$P(y_j) = \sum_{d=1}^{D} \pi_d \prod_{i=1}^{n_j} P(y_{ji}|d). \tag{13.16}$$

As can be seen, the main additional model assumptions are that there are D group-level classes and that the individuals' responses within a group are independent given the group's class membership. Combining the above two equations yields the full equation of a two-level LC model:

$$P(y_j) = \sum_{d=1}^{D} \pi_d \prod_{i=1}^{n_j} \sum_{c=1}^{C} \pi_{c|d} \prod_{k=1}^{K} P(y_{jik}|c). \tag{13.17}$$

As in a LC class model, we include concomitant variables predicting the higher- and lower-level class memberships, either using a simultaneous analysis or a three-step approach. Moreover, the assumption that the y_{jik} are independent of the groups' class memberships given the individuals' class memberships can be tested and relaxed (Nagelkerke et al. 2016). Section 13.3.2 presents an application of the multilevel LC model, with two levels.

13.3 Applications in International Marketing

13.3.1 Introduction

We illustrate the concepts discussed in Sect. 13.2 in the context of international marketing. Ter Hofstede et al. (1999) point out that international marketing has become more important for developing, positioning and selling products. This results from globalization, implying that firms are reacting to international competitors in the local market and competing with local competitors in markets outside their country of origin (Yip 1995). International marketing strategies require thorough understanding of the various national and cross-national markets (Bijmolt et al. 2004; Ter Hofstede et al. 1999). For example, firms that operate internationally may aim to detect segments that occur across multiple countries, allowing the development of internationalized marketing strategies (Ter Hofstede et al. 1999). Conversely, firms operating in a single country can detect and target segments that only occur in their country and are therefore more likely to react positively to a local strategy implemented by a local company. Detection of such cross-national or country-specific segments relies on segmentation techniques that accommodate for the hierarchy in international data (Bijmolt et al. 2004; Paas et al. 2015; Ter Hofstede et al. 1999). Note that international data are hierarchical in the sense that there are units at two levels, consumers or respondents at the lower level and country represents are the higher level unit (Bijmolt et al. 2004).

We discuss two international segmentation applications of mixture modeling, using a LC model, category (4) in Table 13.1, and the multilevel LC model, (category 5). We show how data from multiple countries can be analyzed in different ways, without ignoring similarities and differences across the countries analyzed and thereby taking into regard the hierarchical nature of international data.

13.3.2 International Segmentation Using a Covariate

The first discussed application (Ter Hofstede et al. 1999) involves a LC model that accommodates the incorporation of within- and cross-country heterogeneity by using country membership of the individual respondent as a concomitant variable or covariate, as discussed in Sect. 13.2.6. Ter Hofstede et al. (1999) analyse data on consumer's yoghurt preferences in 11 European Union (EU) countries. Data were part of an EU survey conducted for the European commission. The segmentation basis concerns variables describing consumer Means-End Chains (MECs). MECs assume that consumers obtain desired ends, represented as values through the attributes of specific types of yoghurt. In MECs product attributes are linked to values via benefits (Gutman 1982). Thus, in this hierarchy there are two key links: attribute-benefit (AB) and benefit-value (BV). As an example of an AB link, Ter Hofstede et al. (1999) find that the product attribute *low fat* is strongly linked to the benefit *good health.* A related BV-link connects *good health* to the value *security.* The AB and BV links vary in strength from 0 to 1. Similarities and differences between consumers, concerning strengths of the links, are used to segment these individuals.

In the resulting LC model (category 4) Ter Hofstede et al. (1999) obtain four segments, using information criteria (see Sect. 13.2.5), with varying strengths in the links. As an example, their segment 2 is defined by consumers who chose yoghurt mostly accruing to fulfillment of the value *fun and enjoyment.* Through BV-links we find that the value *fun and enjoyment* is linked to the following benefits: *convenient to use, good taste, good quality, good health, good for digestion* and *diet.* In turn the AB-links show that the abovementioned segment 2 benefits are strongly linked to the attributes: *individually packed, with fruit, high priced, mild, organically produced, biobifidus* and *low fat.* We refer to Ter Hofstede et al. (1999) for a more comprehensive discussion of segment two and the other three segments.

Most relevant for the current discussion is that differences in the occurrence of the four segments across the 11 analyzed EU countries are accommodated for using a country-covariate in the LC model (see Sect. 13.2.6), which leads to different segment sizes across the countries. Note that Ter Hofstede et al. (1999) included other covariates in their model, which are not discussed in our chapter. Table 13.6 shows segment sizes in the 11 analyzed countries. Large proportions of consumers are in segment 4 across all analyzed countries. Therefore, a cross-national marketing strategy can be developed targeting segment 4 across the 11 EU countries analyzed. Contrarily, the previously discussed segment 2 with the dominant fun and enjoyment value is particularly large in Germany and is also relatively large in Portugal and France. Strategies aimed at targeting this segment are most important for the first mentioned country and can possibly also be applied in France and Portugal.

Table 13.6 Occurrence of segments in Ter Hofstede et al study[a]

Country	$p(S_1)^a$	$p(S_2)$	$p(S_3)$	$p(S_4)$
Belgium	12.2	17.5	8.5	61.8
Denmark	47.6	2.6	27.0	22.8
France	2.4	21.8	3.3	72.4
Germany	3.2	45.1	26.3	25.4
Great Britain	41.2	7.0	26.0	25.9
Greece	28.2	13.4	6.5	52.0
Ireland	40.6	12.1	17.9	29.5
Italy	5.9	10.2	5.1	78.8
Netherlands	31.5	14.3	17.9	36.3
Portugal	35.2	27.8	4.9	32.1
Spain	24.1	8.5	3.8	62.6

[a]$p(S_1)$ = proportion of segment 1, etc.
Source: Ter Hofstede et al. (1999, p. 8)

13.3.3 Multilevel International Segmentation

The analysis reported by Ter Hofstede et al. (1999) can be applied to international data with any number of countries. However, the interpretation of the covariate effects becomes cumbersome as the number of higher-level units, such as countries, increases. Under such circumstances, it may be more insightful to simultaneously cluster lower-level units, consumers, and higher-level units, countries, using a multilevel LC model (category 5). Bijmolt et al. (2004) applied this model to consumer ownership data on eight financial products across 15 EU countries. Two countries are split over two regions, i.e., Germany over East and West Germany and Great Britain over Northern Ireland versus the rest, resulting in 17 higher-level units. Paas et al. (2015) reported similar, less extensive analyses.

Bijmolt et al. (2004) apply the multilevel LC model to the Eurobarometer 56.0 database, resulting in 14 consumer-level segments and seven higher-level segments for categorizing the 17 countries and regions, using information criteria (see Sect. 13.2.5). That is, models with up to 15 lower level classes, for clustering respondents, and eight higher level classes, for clustering countries, were estimated. Amongst the 120 estimated model the multilevel LC model with 14 respondent segments and seven higher level country-segments led to the lowest value on the information criterion, CAIC. Hence this model has the optimal fit to the data and was selected as the final model.

The 14 consumer-level segments are defined by differing propensities for owning each of the eight analyzed financial products. For example, in the highly active respondent-level segment 14, we find 100% of the respondents owning the current account, 85.7% a savings account, 83.3% a credit card, 87.1% other bank card, 100% a cheque book, 60.3% an overdraft, 89.3% a mortgage and 39.2% a loan. Contrarily, in segment 1 we find that 4.9% of the respondents owns the current account, 38.7% a savings account, 0.0% a credit card, 0.2% other bank card, 8.5% a cheque book, 0.0% an overdraft, 0.8% a mortgage and 2.2% a loan. Covariate effects on the 14 respondent-level segments are incorporated in the model, as discussed in Sect. 13.2.6. Bijmolt et al. (2004) find that respondents aged 30–59, with above average incomes and with a partner are overrepresented in the consumer segments that are characterised by high penetrations of the products, such as segment 14 that is discussed above.

Next to incorporating covariates, Bijmolt et al. (2004) also assessed alternative model specifications, linked to the respondent-level segmentation, such as those discussed in Sect. 13.2.3. Results of previously published studies on developments in consumer financial product portfolios suggest that most consumers will acquire financial products in a similar order, those products relevant for the satisfaction of more basic financial needs before more advanced products (Dickenson and Kirzner 1986; Kamakura et al. 1991; Paas and Molenaar 2005). Bijmolt et al. (2004) test whether such an order of acquisition applies for the eight financial products in their 15-country data set by assessing whether IRT-based assumptions, as those presented in Sect. 13.2.3, lead to better a model, according to the information criteria in Sect. 13.2.5. The model without the restrictions leads to lower information criterion values, CAIC, thus, a common order of acquisition in the Bijmolt et al. (2004) data is not supported.

Bijmolt et al. (2004) also present results of applying a multilevel LC model to internationally collected consumer data. Instead of using covariates to assess similarities and differences in segmentation structures across countries analyzed, the countries themselves are clustered on the basis of these similarities and differences. That is, countries with similar respondent-level segmentation structures are allocated to the same higher-order segment. We present the country clustering reported in Bijmolt et al. (2004) in our Table 13.7. As pointed out by Bijmolt et al. (2004), the classification of countries in Table 13.7 reflects European geography to a certain degree, which supports face validity of the results.

Table 13.7 Higher level country segments[a]

Country segment	Relative size	Country	Prob.	(%)
1	0.256	Belgium, Germany (East and West), The Netherlands Luxembourg	100	81.1
2	0.260	Austria, Denmark, Sweden, Finland Luxembourg	100	18.9
3	0.175	Great Britain, Ireland, Northern Ireland	100	
4	0.119	Italy, Portugal	100	
5	0.064	Spain	100	
6	0.064	Greece	100	
7	0.064	France	100	

[a]Based on Bijmolt et al. (2004, p. 330)

13.4 Software

One of the first LC analysis programs, MLLSA, made available by Clifford Clogg in 1977, was limited to a relatively small number of nominal variables. Today's programs can handle many more variables, as well as other scale types. For example, the LEM program (Vermunt 1997) provides a command language that can be used to specify a large variety of models for categorical data, including LC models. Mplus is a command language based on the structural equation modeling package that implements many types of LC and mixture models. In addition, routines for the estimation of specific types of LC models are available as SAS, R, and Stata packages/macros (see, for example, Lanza et al. 2007; Skrondal and Rabe-Hesketh 2004).

Latent GOLD (Vermunt and Magidson 2000–2016) is a program that was specifically developed for LC analysis, and which contains both an SPSS-like point-and-click user interface and a syntax language. It implements all important types of LC models, such as models for response variables of different scale types, restricted LC models, models with predictors, models with local dependencies, models with multiple discrete latent variables, LC path models, LC Markov models, mixture factor analysis and IRT, and multilevel LC models, as well as features for dealing with partially missing data, performing bootstrapping, performing simulation studies, power computation, and dealing with complex samples.

13.5 Other Implications

We introduced different types of mixture models that can be used for classifying entities, such as consumers. Consecutively we discussed the simple mixture model for a univariate response and extended this to the LC model for multivariate observed responses. Then we discussed the restrictions that may be imposed on the observed responses followed by more technical issues, i.e., parameter estimation and model selection. After this we discussed the LC model for multivariate responses, restricted LC models, LC models with concomitant variables and the multilevel LC model for accommodating data with lower- and higher- level units. The LC model and the multilevel LC model were then illustrated in the context of international segmentation, in which we emphasized the use of a covariate or alternatively a multilevel structure to accommodate for similarities and differences between consumers within and across countries. Last of all software programs applicable for mixture modelling were briefly pointed out.

To conclude this contribution we point out that the marketing literature reports many other applications of the LC model (category 4 in Table 13.1). A selection of these applications is presented in Table 13.8, in order to illustrate some of the possibilities. Note that this list is far from exhaustive. The other category of mixture model discussed in this chapter was the multilevel LC model (category

Table 13.8 Studies based on standard latent class analysis model

Publication	Description
Green et al. JCR[a] (1976)	Modelling consumer adoption of a new telecommunications service
Feick, JMR[b] (1987)	Analysis of behavioral hierarchies in terms of consumer complaining behavior
Grover and Srinivasan, JMR[b] (1987)	Assessing the competitive market structure of different brands in the coffee product category
Kamakura and Novak, JCR[a] (1992)	Identifying segments based on consumer values in the LOV instrument
Kamakura et al. IJRM[c] (1994)	Modeling consumer preferences for bank services
Gupta and Chintagunta, JMR[b] (1994)	Analyzing the relationship between segments characterized by profiles of brand preferences and marketing variable sensitivity in relation to household demographics
Bhatnagar and Ghose, JBR[d] (2004)	Segmentation of web-shoppers based on their purchase behavior across various product categories
Paas and Molenaar, IJRM[c] (2005)	Analysing orders in which consumers acquire financial products—Acquisition Pattern Analysis
Kamakura and Mazzon, IJRM[c] (2013)	Social-economic stratification of consumers to explain consumption of various product categories
De Keyser et al. IJRM[c] (2015)	Clustering respondents on the basis of self-reported after-sales channel usage

Notes: [a]JCR: Journal of Consumer Research, [b]JMR: Journal of Marketing Research, [c]IJRM: International Journal of Research in Marketing, [d]JBR: Journal of Business Research

5 in Table 13.1). We did not find other applications of this model in the marketing literature, besides the application discussed in Sect. 13.3.2. However, applications of multilevel LC models to marketing issues have been presented in statistical journals, e.g., Paas et al. (2015). Thus, this chapter may be concluded by pointing out that the marketing research applications of the various types of multilevel LC models should also be exploited.

References

Bakk, Z., Tekle, F.B., Vermunt, J.K.: Estimating the association between latent class membership and external variables using bias adjusted three-step approaches. Sociol. Methodol. **43**, 272–311 (2013)

Bhatnagar, A., Ghose, S.: Segmenting consumers based on the benefits and risks of internet shopping. J. Bus. Res. **57**, 1352–1360 (2004)

Bijmolt, T.H., Paas, L.J., Vermunt, J.K.: Country and consumer segmentation: multi-level latent class analysis of financial product ownership. Int. J. Res. Mark. **21**, 323–340 (2004)

Bolck, A., Croon, M.A., Hagenaars, J.A.: Estimating latent structure models with categorical variables: one-step versus three-step estimators. Polit. Anal. **12**, 3–27 (2004)

Croon, M.A.: Latent class analysis with ordered latent classes. Br. J. Math. Stat. Psychol. **43**, 171–192 (1990)

Dayton, C.M.: Latent Class Scaling Analysis. Sage, Thousand Oaks, CA (1999)

Dayton, C.M., Macready, G.B.: Concomitant-variable latent class models. J. Am. Stat. Assoc. **83**, 173–178 (1988)

De Keyser, A., Konüs, U., Schepers, J.: Multichannel customer segmentation: does the after-sales channel matter? A replication and extensions. Int. J. Res. Mark. **32**, 453–456 (2015)

Dempster, A.P., Laird, N.M., Rubin, D.B.: Maximum likelihood from incomplete data via the EM algorithm (with discussion). J. R. Stat. Soc. Ser. B. **39**, 1–38 (1977)

Dickenson, J.R., Kirzner, E.: Priority patterns of acquisition of financial assets. J. Acad. Mark. Sci. **14**, 43–49 (1986)

Feick, L.F.: Latent class models for the analysis of behavioral hierarchies. J. Mark. Res. **24**, 174–186 (1987)

Goodman, L.A.: Exploratory latent structure analysis using both identifiable and unidentifiable models. Biometrika. **61**, 215–231 (1974)

Green, P.E., Carmone, F.J., Wachspress, D.P.: Consumer segmentation via latent class analysis. J. Consum. Res. **3**, 170–174 (1976)

Grover, R., Srinivasan, V.: A simultaneous approach to market segmentation and market structuring. J. Mark. Res. **24**, 139–153 (1987)

Gupta, S., Chintagunta, P.K.: On using demographic variables to determine segment membership in logit mixture models. J. Mark. Res. **31**, 128–136 (1994)

Gutman, J.: A means-end model based on consumer categorization processes. J. Mark. **46**(Spring), 60–72 (1982)

Hagenaars, J.A.: Latent structure models with direct effects between indicators: local dependence models. Sociol. Methods Res. **16**, 379–405 (1988)

Hambleton, R.K., Swaminathan, H.: Item Response Theory: Principles and Applications. Sage, Thousand Oaks, CA (1985)

Heinen, T.: Latent Class and Discrete Latent Trait Models: Similarities and Differences. Sage, Thousand Oaks, CA (1996)

Kamakura, W.A., Mazzon, J.A.: Socioeconomic status and consumption in an emerging economy. Int. J. Res. Mark. **30**, 4–18 (2013)

Kamakura, W.A., Novak, T.P.: Value-system segmentation: exploring the meaning of LCV. J. Consum. Res. **19**, 119–132 (1992)

Kamakura, W.A., Ramaswami, S.N., Srivastava, R.K.: Applying latent trait analysis in the evaluation of prospects for cross-selling financial products. Int. J. Res. Mark. **8**, 329–349 (1991)

Kamakura, W.A., Wedel, M., Agrawal, J.: Concomitant variable latent class models for the external analysis of choice data. Int. J. Mark. Res. **11**, 541–464 (1994)

Lanza, S.T., Collins, L.M., Lemmon, D.R., Schafer, J.L.: PROC LCA: a SAS procedure for latent class analysis. Struct. Equ. Model. **14**, 671–694 (2007)

Lazarsfeld, P.F.: The logical and mathematical foundation of latent structure analysis & the interpretation and mathematical foundation of latent structure analysis. In: Stouffer, S.A., et al. (eds.) Measurement and Prediction, pp. 362–472. Princeton University Press, Princeton, NJ (1950)

Leeflang, P.S.H., Wittink, D.R., Wedel, M., Naert, P.A.: Building Models for Marketing Decisions. Kluwer Academic Publishers, Boston (2000)

Lindsay, B., Clogg, C.C., Grego, J.: Semiparametric estimation in the Rasch model and related models, including a simple latent class model for item analysis. J. Am. Stat. Assoc. **86**, 96–107 (1991)

Magidson, J., Vermunt, J.K.: Latent class factor and cluster models, bi-plots and related graphical displays. Sociol. Methodol. **31**, 223–264 (2001)

McLachlan, G.J., Peel, D.: Finite Mixture Models. John Wiley & Sons, New York (2000)

Nagelkerke, E. Oberski, D.L., Vermunt, J.K.: Goodness-of-fit measures for multilevel latent class models. Sociol. Methodol. **46**, 252–282 (2016)

Oberski, D.L., van Kollenburg, G.H., Vermunt, J.K.: A Monte Carlo evaluation of three methods to detect local dependence in binary data latent class models. Adv. Classif. Data Anal. **7**, 267–279 (2013)

Paas, L.J., Bijmolt, T.H.A., Vermunt, J.K.: Long-term developments of respondent financial product portfolios in the EU: a multilevel latent class analysis. Metron. **73**, 249–262 (2015)

Paas, L.J., Molenaar, I.W.: Analysis of acquisition patterns: a theoretical and empirical evaluation of alternative methods. Int. J. Res. Mark. **22**, 87–100 (2005)

Paas, L.J., Sijtsma, K.: Nonparametric item response theory for evaluating the dimensionality of marketing measurement scales: a SERVQUAL application. Mark. Lett. **19**, 157–170 (2008)

Proctor, C.H.: A probabilistic formulation and statistical analysis of Guttman scaling. Psychometrika. **35**, 73–78 (1970)

Rossiter, J.R., Bellman, S.: Marketing Communications: Theory and Applications. Prentice Hall, Frenchs Forest (2005)

Rost, J.: Rasch models in latent classes. An integration of two approaches to item analysis. Appl. Psychol. Meas. **14**, 271–282 (1990)

Sijtsma, K., Molenaar, I.W.: Introduction to Nonparametric Item Response Theory. Sage, Thousand Oaks, CA (2002)

Skrondal, A., Rabe-Hesketh, S.: Generalized Latent Variable Modeling: Multilevel, Longitudinal and Structural Equation Models. Chapman & Hall/CRC, London (2004)

Smith, W.R.: Product differentiation and market segmentation as alternative marketing strategies. J. Mark. **21**, 3–8 (1956)

Ter Hofstede, F., Steenkamp, J-B.E.M., Wedel, M.: International segmentation based on consumer-product relations. J. Mark. Res. **36**, 1–17 (1999)

Vermunt, J.K.: LEM: A general program for the analysis of categorical data. Department of methodology and statistics, Tilburg University, The Netherlands (1997)

Vermunt, J.K.: The use restricted latent class models for defining and testing nonparametric and parametric IRT models. Appl. Psychol. Meas. **25**, 283–294 (2001)

Vermunt, J.K.: Multilevel latent class models. Sociol. Methodol. **33**, 213–239 (2003)

Vermunt, J.K.: Latent class modeling with covariates: two improved three-step approaches. Polit. Anal. **18**, 450–469 (2010)

Vermunt, J.K., Magidson, J.: Technical Guide for Latent GOLD 5.0: Basic, Advanced, and Syntax. Statistical Innovations Inc., Belmont, MA (2000–2016)

Vermunt, J.K., Magidson, J.: Latent class cluster analysis. In: Hagenaars, J., McCutcheon, A. (eds.) Applied Latent Class Analysis, pp. 89–106. Cambridge University Press, Cambridge (2002)

Wedel, M., Kamakura, W.A.: Market Segmentation: Conceptual and Methodological Foundations, 2nd edn. Kluwer, Dordrecht (2000)

Yip, G.S.: Total Global Strategy. Prentice Hall, Englewood Cliffs, NJ (1995)

Chapter 14
Hidden Markov Models in Marketing

Oded Netzer, Peter Ebbes, and Tammo H. A. Bijmolt

14.1 Introduction: Capturing Dynamics

Hidden Markov models (HMMs) have been used to model how a sequence of observations is governed by transitions among a set of latent states. HMMs were first introduced by Baum and co-authors in late 1960s and early 1970 (Baum and Petrie 1966; Baum et al. 1970), but only started gaining momentum a couple decades later. HMMs have been applied in various domains such as speech or word recognition (Rabiner et al. 1989), image recognition (Yamato et al. 1992), economics (Hamilton 1989, 2008), finance (Mamon and Elliott 2007), genetics (Eddy 1998), earth studies (Hughes and Guttorp 1994), and organization studies (Wang and Chan 2011). Over the last decade the number of applications of HMMs in marketing has grown substantially (see Sect. 14.4).

In the context of marketing, HMMs are often used to model a time series of customer or firm behavior such as customer choices or firm sales. These observations evolve over time following a latent Markovian process. That is, the firm or customer transition over time (in a Markovian manner) among a set of latent states, and given each one of the states the customer or firm (probabilistically) behaves in a particular fashion. The observations provide only a noisy measure of the underlying state. The main objective in utilizing a HMM is often to capture the

O. Netzer (✉)
Columbia Business School, Columbia University, 3022 Broadway, Uris Hall 520, New York, NY 10027, USA
e-mail: onetzer@gsb.columbia.edu

P. Ebbes
Department of Marketing, HEC Paris, 1, rue de la Libération, Jouy-en-Josas 78351, France

T.H.A. Bijmolt
Department of Marketing, University of Groningen, Groningen, The Netherlands

P.S.H. Leeflang et al. (eds.), *Advanced Methods for Modeling Markets*, International Series in Quantitative Marketing, DOI 10.1007/978-3-319-53469-5_14 dynamics in customer behavior over time. For simplicity we will describe the HMM in this chapter in the context of capturing dynamics in customer behavior and how firm actions may influence these behaviors. We note that HMMs in marketing are not limited to modeling consumer behavior, and have been applied in B2B contexts where the unit of analysis is a firm (Sect. 14.4).

Markovian models (see Vol. I, Sect. 8.2.4) have been used in marketing to capture dynamics in customer behavior since the mid-1960s (e.g., Ehrenberg 1965; Leeflang 1974). In these models the customer's behavior at time t is assumed to be a function of the customer's behavior at time $t-1$, and according to a typical Markov model, depends only on the customer's behavior at time $t-1$ and not the customer's behavior in earlier time periods. This type of Markovian relationship between current customer behavior and previous behavior has been often referred to in marketing and economics as state dependence (e.g., Chintagunta 1998; Dubé et al. 2010; Keane 1997; Seetharaman 2004).

To illustrate the notion of state dependence, consider a customer choice between brand A and brand B. State dependence suggests that the customer may have a different utility for brand A depending on whether brand A or brand B was previously chosen. For example, positive state dependence suggests that the customer's utility from choosing brand A will be higher if the customer purchased brand A (rather than brand B) in the previous time period. A related construct called variety seeking would predict the opposite effect, such that following a purchase of brand A the utility the customer obtains from choosing brand A again will be lower than its utility had the customer purchased brand B instead. For example, consider the Markov process of purchase probabilities of brands A and B in Fig. 14.1.

Based on Fig. 14.1, the probability of buying brand A given that brand A was previously chosen is 0.7, i.e. $P(A_t|A_{t-1})=0.7$, and the probability of buying brand B given that brand A was previously chosen is 0.3, i.e. $P(B_t|A_{t-1})=0.3$. Similarly, the probability of buying brand B given that brand B was previously chosen is 0.8, i.e. $P(B_t|B_{t-1})=0.8$, and the probability of buying brand A given that brand B was previously chosen is 0.2, i.e. $P(A_t|B_{t-1})=0.2$. Thus, this example demonstrates positive state dependence as staying with the same brand from one period to the next is considerably more likely than switching to the other brand. The model of customer behavior as depicted in Fig. 14.1 is fairly simplistic. This model assumes that the customer's choice in the current period dependent *only* on the customer's choice in the previous period. This is a result of two modeling assumptions:

Fig. 14.1 A Markov model of brand choice

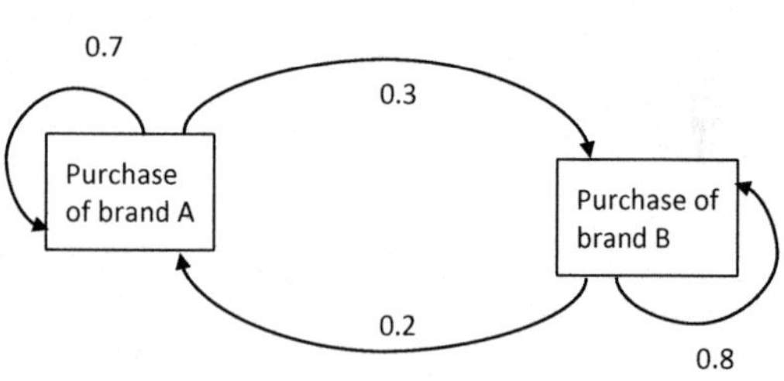

1. that the state of the world is defined purely based on the customer's observed purchase in the previous period, and
2. the Markovian assumption that only the last purchase and not the purchases before the last matter.

The first assumption could be relaxed by adding observed variables that may affect the customer behavior such as advertising or price as covariates in the model (Leeflang 1974). The second assumption could be relaxed by defining the state by a longer history of purchases such as a running average of past purchases or a weighted sum of past purchases (e.g., Guadagni and Little 1983).

An additional limitation of the model depicted in Fig. 14.1, or its extensions described above, is that these models assume that the customer state can be fully characterized by the observed behavior. However, the customer decision of which product to purchase is often governed by an underlying latent state of preference for different brands. While the customer may switch brands at times due to stock out or a visitor from out of town without changing her intrinsic preferences, the underlying preferences are likely to be relatively sticky reflecting the long-term customer behavior. HMMs offer a solution to this difficulty by proposing a model of *latent* customer preference and the transitions among them. In the context of the example described in Fig. 14.1, one could model the customer behavior using a HMM as shown in Fig. 14.2.

In the model described in Fig. 14.2, the two states represent the customer latent preference states for brand A and brand B and are represented through ovals. Unlike Fig. 14.1, the states in Fig. 14.2 are unobserved. Given the customer's latent preference state the customer probabilistically choses the brands (the observed

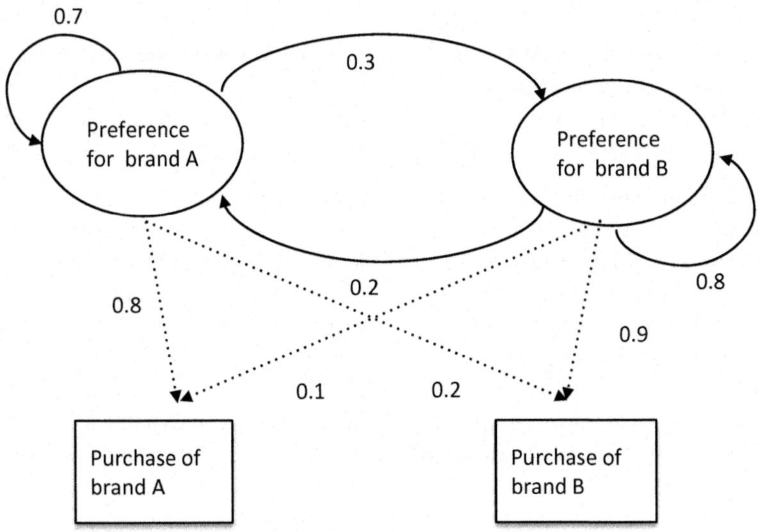

Fig. 14.2 A hidden Markov model of brand choice

purchases). For example, a customer who is in a state of a high preference for brand B does not choose brand B with probability 1 but rather with probability 0.9, for example, because the customer may occasionally have a visitor from out of town that prefers brand A. Similarly, when the customer is in the preference for brand A state she has a probability of 0.8 to choose brand A and a probability of 0.2 to choose brand B. Thus, in a HMM the observed behavior (purchases) serve as a noisy measure of the customer's true state. Additionally, the customer may change her preference for the brands over time. Such preference evolution will follow a Markovian process. In the example in Fig. 14.2, the customer has an 80% chance of staying in the preference for brand B state from one period to another and a 20% of transition to the brand A preference state. We call these the transition probabilities. In the example in Fig. 14.2, the transition probabilities for a customer in the preference for brand A state are [0.7 0.3] and in the preference for brand B state [0.2 0.8]. Because the states in Fig. 14.2 are fairly sticky, once a customer transitions to a different preference state she is likely to stay there for a while.

One may wonder how the latent preference states can be identified from a sequence of observed purchases. If the researcher observes a sequence of purchases that involves mainly purchases of brand A (though the customer may occasionally purchase brand B), the researcher will infer that the customer belongs to the brand A preference state. If at some point the customer starts buying more frequently brand B, the researcher may infer that the customer has transitioned to the brand B preference state. If the researcher also observes some marketing actions along with the observed purchases, she can relate these to the transition probabilities between the underlying preference states in order to understand their effect on shifting consumers' preferences.

Thus, the HMM in Fig. 14.2, and HMMs in general, have two main components:

1. a stochastic state dependent distribution—given a state the observations are stochastically determined, and
2. a state Markovian evolution—the system can transition from one state to another according to a set of transition probabilities.

Note that if the customer chooses brand A (B) with probability 1 when she is in preference state A (B), the HMM in Fig. 14.2 collapses to the observed Markov process in Fig. 14.1. Thus, the distinction between a HMM and an observed Markov process model is that in a HMM the states are only stochastically observed by the sequence of observations, whereas in a Markov model the observations deterministically determine the states.

An alternative way of thinking about a HMM of customer purchase behavior, is to think about a HMM as an approach to incorporate time dynamics in customer preferences and responses to marketing actions. Consider for example a customer that has the following utility function, as is commonly described in marketing and economic choice models:

$$u_{ijt} = X'_{ijt}\beta_{it} + \varepsilon_{ijt} \tag{14.1}$$

for $i = 1, 2, \ldots, N$, $j = 1, 2, \ldots, J$, and $t = 1, 2, \ldots, T$. In this model u_{ijt} is customer i's utility for product j at time t, X_{ijt} is a $P \times 1$ vector of time-varying, customer-specific, covariates relevant for product j and customer i, such as price and advertising, β_{it} is a $P \times 1$ vector of customer-specific and time varying response parameters, and ε_{ijt} is an error term, capturing unobserved shocks. In the model described in Eq. (14.1) the vector β_{it} varies across customers and time, thus capturing full heterogeneity and dynamics in customer preferences and customer responses to the covariates in X_{ijt}.

Estimating such model without putting any structure on the heterogeneity distribution across customers or across time (or both), is largely impractical for most empirical applications in marketing, because we often observe at most one observation per customer per time period. Two main approaches have been suggested in the literature to capture unobserved, cross-customer, heterogeneity in β_{it}, but without capturing dynamics (i.e. $\beta_{i1} = \beta_{i2} = \ldots = \beta_{iT}$). The first approach is a latent class or finite mixture approach (see Chap. 13 on Mixture Models) in which, instead of estimating a preference vector (β_i) for each individual, the researcher estimates a smaller set of vectors $\widetilde{\beta}_s$, where $s = 1, 2 \ldots, S$, and $S \ll N$. Here, the S latent classes are sometimes interpreted as segments (e.g., Wedel and Kamakura 2000). Another approach is the random-effects approach in which a multivariate distributional structure is assumed to describe the heterogeneity in β_i in the population of customers (e.g., $\beta_i \sim N(\mu_\beta, \Sigma_\beta)$) (see Chap. 16 on Bayesian Models). Here, each customer is assumed to be unique in its preferences (i.e. form its own segment of size 1), but the preferences are drawn from a population distribution.

In a similar manner one can define a distribution for how the vector of parameters β_{it} varies over time. HMMs can be thought of as the dynamic analogue to the latent class or finite mixture approach, whereas dynamic linear models (DLMs) based on the Kalman filter approach (see Chap. 5 on State Space Models) can be seen as the dynamic analogue to the random-effects approach.

Now that we have introduced the basic intuition behind the HMM and its relationship to other models in marketing, we detail the components of the HMM, the modeling considerations that one needs to take into account when building a HMM, as well as the importance of accounting for cross-customer heterogeneity when estimating a HMM. These topics are extensively discussed in Sect. 14.2. Estimating a HMM is the topic of Sect. 14.3. In Sect. 14.4 an overview of applications of HMMs in marketing is given. Section 14.5 provides a detailed description of a HMM-marketing application.

14.2 Building a HMM

14.2.1 Introduction

A HMM describes the customer's transition among a finite set of latent states over time and the stochastic process that converts the customer's state of the world to the observed behavior. Figure 14.3 extends Fig. 14.2 to a more general HMM of customer behavior.[1]

As can be seen in Fig. 14.3, the customer can transition over time among the K hidden states. As discussed before, the states follow a Markovian process. However, because the researcher generally does not observe the customer's latent state, we must convert the set of latent states at time t to the set of observed behaviors using a state dependent distribution. Although not explicitly shown here, covariates can affect both the customer's likelihood of transitioning among states as well as the customer observed behaviors given a state (e.g., Netzer et al. 2008).

It is important to note that in the context of modeling customer behavior we often assume that the customer observes all of the components in Fig. 14.3. That is, the customer knows her latent state, knows the likely behavior given a state and of course observes her actions given a state. The researcher on the other hand, observes only a sequence of observations. Hence, the hidden states, the transitions among them, the distribution of customer behavior given a state, and even the number of states (K), are parameters to be inferred or estimated from the available data.

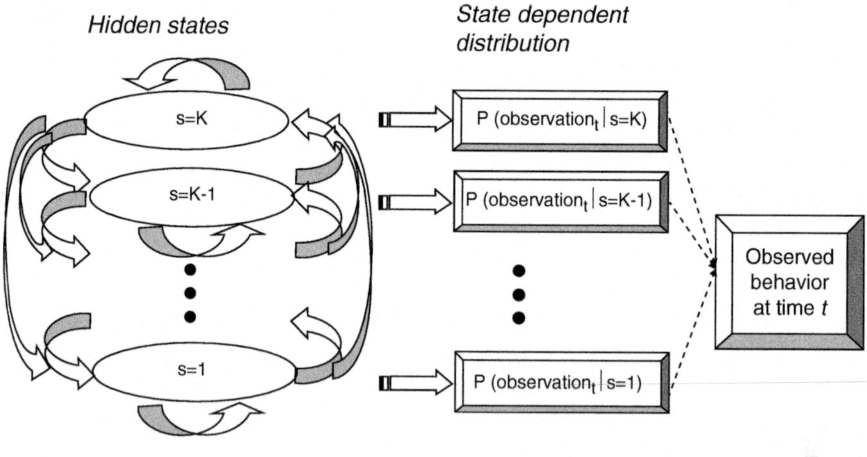

Fig. 14.3 An illustration of a general hidden Markov model

[1]Compare to Vol. I, Sect. 8.2.4.2.

14.2.2 The Basic Components of a HMM[2]

14.2.2.1 Introduction

We consider typical marketing data where we observe a time series of observations (e.g., choices), say $\{Y_{i1}, Y_{i2}, \ldots, Y_{iT}\}$, for a set of customers ($i = 1, \ldots, N$). Y_{it} may be a discrete or continuous variable, and may be univariate or multivariate. In a HMM, we assume that the probability distribution of Y_{it} depends on the realization of an unobserved (i.e. latent or hidden) discrete stochastic process S_{it}, with a finite state space $\{1, \ldots, K\}$. Hence, while we observe Y_{it} directly, we can only observe S_{it} indirectly through its stochastic outcome or noisy measure Y_{it}.

In the HMM the state membership S_{it} is assumed to satisfy the Markov property such that $P(S_{it+1}|S_{it}, S_{it-1}, \ldots, S_{i1}) = P(S_{it+1}|S_{it})$. That is, the state customer i is at in time period $t+1$ only depends on what state she is at in time period t. While higher order HMMs are possible, i.e. where the conditioning extends beyond the most recent time period, the first order assumption is often made for convenience and is often sufficient to capture the dynamics in the data. It should be noted that even though the state transitions are assumed to follow a first-order Markov process, the sequence of observations can follow any order of autocorrelation, depending on the values of the state transition probabilities.

The basic HMM for customer i transitioning among K states over T time periods can be written as (see Sect. 14.2.3 for an intuitive derivation of the following equation for a simple example with three time periods and two states):

$$P(Y_{i1}, Y_{i2}, \ldots, Y_{iT}) = \sum_{s_1=1,2,\ldots,K} P(S_{i1} = s_1) \prod_{\tau=2}^{T} P(S_{i\tau} = s_\tau | S_{i\tau-1} = s_{\tau-1}) \times \prod_{\upsilon=1}^{T} P(Y_{i\upsilon} | S_{i\upsilon} = s_\upsilon). \tag{14.2}$$

Hence, a standard HMM as presented in Eq. (14.2) consists of three main components, each of which we will discuss in more detail below:

- *The initial state distribution* $P(S_{i1} = s_1), s_1 = 1, 2, \ldots, K$, which may be represented by a $1 \times K$ row vector π.
- *The transition probabilities* $P(S_{it+1} = s_{t+1}|S_{it} = s_t)$ for $s_{t+1}, s_t = 1, 2, \ldots, K$, which may be represented by a $K \times K$ transition matrix Q.
- *The state-dependent distributions* of observed activity $P(Y_{it}|S_{it} = s_t)$, $s_t = 1, 2, \ldots, K$, which may be represented by a $K \times K$ matrix $M_{i\tau}$, that has the elements $P(Y_{it}|S_{it} = s_t)$ on the diagonal and zeros on the off-diagonal.

---

[2]This and the following sections build on Zucchini and MacDonald (2009). We adapt and extend their framework to a context typical for marketing where we have panel data. Zucchini and MacDonald (2009) mostly consider applications of HMMs for a single time series.

We refer the interested reader to Zucchini and MacDonald (2009) for further details of the modeling aspects of the HMM. Specification of these three components will be discussed next.

14.2.2.2 The Initial State Distribution

The initial state distribution describes the state membership at the beginning of the time series. Here, the researcher needs to choose how to specify the vector of initial state probabilities $\pi = \{\pi_1, \pi_2, \ldots, \pi_K\}$, where π_k is the probability of the customer being in state k at the first time period ($\pi_k = P(S_{i1} = s_1), s_1 = 1, 2, \ldots, K$). One possibility is to assume a-priori, based on theoretical grounds, that all customers start at one particular state. For example, in the context of a prescription of a new pharmaceutical drug, Montoya et al. (2010) assume that all physicians, prior to the introduction of the drug, start at the lowest state of prescription behavior (i.e. $\pi = \{1, 0, \ldots, 0\}$). However, this requires strong prior knowledge regarding the initial process.

Another option is to assume that the process started from its stationary distribution. In this case we would estimate π from solving the systems of equations $\pi = \pi Q$, where Q is the $K \times K$ transition probabilities matrix. This constraint is reasonable if the customer has had a long history of transactions with the firm prior to the start of the observation period (e.g., Netzer et al. 2008). A necessary condition to be able to calculate such stationary distribution is that the transition matrix is ergodic or irreducible. That is, it is possible to eventually get from every state to every other state with a positive probability.

Finally, in the most general form, one could estimate π directly using a vector of $K-1$ parameters. While this approach is most flexible, its primary drawback is that it increases the risk of local maxima, particularly when estimating the HMM using a Maximum Likelihood or an Expectation Maximization (EM) approach (Zucchini and MacDonald 2009).

14.2.2.3 The Transition Matrix Q

The conditional probabilities $P(S_{it+1}|S_{it})$ are called the transition probabilities and can be represented by a $K \times K$ transition matrix of conditional probabilities, Q. Each row in Q contains the conditional probabilities that the customer would be in any of the K latent states in the next time period, given the customer's current state. Thus, each element of the matrix Q needs to be in between 0 and 1, and the row-sum of each row in Q needs to equal 1. One can represent the transition matrix Q as in Fig. 14.4.

In the transition matrix Q depicted in Fig. 14.4, q_{11} is the conditional probability $P(S_{it+1} = 1|S_{it} = 1)$, Similarly, q_{12} is the conditional probability $P(S_{it+1} = 2|S_{it} = 1)$, and, in general, $q_{s_t s_{t+1}} = P(S_{it+1} = s_{t+1}|S_{it} = s_t)$ for $s_{t+1}, s_t = 1, 2, \ldots, K$.

State at t \ State at t+1	1	2	...	K
1	q_{11}	q_{12}	...	q_{1K}
2	q_{21}	q_{22}	...	q_{2K}
⋮	⋮	⋮	⋱	⋮
K	q_{K1}	q_{K2}	...	q_{KK}

Fig. 14.4 A schematic representation of the transition probability matrix Q of a HMM

In most applications outside of marketing the states are considered to be "states of the world" and therefore the transition matrix is not dependent on time. In such a case the HMM is a homogenous HMM with $Q_t = Q$ for $t = 1, 2, \ldots, T$, and Q can be represented as in Fig. 14.4. In marketing, however, the states are often states of customer behavior, which could be affected by the firm's actions. In such cases the transition matrix Q may depend on time and/or on time varying covariates, in which case we would write Q_t instead of Q. The resulting HMM is referred to as a non-homogeneous HMM (e.g., Netzer et al. 2008). Furthermore, if the transition matrix depends on how long the customer has been in the state, then the HMM is referred to as a semi-HMM (e.g., Montgomery et al. 2004).

As the number of states increases, the number of transition parameters grows at a rate of approximately the square of the increase in the number states. Therefore, it is sometimes beneficial to impose restrictions on the transition matrix. For example, one could impose that transitions are allowed only among adjacent states. In such case, only q_{jj}, q_{jj-1}, and q_{jj+1} (for $j = 2, 3, \ldots K-1$) along with q_{11}, q_{12}, q_{KK-1}, and q_{KK} are estimated, and the other transition matrix elements are set to 0. Alternatively, restrictions on Q could arise from the desire to capture a particular customer behavior. For example, customer churn could be captured by an absorbing state. In order to create a HMM with an absorbing state, one would restrict in the transition matrix Q all probabilities in the row of the absorbing state to zero except the probability on the diagonal, which is set equal to one.

14.2.2.4 The State Dependent Distributions

In a HMM, given the customer's state S_{it}, the observed behavior Y_{it} is a noisy measure and a probabilistic outcome of the state. If the customer's latent state S_{it} is known, the probability distribution of Y_{it}, $P(Y_{it}|S_{it})$, only depends on the current state. Thus, the temporal dependencies across observations are only driven by the customer's state membership over time and conditional on the customer's state the conditional probabilities $P(Y_{it}|S_{it})$ are independent over time.

The state dependent distribution is probably the most flexible component of the HMM as it can be fully adapted to capture the distribution of the observed outcome Y_{it}. For example, if the observed behavior is a binary outcome one can use a binary logit or binary probit distribution (e.g., Netzer et al. 2008), for multinomial choice one can use a multinomial logit or multinomial probit (e.g., Schweidel et al.

2011), for count data one can use a Poisson distribution (e.g., Ascarza and Hardie 2013), and for continuous Y_{it} one can use a normal distribution (e.g., Ebbes et al. 2010). In cases in which multiple outcomes are observed given a state one can use any combination of the above (e.g., Ebbes et al. 2010; Ebbes and Netzer 2017; Zhang et al. 2014). For example, Ebbes and Netzer (2017) consider a combination of different user behaviors on the social network website LinkedIn, consisting of activities that are discrete. They modeled this as a binary logit model (e.g., the user updated her profile page or not), and activities that are continuous as a Tobit-regression model (e.g., how many pages did the user visit).

The state dependent distributions are often specified as a generalized linear model, with or without covariates, where the (regression) parameters are state dependent. For instance, if we have just one dependent variable which indicates a binary choice, and we have P time-varying covariates given by the $P \times 1$ vector X_{it} (including an intercept), then $P(Y_{it}|S_{it} = s_t)$ could be modeled as a binary logit model, given by:

$$m_{its} = P\left(Y_{it}|S_{it} = s_t, X_{it}\right) = \frac{\exp\left(X'_{it}\beta_{s_t}\right)}{1 + \exp\left(X'_{it}\beta_{s_t}\right)}. \tag{14.3}$$

The state dependent distributions differ across states according to K vectors of regression coefficients β_{s_t}, one vector for each state $s_t = 1, 2, \ldots, K$. We can define a matrix M_{it} that collects the state dependent probabilities of consumer i in time t as a $K \times K$ diagonal matrix:

$$M_{it} = \begin{bmatrix} m_{it1} & \cdots & 0 \\ \vdots & \ddots & \vdots \\ 0 & \cdots & m_{itK} \end{bmatrix}.$$

If the state dependent distributions differ across states not only in terms of the value of the distribution parameters but also in the distributional functional form, then the model is sometimes called a hidden Markov mixture of experts. For example, in the context of behavioral games, Ansari et al. (2012) build a hidden Markov mixture of experts in which one of the states represents reinforcement learning and the other state represents belief learning.

The state dependent distributions in the HMM are rather modular, and depending on the behavior modeled, one can consider almost any general distribution or a mix of distributions, to capture the nature of the observed dependent variable(s).

14.2.3 *The HMM Likelihood Function*

14.2.3.1 Likelihood Function

In this section we put together the three components of the HMM, namely, the initial state distribution, the transition matrix, and the state dependent distribution to form the HMM likelihood function of observing the sequence of observations. To build the intuition for the likelihood function (and Eq. (14.2)), we start with a simple example, where we have two states ($K=2$) and three time periods ($T=3$). For customer i, we therefore observe Y_{i1}, Y_{i2}, and Y_{i3} and this customer is in (latent) states S_{i1}, S_{i2},and S_{i3}, in periods 1, 2 and 3, respectively. The joint probability of data and latent states is given by $P(Y_{i1}, Y_{i2}, Y_{i3}, S_{i1}, S_{i2}, S_{i3})$, and can be written as follows[3]:

$$\begin{aligned} P\left(Y_{i1}, Y_{i2}, Y_{i3}, S_{i1}, S_{i2}, S_{i3}\right) &= P\left(Y_{i3}, S_{i3}, Y_{i2}, S_{i2}, Y_{i1}, S_{i1}\right) \\ &= P\left(Y_{i3}|S_{i3}, Y_{i2}, S_{i2}, Y_{i1}, S_{i1}\right) \times P\left(S_{i3}|Y_{i2}, S_{i2}, Y_{i1}, S_{i1}\right) \\ &\quad \times P\left(Y_{i2}|S_{i2}, Y_{i1}, S_{i1}\right) \times P\left(S_{i2}|Y_{i1}, S_{i1}\right) \\ &\quad \times P\left(Y_{i1}|S_{i1}\right) P\left(S_{i1}\right). \end{aligned} \tag{14.4}$$

Here is where the Markov property together with the fact that the state dependent distributions are conditionally independent help simplifying the previous product of conditional probabilities:

1. $P(Y_{i3}|S_{i3}, Y_{i2}, S_{i2}, Y_{i1}, S_{i1}) = P(Y_{i3}|S_{i3})$—the distribution of Y_{13} only depends on the current state S_{i3} and not on pervious states nor previous observations;
2. $P(S_{i3}|Y_{i2}, S_{i2}, Y_{i1}, S_{i1}) = P(Y_{i3}|S_{i2})$—the state membership in $t=3$ *only* depends on the customer's previous State S_{i2} (the Markov property);
3. $P(Y_{i2}|S_{i2}, Y_{i1}, S_{i1}) = P(Y_{i2}|S_{i2})$—following the same rational as 1;
4. and, $P(S_{i2}|Y_{i1}, S_{i1}) = P(S_{i2}|S_{i1})$—following the same rational as 2.

Hence, the likelihood of observing the set of observations and states can be more succinctly written as:

$$\begin{aligned} P\left(Y_{i1}, Y_{i2}, Y_{i3}, S_{i1}, S_{i2}, S_{i3}\right) &= P\left(S_{i1}\right) P\left(Y_{i1}|S_{i1}\right) P\left(S_{i2}|S_{i1}\right) \\ &\quad P\left(Y_{i2}|S_{i2}\right) P\left(S_{i3}|S_{i2}\right) P\left(Y_{i3}|S_{i3}\right). \end{aligned} \tag{14.5}$$

However, in practice, we do not observe the customer states. That is, we observe the customer's activity (Y_{i1}, Y_{i2}, and Y_{i3}) but not the customer's state in each time period

[3] Here we use a general product rule to calculate the probability of the joint distribution using conditional probabilities. For example, Under the general product rule the joint distribution of four 'events' (B_1, B_2, B_3, B_4) can be written as the product of conditional distributions as follows: $P(B_1, B_2, B_3, B_4) = P(B_1|B_2, B_3, B_4)P(B_2|B_3, B_4)P(B_3|B_4)P(B_4)$.

(S_{i1}, S_{i2}, and S_{i3}). Thus, to obtain the likelihood for the observed data, we need to "integrate" the latent states, across all state paths that the customer could take over time:

$$\begin{aligned}
P(Y_{i1}, Y_{i2}, Y_{i3}) &= \sum_{s_1=1}^{2}\sum_{s_2=1}^{2}\sum_{s_3=1}^{2} P(Y_{i1}, Y_{i2}, Y_{i3}, S_{i1}=s_1, S_{i2}=s_2, S_{i3}=s_3) \\
&= \sum_{s_1,s_2,s_3} P(S_{i1}=s_1) \times P(Y_{i1}|S_{i1}=s_1) \times P(S_{i2}=s_2|S_{i1}=s_1) \\
&\quad \times P(Y_{i2}|S_{i2}=s_2) \times P(S_{i3}=s_3|S_{i2}=s_2) \times P(Y_{i3}|S_{i3}=s_3) \\
&= \sum_{s_1,s_2,s_3} P(S_{i1}=s_1) \times P(S_{i2}=s_2|S_{i1}=s_1) \times P(S_{i3}=s_3|S_{i2}=s_2) \\
&\quad \times P(Y_{i1}|S_{i1}=s_1) \times P(Y_{i2}|S_{i2}=s_2) \times P(Y_{i3}|S_{i3}=s_3) \\
&= \sum_{s_1,s_2,s_3} P(S_{i1}=s_1) \prod_{\tau=2}^{3} P(S_{i\tau}=s_\tau|S_{i\tau-1}=s_{\tau-1}) \\
&\quad \times \prod_{\upsilon=1}^{3} P(Y_{i\upsilon}|S_{i\upsilon}=s_\upsilon)
\end{aligned} \tag{14.6}$$

where $s_\tau = 1$ or 2 for $\tau = 1, 2, 3$. One limitation with the likelihood function as presented here, is that the summation over all possible states' paths that the customer could take, involves K^T terms in the summation, which can create a computational burden when the number of time periods and states increase (see also Eq. (14.2)). Zucchini and MacDonald (2009, p. 37) show that the HMM likelihood function can be written in a more convenient matrix form instead. Extending the simple example to a more general case with K states and T time periods, and using matrix notation, we can write the HMM likelihood function for customer i as:

$$L_{iT} = P(Y_{i1}, Y_{i2}, \ldots, Y_{iT}) = \pi M_{i1} Q M_{i2} \ldots Q M_{iT} \iota \tag{14.7}$$

where π, M_{it}, and Q are defined as above and ι is a $K \times 1$ vector of ones. The likelihood function (14.7) also provides the intuition for the HMM process. The process starts with customer i belonging to a particular latent state k, which follows the initial state distribution π. Given her state in period 1 the customer behaves in particular manner, as described by the probabilities M_{i1}. Next, the customer may transition from her state at time period 1 to her state at time period 2 (as described by the transition probabilities Q). Subsequently, given the state the customer transitioned to in period 2 (which may be the same state as her state in period 1), M_{i2} captures customer behavior in period 2, followed by another state transition between period 2 and period 3 according to the probabilities in the transition matrix Q. This process repeats itself until we reach the final behavior of customer i in time period T.

The likelihood for the complete sample of customers $i = 1, 2, \ldots, N$ is given by the following product: $L_T = \prod_{i=1}^{N} L_{iT}$. In Sect. 14.3, we discuss several approaches to estimate the HMM parameters after observing the data.

14.2.3.2 The Forward and Backward Probabilities

For the purpose of state recovery, prediction, and estimation, it is useful to split the likelihood function in (14.7) into forward and backward components.

Let the $1 \times K$ row vector α_{it} be defined as follows: $\alpha_{it} = \pi M_{i1} \prod_{s=2}^{t} QM_{is}$. Thus, we can rewrite the likelihood function up to time T as $L_{iT} = \alpha_{iT}\iota$, which can be obtained recursively as $\alpha_{it} = \alpha_{it-1} QM_{it}$ $(t \geq 2)$ with, for $t = 1$, $\alpha_{i1} = \pi M_{i1}$. The row vector α_{it} is called the vector of *forward* probabilities. Furthermore, it can be shown (e.g., Zucchini and MacDonald 2009, p. 60) that the j-th element of α_{it}, say $\alpha_{it}(j)$, is the joint probability $P(Y_{i1}, Y_{i2}, \ldots, Y_{it}, S_{it} = j)$.

Similarly, one can define a $1 \times K$ vector of *backward* probabilities β_{it}. This vector captures the last $T - t$ terms of the HMM likelihood recursion, that is $\beta'_{it} = \left(\prod_{s=t+1}^{T} QM_{is}\right)\iota$, for $t = 1, 2, \ldots, T$, with $\beta'_{iT} = \iota$. It can be shown (e.g., Zucchini and MacDonald p. 61) that the j-th element of this vector, say $\beta_{it}(j)$, is the conditional probability $P(Y_{it+1}, Y_{it+2}, \ldots, Y_{iT} | S_{it} = j)$. This is, the probability of observing $Y_{it+1}, Y_{it+2}, \ldots, Y_{iT}$, given that customer i is in state j in time period t.

In fact, the forward and backward probabilities can be combined to give the joint probability $P(Y_{i1}, Y_{i2}, \ldots, Y_{iT}, S_{it} = j)$ as the product of the two, i.e. $\alpha_{it}(j)\beta_{it}(j)$. Then,

$$P(Y_{i1}, Y_{i2}, \ldots, Y_{iT}) = \sum_{j=1}^{K} P(Y_{i1}, Y_{i2}, \ldots, Y_{iT}, S_{it} = j) = \sum_{j=1}^{K} \alpha_{it}(j)\beta_{it}(j) = \alpha_{it}\beta'_{it}. \tag{14.8}$$

Hence, another way to compute the likelihood L_{iT} is through any of the $t = 1, 2, \ldots, T$ combinations $\alpha_{it}\beta'_{it}$. The likelihood function given in (14.7) is a special case of the product of the forward-backward probabilities for $t = T$, where we only need the forward probabilities (as $\beta'_{iT} = \iota$).

When the time series is long the calculation of the forward and backward probabilities can suffer from underflow. Zucchini and MacDonald (2009, Sect. 3.2) discuss appropriate scaling of these probabilities to avoid underflow.

14.2.4 *HMM State Recovery and Prediction*

In some cases, HMMs are primarily used as a predictive model with the objective of predicting customer behavior (Y_{it}) in future time period $t = T + h$, $h > 0$. One advantage of using HMMs for that purpose is that it is easy to predict a few periods ahead. For example, Paas et al. (2007) present a HMM for household ownership of

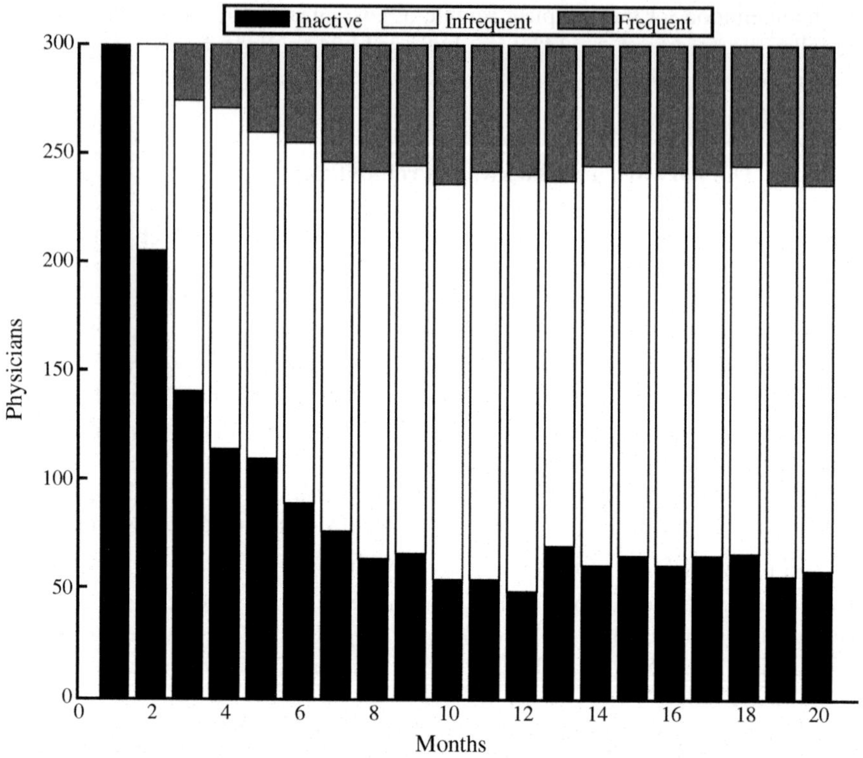

Fig. 14.5 An example of customer state membership evolution from Montoya et al. (2010) *Source*: Montoya et al. (2010, p. 916)

financial products and use the HMM to predict future acquisitions of such products. In other cases the primary objective of the HMM is to recover the customer's state (S_{it}) at each time period. For example, Ebbes and Netzer (2017) use a HMM and observations on users' activity on LinkedIn with the primary objective of inferring which users are in a state of a job search. State recovery can also be used to capture how the firm's customer base has evolved over time. Figure 14.5 depicts such an example from Montoya et al. (2010). Following the introduction of a new drug, and marketing efforts by the firm, the physicians' base has transitioned from the inactive prescription state prior to the introduction of the drug to a majority of the physicians in an infrequent prescription state, and approximately 20% of the physicians in a frequent prescription state. Note that it took the physicians' base approximately eight months post the introduction of the drug to stabilize on the prescription state membership.

Both predictions and state recovery are closely related to the HMM likelihood function and forward/backward probabilities described in Sect. 14.2.3.2.

14.2.4.1 Recovering State Membership

Two main approaches have been suggested for recovering the state membership distribution: filtering and smoothing.[4] Filtering utilizes only the information known up to time *t* to recover the individual's state at time *t*, while smoothing utilizes the full information available in the data to predict the customer state at any point in time during the observed data period. The smoothing approach is quite common in fields such as speech recognition where one wants to infer the meaning of a particular word both by words that appeared prior to the focal word and words that appeared after the focal word. In most marketing applications, the researcher is more interested to infer a customer state only based on the history of the observed behavior and not based on future behavior and hence the filtering approach is more common.

The smoothing state membership probabilities can be computed using the Bayes formula:

$$P(S_{it}=j|Y_{i1},Y_{i2},\ldots,Y_{iT})=\frac{P(Y_{i1},Y_{i2},\ldots,Y_{iT},S_{it}=j)}{P(Y_{i1},Y_{i2},\ldots,Y_{iT})} \tag{14.9}$$

which can be further simplified using the forward and backward probabilities discussed in the previous section as follows:

$$P(S_{it}=j|Y_{i1},Y_{i2},\ldots,Y_{iT})=\frac{\alpha_{it}(j)\beta_{it}(j)}{L_{iT}}. \tag{14.10}$$

Similarly, the filtering probabilities can be written as:

$$P(S_{it}=j|Y_{i1},Y_{i2},\ldots,Y_{it})=\frac{P(Y_{i1},Y_{i2},\ldots,Y_{it},S_{it}=j)}{P(Y_{i1},Y_{i2},\ldots,Y_{it})} \tag{14.11}$$

which can be computed using the forward probabilities as:

$$P(S_{it}=j|Y_{i1},Y_{i2},\ldots,Y_{it})=\frac{\alpha_{it}(j)}{L_{it}}. \tag{14.12}$$

Another approach related to recovering state membership attempts to recover the most probable sequence of states given the full information in the data. Unlike smoothing, which predicts state membership at one point in time, this approach decodes the best hidden *state path* given a sequence of observations. In principle the most likely path could be discovered by running the forward algorithm for each possible sequence of states, and then find the path which corresponds to the highest probability. Clearly, this would easily become impossible given the potentially large number of state sequences. Instead, for this task one could use

[4]Compare also Sects. 5.4.2 and 5.4.3 for corresponding approaches.

the Viterbi algorithm which is a recursive algorithm (leveraging the forward and backward probabilities algorithm) akin to dynamic programing algorithms (Jurafsky and Martin 2008; Viterbi 1967). If the main purpose of the analysis is to recover and interpret the sequence of state membership, it is recommended to test the accuracy of the Viterbi algorithm using simulation (Zucchini and MacDonald 2009, pp. 84–86). For marketing applications, one could potentially compute one such sequence for each customer. For instance, in the context of the preference example for brands A and B discussed earlier in this chapter, the Viterbi algorithm would allow a manager to infer the most probably sequence of preference states that a customer took during the observation window.

14.2.4.2 Predicting Future Activity

In some applications of HMMs, the researcher is interested in predicting future values of the observed variable Y_{it}. Hence, we want to compute the probability of observing customer i's activity in the time period $T+h$, $h>0$, given the activity we have observed until time T. This probability is derived from Bayes theorem, i.e.

$$P\left(Y_{iT+h}|Y_{i1}, Y_{i2}, \ldots, Y_{iT}\right) = \frac{P\left(Y_{i1}, Y_{i2}, \ldots, Y_{iT}, Y_{iT+h}\right)}{P\left(Y_{i1}, Y_{i2}, \ldots, Y_{iT}\right)}. \tag{14.13}$$

The denominator of the above equation is simply L_{iT} given in (14.7). The numerator can be computed by multiplying the customer's forward probabilities by h transition matrices and by the customer's state dependent distribution in period $T+h$ (see also Zucchini and MacDonald 2009, p. 33 and p. 37). That is,

$$P\left(Y_{i1}, Y_{i2}, \ldots, Y_{iT}, Y_{iT+h}\right) = \pi M_{i1} Q M_{i2} \ldots Q M_{iT} Q Q \ldots Q M_{iT+h} \iota = \alpha_{iT} Q^h M_{iT+h} \iota. \tag{14.14}$$

The predicted customer behavior in period $T+h$ can be written as:

$$P\left(Y_{iT+h}|Y_{i1}, Y_{i2}, \ldots, Y_{iT}\right) = \frac{\pi M_{i1} Q M_{i2} \ldots Q M_{iT} Q^h M_{iT+h} \iota}{\pi M_{i1} Q M_{i2} \ldots Q M_{iT} \iota} = \frac{\alpha_{iT} Q^h M_{iT+h} \iota}{\alpha_{iT} \iota}. \tag{14.15}$$

This expression can be computed as a by-product in likelihood estimation.

14.2.5 Accounting for Cross-customer Heterogeneity

One of the aspects that differentiates HMMs in marketing from HMMs in other fields is that in other fields there is usually one single long sequence of observations (e.g., pixels in an image or the GDP in the United States over the past few decades) and the HMM is estimated for a single time series using the entire sequence of observations. In marketing, on the other hand, we often have a panel data structure in which we observe multiple sequences of observations, one for each customer, allowing for different customers to possibly have heterogeneous preferences and behaviors.

The idea that customers are different in terms of preferences and behavior has a long history in marketing. Modeling consumer heterogeneity has been the central focus of many econometric marketing applications (see Chap. 8 in Vol. I and Chap. 13 in this volume). Voluminous research has demonstrated the bias that may arise from not accounting for heterogeneity across customers. Moreover, in many marketing applications the researcher is interested in targeting individual consumers based on their individual preferences, which would require a detailed understanding of customer heterogeneity.

Accounting for cross-customer heterogeneity is even more important in the context of dynamic models, such as the HMM. Heckman (1981) demonstrates that estimating a random utility homogenous choice model based on a heterogeneous sample may lead to a strong spurious state dependence, even when the actual choices were independent over time. Similarly, a model that accounts for heterogeneity but ignores state dependence may overestimate the degree of heterogeneity (Keane 1997). In the context of HMMs, not accounting for cross-customer heterogeneity forces the states to capture both heterogeneity (similar to latent class model) and dynamics. To see this, imagine a group of customers who are static in their preferences (a HMM estimated for these customers should lead to an identity transition matrix as customers do not switch states over time) and a second group of customers who have a 60% chance of staying in their previous preference state and 40% chance of transitioning to another preference state at each time period. A homogenous HMM estimated using data from both groups of customers would lead to a single transition matrix, that is an "average" of an identity matrix and a matrix reflecting the switching behavior of the second group. Consequently, the estimated transition matrix would suggest that *all* customers are dynamic in their preferences (including the first group with static preferences), whereas at the same time, the estimated transition matrix overstates the stickiness of the states (i.e. the likelihood of staying in the same state from one period to another) for the second, dynamic group of customers.

With long enough time series per customer, in principle, one could estimate a separate HMM for each customer. This would give a unique set of estimated parameters for each customer. That is, each customer would have its own estimated initial state probabilities (π_i), transition probability matrix (Q_i), and parameters of the state-dependent activity distribution (M_{it}). Because typically the number of observations per customer are insufficient to estimate a unique HMM for each customer, data can be pooled across customers by including customer-level heterogeneity in the HMM. For instance, random-effect parameters can be included in a HMM and estimated using either a Hierarchal Bayes MCMC estimation or a simulated Maximum Likelihood approach (Train 2009, Sect. 6.8.7 in Vol. I and Chap. 16 in this volume). Alternatively, the heterogeneity across customers can be captured using a latent class approach (Kamakura and Russell 1989; Chap. 13 in this volume). One could also account for observed heterogeneity by including covariates, such as demographics in the model. However, because observed heterogeneity covariates often capture only limited degree of heterogeneity, we recommend controlling for unobserved heterogeneity as well.

In the most general case one could allow of cross-customer heterogeneity in each of the three HMM components: initial state distributions (π_i), transition matrix (Q_i), and state-dependent distribution (M_{it}). Capturing heterogeneity in π_i and Q_i but not in M_{it} allows different customers to have different level of stickiness to the states but assume that, given a state, all customers have the same preference structure, exhibit similar behavior, or respond in a similar manner to marketing actions. The attractiveness of such an approach is that the interpretation of the states becomes easier, because the states now mean the same thing for all customers. On the other hand, allowing for heterogeneity in the state-dependent distribution (M_{it}), implies that what a "high state" is for one customer may be very different from what a "high state" is for another customer. A limitation of not accounting for heterogeneity in the state-dependent distribution is that if the behavior given a state is highly heterogeneous and has a wide support (e.g., food expenditure which can vary substantially among customers given their household size and income), not accounting for heterogeneity in the state-dependent distribution could lead to confusion between heterogeneity and dynamics, as some states will capture heterogeneity in addition to dynamics.

Finally, to the best of our knowledge, all HMMs in marketing (and in other fields) assumed the same number states for all customers (even if heterogeneity in the model parameters is allowed). Failure to account for heterogeneity in the number of states leads to a mis-specified model for customers for whom the number of states does not match their dynamic behavior. Padilla et al. (2017) attempt to relax this assumption and allow for heterogeneity in the number of states across customers.

In sum, when one estimates a HMM for a heterogeneous set of consumers, we encourage researchers to carefully account for unobserved heterogeneity in order to disentangle heterogeneity from dynamics. It is almost always advisable to allow for heterogeneity in the transition matrix (Q_i) and the initial state distribution (π_i) and wherever possible or needed also in the state-dependent distributions (M_{it}).

14.2.6 Non-homogenous HMMs[5]: Time-Varying Covariates in the Transition Matrix

In most non-marketing applications the states of the HMM are exogenous states of the world. Accordingly, the transition matrix in these applications is rarely a

[5]In the context of HMMs the convention is to call a non-homogenous HMM a HMM with a time variant transition matrix (Q_t). This is not be confused with a heterogeneous HMM, in which the transition matrix, and possibly other model parameters, can vary across consumers (Q_i) and from a non-stationary HMM in which the state transition are a function of time itself.

function of covariates. However, in marketing, because the states of the HMM are often customer behavior states, the firm may believe that it can affect customers' transitions among states. Therefore, marketing applications of HMMs often allow the transition matrix to be a function of covariates such as marketing actions. Indeed, until the diffusion of HMMs to marketing, HMMs rarely incorporated time-varying covariates in the transition matrix (see Hughes and Guttorp 1994 for an exception). Early work on HMMs in marketing (e.g., Montoya et al. 2010; Netzer et al. 2008; Paas et al. 2007) proposed non-homogenous HMMs in which the transitions among the states were a function of customer activities or marketing actions. In these cases the transition probabilities in Q_i are both customer and time specific, which can be modeled by standard (or ordered) logit models. For instance, $P(S_{it} = s_t | S_{it-1} = s_{t-1}) = f(Z_{it})$, where $f(Z_{it})$ is the logit function and Z_{it} is a vector of covariates that are specific to customer i and time period t, and $s_t, s_{t-1} = 1, 2, \ldots, K$. Now, the elements of the transition matrix are both a function of time and customer, and we write Q_{it}.

As discussed earlier, one could also add covariates in the state dependent distributions. These covariates would affect the customer behavior, conditional on the customer's state. The choice of which covariates should go in the transition matrix and which should go in the state-dependent distribution is a researcher decision. In general, covariates that are included in the transition matrix should be covariates that are postulated to have a long-term effect on the customer's behavior. The rational is that these covariates create a regime shift in the customer behavior by transitioning the customer to a different, and often sticky, state of customer behavior. Covariates that are included in the state-dependent distribution, by definition affect the customer behavior only in the current time period, conditional on the customer state, and therefore have a short-term effect. In the context of pharmaceutical drugs prescriptions by physicians, Montoya et al. (2010) demonstrate that including detailing and sampling to physicians covariates in both in the transition probabilities and the state dependent distribution can capture both the short- and long-term effects of these marketing activities.

14.2.7 Selecting the Number of States and Model Selection

The first order of business in estimating a HMM is to select the number of hidden states (K). The number of states could either be estimated from the data or defined based on theoretical grounds. If the researcher has a strong theoretical basis with respect to the number and the interpretation of each of the states, then the researcher could determine the number of states a-priori. For example, Ansari et al. (2012) choose a-priori two states which correspond to reinforcement and belief learning over repeated rounds of a behavioral game.

A more common approach is to use model selection procedures to choose the number of states based on the fit of the model to the data. The approach involves estimating a range of models with increasing number of states K until the point at which adding an additional state does not further improve or leads to a worse model selection criterion value. Increasing the number of hidden states adds flexibility and parameters to the model and, hence, will always improve model fit as measured by the likelihood. However, as the number of model parameters increases, the key issue is whether the improvement in model fit is large enough relative to the increase in the number of parameters. Accordingly, one often uses panelized model selection fit measures, such as information criteria, which balance model fit and model parsimony.

Information criteria add a penalty to the model fit ($-2 \times \textit{loglikelihood}$) on the basis of the number of parameters g. A typical and fully specified HMM with no covariates and a single parameter state dependent distribution has $K-1$ parameters in π, $K \times (K-1)$ parameters in Q, and K parameters in M, leading to $g = (K+1)\ (K-1) + K$ parameters. The Akaike Information criterion (AIC) equals: $-2 \times \textit{loglikelihood} + 2 \times g$, the Bayesian Information Criterion (BIC) equals $-2 \times \textit{loglikelihood} + g \times \ln(n)$, and the Consistent Akaike Information criterion (CAIC) equals: $-2 \times \textit{loglikelihood} + g \times (\ln(n) + 1)$, where n denotes the sample size (which for the case of panel data equals to $N \times T$, where $i = 1, 2, \ldots, N$ is the number of customers and $t = 1, 2, \ldots, T$ is the number of time periods per customer). The choice among alternative model specifications can be made by selecting the model with the minimum value of a specific information criterion.

For reasonable sample sizes, the penalty per additional parameter is typically much larger for BIC and CAIC than for AIC. Accordingly, the AIC tends to favor models with many, oftentimes too many, states. Accordingly, the BIC is commonly the preferred criterion to determine the number of states (Bartolucci et al. 2014).

When one estimates the model based on Bayesian estimation procedures, typical Bayesian model selection criteria such as the Log Marginal Density and the Bayes Factor are often used. These criteria could be calculated from the output of the MCMC procedure (see Chib 1995, 2001 for details). It has been shown that the BIC measure in classical estimation asymptotically approximates the Log Marginal Density (Congdon 2002, p. 473). Alternatively, because the Log Marginal Density and the Bayes Factor, sometimes recommend non-parsimonious models, researchers have used a modified Deviance Information Criterion (Celeux et al. 2006), cross validation approaches, and posterior predictive checks for model selection. Another advantage of these model selection criteria is that they do not require the calculation of g (the number of parameters), as for e.g., AIC or BIC, which is often cumbersome in particular if the researcher accounts for cross-customer heterogeneity through random coefficients.

Several studies have proposed model selection criteria that are specific for HMM estimation. Bacci et al. (2014) propose a classification-based or entropy-based criterion, which examines the posterior probabilities of state membership of each of the customers. The idea behind these measures is that if the states of the HMM are well-separated, the posterior probabilities of state membership are close to one, resulting in an entropy that is close to zero. They find that most decision criteria tend to work reasonably well, and their performance improves if the sample size or the number of time periods increases. When the number of states is large, BIC, and the classification-based criteria tend to underestimate the correct number of states.

Smith et al. (2006) build on the Kullback–Leibler (KL) divergence criterion and propose a Markov Switching Criterion (MSC), which is specifically suited for states selection in Markov and latent Markov models. Using simulations, they find that the MSC preforms well in term of retaining the correct number of states and, unlike measures such as the AIC, avoids overstating the true number of states. We encourage future research to explore the use of the reversible jump algorithm (e.g., Ebbes et al. 2015; Green 1995) to simultaneously estimate the HMM with varying number of states and select the best fitting model.

Similar model selection criteria to the ones described in this section can be used to select among different model specifications other than selecting the number of latent states K, such as whether and which covariates to include in the transition probabilities or in the state dependent distribution.

14.3 Estimating a HMM

14.3.1 Introduction

As discussed above, a HMM has three main components leading to three sets of parameters to be estimated:

1. the initial state probabilities π_i;
2. the transition probability matrix Q_i, and
3. parameters of the state dependent distributions M_{it}.

In this section we retain the subscript i for π and Q implicitly assuming that we would like to control for cross-customer heterogeneity, either by estimating a separate HMM for each customer, or by estimating one HMM by pooling across customers while including customer-specific unobserved and/or observed heterogeneity through covariates.

Three main approaches have been proposed to estimate the model parameters of a HMM:

1. Maximum Likelihood estimation by the Expectations Maximization (EM) algorithm;
2. Maximum Likelihood estimation by directly optimizing the likelihood function, and
3. Bayesian estimation.

We will briefly discuss each approach in turn, focusing on the essentials, and provide references for further details of the implementations. We note that several software packages are available to estimate basic HMMs (e.g., R-HMM in CRAN, Latent GOLD),

14.3.2 The Expectation Maximization (EM) Algorithm

A popular way to estimate a HMM is through the EM algorithm, also known as the Baum-Welch forward-backward algorithm (Baum et al. 1970; Baum 1972; Dempster et al. 1977; Welch 2003). The main idea behind the EM algorithm is to treat the state memberships, which are unobserved, as missing data. The algorithm then iteratively finds the parameters that maximize the likelihood function by an E step and an M step. The E step is designed to obtain the conditional expectations of the missing data (here, the state memberships). Then, in the M step, the complete data log likelihood is maximized. The complete data now comprises the observed data and the conditional expectations of the missing data. Generally, the complete data log-likelihood function can be easily maximized, often much more straightforwardly then the (log) likelihood function of only the observed data.

To derive the EM algorithm for HMMs, we start with the complete data likelihood function. Extending the three-time periods and two states example used in Sect. 14.2.3 to motivate the construction of the likelihood function, we can write the complete data log-likelihood function of observing the customer states and the customer behavior at each time period t, $t = 1, 2, \ldots, T$, as[6]:

$$\log P\left(y_1, y_2, \ldots, y_T, s_1, s_2, \ldots, s_T\right) = \log\left(\pi_{s_1}\right) + \sum_{t=2}^{T} \log\left(q_{s_{t-1}s_t}\right) + \sum_{t=1}^{T} \log\left(m_{ts_t}\right) \tag{14.16}$$

where, $y_1, y_2, \ldots, y_T, s_1, s_2, \ldots, s_T$ are the realizations of the customer's state and activities at each time period. π_{s_1} is the s_1-th element of the initial state distribution vector π, which corresponds to the state the customer is at in time period 1. Similarly, $q_{s_{t-1}s_t}$ is the element from the transition matrix Q that corresponds to the customer probability of transitioning from her state at time $t-1$ to her state at time t, and m_{ts_t} is the s_t-diagonal element from the matrix M_t that corresponds to the customer's state dependent distribution given the customer state at time t (s_t).

To implement the EM algorithm, it would be more convenient to represent the state assignments by the $K \times 1$ dummy vector $v_t = (v_{t1}, v_{t2}, \ldots, v_{tK})$ where $v_{tj} = 1$ if $s_t = j$, and 0 otherwise, and the $K \times K$ dummy matrix W_t, with elements $w_{tij} = 1$ if $s_{t-1} = i$ and $s_t = j$, and 0 otherwise. We can now rewrite the complete data log likelihood in (14.16) as:

$$\log P\left(y_1, y_2, \ldots y_T, s_1, s_2, \ldots, s_T\right) = v_1'\tilde{\pi} + \sum_{t=2}^{T} \iota'\left(W_t \circ \tilde{Q}\right)\iota + \sum_{t=1}^{T} v_t'\tilde{m}_t \tag{14.17}$$

[6]For ease of exposition we drop in the description of the EM algorithm the subscript i for customer. Estimating a HMM with heterogeneous parameters across customers using the EM algorithm is challenging, as it would involve integrating out (in the M step) the unobserved heterogeneity.

where, $\tilde{\pi}$ is a $K \times 1$ vector such that, $\tilde{\pi} = \log(\pi)$, $\tilde{Q}$ is a $K \times K$ matrix defined by $\log Q$, $\circ$ denotes the Hadamard matrix product, and $\tilde{m}_t$ is a $K \times 1$ vector with the log of the diagonal elements of M_t.

If one observes panel data structure with multiple observations per person, the total sample complete data log likelihood (SCDLL), ignoring unobserved heterogeneity across customers, would be the sum of (14.17) across all customers $i = 1, 2, \ldots, N$, i.e.:

$$\text{SCDLL} = \sum_{i=1}^{N} \log P\left(y_{i1}, y_{i2}, \ldots, y_{iT}, s_{i1}, s_{i2}, \ldots, s_{iT}\right). \tag{14.18}$$

From Eq. (14.17) it can be seen that the complete data log likelihood has three additive terms: a term involving the initial states, a term involving the transitions, and a term involving the state dependent distributions. Therefore, maximizing this function boils down to maximizing each of these terms separately. For the first two terms involving the initial state and transition probabilities, it is possible to obtain closed-form expressions. For the last term, closed-form expressions exist for many common specifications of the state-dependent distribution (e.g., a normal distribution), otherwise numerical maximization will be necessary.

In the E step, the quantities v_t and W_t are "estimated" by their conditional expectations, given the observed data and the current parameter estimates, using the forward and backward probabilities, see e.g., Zucchini and MacDonald (2009, p. 65):

$$\widehat{v}_t(j) = P\left(S_t = j | y_1, y_2, \ldots, y_T\right) = \alpha_t(j)\beta_t(j)/L_T \tag{14.19}$$

and

$$\widehat{W}_t\left(j,k\right) = P\left(S_{t-1} = j, S_t = k | y_1, y_2, \ldots, y_T\right) = \alpha_{t-1}(j)Q_i\left(j,k\right)P\left(y_t|k\right)\beta_t(k)/L_T \tag{14.20}$$

for $j, k = 1, \ldots, K$. The intuition behind the estimates of $\widehat{v}_t(j)$ and $\widehat{W}_t\left(j,k\right)$ is that $\widehat{v}_t$ is the likelihood that the customer visits each state and $\widehat{W}_t\left(j,k\right)$ is the customer's likelihood of transitioning from state j to state k.

Then, in the M step of the EM algorithm the complete data log likelihood is maximized after replacing v_t and W_t by their updated quantities $\widehat{v}_t$ and $\widehat{W}_t$, which gives a set of updated parameter estimates. The E and M steps are repeated sequentially until the change in the estimated parameter values or the likelihood function does not further improve beyond some threshold value.

The EM algorithm can suffer from local maxima. Additionally, the calculation of the forward and backward probabilities can suffer from under flow. We briefly discuss these challenges in the next subsection (further details are provided in Sect. 3.2 in Zucchini and MacDonald 2009).

14.3.3 Directly Maximizing the Likelihood Function

In Sect. 14.2 we derived the likelihood function for the general HMM for a sample of N customers and T time periods. The sample likelihood is given by $L_T = \prod_{i=1}^{N} L_{iT}$ and can be computed recursively using the forward probabilities α_{it}. Rather than using the EM algorithm discussed in the previous section, the likelihood function can be maximized directly using numerical optimization routines in order to estimate the HMM parameters. The main obstacles are under and overflow challenges in computing the likelihood, constraining the probabilities such that they sum up to one and are all non-negative, and the risk of local maxima. Similar to the forward and backward probabilities discussed earlier, the customer log likelihood (e.g., Eq. (14.7)) is comprised of multiplications of probabilities over time and states, leading to a risk of underflow. For details of the likelihood scaling, we refer the reader to Zucchini and MacDonald (2009, Sect. 3.2).

Both the initial state probabilities and the transition matrix parameters are probabilities. Thus, each one of these parameters needs to be between 0 and 1, and the vector of initial probabilities and each row of the transition matrix needs to sum to one. This can be achieved by running a constraint optimization, or by optimizing the likelihood not in the actual parameters (e.g., $\pi_1, \pi_2, \ldots, \pi_K$) but in transformed parameters (say) $\lambda_1, \lambda_2, \ldots, \lambda_{K-1}$. We need one parameter less than the number of states K, as the sum of the probabilities is 1. Now, the actual parameters are parameterized as:

$$\pi_j = \frac{\exp(\lambda_j)}{1 + \sum_{j=1}^{K-1} \exp(\lambda_j)} \tag{14.21}$$

for $j = 1, 2, \ldots, K-1$ and $\pi_K = 1 - \sum_{j=1}^{K-1} \pi_j$ (implicitly we set $\lambda_K = 0$). Similarly, this reparametrization may be done for each row in the transition probability matrix Q.

As with many numerical optimization problems, the likelihood function of the HMM is often multimodal and therefore the optimization procedure can get stuck in a local maxima instead of the desirable global maximum point. The problem of a multimodal likelihood function and the risk of local maxima is higher when one estimates the initial state probabilities rather than fixing these a-priori, or assuming these to be at the stationary distribution (see Sect. 14.2.2). Unfortunately, there is no simple approach to guarantee a global maximum, when applying numerical optimization for multimodal distributions. We advise researchers to use theory and judgment in selecting the initial starting values and explore a wide range of starting values. If different starting values result in different maxima, one should select the Maximum Likelihood solution that leads to the highest value of the log-likelihood.

One of the limitations of classical likelihood optimization (either through the EM algorithm or by directly optimizing the likelihood function) is that it is not obvious how to incorporate in these methods random-effect parameters to capture cross-customer unobserved heterogeneity. One could still use these methods to capture unobserved heterogeneity using the latent class approach and/or include covariates to control for observed heterogeneity. The two Bayesian estimation approaches we discuss next allow for a more natural incorporation and estimation of cross-customer unobserved heterogeneity.

14.3.4 Bayesian Estimation

14.3.4.1 Introduction

HMMs may also be estimated in a Bayesian framework (Chap. 16). We take a pragmatic point of view whether one should consider estimating a HMM in a Bayesian framework or in a classical statistics framework using the EM algorithm or a direct Maximum Likelihood approach. While the EM algorithm and the Maximum Likelihood approach are often easier to implement and required shorter computational time, the Bayesian approach is less susceptible to a local maxima problem. More importantly, if one wishes to estimate cross-customer heterogeneity, which we highly recommend when estimating HMMs across multiple customers (Sect. 14.2.5), the Bayesian approach seems the natural way to estimate the model parameters.

We discuss two Bayesian approaches to estimate a HMM in a Bayesian framework, both of which are based on Markov Chain Monte Carlo (MCMC) estimation:

1. a direct approach using the complete likelihood through a Metropolis-Hastings step, and
2. a data-augmentation approach by treating the unobserved states as missing data.

In both approaches one needs to address label switching, which we briefly discuss at the end of this section.

14.3.4.2 Sampling the Posterior Distribution Using the Metropolis-Hastings (MH) Algorithm

This approach uses a standard Hierarchical Bayes estimation procedure, where we distinguish between two main sets of parameters: random effect parameters (say θ_i) that are particular to each customer i (Sect. 14.2.5) and parameters (say ψ) that are common to all customers. Heterogeneity is introduced in the model by assuming a prior distribution for the random effects parameters (e.g., $\theta_i \sim MVN(\bar{\theta}, \Omega)$). As is common in most marketing applications, the Bayesian model specification is completed by assuming standard diffuse and wherever possible, conjugate priors for all model parameters. Then, the MCMC algorithm is operationalized by sequentially drawing from a set of full conditional posterior distributions. Because the full conditional distribution constructed from the HMM likelihood function (Eq. (14.7) with cross-customer heterogeneity) combined with the priors does not have a closed form, an acceptance-rejection MH step is needed to estimate the parameters ψ and possibly θ_i. At each iteration of the MCMC algorithm, we would draw a candidate value for the parameters from a proposal distribution, which then is accepted with a certain probability. If it is accepted, then the likelihood function is updated with new parameters. If it is not accepted, then the current value for the parameters is retained. After running the algorithm for a long time, we end up with a sequential sample from the posterior distribution of the parameters of the HMM. Because the sequentially generated draws from the posterior distribution can be highly correlated, we found the adaptive MH algorithm as described in Atchadé and Rosenthal (2005) to be quite useful in reducing the autocorrelation and achieving convergence faster. The Atchadé and Rosenthal (2005) algorithm automatically adjusts the tuning parameter (the variance of the proposal density) of the MH algorithm. We refer to reader to Chap. 16 for more general information about the MH algorithm. Further details on the estimation of HMMs using the MH approach can also be found in Appendix A of Netzer et al. (2008).

14.3.4.3 Sampling the Posterior Distribution Using Gibbs Sampling and Data Augmentation

Similar to the EM algorithm to maximize the likelihood function (Sect. 14.3.2), this second Bayesian approach uses data augmentation by treating the unobserved states as missing data. In each step of the MCMC algorithm, one draws the customer's state at each time period, given the current set of parameter estimates and observed data. Then, by principle of MCMC estimation, conditional on the customer's state, we need only to sample the parameters of the distribution of the state-dependent behavior, which is often rather straightforward to do using standard Gibbs sampling. This approach was proposed by Scott (2002) and was implemented in marketing in several papers (Ascarza and Hardie 2013; Ebbes et al. 2010).

One of the limitations of the data augmentation approach is that the sampler can "get stuck" in a sticky state, where the customer is continuously being drawn to be in the same state. Frühwirth-Schnatter (2006, Sect. 11.5) provides a very useful summary of various algorithms to mitigate such issues. While these algorithms are more challenging to implement than the MH approach discussed in the previous subsection, it is found that they mix more rapidly, generally implying faster convergence (Scott 2002). Further details on the estimation of HMMs using the Gibbs sampling approach can be found in Scott (2002).

Lastly, similar to classical likelihood optimization for HMMs, Bayesian approaches for HMMs are also susceptible to under/over flow in computing the likelihood function. Fortunately, the same scaling solution referred to above for likelihood estimation can be applied to Bayesian estimation. Furthermore, while less problematic than for numerical maximum likelihood estimation, starting values can also play a role in MCMC estimation, particularly with respect to time to convergence. One option is to run several MCMC chains starting from different randomly chosen starting values. Another approach is to choose "smart" starting values by starting the MCMC algorithm around the robust Maximum Likelihood estimate obtained for the simpler HMM model ignoring cross-customer heterogeneity.

14.3.4.4 Label Switching

Label switching refers to the invariance of the likelihood function of the HMM to a relabeling of the components of the model. This is also an important concern for finite mixture models. While for Maximum Likelihood estimation or EM algorithm label switching only means that the interpretation of the state ordering may vary from one run to another, it is very important to properly address this issue in Bayesian MCMC estimation of HMMs. The reason is that over the course of the sampling in the MCMC draws, the labeling of the unobserved states can shift leading to mixing posterior parameter draws from multiple states. Label switching is particularly problematic when the HMM states are not well separated, as in such situations the sampler is more likely to jump between states. We refer the reader to Frühwirth-Schnatter (2006, Sect. 3.5.5) for a detailed discussion and an illustration.

Label switching can often be detected by investigating the iteration plots of the MCMC sampler. If label switching occurs at some point in the iteration sequence, two sets of parameters will switch their value. One approach to deal with label switching when running an MCMC algorithm is to force a unique labeling by imposing constraints on the parameter space. For instance, the means of a normally distributed variable across the K states may be ordered such that $\mu_1 < \mu_2 <, \ldots < \mu_K$. This could be implemented in the likelihood function by the re-parametrization $\mu_k = \varphi_1 + \sum_{k'=2}^{k} \exp(\varphi_{k'})$ for $k = 2, \ldots, K$, and $\mu_1 = \varphi_1$. Several researchers have criticized this approach (e.g., Celeux 1998), because the choice of the constraints can shape the posterior distribution of the parameters. A second approach is to run an unconstrained MCMC algorithm and apply post-processing where the unique labels are recovered through choosing an ordering of state-specific parameters or through clustering (Celeux 1998; Frühwirth-Schnatter 2001; Richardson and Green 1997). It is advisable to post-process the MCMC run according to different choices of the labels to investigate the consequences on the final solution and interpretation of the state-specific parameters.

14.4 Applications of HMMs in Marketing

Probably the first HMM-like model in marketing was the model of Poulson (1990), in which customers were allowed to change their membership in latent classes over time. HMMs in marketing have been primarily used to model how customers (and sometimes firms) transition among a set of latent states over time. However, it is only in the mid and late 2000s that these models started to diffuse to the marketing literature (see Table 14.1 for a non-comprehensive summary of HMMs

Table 14.1 Non-comprehensive list of marketing papers using HMMs

Article	Capturing unobserved heterogeneity	Estimation	Non homogenous HMM (Covariates in Q)	# of states[a]	State dependent distribution
Poulson (1990)	No	EM algorithm	No	2	Multinomial choice
Brangule-Vlagsma et al. (2002)	No	Maximum Likelihood	Yes	6	Rank-order logit
Liechty et al. (2003)	No	Reversible Jump MCMC	No	2 (theory)	First-order continuous time Markov chain
Montgomery et al. (2004)	Yes, Q, M and π	Reversible Jump MCMC	No	2	Multinomial probit
Du and Kamakura (2006)	No	EM algorithm	No	13	Multivariate (Bernoulli/Normal)
Paas et al. (2007)	No	EM algorithm	Yes	9	Multivariate (Bernoullis)
Moon et al. (2007)	Yes, only in M	MCMC State Augmentation	No	2 (theory)	Linear regression (Normals)
Netzer et al. (2008)	Yes, in Q and π	MCMC Direct Likelihood	Yes	3	Binary logit
Wedel et al. (2008)	No	Reversible Jump MCMC	No	2 (theory)	First-order continuous time Markov chain
Van der Lans et al. (2008a)	Yes, only in Q	MCMC State Augmentation	No	2 (theory)	Categorical—Square-root link function
Van der Lans et al. (2008b)	Yes, only in M	MCMC State Augmentation	No	2 (theory)	Spatial point process
Montoya et al. (2010)	Yes, in Q and M	MCMC Direct Likelihood	Yes	3	Binomial
Ebbes et al. (2010)	No	MCMC State Augmentation	No	3	Multivariate Normal
Schweidel et al. (2011)	Yes, in Q and π	MCMC Direct Likelihood	Yes	4	Multivariate (Markov chain/Multinomial logit)
Park and Gupta (2011)	Yes, only in M	Simulated Maximum Likelihood	Yes	2 (theory)	Multinomial logit
Li et al. (2011)	Yes, Q, M and π	MCMC	Yes	3	Multivariate probit

Kumar et al. (2011)	Yes, only in M	Maximum Likelihood	Yes	3	Multivariate Tobit
Lemmens et al. (2012)	Yes, only in M	EM algorithm	Yes	3	Linear regression (Normal)
Stüttgen et al. (2012)	Yes, in Q and M	MCMC State Augmentation	Yes	2 (theory)	Multivariate (Markov chain/Multinomial)
Ansari et al. (2012)	Yes, Q, M and π	MCMC Direct Likelihood	Yes	2 (theory)	Multinomial logit
Shachat and Wei (2012)	No	EM algorithm	No	3 (theory)	Normal
Ascarza and Hardie (2013)	Yes, in Q and M	MCMC State Augmentation	No	3	Poisson
Romero et al. (2013)	Yes, in M and π	EM algorithm	No	7 and 9	Multivariate (Truncated NBD / Gamma-Gamma)
Shi et al. (2013)	No	MCMC State Augmentation	No	3	2 Layers of Hidden States
Luo and Kumar (2013)	Yes, in Q and M	MCMC State Augmentation	Yes	3	Multivariate Tobit model
Mark et al. (2013)	No	EM algorithm	No	4	Hurdle Poisson
Mark et al. (2014)	No	Maximum Likelihood	No	3	Poisson
Shi and Zhang (2014)	Yes, only in Q	MCMC Direct Likelihood	Yes	3	Type-2 Tobit model
Zhang et al. (2014)	Yes, Q, M and π	MCMC Direct Likelihood	Yes	2	Multivariate (Log-logistic/Log-normal/Binary logit)
Schwartz et al. (2014)	Yes, Q, M and π	MCMC State Augmentation	No	2 (theory)	Bernoulli
Ma et al. (2015)	Yes, Q, M and π	MCMC State Augmentation	Yes	3	Multinomial logit
Zhang et al. (2016)	Yes, only in π	MCMC Direct Likelihood	Yes	4	Normal

[a]"theory" means the number of states were selected based on theoretical grounds rather than based on model fit

in marketing). In the context of customers, the latent states could represent attention (Liechty et al. 2003; Shi et al. 2013; Van der Lans et al. 2008a, 2008b; Wedel et al. 2008), the relationship between the customer and the firm (Ascarza and Hardie 2013; Ma et al. 2015; Netzer et al. 2008; Romero et al. 2013), customers' value system (Brangule-Vlagsma et al. 2002), channel migration (Mark et al. 2014), internet browsing behavior and search (Montgomery et al. 2004; Stüttgen et al. 2012), consumers' choice among portfolio of products (Paas et al. 2007; Schweidel et al. 2011), customer satisfaction (Ho et al. 2006), store loyalty and promotion sensitivity (Shi and Zhang 2014), purchase cycles states (Park and Gupta 2011), latent behavioral learning strategies (Ansari et al. 2012), bidding strategies (Shachat and Wei 2012), and households lifecycle stages (Du and Kamakura 2006). HMMs have also been used to capture how marketing actions could affect the transition among states (Kumar et al. 2011; Li et al. 2011; Luo and Kumar 2013; Montoya et al. 2010; Netzer et al. 2008; Zhang et al. 2014).

In the most general sense the latent attrition models (e.g., Fader et al. 2010; Schweidel and Knox 2013) can thought of as a special case of a HMM with two states, where attrition is an absorbing state. This model has been extended to allow for an always share model (Ma and Büschken 2011). Schwartz et al. (2014) explore the relationship between the HMM and several of its constraint versions such as the latent attrition model.

One common theme across most of the above applications of HMMs in marketing is that the customer behavior was governed by an underlying state that is unobserved to the researcher. Further, the customer can transition to among states over time. Such states were often the state of customer attention to marketing information, the customer's strategy of making choices, her lifecycle stage, or her loyalty, trust, satisfaction level, or, more generally, her relationship status with the firm. Research has often investigated the customers' transitions among these states and how the context of the decision and the firm's actions affect customers' transitions to states that are more favorable to the firm or lead to higher welfare.

In some marketing applications the unit of analysis was not the consumer. Luo and Kumar (2013) and Zhang et al. (2014, 2016) have all used HMMs to investigate the relationship between buyers and sellers in the context of B2B relationships. Ebbes et al. (2010) looked at how firms' (banks') competitive landscape changed over time. Moon et al. (2007) used a HMM to uncover firms' latent competitive promotions. Lemmens et al. (2012) looked at evolving segments of countries in the context of new product growth.

Several aspects make the application of HMMs in marketing different from applications in other fields. First, HMMs in marketing often leverage the latent structure as a means to capture the data generating process of the customer's behavior, and use this in order to understand and predict the outcome of the customer behavior, whereas in many of the HMM applications outside of marketing the objective is mostly to recover the underlying state (e.g., words in speech recognition). An exception in marketing is Ebbes and Netzer (2017) who use HMMs to identify the latent job seeking state using social media data.

Second, as discussed in Sect. 14.2.5, because most HMM applications in marketing involve multiple time series for different consumers, capturing heterogeneity is very important. Indeed, as can be seen in Table 14.1, most marketing applications have captured unobserved heterogeneity using a random-effect or latent class approach. Finally, one of the main reasons to apply a HMM in marketing is to investigate what customer or firm behavior can create a regime shift (i.e. a transition among states) in the customer behavior. Accordingly, non-homogeneous HMMs that incorporate time-varying covariates in the transition matrix are much more common in marketing relative to other fields. For example, Montoya et al. (2010), have looked at how detailing and sampling can affect physicians' drug prescription and found that detailing can help transition physicians from a low prescription state to a higher one, whereas sampling was mainly useful in keeping physicians in the high prescription state. In the context of B2B buyer-seller relationships Luo and Kumar (2013) find that direct mail and phone calls can help transition a buyer from a lower to a higher state of purchase behavior. One of the main benefits of using HMMs in marketing is to disentangle the short-term and long-term effects of marketing activities through the incorporation of these variables in the transition probabilities and in the state-dependent distributions.

From the above discussion it is clear that the body of literature that utilizes HMMs to capture marketing dynamics is sizeable and growing. We expect to see many more applications of these useful models, to model latent and dynamic customer behavior. For example, as behavioral researchers in marketing increase their use of repeated observational experiments and secondary data, HMMs can be used to capture the dynamics of customer behavior in areas such as arousal, fatigue, or goal pursuit.

14.5 An Illustrative Application of HMM

To illustrate several of the considerations involved in building and estimating a HMM in marketing, we describe a typical marketing application of HMMs involving the customer relationship management (CRM) between a business-to-business (B2B) company and its industrial clients. For this illustration we use simulated data.

14.5.1 Description of the Data

We consider a B2B firm that has CRM data for $N = 1{,}080$ customers. Based on the sales to these customers and their total category expenditures, the firm computed the Share-Of-Wallet (SOW) at the customer-level for 20 consecutive months (time periods), i.e. $T = 20$. In addition, the customer database contains time-varying marketing mix variables such as price, sales representative visits, and a direct mail.

Table 14.2 Data of the first 22 observations

Observation	Customer ID	Period	SOW	Price	Sales visit	Direct mail
1	1	1	63.60	4.00	1	0
2	1	2	45.10	4.48	1	1
3	1	3	43.56	4.36	1	0
4	1	4	36.93	4.34	0	0
5	1	5	19.37	5.50	1	0
6	1	6	60.62	4.29	0	0
7	1	7	71.45	3.86	0	0
8	1	8	53.95	5.87	1	0
9	1	9	42.99	4.55	1	1
10	1	10	41.71	5.82	1	1
11	1	11	28.77	2.17	0	0
12	1	12	18.30	4.91	1	0
13	1	13	23.06	4.56	0	0
14	1	14	22.77	5.76	1	0
15	1	15	15.11	5.06	1	0
16	1	16	24.96	2.53	1	0
17	1	17	30.17	4.66	1	1
18	1	18	14.43	3.76	1	0
19	1	19	28.46	5.55	1	1
20	1	20	18.48	5.65	1	0
21	2	1	34.39	5.99	0	1
22	2	2	37.49	6.48	0	1

Table 14.2 shows the structure of the database (the first 22 observations). Such panel data structures are commonly used in HMM applications in marketing. The variable CustomerID is used to identify all observations that belong to the same customer (index i), and the variable Period will be used to identify the consecutive time periods (index t in Sect. 14.2).

14.5.2 The Basic Model Setup

The firm is interested in inferring the states of loyalty (SOW) between the firm and its clients. Importantly, the firm would like to know to which loyalty state each customer belongs to during each time period, and how the firm could potentially increase the SOW using its marketing mix.

In the HMM, SOW is the observed variable Y_{it}. The last three columns in Table 14.2 present the covariates X_{it} that can affect the SOW of each client at each time period. In other words, the covariates X_{it} have a short-term effect on customer behavior. Thus, the SOW of a customer in a specific time period, conditional on the customer's state, depends on the price level, whether or not the customer was visited by a sales representative, and whether or not the customer received a direct mailing:

$$SOW_{its} = \beta_{0s} + \beta_{1s}Price_{it} + \beta_{2s}SalesVisits_{it} + \beta_{3s}DirectMail_{it} + \epsilon_{its}. \quad (14.22)$$

In Eq (14.22), we allow for multiple states of SOW with different effects of marketing actions in each state. Therefore, the regression parameters (β_{0s}, β_{1s}, β_{2s}, and β_{3s}) in (14.22) are state-specific and have a subscript s. We simulated the customer data consisting of three hidden states (i.e. $K=3$ and $s=1,2,3$), with initial state probabilities (π) of 0.43, 0.40, and 0.17, and the following values for the regression parameters for each of the three states:

1. Low SOW ($\beta_{01}=30$), marketing effects (price: $\beta_{11}=-2.5$; sales visit: $\beta_{21}=0$; DM: $\beta_{31}=2.5$);
2. Medium SOW ($\beta_{02}=60$), marketing effects (price: $\beta_{12}=-1.5$; sales visit: $\beta_{22}=0$; DM: $\beta_{32}=1$);
3. High SOW ($\beta_{03}=85$), marketing effects (price: $\beta_{13}=-0.5$; sales visit: $\beta_{23}=0$; DM: $\beta_{33}=0$).

We take ϵ_{its} to be i.i.d. following a normal distribution. Therefore, each diagonal element of the 3×3 state-dependent distribution matrix (M_{it}) is a univariate normal distribution with mean $\beta_{0s} + \beta_{1s}Price_{it} + \beta_{2s}SalesVisits_{it} + \beta_{3s}DirectMail_{it}$ and standard deviation σ_s, for $s=1,2,3$. Additionally, the model includes the transition matrix (Q), which we will further discuss below in the results section.

We estimate two versions of the HMM:

1. a basic HMM with a homogeneous transition matrix (no covariate effects) but with effect of covariates on the state-dependent distribution of SOW;
2. a non-homogenous (effects of a covariate (sales visits) in the transition matrix) and heterogeneous (cross-customer heterogeneity using a Latent Class approach) HMM.

14.5.3 *Estimation of HMMs Using Latent Gold*

We use the software program Latent Gold 5.1 (Vermunt and Magidson 2015), distributed by www.statisticalinnovations.com, to estimate the two HMMs. Latent Gold 5.1 for HMM includes a module for estimating basic HMMs, which can be accessed either through the menu (model option Markov) or through the syntax. To set up a HMM in Latent Gold, the observed variable(s) Y_{it} (here: SOW) has to be selected as Indicator. Next, the state-dependent distribution that corresponds to this variable has to be selected. Latent Gold allows for the following options: continuous, count, ordinal and nominal, which indirectly specifies the underlying distribution of Y_{it} (see Sect. 14.2.2). In this application, SOW is a continuous variable, which will be modeled as a Normal distribution by Latent Gold. In addition, Latent Gold allows the user to include covariates X_{it}, which can have an impact on the initial state, the transition probabilities and/or the state-dependent distribution. As discussed in Sect. 14.2.6, when covariates are included in the transition probabilities, they are postulated to create a regime shift in the customer behavior and have a long-term impact, whereas covariates that are included in the state-dependent distribution only affect the customer behavior in the current time period, and therefore have a short-term impact. As mentioned previously, in this application, we first include the marketing mix covariates in the state-dependent distribution of SOW only, assuming they only have a short-term impact on customer behavior. Later on we extend that model and include some of these variables in the transition probability matrix as well, to investigate their effect on long-term customer behavior. Several of the other model specifications described in this chapter can be estimated as well. For detailed information on how to specify various HMMs in Latent Gold, we refer to the Latent Gold manual (Vermunt and Magidson 2015). In Latent Gold, parameter estimates are obtained by means of the EM algorithm (see Sect. 14.3.2). For estimation of HMMs using Bayesian approaches, or for specific, more advanced, specifications of HMMs, we recommend using other statistical programing tools such as R or Matlab.

14.5.4 *Results of Alternative Specifications of the HMMs*

14.5.4.1 Results for a Basic HMM

First, we estimate a basic HMM with a homogeneous transition matrix and covariates in the state dependent distribution. Model estimates are obtained for 1 to 6 hidden states, requiring the estimation of, respectively, 5 to 65 parameters (including estimates for the initial state probabilities, the transition probabilities matrix, the parameters of the Normal distribution of SOW for each state, given the covariates price, sales visits and direct mail). We compare various information criteria across these solutions to determine the most appropriate number of states K, see Table 14.3. Minimum values of BIC and CAIC are obtained for an HMM with 3 hidden states, which corresponds to the true number of states in this simulated data example. AIC is minimized for 6 hidden states, reflecting the common finding that AIC tends to overestimate the number of states (see Sect. 14.2.7). Therefore, we choose the HMM with three hidden states and we present the detailed estimation results for this model in Table 14.4.

Most estimated parameter values closely match their true values underlying the data generation procedure described in Sect. 14.5.2. The estimates for the intercept range from 35.84 for customers in State 1 to 84.74 for customers in State 3. The three states also differ substantially in terms of their response to marketing actions: customers in State 1 (the low SOW state as indicated by the intercept) are the most sensitive to price and direct mail. Price has a negative effect on SOW in all states (all p-values < 0.01), with the largest effect in State 1. Furthermore, the effect of

Table 14.3 Information criteria for the HMMs with state-dependent covariate effects on SOW

Number of states	Number of parameters	AIC	BIC	CAIC
1	5	200151.28	200176.20	200181.20
2	13	188460.35	188525.15	188538.15
3	23	179899.53	**180014.18**	**180037.18**
4	35	179898.79	180073.25	180108.25
5	49	179786.49	180030.74	180079.74
6	65	**179733.66**	180057.67	180122.67

Note: Figures in bold are the minimum values for AIC/BIC/CAIC

Table 14.4 Estimation results (parameter estimates and standard errors) of the HMM with state-dependent covariate effects on the observed variable (SOW), with three states ($K = 3$)

	Initial state distribution		
State ($t = 0$)	1	2	3
Probability	0.44 (0.02)	0.40 (0.02)	0.16 (0.01)
	Transition probability matrix		
	State (t)		
State ($t-1$)	1	2	3
1	0.80 (0.01)	0.14 (0.01)	0.06 (0.01)
2	0.09 (0.01)	0.80 (0.01)	0.11 (0.01)
3	0.07 (0.01)	0.10 (0.01)	0.83 (0.01)
	State-dependent distribution parameters of the observed variable for each State (t)		
	1	2	3
Intercept (β_0)	35.84 (0.62)	59.17 (0.61)	84.74 (0.59)
Price (β_1)	−2.65 (0.12)	−1.43 (0.11)	−0.55 (0.11)
Sales visit (β_2)	−0.25 (0.23)	0.65 (0.23)	0.49 (0.24)
Direct Mail (β_3)	2.55 (0.25)	1.36 (0.25)	−0.04 (0.25)

direct mail on SOW is significant and positive for States 1 and 2 (p-values < 0.01) and not significant for State 3 ($p = 0.88$).

Interestingly, the estimated effect of sales visits is relatively small, though significantly positive in States 2 and 3 ($p < 0.01$ and $p = 0.04$, respectively). We note that the *true* effect of sales visits on SOW is 0 in each state, i.e. there is *no* short-term effect of sales visits on SOW, and this bias in the estimated effect of sales visit on SOW is due to a model misspecification. As we will demonstrate below, sales visits have a significant positive effect on the transition among states, stimulating customers to switch to a state with higher SOW. In other words, sales visits have a long-term effect but no short-term effect on customer behavior. Hence, the long-term effect of sales visits on SOW is wrongfully captured by the short-term effect of sales visits on SOW in the state-dependent distribution in this particular HMM, leading to a potentially misinterpretation by the manager of the usefulness of sales visits on short-term behavior.

Examining the estimates for the initial state distribution and transition probability matrix, we see that customers are most likely to start in the low and medium SOW states (States 1 and 2). Subsequently, the customers have a fairly high probability of staying in the same state from one time period to the next, as the estimated diagonal elements of the transition probability matrix are fairly high (80% or higher), suggesting that the states are "quite sticky" across customers. While the estimated parameters for the initial state distribution are fairly close to their true values, we will demonstrate below that the stickiness in the transition probabilities is overestimated by this simple HMM, because cross-customer heterogeneity is not appropriately accounted for.

14.5.4.2 Results for a Non-homogenous, Heterogeneous HMM

We will now use the same simulated data to estimate a non-homogenous (covariates in the transition probability matrix) and heterogeneous (latent class approach to capture cross-customer heterogeneity) HMM with Latent Gold. This can be done in Latent Gold by specifying the number of latent classes in the Advanced Menu option, or by defining a latent variable "Class" and including it in the "equation" lines in a Latent Gold syntax file. We allow for cross-customer heterogeneity in the model parameters only in the transition probability matrix. In addition, we include the sales visits covariate in the transition probabilities such that sales visits have a potential long-term effect on customer behavior. Including sales visits as a covariate to the transition probability matrix adds $K \times (K-1)$ additional parameters to the model, where K is the number of states in the HMM. Allowing for the transition probability matrix to be heterogeneous through (say) S latent classes, multiplies the number of transition matrix parameters by S, because we now have one transition matrix for each of the S latent class segments.

In addition to determining the number of states, we now also need to determine the number of latent classes. For brevity, we only estimate HMMs with two and three latent classes and with one to six latent states, and compare the relative fit of these 12 model specifications.[7] The minimum CAIC rule suggests the model with three hidden states and two latent classes as most appropriate (Table 14.5), which corresponds to the true number of latent states and latent classes with which the data was generated. In addition, the CAIC values are lower than those of the previous homogenous HMM with three latent states (see Table 14.3), which indicates that accommodating cross-customer heterogeneity in the transition matrix, by means of a latent class structure, and that including the covariate sales visits in the transition probabilities, is warranted. Therefore, we present the detailed estimation results of the HMM with two latent classes and three hidden states in Table 14.6.

The estimates for the parameters of the state-dependent distributions of the HMM with heterogeneity and covariates in the transition matrix, are quite similar to those

---

[7]In general one may wish to vary the number of latent classes from 1 to a larger number than 3.

Table 14.5 Information criterion CAIC for the HMMs with heterogeneity and covariates in the transition matrix

Number of states	Number of latent classes	
	2	3
1	200189.19	200197.17
2	188363.87	188401.11
3	**179771.97**	179860.98
4	179957.21	180136.37
5	180182.21	180448.84
6	180488.81	180965.82

Note: Figure in bold is the minimum value for CAIC

obtained from the simple homogenous HMM (Tables 14.4 and 14.6). Importantly, all estimated parameter values now closely match the true values underlying the data generation procedure, including the null-effect of sales visits. More specifically, the estimated values for the intercepts are very close to the true values (35, 60 and 85), and similarly for the estimated price effects (all p-values < 0.01; true values -2.5, -1.5, and -0.5). The estimated effects of direct mail are significant and positive for States 1 and 2 (p-values < 0.01; true values 2.5 and 1.0), and not significant for State 3 ($p = 0.76$; true value 0.0). In other words, looking at short-term customer behavior, the customers in the low SOW state (state 1) are most sensitive to price and respond positively to direct mail. On the other hand, the customers in the high SOW state, are least sensitive to price, and direct mail is not an effective marketing instrument for these type of customers to increase their SOW.

Lastly, considering the sales visits covariate, the estimated direct effects of sales visits on SOW are very small and not significant anymore for each of the three states (true values 0.0 for each state; p-values 0.09, 0.64 and 0.50, respectively). This highlights the importance of specifying the correct heterogeneity in HMMs. Apparently, the sales visit covariate picked up spurious correlation in the basic homogenous HMM (Table 14.4). As such, the manager would incorrectly conclude that sales visits have a short-term, positive, effect on behavior. In fact, as we will see next, sales visits have a long-term effect on behavior by moving customers to a higher SOW state, i.e. inducing a (positive) regime shift among customers.

Before we discuss the long-term effect of sales visits on behavior, we will first discuss the results for the latent class approach that was used to capture unobserved cross-customer heterogeneity. As mentioned before, the best model to capture cross-customer heterogeneity (according to the model selection criteria) is a HMM with two latent classes. As indicated in Table 14.6, the two latent classes are estimated to represent 72 and 28 percent of the customers, respectively. As we only included heterogeneity in the transition probability matrix, we would get two estimated transition probability matrices, one for each latent class. Because we also included the sales visit covariate in the transition probabilities, where sales visit is a dummy variable, we estimated two transition probability matrices, one for sales visit and one for no sales visit, for each latent class. These four matrices are also given in Table 14.6.

Table 14.6 Estimation results (parameter estimates and standard errors) of the HMM with heterogeneity and covariates in the transition matrix, with three states and two latent classes

			Initial state distribution				
State ($t = 0$)			1	2	3		
Probability			0.44 (0.02)	0.40 (0.02)	0.16 (0.01)		
			Transition probability matrix				
		Latent Class 1 size: 0.72			Latent Class 2 size 0.28		
No Sales Visit	State ($t-1$)	1	2	3	1	2	3
	1	0.80 (0.01)	0.16 (0.01)	0.04 (0.01)	0.74 (0.01)	0.17 (0.01)	0.09 (0.01)
	2	0.16 (0.01)	0.75 (0.01)	0.09 (0.01)	0.08 (0.02)	0.82 (0.03)	0.10 (0.02)
	3	0.15 (0.02)	0.22 (0.02)	0.63 (0.03)	0.04 (0.01)	0.06 (0.02)	0.90 (0.03)
Sales visit	1	0.84 (0.01)	0.11 (0.01)	0.06 (0.01)	0.59 (0.05)	0.25 (0.04)	0.16 (0.03)
	2	0.05 (0.01)	0.82 (0.01)	0.14 (0.01)	0.09 (0.01)	0.80 (0.02)	0.11 (0.01)
	3	0.06 (0.01)	0.04 (0.01)	0.90 (0.01)	0.04 (0.01)	0.09 (0.01)	0.87 (0.01)
		State-dependent distribution parameters of the observed variable (SOW) for each State (t)					
		1	2		3		
Intercept (β_0)		36.00 (0.62)	59.68 (0.61)		85.06 (0.59)		
Price (β_1)		−2.66 (0.12)	−1.47 (0.11)		−0.56 (0.11)		
Sales visit (β_2)		−0.40 (0.24)	0.16 (0.23)		0.11 (0.24)		
Direct Mail (β_3)		2.56 (0.25)	1.33 (0.25)		−0.08 (0.25)		

Importantly, the four estimated transition probability matrices are quite different between the two classes and depending on whether a sales visit was made in a particular time period. Two points are worth noting regarding the estimated transition probability matrices. First, we see that, for customers in the first segment (latent class 1), sales visits have a substantial (and significant) impact on transitioning customers between the middle and the high SOW states (i.e. between States 2 and 3) and on keeping them in the high SOW state (State 3). For example, following a sales visit, an average Segment 1 customer in the highest SOW state (State 3) has a 90% chance of staying in that state in the next period, but only a 63% chance of staying in that state in the next period without a sales visit. Second, for customers in the second segment (latent class 2), sales visits are mostly effective as an acquisition tool, transitioning them from the low (State 1) to the middle (State 2) SOW state, whereas high SOW customers (State 3) are not much affected by sales visits in the long-run.

The importance of accounting for cross-customer heterogeneity in a HMM, through an unobserved heterogeneity approach (e.g., latent classes), and of including time varying covariates (e.g., sales visits), are clearly shown in this example. If we compare the estimation results for the transition probability matrices of the non-homogenous, heterogeneous HMM in Table 14.6 and the basic homogenous HMM in Table 14.4, we see that the stickiness of customers to their state is considerably overestimated by the basic homogenous HMM. A manager estimating a homogeneous HMM may wrongfully conclude that little can be done to move customers up to a more favorable (i.e. higher) SOW state. In fact, the results of the non-homogenous, heterogeneous HMM show that sales visits can be an effective marketing tool, to either reduce the chance that customers move from a high SOW state to a lower SOW state (latent class 1), or to move customers up from a low SOW state to a higher SOW state (latent class 2). In other words, sales visits have the potential to make customers more "sticky" in staying in a higher SOW state, and by using sales visits the firm has the chance to favorably (for the firm) influence customers' long term behavior towards higher SOW. Such insights would not have been possible using the basic homogenous HMM that ignores cross-customer heterogeneity.

This empirical application demonstrates the considerations involved in specifying the HMM and structuring the data. We also discuss how to estimate the model and how to choose the number of latent states. Importantly, we highlight the relevance of accounting for cross-customer heterogeneity. Our illustration demonstrates the type of insights that can be generated from interpreting the model's parameter estimates, and, in particular, the effect of marketing actions on the transitions among states and on the state dependent behavior.

14.6 Conclusions

In this chapter we have provided an overview of HMMs with a particular focus on the unique aspects of HMMs applied to marketing problems. HMMs are a flexible class of models that can be used to model dynamics in a sequence of observations. While HMMs have been developed and applied in many fields other than marketing, their application and implementation in marketing requires further development. In particular, the availability of "panel data" in marketing implies that we have multiple time series (one for each customer), which requires special attention as the basic HMMs have traditionally been developed for applications where there is only one (often very long) time series (see e.g., Zucchini and MacDonald 2009 for such HMM applications in various fields). Particularly, addressing customer-specific heterogeneity is a primary concern when applying HMMs to a marketing problem with possibly heterogeneous agents, as we know from extant literature in marketing (see also Chap. 13). Improperly accounting for such heterogeneity can lead to misleading insights regarding the dynamics underlying the behavioral process. Indeed, as we report in Table 14.1 almost all HMM applications in marketing have accounted for heterogeneity in one form or another.

Another important difference in HMM applications in marketing relative to other fields is the notion that firms can (and would like to) nudge customers' behavior in a way that would be profitable to the firm. In a HMM application context, this often means that the firm would like to move the customer from one state to another (e.g., from a low loyalty state to a high loyalty state). Or, in another application context, the firm may want to prevent the customer from drifting down from an active state to a passive or churn state. Such research questions can be addressed by extending the basic HMMs and including marketing activity into the model. Specifically, this can be done by developing non-homogenous HMMs that relate the probabilities in the transition matrix to marketing actions. Such HMMs can capture a long-term or a regime shift effect of marketing actions on customer behavior. Indeed, non-homogenous HMMs are quite common in marketing but are fairly rare outside of marketing.

In our experience there are aspects of HMMs in marketing that are worthwhile further research. First, building on the notion of heterogeneity, it is possible that customers are different not only in terms of the way they transition among states or how they behave given a state, but also in the number of states they transition among. In other words, instead of developing a HMM with K states, one could consider a HMM with K_i states, i.e. a different number of states for each customer. Such a model would greatly complicate the model selection problem, as we would now need to select the number of states at the customer level (see Padilla et al. 2017). Reversible jump algorithms (e.g., Ebbes et al. 2015) can be a useful avenue to address these issues. Similarly, a fruitful avenue of research could explore the topic of state generation. A customer could be moving among a set of states for a while and due to an exogenous to the customer event (e.g., introduction of a new product) or an endogenous to the customer event (e.g., getting married), she may start visiting a state she has never visited before. Modeling such state generation could help to better understand the evolution of customers over time.

A second fruitful area of research in applying HMMs in marketing may be in the context of data fusion. Because HMMs model a latent state that evolves over time, one can use the latent state for data fusion by merging together different sets of information at different time intervals, using their common latent state. For instance, Ebbes and Netzer (2017) merge survey data collected at specific time intervals with continuously observed customer activity data.

Third, in most HMM applications in marketing the interpretation of the states have been empirically inferred from the estimation results. However, psychological and consumer behavior research in marketing often has a strong a-priori theory regarding what could in fact be the meaning of underlying states. Research in this area typically conducts experiments with a particular manipulation aimed at transitioning an individual from one behavioral state to another (e.g., affective states). Therefore, we encourage future researchers to use HMMs in the context of behavioral experiments with repeated observations to identify the latent behavioral states and the transitions among them, as a function of the experimental design.

One natural question to ask is when to use a discrete version of dynamics such as HMMs and when to use a more continuous version of dynamics such as state-space dynamics as in Kalman filter-type approaches (See Chap. 5). There are several notable advantages of HMMs over their continuous counterparts. First, HMMs are particularly useful in capturing dynamics when the underlying dynamics are reflective of regime shift dynamics, as opposed to a gradual dynamics. On the other hand, when the underlying dynamic process is more gradual we recommend using the continuous state-space approaches. Second, HMMs capture dynamics in a semi-parametric manner and are therefore more flexible than most of the continuous state-space approaches, which often rely on specific distributional and parametric assumptions (e.g., the change from one period to another is drawn from a normal distribution). Third, from an interpretation point of view, relative to continuous dynamic models, applications of HMMs in marketing are attractive because they are easily interpretable and often lead to easy to communicate managerial insights (similar to segmentation studies) such as "marketing action X shifts customers from a low state of activity to a high state of activity." Finally, if one estimates a HMM on a truly continuous dynamics process, the HMM would approximate the continuous dynamic process well by letting the number of states K grow. This, of course, comes at a cost, as for such cases the HMM is less parsimonious than a continuous dynamics state-space model. Therefore, if the number of states recommend by the model selection criteria becomes large, we suggest the researcher to explore also continuous dynamics state-space models. Future research could investigate the similarities and differences between HMMs and other state-space models in marketing problems.

References

Ansari, A., Montoya, R., Netzer, O.: Dynamic learning in behavioral games: a hidden Markov mixture of experts approach. Quant. Mark. Econ. **10**, 475–503 (2012)

Ascarza, E., Hardie, B.G.: A joint model of usage and churn in contractual settings. Mark. Sci. **32**, 570–590 (2013)

Atchadé, Y.F., Rosenthal, J.S.: On adaptive Markov chain Monte Carlo algorithms. Bernoulli. **11**, 815–828 (2005)

Bacci, S., Pandolfi, S., Pennoni, F.: A comparison of some criteria for states selection in the latent Markov model for longitudinal data. ADAC. **8**, 125–145 (2014)

Bartolucci, F., Farcomeni, A., Pennoni, F.: Latent Markov models: a review of a general framework for the analysis of longitudinal data with covariates. TEST. **23**, 433–465 (2014)

Baum, L.E.: An equality and associated maximization technique in statistical estimation for probabilistic functions of Markov processes. Inequalities. **3**, 1–8 (1972)

Baum, L.E., Petrie, T.: Statistical inference for probabilistic functions of finite state Markov chains. Ann. Math. Stat. **37**(6), 1554–1563 (1966)

Baum, L.E., Petrie, T., Soules, G., Weiss, N.: A maximization technique occurring in the statistical analysis of probabilistic functions of Markov chains. Ann. Math. Stat. **41**, 164–171 (1970)

Brangule-Vlagsma, K., Pieters, R.G., Wedel, M.: The dynamics of value segments: modeling framework and empirical illustration. Int. J. Res. Mark. **19**, 267–285 (2002)

Celeux, G.: Bayesian inference for mixture: the label switching problem. In: Payne R. and Green P. Compstat, pp. 227–232. Physica-Verlag, Heidelberg (1998)

Celeux, G., Forbes, F., Robert, C.P., Titterington, D.M.: Deviance information criteria for missing data models. Bayesian Anal. **1**, 651–674 (2006)

Chib, S.: Marginal likelihood from the Gibbs output. J. Am. Stat. Assoc. **90**, 1313–1321 (1995)

Chib, S.: Markov Chain Monte Carlo methods: computation and inference. In: Heckman, J.J., Leamer, E. (eds.) Handbook of Econometrics, pp. 3569–3649. Elsevier, Amsterdam (2001)

Chintagunta, P.K.: Inertia and variety seeking in a model of brand-purchase timing. Mark. Sci. **17**, 253–270 (1998)

Congdon, P.: Bayesian Statistical Modelling, 2nd ed. Wiley series in probability and statistics. Chichester, UK (2002)

Dempster, A.P., Laird, N.M., Rubin, D.B.: Maximum likelihood from incomplete data via the EM algorithm. J. R Stat. Soc. Series B Methodol. **39**(1), 1–38 (1977)

Du, R.Y., Kamakura, W.A.: Household life cycles and lifestyles in the United States. J. Mark. Res. **43**, 121–132 (2006)

Dubé, J.P., Hitsch, G.J., Rossi, P.E.: State dependence and alternative explanations for consumer inertia. RAND J. Econ. **41**, 417–445 (2010)

Ebbes, P., Grewal, R., DeSarbo, W.S.: Modeling strategic group dynamics: a hidden Markov approach. QME. **8**, 241–274 (2010)

Ebbes, P., Liechty, J.C., Grewal, R.: Attribute-level heterogeneity. Manag. Sci. **61**, 885–897 (2015)

Ebbes, P., Netzer, O.: Using hidden Markov models to identify and target job seekers for social network data. Working paper (2017)

Eddy, S.R.: Profile hidden Markov models. Bioinformatics. **14**, 755–763 (1998)

Ehrenberg, A.S.: An appraisal of Markov brand-switching models. J. Mark. Res. **2**, 347–362 (1965)

Fader, P.S., Hardie, B.G., Shang, J.: Customer-base analysis in a discrete-time noncontractual setting. Mark. Sci. **29**, 1086–1108 (2010)

Frühwirth-Schnatter, S.: Markov chain Monte Carlo estimation of classical and dynamic switching and mixture models. J. Am. Stat. Assoc. **96**, 194–209 (2001)

Frühwirth-Schnatter, S.: Finite Mixture and Markov Switching Models. Springer, New York (2006)

Green, P.J.: Reversible jump Markov chain Monte Carlo computation and Bayesian model determination. Biometrika. **82**, 711–732 (1995)

Guadagni, P.M., Little, J.D.: A logit model of brand choice calibrated on scanner data. Mark. Sci. **2**, 203–238 (1983)

Hamilton, J.D.: A new approach to the economic analysis of nonstationary time series and the business cycle. Econometrica. **57**(2), 357–384 (1989)

Hamilton, J.D.: Regime switching models. In: Durlauf, S.N., Blume, L.E. (eds.) The New Palgrave Dictionary of Economics, 2nd edn. Palgrave Macmillan. The New Palgrave Dictionary of Economics Online. Palgrave Macmillan. 08 September (2008)

Heckman, J.J.: Heterogeneity and state dependence. In: Studies in Labor Markets, Sherwin Rosen, 91–140. University of Chicago Press, Chicago, IL (1981)

Ho, T.H., Park, Y.H., Zhou, Y.P.: Incorporating satisfaction into customer value analysis: optimal investment in lifetime value. Mark. Sci. **25**, 260–277 (2006)

Hughes, J.P., Guttorp, P.: A class of stochastic models for relating synoptic atmospheric patterns to regional hydrologic phenomena. Water Resour. Res. **30**(5), 1535–1546 (1994)

Jurafsky, D., Martin, J. H.: Speech and Language Processing, 2nd edn. Prentice Hall, Englewood Cliffs, NJ (2008).

Kamakura, W.A., Russell, G.: A probabilistic choice model for market segmentation and elasticity structure. J. Mark. Res. **26**, 379–390 (1989)

Keane, M.P.: Modeling heterogeneity and state dependence in consumer choice behavior. J. Bus. Econ. Stat. **15**, 310–327 (1997)

Kumar, V., Sriram, S., Luo, A., Chintagunta, P.K.: Assessing the effect of marketing investments in a business marketing context. Mark. Sci. **30**, 924–940 (2011)

Leeflang, P.S.H.: Mathematical Models in Marketing. Stenfert Kroese, H.E., Leiden, The Netherlands (1974)

Lemmens, A., Croux, C., Stremersch, S.: Dynamics in the international market segmentation of new product growth. Int. J. Res. Mark. **29**, 81–92 (2012)

Li, S., Sun, B., Montgomery, A.L.: Cross-selling the right product to the right customer at the right time. J. Mark. Res. **48**, 683–700 (2011)

Liechty, J., Pieters, R., Wedel, M.: Global and local covert visual attention: evidence from a Bayesian hidden Markov model. Psychometrika. **68**, 519–541 (2003)

Luo, A., Kumar, V.: Recovering hidden buyer-seller relationship states to measure the return on marketing investment in business-to-business markets. J. Mark. Res. **50**, 143–160 (2013)

Ma, S., Büschken, J.: Counting your customers from an "always a share" perspective. Mark. Lett. **22**(3), 243–257 (2011)

Ma, L., Sun, B., Kekre, S.: The Squeaky wheel gets the grease—An empirical analysis of customer voice and firm intervention on Twitter. Mark. Sci. **34**, 627–645 (2015)

Mamon, R.S. Elliott, R.J. (eds.): Hidden Markov Models in Finance, vol. 104. Springer, New York (2007)

Mark, T., Lemon, K.N., Vandenbosch, M.: Customer migration patterns: evidence from a North American retailer. J. Mark. Theory Pract. **22**, 251–270 (2014)

Mark, T., Lemon, K.N., Vandenbosch, M., Bulla, J., Maruotti, A.: Capturing the evolution of customer-firm relationships: how customers become more (or less) valuable over time. J. Retail. **83**, 231–245 (2013)

Montgomery, A.L., Li, S., Srinivasan, K., Liechty, J.C.: Modeling online browsing and path analysis using clickstream data. Mark. Sci. **23**, 579–595 (2004)

Montoya, R., Netzer, O., Jedidi, K.: Dynamic allocation of pharmaceutical detailing and sampling for long-term profitability. Mark. Sci. **29**, 909–924 (2010)

Moon, S., Kamakura, W.A., Ledolter, J.: Estimating promotion response when competitive promotions are unobservable. J. Mark. Res. **44**(3), 503–515 (2007)

Netzer, O., Lattin, J.M., Srinivasan, V.: A hidden Markov model of customer relationship dynamics. Mark. Sci. **27**, 185–204 (2008)

Paas, L.J., Vermunt, J.K., Bijmolt, T.H.: Discrete time, discrete state latent Markov modelling for assessing and predicting household acquisitions of financial products. J. R. Stat. Soc. A. Stat. Soc. **170**, 955–974 (2007)

Padilla, N., Montoya, R., Netzer O.: Heterogeneity in HMMs: allowing for heterogeneity in the number of states. Working paper, Columbia University (2017)

Park, S., Gupta, S.: A regime-switching model of cyclical category buying. Mark. Sci. **30**, 469–480 (2011)

Poulson, C.S.: Mixed Markov and latent Markov modelling applied to brand choice behavior. Int. J. Res. Mark. **7**, 5–19 (1990)

Rabiner, L.R., Lee, C.H., Juang, B.H., Wilpon, J.G.: HMM clustering for connected word recognition. In: Acoustics, Speech, and Signal Processing, 1989. ICASSP-89., 1989 International Conference on (405–408). IEEE (1989), May.

Richardson, S., Green, P.J.: On Bayesian analysis of mixtures with an unknown number of components (with discussion). J. R. Stat. Soc. Ser. B (Stat Methodol.) **59**, 731–792 (1997)

Romero, J., Van der Lans, R., Wierenga, B.: A partially hidden Markov model of customer dynamics for CLV measurement. J. Interact. Mark. **27**, 185–208 (2013)

Schwartz, E.M., Bradlow, E.T., Fader, P.S.: Model selection using database characteristics: developing a classification tree for longitudinal incidence data. Mark. Sci. **33**, 188–205 (2014)

Schweidel, D.A., Bradlow, E.T., Fader, P.S.: Portfolio dynamics for customers of a multiservice provider. Manag. Sci. **57**, 471–486 (2011)

Schweidel, D.A., Knox, G.: Incorporating direct marketing activity into latent attrition models. Mark. Sci. **32**, 471–487 (2013)

Scott, S.L.: Bayesian methods for hidden Markov models: recursive computing in the 21st century. J. Am. Stat. Assoc. **97**, 337–351 (2002)

Seetharaman, P.B.: Modeling multiple sources of state dependence in random utility models: a distributed lag approach. Mark. Sci. **23**, 263–271 (2004)

Shachat, J., Wei, L.: Procuring commodities: first-price sealed-bid or English auctions? Mark. Sci. **31**, 317–333 (2012)

Shi, S.W., Wedel, M., Pieters, F.G.M.: Information acquisition during online decision making: a model-based exploration using eye-tracking data. Manag. Sci. **59**, 1009–1026 (2013)

Shi, S.W., Zhang, J.: Usage experience with decision aids and evolution of online purchase behavior. Mark. Sci. **33**, 871–882 (2014)

Smith, A., Naik, P.A., Tsai, C.-L.: Markov-switching model selection using Kullback–Leibler divergence. J. Econ. **134**(2), 553–577 (2006)

Stüttgen, P., Boatwright, P., Monroe, R.T.: A satisficing choice model. Mark. Sci. **31**(6), 878–899 (2012)

Train, K.E.: Discrete Choice Methods with Simulation. Cambridge University Press, Cambridge (2009)

Van der Lans, R., Pieters, R., Wedel, M.: Competitive brand salience. Mark. Sci. **27**, 922–931 (2008a)

Van der Lans, R., Pieters, R., Wedel, M.: Eye-movement analysis of search effectiveness. J. Am. Stat. Assoc. **103**, 452–461 (2008b)

Vermunt, J.K., Magidson, J.. Upgrade Manual for Latent GOLD 5.1. Statistical Innovations, Inc., Belmont, MA (2015)

Viterbi, A.J.: Error bounds for convolutional codes and an asymptotically optimum decoding algorithm. IEEE Trans. Inf. Theory. **13**, 260–269 (1967)

Wang, M., Chan, D.: Mixture latent Markov modeling: identifying and predicting unobserved heterogeneity in longitudinal qualitative status change. Organ. Res. Methods. **14**(3), 411–431 (2011)

Wedel, M., Kamakura, W.A.: Market Segmentation Conceptual and Methodological Issues. Kluwer Academic Publishing, Boston (2000)

Wedel, M., Pieters, R., Liechty, J.: Attention switching during scene perception: how goals influence the tie course of eye movements across advertisements. J. Exp. Psychol. **14**, 129–138 (2008)

Welch, L.R.: Hidden Markov models and the Baum-Welch algorithm. IEEE Inform. Theory Soc. Newsletter. **53**, 10–13 (2003)

Yamato, J., Ohya, J., Ishii, K.: Recognizing human action in time-sequential images using hidden markov model. In: Computer Vision and Pattern Recognition, 1992. Proceedings CVPR'92., 1992 IEEE Computer Society Conference, 379–385. IEEE June (1992)

Zhang, J.Z., Netzer, O., Ansari, A.: Dynamic targeted pricing in B2B relationships. Mark. Sci. **33**, 317–337 (2014)

Zhang, J.Z., Watson IV, G.F., Palmatier, R.W. Dant, R.P.: Dynamic relationship marketing. J. Mark. **80**(5), 53–75 (2016)

Zucchini, W., MacDonald, I.L.: Hidden Markov Models for Time Series: An Introduction Using R, vol. 150. CRC, Boca Raton, FL (2009)

Part IV
Estimation Issues

Chapter 15
Generalized Method of Moments

Tom J. Wansbeek

15.1 Introduction

The generalized method of moments (GMM) is a conceptually simple and flexible estimation method that has come to play an increasingly prominent role in empirical research in economics over the last 30 years. Application of GMM requires the availability of so-called moment equations or moment conditions. There should be at least as many moment equations as there are parameters to be estimated. If this condition is satisfied (plus some regularity conditions), application of GMM is in principle straightforward and delivers estimators for the parameters that are consistent and asymptotically normal. If desired, the estimators can in addition be made asymptotically efficient given the available moment equations, that is, have the lowest achievable variance or highest precision asymptotically.

The chapter is introductory, with an emphasis more on elucidating the relevant concepts rather than on mathematical rigor. Although it is introductory, the use of matrix algebra is unavoidable. Section A.6 of Vol. I gives a succinct introduction to matrix algebra Excellent, elaborate treatments of GMM are given in econometric textbooks like Hayashi (2000), Cameron and Trivedi (2005), and Wooldridge (2010). Some parts of this chapter are based on Chap. 9 of Wansbeek and Meijer (2000). Hall (2005) is a monograph dedicated to the topic and Hall (2013) and Hall (2015) are recent summaries. Much of the underlying theory is discussed in depth and generality by Newey and McFadden (1994). Although the ideas underlying

T.J. Wansbeek (✉)
Department of Economics, Econometrics & Finance, Faculty of Economics and Business, University of Groningen, Groningen, The Netherlands
e-mail: t.j.wansbeek@rug.nl

P.S.H. Leeflang et al. (eds.), *Advanced Methods for Modeling Markets*,
International Series in Quantitative Marketing, DOI 10.1007/978-3-319-53469-5_15

GMM have a long and varied history, starting with Pearson (1894), Hansen (1982) is generally considered as the seminal paper launching GMM in econometrics, earning its author a (shared) Nobel prize in economics in 2013.

In this chapter we summarize the main issues around GMM. We first give the basic idea behind GMM in Sect. 15.2. There, we also consider the simpler, special case of the method of moments (MM) and compare GMM with the method of maximum likelihood (ML). Section 15.3 offers an array of cases that illustrate where moment equations may come from. We then present the basic GMM theory in Sect. 15.4 and a number of important extensions in Sect. 15.5. A leading special case of GMM estimation is instrumental variables (IV) estimation, which is the subject of Sect. 15.6. We show how to obtain IVs, through some examples. In Sect. 15.7 we consider the empirically important case of weak instruments.

15.2 The Basic Idea of GMM

In this section we present some of the basic ideas of GMM. We explain the notion of moment equations and discuss the simpler case of MM. We next comment on the link between GMM and the method of maximum likelihood (ML).

15.2.1 Moment Conditions

Assume we have a model with m parameters that we want to get to know. We call the parameters $\theta_1, \ldots, \theta_m$ and collect them in the m-vector θ. We have a sample of size n of data generated by the model. For each $i = 1, \ldots, n$ we observe $p \geq m$ variables $x_{1i}, \ldots, x_{pi}$, collected in the p-vector x_i. Ideally, the x_i are independently and identically distributed (i.i.d.) but there is quite a bit of flexibility. The expectation of x_i is a function $g(\theta)$ of the parameters, so $\mathrm{E}[x_i - g(\theta)] = 0$. A simple example is the case of a sample $x_1, \ldots, x_n$ from the normal distribution with mean μ and variance σ^2. To estimate these parameters it is obvious to use the x_i and x_i^2. Then $x_i = (x_i, x_i^2)'$, $\theta = (\mu, \sigma^2)'$, and $g(\theta) = (\mu, \mu^2 + \sigma^2)'$.

Instead of considering $\mathrm{E}[x_i - g(\theta)] = 0$, we may directly consider the more general form $\mathrm{E}[h_i(\theta)] = 0$, with $h_i(\theta)$ a function of θ; the subscript i indicates dependence on data. Following Wansbeek and Meijer (2000), we call $\mathrm{E}[x_i - g(\theta)] = 0$ the separated form and $\mathrm{E}[h_i(\theta)] = 0$ the inclusive form.

When the moment equations are given, we can leave the estimation job to the generalized method of moments (GMM). It will deliver an estimator $\hat{\theta}$ of θ that is consistent, asymptotically normal and, if we so choose, asymptotically efficient, at least as far as the moment equations $\mathrm{E}[h_i(\theta)] = 0$ allow. Also, GMM produces a consistent estimator of the asymptotic variance of $\hat{\theta}$.

Estimating m parameters requires the availability of m moment equations. When there are more available, we can using this additional information to increase the precision of the estimation process. That is, we can obtain an estimator with a lower asymptotic variance. Moreover, we can use the surplus moment equations to see if they “tell the same story”; we have some scope for specification testing.

15.2.2 The Method of Moments

As the name indicates, GMM is a generalization of the method of moments (MM), conceptually the simplest approach to parameter estimation. MM is as follows. Suppose we have a random sample $x_1, \ldots, x_n$ from a distribution with density $f(x;\theta)$, with θ a single parameter. The idea of MM is to equate the first sample moment (the sample mean) and the first population moment (the expectation of x), and solve the implied equation for θ to yield the MM estimator $\hat{\theta}$. For example, when the sample is from the gamma distribution, with density $f(x) = x^{\theta-1}e^{-x}/\Gamma(\theta)$, there holds $\mathrm{E}[x_i] = \theta$. Hence the MM estimator $\hat{\theta}$ of θ is $\bar{x}$, the sample mean. The ML estimator is the solution of the nonlinear equation $n^{-1}\sum_{i=1}^{n}\log y_i = \Gamma'(\hat{\theta})/\Gamma(\hat{\theta})$. This estimator is computationally more burdensome but is more precise.

When there would be m parameters instead of a single one, equate the first m population moments $\mathrm{E}[x_i^k]$, expressed as a function of the parameters, and the first m sample moments $n^{-1}\sum_{i=1}^{n} x_i^k$, for $i = 1, \ldots, m$ and solve the system. In the example of the normal distribution above, we had $m = 2$ and the MM estimators of μ and σ^2 follow from:

$$\hat{\mu} = n^{-1}\sum_i x_i \tag{15.1}$$

$$\hat{\mu}^2 + \hat{\sigma}^2 = n^{-1}\sum_i x_i^2 \tag{15.2}$$

unsurprisingly yielding the sample mean as the MM estimator for μ and the sample variance (with denominator n, not $n-1$) as the MM estimator for σ^2.

In this example we used the first and second moment, and in the example on the gamma distribution we used the first moment. Using moments comes in naturally, as they are object of the form $\mathrm{E}[x_i^r]$, readily spawning moment equations. The name “method of moments” may suggest that it should be based on moments in this strict sense, but that is not the case, “anything goes” for MM (and GMM, for that matter) as long as it yields moment equations.

The main virtue of the MM estimator is its consistency. Take for simplicity the case of a single parameter. Let $\mathrm{E}[x_i] = g(\theta)$, with $g(\cdot)$ known, continuous and one-to-one, then the MM estimator follows by solving the equation $\bar{x} = g(\hat{\theta})$ so $\hat{\theta} = g^{-1}(\bar{x})$. Using the continuous mapping theorem saying that the plim of a function is the function of the plim and replacing plim by lim E, which is allowed under general conditions then yields:

$$\begin{aligned}\operatorname*{plim}_{n\to\infty}\hat{\theta} &= \operatorname*{plim}_{n\to\infty} g^{-1}(\bar{x}) = g^{-1}(\operatorname*{plim}_{n\to\infty}\bar{x}) = g^{-1}(\lim_{n\to\infty}\mathrm{E}[\bar{x}]) = g^{-1}(\lim_{n\to\infty} g(\theta)) \\ &= g^{-1}(g(\theta)) = \theta. \end{aligned} \tag{15.3}$$

Another feature of the MM estimator is that its asymptotic distribution is easily established. When $\bar{x}$ has an asymptotically normal distribution with a variance that can be estimated consistently, which usually is the case, the asymptotic variance of $\hat{\theta}$ follows readily through the delta method.

15.2.3 GMM and ML

GMM can never beat the method of maximum likelihood (ML), the gold standard in estimation, as ML delivers estimators that are not only consistent and asymptotically normal but also asymptotically efficient; Sect. 6.4 in Vol. 1 gives an introduction to ML. The efficiency of ML holds overall, not just as far as the moment equations that we have chosen to work with, $\mathrm{E}[h_i(\theta)] = 0$, allow. So, ML gives more precise results than GMM. This raises the question why we do not always do ML. The answer depends on the situation. The application of ML requires the full specification of the model as we cannot write down the likelihood function otherwise. When we can do so and are confident that we do not make a specification error, ML is superior and should be used, not GMM, and the only exception could be computational as ML is often more demanding than GMM. However, even in the simplest models one might not be too certain about specification. For example, in a simple linear regression to be estimated with cross-sectional data, heteroskedasticity is likely to occur. For ML estimation, one has to specify this heteroskedasticity parametrically. However, there is seldom a theoretical basis for such a specification, making the job an ad hoc one, and a specification error is the likely result. When the specification is correct, ML yields a superior outcome in terms of efficiency, but it can be inconsistent when the specification is not correct. The GMM result is less efficient but robust against misspecification, up to a point.

So, the trade-off that a researcher has to make when choosing between GMM and ML is between the higher precision offered by ML and the inconsistency of estimators when some elements of the model happen to be misspecified. GMM has a certain robustness as we do not have to specify the model completely and can leave unspecified aspects that do not interest us or that we can not specify with confidence. GMM is a semiparametric method, so to speak, as it allows for parameter estimation in a model that need not be fully specified, unlike with ML.

15.3 Where Do Moment Equations Come From?

In this section we group a number of quite diverse examples to give a feel for where moment equations may come from. We show for each example what θ and $h_i(\theta)$ are. Taken together, the examples underline the versatility and the unifying nature of GMM, precluding the need for specific estimation methods.

15.3.1 *Linear Regression*

Linear regression is still the workhorse in quantitative research in economics and management. We show how it can be couched in GMM terms. The simplest regression model is the model with only an intercept. This is already insightful, so we start with that.

Suppose we have a sample $x_1, \ldots, x_n$ from $N(\mu, \sigma^2)$, the normal distribution with parameters μ and σ^2. Our interest is in estimating μ. This can be put in MM terms by taking $h_i(\mu) = x_i - \mu$. So the MM estimator is $\bar{x}$, which is also the ML estimator. Now suppose that we have heteroskedasticity, meaning that the variances vary over observations while the mean is the same, so the sample is now from $N(\mu, \sigma_i^2)$. The moment equation remains the same and MM still produces $\bar{x}$ as the estimator for μ. Also, under some regularity conditions on the asymptotic sequence of the variances, we can easily derive a consistent estimator of the asymptotic variance of the estimator. In the entire process, we do not have to specify a model for the variances σ_i^2.

This is unlike the situation when we want to find the ML estimator of μ. Then we have to become explicit about σ_i^2. If the model for σ_i^2 is correctly specified, we will be rewarded with a more precise estimator of μ, essentially since such a model offers the opportunity to give a higher weight to x_i in the estimation process when σ_i^2 is low and hence x_i is quite informative about μ, and a lower weight in the opposite case.

The regression model $y_i = \alpha + x_i\beta + u_i$ is a direct extension. Usually in a regression model, the parameter of interest is β but there are two more parameters, the intercept α and μ, the mean of the x_i. We allow for heteroskedasticity and have no clue about its form, apart from some regularity conditions. Since we have three parameters we need at least three moment equations. Two are obvious, $\mathrm{E}[x_i - \mu] = 0$ and $\mathrm{E}[y_i - \alpha - x_i\beta] = 0$. The most interesting moment equation comes from $\mathrm{E}[u_i \mid x_i] = 0$ implying $\mathrm{E}[x_i u_i] = 0$, assuming of course that this holds; if not, a way out can be through instrumental variables, to be discussed in Sect. 15.6. We can rewrite this moment equation as $\mathrm{E}[x_i y_i - x_i\alpha - x_i^2\beta] = 0$. So we have $\mathrm{E}[h_i(\theta)] = 0$, with:

$$h_i(\theta) = \begin{pmatrix} x_i - \mu \\ y_i - \alpha - x_i\beta \\ x_i y_i - x_i\alpha - x_i^2\beta \end{pmatrix} \tag{15.4}$$

with $\theta = (\alpha, \beta, \mu)'$. Notice that we need the general form $h_i(\theta)$ here since we cannot separate data and parameters as in $\mathrm{E}[x_i - g(\theta)]$. The implied MM estimator of β is easily seen to be the ordinary least squares (OLS) estimator, and the estimator of its variance can be shown to be the heteroskedasticity-robust estimator as popularized by White (1980).

Under homoskedasticity, this is also the ML estimator. Just as in the case of estimating the mean μ above, the advantage of MM over ML lies in its robustness; we need again some regularity conditions on the process generating the σ_i^2 but do not have to specify a particular parametric form for the way σ_i^2 depends on x_i. In the earlier econometrics literature an assumption was made like $\sigma_i^2 = \exp(\delta_0 + \delta_1 x_i)$, with δ_0 and δ_1 additional parameters to be estimated. With such a specification given, the (now) five parameters can be estimated by ML. If the specification would be the correct specification, ML would give more precise results than MM, but usually such an assumption is ad hoc and, when not true, leads to an inconsistent estimator of β in particular. Application of MM avoids this.

15.3.2 Consumption-Based CAPM

Moment equations can sometimes be derived from economic theory directly. A classical case is the consumption-based capital asset-pricing model (CAPM), cf. Hansen and Singleton (1982) and Jagannathan et al. (2002).

To concentrate on the essential GMM aspect of the case, we consider the simplest case. It concerns an agent who chooses current ($t = 1$) and future ($t > 1$) consumption such that the expected utility is optimized:

$$\max \sum_{t=1}^{\infty} \beta^t \, \mathrm{E}[u(c_t)|z_1] \tag{15.5}$$

where $u(\cdot)$ is the utility function, c_t is consumption at time t, and z_t contains the relevant variables available at time t; β is a time-preference parameter. There are n assets available for investment, indexed by i, with (random) returns r_{it}. When the utility function is of the constant relative risk aversion type, there holds $u(c) = c^{1-\gamma}/(1-\gamma)$ if $\gamma \neq 0$ and $u(c) = \ln(c)$ if $\gamma = 1$. The solution to the optimization problem is:

$$\mathrm{E}[\beta(c_{t+1}/c_t)^{-\gamma} r_{i,t+1}|z_t] = 1. \tag{15.6}$$

Apart from the conditioning on z_t, this is a moment equation as before. As we will discuss in Sect. 15.5.2, the law of iterated expectation shows that (15.6) implies:

$$\mathrm{E}[\{1 - \beta(c_{t+1}/c_t)^{-\gamma} r_{i,t+1}\} f_t(z_t)] = 0 \tag{15.7}$$

where the k-vector $f_t(z_t)$ is any function of z_t. Collecting the $r_{i,t+1}$ in the n-vector r, (15.7) written for all assets together is:

$$\mathrm{E}[h_t(\theta)] = \mathrm{E}[\{\iota_n - \beta(c_{t+1}/c_t)^{-\gamma} r_{t+1}\} \otimes f_t(z_t)] = 0 \tag{15.8}$$

where ι_n is a vector of ones. This is a set of kn moment equations, indexed by t, with parameter vector $\theta = (\beta, \gamma)'$.

In the area of marketing, an example of deriving moment conditions from a dynamic optimization problem is provided by Vitorino (2014), to analyze the effect of advertising on firm value.

15.3.3 Quadratic Regression with Measurement Error

We now turn to the quadratic regression model with a single, normally distributed regressor. Although the applicability of this model is limited, the example is meant to illustrate the highly practical way in which empirical researchers often think about GMM, which is to count the number of parameters and derive at least as many moment equations.

Regression models with measurement error in a regressor have since long been a source of inspiration for statisticians and econometricians since the model, in its basic form of linearity, normality and independence of observations is not identified; no consistent estimator exists for the model parameters, most notably not for the regression coefficients. The problem can vanish when the model is not linear anymore. A simple case is the quadratic regression model where we only observe a proxy x_i for the regressor ξ_i,

$$\begin{aligned} y_i &= \alpha + \beta\xi_i + \gamma\xi_i^2 + u_i \\ x_i &= \xi_i + v_i \end{aligned}$$

for $i = 1, \ldots, n$, where u_i, ξ_i and v_i are assumed mutually i.i.d. normal with mean 0 and variances σ_u^2, σ_ξ^2 and σ_v^2, respectively. The normality assumption on ξ_i would be a stretch in empirical applications but serves us well in this illustrative example. Without loss of generality, x_i and y_i are assumed to have mean 0; notice that $\mathrm{E}[y_i] = 0$ implies $\alpha = -\gamma\sigma_\xi^2$. We can estimate β and γ by regressing y_i on x_i and x_i^2 and a constant, but the result is inconsistent.

Consistent estimation can be done by GMM. We find moment equations by inspecting the moments of x_i and y_i up till three. This choice by itself has no deep meaning and is motivated only by the sheer fact that we then get enough moment equations. We disregard the first moments since they are 0 anyhow, as is the third moment of x_i due to the assumed normality of ξ_i and v_i implying normality of x_i as well. This leaves us with the task of deriving the expectation of $x_i^2, y_i^2, x_iy_i, x_i^2y_i, x_iy_i^2$

and y_i^3. By some straightforward computations we obtain six moment equations $\mathrm{E}[h_i(\theta)] = 0$, with:

$$h_i(\theta) = \begin{pmatrix} x_i^2 - \sigma_\xi^2 - \sigma_v^2 \\ y_i^2 - \beta^2\sigma_\xi^2 - 2\gamma^2(\sigma_\xi^2)^2 - \sigma_u^2 \\ x_i y_i - \beta\sigma_\xi^2 \\ x_i^2 y_i - 2\gamma\sigma_\xi^4 \\ x_i y_i^2 - 4\beta\gamma\sigma_\xi^4 \\ y_i^3 - 6\gamma^3(\sigma_\xi^2)^3 - 6\beta\gamma^2(\sigma_\xi^2)^2 \end{pmatrix}. \tag{15.9}$$

There are five parameters, $\theta = (\beta, \gamma, \sigma_u^2, \sigma_\xi^2, \sigma_v^2)'$. So we should have enough material for consistent estimation. Formally speaking, the order condition for parameter identification is satisfied, where (give or take some mathematical details) identification means the existence of a consistent estimator. Whether the parameters are really identified depends on the rank condition for identification being satisfied. Here we can circumvent the issue by just constructing a consistent estimator thus showing identification. This can be done by dropping the sixth moment equation. We are left with five moment equations and five parameters, and the system can be solved easily; the solution by itself is not interesting and is omitted.

The derivation of the moment equations is greatly simplified by the assumed normality of ξ_i, which implies that all its even moments are a function of a single parameter, σ_ξ^2, and all its odd moments are 0. It can be shown that the model is also identified if ξ_i is not normally distributed and can still be estimated by MM, but more moment equations are required; see e.g. Wang and Hsiao (2011).

15.3.4 Regression with Measurement Error

Here we consider regression with measurement error again, but now for the simplest linear case, to illustrate yet another aspect of GMM, which is the ease of deriving the asymptotic variance of an estimator. The model is:

$$y_i = \beta\xi_i + \varepsilon_i \tag{15.10}$$

$$x_i = \xi_i + v_i \tag{15.11}$$

so the same model as above but without the quadratic term and without the intercept α; all variables are demeaned, to concentrate on the essentials. It is simple to derive that the OLS estimator obtained by regressing y on x is inconsistent:

$$\operatorname*{plim}_{n\to\infty} \hat{\beta}_{\text{OLS}} = \operatorname*{plim}_{n\to\infty} \frac{\sum_i x_i y_i}{\sum_i x_i^2} = \beta\frac{\sigma_\xi^2}{\sigma_x^2}. \tag{15.12}$$

So OLS is biased towards 0.

We consider the case that the measurement error variance is known, so $\sigma_v^2 = c$, say. By some simple algebra we obtain:

$$E(y_i^2) = \beta^2\sigma_\xi^2 + \sigma_\varepsilon^2 \quad (15.13)$$

$$E(y_i x_i) = \beta\sigma_\xi^2 \quad (15.14)$$

$$E(x_i^2) = \sigma_\xi^2 + c. \quad (15.15)$$

This is a system of three equations in three unknown parameters, so we have a case of MM. Solving these equations readily yields:

$$\beta = \frac{E(y_i x_i)}{E(x_i^2 - c)} \quad \text{so} \quad \hat{\beta}_{\text{MM}} = \frac{\sum_i x_i y_i}{\sum_i (x_i^2 - c)} \quad (15.16)$$

the latter being consistent as can be proven directly but also follows from the general result that MM estimators are consistent. This all is obvious, but it is less obvious what the asymptotic variance of $\hat{\beta}_{\text{MM}}$ is. GMM theory provides a simple answer, which we will apply in Sect. 15.4 to this particular case to illustrate the general idea.

15.3.5 Structural Equation Models

Research in marketing is often based on models involve latent variables like attitudes, sentiments and perceptions, which are by definition not directly observable. The way to treat these variables is to embed them in a model including observable variables, where causal links may go either way. Such a model is a structural equation model (SEM). They are discussed at length in Chap. 11. Here we restrict our attention to the issue of estimating SEMs as a special case of GMM.

To estimate SEMs, the usual approach is to derive the implications of the model for the variances and covariances of the observables. A SEM implies a parametric structure on the covariance matrix of the observables, $\Sigma(\theta)$. From the data, the corresponding empirical covariance matrix S can be derived. So $E[S - \Sigma(\theta)] = 0$. Stacking the elements of these matrices in vectors $\sigma(\theta)$ and s, respectively, while omitting the elements that occur twice because of the symmetry gives the moment equations $E[s - \sigma(\theta)] = 0$. So GMM provides the natural context to think about estimating SEMs and provides the right tools for estimation.

A simple model to illustrate the essence of SEMs and their link with GMM is the classical model from sociology to investigate the stability of the sense of alienation over time, due to Wheaton et al. (1977). The data are from 1967 and 1971, and the parameter of interest is the autocorrelation parameter driving an individual's sense of alienation from 1967 to 1971. Alienation, to give it a short-hand name, is a latent variable, and its measurement takes place through indicators, that is, variables that can be observed (through questionnaires, in this case) and that are considered to be causally driven by alienation. In each year, there are two indicators, called anomia and powerlessness in equally short-hand language; see Wheaton et al. (1977) for a discussion of the substance of these notions.

So, there are two latent variables, Alien67$_i$ and Alien71$_i$ and there are four observable variables:

$$x_i = (x_{1i}, x_{2i}, x_{3i}, x_{4i})' = (\text{anomia67}_i, \text{pwless67}_i, \text{anomia71}_i, \text{pwless71}_i)'. \quad (15.17)$$

The variables are transformed to have mean 0. A simplified version of the model due to Wheaton et al. (1977) is:

$$\text{Alien71}_i = \beta \ \text{Alien67}_i + e_i$$

where β is the autocorrelation parameter of interest. The measurement equations linking the latent variables to the observable variables are:

$$\text{anomia67}_i = \text{Alien67}_i + \varepsilon_{1i} \quad (15.18)$$

$$\text{pwless67}_i = \lambda_1 \text{Alien67}_i + \varepsilon_{2i} \quad (15.19)$$

$$\text{anomia71}_i = \text{Alien71}_i + \varepsilon_{3i} \quad (15.20)$$

$$\text{pwless71}_i = \lambda_2 \text{Alien71}_i + \varepsilon_{4i}. \quad (15.21)$$

For reasons of identification, two of the four coefficients have been set at one. We assume the error terms $e_i, \varepsilon_{1i}, \ldots \varepsilon_{4i}$ to be with i.i.d., each with its own variance. There are four observed variables, anomia67$_i$, pwless67$_i$, anomia71$_i$pwless71$_i$, so there are ten variances and covariances available. There are nine parameters:

$$\theta = (\beta, \lambda_1, \lambda_2, \sigma_e^2, \sigma_{\varepsilon_1}^2, \sigma_{\varepsilon_2}^2, \sigma_{\varepsilon_3}^2, \sigma_{\varepsilon_4}^2, \phi)' \quad (15.22)$$

with $\phi \equiv$ var(Alien67$_i$). Letting for brevity $\pi \equiv$ var(Alien71) $= \beta^2\phi + \sigma_e^2$, we obtain as the population covariance matrix of the observable variables:

$$\Sigma = \begin{pmatrix} \phi + \sigma_{\varepsilon_1}^2 & & & \\ \lambda_1\phi & \lambda_1^2\phi + \sigma_{\varepsilon_2}^2 & & \\ \beta\phi & \lambda_1\beta\phi & \pi + \sigma_{\varepsilon_3}^2 & \\ \beta\lambda_2\phi & \lambda_1\lambda_2\beta\phi & \lambda_2\pi & \lambda_2^2\pi + \sigma_{\varepsilon_4}^2 \end{pmatrix}. \quad (15.23)$$

To see this, consider e.g. element (4,1) of this matrix:

$$\begin{aligned} \text{E}[(\text{pwless71}_i)(\text{anomia67}_i)] &= \text{E}[(\lambda_2 \text{Alien71}_i + \varepsilon_{4i})(\text{Alien67}_i + \varepsilon_{1i})] \\ &= \lambda_2 \, \text{E}[(\text{Alien71}_i)(\text{Alien67}_i)] \\ &= \lambda_2 \, \text{E}[(\beta \ \text{Alien67}_i + e_i)(\text{Alien67}_i)] \\ &= \beta\lambda_2\phi. \end{aligned} \quad (15.24)$$

The observed counterpart of Σ is:

$$S = \begin{pmatrix} 11.834 & & & \\ 6.947 & 9.364 & & \\ 6.819 & 5.091 & 12.532 & \\ 4.783 & 5.028 & 7.495 & 9.986 \end{pmatrix}. \tag{15.25}$$

Stacking the unique elements into a vector we get:

$$h_i(\theta) = \begin{pmatrix} x_{1i}^2 - \phi - \sigma_{\varepsilon_1}^2 \\ x_{1i}x_{2i} - \lambda_1\phi \\ \vdots \\ x_{4i}^2 - \lambda_2^2\pi - \sigma_{\varepsilon_4}^2 \end{pmatrix}. \tag{15.26}$$

Since there are nine parameters but ten moment equations, there is some scope for specification testing since the assumptions underlying the specification of the model impose a structure on Σ that can be confronted with the data. Inspection of the precise form of Σ shows that its lower left two-by-two block has rank one. As $\Sigma_{32}/\Sigma_{21} = \lambda_1\beta\phi/\lambda_1\phi = \beta$, a quick-and-dirty MM estimate of the autocorrelation parameter β is $S_{32}/S_{21} = 5.091/6.947 = 0.73$.

15.3.6 The Market for Differentiated Products

There is no "generic" case of GMM in marketing, but analyzing markets for differentiated product is certainly a popular area of applying GMM. The theory begins with the analysis of individual choice. There, the additive random utility model (ARUM) has gained great popularity. With ARUM, the utility to individual i of alternative j, with $j = 1, \ldots, q$, is:

$$u_{ij} = m_{ij} + e_{ij} \tag{15.27}$$

where m_{ij} is a parametric function of observables that vary over individual consumers or alternatives or both, and e_{ij} is unobservable. We assume that individuals choose the alternative with the highest utility. We do not observe the separate utilities per product but only know which alternative has been chosen. We assume that the e_{ij} are i.i.d with a Type-I Extreme Value distribution. This is an unusual assumption but it can be motivated by an argument, due to Jaibi and Ten Raa (1998). This argument is similar to the argument underlying the use of the normal distribution. Just like the central limit theorem is the limit distribution of means, the Type-I Extreme Value distribution is the limit distribution of maxima. The underlying idea is that a discrete choice follows on utility-maximizing choices made at a lower level. Given this distributional assumption, we can use an elegant mathematical result to the extent that the probability π_{ij} that u_{ij} is the maximum of all $u_{i1}, \ldots, u_{iq}$, has a simple, closed-form expression:

$$\pi_{ij} = \frac{\exp(m_{ij})}{\sum_{k=1}^{q} \exp(m_{ik})} \tag{15.28}$$

thus spawning the multinomial logit model, cf. Vol. I, Sect. 8.2.3 and Chap. 2 of this volume. Estimation can be done by ML since the model is fully specified; the relevant distribution is the multinomial distribution. This simple model is a good point of departure in many directions.

One such direction is the analysis of markets for differentiated products, distinguished by their characteristics. Again starting with the simplest case to capture the essence, let $m_{ij} = \alpha(y_i - p_j) + x_j'\beta + \xi_j$ so:

$$u_{ij} = \alpha(y_i - p_j) + x_j'\beta + \xi_j + e_{ij} \tag{15.29}$$

with y_i income of individual i, p_j price of product j, and x_j a constant and a vector of other observable characteristics of product j while its other characteristics are grouped in the unobservable ξ_j. There is also an "outside good", labeled 0, corresponding with not buying any of the q products, with utility $u_{i0} = e_{i0}$ after standardization. The implied logit model for the individual probabilities does not depend on i as the term αy_i cancels out and $\pi_{ij} = \pi_j$. When the number of individuals in the data set is large, we may take $\pi_j = s_j$, the observed market share of product j, and there holds:

$$s_j = \frac{\exp(-\alpha p_j + x_j'\beta + \xi_j)}{1 + \sum_{k=1}^{q} \exp(-\alpha p_k + x_k'\beta + \xi_k)} \quad \text{so} \quad s_0 = \frac{1}{1 + \sum_{k=1}^{q} \exp(-\alpha p_k + x_k'\beta + \xi_k)}. \tag{15.30}$$

When the ξ_j are taken to be random and hence play the role of an error term, this is a nonlinear regression model, complicating things. Another complication is a matter of endogeneity; industrial-organization models predict p_j and ξ_j to be correlated, so nonlinear regression without proviso for this correlation will produce an inconsistent estimator. Both problems can be solved jointly by a simple transformation:

$$\log s_j = \log s_0 - \alpha p_j + x_j'\beta + \xi_j \tag{15.31}$$

for $j = 1, \ldots, q$. We can neglect the term $\log s_0$ and redefine the first element of β accordingly. As we will discuss in detail in Sect. 15.6, the problem of p_j and ξ_j being correlated can be solved when there are variables z_j available that correlate with x_j but not with ξ_j. With:

$$h_j(\alpha, \beta) = \begin{pmatrix} x_j \\ z_j \end{pmatrix} \xi_j = \begin{pmatrix} x_j \\ z_j \end{pmatrix} (\log s_j + \alpha p_j - x_j'\beta) \tag{15.32}$$

there then holds $\mathrm{E}[h_j] = 0$, and GMM is in business.

This simple model, due to Berry (1994), is the point of departure for a range of more realistic and more complicated models, popular in industrial organization and marketing, to handle differentiated products. A major extension is the inclusion of individual characteristics beyond y_i. They have to be integrated out of the π_{ij} in order to obtain the aggregate market shares s_j and the simple transformation to a linear model is no longer available. The moment equations based on $\mathrm{E}[x_j\xi_j] = 0$ and $\mathrm{E}[z_j\xi_j] = 0$ still hold, so GMM can still be used, but it is now computationally demanding. Usually the data have more dimensions and cover a number of time periods or markets, which can greatly improve statistical inference. The BLP model due to Berry et al. (1995) has become the core model, offering results on the computational aspects and proposals to find candidates for z_j from the supply side of the market under investigation. We discussed this model in Sect. 7.2.2. Nevo (2000) is a good introduction. An alternative approach by the method of maximum likelihood rather than GMM is advocated by Park and Gupta (2012). Applications in marketing include Narayanan et al. (2005) and Albuquerque and Bronnenberg (2009).

15.3.7 Generated Regressors

Our final example illustrating the versatility of GMM is about generated regressors, that is, regressors that are a function of unknown parameters. Estimation is usually in two steps. In the first step the parameters are estimated and the estimate substituted in the regressor. The result is called a generated regressor. Regression takes place as usual in the second step. When the first-stage estimator is consistent, it is intuitively clear that the estimator in the second step will be consistent, but the technical details are still tricky and deriving the asymptotic distribution of the estimators is nontrivial. However, when we can write the two-step procedure as a case of MM, we get all desired results right away. We illustrate this with the sample selection model, or Type-2 Tobit model, due to Heckman (1979), following Newey (1984) and Meijer and Wansbeek (2007).

The sample selection model consists of two equations for the latent response variables y_{1i}^* and y_{2i}^*,

$$y_{1i}^* = z_i'\gamma + u_{1i} \tag{15.33}$$

$$y_{2i}^* = x_i'\beta + u_{2i} \tag{15.34}$$

where z_i and x_i are observed and u_{1i} and u_{2i} are error terms, assumed bivariate normal with mean 0, with $\mathrm{E}[u_{1i}^2]$ normalized at one, $\sigma^2 \equiv \mathrm{E}[u_{2i}^2]$ and $\tau \equiv \mathrm{E}[u_{1i}u_{2i}]$. We only observe the sign of y_{1i}^* and hence observe d_i, with $d_i = 1$ if $y_{1i}^* > 0$ and $d_i = 0$ otherwise. We only observe y_{2i}^* if $d_i = 1$ and then set $y_i = y_{2i}^*$.

The first equation is a probit equation, with $p_i \equiv \mathrm{E}[d_i] = \Pr(d_i = 1) = \Phi(z_i'\gamma)$, where $\Phi(\cdot)$ is the standard normal distribution function. For the second equation there holds, using the properties of the truncated normal distribution:

$$\mathrm{E}[y_i \mid d_i = 1] = x_i'\beta + \lambda_i\tau = (x_i', \lambda_i)\begin{pmatrix}\beta \\ \tau\end{pmatrix} \equiv w_i'\alpha \tag{15.35}$$

where $\lambda_i \equiv \phi(z_i'\gamma)/\Phi(z_i'\gamma) \equiv \phi_i/p_i$, with $\phi(\cdot)$ the standard normal density. If λ_i were observed, least squares of y_i on x_i and λ_i would give consistent estimators of α, and thus of β and τ. However, λ_i depends on the unknown γ. It can be estimated by probit and the result plugged in λ_i to obtain the generated regressor $\hat{\lambda}_i \equiv \phi(z_i'\hat{\gamma})/\Phi(z_i'\hat{\gamma})$.

Now consider, for all i (after setting the as yet undefined y_i for $d_i = 0$ equal to 0 or whatever):

$$h_i(\gamma, \alpha) = \begin{pmatrix} h_{1i}(\gamma) \\ h_{2i}(\gamma, \alpha) \end{pmatrix} = \begin{pmatrix} z_i\phi_i(d_i - p_i)/[p_i(1 - p_i)] \\ w_i d_i(y_i - w_i'\alpha) \end{pmatrix}. \tag{15.36}$$

There holds $\mathrm{E}[h_i(\gamma)] = 0$. To see this, notice that $\mathrm{E}[d_i - p_i \mid z_i] = 0$ implies the first set of moment equations. The second set follows from the exogeneity of w_i. We have as many moment equations as we have parameters so we can do MM.

The sample average $\bar{h}_1(\gamma)$ is the score vector of the probit model. So, solving $\bar{h}_1(\gamma) = 0$ produces the probit ML estimator $\hat{\gamma}$. Next, substitute $\hat{\gamma}$ for γ in $h_{2i}(\gamma, \alpha)$ so solving $\bar{h}_2(\gamma, \alpha) = 0$ amounts to solving $\bar{h}_2(\hat{\gamma}, \alpha) = 0$. Thus:

$$\bar{h}_2(\hat{\gamma}, \alpha) = n^{-1}\sum_{i=1}^{n} \hat{w}_i d_i(y_i - \hat{w}_i'\alpha) = n^{-1}\sum_{\{d_i=1\}} \hat{w}_i(y_i - \hat{w}_i'\alpha) = n^{-1}\hat{W}_1'(y_1 - \hat{W}_1\alpha) \tag{15.37}$$

where $\hat{W}_1$ is the matrix with rows $\hat{w}_i' = (x_i', \hat{\lambda}_i)$ and y_1 is the vector with corresponding elements y_i, both for the subset with $d_i = 1$ only. The solution is just OLS on the model with the generated regressor. So the two-step estimator can be seen as a case of MM with all its known properties, precluding the need for a specific analysis of its statistical properties.

15.4 The Basic Theory of GMM

After illustrating the versatility of GMM we turn to theory. We define the GMM estimator and then derive its properties. Estimation by GMM involves a weight matrix, to be chosen by the researcher. We discuss which choice is optimal, and how to estimate it consistently. Although the treatment is made as simple as possible, it is technical and requires elaborate use of matrix algebra. The appendix to Vol. I provides the necessary background.

15.4.1 GMM Defined

Let the data consist of n observations $x_i, i = 1, \ldots, n$, each being a p-dimensional random variable. In the simplest case, the x_i are independent, which usually holds when the observations are from a cross-section, but the standard GMM theory still holds when the observations are observations over time and are generated by a "weakly stationary ergodic stochastic process", which roughly means that the observations may be dependent over time but any dependence that may exist between two observations should vanish fast enough, in a technical sense, the further these two observations are apart over time. We are interested in estimating an m-dimensional parameter θ from this process, with $m \leq p$. We assume that the expectation of x_i is a known function of θ:

$$\mathrm{E}[x_i] = g(\theta). \tag{15.38}$$

The idea behind GMM is to replace the population average $\mathrm{E}[x_i]$ by its sample analog $\bar{x} \equiv n^{-1} \sum_{i=1}^{n} x_i$ and the population quantity $g(\theta)$ by its sample analog $g(\hat{\theta})$ and try to solve the resulting equation system $\bar{x} = g(\hat{\theta})$ for $\hat{\theta}$. This fails when $p > m$. The approach then is to solve $\bar{x} \approx g(\hat{\theta})$ as well as possible, by minimizing the distance, somehow measured, between $\bar{x}$ and $g(\theta)$ over θ. Hence the GMM estimator $\hat{\theta}$ is defined as the minimizer of:

$$\bar{q}(\theta) \equiv [\bar{x} - g(\theta)]' \hat{W} [\bar{x} - g(\theta)] \tag{15.39}$$

with $\hat{W}$ a weight matrix of order $p \times p$, chosen by the researcher. The hat on W indicates that it may depend on data.

The moment equations we consider are of the form $\mathrm{E}[x_i] = g(\theta)$ or $\mathrm{E}[x_i - g(\theta)] = 0$, with a separation between data and parameters. As we already observed in the opening paragraph of this chapter, we can consider a more general form of moment equations, $\mathrm{E}[h_i(\theta)] = 0$, the subscript i suggesting the dependence on the data. We saw that we needed this more general form when discussing regression. The more general form does not introduce any complications.

With $\bar{h}(\hat{\theta}) \equiv n^{-1} \sum_{i=1}^{n} h_i(\hat{\theta})$, the GMM estimator is the minimizer of:

$$\bar{q}(\theta) \equiv \bar{h}(\theta)' \hat{W} \bar{h}(\theta). \tag{15.40}$$

Most of the GMM theory can be cast in the inclusive form but some results apply only to the separated form. GMM in the separated form is also known as minimum-distance estimation. Write $\hat{h}$ as short-hand for $\bar{h}(\hat{\theta})$ and $\hat{G} \equiv \bar{G}(\hat{\theta})$, with $\bar{G}(\theta) \equiv \partial \bar{h}(\theta) / \partial \theta'$, a matrix of order $p \times m$. Then the first-order condition for a minimum is $\hat{G}' \hat{W} \hat{h} = 0$. The solution is the GMM estimator $\hat{\theta}$ of θ. Under certain conditions, it is consistent and asymptotically normal. As we will see, $\hat{W}$ can be chosen such that the estimator is asymptotically efficient given the moment equations employed.

15.4.2 Illustration

To illustrate these notions we return to the case of linear regression model with model with known measurement error variance shown in Sect. 15.3.4. To translate this in the current terms, we notice that this case is of the separated form and we have $\theta = (\beta, \sigma_\xi^2, \sigma_\varepsilon^2)'$ and:

$$x_i = \begin{pmatrix} y_i^2 \\ y_i x_i \\ x_i^2 \end{pmatrix} \quad g(\theta) = \begin{pmatrix} \beta^2\sigma_\xi^2 + \sigma_\varepsilon^2 \\ \beta\sigma_\xi^2 \\ \sigma_\xi^2 - c \end{pmatrix} \quad h_i(\theta) = \begin{pmatrix} y_i^2 - \beta^2\sigma_\xi^2 - \sigma_\varepsilon^2 \\ y_i x_i - \beta\sigma_\xi^2 \\ x_i^2 - \sigma_\xi^2 - c \end{pmatrix} \tag{15.41}$$

hence:

$$\bar{h}(\theta) = \begin{pmatrix} \sum_i y_i^2/n - \beta^2\sigma_\xi^2 - \sigma_\varepsilon^2 \\ \sum_i y_i x_i/n - \beta\sigma_\xi^2 \\ \sum_i x_i^2/n - \sigma_\xi^2 - c \end{pmatrix} \quad \text{so} \quad \bar{G}(\theta) = \frac{\partial \bar{h}(\theta)}{\partial \theta'} = -\begin{pmatrix} 2\beta\sigma_\xi^2 & \beta^2 & 1 \\ \sigma_\xi^2 & \beta & 0 \\ 1 & 0 & 0 \end{pmatrix}. \tag{15.42}$$

Notice that $|\bar{G}(\theta)| = \beta$, so $\bar{G}(\theta)$ is of full rank whenever $\beta \neq 0$. Below we discuss the relevance of this.

15.4.3 Asymptotic Properties

In order to establish these results, we make a few assumptions about the asymptotic behavior at the true value of θ. First, under weak conditions, $\bar{h}(\theta)$ converges to 0 in probability and, by the central limit theorem:

$$n^{\frac{1}{2}}\, \bar{h}(\theta) \xrightarrow{d} N_p(0, \Psi) \tag{15.43}$$

for some positive definite $p \times p$ matrix $\Psi > 0$. In the i.i.d. case:

$$\Psi = \text{var}[n^{\frac{1}{2}}\bar{h}(\theta)] = n\,\text{E}[\bar{h}(\theta)\bar{h}(\theta)'] = n^{-1}\,\text{E}[\bar{h}(\theta)\bar{h}(\theta)']. \tag{15.44}$$

Next, $\hat{W}$ converges in probability to a nonrandom symmetric positive definite matrix W. Finally, we assume that $\bar{G}(\theta)$ converges in probability to G, say, of full rank. The latter assumption is the most incisive and is about local identification. To give a feel for what it means, consider the case of the linear regression model $y_i = x_i'\beta + u_i$. OLS estimation is based on the moment equation $h_i(\beta) = x_i y_i - x_i x_i'\beta$ so:

$$\bar{h}(\beta) = n^{-1}\sum_{i=1}^{n}(x_i y_i - x_i x_i'\beta) = n^{-1}(X'y - X'X\beta) \tag{15.45}$$

in self-evident matrix notation. So $\bar{G}(\beta) = -n^{-1}X'X$. Identification means that this matrix converges to a matrix of full rank. Basically, X should be of full column rank, which is of course a well-known requirement for β to be estimable. With G of full column rank there holds:

$$n^{1/2}(\hat{\theta} - \theta) \xrightarrow{d} N(0, V_W) \tag{15.46}$$

with asymptotic covariance matrix V_W:

$$V_W \equiv (G'WG)^{-1}G'W\Psi WG(G'WG)^{-1}. \tag{15.47}$$

In case $m = p$, so there are as many moment equations as there are parameters, GMM becomes MM and G becomes a square matrix. This allows for a drastic simplification of V_W as W drops out; there is no need to weight moment equations anymore. Omitting the now redundant subscript W we get $V = G^{-1}\Psi(G')^{-1}$.

The expression for V_W means that the variance of $\bar{h}$ carries over into the variance of $\hat{\theta}$ by a simple transformation. This result is closely connected to the delta method to find the asymptotic variance of a transformation of a random vector. When $y = Ax$, say, with A nonrandom and x and y random, with $\text{var}(x) = \Psi$, there holds $\text{var}(y) = A\Psi A'$. Notice that A is the Jacobian, $A = \partial y/\partial x'$. When the transformation is nonlinear we have basically the same structure. Let $\hat{\lambda}$ be a consistent estimator of a parameter vector λ, with asymptotic variance Ψ. Then $f(\hat{\lambda})$ is a consistent estimator of $f(\lambda)$, with asymptotic covariance matrix $A\Psi A'$, where now $A = \partial f(\lambda)/\partial \lambda'$, evaluated at the true parameter value. In the GMM case, the Jacobian is $(G'WG)^{-1}G'W$.

15.4.4 Optimality

There is still the matter of choice of $\hat{W}$. The asymptotic variance V_W of $\hat{\theta}$ depends on W and we want to choose W such that V_W is minimal. More precisely, we want to find a W^* such that $V_W \geq V_{W^*}$, where we use the notation $A \geq B$ to indicate that $A - B$ is a positive semidefinite matrix, for symmetric matrices A and B. One implication of $A \geq B$ concerns the diagonal elements, $A_{ii} \geq B_{ii}$. So when using the optimal W^* we make sure that each of the parameters collected in the vector θ is estimated with maximum precision.

To find the optimal solution, let H be such that $G'\Psi^{-1}H = 0$ and $F \equiv (\Psi^{-1}G, \Psi^{-1}H)$ is a square matrix of full rank. Then:

$$\Psi = G(G'\Psi^{-1}G)^{-1}G' + H(H'\Psi^{-1}H)^{-1}H'. \tag{15.48}$$

To see this, premultiply both sides by F' and postmultiply both sides by F, to obtain an identity. Since $H(H'\Psi^{-1}H)^{-1}H' \geq 0$, we have $\Psi \geq G(G'\Psi^{-1}G)^{-1}G'$, one form of the Cauchy-Schwarz inequality. Premultiply both sides by $(G'WG)^{-1}G'W$ and postmultiply both sides by its transpose to obtain:

$$(G'WG)^{-1}G'W\Psi WG(G'WG)^{-1} \geq (G'\Psi^{-1}G)^{-1}. \tag{15.49}$$

Equality holds when W is chosen such that $W = \Psi^{-1}$ (or proportional to it); the weight matrix is the inverse of the covariance matrix of $\bar{h}$. This result is intuitively appealing and basically tells us that, for an optimal result, moments have to be weighted inversely proportional to their variance. The asymptotic covariance matrix can obviously be estimated consistently by $(\hat{G}'\hat{\Psi}^{-1}\hat{G})^{-1}$, with $\hat{G} \equiv \bar{G}(\hat{\theta})$ and $\hat{\Psi}$ a consistent estimator of Ψ.

It should be stressed that the optimality is asymptotic. Choosing $W = \Psi^{-1}$ instead of crudely $\hat{W} = I_p$ leads to the lowest asymptotic variance. The asymptotic results may, however, be a poor guide to what happens when the sample is small. The fact that W now depends on the data introduces a source of random fluctuation that may bias $\hat{\theta}$ and that makes the asymptotic variance a poorer reflection of the second-order properties of $\hat{\theta}$, see e.g. Hansen et al. (1996) and Doran and Schmidt (2006).

15.4.5 Estimating Ψ with Independent Observations

There are several ways to obtain a consistent estimator of Ψ. We start with the separated case, where the moment equations are of the form $\mathrm{E}[x_i - g(\theta)] = 0$. Two obvious choices are:

$$\hat{\Psi}_1 \equiv n^{-1}\sum_{i=1}^{n}[x_i - g(\tilde{\theta})][x_i - g(\tilde{\theta})]' \quad \text{and} \quad \hat{\Psi}_2 \equiv n^{-1}\sum_{i=1}^{n}[x_i - \bar{x}][x_i - \bar{x}]' \tag{15.50}$$

where $\tilde{\theta}$ is an initial consistent estimator of θ, usually a GMM estimator based on a nonoptimal weight matrix such $\hat{W} = I_p$, the unit matrix of order equal to the number of moment equations. Both estimators use the second moment of the vector of observations as a consistent estimator of their variance but deal with the problem that the mean of x_i is unknown in a different way; $\hat{\Psi}_1$ uses an initial consistent estimator and $\hat{\Psi}_2$ uses the sample mean, making it robust to model misspecification.

Estimators of Ψ for the inclusive case are obtained by some adaptation. For the matrix $\hat{\Psi}_1$, notice that $[x_i - g(\tilde{\theta})]$ is a special case of $h_i(\tilde{\theta})$. Hence, now:

$$\hat{\Psi}_1 \equiv n^{-1}\sum_{i=1}^{n} h_i(\tilde{\theta})h_i(\tilde{\theta})'. \tag{15.51}$$

The generalization of $\hat{\Psi}_2$ is slightly less immediate since estimating the mean of the h_i requires an initial consistent estimator of θ. We get:

$$\hat{\Psi}_2 \equiv n^{-1} \sum_{i=1}^{n} [h_i(\tilde{\theta}) - \bar{h}(\tilde{\theta})][h_i(\tilde{\theta}) - \bar{h}(\tilde{\theta})]'. \tag{15.52}$$

If $h_i(\theta) = x_i - g(\theta)$, the expression reduces to the expression for the separated case, which justifies the use of the same notation; the initial estimator drops out.

To continue the illustrative example from Sect. 15.4.2, we find for the MM estimator of β that corrects for the presence of measurement error:

$$\widehat{\text{var}}(\hat{\beta}_{\text{MM}}) = n^{-1}(2\hat{\beta}_{\text{MM}}\hat{\sigma}_\xi^2, \hat{\beta}_{\text{MM}}^2, 1)\hat{\Psi}_2(2\hat{\beta}_{\text{MM}}\hat{\sigma}_\xi^2, \hat{\beta}_{\text{MM}}^2, 1)' \tag{15.53}$$

where $\hat{\sigma}_\xi^2 = \sum_i (x_i - c)^2/n$ is a consistent estimator of σ_ξ^2 and $\hat{\Psi}_2$ follows directly from its definition, with x_i as in (15.41).

In Sect. 15.3.5 we discussed structural equation models, SEMs, and indicated how GMM provides the natural context for estimation by confronting the observed covariance matrix S with its expectation $\Sigma(\theta)$. The moment equations are $\text{E}[s - \sigma(\theta)] = 0$, the stacked versions of S and $\Sigma(\theta)$ where the elements that are redundant due to symmetry have been omitted. An often used approach is the asymptotically distribution free (ADF) estimator, based on weighting with fourth moments (since the data used are second moments), also called weighted least squares (WLS). Another approach is the generalized least squares (GLS) estimator, not to be confused with the GLS estimator from regression analysis. This approach is valid when the underlying data are normally distributed. Then the covariance matrix of the sample moments are highly structured and is a function of Σ; no new parameters are involved, just as in the one-dimensional case where $x \sim N(0, \sigma^2)$ means $\text{E}[x^4] = 3(\sigma^2)^2$. Estimating Σ by S and substitution in the criterion function leads, after a bit of rewriting, to the result that $\hat{\theta}$ is the minimizer of $\text{tr}[(S - \Sigma(\theta))S^{-1}]^2$.

15.4.6 Estimating Ψ When There Is Heteroskedasticity and Autocorrelation

In estimating Ψ, we had assumed that the data are i.i.d. In many econometric applications of GMM, starting with the seminal Hansen (1982) paper, the data are time-series data, where no independence can be assumed. Also, with cross-sectional data, one may want to avoid the hypothesis of homoskedasticity. In fact, GMM owes much of its popularity to its relatively easy application in time-series models. The estimation of Ψ is slightly more complicated then. A main result is due to Newey and West (1987), who proposed the heteroskedasticity and autocorrelation consistent (HAC) estimator:

$$\hat{\Psi} \equiv \hat{\Psi}_0 + \sum_{j=1}^{r} [1 - j/(r+1)](\hat{\Psi}_j + \hat{\Psi}_j') \tag{15.54}$$

where $\hat{\Psi}_0$ taken to be $\hat{\Psi}_1$ or $\hat{\Psi}_2$ as before, and $\hat{\Psi}_j$ is taken $\hat{\Psi}_{j1}$ or $\hat{\Psi}_{j2}$, with:

$$\hat{\Psi}_{j1} \equiv n^{-1} \sum_{i=j+1}^{n} h_i(\tilde{\theta}) h_{i-j}(\tilde{\theta})' \quad \text{and} \tag{15.55}$$

$$\hat{\Psi}_{j2} \equiv n^{-1} \sum_{i=j+1}^{n} [h_i(\tilde{\theta}) - \bar{h}(\tilde{\theta})][h_{i-j}(\tilde{\theta}) - \bar{h}(\tilde{\theta})]' \tag{15.56}$$

with $\tilde{\theta}$ an initial consistent estimator. Let $\Psi_j \equiv \lim_{n\to\infty} n^{-1} \sum_{i=j+1}^{n} \mathrm{E}[h_i(\theta) h_{i-j}(\theta)']$. Then $\Psi = \Psi_0 + \sum_{j=1}^{\infty} (\Psi_j + \Psi_j')$. So consistency requires that the weight factor $1 - j/(r+1)$ converges to one.

15.4.7 *Testing for Model Adequacy*

One test that is of particular interest in the context of GMM estimation is an overall test, the J-test, of model adequacy based on the distance of the estimated moment vector $\hat{h}$ from 0. If the model is correctly specified this distance should not be too large. In the case of model misspecification, a larger value of $\hat{h}$ may result. The null hypothesis is $\mathrm{E}[\bar{h}(\theta)] = 0$ and the alternative hypothesis is $\mathrm{E}[\bar{h}(\theta)] \neq 0$.

Under optimal weighting using a consistent estimator of Ψ, n times the minimum of the GMM objective function can be shown to be asymptotically chi-squared distributed with $p - m$ degrees of freedom under the hypothesis of correct model specification:

$$\chi^2 \equiv n\bar{q}(\hat{\theta}) \xrightarrow{d} \chi^2_{p-m}. \tag{15.57}$$

The statistic χ^2 is called the chi-square test statistic, frequently abbreviated as chi-square statistic or simply chi-square. Using it requires a certain degree of overidentification, i.e. $p > m$. Under nonoptimal weighting testing is much more complicated, cf. Wansbeek and Meijer (2000, Chap. 10).

15.5 Further Issues Around GMM

The above constitutes the basics of GMM theory. Much more can be said about GMM. This section contains some selected topics. The first one is the effect of adding moment equations to those already considered, potentially leading to more precise inference. One context where this is relevant is the presence of a conditional moment equation, which allow us to generate an arbitrary number of additional moment equations. There is, however a bound to the efficiency that can be obtained. We conclude by briefly discussing estimation with combined data from different groups.

15.5.1 Adding Moment Equations

The question is whether more moment equations lead to more precise estimation. The answer is a qualified yes. This is easily seen when approaching the question from the other end, that is, does the asymptotic variance increase when we omit moment equations? We have p moment equations, and under optimal weighting the asymptotic variance is $(G'\Psi^{-1}G)^{-1}$. When we work with the first p_1 moment equations only, the asymptotic variance is $(G_1'\Psi_{11}^{-1}G_1)^{-1}$, with G_1 the matrix with the first p_1 rows of G and Ψ_{11} the upper $p_1 \times p_1$ block of Ψ. Let L be the $p \times p_1$ matrix with the first p_1 columns of the $p \times p$ identity matrix, then $G_1 = L'G$ and $\Psi_{11} = L'\Psi L$. Then, according to the Cauchy-Schwarz inequality as given in Sect. 15.4.4:

$$G_1'\Psi_{11}^{-1}G_1 = G'L(L'\Psi L)^{-1}L'G \leq G'\Psi^{-1}G. \tag{15.58}$$

Taking the inverse of $G_1'\Psi_{11}^{-1}G_1$ and $G'\Psi^{-1}G$ reverses the inequality sign. This establishes the increase in variance when moment equations are left out. Equivalently, adding moment equations leads to a lower variance.

Notice, however, that this is based on the expression $(G'\Psi^{-1}G)^{-1}$, which is the asymptotic variance under optimal weighting. The conclusion only holds for optimal GMM. When the weighting is not optimal, the expression for the asymptotic variance is more complicated and the argument does not hold anymore. Then, adding moment equations can actually increase the asymptotic variance.

It is of some interest to have a closer look at the difference in variance. With the notation:

$$G = \begin{pmatrix} G_1 \\ G_2 \end{pmatrix} \quad \text{and} \quad \Psi = \begin{pmatrix} \Psi_{11} & \Psi_{12} \\ \Psi_{21} & \Psi_{22} \end{pmatrix} \tag{15.59}$$

application of the expression for the inverse of a partitioned matrix yields:

$$G'\Psi^{-1}G = G_1'\Psi_{11}^{-1}G_1' + B'(\Psi_{22} - \Psi_{21}\Psi_{11}^{-1}\Psi_{12})^{-1}B \geq G_1'\Psi_{11}^{-1}G_1 \qquad (15.60)$$

with $B \equiv G_2 - \Psi_{21}\Psi_{11}^{-1}G_1$. Using more moment equations actually lowers the asymptotic variance when $B \neq 0$. When $B = 0$, the second set of moment equations is said to be redundant with respect to the first set, cf. Breusch (1999). This happens trivially when the second set of moment equations is a linear combination of the first one. Another observation is that we do not require G_2 to be nonzero. When the second set of moment equations does not depend on parameters, $G_2 = 0$, but that still does not imply $B = 0$; moment equations need not depend on parameters to contribute to the precision of the estimation process. This somewhat surprising finding is due to Qian and Schmidt (1999).

15.5.2 Conditional Moment Equations and the Efficiency Bound

A typical point of departure for GMM is a conditional moment equation, which is something of the form $\mathrm{E}[u_i \mid z_i] = 0$; see Sect. 15.3.2 for an example. The regression case discussed in Sect. 15.3.1 provides one example, where u_i is the error term of a regression and z_i is an exogenous regressor. Another example was provided by the probit model mentioned in Sect. 15.3.7, where u_i is $d_i - p_i$, where d_i is a random dummy variable and p_i is the probability of d_i being one.

The nice thing about conditional moment equations is that they can be used to find many moment equations of the usual, unconditional kind. To see this, let $f(z_i)$ be a vector of functions of z_i. Then, using the law of iterated expectation:

$$\mathrm{E}[f(z_i)u_i] = \mathrm{E}[\mathrm{E}[f(z_i)u_i \mid z_i]] = \mathrm{E}[f(z_i)\,\mathrm{E}(u_i \mid z_i)] = 0 \qquad (15.61)$$

for any $f(\cdot)$. There is no limit to the number of moment equations $h_i = f(z_i)u_i$, with u_i a function of θ, that can be added.

Yet there is a limit to the gain in efficiency that can be had. Choose some $f(\cdot)$. Collect the u_i in the n-vector u and let $F \equiv [f(z_1), \ldots, f(z_n)]'$ and $Z \equiv (z_1, \ldots, z_n)'$. Then we have $\mathrm{E}[F'u] = 0$. Let $\Omega \equiv \mathrm{E}[uu' \mid Z]$, then $\mathrm{var}(F'u|Z) = F'\Omega F$. Since Ω is of order $n \times n$, it can generally not be consistently estimated, but an appropriate estimator $\hat{\Omega}$ makes $F'\hat{\Omega}F$ a consistent estimator of $F'\Omega F$. Hence, the GMM estimator of θ is found by minimizing $u'F(F'\hat{\Omega}F)^{-1}F'u$. This estimator has conditional asymptotic covariance matrix:

$$\mathrm{avar}(\hat{\theta} \mid Z) = \operatorname*{plim}_{n\to\infty} n(D'F(F'\Omega F)^{-1}F'D)^{-1} \qquad (15.62)$$

where $D \equiv \mathrm{E}[\partial u/\partial\theta' \mid Z]$. From the Cauchy-Schwarz inequality from Sect. 15.4.4 we know:

$$D'\Omega^{-1}D \geq D'F(F'\Omega F)^{-1}F'D. \tag{15.63}$$

On inversion this shows a lower limit to the asymptotic variance, however we expand the number of instruments in F. When $F = \Omega^{-1}DQ$ with Q a square, nonsingular matrix, the inequality becomes an equality and the lower limit to the variance (or GMM bound) is reached. This indicates the way to construct optimal instruments.

15.5.3 Continuous Updating

In the inclusive case, an initial consistent estimator $\tilde{\theta}$ is needed for consistent estimation of Ψ. The inverse of $\hat{\Psi}$ is next used as a weight matrix to obtain an asymptotically optimal estimator of θ. Hence, this estimate is computed in a two-step procedure. Evidently, we can repeat the process, that is, update $\hat{\Psi}$ with the new estimator of θ, to obtain a new estimator of θ. This may be more efficient in a finite sample setting since the two-step GMM estimator is more efficient than the initial estimator. We can iterate until convergence, and one might guess that this produces an estimator that minimizes:

$$\bar{q}(\theta) \equiv \bar{h}(\theta)'\hat{W}(\theta)\bar{h}(\theta) \tag{15.64}$$

over θ, where we wrote the dependence of W on θ explicitly. This guess is, however, not the case. Yet, we can certainly consider an estimator of θ thus defined. This estimator is called the continuous-updating GMM estimator (CUE), introduced by Hansen et al. (1996). It is asymptotically equivalent to the optimal GMM estimator and its iterated version, as the weight matrices converge to Ψ^{-1} in both cases. Yet the estimators behave differently in finite samples. There is quite a bit of evidence from Monte Carlo studies that the CUE outperforms the two-step GMM estimator in the sense that it has lower median bias and a better coverage rate for the J-test for overidentifying restrictions. CUE is a generalization of the limited-information maximum likelihood estimator (LIML), to be discussed in Sect. 15.7.3.

15.5.4 Multiple Groups

In empirical practice, we want to combine data from different sources, to estimate the same parameters. We may have the same model, with data from different sources, or we may just have different models that only share some parameters. Joint estimation is obviously desirable from an efficiency point of view. Such analysis with different groups can be done in a simple way.

If the samples from the various groups are drawn independently, the criterion function to be minimized for GMM estimation is simply the sum of the criterion functions for the groups, weighted with weights proportional to their sample size.

Let $j = 1, \ldots, J$ index groups. Let n_j is the sample size in the jth group and $n \equiv n_1 + \ldots + n_J$. There holds for the overall criterion:

$$\bar{q}(\theta) \equiv \sum_{j=1}^{J} (n_j/n)\, \bar{q}_j(\theta) = [\bar{h}_1(\theta)', \ldots, \bar{h}_J(\theta)'] \begin{pmatrix} (n_1/n)\hat{W}_1 & & \\ & \ddots & \\ & & (n_J/n)\hat{W}_J \end{pmatrix} \begin{pmatrix} \bar{h}_1(\theta) \\ \vdots \\ \bar{h}_J(\theta) \end{pmatrix} \tag{15.65}$$

in self-evident notation. This fully fits in the standard GMM mold. So estimation and inference then proceed as usual, and combining information from different groups turns out to be quite easy.

Albuquerque and Bronnenberg (2009) provide an example in marketing. The estimate a model for new-product demand in consumer packaged goods categories, combining market-level time-series data with summaries of household purchase behavior.

15.6 Instrumental Variables

GMM is quite general, and nests many special cases. A major one is instrumental variables (IV) estimation. For an introduction, see Sect. 6.6 in Vol. 1 and Sect. 18.3 in this volume, and for an extensive and incisive discussion from a marketing point of view see Rossi (2014). The reason to discuss IV here is that the we can bring general GMM theory to bear on IV, hence obtaining IV theory at no additional cost.

IV theory becomes relevant when, in the linear regression model $y_i = x_i'\beta + u_i$ the assumption $\mathrm{E}[x_i u_i] = 0$ does not hold. This can occur in a wide array of cases; below, in Sect. 15.6.1, we give a number of examples. When $\mathrm{E}[x_i u_i] \neq 0$, we can still estimate β by OLS but the estimator is inconsistent. In the case of a single regressor and $\mathrm{E}[x_i u_i] > 0$, above-mean values of x_i have a tendency to go together with $u_i > 0$, and below-mean values of x_i tend to correspond with $u_i < 0$, leading to an upward bias of OLS.

A way out of the problem of inconsistent OLS is offered when there are variables available collected in the vector z_i that correlate with x_i but not with u_i. So $\mathrm{E}[z_i u_i] = 0$, and after substituting out u_i we obtain $\mathrm{E}[z_i(y_i - x_i'\beta)] = 0$ as a set of moment equations. When z_i has at least as many elements as x_i, we estimate β consistently by GMM. Following Reiersøl (1941), the variables constituting z_i are called instrumental variables, or instruments for short. To qualify for an instrument, a variable needs to pass the two hurdles of instrument validity, that is, no correlation with the error term, and instrument strength, that is, sufficient correlation with the problematic regressor.

By way of motivating examples, we first present a number of cases where a correlation between a regressor and the error term may arise. We indicate where instruments may come from. We then develop the theory around IV estimation by taking it as a special case of GMM. We next return to the issue of finding instruments. There is not a general recipe for all cases, and the researcher's creativity is challenged. We give some solutions that have actually been found. One solution, due to Angrist and Krueger (1991), was not only inspiring per se but also led to an interest in the case where there are many instruments that yet together correlate only weakly with the variable it is supposed to instrument. We indicate the issue and discuss one specific solution, the limited-information maximum likelihood estimator.

15.6.1 Motivating Examples

We now present a number of situations where $\mathrm{E}[x_i u_i] = 0$ does not hold. We concentrate on the bare essentials, indicate why regressor and error term are correlated, and suggest appropriate instrumental variables. Variables are taken into deviations from their mean so we don't get distracted by intercepts.

15.6.1.1 Simultaneity

Economic theory predicts that, under certain assumptions, firms set their advertising budgets such that there is a constant ratio between advertising outlay and sales. At the same time, advertising is meant to increase sales. So, advertising and sales are simultaneously determined, as was already noted by Bass and Parsons (1969). Following Berndt (1991), a very simple and stylized model describing the simultaneous determination of advertising and sales for a firm at time t is:

$$s_t = \beta a_t + \gamma r_t + u_t \tag{15.66}$$

$$a_t = \delta s_t + \zeta z_t + v_t \tag{15.67}$$

where s_t is sales at time t, a_t advertising, the two being the endogenous variables, and r_t is the price of output at time t and z_t the price of advertising, the two assumed exogenous, that is, determined outside the model. The error terms are u_t and v_t and may be correlated with each other. Theory predicts $\beta > 0$ and $\delta > 0$, and $\gamma < 0$ and $\zeta < 0$. Since, according to (15.67), a_t depends on v_t and v_t is correlated with u_t, we have $\mathrm{E}[a_t u_t] \neq 0$ and estimating (15.66) by OLS yields inconsistent estimators of β and γ. Likewise, $\mathrm{E}[s_t v_t] \neq 0$, invalidating OLS estimation in (15.67). Consistent estimation is possible by using z_t as an instrumental variable in (15.66) and r_t in (15.67).

15.6.1.2 Dynamic Panel Data Model

The model has two parts, an autoregressive equation and a split-up of the error term into an individual effect α_i and an overall white noise error term:

$$y_{it} = \gamma y_{i,t-1} + u_{it} \tag{15.68}$$

$$u_{it} = \alpha_i + \varepsilon_{it}. \tag{15.69}$$

The model is extremely popular as it disentangles two sources of persistence of a phenomenon over time, heterogeneity through the time-constant individual effect α_i, and state dependence through the autoregressive parameter γ. The model formulation implies that the individual effect is correlated with y_{is} for all s including $s = t - 1$, so the regressor is correlated with the error term since it includes the individual effect. To find instruments, take first differences to obtain:

$$y_{it} - y_{i,t-1} = \gamma(y_{i,t-1} - y_{i,t-2}) + (\varepsilon_{it} - \varepsilon_{i,t-1}). \tag{15.70}$$

The source of correlation, α_i, has now been removed from the model. Due to the assumed lack of correlation of the ε_{it} over time we can use $y_{i,t-2}, y_{i,t-3}, \ldots$ as instruments. The basic idea is due to Anderson and Hsiao (1981) and has been extended to Arellano and Bond (1991); the Arellano-Bond estimator has become a household name.

15.6.1.3 Endogeneity in a Static Panel Data Model

Another important case is the static panel data model with two regressors, one varying over time and the other time-constant; the individual effect is correlated with the latter but not with the former:

$$y_{it} = \beta x_{it} + \gamma s_i + u_{it} \tag{15.71}$$

$$u_{it} = \alpha_i + \varepsilon_{it}. \tag{15.72}$$

A leading example is the wage equation, where y_{it} is log wage and s_i is the level of schooling, optimized by the agent with regard to all information, including time-constant individual traits like intelligence captured by α_i. Regression without proviso for this correlation leads to inconsistent results. One way out is to transform the model into first differences over time. This solves the problem due to the correlation between s_i and α_i since both are eliminated from the model but precludes estimation of γ as it disappeared jointly with s_i. A simple solution retaining s_i is to use the mean over time $\bar{x}_i$ of the x_{it} as instrument for s_i, as was first noted by Hausman and Taylor (1981).

15.6.1.4 Measurement Error

The model is $y_i = \beta\xi_i + u_i$ but ξ_i is observed with error, so $x_i = \xi_i + v_i$, with v_i the measurement error, a random variable uncorrelated with everything else. Elimination of ξ_i from the model by substitution of $\xi_i = x_i - v_i$ yields:

$$y_i = \beta x_i + w_i \tag{15.73}$$

$$w_i \equiv u_i - \beta v_i. \tag{15.74}$$

So, x_i and w_i share the measurement error v_i, so they are correlated, making the OLS estimator of β inconsistent. The inconsistency is negative if $\beta > 0$ and positive if $\beta < 0$ hence towards 0 in both cases; measurement error causes an "attenuation" in the estimate if not accounted for. In this model, there holds:

$$\mathrm{E}[(x_i y_i)x_i] = \mathrm{E}[(\xi_i\beta + u_i)(\xi_i + v_i)^2] = \beta\,\mathrm{E}[\xi_i^3] \quad \text{and} \tag{15.75}$$

$$\mathrm{E}[(x_i y_i)u_i] = \mathrm{E}[(\xi_i + v_i)(\xi_i\beta + u_i)(u_i - v_i\beta)] = 0, \tag{15.76}$$

so $x_i y_i$ can be used as an instrumental variable if the distribution of ξ_i is asymmetric and $\mathrm{E}[\xi_i^3]$ does not vanish.

15.6.1.5 Omitted Variables

The above cases might be called "technical", with a correlation between the regressor and the error term implied by the structure of the model. Now something different, although the difference is a bit contrived. We now look at a case that we may call "structural". Let the model be $y_i = \beta_1 x_{1i} + \beta_2 x_{2i} + u_i$ but x_{2i} is omitted; the model estimated is $y_i = \beta_1 x_{1i} + w_i$, where $w_i = u_i + \beta_2 x_{2i}$. So the regressor x_1 and the error term w_i are correlated when x_{1i} and x_{2i} are correlated. If the correlation is positive, $\hat{\beta}_1$ is too high. The effect of x_{1i} on y_i is overstated as it partly takes over the effect of the omitted x_{2i}. This effect is known as omitted variable bias.

A particular way of giving substance to omitted variable bias is by invoking the neoclassical paradigm. The generic case is that some regressor, x_i, say, is considered the outcome of optimizing behavior on behalf of economic agent i. So x_i is a function of all variables in the information set available to agent i. This set is much larger than an econometrician can ever measure and incorporate in the model. Most variables remain unobserved. This case of "asymmetric information" need not be a problem when these variables only enter the model through x_i, but that is a long shot; some of them will have a direct influence on the dependent variable y_i themselves, leading to correlation between x_i and the error term.

A leading example is the wage equation, where y_i is hourly wage, x_i the level of education (optimized by the agent), and the information set includes unobservables like ability. Ability has a double effect on earnings. It will affect hourly wage in a direct way, and it will affect the level of education and hence affect hourly wage in an indirect way. Doing OLS produces an estimate of the returns to education that will be too high when considered the effect of education on earnings only, since it also includes the indirect (through education) effect of ability on earnings.

There is no general recipe for finding instruments. Creativity is required. In Sect. 15.6.4 we give some examples.

15.6.2 IV as GMM

As we noticed above, the availability of instruments leads to moment equations of the form $\mathrm{E}[z_i(y_i - x_i'\beta)] = 0$. So in terms of the GMM theory of the previous section we have $h_i(\beta) = z_i(y_i - x_i'\beta)$, and hence, on collecting the instruments in $Z \equiv (z_1, \ldots, z_n)'$:

$$\bar{h}(\beta) = n^{-1}\sum_{i=1}^{n} z_i(y_i - x_i'\beta) = n^{-1}Z'(y - X\beta). \tag{15.77}$$

If we like, we can stop here and let GMM take over, producing a consistent and asymptotically efficient estimator of β. There is an elaborate history of IV estimation of the linear model long before GMM entered the scene but we can leave that alone if we are only interested in consistent and efficient estimation.

Yet it is useful and insightful to elaborate things a bit, exploiting the specific structure of the case. Let us first consider the "just-identified" case where there are as many instruments as there are regressors, so the context is MM rather than GMM. Then $Z'X$ is a square matrix, and we can solve the estimating equations $\bar{h}(\hat{\beta}) = 0$ to yield:

$$\hat{\beta} \equiv (Z'X)^{-1}Z'y. \tag{15.78}$$

An intuitive way to look at this is as follows. The model $y = X\beta + u$ implies $Z'y/n = Z'X\beta/n + Z'u/n$. Since $Z'u/n$ vanishes in the limit, solving $Z'y = Z'X\hat{\beta}$ should give a sensible estimator of β.

We now consider the "overidentified" case where there are more instruments than regressors. To do GMM, choose a weight matrix $\hat{W}$ and minimize:

$$\bar{q}(\beta) = \bar{h}(\beta)'\hat{W}\bar{h}(\beta) = (y - X\beta)'Z\hat{W}Z'(y - X\beta) \tag{15.79}$$

yielding:

$$\hat{\beta} = (X'Z\hat{W}Z'X)^{-1}X'Z\hat{W}Z'y. \tag{15.80}$$

It is simple to see that this reduces to (15.78) when $X'Z$ is a square, invertible matrix. From the general GMM theory, the asymptotic distribution of $\hat{\beta}$ is given by:

$$n^{1/2}(\hat{\beta} - \beta) \xrightarrow{d} N(0, (G'WG)^{-1}G'W\Psi WG(G'WG)^{-1}) \tag{15.81}$$

with:

$$G = \operatorname*{plim}_{n\to\infty} \bar{G}(\beta) = \operatorname*{plim}_{n\to\infty} \partial\bar{h}(\beta)/\partial\beta' = -\operatorname*{plim}_{n\to\infty} n^{-1}Z'X \tag{15.82}$$

$$\Psi = \operatorname*{plim}_{n\to\infty} n^{-1}\sum_{i=1}^{n} \mathrm{E}[u_i^2 z_i z_i'] = \operatorname*{plim}_{n\to\infty} n^{-1}\,\mathrm{E}[Z'\Delta Z] \tag{15.83}$$

with Δ the diagonal matrix with the u_i^2 on the diagonal. So the estimated variance of $\hat{\beta}$ is given by:

$$\widehat{\mathrm{var}}(\hat{\beta}) = (X'Z\hat{W}Z'X)^{-1}X'Z\hat{W}\hat{\Psi}\hat{W}Z'X(X'Z\hat{W}Z'X)^{-1} \tag{15.84}$$

where $\hat{\Psi} = n^{-1}\sum_{i=1}^{n}\hat{u}_i^2 z_i z_i' = n^{-1}Z'\hat{\Delta}Z$ a consistent estimator of Ψ, with $\hat{u}_i = y_i - x_i'\hat{\beta}$ the residuals. This estimator of Ψ assumes independence across observations but is resistant against heteroskedasticity. An optimal GMM estimator is obtained in the usual way, that is to proceed in two steps. In the first step an initial consistent estimator for β is found, like the 2SLS estimator discussed below, which is used to find $\hat{\Psi}$. Then in the second step we let $\hat{W} = \hat{\Psi}^{-1}$ and obtain the asymptotically efficient estimator of β in the second step, with estimated variance $\widehat{\mathrm{var}}(\hat{\beta}) = (X'Z\hat{\Psi}^{-1}Z'X)^{-1}$.

15.6.3 *Further Issues Around IV*

These are the main results on IV estimation. There are many comments that can be made and extensions that can be given. Here we collect a number of them.

This asymptotic result may be inadequate for small samples; the asymptotic distribution may be a poor guide to the exact distribution of $\hat{\beta}$. Standard errors can be severely underestimated due to extra variation when going from Ψ to $\hat{\Psi}$. Windmeijer (2005) has noticed that the difference between the two can be estimated and proposes a correction term, leading to more accurate inference.

An important issue with IV concerns identification. It requires that:

$$G = \operatorname*{plim}_{n\to\infty} \bar{G}(\theta) \equiv \partial\bar{h}(\theta)/\partial\theta' = -\operatorname*{plim}_{n\to\infty} n^{-1}Z'X \tag{15.85}$$

is of full column rank. As G is not known and has to be estimated, this amounts to a test on the rank of $n^{-1}Z'X$, which amounts to a test on the rank of the random matrix $Z'X$. Such a test, under quite general conditions, has been presented by Kleibergen and Paap (2006). The null hypothesis is that the rank of this matrix (or rather, in their approach of $(Z'Z)^{-1}Z'X)$ has a rank deficiency of one, and the alternative hypothesis is that it is of full rank.

When there is no endogeneity issue, we can take $Z{=}X$ and $\hat{\beta}$ in (15.80) reduces to the OLS estimator. From (15.84), it has asymptotic variance $(X'X)^{-1}X'\hat{\Delta}X(X'X)^{-1}/n$. This is the robust variance estimator due to White (1980). So only the estimator of the variance takes heteroskedasticity into account, but not the estimator of β itself. We thus seem to miss the opportunity adapt the estimator itself, and not just the estimator of its variance, for heteroskedasticity of unknown form. We thus may miss some potential efficiency gain. To have an estimator taking heteroskedasticity into account as yet, one might consider the GLS estimator $\hat{\beta} = (X'\hat{\Delta}^{-1}X)^{-1}X'\hat{\Delta}^{-1}y$, but properties of this estimator are hard to obtain, cf. Wansbeek (2004). Another, and more sensible way out is to take Z equal to X but with a column added containing another exogenous variable, for example some nonlinear function of X. By doing so, (15.80) does not reduce to (15.78) anymore and $\hat{W}$, with this optimal choice $\hat{\Psi}^{-1}$, are maintained, cf. Cragg (1983). So instruments are not invoked to solve an inconsistency problem with estimating β due to endogeneity problem but an efficiency problem due to heteroskedasticity.

A leading special case is the case where the u_i are homoskedastic, $\mathrm{E}[u_i^2 z_i z_i'] = \sigma^2 z_i z_i'$, leading to the simpler estimator $\hat{\Psi} = \hat{\sigma}^2 n^{-1}\sum_{i=1}^n z_i z_i' = \hat{\sigma}^2 n^{-1}Z'Z$, with $\hat{\sigma}^2 = (n-k)^{-1}\sum_{i=1}^n \hat{u}_i^2$. Then, with $P_Z \equiv Z(Z'Z)^{-1}Z'$:

$$\hat{\beta} = [X'Z(Z'Z)^{-1}Z'X]^{-1}X'Z(Z'Z)^{-1}Z'y = (X'P_ZX)^{-1}X'P_Zy \tag{15.86}$$

with estimated variance $\widehat{\mathrm{var}}(\hat{\beta}) = \hat{\sigma}^2(X'P_ZX)^{-1}$. The important element here is the matrix P_Z. This matrix is idempotent, $P_Z^2 = P_Z$. So we can write, with $\hat{X} \equiv P_ZX$:

$$\hat{\beta} = (X'P_ZX)^{-1}X'P_Zy = [(P_ZX)'(P_ZX)]^{-1}(P_ZX)'y = (\hat{X}'\hat{X})^{-1}\hat{X}'y. \tag{15.87}$$

So $\hat{\beta}$ is the OLS estimator of y on $\hat{X}$. This hugely popular estimator is the two-stage least squares (2SLS) estimator, the first stage being the computation of P_ZX from X and the second stage the regression of y on P_ZX. We discussed this estimator in Sect. 6.3 of Vol. I. Theil (1953) is usually credited to be the source of 2SLS, although Anderson (2005) argues that Anderson and Rubin (1950) used what is "essentially" the 2SLS estimator in the derivation of the asymptotic distribution of the limited information maximum likelihood (LIML) estimator.

As the matrix P_Z is an idempotent matrix, it can be seen mathematically as a projection matrix, in this case projection onto the space spanned by the columns of Z. Intuitively, these columns are orthogonal to u, at least in expectation, and what 2SLS does is to project X onto the Z space, hence "cleaning" X of any correlation with u. The detour through Z breaks the correlation. Figure 15.1 gives a symbolic illustration.

The approach is easily extended to cover the case of panel data. Let T be the number of observations over time and redefine y, X and Z to have nT rather than n

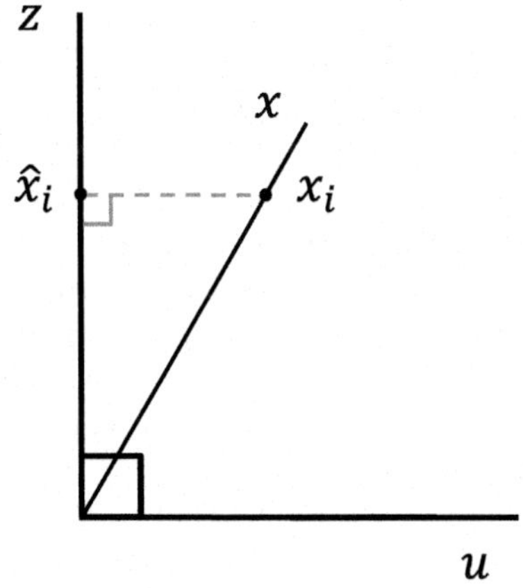

Fig. 15.1 IV estimation as a projection

rows. In particular, let Z consist of n blocks Z_i, each with T rows. The error term is now a T-vector u_i instead of a scalar u_i. Let:

$$\Psi = \operatorname*{plim}_{n\to\infty} n^{-1} \sum_{i=1}^{n} \mathrm{E}[Z_i' u_i u_i' Z_i] = \operatorname*{plim}_{n\to\infty} n^{-1}\, \mathrm{E}[Z' \Delta Z] \tag{15.88}$$

with Δ redefined as the block-diagonal matrix with blocks $u_i u_i'$. After this adaptation the sequel is much the same. The approach hedges against heteroskedasticity over i and takes care of any covariance structure over time, so there is no need for a special treatment of random effects; fixed effects can be eliminated by e.g. taking first differences. The above approach then still holds with the remark that there are only $T - 1$ observations over time left.

15.6.4 How to Obtain Instruments?

Having thus settled the question how the method of instrumental variables offers a general way out of a predicament, another question offers itself. That is, how to obtain instruments? In the examples above we offered answers for specific cases where instruments could be found by exploiting the model structure, but in other cases instruments have to be sought outside the model. This requires creativity, insight in the institutional setting of the case, or just "by being clever" Wooldridge (2010, p. 93), always keeping in mind that "all instruments arrive on the scene with a dark cloud of invalidity hanging overhead" Murray (2006). Sometimes there are variables left in the data set that are good instruments. Sometimes the search is harder. The literature (see also Sect. 18.3) offers many examples, sometimes quite funny or surprising ones. For example, when estimating demand functions at the country level, Theil and Finke (1983) question the assumption that income, a major regressor, is measured without error. They use the distance of a country's capital from the equator as an instrument and motivate this by the consideration that "poverty is considered as being approximately a tropical problem." Here are some examples from marketing.

Angrist et al. (2000) set out to estimate the demand for whiting at the Fulton fish market in New York. Since price and quantity are simultaneously determined, regressing quantity on price produces an inconsistent result since price is endogenous. The problem can be solved by using an instrument that shifts supply, for which the authors use the weather conditions at sea. The idea of using a supply shifter to identify a demand equation has a long history and goes back to Wright (1928), according to Stock and Trebbi (2003), in a paper titled "Who invented instrumental variable regression?"

Ashworth and Clinton (2007) investigate whether advertising exposure affects voting at presidential elections in the U.S. Individuals who are more exposed to advertising are more inclined to vote. But individuals who are more interested in elections might seek more information, causing an endogeneity problem when voting is regressed on exposure. The authors solve this by using residence in a "battleground state" as instrument, as it is likely to be correlated with advertising exposure but not with the error term reflecting individual characteristics that influence voting.

Gu et al. (2012) analyze the impact of the number of online reviews (or "word of mouth", WOM) on retailer sales. Regression sales on WOM suffers from an endogeneity problem because of simultaneity. WOM will influence sales, but you need to have bought a product before you can write a review on it. The authors use the seven-day lagged value of WOM as an instrument as it will be correlated with current WOM, while current sales shocks cannot influence past WOM.

Narayanan and Nair (2013) analyze the adoption of the Toyota Prius Hybrid in California. The data are at the individual level, so the dependent variable y_i is 0-1, indicating the choice made. Individual i's choice may be influenced by the "installed base", in particular the number of cars of the same type bought in the neighborhood prior to the purchase by i. Regressing the y_i on the installed base suffers from an endogeneity problem as the installed base is likely to be correlated to the error term as the taste for hybrid cars enters both. To solve the problem, the authors use the installed base of Honda Civic Hybrids as instrument. The Honda Civic Hybrid is in appearance hardly distinguishable from its non-hybrid counterpart. Hence, consumers can hardly track the installed based of Honda Civic hybrids, and the number of local adopters may not affect a consumer's belief about hybrid quality in general.

Germann (2015) investigate whether the presence of a chief marketing officer (CMO) has an effect on a firm's financial performance. This can be assessed by regressing some measure of financial performance, like Tobin's Q, on the dummy variable indicating the presence of a CMO plus control variables. The decision to hire a CMO is based on unobserved firm-specific variables like strategy and organizational culture, leading to an omitted variables problem. This is solved by using the incidence of CMO's among firms with the same two-digit SIC code as an instrument. It should be valid as similar firms face similar conditions and will hence come to a similar decision about a CMO, so the instrument is likely to be correlated with the endogenous variable, while the relevant firm-specific variables are unlikely to be easily observed and imitated by others, so the instrument is not likely to be correlated with the error term.

15.7 Many and Weak Instruments

15.7.1 Choice of Instruments

Arguably the most influential example of a creative choice of instrumental variables in economics comes from Angrist and Krueger (1991). They are concerned with the wage equation and search for instruments for the most interesting but endogenous regressor, which is the level of education and in particular the years of schooling. They notice that in many states of the U.S. the law requires children to go to school in the year they turn six and allows them to leave school when they turn 16. So, children born early in the year have to wait till September while children born later in the year go to school even before they turn six. Since leaving school can be done on the day of turning 16, years of schooling will be positively correlated with timing of birth in the year. This suggests using dummy variables indicating the quarter of birth as instruments.

Their approach gave a boost to the search of natural experiments (like an exogenously given legislative context) to find instruments and to further develop the notion of causality in a field like economics where real-life experiments are mostly prohibitively expensive if not just impossible; see e.g. Angrist and Pischke (2009).

Angrist and Krueger (1991) also had an impact in another direction. This concerns instrument strength, or rather the possible lack of it. In this section we first sketch the problems that may arise and some of the mathematics around it, and next discuss one solution, which is the limited-information maximum likelihood (LIML) estimator, which predates 2SLS but has been revitalized recently to cope with many and weak instruments.

15.7.2 The Effect of Weak and Many Instruments

In their study, Angrist and Krueger (1991) distinguish four quarters of birth, leading to three instruments. The number of instruments can be greatly expanded by interacting these with state of residence and year of birth, leading to hundreds of instruments. Increasing the number of instruments reduces the asymptotic variance of $\hat{\beta}$. The huge number of observations, hundreds of thousands, suggests that asymptotic theory is a good guide to actual behavior. In particular, the consistency of the IV estimator suggests that the estimated value of β is close to the true value, while the asymptotic variance should give an adequate reflection of the estimate's precision. However, a series of papers from the early 1990s onwards, showed that 2SLS estimates can be highly misleading in empirically relevant cases; see e.g. Bound et al. (1995). The bias is highest when the instruments are weak, that is, correlate poorly with the endogenous regressors, and when there are many of them relative to the number of endogenous regressors; otherwise phrased, when the degree of overidentification is high.

The theory on the distribution of IV estimators is mostly asymptotic. It provides a good approximation to the actual distribution of the estimator when the instruments correlate well with the endogenous regressors but the quality of the approximation deteriorates when the instruments are weak. Also, the quality of the approximation increases with the number of observations but even a very large number may not be enough for a good approximation when the instruments are weak. Also, more instruments mean more moment equations hence a lower asymptotic variance, but this is not without problems.

There are, in fact, two problems with 2SLS. The first one is that it is biased towards OLS, more precisely, to the probability limit of the corresponding OLS estimator. The other one is that the reported standard errors are too low, which may lead to overrejection of the hypothesis that a particular element of β is 0; one might conclude that there is a significant effect of a variable of interest on the target variable while in fact there may be none.

For the sake of exposition we consider the case of a single regressor only. We add to the model $y_i = x_i\beta + u_i$ a relation linking the regressor to the k instruments, $x_i = z_i'\pi + v_i$. Endogeneity of x_i means that σ_{uv}, the covariance between u_i and v_i, can be nonzero. In matrix format, $y = x\beta + u$ and $x = Z\pi + v$. Let $F = \pi'Z'Z\pi/k\sigma_v^2$. Its estimated counterpart is the usual statistic to test, in a regression equation, whether all regression coefficients are equal to 0, so in our case the statistic is informative about instrument strength. With a bit of algebra it can be shown that the 2SLS estimator $\hat{\beta}$ satisfies:

$$\mathrm{E}[\hat{\beta} - \beta] \approx \sigma_{uv}/[\sigma_v^2(F + 1)]. \tag{15.89}$$

So, the weaker the instruments are and hence the lower F is, the more the bias of $\hat{\beta}$ goes to σ_{uv}/σ_v^2. Now, the bias of the OLS estimator goes to σ_{uv}/σ_x^2, which goes to σ_{uv}/σ_v^2 when $\pi \approx 0$. So, with weak instruments, 2SLS tends to OLS. We can also look at the effect of many instruments; adding worthless instruments increases the bias as k goes up so $F = \pi'Z'Z\pi/k\sigma_v^2$ goes down. If there is just one instrument, 2SLS can be shown to be median unbiased.

15.7.3 Limited Information Maximum Likelihood

One way towards better inference with many and weak instruments is to say that there is nothing wrong with using asymptotic theory by itself as a basis for inference, but the way to infinity needs adaptation to take into account that there are many and weak instruments. This leads us away from GMM to the limited-information maximum likelihood (LIML) estimator due to Anderson and Rubin (1949, 1950), which predated the 2SLS estimator but never acquired anything like its popularity. We go back to the multiple regression case and write, in matrix form $y = X\beta + u$ and $X = Z\Pi + V$. The errors u_i and v_i', the ith element of u and ith row of V, are assumed i.i.d. normal over i, with:

$$\begin{pmatrix} u_i \\ v_i \end{pmatrix} \sim N(0, \Omega), \quad \text{with} \quad \Omega = \begin{pmatrix} \sigma^2 & \omega' \\ \omega & \Omega_v \end{pmatrix}. \tag{15.90}$$

The crucial parameter here is ω as it is equal to $\mathrm{E}[x_i u_i]$. After some algebraic operations, the LIML estimator turns out to be the minimizer of $u'P_Z u/u'M_Z u$, with $M_Z \equiv I_n - P_Z$ and $u = y - X\beta$. Let $s^2(\beta) \equiv u'M_Z u/n$ be the estimator of σ^2 as a function of β. Then we can write the LIML criterion as $(y - X\beta)'Z[s^2(\beta)Z'Z]^{-1}Z'(y - X\beta)$, to be minimized over β. This criterion is the GMM criterion for IV estimation with optimal weighting, with minimization also over the parameter in the weight matrix. So the LIML estimator is a continuous-updating estimator (CUE, see Sect. 15.5.3), and the LIML estimator that results from the minimization:

$$\hat{\beta} = [X'(P_Z - \hat{\lambda} M_Z)X]^{-1}X'(P_Z - \hat{\lambda} M_Z)y \tag{15.91}$$

with $\hat{\lambda}$ the smallest value for which $(y, x)'(P_Z - \hat{\lambda} M_Z)(y, x)$ is singular, is almost median unbiased, as befits a CUE estimator. That solves one problem with 2SLS.

As we mentioned in Sect. 15.7.2, another problem with 2SLS with weak and many instruments is the reported standard errors, based on the usual asymptotic theory, are too low. To remedy this, Bekker (1994) proposed to consider alternative asymptotics, where not only $n \to \infty$ but also the number of instruments k increases along with n in order to better reflect reality. In particular, $k/n = \alpha + o(n^{-1/2})$ for some $\alpha \geq 0$. Moreover, $\Pi'Z'Z\Pi/n \to Q > 0$, guaranteeing that the instruments are still well-behaved even though their number grows beyond bound. Under such many-instruments asymptotics, 2SLS is inconsistent but LIML is consistent. This inconsistency of 2SLS reflects the bias towards OLS discussed above. The asymptotic distribution of LIML under many-instruments asymptotics can be shown to be:

$$n^{1/2}(\hat{\beta} - \beta) \xrightarrow{d} N(0, \sigma_u^2 Q^{-1}(Q + \lambda \Omega_{v|u})Q^{-1}) \tag{15.92}$$

with $\lambda \equiv \alpha/(1 - \alpha)$ and $\Omega_{v|u} \equiv \Omega_v - \omega\omega'/\sigma^2$. With the usual large-$n$ asymptotics, $\alpha = 0$ and hence $\lambda = 0$, so the asymptotic variance is simply $\sigma^2 Q^{-1}$, with

$Q = \text{plim}_{n\to\infty} X'P_Z X/n$. This is also the asymptotic variance of 2SLS. Notice that going over from large-n asymptotics to many-instruments asymptotics leads to a higher asymptotic variance since $Q^{-1}(Q + \lambda\Omega_{v|u})Q^{-1} > Q^{-1}$. The difference is relevant when λ cannot be neglected (many instruments) or when $\Omega_{v|u}$ cannot be neglected (weak instruments). To make the expression operational, we take for σ_u^2 the usual estimator, we estimate λ by $\hat{\lambda}$ from LIML, and take:

$$\hat{Q} = (n-m)^{-1} X'(P_Z - \hat{\lambda} M_Z)X \tag{15.93}$$

$$\hat{\Omega}_{v|u} = (n-m)^{-1}(1+\hat{\lambda})X'(I_n - R(R'R)^{-1}R')X \tag{15.94}$$

with $R \equiv (Z, \hat{u})$ and $\hat{u}$ the vector of residuals; for large n, $\hat{\lambda}$ tends to 0 and the familiar expression for the asymptotic variance of the 2SLS estimator remains. These estimators are consistent under many-instruments asymptotics. Squares of the diagonal elements give the Bekker standard errors. A drawback of LIML is its sensitivity to heteroskedasticity. Bekker and Crudu (2015) present an estimator that is closely related to LIML and JIVE and that avoids this sensitivity.

15.8 Software

GMM has its roots in economics. Most economists use Stata, Eviews or R, where GMM is well-developed. In SPSS there is not a general GMM module.

In Stata, the command gmm performs GMM estimation, with a wide array of options, for single and multiple equation models. The moment equations can be of the form $E[z_i u_i(\theta)]$, with z_i a vector of instruments and $u_i(\theta)$ an error term, but can also be of the more general form $E[h_i(\theta)] = 0$, where the user has to do a bit of programming to provide $h_i(\theta)$. The user can provide the expression for the matrix of derivatives $\partial h_i(\theta)/\partial\theta'$ or relies on numerical derivatives computed by the program. Eviews can handle moment equations of the form $E[z_i u_i(\theta)]$. The GMM package gmm in R provides wide flexibility, see e.g. Chaussé (2010).

Acknowledgements The author is grateful to Erik Meijer for his ever incisive and stimulating comments. He benefited greatly from comments and suggestions by Jochem de Bresser, Marnik Dekimpe, Pim Heijnen, Peter Leeflang, Laura Spierdijk, Roberto Wessels and the students in my Applied Econometrics course.

References

Albuquerque, P., Bronnenberg, B.J.: Estimating demand heterogeneity using aggregated data: an application to the frozen pizza category. Market. Sci. **28**, 356–372 (2009)

Anderson, T.W.: Origins of the limited information maximum likelihood and two-stage least squares estimators. J. Econ. **127**, 1–16 (2005)

Anderson, T.W., Hsiao, C.: Estimation of dynamic models with error components. J. Am. Stat. Assoc. **77**, 598–606 (1981)

Anderson, T.W., Rubin, H.: Estimator of the parameters of a single equation in a complete system of stochastic equations. Ann. Math. Stat. **20**, 46–63 (1949)

Anderson, T.W., Rubin, H.: The asymptotic properties of estimates of the parameters of a single equation in a complete system of stochastic equations. Ann. Math. Stat. **21**, 570–582 (1950)

Angrist, J.D., Krueger, A.B.: Does compulsory school attendance affect schooling and earnings? Q. J. Econ. **106**, 979–1014 (1991)

Angrist, J.D., Pischke, J.-S.: Mostly Harmless Econometrics. Princeton University Press, Princeton (2009)

Angrist, J., Graddy, K., Imbens, G.: The interpretation of instrumental variables estimators in simultaneous equations models with an application to the demand for fish. Rev. Econ. Stud. **67**, 499–527 (2000)

Arellano, M., Bond, S.: Some tests of specification for panel data: Monte Carlo evidence and an application to employment equations. Rev. Econ. Stud. **58**, 277–297 (1991)

Ashworth, S., Clinton, J.D.: Does advertising exposure affect turnout? Q. J. Polit. Sci. **2**, 27–41 (2007)

Bass, F.M., Parsons, L.J.: Simultaneous equation regression analysis of sales and advertising. Appl. Econ. **1**, 103–124 (1969)

Bekker, P.A.: Alternative approximations to the distributions of instrumental variable estimators. Econometrica **62**, 657–681 (1994)

Bekker, P.A., Crudu, F.: Jackknife instrumental variable estimation with heteroskedasticity. J. Econ. **185**, 332–342 (2015)

Berndt, E.R.: The Practice of Econometrics. Addison-Wesley, Reading, MA (1991)

Berry, S.: Estimating discrete-choice models of product differentiation. RAND J. Econ. **25**, 242–262 (1994)

Berry, S., Levinsohn, J., Pakes, A.: Automobile prices in market equilibrium. Econometrica **63**, 841–890 (1995)

Bound, J., Jaeger, D., Baker, R.: Problems with instrumental variables estimation when the correlation between the instruments and the endogenous variables is weak. J. Am. Stat. Assoc. **90**, 443–450 (1995)

Breusch, T., Qian, H., Schmidt, P., Wyhowski, D.J.: Redundancy of moment conditions. J. Econ. **91**, 89–111 (1999)

Cameron, A.C., Trivedi, P.K.: Microeconometrics. Cambridge University Press, New York (2005)

Chaussé, P.: Computing generalized method of moments and generalized empirical likelihood with R. J. Stat. Softw. **34**(11), 1–35 (2010)

Cragg, J.: More efficient estimation in the presence of heteroskedasticity of unknown form. Econometrica **51**, 751–763 (1983)

Doran, H.E., Schmidt, P.: GMM estimators with improved finite sample properties using principal components of the weighting matrix, with an application to the dynamic panel data model. J. Econ. **133**, 387–409 (2006)

Germann, F., Ebbes, P., Grewal, R.: The chief marketing officer matters! J. Market. **79**(3), 1–22 (2015)

Gu, B., Park, J., Konana, P.: The impact of external word-of-mouth sources on retailer sales of high-involvement products. Inf. Syst. Res. **23**, 182–196 (2012)

Hall, A.R.: Generalized Method of Moments. Oxford University Press, Oxford (2005)

Hall, A.R.: Generalized method of moments. In: Hashimzade, N., Thronton, M.A. (eds.) Handbook of Research Methods and Applications in Empirical Macroeconomics, pp. 313–333. Edward Elgar, Cheltenham (2013)

Hall, A.R.: Econometricians have their moments: GMM at 32. Econ. Rec. **91**(Suppl. S1), 1–24 (2015)

Hansen, L.P.: Large sample properties of generalized method of moments estimators. Econometrica **50**, 1029–1054 (1982)

Hansen, L.P., Singleton, K.J.: Generalized instrumental variables estimation of nonlinear rational expectations models. Econometrica **50**, 1269–1286 (1982)

Hansen, L.P., Heaton, J., Yaron, A.: Finite-sample properties of some alternative GMM estimators. J. Bus. Econ. Stat. **14**, 262–280 (1996)

Hausman, J.A., Taylor, W.E.: Panel data and unobservable individual effects. Econometrica **49**, 1377–1398 (1981)

Hayashi, F.: Econometrics. Princeton University Press, Princeton (2000)

Heckman, J.J.: Sample selection bias as a specification error. Econometrica **47**, 153–161 (1979)

Jagannathan, R., Skoulakis, G., Wang, Z.: Generalized method of moments: applications in finance. J. Bus. Econ. Stat. **20**, 470–481 (2002)

Jaibi, M.R., Ten Raa, M.H.: An asymptotic foundation for logit models. Reg. Sci. Urban Econ. **28**, 75–90 (1998)

Kleibergen, F., Paap, R.: Generalized reduced rank tests using the singular value decomposition. J. Econ. **133**, 97–126 (2006)

Meijer, E., Wansbeek, T.J.: The sample selection model from a method of moments perspective. Econ. Rev. **26**, 25–51 (2007)

Murray, M.P.: Avoiding invalid instruments and coping with weak instruments. J. Econ. Perspect. **20**, 111–132 (2006)

Narayanan, S., Nair, H.S.: Estimating causal installed-base effects: a bias-correction approach. J. Market. Res. **50**, 70–94 (2013)

Narayanan, S., Manchanda, P., Chintagunta, P.K.: Temporal differences in the role of marketing communication in new product categories. J. Market. Res. **42**, 278–290 (2005)

Nevo, A.: A practitioner's guide to estimation of random coefficients logit models of demand. J. Econ. Manag. Strateg. **9**, 513–548 (2000)

Newey, W.K.: A method of moments interpretation of sequential estimators. Econ. Lett. **14**, 201–206 (1984)

Newey, W.K., McFadden, D.: Large sample estimation and hypothesis testing. In: Griliches, Z., Intriligator, M. (eds.) Handbook of Econometrics, vol. 4. North Holland, Amsterdam (1994)

Newey, W.K., West, K.D.: A simple positive-definite, heteroskedasticity and autocorrelation consistent covariance matrix. Econometrica **55**, 703–708 (1987)

Park, S., Gupta, S.: Comparison of SML and GMM estimators for the random coefficient logit model using aggregate data. Empir. Econ. **43**, 1353–1372 (2012)

Pearson, K.: Contributions to the mathematical theory of evolution. Philos. Trans. R. Soc. Lond. Ser. A **185**, 71–110 (1894)

Qian, H., Schmidt, P.: Improved instrumental variables and generalized method of moments estimators. J. Econ. **91**, 145–169 (1999)

Reiersøl, O.: Confluence analysis by means of lag moments and other methods of confluence analysis. Econometrica **9**, 1–24 (1941)

Rossi, P.E.: Even the rich can make themselves poor: a critical examination of IV methods in marketing applications. Market. Sci. **33**, 655–672 (2014)

Stock, J.H., Trebbi, F.: Who invented instrumental variable regression? J. Econ. Perspect. **17**, 177–194 (2003)

Theil, H.: Repeated Least Squares Applied to Complete Equation Systems. Central Planning Bureau, The Hague (1953)

Theil, H., Finke, R.: The distance from the equator as an instrumental variable. Econ. Lett. **13**, 357–360 (1983)

Vitorino, M.A.: Understanding the effect of advertising on stock returns and firm value: theory and evidence from a structural model. Manag. Sci. **60**, 227–245 (2014)

Wang, L., Hsiao, C.: Method of moments and identifiability of semi-parametric nonlinear errors-in-variables models. J. Econ. **165**, 30–44 (2011)

Wansbeek, T.J.: Correcting for heteroskedasticity of unspecified form – problem 04.1.2. Econ. Theory **20**, 224 (2004)

Wansbeek, T.J., Meijer, E.: Measurement Error and Latent Variables in Econometrics. North-Holland, Amsterdam (2000)

Wheaton, B., Muthén, B., Alwin, D., Summers, G.: Assessing reliability and stability in panel models. In: Heise, D.R. (ed.) Sociological Methodology 1977, pp. 84–136. Jossey-Bass, San Francisco (1977)
White, H.L.: A heteroskedasticity-consistent covariance matrix estimator and a direct test for heteroskedasticity. Econometrica **48**, 817–838 (1980)
Windmeijer, F.: A finite sample correction for the variance of linear efficient two-step GMM estimators. J. Econ. **126**, 25–51 (2005)
Wooldridge, J.M.: Econometric Analysis of Cross Section and Panel Data, 2nd edn. MIT Press, Cambridge (2010)
Wright, P.G.: The Tariff on Animal and Vegetable Oils. Macmillan, New York (1928)

Chapter 16
Bayesian Analysis

Elea McDonnell Feit, Fred M. Feinberg, and Peter J. Lenk

16.1 Why Bayes?

In this chapter, we provide an introduction to Bayesian analysis and its application to economics and marketing. An outline of the chapter follows. In this section, we provide some motivation for why marketing analysts would want to adopt the Bayesian approach. Since the Bayesian approach to inference is not familiar to the typical marketing student, Sect. 16.2 provides the reader with the foundations necessary to properly understand Bayesian analysis, using the familiar linear regression model as an example. By the end of that section, readers will understand all the key concepts in Bayesian analysis: prior and posterior distributions, Bayesian updating, how to construct a Gibbs sampler to generate draws from the posterior distribution and how to interpret those posterior draws and how to compare models. Section 16.3 illustrates how one would use software packages that sample from the posterior for common models, providing readers with the foundation needed to be a "smart user" of such packages. Section 16.4 provides more detail and examples of how those packages are created, preparing the reader to write his or her own Bayesian samplers for new, complex models. The section develops an example from labor economics and presents a series of three models of increasing complexity to highlight the flexibility of Bayesian analysis to address econometric problems. In the final section, we provide a review of the wide variety of marketing models that have been analyzed using Bayesian methods. Readers who are completely new to

E.M. Feit (✉)
LeBow College of Business, Drexel University, 3220 Market Street, Philadelphia, PA 19104, USA
e-mail: efeit@drexel.edu

F.M. Feinberg • P.J. Lenk
Ross School of Business, University of Michigan, 701 Tappan St., Ann Arbor, MI 48109, USA

P.S.H. Leeflang et al. (eds.), *Advanced Methods for Modeling Markets*,
International Series in Quantitative Marketing, DOI 10.1007/978-3-319-53469-5_16

Bayesian analysis may prefer to begin with the introduction to Bayesian Estimation provided in Vol. I, Sect. 6.8 and then move on to the more in-depth coverage in this chapter.

Bayesian inference has become a staple of marketing research both in the literature and in practice. It became an important tool largely due to researchers' interest in understanding consumer heterogeneity. The first major use of Bayesian analysis in marketing was to allow for random coefficients across respondents commonly referred to as hierarchical Bayes modeling (Allenby and Lenk 1994; Allenby and Rossi 1998; Lenk 1992; Lenk and Rao 1990; Lenk et al. 1996). Hierarchical Bayes allows researchers to understand the distribution of preferences across the population, something of great importance when optimizing product portfolios. While random coefficients models can certainly be estimated under other paradigms, the hierarchical Bayes approach makes it feasible to estimate any model the researcher may wish to posit, as well as to obtain parameter estimates for individual consumers, allowing marketers to target those individuals. The appeal of hierarchical Bayes led it to be quickly adopted in practice; for example the Sawtooth Software Choice-Based Conjoint—Hierarchical Bayes (CBC-HB) package was released in 2003 and rapidly became the de facto standard for conjoint analysis, putting Bayesian analysis in the hands of thousands of marketing practitioners.

Hierarchical Bayes models are most suited to data sets that are "broad, but shallow," that is where there are a large number of customers or subjects and relatively few observations for each customer. For instance, Zappos would like to infer its customer preferences for different styles and brands of shoes to better meet customer's needs, personalize promotions, compute life-time value, optimize web pages and mobile marketing, manage inventory, and forecast demand. Some customers are frequent shoppers with tens or hundreds of purchases a year. For these customers, it would be possible to infer their preferences and responsiveness to marketing with standard statistical methods because of their extensive purchase history. However, the majority of customers have fewer purchases, too few to estimate individual-specific parameters with classical methods. Hierarchical Bayes models shine in these circumstances because they allow the flexibility to estimate parameters for each customer from the relatively thin data by partially pooling information across customers. This results in parameter estimates for each individual that are somewhere between what the individual's data would suggest and what the population distribution would suggest, a phenomena referred to as Bayesian "shrinkage."

However, the appeal of Bayesian analysis goes far beyond hierarchical models. Bayesian analysis, and specifically Bayesian Markov chain Monte Carlo (MCMC) methods, allow researchers to specify nearly any model they might choose and have facilitated the development of a wide range of models for analyzing marketing data. For instance, they have been applied to joint models of supply and demand (Manchanda et al. 2004). Bayesian methods are also particularly useful for dealing with any type of latent variable including structural equation models (Ansari et al. 2000a, 2000b and Chap. 11 in this volume), two-stage models of choice (Gilbride and Allenby 2004), hidden Markov models (Netzer et al. 2008 and Chap. 14), and state space models (Bruce 2008; Zantedeschi et al. 2016 and Chap. 5). The Bayesian approach to inference is also particularly well suited to addressing missing data problems (Feit et al. 2013; Van Heerde et al. 2007; Ying et al. 2006; Zeithammer and Lenk 2006), as Bayesian analysis treats all unknown quantities, including parameters, latent variables and missing data, the same. The Bayesian MCMC machinery also makes it easy to combine any one of these approaches with random coefficients to accommodate consumer heterogeneity, and most of the applications in the literature do so.

Two features of Bayesian analysis make it particularly well suited to work in practice. First, Bayesian analysis allows decision makers to bring knowledge to the analysis that goes beyond the data. This is done through the prior and the model specification, which we discuss in more detail in Sect. 16.2. For managers who want to make the best possible marketing decisions, it is only sensible to bring this prior knowledge into the analysis (cf. Allenby et al. 1995, 1998). For instance, a manager may know that customers of the "value brand" are more price sensitive than customers of the "premium brand". Additionally, prior distributions facilitate the estimation of models even when there is not enough data for other approaches to have reliable estimators, or any estimators at all. This situation can occur even with large datasets when the model is complex, so that the number of observations is small relative to the number of parameters (Lenk and Orme 2009). In fact, many machine learning methods add a penalty term to the objective function to "regularize" the problem and obtain stable estimators. These penalty terms were originally motivated from prior distributions (Good and Gaskins 1971, 1980; Kimeldorf and Wahba 1970). More recently, the rise of systems for rapidly collecting large volumes of consumer data has increased interest in practice for real time analysis through marketing "dashboards" (Vol. I, Sect. 10.5.3). Unlike most other statistical approaches, Bayesian analysis can be performed sequentially with regular model updates as new data arrives (cf. Scott 2010).

In the next section, we provide the foundations of Bayesian inference in a way that we hope both gives the reader an appreciation for the important theoretical underpinnings and a sense of what is required to use it in practice. In Sect. 16.3, we illustrate the use of modern software to conduct Bayesian analysis. In the Sects. 16.4 and 16.5, we provide an overview of the use of Bayesian inference in marketing over the past two decades, pointing the reader toward the relevant literature.

16.2 Basically Bayes

16.2.1 Basic Concepts

The goal of this section is to present succinctly the basic concepts of Bayesian inference. Readers that are mainly interested in implementing Bayesian models can jump to Sect. 16.3; however, those who skip ahead will probably find their way back to this section as their appetite for Bayes grows. Bayesian inference (Bayes 1763[1]), provides a unified approach to inference, hypothesis testing, and prediction that is independent of particular model specifications. This unified framework frees researchers from having to improvise new methods of analysis for new models. Instead, Bayesians can focus their full attention on constructing models that best represent salient features of the phenomenon under consideration, knowing that the machinery of Bayesian inference will allow any model to be estimated as accurately as the data and model permit. In contrast, other inferential approaches are often strongly tied to classes of models or special cases: least-squares for regression models, iteratively weighted least squares for generalized linear models (see Chap. 13), two-stage least squares for endogeneity corrections (see Chap. 18), EM for mixture models (Chap. 13), hidden Markov models (Chap. 14), method of simulated likelihood for random effects, Kalman filtering for state-space models (Chap. 5), and so on. Often these estimation methods become strongly associated with particular models because researchers designed the method for the models, and statistical software reinforces the pairings between models and estimation methods. In contrast, Bayesian inference consists of general principles that researchers can apply to *any* model. In fact, all of the estimation methods listed above can be derived from Bayesian inference as special cases using appropriate approximations.

A Bayesian's first step is to specify a probability model for the data and all other sources of uncertainty. For instance, a researcher models yearly income as a function of education, work experience, and other factors. The linear model provides the probability specification for the data assuming fixed independent variables and a set of unknown parameters relating income to those independent variables. A Bayesian researcher also gathers additional information about the problem that the researcher believes to be valid and relevant and uses this information to specify prior distributions for the unknown parameters. These prior distributions reflect his or her beliefs about reasonable values for the parameters. For example, the annual salary return of an additional year of college education is highly likely to be between −\$100,000 and \$100,000 based on previous studies or serious consideration about the likely magnitude of marginal returns.

This specification of prior distributions for parameters often receives the most criticism from non-Bayesians as being "subjective." It is true that prior distributions often reflect subjective beliefs, but then again, so do many other aspects of the research paradigm, including measurement, sampling, data cleaning, and model specification. "Subjective" need not mean "arbitrary." Prior specifications are often innocuous provided that they do not overly constrain the model: the data will dominate prior distributions that are not too restrictive. A "tight" prior specification that the marginal return for a year of college is between 0 and \$10 would seriously

[1]It may seem extreme to cite such an ancient reference. However, Rev. Thomas Bayes' essay, as presented by Richard Price to the Royal Society, is a remarkably sophisticated and modern treatise about probability and inference if one updates its eighteenth century notation to twenty-first century standards. It no doubt languished in the archives for centuries because it was that far ahead of the science of the time.

distort the eventual estimates and no amount of data would change the researcher's extreme, a priori beliefs. However, prior distributions for parameters receive the same external scrutiny by other researchers as other parts of the research paradigm, such as measurement and sampling, and such a tight prior would not hold up against expert scrutiny. Subjective probabilities are not incontestable and most scientists would agree that we don't completely understand the relationship between education and income, and so our analysis should use a prior that reflects this uncertainty.

The researcher may also want to introduce out-of-sample information that he or she believes to be true based on theory or generally held beliefs. For instance, people may decide how much education to pursue based on their beliefs regarding expected returns for education. If so, education is stochastic and not fixed, and the researcher should use this information by expanding the probability model to account for potentially "endogeneous selection" of education level. The researcher imposes this constraint based on his or her subjective understanding of the relationship between income and education. (See Li and Tobias 2011 for a Bayesian analysis of this problem.)

Once the researcher specifies a proper probability model for the data and prior distributions for all parameters, inference follows from the rules of probability, in particular, conditional probability. The basic idea is to update one's beliefs about the unknown parameters given the data and the model specification. Not surprisingly, the probability updating relies on Bayes Theorem (see Sect. 6.8, Vol. I). If the reader recalls Bayes Theorem from an introductory statistics or probability class, it may not seem a fruitful approach to solve general inference problems. Even though these computations are simple in the abstract, budding Bayesians often find them intimidating in practice because of the resulting flood of notation and because they are not used to thinking about conditional probabilities. However, even standard regression models are conditional probability statements: they tell you the distribution of "y" values conditional on knowing "x" values and the model's parameters. In addition, most Bayesian analyses require integration, which is a topic that many social scientists are not comfortable with. Fear not: Bayesian software solves the integrals, allowing the user to focus on what is being integrated and why.

The goal of this section is to highlight the standard elements of Bayesian inference. The first challenge is to construct a probability model of all salient aspects of the phenomenon under study. Bayesians are not allowed to cheat by leaving random or unknown quantities unspecified. The payoffs are that the analysis will be *coherent* (De Finetti 1937): Bayesian analyses will not be self-contradictory, which can happen with classical inference; and *consistent* (Doob 1949): under general conditions Bayes estimates converge to their true values in probability (i.e., the chance of substantial deviation gets smaller and smaller with more data). Additionally, Bayesian inference meets many standard statistical optimality criteria, as summarized in Berger (1985) and Bernardo and Smith (1994). De Groot (1970) showed that Bayes estimators are (nearly) admissible: given an estimation criterion, such as squared error loss, there do not exist alternative estimators that will uniformly improve on Bayesian ones[2]. Bayesian inference guarantees the best possible use of the data given the model. For instance, Zellner (1988) shows that Bayesian analysis preserves the information content of the inputs: the data and prior information. "Bad" results are due to other aspects of the research design, such as data collection, model specification, or hypothesis generation, and not the estimation method.

16.2.2 Example of Bayesian Inference (Linear Regression with Known Variance)

In this section, we walk through the steps of Bayesian analysis using a linear regression. Through this example, readers will see how models and priors are specified, how those prior distributions are updated with data to find the posterior and how we analyze the posterior distribution to make statements about the likely values of the parameters. To simplify the discussion for novices, we will focus on the linear model with just one slope parameter and make the unrealistic assumption that the variance of the linear model is known. In subsequent sections, we will address the more realistic case where the variance is unknown.

16.2.2.1 Introduction

For a concrete example, consider a simple regression model where y is, say, annual income and x is number of years of education. The data consist of a random sample of n observations of (x_i, y_i) for $i = 1, 2, \ldots, n$. Further, to simplify the analysis, suppose that both variables have been centered so that their means and the intercept are 0[3]. Then the simple regression model is $y_i = \beta x_i + \varepsilon_i$ where β is the unknown regression coefficient and ε_i is a random error (random shock or innovation) for subject i. We make the standard assumption that the random errors are a random sample from a normal distribution with mean 0 and standard deviation σ. To further simplify the analysis, we further assume that $E(x\varepsilon) = 0$: the amount of education is exogenous (uncorrelated with the random shocks) to annual income.

For this first example, we assume that the standard deviation σ is known. The reason for assuming a known standard deviation σ at this point is to simplify the discussion and to focus attention on one parameter, the unknown slope β. That way,

---

[2]A surprising result is that our old friend, the sample mean, is not admissible under squared error loss in three or more dimensions (Stein 1956 and James and Stein 1961)!

[3]Suppose that $y = \alpha + \beta x + \varepsilon$ with $E(\varepsilon) = 0$, $E(x\varepsilon) = 0$, and $\beta \neq 0$. Then $E(y|\,x) = \alpha + \beta x$. Further suppose that $E(y) = E(x) = 0$. Then $E(y) = E[E(y|\,x)] = \alpha + \beta E(x)$. Since $E(y) = E(x) = 0$, then $\alpha = 0$.

we can graph prior and posterior distributions without the further complication of unknown σ. Later, we will estimate σ.

This standard linear model is actually making a conditional probability statement: "y_i given x_i, β, and σ" is normally distributed with conditional mean βx_i and conditional standard deviation σ. More succinctly, we write:

Data Model $$y \mid x_i, \beta, \sigma \sim N\left(\beta x_i, \sigma^2\right) \quad (16.1)$$

which we read as, "y_i conditional on x_i, β, and σ is distributed normally with mean βx_i and variance σ^2." The likelihood function of the slope gives the information contained in the data about different values of the slope:

Likelihood $$\begin{aligned} L(\beta) &= \prod_{i=1}^{n} f\left(y_i|\beta x_i, \sigma\right) \\ &= \left(2\pi\sigma^2\right)^{-\frac{n}{2}} \exp\left[-\frac{1}{2\sigma^2}\sum_{i=1}^{n}\left(y_i - \beta x_i\right)^2\right] \end{aligned} \quad (16.2)$$

where $f(y_i|\, \beta x_i, \sigma)$ is the normal density function for y given mean βx_i and standard deviation σ. Note that, although this formula contains many symbols and quantities, they are all *known*, except for the slope (β); so, the likelihood here is a function of the unknown slope, β, alone.

Readers familiar with non-Bayesian estimation may know that maximum likelihood estimation finds the value of the slope that maximizes $L(\beta)$ and results in the maximum likelihood estimate (MLE)[4] for β:

$$\widehat{\beta} = \sum_{i=1}^{n} x_i y_i \Big/ \sum_{i=1}^{n} x_i^2 \,. \quad (16.3)$$

The standard error of the MLE is:

$$se\left(\widehat{\beta}\right) = \left(\sigma^2 \Big/ \sum_{i=1}^{n} x_i^2\right)^{\frac{1}{2}} \quad (16.4)$$

and measures the sampling variance of the MLE. These are fine estimates, and we advocate their use. MLE and Bayesian analysis are close cousins; they are both based on the likelihood function. The benefit of considering the Bayesian analysis is that it generalizes to complex models where the MLE and other types of estimates are not easily obtained, behave poorly, or may not exist. While many introductory statistics books skip over these more complex models, researchers in all social sciences, including economics and marketing, quickly run into them.

The model with only the likelihood is not complete for Bayesian analysis. The slope is an unknown parameter, and we must therefore provide a prior distribution

[4]The MLE is also the least-squares estimate that minimizes sums-of-squares errors: $\sum_{i=1}^{n}\left(y_i - \beta x_i\right)^2$. Compare with Sect. 6.4.1, Vol. I and Sect. 1.4.1 in this volume.

for it. The simplest, tractable prior distribution that is also flexible is the widely used normal distribution with mean b_0 and standard deviation v_0:

$$\textit{Prior Distribution} \qquad \beta \sim N\left(b_0, v_0^2\right). \tag{16.5}$$

The "0" subscript indicates that these are the prior parameters, that is, specified before observing the data (sample size = 0). The complete specification for the data and the slope is the joint probability distribution, obtained by simply multiplying the prior density and the likelihood:

$$\textit{Joint Distribution} \quad P\left(y_1, \ldots, y_n, \beta|\sigma\right) = f\left(\beta|b_0, v_0\right) \prod_{i=1}^{n} f\left(y_i|\beta x_i, \sigma\right). \tag{16.6}$$

This specifies the joint probability of $y_1, \ldots, y_n, \beta$ prior to observing the data. We add "given σ" to the joint probability to emphasize that this first example model depends on the known σ, i.e., that it is "given" to us, not estimated from the data. We simplify notation by dropping $x_1, \ldots, x_n$ in the conditional argument because they are exogeneous and we treat them as fixed constants.

The goal of Bayesian inference is to compute the posterior distribution of β given the sample information (i.e., the data). Operationally, this is easy to do by writing the joint distribution as a function of β and dividing by its integral, so that the posterior distribution integrates to one:

$$\textit{Posterior Distribution} \quad P\left(\beta|y_1, \ldots, y_n, \sigma\right) = \frac{P\left(y_1, \ldots, y_n, \beta|\sigma\right)}{\int P\left(y_1, \ldots, y_n, b|\sigma\right)\, db} \tag{16.7}$$

where b is the dummy variable of integration for integrating over all possible values of β in the integral of the denominator. Any factor in the joint distribution that does not depend on β can be ignored because it will cancel in the numerator and denominator of the posterior distribution. Being a rather lazy and slovenly tribe[5], Bayesians write the posterior distribution as proportional to the joint distribution:

$$P\left(\beta|y_1, \ldots, y_n, \sigma\right) \propto P\left(y_1, \ldots, y_n, \beta|\sigma\right) = f\left(\beta|b_0, v_0\right) \prod_{i=1}^{n} f\left(y_i|\beta x_i, \sigma\right) \tag{16.8}$$

and ignore the integration constant in the denominator; as we will see later, this is an excellent bookkeeping device that helps avoid accumulating constants that do not affect the analysis. Substituting in for the prior $f(\beta|\, b_0, v_0)$ and the likelihood $\prod_{i=1}^{n} f\left(y_i|\beta x_i, \sigma\right)$, we get:

$$P\left(\beta|y_1, \ldots, y_n, \sigma\right) \;\propto\; \exp\left[-\frac{1}{2v_0^2}(\beta - b_0)^2 - \frac{1}{2\sigma^2}\sum_{i=1}^{n}(y_i - \beta x_i)^2\right]. \tag{16.9}$$

[5]But amazingly good looking (for statisticians).

Inside the exponential is a linear function of β^2 and β (i.e., is quadratic in β), which alerts us that the posterior distribution is a normal distribution. Our work is almost done: to put this normal distribution in standard form, we need to dust-off our high school algebra about expanding and completing quadratic functions, ignoring all factors that are not a function of β in each line:

$$P(\beta|y_1,\ldots,y_n,\sigma)$$
$$\propto \exp\left[-\frac{1}{2v_0^2}\left(\beta^2-2\beta b_0+b_0^2\right)-\frac{1}{2\sigma^2}\sum_{i=1}^{n}\left(y_i^2-2\beta x_i y_i+\beta^2 x_i^2\right)\right]$$
$$\propto \exp\left\{-\frac{1}{2}\left[\beta^2\left(\frac{1}{v_0^2}+\frac{1}{\sigma^2}\sum_{i=1}^{n}x_i^2\right)-2\beta\left(\frac{b_0}{v_0^2}+\frac{1}{\sigma^2}\sum_{i=1}^{n}x_i y_i\right)\right]\right\}. \tag{16.10}$$

After completing the squares in β in the exponent, we can see that the posterior distribution is also a normal distribution with a mean and a variance that are functions of the prior and the data:

$$\beta \mid y_1,\ldots,y_n,\sigma^2 \sim N\left(b_n, v_n^2\right)$$
$$b_n = v_n^2\left(\frac{b_0}{v_0^2}+\frac{1}{\sigma^2}\sum_{i=1}^{n}x_i y_i\right)$$
$$v_n^2=\left(\frac{1}{v_0^2}+\frac{1}{\sigma^2}\sum_{i=1}^{n}x_i^2\right)^{-1} \tag{16.11}$$

where b_n is the posterior mean, and v_n is the posterior standard deviation. The subscript "n" indicates we have observed n observations. In this case, the prior distribution we chose for β is called "conjugate" because both the prior and posterior distributions are in the same family of distributions: normal distributions. Examples of conjugate distributions are given in Table 16.1. Being able to write the posterior out in this way affords us the opportunity to gain some insight into how the prior and the data combine (which is not possible for most models).

The equations for the posterior mean and variance are formidable expressions, but they can be written more simply and intuitively if the MLE exists. The posterior variance becomes:

$$v_n^2 = 1\Big/\frac{1}{v_0^2}+\frac{1}{se(\hat{\beta})^2}. \tag{16.12}$$

In the Bayesian literature, the inverse of the variance is called the "precision." If the variance is large, the precision is small. So, the precision of the posterior distribution, v_n^{-2}, is the sum of the prior precision v_0^{-2} and the precision of the MLE

Table 16.1 Common conjugate distributions

Likelihood	Parameter	Conjugate Prior
Binomial	Probability	Beta
Negative binomial	Probability	Beta
Gamma	Rate	Poisson
Multinomial	Probability vector	Dirichlet
Beta	Probability	Geometric
Exponential	Rate	Gamma
Normal with known variance	Mean	Normal
Normal with known mean	Variance	Inverse Gamma
Multivariate Normal with known covariance matrix	Mean vector	Multivariate Normal
Multivariate Normal with known mean vector	Covariance matrix	Inverse Wishart

$se\left(\widehat{\beta}\right)^{-1}$. If $\sum_{i=1}^{n} x_i^2$ goes to infinity as n increases, the standard error of the MLE goes to 0, as does the posterior variance.

The posterior mean can be written as a weighted or convex sum of the prior mean and the MLE. The weights are positive and sum to one, and they depend on the precisions:

$$b_n = (1 - w_n)\, b_0 + w_n \widehat{\beta} \tag{16.13}$$

$$w_n = \frac{1}{se\left(\widehat{\beta}\right)^2} \bigg/ \left(\frac{1}{v_0^2} + \frac{1}{se\left(\widehat{\beta}\right)^2}\right). \tag{16.14}$$

The posterior mean "pulls" or, as we usually say, *shrinks* the MLE towards the prior mean, where the amount of shrinkage depends on the relative precisions of the prior distribution and the MLE. The posterior mean puts more weight on the prior mean if the data are relatively less informative (larger standard error of the MLE) or the prior information is relatively more informative (smaller prior variance), while it puts more weight on the MLE as the data become more informative about β or the sample size increases. Diaconis and Ylvisaker (1979) generalize this neat trick to all exponential families[6] of distributions: the posterior mean is a convex function of the prior mean and the MLE when using conjugate priors. While this result arises directly from the rules of conditional probability, it is also intuitively sensible.

Figure 16.1 plots the prior and posterior densities for the slope and the likelihood function for a simulation study. The data are simulated from: $y_i \sim N(5x_i, 225)$ and $x_i \sim N(0, 9)$. The likelihood functions and the prior and posterior densities are graphed on different scales because likelihood functions need not integrate to one.

[6]Exponential families include almost every distribution we can easily write down, except the uniform and t-distribution.

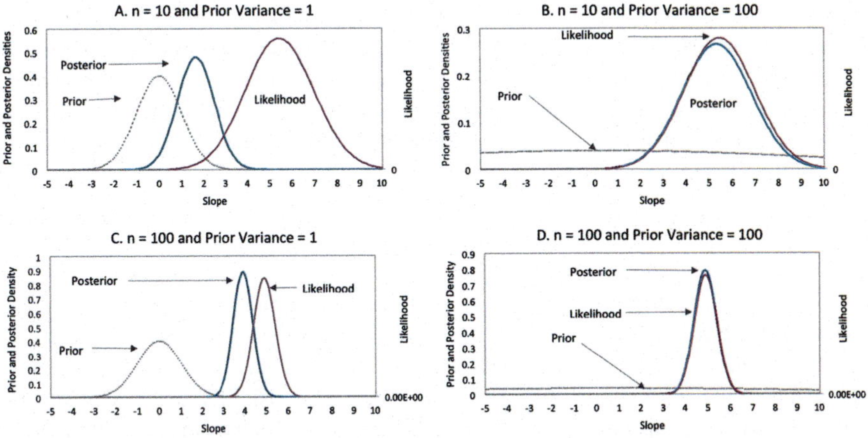

Fig. 16.1 Prior and posterior densities and likelihood function for the slope. (**a**) $n = 10$ and Prior Variance $= 1$, (**b**) $n = 10$ and Prior Variance $= 100$, (**c**) $n = 100$ and Prior Variance $= 1$, (**d**) $n = 100$ and Prior Variance $= 100$

As you can see in Fig. 16.1, we have chosen a prior with mean 0, which is a standard choice and is consistent with the null hypothesis of no effect. The resulting posterior mean will be closer to 0 than the MLE is to 0. Figure 16.1 shows the prior, the posterior and the likelihood under four different conditions: low and high information in the sample data, which we manipulate by changing the sample size n, and low and high information in the prior distribution, which we manipulate by changing the prior variance v_0. Panels A and B use 10 observations (low sample information), and panels C and D use 100 observations (high sample information). Panels A and C set the prior variance to 1 (high prior information), and panels B and D set the prior variance to 100 (low prior information). When we set the prior variance to 1 we say that the prior is "tight," and it greatly effects the posterior distribution even with 100 observations in the data. In panels A and C the posterior distribution is between the prior distribution and the likelihood function, and the posterior distribution moves closer to the likelihood function for the larger sample size. The prior distributions in panels B and D are less informative (higher prior variance) than those in panels A and C. The less informative prior distribution has less of an effect on the posterior distributions, which tend to be closer to the likelihood function. With 100 observations, the likelihood function is nearly proportional to the posterior distribution because the prior distribution is nearly flat between 3 and 7, which is the support of the likelihood function.

16.2.2.2 Posterior Summary Statistics

In addition to graphing the posterior densities, it is common to report summary statistics including the posterior mean and the posterior standard deviation to help the analyst get a quick sense of the location and spread of the posterior distribution. Many who are new to Bayesian analysis will treat the posterior means as they would frequentist parameter estimates and the posterior standard deviations as frequentist standard errors. This practice is largely benign; however, proper Bayesian estimates are always defined relative to a loss function. For example, squared-error loss between the slope β and its estimator d is:

$$\Lambda\,(\beta, d) = (\beta - d)^2.$$

The Bayes estimator or "Bayes rule" minimizes the posterior expectation of the loss function: $\mathrm{E}[\Lambda(\beta, d)|y_1, \ldots, y_n]$. The posterior mean is the Bayes rule for squared-error loss, and the posterior variance is the posterior expectation of the loss function evaluated at the posterior mean, also called "posterior risk." Other loss functions will lead to different parameter estimates. For example, the absolute error loss $\Lambda(\beta, d) = |\beta - d|$ leads to the median of the posterior distribution as the Bayes estimator. MAP estimators (maximum a posteriori) are receiving increasing interest and are based on 0/1 loss functions where the analyst loses nothing if he or she correctly estimates the parameter and loses 1 if not. MAP estimators are maximizers of the posterior distributions. Lasso regression is mathematically equivalent to MAP with Laplace or double exponential prior distributions on the regression coefficients and a uniform prior distribution on the error variance.

To obtain a proper posterior estimate, a Bayesian analyst should examine the decision problem at hand and choose an appropriate loss function, rather than simply choosing squared error loss and the posterior mean out of convenience or habit. In economics and marketing, the loss function could reflect actual monetary values. For instance, miss-estimating the creditworthiness of a loan application can result in financial losses with over-estimation (making a bad loan) being worse than under-estimation (rejecting a good loan). A proper Bayesian analysis using a realistic loss function may provide a point estimator for the creditworthiness parameter that tends to underestimate creditworthiness as a way to protect against asymmetrical losses.

The posterior standard deviation conveys the degree of uncertainty in the posterior distribution and is similar in intent, if not meaning, to standard errors. Posterior uncertainty in the parameters can also be summarized other ways besides the posterior standard deviations; for instance, posterior quantiles, e.g., the 2.5th and 97.5th percentiles of the posterior distribution, will reveal asymmetry in the posterior. (The posteriors depicted in Fig. 16.1 are symmetric, but we will see an example of an asymmetric posterior in Sect. 16.2.4; see Fig. 16.2). In cases where the posterior is highly diffuse, it may be counterproductive to report a posterior mean, as, in our experience, it often gives decision makers a false sense of certainty about the parameters.

16.2.2.3 Highest Posterior Distribution Intervals

After laboring to obtain the posterior distribution, we can use it for all sorts of inferences. Bayesians can do what is forbidden in other approaches to inference: we can give probability statements about the slope given the data. For instance, the 95% Bayesian highest posterior distribution (HPD) interval for the slope with known $\sigma = 15$ is: $b_n \pm 1.96 * v_n$, which looks very similar to the traditional 95% confidence intervals: $\widehat{\beta} \pm 1.96 * se(\widehat{\beta})$. However, their interpretations are vastly different. Bayesians say, "there is a 95% probability that the slope is in the 95% HPD interval, given the data." In this example, the HPD interval is symmetric about the posterior mean because the posterior distribution is normal. In general, the HPD is not symmetric if the posterior distribution is skewed. It can even have multiple regions if the posterior distribution has more than one mode.

In contrast, the classical or frequentist branch of statistics bases inference on repeated random sampling from the population and sampling distributions. Frequentists resort to describing confidence intervals in terms of repeated sampling: "95% of all possible random samples will result in 95% confidence intervals that contain the true slope." For frequentists, both the true slope and the observed confidence interval are constants, so for the particular sample, either the observed interval covers or does not cover the true slope, so they cannot use the confidence interval to make direct *probability statements* about the slope: the slope is either in the CI, or it's not. The Bayesian HPD is more useful to decision makers, who want to know what values the slope might take, rather than how alternative samples of the data might have turned out.

16.2.2.4 Hypothesis Tests

A decision maker might want to know the probability that education increases income. Bayesians answer this question directly by computing the posterior probability that the slope β is greater than a given threshold, and this is called hypothesis testing. For instance, a one sided test of $H_0 : \beta \leq 0$ (education does not improve income) versus $H_a : \beta > 0$ (education does improve education) with 95% confidence has the decision rule: reject H_0 if $P(\beta > 0 \mid \text{Data})$ is greater than 0.95. That is, we conclude that education affects income if most of the mass of the posterior distribution is larger than 0. Here, the posterior probability of H_0 is $P(\beta \leq 0 \mid \text{Data})$, and the posterior probability of H_a is $P(\beta > 0 \mid \text{Data})$. In Fig. 16.1.A, the posterior probability that $\beta > 0$ is 0.976. Similarly, for a two-sided test: reject $H_0 : \beta = 0$ if $P(\beta > 0 \mid \text{Data})$ is greater than 0.975, or $P(\beta < 0 \mid \text{Data})$ is greater than 0.975. That is, reject H_0 if most of the mass of the posterior distribution is on either side of 0. Bayesian hypothesis testing really is very straightforward without convoluted explanations, such as "The p-value is the probability under the null hypothesis of observing a random sample with a test statistic that favors the alternative hypothesis more than the observed test statistic[7]."

16.2.2.5 Predictions About Future Observations

Predictive analysis is particularly important in marketing and economics; we often need to predict what will happen, say, from a sales promotion or a change in Federal Reserve interest rates. Predictive analysis flows naturally from the predictive distribution of the next observation y_{n+1} given x_{n+1} and the data $y_1, \ldots, y_n$. The predictive distribution integrates the distribution of y_{n+1} given x_{n+1} and β over the posterior distribution of β, resulting in a full probability distribution for y_{n+1}:

$$f\left(y_{n+1} | x_{n+1}, y_1, \ldots, y_n, \sigma\right) = \int f\left(y_{n+1} | \beta x_{n+1}, \sigma\right) P\left(\beta | y_1, \ldots, y_n, \sigma\right) d\beta. \quad (16.15)$$

This integral is easily solved for the linear model with normally distributed errors by writing the posterior distribution of β as $\beta = b_n + \delta$ where $\delta \sim N\left(0, v_n^2\right)$. Then substitute this equation for β into $y_{n+1} = \beta x_{n+1} + \varepsilon_{n+1}$ where $\varepsilon_{n+1} \sim N(0, \sigma^2)$ to obtain $y_{n+1} = b_n x_{n+1} + \varepsilon'_{n+1}$ where $\varepsilon'_{n+1} \sim N\left(0, (x_{n+1} v_n)^2 + \sigma^2\right)$. The mean of the predictive distribution multiplies x_{n+1} by the posterior mean of β, and the predictive variance is larger than the random shock variance to account for the uncertainty about the slope.

While we can compute the predictive distribution for y_{n+1} in closed form for this small example, for more complicated models, we often estimate the integral with Monte Carlo integration. First, draw random samples for β from the posterior, $(\beta | y_1, \ldots, y_n, \sigma)$. Second, draw random samples of y from $f(y_{n+1} | \beta x_{n+1}, \sigma)$ where the density is computed at the values of β from the first random sample. In this way, we "integrate" over the posterior just by taking averages across its sample. Section 16.2.4 discusses Monte Carlo methods in more detail. The main point here is that Bayesian prediction follows directly and easily from the model specification and Bayes Theorem and accounts for all sources of uncertainty, including uncertainty in the model parameters.

[7]Frequentists often use the subjunctive mood when describing inference or hypothesis testing: "The null hypothesis would be rejected in 5% of all random samples if it were true." Bayesian use the indicative mood: "The posterior probability of the null hypothesis is 0.05 given our data and model."

16.2.3 Second Example of Bayesian Inference (Linear Regression with Known Slope and Unknown Variance)

In the simple example in the previous subsection, we assumed that the *standard deviation* σ of the random shock is *known* to simplify the presentation. We can consider a second example where the slope β is assumed to be *known*, and σ is *unknown*. While this is a very impractical case, in the next subsection, we will put the two cases together to demonstrate modern computational methods.

The customary prior distribution for the variance is the inverse Gamma (*IG*) (or, equivalently, the customary prior distribution for the precision is the Gamma.):

$$\sigma^2 \sim IG\left(\frac{r_0}{2}, \frac{s_0}{2}\right) \text{ for } r_0 > 0, \text{and } s_0 > 0. \tag{16.16}$$

The inverse Gamma distribution has the following density:

$$g\left(\sigma^2 | \frac{r_0}{2}, \frac{s_0}{2}\right) = \left[\left(\tfrac{s_0}{2}\right)^{\frac{r_0}{2}} \Big/ \Gamma\left(\tfrac{r_0}{2}\right) \left(\sigma^2\right)^{-\left(\frac{r_0}{2}+1\right)}\right] \exp\left(-\frac{s_0}{2\sigma^2}\right) \text{ for } \sigma^2 > 0 \tag{16.17}$$

where $\Gamma(x)$ is the Gamma function, a generalization of the factorial such that $\Gamma(n) = (n-1)!$, when n is an integer. The mean and variance of the inverse Gamma prior distribution for σ^2 are:

$$\mathrm{E}\left(\sigma^2\right) = \frac{s_0}{r_0 - 2} \text{ if } r_0 > 2 \text{ and } \mathrm{Var}\left(\sigma^2\right) = \left[\mathrm{E}\left(\sigma^2\right)\right]^2 \frac{2}{r_0 - 4} \text{ if } r_0 > 4. \tag{16.18}$$

Specifying of the inverse Gamma's prior parameters to represent the analyst's subjective beliefs about the variance can be tricky. One approach is to specify the prior mean and variance of σ^2 and solve for r_0 and s_0:

$$r_0 = 2\left[\mathrm{E}\left(\sigma^2\right)\right]^2 \Big/ \mathrm{Var}\left(\sigma^2\right) + 4 \text{ and } s_0 = (r_0 - 2)\,\mathrm{E}\left(\sigma^2\right). \tag{16.19}$$

As we saw in the first example, the next step in Bayesian analysis is to write down the joint distribution of the data and the unknown parameters. In this case, β is known and σ is unknown:

$$P\left(y_1, \ldots, y_n, \sigma^2 | \beta\right) = g\left(\sigma^2 | \frac{r_0}{2}, \frac{s_0}{2}\right) \prod_{i=1}^{n} f\left(y_i | \beta x_i, \sigma\right). \tag{16.20}$$

The posterior distribution of the variance is:

$$P\left(\sigma^2 | y_1, \ldots, y_n, \beta\right) \propto \left(\sigma^2\right)^{-\left(\frac{r_0+n}{2}+1\right)} \exp\left[-\frac{s_0}{2\sigma^2} - \frac{1}{2\sigma^2} \sum_{i=1}^{n} (y_i - \beta x_i)^2\right] \tag{16.21}$$

which we can recognize as an inverse Gamma density:

$$\begin{aligned}\sigma^2 \mid y_1, \ldots, y_n, \beta &\sim IG\left(\frac{r_n}{2}, \frac{s_n}{2}\right)\\ r_n &= r_0 + n \\ s_n &= s_0 + \sum_{i=1}^{n} (y_i - \beta x_i)^2.\end{aligned} \tag{16.22}$$

Similar to the normal prior for the slope, the inverse Gamma distribution for the variance is conjugate, which simply means that the posterior distribution is also inverse Gamma. A point of confusion might be that variance of the error term in the linear model, σ^2, has a posterior distribution, which, like most distributions, has a variance. The variance of the posterior is related to our posterior uncertainty about what values σ^2 might take. As we might expect, as we amass more data, the posterior variance of σ^2 goes to 0 at rate $1/n$ as n goes to infinity.

Of course, this does not mean that the posterior expected value of σ^2 goes to zero. As a special case of the theorem of Diaconis and Ylvisaker (1979), we can write the posterior mean of σ^2 as a convex function of the prior mean $s_0/(r_0-2)$ and the MLE $\widehat{\sigma}^2$:

$$\begin{aligned}\mathrm{E}\left(\sigma^2 | y_1, \ldots, y_n, \beta\right) &= \tfrac{s_n}{r_n-2} = \tfrac{s_0+\sum_{i=1}^{n}(y_i-\beta x_i)^2}{r_0+n-2}\\ &= (1-w_n)\tfrac{s_0}{r_0-2} + w_n\widehat{\sigma}^2 \\ w_n &= \tfrac{n}{r_0+n-2}\end{aligned} \tag{16.23}$$

where the MLE is:

$$\widehat{\sigma}^2 = \frac{1}{n}\sum_{i=1}^{n} (y_i - \beta x_i)^2. \tag{16.24}$$

As the sample size becomes large, more weight is given to the MLE, and the posterior variance goes to zero. So the posterior distribution converges in probability to a point mass at the true variance as n gets large.

16.2.4 Bayesian MCMC Example (Linear Regression with Unknown Slope and Variance)

16.2.4.1 Basics of MCMC

We have covered the unrealistic case of estimating the slope given the error variance is known and the even more unrealistic case of estimating the error variance when the slope is known. What about the realistic problem of estimating them together? Assuming, as before, a normal prior for the slope and an inverse Gamma prior for the variance, the joint distribution of the data and the priors for the slope and error variance is:

$$P\left(y_1,\ldots,y_n,\beta,\sigma^2\right) = f\left(\beta|b_0,v_0\right) g\left(\sigma^2|\frac{r_0}{2},\frac{s_0}{2}\right) \prod_{i=1}^{n} f\left(y_i|\beta x_i,\sigma\right). \tag{16.25}$$

The posterior distribution of the slope and error variance is:

$$P\left(\beta,\sigma^2|y_1,\ldots,y_n\right) = \frac{P\left(y_1,\ldots,y_n,\beta,\sigma^2\right)}{\int\int P\left(y_1,\ldots,y_n,b,s^2\right) ds^2\, db} \tag{16.26}$$

where b and s^2 are dummy variables of integration for the slope and error variance in the integrals of the denominator. Even in this common and fairly simple case, the posterior distribution does not have a convenient closed-form expression. That is, it does not fall into a standard class of distributions[8].

Instead of walking through more examples of prior to posterior analyses that result in standard distributions, we next consider a numerical method, Markov chain Monte Carlo (MCMC), for analyzing Bayesian models. The key to understanding the use of Monte Carlo simulations in Bayesian analysis is the following. As mentioned earlier, Bayesian inference requires integrating functions over the posterior distribution. While it was possible to solve this integral in closed form in our first two examples, this is generally not so. However, if you have a random number generator capable of drawing from the posterior distribution, then a simple and fast approximation to the posterior mean can be obtained by generating random draws from the posterior and averaging them together. The approximation is called Monte Carlo integration. Posterior means and variances, posterior probabilities, and predictive distributions can all be computed by averaging over the random draws from the posterior distribution. For instance, if you want to compute the posterior mean of $S(\beta)$ where S is any function of β, then independently generate a chain of random deviates $\beta_1, \beta_2, \ldots, \beta_m$ by using the random number generator; compute S at each random draw; and average the $S(\beta_j)$ together:

$$\mathrm{E}\left[S\left(\beta\right)|y_1,\ldots,y_n\right] \approx \frac{1}{m}\sum_{j=1}^{m} S\left(\beta_j\right). \tag{16.27}$$

For example, if β is the coefficient on education in a regression relating education to income, then $S(\beta)$ could be the returns to education. You can make the Monte Carlo approximation as accurate as desired by using large m by the strong law of large numbers. The standard error of the approximation (comparing the Monte

[8]If we modify the prior distributions slightly, they are conjugate and have a closed form. The modification conditions the slope on the error variance: $\beta\,|\,\sigma^2 \sim N\left(b_0,\sigma^2 v_0^2\right)$ and $\sigma^2 \sim IG\left(\frac{r_0}{2}, s_0/2\right)$. This results in a "scale free" model: you can multiply y and x by a constant without changing the prior distributions. Instead of pursuing the algebra for this specification, we think it is a better use of time to introduce numerical methods.

Carlo approximation to the integral over the posterior distribution, not to the true parameter), is proportional to $m^{-1/2}$, since the draws are mutually independent. This approach also scales well to multiple dimensions when S is a function of two or more parameters. Other approximation methods, which were designed before the age of modern computation, compute S times the posterior probability over a grid of values for β and then average them. These grid methods work well if S a function of a few parameters, but the number of computations becomes practically impossible to implement even on fast computers when S is a function of a large number of parameters, which is very common in standard models. Fortunately, Monte Carlo methods easily approximate integrals that were impossibly hard to evaluate in Thomas Bayes' times.

The key innovation that ignited the explosion of Bayesian computation was MCMC, or Markov chain Monte Carlo. Gelfand and Smith (1990) and Geman and Geman (1984) reintroduced MCMC, which was originally described by Hastings (1970) and Metropolis et al. (1953). Essentially, MCMC is a highly flexible approach to creating a computer program that will produce random draws from the posterior distribution for nearly any model. MCMC starts by using the wrong-but-convenient random number generator and cleverly ends with random draws from the correct random number generator. It does this by creating a Markov chain that transverses the support of the posterior distribution. A Markov chain is a sequence of random numbers where the subsequent draws depend only on the current draw and are independent of earlier draws. At each iteration, MCMC generates a random draw in an intelligent way, such that the resulting sequence of numbers is a Markov chain whose stationary (limiting) distribution is the desired posterior distribution. The MCMC draws, after an initial "burn-in" period, during which the parameter draws move towards regions of the parameter space where the posterior density is large, act as though they are generated from the posterior distribution. The Markov chain tours around the support for the posterior distribution and visits region of the parameter space in proportion to the posterior distribution. If the reader is not familiar with Markov chains, suffice it to say that Hastings (1970), Metropolis et al. (1953), and other mathematicians have worked out the details, and MCMC had great success in analyzing a wide variety of complex models.

"Gibbs sampling[9]" is the simplest instance of MCMC. The key is to decompose the posterior distribution into a sequence of distributions for subsets of the parameters. These sub-distributions are called "full conditional distributions." Gibbs sampling then sequentially makes random draws from each full conditional distribution given the current values of other parameters. The advantage to drawing from the full conditionals is that it is often easier to generate random draws from these simpler distributions and standard statistical programming languages (e.g., R, Matlab, C++, or Gauss) often have built-in random number generators for common full conditional distributions such as the normal or Gamma distribution.

[9]It is strange nomenclature. Metropolis et al. (1953) generated random variables from the Gibbs distribution, which describes the distribution of energy states for a system of atoms. Because they were sampling from a Gibbs distribution, this special case is called "Gibbs sampling" even when it is not applied to a Gibbs distribution.

Our example linear model with unknown slope and error variance is just such an example. Recall that we could not sample from both parameters concurrently, since their joint posterior was not of a standard form (that is, random number generators don't have it built-in). Instead, we construct a way to sample parameters *sequentially*. The first step in constructing the Gibbs sampler for our example model is to divide the parameters into groups, which is easy to do since we only have two parameters[10]. The second step is to compute the full conditional distributions:

1. β given σ^2 and $y_1, \ldots, y_n$; and
2. σ^2 given β and $y_1, \ldots, y_n$.

We drop $x_1, \ldots, x_n$ in the conditional statement to simplify notation.

In computing the full conditional distribution for the slope, we pretend we know the error variance, and in computing the full conditional distribution for the error variance, we pretend we know the slope. The two, full conditional distributions are:

$$\beta \mid y_1, \ldots, y_n, \sigma^2 \sim N\left(b_n, v_n^2\right) \tag{16.28}$$

$$\sigma^2 \mid y_1, \ldots, y_n, \beta \sim IG\left(\frac{r_n}{2}, \frac{s_n}{2}\right) \tag{16.29}$$

where the posterior parameters are given in Eqs. (16.11) and (16.22). There are standard routines in most statistical libraries to draw from the normal distribution and the Gamma distribution. The inverse Gamma draw is just 1 divided by the Gamma draw. The full conditional distribution for β depends on σ^2, since b_n and v_n depend on σ. Similarly, the full conditional distribution for σ^2 depends on β through s_n. Using these full conditionals, we can define our MCMC algorithm as follows. The subscripts on the parameters indicate the iteration of the MCMC sampler.

1. initialize the parameters: β_0 and σ_0^2;
2. at iteration j of the algorithm:

   generate β_j from the full conditional distribution of β given σ_{j-1}^2;
   generate σ_j^2 from the full conditional distribution of σ^2 given β_j;

3. repeat step 2 until:
   the draws forβ and σ^2 converge to the joint posterior distribution of β and σ^2;
4. after convergence, keep generating β and σ^2 until there are enough draws to estimate integrals accurately;
5. approximate posterior integrals for any function, $S[\beta, \sigma]$. Drop the first B draws that occur before convergence in 3 from the Monte Carlo approximation of the integral:

$$\widehat{\mathrm{E}}\left(S\left[\beta, \sigma\right] \mid y_1, \ldots, y_n\right) = \frac{1}{G-B} \sum_{j=B+1}^{G} S\left[\beta_j, \sigma_j\right] \tag{16.30}$$

where the total number of iterations is G, and the MCMC chain has reached the stationary distribution during the first B iterations.

[10]In multivariate regression models, β would be the vector of regression coefficients.

Figure 16.2 presents the output of the MCMC for $n = 10$ observations of (y_i, x_i). The prior parameters for the slope are $b_0 = 0$, $v_0{}^2 = 100$, which are the values used in Fig. 16.1b and d. To determine the prior parameters for the error variance, σ^2, we choose "diffuse" or relatively "non-informative" values, setting the prior mean of σ^2 to 400, and the prior variance of σ^2 to 1,000,000. We then solve for the parameters for the inverse Gamma distribution: $r_0 = 4.16$, and $s_0 = 864$. The chain was initialized at $\beta_0 = 0$ and $\sigma_0^2 = 1$. The MCMC generated values for σ^2, but we will graph and report statistics for σ. Figure 16.2c graphs the traces (plots of the random draws versus the iteration number) for 1000 iterations.

Convergence to the posterior distribution does not mean that the traces become constant. If the traces become constant, then the chain has become stuck, and there is something horribly wrong with the MCMC sampler. The traces should become stationary (no apparent trend and relatively constant variation), yet still wobble, because they are random draws from the posterior distribution. It is typical to have a few, large values from the inverse Gamma distribution because it has positive skew and long tails (algebraically, not exponentially, decreasing density for large positive values). Figure 16.2c indicates that the chain rapidly converges to the posterior distribution, and we drop the first 50 draws when approximating integrals. Figure 16.2a plots the draws of the standard deviation versus the draws of the slope. The MCMC starts in the lower left-hand corner at (0,1). The MCMC sampler transverses the support of the posterior distribution and visits areas of high posterior probability more frequently. Figures 16.2b and d plot histograms of the draws from iteration 51 to 1000. Note that the histogram in Fig. 16.2d shows that the posterior of σ is asymmetric.

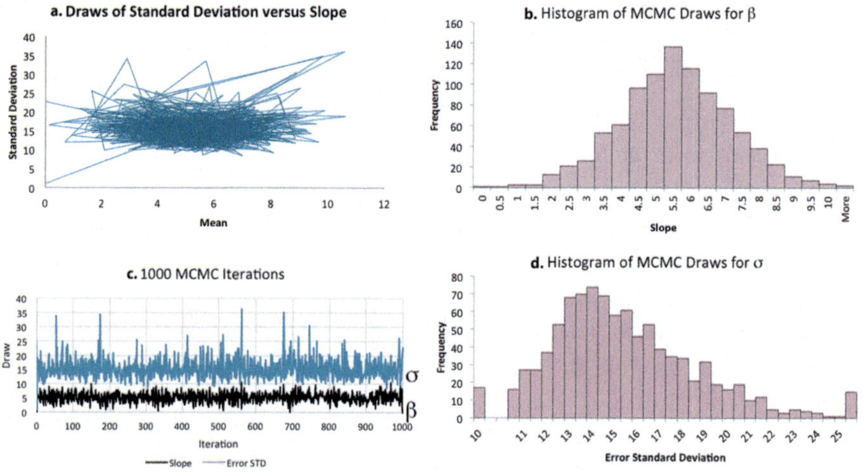

Fig. 16.2 MCMC when the true model is $y = N(5x, 225)$ and $n = 10$
Note: (**a**) Trace of 1000 iterations for the mean and standard deviation, (**b**) Histogram of the draws for the slope, (**c**) Scatter plot of the draws for the standard deviation versus the slope, (**d**) Histogram of the draws for the standard deviation

Table 16.2 MCMC Estimates of the posterior means and standard deviations

	Slope	Error (Standard Dev.)
True values	5.0000	15.0000
Posterior mean	5.3258	15.2391
Posterior STD DEV	1.6144	3.3932
2.5th%-tile	2.0785	10.2697
97.5th%-tile	8.4816	22.8224
P(Slope > 0 | Data)	0.9989	
P(Slope > 5 | Data)	0.5905	

We can use the posterior draws to make statements about the likely values of β and σ, to test hypotheses about the parameters or functions of the parameters, and to make predictions for new data points. For instance, we approximate the posterior means by averaging the draws from the MCMC sampler, and we approximate the posterior standard deviations by computing the standard deviation of the draws. In Table 16.2, these posterior summaries are compared to the true values used to generate the data. The posterior means are close to the true values relative to the posterior standard deviations. Using the posterior draws from our MCMC sampler, we can test the hypothesis that the slope is greater than 0. $P(\beta > 0|y_1, \ldots, y_n)$ is simply estimated by finding the proportion of draws for β that are larger than 0. Because 99.80% of the draws are larger than 0, we would conclude that the slope is larger than 0. If we wish to test the null hypothesis that the slope is equal to 5 versus the alternative that it is not equal to 5, we use the draws to estimate $P(\beta > 5|y_1, \ldots, y_n) = 0.5905$ and $P(\beta < 5|y_1, \ldots, y_n) = 0.4095$. We fail to reject the null because 5 is in the fat-part of the posterior distribution. We can also see this in the histogram for the slope in Fig. 16.2b, which is mound-shaped with a mode near 5.

In regular Monte Carlo, the draws from the random number generator are mutually independent from one draw to the next. In MCMC, the draws are correlated over iterations, which is called auto-correlated. The auto-correlation occurs in MCMC because the draws at iteration j depend on the draws from iteration $j-1$. Auto-correlation adversely impacts the performance of the numerical approximations: the standard error of the MCMC approximation (comparing the MCMC approximation to the integral of the posterior distribution, not to the true parameters) can be slower than $(G-B)^{-1/2}$where $G-B$ is the number of draws used in the MCMC approximation (recall that B refers to burn-in, G to total number of Gibbs draws). Auto-correlation can be very high for poorly designed MCMC procedures, in which case you will need a very large number of iterations to obtain good results. If the auto-correlation is small, we say that the MCMC "mixes well."

Figure 16.3 displays the auto-correlation functions (ACF, introduced in Chap. 3) and cross auto-correlation functions for the iterations after 50. Figure 16.3 paints a happy picture for our example: other than lag 0, where ACF(0) is always 1, most of the correlations are within the blue dotted lines and very close to zero, which indicate that they are not significantly different from zero at the 0.05 level of

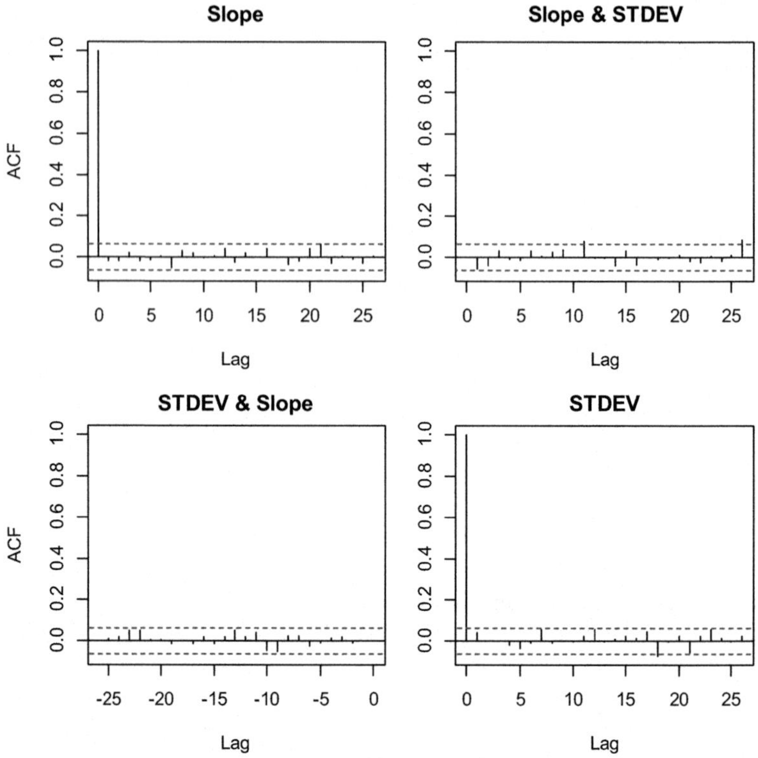

Fig. 16.3 Auto-correlation Functions (ACF) and Cross Auto-correlations of the draws from the Slope and Error Standard Deviation (STDEV). Plots were made with R's `acf()` function

significance. (In fact, most of the auto-correlations are so close to zero that they are difficult to see in Fig. 16.3.) This result indicates that MCMC for our simple problem is nearly the same as standard Monte Carlo where the draws are independent, although this may be because we are sampling for just two parameters with data conforming closely to the model. To reiterate, we are checking the performance of the numerical approximations from MCMC, and not the performance of the Bayes estimators, such as the posterior mean. Much of the modern literature on Bayesian inference focuses on the performance of the MCMC approximations, not directly on Bayes inference. This literature assumes that Bayes estimators are correct (in fact, the gold standard), and it is testing how close the MCMC or other approximation gets to that gold standard. Numerical approximations are an evolving field, and, unless updated frequently, chances are your MCMC software is either out-of-date or will not always give good answers.

Prediction also is easy once you have the sample of draws $\{\beta_j, \sigma_j\}$ from MCMC. First, generate a sample of future observations for y_{n+1} at x_{n+1} by: $y_{j,n+1} \sim N\left(\beta_j x_{n+1}, \sigma_j^2\right)$ for $j = B+1, \ldots, G$. That is, for each draw of the MCMC, compute a draw from the distribution of y evaluated at the draw from the posterior distribution of the parameters. (Note that the posterior distribution is multivariate, and so you should keep each pair of $\{\beta_j, \sigma_j\}$ as a pair.) Then you can use these draws of y to approximate the expected value of different functions. For example, suppose the researcher is interested in the return on education, R, for x_{n+1} years of education and other variables, z, such as degree, cost of college, field of study, discount rate, etc. Then:

$$\widehat{\mathrm{E}}\left[R\left(y_{n+1}, x_{n+1}, z\right) | y_1, \ldots, y_n\right] = \frac{1}{G-B} \sum_{j=B+1}^{G} R\left(y_{j,n+1}, x_{n+1}, z\right). \tag{16.31}$$

The return on education function R can be as complex as one needs, yet the predicted return on education is a simple average of different realizations of that function given the draws from MCMC. Moreover, the uncertainty in the prediction can be summarized simply as the standard deviation of $R(y_{j,n+1}, x_{n+1}, z)$ for the $G-B$ draws of y_{n+1}. Other approaches to prediction entail complex approximations to R to obtain possibly inaccurate, large-sample approximations for the prediction standard error. Bayesians have an easy-to-implement, accurate, "exact" method (that is, given a suitably large set of draws from the stationary distribution of the posterior). Why then are large-sample approximations so popular, when exact Bayesian analysis is straightforward? A perverse reason may be that large-sample approximations often under-estimate uncertainty and thereby give smaller standard errors. Inaccurate claims of significant results can then arise due to misuse of large-sample classical approximations.

Two much-studied issues in the literature are the length of the "burn-in" period B before the MCMC chain starts acting as though it is generating random numbers from the posterior distribution, and the number of draws $G-B$ to use in approximations after burn-in. There are a large number of convergence criteria. None of them will work in all situations, and they vary in implementation difficulty. Posterior distributions that have disjoint regions can fool all of the criteria: the chains can become stationary but not visit all of the different regions. Cowles and Carlin (1996) provide an outstanding review, and Gelman and Rubin (1992) provide a diagnostic statistic that is implemented in the R package `Coda`. In practice, we find that starting several chains from different starting points and then comparing traceplots to see if the chains have reached the same stationary distribution will detect gross convergence failures.

16.2.4.2 More Advanced MCMC Techniques for Other Models

Generalizing from our linear model example, to create a Gibbs sampler we partition all of the model parameters Θ into K mutually exclusive and exhaustive subsets $\theta_1, \ldots, \theta_K$. We typically choose this partition in a way that is consistent with the structure of the statistical model: fixed-effects parameters, random-effects parameters, covariance matrices, and so on. In a wonderful abuse of notation that is commonly used in the literature, we write θ_{-k} for all of the parameters except θ_k. The full conditional for θ_k is $P(\theta_k|\,\theta_{-k}, y_1, \ldots, y_n)$. We first initialize the parameter to a starting value. At iteration j of Gibbs sampling, we generate θ_k from its full conditional distribution where θ_{-k} is evaluated at the current values of the other parameters from either the $(j-1)$th or jth iteration. We repeat this until the chain starts to act like it is producing draws from the posterior. We then save these draws to use in approximating integrals.

If the full conditionals do not have a convenient random number generator, then a Metropolis step is required. Basically, one generates a candidate value of θ_k from a proposal distribution g, and either keeps the candidate or rejects it and keeps the previous draw of θ_k according to probabilities that filter out the candidates to get the correct stationary distribution. The acceptance probabilities are:

$$\alpha\left(\theta_k, \theta_k^*\right) = \min\left\{\frac{P\left(\theta_k^*|\theta_{-k}, y_1, \ldots, y_n\right) g\left(\theta_k|\theta_k^*, \theta_{-k}\right)}{P\left(\theta_k|\theta_{-k}, y_1, \ldots, y_n\right) g\left(\theta_k^*|\theta_k, \theta_{-k}\right)}, 1\right\} \tag{16.32}$$

where the proposal density g for generating the candidate θ_k^*, can depend on current values of the parameters. The candidate θ_k^* value is randomly accepted (the chain jumps to the new value) with probability $\alpha\left(\theta_k, \theta_k^*\right)$, and the current value is kept (the chain stays at the current value) with probability $1-\alpha\left(\theta_k, \theta_k^*\right)$. It is not intuitive, but this screening operation results in a sequence of draws from the posterior distribution.

The most popular Metropolis proposal distribution is a normal random walk: the candidate is drawn from a normal distribution whose mean is equal to the current value of θ_k. The performance of random walk MCMC is sensitive to the variance of the random walk. If the variance is too big, the chain will frequently reject the candidates and be stuck at one value for many iterations, and the auto-correlation will be large. If the variance is too small, the chain frequently accepts the candidate, but the auto-correlation will be large because the step size from one draw to the next is small.

All modern texts on Bayesian statistics will have a long section on general MCMC methods that cover both Gibbs sampling and Metropolis steps in more detail than we can here; see, for example, Gelman et al. (2014) or Kruschke (2015).

16.2.5 Model Selection

Model selection is the process of choosing a model (including the likelihood and the priors). Bayesian theory on model selection is conceptually very simple:

1. Write down all of the models that you think could be true, including the likelihood function and the prior distributions of the parameters. Suppose that the researcher is entertaining M models. For $m = 1, \ldots, M$:

a. the conditional distribution of the data given the parameters θ_m for model m is $f_m(\text{Data}|\ \theta_m)$;
b. the prior density for θ_m is $g_m(\theta_m)$;
c. the posterior density of θ_m for model m is:

$$g_m\left(\theta_m|\text{Data}\right) = \frac{f_m\left(\text{Data}|\theta_m\right) g_m\left(\theta_m\right)}{P_m\left(\text{Data}\right)}$$

$$P_m\left(\text{Data}\right) = \int f_m\left(\text{Data}|\theta_m\right) g_m\left(\theta_m\right) d\theta_m \tag{16.33}$$

where $P_m(\text{Data})$ is the probability of the data or the integrated likelihood under model m. It is the normalizing constant for the posterior density. Usually, we ignore the normalizing constant when computing the posterior distributions. It has a central role in model selection, so we need to keep track of it.

2. Specify the prior probability of each model: $P(\text{Model } m) = p_m$ for $m = 1, \ldots, M$. Most academic studies assume that these prior probabilities are equal for the M models so as not to bias the analysis towards a favorite. In real applications, the researcher may know from past experience or theory that some models are more tenable than others.
3. Write down the misclassification costs for the models. If these are equal, they can be ignored in the analysis. Most academic studies assume equal misclassification costs, and we will do the same here. Real applications often have unequal misclassification costs. For example, using a model that excludes important variables can result in biased estimates if the excluded variables are correlated with the variables in the model, while using models with unimportant variables are inefficient in terms of estimation accuracy. The cost of incorrectly selecting a biased model may be higher than incorrectly selecting an inefficient model. Inefficient estimators are less of an issue for large datasets, while the biased estimators are inconsistent. Large sample sizes cannot compensate for the bias due to model misspecification.
4. After observing the data, compute the posterior probability of each model according to Bayes Theorem:

$$P\left(\text{Model } m \mid \text{Data}\right) = \frac{p_m P_m\left(\text{Data}\right)}{\sum_{j=1}^{M} p_j P_j\left(\text{Data}\right)} \text{ for } m = 1, \ldots, M \tag{16.34}$$

where $P_m(\text{Data})$ is the probability of the data or the integrated likelihood under model m.
5. Select the best model according to the posterior probabilities of the models.

a. If the models have different misclassification costs, pick the model with smallest posterior misclassification costs. This criterion is similar to classical *discriminant* analysis, which uses Bayes Theorem, to classify observations into one of G groups based on observed covariates.

b. If the misclassification costs are equal, pick the model with maximum posterior probability.
c. If the prior probabilities of the models are equal, select the model with maximum log integrated likelihood: $LIL(m) = \ln[P_m(\text{Data})]$.

Bayesian model selection is remarkably simple, general and effective in theory. Unfortunately, $LIL(m)$ is remarkably hard to compute accurately in practice. Newton and Raftery (1994) proposed a "harmonic mean" approximation of $LIL(m)$ by using the draws from the MCMC sampler. The method is easy to implement if the likelihood is easy to compute. It is based on the identity:

$$\int \frac{g_m(\theta_m|\text{Data})}{f_m(\text{Data}|\theta_m)} d\theta_m = \frac{\int g_m(\theta_m)\, d\theta_m}{P_m(\text{Data})} = \frac{1}{P_m(\text{Data})} = \exp\left[-LIL(m)\right]. \quad (16.35)$$

Let $\{\theta_{mj}\}$ be the MCMC draws from the posterior distribution for model m. The Newton and Raftery approximation is:

$$\widehat{LIL}_{NR}(m) = -\ln\left[\frac{1}{T-B}\sum_{j=B+1}^{T}\frac{1}{f_m\left(\text{Data}|\theta_{m,j}\right)}\right]. \quad (16.36)$$

Unfortunately, the approximation has infinite variance; its MCMC approximation is biased, and it tends to pick models that are too complex[11] (Lenk 2009).

Other approximations that work well are computationally intensive. Gelfand and Dey (1994) provide a general approximation that uses an auxiliary density h_m for θ_m. The auxiliary density can be arbitrary as long as it integrates to one on the posterior support of θ_m. The approximation is based on the following identity:

$$\int \frac{h_m(\theta_m)\, g_m(\theta_m|\text{Data})}{f_m(\text{Data}|\theta_m)\, g_m(\theta_m)} d\theta_m = \frac{\int h_m(\theta_m)\, d\theta_m}{P_m(\text{Data})} = \frac{1}{P_m(\text{Data})} = \exp\left[-LIL(m)\right]. \quad (16.37)$$

For the approximation to work, the tails of h_m have to decrease at the same rate or faster than the tails of the posterior distribution. The Gelfand and Dey approximation is:

$$\widehat{LIL}_{GD}(m) = -\ln\left[\frac{1}{T-B}\sum_{j=B+1}^{T}\frac{h_m\left(\theta_{m,j}\right)}{f_m\left(\text{Data}|\theta_{m,j}\right) g_m\left(\theta_{m,j}\right)}\right]. \quad (16.38)$$

The closer that the auxiliary density h_m matches the posterior distribution, the more accurate the approximation will be. A common choice for unrestricted parameters is multivariate normal distributions. The mean parameter for the multivariate normal

[11] In fairness to Newton and Raftery (1994), their method is not the main focus of their paper.

distribution is set to the MCMC estimate of the posterior mean, and its covariance is set to the MCMC estimate of the posterior covariance. For parameters with limited range, one can define h_m to be in the same family as the prior distribution, and set its parameters by the method of moments using the MCMC draws as "data." A pro tip is to shrink the variance of h_m by dividing it by, say, 4. Shrinking the covariance ensures that the tails of h_m decline at least as fast as the tails of the posterior distribution.

Chib (1995) provides a third approach to computing the marginal likelihood and can be easier to compute than Gelfand and Dey if the MCMC algorithm only uses Gibbs sampling, but it is not suitable for general MCMC using Metropolis-Hastings.

Schwartz Information Criterion (Schwartz 1978) or Bayes Information Criterion (introduced in Sect. 5.6.3 in Vol. I) is a large sample approximation to *LIL* and is used as a fit statistic in many statistical software packages including SAS, JMP, and R. It balances model fit with model complexity: $\text{SIC}(m) = -2L_m(\theta_m) + k_m \ln(n)$ where k_m is the number of parameters for model m. The fit criterion is the maximum of the traditional log-likelihood function $L_m\left(\widehat{\theta}_m\right)$ where $\widehat{\theta}_m$ is the MLE, and model complexity is a function of the number of parameters. SIC works remarkably well in identifying the variables in regression models or the specification of ARIMA models. In more complex models, such as hierarchical Bayes or latent variable models, the number of parameters is not always well defined and the approximation often fails due to relatively small n compared to the number of parameters. SIC(m) is consistent: as the sample size *increases*, it will select the true model. A popular competitor is Akaike Information Criterion: $\text{AIC}(m) = -2L_m(\theta_m) + 2k_m$ (Akaike 1974). AIC under-penalizes complexity, is not consistent, and tends to choose models that are too complex. An argument for AIC(m) is that it picks the correct model if the number of parameters grows, which is not unreasonable in practice: the more data we have, the more variables we will want to include in regression models. Corrected AIC (cAIC) modifies AIC to have a larger penalty term as in SIC. An alternative and popular approach, DIC (Spiegelhalter et al. 2002), is based on information arguments and not derived from Bayes theorem. DIC is reported in the popular WinBugs package.

16.2.6 Repeated Inference

A final feature of Bayesian inference that we should mention is the ease of conducting repeated inference. Unlike in frequentist frameworks, Bayesian inference can be repeated as more data becomes available. For instance, if we were to get a second sample of data on incomes and education for our linear model, we would simply posit our new prior to be the posterior we obtained from the first sample. We would then conduct the analysis just as before, combining the likelihood of the new data with our new prior to obtain a posterior. This approach is completely coherent; in fact, assuming the same original prior, we obtain the exact same posterior whether we do the analysis sequentially versus combining the two data sets into one and doing the posterior updating just once. This makes Bayesian analysis very appealing in marketing and other business settings where data are often updated daily or even more frequently and analysis is provided in near real-time to managers through online interfaces.

16.2.7 Subjective Probability and Inference

By this point, the reader should have a notion of how Bayesian analysis works, it is a good point to step back and discuss some of the important foundations that make Bayesian analysis a complete, coherent, and elegant approach to statistical inference. The subjective interpretation of probability should have particular appeal to researchers with an economics background because it can be derived from Von Neumann and Morgenstern (1944), who propose a normative model for decision making under uncertainty. Their theory takes a person's preferences for risky decisions as the fundamental object of study. They provide axioms for "rational" choice. For instance, if decision A is preferred to decision B, and if decision B is preferred to decision C, then decision A must also be preferred to decision C. If the ordering of a person's preferences follow the axiom's of rationality, then there exists a utility function on the outcomes of the decisions such that the ordering of decisions based on expected utility is the same as the person's preference ordering. The theory does not assume that subjects actually have utility functions and compute expectations. However, an economist or psychologist could estimate the appropriate utility function based on observed preferences if the axioms hold. In their treatment, probabilities of random outcomes are exogenous to the person's preferences: they assume that the probabilities are given to the person, as in gambles with known probabilities and payouts, or that there exists an external randomization device to calibrate the likelihood of events.

Savage (1954) extended the axioms of rational choice to endogenize probability: a person's preferences for risky choices determine both the utilities for outcomes and the probabilities for events. These probabilities are subjective: they are derived from the person's preferences and not from data generating mechanisms. These subjective probabilities may or may not include information about processes that produced the random events. In fact, the theory does not assume that people use probabilities, utility, or expected utility. It only says that rational preferences can be represented mathematically by expected utilities for the appropriate utility and probability functions. Having established subjective probability from preferences, Savage solves the inference problem by using Bayes Theorem to update these subjective beliefs as new data become available.

For instance, a marketing manager may have subjective beliefs about the demand of a new product before launch. These beliefs could include demand for previous product launches, knowledge about market conditions, and test market data for the new product. After the product launch, he or she observes realized demand. Using Bayes Theorem, the manager can update his or her beliefs about future demand

and, if need be, change the marketing mix to meet business objectives. It would be a mistake to ignore the manager's prior beliefs and only react to the early sales of the product, which can be very volatile depending on market conditions. It is easy to become unrealistically optimistic to favorable, early sales and change marketing and production plans to meet accelerated demand that does not materialize. Similarly, the manager should not become too pessimistic in response to low, early sales and cut losses by withdrawing marketing support, which can lead to a self-fulfilling prophecy. A better approach is to temper the early sales information after launch with the prior information and not to over-react. This approach seems obvious, yet other modes of inference would ignore the subjective prior information for the chimera of "objectivity."

In this section, we have provided a foundation for understanding Bayesian analysis, although we have only scratched the surface. Readers who want to know more about the theory underlying Bayesian inference and the mechanics of MCMC should consult one of the many textbooks available in Bayesian inference such as Gelman et al. (2014). In the interest of exposing readers to more of the practicalities of Bayesian inference, the next section illustrates a few applications using MCMC software. The following section then provides an example of how to build a Gibbs sampler from scratch for more complex models than the linear model with a single slope parameter.

16.3 Using Bayesian MCMC Routines

16.3.1 Introduction

As we discussed in the previous section, the key computational step in most Bayesian methods is to use MCMC methods to generate random draws from the posterior distribution and then use these posterior draws to estimate posterior means, HPDs, hypothesis tests, and predictions. Those who pioneered Bayesian analysis derived the full conditionals for their desired model and then coded an MCMC algorithm to produce samples from the posterior directly from the full conditionals. While these algorithms can be programmed in general purpose languages such as FORTRAN and C, those who use this "roll-your-own" approach to Bayesian computation have typically adopted statistical programming languages such as Gauss, Matlab, C++ with the Gnu Scientific Library, and R. These statistical programming languages typically have efficient, built-in random number generators for common distributions like the uniform and the normal, as well as efficient matrix algebra routines, which are useful in developing an MCMC routine for drawing from the posterior of your desired model.

For those who do not wish to derive and program full conditionals, an alternative is to find a well-developed MCMC routine for the model that you wish to use. Easy-to-use software is available for many common models. Both STATA and

SAS offer routines for MCMC for common models including linear regression, generalized linear models like logistic regression, finite mixture models and survival models. There are also several contributed packages for R that provide routines for generating posterior samples from popular models including `MCMCpack` (Martin et al. 2011), `BayesFactor` (Morey et al. 2015) and `bayesm` (Rossi, 2015). These packages are regularly updated and new models frequently added. These software packages typically provide fast and reliable MCMC routines for drawing a posterior sample, as well as tools for analyzing that posterior sample. While these packages are often very easy to use, they, of course, limit the user to the priors and likelihoods that have been chosen by the developer. They also sometimes attempt to present Bayesian analysis in a "frequentist style," which can be confusing and potentially misleading to those new to Bayesian analysis. Despite these limitations, these packages make it easy to generate and analyze posterior samples. In this section, we will illustrate the use of such packages, using the `MCMCpack` package from R as an example.

The ideal tool for Bayesian analysis would generate a posterior sample for *any* model and priors that the user might specify, without requiring the user to think about the details of the MCMC sampler. Several efforts have been undertaken to develop such a tool, including the Bayesian inference Using Gibbs Sampling (BUGS) project (Lunn et al., 2000), the Just Another Gibbs Sampler (JAGS) project (Plummer, 2015) and Stan (Carpenter et al., 2017). Each of these tools allows users to specify a very wide variety of models using a modeling language. Once the model is specified, the tool automatically creates an MCMC algorithm to draw samples from the posterior for that model. The promise of these tools is that they will allow users to focus on the most important elements of Bayesian analysis—choosing a model and prior that suits the data and reflects prior beliefs—without having to create or find code for an MCMC sampler for each model they might consider. Changing the model is often a matter of changing one or two lines in the model formulation. However, these tools are still somewhat in their adolescence, and sometimes the MCMC routine that is produced for a particular model may not converge rapidly or mix well. When this happens, the user has little recourse. Thus, these tools are often useful when prototyping a new model, but are not as efficient as the routines that are optimized for particular models.

In Sects. 16.3.2 and 16.3.3, we focus on the application of routines for specific models and priors, focusing on two functions from the `MCMCpack` package in R.

16.3.2 Bayesian Analysis for the Linear Model with MCMCpack

We begin by replicating the analysis of Sect. 16.2.4, using the `MCMCregress()` function from the `MCMCpack`. While this section is most useful for R users, we also think that seeing the process and syntax of modern Bayesian analysis will be useful for readers who use other tools.

We will assume that the reader has installed R and knows how to get to the R console. To use the `MCMCpack` package, it first must be installed in using the command `install.packages("MCMCpack")`. This only needs to be done once; after that, each time the `MCMCpack` package is used it has to be loaded using the command `library(MCMCpack)`. These commands are typed into the R console as:

```
> install.packages('MCMCpack')# only needed once for each R installation
> library(MCMCpack)
```

Next, the data from Sect. 16.2.4 is loaded into the data frame `exdata` using the command `read.csv()`.

```
>   exdata <- read.csv("BayesChapData.csv", header=TRUE)
```

After that the `MCMCregress()` function can be called to produce a set of posterior draws from the model.

```
>   post1 <- MCMCregress(Yi ~ Xi - 1, data=exdata[1:10,],
+                        b0=0, B0=1/100, sigma.mu=400, sigma.var=1000000,
+                        burnin=1000, mcmc=10000, seed=20030601,
+                        marginal.likelihood="Chib95")
```

The command above runs the MCMC algorithm to produce the posterior draws and then puts these draws in an object called `post1`. This function call looks a bit daunting, because there are a number of inputs required for the algorithm, but they correspond exactly to the inputs we discussed in Sect. 16.2.4. The inputs on the first line describe the linear model that we want to estimate, which is `Yi~Xi-1`, meaning we want to regress `Yi` on `Xi` without an intercept (`-1`) resulting in the model $Y_i = \beta X_i + \epsilon_i$ where $\epsilon_i \sim N(0, \sigma^2)$. (Model formulas like this are a standard part of R syntax and are used in most modeling functions.) `data=exdata[1:10,]` tells the function to look for `Yi` and `Xi` in the first 10 rows of the exdata object; that is, we want to compute the posterior based on only the first 10 observations.

The next line indicates the parameters of a normal prior for the slope and an inverse Gamma for the error variance. The mean and precision (i.e., 1/variance) for the normal prior are specified as `b0=0` and `B0=1/100` meaning our prior on the slope is normal with mean 0 and variance 100, as it was in Sect. 16.2.4. Similarly, the prior on the error variance is specified in terms of the mean and variance of the inverse Gamma (`sigma.mu=400` and `sigma.var=1000000`). Although many routines including `MCMCregress()` will use default priors when the user does not specify a prior, we highly recommend that the user specify priors explicitly, as this is an important part of Bayesian analysis. It is also a limitation of these types of tools that you can not specify a prior with a different distributional form such as a uniform prior. Priors with different distributional forms would lead to different full conditional distributions and different code.

The third line in the command above specifies how many posterior draws should be produced by the MCMC algorithm, i.e., how many times we should repeat the Gibbs sampling steps. In this case, we have specified that the algorithm should first produce $B = 1000$ burn-in draws and then $G - B = 10{,}000$ more draws that we will use for analyzing the posterior. Since this is a stochastic algorithm, it will produce a slightly different set of posterior draws any time it is called. We prevent this by setting a specific random number seed (`seed=20030601`), which ensures that we will get repeatable results from the stochastic MCMC algorithm. This is a good practice when testing the computations across runs for the same model.

Finally, on the last line, we indicate that we want to compute the log marginal likelihood, which is the same as "log integrated likelihood" or LIL, using the method of Chib (1995). This will allow us to do model comparisons later.

We can examine the first few rows of the draws in `post1` using the `head()` function.

```
>   head(post1)
```

```
Markov Chain Monte Carlo (MCMC) output:
```

```
Start = 1001
End = 1007
Thinning interval = 1
          Xi       sigma2
[1,] 5.961533 294.5271
[2,] 7.646806 356.6829
[3,] 6.462444 114.9422
[4,] 6.631381 315.2794
[5,] 7.091786 347.9395
[6,] 4.944335 221.2036
[7,] 5.326958 177.9925
```

We can see that `post1` now contains draws for the slope (labeled `Xi`, which is shorthand for "the coefficient on X_i", i.e., β) and the error variance (labeled `sigma2`, i.e., σ^2). Each row represents one draw from the posterior distribution produced by one iteration of the MCMC algorithm.

With these posterior draws in hand, we can use them to investigate the posterior of the parameters. For example, we can use the `plot()` command to produce the plot in Fig. 16.4.

```
>   plot(post1)
```

The resulting plot appears in in a separate window in R. Quick inspection of the traceplots in Fig. 16.4 suggests that the chain converged and is producing draws from the posterior. The density plots give us a nice visualization of the posterior

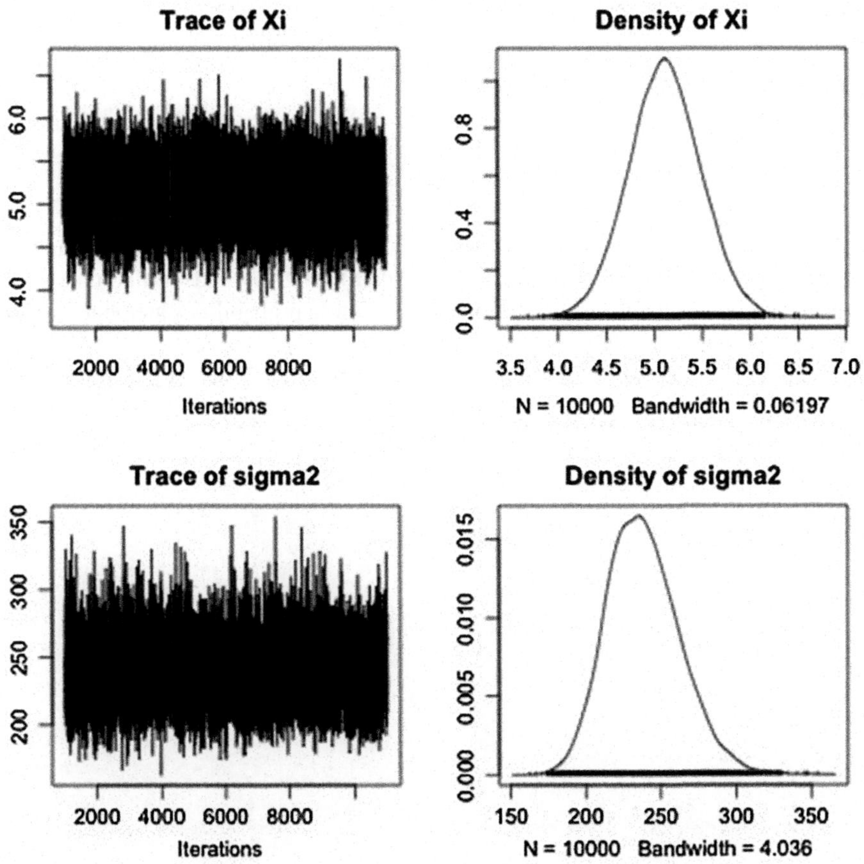

Fig. 16.4 Plots of MCMC draws produced by R

distribution for the model parameters, akin to the histograms in Fig. 16.4. To produce an autocorrelation plot like that in Fig. 16.3, we use the command:

```
>   acf(post1)
```

We can also compute summaries of the draws. For example, to understand the posterior of β we can compute the mean and the standard deviation of the draws in the `Xi` column:

```
>   mean(post1[,"Xi"])
     [1] 5.316856
>   sd(post1[,"Xi"])
     [1] 1.552501
```

The results that we get are comparable to the first column in Table 16.1, although they are not exactly the same; because the MCMC algorithms that produce the draws are stochastic, you will get a slightly different answer each time unless you set a random number seed. We can estimate the probability that the parameter β is greater than zero or greater than 5, simply by counting the number of posterior draws in `post1` that exceed the threshold.

```
>   mean(post1[,"Xi"]>0)
     [1] 0.999
>   mean(post1[,"Xi"]>5)
     [1] 0.5904
```

Based on the posterior draws produced by `MCMCregress()` we are highly confident that β is greater than zero ($p(\beta > 0|\text{ data}) \approx 0.999$), and we find that there is a 59.04% chance that β is greater than 5. Note these probability statements are all conditional on our model, priors and data.

While we can continue to summarize the draws using standard R functions, `MCMCpack` provides a convenient function for summarizing all the draws in `post1`:

```
>   summary(post1)

Iterations = 1001:11000
Thinning interval = 1
Number of chains = 1
Sample size per chain = 10000

1. Empirical mean and standard deviation for each variable,
   plus standard error of the mean:
                    Mean          SD Naive       SE             Time-series SE
Xi                  5.317         1.553          0.01553               0.01553
sigma2  245.698   114.523         1.14523        1.20311

2. Quantiles for each variable:
                2.5%        25%          50%           75%          97.5%
Xi              2.189       4.337        5.329         6.326        8.393
sigma2        109.162     169.630      218.557       291.200      539.307
```

While at first glance this might look like the output from a frequentist regression package (e.g., `lm()`), closer inspection reveals some important differences. First, the summary output tells you a bit about the MCMC algorithm that produced the draws. In this case, it reminds us that we have 10,000 draws, which were taken from iterations 1001 to 11000 of the MCMC chain. This can be useful when diagnosing problems with the MCMC algorithm. After that, the summary output gives us the mean and standard deviation of the posteriors for each parameter (similar to Table 16.2 in the previous section). The `Naive SE` and the `Time-series SE` tell us how close the MCMC approximation of the posterior mean is to the true Bayes estimator; the fact that the `Naive SE` and the `Time-series SE` are similar reflects that fact that the chain has little autocorrelation. In the lower panel, the summary output also shows quantiles for the posterior draws for each parameter.

Up to this point, we have been summarizing the posterior separately for the two parameters, but we should point out that the posterior is multidimensional, that is, each draw from the sampler is a multidimensional vector from the posterior. This means that we can scatter plot the posterior draws for β (i.e., the coefficient on `Xi`) against the posterior draws for σ^2:

```
>   plot(x=as.vector(post1[,"Xi"]), y=as.vector(post1[,"sigma2"]),
    + xlab="Posterior draw of beta", ylab="Posterior draw of sigma2")
```

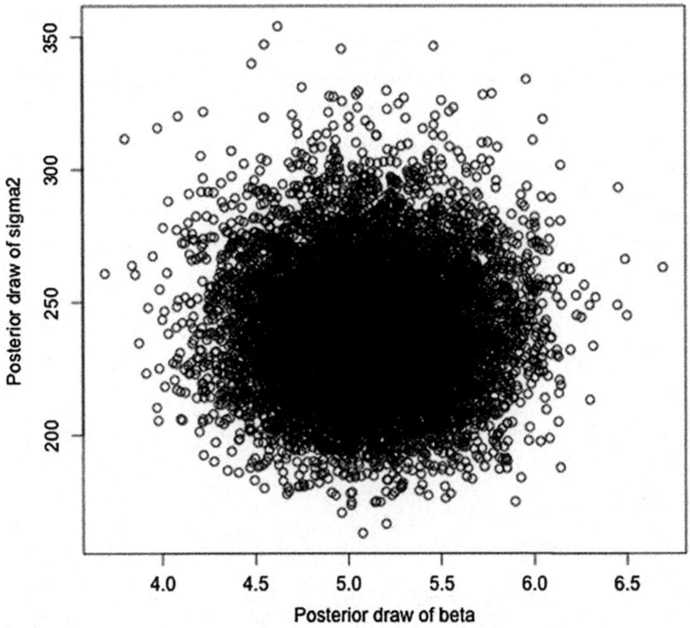

Fig. 16.5 Scatterplot of posterior draws shows that the posterior for the two parameters is not correlated

The resulting plot is shown in Fig. 16.5.

It can also be useful to compute the posterior correlation between the two parameters, which can be done using the `cor()` function in R:

```
>   cor(post1)
               Xi            sigma2
Xi             1.00000000    -0.03596884
sigma2        -0.03596884     1.00000000
```

In this case, the posterior correlation is near zero, meaning that our posterior beliefs about the parameters are independent. However, for other models and data, we may find strong posterior correlations between the parameters. For instance, if we have two independent variables in the regression that are highly correlated with each other, i.e., we have multicollinearity, this will result in posterior correlations between the coefficients on those two independent variables. Put another way, if two independent variables are highly correlated, the data does not provide information about which of those two is affecting the outcome, and so the posterior will reflect the fact that it could be that the first covariate affects the outcome and not the second, or vice versa, or somewhere in between. So, it is a good practice to compute the posterior correlations and investigate any that are unusually large.

We can repeat the key steps in Bayesian analysis by fitting a different model to the same data and then summarizing the posterior draws. For the second model, we estimate a linear regression that includes an intercept (whereas in the previous model, we assumed that intercept was zero.) We do this by removing the "−1" from the model formula. Note that producing the draws and then summarizing them requires just 5 lines of R code.

```
> post2 <- MCMCregress(Yi ~ Xi, data=exdata[1:10,],
  + b0=0, B0=1/100, sigma.mu=400, sigma.var=1000000,
  + burnin=1000, mcmc=10000,
  + marginal.likelihood="Chib95")
> summary(post2)
  Iterations = 1001:10991
  Thinning interval = 10
  Number of chains = 1
  Sample size per chain = 1000

1. Empirical mean and standard deviation for each variable,
   plus standard error of the mean:
              Mean      SD  Naive SE  Time-series SE
(Intercept)  5.518   4.204   0.13293         0.13293
Xi           5.636   1.535   0.04854         0.04854
sigma2     224.149 102.100   3.22869         3.22869

2. Quantiles for each variable:
              2.5%     25%      50%      75%    97.5%
(Intercept) -2.884   3.079    5.589    8.064   13.601
Xi           2.502   4.628    5.664    6.618    8.664
sigma2      99.468 154.139  202.680  265.658  487.224
```

The output of `summary()` shows that the posterior draws for the intercept which was added to the model ranges from the 2.5% quartile at −2.884 to the 97.5% quartile at 13.601, so there is posterior support for zero, which was the true value of the intercept used to generate the data. Our posteriors for β and σ^2 have also shifted somewhat between the first model and the second.

Once there are two models, a natural question is, "Which model is better?" We can compare the two models using the Bayesian approach to model comparison described in Sect. 16.2.5. `MCMCpack` provides a function called `BayesFactor()`, which takes as input the two posterior draws objects and reports the log marginal likelihood for each model. Note that the log marginal likelihood was actually computed when we ran `MCMCregress()` and is stored in the `post1` and `post2` objects. This happened because we included the input `marginal.likelihood="Chib95"` in `MCMCregress()`. `MCMCregress()` provides several other approaches to computing the marginal likelihood that are outside the scope of this chapter. `BayesFactor()` recovers the stored log marginal likelihood for each model and reports the original call to `MCMCregress()` in the lower half of the output.

```
> BayesFactor(post1, post2)
The matrix of Bayes Factors is:
          post1     post2
post1     1.00      0.933
post2     1.07      1.000

The matrix of the natural log Bayes Factors is:
        post1       post2
post1   0.0000     -0.0689
post2   0.0689      0.0000

 post1 :
   call =
MCMCregress(formula = Yi ~ Xi - 1, data = exdata[1:10, ], burnin = 1000,
      mcmc = 10000, seed = 20030601, b0 = 0, B0 = 1/100, sigma.mu = 400,
      sigma.var = 1e+06, marginal.likelihood = "Chib95")

      log marginal likelihood =  -42.98895

 post2 :
   call =
MCMCregress(formula = Yi ~ Xi, data = exdata[1:10, ], burnin = 1000,
      mcmc = 10000, thin = 10, b0 = 0, B0 = 1/100, sigma.mu = 400,
      sigma.var = 1e+06, marginal.likelihood = "Chib95")

      log marginal likelihood =  -42.92005
```

In this case, we can see that the log marginal likelihoods are similar for both models (–42.98895 versus –42.92005). Following the rules from Sect. 16.2.5, we would choose the second model that includes the intercept. Even though this is not the true model, this is hard to discern with just 10 data points. As its name suggests, the output of `BayesFactor()` also reports the Bayes factor, which is simply the ratio of the marginal likelihoods of the two models. In this case, the Bayes factor comparing the second model to the first is 1.07, which suggests that we have very weak evidence in favor of the model with the intercept (based on these 10 data points).

A more realistic model comparison might use more data. If we repeat this analysis with 200 simulated data points, the log marginal likelihood is higher for the model that does not include the intercept (−835.3955 versus −837.0764, Bayes factor of 5.37). (We leave computing posterior samples and log-marginal likelihoods with more data as an exercise for the reader.) Following the rules specified in Sect. 16.2.5 again, we would choose the first model (which was the true model used to generate the data). Similarly, if we compute the log marginal likelihood for a model with strong priors that are inconsistent with the data such as a mean on β of 10 with a variance of 1/100 (precision of 100), we will obtain a much lower log marginal likelihood of −893.6426 with a Bayes factor of 58.2 versus the first model, suggesting we have strong evidence that our first model is more consistent with the data than a model with tight priors on β centered at 10.

By this point we hope to have convinced the reader that it is relatively simple to use packages like MCMCpack to conduct Bayesian analysis. In fact, much of the software is sufficiently well-developed, that Bayesian estimation of common models is no more difficult than frequentist analysis. In many ways, the commands and output are very similar and easy-to-learn. The greater challenge is in learning to think about data analysis in the Bayesian way.

Some readers may want to know exactly what is happening when MCMCregress() is called. For those readers, we provide a bit of R code illustrating how the Gibbs sampler described in Sect. 16.2.4.1 is translated to R code. We use the same notation for the priors as used in the inputs to MCMCregress(), so one could imagine that this is what the code looks like "inside" the MCMCregress() function. MCMCregress() is actually implemented in C to speed computation and would contain a lot more error checking, but the code below gives the general sense of how the Gibbs sampler is constructed. The only tricky bit is that R uses a different parameterization for the Gamma distribution than the one we described in Sect. 16.2.

```
# Code for Gibbs Sampler
draws.beta <- rep(NA, mcmc)# storage for draws
draws.sigma2 <- rep(NA, mcmc)# storage for draws
beta <- 0
sigma2 <- 1
for (i in 1:(burnin+mcmc)) {

      # Draw beta conditional on sigma2
      v2 <- (B0 + sum(Xi*Xi)/sigma2)^(-1)
      b  <- v2*(b0*B0 + sum(Xi*Yi)/sigma2)
      beta <- rnorm(1, mean=b, sd=sqrt(v2))
      # Draw sigma2 conditional on beta
      r0 <- sigma.mu^2/sigma.var + 4
      s0 <- (r0-2)*sigma.mu
      r  <- r0 + length(Yi)# r0 computed from sigma.mu and sigma.var
      s  <- s0 + sum((Yi - beta*Xi)*(Yi - beta*Xi))

      # note R uses a different parameterization of the Gamma
      sigma2 <- s/(2*rgamma(1, shape=r/2, scale=1))

      # After burnin store the draws
      if (i > burnin) {
      draws.beta[i-burnin] <- beta
      draws.sigma2[i-burnin] <- sigma2
      }
}
```

We hope this brief introduction gives the reader a sense of what is involved in developing a Gibbs sampler. Section 16.4 discusses the development of a Gibbs sampler in more detail, but first, Sect. 16.3.3 illustrates the use of another MCMCpack function to estimate a more complex hierarchical model. As we have discussed, one of the great advantages of adopting Bayesian MCMC is that it allows the user to estimate a wide variety of models. This stems from the fact that the

Gibbs sampler is highly modular. This structure makes it easy to build on these simple models, adding features like random coefficients, which are then drawn in another block within the Gibbs sampler. This modularity is what makes it possible to create an algorithm to sample from the posterior for nearly any model using MCMC methods.

16.3.3 Hierarchical Regression with MCMCpack

For our next analysis, we turn to a hierarchical Bayes model, which is one of the models that made Bayesian methods popular in marketing. To illustrate this model, we use data from a conjoint study taken from Lenk et al. (1996). In this study, MBA students were given a series 20 of hypothetical computer profiles described in terms of their various features: was there a help support HotLine, RAM, Screen size, CPU, etc. The students rated each profile on a scale of 1:10. (See Lenk et al. 1996 for more detail.) We can read in the data and inspect the first few rows:

```
>   c.data <- read.csv("ComputerConjointData.csv")
>   head(c.data)

  Question LIKE id HotLine RAM   Screen CPU  HardDisk CD Cache Color
1 1           6  1 yes     small large  fast small    no big   white
2 1           5  2 yes     small large  fast small    no big   white
3 1          10  3 yes     small large  fast small    no big   white
4 1          10  4 yes     small large  fast small    no big   white
5 1           8  5 yes     small large  fast small    no big   white
6 1           3  6 yes     small large  fast small    no big   white

  Channel           Warranty  Software  Guarantee  Price
1 mail-order        long      yes       yes        no
2 mail-order        long      yes       yes        no
3 mail-order        long      yes       yes        no
4 mail-order        long      yes       yes        no
5 mail-order        long      yes       yes        no
6 mail-order        long      yes       yes        no
```

These first 6 rows show the ratings of the first 6 respondents for the first computer profile. The `LIKE`-variable, at least in principle, may range from 0 to 10.

```
>   summary(c.data$LIKE)

Min.   1st Qu.  Median  Mean   3rd Qu.  Max.    NA's
0.000  3.000    5.000   4.773  7.000    10.000  22
```

Our analysis goal is to determine the relationship between the features of the computers and the ratings. A natural model for this data is a linear model where the ratings are a function of the features of each product. The 1–10 scale for likelihood of purchase is sufficiently granular that we treat it as a continuous variable instead of an ordinal one. In specifying our model, we will assume that respondent i's rating for profile j is a function of the vector of computer features, x_j, times a vector of parameters, β_i, plus a normally distributed error term:

$$y_{ij} = \beta_i x_j + \epsilon_{ij} \quad (16.39)$$

$$\epsilon_{ij} \sim N\left(0, \sigma^2\right). \quad (16.40)$$

To simplify notation, we assume that x_i includes a column of 1's to represent the intercept. Lenk et al. (1996) also allow the error variance to depend on the subject, thus accommodating subject-specific scale usage in their ratings.

We also believe that different survey respondents may find different features more or less important and may use the ratings scale differently. For instance, just inspecting the data, we find that the mean of the ratings provided by respondent 4 is 4.865, while the mean for respondent 9 is 2.75 (not shown), which strongly suggests that respondents are using the scale differently. Thus we assume a probability model for ratings that allows for each respondent to have his or her own coefficient vector, β_i, which we will assume is multivariate normally distributed across students:

$$\beta_i \sim N_k\left(\mu_\beta, V_\beta\right) \quad (16.41)$$

where μ is a mean vector and V is a covariance matrix. To complete the model, we specify distributions[12] for the unknowns σ^2, μ and V:

$$\sigma^2 \sim IG\left(\nu, 1/\delta\right) \quad (16.42)$$

$$\mu_\beta \sim N_k\left(\mu_0, V_0\right) \quad (16.43)$$

$$V \sim IW\left(r, rR\right) \quad (16.44)$$

where IW is the inverse Wishart distribution, which is a multivariate generalization of the inverse Gamma distribution.

[12] Some Bayesians refer to the distribution on $\beta_i|\mu_\beta, V_\beta$ as the "prior" and the distributions $\mu|\mu_0, V_0$ and $V|r, R$ as "hyperpriors." Others view $\beta_i|\mu_\beta, V_\beta$ as part of the random-coefficients "model." While this occasionally causes some confusion among Bayesians, the difference is unimportant in practice, as both the probability model and the priors should be carefully considered and should represent the analyst's subjective beliefs. In this chapter we have avoided making a strong distinction between models and prior.

MCMCpack provides a Gibbs sampler for drawing posterior samples from this model. We can access it by calling MCMChregress, where the additional "h" stands for hierarchical.

```
c.post <- MCMChregress(fixed = LIKE ~ . - Question - id,
    random = ~ . - Question - id - LIKE,
    group="id", data=c.data,
    burnin=1000, mcmc=10000, thin=10,
    mu.zero=0, V.zero=1000000, r=14, R=diag(0.5, 14),
    nu=0.001, delta=0.001)$mcmc
```

Again, we have to specify which variables to include in the regression, and which of those we want to be "random" or heterogeneous across the population. We do this with the R formula notation LIKE ~ . − Question − id, which is shorthand for "use all the variables in the data as independent variables except Question and id." To complete the model specification, we also have to specify which variable describes the grouping in the data (i.e., the index i.) For this analysis, we group by student, which is stored in the variable id. As before, we also specify the number of burn-in draws (burnin) and number of MCMC draws (mcmc). We also specify a new input called thin, which tells the function to store the draw from every 10th iteration of the sampler. Finally, on the last two input lines specify the parameters of the priors using the same notation as above (i.e., mu.zero means μ_0).

This sampler takes much, much longer to run and when we inspect the result we can see why. If we inspect the dimensions of the output, we can see that there are 1000 rows and 3026 columns.

```
>   dim(c.post)
    [1] 1000 3026
```

The 1000 rows represent the 1000 draws that the sampler stored (10,000 thinned to every 10th draw). The 3026 columns represent the large number of parameters that have been drawn by the sampler: 14 β_i parameters for each of 201 respondents, 14 parameters in μ, $14 \times 14 = 196$ parameters in V, one parameter for σ^2 and one column to store the deviance.

As you can see, the Bayesian machinery works fine, albeit a bit slowly when there are a large number of parameters. Thinning is not necessary, but it reduces the requirements for storing the draws and the computational cost of computing any posterior integrals over the draws.

We can summarize the draws in parts, using a bit of R code to pull out the columns from c.post with particular names. For instance, the posterior draws for μ_β are in columns that include the prefix "beta" in the name and can be obtained and summarized as follows:

```
>   summary(c.post[,grep("beta.", dimnames(c.post)[[2]])])


Iterations = 1001:10991
Thinning interval = 10
Number of chains = 1
Sample size per chain = 1000

1. Empirical mean and standard deviation for each variable,
   plus standard error of the mean:

                              Mean       SD         Naive SE       Time-series SE
beta.(Intercept)              5.94332    0.3422     0.010821       0.010821
beta.HotLineyes               0.21166    0.2014     0.006369       0.006369
beta.RAM8MB                  -0.59332    0.1912     0.006047       0.006047
beta.Screen17in               0.36779    0.1873     0.005922       0.005922
beta.CPU50MHz                -0.84812    0.1933     0.006112       0.005282
beta.HardDisk730MB            0.28345    0.1899     0.006006       0.006006
beta.CDyes                    0.95711    0.1937     0.006126       0.006126
beta.Cache256MB               0.09340    0.1848     0.005844       0.005844
beta.Colorblack              -0.02387    0.1844     0.005830       0.005830
beta.Channelstore             0.21310    0.1886     0.005963       0.005963
beta.Warranty5yr             -0.26236    0.1979     0.006258       0.005079
beta.Softwarenot_bundled     -0.37268    0.1929     0.006099       0.006407
beta.Guaranteenone           -0.22805    0.1981     0.006266       0.006266
beta.Price$3500              -2.28038    0.1848     0.005844       0.005844
```

These parameters represent the population average effect of each feature on the ratings of the computers. For instance, adding a CD drive (`beta.CDyes`) increases the rating on average by 0.95711, while increasing the price to $3500 (from $2000) decreases the rating on average by −2.28038.

The sampler has also stored posterior draws of $\beta_i - \mu_\beta$ for each of the 201 students who answered the survey. That is, the sampler records the posterior draws of the deviation of each student from the population average. We can inspect the posterior mean and standard deviation for `id` 152:

```
>   summary(c.post[,grep(".152", dimnames(c.post)[[2]])])


Iterations = 1001:10991
Thinning interval = 10
Number of chains = 1
Sample size per chain = 1000

1. Empirical mean and standard deviation for each variable,
   plus standard error of the mean:

                              Mean       SD         Naive SE       Time-series SE
b.(Intercept).152             0.31102    1.0091     0.03191        0.03423
b.HotLineyes.152             -0.92546    0.6278     0.01985        0.02190
b.RAM8MB.152                  0.74625    0.5821     0.01841        0.01745
b.Screen17in.152             -0.02246    0.5498     0.01739        0.01832
b.CPU50MHz.152                0.13130    0.5785     0.01829        0.01829
b.HardDisk730MB.152           0.45989    0.5899     0.01865        0.01973
b.CDyes.152                  -0.36206    0.5786     0.01830        0.01920
b.Cache256MB.152              0.49790    0.6082     0.01923        0.01923
b.Colorblack.152             -0.57249    0.5499     0.01739        0.01821
b.Channelstore.152           -0.17108    0.5655     0.01788        0.01942
b.Warranty5yr.152             0.29848    0.6195     0.01959        0.01959
b.Softwarenot_bundled.152     0.01725    0.5498     0.01739        0.01830
b.Guaranteenone.152           0.34028    0.6071     0.01920        0.01920
b.Price$3500.152              0.50154    0.5904     0.01867        0.01867
```

Looking at the individual-level estimates for student 152, we can see that his/her coefficient for `b.Price$3500` is 0.50154, which means that their ratings are less sensitive to price on average. We would expect this respondent's ratings to drop by $0.50154 + (-2.28038) = -1.77884$ when the price goes up to $3500. Similarly, respondent 152 is more sensitive to the RAM than the population average and prefers the beige `Color` to black. The posterior standard errors are also large for the respondent-level parameters, reflecting our greater posterior uncertainty about how specific features affect respondent 152's ratings, versus how they affect the population on average.

Finally, we can also inspect the posterior means and standard deviations for the parameters in V and for σ^2. In the interest of conserving space, we omit the results.

```
>   summary(c.post[,grep("VCV.", dimnames(c.post)[[2]])])
>   summary(c.post[,grep("sigma2", dimnames(c.post)[[2]])])
```

Having obtained this posterior sample for the model parameters using `MCMChregress`, we can proceed with other aspects of Bayesian analysis including hypothesis testing and making probability statements about parameters or other quantities of interest. For instance, to predict what rating student number 152 would give to a new computer, we first create the new computer. For convenience, we will take the computer that is listed in the 1003rd row of the original data. We also convert that to a coded x vector using the R function `model.matrix()`, which codes out factor variables.

```
>   new.comp <- c.data[1003,4:16]
>   new.comp

       HotLine    RAM          Screen     CPU        HardDisk   CD      Cache
1003   yes        16MB         14in       100MHz     730MB      no      128MB
       Color      Channel      Warranty   Software   Guarantee  Price
       black      mail-order   3yr        bundled    none       $3500

>   x <- model.matrix(~ ., data=new.comp)
>   x

(Intercept)  HotLineyes  RAM8MB  Screen17in  CPU50MHz  HardDisk730MB   CDyes  Cache256MB
Colorblack
1003            1          0       0           0        1              0       0     1
    Channelstore Warranty5yr Softwarenot_bundled Guaranteenone Price$3500
1003 0           0           0                   1             1
```

Next, to compute the posterior predictive distribution for the rating that student 152 would give to this computer, we take a draw from the normal distribution for the rating that conditions on the parameters β and σ^2.The key to this calculation is that we do it for *each of the saved draws* in `c.post`.

```
>    rating.post <- rep(NA, nrow(c.post)) # storage for new draws
>    for (j in 1:nrow(c.post)) {
      + beta.ij <- c.post[j, grep(".152", dimnames(c.post)[[2]])] +
      + c.post[j, grep("beta.", dimnames(c.post)[[2]])] # beta for
        id 152
      + sigma2.j <- c.post[j,grep("sigma2", dimnames(c.post)[[2]])]
      + rating.post[j] <- rnorm(1, mean=sum(beta.ij*x),
        sd=sqrt(sigma2.j))
      + }
>    summary(rating.post)
Min.      1st Qu.   Median   Mean    3rd Qu.   Max.
-3.200    2.512     3.963    4.042   5.603     11.610
```

The result—1000 draws from the posterior predictive distribution for the rating that 152 will give this new computer—can be summarized like any other posterior distribution. In this case, our posterior suggests that the most likely rating is about 4, but there is a fairly large posterior range. Notice that, as we discussed in Sect. 16.2, this prediction accounts for both the posterior uncertainty in the parameters (through the draws) *and* error in the response equation (through the random normal draw with variance σ_j^2.) We can use these draws to make probability statements about the likely values of the rating. For instance, by counting the number of draws that are greater than 7, we can estimate that there is an 11% chance that the student would give this new computer a rating greater than 7.

```
>   mean(rating.post>7)
    [1] 0.11
```

Using the simple process we have illustrated here, the analyst can produce samples for any function of the parameters and then use those samples to test hypotheses and make probability statements about those unknown quantities.

In this section, we have:

1. demonstrated how researchers use the simulated draws from MCMC to make inferences;
2. introduced Hierarchical Bayes models that have become standard tools in both academic and commercial research, and
3. illustrated software for estimating these models with MCMC.

It goes beyond the scope of this section to study how MCMC samples are constructed. An online appendix shows how Gibbs samplers are constructed for:

- the linear model with one coefficient;
- the linear model with instrumental variables, and
- a Heckman selection model.

The appendix on Gibbs Sampling can be downloaded from http://www.modelingmarkets.com.

16.4 Applications of Bayesian Inference in Marketing

16.4.1 Introduction

Bayesian methods were brought into marketing among others to address an important, ubiquitous problem: finding a way to incorporate parametric heterogeneity, i.e., not forcing every customer to have the same set of parameters. This was (and is) considered critical because we know from vast experience that different people *respond* differently to various stimuli—in particular, marketing stimuli—like advertising, in-store promotion, displays, coupons, not to mention "environmental" factors that marketers cannot control directly, like the state of the economy. And coefficients allow us to represent how a target consumer responds (y) to a change in some observable (x), which in turn allows us to try to *optimize* our marketing expenditures conditional on real-world data and a suitably flexible model. Although heterogeneity was representable, usually using a latent class approach (Kamakura and Russell 1989) well before the advent of Bayesian methods in marketing, estimation was tedious and often unsuccessful, due to convergence problems and local maxima. It's no exaggeration to say that Bayesian methods revolutionized our ability to accurately, flexibly model individual consumers' reaction to marketing and fine-tune marketing programs using available data.

A full coverage of Bayesian methods and applications used in academic marketing would take a book. And in fact, such a book exists, the aptly titled "Bayesian Statistics and Marketing", by Rossi et al. (2012), which covers the application of Bayesian methodology to statistical issues arising in marketing, although at a level that would make it more suitable for "second course" in Bayesian methods than an introduction. The book is accompanied by an R package, `bayesm`, frequently updated by the authors, and allowing users to avail of code for some of the most common models in the marketing literature, including Bayesian Regression (with multivariate DVs); SUR; binary/ordinal probit; multinomial logit (MNL) and probit (MNP); multivariate probit (MVP); mixtures of normals; Dirichlet process prior density estimation; a suite of hierarchical models (linear, MNL, NBD); choice-based conjoint; linear IV models; scale usage heterogeneity; BLP type models; and more. This may look like alphabet soup to the uninitiated reader, but the acronyms indicate a model whose worth has been vetted through frequent use. Below, we will introduce many of these, but the point is that new users can already avail of a suite of code to run models that appeared relatively recently in the marketing literature.

Our purpose in this section is to discuss how Bayesian methods have been *used* in marketing, and as such our treatment will be largely non-technical. Academic research prides itself on pushing the bar as far as technology (usually, processing speed) will allow, and by now many of the methods being applied have derivations that seem complex even to experts. As such, we will try to give a feel for how the actual "modeling" goes—what is being captured, what is being estimated—but not the fearsome notation or full conditional derivations that allow the Bayesian magic to happen.

16.4.2 Hierarchical Models and "HB" (Hierarchical Bayes)

We start with one of the most powerful and common methods used throughout social science: hierarchical models. The interested reader will find a host of dedicated books on this topic alone, including the classic by Raudenbush and Bryk (2002), as well as a host of more recent treatments, some with substantial Bayesian content, like Gelman and Hill (2006). There are many ways to introduce hierarchical modeling, but for our purposes, we can focus on *Hierarchical Bayes models*, which are simply "hierarchical" models estimated using Bayesian techniques. As the name would imply, such models posit a "hierarchy" of effects, and thereby have "levels", often called "Level 1", "Level 2", etc. The key insight is that we have already seen many examples of such "Level 1" models, which in marketing specifically are usually regression models for each individual (where "regression" can mean *any* form of regression, as in Generalized Linear Models, discrete choice models, etc.) So, in marketing, we are usually fixated on "Level 1" being the individual, usually the consumer.

And therein lies the problem: we have no realistic way of using data on just one consumer to estimate that consumer's parameters! Imagine a typical scenario arising in by far the most common modeling application in marketing: the analysis of supermarket scanner data (usually from a *panel* of consumers who have agreed to have their purchases tracked over time). We might have, over the course of several years, data on a few dozen purchases of most product types, with perishable (but often non-branded) items like milk and eggs being bought on most such trips, and stockable branded items like coffee or sugar being bought far less frequently. The marketing analyst wishes to relate a huge number of variables, often numbering in the hundreds—prices, promotion levels, shelf displays, coupon activity, circular features, local advertising levels, time of store visit, general economic activity, etc.—to a particular consumer's choices among what could be tens or even hundreds of options (e.g., in breakfast cereals or frozen entrees). How would it be possible to estimate these hundreds of parameters, including "fixed effects" for each brand, based on a relative handful of shopping outcomes in a specific category for that particular consumer? To relate it back to simple regression, what would you do if you had 20 outcomes but needed to estimate 300 coefficients? We simply don't want to give up.

This is where hierarchical models come in. Our Level 1 model is for each particular consumer, but we can unify and unite them by "going up a level" to Level 2, *which gives us a model for the coefficients themselves.*

To make things concrete and simple, consider a model with just two such levels, a lower and a higher, although there can be any number in practice. As mentioned earlier, our (lower) "Level 1" can be any type of regression, so assume it's just a linear regression, with one covariate, and all the "usual assumptions" (like the ones laid out earlier in this chapter); that is:

$$y_i = \alpha_j + \beta_j x_i + \varepsilon_i. \quad (16.45)$$

Our task would be to estimate a separate slope (β_j) and intercept (α_j) for each individual, j (we denote observations by i, individuals by j). Even with just one covariate, estimating two quantities per individual would be inadvisable, due to instability, if we had (say) just three observations per person, or perhaps even more for just some people. Instead of saying "our data are inadequate", hierarchical approaches leverage a key idea: one can write a *model* linking up each person's parameters. Such a model can be as simple as another regression, and so might look like the following, where z_j is a vector of information about individual j, like her income, age, years of education, etc.:

$$\beta_j = \varphi z_j + \delta_j. \tag{16.46}$$

What this does is relate an individual's slope (β_j), to a coefficient (φ) and error (δ) *that do not vary across the population.* In this way, we have "projected" the large number of slopes—one for each individual—onto a much smaller "space" of values: φ and an estimated variance for δ. This is called *slope heterogeneity*, and not only tells us that the slopes β_j vary across individuals (j), but tries to relate that variation to some facts about those people (z_j). We would also ideally try to explain *intercept heterogeneity* as well, using a model for α_j as well.Hierarchical models have become widely used tools in marketing for at least three reasons:

- they assign different coefficients to each customers—that is, heterogeneity—even when we cannot estimate separate regressions for each;
- they help explain *patterns* in heterogeneity: which aspects of consumers are related to their marketing sensitivities;
- they "borrow" information for other customers to obtain better estimates ("shrinkage") for a target customer.

The third point bears closer scrutiny. Suppose we have a new customer, about whom we have no data at all, but want to know how receptive she might be to an offer for a new credit card. If we know some demographic information about her—age, income, location, education, marital status, etc.—we could use our Level 2 model to provide a *confidence interval* for her receptiveness (i.e., coefficient) to the offer. Since we are Bayesians, we would also be able to *update* that sensitivity once we observed some data about her reactions to other offers she receives. The uncertainty in the estimate would come from the variance of the Level 2 "error" (δ) distribution, to which we turn our attention in the following subsection.

Estimating hierarchical models can be challenging, particularly when there are many "random coefficients" in the Level 2 (or higher) model and one also wishes to allow them to covary, so that an empirical covariance matrix must be calculated. Such matrices can have an enormous number of entries, roughly on the order of the number of random coefficients squared (divided by 2). Frequentist (i.e., non-Bayesian) methods, even specialized algorithms, can have trouble with such high-dimensional estimation, getting stuck at local maxima. While Bayesian estimation isn't immune to such issues, the Bayesian analyst can use the prior or—if relying on Metropolis-Hastings or other "tunable" methods of hopping about the posterior distribution—the search algorithm itself to visit far-flung regions of the parameter space.

Bayesian methods have therefore become by far the most common path to estimating complex marketing models involving parametric heterogeneity. Surveying the various applications of "HB" (Hierarchical Bayes) methods even in quantitative marketing in the past decade alone could be the subject of a long review article; readers interested in pioneering applications through the early years of the 21st century will find them detailed by Rossi and Allenby (2003). Instead we focus on providing some sense of the depth and variety of HB applications, to heterogeneity in particular. As mentioned earlier, arguably the first of these was to *conjoint* models. Such models are perhaps the most widely industrially deployed in all of quantitative marketing, having been pioneered in the 1960s in psychometrics and both adapted and refined for marketing applications in the subsequent decade, notably by Paul Green and collaborators. The main idea is confronting lab participants with product descriptions (or mock-ups) that have been carefully designed to allow the analyst to figure out the value, to each participant, of important product attributes, like a tablet's having a dedicated stylus or a car's coming with a built-in navigation system. Two problems immediately confronted the many users of conjoint: time constraints prevented showing many hypothetical products in one lab session; and it was critical to understand not only how much attributes were valued *on average*, but to measure them *for each participant*. Not doing so would completely leave unanswered critical design questions, like whether car buyers favoring sports cars *also* favored red exteriors or leather trim. In other words: understanding heterogeneity. We revisit this central topic in several of the forthcoming sections.

16.4.3 Mixture Models

As mentioned previously, a critical aspect of using and interpreting hierarchical and HB models concerns the "error" (δ) distribution in the Level 2 (or higher) model. One might think that we need explanatory variables (z_j) in our Level 2 model, but this is not so. In the absence of such covariate information, the Level 2 "error" (δ) distribution describes how (but not "why") coefficients are distributed *across the population*. The beauty of this is that the analyst can choose a particular distribution, based on judgment and experience, and this will serve as the "heterogeneity distribution". As we shall see below, this can have many forms. By far the most popular assumption—and one quietly imposed in most non-Bayesian software for hierarchical models—is that all "random coefficients" are described jointly by a multivariate normal distribution (MVN). This is called "continuous heterogeneity", to be contrasted with "discrete heterogeneity" in the form of latent classes. Once the analyst decides which distribution the error should have, estimation (from specialized software or purpose-written code as described in Sects. 16.3 and 16.4) determines the individual-level β_j—each of which has a distribution of its own, as all unknown quantities do in Bayesian estimation—which can then be used to make predictions. These predictions are nearly always superior to those arising from homogeneous (i.e., everyone has the same parameters) models.

Among the first to systematically consider how to accommodate heterogeneity in marketing models were Allenby and Rossi (1998). Their research is an example of *finite mixture models*, a major topic in statistics that is an active topic of study (for more information on mixture models in general, see Lenk and DeSarbo 2000; McLachlan and Peel 2004; Wedel and Kamakura 2000, and Chap. 13). The general idea is that the overall population can be decomposed into several subpopulations, which can be identified using data; but, importantly, which subpopulation a particular data point belongs to can only be inferred probabilistically. That is, classification is not perfect. In marketing, we might wish to break the population into "promotion sensitive" and "promotion insensitive", but realize a particular household doesn't always react to a promotion, or never react to it: it's somewhere in the middle. Bayesian methods are particularly valuable in detecting such mixtures, since they are *latent*: because we cannot observe directly the "sensitivity parameter" of a particular household, we cannot calculate an exact distribution of such values. The Gibbs samplers like those described in Sects. 16.2 and 16.3 can sample for this latent distribution, then sample for the parameters of individual households, then again for the latent distribution, etc., until stable values (of parameters) are achieved for each.

In classical estimation, finding even a modest number of latent classes can be very difficult, due to local maxima and the large parameter space. But Bayesians can avail of what looks like a special trick, one that turns out to be integral to the entire enterprise: which latent class a household falls into can be viewed as *missing data*. We simply don't know the value of this label, and need to infer it. And, because in Bayesian analysis there are only two kinds of quantities—those we observe (data) and those we don't (parameters)—*we can treat these missing latent class labels as parameters*, and simply sample for them. By doing so thousands of times, we can calculate their distribution; but, on each pass of the sampler, we need only sample for a household's coefficients for the latent class it's assigned to on that pass, vastly simplifying calculations. Discrete and continuous heterogeneity can be combined into "finite mixture models", which in most applications look like a group of normal distributions that together characterize the population. Note that the usual normal heterogeneity and latent classes are both special cases of finite mixture models: with first using just one normal in the mixture, the second setting the within-normal covariance matrices to zero. Estimating such normal mixtures can be challenging when the number of components isn't known in advance (which, in general, it is not). But even here, Bayesian methods—nonparametric ones, as discussed later—have been greatly helpful. For example, Kim et al. (2004) showed how to use the Dirichlet Process Prior to *simultaneously* explore different numbers of normal distributions in the mixture, so that a particular (discrete choice) model could be run only once; they apply the method to liquid detergent data, showing how to reduce the large number of revealed "clusters" to four managerially meaningful ones.

16.4.4 Missing Data

Missing data have played a key role in other marketing contexts. In product recommendation systems, one can view items that are not rated as "missing values", to be filled in by some algorithm. A Bayesian approach to this problem was taken by Ying et al. (2006), who extended the Heckman selectivity framework to include ordinal ratings that were heterogeneous across consumers, and used MCMC to "stochastically sample over" a vast number of missing ratings. In this way, the missing data are clearly "informative", in the sense that they are *nonignorable*: estimating a model without them can provide biased estimates of key quantities (for more detail on ignorability in marketing applications, see Zanutto and Bradlow 2006). When missing data are "ignorable"—either "missing completely at random" or "missing at random" in the nomenclature of Little and Rubin (2002)—model estimation can proceed without them, either classically or via Bayesian techniques. When missing data are nonignorable, they must be sampled over somehow, and Bayesian methods provide a powerful, general way to do so. For example, a key task in many marketing applications is *data fusion*: trying to tie together different data sets. If there is overlap in the people appearing in each data set, the goal of data fusion would be to figure out "who is who", to allow the most statistical power in relating the data sets. Gilula et al. (2006) place this problem squarely in the Bayesian tradition by viewing the generic fusion problem as one of making "inferences about the joint distribution of two sets of variables without any direct observations of the joint distribution", when one instead has information for each data set, which contain some common variables allowing them to be linked. They posit a fully Bayesian approach that directly estimates the joint distribution of key marketing quantities, in their case media viewing and product purchase.

A related domain application with deep roots in marketing is trying to join sources of data from experiments and the field, e.g., conjoint studies and actual purchases. Bayesian methods allow such fusion even when the "overlapping" variables are few. For example, Feit et al. (2010) demonstrated an HB-based method for combining choice-based conjoint data with individual-level purchase data to produce preference parameter estimates more consistent with the market than using only the former. Their method works even when there are differences in how the two samples are conducted (e.g., one of them "skews older") and their application to minivan purchases relied on just two common variables to integrate over some two dozen "missing variables" in the conjoint exercise data. Feit et al. (2013) tackled a common problem in data collected across multiple platforms: they exist at different levels of aggregation, merging them for "consumer insights" is nontrivial. They take a Bayesian data-fusion approach that can combine individual-level usage data (available for most digital platforms) with aggregate data on usage over time (available for traditional platforms). They show how such a method can disentangle the unique information from various sources, such as gauging the interplay between online and brick-and-mortar purchasing behavior.

Many of these models could simply not be fit, or estimated with great difficulty, if analysts needed to work with the likelihood only for the observed data. By writing down a model for missing data, and integrating over that missing data, conditional distributions that would have a very ugly, complex form can usually be transformed to "nice" distributions, i.e., those with known, easy-to-sample-from densities. A major advance in this area was the advent of methods that sampled over an *unidentified space*—one in which the "best" parameters can take on many values—and only work out the correct ones later. For example, if one ran a regression using x and $2x$ as independent variables, a classical regression program would say "Error!" Interestingly, in Bayesian estimation, this is possible: one could sample for the coefficients of both x and $2x$, and later "post-process" the results to get the true coefficient of x (in this case, one would add the draws for both variables together, and multiply by 3). This strategy was brought into marketing by Edwards and Allenby (2003), in their analysis of multiple response ("pick any of J") data. Such data are naturally analyzed using a multivariate binomial probit model, which requires the estimation of a covariance matrix with unit-diagonal elements (i.e., a correlation matrix). Such a covariance matrix does not have a conjugate prior, nor a simple, named density (like the Inverse Wishart mentioned earlier in this chapter) to sample from. Instead, the authors proposed simply "making believe" that the diagonal entries were not 1, and imposing that constraint *after* the model was estimated. This has proved to be an enormously powerful insight with broad application within marketing and elsewhere, although one needs to be careful about the role of priors in unidentified models.

16.5 A Selection of Applications of Bayesian Methods in Marketing

16.5.1 Introduction

Among the earliest applications was the study of Lenk and Rao (1990), who took the famous model of Bass (1969) (Chap. 10) and wrote down a (nonlinear) likelihood, combined it with a heterogeneity across new product introductions, and showed that this helped improve early forecasting for such introductions. Talukdar et al. (2002) extended this work by using random effects specification for the three pivotal coefficients coefficients of the Bass model (innovation, imitation, and market potential); a key finding is that the variables included hierarchically (i.e., "observed" heterogeneity)—specifically, macroeconomic covariates—had great explanatory power relative to what was left unexplained ("unobserved" heterogeneity).

In what follows we discuss:

- the analysis of scanner data using HB (Sect. 16.5.2);
- HB and forecasting (Sect. 16.5.3);
- HB and psychometrics (Sect. 16.5.4);
- State-space and hidden Markov models (Sect. 16.5.5).

16.5.2 Scanner Panel Data

Since the landmark article of Guadagni and Little (1983), the analysis of scanner panel data has been among the most fruitful and common in both academic research and managerial application. That article was notable for its masterful work-around for heterogeneity: the creation of "loyalty variables" that tracked the supposed loyalty of each household to each brand and size, over time, using just one *homogeneous* parameter for each. Although these required time-consuming searches for optimal carry-over parameters, it allowed a quick and remarkably effective method to overcome computational difficulties in incorporating *unobserved* parametric heterogeneity. An early explication of these ideas is Blattberg and George (1991), who consider retailers or manufacturers wishing to estimate price or promotional elasticities using scanner data. Recognizing that such elasticities vary considerably among chains and brands, they found that individual models suffered from too little data for sensible estimates to emerge, but homogeneous models missed the all-important variation. They applied shrinkage-based methods that "borrowed" stability across both chains and brands, improving both estimation accuracy and predictive power. The estimation picture changed again due to the advent of HB methods, ushered in by, among others, Allenby and Lenk's (1994) extension of the usual discrete choice model used for scanner data analysis to allow for both autocorrelated errors and consumer heterogeneity, finding both to be substantial in a panel data set on ketchup purchases. Montgomery (1997) followed suit with an HB model for *store-level* scanner data, and allowed demographic variables to help set store-level pricing strategies. Montgomery and Rossi (1999) showed how to estimate price elasticities—a major objective in scanner studies—that are consistent with economic theory or other experience-based beliefs by using a prior distribution, yet another way of using the prior to achieve an important modeling objective.

As the field developed and computational power increased, analysts went beyond merely looking at a single category, focusing on "market basket" analysis. For example, Manchanda et al. (1999) examined purchase incidence using multicategory demand data, modeling them via multivariate probit model; MVP models are notoriously tricky, due to scale identification problems, but was handled here by a Metropolis-Hastings step for the latent error covariance matrix. In a similar vein, Seetharaman et al. (1999) examined how state-dependence—the well-established tendency for consumers to stick with ("inertia") or avoid ("variety-seeking") their last-purchased brand—worked across (five) product categories, using an MNP model and a Bayesian variance components approach to capture the covariation of household state dependence across categories.

As the field progressed, more powerful methods were brought to bear on the very nature of the relationship between marketing variables and outcomes. Such approaches fall under the general rubric of "Bayesian Nonparametrics", which in simple terms are models with a number of parameters that is unknown in advance, estimated by Bayesian methods. Such models allow an arbitrary degree of complexity in various reaction functions—like consumer utility, demand, advertising effects, etc.—that are dictated by the data; larger data sets can lead to the detection of greater complexity. One popular way of accommodating such complexity is the use of *spline* functions, which can take many forms, but most commonly are simple curves (linear, quadratic, etc.) joined up at specific points, called knots, that need to be determined; they can be set by the analyst or determined by the estimation algorithm (see also Chap. 17). In any early application, Kalyanam and Shively (1998) used "stochastic splines" in an HB setting to capture market response functions that may not only be nonlinear, but nonmonotonic, finding substantial irregularities in own-price response for most of the brands examined, including kinks consistent with segmentation effects. Similarly, Kim et al. (2007) used truncated-power-basis splines to estimate individual-level, utility functions in discrete choice models; the method was nonparametric because the number and location of knots was unknown, requiring use of birth-death processes and Bayesian reversible jump methods for estimation. They found substantial non-linearity and some non-monotonicity in consumer utility functions for both conjoint and scanner data applications. This is reminiscent of Shively et al. (2000), who also explored nonparametric approaches to identifying latent relationships in hierarchical models, in particular the covariate specification in the heterogeneity distribution of, also finding evidence of highly nonlinear relationships.

Shortly after the initial development of discrete choice models, a practical problem emerged: it was nonsensical to presume that consumers could acquaint themselves with the characteristics of dozens or hundreds of potential choices, then "crunch the numbers" to arrive at a final, presumably optimal selection from the full set. In a landmark contribution, Swait (1984) put forth a model of *choice set formation*, which built on earlier conceptual and behavioral work on "consideration sets": the subgroup of items that consumers actively focus on when making a choice. Swait's model was computationally costly, due to a combinatorial explosion in the number of possible choice sets for k items, roughly 2^k. It was therefore some time before this critical concept could be incorporated into choice models using Bayesian machinery. Chiang et al. (1998) accommodated heterogeneity in consideration set and brand choice, using MCMC methods, applied to scanner panel data. They demonstrated that ignoring consideration set heterogeneity distorts the estimation of key marketing quantities (e.g., understates marketing mix impact and overstates the importance of preferences and past purchases), even in a fully heterogeneous preference model. This line of work was substantially extended by Van Nierop et al. (2010), who posited a very general framework for consideration set modeling, specifically tailored to capture unobserved consideration from discrete choice data and not subject to the "curse of dimensionality" and amenable to Bayesian estimation. Uncommon for research in this area, they presented experimental data showing that "latent consideration sets" can be reliably retrieved from choice data alone, establishing the validity of Bayesian methods for doing so.

16.5.3 Forecasting

Academic marketing has focused on forecasting—in particular, sales forecasting—since its inception. One of its earliest successes was the Bass (1969) model, which predicted aggregate first-time sales based either on analogous products or a relatively small proportion of eventual sales being observed (see Chap. 10). It was natural that Bayesian methods would be applied to, and ultimately improve, this critical area of marketing practice. This section started by mentioning Lenk and Rao's (1990) extension of the Bass model using Bayesian methods, but they were hardly alone. For example, Neelameghan and Chintagunta (1999) showed how to use Bayesian methods—specifically, a Poisson model with log-normal heterogeneity (i.e., a very early departure from the usual heterogeneity distributional assumptions)—to forecast new product performance both domestically and internationally. Bradlow and Fader (2001) apply Bayesian techniques to forecast the entire lifetime a song spends on the Billboard "Hot 100", using a (generalized gamma) time-series model for ranked items that can incorporate key covariates, like artist history, to capture additional sources of variation across songs and over time. Their model is notable for its flexibility, allowing for exponential, Weibull, lognormal, gamma (etc.) contours for a song to take through the chart, and estimated via MCMC. Similarly, Lee et al. (2003) formulate a Bayesian model for prelaunch sales forecasting of music albums, using a hierarchical logistic diffusion model to integrate various album attributes and marketing variables effects to forecast adoption dynamics. Specialized models have taken advantage of specific data sources to engage in forecasting. For example, Moe and Fader (2002) used advance purchase orders to forecast new product sales, via a hierarchical diffusion framework based on a mixture of Weibulls applied to data from music album sales. It is also possible to use information on what people *say* they will purchase to forecast sales, via so-called "purchase intention" survey measures, although these can be notoriously misleading. Van Ittersum and Feinberg (2010) survey this literature and propose a Bayesian model for "timed intent", where consumers specify when, specifically, they expect to purchase a product over a given horizon, showing that it significantly outpredicts other intent measures. An overview of time series methods in marketing, including Bayesian approaches, is available in Pauwels et al. (2004). While the evidence in favor of accounting for heterogeneity, via Bayesian methods or otherwise, in forecasting is strong, it is not unequivocal: Andrews et al. (2008) applied the widely-accepted SCAN*PRO model to store-level scanner data, using a variety of techniques (e.g., discrete vs. continuous representations of heterogeneity; hierarchical Bayes vs. finite mixture methods), finding that incorporating store-level heterogeneity did *not* improve the accuracy of marketing mix elasticities, and further that fit and forecasting accuracy saw only modest improvements. Similarly, Andrews et al.'s (2011) extensive simulations (and an estimation approach based on simulated likelihood) demonstrated that only one of seven distinct heterogeneity specifications produced more accurate sales response forecasts using store-level data: a random coefficients framework for within-store heterogeneity.

An area of recent especial interest in forecasting is predicting what consumers will do—visit, click on, purchase, rate—in their online activity. Marketers have studied purchase patterns for decades, but the new, rich, individual-level data available from online tracking allows for a far more nuanced understanding of marketing effects than ever before. Bayesian analysis has played a key role in this literature from its inception. Among the most important applications for online firms is simply figuring out, from the sometimes-in-the-millions set of options consumers can access, which they should be shown. That is, what should the firm recommend? Early work used various forms of *collaborative filtering*, the key operative concept being that, if two customers seem to like some of the same items—books, movies, music, etc.—they each might appreciate items the other has also liked, but they haven't tried yet. An initial foray into such "internet recommendation systems" was Ansari et al. (2000a), who posited a Bayesian random coefficients model integrating multiple sources of information relevant to recommendations: expressed preferences, preferences of *other* consumers, expert evaluations, item characteristics, and individual characteristics. Their model showed the value of MCMC methods applied to rich internet-based data for making product recommendations, over the traditional collaborative filtering approach. Bradlow and Schmittlein (2000) developed a proximity model to assess the performance of six Internet search engines, where proximity estimates the distance between each engine and specific URLs. Their approach was notable for providing an estimate of the number of relevant Web pages *not* found by any of the engines (rough half individually and 10% collectively), and examined how a web page's properties affects its likelihood of turning up using particular search phrases. De Bruyn et al. (2008) took a different path, using preference models from conjoint analysis to create decision aids eliciting customer preferences based on simple demographics, product usage, and self-reports, finding such a system offers relevant recommendations quickly and with low customer input. As mentioned earlier, Ying et al. (2006) show that recommendation systems can be improved (by roughly 10% in their movie-based data set) by systematically including information on which items were *not* rated, under the theory that what consumers don't rate offers information about their preferences as well as those they do. Chung et al. (2009) proposed an "adaptive personalization system" for digital audio players, to automatically download personalized playlists of mobile digital music, in real time, with little to no explicit feedback for song preferences on users' parts. At the heart of the model is sophisticated Bayesian machinery: a hazard model for consumer utility for each song; a Bayesian variable selection procedure to select relevant song characteristics; and "Bayesian model averaging", a common and powerful technique to smooth out predictions across multiple models for greater stability and robustness in real-world applications.

16.5.4 HB and Psychometrics

The range of application of Bayesian methods in quantitative marketing is by now nearly the entire field. Almost no area has been immune to its application and enrichment, including some that have very deep historical roots and would be viewed as venerated, mature tools. Perhaps chief among these is SEM, "structural equation models", as detailed in the seminal papers of Bagozzi and Yi (1988) and Fornell and Larcker (1981), or in the modeling-focused review of Steenkamp and Baumgartner (2000). (See also Chap. 11). SEMs have been applied in a staggering variety of contexts in marketing, to model relationships between unobserved constructs and manifest variables, as well as control for measurement error. An early exploration of the possibilities afforded by a Bayesian approach is Ansari et al. (2000b), who pointed out that SEMs treat data as stemming from a homogeneous population, and developed an HB framework for modeling general forms of heterogeneity in partially recursive SEMs. Their method extends the usual random-coefficient framework to accommodate heterogeneity in both mean and covariance structures and to provide individual-specific estimates of the factor scores and structural coefficients, illustrating it using panel satisfaction data. This is an active area of current research, and has been extended, via Bayesian methods to heterogeneous factor models by Ansari et al. (2002), and surveyed generally for multilevel (i.e., hierarchical) SEMs by Jedidi and Ansari (2001). Another venerated psychometric model is *multidimensional scaling*, supported in every major statistical program in its traditional, homogeneous form. In the first of a series of papers greatly expanding the range of applicability of the method, DeSarbo et al. (1999) present a Bayesian MDS procedure to spatially analyze "revealed" choice (that is, what people actually choose, instead of what they *say* they might choose). In a similar vein, Park et al. (2008) extend Bayesian MDS to accommodate both "vector" ("more is always better, or always worse") and "ideal point" ("there's an internal, Goldilocks amount that's best") preferences a generalized framework for metric dominance data, including both preference and structural heterogeneity, applying it to physicians' prescription behavior for antidepressants.

Another traditional topic in marketing seeing great success in Bayesian application is survey methods in general. It has long been noted that different respondents tend to use rating and other scales in idiosyncratic ways, but there was little that market researchers could do to assess and correct for this. Rossi et al. (2001) proposed a general method for overcoming such "scale usage heterogeneity", via HB models, by assuming consumers' rating scale responses were censored outcomes from a latent MNV distribution, from which heterogeneous scale censoring cutoffs could be estimated. This line of work has been extended in ways that would be unthinkable using classical approaches. For example, Lenk et al. (2006) used HB methods to estimate a "circumplex" model for ordinal ratings data, to account for circular item ordering in psychological testing. Bayesian methods allowed the imposition of constraints on item correlations in a natural way, and the authors derive conjugate priors for key circumplex ("angular") parameters to aid in Bayesian computation.

Bayesian methods are starting to be used for survey design issues as well. In the best of all possible worlds, researchers would present respondents with long surveys containing every question of interest, but this is prevented by respondent fatigue, drop-out, inattention, and high researcher cost. An alternative is splitting questionnaires up into smaller chunks and distributing them across respondents, but this loses critical linking information across questions. To solve this dilemma, Adigüzel and Wedel (2008) proposed a methodology to design "split questionnaires" to minimize information loss in a framework accommodating continuous, rank-ordered, and discrete measurement scales. Moreover, the optimal construction of the split questionnaire—either entire blocks of questions (between-block design) or sets of questions in each block (within-block design)—is speedy, owing to MCMC methods to impute missing values resulting from the design.

Psychologists have also long sought to understand group decision-making, both how individuals influence the preferences (and choices) of a group and vice versa. Bayesian methods have allowed the use of very general heterogeneous models for this purpose. An initial foray in this regard was Arora and Allenby (1999), who measuring the influence of individual preference structures in group decision making, using conjoint data on durable good purchases by each member of a married couple, as well as their joint evaluation. Using HB methods, they show that the model's "inferred" measure of influence leads to more accurate predictions than alternate ones. Similarly, Aribarg et al. (2010) use Bayesian methodology to estimate group preference in the absence of joint data from group members. At the heart of their model is an HB formulation relating joint choices for each group, coupled with a utility aggregation set-up, and is estimated on cell phone purchases for parent-teen dyads, showing strong predictive validity for their joint choices.

16.5.5 State-Space and Hidden Markov Models (HMMs)

By now, we hope it is clear that Bayesian methods shine when there is some latent structure (a model with unknown parameters) that gives rise to what we see in the world (our data), and we must somehow average across—that is, take a representative sample from—the model's parameters to understand the data. Some recent advances have exploited that insight to great advantage, and we briefly mention two of these, due to their conceptual similarity: state-space and hidden Markov models. (See Chap. 14 for a more in-depth discussion of hidden Markov models.) These were brought into marketing owing to their unique ability to shed light on *dynamic* processes, especially those with unobservable states. To take a simple example, we may observe a household that tends to buy inexpensive white wine, but every now and again purchases much more costly red wine. We may posit that the household has certain "states"—for example, everyday dining vs. having friends over for dinner—that give rise to what we observe in terms of their wine purchases. What we would like to do is have a model of *how these states evolve over time*, but calibrate that model using only observed data.

Among the earliest applications of these ideas in marketing was the adaptation of the Kalman filter methodology by Naik et al. (1998), who addressed media schedule planning under a given budget constraint, and must decide how much, and when to advertise. Their model used real brand-level data from two advertising awareness tracking studies, including spending schedules, estimating model parameters for the Kalman filter by genetic algorithms. Since that time, further studies have confirmed the power of the general methodology, for example, Naik and Raman (2003), who used it to understand synergies in media communication. Recent advances have demonstrated the power of a Bayesian approach, which integrates remarkably naturally with the Kalman filter methodology. For example, Bruce et al. (2012) examine the dynamic nature of marketing communication, like advertising and word-of-mouth, constructing a dynamic linear model for theater-then-video sequential film distribution, and estimating the Kalman filter parameters using MCMC methods.

A powerful, distinct approach was pioneered by Netzer et al. (2008), who modeled customer relationship dynamics using typical transaction data. They estimated a nonhomogeneous *hidden Markov model* to capture transitions among latent states, as a function of time-varying covariates (e.g., customer-firm encounters) that may shift customers among different (unobservable) states (see Chap. 14). As might be expected by now, heterogeneity was incorporated using an HB approach, and applied to longitudinal gift-giving among alumni, who could be (probabilistically) classified as belonging to three relationship states. Importantly, these states could not be observed, or even characterized, in the absence of the model. A similar approach was used by Montoya et al. (2010), who applied an HMM framework to the problem of dynamically allocating detailing and sampling activities across physicians, whose prescription behavior is both dynamic and heterogeneous, both facilitated by a Bayesian estimation approach. They apply the model to a new drug introduction by a major pharmaceutical firm, using it to identify three latent prescription-behavior states and a high degree of dynamic behavior, neither of which, again, would be inferable in the absence of a dedicated model.

References

Adigüzel, F., Wedel, M.: Split questionnaire design for massive surveys. J. Mark. Res. **45**, 608–617 (2008)

Akaike, H.: A new look at statistical model identification. IEEE Trans. Autom. Control. **19**, 716–723 (1974)

Allenby, G.M., Lenk, P.J.: Modeling household purchase behavior with logistic normal regression. J. Am. Stat. Assoc. **89**, 1218–1231 (1994)

Allenby, G.M., Rossi, P.E.: Marketing models of consumer heterogeneity. J. Econ. **89**, 57–78 (1998)

Allenby, G.M., Arora, N., Ginter, J.L.: Incorporating prior knowledge into the analysis of conjoint studies. J. Mark. Res. **32**, 152–162 (1995)

Allenby, G.M., Arora, N., Ginter, J.L.: On the heterogeneity of demand. J. Mark. Res. **35**, 384–389 (1998)

Andrews, R.L., Currim, I.S., Leeflang, P.S.H., Lim, J.: Estimating the SCAN* PRO model of store sales: HB, FM or just OLS? Int. J. Res. Mark. **25**, 22–33 (2008)
Andrews, R.L., Currim, I.S., Leeflang, P.S.H.: A comparison of sales response predictions from demand models applied to store-level versus panel data. J. Bus. Econ. Stat. **29**, 319–326 (2011)
Ansari, A., Essegaier, S., Kohli, R.: Internet recommendation systems. J. Mark. Res. **37**, 363–375 (2000a)
Ansari, A., Jedidi, K., Jagpal, S.: A hierarchical Bayesian methodology for treating heterogeneity in structural equation models. Mark. Sci. **19**, 328–347 (2000b)
Ansari, A., Jedidi, K., Dube, L.: Heterogeneous factor analysis models: a Bayesian approach. Psychometrika. **67**, 49–77 (2002)
Aribarg, A., Arora, N., Kang, M.Y.: Predicting joint choice using individual data. Mark. Sci. **29**, 139–157 (2010)
Arora, N., Allenby, G.M.: Measuring the influence of individual preference structures in group decision making. J. Mark. Res. **36**, 476–487 (1999)
Bagozzi, R.P., Yi, Y.: On the evaluation of structural equation models. J. Acad. Mark. Sci. **16**, 74–94 (1988)
Bass, F.M.: A new product growth model for consumer durables. Manag. Sci. **15**, 215–227 (1969)
Bayes, T.: An essay towards solving a problem in the doctrine of chances. Philos. Trans. R. Soc. Lond. **53**, 370–418 (1763)
Berger, J.: Statistical Decision Theory and Bayesian Analysis. Springer-Verlag, New York (1985)
Bernardo, J., Smith, A.F.M.: Bayesian Theory. John Wiley and Sons, New York (1994)
Blattberg, R.C., George, E.I.: Shrinkage estimation of price and promotional elasticities: seemingly unrelated equations. J. Am. Stat. Assoc. **86**, 304–315 (1991)
Bradlow, E.T., Fader, P.S.: A Bayesian lifetime model for the "Hot 100" Billboard songs. J. Am. Stat. Assoc. **96**, 368–381 (2001)
Bradlow, E.T., Schmittlein, D.C.: The little engines that could: Modeling the performance of World Wide Web search engines. Mark. Sci. **19**, 43–62 (2000)
Bruce, N.I.: Pooling and dynamic forgetting effects in multitheme advertising: tracking the advertising sales relationship with particle filter. Mark. Sci. **27**, 659–673 (2008)
Bruce, N.I., Foutz, N.Z., Kolsarici, C.: Dynamic effectiveness of advertising and word of mouth in sequential distribution of new products. J. Mark. Res. **49**, 469–486 (2012)
Carpenter, B., Gelman, A., Hoffman, M. Lee, D., Goodrich, B., Betancourt, M., Brubaker, M. A., Guo, J., Li, P., and Riddell, A.: Stan: a probabilistic programming language. J. Stat. Softw. **76**(1), (2017)
Chiang, J., Chib, S., Narasimhan, C.: Markov chain Monte Carlo and models of consideration set and parameter heterogeneity. J. Econ. **89**, 223–248 (1998)
Chib, S.: Marginal likelihood from the Gibbs output. J. Am. Stat. Assoc. **90**(432), 1312–1321 (1995)
Chung, T.S., Rust, R.T., Wedel, M.: My mobile music: an adaptive personalization system for digital audio players. Mark. Sci. **28**, 52–68 (2009)
Cowles, M.K., Carlin, B.P.: Markov chain Monte Carlo convergence diagnostics: a comparative review. J. Am. Stat. Assoc. **91**(434), 883–904 (1996)
De Bruyn, A., Liechty, J.C., Huizingh, E.K., Lilien, G.L.: Offering online recommendations with minimum customer input through conjoint-based decision aids. Mark. Sci. **27**, 443–460 (2008)
De Finetti, B.: "La Prévision: Ses Lois Logiques, Ses Sources Subjectives", *Annales de l"Institut Henri Poincaré*, 7: 1–68; translated as "Foresight. Its Logical Laws, Its Subjective Sources", in *Studies in Subjective Probability*, H. E. Kyburg, Jr. and H. E. Smokler (eds.), Robert E. Krieger Publishing Company, New York, 1980 (1937)
De Groot, M.: Optimal Statistical Decisions. John Wiley and Sons, Hoboken, NJ (1970)
DeSarbo, W.S., Kim, Y., Fong, D.: A Bayesian multidimensional scaling procedure for the spatial analysis of revealed choice data. J. Econ. **89**, 79–108 (1999)
Diaconis, P., Ylvisaker, D.: Conjugate priors for exponential families. Ann. Stat. **7**(2), 269–281 (1979)

Doob, J. L. Application of the theory of martingales. In: Actes du Colloque International Le Calcul des Probabilit´es et ses applications, (Lyon, 28 juin–3 juillet 1948), pp. 23–27. CNRS, Paris (1949)

Edwards, Y.D., Allenby, G.M.: Multivariate analysis of multiple response data. J. Mark. Res. **40**, 321–334 (2003)

Feit, E.M., Beltramo, M.A., Feinberg, F.M.: Reality check: combining choice experiments with market data to estimate the importance of product attributes. Manag. Sci. **56**, 785–800 (2010)

Feit, E.M., Wang, P., Bradlow, E.T., Fader, P.S.: Fusing aggregate and disaggregate data with an application to multiplatform media consumption. J. Mark. Res. **50**, 348–364 (2013)

Fornell, C., Larcker, D.F.: Evaluating structural equation models with unobservable variables and measurement error. J. Mark. Res. **18**, 39–50 (1981)

Gelfand, A.E., Dey, D.K.: Bayesian model choice: asymptotics and exact calculations. J. R. Stat. Soc. Ser. B. **56**, 501–514 (1994)

Gelfand, A.E., Smith, A.F.M.: Sampling based approaches to calculating marginal densities. J. Am. Stat. Assoc. **85**, 398–409 (1990)

Gelman, A., Hill, J.: Data Analysis Using Regression and Multilevel/Hierarchical Models. Cambridge University Press, New York, NY (2006)

Gelman, A., Rubin, D.B.: Inference from iterative simulation using multiple sequences (with discussion). Stat. Sci. **7**, 503–507 (1992)

Gelman, A. Carlin, J.B., Stern, H.S., Dunson, D.B., Vehtari, A. and Rubin, D.B.: Bayesian Data Analysis, 3rd edn. CRC Press Taylor and Francis Group, Boca Raton, FL (2014)

Geman, S., Geman, D.: Stochastic relaxation, Gibbs distributions, and the Bayesian restoration of images. IEEE Trans. Pattern Anal. Mach. Intell. **6**, 721–741 (1984)

Gilbride, T.J., Allenby, G.M.: A choice model with conjunctive, disjunctive, and compensatory screening rules. Mark. Sci. **23**, 391–406 (2004)

Gilula, Z., McCulloch, R.E., Rossi, P.E.: A direct approach to data fusion. J. Mark. Res. **43**, 73–83 (2006)

Good, I.J., Gaskins, R.A.: Nonparametric roughness penalties for probability densities. Biometrika. **58**, 255–277 (1971)

Good, I.J., Gaskins, R.A.: Density estimation and bump-hunting by the penalized likelihood method exemplified by scattering and meteorite data. J. Am. Stat. Assoc. **75**, 42–56 (1980)

Guadagni, P.M., Little, J.D.: A logit model of brand choice calibrated on scanner data. Mark. Sci. **2**, 203–238 (1983)

Hastings, W.K.: Monte Carlo sampling methods using Markov chains, and their applications. Biometrika. **57**, 97–109 (1970)

James, W., Stein, C.: Estimation with quadratic loss. In: Proceedings of the Fourth Berelely Symposium on Mathematical Statistics and Probability, pp. 361–379 (1961)

Jedidi, K., Ansari, A.: Bayesian structural equation models for multilevel data. In: Marcoulides, G. A., Schumacker, R. E. (eds.) .New Developments and Techniques in Structural Equation Modeling, pp. 129–157, Psychology Press, Westminster (2001)

Kalyanam, K., Shively, T.S.: Estimating irregular pricing effects: a stochastic spline regression approach. J. Mark. Res. **35**, 16–29 (1998)

Kamakura, W.A., Russell, G.: A probabilistic choice model for market segmentation and elasticity structure. J. Mark. Res. **26**, 379–390 (1989)

Kim, J., Gyo, U.M., Feinberg, F.M.: Assessing heterogeneity in discrete choice models using a Dirichlet process prior. Rev. Mark. Sci. **2**, (2004)

Kim, J.G., Menzefricke, U., Feinberg, F.M.: Capturing flexible heterogeneous utility curves: a Bayesian spline approach. Manag. Sci. **53**, 340–354 (2007)

Kimeldorf, G.S., Wahba, G.: A correspondence between Bayesian estimation on stochastic processes and smoothing by splines. Ann. Math. Stat. **41**, 495–502 (1970)

Kruschke, J.K.: Doing Bayesian Data Analysis. Academic Press, Amsterdam (2015)

Lee, J., Boatwright, P., Kamakura, W.A.: A Bayesian model for prelaunch sales forecasting of recorded music. Manag. Sci. **49**, 179–196 (2003)

Lenk, P.J.: Hierarchical Bayes forecasts of multinomial Dirichlet data applied to coupon redemptions. J. Forecast. **11**, 603–619 (1992)
Lenk, P.J.: Simulation pseudo-bais correction to the harmonic mean estimator of integrated likelihoods. J. Comput. Graph. Stat. **18**(4), 941–960 (2009)
Lenk, P.J., DeSarbo, W.S.: Bayesian inference for finite mixtures of generalized linear models with random effects. Psychometrika. **65**, 93–119 (2000)
Lenk, P.J., Orme, B.: The value of informative priors in Bayesian inference with sparse data. J. Mark. Res. **46**, 832–845 (2009)
Lenk, P.J., Rao, A.G.: New models from old: forecasting product adoption by hierarchical Bayes procedures. Mark. Sci. **9**, 42–53 (1990)
Lenk, P.J., DeSarbo, W.S., Green, P.E., Young, M.R.: Hierarchical Bayes conjoint analysis: recovery of partworth heterogeneity from reduced experimental designs. Mark. Sci. **15**, 173–191 (1996)
Lenk, P., Wedel, M., Böckenholt, U.: Bayesian estimation of circumplex models subject to prior theory constraints and scale-usage bias. Psychometrika. **71**, 33–55 (2006)
Li, M., Tobias, J.L.: Bayesian inference in a correlated random coefficients model: modeling causal effect heterogeneity with an application to heterogeneous returns to schooling. J. Econ. **162**, 345–361 (2011)
Little, R. J., and Rubin, D. B.: Statistical Analysis with Missing Data, 2nd edn. John Wiley and Sons, Hoboken, New Jersey (2002)
Lunn, D.J., Thomas, A., Best, N., Spiegelhalter, D.: WinBUGS — a Bayesian modelling framework: concepts, structure, and extensibility. Stat. Comput. **10**, 325–337 (2000)
Manchanda, P., Ansari, A., Gupta, S.: The "shopping basket": a model for multicategory purchase incidence decisions. Mark. Sci. **18**, 95–114 (1999)
Manchanda, P., Rossi, P.E., Chintagunta, P.K.: Response modeling with nonrandom marketing-mix variables. J. Mark. Res. **41**, 467–478 (2004)
Martin, A.D., Quinn, K.M., Park, J.H.: MCMCpack: Markov Chain Monte Carlo in R. J. Stat. Softw. **42**, 1–21 (2011)
McLachlan, G., Peel, D.: Finite Mixture Models. John Wiley and Sons, New York (2004)
Metropolis, N., Rosenbluth, A.W., Rosenbluth, N.M., Teller, A.H., Teller, E.: Equations of state calculations by fast computing machines. J. Chem. Phys. **21**(6), 1087–1091 (1953)
Moe, W.W., Fader, P.S.: Using advance purchase orders to forecast new product sales. Mark. Sci. **21**, 347–364 (2002)
Montgomery, A.L.: Creating micro-marketing pricing strategies using supermarket scanner data. Mark. Sci. **16**, 315–337 (1997)
Montgomery, A.L., Rossi, P.E.: Estimating price elasticities with theory-based priors. J. Mark. Res. **36**, 413–423 (1999)
Montoya, R., Netzer, O., Jedidi, K.: Dynamic allocation of pharmaceutical detailing and sampling for long-term profitability. Mark. Sci. **29**, 909–924 (2010)
Morey, R.D., Rouder, J.N., Jamil, T.: BayesFactor: Computation of Bayes factors for common designs, R package version 0.9.12-2, http://CRAN.R-project.org/package=BayesFactor (2015)
Naik, P.A., Raman, K.: Understanding the impact of synergy in multimedia communications. J. Mark. Res. **40**, 375–388 (2003)
Naik, P.A., Mantrala, M.K., Sawyer, A.G.: Planning media schedules in the presence of dynamic advertising quality. Mark. Sci. **17**, 214–235 (1998)
Neelameghan, R., Chintagunta, P.K.: A Bayesian model to forecast new product performance in domestic and international markets. Mark. Sci. **18**, 115–136 (1999)
Netzer, O., Lattin, J.M., Srinivasan, V.: A hidden Markov model of customer relationship dynamics. Mark. Sci. **27**, 185–204 (2008)
Newton, M., Raftery, A.: Approximate Bayesian inference with weighted likelihood bootstrap. J. R. Stat. Soc. Ser. B. **56**(1), 3–48 (1994)
Park, J., DeSarbo, W.S., Liechty, J.: A hierarchical Bayesian multidimensional scaling methodology for accommodating both structural and preference heterogeneity. Psychometrika. **73**, 451–472 (2008)

Pauwels, K.H., Currim, I., Dekimpe, M.G., Hanssens, D.M., Mizik, N., Ghysels, E., Naik, P.: Modeling marketing dynamics by time series econometrics. Mark. Lett. **15**, 167–183 (2004)
Plummer, M: Just Another Gibbs Sampler available at http://mcmc-jags.sourceforge.net/ (2015)
Raudenbush, S. W., Bryk, A. S.: Hierarchical Linear Models: Applications and Data Analysis Methods, vol. 1. Sage, Newbury Park, CA (2002)
Rossi, P. Bayesm: Bayesian Inference for Marketing/Micro-Econometrics, R package version 3.0-2, http://CRAN.R-project.org/package=bayesm (2015)
Rossi, P.E., Allenby, G.M.: Bayesian statistics and marketing. Mark. Sci. **22**, 304–328 (2003)
Rossi, P.E., Gilula, Z., Allenby, G.M.: Overcoming scale usage heterogeneity: a Bayesian hierarchical approach. J. Am. Stat. Assoc. **96**, 20–31 (2001)
Rossi, P.E., Allenby, G.M., McCulloch, R.: Bayesian Statistics and Marketing. John Wiley and Sons, Hoboken, NJ (2012)
Savage, J.L.: The Foundations of Statistics. John Wiley and Sons, New York, NY (1954)
Schwartz, G.: Estimating the dimension of a model. Ann. Stat. **6**(2), 461–464 (1978)
Scott, S.L.: A modern look at the multi-armed bandit. Appl. Stoch. Model. Bus. Ind. **26**, 639–658 (2010)
Seetharaman, P.B., Ainslie, A., Chintagunta, P.K.: Investigating household state dependence effects across categories. J. Mark. Res. **36**, 488–500 (1999)
Shively, T.S., Allenby, G.M., Kohn, R.: A nonparametric approach to identifying latent relationships in hierarchical models. Mark. Sci. **19**, 149–162 (2000)
Spiegelhalter, D.J., Best, N.G., Carlin, B.P., Van Der Linde, A.: Bayesian measures of model complexity and fit. J. R. Stat. Soc. Ser. B. **64**, 583–639 (2002)
Steenkamp, J-B.E.M., Baumgartner, H.: On the use of structural equation models for marketing modeling. Int. J. Res. Mark. **17**, 195–202 (2000)
Stein, C.: Inadmissibility of the usual estimator for the mean of a multivariate distribution. In: Proceedings of the Third Berelely Symposium on Mathematical Statistics and Probability, vol. 1, pp. 197–206 (1956)
Swait, J. D.: Probabilistic choice set generation in transportation demand models. Doctoral dissertation, Massachusetts Institute of Technology (1984)
Talukdar, D., Sudhir, K., Ainslie, A.: Investigating new product diffusion across products and countries. Mark. Sci. **21**, 97–114 (2002)
Van Heerde, H., Helsen, K., Dekimpe, M.G.: The impact of a product-harm crisis on marketing effectiveness. Mark. Sci. **26**, 230–245 (2007)
Van Ittersum, K., Feinberg, F.M.: Cumulative timed intent: A new predictive tool for technology adoption. J. Mark. Res. **47**, 808–822 (2010)
Van Nierop, E., Bronnenberg, B., Paap, R., Wedel, M., Franses, P.H.: Retrieving unobserved consideration sets from household panel data. J. Mark. Res. **47**, 63–74 (2010)
Von Neumann, J., Morgenstern, O.: Theory of Games and Economic Behavior. Princeton University Press/John Wiley and Sons, Princeton/New York (1944)
Ying, Y., Feinberg, F., Wedel, M.: Leveraging missing ratings to improve online recommendation systems. J. Mark. Res. **43**, 355–365 (2006)
Wedel, M., Kamakura, W.A.: Market Segmentation, Conceptual and Methodological Foundations. Kluwer Ac. Publishers, Boston (2000)
Zantedeschi, D., Feit, E.M., Bradlow, E.T. Measuring multi-channel advertising effectiveness. *Manag. Sci.*, forthcoming (2016). http://pubsonline.informs.org/doi/abs/10.1287/mnsc.2016.2451?journalCode=mnsc&
Zanutto, E.L., Bradlow, E.T.: Data pruning in consumer choice models. Quant. Mark. Econ. **4**, 267–287 (2006)
Zeithammer, R., Lenk, P.J.: Bayesian estimation of multivariate normal models when dimensions are absent. Quant. Mark. Econ. **4**, 241–265 (2006)
Zellner, A.: Optimal information processing and Bayes's Theorem. Am. Stat. **42**, 278–280 (1988)

Chapter 17
Non- and Semiparametric Regression Models

Harald J. Van Heerde

17.1 Introduction

Many models in marketing are "parametric". Parametric models impose a mathematical function that links the variables, and this mathematical function contains parameters that have to be estimated. Popular examples are the linear regression model (with a dependent variable y and independent variables x), the log-log model (log dependent variable y, log independent variables x), and the semi-log model (log y, untransformed x).

A marketing researcher may consider parametric regression models too inflexible because s/he is not sure what the relationship between dependent and independent variables may look like. Obtaining insight into the correct functional form is essential for marketing decision support (Albers 2012). One option is to use polynomial regression and add squares or higher-order powers of selected independent variables. However, since individual observations can have a large influence on remote parts of a curve and the polynomial terms can be highly correlated, especially when many powers are needed, polynomial regression is potentially quite problematic (Fan and Gijbels 1996).

To explore the functional form of the relationship between independent and dependent variables, it may be useful to consider flexible approaches such as nonparametric regression models and semiparametric regression models. These models differ in the way they approximate the dependent variable. Nonparametric regression models do not impose any functional relationship between the dependent variable and the independent variables. Semiparametric regression models can be

H.J. Van Heerde (✉)
School of Communication, Journalism and Marketing, Massey University, Private Bag 102904, Auckland 0745, New Zealand
e-mail: h.vanheerde@massay.ac.nz

P.S.H. Leeflang et al. (eds.), *Advanced Methods for Modeling Markets*,
International Series in Quantitative Marketing, DOI 10.1007/978-3-319-53469-5_17

considered as being partly parametric (e.g., for a subset of the independent variables) and partly nonparametric (for another subset). We will give ample examples in this chapter.[1]

Note that this chapter only discusses non- and semiparametric *regression* models. Hence, the dependent variable has an interval scale at minimum. As a result, this chapter does not deal with non- and semiparametric models with dependent variables that have binary or nominal scales, such as a brand choice model.[2]

This chapter has the following structure. To explain why we may want to use nonparametric and semiparametric models, Sect. 17.2 summarizes the advantages and disadvantages of parametric regression models. Section 17.3 introduces nonparametric models and gives some marketing examples. As semiparametric models offer a good compromise between parametric and non-parametric models, the rest of the chapter is dedicated to this class of models. Section 17.4 offers an introduction to semiparametric models and Sect. 17.5 elaborates on an application to estimate the "deal effect curve" which is the nonlinear effect of price discounts on sales. The next two sections expand on alternative estimators for semiparametric models: local polynomial regression (Sect. 17.6) and spline regression (Sect. 17.7): Section 17.8 discusses new developments in non- and semiparametric models in the econometrics literature. Section 17.9 offers software suggestions for the estimation of non- and semiparametric models and Sect. 17.10 concludes the chapter.

17.2 Advantages and Disadvantages of the Parametric Regression Model

In a parametric regression model, the modeler approximates reality by a mathematical function that includes parameters. The effects of independent variables on the dependent variable are quantified by regression parameters captured in β, which is a scalar in case of a single independent variable and a vector in case of multiple independent variables. The error terms u have mean zero and variance σ^2. In general, parametric models have a parametric functional form and a parametric distribution of the error term.

The advantages of a parametric modeling lie in a number of optimality properties (Powell 1994). If the assumed functional form is correct, the maximum likelihood estimators of the unknown parameters in the model are consistent. In other words, they converge to the true values if the sample size increases to infinity. The rate at which these parameters converge to these true values is maximal (i.e., the

[1] A related but distinct domain in marketing that uses flexible functional forms are diffusion models (Chap. 10). These models describe how adoption of innovations progresses over time using a flexible function. Examples of these flexible functions include Functional Data Analysis (Sood et al. 2009) and Step and Wait models (Sood et al. 2012).

[2] See, for example, the semiparametric brand choice model by Abe (1995) and the non- and semiparametric brand choice models by Briesch et al. (1997).

estimators are efficient). This implies that the parametric regression model does not require very large sample sizes to obtain parameter estimates with sufficiently low variances. A common rule of thumb is that we need about five or ten observations for each regression parameter.

The disadvantage of parametric modeling is its inflexibility. The model specification is subject to uncertainty regarding the correct parametric specification of the response function. Incorrect specifications typically yield incorrect conclusions about marketing effectiveness and optimal marketing decisions (Albers 2012). We could try to solve this problem by considering different parametric specifications and performing standard specification tests. But this does not necessarily solve the problem because there is no guarantee that any of the parametric specifications considered will be the true one. In fact, there is no guarantee that the true functions belong to any parametric family (Briesch et al. 1997). Thus, the cost of imposing the strong restrictions required for parametric estimation can be considerable (Härdle and Linton 1994).

17.3 The Nonparametric Regression Model

17.3.1 Introduction

In the nonparametric regression approach, we approximate the dependent variable given independent variables without reference to a specific form. Nonparametric regression models can be represented as:

$$y = m(x) + u \tag{17.1}$$

where

y = a $T \times 1$ column vector representing values of the dependent variable,
$m(x)$ = a function of l independent variables x,
u = a $T \times 1$ vector of random disturbance terms.

The function $m(x)$ contains no parameters. It has the l-dimensional vector x with independent variables as its argument.

There are multiple nonparametric estimators for $m(x)$in (17.1). The four major types are (Fan and Gijbels 1996; Härdle 1990)[3]:

- k-nearest neighbor estimator (Sect. 17.3.2);
- kernel estimator (Sects. 17.3.3 and 17.5);
- local polynomial regression (Sects. 17.3.4 and 17.6);
- splines (Sects. 17.3.5 and 17.7).

[3]See also Sect. 19.4.

Because the kernel estimator, local polynomial regression and spline regression are among the most widely used nonparametric regression estimators, we discuss those in more detail in Sects. 17.5–17.7 of this chapter.

17.3.2 k-nearest Neighbor Estimator

The *k-nearest neighbor estimator* uses "nearest neighbor" observations to approximate the dependent variable. More specifically, it bases an estimate of the dependent variable for given values of the independent variables (say: x_0) on the observations in the data set that are most near to x_0. Hence, the method searches among the observations $x_1, \ldots, x_n$ and identifies the k observations that have the shortest (Euclidian) distance to x_0. The value of the dependent variable for x_0 is estimated by taking the unweighed average of the y-values for these k observations. The smaller k, the less smooth the function will look like, but the less bias the approximation has. Conversely, the higher k, the smoother the function but the more bias. All non- and semiparametric models have this trade-off between smoothness and bias.

17.3.3 Kernel Estimator

The intuition behind the kernel method (Nadaraya 1964; Watson 1964) is that it computes a local weighted average of the dependent variable y given the values of the independent variables x_0:

$$\widehat{m}\left(x_0\right) = \sum_{t=1}^{T} w_t\left(x_0\right) y_t \tag{17.2}$$

where $w_t(x_0)$ represents the weight assigned to the t-th observation y_t in the estimation of y for x_0. This weight depends on the distance of x_t from the point x_0, which is described by:

$$w_t\left(x_0\right) = \frac{K\left(\frac{x_t - x_0}{h}\right)}{\sum_{t'=1}^{T} K\left(\frac{x_{t'} - x_0}{h}\right)} \tag{17.3}$$

where $K(\cdot)$ is a kernel function, and h the bandwidth. By substituting (17.3) in (17.2) we obtain the kernel estimator:

$$\widehat{m}\left(x_0\right) = \frac{\sum_{1}^{T} K\left(\frac{x_t - x_0}{h}\right) y_t}{\sum_{t'=1}^{T} K\left(\frac{x_{t'} - x_0}{h}\right)}. \tag{17.4}$$

To implement the kernel estimator, we have to choose the kernel function and the bandwidth parameter. The choice of the bandwidth parameter is more crucial than the choice of the kernel function (Silverman 1996). Generally, the kernel function is a symmetric function around zero, it reaches its maximum at zero, and it integrates to one. A common choice for the kernel is the normal (Gaussian) kernel:

$$K\left(\frac{x_t - x_0}{h}\right) = \frac{1}{\sqrt{2\pi}}\exp\left(\frac{-(x_t - x_0)^2}{2h^2}\right). \tag{17.5}$$

This kernel represents the density function of a normal distribution. The closer $\frac{x_t - x_0}{h}$ is to zero, the larger $K(.)$ is, i.e. the larger observation y_t weighs in the computation of the estimate of y for x_0.

The bandwidth parameter selection is essential in kernel regression. This parameter h controls the smoothness of the kernel function. The smaller it is, the less smooth the kernel function is, and the more weight is put on the nearest observations. To illustrate, the bandwidth parameter in (17.5) can be interpreted as the standard deviation of a normal distribution. The smaller the standard deviation of a normal distribution, the smaller the width of the normal density function. As the bandwidth decreases, the response curve becomes squigglier and the bias of the curve is reduced at the cost of increased variance. A bandwidth parameter of (almost) zero leads to a response curve that connects the observations, resulting in zero bias but maximal variance. An infinite bandwidth parameter leads to a horizontal response curve: maximal bias and zero variance. Hence, the choice of the bandwidth parameter involves a trade-off between bias and variance. Most bandwidth selection techniques try to minimize some mean squared error criterion, i.e., the sum of squared bias and variance of the dependent variable. We refer to Abe (1995) for bandwidth selection techniques.

17.3.4 Local Polynomial Regression

Local polynomial regression approximates the unknown regression function $m(x)$ locally by a polynomial of order d (Fan and Gijbels 1996, p. 57–58). A Taylor expansion gives, for x in the neighborhood of x_0:

$$m(x) \approx m(x_0) + m'(x_0)(x - x_0) + \frac{m''(x_0)}{2!}(x - x_0)^2 + \cdots + \frac{m^{(p)}(x_0)}{p!}(x - x_0)^p. \tag{17.6}$$

A polynomial is fitted locally by a weighted least squares regression problem: Minimize:

$$\sum_{t=1}^{T}\left[\left\{y_t - \sum_{q=0}^{d}\left[\beta_q (x_t - x_0)^q\right]\right\}^2 K_h(x_t - x_0)\right] \tag{17.7}$$

where $K_h(.)$ is a kernel function and h is the bandwidth parameter. Now the estimate for the level of the function is $\widehat{m}(x_0) = \widehat{\beta}_0$, the estimator for the first derivative is $\widehat{m}'(x_0) = \widehat{\beta}_1$, and, the estimator for the vth derivative is $\widehat{m^{(v)}}(x_0) = v!\widehat{\beta}_v$ (Fan and Gijbels 1996, p. 58).

17.3.5 Splines

The spline regression estimator represents $m(x)$ by connecting multiple cubic polynomials (De Boor 2001; Eilers and Marx 1996). The polynomials are connected at observation points x_t in such a way that the first two derivatives of $\widehat{m}(.)$ are continuous (Härdle 1990, p. 57). Kalyanam and Shively (1998) use a special variant of the spline regression estimator to estimate the relationship between price and sales flexibly, viz., a stochastic spline regression. They approximate this response function by a piecewise linear function that has derivatives obtained by draws from a normal distribution. We will return to spline regressions in Sect. 17.7 because they have certain desirable properties.

17.3.6 Advantages and Disadvantages of Nonparametric Regression Models

The big advantage of nonparametric regression models relative to their parametric counterparts is their flexibility. A nonparametric approach does not project the observed data into a "Procrustean bed"[4] of a fixed parameterization (Härdle 1990). Nonparametric modeling imposes few restrictions on the form of the joint distribution of the data, so there is little room for (functional form) misspecification, and consistency of the estimator of the regression curve is established under much more general conditions than for parametric modeling.

Rust (1988) introduced nonparametric regression models to marketing research. He emphasizes that nonlinearity, non-normal errors, and heteroscedasticity are automatically accommodated, as an inherent feature of the method, without the use of special analyses requiring a high level of judgement and knowledge. Conceptually, the primary benefits consist of the relaxation of functional form constraints and the allowance for flexible interactions.

A disadvantage of the nonparametric approach is the convergence rate of the nonparametric estimator. It is usually slower than it is for parametric estimators (Powell 1994), i.e. precise estimation of the nonparametric multidimensional regression

[4]Procrustes is a figure from the Greek mythology. He was a robber and he cut or stretched his victims to fit in his bed.

Table 17.1 Required sample sizes for nonparametric and parametric regression models

Number of independent variables	Sample size nonparametric model	Sample size parametric model
1	4	10
2	19	20
3	67	30
4	223	40
5	768	50
6	2790	60
7	10,700	70
8	43,700	80
9	187,000	90
10	842,000	100

surface requires many observations.[5] In Table 17.1 we show the sample size required for a given number of independent variables (dimensionality) in a nonparametric regression model (for details see Silverman 1986, p. 94)[6] to illustrate "the curse of dimensionality." For comparison purposes, we also include a column for the sample sizes required for parametric regression models, based on the rule of thumb "10 observations per parameter." Based on Table 17.1, we see that even a simple problem of a nonparametric brand sales model with three marketing instruments for three brands as independent variables, for a total of 9 independent variables, requires almost 200,000 observations.

Rust (1988) shows two nonparametric kernel regression applications to marketing research issues. One example is an investigation of how profitability influences the compensation of top marketing executives. In particular, cash salary (y) is studied as a function of net profit (x).

Parametric regression shows little relationship (R^2 of 0.01), but nonparametric regression has an R^2 of 0.31. Moreover, flexible regression reveals some interesting insights about the data. The relationship between profitability and salary is nonlinear, with high salaries going to executives in companies with either large losses or large profits (see Fig. 17.1a).

The data for the second example in Rust (1988) are from a study on the behavior of Hispanic consumers (see Fig. 17.1b). The issue of interest is whether the extent of ethnic identification (x_1) and/or income (x_2) affects usage of Spanish media (y). Conventional regression analysis results in an R^2 of 0.13. Nonparametric regression yields an R^2 of 0.36. The nonparametric approach reveals that income does not affect

[5]For further discussion of parametric versus nonparametric regression models see Härdle (1990, pp. 3–6), and Powell (1994, pp. 2444–2447).

[6]Table 17.1 was derived in a nonparametric density estimation context and not in a nonparametric regression context. However, nonparametric regression is equivalent to estimating the density of the criterion variable given the predictor variables (Härdle 1990, p. 21).

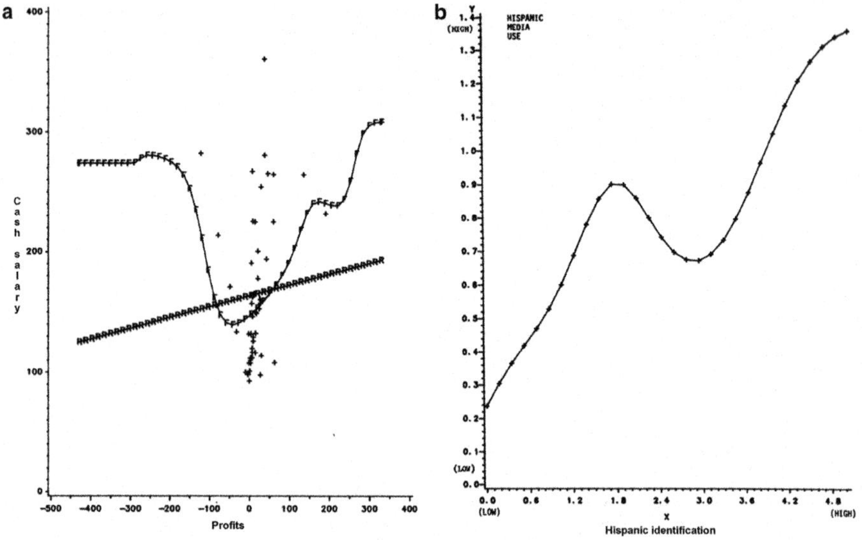

Fig. 17.1 Two nonparametric marketing examples, reproduced from Rust (1988). (**a**) Effect of profitability on salaries of marketing executives. (**b**) Use of Spanish language media as a function of Hispanic ethnic identification

the use of Spanish language media, whereas in the parametric approach it does. In addition, the relationship between degree of Hispanic ethnic identification and usage of Hispanic media is found to be interestingly nonlinear. The use of Hispanic media increases for the Hispanic identification level going from low to medium, then decreases a bit, and then increases again for increasing identification levels.

17.4 The Semiparametric Regression Model

Semiparametric regression models contain components from parametric and nonparametric regression models. Therefore, semiparametric regression models combine the advantages and disadvantages of parametric and nonparametric regression models. They combine the efficiency (low variance) of parametric models and the flexibility of nonparametric models. But semiparametric models are neither as flexible as nonparametric models nor they are not as efficient as parametric models. This midway position of semiparametric models is illustrated in Table 17.2.

We discuss two common examples of semiparametric regression models below: single-index models and semilinear models. The single-index model can be written as:

$$y = m\left(x'\beta\right) + u. \tag{17.8}$$

Table 17.2 Relative positions of the three types of regression models

↑	Parametric regression models	
Efficiency	Semiparametric regression models	Flexibility
	Nonparametric regression models	↓

This semiparametric model has a nonparametric component, i.e., unknown function $m(.)$ and a parametric component, i.e., parameter vector β. This model allows for some flexibility in the effect of x on y. Note that the nonparametric function $m(.)$ operates on $x'\beta$ which is one-dimensional. This dimensionality is lower than the dimensionality of the fully nonparametric regression model, which enhances nonparametric estimation of $m(.)$. In other words, the curse of dimensionality that plagues fully nonparametric models is reduced.[7] The single-index has no application in marketing (yet).

The semilinear model (Robinson 1988) can be written as:

$$y = m\left(x^{(1)}\right) + x^{(2)\prime}\beta. \tag{17.9}$$

Hence the vector of independent variables x is split into two parts, $x^{(1)}$ and $x^{(2)}$. The effect of $x^{(1)}$ on y is modeled nonparametrically, whereas the effect of $x^{(2)}$ on y is modeled parametrically. As $x^{(1)}$ contains fewer independent variables than x itself, the nonparametric function $m(.)$ operates on a vector of a lower dimension than in the fully nonparametric model (17.1). Therefore, the semilinear model is another example of reducing the curse of dimensionality. Robinson (1988) gives the estimation procedure for this model.

17.5 Application of a Semiparametric Model: The Deal Effect Curve

17.5.1 Model Specification

Van Heerde et al. (2001) use a semilinear regression model for the estimation of the deal effect curve. The deal effect curve represents the relationship between sales and price discounts. The marketing literature suggests several phenomena that may contribute to the shape of the deal effect curve (see, for example, Gupta and Cooper 1992). These phenomena can produce severe nonlinearities in the curve, and Van Heerde et al. (2001) argue that those are best captured in a flexible manner. Van

[7] We refer to Lee (1996, pp. 205–210) for estimators for the single-index model.

Heerde et al. (2001) model store-level sales over time as a nonparametric function of own- and cross-item price discounts, and a parametric function of other independent variables (all indicator variables).

The dependent variable of the semiparametric model is log unit sales. Taking log unit sales as the dependent variable instead of unit sales itself makes the interpretation of the effects of the independent variables multiplicative. Moreover, certain interaction effects between the indicator variables are implicitly taken into account if log unit sales is taken.

The price variables are log price indices. The price index is the ratio of actual to regular price for an item in the store. Both actual and regular prices are available in the AC Nielsen data sets. AC Nielsen uses an algorithm to infer regular prices from actual prices and price promotion indicator variables. Price indices less than one represent temporary price cuts. The usage of this variable allows to isolate deal effects. The partial relation between the deal (discount) and sales is called the deal effect relation. Its representation is the deal effect curve. For brand k, $k = 1, \ldots, K$, sold in store i in week t, the specification for the semiparametric model is:

$$\ln S_{ikt} = m\left(\ln PI_{i1t}, \ln PI_{i2t}, \ldots, \ln PI_{iJt}\right) + \sum_{j=1}^{K}\sum_{l=1}^{L} \gamma_{jkl} D_{ijlt} + \alpha_{ik} X_i + \lambda_{tk} W_t + u_{ikt}$$

$$t = 1, \ldots, T \text{ and } i = 1, \ldots, n, \tag{17.10}$$

where

S_{ikt} = ln unit sales (e.g., log number of kgs) for brand k in store i, week t,
$m(.)$ = a nonparametric function,
$\ln PI_{ijt}$ = ln price index (ratio of actual to regular price) of brand j in store i in week t,
D_{ij1t} = an indicator variable for feature advertising: 1 if brand j is featured (but *not* displayed) by store i, in week t; 0 otherwise,
D_{ij2t} = an indicator variable for display: 1 if brand j is displayed (but *not* featured) by store i, in week t; 0 otherwise,
D_{ij3t} = an indicator variable for the simultaneous use of feature and display: 1 if brand j is featured *and* displayed by store i, in week t; 0 otherwise,
X_i = an indicator variable for store i: 1 if the observation is from store i; 0 otherwise,
W_t = an indicator variable (proxy for missing variables and seasonal effects): 1 if the observation is in week t; 0 otherwise,
γ_{jk1} = the own feature multiplier if $j = k$, or cross-feature multiplier if $j \neq k$,
γ_{jk2} = the own display multiplier if $j = k$, or cross-display multiplier if $j \neq k$,
γ_{jk3} = the own feature and display multiplier if $j = k$, or cross-feature and display multiplier if $j \neq k$,

α_{ik} = store i's regular (base) log unit sales for brand k when there are no price cuts nor promotion activities for any of the brands k, $k = 1, \ldots, K$,
λ_{tk} = the seasonal multiplier for week t for brand k,
u_{ikt} = a disturbance term for brand k in store i, week t,
K = the number of brands used in the competitive set,
n = the number of stores in the sample for a major market, and
T = the number of weeks.

The weekly indicator variables are included to account for seasonal effects and the effects of missing variables.

Equation (17.10) is a modification of the SCAN*PRO-model (Wittink et al. 2011).[8] It is a fully flexible model as far as the main effects of the independent variables are concerned, since continuous independent variables (price indices) are modeled nonparametrically. It also includes flexible interaction effects between the price index variables of different items. However, it does not allow for flexible interaction effects between the price index variables and the indicator variables of the parametric part, nor between these indicator variables themselves.

17.5.2 Benchmark Models

Van Heerde et al. (2001) compare the semiparametric model (17.10) to two benchmark models. The first is the SCAN*PRO model:

$$\ln S_{ikt} = \sum_{j=1}^{K} \beta_{jk} \ln PI_{ijt} + \sum_{j=1}^{K} \sum_{l=1}^{L} \gamma_{jkl} D_{ijlt} + \alpha_{ik} X_i + \lambda_{tk} W_t + u_{ikt}, \quad t = 1, \ldots, T \text{ and } i = 1, \ldots, n. \tag{17.11}$$

The second benchmark is Blattberg and Wisniewksi's (B&W) (Blattberg and Wisniewski 1989) model, adapted by excluding regular prices. The B&W model differs from SCAN*PRO in the functional forms assumed for own- and cross-brand deal effects:

$$\ln S_{ikt} = \eta_{kk} (1 - PI_{ikt}) + \sum_{j \neq k}^{K} \eta_{jk} / PI_{ijt} + \sum_{j=1}^{K} \sum_{l=1}^{L} \gamma_{jkl} D_{ijlt} + \alpha_{ik} X_i + \lambda_{tk} W_t + u_{ikt}, \quad t = 1, \ldots, T \text{ and } i = 1, \ldots, n. \tag{17.12}$$

[8]This model is discussed in detail in Vol. I, Sects. 6.8.7 and 7.3.2.

17.5.3 Empirical Setting

Van Heerde et al. (2001) apply the models to weekly store-level scanner data sets for three product categories. The first data set contains the three largest national brands in the US 6.5 oz. canned tuna fish product category. The second data set is for six US brands in a beverage category. The third data set contains the four largest items of a Dutch packaged food product. Only items 3 and 4 have been offered at a discount. Therefore, only the price indices of these two items are included in the nonparametric part of the semiparametric model. All weekly data are from stores belonging to a single chain. Van Heerde et al. (2001) pool data across stores of a given chain, and use the first half of the observations for estimation, leaving an equal number of weeks per store for validation.

Van Heerde et al. (2001) compare the semiparametric model (17.10) to the two parametric benchmark models (17.11) and (17.12) in terms of model fit in the estimation and validation sample. They conclude that the flexible modeling of deal effects may result in considerable gains in in- and out-of-sample fit.

17.5.4 Own-Brand Deal Effect Curves

Figure 17.2 shows the own-item deal effect curves from the semiparametric model graphically. For each category, it also plots the curve for the best-fitting parametric model, which is the B&W model (17.12) for tuna, and SCAN*PRO model (17.11) for the other two categories. The graphs show price indices on the x-axis and predicted sales volumes on the y-axis. For the x-axis the graphs use 300 focal item's price indices, equally spaced between the lowest and highest price indices observed in the estimation sample, while the other items' price indices were fixed at one.

All own-item deal effect curves indicate threshold levels, i.e., there is a minimal price discount required before sales start increasing. For several items (e.g., tuna item 2, beverage item 5, food item 3), we also see a saturation effect: too large price discounts do not yield additional sales.

17.5.5 Cross-Brand Deal Effect Curves

The semiparametric model (17.10) also includes flexible cross-item price discount effects. We show examples of cross-item deal effect curves in Fig. 17.3. The line represents the influence of price discounts for one brand on another brand's sales.

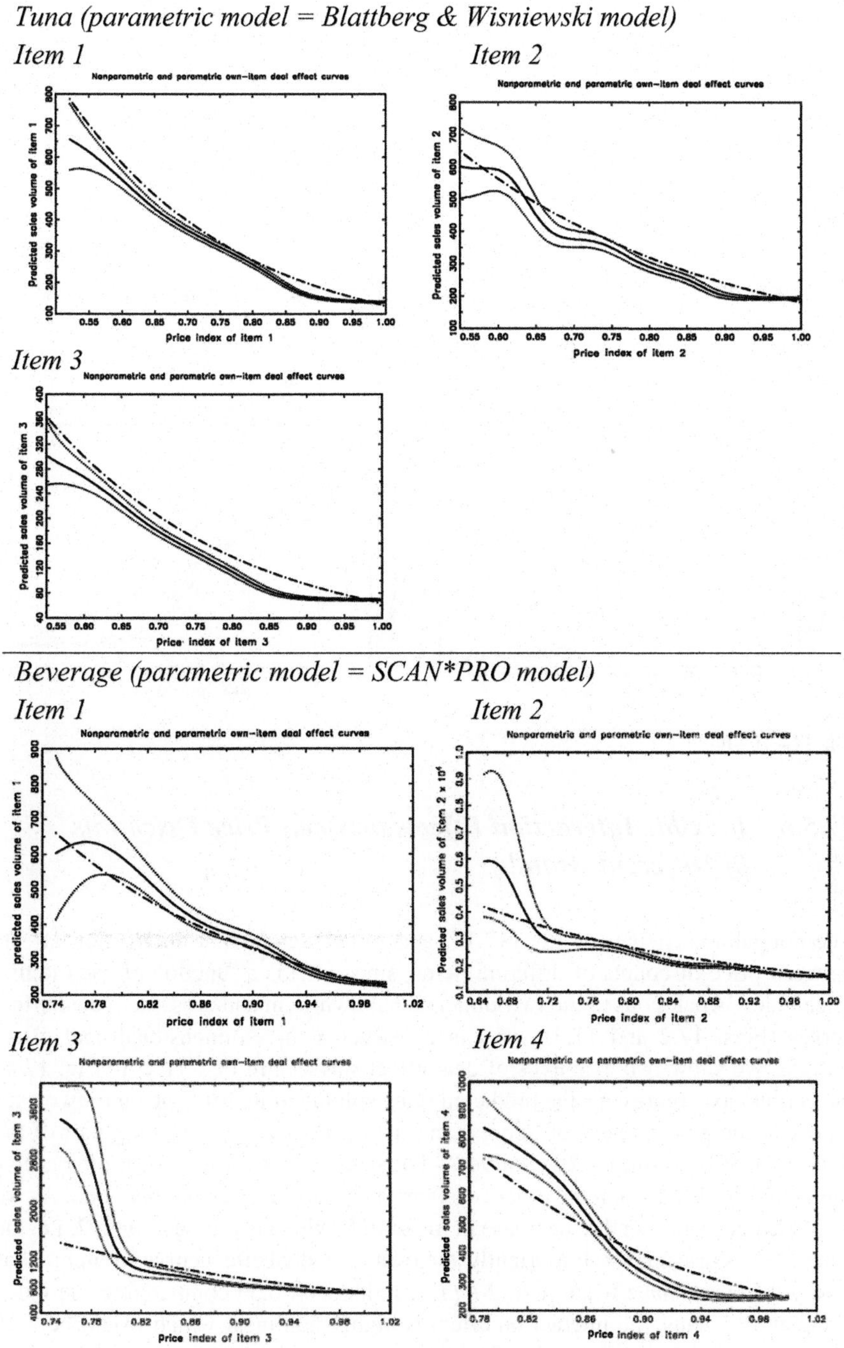

Fig. 17.2 Own-item deal effect curves: semiparametric model (kernel) and parametric model, reproduced from Van Heerde et al. (2001). *Solid line* nonparametric estimate, *dashed line* parametric estimate, *dotted lines* nonparametric confidence bounds (95%)

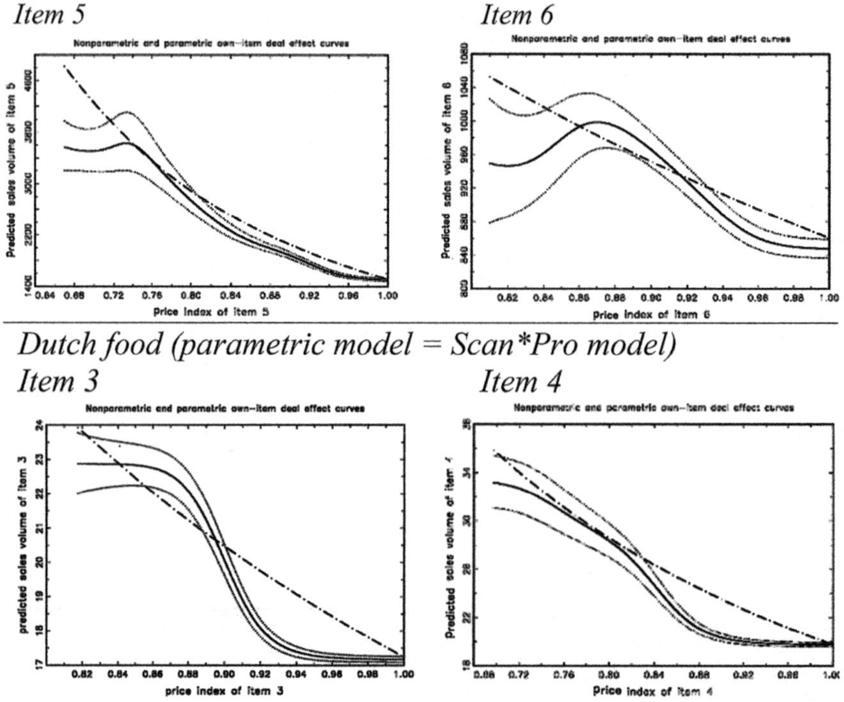

Fig. 17.2 (continued)

17.5.6 *Flexible Interaction Effects between Price Discounts of Different Brands*

The nonparametric part of Eq. (17.10) accommodates flexible interaction effects between price discounts of different items, since *m*(.) is a function of each item's price index. Analogous to the two-dimensional own-item and cross-item deal effect curves (Figs. 17.2 and 17.3), we can construct a three-dimensional deal effect surface. We show two examples of deal effect surfaces in Fig. 17.4. In Fig. 17.4a the vertical axis represents the predicted sales volume of item 1. The other two axes represent the price indices of items 1 and item 2 respectively. The top part of the three-dimensional surface (the curve A–B) is item 1's own-item deal effect, also shown in Fig. 17.2, when the other two items both have a price index of one. As we would expect, sales tend to decrease in magnitude with a decrease in item 2, i.e. the competitor's price index. Importantly, the own-item deal effect curve for item 1 has a very different shape when item 2's price index is at 0.55 compared to the index being at 1.0. Thus, the interaction effect is highly nonlinear which would be very difficult to model parametrically. Substantively, if item 1 is promoted with a deep discount, item 2 can reduce the sales gain considerably if it has a price discount of (at least) 25 percent.

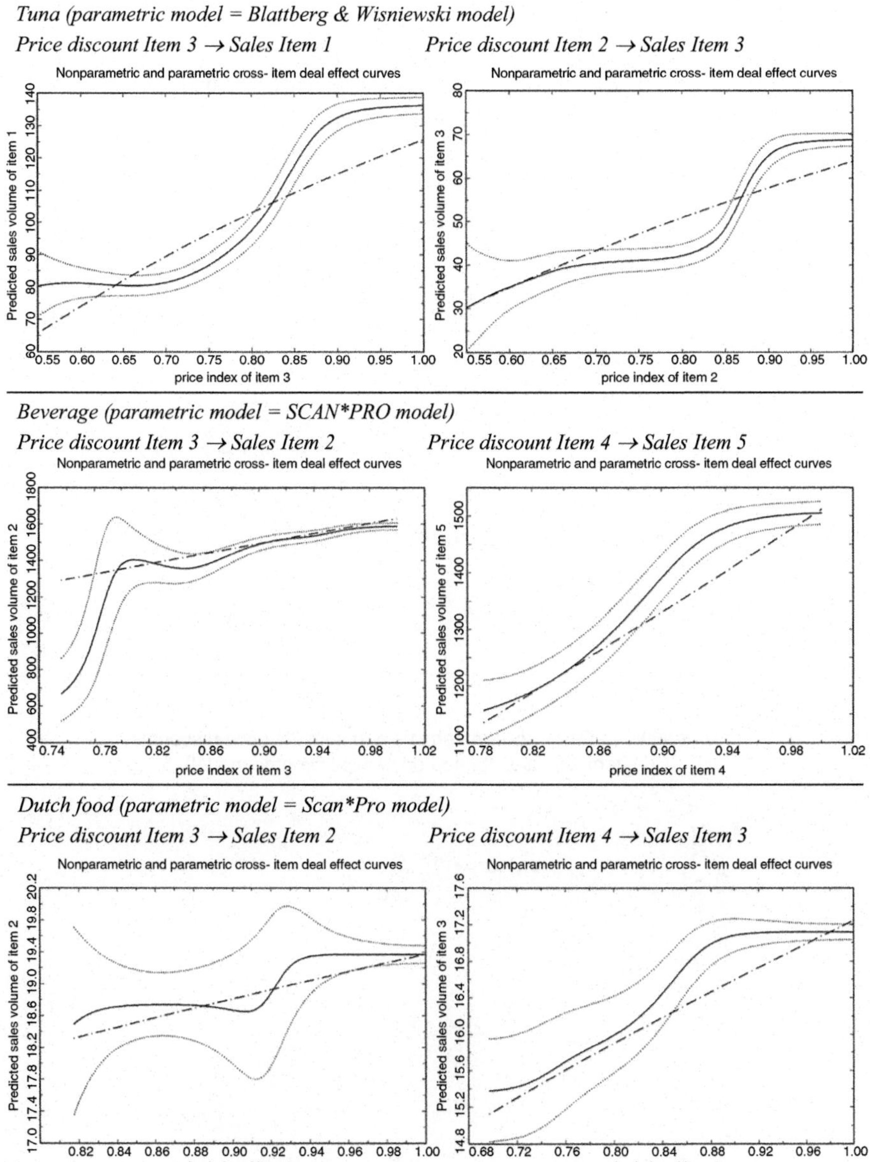

Fig. 17.3 Cross-item deal effect curves: semiparametric model (kernel) and parametric model, reproduced from Van Heerde et al. (2001). *Solid line* nonparametric estimate, *dashed line* parametric estimate, *dotted lines* nonparametric confidence bounds (95%)

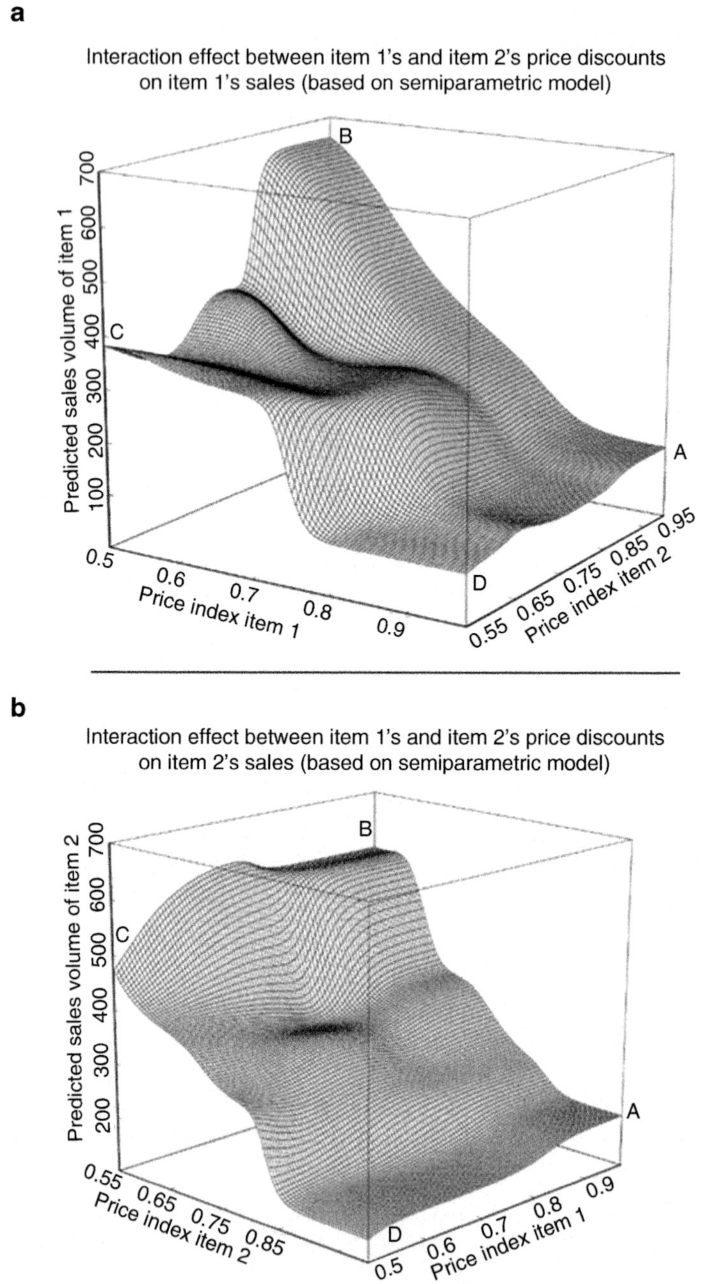

Fig. 17.4 3D tuna deal effect surfaces, reproduced from Van Heerde et al. (2001)

We show the interaction effect for the same price indices on item 2's sales in Fig. 17.4b. Here, the curve A–B represents item 2's own-item deal effect, when items 1 and 3 have a price index of one (see also Fig. 17.2). This curve also tends to decrease in magnitude when the price index of item 1 decreases, but the decrease is not as dramatic as it is in Fig. 17.4a. The own-item deal effect for item 2 is less sensitive to item 1's discounting than vice versa. Thus, the interaction effects appear to be asymmetric.

17.5.7 Flexible Interaction Effects between Price Discount and Feature and Display

Promotion signals such as feature and display have strong effects on item sales (Blattberg et al. 1995, p. G125). However, we know little about the synergies between feature advertising, displays, and price discounts. Inman et al. (1990) and Mayhew and Winer (1992) suggest that "low need for cognition" consumers react to the simple presence of a promotion signal whether or not the price of the promotion is reduced. If these consumers form a large group, the deal effect curve for price discounts accompanied by feature advertising will be shifted upward from the deal effect curve for price discounts without a promotion signal, but it may show less price sensitivity.

The semiparametric model (17.10) allows for flexible interaction effects between own- and cross-item price indices (such as those illustrated in Figs. 17.4a, b) but not between own-item price index and own-item promotion signals. Therefore, Van Heerde et al. (2001) adapt the methodology to estimate these interactions flexibly as well, illustrated for tuna item 1. They split the sample of 1456 tuna observations into four subsamples (Lee 1996, p. 158) with sample sizes as follows: neither feature nor display 1017, feature-only 73, display-only 103, combined use of feature and display 263.

They estimate a separate own-item deal effect curve for each subsample, analogous to model (17.1). Figure 17.5 shows the own-item deal effect curves for tuna item 1 under the four conditions. The figure does not present confidence intervals for the individual curves since they would confound the interpretation of this figure. Importantly, these intervals are only slightly less tight than the one for the overall deal effect curve for this item (Fig. 17.2). The deal effect curve for unsupported price discounts (neither feature, nor display) is similar to the one for item 1 (tuna) in Fig. 17.2. The "feature-only" deal effect curve is almost horizontal. This pattern is consistent with the idea that the response to feature is dominated by "need for cognition" consumers (Inman et al. 1990; Mayhew and Winer 1992) who are not very sensitive to the actual price. A comparison of the "feature-only"- and "display-only" deal effect curves suggests that at the rightmost point (no discount) the effect of feature-only is larger than that of display-only. However, the two curves

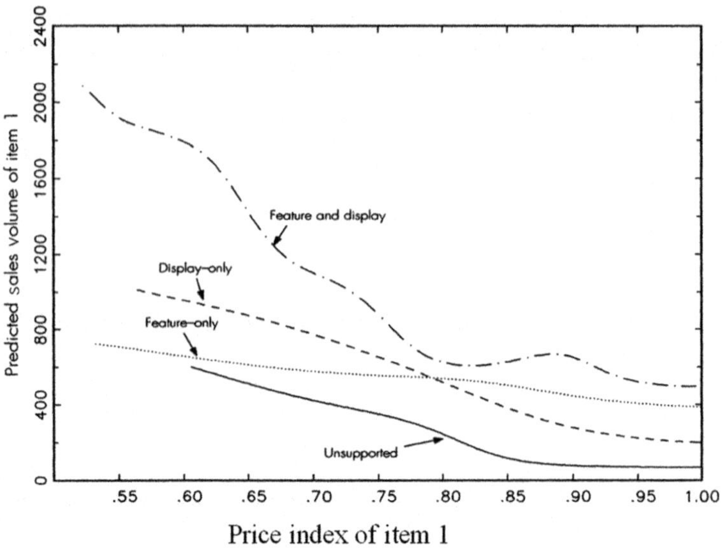

Fig. 17.5 Interaction effects between price, feature, and display for tuna item 1, reproduced from Van Heerde et al. (2001)

intersect at a discount of about 20 percent, after which the deal effect with display exceeds the effect with feature. Thus, feature is more effective (than display) at no/low discount, while display is more effective at high discount. Such a crossover interaction is very difficult to anticipate and almost impossible to diagnose from the residuals of parametric models. Importantly, none of the prevailing parametric models allow for this crossover interaction effect.

Martínez-Ruiz et al. (2006) use semiparametric models to study deal effect curves using daily data. Similar to Van Heerde et al. (2001) they document saturation effects, threshold effects and nonlinear 3D deal effect surfaces.

17.6 Local Polynomial Regression

17.6.1 Boundary Problems for Kernel Estimator

Although these results suggest that the semiparametric model provides more valid deal curves than parametric ones, we have to consider the fact that the kernel method that was used for nonparametric estimation is not without problems. Due to its ease of use, the kernel method is widely used. But its estimates may tend to flatten in the boundaries of the observed ranges of independent variables (Fan 1992). This potential "boundary problem" is avoided by another nonparametric technique, known as local polynomial (LP) regression (Fan 1992). Van Heerde et al.

(2001) apply this technique to assess to what extent boundary problems occur in their applications. The comparisons suggest that the kernel method outperforms the local polynomial method in general but may suffer from boundary effects for small discount values.

17.6.2 Model Specification and Estimation

Local polynomial regression overcome boundary problems. Local polynomial regression is a flexible, design-adaptive, and easy to implement method (see Sect. 17.3.1 in Fan and Gijbels 1996). Let us assume we want to estimate the following semiparametric model with local polynomial regression:

$$y_t = m(x_t) + x_t^{(2)\prime}\gamma + u_t \tag{17.13}$$

where x_t is the independent variable of central interest. In (17.13), $x_t^{(2)}$ is the vector of independent variables that are modeled parametrically and γ is the vector of associated regression parameters.

Model estimation proceeds by fitting for a given level of the independent variable $x = x_0$ the following locally weighted polynomial regression (Fan and Gijbels 1996, p. 274):

$$\sum_{t=1}^{T}\left[\left\{y_t - \sum_{q=0}^{d}\left[\beta_q (x_t - x_0)^q\right] - x_t^{(2)\prime}\gamma\right\}^2 K_h(x_t - x_0)\right] \tag{17.14}$$

where d is the degree of the polynomial and β_q are the parameters that need to be estimated. As before, the Kernel $K_h(x_t - x_0)$ determines the weight of neighboring observations. The estimate for $m(x_t)$ at $x_t = x_0$ equals $\widehat{\beta_0}$.

17.6.3 Application of Local Linear Regression

Van Heerde et al. (2004) use local linear regression to flexibly decompose sales promotions effects into their constituent sources such as cross-brand effects, cross-period effects, and category expansion effects. For local linear regression, $d = 1$ in (17.14). This choice is based on Fan and Gijbels (1996, Sect. 3.3) who argue that for the estimation of main effects the polynomial degree should be one. Van Heerde et al. (2004) use the quartic kernel:

$$K_h(u) = \frac{15}{16}\left(1 - (u/h)^2\right)^2 \mathrm{I}\{|u/h| \le 1\}.$$

The bandwidth parameter is 0.3 for all data sets.

Van Heerde et al. (2004) model non-transformed (non-log) values for sales and price indices to ensure a decomposition that is internally consistent: the decomposition sources add up to the own-promotion effect. The model for own-brand sales, for instance, is specified as:

$$S_{ikt} = m_{own}\left(PI_{iklt}\right) + Z'_{ikt}\gamma_k + u_{ikt} \tag{17.15}$$

where $m(.)$ is a nonparametric function, PI_{iklt} is the price index variable for four types of support: feature-only ($\ell = 2$), display-only ($\ell = 3$), feature and display ($\ell = 4$), and no support ($\ell = 1$). In (17.15), $Z'_{ikt}\gamma_k$ captures the effects of control variables such as cross-price indices, week dummies and store dummies (see Van Heerde et al. 2004 for details).

The key benefit of local linear regression is that it allows for any degree of nonlinearity while maintaining the mathematical consistency of the decomposition for each level of the price index variable:

$$m_{own}\left(PI_{iklt}\right) = m_{cross-brand}\left(PI_{iklt}\right) + m_{cross-period}\left(PI_{iklt}\right) + m_{category\ expansion}\left(PI_{iklt}\right) \tag{17.16}$$

which says that the own effect equals the cross-brand effect plus the cross-period effect and the category expansion effect. Van Heerde et al. (2004) create this decomposition separately for each brand, for each decomposition effect, and for each of the four price index variables.

17.7 Spline Regression

17.7.1 Why Spline Regression?

Kernel regression and local polynomial regression are flexible, but both suffer from the curse of dimensionality. That is, as the number of nonparametrically-modelled independent variables increase, the required number of observations to estimate all nonparametric main and interaction effects reliably grow exponentially (see Sect. 17.3). One solution is to use a semiparametric model and only model a subset of all independent variables nonparametrically, as discussed in Sect. 17.4. However, the implicit assumption of kernel regression and local polynomial regression is that we want to flexibly estimate all main and interaction effects within this subset of independent variables. Very often, we are mainly interested in flexible main effects but have less interest in flexibly estimate interaction effects. If that is the case, we can specific a semiparametric model for brand k, sold in store i in week t that is additive in the nonparametric effects. For example, Steiner et al. (2007) analyze the deal effect curve with this model that includes the additive effect of flexible main effects for price index, $\sum_{j=1}^{J} f_{kj}\left(PI_{ijt}\right)$:

$$\ln S_{ikt} = \alpha_{ik} + \sum\nolimits_{j=1}^{J} f_{kj}\left(PI_{ijt}\right) + \sum\nolimits_{q=2}^{4} \delta_{iq} W_{qt} + u_{ikt}$$
$$t = 1, \ldots, T \text{ and } i = 1, \ldots, n, \quad (17.17)$$

where W_{qt} is a seasonal dummy indicating if week t belongs to the qth quarter, where the first quarter represents the reference quarter. The unknown price response function $f_{kj}(PI_{ijt})$ is approximated by a cubic spline with equally spaced knots within the observed price range. We can write such a spline for the jth price effect in terms of a linear combination of M_j cubic B-splines for Basis functions B_{jm}, $m = 1, \ldots, M_j$:

$$f_{kj}\left(PI_{ijt}\right) = \sum_{m-1}^{M_j} \beta_{jm} B_{jm}\left(PI_{ijt}\right) \quad (17.18)$$

where β_{jm} denotes the regression coefficient to be estimated for the mth B-spline basis (De Boor 2001; Eilers and Marx 1996). The coefficients are determined partly by the data to be fitted, and partly by an additional penalty function that aims to impose smoothness to avoid overfitting (Eilers and Marx 1996). The "penalized B-spline" is called "P-spline" for short. In a marketing application, Sloot et al. (2006) use cubic splines to measure the effect of assortment reduction on category sales.

17.7.2 Monotonicity Constraints

Importantly, the spline estimator used in Steiner et al. (2007) also imposes monotonicity, which means that demand is a strictly decreasing function of price, in line with economic theory. They show that this leads to more plausible deal effect curves than when using unconstrained semiparametric models. Figure 17.6 shows an example from Steiner et al. (2007), with an unconstrained semiparametric deal effect curve on the left-hand side and monotonicity-restricted semiparametric curve on the right-hand side (along with a parametric curve). The left-hand panel suggests a big drop in sales for very low price levels, which is implausible, whereas the right-hand panel shows a more plausible pattern. Haupt and Kagerer (2012) use B-splines and quantile regression with the same objective of estimating monotonicity-restricted nonlinear pricing effects.

17.8 Developments in Non- and Semiparametric Regression Models

The econometrics literature continues to develop non- and semiparametric regression models for various cases. For example, imposing *monotonicity constraints*, which is important in many settings to ensure the face validity of the relationships in

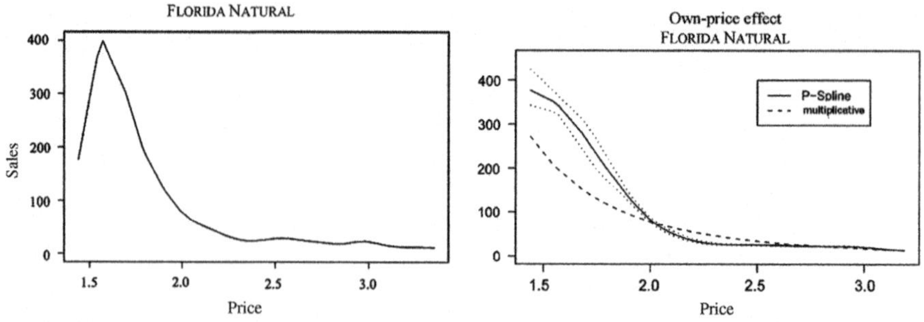

Fig. 17.6 Unconstrained Deal Effect Curve (*left*) and Monotonicity-constrained Deal Effect Curve (*right panel*), reproduced from Steiner et al. (2007)

the model, is further developed in Lee et al. (2014). *Variable selection* is discussed in Su and Zhang (2014) and semiparametric models for *truncated and censored dependent variables* in, e.g., Chen and Zhou (2012) and Čížek (2012). Other papers in econometrics focus on developing nonparametric regression methods for *panel data* (e.g., Lee and Robinson 2015), for the estimation of *gradients* (Henderson et al. 2015), and for the estimation of *confidence intervals for quantiles* (Fan and Liu 2016). Non- and semiparametric models are also expanding into the time series realm, with methods being developed for *cointegration* (Kim and Kim 2010; Park et al. 2010) and for *time-varying parameters* (Zhang 2015). Finally, progress is also made in nonparametric *instrumental variable regression* (e.g., Darolles et al. 2011). These citations are just a snapshot of the developments in non- and semiparametric regression models in econometrics.

17.9 Software for Non- and Semiparametric Regression

There are several software packages to estimate non- and semi-parametric models. SPSS has only limited options in this domain. It offers a function called "LOESS" (for local regression) that implements a local polynomial regression model for one dependent variable y and one independent variable x. The LOESS function can be activated through "Scatter Plot" and next "Add fit line at Total".

Stata has more options than SPSS. Its "Smoothing" package offers "lowess" smoothing (which is similar to LOESS), Kernel-weighted local polynomial smoothing ("lpoly"), and a Robust nonlinear smoother ("smooth") (Gutierrez et al. 2003). Stata also offers the package "bspline" to estimate spline regression models (Newson 2012).

Matrix languages such as Matlab, Gauss and R allow users to program model estimation from scratch. These also have dedicated programs to estimate various non- and semiparametric models. In Matlab, the package "Nonparametric Fitting" offers various methods. Gauss and its add-on Gaussx offer the package "NPE" (nonparametric estimation). Unlike Matlab and Gauss, R (https://cran.r-project.org/) is for free and it has a whole suite of user-developed packages including:

- regpro: Nonparametric Regression;
- np: Nonparametric kernel smoothing methods for mixed data types, providing a variety of nonparametric (and semiparametric) kernel methods that handle a mix of continuous, unordered, and ordered factor data types;
- sm: Smoothing methods for nonparametric regression and density estimation;
- npregfast: for fast non-parametric regression;
- NonpModelCheck: Model Checking and Variable Selection in Nonparametric Regression;
- monreg: Nonparametric Monotone Regression;
- bnpmr: Bayesian monotonic nonparametric regression;
- DPpackage: Bayesian nonparametric modeling in R;
- BNSP: Bayesian Non- and Semi-Parametric Model Fitting;
- SemiPar: Semiparametic Regression;
- AdaptFit: Adaptive Semiparametic Regression;
- AdaptFitOS: Adaptive Semiparametric Regression using spatially adaptive penalized splines with Simultaneous Confidence Bands;
- PCDSpline: Semiparametric regression analysis of panel count data using monotone splines.

A software package that was completely dedicated to non- and semiparametrics is Xplore. Unfortunately, it is no longer further developed, but the latest version is available for free at http://sfb649.wiwi.hu-berlin.de/fedc_homepage/xplore.php.

17.10 Conclusion

Non- and semiparametric models are useful to study the functional form governing the relationship between marketing inputs (e.g., marking mix, service levels) and outputs (e.g., sales, satisfaction). While most application focus on the relationship between price and sales, these models may be applied to other areas of marketing in which the functional form of main- and interaction effects is of crucial interest. Examples include attribute effects in conjoint experiments, main effects of advertising on sales, and interaction effects between price and advertising on sales. The semiparametric approach offers opportunities to study these effects flexibly while controlling for other relevant independent variables. By avoiding imposing a certain parametric functional forms, these models allow the data to speak for themselves, often leading to interesting, nonlinear patterns that can be explored further. The flexibility is a disadvantage too, because of the curse of dimensionality problem (exponential increase in need for observations with an increase in the number of regressor) and the possibility of obtaining implausible, non-monotonic patterns. The advent of linearly additive semiparametric models with monotonicity constraints alleviates these concerns.

References

Abe, M.: A nonparametric density estimation method for brand choice using scanner data. Mark. Sci. **14**, 300–325 (1995)

Albers, S.: Optimizable and implementable aggregate response modeling for marketing decision support. Int. J. Res. Mark. **29**, 111–122 (2012)

Blattberg, R.C., Wisniewski, K.J.: Price-induced patterns of competition. Mark. Sci. **8**, 291–309 (1989)

Blattberg, R.C., Briesch, R., Fox, E.J.: How promotions work. Mark. Sci. **14**, g122–g132 (1995)

Briesch, R.A., Chintagunta, P.K., Matzkin, R.L.: Nonparametric and semiparametric models of brand choice behavior, Working Paper. Department of Marketing, University of Texas at Austin, Austin, TX (1997)

Chen, S., Zhou, X.: Semiparametric estimation of a truncated regression model. J. Econ. **167**(2), 297–304 (2012)

Čížek, P.: Semiparametric robust estimation of truncated and censored regression models. J. Econ. **168**(2), 347–366 (2012)

Darolles, S., Fan, Y., Florens, J.P., Renault, E.: Nonparametric instrumental regression. Econometrica **79**(5), 1541–1565 (2011)

De Boor, C.: A Practical Guide to Splines. Springer, New York, NY (2001)

Eilers, P.H.C., Marx, B.D.: Flexible smoothing with B-splines and penalties (with comments and rejoinder). Stat. Sci. **11**, 89–121 (1996)

Fan, J.: Design-adaptive nonparametric regression. J. Am. Stat. Assoc. **87**, 998–1004 (1992)

Fan, J., Gijbels, I.: Local Polynomial Modeling and Its Applications. Chapman & Hall, Suffolk (1996)

Fan, Y., Liu, R.: A direct approach to inference in nonparametric and semiparametric quantile models. J. Econ. **191**(1), 196–216 (2016)

Gupta, S., Cooper, L.G.: The discounting of discounts and promotion thresholds. J. Consum. Res. **19**, 401–411 (1992)

Gutierrez, R.G., Linhart, J.M., Pitblado, J.S.: From the help desk: local polynomial regression and stata plugins. Stata J. **3**, 412–419 (2003)

Härdle, W.: Applied nonparametric regression. In: Econometric Society Monographs, vol. 19. Cambridge University Press, Cambridge (1990)

Härdle, W., Linton, O.: Applied nonparametric methods. In: Engle, R.F., McFadden, D.L. (eds.) Handbook of Econometrics, vol. 4. Elsevier Science B.V, Amsterdam (1994)

Haupt, H., Kagerer, K.: Beyond mean estimates of price and promotional effects in scanner–panel sales-response regression. J. Retail. Consum. Serv. **19**, 470–483 (2012)

Henderson, D.J., Li, Q., Parmeter, C.F., Yao, S.: Gradient-based smoothing parameter selection for nonparametric regression estimation. J. Econ. **184**(2), 233–241 (2015)

Inman, J., McAlister, L., Hoyer, W.D.: Promotion signal: proxy for price cut? J. Consum. Res. **17**, 74–81 (1990)

Kalyanam, K., Shively, T.S.: Estimating irregular pricing effects: a stochastic spline regression approach. J. Mark. Res. **35**, 16–29 (1998)

Kim, J., Kim, C.S.: Local linear estimation of nonparametric cointegrating regression. J. Econ. Theory Econ. **21**(1), 23–42 (2010)

Lee, M.J.: Methods of Moments and Semiparametric Econometrics for Limited Dependent Variable Models. Springer-Verlag, New York, NY (1996)

Lee, J., Robinson, P.M.: Panel nonparametric regression with fixed effects. J Econ. **188**(2), 346–362 (2015)

Lee, T.-H., Yundong, T., Ullah, A.: Nonparametric and semiparametric regressions subject to monotonicity constraints: estimation and forecasting. J. Econ. **182**(1), 196–210 (2014)

Martínez-Ruiz, M.P., Mollá-Descals, A., Gómez-Borja, M.A., Rojo-Álvarez, J.L.: Using daily store-level data to understand price promotion effects in a semiparametric regression model. J. Retail. Consum. Serv. **13**, 193–204 (2006)

Mayhew, G.E., Winer, R.S.: An empirical analysis of internal and external reference prices using scanner data. J. Consum. Res. **19**, 62–70 (1992)
Nadaraya, E.A.: On estimating regression. Theory Probab. Appl. **9**, 141–142 (1964)
Newson, R.B.: Sensible parameters for univariate and multivariate spline. Stata J. **12**, 479–504 (2012)
Park, J.Y., Shin, K., Whang, Y.-J.: A semiparametric cointegrating regression: investigating the effects of age distributions on consumption and saving. J. Econ. **157**, 165–178 (2010)
Powell, J.L.: Estimation of semiparametric models. In: Engle, R.F., McFadden, D.L. (eds.) Handbook of Econometrics, vol. 4. Elsevier Science B.V., Amsterdam (1994)
Robinson, P.M.: Root-n-consistent semiparametric regression. Econometrica. **56**, 931–954 (1988)
Rust, R.T.: Flexible regression. J. Mark. Res. **25**, 10–24 (1988)
Silverman, B.W.: Density estimation for statistics and data analysis. In: Monographs on Statistics and Applied Probability, vol. 26. Chapman & Hall, London (1986)
Sloot, L.M., Fok, D., Verhoef, P.C.: The short- and long-term impact of an assortment reduction on category sales. J. Mark. Res. **43**, 536–548 (2006)
Sood, A., James, G.M., Tellis, G.J.: Functional regression: A new model for predicting market penetration of new products. Market. Sci. **28**(1), 36–51 (2009)
Sood, A., James, G.M., Tellis, G.J., Zhu, J.: Predicting the path of technological innovation: SAW vs. Moore, Bass, Gompertz, and Kryder. Market. Sci. **31**(1), 964–979 (2012)
Steiner, W.J., Brezger, A., Belitz, C.: Flexible estimation of price response functions using retail scanner data. J. Retail. Consum. Serv. **14**, 383–393 (2007)
Su, L., Zhang, Y.: Variable selection in nonparametric and semiparametric regression models. In: Racine, J., Su, L., Ullah, A. (eds.) The Oxford Handbook of Applied Nonparametric and Semiparametric Econometrics and Statistics, pp. 249–307. Oxford University Press, New York (2014)
Van Heerde, H.J., Leeflang, P.S.H., Wittink, D.R.: Semiparametric analysis of the deal effect curve. J. Mark. Res. **38**, 197–216 (2001)
Van Heerde, H.J., Leeflang, P.S.H., Wittink, D.R.: Decomposing the sales promotion bump with store data. Mark. Sci. **23**, 317–334 (2004)
Watson, G.S.: Smooth regression analysis. Sankhyaā A. **26**, 359–372 (1964)
Wittink, D.R., Addona, M.J., Hawkes, W.J., Porter, J.C.: The estimation, validation, and use of promotional effects based on scanner data. In: Wieringa, J.E., Verhoef, P.C., Hoekstra, J.C. (eds.) Liber Amicorum in Honor of Peter Leeflang, pp. 135–161. University of Groningen, Groningen (2011)
Zhang, T.: Semiparametric model building for regression models with time-varying parameters. J. Econ. **187**(1), 189–200 (2015)

Chapter 18
Addressing Endogeneity in Marketing Models

Dominik Papies, Peter Ebbes, and Harald J. Van Heerde

18.1 Introduction

The marketing literature uses regression models based on observational data for causal inferences. Endogeneity issues are a threat to inferring causal effects. Endogeneity—the correlation between the regressors and the model error term—will lead to inconsistent estimates of the regression effects and potentially erroneous conclusions. We discuss this in more detail in Sect. 18.2. The standard approach to deal with endogeneity is to use an instrumental variables (IV) approach. In Sect. 18.3, we briefly introduce this technique before we highlight key aspects of IV selection.

One recent development in the domain of endogeneity correction is the quest for instrument-free methods that allow researchers to correct for endogeneity without the need to search for and justify IVs. We review these new techniques and highlight their strengths and weaknesses, point out their identifying assumptions, and discuss good practices when using these approaches. These methods are discussed in Sects. 18.4 and 18.5.

D. Papies (✉)
School of Business and Economics, University of Tübingen, Nauklerstr. 47,
Tübingen 72074, Germany
e-mail: dominik.papies@uni-tuebingen.de

P. Ebbes
Department of Marketing, HEC Paris, 1, Rue de la Libération, Jouy-en-Josas 78351, France

H.J. Van Heerde
School of Communication, Journalism and Marketing, Massey University, Private Bag 102904,
Auckland 0745, New Zealand

P.S.H. Leeflang et al. (eds.), *Advanced Methods for Modeling Markets*,
International Series in Quantitative Marketing, DOI 10.1007/978-3-319-53469-5_18

Section 18.6 then moves on to several extensions of IV estimation and we consider the cases of multiple endogenous regressors, interactions that involve endogenous regressors, including squared terms, and binary endogenous regressors.

An important theme in this chapter is that we should only try to correct for endogeneity if there is a real concern that endogeneity is an important problem. Including a rather complete set of control variables in the regression model is of paramount importance. In several instances, controlling for endogeneity can lead to more biased estimates, less significant estimates, and inferior predictions. Section 18.7 reflects this discussion in more detail.

Our goal is to provide a mostly non-technical but comprehensive discussion of endogeneity problems and their solutions. While we discuss recent and advanced topics in IV estimation, our focus is on providing guidelines and best practices when it comes to addressing an endogeneity problem in marketing models.

18.2 Endogeneity: Consequences and Caveats

18.2.1 What Is Endogeneity?[1]

Market response modeling is centered around the estimation of the effects of marketing activities on performance. However, marketing managers are often strategic in their use of marketing activities and adapt them in response to factors unobserved by the researcher. From an econometrician's perspective, these management decisions are endogenous to their expected effects on market performance. Empirical market response models that seek to estimate the causal effect of marketing instruments need to account for such strategic planning of marketing activities, or otherwise may suffer from an endogeneity problem, leading to biased estimates of the effects of the marketing activities on performance.

To illustrate the problem, consider a city with just one hotel. Suppose we have data on hotel prices and demand for rooms for this hotel. What may be unknown to a researcher is that the city has hosted a few major events throughout the year, and the hotel manager capitalized on these events by raising prices during days of peak demand. If the researcher now estimates a regression model for the effect of price on demand, the estimated effect will be distorted because she did not include the major events in the model. That is, during these events, there will be observations with high prices and high demand, which goes against the commonly assumed downward-sloping demand curve and which will bias the negative effect of price on demand toward zero. This is the essence of the endogeneity problem: distorted estimates due to a correlation between an independent variable (price in the example) and unobserved factors that are part of the error for demand (major events in this case).

---

[1]See also Vol. I, Sects. 6.5–6.7.

In mathematical terms we can consider a simple demand model, in which y_t is the market response (e.g., demand), and p_t is the price for rooms in week t. We are interested in estimating[2] the effect of price on demand (β_p):

$$y_t = \beta_0 + \beta_p p_t + \varepsilon_t. \quad (18.1)$$

We might be tempted to estimate this equation using Ordinary Least Squares (OLS). When we do so, we implicitly assume that price is exogenous. However, an endogeneity problem arises when price is correlated with the error of the demand equation, i.e., when $\mathrm{Cov}(p_t \varepsilon_t) \neq 0$, and we say that price is endogenous. The implication then is that the OLS estimates are "distorted", or in more formal terms, they are biased (i.e., have an expectation that is unequal to their true values) and they are inconsistent (i.e., they do not converge to their true values when the sample size grows to infinity).

In this stylized example, we have an endogeneity problem because the major events were omitted from the model. If the researcher had observed one or more variables describing the major events, she should have included these as control variables in the model (e.g., dummy variables for the weeks during which the event took place), and this would have taken care of the omitted variable problem. Unfortunately, in many applications it is impossible to enumerate all possible demand drivers, measure them, and include them in the model. Thus, the problem of endogeneity can often not be addressed by control variables alone.

A second example is where we have a cross-section of observations. Suppose we observe demand for hotels ($i = 1, \ldots, I$) for a city for one given year (one observation per hotel). Now y_i is annual demand and p_i is the price for rooms in hotel i (for simplicity, let's assume prices are set on a yearly basis). We are interested in estimating the effect of price on demand (β_p):

$$y_i = \beta_0 + \beta_p p_i + \varepsilon_t. \quad (18.2)$$

Hotels differ in quality levels, which are not observed by the researcher. Higher-quality hotels will be in higher demand and they are therefore able to charge higher prices. This can again lead to a correlation between price and the error term, which captures unobserved quality, i.e., we have an endogeneity problem. There may be several other ways in which price and the error term in Eq. (18.1) or (18.2) are correlated, so that an endogeneity problem can still arise even if all omitted variables are controlled for (Bascle 2008). One way is when price is measured with error, such that we have a measurement error problem. Another way is when price and demand are determined simultaneously, as it is the case, for example, in an auction for commodities.

Endogeneity has arguably become the number one issue in empirical marketing studies since the late 1990s. The reason is that valid causal effects are often the

[2]For sake of exposition we assume here that the observations are independent across time and we do not consider autocorrelations in the errors (e.g., Verbeek 2012, Chap. 4).

desired outcomes of a market response model. A researcher would likely want to tell a manager: "If you change the marketing variable by $x\%$, the performance changes by $y\%$". To make such a statement, consistently estimated parameters that do not have an endogeneity bias are essential. In *experimental studies* in which the researcher has full control over how the values of the regressors are set (i.e., random variation of prices), estimating valid causal effects is usually straightforward, and endogeneity is *not* an issue.

In many empirical applications, however, experimental studies are infeasible, and the researcher has to rely on observational data. Here, the researcher does not have full control over how the values of the regressors are set, but she observes variation in the marketing instruments, but the source of the variation is beyond her control. In these situations, causal statements (e.g., changing a marketing instrument by $x\%$ leads to a performance change of $y\%$) can only be made with the help of identifying assumptions (e.g., Pearl 2009). We explore different methods, their underlying assumptions, and the research implications of these assumptions in this chapter.

18.2.2 How Strong are Endogeneity Biases?

Most academic marketing papers focus on causal effects and hence endogeneity considerations are relevant. This will not only be apparent in the cases we discuss in this chapter, but also is evident in *meta-analyses* on marketing effectiveness.

Bijmolt et al. (2005) study 1851 *price elasticities* that were published across 40 years in 81 articles, and report an average elasticity of -2.62. One of the factors that drives price elasticity estimates is whether or not the estimation method accounts for endogeneity. Demand is substantially more price elastic when controlling for endogeneity (elasticity $= -3.74$) than when endogeneity is ignored (elasticity $= -2.47$). In other words, without endogeneity controls, the price elasticity estimate is biased toward zero, similar to the hotel example from before. In general, the sign of an omitted variable bias is the sign of the correlation between the included and excluded variable. Using this logic, a positive bias in the elasticity implies there must be a positive correlation between price and the unobserved demand shock: manager raising prices in case of a positive shock in demand.

The meta-analysis of *advertising elasticity* by Sethuraman et al. (2011) also shows a significant effect of endogeneity correction. The average short-term advertising elasticity is 0.12 across 751 estimates from 56 studies published between 1960 and 2008. They find the advertising elasticity is lower when endogeneity is not incorporated than when it is accounted for. In other words, the omission of endogeneity leads to a *negative bias* in the estimates, which is consistent with Villas-Boas and Winer (1999). This negative bias is consistent with a negative correlation between advertising and the unobserved demand shock: a manager increasing advertising in case of a shortfall in demand.

Albers et al. (2010) analyse 506 *personal selling elasticities* from 75 articles and find an average personal selling elasticity of 0.34. Interestingly, the mean predicted elasticity when endogeneity is not taken into account is 0.37, while it is 0.28 when endogeneity is controlled for. That is, the personal selling elasticity is *overestimated* when endogeneity is not incorporated, which is in contrast with the direction of the endogeneity bias for advertising.[3]

The previous discussion illustrates the two main points of this chapter. First, in many empirical settings, endogeneity matters, and ignoring it may lead to erroneous conclusions. Second, the magnitude and direction of the endogeneity bias (i.e., whether the correlation between the error and the endogenous regressors is positive or negative) is not always apparent but depends on the way managers react to unobserved demand shocks. However, while there are several ways to address endogeneity as we discuss in this chapter, none of these are perfect. In certain cases, it may be even better not to correct for endogeneity at all, as "the cure may be worse than the disease" (Bound et al. 1993). We will elaborate on these cases throughout the rest of the chapter.

18.2.3 Caveats in Addressing Endogeneity

Importantly, if the goal of the market response is purely *predictive*, i.e., to provide forecasts for future observations, the advice is not to correct for endogeneity (Ebbes et al. 2011). The reason is that any endogeneity correction in a linear regression model will tilt the fit line away from the best fitting OLS model, both in- and out of sample. We elaborate more on this caveat in Sect. 18.3.5.5.

A second caveat is that "treating variables as endogenous variables" is not the same as "correcting for endogeneity." VAR models and other vector-based time series models (VARX, VEC) treat multiple variables as endogenous. For example, sales and price may be stacked in a bivariate vector in a VAR model (see Chap. 4). This vector becomes the endogenous (dependent) variable, which is explained by lagged values of the same vector. VAR models can be used to study the dynamic relationship between price and sales. The current-period effect between price and sales is captured through the covariance of their error terms. This means that the effect is bidirectional (e.g., sales affects price as much as price affects sales). There is nothing in a VAR model that tries to correct for endogeneity bias when inferring the effect of one variable on another. To correct for endogeneity in VAR(X) or VEC models certain assumptions need to be imposed (e.g., structural VAR models, Gijsenberg et al. 2015) and/or IVs need to be employed (e.g., Van Heerde et al. 2013).

[3]See also Kremer et al. (2008).

18.3 Instrumental Variable (IV) Estimation

18.3.1 How IV Works

If a researcher (or reviewer) has strong theory- or evidence-based arguments that there is a relevant correlation between one or more regressors and the model error term, then the most common method to estimate the parameters of interest is through IV estimation. The general idea behind IV estimation is that the observed variation in the independent variable can be decomposed into an exogenous part and an endogenous part.

Figure 18.1 provides a stylized illustration. The full set of observations (left panel) are the split into those representing exogenous variation, i.e., independent of the error term in demand (middle panel) and those representing endogenous variation, i.e., correlated with the error term in demand. To estimate the regression effects, the IV approach uses—instead of the observed variation in the endogenous regressor—only the exogenous variation (middle panel).

Rather than literally splitting observations, IV isolates the exogenous variation by using an auxiliary (=additional) regression, called the "first-stage regression". To illustrate more concretely how the IV approach works, let us revisit our main equation of interest, which is a market response model for the hotel market with price as the only regressor[4]:

$$y_i = \beta_0 + \beta_p p_i + \varepsilon_i. \tag{18.3}$$

The endogeneity problem arises because p_i is correlated with the error of the demand equation, i.e., $\mathrm{Cov}(p_i\, \varepsilon_i) \neq 0$. In the IV approach, we introduce an auxiliary regression and regress the endogenous regressor p_i on all variables in the market response model (18.3) that are not correlated with the error term and an additional

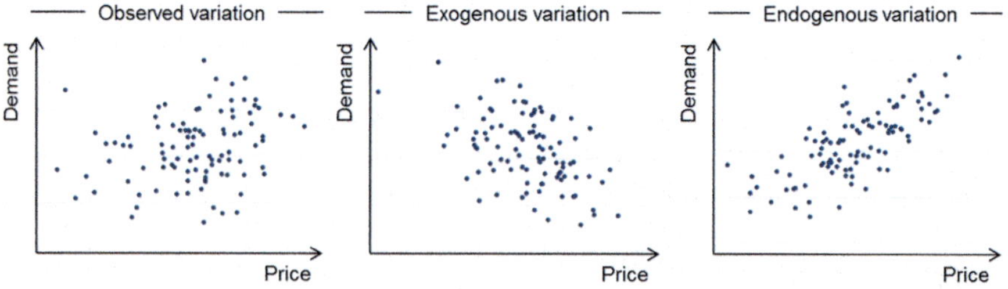

Fig. 18.1 Decomposing the variation in the independent variable, where observed variation = exogenous variation + endogenous variation

[4]We use the cross sectional case (Eq. 18.2) as the leading example. The same logic applies to a time series case (Eq. 18.1), which would in addition require a discussion of dealing with potential autocorrelation, which is beyond the scope of this chapter.

variable z that is not part of the market response model (18.3). This additional variable z_i is called an "instrumental variable". As will become clear below, this variable has to capture the exogenous variation in price, and thus must not be correlated with the error term. In our simple illustration in (18.3), there are no further exogenous variables, and hence the first stage regression becomes:

$$p_i = \gamma_0 + \gamma_z z_i + \theta_i. \tag{18.4}$$

The most common IV estimator is the two-stage least squares (2SLS) approach, which can be computed in two simple steps. First, we estimate (18.4) with OLS and use the OLS estimates from (18.4) to compute predicted values for p_i using the fitted model. Second, we replace p_i in (1) with these predicted values ($\widehat{p}_i = \widehat{\gamma}_0 + \widehat{\gamma}_z z_i$) resulting in:

$$y_i = \beta_0 + \beta_p \widehat{p}_i + \varepsilon_i. \tag{18.5}$$

The β_p estimated from (18.5) using OLS is now a consistent estimate for the effect of p_i on y_i. The resulting estimator $\widehat{\beta_p}$ is the 2SLS estimate for β_p.

So why does the IV approach work? In step 1, we compute the predicted values for p_i *using only exogenous variables*. Hence, by construction, $\widehat{p}_i$ is exogenous. Then in step 2, we replace the endogenous price by the exogenously predicted price. This variable is not correlated with the error term, and we can therefore simply use OLS to estimate the effect of price. Of course, we need to make sure that the predicted price is "meaningful" and the exogenous variables, particularly the IV, needs to have sufficient predictive power to predict price, otherwise we are substituting a useless variable in step 2 in the main equation that has little to do with the original (endogenous) price variable. We can also see that we need an additional variable z that does not appear in Eq. (18.3), because otherwise $\widehat{p}_i$ will be perfectly collinear with the other exogenous variables in the main equation, and the OLS regression in the second stage will not work either.

Figure 18.2 graphically shows for 10 hypothetical observations the three variables at play here: observed price (=p) as a solid black line, the instrumental variable z as a solid grey line, and the predicted price variable as a dashed black line. Under the assumption that z is a valid instrument, the extent to which it correlates with price represents the exogenous variation in price. In the example, it varies in steps: first 100, then 200, then 125, and finally 175. This is the type of variation we would like to use to estimate the model with. The remaining variation in price is endogenous, which we would like to remove. The way we do this is by regressing price on z, leading to $\widehat{p}_i$ (="p-hat"), which is the dashed black line in Fig. 18.2. $\widehat{p}_i$ represents exogenous variation in price, and it follows the same pattern as the IV. In the model, we use $\widehat{p}_i$ instead of p to capitalize on the exogenous variation in price.

We would like to be very clear: *2SLS only works if we have a suitable instrumental variable(s) Z*. Therefore, we must impose and accept two main assumptions for z_i to be suitable. The first assumption is that the instrument is strong, i.e., z_i must be strongly related to p_i. The second assumption is that the instrument is

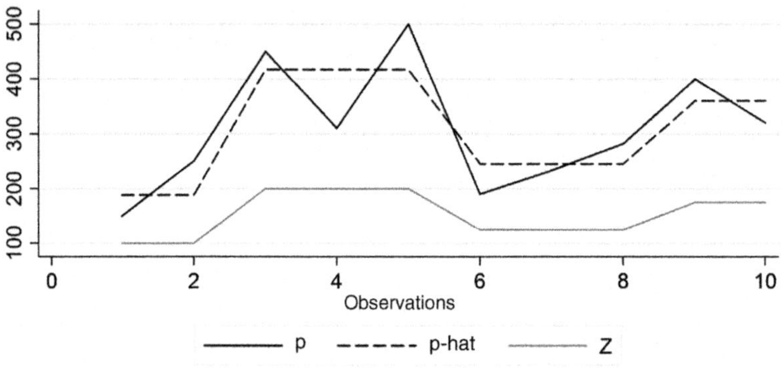

Fig. 18.2 Exogenous variation in *p*

valid (=exogenous), i.e., z must be uncorrelated with the structural error ε_i from the main Eq. (18.3). We use the terms "valid IV" and "exogenous IV" interchangeably in this chapter. In practical applications, the assumption of valid IV is arguably the most problematic assumption, as it cannot be tested directly. Thus, it truly is an assumption. We will explore these two assumptions in detail in the following sections.

The IV estimator is a standard estimator that is implemented in many statistical and econometrical software packages. In Stata, for instance, the IV approach above could be carried out with "ivreg":

$$\text{ivreg y } (\text{p} = \text{z})\text{, first.}$$

We recommend using this or similar estimation packages from the shelf instead of manually following the three steps we outline above. Manually performing these steps is prone to mistakes, and the standard errors for $\widehat{\beta}_0$ and $\widehat{\beta}_p$ will be incorrect. In case we have to conduct the 2SLS steps manually and want to obtain correct standard errors, we have to calculate the residuals based on the observed independent variable(s) p_i rather than the predicted independent variable(s) $(\widehat{p}_i)$ (Wooldridge 2010, p. 97 and p. 101):

$$\widehat{\varepsilon}_i = y_i - \left(\widehat{\beta}_0 + \widehat{\beta}_p p_i\right). \tag{18.6}$$

Next, the standard error of the estimate is calculated as $\hat{\sigma}^2 = \sum_{i=1}^{n} \widehat{\varepsilon}_i^2 / (N - K)$, where N is the number of observations and K is the number of independent variables (in our example $K = 2$). The covariance matrix of $\widehat{\beta}_p$ is calculated as $\widehat{\Sigma} = \hat{\sigma}^2 \left(\widehat{X}'\widehat{X}\right)^{-1}$ where $\widehat{X}$ is a matrix with the observations in rows and in the columns, in our example, a vector of ones and the values $\widehat{p}_i$ (Wooldridge 2010, p. 102). The standard error is the square root of the diagonal of $\widehat{\Sigma}$.

In the IV approach we achieve identification (i.e., we identify a causal effect of p on y) by relying on additional exogenous information by means of the exclusion restriction: we exclude the exogenous instrument from the main equation. In the previous example, we computed the 2SLS estimator. However, there are two other estimation approaches that leverage the IV in the presence of an endogenous regressor: the control function (CF) approach (Sect. 18.3.2) and the Limited Information Maximum Likelihood (LIML) approach, which is used to estimate a simultaneous system of equations (Sect. 18.3.3).

18.3.2 Control Function Approach

The approach that is closest in nature to 2SLS is the so-called control function (CF) approach (Ebbes et al. 2011; Petrin and Train 2010; Wooldridge 2015). For the linear model, the CF approach is exactly equivalent to 2SLS. However, the CF approach is better suited for addressing endogeneity for a non-continuous dependent variable (Sect. 18.6.4) and offers an alternative for addressing endogenous interaction effects (Sect. 18.6.1.2) and squared terms (Sect. 18.6.1.3).

So how does the CF approach look like for the linear model? After fitting the first-stage regression the way we described above for the 2SLS estimator, we use the predicted values p_i to compute the fitted residuals $\widehat{\theta}_i = p_i - \widehat{p}_i$ and subsequently include these as an *additional* regressor in the main Eq. (18.2), resulting in:

$$y_i = \beta_0 + \beta_p p_i + \beta_c \widehat{\theta}_i + \varepsilon_i. \tag{18.7}$$

The idea is that the control function ($\widehat{\theta}_i$) captures the endogenous part of p_i. That new variable is then included, resulting in Eq. (18.7). In Eq. (18.7) we are now "controlling for" the unobserved variation that makes price endogenous. Subsequently, we can estimate (18.7) with OLS to obtain a consistent estimate of β_p. In contrast, the 2SLS approach eliminates the endogenous variation in p_i by using $\widehat{p}_i$ instead of p_i in Eq. (18.5). Interestingly, in linear models, both approaches will yield the exact same results when the same IV is used. Not surprisingly, both approaches require the same two main assumptions for z_i: z_i must be a strong and valid (exogenous) instrument.

Two additional remarks are warranted. First, the inclusion of $\widehat{\theta}_i$ in (18.7) is a computationally easy version of the Hausman test for the presence of endogeneity that we will discuss in Sect. 18.3.5.3.

Second, the OLS sampling standard errors for $\widehat{\beta}_p$ ($= s.e._{\widehat{\beta}_p}^{OLS}$) from (18.7) will be incorrect because $\widehat{\theta}_i$ is an estimated quantity (Karaca-Mandic and Train 2003; Petrin and Train 2002, footnote 3). For the general CF approach (across linear and nonlinear models), we should use a bootstrap approach to approximate the correct standard errors.[5] In such an approach, $\widehat{\theta}_i$ needs to be sampled repeatedly, and for each sampled value of $\widehat{\theta}_i$, the regression model (18.7) is estimated. More specifically, we take M bootstrap samples to estimate the first-stage regression (18.4). Each bootstrap sample has N observations, which are sampled, with replacement, from the original set of N observations. Each bootstrap sample is used to estimate Eq. (18.4), which leads to M sets of fitted residuals, denoted as $\widehat{\theta}_i^{(m)}$, for $i = 1, \ldots, N$, and $m = 1, \ldots, M$. The fitted residuals of bootstrap sample m are subsequently used in the following equation, which is estimated with OLS:

$$y_i = \beta_0 + \beta_p p_i + \beta_c \widehat{\theta}_i^{(m)} + \varepsilon_i. \tag{18.8}$$

Each bootstrap sample results in a different point estimate for β_p, denoted by $\widehat{\beta}_p^{(m)}$, $m = 1, \ldots, M$. The standard deviation among this set of M estimates,

$$s.e._{\widehat{\beta}_p}^{bootstrap} = \sqrt{\frac{1}{M-1}\sum_{m=1}^{M}\left(\widehat{\beta}_p^{(m)} - \overline{\widehat{\beta}}_p\right)^2} \tag{18.9}$$

with $\overline{\widehat{\beta}}_p = \frac{1}{M}\sum_{m=1}^{M}\widehat{\beta}_p^{(m)}$, is now combined with the OLS standard error from Eq. (18.7) to obtain the corrected standard error for $\widehat{\beta}_p$:

$$s.e._{\widehat{\beta}_p}^{corrected} = \sqrt{\left(s.e._{\widehat{\beta}_p}^{OLS}\right)^2 + \left(s.e._{\widehat{\beta}_p}^{bootstrap}\right)^2}. \tag{18.10}$$

Karaca-Mandic and Train (2003, footnote 3) note that this bootstrapping approach is a reasonable approximation of the standard errors that can also be derived via an asymptotic formula. We note that this approach is *not* the same as computing the residuals from (18.4) once and then bootstrapping by sampling repeatedly from (18.7).

18.3.3 Simultaneous Equations

An alternative way of addressing the endogeneity problem is to directly model the correlation between the error term of the endogenous regressor Eq. (18.4)

[5] For the linear model, we do not need the bootstrap method. We can calculate $\widehat{\varepsilon}_i = y_i - \left(\widehat{\beta}_0 + \widehat{\beta}_p p_i\right)$ (hence we exclude the control function in the calculation of the residuals). Next, the standard error of the estimate is calculated as $\hat{\sigma}^2 = \sum_{i=1}^{n} \widehat{\varepsilon}_i^2 / (N - K)$, where N is the number of observations and K is the number of independent variables. The covariance matrix of $\widehat{\beta}_p$ is calculated as $\widehat{\Sigma} = \hat{\sigma}^2 (X'X)^{-1}$ where X is a matrix with the observations in rows and in the columns, in our example, a vector of ones and the values p_i and $\widehat{\theta}_i$. The standard error is the square root of the diagonal of $\widehat{\Sigma}$.

and the error term of the main Eq. (18.3). This can be achieved through a system of equations consisting of Eqs. (18.3) and (18.4), which we then estimate simultaneously, correlating the errors of both equations. We would typically assume a multivariate normal error term, which would then lead to the Limited Information Maximum Likelihood estimator (LIML).

A limitation of LIML is the multivariate normality assumption, which is not required in 2SLS or CF estimation. Again, many statistical and econometrical software packages offer estimation commands for LIML. In Stata for instance, one approach that is an approximation of a ML estimator is to use an iterative flavor of "sureg" in combination with the "isure" option to estimate the equations simultaneously (Gao and Lahiri 2000; Pagan 1979):

$$\text{sureg }(\text{y} = \text{p})\,(\text{p} = \text{z})\,,\text{isure}.$$

Again, in order to obtain consistent estimates using LIML, we must rely on the same assumption regarding the instruments (i.e., strength and exogeneity) as in the classical IV case.

Similar approaches to the ones that we describe above can also be implemented in a *Bayesian framework* (for a discussion, see e.g., Kleibergen and Zivot 2003 and Chap. 16). Several authors use Bayesian simultaneous equations to control for endogeneity (e.g., Ataman et al. 2008, 2010). Again, the IVs must be strong and exogenous, and we are therefore making the same assumptions as in the classical IV case. Also in the Bayesian context, the simultaneous equation approach requires an assumption on the distribution of the error term, and multivariate normality is the typical choice (e.g., Ataman et al. 2008, 2010).

There are also spatial approaches to deal with endogeneity using simultaneous equations. Bronnenberg and Mahajan (2001) argue that the unobserved actions of retailers cause a measurable joint spatial dependence among the marketing variables and sales. They construct a covariance matrix between these variables based on spatial proximity of stores and use this to obtain consistent estimates. Van Dijk et al. (2004) argue that store similarity (rather than store proximity) could underlie the spatial dependence between shelf space and sales. They use store characteristics to construct the covariance matrix between these variables to obtain a consistent estimate for the shelf space elasticity.

18.3.4 Simulation

To illustrate the basic IV approach and the different estimators that we discussed, we present a brief simulation study that considers a cross-sectional case. Suppose a researcher has cross-sectional sales data for $i = 1, \ldots, 175$ hotels in a certain local geographic region (e.g., an island in a remote area). The researcher observes only sales for 1 year as well as room prices that each hotel charges in that year (there is no variation within the year). The researcher does not observe the overall service quality of the hotels, but managers and consumers do observe quality. When the service quality of the hotel is high, the hotel manager tends to charge a higher price. Let us assume the researcher wants to estimate the simple demand model in Eq. (18.3). An endogeneity issue arises because the researcher does not observe quality, which is then an omitted variable that becomes part of the error term ε_i. As managers set prices using information on quality, there now is a positive correlation between the observed price p_i and the error term ε_i. We would expect OLS to be biased upward (Bijmolt et al. 2005) so that, as the price effect β_p is negative, the OLS estimate of price is less negative (or potentially even positive). We expect an upward bias in OLS because we now observe higher demand with higher prices, given this price setting behavior.

We simulated 500 datasets (details on the simulation settings are available upon request) and compute for each dataset the four estimators discussed before: OLS, IV, CF and LIML. Here we consider a case where we have a valid IV which explains about 33% of the variance in price (the correlation between the instrument and price is about 0.58). The true price effect is −1. The results (Table 18.1) show that OLS in this example is biased upward by about 20%. The three IV estimators perform equally well and recover the true value. In this case where we have a linear model, the CF and the 2SLS approach are identical, and with exact identification 2SLS and LIML are equivalent, and hence the identical rows. We can also see that the three IV estimators are less efficient than OLS as they have wider confidence intervals.[6]

18.3.5 Selecting the IVs

The consistency of any IV-based estimate (including 2SLS, the CF and LIML) critically depends on the *strength* of the IV. Furthermore, it also critically depends on whether the IV is exogenous. The proper selection of one or more IVs is therefore *the* critical decision in the implementation of an IV approach. In many settings it is

Table 18.1 Simulation results IV

Estimator	True value	Mean estimate	SD	95% CI	
OLS	−1	−0.834	0.060	−0.955	−0.714
2SLS	−1	−1.008	0.113	−1.235	−0.781
CF	−1	−1.008	0.113	−1.235	−0.781
LIML	−1	−1.008	0.113	−1.235	−0.781

Correlation between IV and price = 0.58. Correlation between IV and error term = 0.00

[6]Strictly speaking, "efficiency" refers to asymptotic standard errors. An efficient estimator has the lowest standard errors within a class of estimators when the sample size goes to infinity. In this chapter we use the term "efficiency" somewhat loosely as a synonym for "low standard errors" or "tight confidence intervals."

appropriate to follow a three-step approach when implementing an IV estimation. First, we should assess the strength of candidate instruments, i.e., the degree to which the instruments are correlated with the endogenous regressor (Sect. 18.3.5.1). Second, if the instruments are sufficiently strong, we can proceed to assess whether they are exogenous (Sect. 18.3.5.2). Once these two requirements are fulfilled, we would believe the IV is suitable and the researcher can formally assess whether the IV estimates differ from non-corrected estimates such as OLS (Sect. 18.3.5.3).

18.3.5.1 Instrument Strength

An instrument is strong if it is correlated with the endogenous regressor. Intuitively, this means that z must have a strong and significant effect on p in (18.4). A weak or insignificant estimate for γ in the first-stage regression is a cause for concern and most likely means that the instrument is not sufficiently strong. The most important source for understanding whether an instrument is strong or not is a good understanding of how the data at hand came about. Theory should provide a clear prediction of why and how the instrument affects the endogenous variable and we must have a clear understanding of why there is exogenous variation is the endogenous regressor. For example, see Germann et al. (2015, p. 8) for a detailed theoretical development in the context of estimating the effect of a chief marketing officer (CMO) on firm performance.

Bound et al. (1995) provide a demonstration of the role of instrument strength. They reanalyze a paper by Angrist and Krueger (1991) and replace the original instrument (quarter of birth) by randomly generated quarter of birth. This random instrument generates the same results as the original instruments, which casts strong doubts on the appropriateness of the original instruments.

Several tests exist to *formally* assess the strength of an instrument. These tests typically measure the extent to which the R^2 of the first stage regression changes due to the inclusion of the instrument. Loosely speaking, these tests compare the R^2 from a first stage regression *without* the instrument(s) to a first stage regression *including* the instrument(s). The R^2 from the latter should be significantly larger. A popular way of assessing the strength of an instrument is to assess the change in R^2 with an F-test that also considers the number of instruments required to achieve this change in R^2. Stock et al. (2002) highlight the importance of using instruments that produce a sufficiently large F-statistic. Failure to use strong instruments may result in severe biases of the estimated coefficients (Rossi 2014).

One situation in which the application of a standard (univariate) F-test will not work is when two or more regressors, say, advertising and price, are treated as endogenous. In this case, two IVs are required. If we assume that one instrument predicts advertising as well as price, and the other instrument is a weak predictor of both, then two separate F-tests for the two first-stage regressions will not uncover the resulting identification problem. A multivariate F-test may be used instead when there is more than one endogenous variable, which we will discuss in Sect. 18.6.1.

We urge researchers to report three key statistics to allow readers to assess instrument strength: the R^2 of the first-stage regression without IVs, the R^2 of the first-stage regression with IVs, and the appropriate incremental F-statistic.

18.3.5.2 Simulation (effects of weak instrument)

In the following simulation study, we illustrate the problems arising from a weak instrument, and we continue our previous example with data for 175 hotels. As before, we suspect there is an endogeneity problem. While the researcher has an IV that she believes is exogenous, the correlation between the instrument and the endogenous regressor price is weak. In our simulation study, we set the correlation between price and the instrument to 0.03. For instance, the IV may be the cost of cleaning supplies, which turns out to be only a small portion of the total cost a hotel incurs. Therefore, the IV has barely any influence on setting the prices of a hotel rooms, and weakly correlates with the endogenous variable price.

From Table 18.2 we can see that the performance of the IV approaches decreases dramatically compared to Table 18.1 (where we have a strong IVs). Across the simulated datasets, the IV estimators exhibit a very strong bias with a very large variation in the sampling distributions, indicating strong loss of efficiency of the IV models due to the weak instrument. The LIML estimator behaves slightly better under weak instruments than 2SLS and CF. The bias in the OLS estimator is of the same direction and magnitude as in the previous example (Table 18.1). Hence, when we have very weak instruments, this is one example where the "cure" (IV-based methods) may be worse than the "disease" (OLS).

18.3.5.3 Instrument Exogeneity

A valid instrument is uncorrelated with the error from the main equation, i.e., $\text{Cov}(z\,\varepsilon) = 0$. Unfortunately—and this is arguably the largest drawback of IV—this assumption cannot be tested directly. Therefore, it is of critical importance to provide theoretical arguments that can support this assumption. It is impossible to overstate the relevance of proper theoretical arguments in this context. The consistency of the coefficient that we are interested in depends on whether this

Table 18.2 Simulation results with very weak but valid instrument

Estimator	True value	Mean estimate	SD	95% CI	
OLS	−1	−0.830	0.060	−0.950	−0.71
2SLS	−1	2.060	66.502	−130.944	135.064
CF	−1	2.060	66.502	−130.945	135.065
LIML	−1	−1.289	3.011	−7.310	4.732

Correlation between IV and price = 0.03. Correlation between IV and error term = 0.00

assumption is met. In other words: whether or not the IV estimate of β_p in (18.3) is the causal effect of p on y depends on whether we can provide convincing theoretical arguments that z is uncorrelated with ε. Any IV analysis should be accompanied by such a theoretic discussion. For instance, Germann et al. (2015, p. 8) provide extensive theoretic support for why their IV (CMO prevalence) is exogenous. They first provide an analysis of what omitted variables could affect the dependent variable, and then provide theoretical support for the exogeneity of their instrument, drawing on theories in organizational processes and culture (see also Levitt 1996).

In many situations, it is useful to think of an endogeneity problem in a marketing model as an omitted variable problem, where the omitted variable is related to both the dependent variable and the (endogenous) independent variable. To provide theoretical reasons for or against an endogeneity problem, it is helpful to describe the process that is unobserved but related to, for instance, price and demand in the hotel case, or CMO presence and firm performance in the case of Germann et al. (2015). The argument of instrument validity then becomes traceable for the observer. Returning to the hotel example, we argued that an endogeneity problem arises because quality remains unobserved to the researcher, but hotels sets prices based on quality. When we try to find an IV for this situation, the argument always needs to refer to the question of whether a candidate IV is correlated with unobserved factors driving demand. For example, cost of cleaning supplies (which we used as an IV for price) is unlikely to be related to the unobserved factors that drive demand for hotel room, such as quality, and hence the IV is valid. However, it turned out to be weak as well. We will give additional guidance for finding IVs in Sect. 18.3.6.

Many researchers feel uncomfortable with the fact that the central assumption of a model is untestable (e.g., Rossi 2014), and indeed, there is no direct way of testing whether the IV in (18.4) is valid. However, in the special case where more IVs than endogenous variables are available (i.e., the model is over-identified), over-identification-tests can shed some light on the adequacy of instruments. The test utilizes the notion that the residuals from the second stage regression (Eq. 18.5) should be unrelated to the instruments. To assess this, we would store the residuals from estimating (18.5), i.e., $\widehat{\varepsilon}_i$, and regress these on all exogenous regressors including all the IVs (in the previous explanations, we mostly considered a single IV, such that z_i and γ_z are scalars; when we have multiple IVs, then z_i and γ_z become vectors). The resulting R^2 multiplied by the number of observations is χ^2-distributed and can be used to test the null hypothesis of valid instruments. A large p-value indicates that the null of valid instruments cannot be rejected and "we can have some confidence in the set of instruments used up to a point" (Wooldridge 2010, p. 135). This test is sometimes also called the Sargan test[7]; the Hansen J-test is similar but allows for heteroskedastic errors (e.g., Bascle 2008).

[7]See Vol. I, p. 210.

So, up to what point can we have confidence in this test for instrument validity? It is important to use this test with caution and to realize its limitations. First, the test can only be conducted when we have over-identification, i.e., we have a larger number of (strong) instruments than endogenous regressors. Second, the test will not tell us which instrument is suspect, it will only test the set of instruments. This means that if we reject the null hypothesis that the IVs are exogenous, we have to reject the complete set of instruments. Hence, we will not know which specific instrument caused the test to reject. Third, we must assume that at least one candidate IV is exogenous, otherwise the test yields inconsistent and biased estimates (Murray 2006). Some of these problems become less severe when at least two more instruments than needed for identification are available (e.g., Bascle 2008). Irrespective of these refinements, we urge researchers not to rely on this test as the sole measure for assessing the validity of instruments. Instead, theoretical arguments for the validity are much more important. See also Murray (2006) for more advice on this issue.

18.3.5.4 Simulation (effects of invalid instrument)

In the following simulation, we illustrate the problems arising from an invalid instrument. We consider the same case as before where unobserved quality is the problem, leading to a correlation between price and the error. Now we use a different instrument: number of personnel employed per hotel room. This is a strong IV because it will correlate with the price the hotel charges. However, it is an invalid IV because higher quality hotels tend to employ more staff, which will result in a better experience to guests, which leads to more demand (ceteris paribus). Hence this IV will be correlated with the model error term ε_i, which means it is not valid.

In the simulation study, we make the instrument invalid by setting the correlation between the instrument and the error term to 0.1, while keeping the instrument strong (correlation of 0.53 between IV and price). The true parameter values are chosen such that the bias in OLS is about the same as in the previous simulation examples. We can see from Table 18.3 that the IV estimators are now biased, with approximately the same direction and magnitude as OLS. Hence, the researcher would conclude for instance that there is no endogeneity bias in OLS (as the difference between OLS and IV is empirically negligible), whereas there is a considerable endogeneity bias as all estimators underestimate price sensitivity by about 20%.

The bias from an endogenous IV in the IV approach is exacerbated when the instrument is also weak (Bound et al. 1995). In the previous case, we had an endogenous IV which was fairly strong, as the correlation between the endogenous

Table 18.3 Simulation results with invalid but strong instrument

Estimator	True value	Mean estimate	SD	95% CI	
OLS	−1	−0.823	0.065	−0.952	−0.694
2SLS	−1	−0.833	0.136	−1.105	−0.561
CF	−1	−0.833	0.136	−1.105	−0.561
LIML	−1	−0.833	0.136	−1.105	−0.561

Correlation between IV and price = 0.53. Correlation between IV and error term = 0.10

Table 18.4 Simulation results with invalid and weak instrument

Estimator	True value	Mean estimate	SD	95% CI	
OLS	−1	−0.800	0.074	−0.948	−0.652
2SLS	−1	−0.568	0.535	−1.637	0.502
CF	−1	−0.568	0.535	−1.637	0.502
LIML	−1	−0.561	0.435	−1.432	0.309

Correlation between IV and price = 0.25. Correlation between IV and error term = 0.10

instrument and the endogenous regressor was 0.53. We now reduce the strength and set the correlation between the instrument and the regressor to 0.25. We keep the correlation between the instrument and the error term at 0.10. That is, the instrument is invalid (endogenous) to the same extent as before but has now a medium correlation with price (it is certainly not weak). We see that the IV approaches (2SLS, CF, LIML) are now *more biased* than OLS and also much less efficient (Table 18.4). Here, the researcher could wrongfully conclude that the OLS estimator has a *downward* bias whereas, in fact, it has an *upward* bias. Hence, having an endogenous IV which is only moderately strong definitely again represents a case "where the cure is worse than the disease".

18.3.5.5 Test for Presence of Endogeneity

Once we have verified that the instruments are sufficiently strong and we argued that they are valid, we can proceed with a Hausman test for the presence of endogeneity (Verbeek 2012, p. 152).[8] The essence of this test (also known as the Durbin-Wu-Hausman test) is to test whether there is a significant difference between the uncorrected set of parameter estimates and the endogeneity-corrected set (Wooldridge 2010, p. 130). The null hypothesis is that there is no difference, and a rejection of the null indicates a significant difference. If we trust the instrument,

[8]See also Sect. 6.7, Vol. I.

we may conclude that the endogeneity-corrected estimates are preferred. The equivalent test is for the significance of the control function term β_c in Eq. (18.7) as explained in Sect. 18.3.2.

Importantly, we cannot use standard model fit criteria (e.g., R^2 or holdout sample fit) to assess whether endogeneity correction is successful (Ebbes et al. 2011). When we use 2SLS estimation or any other endogeneity-correcting approach, we sacrifice fit in the hopes to obtain (more) consistent parameter estimates. The OLS line is the line that minimizes the sum of squared residuals, and 2SLS will tilt the fit line with the aim of obtaining a consistent estimate of the true slope. This happens at the expense of no longer minimizing the sum of squared residuals. This is the case both in- and out-of-sample: the OLS fitted line should beat the 2SLS fitted line. Unlike other advances in marketing modeling over the last decades (e.g., unobserved parameter heterogeneity, nonlinear functional forms), the success or failure of 2SLS cannot be assessed from the in- and out of sample fit. Only when there are two competing endogeneity-correcting approaches that are in theory equally valid, we can use in- and out-of-sample fit as a criterion for which approach should be preferred (Ebbes et al. 2011).

18.3.6 Where to Find Suitable Instruments

When we face an endogeneity problem that we believe is substantial enough such that it warrants the use of IVs, the question arises which variables can serve as potential instruments. We will consider a set of potential sources.

18.3.6.1 Lagged Variables

Quite frequently, researchers rely on lagged values of the potentially endogenous regressor as instruments, e.g., lagged prices (e.g., Rossi 2014; Villas-Boas and Winer 1999). The appeal is that lagged marketing variables are often strong predictors of current marketing variables, and hence they will typically satisfy the condition of being a strong IV.

However, are lagged regressors also valid instruments? Rossi (2014) argues that lagged prices will be invalid in a setting in which frequent sales promotions and consumer stockpiling co-occur. The household's inventory, and therefore demand, will then be related to past prices. Similarly, we can argue that reference prices (Winer 1986), which are formed on the basis of past prices, may invalidate lagged prices as instruments. More generally, lagged regressors will only be valid instruments if unobserved demand shocks are restricted to the current period. Since this will often not be the case in marketing we recommend considerable caution in using lagged regressors as instruments in general.

Is there something we can do to make lagged variables more valid instruments? We believe there may be two approaches to achieve this. The first approach is to use longer lags as IVs. For example, rather than using last period's values, go back two, three or more periods. The longer the lag, the less likely that the regressor was set deliberately based on a future demand shock, making the instrument more valid. For example, Ataman et al. (2010) use the Sargan test to lag the IV sufficiently long until the exclusion restriction is satisfied. At the same time, the strength of the IV will likely suffer from longer lags because it becomes more removed from the current period endogenous regressor. Using (longer) lags as IVs also breaks down in case of (severe) autocorrelation in the error term of the main equation, because it means that any contemporaneous correlation between the regressor term and the error term (a.k.a. endogeneity) carries over into the future, making the lagged regressor less valid yet again as an IV, because the assumption that it is exogenous cannot be maintained.

The second approach where a case for using lagged regressors as IVs could be made is when the mechanism through which these lagged regressors affect current demand is explicitly included in the model. Following up on the example of price promotions, a price promotion may lead to consumer stockpiling, which means that the consumer needs to buy less of the product in the next period. Using a lagged price promotion variable as an IV for current price promotion is not valid, because lagged price promotion is (negatively) correlated with current demand because of the consumer stockpiling, which is often an unobserved variable in many models. However, we may be able to observe or model a consumer's inventory and use it as a control variable in the demand equation. This is in line with consumer theory that says that lagged price promotion affects demand via a consumer's inventory. Once we control for inventory, the lagged price promotion variable is no longer (or much less) correlated with the current demand error term, making it a more valid IV. Of course, this argument does hinge upon the correct measurement or approximation of inventory.

This general principle of including the relevant mechanism as an explicit term in the demand model to justify the validity of lagged regressors as an IV can also be applied in other cases, as long as the relevant mechanism(s) is (are) sufficiently well represented in the model. For example: advertising affects demand via brand equity, and it has a direct effect on demand as well. Suppose the entire dynamic (over-time) effect of advertising goes via brand equity, and there is no autocorrelation in the demand error term. We now may want to estimate a model that regresses demand on advertising and brand equity, while accounting for the possible endogeneity in advertising. We can now argue that, since we include the key mechanism through which lagged advertising affects demand in the model (i.e., brand equity), we resolve the omitted variable problem that made the IV potentially invalid. Hence, the IV will have little correlation with the demand error term and that it therefore can serve as a valid IV for current advertising.

In sum, while do not explicitly recommend the use of lagged regressors as IVs, we do not see reasons to dismiss them in general. Rather, if the researcher can provide solid theoretical arguments speaking to the *strength* and *exogeneity* of the IV, then lagged regressors may be appropriate IVs in an IV regression.

18.3.6.2 Costs

Several publications rely on costs as an instrument for endogenous price. Rooderkerk et al. (2013) for instance tackle price endogeneity of liquid detergent and use costs for key ingredients (alkalines and chlorines), packaging (i.e., plastics) as well as transportation (i.e., diesel) as instruments. The idea behind costs as instrument is that firms will adjust price in response to cost shocks, but costs are unobserved by consumers, and may therefore be unrelated to unobserved demand shocks. In a similar vein, Dinner et al. (2014) use the price index for advertising from the American Bureau of Labor Statistics as an IV for advertising.

There are, however, at least two caveats that researchers should be aware of when using costs as IVs. First, costs are often difficult to observe. For example, for strategic reasons, many firms are reluctant to reveal the wholesale costs they face. In that case, researchers have to use external, more aggregate sources to approximate costs, such as quarterly statistics available from national statistics agencies (e.g., Dinner et al. 2014; Rooderkerk et al. 2013). These cost data are likely to be valid instruments (as they most likely have little relation with unobserved factors shaping demand of the focal product). Their strength, however, may be compromised because they are far removed from the focal endogenous regressor. What's more, oftentimes they are not measured at the same frequency (e.g., a weekly observed endogenous regressor and a quarterly observed price index from the Central Bureau of Statistics), which limits their ability to explain variation in the regressor.

Second, consider the case of a retailer setting prices in an endogenous manner. If manufacturers or other suppliers of goods to this retailer are aware of these unobserved demand shocks and adjust their prices accordingly, the retailer's costs will be correlated with the unobserved demand shocks, and costs become invalid instruments (Rossi 2014). How can upstream firms have knowledge of demand shocks? Rossi (2014) gives the example that manufacturers anticipate advertising and promotional campaigns. Further, let us consider hotel prices in a small US college town with a popular college football team. Hotel prices will soar on football weekends, but costs may also increase on this weekends because of overtime pay or because staff may require higher wages (Otter et al. 2011). As a last example, prices for music downloads may be endogenous because retailers adjust their prices to unobserved shocks in artists' popularity. Music labels, however, may be aware of shock in popularity and adjust the prices that download stores have to pay to labels in response to these shocks.

In sum, costs are among the most promising candidates when looking for valid instruments. In each instance, however, a researcher has to carefully assess whether the exogeneity assumption is reasonable and whether they are indeed sufficiently strong.

18.3.6.3 Different Markets, Industries or Brands

In many situations, unobserved demand shocks may be restricted to local markets, but firms share costs structures across different markets (Hausman 1996). In these cases, prices from other markets may be suitable instruments (e.g., Rooderkerk et al. 2013). However, this only holds if unobserved demand shocks are indeed restricted to local markets, which is unlikely to be the case when national advertising expenditures are an important element of the marketing mix (Rossi 2014), and Hausman's (1996) approach has been questioned (see comments to Hausman 1996). Nevo (2001) also contains a detailed discussion of these considerations.

A similar strategy relies on the use of different brands, firms, or categories. Van Heerde et al. (2013), for instance, use the marketing instruments from brands in other categories as instruments for the focal brand's marketing activities. The assumptions underlying this approach are the same as above: the different brands or categories share common cost structures, but the unobserved demand shocks are restricted to the focal brands. It is important to choose these "other" brands, firms, or categories sufficiently different from the focal market (to ensure instrument validity) yet not too far away (to ensure instrument strength). For example, while the IVs used by Dinner et al. (2014) are advertising expenditures by (low-end) retailers that compete in a very different price tier as IVs for the focal (high-end) retailer's advertising (to ensure instrument validity), they are from the same broad industry (clothing and apparel retailing) to ensure instrument strength.

Germann et al. (2015, p. 8) use CMO prevalence as the primary IV for estimating the effect of CMO presence on firm performance. They compute CMO prevalence from the sample firms' peers, which are firms that operate in the same primary two-digit Standard Industrial Classification (SIC) code(s) as the focal firm. They provide theoretical arguments using organizational theory and argue that this instrument meets the exclusion restriction in the context of their study, although they recommend to include time fixed effects to capture shocks that are common across industries (such as economy wide boom), which could influence both firm performance (their dependent variable) and CMO prevalence (their IV). They also investigate a robustness specification where they include time fixed effects interacted with industry-specific fixed effects to control for possible time unobserved shocks at the industry level, that could invalidate the instrument. Hence, carefully argued robustness analyses can also help providing theoretic support for the IVs.

18.4 Panel Data

18.4.1 Introduction: Endogeneity and Panel Data

As has become apparent above, correcting for endogeneity comes at a cost (Rossi 2014). It is hard to find suitable instruments. Furthermore, the IV estimator is generally less efficient than OLS, in particular when the instruments are weak. On top of that, it will be biased when the instrument is invalid. This implies that researchers should only consider an IV approach to endogeneity correction if other options are infeasible or insufficient.

Another opportunity lies in panel data, where we have multiple time series observations per response unit. In some cases, these can be used to control for endogeneity without needing observed IVs. For that reason, we recommend that researchers carefully assess if they can address endogeneity concerns by exploiting the panel structure of the data. A panel data structure is very common in marketing, where we observe data across a cross-section (e.g., consumers, firms, brands, stores, countries) as well as across time (e.g., purchase occasions, days, weeks, months, quarters, years).[9]

Consider the following demand model, where we extend Eq. (18.3) by a time dimension (e.g., we observe weekly sales and prices per hotel). y_{it} is then demand for hotel i in week t:

$$y_{it} = \beta_0 + \beta_p p_{it} + \alpha_i + \lambda_t + \varepsilon_{it}. \tag{18.11}$$

We can now think of the error as containing three separate components. One component varies across hotels and time: ε_{it}. Another component varies across hotels but not across time, i.e., these are unobserved hotel characteristics that affect a hotel's demand (α_i). These could be the hotel's location, quality of the facility, or the management quality, as these aspects may often be considered fairly stable for a period of time (e.g., for the duration of the panel). Lastly, there may be a component (λ_t) that varies across time but not across hotels. An example is seasonality or holidays affecting demand for hotels. When the factors α_i and λ_t are not explicitly accounted for in the estimation, they will be part of the (total) error term $\tilde{\varepsilon}_{it} = \alpha_i + \lambda_t + \varepsilon_{it}$. If these factors α_i and λ_t are correlated with price, then an endogeneity problem arises because now prices are correlated with the total error $\tilde{\varepsilon}_{it}$.

Fortunately, the panel structure of the data allows us to eliminate two of these unobserved components and any endogeneity problem arising from these. We first illustrate this idea for the case of a model in which there is an unobserved component α_i but no λ_t. By estimating (18.11) with fixed effects (FE), for example by including one dummy variable per hotel, all time-invariant hotel characteristics are controlled for. Because in most marketing applications we often have large cross-sections

[9]See Sect. 4.5, Vol. I.

leading to a model with many fixed effects, a simpler (yet equivalent) approach is to use a "within-transformation" that eliminates α_i. As such, we need to calculate the mean demand and mean price across t for each i, i.e., $\overline{y}_i$ and $\overline{p}_i$, by averaging (18.11) resulting in[10]:

$$\overline{y}_i = \beta_p \overline{p}_i + \alpha_i + \overline{\varepsilon}_i. \tag{18.12}$$

We then take the difference between (18.11) and (18.12):

$$(y_{it} - \overline{y}_i) = \beta_p (p_{it} - \overline{p}_i) + (\varepsilon_{it} - \overline{\varepsilon}_i). \tag{18.13}$$

It becomes apparent that the within-transformation removes the hotel-specific unobserved effect (α_i) and potential distortions that arise from its correlation with p_i. We can now simplify (18.13) by defining $\ddot{y}_{it} = (y_{it} - \overline{y}_i)$; $\ddot{p}_{it} = (p_{it} - \overline{p}_i)$; $\ddot{\varepsilon}_{it} = (\varepsilon_{it} - \overline{\varepsilon}_i)$:

$$\ddot{y}_{it} = \beta_p \ddot{p}_{it} + \ddot{\varepsilon}_{it}. \tag{18.14}$$

We can now consistently estimate (18.14) with OLS under the assumption that $\ddot{\varepsilon}_{it}$ is uncorrelated with $\ddot{p}_{it}$. Vis-à-vis our hotel example, this assumption implies that there are no *time-varying* unobserved demand shocks that managers take into account when setting prices, and that potential price endogeneity in this case arises solely from time-invariant hotel characteristics such as quality.[11]

A similar reasoning applies when a time-varying unobserved component is present that is constant across hotels (λ_t). In that case, we can use a within-transformation to remove the time component and estimate the resulting transformed model with OLS. We can also simultaneously correct for both the cross-sectional component α_i and the time-varying component λ_t, for instance by estimating Eq. (18.14) including time fixed effects; we refer to Verbeek (2012, Chap. 10) for details.

We note that another approach commonly discussed in panel applications is the *random effects* estimator that takes the unobserved intercepts α_i as random variables. We note that this approach does not account for endogeneity, and it has even slightly stronger exogeneity assumptions regarding the identification of

[10]This part relies heavily on Wooldridge (2010, p. 300). We recommend this as further reading for those interested in more details. Another very useful econometric resource is Verbeek (2012; Chap. 10).

[11]It is important to realize that the panel structure of data does not necessarily refer to repeated observations over time alone. It can also encompass other cases of a nested or multi-level data structure, e.g., brands are observed across multiple stores, schools contain multiple classes, which contain multiple students. The estimation approach applies to these cases as well (e.g., Ebbes et al. 2004; Kim and Frees 2006, 2007).

the regression effects than OLS. An (informal) discussion on the main identifying assumptions of panel model applications in marketing is given by Germann et al. (2015, Table 2).

We now illustrate these panel data approaches in a simulation study, in which we have a panel data with 52 weeks for 175 hotels. We consider four scenarios. In *scenario 1*, there are no unobserved differences between hotels (i.e., $\alpha_i = 0$); λ_t is a common weekly demand shock (e.g., a home football game) that is observed by hotel managers and used to set prices, but it is not observed by researchers, hence $\text{Cov}(p_{it}\,\lambda_t) \neq 0$[12]:

$$y_{it} = \beta_0 + \beta_p p_{it} + \lambda_t + \varepsilon_{it}. \tag{18.15}$$

In *scenario 2*, the hotels exhibit unobserved (to the researcher) quality aspects (α_i) The quality information drives demand but is also used to set prices: $\text{Cov}(p_{it}\,\alpha_i) \neq 0$. There are no time shocks: $\lambda_t = 0$. The demand model now is:

$$y_{it} = \beta_0 + \beta_p p_{it} + \alpha_i + \varepsilon_{it}. \tag{18.16}$$

Scenario 3 is the combination of the previous two with unobserved shocks that are common to all hotels, and unobserved shocks that are hotel specific, but time invariant, and the firm sets prices based on both types of shocks: $\text{Cov}(p_{it}\,\lambda_t) \neq 0$ and $\text{Cov}(p_{it}\,\alpha_i) \neq 0$:

$$y_{it} = \beta_0 + \beta_p p_{it} + \alpha_i + \lambda_t + \varepsilon_{it}. \tag{18.17}$$

Scenario 4 is the same as scenario 3 in that it combines the two previous demand shocks of scenarios 1 and 2. In addition, we now assume that the price is also set based on demand shocks that vary across hotel and time, i.e., $\text{Cov}(p_{it}\,\lambda_t) \neq 0$, $\text{Cov}(p_{it}\,\alpha_i) \neq 0$ and $\text{Cov}(p_{it}\,\varepsilon_{it}) \neq 0$.

As before, we simulate 500 datasets (details are available upon request) and estimate the following approaches: OLS, OLS with week dummies, FE, FE with week dummies, and 2SLS. We omit the CF approach and LIML as these perform at a similar level as 2SLS. We assume that the researcher observes a cost instrument that she obtained from the local chamber of commerce that provided her with weekly data of labor cost for maintenance and cleaning staff. Hence, his instrument captures cost at a weekly level, but is the same for all hotels. After plotting a time series of Sales, Price and Cost for one hotel, she observes that cost increases throughout the year following a step function; prices tend to increase, and sales have a small negative trend because of the price increase. This pattern is representative for the other hotels.

[12]For scenarios 1–3, we assume $\text{Cov}(p_{it}\,\varepsilon_{it}) = 0$.

18.4.2 Results for Scenario 1: Only Time Shocks

When the endogeneity comes from time unobserved shocks only, just including time dummies in OLS (or FE or Random Effects (RE)) recovers the true parameters well (Table 18.5). We note that we have employed the cross-sectional 2SLS approach, ignoring the panel structure in the data. This approach yields estimates that are approximately unbiased but are not efficient.[13] Hence, we conclude that in such a scenario, the recommended course of action is the *inclusion of time dummies* rather than 2SLS.

18.4.3 Results for Scenario 2: Only Cross-Sectional Shocks

When the unobserved component is purely cross-sectional, *2SLS will resolve the endogeneity problem* (see Table 18.6). It requires, however, the availability of suitable instruments. FE, in contrast, does not require instruments but works equally well and is slightly more efficient.

18.4.4 Results for Scenario 3: Both Time and Cross-Sectional Shocks

When there are both omitted time varying and time-invariant omitted variables (i.e., a combination of scenarios 1 and 2), we see that the *FE approach with time dummies*

Table 18.5 Simulation results scenario 1 (only unobserved time shocks)

Estimator	True value	Mean estimate	SD	95% CI	
OLS	−1	−0.834	0.066	−0.967	−0.702
2SLS	−1	−1.011	0.128	−1.268	−0.754
OLS with time fixed effects	−1	−1.000	0.011	−1.022	−0.979
FE (cross-sectional)	−1	−0.833	0.067	−0.967	−0.699
FE (cross-sectional) and time fixed effects	−1	−1.000	0.011	−1.022	−0.979
RE (cross-sectional)	−1	−0.835	0.066	−0.967	−0.703
RE (cross-sectional) and time fixed effects	−1	−1.000	0.011	−1.022	−0.979

[13]We also note that in this example the instrument only varies across time and not across hotels, similar to the omitted variable. Hence, in separating out the exogenous and endogenous variation which are both constant across hotels we only have the time dimension of the data.

Table 18.6 Simulation results scenario 2 (only unobserved cross-sectional shocks)

Estimator	True value	Mean estimate	SD	95% CI	
OLS	−1	−0.832	0.052	−0.937	−0.728
2SLS	−1	−1.001	0.012	−1.025	−0.977
OLS with time fixed effects	−1	−0.717	0.026	−0.770	−0.665
FE (cross-sectional)	−1	−1.000	0.007	−1.014	−0.986
FE (cross-sectional) and time fixed effects	−1	−1.000	0.011	−1.021	−0.979
RE (cross-sectional)	−1	−0.976	0.011	−0.998	−0.953
RE (cross-sectional) and time fixed effects	−1	−0.953	0.012	−0.978	−0.928

Table 18.7 Simulation results scenario 3 (both unobserved time and cross-sectional shocks)

Estimator	True value	Mean estimate	SD	95% CI	
OLS	−1	−0.827	0.069	−0.964	−0.689
2SLS	−1	−1.012	0.129	−1.271	−0.754
OLS with time fixed effects	−1	−0.776	0.039	−0.855	−0.698
FE (cross-sectional only)	−1	−0.892	0.069	−1.030	−0.755
FE (cross-sectional) and time fixed effects	−1	−1.000	0.011	−1.022	−0.979
RE (cross-sectional only)	−1	−0.888	0.068	−1.025	−0.751
RE (cross-sectional) and time fixed effects	−1	−0.990	0.011	−1.011	−0.968

is the only panel approach that is approximately unbiased. This approach controls for both the unobserved demand shocks at the hotel level (by applying the within-transformation) as well as unobserved demand shocks that are time varying (but constant across hotels) by including time-fixed effects. The RE approach with time dummies is also performing very well, but still suffers a bit from the demand shocks at the hotel level. In the presence of a good IV (as we have here), the 2SLS approach also yields approximately unbiased results but is inefficient. As before, we have employed the cross-sectional 2SLS approach, ignoring the panel structure in the data. Here we could improve on its efficiency by appropriately accounting for the correlated error structure within hotels (Tables 18.7 and 18.8).

18.4.5 Results for Scenario 4: Both Time and Cross-Sectional Shocks, Plus a Correlation Between Price and the Error Term

In this scenario, we need an observed IV as neither controlling for time (week dummies) nor controlling for unobserved hotel random intercepts (fixed effects) is

Table 18.8 Simulation results scenario 4 (both unobserved time and cross-sectional shocks, and a correlation between price and the error term)

Estimator	True value	Mean estimate	SD	95% CI	
OLS	−1	−0.818	0.067	−0.952	−0.685
2SLS	−1	−1.003	0.087	−1.178	−0.829
OLS with time fixed effects	−1	−0.705	0.035	−0.775	−0.635
FE (cross-sectional only)	−1	−0.875	0.064	−1.002	−0.748
FE (cross-sectional) and time fixed effects	−1	−0.799	0.010	−0.820	−0.779
RE (cross-sectional only)	−1	−0.873	0.064	−1.000	−0.745
RE (cross-sectional) and time fixed effects	−1	−0.795	0.010	−0.816	−0.774

sufficient. The *2SLS approach works very well here* as it can account for endogeneity coming from time and cross-sectional shocks, as well as for endogeneity coming from the correlation between price p_{it} and the error term ε_{it}. We could potentially further improve the 2SLS approach by including week dummies to reduce its standard error. We note that the cost instrument we use here, although constant across hotels, is relatively strong (the correlation between the instrument and price is about 0.64). In the absence of such a high quality instrument, none of the other approaches (OLS, FE or RE) would estimate the price effect well, despite the presence of panel data.

In sum, our simulation examples show that:

- the fixed-effects approach with time dummies is a very robust approach across three of the four scenarios (scenarios 1–3);
- only when the endogeneity arises at the lowest level in the model ($\text{Cov}(p_{it}\, \varepsilon_{it}) \neq 0$ as in scenario 4), we need an observed instrument.

We need to wonder in which situations we may have situations like scenario 4 (Rossi 2014). Marketing researchers, in many cases, have access to rich data that usually contain a time and cross-sectional dimension (see also the discussion in Germann et al. 2015). Therefore, it is our recommendation that researchers attempt to address endogeneity concerns by exploiting the panel structure of their data. Under the assumptions that we outlined, this will address potential endogeneity concerns. Because these assumptions—as most identifying assumptions—are untestable, researchers need a strong theory and understanding of the data generating process in order to judge how reasonable this assumption is. If the assumption is reasonable that the endogeneity is concentrated in the cross-section (i.e., time-invariant, at the hotel level) or time-dimension (i.e., at the week level, invariant across hotels), researchers should rely on fixed-effects estimation. If one believes that this assumption is too strong, i.e., that the idiosyncratic component ε_{it} is correlated with a regressor after including control variables and fixed effects (e.g., for time, cross-sectional units, or both), only then the analysis should be complemented with more advanced but potentially costly methods, such as an IV approach.

18.5 IV-Free Methods

18.5.1 Introduction to IV-Free Methods

The difficulty of finding suitable instruments (e.g., Rossi 2014; Stock et al. 2002) has sparked researchers' interest in finding ways of accounting for endogeneity in observational data without the need to use observed instruments. At least two approaches have been discussed in the marketing literature.[14]

Ebbes et al. (2005) develop the method of latent instrumental variables (LIV) that provides identification through latent, discrete components in the endogenous regressors. Similar to the observed IV approach, the LIV approach shares the underlying idea that the endogenous regressor is a random variable that can be separated into two components, i.e., $p = \theta + \nu$, where θ represents the exogenous variation and ν the endogenous variation. The endogenous component is correlated with the error term of the main regression equation through a bivariate normal distribution. The LIV model can be estimated using a maximum likelihood approach, as we will discuss in more detail below.

Park and Gupta (2012) introduce a method that directly models the correlation between the endogenous regressor and the error using Gaussian copulas. Simply put, the copula connects the marginal distributions of two or more variables that follow any distribution (e.g., normal, non-normal). Park and Gupta (2012) add a copula term to the model that represents the correlation between the endogenous variable and the error term. By including this term, the effect of the endogenous regressor can be estimated consistently. Both latent IV and Gaussian copulas exploit non-normality in the endogenous regressor, and normality of the error term(s). We will now discuss these two methods in more detail.

18.5.2 The Latent Instrumental Variables (LIV) Approach

18.5.2.1 LIV Approach

Similar to observed IV methods, the LIV approach decomposes the endogenous variable into two parts: a source of exogenous information and an endogenous error term. Without an observed IV to provide exogenous identifying information, the LIV method requires distributional assumptions for the exogenous source (the latent instrument) and the endogenous error term. Ebbes et al. (2005) approximate the unobserved instrument by a latent discrete variable. That is, in the basic LIV model

[14]In addition to the two approaches we discuss here, framed as a potential solution to measurement error, Lewbel (1997) introduced a method that obtains identification from higher moments when the endogenous regressor is skewed. Ebbes et al. (2009) provide a detailed analysis.

the main regression equation for Y is augmented with a linear, additive, specification for the endogenous regressor:

$$y_i = \beta_0 + \beta_p p_i + \varepsilon_i \tag{18.18}$$

$$p_i = \pi \tilde{z}_i + \nu_i \tag{18.19}$$

where π is a $1 \times L$ vector of latent category means, which are different, and $\tilde{z}_i$ is an unobserved $L \times 1$ indicator variable. The probability of category $l = 1, 2, \ldots, L$ is λ_l, with $\sum_{l=1}^{L} \lambda_l = 1$, $\lambda_l > 0$, and $L > 1$. The endogenous error term ν_i is correlated with the error term ε_i. With bivariate normally distributed error terms, it can be shown that the resulting LIV model belongs to the class of normal mixture models with L components. As such, the LIV approach is a parametric, likelihood based, approach. The parameters of the LIV model can be estimated through maximum likelihood estimation by numerically optimizing the likelihood function. The likelihood equation for observation i of the basic LIV model is given in Eq. (5) of Ebbes et al. (2005). Ebbes et al. (2005, 2009) show that identification of the LIV model requires that the latent instrument has a non-normal distribution, assuming bivariate normally distributed error terms ε_i and ν_i. Based on a set of simulation studies, they conclude that, when applied sensibly, the LIV approach may be a useful alternative in situations where an endogenous regressor is present but no good quality observed IVs are available.

The LIV approach has recently been applied, and extended beyond the linear (cross-sectional) regression model, in several studies in marketing, among which e.g., Abhishek et al. (2015); Grewal et al. (2010, 2013); Lee et al. (2015); Ma et al. (2014); Narayan and Kadiyali (2015); Rutz et al. (2012); Rutz and Trusov (2011); Sabnis and Grewal (2015); Saboo and Grewal (2012); Sonnier et al. (2011); Srinivasan et al. (2013), and Zhang et al. (2009).

Good practice using LIV requires at least the following tasks for the researcher (Ebbes et al. 2005). First, like traditional IV, the LIV approach assumes that p_i can be decomposed in a linear way in two parts: an exogenous part and an endogenous part. This is an assumption that cannot be tested for. Hence, the development of theoretical arguments based on an analysis of the problem motivating the investigation of endogeneity remains crucial, as is standard in traditional IV estimation, and should precede the application of LIV. Second, when a researcher finds evidence of endogeneity using LIV, we suggest that the researcher contrasts the LIV estimates and implications with traditional approaches, such as OLS. Here, the magnitude and direction of the differences should conform to theoretical predictions. Third, the LIV approach should be fitted with a range of choices for L (the number of categories of the latent instrument). We suggest that the researcher fits at least $L = 2, 3, 4$ and 5. When the estimated coefficient β_p varies strongly for different choices of L, then the latent instrument is likely ill-defined, and the approach may not be suitable. Fourth, the researcher should always investigate normality of the error term, particularly ε_i. One can start with the OLS residuals, followed by an analysis of the fitted residuals from the LIV model. And, lastly, the LIV approach exploits non-normality of the endogenous regressor. Hence, one should always test that the endogenous regressor is not normally distributed.

18.5.2.2 Simulation (LIV Approach)

We consider the same panel data example as in the previous section. Suppose that the researcher observes for 1 year weekly sales and price data of 175 hotels, where price is endogenous because it is correlated with the model error term ε. For simplicity, we do not consider time and cross sectional shocks. The researcher knows that prices are also set based on cost, where cost is largely unaffected by local market drivers. If she had access to cost data, she would have used cost as an observed IV. Hence, she believes that prices also exhibit exogenous variation. She will use the LIV approach to capture the exogenous variation and estimate the regression parameters.

We simulate 500 datasets, and take a Gamma (1,1) distribution for the true, but unobserved instrument. Note that the LIV approach is misspecified, as the "true" instrument is not discrete. However, Ebbes et al. (2009) show that this is not problematic for LIV. The correlation of this unobserved instrument with price is 0.58 (which corresponds to an R^2 square of 0.33). This true instrument is not used in estimating the LIV model parameters because the researcher would not have access to it. Instead, the LIV methods tries to infer the latent IV. The results for OLS and the LIV approach with $L = 2, 3, 4$ are given Table 18.9.

Hence, the LIV approach works well when there exists exogenous variation that is not normally distributed. When we test for the non-normality of the endogenous regressor p, we reject normality in 100% of the cases. We see that the LIV2, LIV3, and LIV4 results are similar, but taking more categories results here in some small efficiency gains. Furthermore, residual checks for ε_i using the LIV fitted residuals show that these are normally distributed (we used the Anderson-Darling test, and examined the skewness and kurtosis of the fitted residuals).

Table 18.9 Simulation results LIV approach

Estimator	Mean estimate	SD	95% CI	
OLS	−0.833	0.009	−0.850	−0.816
LIV2	−0.999	0.040	−1.079	−0.920
LIV3	−0.999	0.039	−1.077	−0.921
LIV4	−1.000	0.038	−1.076	−0.923

Table 18.10 Illustration of the Gaussian copula method

Column 1: Endogenous regressor p sorted from low to high	Column 2: Empirical cumulative density function $H(p)$	Column 3: The inverse normal CDF of the cumulative density function $p^* = \Phi^{-1}(H(Pp))$
100	0.01	−2.32
105	0.02	−2.05
–	–	–
390	0.99	2.32
400	1.00 → 0.99	2.32

18.5.3 Gaussian Copula

Park and Gupta (2012) propose to correlate the normally distributed error term with the non-normally distributed endogenous regressor directly through a copula structure. Hence, they treat the endogenous variable as a random variable from any (non-normal) marginal population distribution, which is correlated with the normal error term of the main equation through a copula.

The Gaussian copula method to correct for endogeneity (Park and Gupta 2012) is rather simple to implement through a CF approach[15] and has been used in a number of recent marketing papers (e.g., Burmester et al. 2015; Datta et al. 2015). Similar to the CF approach, it boils down to adding an extra term to the regression model of interest. This term is $p^* = \Phi^{-1}(H(p))$, where $H(p)$ is the empirical cumulative density function (CDF) of p, and Φ^{-1} is the inverse normal CDF.

Table 18.10 shows how it works for an example case with $N = 100$. First, we sort the observations for the endogenous regressor p from low to high in column 1. Suppose the minimum p observed is 100, next is 105, and the highest two values are 390 and 400, respectively. Column 2 contains $H(p)$, which is the probability mass of observing a value less than or equal to that value. So for the lowest observation it is $1/N = 0.01$, and for the second-lowest observation it is $2/N = 0.02$, and so forth. For the highest observation ($p = 400$), $H(p)$ is 1.00, which has to be set to a value just below that $(1-(1/N) = 0.99)$ to avoid an error in the next step. The next step (column 3) is to calculate the inverse normal CDF: $p^* = \Phi^{-1}(H(p))$.

This p^* term is the copula CF term, and it controls for the correlation between the error term and the endogenous regressor. In the spirit of the CF approach, we add this to the main Eq. (18.3) while keeping the original endogenous regressor p_i in the equation:

$$y_i = \beta_0 + \beta_p p_i + \beta_c p_i^* + \varepsilon_i. \tag{18.20}$$

[15] We thank Sungho Park for sharing his Gauss code with us.

We can now consistently estimate Eq. (18.20) with OLS. The parameter estimate of central interest is $\widehat{\beta}_p$. The estimate of $\widehat{\beta}_c$ allows us to test whether there is significant presence of endogeneity, which is the Hausman test discussed before.

The OLS standard errors, however, are incorrect because p_i^* is an estimated quantity. Park and Gupta (2012) suggest to use bootstrapping. Each bootstrap sample ($m = 1, \ldots, M$) has N observations drawn with replacement from the original N observations. Next, for each bootstrap sample m, we estimate Eq. (18.21) with OLS:

$$y_i^{(m)} = \beta_p p_i^{(m)} + \beta_c p_i^{*(m)} + \varepsilon_i \tag{18.21}$$

where each sample $m = 1, \ldots, M$ leads to a different point estimate for β_p, denoted by $\widehat{\beta}_p^{(m)}$. The standard deviation among this set of M estimates is now used as the standard error:

$$s.e._{\widehat{\beta}_p}^{corrected} = \sqrt{\frac{1}{M-1}\sum\nolimits_{m=1}^{M}\left(\widehat{\beta}_p^{(m)} - \overline{\widehat{\beta}}_p\right)^2} \tag{18.22}$$

where $\overline{\widehat{\beta}}_p = \frac{1}{M}\sum_{m=1}^{M}\widehat{\beta}_p^{(m)}$.

Given how simple the endogeneity correction via Gaussian copulas is, the question arises whether this method exhibits serious downsides. First and foremost, the key identifying assumption is the non-normal distribution of the endogenous regressor. Our simulations below show that the method fails if the distribution of the endogenous regressor is "too normal". Hence, we urge researchers to carefully establish that the endogenous regressor is truly non-normal (e.g., through visual inspection and tests such as the K-S-test or Shapiro-Wilk-test).

Our simulations show that—conditional on a non-normal endogenous regressor and normal structural error—the method resolves the endogeneity bias and is about as efficient as IV. Table 18.11 contains the results of a small simulation study in which we continue the example from Sect. 18.5.2.2, where the endogenous regressor is non-normally distributed. In our example, the endogenous regressor follows either a Gamma, F, χ^2, t, or Poisson distribution, and we vary each distribution across a set of three different shape parameters and perform 500 replications. This leads to a

Table 18.11 Simulation results Gaussian copulas method across all simulated cases

Estimator	Mean estimate	SD	95% CI	
OLS	−0.820	0.101	−0.822	−0.817
Copula corrected estimate	−0.995	0.071	−0.997	−0.993

total of 7500 datasets. We discard 56 datasets in which a Shapiro-Wilk-test does not reject the null hypothesis of a normal distribution with $p < 0.05$.[16]

Similarly, as in the case of latent instruments, we highlight the relevance of assessing the distributional assumptions, i.e., we *must* ascertain that the endogenous regressor is not normally distributed and that the error is approximately normal.

18.6 Advanced Topics in IV Estimation

When estimating more complex applied models that go beyond the standard textbook case (e.g., multiple endogenous marketing instruments), IV estimation offers challenges that are often not well understood. We will cover several of those.

18.6.1 Multiple Endogenous Regressors, Interactions, and Squared Terms

18.6.1.1 Multiple Endogenous Regressors

So far, we have mostly only considered cases with one endogenous regressor, and one IV. However, the IV problem can easily be extended to a case with more than one endogenous regressor. Consider the following model:

$$y = \beta_0 + \beta_1 p_1 + \beta_2 p_2 + \beta_3 w + \varepsilon_1 \tag{18.23}$$

where both p_1 and p_2 are potentially endogenous. We now require at least two IVs, and two first stage regressions, which both contain *all* exogenous information (i.e., *all* exogenous regressors w and *all* instruments z):

$$p_1 = \gamma_0 + \gamma_1 z_1 + \gamma_2 z_2 + \gamma_3 w + \theta_1, \text{ and} \tag{18.24}$$

$$p_2 = \eta_0 + \eta_1 z_1 + \eta_2 z_2 + \eta_3 w + \theta_2. \tag{18.25}$$

Equations (18.24) and (18.25) show that both first-stage regressions share the same set of predictors. It is important to realize that each instrument needs to be uniquely associated with one endogenous regressor, i.e., in this case of two endogenous regressors one instrument, say z_1, must be strongly correlated with p_1, and the other instrument z_2 must now be strongly correlated with p_2. We can still have that, in

[16]The standard deviation of the OLS estimates in Table 18.11 appears large. The reason is that the distribution of the estimates is not normal, which is due to outliers that arise because of the non-normal distribution of the endogenous regressor.

addition, z_2 also correlates with p_1 and z_1 also correlates with p_2. But we cannot have that z_1 correlates with both p_1 and p_2, while z_2 correlates with none. Nor can we have that z_1 and z_2 correlate with p_1 and neither correlates with p_2.

This explains why it is not sufficient in the case of more than one endogenous regressor to perform independent tests for the strength of instruments (e.g., F-tests) for both first stage regressions. Rather, we have to use a multivariate F-test (e.g., the Angrist-Pischke-F-test, Angrist and Pischke 2009, p. 217–218 or the more recent Sanderson-Windmeijer-F-test, Sanderson and Windmeijer 2015). Importantly, we recommend using an estimator that produces IV estimates directly, such as the ivreg or ivreg2 command in Stata. The required code makes it directly obvious that we use the same IVs (z_1 and z_2) for both endogeneous regressors (p_1 and p_2):

$$\text{ivreg2 y w } (\text{p1 p2} = \text{z1 z2})\text{, first.}$$

The option "first", specified behind the comma, produces an output for the first-stage regressions that includes a multivariate F-test as well as an over-identification (Sargan) test if the number of IVs exceeds the number of endogenous variables. This output should routinely be examined and discussed in any IV analysis.

18.6.1.2 Interaction Terms

In marketing we are often interested in estimating interactions that involve an endogenous regressor. Consider for example a case where we expect that the price effect changes over time. We can capture this effect by interacting price with a (exogenous) seasonal dummy, say, w as follows:

$$y = \beta_0 + \beta_1 p_1 + \beta_2 w + \beta_3 p_1 w + \varepsilon_1. \tag{18.26}$$

To obtain consistent estimates we must treat the interaction $p_1 w$ as a separate endogenous regressor with its own first stage regression and its own instrument:

$$p_1 = \gamma_0 + \gamma_1 z_1 + \gamma_2 w + \gamma_3 z_1 w + \theta_1 \tag{18.27}$$

$$p_1 w = \eta_0 + \eta_1 z_1 + \eta_2 w + \eta_3 z_1 w + \theta_2. \tag{18.28}$$

We use z_1 as the instrument for p_1 and the interaction between w and z_1 as the instrument to identify the interaction $p_1 w$. Again, we use the same set of regressors in both first stage regressions (Wooldridge 2015, p. 429). Note that the implication is that we would need to argue that $z_1 w$ is a valid instrument for $p_1 w$, just like with any IV.

However, we can also use the CF approach that we discussed above to make life a bit easier when dealing with interactions that involve endogenous regressors (Wooldridge 2015, p. 428). If we wish to estimate (18.26) while controlling for the endogeneity of p_1 and $p_1 w$ by means of a control function, it is sufficient

(Wooldridge 2015, p. 428) to only estimate one first stage regression (18.29) and add the fitted residuals as additional regressor to (18.26) as shown in (18.30):

$$p_1 = \gamma_0 + \gamma_1 z_1 + \gamma_2 w + \theta \tag{18.29}$$

$$y = \beta_0 + \beta_1 p_1 + \beta_2 w + \beta_3 p_1 w + \widehat{\theta} + \varepsilon_1. \tag{18.30}$$

It is important to keep in mind that in this control function approach, the standard errors need to be derived using bootstrapping as described in Sect. 18.3.2.

This approach is also feasible if we would implement the Gaussian copula approach (see above) in an application with an interaction term. Here, including just the one correction term (p^*) will be sufficient to address the regressor's endogeneity as well as the endogeneity in the interaction term.

18.6.1.3 Squared Terms

Similar considerations arise when we have to deal with squared terms of endogenous regressors, for instance if we wish to test whether (endogenous) price has a nonlinear effect on sales due to e.g., saturation:

$$y = \beta_0 + \beta_1 p_1 + \beta_2 p_1^2 + \beta_3 w + \varepsilon_1. \tag{18.31}$$

We *cannot* estimate one first-stage regression for p_1, compute the predicted values $\widehat{p_1}$ and $\widehat{p_1^2}$, and use these two terms in the second stage regression instead of p_1 and p_1^2, imitating a 2SLS approach. This is occasionally termed the "forbidden regression" (Wooldridge 2010, p. 267). Instead, we can choose one of the following three approaches. The first two approaches have in common that they treat p_1 and p_1^2 as two separate endogenous variables, which accordingly require two separate first-stage regressions and two different instruments (Wooldridge 2010, p. 266). Approach 1 uses the squared instruments as additional source for identification:

$$p_1 = \gamma_0 + \gamma_1 z_1 + \gamma_2 z_1^2 + \gamma_3 w + \theta_1 \tag{18.32}$$

$$p_1^2 = \eta_0 + \eta_1 z_1 + \eta_2 z_1^2 + \eta_3 w + \theta_3. \tag{18.33}$$

Approach 2 includes the square of the projection of the endogenous regressor on the instrument as the instrument for the squared endogenous regressor:

$$p_1 = \gamma_0 + \gamma_1 z_1 + \gamma_3 w + \theta_1 \tag{18.34}$$

$$p_1^2 = \eta_0 + \eta_1 z_1 + \eta_2 \widehat{p_1^2} + \eta_3 w + \theta_2 \tag{18.35}$$

where $\widehat{p_1^2}$ is the squared predicted dependent variable after estimating (18.34).

Lastly, we could consider the square of p_1 as in interaction with itself, such that we could apply the CF approach discussed above for interactions. That is, we would include the residuals of a first-stage regression from (18.34), and include these as an additional regressor in (18.31).

18.6.2 Binary or Categorical Endogenous Regressor

Suppose we are interested in the effect of a binary endogenous variable d_1 on y:

$$y = \beta_0 + \beta_1 d_1 + \varepsilon. \tag{18.36}$$

To obtain a consistent estimate for this effect, researchers have different options. The easiest option arises from the fact that IV does not make any assumption on the nature of the endogenous regressor. Hence, we can just use the 2SLS approach discussed above and not worry about the binary nature of the endogenous regressor (Wooldridge 2010, p. 90). Leenheer et al. (2007) use this approach to study the effect of loyalty program membership (an endogenous 0–1 variable) on share of wallet.

This approach, however, may be less efficient than the following three alternatives. A first alternative approach uses a probit model[17] in the first stage, $P(d_1 = 1) = \Phi(\eta z)$, instead of a linear model, and then uses the fitted probabilities, $\widehat{P}(d_1 = 1)$, *as an instrument* for the endogenous binary regressor (Wooldridge 2010, p. 939), i.e., $d_1 = \delta_0 + \delta_1 \widehat{P}(d_1 = 1)$. The predicted values computed from the *linear* regression, $\widehat{d}_1 = \widehat{\delta}_0 + \widehat{\delta}_1 \widehat{P}(d_1 = 1)$ are then used in the main equation:

$$y = \beta_0 + \beta_1 \widehat{d}_1 + \varepsilon_1. \tag{18.37}$$

In other words, the fitted probabilities from the first stage probit are used as IVs for d_1. Note that this approach is *not* equivalent to as using the predicted probabilities $\widehat{P}(d_1 = 1)$ as a regressor in the main equation, which will lead to inconsistent estimates and should thus be avoided (Wooldridge 2010, p. 941).

A second alternative approach also fits a first stage probit but includes a generalized residual as control function (e.g., Germann et al. 2015; Wooldridge 2010, p. 949), which is given by $\left(d_1 \widehat{\lambda}(\widehat{\eta}z) - (1 - d_1)\widehat{\lambda}(-\widehat{\eta}z)\right)$, where $\widehat{\lambda}(.) = {}^{\varphi(.)}/_{\Phi(.)}$ is the inverse Mills ratio, i.e., the ratio of the normal pdf and cdf.[18]

A third alternative approach is also in the spirit of the CF approach, which uses the first-stage probit (or other non-linear estimators) to compute the probit residuals, $\widehat{\zeta} = x_1 - \widehat{P}(x_1 = 1)$, and include these as additional regressors in the main equation:

[17] See Vol. I, Sect. 8.2.2.1.

[18] See, for example, Franses and Paap (2001, p. 138).

$$y = \beta_0 + \beta_1 p_1 + \beta_2 \widehat{\xi} + \varepsilon_1. \tag{18.38}$$

This approach is known as the two-stage residual inclusion (2SRI) and is discussed in detail in Terza et al. (2008). Danaher et al. (2015) provide an application of 2SRI in marketing to a setting where the endogenous variable of interest is whether or not consumers obtained a mobile coupon.

We are not aware of any study that compares the various approaches of dealing with binary or categorical endogenous variables.

18.6.3 Selection Models

A case that is closely related to a binary endogenous variable is a selection model. The key difference, however, is that in a selection model the binary variable is *not* an independent variable in the main equation, but it determines whether the regressand of interest is observed or not. Specifically, consider the following main equation for y_1:

$$y_1 = \beta_0 + \beta_1 w_1 + \varepsilon_1. \tag{18.39}$$

However, y_1 is only observed when a binary variable, y_2 equals 1. Suppose we have the following model for y_2:

$$y_2 = 1|\delta_0 + \delta_1 w_2 + \varepsilon_2. \tag{18.40}$$

One example is a household's weekly expenditure in a supermarket. First the household needs to choose to buy something in the supermarket ($y_2 = 1$) and conditional on this decision, the household decides to spend a certain monetary amount y_1 (Van Heerde et al. 2008). The error terms ε_1 and ε_2 follow a bivariate normal distribution with a nonzero correlation. Estimating Eq. (18.39) without taking into account the selection process leads to biased estimates (Wooldridge 2010, p. 804). Instead, we first need to estimate a probit model for Eq. (18.40):

$$P(y_2 = 1) = \Phi(\delta_0 + \delta_1 w_2). \tag{18.41}$$

Next, we calculate the "inverse Mills ratio" (Wooldridge 2010, p. 805):

$$\widehat{\lambda} = \varphi\left(\widehat{\delta_0} + \widehat{\delta_1} w_2\right) / \Phi\left(\widehat{\delta_0} + \widehat{\delta_1} w_2\right) \tag{18.42}$$

where $\varphi(.)$ is the pdf of the standard normal distribution. Finally, we add the inverse Mills ratio to the main equation:

$$y_1 = \beta_0 + \beta_1 w_1 + \beta_2 \widehat{\lambda} + \varepsilon_1. \tag{18.43}$$

Equation (18.43) can be estimated consistently with OLS. Note that w_2 in (18.41) and (18.42) is not an instrument in the sense that we have to make equally strong assumptions as in the case of IVs when estimating IV. Rather, we choose w_2 to avoid that the predicted probabilities from (18.41) and, hence, the "inverse Mills ratio", is a linear combination of the regressors in (18.39) as these would lead to problems of multicollinearity (Wooldridge 2010, p. 806). We refer to Wooldridge (2010, Chap. 19) for more detail on selection models.

18.6.4 Limited Dependent Variables

In many marketing settings, the dependent variable is not a continuous measure such as sales, but it has a more limited distribution, i.e., it can only assume discrete values or it can only obtain values within a certain range. Examples include:

- a binary dependent variable (e.g., does the consumer buy or not);
- a multinomial dependent variable (which brand does the consumer buy);
- a bivariate binary dependent variable (does the consumer buy online (yes or no) and/or offline (yes or no);
- a truncated dependent variable (monetary amount spent, which has to be nonnegative);
- a fractional dependent variable (share of wallet, between 0 and 1);
- a discrete dependent variable (how many hotel nights does a consumer book).[19]

Such "limited-dependent" variables are very common in marketing applications, and very often, there are endogeneity concerns surrounding the independent variables. To address these concerns, the CF approach is the recommended course of action (Petrin and Train 2010). For example, suppose the dependent variable is brand choice, and price is the endogenous regressor. We can set up a utility model for brand choice:

$$\textit{Utility}\,(\text{brand}\, j) = \beta_{0j} + \beta_1 p_j + \varepsilon_j. \tag{18.44}$$

To account for the endogeneity of p_j, we estimate a first-stage regression that follows the same reasoning as in the standard IV case (i.e., valid and strong instruments),

$$p_j = \gamma z_j + \theta_j \tag{18.45}$$

and save the residuals $\widehat{\theta}_j = p_j - \widehat{\gamma} z_j$. We add these residuals to the utility equation as the control function term:

$$\textit{Utility}\,(\text{brand}\, j) = \beta_{0j} + \beta_1 p_j + \beta_2 \widehat{\theta}_j + \varepsilon_j. \tag{18.46}$$

[19]Compare Sects. 8.2 and 8.5, Vol. I.

In addition, the researcher has to make an assumption on the distribution of ε_j. If we assume a multivariate normal distribution, Eq. (18.45) is estimated as a probit model follows. In case ε_j has an Extreme Value distribution, the logit model follows (Petrin and Train 2010). As described in Sect. 18.3.1, the standard errors for the estimates of Eq. (18.46) need to be corrected for the fact that $\widehat{\theta_j}$ is an estimated quantity. The bootstrap approach discussed in Sect. 18.3.2 for the control function can be implemented for this brand choice model in the same manner, as well as in many other nonlinear or limited dependent variable models.

Andrews and Ebbes (2014) investigate the properties of IV approaches in logit-based demand models for store-level data. Their study highlights the robust performance of the CF approach as proposed by Petrin and Train (2010). They also find good properties of readily available panel based instruments that can be computed from the data at hand. These store-mean centered instruments are used in a first-stage regression for price, and the residuals are then included in the logit based demand model as control functions. The validity of these readily available instruments rests on the same assumptions as fixed effects approaches discussed before, i.e., that the common unobserved demand shocks are common to stores. However, as standard fixed effects approaches are only available for linear regression models, the approach proposed in Andrews and Ebbes (2014) demonstrates how the fixed effects approach can potentially be extended to logit based panel data models without having to estimate a large set of (store-level) intercepts.

18.7 Discussion

18.7.1 Endogeneity: A Thorny Issue

Endogeneity is, as Van Heerde et al. (2005) put it, often used as a crutch by reviewers to justify recommending that a marketing article should be rejected. The issue is that endogeneity can potentially invalidate causal inferences. Outsiders can always raise this concern for observational data and it can never be fully excluded based on arguments alone or based on statistical grounds. Correcting for endogeneity requires additional assumptions and conditions, it can make the problem worse and we are never sure which estimate is the true one. Finally, correcting for endogeneity leads to worse in- and out-of-sample fit (Ebbes et al. 2011). In sum, endogeneity is truly a thorny issue.

While we agree that endogeneity is a potentially very serious issue, we do also believe that it is key to establish a best practice around it. First, as a researcher, we have to think carefully what aspect of the variation in the regressor is potentially endogenous. Very often in marketing, endogeneity problems arise from omitted variables. A first advice therefore is to think through exactly what information is missing, and then make every effort to collect data and add additional control variables to the model.

For example, in the hotel example discussed throughout this chapter, endogeneity arose because of (1) unobserved demand shocks due to major events and (2) firms capitalizing on unobserved quality differences. Rather than right away jumping to an IV-based or IV-free approach to address endogeneity, our advice is to collect additional data. This is in line with Germann et al. (2015, p. 4) who suggest to start with "rich data models" before considering IV estimation. The main goal is to collect an extensive set of data such that the most relevant control variables that correlate with the dependent and independent variables is included. Of course such an approach is only feasible if such an extensive set of control variables were available. Similarly, Rossi (2014) argues that a convincing argument must be made that there is a serious endogeneity problem given the set of control variables, as in absence of good IVs, the researcher is *better off* trying to measure these unobservable variables and *including them* in the model. Drawing on the hotel example that we used throughout this chapter, an event calendar showing the major events allows us to capture these events through dummy variables. Including such dummies in the model would address the endogeneity arising from managers raising prices during these events. Quality ratings from websites such as TripAdvisor allow us to make the previously unobserved quality differences observable, and including them in the model would alleviate much, if not all, of the endogeneity problem due to manager setting prices based on quality differences.

Second, in a panel data setting, if the endogeneity concern arises because firms set their marketing instruments based on cross-sectional differences, (firm) fixed effects fully address this problem. Similarly, if the endogeneity arises because firm set their marketing instruments based on seasonal patterns, fixed time effects can completely take care of the problem. These fixed effects can be considered as control variables that can take care of some of the most pressing endogeneity issues in panel data.

Third, it is crucial that the researcher describes potential endogeneity problems in the order of importance and indicates which control variables are included to address the problem. Researchers should combine this with a clear statement regarding their identifying assumption, i.e., under which assumption the estimates can be treated as causal. Fourth, it is easier to raise endogeneity concerns than to invalidate them, i.e., the proof of burden rests with the researcher. Therefore, reviewers should not raise these concerns lightly, and not raise them without explicitly providing strong arguments why the problem may be substantial. Further, reviewers should acknowledge that carefully chosen control variables—as described above—can often address a very large part of the endogeneity problem. Of course, a reviewer can always argue for more far-fetched endogeneity issues, but the question then becomes whether it is truly worth addressing these because the cure (ill-chosen IVs for example) can be worse than the disease (the remaining bias after controlling for a variety of endogeneity mechanisms), as we have shown over and over again in this chapter.

Using IV also affects the way we have to think about the coefficient of interest reflecting a causal effect in the sense that it is an average treatment effect. Strictly speaking, we can only consider the estimate an average treatment effect if all units (e.g., hotels, brands) respond to the instrument in the same way. Coming back to our hotel example, this would imply that all hotels increase their prices with the same amount in response to a one unit increase in cost. We could not interpret the price coefficient as causal, for instance, when some hotels would and others would not react to cost shocks. Intuitively speaking, there is no exogenous variation in price that is captured by the cost instrument for some hotels, and for those hotels the price effect in the demand model becomes essentially un-identified. Consequently, the estimated price effect in the demand model using 2SLS cannot be interpreted as average treatment effect anymore. We recommend that these aspects are taken into consideration when interpreting the results of an IV model, and refer the reader to Bascle (2008) for more details.

Some may wonder whether we should use IV at all, given the limitations and recent discussions (e.g., Rossi 2014). IVs need to satisfy two conditions that are essentially polar opposites: they need to be strong (be a strong predictor of the endogenous regressor) but exogenous at the same time (so not correlated at all with the error term of demand). Hence, theoretical arguments that make an instrument exogenous, also work to make the instrument weak (and vice versa). Importantly, only the strength condition can be statistically tested. While we can provide some statistical evidence for the exogeneity assumption (if we have more IVs than endogenous regressors), this can be done only to a limited extent and some even argue exogeneity cannot be tested at all (Rossi 2014).

IV-free methods such as the LIV approach or the Gaussian copulas rely yet on different conditions that are not always satisfied (e.g., the regressor may have a normal distribution whereas it should not, or assumptions regarding the structural error terms are violated).

It is important to notice that every non-experimental empirical research study that seeks to make causal inferences must rest on identifying assumptions that are not testable without experiments (Pearl 2009). Therefore, when we use an IV approach, we replace one assumption (the error is uncorrelated with the independent variable) by a new assumption (the instrument is uncorrelated with the error). Only theory and conceptual arguments are the means that can tell us which approach is more appropriate. Recognizing that there are many potential models available to deal with endogeneity, Germann et al. (2015) suggest that researchers explore the meaning of the various models' identifying assumptions in light of their context and then determine the appropriate specifications, as opposed to mechanically estimating many potential models and then only reporting the model or models that provide the most desirable results. In that sense, researchers should see themselves as "regression engineers" instead of "regression mechanics" (Angrist and Pischke 2009), and researchers should understand and discuss the meaning of the model identifying assumptions for their particular context (Germann et al. 2015, pp. 10–11). This could include a discussion of a subset of models whose identifying assumptions make the most sense given the researcher's problem context. In particular robust findings would strengthen the beliefs in the findings and conclusions. But Germann et al. (2015) also note that if the findings are not robust, then a discussion of the identifying assumptions is needed to assess which results, if any, to believe and whether an altogether different approach is needed.

18.7.2 What Should be Reported

We believe that an empirical study in marketing should report the following to address endogeneity concerns:

1. What are the core potential endogeneity problems and which control variables in the model are included to avoid the problem? As discussed in Sect. 18.7.1, these can be dummies for special events, variables capturing quality differences or cross-sectional and time fixed effects, and many more. All potential solutions to endogeneity problems should be accompanied by clear statements on the identifying assumptions. Germann et al. (2015) discuss for many common regression models in marketing the respective identifying assumptions (e.g., Table 2 in Germann et al. 2015).
2. What remaining potential endogeneity problem is there? If there is not a plausible problem, there is no need to address it.
3. If there is a potential endogeneity problem, consider an IV approach or an IV-free approach, or ideally a combination of observed IV and IV-free approaches to check the robustness of the findings (e.g., Grewal et al. 2010 and Narayan and Kadiyali 2015 use an LIV approach to assess robustness of their findings). For the IV-based approaches (including control functions), strong and detailed theoretical arguments for the validity of the IVs should be provided. In the case of over-identification, they may be augmented with Sargan or Hanssen J-tests. For the strength of the IVs, the appropriate statistics must be reported (see Sect. 18.3.1). Finally, the Hausman test for the presence of endogeneity should be reported. Actually, if the Hausman test says there is no significant endogeneity issue, the advice is to use the non-corrected estimates (e.g., OLS) as the focal result.

For the IV-free approach, the underlying assumption must be investigated (e.g., for both the LIV and the Gaussian Copula approaches, the endogenous regressor is non-normally distributed, and the structural error term(s) are normally distributed). We have discussed good practices for both approaches in this chapter.

Figure 18.3 gives a roadmap on how to address endogeneity issues in marketing, following the guidelines we have laid out in this chapter. In the presence of panel data, the roadmap discussed in Germann et al. (2015, pp. 3–11), which considers rich data models, unobserved effects models, IV models, and panel internal instrument models, provides more details.

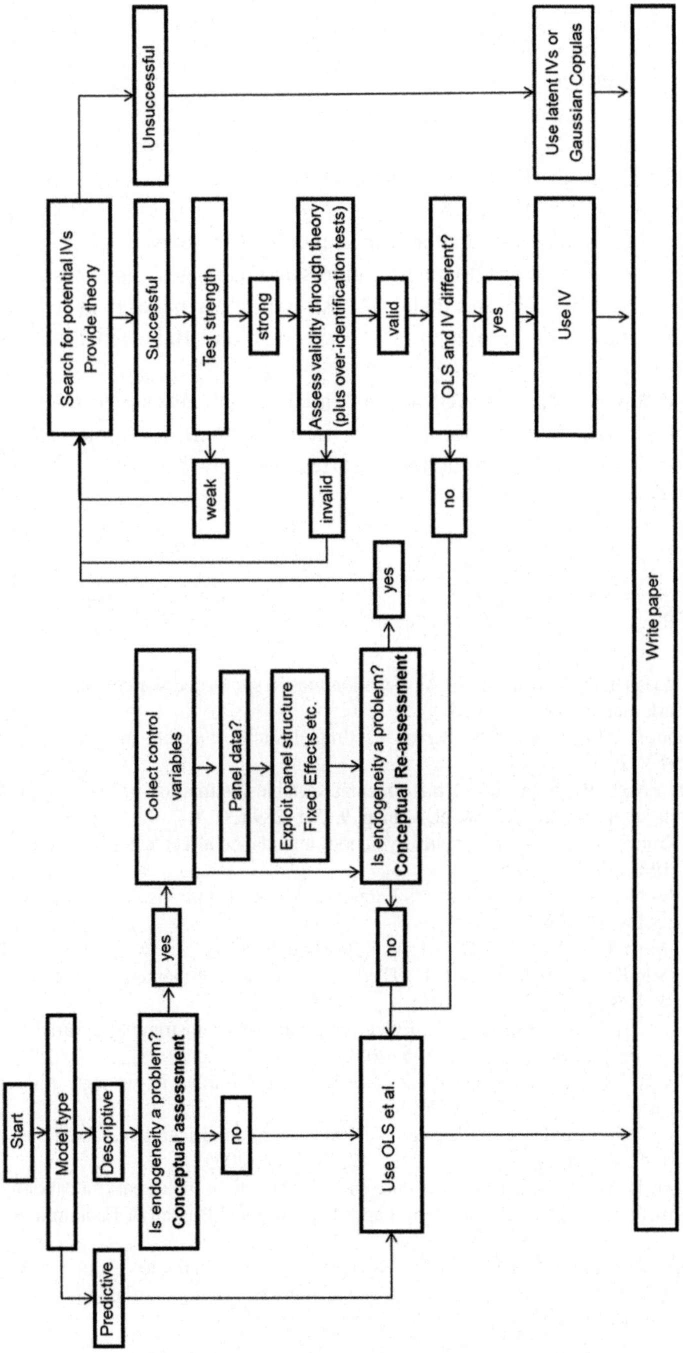

Fig. 18.3 Roadmap for addressing endogeneity concerns in empirical marketing studies

18.7.3 Software

To the best of our knowledge, Stata is the commercial package that has the most complete and up to date set of procedures to deal with endogeneity concerns. The Stata package ivreg2 has a very comprehensive set of tests and estimation methods. We refer to Baum et al. (2007) for details. Further, researchers can write their own code in Stata, e.g., for the Gaussian Copula approach to correct for endogeneity.

R is a free-of-charge statistical software platform that is open source (https://www.r-project.org/). Here, researchers can implement the relevant estimators themselves, or use one of several endogeneity-addressing packages, e.g., on standard IV estimation (ivmodel, ivpack, and tosls), IV estimation for panel data (ivpanel and ivfixed), IV estimation for probit models (ivprobit), and Bayesian IV estimation (ivbma).

Matrix languages such as GAUSS and Matlab are ideally suited to implement estimation procedures that are not available from the shelf. Examples include the Gaussian Copula and LIV approaches to correct for endogeneity—both of which we have programmed in GAUSS ourselves.

References

Abhishek, V., Hosanagar, K., Fader, P.S.: Aggregation bias in sponsored search data: the curse and the cure. Mark. Sci. **34**, 59–77 (2015)

Albers, S., Mantrala, M.K., Sridhar, S.: Personal selling elasticities: a meta-analysis. J. Mark. Res. **47**, 2840–2853 (2010)

Andrews, R.L., Ebbes, P.: Properties of instrumental variables estimation in logit-based demand models: finite sample results. J. Model. Manag. **9**, 261–289 (2014)

Angrist, J.D., Krueger, A.B.: Does compulsory school attendance affect schooling and earnings? Q. J. Econ. **106**, 979–1014 (1991)

Angrist, J.D., Pischke, J.S.: Mostly Harmless Econometrics. An Empiricist's Companion. Princeton University Press, Princeton (2009)

Ataman, M.B., Mela, C.F., Van Heerde, H.J.: Building brands. Mark. Sci. **27**, 1036–1054 (2008)

Ataman, M.B., Van Heerde, H.J., Mela, C.F.: The long-term effect of marketing strategy on brand sales. J. Mark. Res. **47**, 866–882 (2010)

Baum, C.F., Schaffer, M.E., Stillman, S.: Enhanced routines for instrumental variables/GMM estimation and testing. Stata J. **7**, 465–506 (2007)

Bascle, G.: Controlling for endogeneity with instrumental variables in strategic management research. Strateg. Organ. **6**, 285–327 (2008)

Bijmolt, T.H.A., Van Heerde, H.J., Pieters, R.G.M.: New empirical generalizations on the determinants of price elasticity. J. Mark. Res. **42**, 141–156 (2005)

Bound, J., Jaeger, D.A., and Baker, R.: The cure can be worse than the disease: a cautionary tale regarding instrumental variables, Working Paper **137**, National Bureau of Economic Research (1993)

Bound, J., Jaeger, D.A., Baker, R.M.: Problems with instrumental variables estimation when the correlation between the instruments and the endogenous explanatory variable is weak. J. Am. Stat. Assoc. **90**, 443–450 (1995)

Bronnenberg, B.J., Mahajan, V.: Unobserved retailer behavior in multimarket data: joint spatial dependence in market shares and promotion variables. Mark. Sci. **20**, 284–299 (2001)

Burmester, A.B., Becker, J.U., Van Heerde, H.J., Clement, M.: The impact of pre- and post-launch publicity and advertising on new product sales. Int. J. Res. Mark. **32**, 408–417 (2015)

Danaher, P.J., Smith, M.S., Ranasinghe, K., Danaher, T.S.: Where, when, and how long: factors that influence the redemption of mobile phone coupons. J. Mark. Res. **52**, 710–725 (2015)

Datta, H., Foubert, B., Van Heerde, H.J.: The challenge of retaining customers acquired with free trials. J. Mark. Res. **52**, 217–234 (2015)

Dinner, I.M., Van Heerde, H.J., Neslin, S.A.: Driving online and offline sales: the cross-channel effects of traditional, online display, and paid search advertising. J. Mark. Res. **51**, 527–545 (2014)

Ebbes, P., Böckenholt, U., Wedel, M.: Regressor and random-effects dependencies in multilevel models. Statistica Neerlandica. **58**(2), 161–178 (2004)

Ebbes, P., Papies, D., Van Heerde, H.J.: The sense and non-sense of holdout sample validation in the presence of endogeneity. Mark. Sci. **30**, 1115–1122 (2011)

Ebbes, P., Wedel, M., Böckenholt, U.: Frugal IV alternatives to identify the parameter for an endogenous regressor. J. Appl. Econ. **24**, 446–468 (2009)

Ebbes, P., Wedel, M., Böckenholt, U., Steerneman, T.: Solving and testing for regressor-error (in)dependence when no instrumental variables are available: with new evidence for the effect of education on income. Quant. Mark. Econ. **3**, 365–392 (2005)

Franses, P.H., Paap, R.: Quantitative Models in Marketing Research. Cambridge University Press, Cambridge (2001)

Gao, C., Lahiri, K.: Further consequences of viewing LIML as an iterated Aitken estimator. J. Econ. **98**, 187–202 (2000)

Germann, F., Ebbes, P., Grewal, R.: The chief marketing officer matters! J. Mark. **79**(3), 1–22 (2015)

Gijsenberg, M.J., Van Heerde, H.J., Verhoef, P.C.: Losses loom longer than gains: modeling the impact of service crises on perceived service quality over time. J. Mark. Res. **52**, 642–656 (2015)

Grewal, R., Chandrashekaran, M., Citrin, A.V.: Customer satisfaction heterogeneity and shareholder value. J. Mark. Res. **47**, 612–626 (2010)

Grewal, R., Kumar, A., Mallapragada, G., Saini, A.: Marketing channels in foreign markets: control mechanisms and the moderating role of multinational corporation headquarters–subsidiary relationship. J. Mark. Res. **50**, 378–398 (2013)

Hausman, J. A.: Valuation of new goods under perfect and imperfect competition. In: Bresnahan, T. F., Gordon R. J. (eds.) The Economics of New Goods, pp. 207–248. University of Chicago Press, Cambridge (1996)

Karaca-Mandic, P., Train, K.: Standard error correction in two-stage estimation with nested samples. Econ. J. **6**, 401–407 (2003)

Kim, J.-S., Frees, E.W.: Omitted variables in multilevel models. Psychometrika. **71**, 659–690 (2006)

Kim, J.-S., Frees, E.W.: Multilevel modeling with correlated effects. Psychometrika. **72**, 505–533 (2007)

Kleibergen, F., Zivot, E.: Bayesian and classical approaches to instrumental variable regression. J. Econ. **114**, 29–72 (2003)

Kremer, S.T.M., Bijmolt, T.H.A., Leeflang, P.S.H., Wieringa, J.E.: Generalizations on the effectiveness of pharmaceutical promotional expenditures. Int. J. Res. Mark. **25**, 234–246 (2008)

Lee, J.-Y., Sridhar, S., Henderson, C.M., Palmatier, R.W.: Effect of customer-centric structure on long-term financial performance. Mark. Sci. **34**, 250–268 (2015)

Leenheer, J., Van Heerde, H.J., Bijmolt, T.H.A., Smidts, A.: Do loyalty programs really enhance behavioral loyalty? An empirical analysis accounting for self-selecting members. Int. J. Res. Mark. **24**, 31–47 (2007)

Levitt, S.D.: The effect of prison population size on crime rates: evidence from prison overcrowding litigation. Q. J. Econ. **111**, 319–351 (1996)

Lewbel, A.: Constructing instruments for regressions with measurement error when no additional data are available, with an application to patents and R&D. Econometrica. **65**, 1201–1213 (1997)
Ma, L., Krishnan, R., Montgomery, A.L.: Latent homophily or social influence? An empirical analysis of purchase within a social network. Manag. Sci. **61**, 454–473 (2014)
Murray, M.P.: Avoiding invalid instruments and coping with weak instruments. J. Econ. Perspect. **20**, 111–132 (2006)
Narayan, V., Kadiyali, V.: Repeated interactions and improved outcomes: an empirical analysis of movie production in the United States. Manag. Sci. **62**, 591–607 (2015)
Nevo, A.: Measuring market power in the ready-to-eat cereal industry. Econometrica. **69**, 307–342 (2001)
Otter, T., Gilbride, T.J., Allenby, G.M.: Testing models of strategic behavior characterized by conditional likelihoods. Mark. Sci. **30**, 686–701 (2011)
Park, S., Gupta, S.: Handling endogenous regressors by joint estimation using copulas. Mark. Sci. **31**, 567–586 (2012)
Pagan, A.: Some consequences of viewing LIML as an iterated Aitken estimator. Econ. Lett. **3**, 369–372 (1979)
Pearl, J.: Causality: Models, Reasoning, and Inference. Cambridge University Press, Cambridge (2009)
Petrin, A., Train, K.: Omitted product attributes in discrete choice models, Working paper, University of Chicago and University of California, Berkeley (2002)
Petrin, A., Train, K.: A control function approach to endogeneity in consumer choice models. J. Mark. Res. **47**, 3–13 (2010)
Rooderkerk, R.P., Van Heerde, H.J., Bijmolt, T.H.A.: Optimizing retail assortments. Mark. Sci. **32**, 699–715 (2013)
Rossi, P.: Even the rich can make themselves poor: a critical examination of IV methods in marketing applications. Mark. Sci. **33**, 655–672 (2014)
Rutz, O.J., Bucklin, R.E., Sonnier, G.P.: A latent instrumental variables approach to modeling keyword conversion in paid search advertising. J. Mark. Res. **49**, 306–319 (2012)
Rutz, O.J., Trusov, M.: Zooming in on paid search ads—a consumer-level model calibrated on aggregated data. Mark. Sci. **30**, 789–800 (2011)
Sabnis, G., Grewal, R.: Cable news wars on the internet: competition and user-generated content. Inf. Syst. Res. **26**, 301–319 (2015)
Saboo, A.R., Grewal, R.: Stock market reactions to customer and competitor orientations: the case of initial public offerings. Mark. Sci. **32**, 70–88 (2012)
Sanderson, E., Windmeijer, F.: A weak instrument-test in linear IV models with multiple endogenous variables. J. Econ. **190**, 212–221 (2015)
Sethuraman, R., Tellis, G.J., Briesch, R.A.: How well does advertising work? Generalizations from meta-analysis of brand advertising elasticities. J. Mark. Res. **48**, 457–471 (2011)
Sonnier, G.P., McAlister, L., Rutz, O.J.: A dynamic model of the effect of online communications on firm sales. Mark. Sci. **30**, 702–716 (2011)
Srinivasan, R., Sridhar, S., Narayanan, S., Sihi, D.: Effects of opening and closing stores on chain retailer performance. J. Retail. **89**, 126–139 (2013)
Stock, J.H., Wright, J.H., Yogo, M.: A survey of weak instruments and weak identification in generalized method of moments. J. Bus. Stat. Econ. Stat. **20**, 518–529 (2002)
Terza, J.V., Basu, A., Rathouz, P.J.: Two-stage residual inclusion estimation: addressing endogeneity in health econometric modeling. J. Health Econ. **27**, 531–543 (2008)
Van Dijk, A., Van Heerde, H.J., Leeflang, P.S.H., Wittink, D.R.: Similarity-based spatial methods for estimating shelf space elasticities from correlational data. Quant. Mark. Econ. **2**, 257–277 (2004)
Van Heerde, H.J., Dekimpe, M.G., Putsis, W.P.J.: Marketing models and the Lucas critique. J. Mark. Res. **42**, 15–21 (2005)
Van Heerde, H.J., Gijsbrechts, E., Pauwels, K.H.: Winners and losers in a major price war. J. Mark. Res. **45**, 499–518 (2008)

Van Heerde, H.J., Gijsenberg, M.J., Dekimpe, M.G., Steenkamp, J-B.E.M: Price and advertising effectiveness over the business cycle. J. Mark. Res. **50**, 177–193 (2013)

Verbeek, M.: A Guide to Modern Econometrics, 4th edn. Wiley, Hoboken (2012)

Villas-Boas, J.M., Winer, R.S.: Endogeneity in brand choice models. Manag. Sci. **45**, 1324–1338 (1999)

Winer, R.S.: A reference price model of brand choice for frequently purchased products. J. Consum. Res. **13**, 250–256 (1986)

Wooldridge, J.M.: Econometric Analysis of Cross Section and Panel Data, 2nd edn. MIT, Cambridge (2010)

Wooldridge, J.M.: Control function methods in applied econometrics. J. Hum. Resour. **50**, 420–445 (2015)

Zhang, J., Wedel, M., Pieters, R.: Sales effects of attention to feature advertisements: a Bayesian mediation analysis. J. Mark. Res. **46**, 669–681 (2009)

Part V
Expected Developments

Chapter 19
Machine Learning and Big Data

Raoul V. Kübler, Jaap E. Wieringa, and Koen H. Pauwels

19.1 Introduction

The last 10 years saw a remarkable increase of data available to marketers. What was considered 5 years ago as big data (see e.g., Vol. I, Sect. 3.5.6) was based on hundreds of thousands of observations (e.g., Reimer et al. 2014). Today this is considered by data scientists as an average sample size. Consumer handscan panels and regular brand tracking allowed us to build models combining consumer actions with mindset metrics (e.g., Hanssens et al. 2014; Van Heerde et al. 2008). And of course, click stream data inspired a brave new world of modeling (prospective) customers' online decision journeys (Bucklin and Sismeiro 2003; Pauwels and Van Ewijk 2014). Within the last two years we see social media interaction data coming more and more into marketing research (see e.g., Borah and Tellis 2016; Ilhan et al. 2016). Through this source marketers get access to customer and user generated content. Especially service and fast mover consumer goods as entertainment brands enjoy a high volume of interactions (see e.g., Henning-Thurau et al. 2014) in different social media channels that is linked with the company's future sales performance. Social media again boosts the number of data available to marketers. Instead of now facing hundreds of thousands of observations, researchers are very likely to encounter millions of comments, likes and shares in even short observation periods. Combining this new data with existing sources, will provide

R.V. Kübler (✉)
Department of Marketing, Özyeğin University, Istanbul, Turkey
e-mail: raoul.kubler@ozyegin.edu.tr

J.E. Wieringa
Department of Marketing, University of Groningen, Groningen, The Netherlands

K.H. Pauwels
Department of Marketing, Northeastern University, Boston, USA

P.S.H. Leeflang et al. (eds.), *Advanced Methods for Modeling Markets*,
International Series in Quantitative Marketing, DOI 10.1007/978-3-319-53469-5_19

new opportunities and further develop marketing research (Sudhir 2016). Verhoef et al. (2016) provide many examples how big data (analytics) can be used to create value for customers and firms.

This new data is rich with information and thus provides many insights and stimulating research opportunities for marketing researchers. Big data caught a lot of attraction in customer identification and customer classification. Especially in online marketing, marketers like to use big data to teach models predicting the likelihood that an incoming customer belongs to a specific segment given that the customer shares common socio-demographic co-variates such as e.g., age and gender. In other cases previous browsing or buying behavior is used to determine the likelihood that an incoming consumer will be clicking on an advertisement or buying a product from a web store. Profit-optimizing algorithms can then use this prediction to determine a maximum bid for the advertisement. The algorithm specifically determines for each new customer or web site visitor how much a company is willing to pay to show an advertisement to this customer. This is done in real-time with different algorithms bidding in milliseconds for ad-space. In consequence, advertising content and space gets customized to consumer needs. Algorithms use insights from similar customers with an identical or at least related buying or browsing history to make such predictions. Linking information from an incoming customer with insights from predictive models or Machine Learning thus helps managers to classify customers and to make advertising decisions in real-time. Similarly, we see data driven systems in sales, which use historic data and predictive modeling to make predictions how an incoming customer will react to a specific offer or a customized price.

Predictive modeling is nothing new to marketing research. Researchers as well as practitioners have used a wide array of models discussed in Vol. I and in the present volume to predict future consumer behavior. With the recent growth of data, these models however show some limitations. Especially larger models with many variables, millions of observations and sophisticated specifications of inter-variable relations, accounting for data-phenomena like interactions and endogeneity turn out to require a lot of computational power and therefore take rather long time in terms of estimation and prediction time. This means that such models are not well suited for applications where decisions need to be taken in shortest time possible, like in e.g., real-time bidding or any other sort of digital customization.

Machine Learning provides an alternative approach to predictive modeling. It arose from computer sciences and informatics. Machine Learning is commonly believed to better able to deal with larger and more complex data sets than most predictive models from a statistics background.

Given the popularity of real-time decision making in online advertising and the ability of Machine Learning to make predictions in shortest-time possible, the majority of Machine Learning based applications in marketing are so far dealing with *classification tasks*. Classification thereby is not necessarily bound to a digital marketing or online advertising context. Machine Learning based classification is also very frequently applied to on- and offline customer segmentation, customer identification or the prediction of future customer and consumer behavior given membership in a specific group or class. We thus decided to limit this chapter largely to classification applications of Machine Learning in marketing, as we believe that this field is right now of largest interest for marketing scholars. However, Machine Learning algorithms are not necessarily limited to classification tasks; most can also deal with continuous dependent variables.

In this chapter we first address several issues and challenges that come with big data and how Machine Learning helps overcoming these issues (Sect. 19.2). Then we continue with a basic introduction of Machine Learning (in Sect. 19.3). We will discuss the communalities of Machine Learning with traditional statistical tools and how and where Machine Learning differs from traditional models previously described in Vol. I and in the present volume. While introducing the reader to the basic concept of Machine Learning we will distinguish between two general forms of Machine Learning. Algorithms that are used to discover patterns or structure in the data are commonly referred to as *unsupervised learning*. These are introduced in Sect. 19.4. Algorithms that use pre-coded data with pre-determined patterns to classify new observations into pre-determined categories—commonly referred to as *supervised learning* (Sect. 19.5).

In case of unsupervised learning we will discuss *k*-nearest neighbor algorithms and entropy based segmentation techniques. In case of supervised learning techniques we will discuss Support Vector Machines, Naive Bayes classification, Tree-Decision models—with different subforms and specifications of trees—and Neural Networks. In addition we discuss different ways to assess the quality of a Machine Learning based model and discuss issues arising from overfitting models (Sect. 19.6).

We then continue with an overview of existing marketing research studies using Machine Learning and highlight possible future applications of Machine Learning in marketing research (Sect. 19.7). The chapter concludes with an overview of existing software (Sect. 19.8) and coding solutions available to marketing researchers (Sect. 19.9) and a worked out example of all discussed machine-learning techniques using R (Sect. 19.10).

19.2 Big Data: Bone and Bane

The increase of available data is bone and bane together. On the one hand the newly available data brings remarkable new opportunities to measure, model and analyze consumer behavior. On the other hand the immense size of such data brings serious challenges for researchers. Beside data collection and data storage (Sect. 19.9), the analysis of big data has its own intricacies. Analyzing larger sets of consumer panel data may already require significant computational power: sophisticated dynamic and choice models, especially in case of a Bayesian approach, take significant estimation time. More and more researchers report that the estimation of a single model took days and weeks, even though computational power significantly increased in the last decade.

Such problems only worsen when the amount of available data increase further, and they are not offset by the increase of computational power. One way to handle this problem is sub-sampling. Instead of analyzing the whole sample, researchers may want to randomly draw observations from the large data sample and analyze only a representative sample of the original sample. Such an approach has a long tradition in social sciences, but becomes less favorable in a big data setting. With the increase of available data and the desire to combine data from various data sources the amount of noise within the data also increases. Data from different sources may partially be miss-aligned, there may be coding issues, faulty data collection mechanisms, or non-representative sources may negatively affect the quality of some observations and may leave others unaffected. In case of subsampling (even with random sampling) the amount of noise may lead to critical biases, which may endanger the reliability and validity of findings and prevent generalizing from the subsample to the whole data set. Big Data scientists refer to this issue as "*n* equals all" paradox (Mayer-Schönberger and Cukier 2013). Noise may cause harm in case of smaller (sub) samples, but is usually outperformed in presence of very large data sets that contain all sort of observations available to a researcher.

Due to the performance issues of the traditional marketing models used so far, marketing research is more and more borrowing new estimation techniques and modeling approaches from computer sciences to address the challenges of larger data sets. Computer scientists have a longer tradition dealing with big data and developed a rich set of techniques capable to deal with big data. These techniques are collectively commonly referred to as Machine Learning algorithms.

19.3 Basic Concept of Machine Learning

Machine Learning and Predictive Statistics share common methodologies such as e.g., regression analysis, resampling, classification, and non-linear methods. Especially logistic regression (see Chap. 8 of Vol. I and Chap. 2 of the present volume) is heavily applied in Machine Learning. However, both fields arose from different sources. Statistics is largely applied in social sciences, economics and other related fields. Machine Learning originated in computer sciences. Wasserman (2012) emphasizes how the two different backgrounds lead to two different philosophies. He claims that statistics in general is applied to low dimensional problems emphasizing formal statistical inferences (i.e., hypothesis testing, confidence intervals, optimal estimators, etc.). In contrast, Machine Learning is more outcome-oriented and focuses on accurate prediction making. This practicability is largely due to the fact that data in computer sciences origins from high dimensional problems with many observations and an indefinite number of variables. Machine Learning can hence be perceived as being less restrictive and less formal than classic statistics. It is more focused on system- and software-based solutions to make problem-specific predictions.

The basic concept behind Machine Learning is using pre-classified training data to teach a machine through an algorithm an inferred function with which the machine is able to classify unseen new data. Machine Learning is therefore very close to what we call in marketing research forecasting or predictive modeling.

What is referred to as training in Machine Learning corresponds to the estimation of parameters in marketing research. Marketing analysts may for example run a regression analysis explaining S_t, sales in period t, by sales in the previous period, S_{t-1}, advertising and price in period t, (A_t and P_t), as well as by their lagged effects (A_{t-1} and P_{t-1}). Chapters 4, 5 and 6 of Vol. I explain in detail how such a model can be estimated with Ordinary Least Squares (OLS). This will result in an estimated coefficient for each independent variable that is included to explain its effect on sales, as in the following example:

$$\widehat{S}_t = 12.89 + 0.4\,S_{t-1} + 0.12\,A_t - 0.5\,P_t + 0.03\,A_{t-1} + 0.2\,P_{t-1}. \qquad (19.1)$$

A manager interested in future sales can now easily forecast sales by substituting the corresponding values for advertising and price for the different periods and multiply them with the estimated coefficients.

Machine Learning uses a similar approach. Instead of estimating parameters for each independent variable, Machine Learning algorithms assign weights to the input factors. With the help of training data (i.e., data with a known outcome)—as depicted in Fig. 19.1–an algorithm learns to find patterns within the training data, which allows him later to predict the outcome of a variable given some new data. The algorithm uses an observation's attributes or features to predict its label or category. The learning ability of Machine Learning algorithms corresponds to what we refer to as fitting in statistics. We conclude that, despite the different philosophies and backgrounds, statistics and Machine Learning have very much in common and have similar DNA.

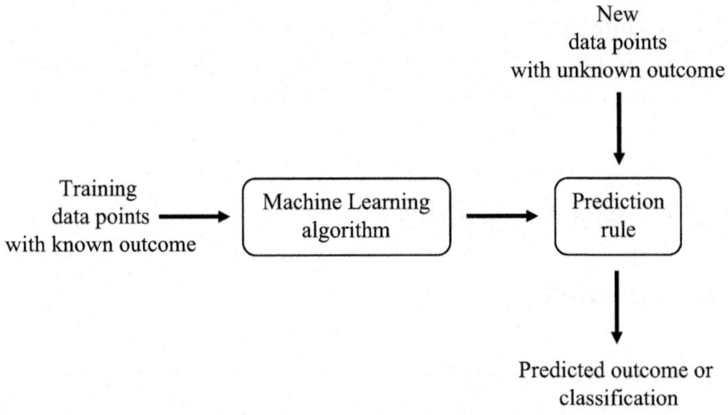

Fig. 19.1 Classification process in Machine Learning

A common application of Machine Learning most people get in touch with on a daily basis is spam detection. Machine Learning-based spam detectors use large sets of pre-classified mails to learn which words and word combinations (attributes) drive the likelihood that a mail belongs to the "spam" category. After the learning stage, the learned rules are applied to the words and word combinations of new incoming mail to determine whether it is "spam" or "ham". Similar to the above discussed regression equation, the algorithm assigns weights (i.e., probability scores) to each word occurrence or word combination. It then calculates a total probability score for an email, given its content and uses its learned prediction rule to determine if the mail is over the particular threshold, in which case it is classified as spam.

There are two types of Machine Learning: *supervised* and *unsupervised* learning. In case of *supervised learning* the algorithm is trained with data that contains both the inputs (e.g., the words and the word combinations in the spam detection example), as well as the desired output (i.e., the correct labels "spam" or "ham" for each email in the training set). With the known outcome labels in the training data, the algorithm aims to determine a rule that maps attributes of an observation (inputs of the rule) to a label or category (output of prediction rule). Examples of classification or predictions tasks that make use of supervised learning are face recognition (Viola and Jones 2004), sentiment analysis (Pang and Lee 2008), language detection (Martin and Jurafsky 2000), fraud detection (Chan and Stolfo 1998) or medical diagnosis (Cruz and Wishart 2006).

In case of *unsupervised learning*, there is no desired output in the training data. Consequently, the algorithm involved cannot "learn" how to classify or predict new data points. Instead, unsupervised learning commonly aims at identifying a structure within the data. Unsupervised learning is usually used in data mining procedures where the interest is more in finding patterns or phenomena within the data than in assigning labels to observations. Examples of unsupervised learning applications are pattern recognition (Fayyad 1996), cluster identification (Gamon et al. 2005), opinion mining (Sidorov et al. 2012), referrals and collaborative filtering (Melville et al. 2002) or feature learning (Blum and Langley 1997).

In the following two sections we first discuss several unsupervised algorithms and then focus on a number of supervised algorithms.

19.4 Unsupervised Algorithms

19.4.1 Introduction

Identifying underlying structures in data is nothing new in marketing. Different forms of cluster analysis like hierarchical clustering, *k*-means clustering or simple factor analysis are already commonly used in marketing to identify e.g., customer segments or patterns of similar usage behavior. These methods are also frequently applied in other fields of data science and big data analytics. They are commonly also attributed with Machine Learning. However, the most commonly applied unsupervised Machine Learning technique is nearest neighbors (NN). The popularity of NN approaches is largely due to the high efficiency of the algorithm. NN does not consume a lot of computational power and is therefore easy to apply—even in case of very large datasets—and returns results in almost real-time. Another important concept in unsupervised learning is entropy. Entropy measures in-group homogeneity and helps segmenting heterogeneous data into homogeneous subgroups. In the following we give a detailed description of the two main concepts before we move on to supervise learning techniques.

19.4.2 Nearest Neighbors (NN-Classification)

As explained in the preceding section, in unsupervised learning problems, we aim to identify structure in a set of data points. Many of the applications of unsupervised learning the output of the algorithm is a grouping of objects, based on similarity, where similar objects share similar features. In order to group similar items together, one needs to measure similarity across features and objects, and it appears reasonable to place objects with high level of similarity in the same group. Similarity is usually quantified by means of some kind of distance measure, where very similar objects will have a smaller distance to each other than dissimilar ones.

In the marketing research literature, many types of distance measures are available to accommodate different types of feature measurement. There are measures for calculating distances between objects based on continuous measurements of features of objects (e.g., measuring distance between customers based on their income), as well as distance measures that are based on categorical measurements of features (e.g., distance between customers based on whether they own a car, live in a rural area, their gender etc.). Here we consider the simple case where there are continuous measurements of object features.

Suppose that there are two objects A and B, and that we have data on n features of A and B. Let us denote the value of feature $1, 2, \ldots, n$ for object A by $f_{1,A}, f_{2,A}, \ldots, f_{n,A}$, respectively, and values for the same features for object B by $f_{1,B}, f_{2,B}, \ldots, f_{n,B}$. The Euclidian distance between A and B based on these n features is defined as:

$$d(A, B) = \sqrt{(f_{1,A} - f_{1,B})^2 + (f_{2,A} - f_{2,B})^2 + \cdots + (f_{n,A} - f_{n,B})^2}. \qquad (19.2)$$

To illustrate this, we present several features of 5 physicians in Table 19.1. For each physician we know the age, the number of patients, how many people are working in their medical practice and whether the physician is prescribing branded drugs or generic products. Consider a sixth physician: Dr. Pierce, age 37, with 500 patients, and a practice size of 2. Based on the features age, number of patients, and practice size, the distance between Dr. Hunnicut and Dr. Pierce can be computed as

Table 19.1 Features of several physicians

Physician	Age	Nr. of patients	Practice size	Branded	Distance to Dr. Pierce
Hunnicut	35	350	3	Yes	15.16
Trapper	22	500	2	No	15.00
Potter	63	2000	1	No	152.23
Burns	59	1700	1	No	122.00
Winchester	25	400	4	Yes	15.74

$\sqrt{(35-37)^2+(350-500)^2+(3-2)^2} = 15.16$. The last column of Table 19.1 shows the distance between Dr. Pierce and all of his colleagues, based on the features age, number of patients, and practice size.

It is important to note that the distance does not allow for any quality comparisons or any other sort of interpretation. Dr. Potter is neither better nor worse than Dr. Trapper or Dr. Hunnicut. The distance is just displaying how similar or dissimilar the physicians are to Dr. Pierce based on a selection of features.

Given the similarity information we can now also see if there is a pattern in description behavior. The closest colleagues to Dr. Pierce are Dr. Trapper, Dr. Hunnicut and Dr. Winchester. Dr. Burns and Dr. Potter are rather dissimilar to Dr. Pierce with a Euclidean Distance almost 10 times higher than the other three. The most similar objects are commonly referred to as nearest-neighbors. If we now look at the prescription behavior of Dr. Pierce's nearest neighbors, we see that two prescribe branded drugs and only one (Dr. Trapper) does not. By majority count, we could predict that Pierce is also prescribing branded drugs. A sales person representing the pharmaceutical company that produces the branded drug might find this information useful.

The Euclidean distance is formally referred to as L2-norm. It is the most widely applied distance measure in data science (see Provost and Fawcett 2013). However, there are also other distance measures such as the Manhattan distance measure (L1-norm) that simply sums the absolute differences along the features of objects A and B. In text classification tasks Jaccard and Cosine distance measures are widely applied. These two measures account for how many items A and B share in common in relation to the total quantity of available items (Levandowsky and Winter 1971).

A common problem here is the question of how many neighbors to include into the prediction. In the example we used a majority approach for the 3 nearest neighbors. The choice was arbitrary and mostly driven by the feeling that the three colleagues with distance scores around 15 are very similar to Dr. Pierce and should be used for the prediction. This is a common issue with k-Nearest-Neighbor (NN) classification. The higher the value of k, the more the estimation gets smoothed out. In the most extreme case k equals n, so that the entire data set is used for class prediction and that the new observation will be assigned to the majority class. In case of $k = 1$, a 1-NN classifier will develop very specific rules and will deliver very erratic boundaries perfectly depicting the training data. Such 1-NN classifiers are very sensitive to overfitting, an issue that we discuss later in this chapter.

19.4.3 Entropy

Whereas neighboring helps assigning people into groups or predicting peoples' behavior given previous observations from similar people, it does not allow determining which factors or features help best to make good predictions. Neighboring approaches are good in assessing total similarity. When it comes to determining the features that make objects differ from each other, other measures perform better.

In marketing, assigning observations into groups is known as segmentation. A key task in segmentation is to divide a heterogeneous number of objects in homogeneous subgroups (Wedel and Kamakura 2000 and Chap. 11). Homogeneity is closely related to the concept of purity. The most common purity measure is called entropy and was first introduced into information theory by Shannon (1948). Entropy is measuring disorder, and refers to the degree of heterogeneity within a group. A high entropy score indicates that all group members share many different features, and a low entropy score indicates a high degree of common features amongst group members. Entropy is hence measuring how homogenously a group is composed. Provost and Fawcett (2013) give a formal definition of entropy as displayed in Eq. (19.3):

$$\text{Entropy} = -p_1 \log_2 (p_1) - p_2 \log_2 (p_2) - \cdots - p_n \log_2 (p_n)\,. \tag{19.3}$$

Each p_i represents the probability—measured as the relative frequency—of feature i being within the observed set ($i = 1, \ldots, n$). Each p_i gets multiplied with its logarithm taken at base 2.

With entropy as a means to measure within-group homogeneity, the information gain can be calculated that a feature provides for splitting groups. Entropy allows us deciding which variables are the best to split groups into more homogenous subgroups. More formally speaking and as shown in (19.4), a feature's information gain is the change in entropy caused by the presence of this feature when splitting up observations into resulting n new groups:

$$\begin{aligned} \text{IG}\,(\text{parent, child}) = \text{Entropy(parent)} - [p\,(\text{child}_1) \times \text{Entropy}\,(\text{child}_1) \\ + \cdots + p\,(\text{child}_n) \times \text{Entropy}\,(\text{child}_n)]\,. \end{aligned} \tag{19.4}$$

The information gain is the difference between the entropy of the old segmentation (without the new feature often referred to as parenting group) and the sum of the with the group size ($p(\text{new}_n)$) weighted entropy scores of the resulting new subgroups (often referred to as child groups) new_n.

To illustrate the concept of information gain, let us go back to Table 19.1. This time we are not interested in predicting Dr. Pierce's prescription behavior but try to gain insights into which of the three features age, number of patients, and practice size helps most to predict whether a physician is prescribing branded drugs or generics.

To do so we first calculate the entropy score for the whole group regarding the description behavior. We have observations for 5 physicians. From the five physicians, two prescribe branded drugs and three generics. This leads to the following probabilities:

$$p\,(\text{branded}) = 2/5 = 0.4, \text{and} \tag{19.5}$$

$$p\,(\text{generics}) = 3/5 = 0.6. \tag{19.6}$$

The resulting entropy score according to formula (19.3) is:

$$\text{Entropy}\,(\text{start}) = -\,[0.4 \times \log_2(0.4) + 0.6 \times \log_2(0.6)] \approx 0.971. \tag{19.7}$$

Now we split up the group according to the feature "practice size", creating two new groups. One consists of physicians that work alone, and the other of physicians that work in larger practices. The group "Practice size ≤ 1" consists of Dr. Potter and Dr. Burns who both only prescribe generics. The group "Practice size > 1" consists of Dr. Trapper, Dr. Hunnicut and Dr. Winchester from which two prescribe branded drugs and one prescribes generics. Consequently:

$$\text{Entropy}\,(\text{Practice size} \leq 1) = 1 \times \log_2(1) + 0 \times \log_2(0) = 0, \ \textit{and} \tag{19.8}$$

$$\text{Entropy}\,(\text{Practice size} > 1) \approx 0.33 \times \log_2(0.33) + 0.67 \times \log_2(0.67) \approx 0.915. \tag{19.9}$$

The information gain from differentiating between physicians that work alone and those that work in larger practices is then:

$$\begin{aligned} \text{IG} &= \text{Entropy}\,(\text{start}) - [p\,(\text{Practice size} \leq 1) \times \text{Entropy}\,(\text{Practice size} \leq 1) \\ &\quad + p\,(\text{Practice size} > 1) \times \text{Entropy}\,(\text{Practice size} > 1)] \\ &\approx 0.971 - [2/5 \times 0 + 3/5 \times 0.915] \approx 0.422. \end{aligned} \tag{19.10}$$

Figure 19.2 depicts a tree model of this segmentation with the corresponding entropy scores and distribution scores

Instead of setting an arbitrary cut-off like 1, one can also build up four groups, one for each practice size. Each group has an entropy score of 0, so that the IG of such a split would be 0.971. Figure 19.3 shows the resulting tree with the subgroups and the corresponding entropy values.

As the information gain score is higher for the 4 group solution, one should rather use all four dimensions of the feature instead of relying on a single cut-off. Nevertheless we will later see that in this particular case the information gain is due to over-fitting, as the split-off is perfectly describing the training data and it is highly doubtable that such a division will be generalizable.

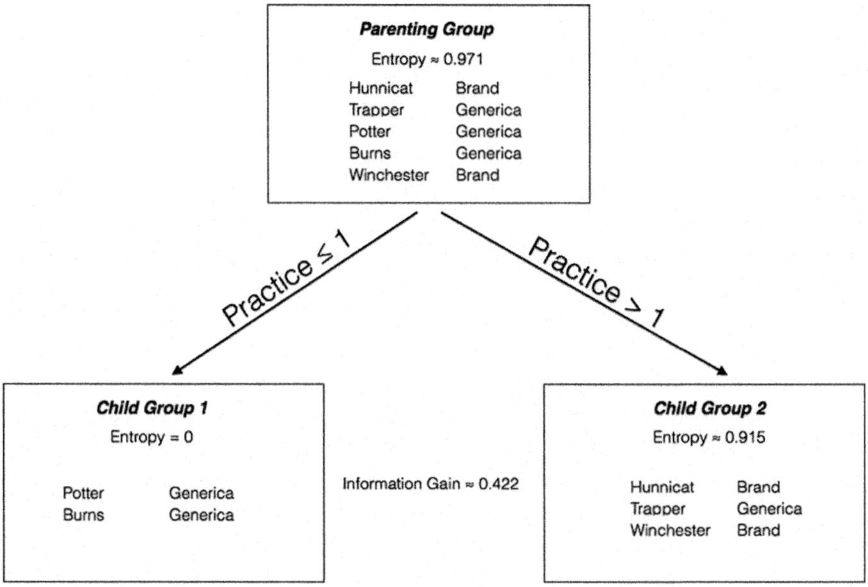

Fig. 19.2 Segmentation split with "Practice size > 1"

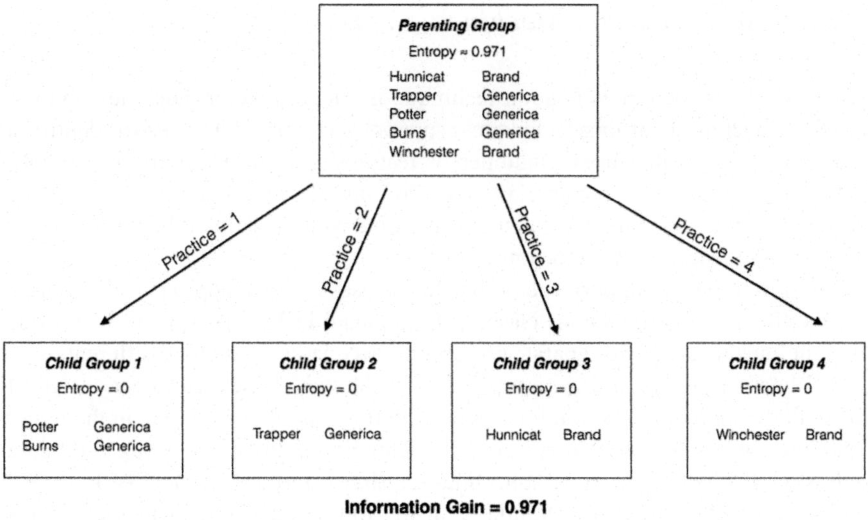

Fig. 19.3 Segmentation split on all possible values of "Practice size"

19.5 Supervised Learning

19.5.1 Introduction

Supervised learning is less about identifying hidden patterns or structures within data. It is more about inferring probabilities from training data to determine how certain features help predicting class membership or future behavior of freshly incoming data. Questions like, which customer behavior helps best to predict churn (Xia and Jin 2008), which types of user-generated content indicate consideration or buying intention (Kübler et al. 2016), or which types of engine signals predict a major breakdown of a car engine within the next 2 weeks (Schlangenstein 2013), are common questions addressed by supervised learning techniques. Supervised learning uses a wide array of algorithms that continuously grows. Nevertheless one can distinguish 4 main kinds of supervised learning techniques, which are prevalent in Machine Learning and data science: Support Vector Machines, Classification and Regression Trees (CRT), Naïve Bayes, and Neural Networks. For each technique researchers developed extensions and modifications, which address specific data specifications and needs. We will present for all four approaches the main concept and introduce the most common extensions.

19.5.2 Support Vector Machines (SVM)

A frequently applied classification technique is support vector machines. Similar to other Machine Learning techniques, support vector machines try to identify a function $f(x_i) = y_i$ that uses a number of features x_i from a training set to split observations into two separate classes y_i. For any new observation n—out of the training sample—the function can then determine with the help of the features x_n to which class the new object n belongs.

To split groups, support vector machines use a linear approach to separate observations into homogenous classes. As depicted in Fig. 19.4, there is not one straight line that is able to separate groups into two classes, but many different ones.

All lines in Fig. 19.4 allow a separation of the two classes. However not all of them allow optimal prediction for newly incoming data. For example, in the upper left situation a new observation originally belonging to the green group and being only slightly right of the separating line—as shown in the left panel of Fig. 19.5 will be misclassified as red. Similarly in the lower left situation in Fig. 19.4 a new observation from the red group being only marginally left of the line will be misclassified as belonging to the green class (right panel of Fig. 19.5).

The difficulty with linear classification is to find a line that "best" separates the observed classes and allows the "best" possible prediction of newly incoming data. As shown in the lower right example in Fig. 19.5 such an "optimal" solution maximizes the distance between both classes and is located somehow in the

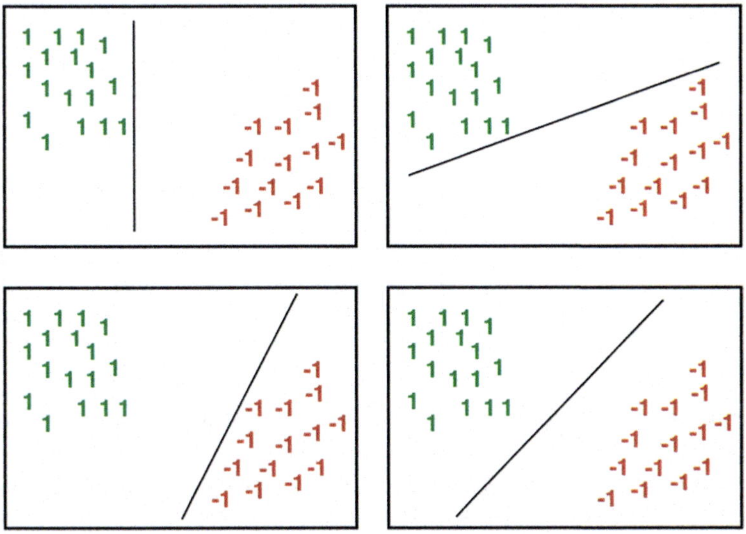

Fig. 19.4 Different possible separation lines

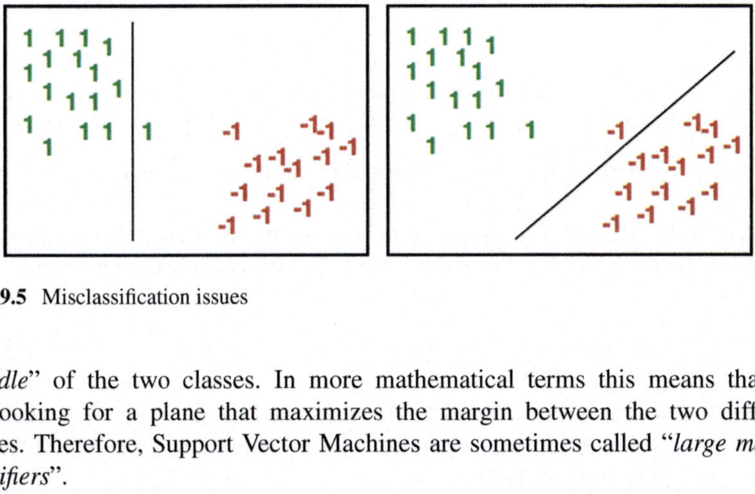

Fig. 19.5 Misclassification issues

"*middle*" of the two classes. In more mathematical terms this means that we are looking for a plane that maximizes the margin between the two different classes. Therefore, Support Vector Machines are sometimes called "*large margin classifiers*".

In case of a linear separation problem with the two classes 1 and -1—as shown in Figs. 19.4 and 19.5–we can formally define the separating plane with the help of Eqs. (19.11) and (19.12):

$$\omega \cdot x + b = 1 \tag{19.11}$$

$$\omega \cdot x + b = -1. \tag{19.12}$$

As shown in Fig. 19.6, Eqs. (19.11) and (19.12) express the two boarders on the edges of the hyperplane that separates the two classes 1 and -1. These two vectors

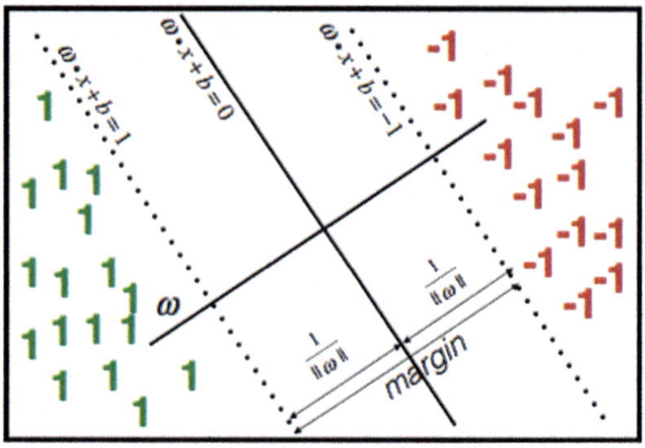

Fig. 19.6 Hyperplane with support vectors

are commonly referred to as *support vectors.* ω represents a normalized vector to the hyperplane and b the offset of the vector from the origin. As shown in Fig. 19.6, we can combine b and ω to express the distance between the two support vectors which is $\frac{2}{||\omega||}$. To find the hyperplane that maximizes the distance $\frac{2}{||\omega||}$ between the two support vectors we thus need to minimize $||\omega||$.

Simultaneously, we do not want any observation of the training data to fall into the margin of the hyperplane. We need thus to re-formulate Eqs. (19.11) and (19.12) as:

$$\omega \cdot x + b \geq 1 \text{ for all observations belonging to class 1} \quad (19.13)$$

$$\omega \cdot x + b \leq -1 \text{ for all observations belonging to class} - 1. \quad (19.14)$$

Equations (19.13) and (19.14) therefore express the rule for the margin that is separating the two classes. This leads to the following optimization problem:

$$\min \frac{1}{2} ||\omega^2|| \text{ under the condition } y_i\,(\omega x_i - b) \geq 1 \text{ for all } i = 1 \ldots n. \quad (19.15)$$

Commonly this is achieved with the help of a simple Lagrange approach where one tries to maximize the Lagrange operator α while minimizing b and ω (for more details see Vapnik 1995, p. 182).

A SVM algorithm starts with estimating the Lagrange operator α_i for the two support vectors. Then the algorithm uses the information from the two support vectors to determine the separating "middle" vector ω of the hyperplane with $\omega = \sum_{i=1}^{N} \alpha_i y_i x_i$.

This approach however only works with linearly separable data. For data that cannot be linearly split into groups different extensions of SVMs have been developed. First of all, one may relax the rules for the margin and allow few "misclassified" observations to be within the margin like shown in Fig. 19.5. Such approaches are commonly called *soft margin machines* (Cortes and Vapnik 1995). In this case the minimization problem depicted in Eq. (19.15) is extended with a slack

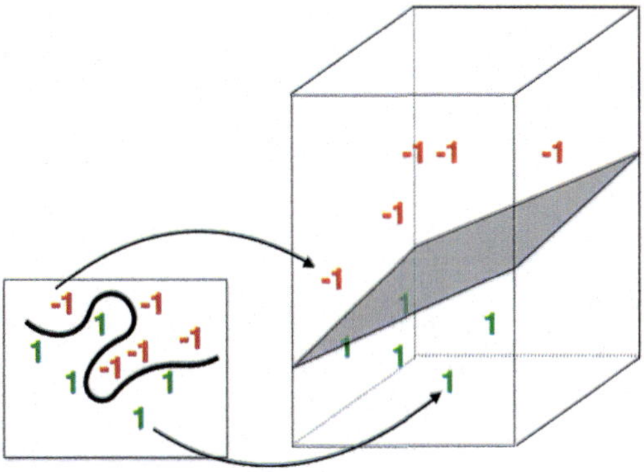

Fig. 19.7 Multi-dimensional split with kernel

variable that allows some observations—like outliers or false measurements—to be within the separating margin, so that the optimization problem re-formulates to:

$$\min \frac{1}{2} \, ||\omega^2|| + C \sum_{i=1}^{n} \xi_i \text{ under the condition} \tag{19.16}$$

$$y_i \left(\omega x_i - b \right) \geq 1 - \xi_i \text{ and } \xi_i \geq 0 \tag{19.17}$$

Here C is a constant that balances the width of the margin and the amount of misclassification of data points, and ξ_i represents the misclassification of observation i. The extension can be interpreted as some sort of cost function. By minimizing Eq. (19.16), the degree of separation and the degree of misclassification are jointly optimized.

This approach however is still based on a linear separation function. Many problems are not separable with a linear approach. For these cases one may split up the data in a more dimensional space to find a plane that then helps to separate the data into groups, like illustrated in Fig. 19.7. Such approaches are known as *Kernel based support vector machines* and got first introduced by Boser et al. (1992).

Kernel functions take in general the form displayed in Eq. (19.18):

$$K\left(x_i, x_j\right) = \phi\left(x_i\right) \cdot \phi\left(x_j\right) \tag{19.18}$$

where $\phi(x)$ depicts a function that is mapping the data into another space. The kernel function applies some transformation to the feature vectors x_i and x_j and combines the features using a dot product, which takes the vectors of the two input features and returns a single number.[1] Doing so, one can apply different forms of transformation. Kernel functions hence take different forms with the most basic one using a *linear combination* that simply forms the dot products of the different input features like shown by Cover (1965) and displayed in Eq. (19.18a):

[1]See also Chap. 17.

$$K\left(x_i, x_j\right) = x_i \cdot x_j. \tag{19.18a}$$

Polynomial Kernels of degree d use a simple non-linear transformation of the data like displayed in Eq. (19.18b):

$$K\left(x_i, x_j\right) = \left(x_i \cdot x_j + 1\right)^d. \tag{19.18b}$$

The multi-dimensional transformation allows a linear separation if the dimension d of the higher dimensional space is large enough, so that one can again rely on the basic SVM approach represented by Eqs. (19.18a) and (19.18b). Other common kernel transformations use a sigmoid or Gaussian transfer function (similar to the ones discussed below in the neural network section). Even though the transformation ϕ may lead to an infinite dimensional space, kernel extensions of SVMs usually generalize quite well, while being robust to over-fitting issues. However, non-linear Kernels usually require more testing efforts and commonly results in longer training times. Such Kernel extensions are therefore frequently used for more complex classification tasks such as e.g., image or face recognition (Osuna et al. 1997) or sentiment analysis (Kübler et al. 2016).

19.5.3 Decision Tree Models

19.5.3.1 Introduction

The basic idea of decision trees is to start out with the complete training set, and determine a series of splits to create more homogenous sub-groups, with the goal of creating a classification that is as good as possible, with a minimum number of splits. At each split, a variable is selected that forms the basis for a decision rule that drives the split. For example: at the first split, the set of physicians may be split up according to the practice size (as described earlier). Variable selection can be based on the previously described concept of entropy and information gain.[2] In most cases, a "greedy" strategy is followed, where the variable and the thresholds for the associated decision rule are selected that result in the greatest improvement in the classification. Hence, in the physician example, the first split will only be according to the "Practice Size $\leq$ 1" rule if that split results in the best partition of physicians that prescribe branded drugs and physicians that prescribe branded drugs. At each step in the creation of a decision tree, it is determined whether additional splits will lead to better classifications. Splitting the root set into two sets according to practice size already leads to a group—the one on the left–that only consists of physicians

[2]Some tree-structured models use different splitting algorithms such as Gini-Impurity (see e.g., Kuhn and De Mori 1995) or Variance Reduction (see e.g., Gascuel 2000). Despite formal differences, the main concept behind this is still to improve in group homogeneity by comparing purity before and after the split.

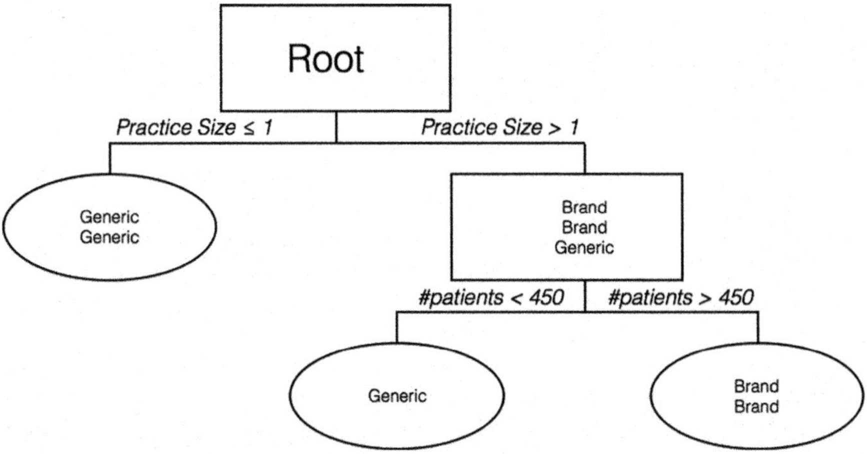

Fig. 19.8 Example of a decision tree model

who prescribe generics. The other group is still mixed and contains both sorts of physicians. Please note that a split does not necessarily immediately lead to pure groups. In most cases splits will lead to purer but not entirely pure groups, and for each group that is created at a given step, it is determined whether other attributes of splits at other levels of the same attribute lead to better and purer classifications. The resulting groups that are not split further are commonly called leaves or end nodes. Each leaf is based on a sequence of classification rules such as: "If practice size > 1 and number of patients > 500 THEN p(physician = prescribes generics) = 1".

A tree by default accommodates interaction effects and nonlinearities. For example, as shown in Fig. 19.8, the number of patients only plays a role in case a physician works in a practice with a size larger than one. Similarly, a tree can account for nonlinearities by splitting on the same variable twice (e.g., first split on #patients > 400, and in a later step on #patients > 1000), where the effect sizes are not restricted to be linear. Having suitable training data with enough attributes one can develop larger models with more nodes and leaves accounting for many interactions between the different available variables.

The developed rules can then easily be used for predictions with data for which one does not know the classification. Tree-structured models are popular in practice, as they are easy to follow and to understand. As they are robust to many data problems and rather efficient in determining classes, they are included in many status-quo data mining packages.

Rules for decision trees with binary outcomes are largely based on the concept of entropy when calculating the information gain of a split using a feature.

Decision Tree learning models can also be applied to continuous outcome variables such as e.g., buying volume, or click and usage frequencies. In these cases two other measures for impurity are commonly used: Gini Impurity and Variance Reduction. Both concepts similarly measure impurity within the resulting groups of a split. The information gain can then be calculated similarly to the entropy-based approach. Most commonly in case of continuous variables impurity is measured with the help of variance reduction. Here one compares how much the variance within a leaf is decreased given a split variable compared to other split variables. For more details on all measures of impurity see Breiman et al. (1984).

Tree models using classical impurity measures as discussed above are commonly referred to as Classification and Regression Trees (CART) models. Beside these classic split rules, trees can also be grown with the help of other decision criteria. Another popular approach here consists of models that make splitting decisions at each leaf based on classic statistical tests like e.g., chi-square tests (in case of a dichotomous dependent variable) or F-tests (in case of a continuous dependent variable). Using Chi-square tests is another way to see how well groups can be separated. Tree models using such chi-square tests are commonly referred to as Chi-squared Automatic Interaction Detector (CHAID) models. They have been introduced by Kass (1980). CHAID models rely on a three-step process to build up a tree: merging, splitting and stopping. In the first step the algorithm cycles through all predictors testing for significant differences between outcome categories with respect to the dependent variable. If the difference for a given pair of predictor categories is not statistically significant (according to a threshold determined by the research commonly called alpha-to-merge value) the algorithm *merges* the predictor categories and repeats this step. For all pairings with a significant difference, the algorithm will continue to calculate a p-value (based on a Bonferroni adjustment). It then continues to find the pairing with the highest similarity, which is indicated by the lowest statistical difference i.e., the highest p-value. This pairing is then used to *split* the leaf. The algorithm *stops* growing the tree in case that the smallest p-value for any predictor is greater than a pre-set threshold commonly called alpha-to-split value. CHAID models can deal with different types of dependent variables. Ritschard (2010) shows how to transform continuous dependent variables into categorical variables and how to adapt the chi-square and F-tests.

CHAID models deliver powerful and convenient alternatives to traditional CART models. However, merging and stopping decisions are largely affected by the alpha-values the researcher has to pre-determine. Biggs et al. (1991) therefore introduced an extension of the basic CHAID model that continues the merging process until only two categories remain for each predictor. Splitting and stopping decisions are taken in the same way than in case of the basic CHAID model. However, through the exhaustive merging process (until only two categories remain), these models do not need an alpha-to-merge variable. Therefore such models are commonly referred to as *Exhaustive CHAID* models.

Compared to ordinary CART models, CHAID models take more computational time and computational power. This is even more the case for exhaustive CHAID models, which use more combinations of predictors during the merging stage. Especially in case of data sets with many (continuous) variables and many observations this may become a serious limiting issue.

QUEST (Quick, Unbiased, Efficient, Statistical Tree) is another approach to tree growing (Loh and Shih 1997). QUEST relies on Fisher's Linear Discriminant

Analysis (LDA) (Fisher 1936) for splitting leaves. LDA resembles classic logistic regression techniques as it also depicts a dependent categorical variable through a combination of independent continuous variables. QUEST uses LDA to determine the dominant predictor at each leave and then continuous growing the tree. QUEST turns out to be most efficient in terms of computational resources. However, QUEST is only able to cope with binary outcomes.

One important issue of decision tree models is the problem of overfitting. The temptation of classifying the training data perfectly with a fully developed tree is high. However, it turns out that such trees commonly do rather poor in predicting class-membership for out-of-sample data. Therefore it is essential to understand how to judge the prediction effectiveness of the classification model to be able to understand how detailed a tree model should be developed. We will come to this aspect later when we discuss overfitting. So far it is important to note that using only one tree model may lead to very specific prediction outcomes that are unique to the training data. This brings the researcher in a dilemma. On the one hand, using loose stopping criteria when growing trees will help developing sophisticated, large trees, which account for many factors. This however, may immediately lead to overfitting. On the other hand, a too tight stopping criterion will lead to a tree that is too general, which does not provide enough insights and whose predictive power is underdeveloped. A key question in tree development is therefore, how far does one want to develop a tree and which kind of stopping criterion does one need to prevent a tree model from overfitting.

One way to deal with this question is pruning (Breiman et al. 1984). *Pruning* approaches develop trees with the loosest possible stopping criterion. The resulting, overfitting tree is then cut back by removing leaves, which are not contributing to the generalization accuracy (Rokach and Maimon 2007). Pruning can follow a top-down or a bottom-up approach. The decision to cut off a leaf is taken according to different decision-criteria, which focus on the overall contribution of a leaf to the generalizability of the tree. A very common pruning approach is reduce-error-pruning as described by Quinlan (1987). While going–from the bottom to the top–through each leaf, reduce-error-pruning checks, whether replacing a leaf with the most frequent category does not reduce the tree's accuracy. If this is true, the leaf gets pruned. There is a wide variety of pruning approaches described in Rokach and Maimon (2007), with more sophisticated approaches like Cost–Complexity Pruning, Minimum Error Pruning, Pessimistic Pruning, Error–based Pruning, Minimum Description Length (MDL) Pruning, Minimum Message Length Pruning, and Critical Value Pruning. Esposito et al. (1997) show by comparing different pruning approaches that there is no golden rule or no approach that outperforms other approaches. Although that pruning is important to avoid over- or underfitting models, it is in the responsibility of the researcher to identify the approach that fits best to his or her data. Another way to deal with overfitting is combining different tree models together aggregating decision rules across different tree models. Such combination approaches are commonly referred to as ensemble methods.

Table 19.2 Tree overview

	CART	CHAID	QUEST
Split procedure			
Univariate	X	X	X
Linear combination	X		X
Number of branches			
Always 2	X		X
More than 2		X	
Tree size control			
Stopping rule		X	
Pruning	X		X
Computational power and estimation time	*	**	***

Note: * low performance, ** ordinary performance, *** good performance

The most common ensemble methods are *Bagging Decision Trees, Random Forest Classifiers, and Boosted Decision Trees*. Table 19.2 gives an overview of the three different tree forms CART, CHAID and QUEST.

19.5.3.2 Bagging Decision Trees

Bagging Decision Trees were first introduced into Machine Learning by Breiman (1996). The approach is very similar to what is known in classic statistics as bootstrapping. In this procedure, a number (say *N*) of data sets are created, consisting of random draws with replacement from the main training set. Usually these newly created data sets are of the same size as the full training set, so that some observations appear more than once in any of these data sets. Each set is then used to train a decision tree. When a new data point needs to be classified, the *N* resulting trees each generate a classification for the new data point. The results of each tree are then aggregated when assigning the final category for the new observation. This is typically done by means of a majority vote over the *N* classifications.

Bagging is a combination of *bootstrapping* and *aggregation*. Even though each subset tree may overfit, results show that the mean model delivers acceptable generalizable results. The improved model performance is caused by a decrease of variance within the model that comes without an increase of the bias. While the predictions of a single tree are highly sensitive to noise in the training set and thus to overfitting, the average of many trees is not, as long as the trees are not correlated. Dietterich (2000) shows that bagging is especially suitable when the training data features a high level of noise. Comparing all types of CRT extensions, bagging turns out to be the classifier that delivers the best performance in case of training data that features many outliers and other issues.

19.5.3.3 Random Forests

Such strong correlation may however occur, if one or a few features are very strong predictors for an outcome variable. As these features will be selected in many of the n trees, correlation will be high between trees. Ho (2002) introduces a solution to this, by adapting the bagging procedure by modifying the learning algorithm. The adapted algorithm selects, at each feature split in the learning process, a random subset of the features following a random subspace method. Learning algorithms combining random subspace sampling on feature level with a bagging subsample approach are commonly called *Random Forest Classifiers*. For more details see Skurichina (2002).

As Random Forest Classifiers and Bagging Decision Trees rely on mean-aggregations when combining the results from different models, they are also commonly referred to as *averaging ensemble methods*. Dietterich (2000) shows that with normal training data, random forests deliver results that are as good as those of Bagging Regression Trees.

19.5.3.4 Boosting Decision Trees

Another approach that does not belong to the class of averaging ensemble methods is boosting. In *boosting methods*, estimators are built sequentially. Contrary to bagging and Random Forest, boosting does not use resampling methods to generate new classifications, instead it works with reweighted versions of the original training set. The algorithm starts out with the original version of the training data set, where each observation has the same weight. The weights for the second step are determined based on the misclassifications that result when applying a tree to the data. Contrary to expectations, the misclassified observations receive a higher weight in the next step of the boosting algorithm. The idea is that a stronger focus on the misclassified data points increase accuracy of subsequent steps in the algorithm. The final classification is based on a weighted vote across the sequential classifications, where better classifications get a higher weight.

Boosting is especially suitable in case of different types of predictor variables and in presence of missing data. Boosting further allows outliers and does not require any form of data transformation. It can further fit complex nonlinear relationships. For a more detailed description of boosting see Hastie et al. (2009) and Elith et al. (2008). Even though the latter comes from a non-business background it gives a very detailed and profound guide to optimally boost different kinds of tree models. Dietterich (2000) finds boosting regression trees to outperform random forests and classic bagging trees in case of non-skewed data.

19.5.3.5 Naive Bayes

Another popular approach to data classification is Naive Bayes (NB) classification. Similar to the types of classifiers that we discussed so far, NB tries to infer information from training data and to build rules that the (co)-occurrence of certain features determines the membership in different classes. Contrary to most sampling and simulation based approaches of Bayesian statistics in marketing, NB classifiers use a rather simple approach to determine the probabilities for class membership. As we will later see, this is however not the main reason that they are commonly referred to as being naive. All NB classifiers rely on the basic Bayesian Theorem presented in Eq. (19.19):

$$p\left(A|B\right) = \frac{p\left(B|A\right) \times p(A)}{p(B)} \tag{19.19}$$

where $p(A|\,B)$ represents the probability that we can classify an observation to class A, given that we observe behavior B. In Bayesian language this is referred to as the posterior. Bayes rule decomposes this posterior into three parts. The first part, $p(B|\,A)$, expresses the probability that the attribute B occurs, given that the observation belongs to class A. The second part, $p(A)$, is the general probability of occurrence of class A, and the third part ($p(B)$) is the general probability of occurrence of B (see also Chap. 16).

Bayes Theorem can be adapted to all types of classification problems where we observe a certain numbers of features for different items and where we want to determine the probability that an item belongs to a certain class.

As with other Machine Learning methods we use a training sample consisting of n items belonging to k classes $C_1, \ldots, C_k$ to infer the class determining probabilities. Each item in the training sample can then be represented by an m−dimensional vector $X = \{x_1, x_2, x_3, \ldots, x_m\}$ denoting values of the m attributes of the item.

For every new observation of X, the classifier will predict that the observation belongs to the class that results with the highest a posteriori probability depending on the presence of X as depicted in Eq. (19.20):

$$p\left(C_i|X\right) > p\left(C_j|X\right) \text{ for } 1 \leq j \leq k \text{ and } i \neq j. \tag{19.20}$$

X can thus only be classified as belonging to class C_i if $p(C_i|\,X)$ is highest among all k posterior probabilities, which is referred to as the maximum posteriori hypothesis. To achieve this we can use Bayes Theorem from Eq. (19.19) that leads us to:

$$p\left(C_i|X\right) = \frac{p\left(X|C_i\right) \times p\left(C_i\right)}{p(X)} \tag{19.21}$$

which expresses the probability of X belonging to class C_i as the product of the probability of X occurring in presence of C_i and the general probability of class C_i divided by the general probability of the occurrence of X. As $p\ (X)$ is the same for all classes, only the numerator needs to be maximized. Thereby $p(C_i)$ can be determined by two approaches. First of all, one may use the frequency of C_i to calculate the respective class probability. So that $p(C_i)$ equals:

$$p\left(C_i\right) = \frac{\text{frequency}\left(C_i\right)}{n} \tag{19.22}$$

If the necessary frequency information is lacking, one commonly assumes that all classes are equally likely which leads to $p(C_1) = p(C_2) = \ldots = p(C_k)$, which then implies that we only need to maximize $p(X|\, C_i)$ as $p(C)$ is the same for all classes.

In order to be able to easily compute $p(X|\, C_i)$ the naive assumption of class conditional independence needs to be made—which finally explains the name of this classifier. Class conditional independence does only require that the values of the attributes are conditionally independent. This can be expressed as follows:

$$p\left(X|C_i\right) \approx \prod_{l=1}^{m} p\left(x_l|C_i\right). \tag{19.23}$$

In case of categorical attributes, $p(x_l|\, C_i)$ can be calculated by dividing the number of items in class C_i sharing value x_l by the total number of items in class C_i. When the attributes are continuous, one commonly assumes a Gaussian distribution of the values with a standard deviation δ and a mean γ:

$$g\left(x, \gamma, \delta\right) = \frac{1}{\delta\sqrt{2\pi}} \exp\left(-\frac{(x-\gamma)^2}{2\delta^2}\right) \tag{19.24}$$

which results in:

$$p\left(x_l|C_i\right) = g\left(x_l, \gamma_{C_i}, \delta_{C_i}\right). \tag{19.25}$$

Using the attribute-specific probabilities, together with the class-specific probabilities from Eq. (19.24), one can calculate the probabilities for each class C_i given a combination of attributes for each new X. The corresponding class label for a vector of observations X is then C_i if $p(X|\, C_i)p(C_i) > p(X|\, C_j)p(C_j)$ for all $j \neq i$.

Naive Bayes classifiers belong to the most efficient Machine Learning algorithms. Thanks to the naive assumption of class conditional independence all necessary probabilities can easily and quickly be inferred from the training data. This allows the algorithm to work rather fast without consuming too much computational power. Popular applications of Naive Bayes classifiers are email spam filters, customer class predictions and collaborative filtering applications.

Fig. 19.9 Schematic model of an artificial neuron

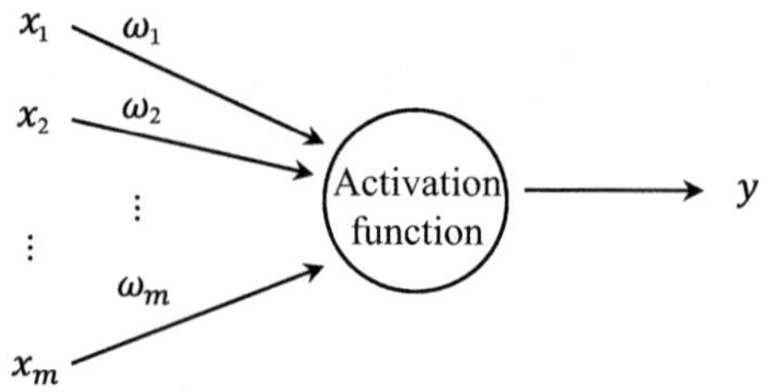

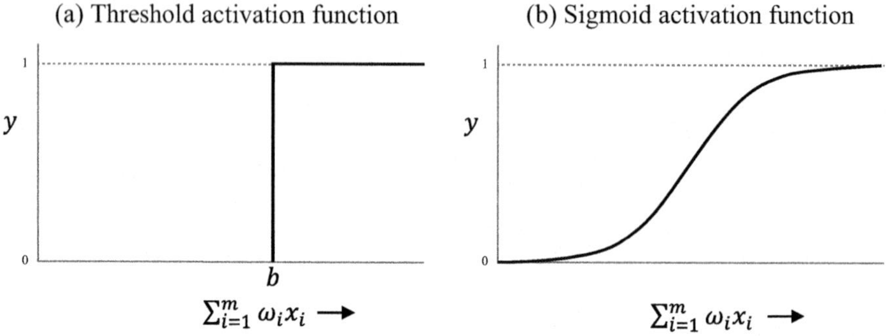

Fig. 19.10 Two types of activation functions

19.5.3.6 Neural Networks

Neural Networks constitute another well-known type of Machine Learning algorithms. Their name, but also their approach, are inspired by how the human brain works. Just as the neurons in a human brain, a neural network consists of a number of interconnected elements that transform inputs (which possibly come from other elements) to outputs. A schematic version of an artificial neuron is depicted in Fig. 19.9, where inputs $x_1, \ldots, x_m$ are weighted according to $\omega_1, \ldots, \omega_m$. Their weighted sum is processed by some activation function, and this results in a binary outcome y. Such an artificial neuron is called a perceptron.

Artificial neurons may have different activation functions that transfer the weighted inputs to outputs. The most basic version is a threshold function, where $y = 0$ if $\sum_{i=1}^{m} \omega_i x_i \leq b$, and $y = 1$ if $\sum_{i=1}^{m} \omega_i x_i > b$. The threshold activation function is illustrated in Fig. 19.10a.

When training the neural network with a training data set, the algorithm determines values for ("learns") the weights $\omega_1, \ldots, \omega_m$ and the threshold b, such that the output y is correctly classified. However, the step change in Fig. 19.10a hinders effective learning, as a small change in one of the ω's or in the b may result in a sudden jump in y from 0 to 1. Learning will occur much quicker if small changes in the parameters lead to small changes in the output. Hence, so-called sigmoid neurons were developed, where the activation function is a logistic function of $\sum_{i=1}^{m} \omega_i x_i$, as depicted in Fig. 19.10b. The value of y in a sigmoid neuron is determined as $y = 1/\left(1 + \exp\left(-b \sum_{i=1}^{m} \omega_i x_i\right)\right)$, where b controls the steepness of the resulting S-shaped curve.

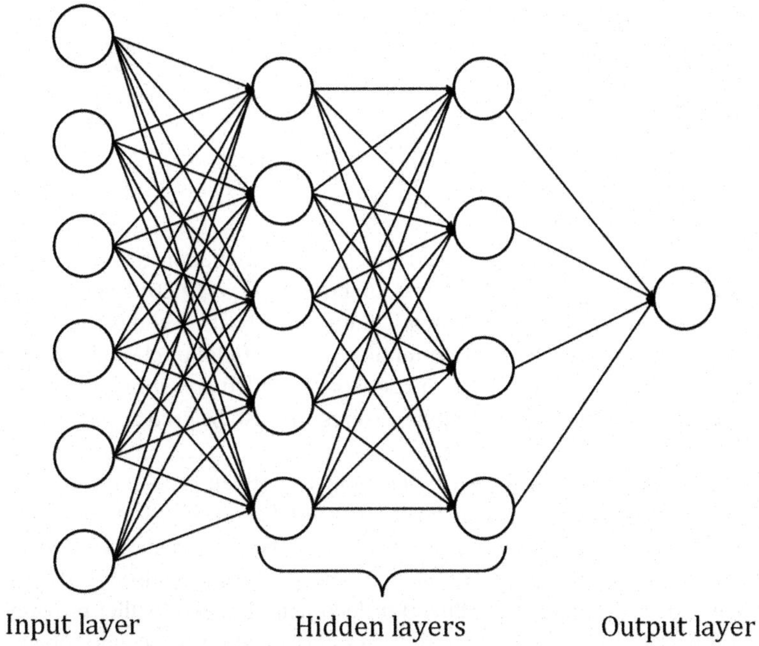

Fig. 19.11 Structure of a neural network

In a neural network the artificial neurons are organized in three types of layers, as illustrated in Fig. 19.11. Input layers are the first neurons to process incoming information. They "fire" their output to a second layer of neurons, which process this information as their inputs and pass their output on to the next layer. The third type of layers is the output layer that uses the incoming output of the preceding layer as input to make the final prediction.

The nodes in the hidden layers differ from those in the input layer and in the output layer because neither their inputs nor their outputs are directly observable. In contrast, the inputs of the nodes in input layer and the output(s) of the nodes in the output layer are directly observed.

When a neural network has more hidden layers, the network is said to be *deeper*. Given that deeper neural networks can build up a more complex hierarchy in the nodes in the network, they often perform (much) better than shallow networks, e.g., those with one hidden layer. Obviously, deep learning comes at the cost of additional training time.

In order for a neural network to yield accurate classifications for its output, the network needs to learn from the training set and obtain appropriate values for the weights in the network. One way to train a neural network in a supervised way is to adjust the weights based on the deviations of the output of the network and the true values of outputs in the training set. The deviations from the true values can be expressed in terms of a loss function, for example in a Mean-

Squared-Error (MSE) sense. If we let x_j denote the j-th m-dimensional vector of inputs: $x_j = \{x_{1j}, x_{2j}, x_{3j}, \ldots, x_{mj}\}$ and y_j the corresponding true output value, where $j = 1, \ldots, n$, we can write the MSE loss function as:

$$C = \frac{1}{n} \sum_{j=1}^{n} \left(y_j - \widehat{y}\left(x_j\right)\right)^2 \tag{19.26}$$

where $\widehat{y}\left(x_j\right)$ denotes the artificial neural network's prediction for y_j based on the input vector x_j. The gradient of the loss function in Eq. (19.26) can be calculated with respect to the weights in the network. Subsequently, the weights can be updated using a gradient descent method to minimize the loss function. Using the feedback of errors in the training set to train the network is called *backpropagation.* Instead of using a MSE loss function, entropy measures can also be used as the basis for the loss function.

When applying an artificial neural network to a given problem, the researcher needs to decide on the number of layers, the number of nodes in each layer, the activation function, etc. Many approaches were developed in the last decade, and rules of thumb are hard to give. For an overview we refer to Nielsen (2015).

Hinton (2007) provides algorithms for deep neural networks that provide good prediction results for visual recognition and classification (especially objects and scenes in images and video). However, Nguyen et al. (2015) show that such algorithms can easily be fooled.

19.6 Performance Judgment and Overfitting

A common problem while developing a model is the question about how many attributes to include into the model. The more attributes are included, the better we are able to classify our training data set. For example, the more attributes we include into a tree model, the higher the likelihood that we are can perfectly classify all cases in our training set. As we are generally aiming at maximizing the degree of explained variance, we might be tempted to include the maximum number of variables into our models. However, when it comes to forecasting, such an attitude brings severe caveats. The more specific our model is to our training data, the less it will be able to generalize to new data points. By enforcing a near-perfect fit of our training data set, we sacrifice generalizability. In data science this trade issue is called overfitting (Dietterich 1995). All models in Machine Learning suffer from overfitting issues at some point. It is the responsibility of the researcher to determine the right balance between the number of included variables and the generalizability of the model.

To examine overfitting issues researchers may rely on hold out data, by splitting the training set into two sets (preferably taking 75% and 25% of the initial data set).

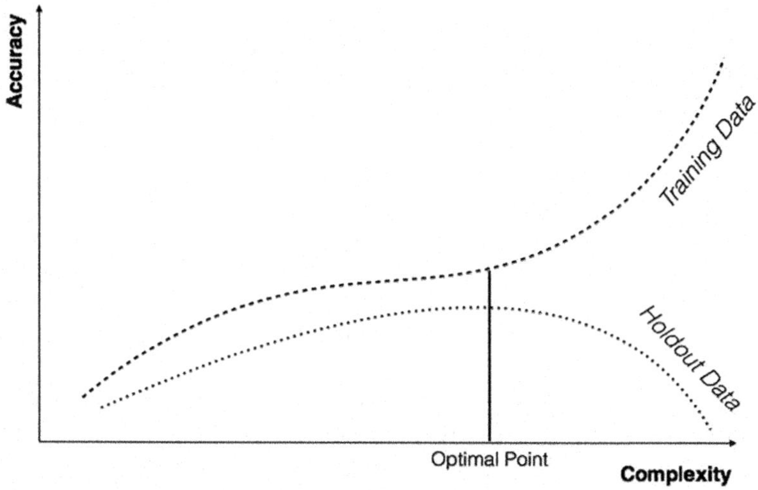

Fig. 19.12 The tradeoff between complexity and accuracy

With the larger set (still called training set) we train our algorithm.[3] The smaller set is called hold-out set. For each observation in the hold out set we know class membership. After training our model with the help of our training set, we can then use the results to predict class membership for each observation in our hold out set. As we already know the real class memberships we can control the predictive power of our model by comparing the predicted and the real class membership. As depicted in Fig. 19.12 it is upon the researcher to find the sweet spot between complexity and predictive power of a model. For a more detailed description how to achieve this, we recommend to have a look at Provost and Fawcett (2013, p. 116) for tree decision models, at Montgomery and Peck (1992) for support vector machines, and Cheng and Greiner (1999) for Naive Bayes.

19.7 Machine Learning and Marketing

Despite calling methods differently marketing research has a long tradition in using unsupervised techniques such as e.g., cluster analysis to identify different customer segments or multidimensional scaling to map latent consumer perceptions of companies.

Latent Class Analysis (Chap. 11) is an example of how marketing research is combining unsupervised and supervised techniques together. In case of a latent

---

[3]Compare the split in data into an estimation (training set) and a validation sample (hold out set): Vol. I, Sect. 5.7.

class regression model, the model tries to predict the impact of a set of independent variables (in Machine Learning language attributes) on an outcome variable. The model thereby accounts for unobserved heterogeneity within the data and estimates different coefficients for the various latent segments within the data, which it identifies during estimation (see Wedel and Kamakura 2000). The estimation of coefficients hereby represents the supervised approach, whereas the identification of homogenous sub patterns represents unsupervised learning.

Another common form of supervised learning in marketing and computer science is logistic regression. Using sample data, a logistic regression determines (see Chap. 8 in Vol. I, and Chap. 2 of the present volume) the impact of different attributes on the likelihood that an observation takes a binary label (i.e., whether a customer clicks on a banner or not).

Except for these overlapping techniques, Machine Learning has not yet been very frequently applied in marketing research. This is somehow surprising, as many supervised learning Machine Learning techniques are well suited for marketing purposes as underlined by several successful use cases.

Especially when it comes to classification, Machine Learning provides powerful and mostly more efficient techniques to solve marketing problems. This is especially the case in online marketing where decisions need to be taken as fast as possible—sometimes even real time–and a lot of data and variables are available. Product referrals such as Amazon's "People who bought…" mechanism as well as Netflix's movie recommendation system are built upon Machine Learning algorithms. Using a customer's profile and comparing this profile to other customer profiles, algorithms decide whether a product or a movie might be of interest for a customer or not and whether the site should recommend this product to the incoming customer (see e.g., Linden et al. 2003; Marlin 2004). The Machine Learning algorithm uses previous customer behavior data to learn which factors determine interest in a specific product and then uses the incoming customers information to predict interest (Anderson 2002). Such live applications have the advantage that they can update the training data with every new transaction and refine their learning skills. This increases the quality of the algorithm more and more and should lead to better predictions in the long run.

Machine Learning can also be used in online advertising and targeting. Online banner advertising as well as Search Engine Advertising are using real time auction systems to sell ad space. Given a customer's profile advertisers make an offer and the customer with the highest bid gets the ad space. Advertisers have hence to decide in milliseconds how much an incoming customer is worth and how much money they want to invest. To judge the individual profitability of an incoming customer, Machine Learning algorithms make predictions whether a customer will click on the displayed ad, whether the customer will stay in the related store and whether and how much he will buy in the store (Jaworska and Sydow 2008). Similarly to referral or collaborative filtering algorithms, a machine will here use labeled data from previous customers where the outcome is known as training data. Comparing customer specific features such as e.g., previous site visits, shopping history, clicking behavior, gender or estimated income the machine will assign the customer a clicking, visiting and buying likelihood (Pandey et al. 2011; Wang et al. 2011). This information can then be used to make a profit-optimizing bid for the ad space (see e.g., Perlich et al. 2012; Skiera and Abou Nabout 2013).

Machine Learning based classification does not necessarily need to be based on online data or used for the prediction of online behavior. Machine Learning can also be used for classic marketing tasks such as customer discovery (Wu et al. 2005), customer segmentation (Reutterer et al. 2006), customer (Kim et al. 2005) and behavioral targeting (Chen et al. 2009; Li et al. 2009; Liu and Tang 2011; Tang et al. 2011), and database marketing (Bennett et al. 1999). In these cases, Machine Learning algorithms try to assign new consumers or customers to pre-determined clusters according to consumer specific features. Customer databases and data on previously observed customer behavior are used to train algorithms and make label assignments. Such segmentations may help marketers to optimize marketing efforts, to allocate resources or adapt pricing between different types of consumers. Previous data on customers' response to offers or direct mailings can train a machine to use customer specific features such as company size, previous ordering behavior, or industry to determine the right price or framing for an offer in a B2B context or help sales people (Guido et al. 2011; Kim and Street 2004). Similarly, machines use consumer specific features to individualize coupons (Buckinx et al. 2004). In user-orientated industries such as telecommunication, machines help marketers to predict churn behavior (Xia and Jin 2008). Using previous call behavior, network strength and size as well as previous response to promotions as features the machine learns to predict churn behavior. The machine then assigns to each customer in the database a churn likelihood. Depending on a customer's profitability and his churn likelihood managers can determine the profit-maximizing investment to retain the customer.

Another prominent field of applied Machine Learning is *Natural Language Processing* (NLP). With the help of Machine Learning algorithms researchers try to determine text sentiments. With the help of pre-labeled texts (i.e., positive and negative) the machine learns to understand how the occurrence of certain words or word combinations determines the favorability of a text. Documents for each labeled category get stripped into a *Term Document Matrix* (TDM). Each column of the matrix corresponds to any word that occurs at least one time in the whole training data set. The rows account for the different documents. With the help of a binary variable the TDM indicates whether a word occurs in the particular document or not. The algorithm then infers categorization rules treating the words as features. Incoming new, unlabeled text can then been assigned to the two categories given the occurrence of words in the unlabeled text and the corresponding probability of these words to assign a document into one or the other category (label). NLP has a long tradition in linguistics and is also frequently applied in computer sciences and political sciences. With the increase of available User Generated Content (UGC) from online sources like Twitter, Facebook, YouTube, Amazon or any other website marketing research is also gaining interest in this topic. Especially since latest research shows that sentiments within UGC can predict sales (Henning-Thurau et al. 2014) and have a positive impact on consumer's likelihood to buy products online (Chevalier and Mayzlin 2006). Latest applications use UGC as an indicator of brand strength replacing traditional survey based methods with self-collected online data from social networks and other online sources (see e.g., Borah and Tellis 2016; Homburg et al. 2015; Schweidel and Moe 2014). Many and more detailed applications of Machine Learning models and big data are discussed in Verhoef et al. (2016).

19.8 Software

With Machine Learning originating from different academic fields there is a wide array of tools and software available for usage. Table. 19.3 gives an overview over the most common software solutions and language based packages for the different types of Machine Learning algorithms. However, please note that due to the fast developments in the field presenting a complete list of options is impossible.

Most of the main software players in the market—like Matlab or SAS–offer standard tools or plugins, which cover the established forms of Machine Learning. These tools already provide a remarkable range of standard options for data analysis. Matlab and SAS both share high prices. Instead researchers may want to rely on open access or free applications like Weka and Knime. Both tools are developed for easy data analysis and offer all common types of Machine Learning approaches. Especially Weka has a minimum learning curve and makes it easy for beginners to dig into Machine Learning. However, this comes at the cost of performance. Especially larger data sets and low computational power makes Weka less efficient. In case one seeks for more customized solutions or faces data-specific issues, developing own code or adapting existing scripts becomes an option. Language wise, there are two major options in the field: R and Python. Python originates from computer sciences and seems to have a larger established user base with more packages and scripts available. Nevertheless, R, which originates from statistics, also features a wide array of packages that allow researchers to apply machine-learning techniques to data. Both languages are however the prevalent tools in the market and offer solutions to almost any sort of problem. The choice therefore becomes a matter of taste. People familiar with one of the two languages will prefer working with their initial choice. Researchers coming into contact for the first time with both options may want to think about future applications.

In some rare cases Python and R both may not be able to deliver suitable solutions (most likely in case of very large data sets with billions of observations). Then one may think about using Java or C to code Machine Learning algorithms. Both languages also feature a large user base and popular online sites like Github or stackoverflow provide excellent guidance to start.

Beside available software or code, data size is another limitation. Although that most current computers share high memories, powerful CPUs and a large amount of working space, analyzing billions of observations can easily become an issue with computing times going easily up to days and even weeks. In this case, one may consider cloud computing solutions that bundle computers into networks and facilitate and speed up estimations like server or cloud based solutions.

Table 19.3 Overview of software and language packages

	kNN	Tree	SVM	NB	Neural network	Script interface	Cloud
Knime	Yes	Yes	Yes	Yes	Yes	Python	Yes
Matlab	Yes	Yes	Yes	Yes	Yes	–	Via simulink
SAS	Yes	Yes	Yes	Yes	Yes	R & Python	Yes
Weka	Yes	Yes	Yes	Yes	Yes	–	
Python	SciKit learn	Decision tree classifier	SVC NuSVC linear SVC	PyBrain FANN neurolab	SciKit learn	–	Server based
R	KKNN FNN	rpart Tree party maptree	e1071 SVMpath kernlab shogun	e1071 klaR	neuralnet	–	Server based R-studio

19.9 Data Collection, Data Storage and Data Processing

Given that big data is relying on data from a wide set of sources, variables usually come in different formats. Think about the structure of a social media site. Sites usually consist of different levels. The upper level consists of the site owner's own posts. For each post there is information on number of likes, comments and shares. The same is true for posts from other people on the site. This is already another level. For each type of post we have then again comments with information on the number of likes and shares. Latest social media sites even introduce a new level of interaction by allowing comments to comments on a fourth interaction level. Similarly companies are collecting information from a rich set of sources. This information can also only be partly structured in a meaningful structural way. This does not only create overview problems, but also complicates quality and consistency check-ups, which leads to increases "messiness" of the data.

Imagine a researcher that wants to combine social media data with other—non-social media variables—like e.g., financial numbers, stock price changes or trading volume. In many cases, information have different levels of time aggregation. This becomes another issue when matching such variables. Sales information is, for example, often only available in daily format, whereas social media data usually comes in a continuous time series. Messiness is hence not only caused by data imperfection of some variables, but also through heterogeneity between variables. The more different the variables are, the more this becomes an issue.

Spreadsheet-like storing solutions are thus unsuitable for depicting larger and very heterogeneous data sets. To get a more flexible working environment that can deal with many different variables in various formats and diverse structures, data scientist usually rely on databases. Databases assign an index to each object. This allows storing homogenous subsets of data or individual variables in their own format. Some variables might be stored as data frames or spreadsheets, others as lists or in any suitable format. Databases are therefore better able to deal with messiness than spreadsheets and are well-suited for big data research.

Researchers have the choice between different types of databases and related languages. The current database language standard is Structured Query Language (SQL). However, as pointed out above, not all big data are structured. Data scientists hence prefer so-called noSQL languages that do not require the data to come in a pre-determined format. NoSQL databases like Hadoop or MongoDB are therefore the current gold standard for big data projects. They allow splitting data over different servers in the cloud and have cloud-computing and data mapping procedures available to generate analyses results and insights from these data.

Another common data format used in Big Data research is JSON. JSON is also able to account for different hierarchies and levels of data. Commonly social media data is stored in JSON format. JSON can easily be read into all types of software and helps to efficiently re-arrange data in a needed format. So-called stream in functions allow loading JSON data directly from the online source into the running analysis and is therefore especially efficient for big data analysis and cloud computing. The predecessor of JSON was XML, another unstructured data standard, similar to JSON. XML is still present in many domains and researchers commonly have the choice between both standards when extracting data from online APIs. In both cases the main challenge is to access the right information in the unstructured data sets and to flatten information into structured (mostly data frame based) formats that can be accessed and analyzed with the common research tools. Despite the fact that there are also a rich set of tools to import and work with XML data sets, the authors recommend to use JSON whenever possible, as most analysis tools like R or Python offer better compatibility and better working solutions (like the jsonlite or jsonio packages in R) for JSON than for XML.

Beside storage issues, size does also pose problems for data analysis. Estimation time for basic models increases by exponent 3 when doubling the data size. This can already become a severe limitation. The first author of this chapter experienced running times of more than 2 days for a basic sentiment analysis with a training data set of 300,000 tweets and a to classify set of approx. 800,000 Facebook comments. Increasing working space and CPU power, as well as splitting tasks between kernels (like e.g., with the doparallel package in R) is only little help. Once the data set is over 1GB of size one might consider cloud computing solutions like e.g., Amazon's Web Service or IBM's cloud service to save time and resources.

19.10 An Empirical Illustration of the Machine Learning Algorithms

To illustrate the algorithms that we discuss in this chapter, we apply all techniques, one by one, to the same data set and compare various performance measures. We work with a data set that can be used to predict customer churn in the telecommunications sector (see also Vol. I, Sect. 9.6.2). The data contains 21 variables, including demographics of 3333 customers as well as their usage of the services that the telco provides. The focal variable is a binary indicator, where a value of 1 indicates that a customer terminated his or her contract, and 0 that he or she stayed with the provider. In Table 19.4 we provide descriptives of the data.

The data are not based on a real life application but are generated in such a way that it reflects reality. The data set is available in the C50 package of R.

In order to make a fair comparison between the different algorithms, we offer the same set of explanatory variables to each algorithm for predicting churn. We do not include the nominal variables as explanatory variables because a priori we do not expect an effect of these variables. There are 12 variables that reflect calling activity. Calling activity during daytime is captured in DayMins, DayCalls and DayCharge. Similarly, there are three variables for calling activity during evenings, for calling activity during nighttime and for international calling activity. For each of these four types of calling activity, we select only one variable: the variable that indicates the costs of the corresponding calling activity. Hence, we only include DayCharge, EveCharge, NightCharge and IntlCharge. Consequently, we use each of the algorithms to estimate the following model:

Table 19.4 Descriptives of the data

Variable	Description	Scale	Min	Max	Mean	StdDev
State	State where customer lives in	Nominal	–	–	–	–
AccountLength	Length of customer relationship (in months)	Numeric	1	243	101.1	39.8
AreaCode	Customer's area code	Nominal	–	–	–	–
Phone	Customer's phone number	Nominal	–	–	–	–
IntlPlan	Subscription to International plan (0 = no, 1 = yes)	Binary	0	1	0.1	0.3
VMailPlan	Subscription to voicemail plan (0 = no, 1 = yes)	Binary	0	1	0.3	0.4
VMailMsg	Number of voicemail messages	Integer	0	51	8.1	13.7
DayMins	Minutes called during day time	Numeric	0	350.8	179.8	54.5
DayCalls	Number of calls during day time	Integer	0	165	100.4	20.1
DayCharge	Costs of calls during day time	Numeric	0	59.64	30.6	9.3
EveMins	Minutes called during the evening	Numeric	0	363.7	201.0	50.7
EveCalls	Number of calls during the evening	Integer	0	170	100.1	19.9
EveCharge	Costs of calls during the evening	Numeric	0	30.91	17.1	4.3
NightMins	Minutes called during night time	Numeric	23.2	395	200.9	50.6
NightCalls	Number of calls during night time	Integer	33	175	100.1	19.6
NightCharge	Costs of calls during night time	Numeric	1.04	17.77	9.0	2.3
IntlMins	Minutes called in international calls	Numeric	0	20	10.2	2.8
IntlCalls	Number of international calls	Integer	0	20	4.5	2.5
IntlCharge	Costs of international calls	Numeric	0	5.4	2.8	0.8
CusServCalls	Number of calls to the customer service center	Integer	0	9	1.6	1.3
Churn	Indicator for churn (0 = stay, 1 = churn)	Binary	0	1	0.1	0.4

$$\begin{aligned} Churn_i = f\,(&Accountlength_i, IntlPlan_i, VMailPlan_i, VMailMsg_i, DayCharge_i,\\ &EveCharge_i, NightCharge_i, IntlCharge_i, CusServCalls_i)\,. \end{aligned} \tag{19.27}$$

We randomly split up the data in two parts: 75% of the data is used to train each algorithm, and 25% is used to evaluate the out-of-sample performance of each algorithm (see also Vol. I, Sect. 5.7).

For evaluating the performance of each model, we compare the out-of-sample Top Decile Lift and the out-of-sample Gini coefficient (see Vol. I, Sect. 9.6.2.3).

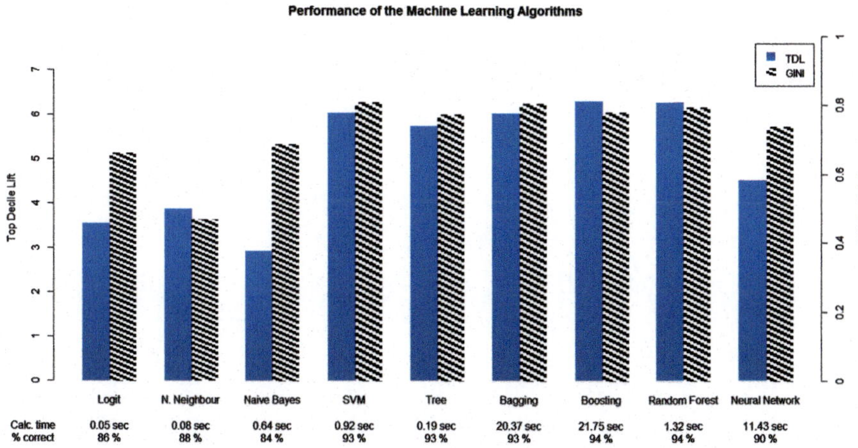

Fig. 19.13 Performance of the Machine Learning Algorithms. *TDL* Top Decile Lift = fraction of churners in the top-decile divided by the fraction of churners in the whole set. The higher the TDL the better the ability of a model to identify those customers that have a high churn probability. *Gini* measure to identify churners and non-churners. The higher the Gini the better the performance of the churn model

Furthermore, we calculate the percentage of correct classifications, and we determine the calculation time. Figure 19.13 summarizes the results.

We observe that there are substantial differences in the performance with respect to the Top Decile Lift. Support Vector Machines and the Tree methods (including Bagging, Boosting, and Random Forests) outperform the other algorithms with Top Decile Lift values close to or exceeding 6, where the majority of the other algorithms have values well below 4. The same algorithms also have the highest Gini Coefficients, but the differences are not as pronounced as with Top Decile Lift. We draw the same conclusion The percentage of correctly classified customers in the evaluation sample follows the pattern of the Top Decile Lift. Interestingly, the Nearest Neighbor algorithm, which has the lowest Gini coefficient, does not have the lowest percentage of correctly classified customers.

In terms of computation time, we observe that the Bagging and the Boosting algorithms require the most calculation time, about twice as much as number three: the Neural Network algorithm. SVM and Random Forest share rank four and five, with about a tenth of the calculation time of the Neural Network Algorithm. Naive Bayes ranks six, and logit and Nearest Neighbour are the fastest algorithms to estimate. The logit model, which we included as benchmark model, is about 435 as fast as the Boosting algorithm.

If we balance calculation time and performance, we see that the Support Vector Machine algorithm and Random Forest couple best performance with fast calculation time. Compared to the worst performing algorithms, a gain in Top Decile Lift of factor 2 is possible for the data that we consider in this section.

For illustration purposes, we depict in Fig. 19.14 the lift curves for the best performing algorithm in terms of Top Decile Lift (Random Forest) and the worst performing algorithm (Naive Bayes).

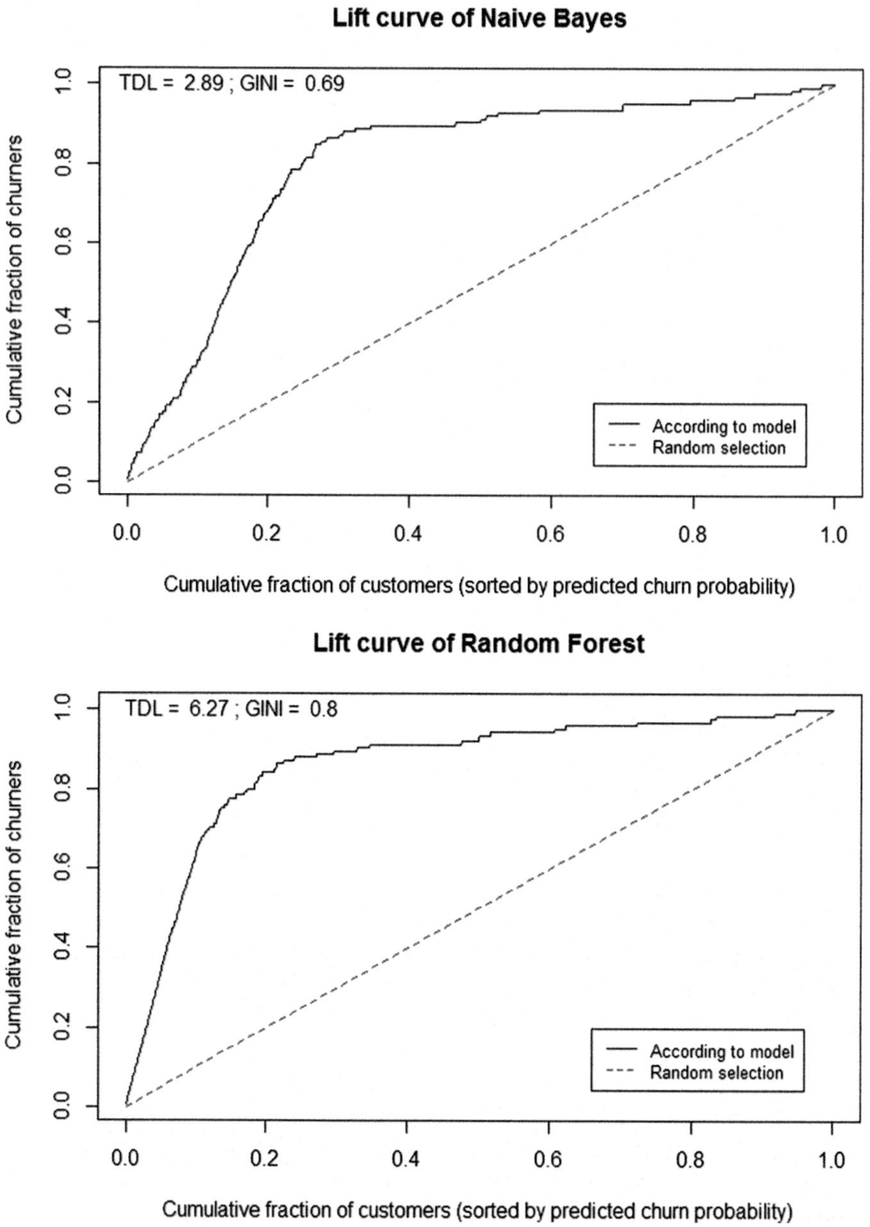

Fig. 19.14 Lift curves of the Naive Bayes and Random Forest algorithms

The R-code that was used for the analyses in this section is available from the authors upon request.

References

Anderson, C.R.: A Machine Learning Approach to Web Personalization. University of Washington Press, Washington, DC (2002)

Bennett, K.P., Wu, D., Auslender, L.: On support vector decision trees for database marketing. Neural Netw. **2**, 904–909 (1999)

Biggs, D., De Ville, B., Suen, E.: A method of choosing multi-way partitions for classification and decision trees. J. Appl. Stat. **18**, 49–62 (1991)

Blum, A.L., Langley, P.: Selection of relevant features and examples in machine learning. Artif. Intell. **97**, 245–271 (1997)

Borah, A., Tellis, G.J.: Halo (spillover) effects in social media: do product recalls of one brand hurt or help rival brands? J. Mark. Res. **53**, 143–160 (2016)

Boser, B.E., Guyon, I.M., Vapnik, V.N.: A training algorithm for optimal margin classifiers. In: Proceedings of the Fifth Annual Workshop on Computational Learning Theory—COLT, pp. 144–146 (1992)

Breiman, L.: Bagging predictors. Mach. Learn. **24**, 123–140 (1996)

Breiman, L., Friedman, J.H., Olshen, R.A., Stone, C.J.: Classification and Regression Trees. Wadsworth & Brooks/Cole Advanced Books & Software, Monterey, CA (1984)

Buckinx, W., Moons, E., Van den Poel, D., Wets, G.: Customer-adapted coupon targeting using feature selection. Expert Syst. Appl. **26**, 509–518 (2004)

Bucklin, R.E., Sismeiro, C.: A model of web site browsing behavior estimated on clickstream data. J. Mark. Res. **40**, 249–267 (2003)

Chan, P.K., Stolfo, S.J.: Toward scalable learning with non-uniform class and cost distributions: a case study in credit card fraud detection. KDD. **98**, 164–168 (1998)

Chen, Y., Pavlov, D., Canny J.F.: Large-scale behavioral targeting. In: Proceedings of the 15th International Conference on Knowledge Discovery and Data Mining ACM (2009)

Cheng, J., Greiner, R.: Comparing Bayesian network classifiers. In: Proceedings of the Fifteenth Conference on Uncertainty in Artificial Intelligence, pp. 101–108 (1999)

Chevalier, J.A., Mayzlin, D.: The effect of word of mouth on sales: online book reviews. J. Mark. Res. **43**, 345–354 (2006)

Cortes, C., Vapnik, V.: Support-vector networks. Mach. Learn. **20**, 273–297 (1995)

Cover, T.M.: Geometrical and statistical properties of systems of linear inequalities with applications in pattern recognition. IEEE Trans. Electron. Comput. **14**, 326–334 (1965)

Cruz, J.A., Wishart, D.S.: Applications of machine learning in cancer prediction and prognosis. Cancer Informat. **2**, 105–117 (2006)

Dietterich, T.: Overfitting and undercomputing in machine learning. Complicat. Surg. **27**, 326–327 (1995)

Dietterich, T.G.: An experimental comparison of three methods for constructing ensembles of decision trees: bagging, boosting, and randomization. Mach. Learn. **40**, 139–157 (2000)

Elith, J., Leathwick, J.R., Hastie, T.: A working guide to boosted regression trees. J. Anim. Ecol. **77**, 802–813 (2008)

Esposito, F., Malerba, D., Semeraro, G., Kay, J.: A comparative analysis of methods for pruning decision trees. IEEE. **19**, 476–491 (1997)

Fayyad, U.M.: Data mining and knowledge discovery–making sense out of data. Intell. Syst. Appl. **11**, 20–25 (1996)

Fisher, R.A.: The use of multiple measurements in taxonomic problems. Ann. Eugenics. **7**, 179–188 (1936)

Gamon, M., Aue, A., Corston-Oliver, S., Ringger, E.: Pulse: mining customer opinions from free text. In: A.F. Famili, J.N. Kok, J.M. Pena, A. Siebes, A. Feelders (eds.): Advances in Intelligent Data Analysis VI. Springer Berlin 121–132 (2005)

Gascuel, O.: On the optimization principle in phylogenetic analysis and the minimum-evolution criterion. Mol. Biol. Evol. **17**, 401–405 (2000)

Guido, G., Prete, M.I., Miraglia, S., De Mare, I.: Targeting direct marketing campaigns by neural networks. J. Mark. Manag. **27**, 992–1006 (2011)

Hanssens, D.M., Pauwels, K.H., Srinivasan, S., Vanhuele, M., Yildirim, G.: Consumer attitude metrics for guiding marketing mix decisions. Mark. Sci. **33**, 534–550 (2014)

Hastie, T., Tibshirani, R., Friedman, J.H.: Boosting and Additive Trees. The Elements of Statistical Learning (2nd ed.). Springer, New York (2009)

Henning-Thurau, T., Wiertz, C., and Feldhaus, F.: Does twitter matter? The impact of microblogging word of mouth on consumers' adoption of new movies. J. Acad. Mark. Sci. **43**, 375–394 (2014)

Hinton, G.E.: Learning multiple layers of representation. Trends Cogn. Sci. **11**, 428–434 (2007)

Ho, T.K.: A data complexity analysis of comparative advantages of decision forest constructors. Pattern. Anal. Applic. **5**, 102–112 (2002)

Homburg, C., Ehm, L., Artz, M.: Measuring and managing consumer sentiment in an online community environment. J. Mark. Res. **52**, 629–641 (2015)

Ilhan E., Pauwels, K.H., Kübler, R.V.: Dancing with the enemy: broadened understanding of engagement in rival brand dyads, MSI Working Paper Series (2016)

Jaworska, J., Sydow, M.: Behavioral targeting in on-line advertising: An empirical study. In: Web Information Systems Engineering-WISE 2008, pp. 62–76. Springer, Berlin (2008)

Kass, G.V.: An exploratory technique for investigating large quantities of categorical data. Appl. Stat. **28**, 119–127 (1980)

Kim, Y., Street, W.N.: An intelligent system for customer targeting: a data mining approach. Decis. Support. Syst. **37**, 215–228 (2004)

Kim, Y., Street, W.N., Russell, G.J., Menczer, F.: Customer targeting: a neural network approach guided by genetic algorithms. Manag. Sci. **51**, 264–276 (2005)

Kübler, R.V., Colicev, A., Pauwels, K.H.: User generated content as a predictor for brand equity. In: Proceedings of the Informs Marketing Science Conference (2016)

Kuhn, R., De Mori, R.: The application of semantic classification trees to natural language understanding. Trans. Pattern Anal. Mach. Intell. **17**, 449–460 (1995)

Levandowsky, M., Winter, D.: Distance between sets. Nature. **234**, 34–35 (1971)

Li, T., Liu, N., Yan, J., Wang, G., Bai, F., Chen, Z.: A Markov chain model for integrating behavioral targeting into contextual advertising. In: Proceedings of the Third International Workshop on Data Mining and Audience Intelligence for Advertising, pp. 1–9 (2009)

Linden, G., Smith, B., York, J.: Amazon.com recommendations: item-to-item collaborative filtering. Internet Comput. **7**, 76–80 (2003)

Liu, K., Tang, L.: Large-scale behavioral targeting with a social twist. In: Proceedings of the 20th ACM International Conference on Information and Knowledge Management, pp. 1815–1824 (2011)

Loh, W.Y., Shih, Y.S.: Split selection methods for classification trees. Stat. Sin. **117**, 815–840 (1997)

Marlin, B.: Collaborative filtering: a machine learning perspective. Dissertation University of Toronto (2004)

Martin, J.H., Jurafsky, D.: Speech and Language Processing. Prentice-Hall, Pearson, GA (2000)

Mayer-Schönberger, V., Cukier, K.: Big Data: A Revolution That Will Transform How We Live, Work and Think. John Murray, London (2013)

Melville, P., Mooney, R.J., Nagarajan, R.: Content-boosted collaborative filtering for improved recommendations. AAAI/IAAI. **23**, 187–192 (2002)

Montgomery, D.C., Peck, E.A.: Introduction to Linear Regression Analysis. Springer, Berlin (1992)

Nguyen, A., Yosinski, J., Clune, J.: Deep neural networks are easily fooled: high confidence predictions for unrecognizable images. In: IEEE Conference on Computer Vision and Pattern Recognition, pp. 427–436 (2015)

Nielsen, M.A.: Neural Network and Deep Learning. Determination Press (2015)

Osuna, E., Freund, R., Girosit, F.: Training support vector machines: an application to face detection. In: Proceedings of Computer Vision and Pattern Recognition Conference, pp. 130–136 (1997)
Pandey, S., Aly, M., Bagherjeiran, A., Hatch, A., Ciccolo, P., Ratnaparkhi, A., Zinkevich, M.: Learning to target: what works for behavioral targeting. In: Proceedings of the 20th ACM International Conference on Information and Knowledge Management, pp. 1805–1814 (2011)
Pang, B., Lee, L.: Opinion mining and sentiment analysis. Found. Trends Inf. Retr. **2**, 1–135 (2008)
Pauwels, K.H., Van Ewijk, B.: Do online behavior tracking or attitude survey metrics drive brand sales? An integrative model of attitudes and actions on the consumer boulevard. Mark. Sci. Inst. Rep. **4**, 13–118 (2014)
Perlich, C., Dalessandro, B., Hook, R., Stitelman, O., Raeder, T., Provost, F.: Bid optimizing and inventory scoring in targeted online advertising. In: Proceedings of the 18th ACM SIGKDD International Conference on Knowledge Discovery and Data Mining, pp. 804–812 (2012)
Provost, F., Fawcett, T.: Data Science for Business: What You Need to Know About Data Mining and Data-Analytic Thinking. O'Reilly Media, Quinlan, TX (2013)
Quinlan, J.R.: Simplifying decision trees. Int. J. Man-Mach. Stud. **27**, 221–234 (1987)
Reimer, K., Rutz, O.J., Pauwels, K.H.: How online consumer segments differ in long-term marketing effectiveness. J. Interact. Mark. **28**, 271–284 (2014)
Reutterer, T., Mild, A., Natter, M., Taudes, A.: A dynamic segmentation approach for targeting and customizing direct marketing campaigns. J. Interact. Mark. **20**, 43–57 (2006)
Ritschard, G.: CHAID and earlier supervised tree methods, accessed online June 12, 2016 at http://www.unige.ch/ses/dsec/repec/files/2010_02.pdf (2010)
Rokach, L., Maimon, O.: Data mining with decision trees: theory and applications. World Scientific (2007)
Schlangenstein, M.: UPS crunches data to make routes more efficient, save gas, Bloomberg, accessed online, June 7, 2016 at http://www.bloomberg.com/news/articles/2013-10-30/ups-uses-big-data-to-make-routes-more-efficient-save-gas (2013)
Schweidel, M., Moe, W.: Listening in on social media: a joint model of sentiment and venue format choice. J. Mark. Res. **51**, 387–399 (2014)
Shannon, C.E.: A note on the concept of entropy. Bell Syst. Tech. J. **27**, 379–423 (1948)
Sidorov, G., Miranda-Jiménez, S., Viveros-Jiménez, F., Gelbukh, A., Castro-Sánchez, N., Velásquez, F., Gordon, J.: Empirical study of machine learning based approach for opinion mining in tweets. In: Famili, A.F., Kok, J.N., Pena, J.M., Siebes, A., Feelders, A. (eds.) Advances in Intelligent Data Analysis VI, pp. 1–14. Springer, Berlin (2012)
Skiera, B., Abou Nabout, N.: Practice prize paper-PROSAD: a bidding decision support system for profit optimizing search engine advertising. Mark. Sci. **32**, 213–220 (2013)
Skurichina, M.: Bagging, boosting and the random subspace method for linear classifiers. Pattern. Anal. Applic. **5**, 121–135 (2002)
Sudhir, K.: The exploration-exploitation tradeoff and efficiency in knowledge production. Mark. Sci. **52**, 1–14 (2016)
Tang, J., Liu, N., Yan, J., Shen, Y., Guo, S., Gao, B., Zhang, M.: Learning to rank audience for behavioral targeting in display ads. In: Proceedings of the 20th ACM International Conference on Information and Knowledge Management, pp. 605–610 (2011)
Van Heerde, H.J., Gijsbrechts, E., Pauwels, K.H.: Winners and losers in a major price war. J. Mark. Res. **45**, 499–518 (2008)
Vapnik, V.N.: The Nature of Statistical Learning Theory. Springer, Berlin (1995)
Verhoef, P.C., Kooge, E., Walk, N.: Creating Value with Big Data Analytics. Rootledge, New York, NY (2016)
Viola, P., Jones, M.J.: Robust real-time face detection. Int. J. Comput. Vis. **57**, 137–154 (2004)
Wang, C., Raina, R., Fong, D., Zhou, D., Han, J., Badros, G.: Learning relevance from heterogeneous social network and its application in online targeting. In: Proceedings of the 34th International ACM SIGIR Conference on Research and Development in Information Retrieval, pp. 655–664 (2011)

Wasserman, L.: Statistics and Machine Learning, accessed online June, 5 2016 at https://normaldeviate.wordpress.com/2012/06/12/statistics-versus-machine-learning-52 (2012)
Wedel, M., Kamakura, W.A.: Market Segmentation: Conceptual and Methodological Foundations. Kluwer Academic, Boston, MA (2000)
Wu, C.H., Kao, S.C., Su, Y.Y., Wu, C.C.: Targeting customers via discovery knowledge for the insurance industry. Expert Syst. Appl. **29**, 291–299 (2005)
Xia, G.E., Jin, W.D.: Model of customer churn prediction on support vector machine. Syst. Eng. Theory Prac. **28**, 71–77 (2008)

Chapter 20
The Future of Marketing Modeling

Koen H. Pauwels, Peter S.H. Leeflang, Tammo H.A. Bijmolt, and Jaap E. Wieringa

20.1 Overview

Giving all the changes to business and marketing just since the start of this century, is there a future for marketing modeling?

The Marketing Science Institute, a leading organization bridging marketing academia and practice, holds a bi-annual survey of all its 70 member companies to reveal those topics of most interest to marketing practice. Surveyed managers are specifically instructed to identify:

1. "big pressing issues for the next 2–3 years: if we knew more, we'd be more effective";
2. "issues that we may not be thinking about now, that will emerge as critical in the next decade".

What was the first identified priority for 2016–2018? "Quantitative models to understand causality, levers and influence in a complex world". That topic includes:

1. understanding the effect and value of marketing actions;
2. attribution, causality and ROI;
3. identifying critical paths to purchase in B2B environments;
4. better models.

This should sound familiar by now to the reader of this book: the need for better marketing models continues unabated. Still, the form these models will take may

K.H. Pauwels (✉)
Department of Marketing, Northeastern University, Boston, USA
e-mail: k.pauwels@northeastern.edu

P.S.H. Leeflang • T.H.A. Bijmolt • J.E. Wieringa
Department of Marketing, University of Groningen, Groningen, The Netherlands

P.S.H. Leeflang et al. (eds.), *Advanced Methods for Modeling Markets*,
International Series in Quantitative Marketing, DOI 10.1007/978-3-319-53469-5_20

differ in the future, depending on their purpose. In our opinion, the abundance of big data (Chap. 19) and advances in analytics will lead to a distinction between models for *short-term performance* and models for *long-term performance*. This distinction is important as recent research shows that such different performance metrics are quite distinct, i.e. not highly correlated (e.g. Katsikeas et al. 2016; Pauwels and Van Ewijk 2013).

Short-term performance refers to conversion such as click-though, website visits, check-out conversion and short-term sales. Such "direct metrics" are over-represented on popular online marketing dashboards such as Google Analytics (Scott 2016). In Vol. I, Sect. 10.5.3 we discussed dashboards for marketing decision making. For such short-term metrics, we believe analytics has changed in focus from prediction to *classification*: the real-time interactions with an individual consumer favor simple models that can quickly classify an individual on expected conversion value to the company, based on hundreds of data points on the individual and millions of data on other individuals like her. Wedel and Kannan (2016) call this "Small Stats on Big data". Examples of such techniques abound in the areas of "Computer Science" and "Data Science". In Chap. 19 we discussed the machine learning models that offer opportunities to analyze big data.

In contrast, long-term performance, driven by journey/funnel constructs such as Salience, Consideration, Brand Love, Satisfaction, Word of Mouth and Loyalty, will likely continue to require the *prediction*-focused models of the past, supplemented with other data sources and models for better *explanation*. Wedel and Kannan (2016) call this "Big Stats on Small Data", but foresee an integration of techniques in the near future. For example, Reimer et al. (2014) first use a latent class model to classify millions of consumer into four segments of vastly different sizes (segment 1 of low-value lurkers is 62% of the population, while only 2.5% is classified as high-value segment 4), and then analyze long-term purchasing patterns and how marketing affect them. They find that lower-value segments are more affected by discounts, while high-value customers by offline and online marketing communication separately and in synergy.

The remainder of this chapter is structured as follows. First, we take the reader "back to the future" with a recent history of modeling development (Sect. 20.2).[1] Next, we discuss current and future models for big data and short-term performance (Sect. 20.3) and then contrast this to future models for causality and long-term performance (Sect. 20.4). Finally, we discuss the substantive marketing applications most likely to see accelerated growth in the future (Sect. 20.5).

---

[1]Other publications that discuss model developments are Bijmolt et al. (2010) with an emphasis on the role of models for customer engagement; Leeflang (2011); Leeflang and Hunneman (2010); Roberts et al. (2014).

20.2 Back to the Future: A Recent History of Modeling Developments

To understand the present and future, it is important to understand the history and evolution of marketing modeling. Wedel and Kannan (2016) distinguish the stages of[2]:

1. describing observable market conditions through simple statistical approaches;
2. developing models for diagnostics based on theories of human behavior;
3. evaluating marketing policies, predicting their effects and supporting marketing decision making using statistical, econometric and operation research models.

These twentieth century developments are discussed in detail in Winer and Neslin (2014).

As to the twenty-first century, in their paper "Building Models for Marketing Decisions: Past, Present and Future", Leeflang and Wittink (2000) predicted the evolution from Decision Support Systems to Dashboard Metrics (e.g. Pauwels et al. 2009), database marketing models, big data (e.g. Verhoef et al. 2016), combining econometric models with experiments (e.g. Drechsler et al. 2017; Venkatraman et al. 2015), and an explicit modeling of the steps in the consumer decision process (e.g. Pauwels and Van Ewijk 2013) and its impact on firm value. Moreover, the turn-of-the-century focus on eCommerce was correctly predicted to give way to modeling electronic word-of-mouth though both econometric models, spatial (social network) models and agent-based models. Private bargaining led to pay-what-you-want business models and real-time auctions, while consumer infobots (e.g.) evolved to search engine and app platforms. Finally, the two main modeling issues of *endogeneity* and *heterogeneity* have seen much more coverage in the last decade.

First, *endogeneity* has been linked to estimation bias in several meta-analyses (Bijmolt et al. 2005; Kremer et al. 2008; Sethuraman et al. 2011). This has motivated both Instrumental Variables (IV) approaches (including the Control Function and Limited Information Maximum Likelihood) as well as growing criticism on IV (e.g. Rossi 2014) and the use of IV-free approaches, such as Gaussian Copulas (Chap. 18), dynamic system models (Chap. 4) and Latent Instrumental Variables (Chap. 18). For the future, we expect these model refinement trends to continue, and to be complemented by approaches that manipulate variables directly, such as (field or lab) experiments.

Second, accounting for *heterogeneity* has been shown to improve model fit and forecasting accuracy (e.g. Andrews et al. 2008; Andrews and Currim 2009). This has renewed advancements in mixture models (Chap. 13), and in individual demand models for purchase timing/incidence, brand choice and purchase quantity. In the hidden Markov Models (Chap. 14) we also observe increasing opportunities to account for heterogeneity.

[2]Alternative stages of development are discussed in Leeflang et al. (2000) and Wierenga (2008, Chap. 1).

20.3 Big Data, Small Stats and Short-Term Performance

Starting from Banko and Brill (2001), evidence is mounting that adding more data may be more beneficial than adding model complexity for the goal of short-term prediction. This observation is rooted in the *bias-variance tradeoff* (Wedel and Kannan 2016). Bias; i.e. not representing the true data generating process, is a more serious concern for simpler models. Variance, i.e. random variation in the data due to sampling and measurement error, is a more serious concern for more complicated models, as those tend to over-fit. More data reduces the potential bias in simple models, especially when they are averaged in bagging or boosting techniques (Hastie et al. 2009). Moreover, simple models can generate causal inferences in (more easily conducted online) field experiments, where the data generating process is under the researchers' control (Hui et al. 2013a).

Does this mean that *more complicated models* are no longer needed? No, as data variety increases (see Chap. 19), the underlying data generating process expands (Wedel and Kannan 2016). To fully capture the rich information value of consumer hobbies, statements, information search, actions, etc., more complex models are needed. However, these models come at greater computational costs. Solutions to this problem involve data reduction, faster algorithms, model simplification and/or computational solutions.

Sampling and statistical inference is a key point of contention in the realm of big data and short-term performance. Many researchers, including Wedel and Kannan (2016) argue that classical sampling-based inference becomes mute because "in many cases big data captures an entire population". In such cases, asymptotic confidence regions degenerate to point-masses under the weight of these massive data and the *p*-value, i.e. the probability of obtaining an effect in repeated samples that is at least as extreme as the effect in the data at hand, loses its meaning (Naik et al. 2008).

Despite the fact that "in many cases big data captures the entire population of customers" (Wedel and Kannan 2016), such data might still have limitations. First, even for the company's current customers, data is typically only available on their transactions with the company, not on their other transactions or on what the customers think or feel. On the latter, even the shortest survey has a less-than-perfect response rate and few people take the time to talk about the industry on social media (Pauwels 2014). Second, companies are typically also interested in prospective and churned customers, for which detailed transactions and mindset data are almost never available for the entire population. In other words, sampling issues still require attention in most of the applications we envision in the coming five years. Therefore, researchers should pay special attention to what classical "independent" sampling may miss, such as rare events in the tail of high-dimensional data (Naik and Tsai 2004) and the properties of social networks (snowball, or random forest samples in Ebbes et al. 2015).

A key aspect new to modeling is the large amount of *unstructured data.* Recent papers focused on developing data-summarizing metrics to structure data on text mining, eye-tracking, and pattern recognition. Once a data structure is put in place using metrics, explanatory, prediction and optimization models can be built. Although, especially in practice, applications of predictive and prescriptive approaches for unstructured data still are scarcely available. Analyzing unstructured data in marketing seems to primarily boil down to placing some structure on the unstructured data, and express the information that it contains in appropriate (structured) metrics as discussed in Chap. 19.

Big *structured data* comprises four main dimensions—Variables, Attributes, Subjects, and Time (VAST: Naik et al. 2008). When any of these dimensions becomes too large for the model, we can use solutions from Big Data Analytics such as (Wedel and Kannan 2016):

1. developments in high performance computing, including MapReduce frameworks for parallel processing, grid and cloud computing, and computing on graphic cards;
2. simpler descriptive modeling approaches such as probability models, or computer science and machine learning approaches that facilitate closed form computations, possibly in combination with model averaging and other divide and conquer strategies to reduce bias;
3. speed improvements in algorithms provided by Variational Inference, Scalable Rejection Sampling, re-sampling and re-weighting, Sequential MCMC, and parallelization of likelihood and MCMC algorithms;
4. application of aggregation, data fusion, selection, and sampling methods that reduce the dimensionality of data.

Work in practice often deploys a combination of 1 and 2, focusing on *exploration, description and classification* to generate real-time actionable insights such as "how much should I bid on displaying an online ad to this prospective consumer"? ("*Small Stats on Big Data*")[3]. In contrast, most academic research focuses on 3 and 4: rigorous and comprehensive process models that allow for statistical inference on underlying causal behavioral mechanisms and optimal decision making, mostly calibrated on small to moderately sized structured data. Wedel and Kannan call this "*Big Stats on Small Data.*" Future solutions will likely aim to combine all 4 above solutions, mixing and matching to fit the specific data and research goals in question. In our opinion, such an important goal distinction is between the current big data focus on short-term performance versus the focus on causality and long-term performance.

[3]See Wedel and Kannan (2016).

20.4 Causality and Long-term Performance

Despite the success in the above discussed techniques for short-term predictions, they typically do not offer insights in causality (key among MSI priorities) nor do they lead to empirical generalizations (a main goal for academics and practitioners alike). As to the former, causal insights are typically answers to why questions such as:

1. why did the consumer visited our website, but did not buy?
2. why do some consumers prefer a competitor brand to ours, and vice versa?
3. why are some consumers heavy (or light) purchasers of our category?
4. why are some of our marketing actions giving huge short-term sales boosts and are they eroding our brand equity?

To address questions such as these, data mining and predictive analytics is not enough and expertise in causal analysis is required. Causal analysis does not necessarily attempt to "prove" cause-and-effect relationships but, instead, assesses plausible reasons for patterns in the data we have observed (Gray 2016).

Combined with other techniques, new models can leverage unstructured data to develop deep insights into the economics and psychology of consumer behavior (Wedel and Kannan 2016). The internet nowadays but also other "techniques" provide great online enhancements of the following research tools:

1. *Surveys* have become much easier to administer with the advances in technology enabling online and mobile data collection (Amazon's MTurk). Very short online surveys allow companies such as First Tennessee Bank (Pauwels 2014) to continuously track consumer satisfaction with each of their many touch points.
2. *Netnography* (Kozinets 2001) scales up qualitative research to online brand communities, forums and consumer-to-consumer interactions and informs the machine learning coding (see Chap. 19) of conversation topics and emotions (e.g. Ilhan et al. 2016; Pauwels et al. 2016).
3. *Field experiments* are much easier and cheaper to scale up, sometimes to millions of prospective customers (e.g. Blake et al. 2015; Li and Kannan 2014; Tadelis and Zettelmeyer 2015). This enables companies to A/B test advertising messages, optimize website design and target promotions (Hui et al. 2013b).
4. *Lab experiments* now allow online administration and collection of audio, video, eye-tracking, face-tracking (Stüttgen et al. 2012; Teixeira et al. 2010), neuromarketing data obtained from EEG and brain imaging (Telpaz et al. 2015).
5. *Real-time experience tracking* (RET). This method asks a panel of consumers to send a structured text message (SMS) by mobile phone whenever they encounter one of a set of competitive brands within a category (Baxendale et al. 2015).
6. *Video-tracking* (Hui et al. 2013a; Zhang et al. 2014). Over the past decades we observe that models are calibrated at more and more disaggregate levels. Hence we observe a trend in model building that attention is shifting from aggregate models to models for segments and models that specify individual behavior. The next step is that we model different states (Chap. 14) and/or

stages in consumer decision-making. Earlier (Chap. 10) we called this micro-micro marketing. Examples are Van Ittersum et al. (2013) (influence of smart shopping carts), Gilbride et al. (2015) (role of within-trip dynamics in unplanned and planned purchase behavior), Inman et al. (2009) and Hui et al. (2013b).
7. *Path data* (records of consumers in a spatial configuration) (Hui et al. 2009a, 2009b).

Mixing and matching such rich methods and data should enable researchers to build models that are both causal and scalable, both simple and comprehensive, both rigorous and relevant to decision makers.

As to *causal models*, we observe continued growth of multivariate time series models, such as Structural Vector Autogression (e.g. De Haan et al. 2016), state-space models (Chap. 5), spatial models (Chap. 6), hierarchical models and structural models (Chap. 7). Moreover, we expect growth in models with latent variables, such as hidden Markov (Chap. 14), mixture models (Chap. 13), variance-based structural equation (Partial Least Squares) models (Chap. 12) and covariance-based structural equation models (Chap. 11).

Likewise, estimation methods will continue to see advancements in:

1. the General Method of Moments (Chap. 15);
2. Bayesian estimation (Chap. 16);
3. machine learning techniques (Macy and Willer 2002; Chap. 19);
4. agent based modeling (see e.g. Delre et al. 2016; Van Eck et al. 2011);
5. matching techniques (e.g. Gensler et al. 2012, 2013; Mithas and Krishnan 2008).

As to empirical generalizations, big data analytics' black box nature, which allows routine application with limited analyst intervention, limits their ability to transcend a specific setting. Yet, both marketing scientists and practitioners value the development of empirical generalizations: "laws" on the effectiveness of marketing instruments, on consumer behavior, etc. that are valid for a broad range of markets and product categories. Over the last few decades, tens of such empirical generalizations have been examined often by means of meta-analysis. For an excellent and recent overview of such generalizations, we refer to Hanssens (2015). The increasing availability of data sets will lead to new empirical findings. On the one hand, the analysis of one huge and broad database may lead directly to an empirical generalization on a specific topic. On the other hand, results from multiple studies can be combined in a meta-analyses and thereby lead to generalizations. Existing meta-analyses might become outdated and could be extended and updated when substantial numbers of new empirical results have become available, e.g. on price elasticity by Bijmolt et al. (2005). In addition, such meta-analyses might be on relatively new topics, e.g. online Word-of-Mouth (Babiç et al. 2016).

20.5 Application areas

The methods discussed in this volume offer ample and promising opportunities for modeling markets in several areas of application. The impact of academic developments on marketing practice has empirically been demonstrated by Roberts et al. (2014). Through interviews among managers, they found a significant impact of several analytics tools on firm decision making. In particular, Roberts et al. (2014) found that:

1. the impact of marketing science is perceived to be largest on decisions on:
   - management of brands;
   - pricing;
   - new product;
   - product portfolios, and
   - customer/market selection; and that
2. tools such as segmentation, survey-based choice models, marketing mix models and pre-test market models have the largest impact on market decisions.

For the future, Wedel and Kannan (2016) see as key application domains:

1. customer relationship management (CRM) to help acquisition, retention and satisfaction of customers to improve their lifetime value to the firm (Chap. 9 in Vol. I);
2. allocate the marketing budget to enhance marketing effectiveness (Albers 2012);
3. capture consumer heterogeneity to personalize for each individual consumer;
4. privacy and security, an area that is of growing concern to firms and regulators (Martin et al. 2017; Peltier et al. 2009).

A thorough analysis of the marketing literature reveals important growth in the applications of marketing models, along three dimensions:

1. the industries and markets studied;
2. the marketing mix intstrument and other relevant decision elements considered as explanatory (decision) variables, and
3. the outcomes used as dependent variables.

First, traditionally marketing modelling strongly focused on the fast-moving-consumer-goods and durable goods industries in North-American or European markets, partly due to availability of data. Nowadays, marketing models are being applied to a broader range of industries and markets. This development started with applications in financial services and other service industries (e.g. Gensler et al. 2012, 2013; Xue et al. 2011). In addition, market models have been applied recently within the entertainment industry (see the special issue, Vol. 33, nr. 2 of the International Journal of Research in Marketing), the health care industry (see Ding et al. 2014).

Next to a broader range of industries, marketing modeling has also expanded geographically. For example, models have been applied to specific issues dealing with emerging markets (e.g. Kamakura and Mazzon 2013; Pauwels et al. 2013 and the special issues of the International Journal of Research in Marketing (Vol. 30, nr. 1) and Marketing Science (Vol. 34, nr. 4)). Often, a specific industry or market will have specific characteristics of the decision making process or the market structure, which may stimulate marketing modellers to adapt existing methods. For example, the fact that going to a movie is oftentimes a group decision due to the joint consumption nature of the product. Hence, we expect that the broadening will continue and that future model development will be driven partly by the requirements based on the structure of the specific industry and/or market.

Second, with respect to the marketing mix instruments, the modeling literature has been dominated by research on (price) promotion and advertising effects. Nowadays, marketing, and firm in general, has to deal with durability of its decisions. A larger stream of quantitative research has examined the antecedents and consequences of social responsibility and cause-related marketing (e.g. Habel et al. 2016; Kang et al. 2016). In addition, technological developments has extended the toolbox of marketing which now include communication through social media (e.g. Borah and Tellis 2016; Kumar et al. 2016; Schweidel and Moe 2014) and electronic Word-of-Mouth (see Babiç et al. 2016 for an overview). Finally, the role of marketing managers or even entire marketing departments on business performance has been examined (Feng et al. 2015; Germann et al. 2015; Hattula et al. 2015; Verhoef and Leeflang 2009).

Third, most traditional marketing models have used some type of sales, market share or purchase variable as the outcome variable. In recent years, it has been acknowledged that the influence of marketing goes beyond sales. Therefore, scholars have studied the effects of marketing on customer engagement (e.g. Ilhan et al. 2016; Van Doorn et al. 2010), firm value and shareholder value (e.g. Edeling and Fischer 2016; McAlister et al. 2016; Schulze et al. 2012; Srinivasan and Hanssens 2009), product returns (Minnema et al. 2016) and non-sales aspects throughout the customer journey (Trusov et al. 2009).

We believe that the methods which are discussed in the present volume offer ample and promising opportunities modeling markets in these areas of application.

References

Albers, S.: Optimizable and implementable aggregate response modeling for marketing decision support. Int. J. Res. Mark. **29**, 111–122 (2012)

Andrews, R.L., Currim, I.S.: Multi-stage purchase decision models: accommodating response heterogeneity, common demand shocks, and endogeneity using disaggregate data. Int. J. Res. Mark. **29**, 197–206 (2009)

Andrews, R.L., Currim, I.S., Leeflang, P.S.H., Lim, J.: Estimating the SCAN*PRO model of store sales: HB, FM, or just OLS? Int. J. Res. Mark. **25**, 22–33 (2008)

Babiç, A., Sotgiu, F., De Valck, K., Bijmolt, T.H.A.: The effect of electronic word of mouth on sales: a meta-analytic review of platform, product, and metric factors. J. Mark. Res. **53**, 297–318 (2016)

Banko, M., Brill, E.: Scaling to very very large corpora for natural language disambiguation. Annu. Meet. Assoc. Comput. Linguist. **39**, 26–33 (2001)

Baxendale, S., MacDonald, K., Wilson, H.N.: The impact of different touchpoints on brand consideration. J. Retail. **91**, 235–253 (2015)

Bijmolt, T.H.A., Van Heerde, H.J., Pieters, R.G.M.: New empirical generalizations on the determinants of price elasticity. J. Mark. Res. **42**, 141–156 (2005)

Bijmolt, T.H.A., Leeflang, P.S.H., Block, F., Eisenbeiss, M., Hardie, B.G.S., Lemmens, A., Saffert, P.: Analytics for customer engagement. J. Serv. Res. **13**, 341–356 (2010)

Blake, T., Nosko, C., Tadelis, S.: Consumer heterogeneity and paid search effectiveness: a large-scale field experiment. Econometrica. **83**, 155–174 (2015)

Borah, A., Tellis, G.J.: Halo (spillover) effects in social media: do product recalls of one brand hurt or help rival brands? J. Mark. Res. **53**, 143–160 (2016)

De Haan, E., Wiesel, T., Pauwels, K.H.: The effectiveness of different forms of online advertising for purchase conversion in a multiple-channel attribution framework. Int. J. Res. Mark. **33**, 491–507 (2016)

Delre, S.A., Broekhuizen, T.L.J., Bijmolt, T.H.A.: The effects of shared consumption on product life cycles and advertising effectiveness: the case of the motion picture market. J. Mark. Res. **53**, 608–627 (2016)

Ding, M., Eliashberg, J., Stremersch, S.: Innovation and Marketing in the Pharmaceutical Industry. Springer, New York, NY (2014)

Drechsler, S., Leeflang, P.S.H., Bijmolt, T.H.A., Natter, M.: Multi-unit price promotions and their impact on purchase decision and sales. Eur. J. Mark. **51**, 1049–1074 (2017)

Ebbes, P., Huamg, Z., Rangaswamy, A.: Sampling designs for recovering local and global characteristics of social networks. Int. J. Res. Mark. **33**, 578–599 (2015)

Edeling, A., Fischer, M.: Marketing's impact on firm value: generalizations from a meta-analysis. J. Mark. Res. **53**, 515–534 (2016)

Feng, H., Morgan, N.A., Rego, L.L.: Marketing department power and firm performance. J. Mark. **79**(5), 1–20 (2015)

Gensler, S., Leeflang, P.S.H., Skiera, B.: Impact of online channel use on customer revenues and costs to serve: considering product portfolios and self-selection. Int. J. Res. Mark. **29**, 192–201 (2012)

Gensler, S., Leeflang, P.S.H., Skiera, B.: Comparing methods to separate treatment from self-selection effects in an online banking setting. J. Bus. Res. **66**, 1272–1278 (2013)

Germann, F., Ebbes, P., Grewal, R.: The chief marketing officer matters! J. Mark. **79**(3), 1–22 (2015)

Gilbride, T.J., Inman, J.J., Stilley, K.M.: The role of within-trip dynamics in unplanned versus planned purchase behavior. J. Mark. **79**(3), 57–73 (2015)

Gray, K.: Causal analysis: the next frontier in analytics? Blog available athttps://www.linkedin.com/pulse/causal-analysis-next-frntier-analytics-kevin-gray?articleId=7747068731631148201 (2016)

Habel, J., Schons, L.M., Alavi, S., Wieseke, J.: Warm glow or extra charge? The ambivalent effect of corporate social responsibility activities on customers perceived price fairness. J. Mark. **80**(1), 84–105 (2016)

Hanssens, D.M.: Empirical Generalizations about Marketing Impact, 2nd edn. Marketing Science Institute, Cambridge, MA (2015)

Hastie, T., Tibshirani, R., Friedman, J.H.: Boosting and additive trees. In: The Elements of Statistical Learning, 2nd edn, pp. 337–384. Springer, New York, NY (2009)

Hattula, J.D., Schmitz, C., Schmidt, M., Reinecke, S.: Is more always better? An investigation into the relationship between marketing influence and managers' market intelligence dissemination. Int. J. Res. Mark. **32**, 179–186 (2015)

Hui, S.K., Fader, P.S., Bradlow, E.T.: Path data in marketing: an integrative framework and prospectus for model building. Mark. Sci. **28**, 320–335 (2009a)

Hui, S.K., Fader, P.S., Bradlow, E.T.: The traveling salesman goes shopping: the systematic deviations of grocery paths from TSP Optimality. Mark. Sci. **28**, 566–572 (2009b)

Hui, S.K., Huang, Y., Suher, J., Inman, J.J.: Deconstructing the "first moment of truth": understanding unplanned consideration and purchase conversion using in-store video tracking. J. Mark. Res. **50**, 445–462 (2013a)

Hui, S.K., Inman, J.J., Huang, Y., Suher, J.: The effect of in-store travel distance on unplanned spending: applications to mobile promotion strategies. J. Mark. **77**(2), 1–16 (2013b)

Ilhan B.E., Pauwels, K.H., and Kübler, R.: Dancing with the enemy: broadened understanding of engagement in rival brand dyads. MSI Report 16–107 (2016)

Inman, J.J., Winer, R.S., Ferraro, R.: The interplay among category characteristics, customer characteristics, and customer activities on in-store decision making. J. Mark. **73**(5), 19–29 (2009)

Kamakura, W.A., Mazzon, J.A.: Socioeconomic status and consumption in an emerging economy. Int. J. Res. Mark. **30**, 4–18 (2013)

Kang, C., Germann, F., Grewal, R.: Washing away your sins? Corporate social responsibility, corporate social irresponsibility, and firm performance. J. Mark. **80**(2), 59–79 (2016)

Katsikeas, C.S., Morgan, N.A., Leonidou, L.C., Hult, T.M.: Assessing performance outcomes in marketing. J. Mark. **80**(2), 1–20 (2016)

Kozinets, R.V.: Netnography: Doing Ethnographic Research Online. Sage, London (2001)

Kremer, S.T.M., Bijmolt, T.H.A., Leeflang, P.S.H., Wieringa, J.E.: Generalizing the effectiveness of pharmaceutical promotional expenditures. Int. J. Res. Mark. **25**, 234–246 (2008)

Kumar, A., Bezawada, R., Rishika, R., Janakiraman, R., Kannan, P.K.: From social to sale: The effects of firm-generated content in social media on customer behavior. J. Mark. **80**(1), 7–25 (2016)

Leeflang, P.S.H.: Paving the way for "distinguished marketing". Int. J. Res. Mark. **28**, 76–88 (2011)

Leeflang, P.S.H., Hunneman, A.: Modeling market response: trends and developments. Mark. J. Res. Manag. **6**, 71–80 (2010)

Leeflang, P.S.H., Wittink, D.R.: Building models for marketing decisions: past, present and future. Int. J. Res. Mark. **17**, 105–126 (2000)

Leeflang, P.S.H., Wittink, D.R., Wedel, M., Naert, P.A.: Building Models for Marketing Decisions. Kluwer Academic Publishers, Boston, MA (2000)

Li, H., Kannan, P.K.: Attributing conversions in a multichannel online marketing environment: an empirical model and a field experiment. J. Mark. Res. **51**, 40–56 (2014)

Macy, M.W., Willer, R.: From factors to actors: computational sociology and agent-based modeling. Annu. Rev. Sociol. **28**, 143–166 (2002)

Martin, K.D., Borah, A., Palmatier, R.W.: Data privacy: Effects on customer and firm performance. J. Mark. **81**(1), 36–58 (2017)

McAlister, L., Srinivasan, R., Jindal, N., Cannella, A.A.: Advertising effectiveness: the moderation effect of firm strategy. J. Mark. Res. **53**, 207–224 (2016)

Minnema, A., Bijmolt, T.H.A., Gensler, S., Wiesel, T.: To keep or not to keep: effects of online customer reviews on product returns. J. Retail. **92**, 253–267 (2016)

Mithas, S., Krishnan, M.S.: From association to causation via a potential outcomes approach. Inf. Syst. Res. **20**, 1–19 (2008)

Naik, P.A., Tsai, C.: Isotonic single-index model for high-dimensional database marketing. Comput. Stat. Data Anal. **47**, 775–790 (2004)

Naik, P.A., Prasad, A., Sethi, S.P.: Building brand awareness in dynamic oligopoly markets. Manag. Sci. **54**, 129–138 (2008)

Pauwels, K.H.: It's not the size of the data: it's how you use it: smarter marketing with analytics and dashboards. Am. Manag. Assoc. (2014)

Pauwels, K.H., Aksehirli, Z., Lackman, A.: Like the ad or the brand? Marketing stimulates different electronic word-of-mouth content to drive online and offline performance. Int. J. Res. Mark. **33**, 639–656 (2016)

Pauwels, K.H., Ambler, T., Clark, B., LaPointe, P., Reibstein, D., Skiera, B., Wierenga, B., Wiesel, T.: Dashboards as a service: why, what, how and what research is needed? J. Serv. Res. **12**, 175–189 (2009)

Pauwels, K.H., Erguncu, S., Yildirim, G.: Winning hearts, minds and sales: how marketing communication enters the purchase process in emerging and mature markets. Int. J. Res. Mark. **30**, 57–68 (2013)

Pauwels, K.H., Van Ewijk, B.: Do online behavior tracking or attitude survey metrics drive brand sales? An integrative model of attitudes and actions on the consumer boulevard. MSI. **13**, 1–50 (2013)

Peltier, J.W., Milne, G.R., Phelps, J.E.: Information privacy research: framework for integrating multiple publics, information channels, and responses. J. Interact. Mark. **23**, 191–205 (2009)

Reimer, K., Rutz, O.J., Pauwels, K.H.: How online consumer segments differ in long-term marketing effectiveness. J. Interact. Mark. **28**, 271–284 (2014)

Roberts, J.H., Kayande, U., Stremersch, S.: From academic research to marketing practice: exploring the marketing science value chain. Int. J. Res. Mark. **31**, 127–140 (2014)

Rossi, P.: Even the rich can make themselves poor: a critical examination of IV methods in marketing applications. Mark. Sci. **33**, 655–672 (2014)

Schulze, C., Skiera, B., Wiesel, T.: Linking customer and financial metrics to shareholder value: the leverage effect in customer-based valuation. J. Mark. **76**(2), 17–32 (2012)

Schweidel, M., Moe, W.: Listening in on social media: a joint model of sentiment and venue format choice. J. Mark. Res. **51**, 387–399 (2014)

Scott, S.: How Google analytics ruined marketing. TechCrunch, available at https://techcrunch.com/2016/08/07/how-google-analytics-ruined-marketing/ (2016)

Sethuraman, R., Tellis, G.J., Briesch, R.A.: How well does advertising work? Generalizations from meta-analysis of brand advertising elasticities. J. Mark. Res. **48**, 457–471 (2011)

Srinivasan, S., Hanssens, D.M.: Marketing and firm value: metrics, methods, findings, and future directions. J. Mark. Res. **46**, 293–312 (2009)

Stüttgen, P., Boatwright, P., Monroe, R.T.: A satisficing choice model. Mark. Sci. **31**, 878–899 (2012)

Tadelis, S., Zettelmeyer, F.: Information disclosure as a matching mechanism: theory and evidence from a field experiment. Am. Econ. Rev. **105**, 886–905 (2015)

Teixeira, T.S., Wedel, M., Pieters, R.: Moment-to-moment optimal branding in TV commercials: preventing avoidance by pulsing. Mark. Sci. **29**, 783–804 (2010)

Telpaz, A., Webb, R., Levy, D.J.: Using EEG to predict consumers' future choices. J. Mark. Res. **52**, 511–529 (2015)

Trusov, M., Bucklin, R.E., Pauwels, K.H.: Effects of word-of-mouth versus traditional marketing: findings from an internet social networking site. J. Mark. **73**(5), 90–102 (2009)

Van Doorn, J., Lemon, K.N., Mittal, V., Nass, S., Pick, D., Pirner, P., Verhoef, P.C.: Customer engagement behavior: theoretical foundations and research directions. J. Serv. Res. **13**, 253–266 (2010)

Van Eck, P.S., Jager, W., Leeflang, P.S.H.: Opinion leaders' role in innovation diffusion: a simulation study. J. Prod. Innov. Manag. **28**, 187–203 (2011)

Van Ittersum, K., Wansink, B., Pennings, J.M.E., Sheehn, D.: Smart shopping carts: how real-time feedback influences spending. J. Mark. **77**(6), 21–36 (2013)

Venkatraman, V., Dimoka, A., Pavlou, P.A., Vo, K., Hampton, W., Bollingeer, B., Herschfield, H.E., Ishihara, M., Winer, R.S.: Predicting advertising success beyond traditional measures: new insights from neurophysiological methods and market response modeling. J. Mark. Res. **52**, 436–452 (2015)

Verhoef, P.C., Leeflang, P.S.H.: Understanding the marketing department's influence within the firm. J. Mark. **73**(2), 14–37 (2009)

Verhoef, P.C., Kooge, E., Walk, N.: Creating Value with Big Data Analytics. Rootledge, New York, NY (2016)

Wedel, M., Kannan, P.: Marketing analytics for data rich environments. J. Mark. **80**(6), 97–121 (2016)

Wierenga, B.: Handbook of Marketing Decisions Models. Springer, New York, NY (2008)
Winer, R.S., Neslin, S.A.: The History of Marketing Science. World Scientific, New York, NY (2014)
Xue, M., Hitt, L.M., Chen, P.: Determinants and outcomes of internet banking adoption. Manag. Sci. **57**, 291–307 (2011)
Zhang, X., Li, S., Burke, R.R., Leykin, A.: An examination of social influence on shopper behavior using video tracking data. J. Mark. **79**(5), 24–41 (2014)

Author Index

P.S.H. Leeflang et al. (eds.), *Advanced Methods for Modeling Markets*,
International Series in Quantitative Marketing, DOI 10.1007/978-3-319-53469-5

B

C

D

E

F

G

H

I

J

K

L

M

N

O

P

Q

R

S

W

X

Subject Index

Subject Index (numbers refer to (sub-)sections)

P.S.H. Leeflang et al. (eds.), *Advanced Methods for Modeling Markets*,
International Series in Quantitative Marketing, DOI 10.1007/978-3-319-53469-5

About the Authors

Paulo Albuquerque is Associate Professor of Marketing at INSEAD. He holds a Ph.D. in management from the UCLA Anderson School of Management. Before joining INSEAD, he was an Associate Professor of Marketing and Faculty Director of the MBA program at the Simon Business School, University of Rochester, where he lectured the marketing core and the distribution channels elective class for 8 years. He was selected as an MSI Young Scholar in 2011 and won multiple teaching awards while at the Simon Business School.

Paulo's research interests include several marketing areas, including firm decisions to introduce new products, how products are adopted and how sales spread over different markets, and consumer decisions to search and purchase products online. This diverse research has appeared in several top marketing academic journals, such as *Marketing Science*, the *Journal of Marketing Research*, and *Management Science*. His recent projects include studying the role of social media in political races, the process by which consumers shop in online grocery stores, and how much and for how long consumers use products using data from the online education and gaming industries.

P.S.H. Leeflang et al. (eds.), *Advanced Methods for Modeling Markets*,
International Series in Quantitative Marketing, DOI 10.1007/978-3-319-53469-5

Hans Baumgartner (Ph.D., Stanford University) is Chair of the Marketing Department and Smeal Professor of Marketing in the Smeal College of Business at Pennsylvania State University. His research interests are in the areas of consumer behavior and research methodology. He has published articles on these topics in the *Journal of Consumer Research*, the *Journal of Marketing Research*, *Marketing Science*, the *Journal of Marketing*, the *Journal of Consumer Psychology*, the *International Journal of Research in Marketing*, *Organizational Behavior and Human Decision Processes*, *Psychological Methods*, and the *Journal of Economic Literature*, among others. He currently is an associate editor of the *Journal of Consumer Psychology* and has served as an associate or area editor of the *Journal of Consumer Research* and the *International Journal of Research in Marketing*. During 2009–2010, he was the president of the Society for Consumer Psychology.

Tammo H. A. Bijmolt is Professor in Marketing Research at the Department of Marketing, Faculty of Economics and Business of the University of Groningen, the Netherlands. His research interest covers various topics, including loyalty programs, retailing, e-commerce, advertising, and meta-analysis. Advanced research methods form a major component of most of his research projects. His publications have appeared in leading international journals, such as the *Journal of Marketing*, the *Journal of Marketing Research*, *Marketing Science*, the *Journal of Consumer Research*, the *International Journal of Research in Marketing*, *Psychometrika*, and the *Journal of the Royal Statistical Society* (A). He won the best paper award in 2007 of the *International Journal of Research in Marketing*, in 2011 of the *Journal of Interactive Marketing*, and in 2015 of the *European Journal of Marketing*. He is member of the editorial board of the *International Journal of Research in Marketing* and the *International Journal of Electronic Commerce*. Furthermore, he publishes regularly in Dutch marketing magazines, and his research on loyalty programs has been covered widely in the general media. He is Vice-President of the European Institute of Advanced Studies in Management (EIASM, Brussels).

Bart J. Bronnenberg is Professor of Marketing and a Center Research Fellow both at the Tilburg School of Economics and Management (TiSEM). He is also a Research Fellow of the Centre for Economic Policy Research (CEPR) in London. He holds Ph.D. and M.Sc. degrees in management from INSEAD, Fontainebleau, France, and an M.Sc. degree in industrial engineering from Twente University, the Netherlands. Bart Bronnenberg previously held appointments at the University of Texas in Austin (1994–1998) and the University of California, Los Angeles (1998–2007). His current research covers (1) convenience and retailing, (2) branding and entry barriers, and (3) consumer search behavior and online product search. His publications on these topics have appeared in leading academic journals in business and economics. Jointly with several co-author teams, he won the 2003 and 2008 Paul Green Award, the 2003 IJRM Best Paper Award, and the 2004 John D. C. Little Best Paper Award. He has been a recipient of a 5-year Vici grant from the Dutch Science Foundation, NWO, and a 4-year Marie Curie grant from the European Research Council.

Peter Ebbes is Associate Professor of Marketing at HEC Paris. He holds a Ph.D. from the University of Groningen (the Netherlands). His research focuses on understanding aspects of consumer behavior through data sources now commonly collected by many companies. In his research, he develops novel statistical methods to accommodate the increasing complexity of the consumer marketplace and the growing richness of available data sources. Insights from his studies help to improve marketing decision making, particularly concerning segmentation, targeting, and pricing activities.

Peter's work has been published in *Marketing Science*, *Management Science*, the *Journal of Marketing*, *Quantitative Marketing and Economics* (QME), the *International Journal of Research in Marketing* (IJRM), *Psychometrika*, and other journals. He is the winner of the 2011 IJRM Best Paper Award. He served on the organizing committee of the Advanced Research Techniques (ART) Forum, a conference that brings together quantitative researchers from industry and academia. He also served as secretary/treasurer of the Section on Statistics in Marketing within the American Statistical Association. Peter is currently a member of the American Marketing Association (AMA), the European Marketing Academy (EMAC), INFORMS, the American Statistical Association (ASA), and the Psychometric Society.

His teaching interests include marketing research and analytics, marketing models, and business statistics. Prior to joining HEC Paris in 2012, he taught at the Ohio State University and Pennsylvania State University. Webpage: http://www.hec.edu/Faculty-Research/Faculty-Directory/EBBES-Peter.

J. P. (Paul) Elhorst is Professor of Regional Economics at the University of Groningen, the Netherlands, endowed by the three northern provinces Groningen, Friesland, and Drenthe. He has degrees in economics (Ph.D., University of Amsterdam) and econometrics (M.Sc., University of Amsterdam). He is Editor-in-Chief of *Spatial Economic Analysis*, European editor of *Papers in Regional Science* (2013–2015), and editorial board member of the *Journal of Regional Science*, *Regional Science and Urban Economics*, and *Empirical Economics*. In 2014, he published the book *Spatial Econometrics: From Cross-Sectional Data to Spatial Panels*. He has written more than 100 papers in refereed journals, both in English and Dutch, and supervised seven Ph.D. theses. He is Educational Coordinator of the Bachelor's and Master's in economics at the University of Groningen and expert member of the SER advisory board of the Northern Netherlands. He won the Martin Beckmann Prize for best paper in *Papers in Regional Science* in 2007. Webpage: http://www.rug.nl/staff/j.p.elhorst/

Fred M. Feinberg is the Joseph Handleman Professor of Marketing (Ross School of Business) and Professor of Statistics (Department of Statistics), University of Michigan. He received B.Sc. degrees in mathematics and philosophy from MIT, did graduate work in mathematics at Cornell, and received his Ph.D. from the MIT-Sloan School of Management, under the guidance of John D. C. Little. His research has focused on using statistical models to explain complex decision patterns, Bayesian methods, dynamic programming, as well as the interface between marketing and operations management and engineering design. He has held editorial positions at *Marketing Science* (Associate Editor, 2007–2014; Senior Editor, 2014–2016), the *Journal of Marketing Research* (Associate editor, 2008–2014, 2016–now), and *POMS* (Senior Editor, OM-marketing interface, 2003–2014). He has been a finalist for the O'Dell and Little Best Paper Awards and on the author team receiving the 2011 Best Paper Award from the *International Journal of Research in Marketing*. He is co-author of *Modern Marketing Research: Concepts, Methods, and Cases*, served as Co-Chair for the 2009 ISMS Marketing Science Conference, and is President-Elect of the INFORMS Society for Marketing Science.

Elea McDonnell Feit is Assistant Professor of Marketing at Drexel University and Senior Fellow of Marketing at The Wharton School, University of Pennsylvania. Her research focuses on leveraging customer data to make better product design and advertising decisions, particularly when data is incomplete, unmatched, or aggregated, and often employs Bayesian methods. Much of her career has focused on developing new quantitative methods and bringing them into practice, first working in product design at General Motors and then commercializing new methods at the marketing analytics firm, The Modellers, and most recently she is the Executive Director of the Wharton Customer Analytics Initiative, where she built the academic-industry partnership program. She brings a rich understanding of industry problems to her research, which has been published in *Management Science* and the *Journal of Marketing Research.* She enjoys making analytics and statistics accessible to a broad audience and has recently co-authored a book on *R for Marketing Research and Analytics* with Chris Chapman. She regularly teaches popular tutorials and workshops for practitioners on digital marketing, marketing experiments, marketing analytics in R, discrete choice modeling, and hierarchical Bayes methods as well as undergraduate and MBA classes at Drexel and Wharton. She holds a Ph.D. in marketing from the University of Michigan, an M.S. in industrial engineering from Lehigh University, and a B.A. in mathematics from the University of Pennsylvania.

Dennis Fok is Professor of Applied Econometrics at Erasmus School of Economics, Erasmus University Rotterdam. He specializes in developing models to describe, understand, and predict decisions made by consumers. Among his technical interests are modeling unobserved heterogeneity, marketing econometrics, and Bayesian statistics. His research has been published in journals such as *Marketing Science*, the *Journal of Marketing Research*, the *International Journal of Research in Marketing*, the *Journal of Econometrics*, and the *Journal of Applied Econometrics*.

Harald J. Van Heerde (Ph.D. 1999, University of Groningen, the Netherlands) is Research Professor of Marketing at Massey University, Auckland. His expertise is in the econometric measurement of marketing effectiveness across a wide domain of substantive areas. He has published in the *Journal of Marketing Research* (JMR), the *Journal of Marketing*, *Marketing Science*, and other major marketing journals. He is the recipient of the Long-Term Impact Award (*Marketing Science*), the William O'Dell Long-Term Award (JMR), the Paul Green Award (JMR), and the *International Journal of Research in Marketing* (IJRM) Best Paper Award, and his papers were best paper award finalist on 15 more occasions. Van Heerde serves as an associate editor at *Marketing Science* and as an editorial board member at the *Journal of Marketing*, the *Journal of Marketing Research*, and IJRM. Van Heerde has attracted over NZ$ 2.1 million in research grants from the Netherlands Organisation for Scientific Research, the New Zealand Royal Society Marsden Fund, the Australian Research Council, and the Marketing Science Institute. Van Heerde is academic trustee at AiMark, the Institute for Advanced International Marketing Knowledge.

Professor Jörg Henseler is the Chair of Product-Market Relations at the Faculty of Engineering Technology of the University of Twente, Enschede, the Netherlands. Moreover, Jörg Henseler is Visiting Professor at NOVA Information Management School, Universidade Nova de Lisboa, Portugal, and Distinguished Invited Professor in the Department of Business Administration and Marketing at the University of Seville, Spain. He holds a Ph.D. from the University of Kaiserslautern, Germany. His broad-ranging research interests encompass empirical methods of marketing and design research as well as the management of design, products, services, and brands. His work has been published in *Computational Statistics and Data Analysis*, the *European Journal of Information Systems*, the *International Journal of Research in Marketing*, the *Journal of the Academy of Marketing Science*, the *Journal of Supply Chain Management*, *Long Range Planning*, *MIS Quarterly*, *Organizational Research Methods*, and *Structural Equation Modeling: An Interdisciplinary Journal*, among others. His outstanding teaching performance has earned him repeated recognition as "Teacher of the Year" according to master's in marketing students.

Professor Henseler is a leading expert on partial least squares (PLS) path modeling. He has written dozens of academic articles, edited two books, and chaired two conferences on PLS. On a regular basis, Prof. Henseler provides seminars on PLS path modeling at the PLS School (www.pls-school.com), through which hundreds of scholars and practitioners have been trained in structural equation modeling. Moreover, he chairs the scientific advisory board of ADANCO, a software for variance-based structural equation modeling (www.composite-modeling.com). Webpage: http://www.henseler.com

Raoul V. Kübler (Ph.D. Christian Albrechts University Kiel, Germany) is Assistant Professor of Marketing at Özyeğin University (Istanbul). His research focuses on social media, user-generated content, crisis communication, and advertising creativity. He frequently applies machine learning techniques to large data sets and is an expert in sentiment and content analysis. His research has been published in journals like *Business Research* and the *Journal for Research and Management* (JRM). Before becoming an academician, he worked for more than 10 years in the advertising industry. He was awarded with several research grants from the Marketing Science Institute and the German Research Foundation and was several times a finalist for EMAC's Best Paper Award. In addition, he consulted leading companies like Deezer, PepsiCo, Rausch AG, and Tetra Pak.

Peter S. H. Leeflang is the Emeritus Frank M. Bass Professor of Marketing at the University of Groningen (the Netherlands). He also holds a position as Honorary Professor at Aston Business School (UK). Besides, he had positions at UCLA, Goethe University (Frankfurt), LUISS University (Rome), and the University of St. Gallen (Switzerland). He holds a Ph.D. from Erasmus University. His research interests include modeling markets, sales promotions, new media, competition, and pharmaceutical marketing.

His work has been published in the *Journal of Marketing Research*, the *Journal of Marketing*, *Marketing Science*, the *Journal of the Academy of Marketing Science*, the *International Journal of Research in Marketing* (IJRM), the *Journal of Econometrics*, and *Management Science*, among others. He has (co-)written several books, such as *Building Implementable Marketing Models* (1978), *Building Models for Marketing Decisions* (2000), and *Modeling Markets* (2015). He is one of the founders of the European Marketing Academy (EMAC). He won several awards, among which are the 2010 Inaugural EMAC Distinguished Marketing Scholar Award (the highest award to be presented to a researcher of marketing who is a member of the European Marketing Academy), the 2009 Harold H. Maynard Award (best article in the *Journal of Marketing*), and the 2000 and 1996 awards for the best paper in IJRM. He is also the first winner of the J.B. Steenkamp Award for the paper with the highest impact in IJRM and is the winner of the ISMS Long Term Impact Award for his article with Harald Van Heerde and

Dick Wittink in *Marketing Science*. In the past 40 years, he supervised 40 Ph.D.s in Groningen, Rome, Rotterdam, etc. Professor Leeflang is a supervisory board member for numerous firms and has written studies for the Dutch government and the Dutch parliament. He is a member of the Royal Dutch Academy of Arts and Sciences (1999–now). Webpage: http://www.rug.nl/staff/p.s.h.leeflang/index

Peter J. Lenk is Professor of Technology and Operations and Marketing at the Stephen M. Ross School of Business at the University of Michigan. His primary area of research is Bayesian inference and its applications to business and economics. He has made numerous contributions to semi-parametric models. He has published widely in marketing and statistics journals. He received his Ph.D. in 1984 at the University of Michigan under Bruce Hill, and his dissertation received the Savage Award in 1985. He was a faculty member of the Statistics and Operations Research Department at the Stern School of Business, New York University, from 1984 to 1989, at which time he joined the University of Michigan Business School.

Oded Netzer is Associate Professor of Business at Columbia Business School and an affiliate with Columbia University Data Science Institute. Professor Netzer received a B.Sc. in industrial engineering and management from the Technion (Israel Institute of Technology) and an M.Sc. in statistics and a Ph.D. in business, both from Stanford University. Professor Netzer's research centers on one of the major business challenges of the data-rich environment of the twenty-first century: developing quantitative methods that leverage data to gain a deeper understanding of customer behavior and guide firms' decisions. He focuses primarily on building statistical and econometric models to measure consumer preferences and understand how customer choices change over time and across contexts. Most notably, he has developed a framework for managing firms' customer bases through dynamic segmentation. His research has been published in top journals such as the *Journal of Marketing Research*, *Marketing Science*, *Quantitative Marketing and Economics*, the *Journal of Consumer Psychology*, and the *Journal of Experimental Psychology*. Professor Netzer won multiple awards for his research and teaching. He is the winner of the ISMS John D. C. Little Best Paper Award, the ISMS Frank Bass Outstanding Dissertation Award, George S. Eccles Research Fund Award, and Columbia Business School Dean's Award for Teaching Excellence. Professor Netzer serves on the editorial board of several leading journals.

Ernst C. Osinga is an Assistant Professor of Marketing at the Lee Kong Chian School of Business, Singapore Management University. Prior to joining SMU, Ernst held an Assistant Professor at Tilburg University. He obtained his Ph.D., Cum Laude, from the University of Groningen. His research interests include pharmaceutical marketing, the marketing-finance interface, and online advertising and retailing. His research has been published in the *Journal of Marketing* and *Journal of Marketing Research*. Ernst is the recipient of the Dutch Marketing Science Award and a runner-up for the EMAC McKinsey Award. He received a Veni research grant from the Netherlands Organisation for Scientific Research (NWO). Ernst served as an expert witness for the Court of Amsterdam and provided guidance to large players in the pharmaceutical and advertising industry. He taught courses on marketing models, customer intelligence, and marketing research. He received several teaching recognitions.

Leo J. Paas is an international expert on marketing and analytics. He has published in top-tier academic journals and in applied journals for the business community. A common thread throughout his research is relevance for business. Before joining academia, Leo worked for the ING group, as a database marketer on areas such as data mining, customer lifetime value, and predictive modeling. In 1999, Leo started working as a consultant in Amsterdam, applying his expertise to a wide range of corporates, insurance firms, banks, and mortgage providers. In this same period, Leo also conducted his Ph.D. research in economic psychology, at Tilburg University, the Netherlands. He then joined the Marketing Department of Tilburg University as an assistant professor. In 2005, he became Associate Professor at the Marketing Department of VU University Amsterdam. In 2014, he joined the School of Communication, Journalism and Marketing at Massey University in Auckland as a Professor and Program Leader for the Master's in Business Analytics.

Dominik Papies is a Professor of Marketing at the School of Business and Economics at the University of Tübingen in Germany. He holds a doctoral degree from the University of Hamburg, Germany. His substantive research interests focus on the impact of new technologies on consumer demand and decision making, in particular in the entertainment industry. In the methodological domain, Dominik Papies studies the boundaries of established and the potential of new methods of addressing endogeneity in market response models. His research has been published in the leading journals of the field (e.g., *Marketing Science*, the *International Journal of Research in Marketing*, the *Journal of the Academy of Marketing Science*, *Information Systems Research*). His work has been funded, among others, by the German Research Foundation (DFG) and the Marketing Science Institute.

Koen H. Pauwels is Professor of Marketing at D'Amore-McKim School of Business, Northeastern University, Boston, and Professor at BI Oslo, Norway. He received his Ph.D. from UCLA, where he was chosen "Top 100 Inspirational Alumnus" out of 37,000 UCLA graduates. Next he joined the Tuck School of Business at Dartmouth, where he became tenured Associate Professor and started the Marketing Dynamics conference. Until 2017, Koen was affiliated with Özyeğin University, Istanbul. Prof. Pauwels' publications exceed 40, in journals such as *Harvard Business Review*, *International Journal of Research in Marketing*, *Journal of Advertising Research*, *Journal of Interactive Marketing*, *Journal of Marketing*, *Journal of Marketing Research*, *Journal of Retailing*, *Marketing Science*, and *Management Science*. Koen's awards include the 2010 Google/WPP Research Award, the 2011 Syntec Best Paper in Marketing/Decision Sciences Award, the 2007 O'Dell award for the most influential paper in the *Journal of Marketing Research*, the 2009 and 2011 Davidson awards for the best paper in *Journal of Retailing*, and the 2009 Varadarajan Award for Early Career Contributions to Marketing Strategy Research. Prof. Pauwels authored chapters in 6 books and has (co) written 3 books, including *Marketing Models* and *It's Not the Size of the Data – It's how you use it: Smarter Marketing with Analytics and Dashboards*. Prof. Pauwels is Senior Editor at the *International Journal of Research in Marketing* and consulted large and small companies across three continents, including Amazon, Credit Europe, Eli Lily, General Mills, Heinz, Inofec, Kayak, Knewton, Kraft, Marks & Spencer, Nissan, Sony, Tetrapak, and Unilever.

Rik Pieters is Arie Kapteyn Chaired Professor of Marketing at Tilburg University. He studied social and economic psychology at the Universities of Nijmegen, Tilburg, and Augsburg and did his Ph.D. research at the University of Leiden. On two Fulbright fellowships, he was visiting professor at the University of Missouri and at Pennsylvania State University. He was guest or visiting Professor at University of Innsbruck, University of Florida, University of Auckland and Koç University. His research concerns the effects of marketing mix variables on consumer behavior and on the well-being implications of such behaviors. It has been published in leading journals in statistics, marketing, economics, and psychology. If he doesn't bike, brew beer, or bake bread, he plays the bass and works.

Jeroen K. Vermunt received his Ph.D. degree in social sciences research methods from Tilburg University in the Netherlands in 1996. He is currently a full Professor and Head of the Department of Methodology and Statistics at Tilburg University. In 2005, he received the Leo Goodman Early Career Award from the methodology section of the American Sociological Association, and in 2010, he obtained a prestigious Vici grant from the Netherlands Science Foundation. His work has been published in the main journals in statistics and social science methodology, as well as in applied social science journals, including marketing journals. His research interests include latent class and finite mixture models, IRT modeling, longitudinal and event history data analysis, multilevel analysis, and generalized latent variable modeling. He is the co-developer (with Jay Magidson) of the Latent GOLD software package. Webpage: https://www.tilburguniversity.edu/webwijs/show/j.k.vermunt.htm

Tom J. Wansbeek is Honorary Professor of Statistics and Econometrics at the University of Groningen. He has a Ph.D. from Leiden University and has worked at the Netherlands Central Bureau of Statistics and the University of Amsterdam before and has held visiting positions at the University of Southern California and Zhejiang University. His research interests are in econometrics, psychometrics, linear algebra, statistics, and marketing. He has published two books, on identification and on measurement error, and a variety of articles in journals including *Econometrica*, *Psychometrika*, *Linear Algebra and Its Applications*, the *Journal*

of the American Statistical Association, and *Marketing Science*. He is or was an editorial board member of the *Journal of Econometrics*, the *Journal of Applied Econometrics*, *Econometric Reviews*, and *Statistica Neerlandica*.

Bert Weijters is Assistant Professor of Market Research at Ghent University (Belgium). His main interest lies in methodological research on survey methods, with a focus on response bias (due to response styles, context effects, and comprehension difficulties) and methods for dealing with such bias through questionnaire design and data analysis (using structural equation modeling). In terms of substantive research, his work is situated in consumer behavior, where he has done work on technology-enabled consumption (self-service technologies, digital music consumption, online shopping), branding (brand personality, prototypical brands, etc.), and—more recently—green consumption behavior. His work has been published in the *Journal of Consumer Research*, the *Journal of Marketing Research*, *Psychological Methods*, the *International Journal of Research in Marketing*, the *Journal of Business Ethics*, the *Journal of the Academy of Marketing Science*, *Applied Psychological Measurement*, and other outlets. Webpage: http://www.ugent.be/pp/pao/en/about-us/bert-weijters.htm

Jaap E. Wieringa is Professor of Research Methods in Business at the Department of Marketing of the University of Groningen and Research Director of the Customer Insights Center (RUGCIC). Since 2013, he is a Visiting Research Professor at Exeter Business School. He has an M.Sc. in econometrics (1994) and a Ph.D. in economics (1999) from the University of Groningen.During the years 1998–2000, he was employed as a senior consultant at the Institute for Business and Industrial Statistics (IBIS UvA BV), which is embedded in the University of Amsterdam, and consulted for, among others, DAF Trucks (a PACCAR company), General Electric, Sarah Lee/DE, and Hollandse Signaal Apparaten in Statistical Process Control and Six Sigma projects. On January 1, 2001, he joined the Department of Marketing at the University of Groningen. He has supervised six Ph.D. theses and is currently supervising two Ph.D. students.

During the last 8 years, he is consistently listed (in some years more than once) in the top 5 of best lecturers of the Faculty of Economics and Business. He won the "Best Teacher of the Year" Award of the Faculty of Economics and Business in 2009 and in 2010. He won the web prize of the "Best Teacher of the University of Groningen" in 2011.

He is co-author of several books, including *Modeling Markets*. His publications in marketing include articles in the *Journal of Marketing*, the *Journal of Marketing Research*, the *International Journal of Research in Marketing*, the *Journal of Product Innovation Management*, *Marketing Letters*, *Health Economics*, *Technological Forecasting and Sociological Change*, the *European Journal of Operations Research*, the *Journal of Service Research*, and the *International Journal of Forecasting*. The main focus of his current research is on marketing analytics, marketing dynamics, pharmaceutical marketing, marketing model building, time series analysis, diffusion modeling, and statistical quality control.

Appendix

Table of contents from Modeling Markets

P.S.H. Leeflang et al. (eds.), *Advanced Methods for Modeling Markets*,
International Series in Quantitative Marketing, DOI 10.1007/978-3-319-53469-5

Subject Index from Modeling Markets

Printed by Printforce, the Netherlands